UNIVERSITY CASEBOOK SERIES

STUDIES IN

CONTRACT LAW

FIFTH EDITION

by

EDWARD J. MURPHY
Late John N. Matthews Professor of Law
Notre Dame Law School

RICHARD E. SPEIDEL
Beatrice Kuhn Professor of Law
Northwestern University School of Law

IAN AYRES
William K. Townsend Professor of Law
Yale Law School

WESTBURY, NEW YORK
THE FOUNDATION PRESS, INC.
1997

COPYRIGHT © 1970, 1977, 1984, 1991 THE FOUNDATION PRESS, INC.
COPYRIGHT © 1997 By THE FOUNDATION PRESS, INC.

    615 Merrick Ave.
    Westbury, N.Y. 11590–6607
    (516) 832–6950

Library of Congress Cataloging-in-Publication Data
Murphy, Edward J.
 Studies in contract law / Edward J. Murphy, Richard E. Speidel,
Ian Ayres. — 5th ed.
  p. cm. — (University casebook series)
 Includes index.
 ISBN 1–56662–468–1 (hardcover)
 1. Contracts—United States—Cases. I. Speidel, Richard E.
II. Ayres, Ian. III. Title. IV. Series. '
KF801.A7M75 1997
346.7302—dc21   97–9348

*To the Memory of Edward J. Murphy,
Late John N. Matthews Professor of Law,
Notre Dame Law School.*

*

PREFACE

"Contract law has deep roots in the past, and much of its present structure is shaped by historical precedents. But as is true in all vital fields of law, familiar concepts are being reexamined and new patterns are emerging."

Thus began the preface to the first edition of *Studies in Contract Law* (1970). Over the intervening decades, through four additional editions, we have sought to chronicle these developments in a way that assists teacher and student in exploring this wonderful world of contract law.

For we remain convinced, as remarked in the preface to the third edition (1984), that contract law should continue to be the "centerpiece of the first-year law school curriculum."

The basic purpose, however, is to assist in the *study* of law. This involves not only familiarizing oneself with certain data, but reflecting upon that data in a way that helps to form a first-rate professional competence. A great legal scholar whom we quoted in previous editions, John Henry Wigmore, put it this way: "Every institute and principle of law has a philosophy—as every object in the sunlight has its attendant shadow. In the quest for the rule we must insist on including its reasons, and on lifting them out into the open."

RICHARD E. SPEIDEL
IAN AYRES

May, 1997

*

ACKNOWLEDGMENTS

The authors acknowledge, with gratitude, the kind permission to reprint copyrighted materials of the following authors and publishers: American Bar Association; American Business Law Journal; American Law Institute; Professor Eric Andersen; Professor Randy Barnett; Bobbs-Merrill Company, Inc.; Callaghan and Company; Cambridge Law Review; Case Western Reserve Law Review; Columbia Law Review; Cornell Law Review; Professor Dan B. Dobbs; Professor Martin Domke; Dow Jones & Company Inc.; Professor Melvin A. Eisenberg; Federal Bar Journal; Professor Daniel Fischell; Professor Lawrence M. Friedman; Professor Eric Green; Professor Robert J. Harris; Harvard Law Review; Professor Harold C. Havighurst; Professor Orrin L. Helstad; Indiana Law Journal; Iowa Law Review; W. Stanfield Johnson, Esq.; Journal of Law and Commerce; Journal of Legal Education; Professor Lewis Kornhauser; Professor Charles L. Knapp; Law Book Co. of Australasia Pty. Ltd.; Professor Michael B. Metzger; Michigan Law Review; Minnesota Law Review; Professor Michael J. Phillips; Fred B. Rothman & Co.; New York University Law Review; Robert J. Nordstrom, Esq.; Northwestern University Law Review; Sir David Hughes Parry; Professor Walter F. Pratt, Jr.; Professor Malcolm P. Sharp; Professor Robert H. Skilton; Stanford Law Review; Stevens & Sons, Ltd.; Professor Robert S. Summers; The Business Lawyer; Professor G. H. Treitel; United Features Syndicate; Universal Press Syndicate; University of Chicago Law Review; University of Colorado Law Review; University of Pennsylvania Law Review; South Carolina Law Review; Valparaiso University Law Review; Vanderbilt Law Review; Professor Lawrence Vold; West Publishing Company; Professor James H. White; William and Mary Law Review; Professor Glanville Williams; The Honourable Sir Victor Windeyer; Wall Street Journal; Yale Law Journal.

Professor Speidel is indebted to Ms. Mary V. Carroll, Northwestern University School of Law, class of 1998, for assistance on the Fifth Edition. Todd Cleary, Gideon Parchamovsky and Fred Vars provided research assistance to Professor Ayres.

*

SUMMARY OF CONTENTS

*

TABLE OF CONTENTS

*

TABLE OF CASES

Principal cases are in bold type. Non-principal cases are in roman type. References are to Pages.

TABLE OF UNIFORM COMMERCIAL CODE CITATIONS (1995 OFFICIAL TEXT)

*

STUDIES IN

CONTRACT LAW

*

CHAPTER ONE

INTRODUCTION TO THE STUDY OF CONTRACT LAW

SECTION 1. PRELIMINARY SURVEY OF SUBJECT AND SOURCES

Contract as Binding Promise. This course of study will deal primarily with the legal implications of promise making. Every issue respecting the legal enforcement of a promise is broadly a contracts issue. An authoritative and acceptable working definition is that of Restatement (Second) of Contracts: "A contract is a promise or set of promises for the breach of which the law gives a remedy, or the performance of which the law in some way recognizes as a duty."[1]

The focus upon promise is useful, since a common element in all contracts is promise, defined in the first Restatement as "an undertaking, however expressed, either that something shall happen, or that something shall not happen, in the future."[2] Yet the result of a contract is the creation of a *legal relationship* involving rights and duties of persons.[3] Thus, it may be better to emphasize the result of the promise rather than the promise itself. To an extent the Uniform Commercial Code does this: " 'Contract' means the total legal obligation which results from the parties' agreement as affected by this Act and any other applicable rules of law."[4]

1. Restatement (Second), Contracts § 1 (1981). Paraphrasing Professor Fuller, contract law might be defined as the enterprise or activity of courts, legislative bodies and administrative agencies of subjecting the human conduct of promise making to the "governance" of rules about liability and remedy. *Lon L. Fuller,* The Morality of Law 106 (1963).

2. Restatement, Contracts § 2 (1932). "A promise is a manifestation of intention to act or refrain from acting in a specified way, so made as to justify a promisee in understanding that a commitment has been made," Restatement (Second), Contracts § 2.

3. A useful discussion of terms, emphasizing legal relations arising from contract and prior negotiations, is Goble, *A Redefinition of Basic Legal Terms,* 35 Colum.L.Rev. 535 (1935). See also Sharp, *Promissory Liability,* 7 U.Chi.L.Rev. 1 (1939).

4. Uniform Commercial Code § 1–201(1). Similarly, in defining agreement as the "bargain of the parties in fact," UCC 1–201(3), the UCC moves even farther away from promise as an indispensable foundation word. For example, the word "promise" is used several times in the 1995 official text of UCC Article 2, Sales, see, e.g., UCC 2–206(1)(b), 2–210(4) and 2–313(1)(a), but defined only in Article 3, Commercial Paper, as "an undertaking to pay" and "more than an acknowledgment." UCC 1–102(1)(c). The definition of agreement as a "bargain" without defining the word "bargain," however, suggests that the ordinary usages of that term may be employed. In Restatement (Second) § 4, bargain is defined as "an agreement to exchange promises or to exchange a promise for a performance or to exchange performances."

Contract law thus concerns the promises we make, and it takes but a moment's reflection to be impressed by the broad scope of the subject. Instances are legion in which we repose confidence in the promises of others. Limited to the commercial area alone, every employment agreement, sales contract, promissory note or check, rental or lease agreement, and so on, embodies a promise or contractual undertaking. And lest one conclude too hastily that humankind is totally unregenerate consider that in the vast majority of these cases, people keep these promises. They do what they say they will do. Goods are ordered, delivered, and paid for. Work is performed; wages are paid. Funds are deposited and returned with interest. And so on, through a myriad of economic transactions.

Why Keep Promises? Why do people ordinarily fulfill their contractual obligations? Why the high rate of contract performance? No doubt the fear of legal sanction helps to deter breach. But the matter surely goes beyond mere fear of the law. Indeed, the fear of officially imposed sanction (e.g., a judgment for damages) may be a relatively minor deterrent in many situations. One thinks, for example, of the great Law Merchant tradition of the late medieval period, out of which much of our modern commercial law developed.[5] The merchants themselves administered a remarkably effective system which did not depend upon state enforcement mechanisms or procedures, but relied upon private sanctions such as refusal to deal or boycott.

Obviously, it is often in one's self-interest to keep promises. If one is to have credibility for the future, one must perform one's promises today. Finally, most people believe that promises ought to be kept because it is the right thing to do. It is a part of the way an honest person behaves.

It is not surprising that there emerged in our legal tradition the notion of "sanctity of contract." One writer summarized the prevalence of this attitude as follows:

> [Throughout the development of the English common law] the giving of a promise or the conclusion of an agreement involved a solemn undertaking the breach of which amounted in the eyes of the Church to a sin and in the eyes of the general body of contemporary lawyers to an immoral or unethical act. With the special emphasis placed by the nineteenth-century philosophers and jurists on the importance of freedom and the manifestation and extension of an individual's freedom through contract, it was not surprising that contracts developed a juristic blessedness or halo and were so often regarded as sacred.[6]

In contrast to this unqualified duty perform, Oliver W. Holmes argued that "the duty to keep a contract at common law means a prediction that you

---

5. See, generally, W. Mitchell, An Essay on the Early History of the Law Merchant (1904); L. Trakman, The Law Merchant: The Evolution of Commercial Law (1983).

6. D. Parry, The Sanctity of Contract 17–18 (1959).

must pay damages if you do not keep it—and nothing else."[7] For Holmes, a contractual promise was merely a promise to perform or pay damages.

Why Should Promises Be Legally Enforced? Although there is no record of a legal system that has undertaken to enforce all promises, there is yet to appear an organized society which has repudiated altogether the concept of binding promise or contract. To be sure, criteria of enforcement have varied. Moreover, the sanction imposed for nonperformance has at times been merely social, or religious, rather than an official court command to perform the promise (specific performance) or a judgment awarding monetary damages. Still, the modern who insists "you gave me your word" or "a bargain's a bargain" is not advancing novel doctrine. The Roman Law maxim *pacta sunt servanda* (agreements are to be kept) reflects a characteristic human attitude.[8] In this respect, the ancient Code of Hammurabi, the celebrated Code of Justinian, and the contemporary Uniform Commercial Code are quite alike in fundamental orientation.[9]

The economic importance of promise making and promise keeping can hardly be exaggerated. Dean Roscoe Pound put it this way: "In a developed economic order the claim to promised advantages is one of the most important of the individual interests that press for recognition. * * * Credit is a principal form of wealth. It is a presupposition of the whole economic order that promises will be kept. Indeed, the matter goes deeper. The social order rests upon stability and predictability of conduct, of which keeping promises is a large item."[10]

With good reason, Sir Frederick Pollock, the English legal historian, could maintain: "Enforcement of good faith in matters of bargain and

7. Oliver W. Holmes, *The Path of the Law,* 10 Harv. L. Rev. 457, 462 (1897) (stating that "nowhere is the confusion between legal and moral ideas more manifest than in the law of contract").

8. See Wehberg, *Pacta Sunt Servanda,* 53 Am.J.Int'l L. 795 (1959); Pound, *Promise or Bargain,* 33 Tul.L.Rev. 455 (1959). Professor Harry W. Jones has stressed "the deeply ingrained power that the idea of contract has had, throughout recorded history, on the minds of men and women; the centrality of contract as a basic institution of contemporary society; and the significance of freedom of contract as one of the great 'constitutional' devices for the dispersion of power in a society fearful, as ours has always and rightly been, of too much power in too few hands." Jones, *The Jurisprudence of Contracts,* 44 U.Cin.L.Rev. 43, 44 (1975).

9. See, generally, C. Fried, Contract as Promise: A Theory of Contractual Obligation (1981); Farnsworth, *The Past of Promise: An Historical Introduction to Contract,* 69 Colum.L.Rev. 576 (1969). Hannah Arendt has noted: "[T]he power of stabilization inherent in the faculty of making promises has been known throughout our tradition. We may trace it back to the Roman legal system, the inviolability of agreements and treaties (*pacta sunt servanda*); or we may see its discoverer in Abraham, the man from Ur, whose whole story, as the Bible tells it, shows such a passionate drive toward making covenants that it is as though he departed from his country for no other reason than to try out the power of mutual promise in the wilderness of the world, until eventually God himself agreed to make a Covenant with him. At any rate, the great variety of contract theories since the Romans attests to the fact that the power of making promises has occupied the center of political thought over the centuries." H. Arendt, The Human Condition 243–44 (1958).

10. 3 Pound, Jurisprudence 162–63 (1959).

promise is among the most important functions of legal justice. It might not be too much to say that, next after keeping the peace and securing property against violence and fraud so that business may be possible, it is the most important."[11]

In his book *The Promises Men Live By,* Harry Scherman, an economist, makes this bold assertion: "I do not think there is any single fact more important for men to recognize, with all its implications, than this simple one—*that their individual well-being, as well as that of the whole society, is determined by the volume of exchanges going on in the whole society.*"[12]

The facilitation of economic exchange is a basic policy of commercial law in general and contract law in particular. Enforcing contracts facilitates trade by promoting present reliance on future promise. When the exchanged promises are to be performed at different times, legal enforcement can assure the person who has promised to perform first that she can rely on the subsequent performance by the other side to the agreement. By encouraging a high volume of private exchange and the economic growth and development that results therefrom, the law contributes to both the welfare of the individual participants and the nation as a whole. If legal impediments to voluntary exchange are kept to a minimum, the law plays a market-supporting role by providing a general framework within which private planners can rationally allocate resources. And this, it is believed, is an essential ingredient of a dynamic economic order.

Beyond Economics. One cannot gainsay the importance of freedom of contract to a market economy and the relative superiority of such a system to unproductive command economies which are, seemingly, in decline throughout the world today. But there are more than economic advantages; there are political advantages as well:

> Freedom of contract, together with the right to own property, were core elements in the American vision of personal liberty. * * * The American constitutional scheme places contract liberty well above common law status; it is a guaranteed personal right. Liberty of contract is recognized not as power delegated by the sovereign, but as power originating in and guaranteed to the people.[13]

Private contract is a powerful tool for diffusing power in a society, for dividing decision-making and opportunities between the state on the one hand and private persons on the other.[14] In a sense, contracting parties are lawmakers. By entering into a binding contract, they make law for themselves.[15] They incur obligations which are enforceable by public authority, the courts. As indicated, the amount of legal obligation of this type is staggering. Any analysis of the real government of the people must take note of this extensive network of contractual obligations.

11. 7 Encyclopedia Britannica 35 (11th ed. 1910).

12. H. Scherman, The Promises Men Live By 393 (1983) (emphasis in original).

13. Blum and Wellman, *Participation, Assent and Liberty in Contract Formation,* 1982 Ariz.St.L.J. 901, 907–8.

14. Jones, supra note 8 at 50.

15. Id. at 53.

But even as one acknowledges these enormous practical advantages, one feels the need to press beyond social considerations. The matter goes beyond economics and politics. It touches on the very nature of a human person.[16] In her book *The Human Condition,* Hannah Arendt relates the power to promise to the power to forgive, the one (forgiveness) providing a remedy for a painful past and the other (promise) a remedy for an uncertain future. She explains: "The possible redemption from the predicament of irreversibility—of being unable to undo what one has done * * * is the faculty of forgiving. The remedy for unpredictability, for the uncertainty of the future, is contained in the faculty to make and keep promises. The two faculties belong together in so far as one of them, forgiving, serves to undo the deeds of the past, whose 'sins' hang like Damocles' sword over every new generation; and the other, binding oneself through promises, serves to set up in the ocean of uncertainty, which the future is by definition, islands of security without which not even continuity, let alone durability of any kind, would be possible in the relationships between men."[17]

Only persons forgive; only persons promise. Indeed, Charles Fried insists that "if we decline to take seriously the assumption of an obligation * * *, to that extent we do not take [the promisor] seriously as a person."[18] There are many, of course, who view these awesome powers as conferred by the Creator who both forgives and promises and commands that we do likewise. According to scripture, God has always dealt with people in terms of covenant and covenantal law.

Sources of Contract Law: The Common Law Tradition. The mainstream of our law is that which evolved within the English common law tradition, encompassing mainly the decisions of common law courts, but also, in the larger sense, those of the separate and in many ways competing Chancery Court.[19] As the royal courts expanded and a law common to the entire realm came to be administered, a significant portion of the judicial precedents thus amassed dealt with what we would regard today as the law of contracts. But this is not how these cases were regarded initially. The common lawyer viewed law in terms of remedies available (*viz.,* "writs" which would be granted to redress wrongs) rather than as a body of substantive doctrine or legal principles. There was no law of contracts, as such, but certain actions were available to enforce rights which, in retrospect at least, we see as "contractual" in nature. The development and expansion of the writ system to meet the exigencies of the times account for the remarkable continuity and durability of the common law. Contracts

---

16. Contracts can be used by individuals to escape from disadvantaged status and to protect their lifestyles through wills and trusts, cohabitation agreements and quasimarriage contracts. See Testy, An Unlikely Resurrection, 90 Nw. U. L. Rev. 219 (1995); Kastely, Cogs or Cyborgs?: Blasphemy and Irony in Contract Theories, 90 Nw. U. L. Rev. 132 (1995).

17. H. Arendt, supra note 9 at 237.

18. Fried, supra note 9 at 20–21.

19. See Newman, Equity and Law: a Comparative Study 11–49 (1961).

developed principally from the writ of assumpsit, itself an offshoot of trespass on the case, a "tort" remedy.[20]

While common law judges proceeded modestly on a case by case basis, adjudicating individual controversies brought before them, they did not act in a strictly *ad hoc* manner or without guidelines of any sort. They adhered to a principle of *stare decisis* as regards their own past and were also influenced by other bodies of legal learning, especially Roman Law, Canon Law and the Law Merchant.[21] Of particular interest here is the influence of the Law Merchant, aptly called "the private international [commercial] law of the Middle Ages."[22] Based upon the customs of merchants, and strongly impressed by an international character, the Law Merchant existed as a body of rules and principles pertaining to merchants and mercantile transactions, distinct from the ordinary law of the land. A characteristic of the mercantile courts, which regularly functioned at fairs and markets, was the dispatch with which disputes were settled. Moreover, it is said that this law, eminently practical and adapted to the requirements of commerce, "was characterized by the spirit of equity."[23] By the 16th century, all the great principles that mark the commercial law of modern times had evolved. "By that time every great country in Europe had recognized in commercial cases the principles of representation, the negotiability of bills of exchange, the liability of the real property of the debtor for his debts, the validity, to a certain extent at least, of formless contracts, the necessity of speedy justice, the importance of the principles of equity and the claims of the bona fide possessor to the protection of the law. The legal relations of partners to one another and to the outside world had, in almost every important point, been definitely settled, and a new commercial contract, insurance, had been evolved and the legal principles that were to govern its development clearly marked."[24]

Until well into the eighteenth century a large part of Anglo–American law pertaining to the sale of goods (and indeed commercial law generally) remained that which was fashioned and administered by the merchants themselves. But gradually this mercantile practice was brought within the common law tradition. One of the chief instruments of the assimilation was a very remarkable jurist, Lord Mansfield, who became Lord Chief Justice of the King's Bench in 1756. Holdsworth called him the "greatest lawyer of

20. See also Professor Simpson's exceptional work, A.W.B. Simpson, A History of the Common Law of Contract: The Rise of the Action of Assumpsit (1975). In a book with a provocative title, "The Death of Contract," Professor Grant Gilmore insisted that recent "contract" trends manifest a return to "tort" roots, so much so that traditional emphasis upon "bargained-for exchange" as the prototypical contractual transaction is obsolete, having been largely superseded by theory allowing recovery for "unbargained-for" reliance. For a critical review, see Speidel, *An Essay on the Reported Death and Continued Vitality of Contract,* 27 Stan.L.Rev. 1161 (1975). See also Speidel, *The Borderland of Contract,* 10 N.Ky.L.Rev. 163 (1983).

21. See Re, *The Roman Contribution to the Common Law,* 29 Ford.L.Rev. 447 (1961); Hamburger, *The Development of the Nineteenth–Century Consensus Theory of Contract* 241, Law & Hist.Rev. (1989).

22. Maitland, Select Pleas in Manorial Courts 133.

23. Mitchell, supra note 5 at 16.

24. Id. at 156–8.

the century."[25] Mansfield was a master at adapting the common law to the needs of the age.[26] This was done by both a careful scrutiny of the work of his predecessors and the use of principles developed in other legal systems. He did not always succeed in his efforts, as we shall see, but his accomplishments are impressive. It is interesting to note that one of the tools which he used was a jury of merchants, men who gave him advice on commercial matters. Because of this, some complained that Lombard Street (the merchants) was dictating to Westminster (the judges). In part, of course, this was true. But how fortunate for the common law, especially in view of the fact that during this period the great expansion of trade and commerce made it imperative that the law keep better pace with changing times.[27]

Legislative Codification. Just prior to the turn of this century there began, in England, the legislative codification of large segments of commercial law. One of the early statutes was the English Sale of Goods Act, drafted by Mackenzie D. Chalmers and enacted in 1893. Lord Chalmers admirably executed his mandate from Parliament to "reproduce exactly as possible the existing law," thereby preserving continuity with case precedent. Codification of sales law in the United States began in 1902,[28] when the National Conference of Commissioners on Uniform State Laws entrusted the task of drafting a statute to Professor Samuel Williston. The result was the Uniform Sales Act, approved by the Commissioners in 1906 and recommended to the various State legislatures. The response was highly favorable, over thirty States adopting it. In the main Professor Williston followed the English statute, often copying verbatim Chalmers' language. In treating of contracts for the sale of goods, each statute touched on matters of general contractual import. But since, as noted, a determined effort was made to preserve a continuity with the common law, the basic structure of contract law was not changed.

In 1923 the American Law Institute, whose activities have had a profound effect upon American law and practice, was founded "to promote the clarification and simplification of the law and its better administration of justice and to encourage and carry on scholarly and scientific work."[29] Among the Institute's accomplishments was the preparation of the Restatement of Contracts, a respected work to which frequent reference will be

---

25. Holdsworth, Some Makers of the English Law 161 (1938).

26. Edmund Burke, a contemporary, said of him: "His ideas go to the growing melioration of the law, by making its liberality keep pace with the demands of justice, and actual concerns of the world; not restricting the infinitely diversified occasions of men and the rules of natural justice, but conforming our jurisprudence to the growth of our commerce and of our empire." Id. at 169.

27. Some of the relationships between common law and economic growth in nineteenth century England and America are dis-

cussed in Simpson, *Innovation in Nineteenth Century Contract Law,* 91 L.Q.Rev. 247 (1975); Horwitz, *The Historical Foundations of Modern Contract Law,* 87 Harv.L.R. 917 (1974). See also, Danzig, *Hadley v. Baxendale: A Study of the Industrialization of the Law,* 4 J.Legal Studies 249 (1975).

28. For an interesting history of earlier and largely unsuccessful efforts to codify American law, see J. Honnold, The Life of the Law 100–145 (1964).

29. Restatement, Contracts viii (1932).

made in this book. As the title implies, a restatement purports to be a systematic statement of prevailing law, both decisional and statutory. Work on the Contracts Restatement (and on those covering Torts, Conflict of Laws and Agency) began in 1923, with Professor Williston serving as Reporter. He was a most logical choice for this position, since his monumental treatise on contracts had just recently been published and he was recognized as the leading authority in the United States.[30] Among Williston's advisers on the project was Professor Arthur L. Corbin, himself a renowned authority on contract law and later the author of a major treatise on the subject.[31] The final draft was approved in May, 1932, and it has been a very influential document. A measure of judicial acceptance can be seen in the fact that it has been cited thousands of times by appellate courts.[32] Williston stated that "the endeavor in the Restatement is to restate the law as it is, not as new law."[33] However, the end product had a strong normative aspect as well; many provisions had only marginal case support and were quite obviously advanced as improvements upon prevailing doctrine.

In the early 1960's, the American Law Institute began work on the Second Restatement of Contracts with Professor Robert Braucher as reporter. He served in that capacity until 1971 when he was appointed to the Supreme Judicial Court of Massachusetts. He was succeeded by Professor Allan Farnsworth. Each year from 1963, a new tentative draft of the Second Restatement was produced, sixteen in all, until 1979 when the American Law Institute adopted the entire Restatement (Second). After some final editing, the Restatement was published in 1981. Like the first Restatement, the second Restatement's primary thrust was to restate the law as it is, not as it should be. Nevertheless, it does contain some outright innovations, the most significant of which is the increased recognition of reliance as a basis of liability.[34]

By far the most significant recent event in the development of contract law has been the appearance of the Uniform Commercial Code (UCC), a comprehensive statute dealing with a wide range of commercial transactions. Work on the Code began in the early 1940's, under joint sponsorship of the National Conference of Commissioners on Uniform State Laws and the American Law Institute. The first edition was approved in 1952. A revised edition, known as the 1958 Official Text with Comments, was published in 1958, followed four years later by the 1962 Official Text. The 1995 official text is the latest version. Forty-nine States, plus the District of Columbia and the Virgin Islands, have enacted the UCC. In addition,

---

30. The original edition of Williston on Contracts was published in 1920. The text was revised by Professor Williston, in collaboration with Professor George Thompson, in 1936–38. The third edition, as revised by Professor Walter H.E. Jaeger, is now complete.

31. Professor Corbin's treatise was published in 1950–1, and after his death in 1967 has been updated by supplements prepared by Professor Colin Kelly Kaufman.

32. Goodrich and Wolkin, The Story of the American Law Institute 39 (1961).

33. 3 ALI Proceedings 159 (1925).

34. See Farnsworth, *Ingredients in the Redaction of the Restatement (Second) of Contracts,* 81 Colum.L.Rev. 1 (1981).

Louisiana has adopted Articles 1, 3, 4 and 5. At this writing every article of the UCC but one[35] has been or will be revised.[36] The twenty-first century could herald a new age of codification for domestic and transnational contract law.[37]

The primary architect of the Code was the late Professor Karl Llewellyn,[38] assisted by many others from the ranks of the judiciary, the practicing bar, the law schools and business. Unlike Chalmers and Williston, Llewellyn and colleagues did not feel a special need or obligation to follow previously charted courses. There are many innovations and departures from precedent in an effort to implement the following purposes and policies: "to simplify, clarify and modernize the law governing commercial transactions; to permit the continued expansion of commercial practices through custom, usage and agreement of the parties; to make uniform the law among the various jurisdictions."[39] The statute has no rival in our country in terms of sheer displacement and modification of existing commercial law. It is much more than a mere restatement or an effort "to make uniform the law among the various jurisdictions." Although the desire for uniformity may have been the principal motive for initiation of the project, the Code being designed to replace seven of the uniform acts prepared by one of the sponsoring organizations, and although the practical value of uniformity may well be the major factor in overwhelming legislative acceptance, it is clear that normative elements of law improvement were so dominant as to result in a reorientation of much legal doctrine. The effect of strict application alone is far-reaching; analogic application adds to the potential impact.[40] Throughout this book, we will study, primarily, Article 2 of the UCC (which governs the sale of goods) as a source of more

35. In all probability, there will be a proposal to revise this one exception (Article 7, concerning documents of title).

36. Two recent symposia contain all you might want to know and more about the "new" Uniform Commercial Code. See Symposium, Is the UCC Dead, or Alive and Well?, 26 Loy. L.A. L. Rev 535 (1993); Symposium, Is the UCC Dead, or Alive and Well?: Practitioners' Perspectives, 28 Loy. L.A. L. Rev. 89 (1994).

37. On January 1, 1988, the Convention for the International Sale of Goods (CISG) became effective in the United States. The convention applies to contracts for the sale of goods between parties having a place of business in different countries that are parties to the convention. See, generally, Perillo, *UNIDROIT Principles of International Commercial Contracts: The Black Letter Text and a Review,* 63 Fordham L. Rev. 281 (1994).

This codification trend raises the continuing questions of the circumstances under which contract doctrine should be codified—especially since the UCC is primarily drafted by private groups rather than in formal legislative hearings. See Schwartz & Scott, The Political Economy of Private Legislatures, 143 U. Pa. L. Rev. 595 (1995).

38. For an interesting study of Llewellyn, his life, times, ideas and role in UCC drafting, see W. Twining, Karl Llewellyn and the Realist Movement (1973).

39. Uniform Commercial Code § 1–202(2).

40. See D. Murray, *Under the Spreading Analogy of Article 2 of the Uniform Commercial Code,* 39 Fordham L.Rev. 447 (1971). In 1990, a new Article 2A, entitled "Leases," was approved by Code-sponsoring organizations and proposed for adoption by the states. A lease of goods is treated in a manner analogous to that in Article 2 pertaining to a sale of goods.

modern ideas about contract and examine the not so subtle impact of the Code upon the development of Restatement (Second).

Default vs. Immutable Rules. Most of the rules that you will learn in this course can be altered by the private agreements of the parties. Such rules that the parties can contract around are often called "default" or "gap-filling" rules. Just as computer word processing software establishes a *default* lefthand margin of 1 inch (which individual users can alter by affirmatively reformatting a document), contract law provides default rules about what is sufficient to reach an agreement[41] and about what the parties' obligations are under an agreement.[42] Default rules govern when the parties have remained silent—i.e. in the absence of agreement to the contrary.

Not every contract rule, however, can be contracted around. Some rules are mandatory or "immutable." This distinction between default and immutable rules is emphasized in the very first section of the UCC: "The effect of provisions of this Act may be varied by agreement, except as otherwise provided in this Act and except that the obligations of good faith . . . may not be disclaimed by agreement."[43] Thus, in learning the rules of contract it is essential to identify (i) *whether* particular rules can be contracted around and (ii) *how* private parties might opt for alternative provisions. Indeed, a worthwhile exercise after reading each case is to consider what contractual provisions would be sufficient to reverse the court's decision. If there is no language that could reverse the decision, then the court has in effect created an immutable rule.

Immutable rules are established by both courts and legislatures. The common law (i.e., law made by judges) established immutable limitations on the maximum amount of damages that parties can contract for (restrictions on so-called liquidated damages) and limitations on the maximum length of "covenants not to compete." In the last 60 years, legislative (and administrative) bodies have promulgated a host of immutable rules that restrict freedom of contract. Many matters, e.g., insurance and labor, have in a sense been removed from the free market and many other commercial activities are limited in scope by such things as the antitrust laws.[44] For

41. For example, UCC § 2–206 provides that "unless otherwise unambiguously indicated by the language or circumstances" an offer to buy goods invites acceptance by either a prompt promise to ship or by shipment of the goods itself. The offeror, however, as master of the offer can alter this rule by "unambiguously indicating" that only a particular type of acceptance will be effective.

42. For example, if an agreement fails to specify a price, the UCC fills this gap by establishing the buyer's obligation to pay "a reasonable price." UCC § 2–305(1).

43. UCC § 1–102(2).

44. Some commentators have suggested that the preemption of common-law rules by market-specific statutes and/or by the encroachment of tort has rendered contract law "dead" or transformed it into a residual category. See G. Gilmore, The Death of Contract (1974); L. Friedman, Contract Law in America (1965); Symposium, *The Relevance of Contract Theory,* 1967 Wis.L.Rev. 803–839. Others focusing on the default-nature of law have characterized contract law as an imperialist theory swallowing large segments of the legal landscape. See, e.g., Langbein, The Contractarian Basis of the Law of Trusts, 105 Yale L.J. 625, 630 (1995) ("Contract has be-

example, since 1964, employers have had an immutable duty not to discriminate on the basis of race or gender in making employment decisions. Even the relatively simple construction of a private home is awash with immutable regulatory duties.[45]

As a normative matter, there is "surprising consensus among academics at an abstract level on two normative bases for immutability. Put most simply immutable rules are justifiable if society wants to protect (1) parties within the contract, or (2) parties outside the contract. The former justification turns on parentalism; the latter on externalities. Immutable rules displace freedom of contract. Immutability is justified only if unregulated contracting would be socially deleterious because parties internal or external to the contract cannot adequately protect themselves."[46]

However, even when contract law chooses not to restrict contractual freedom, it must still decide which default rule will govern when the parties are silent and what manifestations are sufficient and/or necessary to displace the default rule. At times, it might be useful to establish defaults which penalize one or both parties to encourage more explicit contracting—as the parties act to contract around the penalty default. For example, the UCC refuses to enforce contracts that omit the quantity to be sold—which effectively establish a default quantity of zero.[47] In stark contrast to the "reasonable price" default, this "zero quantity" default is likely to induce private parties to provide better information about the terms of their agreement.[48]

Appreciating the default nature of much of contract law suggests that contract law is not just created by courts and legislatures, but, perhaps most importantly, by private parties themselves. Indeed, people in their daily interactions may contract around immutable rules as well as default rules by largely ignoring what contract law ordains to be legally enforceable obligation.[49] Important parts of the way parties actually exchange and resolve promissory obligations may be beyond the shadow of the law.[50] "If,

come the dominant doctrinal current in modern American law. In fields ranging from corporations and partnership to landlord and tenant to servitudes to the law of marriage, scholars have come to understand our legal rules as resting mainly on imputed bargains that are susceptible to alteration by actual bargains.").

45. An increasing amount of this regulatory activity has as its avowed purpose the protection of consumers. See, e.g., Macaulay, *Bambi Meets Godzilla: Reflections on Contracts Scholarship and Teaching vs. State Unfair and Deceptive Trade Practices and Consumer Protection Statutes*, 26 Hous. L.Rev. 575 (1989).

46. Ayres & Gertner, Filling Gaps in Incomplete Contracts: An Economic Theory of Default Rules, 99 Yale L.J. 87, 88 (1989).

47. UCC § 2–201(1) ("a contract . . . is not enforceable under this [provision] beyond the quantity of goods shown").

48. See Ayres & Gertner, supra note 46 (arguing that "penalty defaults" by inducing explicit contracting might produce valuable information for parties to the agreement or third parties—such as courts).

49. See Macaulay, *Non-Contractual Relations in Business: A Preliminary Study*, 28 Am.Soc.Rev. 55 (1963); Ellickson, Order Without Law (1991).

50. See Rubin, The Nonjudicial Life of Contract: Beyond the Shadow of the Law, 90 Nw. U. L. Rev. 107, 109 (1995).

because of the high cost of litigation, the increased use of alternative dispute resolution techniques, and the limitations of adjudication, more behavior occurs outside of the 'shadow of the law,' the impact of contract law is reduced, and theories based upon assumptions that people are influenced by the law are weakened."[51]

In sum, contract operates on two levels. The first is the vast area of agreement in fact, where bargains are performed and disputes settled without resort to public agencies of decision. This level may be likened to that large part of the iceberg which is under water. The second level is that of litigated disputes ultimately resolved by courts or other agencies and the results published in reported opinions. This is the "visible" law of contracts, which emerges as courts resolve disputes between private bargainers. This is the body of doctrine which, in theory, influences rational pre-transaction planning and provides standards for the settlement of disputes. A primary thrust of our study of contract law will be to determine what courts, frequently guided or controlled by legislation, do or should do about private efforts,[52] frequently assisted by attorneys,[53] to allocate economic and other resources through bargain and exchange. But since the "visible" law of contracts has been carefully selected, classified and truncated for insertion into your casebook, you should realize that you are studying the top of the iceberg.

Recurring Questions. As you begin to study the multiple problems of contract law and to draw on both legal materials and your own experience and training, several recurring questions should be kept firmly in mind.

1. Which promises will be enforced? If the law will not enforce every promise, what are the conditions which must be met before the force of organized government will support private citizen A's claim against private citizen B?

2. When enforceable, what is the scope and content of promissory obligations? How will courts interpret contractual provisions and the absence of contractual provisions—especially in the light of changed circumstances?

3. How will these promises be enforced? What remedies are available when a contractual promise is breached?

---

51. Speidel, *The Shifting Domain of Contract,* 90 Nw. U.L. Rev. 254, 257 (1995).

52. A staggering development in the last fifty years has been the growth (measured in billions of dollars) of federal government procurement. The law of government contracting governing this procurement is both complex and voluminous. A basic understanding of this area is essential to a contextual understanding of contemporary contract law. For an introduction, see N. Keyes, Gov-

ernment Contracts in a Nutshell (2d ed. 1990).

53. Contracts, as much as any other area of private activity, poses the greatest opportunities for the parties and their attorneys to negotiate and plan for the future and to resolve disputes by agreement without the direct intervention of government. See, in general, Macneil, *A Primer of Contract Planning,* 48 S.Cal.L.Rev. 627 (1975); Gilson, *Value Creation by Business Lawyers: Legal Skills and Asset Pricing,* 94 Yale L.J. 239 (1984).

4. Which of the foregoing answers can the parties contract around? And what contractual language will be sufficient to produce a particular result?

Although by no means exhaustive,[54] the above questions, if conscientiously considered, should contribute substantially to your study of contract law.[55]

A final note. As the Fifth Edition goes to press, the revision of Article 2, Sales of the Uniform Commercial Code is approaching completion. Final approval is expected by the Summer of 1998. One of your co-authors, Richard E. Speidel, is Reporter to that Revision. In the text that follows there are occasional notes discussing proposed changes and, in brackets, references are given to sections in the January, 1997 Draft. The Revision, however, is still in transition and there will undoubtedly be changes in both content and numbering in the final product. Unless otherwise noted, UCC citations are to the 1995 official text.

SECTION 2. INTRODUCTORY CASES AND PROBLEMS

The following materials are designed to accomplish at least three objectives. First, they can be used to begin the development of certain fundamental lawyering skills, such as the analysis and synthesis of judicial decisions and the use of the legislative sources of contract law. Second, they introduce in a fairly straightforward way some recurring concepts and ideas about contract liability and remedy. Third, they provide a general overview of and framework for what comes later in the book. These objectives overlap and, at first, the pursuit of them will appear to be incomplete and somewhat frustrating. But have faith! Each case and each problem will appear again in the pages to follow, to be reviewed and related to new and more diversified materials.

54. For example, it is also useful to pay attention to (i) whether particular laws are standards ("thou must drive safely") or rules ("thou must drive less than 55 miles per hour") and (ii) who decides these questions—judge, jury, legislator, administrator or the parties themselves.

55. The following abbreviations will be used in subsequent references: UCC—Uniform Commercial Code, 1995 Official Text; Restatement—Restatement, Contracts (1932); Restatement (Second)—Restatement (Second), Contracts (1981); Corbin—Corbin on Contracts; Williston—Williston on Contracts (Jaeger ed.); Farnsworth—Farnsworth, Contracts (2d ed. 1990); Calamari and Perillo—Calamari and Perillo, Contracts (3d ed. 1987); Murray—J. Murray, Murray on Contracts (3d ed. 1990); Prosser and Keeton—Prosser and Keeton on Torts (5th ed. 1984); Dobbs—Dobbs, Remedies (1973).

Editorial marks . . . indicate citations omitted in middle of sentence. Editorial marks. . . . indicate citations omitted at end of sentence. Editorial marks * * * indicate text has been omitted.

Bailey v. West

Supreme Court of Rhode Island, 1969.
105 R.I. 61, 249 A.2d 414.

■ PAOLINO, JUSTICE. This is a civil action wherein the plaintiff alleges that the defendant is indebted to him for the reasonable value of his services rendered in connection with the feeding, care and maintenance of a certain race horse named "Bascom's Folly" from May 3, 1962 through July 3, 1966. The case was tried before a justice of the superior court sitting without a jury, and resulted in a decision for the plaintiff for his cost of boarding the horse for the five months immediately subsequent to May 3, 1962, and for certain expenses incurred by him in trimming its hoofs. The cause is now before us on the plaintiff's appeal and defendant's cross appeal from the judgment entered pursuant to such decision.

The facts material to a resolution of the precise issues raised herein are as follows. In late April 1962, defendant, accompanied by his horse trainer, went to Belmont Park in New York to buy race horses. On April 27, 1962, defendant purchased "Bascom's Folly" from a Dr. Strauss and arranged to have the horse shipped to Suffolk Downs in East Boston, Massachusetts. Upon its arrival defendant's trainer discovered that the horse was lame, and so notified defendant, who ordered him to reship the horse by van to the seller at Belmont Park. The seller refused to accept delivery at Belmont on May 3, 1962, and thereupon, the van driver, one Kelly, called defendant's trainer and asked for further instructions. Although the trial testimony is in conflict as to what the trainer told him, it is not disputed that on the same day Kelly brought "Bascom's Folly" to plaintiff's farm where the horse remained until July 3, 1966, when it was sold by plaintiff to a third party.

While "Bascom's Folly" was residing at his horse farm, plaintiff sent bills for its feed and board to defendant at regular intervals. According to testimony elicited from defendant at the trial, the first such bill was received by him some two or three months after "Bascom's Folly" was placed on plaintiff's farm. He also stated that he immediately returned the bill to plaintiff with the notation that he was not the owner of the horse nor was it sent to plaintiff's farm at his request. The plaintiff testified that he sent bills monthly to defendant and that the first notice he received from him disclaiming ownership was "* * * maybe after a month or two or so" subsequent to the time when the horse was left in plaintiff's care.

In his decision the trial judge found that defendant's trainer had informed Kelly during their telephone conversation of May 3, 1962, that "* * * he would have to do whatever he wanted to do with the horse, that he wouldn't be on any farm at the defendant's expense * * *." He also found, however, that when "Bascom's Folly" was brought to his farm, plaintiff was not aware of the telephone conversation between Kelly and defendant's trainer, and hence, even though he knew there was a controversy surrounding the ownership of the horse, he was entitled to assume that "* * * there is an implication here that, 'I am to take care of this horse.'" Continuing his decision, the trial justice stated that in view of the result reached by this court in a recent opinion wherein we held that the instant defendant was liable to the original seller, Dr. Strauss, for the purchase price of this horse,* there was a contract "implied in fact" between the plaintiff and defendant to board "Bascom's Folly" and that this contract continued until plaintiff received notification from defendant that he would not be responsible for the horse's board. The trial justice further stated that "* * * I think there was notice given at least at the end of the four months, and I think we must add another month on there for a reasonable disposition of his property."

In view of the conclusion we reach with respect to defendant's first two contentions, we shall confine ourselves solely to a discussion and resolution of the issues necessarily implicit therein, and shall not examine other subsidiary arguments advanced by plaintiff and defendant.

I

The defendant alleges in his brief and oral argument that the trial judge erred in finding a contract "implied in fact" between the parties. We agree.

* * *

The source of the obligation in a contract "implied in fact," as in express contracts, is in the intention of the parties. We hold that there was no mutual agreement and "intent to promise" between the plaintiff and defendant so as to establish a contract "implied in fact" for defendant to pay plaintiff for the maintenance of this horse. From the time Kelly delivered the horse to him plaintiff knew there was a dispute as to its ownership, and his subsequent actions indicated he did not know with whom, if anyone, he had a contract. After he had accepted the horse, he made inquiries as to its ownership and, initially, and for some time thereafter, sent his bills to both defendant and Dr. Strauss, the original seller.

There is also uncontroverted testimony in the record that prior to the assertion of the claim which is the subject of this suit neither defendant nor his trainer had ever had any business transactions with plaintiff, and had never used his farm to board horses. Additionally, there is uncontradicted evidence that this horse, when found to be lame, was shipped by defendant's trainer not to plaintiff's farm, but back to the seller at Belmont Park. What is most important, the trial justice expressly stated that he believed the testimony of defendant's trainer that he had instructed Kelly that defendant would not be responsible for boarding the horse on any farm.

From our examination of the record we are constrained to conclude that the trial justice overlooked and misconceived material evidence which establishes beyond question that there never existed between the parties an

---

* [See Strauss v. West, 100 R.I. 388, 216 A.2d 366 (1966). The court held that Bascom's Folly was "sound" at the time delivery was tendered by Strauss, that title had passed to West and that West was liable to Strauss for the purchase price of $1,800. Ed.]

element essential to the formulation of any true contract, namely, an "intent to contract." Compare Morrissey v. Piette, R.I., 241 A.2d 302, 303.

II

The defendant's second contention is that, even assuming the trial justice was in essence predicating defendant's liability upon a quasi-contractual theory, his decision is still unsupported by competent evidence and is clearly erroneous.

The following discussion of quasi-contracts appears in 12 Am.Jur., Contracts, § 6 (1938) at pp. 503 to 504:

"* * * A quasi contract has no reference to the intentions or expressions of the parties. The obligation is imposed despite, and frequently in frustration of, their intention. For a quasi contract neither promise nor privity, real or imagined, is necessary. In quasi contracts the obligation arises, not from consent of the parties, as in the case of contracts, express or implied in fact, but from the law of natural immutable justice and equity. The act, or acts, from which the law implies the contract must, however, be voluntary. Where a case shows that it is the duty of the defendant to pay, the law imputes to him a promise to fulfil that obligation. The duty, which thus forms the foundation of a quasi-contractual obligation, is frequently based on the doctrine of unjust enrichment. * * *

"* * * The law will not imply a promise against the express declaration of the party to be charged, made at the time of the supposed undertaking, unless such party is under legal obligation paramount to his will to perform some duty, and he is not under such legal obligation unless there is a demand in equity and good conscience that he should perform the duty."

Therefore, the essential elements of a quasi-contract are a benefit conferred upon defendant by plaintiff, appreciation by defendant of such benefit, and acceptance and retention by defendant of such benefit under such circumstances that it would be inequitable to retain the benefit without payment of the value thereof. Home Savings Bank v. General Finance Corp., 10 Wis.2d 417, 103 N.W.2d 117, 81 A.L.R.2d 580.

The key question raised by this appeal with respect to the establishment of a quasi-contract is whether or not plaintiff was acting as a "volunteer" at the time he accepted the horse for boarding at his farm. There is a long line of authority which has clearly enunciated the general rule that "* * * if a performance is rendered by one person without any request by another, it is very unlikely that this person will be under a legal duty to pay compensation." 1 A Corbin, Contracts § 234.

The Restatement of Restitution, § 2 (1937) provides: "A person who officiously confers a benefit upon another is not entitled to restitution therefor." Comment a in the above-mentioned section states in part as follows:

"* * * Policy ordinarily requires that a person who has conferred a benefit * * * by way of giving another services * * * should not be permitted to require the other to pay therefor, unless the one conferring the benefit had a valid reason for so doing. A person is not required to deal with another unless he so desires and, ordinarily, a person should not be required to become an obligor unless he so desires."

Applying those principles to the facts in the case at bar it is clear that plaintiff cannot recover. The plaintiff's testimony on cross-examination is the only evidence in the record relating to what transpired between Kelly and him at the time the horse was accepted for boarding. The defendant's attorney asked plaintiff if he had any conversation with Kelly at that time, and plaintiff answered in substance that he had noticed that the horse was very lame and that Kelly had told him: "That's why they wouldn't accept him at Belmont Track." The plaintiff also testified that he had inquired of Kelly as to the ownership of "Bascom's Folly," and had been told that "Dr. Strauss made a deal and that's all I know." It further appears from the record that plaintiff acknowledged receipt of the horse by signing a uniform livestock bill of lading, which clearly indicated on its face that the horse in question had been consigned by defendant's trainer not to plaintiff, but to Dr. Strauss's trainer at Belmont Park. Knowing at the time he accepted the horse for boarding that a controversy surrounded its ownership, plaintiff could not reasonably expect remuneration from defendant, nor can it be said that defendant acquiesced in the conferment of a benefit upon him. The undisputed testimony was that defendant, upon receipt of plaintiff's first bill, immediately notified him that he was not the owner of "Bascom's Folly" and would not be responsible for its keep.

It is our judgment that the plaintiff was a mere volunteer who boarded and maintained "Bascom's Folly" at his own risk and with full knowledge that he might not be reimbursed for expenses he incurred incident thereto.

The plaintiff's appeal is denied and dismissed, the defendant's cross appeal is sustained, and the cause is remanded to the superior court for entry of judgment for the defendant.

[Footnotes omitted.]

NOTES

(1) What are plaintiff's theories of recovery? How do they differ?

(2) Suppose West personally delivered "Bascom's Folly" to Bailey's farm, but nothing was said specifically about Bailey caring for the horse or West paying for that care. Would West be liable? If so, on what theory? *quasi-contracts*

(3) What if Bailey found "Bascom's Folly" collapsed along side the highway, took him in and cared for him, and thereafter sought out West. Would the latter be responsible to Bailey for the care given the horse? If so, on what theory? See, generally, Wade, *Restitution for Benefits Conferred Without Request,* 19 Vand.L.Rev. 1183 (1966). "One who, without intent to act gratuitously, confers a measurable benefit upon another, is entitled to restitution, if he affords the other an opportunity to decline the benefit or else has as reasonable excuse for failing to do so. If the other refuses to receive the benefit, he is not

required to make restitution unless the actor justifiably performs for the other a duty imposed upon him by law." Id. at 1212.

(4) Contract is a theory of promissory liability. Without a promise, express or implied, there can be no contract. See Restatement (Second) § 1. But what is a promise? Consider the following attempts at a definition. What are the similarities? Differences?

> Restatement (First) § 1: "A promise is an undertaking, however expressed, either that something shall happen, or that something shall not happen, in the future."

> Sharp, *Promissory Liability,* 7 U.Chi.L.Rev. 1, 4–5 (1939): "What then is a promise? * * * As a matter of every day experience and common usage, a promise has something reliable about it. * * * It may be suggested that a promise is the maker's statement about his future conduct so made that the maker should expect the person to whom it is made mentally to rely on it as dependable. It will be observed that the maker's actual intention is not regarded as important and this is true at least in the courts. * * * Thus we say that the maker of a promise is one who ought to expect another to rely on his statement. * * * The person who says he has relied on another's work has a kind of burden of showing that the other was in the wrong. * * * He has to give affirmative reasons for deciding that the other has not acted in accordance with ordinary standards of business communication, in making his statement."

> Restatement (Second) § 2(1): "A promise is a manifestation of intention to act or refrain from acting in a specified way, so made as to justify a promisee in understanding that a commitment has been made."

See also C. Fried, Contract as Promise 9–14 (1981), who argues that a promise invokes a commitment to a future course of conduct that "absent our commitment is morally neutral." The force of a promise, then, is in the commitment not in what reliance it may induce.

Hamer v. Sidway

Court of Appeals of New York, 1891.
124 N.Y. 538, 27 N.E. 256.

Appeal from an order of the general term of the supreme court in the fourth judicial department, reversing a judgment entered on the decision of the court at special term in the county clerk's office of Chemung county on the 1st day of October, 1889. The plaintiff presented a claim to the executor of William E. Story, Sr., for $5,000 and interest from the 6th day of February, 1875. She acquired it through several mesne (intermediate) assignments from William E. Story, 2d. The claim being rejected by the executor, this action was brought. It appears that William E. Story, Sr., was the uncle of William E. Story, 2d; that at the celebration of the golden wedding of Samuel Story and wife, father and mother of William E. Story, Sr., on the 20th day of March, 1869, in the presence of the family and invited guests, he promised his nephew that if he would refrain from drinking, using tobacco, swearing, and playing cards or billiards for money until he became 21 years of age, he would pay him the sum of $5,000. The nephew assented thereto, and fully performed the conditions inducing the promise. When the nephew arrived at the age of 21 years, and on the 31st day of January, 1875, he wrote to his uncle, informing him that he had performed his part of the agreement, and had thereby become entitled to the sum of $5,000. The uncle received the letter, and a few days later, on the 6th day of February, he wrote and mailed to his nephew the following letter: "Buffalo, Feb. 6, 1875. W.E. Story, Jr.—Dear Nephew: Your letter of the 31st ult. came to hand all right, saying that you had lived up to the promise made to me several years ago. I have no doubt but you have, for which you shall have five thousand dollars, as I promised you. I had the money in the bank the day you was twenty-one years old that I intend for you, and you shall have the money certain. Now, Willie, I do not intend to interfere with this money in any way till I think you are capable of taking care of it, and the sooner that time comes the better it will please me. I would hate very much to have you start out in some adventure that you thought all right and lose this money in one year. The first five thousand dollars that I got together cost me a heap of hard work. You would hardly believe me when I tell you that to obtain this I shoved a jack-plane many a day, butchered three or four years, then came to this city, and, after three months' perseverance, I obtained a situation in a grocery store. I opened this store early, closed late, slept in the fourth story of a building in a room 30 by 40 feet, and not a human being in the building but myself. All this I done to live as cheap as I could to save something. I don't want you to take up with this kind of fare. I was here in the cholera season of '49 and '52, and the deaths averaged 80 to 125 daily, and plenty of small-pox. I wanted to go home, but Mr. Fisk, the gentleman I was working for, told me, if I left them, after it got healthy he probably would not want me. I stayed. All the money I have saved I know just how I got it. It did not come to me in any mysterious way, and the reason I speak of this is that money got in this way stops longer with a fellow that gets it with hard knocks than it does when he finds it. Willie, you are twenty-one, and you have many a thing to learn yet. This money you have earned much easier than I did, besides acquiring good habits at the same time, and you are quite welcome to the money. Hope you will make good use of it. I was ten long years getting this together after I was your age. Now, hoping this will be satisfactory, I stop. * * * Truly yours, W.E. Story. P.S. You can consider this money on interest." The nephew received the letter, and thereafter consented that the money should remain with his uncle in accordance with the terms and conditions of the letter. The uncle died on the 29th day of January, 1887, without having paid over to his nephew any portion of the said $5,000 and interest.

■ PARKER, J. The question which provoked the most discussion by counsel on this appeal, and which lies at the foundation of plaintiff's asserted right of recovery, is whether by virtue of a contract defendant's testator, William E. Story, became indebted to his nephew, William E. Story, 2d, on his twenty-first birthday in the sum of $5,000. The trial court found as a fact that "on the 20th day of March, 1869, * * * William E. Story agreed to and with William E. Story, 2d, that if he would refrain from drinking liquor, using tobacco, swearing, and playing cards or billiards for money until he should become twenty-one years of age, then he, the said William E. Story, would at that time pay him, the said William E. Story, 2d, the sum of $5,000 for such refraining, to which the said William E. Story, 2d, agreed,'' and that he "in all things fully performed his part of said agreement." The defendant contends that the contract was without consideration to support it, and therefore invalid. He asserts that the promisee, by refraining from the use of liquor and tobacco, was not harmed, but benefited; that that which he did was best for him to do, independently of his uncle's promise,—and insists that it follows that, unless the promisor was benefited, the contract was without consideration,—a contention which, if well founded, would seem to leave open for controversy in many cases whether that which the promisee did or omitted to do was in fact of such benefit to him as to leave no consideration to support the enforcement of the promisor's agreement. Such a rule could not be tolerated, and is without foundation in the law. The exchequer chamber in 1875 defined "consideration" as follows: "A valuable consideration, in the sense of the law, may consist either in some right, interest, profit, or benefit accruing to the one party, or some forbearance, detriment, loss, or responsibility given, suffered, or undertaken by the other." Courts "will not ask whether the thing which forms the consideration does in fact benefit the promisee or a third party, or is of any substantial value to any one. It is enough that something is promised, done, forborne, or suffered by the party to whom the promise is made as consideration for the promise made to him." Anson, Cont. 63. "In general a waiver of any legal right at the request of another party is a sufficient consideration for a promise." Pars. Cont. *444. "Any damage, or suspension, or forbearance of a right will be sufficient to sustain a promise." 2 Kent, Comm. (12th Ed.) *465. Pollock in his work on Contracts, (page 166,) after citing the definition given by the exchequer chamber, already quoted, says: "The second branch of this judicial description is really the most important one. 'Consideration' means not so much that one party is profiting as that the other abandons some legal right in the present, or limits his legal freedom of action in the future, as an inducement for the promise of the first." Now, applying this rule to the facts before us, the promisee used tobacco, occasionally drank liquor, and he had a legal right to do so. That right he abandoned for a period of years upon the strength of the promise of the testator that for such forbearance he would give him $5,000. We need not speculate on the effort which may have been required to give up the use of those stimulants. It is sufficient that he restricted his lawful freedom of action within certain prescribed limits upon the faith of his uncle's agreement, and now, having fully performed the conditions imposed, it is of no moment whether such performance actually proved a benefit to the promisor, and the court will not inquire into it; but, were it a proper subject of inquiry, we see nothing in this record that would permit a determination that the uncle was not benefited in a legal sense. Few cases have been found which may be said to be precisely in point, but such as have been, support the position we have taken. In Shadwell v. Shadwell, 9 C.B. (N.S.) 159, an uncle wrote to his nephew as follows: "My dear Lancey:

I am so glad to hear of your intended marriage with Ellen Nicholl, and, as I promised to assist you at starting, I am happy to tell you that I will pay you 150 pounds yearly during my life and until your annual income derived from your profession of a chancery barrister shall amount to 600 guineas, of which your own admission will be the only evidence that I shall receive or require. Your affectionate uncle, Charles Shadwell." It was held that the promise was binding, and made upon good consideration. * * * In Talbott v. Stemmons, 12 S.W.Rep. 297, (a Kentucky case, not yet officially report-ed,) the step-grandmother of the plaintiff made with him the following agreement: "I do promise and bind myself to give my grandson Albert R. Talbott $500 at my death if he will never take another chew of tobacco or smoke another cigar during my life, from this date up to my death; and if he breaks this pledge he is to refund double the amount to his mother." The executor of Mrs. Stemmons demurred to the complaint on the ground that the agreement was not based on a sufficient consideration. The demurrer was sustained, and an appeal taken therefrom to the court of appeals, where the decision of the court below was reversed. In the opinion of the court it is said that "the right to use and enjoy the use of tobacco was a right that belonged to the plaintiff, and not forbidden by law. The abandonment of its use may have saved him money, or contributed to his health; nevertheless, the surrender of that right caused the promise, and, having the right to contract with reference to the subject-matter, the abandonment of the use was a sufficient consideration to uphold the promise." * * * The order appealed from should be reversed, and the judgment of the special term affirmed, with costs payable out of the estate. All concur.

NOTES

(1) Restatement (Second) § 71:

(1) To constitute consideration, a performance or a return promise must be bargained for.

(2) A performance or return promise is bargained for if it is sought by the promisor in exchange for his promise and is given by the promisee in exchange for that promise.

(3) The performance may consist of (a) an act other than a promise, (b) a forbearance, or (c) the creation, modification, or destruction of a legal relation.

(4) The performance or return promise may be given to the promisor or to some other person. It may be given by the promisee or by some other person.

(2) *Enforceable Promise as Contract.* "Unfortunately, contract, like most of the basic terms constituting the intellectual tools of law, is conventionally defined in a circular fashion. By the most common definition, a contract is a promise or set of promises for the breach of which the law gives a remedy or the performance of which the law recognizes as a duty. This amounts to saying that a contract is a legally enforceable promise. But a promise is legally

enforceable only if it is a contract. Thus nothing less than the whole body of applicable precedents suffices to define the term 'contract.'

"Although the definition of contract does not help much in determining what expressions shall be held to impose legal obligations, it does direct attention to a promise as the starting point of inquiry. Both in popular and legal usage, a promise is an assurance, in whatever form of expression given, that a thing will or will not be done. While we must take care to distinguish between statements meant to express merely present intention and those meant to give an assurance as to a future event, this involves no more than the common difficulty of seeking precise meaning in the usually imprecise, and often careless, expressions of ordinary colloquy.

* * *

"However, the fact that a promise was given does not necessarily mean that a contract was made. It is clear that not every promise is legally enforceable. Much of the vast body of law in the field of contracts is concerned with determining which promises should be legally enforced. On the one hand, in a civilized community men must be able to assume that those with whom they deal will carry out their undertakings according to reasonable expectations. On the other hand, it is neither practical nor reasonable to expect full performance of every assurance given, whether it be thoughtless, casual and gratuitous, or deliberately and seriously made.

"The test that has been developed by the common law for determining the enforceability of promises is the doctrine of consideration. This is a crude and not altogether successful attempt to generalize the conditions under which promises will be legally enforced. Consideration requires that a contractual promise be the product of a bargain. However, in this usage, 'bargain' does not mean an exchange of things of equivalent, or any, value. It means a negotiation resulting in the voluntary assumption of an obligation by one party upon condition of an act or forbearance by the other. Consideration thus insures that the promise enforced as a contract is not accidental, casual, or gratuitous, but has been uttered intentionally as a result of some deliberation, manifested by reciprocal bargaining or negotiation. In this view, the requirement of consideration is no mere technicality, historical anachronism, or arbitrary formality. It is an attempt to be as reasonable as we can in deciding which promises constitute contracts. Although the doctrine has been criticized, no satisfactory substitute has been suggested. It is noteworthy that the civil law has a corresponding doctrine of 'causa' which, to the eye of a common-law lawyer, is not much different than consideration.

"Consideration, as essential evidence of the parties' intent to create a legal obligation, must be something adopted and regarded by the parties as such. Thus, the same thing may be consideration or not, as it is dealt with by the parties. In substance, a contractual promise must be of the logical form: 'If . . . (consideration is given) . . . then I promise that. . . .' Of course, the substance may be expressed in any form of words, but essentially this is the logical structure of those promises enforced by the law as contracts."

Loevinger, J. in Baehr v. Penn–O–Tex Oil Corporation, 258 Minn. 533, 537–39, 104 N.W.2d 661, 664–66 (1960).

(3) Was there equivalency of exchange in *Hamer?* Did the promisor gain a pecuniary advantage? Did he derive any "benefit" from the transaction at all, or is enforcement predicated solely upon "detriment" to the promisee? In what way was plaintiff's conduct detrimental?

(4) *Economic Functions of Contract Law.* In the view of Professor (now Judge) Richard A. Posner, the law of contracts performs three economic functions: first, it furnishes "incentives for value-maximizing conduct in the future," i.e., conduct that exploits economic resources in such a way that human satisfaction as measured by aggregate consumer willingness to pay for goods and services is maximized; second, it reduces the "complexity and hence cost of transactions by supplying a set of normal terms which, in the absence of a law of contracts, the parties would have to negotiate expressly"; and third, it furnishes "prospective transacting parties with information concerning the many contingencies that may defeat an exchange, and hence to assist them in planning their exchange sensibly." These economic functions are supported by the doctrine of consideration, which is used to "deny liability for breach of a promise ... where there is no exchange and where, therefore, enforcement of the promise would not advance the economic purpose of the law of contracts which is to facilitate exchange. A truly gratuitous, nonreciprocal promise to confer a benefit is not a part of the process by which resources are moved, through a series of exchanges, into successively more valuable uses." R. Posner, Economic Analysis of Law 68–71 (2d ed. 1977).

(5) *Contract as a Basic Social Institution.* After discussing the "emotive and symbolic power" of the idea of contract and the "moral imperative" that clusters about the phrase *"pacta sunt servanda,"* that "obligations freely agreed to are to be honored and performed," Professor Harry W. Jones has this to say about contract as a "basic social institution, one comparable in importance to such other pervading social institutions as property, the family, even the institution of representative government":

> In a society like ours, people live not by birds in the hand but by promises: for example, anyone's job is an exchange of promises, by him to work and by his employer to pay agreed or understood wages. Investments are essentially promises by corporate powerholders to manage a business in proper ways and to pay dividends as earned. A bank account is a promise to hold and return money deposited; even money is a promise, though rather less reliable than in earlier days, by government to pay something on due presentation.... John Kenneth Galbraith may or may not have been right to characterize our national community as *The Affluent Society;* he would have said something unquestionably true, and perhaps of even greater economic significance, if he had called us the *promissory* society. A promissory society, by definition, is one energized and bound together by the institution of contract.... The law of contract—and "law of contract" here includes what we elsewhere break up into such segments as commercial transactions, partnerships, corporations, labor law and many more—has as its ultimate purpose the security of those reasonable expectations that arise from agreement between seller and buyer, borrower and depositor, stockholder and corporation, employer and organized employees.

Jones, *The Jurisprudence of Contracts,* 44 U.Cin.L.Rev. 43, 47–48 (1975).

Ricketts v. Scothorn

Supreme Court of Nebraska, 1898.
57 Neb. 51, 77 N.W. 365.

■ SULLIVAN, J. In the district court of Lancaster county the plaintiff Katie Scothorn recovered judgment against the defendant Andrew D. Ricketts, as executor of the last will and testament of John C. Ricketts, deceased. The action was based upon a promissory note, of which the following is a copy:

"May the first, 1891. I promise to pay to Katie Scothorn on demand, $2,000, to be at 6 per cent per annum. J.C. Ricketts."

In the petition the plaintiff alleges that the consideration for the execution of the note was that she should surrender her employment as bookkeeper for Mayor Bros. and cease to work for a living. She also alleges that the note was given to induce her to abandon her occupation, and that, relying on it, and on the annual interest, as a means of support, she gave up the employment in which she was then engaged. These allegations of the petition are denied by the executor. The material facts are undisputed. They are as follows: John C. Ricketts, the maker of the note, was the grandfather of the plaintiff. Early in May,—presumably on the day the note bears date,—he called on her at the store where she was working. What transpired between them is thus described by Mr. Flodene, one of the plaintiff's witnesses:

A. Well the old gentleman came in there one morning about 9 o'clock,—probably a little before or a little after, but early in the morn-ing,—and he unbuttoned his vest and took out a piece of paper in the shape of a note; that is the way it looked to me; and he says to Miss Scothorn, "I have fixed out something that you have not got to work any more." He says, "None of my grandchildren work and you don't have to."

Q. Where was she?

A. She took the piece of paper and kissed him; and kissed the old gentleman and commenced to cry.

It seems Miss Scothorn immediately notified her employer of her intention to quit work and that she did soon after abandon her occupation. The mother of the plaintiff was a witness and testified that she had a conversation with her father, Mr. Ricketts, shortly after the note was executed in which he informed her that he had given the note to the plaintiff to enable her to quit work; that none of his grandchildren worked and he did not think she ought to. For something more than a year the plaintiff was without an occupation; but in September, 1892, with the consent of her grandfather, and by his assistance, she secured a position as bookkeeper with Messrs. Funke & Ogden. On June 8, 1894, Mr. Ricketts died. He had paid one year's interest on the note, and a short time before his death expressed regret that he had not been able to pay the balance. In the summer or fall of 1892 he stated to his daughter, Mrs. Scothorn, that if he could sell his farm in Ohio he would pay the note out of the proceeds. He at no time repudiated the obligation. We quite agree with counsel for the defendant that upon this evidence there was nothing to submit to the jury, and that a verdict should have been directed peremptorily for one of the parties. The testimony of Flodene and Mrs. Scothorn, taken together, conclusively establishes the fact that the note was not given in consideration of the plaintiff pursuing, or agreeing to pursue, any particular line of conduct. There was no promise on the part of the plaintiff to do or refrain from doing anything. Her right to the money promised in the note was not made to depend upon an abandonment of her employment with Mayer Bros. and future abstention from like service. Mr. Ricketts made no condition, requirement, or request. He exacted no *quid pro quo*. He gave the note as a gratuity and looked for nothing in return. So far as the evidence discloses, it was his purpose to place the plaintiff in a position of independence where she could work or remain idle as she might choose. The abandonment by Miss Scothorn of her position as bookkeeper was altogether voluntary. It was not an act done in fulfillment of any contract obligation assumed when she accepted the note. The instrument in suit being given without any valuable consideration, was nothing more than a promise to make a gift in the future of the sum of money therein named. Ordinarily, such promises are not enforceable even when put in the form of a promissory note. (Kirkpatrick v. Taylor, 43 Ill. 207; Phelps v. Phelps, 28 Barb. [N.Y.] 121; Johnston v. Griest, 85 Ind. 503; Fink v. Cox, 18 Johns. [N.Y.] 145.) But it has often been held that an action on a note given to a church, college, or other like institution, upon the faith of which money has been expended or obligations incurred, could not be successfully defended on the ground of a want of consideration. (Barnes v. Perine, 12 N.Y. 18; Philomath College v. Hartless, 6 Ore. 158; Thompson v. Mercer County, 40 Ill. 379; Irwin v. Lombard University, 56 O.St. 9.) In this class of cases the note in suit is nearly always spoken of as a gift or donation, but the decision is generally put on the ground that the expenditure of money or assumption of liability by the donee, on the faith of the promise, constitutes a valuable and sufficient consideration. It seems to us that the true reason is the preclusion of the defendant, under the doctrine of estoppel, to deny the consideration. Such seems to be the view of the matter taken by the supreme court of Iowa in the case of Simpson Centenary College v. Tuttle, 71 Ia. 596, where Rothrock, J., speaking for the court, said: "Where a note, however, is based on a promise to give for the support of the objects referred to, it may still be open to this defense [want of consideration], unless it shall appear that the donee has, prior to any revocation, entered into engagements or made expenditures based on such promise, so that he must suffer loss or injury if the note is not paid. This is based on the equitable principle that, after allowing the donee to incur obligations on the faith that the note would be paid, the donor would be estopped from pleading want of consideration." And in the case of Reimensnyder v. Gans, 110 Pa.St. 17, 2 Atl.Rep. 425, which was an action on a note given as a donation to a charitable object, the court said: "The fact is that, as we may see from the case of Ryerss v. Trustees, 33 Pa.St. 114, a contract of the kind here involved is enforceable rather by way of estoppel than on the ground of consideration in the original undertaking." It has been held that a note given in expectation of the payee performing certain services, but without any contract binding him to serve, will not support an action. (Hulse v. Hulse, 84 Eng.Com.Law 709.) But when the payee changes his position to his disadvantage, in reliance on the promise, a right of action does arise. (McClure v. Wilson, 43 Ill. 356; Trustees v. Garvey, 53 Ill. 401.)

Under the circumstances of this case is there an equitable estoppel which ought to preclude the defendant from alleging that the note in controversy is lacking in one of the essential elements of a valid contract? We think there is. An estoppel *in pais* is defined to be "a right arising from acts, admissions, or conduct which have induced a change of position in accordance with the real or apparent intention of the party against whom they are alleged." Mr. Pomeroy has formulated the following definition: "Equitable estoppel is the effect of the voluntary conduct of a party whereby he is absolutely precluded, both at law and in equity, from asserting rights which might perhaps have otherwise existed, either of property, or contract, or of remedy, as against another person who in good faith relied upon such conduct, and has been led thereby to change his position for the worse, and who on his part acquires some corresponding right either of property, of contract, or of remedy." (2 Pomeroy, Equity Jurisprudence 804.) According to the undisputed proof, as shown by the record before us, the plaintiff was a working girl, holding a position in which she earned a salary of $10 per week. Her grandfather, desiring to put her in a position of independence, gave her the note, accompanying it with the remark that his other grandchildren did not work, and that she would not be obliged to work any longer. In effect he suggested that she might abandon her employment and rely in the future upon the bounty which he promised. He, doubtless, desired that she should give up her occupation, but whether he did or not, it is entirely certain that he contemplated such action on her part as a reasonable and probable consequence of his gift. Having intentionally influenced the plaintiff to alter her position for the worse on the faith of the note being paid when due, it would be grossly inequitable to permit the maker, or his executor, to resist payment on the ground that the promise was given without consideration. The petition charges the elements of an equitable estoppel, and the evidence conclusively establishes them. If errors intervened at the trial they could not have been prejudicial. A verdict for the defendant would be unwarranted. The judgment is right and is

Affirmed.

NOTES

(1) In *Ricketts v. Scothorn*, there was no consideration for the grandfather's promise. Katie's act of quitting her job was not bargained for and given in exchange for the written promise to pay $2,000 plus interest. The court, however, concluded that grandfather's executor was estopped or precluded from raising the defense of "no consideration." Why? Because grandfather's promise induced reliance by Katie that made it inequitable for the executor later to claim that there was no consideration. As a result, the promise was enforced in full as if there was consideration.

There are two difficulties with this analysis. First the analysis tends to confuse two types of estoppel, "equitable" and "promissory." As one court put it: "Equitable estoppel ... is based upon a representation of existing or past facts, while promissory estoppel requires the existence of a promise.... Equitable estoppel ... is available only as a 'shield' or defense, while promissory estoppel can be used as a 'sword' in a cause of action for damages." Klinke v. Famous Recipe Fried Chicken, Inc., 94 Wash.2d 255, 616 P.2d 644, 646 (1980). Second, the consequence of the confusion is that some courts have treated reliance induced by a promise as a reason to foreclose an attack on the enforceability of the promise and to limit the remedy to the loss suffered in reliance. See, e.g., Wheeler v. White, 398 S.W.2d 93 (Tex.1965). A more affirmative statement of "promissory" estoppel appears in Section 90 of Restatement (Second):

> A promise which the promisor should reasonably expect to induce action or forbearance on the part of the promisee or a third person and which does induce such action or forbearance is binding if injustice can be avoided only by enforcement of the promise. The remedy granted for breach may be limited as justice requires.

(2) How would *Ricketts* be decided under Section 90?

(3) Was there "agreement" here? Can there ever be contractual obligation without an agreement?

(4) Can the result in *Ricketts,* where the plaintiff's conduct did not benefit the defendant, be reconciled with the results in *Hamer v. Sidway*, where the defendant was benefited in some respect by the plaintiff's conduct?

Williams v. Walker–Thomas Furniture Co.

District of Columbia Court of Appeals, 1964.
198 A.2d 914.

■ QUINN, ASSOCIATE JUDGE. Appellant, a person of limited education separated from her husband, is maintaining herself and her seven children by means of public assistance. During the period 1957–1962 she had a continuous course of dealings with appellee from which she purchased many household articles on the installment plan. These included sheets, curtains, rugs, chairs, a chest of drawers, beds, mattresses, a washing machine, and a stereo set. In 1963 appellee filed a complaint in replevin for possession of all the items purchased by appellant, alleging that her payments were in default and that it retained title to the goods according to the sales contracts. By the writ of replevin appellee obtained a bed, chest of drawers, washing machine, and the stereo set. After hearing testimony and examining the contracts, the trial court entered judgment for appellee.

Appellant's principal contentions on appeal are (1) there was a lack of meeting of the minds, and (2) the contracts were against public policy.

Appellant signed fourteen contracts in all. They were approximately six inches in length and each contained a long paragraph in extremely fine print. One of the sentences in this paragraph provided that payments, after the first purchase, were to be prorated on all purchases then outstanding.

Mathematically, this had the effect of keeping a balance due on all items until the time balance was completely eliminated. It meant that title to the first purchase, remained in appellee until the fourteenth purchase, made some five years later, was fully paid.

At trial appellant testified that she understood the agreements to mean that when payments on the running account were sufficient to balance the amount due on an individual item, the item became hers. She testified that most of the purchases were made at her home; that the contracts were signed in blank; that she did not read the instruments; and that she was not provided with a copy. She admitted, however, that she did not ask anyone to read or explain the contracts to her.

We have stated that "one who refrains from reading a contract and in conscious ignorance of its terms voluntarily assents thereto will not be relieved from his bad bargain." Bob Wilson, Inc. v. Swann, D.C.Mun.App., 168 A.2d 198, 199 (1961). "One who signs a contract has a duty to read it and is obligated according to its terms." Hollywood Credit Clothing Co. v. Gibson, D.C.App., 188 A.2d 348, 349 (1963). "It is as much the duty of a person who cannot read the language in which a contract is written to have someone read it to him before he signs it, as it is the duty of one who can read to peruse it himself before signing it." Stern v. Moneyweight Scale Co., 42 App.D.C. 162, 165 (1914).

A careful review of the record shows that appellant's assent was not obtained "by fraud or even misrepresentation falling short of fraud." Hollywood Credit Clothing Co. v. Gibson, supra. This is not a case of mutual misunderstanding but a unilateral mistake. Under these circumstances, appellant's first contention is without merit.

Appellant's second argument presents a more serious question. The record reveals that prior to the last purchase appellant had reduced the balance in her account to $164. The last purchase, a stereo set, raised the balance due to $678. Significantly, at the time of this and the preceding purchases, appellee was aware of appellant's financial position. The reverse side of the stereo contract listed the name of appellant's social worker and her $218 monthly stipend from the government. Nevertheless, with full knowledge that appellant had to feed, clothe and support both herself and seven children on this amount, appellee sold her a $514 stereo set.

We cannot condemn too strongly appellee's conduct. It raises serious questions of sharp practice and irresponsible business dealings. A review of the legislation in the District of Columbia affecting retail sales and the pertinent decisions of the highest court in this jurisdiction disclose, however, no ground upon which this court can declare the contracts in question contrary to public policy. We note that were the Maryland Retail Installment Sales Act, Art. 83 §§ 128–153, or its equivalent, in force in the District of Columbia, we could grant appellant appropriate relief. We think Congress should consider corrective legislation to protect the public from such exploitive contracts as were utilized in the case at bar.

Affirmed.

Williams v. Walker–Thomas Furniture Co.

United States Court of Appeals, District of Columbia Circuit, 1965.
121 U.S.App.D.C. 315, 350 F.2d 445.

■ J. SKELLY WRIGHT, CIRCUIT JUDGE. Appellee, Walker–Thomas Furniture Company, operates a retail furniture store in the District of Columbia. During the period from 1957 to 1962 each appellant in these cases purchased a number of household items from Walker–Thomas, for which payment was to be made in installments. The terms of each purchase were contained in a printed form contract which set forth the value of the purchased item and purported to lease the item to appellant for a stipulated monthly rent payment. The contract then provided, in substance, that title would remain in Walker–Thomas until the total of all the monthly payments made equaled the stated value of the item, at which time appellants could take title. In the event of a default in the payment of any monthly installment, Walker–Thomas could repossess the item.

The contract further provided that "the amount of each periodical installment payment to be made by [purchaser] to the Company under this present lease shall be inclusive of and not in addition to the amount of each installment payment to be made by [purchaser] under such prior leases, bills or accounts; *and all payments now and hereafter made by [purchaser] shall be credited pro rata on all outstanding leases, bills and accounts* due the Company by [purchaser] at the time each such payment is made." (Emphasis added.) The effect of this rather obscure provision was to keep a balance due on every item purchased until the balance due on all items, whenever purchased, was liquidated. As a result, the debt incurred at the time of purchase of each item was secured by the right to repossess all the items previously purchased by the same purchaser, and each new item purchased automatically became subject to a security interest arising out of the previous dealings.

On May 12, 1962, appellant Thorne purchased an item described as a Daveno, three tables, and two lamps, having total stated value of $391.10. Shortly thereafter, he defaulted on his monthly payments and appellee sought to replevy all the items purchased since the first transaction in 1958. Similarly, on April 17, 1962, appellant Williams bought a stereo set of stated value of $514.95.* She too defaulted shortly thereafter, and appellee sought to replevy all the items purchased since December, 1957. The Court of General Sessions granted judgment for appellee. The District of Columbia Court of Appeals affirmed, and we granted appellants' motion for leave to appeal to this court.

Appellants' principal contention, rejected by both the trial and the appellate courts below, is that these contracts, or at least some of them, are unconscionable and, hence, not enforceable. In its opinion in Williams v. Walker–Thomas Furniture Company, 198 A.2d 914, 916 (1964), the District

---

* At the time of this purchase her account showed a balance of $164 still owing from her prior purchases. The total of all the purchases made over the years in question came to $1,800. The total payments amounted to $1,400. [Footnote of the court.]

of Columbia Court of Appeals explained its rejection of this contention as follows:

[The court quoted the last two paragraphs of Judge Quinn's opinion, reported supra.]

We do not agree that the court lacked the power to refuse enforcement to contracts found to be unconscionable. In other jurisdictions, it has been held as a matter of common law that unconscionable contracts are not enforceable. While no decision of this court so holding has been found, the notion that an unconscionable bargain should not be given full enforcement is by no means novel. In Scott v. United States, 79 U.S. (12 Wall.) 443, 445, 20 L.Ed. 438 (1870), the Supreme Court stated:

"* * * If a contract be unreasonable and unconscionable, but not void for fraud, a court of law will give to the party who sues for its breach damages, not according to its letter, but only such as he is equitably entitled to. * * *"

Since we have never adopted or rejected such a rule, the question here presented is actually one of first impression.

Congress has recently enacted the Uniform Commercial Code, which specifically provides that the court may refuse to enforce a contract which it finds to be unconscionable at the time it was made. 28 D.C.Code § 2–302 (Supp. IV 1965). The enactment of this section, which occurred subsequent to the contracts here in suit, does not mean that the common law of the District of Columbia was otherwise at the time of enactment, nor does it preclude the court from adopting a similar rule in the exercise of its powers to develop the common law for the District of Columbia. In fact, in view of the absence of prior authority on the point, we consider the congressional adoption of § 2–302 persuasive authority for following the rationale of the cases from which the section is explicitly derived. Accordingly, we hold that where the element of unconscionability is present at the time a contract is made, the contract should not be enforced.

Unconscionability has generally been recognized to include an absence of meaningful choice on the part of one of the parties together with contract terms which are unreasonably favorable to the other party. Whether a meaningful choice is present in a particular case can only be determined by consideration of all the circumstances surrounding the transaction. In many cases the meaningfulness of the choice is negated by a gross inequality of bargaining power. The manner in which the contract was entered is also relevant to this consideration. Did each party to the contract, considering his obvious education or lack of it, have a reasonable opportunity to understand the terms of the contract, or were the important terms hidden in a maze of fine print and minimized by deceptive sales practices? Ordinarily, one who signs an agreement without full knowledge of its terms might be held to assume the risk that he has entered a one-sided bargain. But when a party of little bargaining power, and hence little real choice, signs a commercially unreasonable contract with little or no knowledge of its terms, it is hardly likely that his consent, or even an objective manifestation of his consent, was ever given to all the terms. In such a case the usual rule that the terms of the agreement are not to be questioned should be abandoned and the court should consider whether the terms of the contract are so unfair that enforcement should be withheld.

In determining reasonableness or fairness, the primary concern must be with the terms of the contract considered in light of the circumstances existing when the contract was made. The test is not simple, nor can it be mechanically applied. The terms are to be considered "in the light of the general commercial background and the commercial needs of the particular trade or case." Corbin suggests the test as being whether the terms are "so extreme as to appear unconscionable according to the mores and business practices of the time and place.". . . . We think this formulation correctly states the test to be applied in those cases where no meaningful choice was exercised upon entering the contract.

Because the trial court and the appellate court did not feel that enforcement could be refused, no findings were made on the possible unconscionability of the contracts in these cases. Since the record is not sufficient for our deciding the issue as a matter of law, the cases must be remanded to the trial court for further proceedings.

So ordered.

■ DANAHER, CIRCUIT JUDGE (dissenting). The District of Columbia Court of Appeals obviously was as unhappy about the situation here presented as any of us can possibly be. Its opinion in the *Williams* case, quoted in the majority text, concludes: "We think Congress should consider corrective legislation to protect the public from such exploitive contracts as were utilized in the case at bar."

My view is thus summed up by an able court which made no finding that there had actually been sharp practice. Rather the appellant seems to have known precisely where she stood.

There are many aspects of public policy here involved. What is a luxury to some may seem an outright necessity to others. Is public oversight to be required of the expenditures of relief funds? A washing machine, e.g., in the hands of a relief client might become a fruitful source of income. Many relief clients may well need credit, and certain business establishments will take long chances on the sale of items, expecting their pricing policies will afford a degree of protection commensurate with the risk. Perhaps a remedy when necessary will be found within the provisions of the "Loan Shark" law, D.C.Code §§ 26–601 et seq. (1961).

I mention such matters only to emphasize the desirability of a cautious approach to any such problem, particularly since the law for so long has allowed parties such great latitude in making their own contracts. I dare say there must annually be thousands upon thousands of installment credit transactions in this jurisdiction, and one can only speculate as to the effect that these cases will have.

* * *

[Some footnotes omitted.] *no turn of the lower court because of their decision of they weren't enough evidence to make that decision*

NOTES

(1) Did Judge Wright hold that the contracts were unconscionable at the time of contracting? See UCC 2–302 [UCC 2–105 (1997)].

(2) Try to describe the views of Judge Quinn in the lower court and Judges Wright and Danaher in the Court of Appeals on whether a court should declare a contract unconscionable. What are the similarities and differences?

(3) State as clearly as you can Judge Wright's test for determining whether a contract is unconscionable. Would you expect the outcome of its application to vary with whether the contract was between a professional business person and an individual consumer or two business people?

(4) "Properly understood, [the principle of freedom of contract] does not require a court to enforce every contract brought before it. It does, however, demand that the reasons invoked for not enforcing the contract be of one of two sorts. Either there must be proof of some defect in the process of contract formation (be it duress, fraud or undue influence); or there must be, but only within narrow limits, some incompetence of the party against whom the agreement is to be enforced. The doctrine of unconscionability is important in both these respects because it can, if wisely applied, allow the courts to police these two types of problems, and thereby improve the general administration of the contract law. Yet when the doctrine of unconscionability is used in its substantive dimension, be it in a commercial or consumer context, it serves only to undercut a private right of contract in a manner that is apt to do more social harm than good. The result of the analysis is the same even if we view the question of unconscionability from the lofty perspective of public policy. '(I)f there is one thing which more than another public policy requires, it is that men of full age and competent understanding shall have the utmost liberty of contracting, and that their contracts when entered into freely and voluntarily shall be held sacred and shall be enforced by Courts of justice.' (Printing and Numerical Registering Co. v. Sampson, L.R. 19 Eq. 462, 465 (1875))." Epstein, *Unconscionability: A Critical Reappraisal*, 18 J.Law & Econ. 293, 315 (1975).

We will return to these challenging problems in Chapter Four, Section 2(D).

Sullivan v. O'Connor

Supreme Judicial Court of Massachusetts, 1973.
363 Mass. 579, 296 N.E.2d 183.

■ KAPLAN, JUSTICE. The plaintiff patient secured a jury verdict of $13,500 against the defendant surgeon for breach of contract in respect to an operation upon the plaintiff's nose. The substituted consolidated bill of exceptions presents questions about the correctness of the judge's instructions on the issue of damages.

The declaration was in two counts. In the first count, the plaintiff alleged that she, as patient, entered into a contract with the defendant, a surgeon, wherein the defendant promised to perform plastic surgery on her nose and thereby to enhance her beauty and improve her appearance; that he performed the surgery but failed to achieve the promised result; rather the result of the surgery was to disfigure and deform her nose, to cause her pain in body and mind, and to subject her to other damage and expense. The second count, based on the same transaction, was in the conventional form for malpractice, charging that the defendant had been guilty of negligence in performing the surgery. Answering, the defendant entered a general denial.

On the plaintiff's demand, the case was tried by jury. At the close of the evidence, the judge put to the jury, as special questions, the issues of liability under the two counts, and instructed them accordingly. The jury returned a verdict for the plaintiff on the contract count, and for the defendant on the negligence count. The judge then instructed the jury on the issue of damages.

As background to the instructions and the parties' exceptions, we mention certain facts as the jury could find them. The plaintiff was a professional entertainer, and this was known to the defendant. The agreement was as alleged in the declaration. More particularly, judging from exhibits, the plaintiff's nose had been straight, but long and prominent; the defendant undertook by two operations to reduce its prominence and somewhat to shorten it, thus making it more pleasing in relation to the plaintiff's other features. Actually the plaintiff was obliged to undergo three operations, and her appearance was worsened. Her nose now had a concave line to about the midpoint, at which it became bulbous; viewed frontally, the nose from bridge to midpoint was flattened and broadened, and the two sides of the tip had lost symmetry. This configuration evidently could not be improved by further surgery. The plaintiff did not demonstrate, however, that her change of appearance had resulted in loss of employment. Payments by the plaintiff covering the defendant's fee and hospital expenses were stipulated at $622.65.

The judge instructed the jury, first, that the plaintiff was entitled to recover her out-of-pocket expenses incident to the operations. Second, she could recover the damages flowing directly, naturally, proximately, and foreseeably from the defendant's breach of promise. These would comprehend damages for any disfigurement of the plaintiff's nose—that is, any change of appearance for the worse—including the effects of the consciousness of such disfigurement on the plaintiff's mind, and in this connection the jury should consider the nature of the plaintiff's profession. Also consequent upon the defendant's breach, and compensable, were the pain and suffering involved in the third operation, but not in the first two. As there was no proof that any loss of earnings by the plaintiff resulted from the breach, that element should not enter into the calculation of damages.

By his exceptions the defendant contends that the judge erred in allowing the jury to take into account anything but the plaintiff's out-of-pocket expenses (presumably at the stipulated amount). The defendant excepted to the judge's refusal of his request for a general charge to that effect, and, more specifically, to the judge's refusal of a charge that the plaintiff could not recover for pain and suffering connected with the third operation or for impairment of the plaintiff's appearance and associated mental distress.

The plaintiff on her part excepted to the judge's refusal of a request to charge that the plaintiff could recover the difference in value between the nose as promised and the nose as it appeared after the operations. However, the plaintiff in her brief expressly waives this exception and others made by her in case this court overrides the defendant's exceptions; thus she would be content to hold the jury's verdict in her favor.

We conclude that the defendant's exceptions should be overruled.

It has been suggested on occasion that agreements between patients and physicians by which the physician undertakes to effect a cure or to bring about a given result should be declared unenforceable on grounds of public policy. See Guilmet v. Campbell, 385 Mich. 57, 76, 188 N.W.2d 601 (dissenting opinion). But there are many decisions recognizing and enforcing such contracts, see annotation, 43 A.L.R.3d 1221, 1225, 1229–1233, and the law of Massachusetts has treated them as valid, although we have had no decision meeting head on the contention that they should be denied legal sanction. . . . These causes of action are, however, considered a little suspect, and thus we find courts straining sometimes to read the pleadings as sounding only in tort for negligence, and not in contract for breach of promise, despite sedulous efforts by the pleaders to pursue the latter theory. . . .

It is not hard to see why the courts should be unenthusiastic or skeptical about the contract theory. Considering the uncertainties of medical science and the variations in the physical and psychological conditions of individual patients, doctors can seldom in good faith promise specific results. Therefore it is unlikely that physicians of even average integrity will in fact make such promises. Statements of opinion by the physician with some optimistic coloring are a different thing, and may indeed have therapeutic value. But patients may transform such statements into firm promises in their own minds, especially when they have been disappointed in the event, and testify in that sense to sympathetic juries.[2] If actions for breach of promise can be readily maintained, doctors, so it is said, will be frightened into practicing "defensive medicine." On the other hand, if these actions were outlawed, leaving only the possibility of suits for malpractice, there is fear that the public might be exposed to the enticements of charlatans, and confidence in the profession might ultimately be shaken. See Miller, The Contractual Liability of Physicians and Surgeons, 1953 Wash.L.Q. 413, 416–423. The law has taken the middle of the road

---

2. Judicial skepticism about whether a promise was in fact made derives also from the possibility that the truth has been tortured to give the plaintiff the advantage of the longer period of limitations sometimes available for actions on contract as distinguished from those in tort or for malpractice. See Lillich, The Malpractice Statute of Limitations in New York and Other Jurisdictions, 47 Cornell L.Q. 339; annotation, 80 A.L.R.2d 368.

position of allowing actions based on alleged contract, but insisting on clear proof. Instructions to the jury may well stress this requirement and point to tests of truth, such as the complexity or difficulty of an operation as bearing on the probability that a given result was promised. See annotation, 43 A.L.R.3d 1225, 1225–1227.

If an action on the basis of contract is allowed, we have next the question of the measure of damages to be applied where liability is found. Some cases have taken the simple view that the promise by the physician is to be treated like an ordinary commercial promise, and accordingly that the successful plaintiff is entitled to a standard measure of recovery for breach of contract—"compensatory" ("expectancy") damages, an amount intended to put the plaintiff in the position he would be in if the contract had been performed, or, presumably, at the plaintiff's election, "restitution" damages, an amount corresponding to any benefit conferred by the plaintiff upon the defendant in the performance of the contract disrupted by the defendant's breach. See Restatement: Contracts § 329 and comment a, §§ 347, 384(1). Thus in Hawkins v. McGee, 84 N.H. 114, 146 A. 641, the defendant doctor was taken to have promised the plaintiff to convert his damaged hand by means of an operation into a good or perfect hand, but the doctor so operated as to damage the hand still further. The court, following the usual expectancy formula, would have asked the jury to estimate and award to the plaintiff the difference between the value of a good or perfect hand, as promised, and the value of the hand after the operation. (The same formula would apply, although the dollar result would be less, if the operation had neither worsened nor improved the condition of the hand.) If the plaintiff had not yet paid the doctor his fee, that amount would be deducted from the recovery. There could be no recovery for the pain and suffering of the operation, since that detriment would have been incurred even if the operation had been successful; one can say that this detriment was not "caused" by the breach. But where the plaintiff by reason of the operation was put to more pain than he would have had to endure, had the doctor performed as promised, he should be compensated for that difference as a proper part of his expectancy recovery. It may be noted that on an alternative count for malpractice the plaintiff in the *Hawkins* case had been nonsuited; but on ordinary principles this could not affect the contract claim, for it is hardly a defence to a breach of contract that the promisor acted innocently and without negligence. The New Hampshire court further refined the *Hawkins* analysis in McQuaid v. Michou, 85 N.H. 299, 157 A. 881, all in the direction of treating the patient-physician cases on the ordinary footing of expectancy. See McGee v. United States Fid. & Guar. Co., 53 F.2d 953 (1st Cir.) (later development in the *Hawkins* case); . . . .

Other cases, including a number in New York, without distinctly repudiating the *Hawkins* type of analysis, have indicated that a different and generally more lenient measure of damages is to be applied in patient-physician actions based on breach of alleged special agreements to effect a cure, attain a stated result, or employ a given medical method. This measure is expressed in somewhat variant ways, but the substance is that the plaintiff is to recover any expenditures made by him and for other detriment (usually not specifically described in the opinions) following proximately and foreseeably upon the defendant's failure to carry out his promise. Robins v. Finestone, 308 N.Y. 543, 546, 127 N.E.2d 330; . . . . Stewart v. Rudner, 349 Mich. 459, 465–473, 84 N.W.2d 816. Cf. Carpenter v. Moore, 51 Wash.2d 795, 322 P.2d 125. This, be it noted, is not a "restitution" measure, for it is not limited to restoration of the benefit conferred on the defendant (the fee paid) but includes other expenditures, for example, amounts paid for medicine and nurses; so also it would seem according to its logic to take in damages for any worsening of the plaintiff's condition due to the breach. Nor is it an "expectancy" measure, for it does not appear to contemplate recovery of the whole difference in value between the condition as promised and the condition actually resulting from the treatment. Rather the tendency of the formulation is to put the plaintiff back in the position he occupied just before the parties entered upon the agreement, to compensate him for the detriments he suffered in reliance upon the agreement. This kind of intermediate pattern of recovery for breach of contract is discussed in the suggestive article by Fuller and Perdue, The Reliance Interest in Contract Damages, 46 Yale L.J. 52, 373, where the authors show that, although not attaining the currency of the standard measures, a "reliance" measure has for special reasons been applied by the courts in a variety of settings, including noncommercial settings. See 46 Yale L.J. at 396–401.[4]

For breach of the patient-physician agreements under consideration, a recovery limited to restitution seems plainly too meager, if the agreements are to be enforced at all. On the other hand, an expectancy recovery may well be excessive. The factors, already mentioned, which have made the cause of action somewhat suspect, also suggest moderation as to the breadth of the recovery that should be permitted. Where, as in the case at bar and in a number of the reported cases the doctor has been absolved of negligence by the trier, an expectancy measure may be thought harsh. We should recall here that the fee paid by the patient to the doctor for the alleged promise would usually be quite disproportionate to the putative expectancy recovery. To attempt, moreover, to put a value on the condition that would or might have resulted, had the treatment succeeded as promised, may sometimes put an exceptional strain on the imagination of the fact finder. As a general consideration, Fuller and Perdue argue that the reasons for granting damages for broken promises to the extent of the expectancy are at their strongest when the promises are made in a business context, when they have to do with the production or distribution of goods or the allocation of functions in the market place; they become weaker as the context shifts from a commercial to a noncommercial field. 46 Yale L.J. at 60–63.

There is much to be said, then, for applying a reliance measure to the present facts, and we have only to add that our cases are not unreceptive to

---

4. Some of the exceptional situations mentioned where reliance may be preferred to expectancy are those in which the latter measure would be hard to apply or would impose too great a burden; performance was interfered with by external circumstances; the contract was indefinite. See 46 Yale L.J. at 373–386; 394–396.

the use of that formula in special situations. We have, however, had no previous occasion to apply it to patient-physician cases.[5]

The question of recovery on a reliance basis for pain and suffering or mental distress requires further attention. We find expressions in the decisions that pain and suffering (or the like) are simply not compensable in actions for breach of contract. The defendant seemingly espouses this proposition in the present case. True, if the buyer under a contract for the purchase of a lot of merchandise, in suing for the seller's breach, should claim damages for mental anguish caused by his disappointment in the transaction, he would not succeed; he would be told, perhaps, that the asserted psychological injury was not fairly foreseeable by the defendant as a probable consequence of the breach of such a business contract. See Restatement: Contracts, § 341, and comment a. But there is no general rule barring such items of damage in actions for breach of contract. It is all a question of the subject matter and background of the contract, and when the contract calls for an operation on the person of the plaintiff, psychological as well as physical injury may be expected to figure somewhere in the recovery, depending on the particular circumstances. The point is explained in Stewart v. Rudner, 349 Mich. 459, 469, 84 N.W.2d 816. Cf. Frewen v. Page, 238 Mass. 499, 131 N.E. 475; McClean v. University Club, 327 Mass. 68, 97 N.E.2d 174. Again, it is said in a few of the New York cases, concerned with the classification of actions for statute of limitations purposes, that the absence of allegations demanding recovery for pain and suffering is characteristic of a contract claim by a patient against a physician, that such allegations rather belong in a claim for malpractice. See Robins v. Finestone, 308 N.Y. 543, 547, 127 N.E.2d 330; Budoff v. Kessler, 2 A.D.2d 760, 153 N.Y.S.2d 654. These remarks seem unduly sweeping. Suffering or distress resulting from the breach going beyond that

5. In Mt. Pleasant Stable Co. v. Steinberg, 238 Mass. 567, 131 N.E. 295, the plaintiff company agreed to supply teams of horses at agreed rates as required from day to day by the defendant for his business. To prepare itself to fulfill the contract and in reliance on it, the plaintiff bought two "Cliest" horses at a certain price. When the defendant repudiated the contract, the plaintiff sold the horses at a loss and in its action for breach claimed the loss as an element of damages. The court properly held that the plaintiff was not entitled to this item as it was also claiming (and recovering) its lost profits (expectancy) on the contract as a whole. Cf. Noble v. Ames Mfg. Co., 112 Mass. 492. (The loss on sale of the horses is analogous to the pain and suffering for which the patient would be disallowed a recovery in Hawkins v. McGee, 84 N.H. 114, 146 A. 641, because he was claiming and recovering expectancy damages.) The court in the *Mt. Pleasant* case referred, however, to Pond v.

Harris, 113 Mass. 114, as a contrasting situation where the expectancy could not be fairly determined. There the defendant had wrongfully revoked an agreement to arbitrate a dispute with the plaintiff (this was before such agreements were made specifically enforceable). In an action for the breach, the plaintiff was held entitled to recover for his preparations for the arbitration which had been rendered useless and a waste, including the plaintiff's time and trouble and his expenditures for counsel and witnesses. The context apparently was commercial but reliance elements were held compensable when there was no fair way of estimating an expectancy. See, generally, annotation, 17 A.L.R.2d 1300. A noncommercial example is Smith v. Sherman, 4 Cush. 408, 413–414, suggesting that a conventional recovery for breach of promise of marriage included a recompense for various efforts and expenditures by the plaintiff preparatory to the promised wedding. . . .

which was envisaged by the treatment as agreed, should be compensable on the same ground as the worsening of the patient's condition because of the breach. Indeed it can be argued that the very suffering or distress "contracted for"—that which would have been incurred if the treatment achieved the promised result—should also be compensable on the theory underlying the New York cases. For that suffering is "wasted" if the treatment fails. Otherwise stated, compensation for this waste is arguably required in order to complete the restoration of the status quo ante.[6]

In the light of the foregoing discussion, all the defendant's exceptions fail; the plaintiff was not confined to the recovery of her out-of-pocket expenditures; she was entitled to recover also for the worsening of her condition,[7] and for the pain and suffering and mental distress involved in the third operation. These items were compensable on either an expectancy or a reliance view. We might have been required to elect between the two views if the pain and suffering connected with the first two operations contemplated by the agreement, or the whole difference in value between the present and the promised conditions, were being claimed as elements of damage. But the plaintiff waives her possible claim to the former element, and to so much of the latter as represents the difference in value between the promised condition and the condition before the operations.

Plaintiff's exceptions waived.

Defendant's exceptions overruled.

[Some footnotes omitted.]

NOTES

(1) Comment (a) to Section 329 of the first Restatement stated: "In awarding compensatory damages, the effort is made to put the injured party in

6. Recovery on a reliance basis for breach of the physician's promise tends to equate with the usual recovery for malpractice, since the latter also looks in general to restoration of the condition before the injury. But this is not paradoxical, especially when it is noted that the origins of contract lie in tort. See Farnsworth, The Past of Promise: An Historical Introduction to Contract, 69 Col.L.Rev. 576, 594–596; Breitel, J. in Stella Flour & Feed Corp. v. National City Bank, 285 App.Div. 182, 189, 136 N.Y.S.2d 139 (dissenting opinion). A few cases have considered possible recovery for breach by a physician of a promise to sterilize a patient, resulting in birth of a child to the patient and spouse. If such an action is held maintainable, the reliance and expectancy measures would, we think, tend to equate, because the promised condition was preservation of the family status quo. See Custodio v. Bauer, 251 Cal. App.2d 303, 59 Cal.Rptr. 463; Jackson v.

Anderson, 230 So.2d 503 (Fla.App.). Cf. Troppi v. Scarf, 31 Mich.App. 240, 187 N.W.2d 511. But cf. Ball v. Mudge, 64 Wash.2d 247, 391 P.2d 201; Doerr v. Villate, 74 Ill.App.2d 332, 220 N.E.2d 767; Shaheen v. Knight, 11 Pa.D. & C.2d 41. See also annotation, 27 A.L.R.2d 906.

It would, however, be a mistake to think in terms of strict "formulas." For example, a jurisdiction which would apply a reliance measure to the present facts might impose a more severe damage sanction for the wilful use by the physician of a method of operation that he undertook not to employ.

7. That condition involves a mental element and appraisal of it properly called for consideration of the fact that the plaintiff was an entertainer. Cf. McQuaid v. Michou, 85 N.H. 299, 303–304, 157 A. 881 (discussion of continuing condition resulting from physician's breach).

as good a position as that in which he would have been put by full performance of the contract, at the least cost to the defendant and without charging him with harms that he had no sufficient reason to foresee when he made the contract." Compare UCC 1–106(1). Section 344 of Restatement (Second) states the "purposes" of contract remedies as follows:

> Judicial remedies under the rules stated in this Restatement serve to protect one or more of the following interests of a promisee:
>
> (a) his 'expectation interest,' which is his interest in having the benefit of his bargain by being put in as good a position as he would have been in had the contract been performed,
>
> (b) his 'reliance interest,' which is his interest in being reimbursed for loss caused by reliance on the contract by being put in as good a position as he would have been in had the contract not been made, or
>
> (c) his 'restitution interest,' which is his interest in having restored to him any benefit that he has conferred on the other party.

(2) *Relief to Promisee to Redress Breach, not Compulsion of Promisor to Prevent Breach.* "[O]ur system of contract remedies rejects, for the most part, compulsion of the promisor as a goal. It does not impose criminal penalties on one who refuses to perform his promise, nor does it generally require him to pay punitive damages. Our system of contract remedies is not directed at *compulsion* of *promisors* to *prevent* breach; it is aimed, instead, at *relief* to *promisees* to *redress* breach. Its preoccupation is not with the question: how can promisors be made to keep their promises? Its concern is with a different question: how can people be encouraged to deal with those who make promises? . . .

"How do courts encourage promisees to rely on promises? Ordinarily they do so by protecting the expectation that the injured party had when he made the contract by attempting to put him in as good a position as he would have been in had the contract been performed, that is, had there been no breach. The interest measured in this way is called the *expectation interest* and is said to give the injured party the 'benefit of the bargain.' The expectation interest is based not on the injured party's hopes at the time he made the contract, but on the *actual value that the contract would have had to him had it been performed.*" Farnsworth, Contracts, § 12.1, pp. 812–813. (Emphasis added.)

"The basic principle for the measurement of those damages is that of compensation based on the injured party's expectation. He is entitled to recover an amount that will put him in as good a position as he would have been in had the contract been performed. At least in principle, *a party's expectation is measured by the actual worth that performance of the contract would have had to him, not the worth that it might have had to some hypothetical reasonable person.* Damages based on expectation should therefore take account of any circumstances peculiar to the situation of the injured party, including his own needs and opportunities, his personal values, and even his idiosyncracies. . . ." *Id.*, § 12.8, p. 839. (Emphasis added.)

Frankenmuth Mutual Insurance Company v. Keeley, 433 Mich. 525, 558 n. 23, 447 N.W.2d 691, 705, n. 23 (1989) (dissent. op.).

PROBLEM: THE CASE OF THE RECALCITRANT MANUFACTURER

Smirgo, Inc., a manufacturer of bakery equipment, specializes in custom made ovens. Bisko, Inc. operates a medium sized bakery in a highly competitive market and sells primarily to restaurants, hotels and other institutional buyers.

On May 15, Bisko's research people informed the president that a new bread had been developed for the institutional trade. It was described as "revolutionary" and "likely to sell like hotcakes." A business decision was then made by the board of directors to purchase two new custom ovens and make a concerted effort to expand the business. At this time Bisko policymakers knew that Caraway Co., a competitor, was working on the development of a similar bread but had no idea what progress had been made.

On June 1, Smirgo and Bisko entered a written contract for the manufacture and sale of custom made ovens to bake the new bread. The basic design was supplied by Bisko engineers. The agreed price was $30,000, to be paid in full 90 days after Smirgo had delivered both ovens on the promised delivery date, November 1. While Smirgo and Bisko had done business before, this was the first contract for custom made ovens. At the time the contract was signed, the president of Smirgo was informed that the "ovens will be used in a business expansion," "prompt delivery is critical," and "we have a new product coming out." After the contract was signed, Bisko spent $7,500 in readying its plant for the new ovens.

On November 1, the time agreed for delivery, Smirgo informed Bisko that while the new ovens were completed they would not be delivered unless Bisko paid $30,000 cash. There was no justification for this demand; it was clearly a breach of contract since a 90 day credit term had been agreed. On November 2 Bisko discovered that there were three concerns within a hundred mile radius that would manufacture the custom made ovens at an average price of $29,500. The estimated time of delivery was six months, however, and no business concern had the type of oven needed by Bisko in stock. On November 3, Caraway Co. announced that it was marketing an institutional bread almost identical to that developed by Bisko. The next day, the Bisko sales manager informed the president that unless the ovens were obtained within ten days, Bisko would lose an estimated $20,000 in profits on six long-term contracts already made and an estimated $100,000 in profits on contracts under negotiation but not yet signed. During the past 5 years, Bisko's net profits have averaged $100,000 per year.

On the afternoon of November 4, the president of Bisko came to you for legal advice. Assume that Smirgo is in breach of contract and that the Uniform Commercial Code governs this case. Based upon an analysis of UCC Article 2, Part 7, Sections 2–711 through 2–717, and the business situation, what would you advise Bisko to do? Go as far as you can with the relevant statutory provisions. [Sections 2–801 through 2–808 and Sections 2–823 through 2–828 (1997)].

Comment: An Introduction to Contract Remedies

If one party to an enforceable bargain has repudiated or failed without justification to perform, what remedies are available for the aggrieved party? Seven rather general remedial principles are set out below.

First, one's contractual duty to perform is conditioned on the other side not breaching its own contractual promises. Accordingly, breach of contract gives the non-breaching party the option of suspending its performance or cancelling the contract. However, trivial or insubstantial breaches at times will not give the non-breaching party an option to suspend its own performance. When one side to a contract announces that it does not intend to perform a promise which is not yet due (so called, anticipatory repudiation), the aggrieved party normally can both cancel the contract and sue for damages *before* the date agreed for performance.

Second, Anglo–American law has exhibited a preference for monetary damages instead of specific performance (ordering the contract breacher either to perform or go to jail for contempt). Specific performance is normally given only if the non-breaching party can show that the subject matter of the contract is unique or that monetary damages are unlikely to make the non-breaching party whole.

Third, although there are several ways to measure in dollars the loss caused by a breach, a basic assumption is that the aggrieved party should recover both net gains prevented by the breach (expectation) and out-of-pocket expenditures associated with performance (reliance). Recovery for breach is not limited to the value to the defendant of the aggrieved party's performance up to the breach (restitution). Exceptions aside, the purpose of damages for breach of a bargain is to put the aggrieved party in the position that would have been gained if the defendant had fully performed. For whatever reason, there are objectives here that go beyond the reimbursement of induced reliance or the recovery of unjust enrichment.

Fourth, as a corollary, it is stated that the primary purpose of contract remedies is to compensate the aggrieved party for losses suffered rather than to punish the contract breacher. Unlike the law of crimes, deterrence is not a primary objective in contract remedies. One reason for this is economic—it is, perhaps, more efficient to say to the breacher: "You may breach this contract and move your resources to higher levels of utility if you are prepared to compensate the aggrieved party for the losses thereby caused. Thus, as you decide whether to breach, you need consider only the probability that a judgment for compensatory damages will be imposed, not the risk of an additional amount for punishment." There is some evidence, however, that the willingness of courts to award punitive damages for certain breaches of contract is increasing.

Fifth, there are several explicit policies that permeate the process of translating losses caused by the breach into dollars:

(a) The plaintiff must prove, (1) that the breach was the substantial cause of the loss complained of, and (2) the amount of the loss caused with reasonable certainty. Proof problems are more important than causation problems in the law of contracts. Thus, a court, under the uncertainty rubric, can, for example, limit liability for claims for non-economic loss, i.e., mental anguish.

(b) The provable losses caused by the breach must have been reasonably foreseeable to the defendant at the time of contracting. If not, these consequential damages are not recoverable.

(c) The plaintiff has a "duty" after the breach to make all reasonable efforts to avoid the consequences of the breach. If the defendant, who has the burden of proof, establishes a failure to "mitigate damages," this item of recovery, even if caused, certain and foreseeable, may not be recovered.

Sixth, the parties have some power through agreement to expand or narrow the remedies normally available for breach of contract. In addition, they may substitute arbitration or some other dispute resolving mechanism for the judicial process.

Seventh, in addition to compensatory damages, the victorious party may also recover interest on sums of money withheld and, in the discretion of the court, the costs associated with the litigation. But attorney fees are not awarded to the victor in the absence of agreement, statute or, perhaps, a vexatious and unfounded suit brought by the plaintiff. More pointedly, there is no way to compensate either party for what we might call imperfections or inefficiencies in the process of adjudication, such as delay. These transaction costs clearly influence the plaintiff's choice on when to seek judicial remedies and how far to go before considering a settlement.

For a further exploration of these remedial policies, see Chapter Six, Section (2)(A).

CHAPTER TWO

THE BASES OF PROMISSORY LIABILITY

What promises ought to be legally binding? In this chapter we explore the bases of promissory liability, the reasons for enforcing a promise, any promise. Contemporary American law recognizes four types of enforceable promises or contracts, each involving a transaction where something is added to the promise so as to make it legally binding. They are: promise plus consideration (Section 1); promise plus antecedent benefit (Section 2); promise plus unbargained-for reliance (Section 3); and promise plus form (Section 4).

Before turning to specific cases and problems, we reprint Professor Randy Barnett's thoughtful assessment of current theories of contractual obligation. Professor Barnett's own "consent" theory, which focuses upon the promisor's manifestation of intent to be legally bound, is expounded in the article from which the excerpt is taken.

Comment: Assessing Current Theories of Contractual Obligation

[The following is reprinted from the Columbia Law Review.]

Five theories—the will, reliance, efficiency, fairness, and bargain theories—are most commonly offered to explain which commitments merit enforcement and which do not. These theories of contractual obligation actually exemplify three types of contract theories. Will and reliance theories are *party-based*. Efficiency and fairness theories are *standards-based*. The bargain theory is *process-based*. At least some of each theory's weaknesses are characteristics of its type. For this reason, each type of theory shall be separately considered here.

* * *

Will, reliance, efficiency, fairness, and bargain are best understood as core concerns of contract law. A theory of contractual obligation is needed to provide a framework that specifies when one of these concerns should give way to another. Their proper relationship cannot be explained by a theory based solely on any one concern or on some unspecified combination. * * *

A. *Party–Based Theories*

Theories described here as party-based are those that focus on protecting one particular party to a transaction. A more accurate (though more awkward) label is "one-sided party-based." Will theories are primarily concerned with protecting the promisor. Reliance theories are primarily concerned with protecting the promisee. The undue emphasis that the will and reliance theories each place on one specific party creates insoluble problems for each approach.

1. *Will Theories.*—Will theories maintain that commitments are enforceable because the promisor has "willed" or chosen to be bound by his commitment. "According to the classical view, the law of contract gives expression to and protects the will of the parties, for the will is something inherently worthy of respect."[7] In this approach, the use of force against a reneging promisor is morally justified because the promisor herself has warranted the use of force by her prior exercise of will. A promisor cannot complain about force being used against her, since she intended that such force could be used when she made the commitment.[8]

Will theories depend for their moral force upon the notion that contractual duties are binding because they are freely assumed by those who are required to discharge them. Consequently, enforcement is not morally justified without a genuine commitment by the person who is to be subjected to a legal sanction. This position leads quite naturally to an inquiry as to the promisor's actual state of mind at the time of agreement— the so-called "subjective" viewpoint. After all, the theory can hardly be based on *will* if the obligation was *not* chosen by the individual but instead was imposed by law.

It has long been recognized that a system of contractual enforcement would be unworkable if it adhered to a will theory requiring a subjective inquiry into the putative promisor's intent. Where we cannot discern the actual subjective intent or will of the parties, there is no practical problem, since we assume it corresponds to objectively manifested intentions. But where subjective intent can somehow be proved and is contrary to objectively manifested behavior, subjective intent should prevail if the moral integrity and logic of a will theory are to be preserved.

Of course, any legal preference for the promisor's subjective intent would disappoint a promisee who has acted in reliance on the appearance of legally binding intent. Permitting a subjective inquiry into the promisor's intent could also enable a promisor to fraudulently undermine otherwise perfectly clear agreements by generating and preserving extrinsic evidence of ambiguous or conflicting intentions. Such a strategy might create a de

7. Cohen, The Basis of Contract, 46 Harv.L.Rev. 553, 575 (1933).

8. See C. Fried, Contract as Promise 16 (1981) ("An individual is morally bound to keep his promises because he has *intentionally* invoked a convention whose function it is to give grounds—moral grounds—for another to expect the promised performance.") (emphasis added); see also Burrows, Contract, Tort and Restitution—A Satisfactory Division or Not?, 99 Law Q.Rev. 217, 258 (1983) ("It is the acceptance of an obligation that is vital; it is not enough to have represented that facts are true or to have merely declared that one is intending to do something, for in such situations, the will has not committed itself to do anything."). Anthony T. Kronman also categorizes Professor Fried as a "will theorist." See Kronman, A New Champion for the Will Theory (Book Review), 91 Yale L.J. 404, 404 (1981). * * *

facto option in the promisor. The promisor could insist on enforcement if the contract continued to be in her interest, but if it were no longer advantageous, she could avoid the contract, by producing evidence of a differing subjective intent.

Because the subjective approach relies on evidence inaccessible to the promisee, much less to third parties, an inquiry into subjective intent would undermine the security of transactions by greatly reducing the reliability of contractual commitments. Not surprisingly, and notwithstanding the logic of obligation based on "will," the objective approach has largely prevailed. The subjectivist moral component, on which a will theory focuses to justify legal enforcement, conflicts unavoidably with the practical need for a system of rules based to a large extent on objectively manifested states of mind. While a person's objective manifestations generally reflect subjective intentions, a will theorist must explain the enforcement of the objective agreement where it can be shown that the subjective understanding of a party differs from her objectively manifested behavior.

Some will theorists uneasily resolve this conflict by acknowledging that other "interests"—for example, reliance—may take priority over the will. By permitting individuals to be bound by promises never intended by them to be enforceable, such a concession deprives a will theory of much of its force. Requiring the promisor's subjective will to yield always, or almost always, to the promisee's reliance on the promisor's objective manifestation of assent undermines the claim that contractual obligation is grounded in the individual's will and bolsters the view that contractual obligations may be imposed rightfully on unwilling parties. The inability of will theories to explain adequately the enforcement of objective manifestations of intention also accounts in part for the continued interest in reliance-based theories of contractual obligation.

2. *Reliance Theories.*—Theories that explain contractual obligation as an effort to protect a promisee's reliance on the promises of others have the apparent virtue of explaining why persons may be bound by the common meaning of their words regardless of their intentions. Thus, it has become increasingly fashionable to assert that contractual obligation is created by reliance on a promise.[17] A reliance theory is based upon the intuition that we ought to be liable in contract law for our assertive behavior when it creates "foreseeable" or "justifiable" reliance in others, in much the same

---

17. While the literature is replete with suggestions about "the reliance principle," a comprehensive reliance theory of contract has never been systematically presented. Such an approach clearly underlies Gilmore's seminal work, *The Death of Contract.* See, e.g., G. Gilmore, The Death of Contract 71–72, 88 (1974). Atiyah appears to call for a reliance theory, although he also acknowledges that "the voluntary creation and extinction of rights and liabilities" should re-

main one of the "basic pillars of the law of obligations." P. Atiyah, supra note 16, at 779; see also Feinman, Promissory Estoppel and Judicial Method, 97 Harv.L.Rev. 678, 716–17 (1984) ("reliance principle" undermines "classical" contract law doctrines); Henderson, Promissory Estoppel and Traditional Contract Doctrine, 78 Yale L.J. 343, 344 (1969) (rules of promissory estoppel create a contract grounded on effects of reliance).

way that we are held liable in tort law for harmful consequences of other acts.

Reliance theories have nonetheless faced a seemingly insuperable difficulty. As Morris Cohen wrote as early as 1933: "Clearly, not all cases of injury resulting from reliance on the word or act of another are actionable, and the theory before us offers no clue as to what distinguishes those which are." This deficiency has led necessarily to the employment of such phrases as "justifiable" reliance or "reasonable" reliance. These adjectives, however, depend on (usually vague) standards of evaluation that are unrelated to reliance itself, because, whether justified or unjustified, reasonable or unreasonable, reliance is present in any event.

Furthermore, whether a person has "reasonably" relied on a promise depends on what most people would (or ought to) do. We cannot make this assessment independently of the legal rule in effect in the relevant community, because what many people would do in reliance on a promise is crucially affected by their perception of whether or not the promise is enforceable. A reliance theory, therefore, ultimately does no more than pose the crucial question that it is supposed to answer: is this a promise that should be enforced?

The analysis is no different if we ask whether the promisor knew or had reason to know the promise would induce others to act in reliance,[21] even though this formulation lessens a reliance theory's preference for the promisee's interests. Unlike the subject of the prediction required by foreseeability analysis in tort law—the physical consequences that follow from physical actions—the subject of the prediction required by foreseeability analysis in contract law is the actions of a self-conscious person. A prediction that a promise can reasonably be expected to induce reliance by a promisee or third party will unavoidably depend upon whether the promisee or third party believes that reliance will be legally protected. The legal rule itself cannot be formulated based on such a prediction, however, without introducing a practical circularity into the analysis.

Furthermore, if a promise is defined, as in the Restatement (Second) of Contracts, as "a manifestation of intention to act or refrain from acting in a specified way, so made as to justify a promisee in understanding that a commitment has been made,"[23] then it would seem that *every* promisor should reasonably expect to induce reliance. If so, "The real issue is not whether the promisor should have expected the promisee to rely, but

---

21. See, e.g., Restatement (Second) of Contracts § 90(1) (1979). Section 90 qualifies reliance-based recoveries at the level of formation, by requiring both a "reasonable" expectation of reliance and the imposition of sanctions only if "injustice" cannot otherwise be avoided, and, at the level of remedies, by limiting the remedy "as justice requires." Id. Traditionally, however, the legal method employs doctrinal and theoretical analysis (that is consistent with underlying notions of jus-

tice) *to discover* where justice resides in a particular case. See Barnett, Why We Need Legal Philosophy, 8 Harv.J.L. & Pub.Pol. 6–10 (1985). Section 90 obviously begs this question. While it may have been the victim of overly cautious draftsmanship, no more precise formulations have been offered to take its place.

23. Restatement (Second) of Contracts § 2 (1979). * * *

whether the extent of the promisee's reliance was reasonable.'' But this returns us once again to the difficulties of discerning "reasonable" reliance.

By providing an overly expansive criterion of contractual obligation, any theory that bases obligation on detrimental reliance begs the basic question to be resolved by contract theory: which *potentially* reliance-inducing actions entail legal consequences and which do not? A person's actions in reliance on a commitment are not justified—and therefore legally protected—simply *because* she has relied. Rather, reliance on the words of others is legally protected because of some as yet undefined circumstances.

In short, a person, rather than being entitled to legal enforcement because reliance is justified, is justified in relying on those commitments that will be legally enforced. Reliance theories therefore must appeal to a criterion other than reliance to distinguish justified acts of reliance. Such a criterion has yet to be identified. It is suggested below that a consent theory provides such a criterion.

3. *The Problem With Party–Based Theories.*—These difficulties reveal that reliance theories have much in common with will theories. Both sets of theories must resort to definitions of contractual enforcement that do not follow from either will or reliance, but are based on more fundamental principles that are left unarticulated. By failing to distinguish adequately between those commitments that are worthy of legal protection and those that are not, both the will and reliance theories have failed in their basic mission. Consequently, actual contract cases must be resolved ad hoc using vague concepts such as "reasonableness" or "public policy," or by employing clearer but formalistic criteria such as "consideration."

* * *

B. *Standards–Based Theories*

Standards-based theories are those which evaluate *the substance* of a contractual transaction to see if it conforms to a standard of evaluation that the theory specifies as primary. Economic efficiency and substantive fairness are two such standards that have received wide attention.

1. *Efficiency Theories.*—One of the most familiar standards-based legal theories is the efficiency approach associated with the "law and economics" school. Economic efficiency is viewed by some in this school as the maximization of some concept of social wealth or welfare: "the term *efficiency* will refer to the relationship between the aggregate benefits of a situation and the aggregate costs of the situation.... In other words, efficiency corresponds to 'the size of the pie.' "[28] According to this view, legal rules and practices are assessed to see whether they will expand or contract the size of this pie.

---

28. A. Polinsky, An Introduction to Law and Economics 7 (1983); cf. Cooter & Eisenberg, Damages for Breach of Contract, 73 Calif.L.Rev. 1432, 1460 (1985) ("Econo-mists say that a contract is efficient if its terms maximize the value that can be created by the contemplated exchange.").

In its least assertive variation, an economic assessment of law does not constitute a distinct theory of contractual obligation. Rather, economic analysis of legal rules is simply viewed as a "value-free" scientific inquiry that is confined to accounting for or explaining the consequences that result from particular legal rules or schemes. So viewed, economic analysis is not a competing theory of contractual obligation, but only one of many yardsticks for assessing competing legal theories.

Economic analysis may also be viewed as a normative theory of law—that is, economic efficiency is seen as providing the best or only yardstick of law. However, because standard economic analysis begins by assuming that some agreements are enforceable,[33] normative efficiency theories fail to provide a distinction between enforceable and unenforceable commitments. In a world of no transaction costs, it is asserted, individual economizing behavior would—by means of mutually advantageous exchanges of entitlements—ensure that legal entitlements are freely transferred to their highest value use. Because such a hypothetical world presupposes enforceable exchanges of legal entitlements, it cannot (without much more) tell us why or when some promises are enforceable while others are not.

In a world of positive transaction costs, economists who employ a model of "perfect competition" wish to assess the extent to which such costs block the movement of resources to their highest value use and the ways that legal rules and remedies—including those defining the background set of entitlements—can be altered to minimize such "inefficiency." Such an analysis, based on detecting deviations from the background efficiency "norm" of initial entitlements and cost-free exchanges, must ultimately rest on no more than an assumption that such voluntary economizing exchanges are to some extent enforceable. Typically, then, efficiency analyses focus on the real world problems of forced exchanges (tort law) in an effort to make legal solutions to these nonmarket transactions approximate market solutions as closely as possible. Efficiency analyses of voluntary exchanges (contract law) typically focus on issues other than the source of contractual obligation itself, such as appropriate remedies and other enforcement mechanisms, and assume, rather than demonstrate, the enforceability of all voluntary commitments. How we recognize voluntary commitments that ought to be enforced, as opposed to mere social promises that are not enforceable, is not generally discussed.

Moreover, some normative efficiency theories generate additional problems. If we are to enforce only those real world agreements that increase

---

33. What these economists sometimes refer to as "market transactions," see, e.g., Coase, The Problem of Social Cost, 3 J.L. & Econ. 1, 15 (1960) ("The argument has proceeded up to this point on the assumption . . . that there were no costs involved *in carrying out market transactions.*" (emphasis added)), are in fact contracts. See Cheung, Transaction Costs, Risk Aversion, and the Choice of Contractual Arrangements, 12 J.L. & Econ. 23 (1969) ("Every transaction involves a contract."); Furubotn & Pejovich, Property Rights and Economic Theory: A Survey of Recent Literature, 10 J.Econ.Literature 1137, 1141 (1972) ("[T]he standard competitive model envisions a special system where one particular set of private property rights governs the use of *all* resources, and where the exchange, policing and enforcement costs of contractual activities are *zero.*").

the overall wealth of society, then it must be either claimed or assumed that a neutral observer (for example, an economist-judge) has access to this information—that is, knows *which* agreements increase wealth and which do not. Two problems arise from this assumption or claim. The first concerns its truth. Can observers ever have information about value-enhancing exchanges independent of the demonstrated preferences of the market participants? More importantly, can a legal system practically base its decisions on such information? It has been persuasively argued that such knowledge is simply not available independently of the production of information by real markets. If it is not available, then it cannot provide workable criteria to distinguish enforceable from unenforceable promises.

Assuming, however, that such knowledge is available, if we have direct access to information sufficient to know whether particular exchanges are value enhancing or not, why bother with contract law at all? Why not simply have a central authority use this knowledge to transfer entitlements independently of the parties' agreement, particularly given the fact that the need to reach agreements creates transaction costs? Or, why not let judges use this knowledge to ratify "efficient thefts"—that is, give thieves the option of obtaining title to property that they have taken from others without their consent, provided only that the thief pays court-assessed damages equal to the value to the victim of her property? Normative economists are barred by their assumption about available information from responding that we need the market to provide such information.

Observations provided by economic theory about the effects of certain contract rules or principles on the efficient allocation of resources may rightly influence our normative assessment of those rules or principles, particularly when these effects are considered along with the effects such rules and principles would have on private autonomy, or "will," and on reliance. Most notably, the efficient allocation of resources may require a market composed of consensual exchanges that reveal and convey otherwise unobtainable information about personal preferences and economic opportunities. Economic analysis may, therefore, suggest that demonstrated consent plays an important role in the law of contract, provided that efficient allocation of resources is a social activity that should be facilitated by a legal system. From this perspective, the "transaction costs" created by a requirement of consent are no worse from an efficiency standpoint than any other cost of production. The costs of negotiating to obtain the consent of another may be resources well-spent because such negotiations serve to reveal valuable information.

Where the negotiating costs of obtaining consent become so high as to bar exchanges thought to be desirable by observers, at least three conclusions are possible. Each, however, argues against enforcing involuntary transfers. First, in the absence of a consensual demonstration of preferences, we do not really know if the exchange is worthwhile—value enhancing—or not. Second, the inefficiency of government legal institutions that needlessly raise transaction costs may be principally responsible for making these consensual transactions prohibitively expensive. If so, then "government failure" and not "market failure" may be responsible for preventing the exchange and the appropriate response is to eliminate the true source of the inefficiency. Finally, when negotiation costs make consensual agreements too expensive a means of obtaining the vital information about value, several alternative ways exist to generate this information without negotiation—for example, by forming a new company or "firm," by merging one company with another, or by combining products into a single package.

In this analysis, demonstrated consent can be seen as playing an important role in any effort to achieve economic or allocative efficiency. Efficiency notions alone, however, cannot completely explain why certain commitments *should* be enforced unless it is further shown that economic efficiency is the exclusive goal of a legal order. The attempt to provide such a normative theory of wealth maximization, in the area of contract law at least, is fundamentally flawed. * * *

2. *Substantive Fairness Theories.*—Another standards-based school of thought attempts to evaluate the substance of a transaction to see if it is "fair." Substantive fairness theories have a long tradition dating back at least to the Christian "just price" theorists of the Middle Ages and perhaps even to Aristotle. Their modern incarnation in contract law can be found in nineteenth century discussions of the "adequacy of consideration" and, more recently, in some treatments of "unconscionability."[58]

A substantive fairness theory assumes that a standard of value can be found by which the substance of any agreement can be objectively evaluated.[59] Such a criterion has yet to be articulated and defended. Without such a criterion, substantive fairness theories fall back on one or both of two incomplete approaches. On the one hand, such theories tend to focus all their attention on a small fraction of commitments—those that are thought to be so "extreme" as to "shock the conscience" of the courts. Most real world agreements are considered to be presumptively enforceable. On the other hand, such theories tend to become process based—looking for either information asymmetries or what is called "unequal bargaining power."

The first of these responses attempts to find extreme instances of violations of a standard that cannot be articulated—or at least cannot be

58. See, e.g., Restatement (Second) of Contracts § 208 comment c (1979) ("Theoretically it is possible for a contract to be oppressive taken as a whole, even though there is no weakness in the bargaining process. . . .").

59. Cohen noted this problem with what he called "the equivalent theory" of contract. See Cohen, supra note 7, at 581 (Due to problems of measurement, modern law "professes to abandon the effort of more primitive systems to enforce material fairness within the contract. The parties to the contract must themselves determine what is

fair."). As a purely descriptive matter, the idea that exchange occurs because goods are of "equivalent" or equal value captivated economists for centuries, see supra notes 55–56 and accompanying text, until it was shown to be quite false. In fact, exchange occurs because both parties ex ante perceive the value of the goods to be exchanged as unequal. Each subjectively perceives the good or service offered by the other to be of greater value (to an unknowable extent) than what they are willing to trade for it. See C. Menger, Principles of Economics 180 (J. Dingwall & B. Hoselitz trans. 1981).

articulated for most transactions, while the latter represents a retreat from the substantive fairness position altogether. Therefore, at best a substantive fairness approach attempts to deal with a qualitative issue by making either a quantitative or a procedural assessment, but *what* is being measured—the nature of the unfairness—is not disclosed.

Most importantly for this discussion, however, the substantive fairness approach fails to address squarely the most central and common problem of contract theory: which *conscionable* agreements should be enforced and which should not? This after all, is, or ought to be, the starting point of a useful theory of contractual obligation that purports to discern which commitments merit legal enforcement. In sum, the substantive fairness approach provides neither meaningful standards nor predictable results. Both the extreme indeterminacy and the focus on aberrant cases inherent in a principle of substantive fairness prevent it from providing the overarching account of contractual obligation that contract theory requires.

3. *The Problem With Standards–Based Theories.*—All standards-based theories face two problems, one that is obvious and another that is more subtle. The obvious problem, which has already been discussed, is identifying and defending the appropriate standard by which enforceable commitments can be distinguished from those that should be unenforceable. The more subtle problem arises from the fact that standards-based contract theories are types of what Robert Nozick has called "patterned" principles of distributive justice:

> [A] principle of distribution [is] *patterned* if it specifies that a distribution is to vary along with some natural dimension, weighted sum of natural dimensions, or lexicographic ordering of natural dimensions. . . .
>
> Almost every suggested principle of distributive justice is patterned: to each according to his moral merit, or needs, or marginal product, or how hard he tries, or the weighted sum of the foregoing, and so on.[67]

The problem created by such patterned theories of justice—including theories based on some notion of efficiency—is that they require constant interferences with individual preferences. "Render possessions ever so equal, man's different degrees of art, care, and industry will immediately break that equality."[68] The maintenance of a pattern, therefore, requires either that persons be stopped from entering the contracts they desire, or that those in power "continually (or periodically) interfere to take from some persons resources that others for some reason chose to transfer to them."

Such interferences are at least presumptively suspect. They may sometimes even be objectionable according to the particular standard that is being used to justify the intervention. For example, inefficiency might be

67. R. Nozick, Anarchy, State and Utopia 156–57 (1974).

68. D. Hume, supra note 10, at 25.

shown to be the ultimate result of interventions to achieve "efficiency" that thwart individual preferences in this way. And a system in which judges may—in the absence of fraud, duress, or some other demonstrable defect in the formation process—second-guess the wisdom of the parties may create more substantive unfairness than it cures. More fundamentally, a theory of rights might support the conclusion that such interferences are unjust and wrong.

C. *Process–Based Theories*

Process-based theories shift the focus of the inquiry from the contract parties and from the substance of the parties' agreement to the manner in which the parties reached their agreement. Such theories posit appropriate procedures for establishing enforceable obligations and then assess any given transaction to see if these procedures were followed. The best known theory of this sort is the bargain theory of consideration.

1. *The Bargain Theory of Consideration.*—The origin of the modern doctrine of consideration can be traced to the rise of the action of assumpsit. When the voluntary assumption of obligation came to be viewed as the basis of contractual enforcement, no one seriously suggested that *every* demonstrable agreement could or should be legally enforced. The number of agreements made every day are so numerous that for reasons of both practice and principle some distinction, apart from that made by purely evidentiary requirements, must be made between enforceable and unenforceable agreements.

The doctrine of consideration was devised to provide this distinction. Where consideration is present, an agreement ordinarily will be enforced. And, most significantly, where there is no consideration, even if the commitment is clear and unambiguous, enforcement is supposed to be unavailable. In the nineteenth century, the "bargain theory of consideration" was promoted by some—most notably Holmes and Langdell—as a way of answering the problem of which commitments merit legal protection. Today it is probably the predominant theory of consideration and is embodied in section 71 of the Restatement (Second) of Contracts:

> (1) To constitute consideration, a performance or a return promise must be bargained for.

> (2) A performance or return promise is bargained for if it is sought by the promisor in exchange for his promise and is given by the promisee in exchange for that promise.

This approach attempts to discern "mutuality" of inducement from the motives and acts of both parties to the transaction. It is not *what* is bargained for that is important; what solely matters is that each person's promise or performance is induced by the other's.

The difficulties presented by the doctrine of consideration depend on which way the concept is viewed. If the doctrine is interpreted restrictively, then whole classes of "serious" agreements will be thought to be lacking consideration. In his recent discussion of consideration, Charles Fried lists four kinds of cases—promises to keep an offer open, to release a debt, to modify an obligation, and to pay for past favors—where promisees have traditionally had considerable difficulty obtaining legal relief for nonperformance because bargained-for consideration is lacking, although it is generally conceded that the parties may have intended to be legally bound and that enforcement should therefore be available. To these may be added unbargained-for promises to assume the obligations of another, to convey land, to give to charities, and those made by bailees and within the family.

In each of these types of cases, a promise is made and then broken. The promisee then seeks to base his cause of action on the promise. In many of these cases, the promise is a serious and unambiguous one. In each situation, however, there is no "bargain" and therefore no consideration for the promise.

Such cases as these invite attempts by judges and others to expand the concept of consideration beyond the bargain requirement. Any such attempt to capture these and other types of cases will, however, run afoul of an opposing difficulty. If the web of consideration doctrine is woven too loosely, it will increasingly capture "social" agreements where legal enforcement is not contemplated—for example, promises of financial assistance between family members. Thus, any expanded concept of consideration threatens to undermine the doctrine's traditional function: distinguishing enforceable from unenforceable agreements in a predictable fashion to allow for private planning and to prevent the weight of legal coercion from falling upon those informal or "social" arrangements where the parties have not contemplated legal sanctions for breach.

Each strategy to deal with the problems generated by a doctrine of consideration, therefore, wreaks havoc in its own way with a coherent theory of contractual obligation. With a restrictive definition like that of bargain, serious promises which merit enforcement are left unenforced. With an expansive formulation, informal promises that are thought to be properly outside the province of legal coercion will be made the subject of legal sanctions. The most recognized problem with the bargain theory is that it appears to have erred too far in the direction of under-enforcement. However, the bargain theory suffers in a more fundamental way from its purely process-based character.

2. *The Problem With Process–Based Theories.*—The problem with process-based theories is not simply that they must strike a balance between over-and under-enforcement. Such trade-offs cannot be completely avoided in any system that bases decision-making on rules and principles of general application. The real problem with process-based theories like the bargain theory of consideration is that they place insurmountable obstacles in the way of minimizing such difficulties of enforcement.

First, a process-based theory's *exclusive* focus on the process that justifies contractual enforcement conceals the substantive values that must support any choice of process. By obscuring these values, process-based theories come to treat their favored procedural devices as ends, rather than as means. Then, when the adopted procedures inevitably give rise to problems of fit between means and ends, a process-based theory that is divorced from ends cannot say why this has occurred or what is to be done about it. This inherent weakness of process-based theories has plagued the bargain theory of consideration.

The bargain theory, which was devised to limit the applicability of assumpsit, fails to ensure the enforcement of certain reasonably well-defined categories of unbargained-for, but "serious" commitments. Then, when courts are moved to enforce such commitments, the principal theory of consideration to which they adhere cannot account for these "exceptions" to the normal requirement of a bargain without appealing to concepts more fundamental than bargaining. Ironically, the rise of assumpsit—the source of the need for the consideration doctrine—was itself due to the inability of the then existing process-based writ system to accommodate enforcement of informal, but serious promises.

Second, an exclusively process-based theory cannot itself explain why certain *kinds* of commitments are not and should not be enforceable. For example, it is widely recognized that agreements to perform illegal acts should not be enforceable. Similarly, slavery contracts are also thought to be unenforceable per se. If, however, agreements of these types were reached in conformity with all "rules of the game," a theory that looks only to the rules of the game to decide issues of enforceability cannot say why such an otherwise "proper" agreement should be unenforceable.

These two types of problems, however, are not confined to process-based theories. As was seen above, party-based theories based on will and reliance are also plagued by an inability to account for and explain certain "exceptional" agreements that are enforceable without recourse to their animating principles. And theories based on principles of will, reliance, or efficiency have as hard a time as process-based theories explaining why certain agreements are unenforceable due to so-called "public policy" exceptions to their respective norms of contractual obligation.

Notwithstanding the weaknesses inherent in process-based theories, such theories offer significant advantages over both party-based and standards-based theories. By employing a neutral criterion for determining contractual enforcement, a process-based theory can better protect both the contractual intent and the reliance of both parties than one-sided party-based theories, provided it identifies features of the contractual process that normally correspond to the presence of contractual intent and substantial reliance. By identifying judicially workable criteria of enforcement, process-based theories can avoid the difficulties of extreme indeterminacy that were seen to plague standards-based theories. They can, in short, better provide the traditionally acknowledged advantages of a system of generally applicable laws, such as facilitating private planning and helping to ensure equal treatment of similarly situated persons. Perhaps it is these advantages that have permitted a process-based theory like the bargain theory to survive its frequent detractors.

The significant administrative advantages of process-based theories suggest that the best approach to contractual obligation is one that preserves a procedural aspect of contract law, while recognizing that such procedures are *dependent* for their ultimate justification on more fundamental, substantive principles of right that occasionally affect procedural analysis in two ways. First, these principles might suggest specific improvements in procedures governing contract formation that are appropriate in the event that previously adopted procedures have created well-defined problems of under-enforcement. Second, these principles might serve to deprive certain procedurally immaculate agreements of their normal moral significance, thereby ameliorating identifiable problems of over-enforcement.

Barnett, *A Consent Theory of Contract,* 86 Colum.L.Rev. 269, 271–291 (1986). [Some footnotes omitted. Copyright © 1986 by Directors of the Columbia Law Review Association, Inc. All Rights Reserved. Reprinted by permission.]

SECTION 1. BARGAIN CONTRACT: PROMISE PLUS CONSIDERATION

(A) BARGAIN REQUIREMENT

Restatement (Second) § 71 defines consideration as follows:

(1) To constitute consideration, a performance or a return promise must be bargained for.

(2) A performance or return promise is bargained for if it is sought by the promisor in exchange for his promise and is given by the promisee in exchange for that promise.

(3) The performance may consist of: (a) an act other than a promise, or (b) a forbearance, or (c) the creation, modification, or destruction of a legal relation.

(4) The performance or return promise may be given to the promisor or to some other person. It may be given by the promisee or by some other person.

This formulation, which has changed little from the first Restatement, has been described by Professor Patterson as including both "a thing (promise or performance) that the promisor bargains for * * * [and] the process of bargaining for it. * * * Consideration * * * implies that something happened, a bargain or exchange." Patterson, *An Apology for Consideration,* 58 Colum.L.Rev. 929, 932–933 (1958). And, in the words of Professor Braucher, the first Reporter of Restatement (Second), the requirement that a promise or performance must be bargained for benefits the community by providing "opportunities for freedom of individual action and exercise of judgment and as a means by which productive energy and product are apportioned in the economy." Restatement (Second) § 72, Comment b. See Braucher, *Freedom of Contract and the Second Restatement,* 78 Yale L.J. 598, 599–602 (1969). Thus, there is not much doubt—in this country at least—that the bargain theory is the "generally accepted idea of consideration." Williston § 100. The interesting questions concern historical origins, application in particular cases, exclusivity as a basis for liability and contemporary utility. We will treat some of these questions in this section.

What are the historical origins of the bargain requirement? In his stimulating book, The Death of Contract, Professor Grant Gilmore argues that the bargain requirement miraculously arose from the pages of O.W. Holmes' classic, The Common Law. Between the merger of debt and assumpsit at the beginning of the 17th century (see infra at 81) and 1880, the date of The Common Law, consideration for a promise had come to be defined as either a detriment to the plaintiff or a benefit to the defendant. According to Gilmore, Holmes, with hardly any support from the precedents or historical materials, promoted the definition to something bargained for and given in exchange for the promise. According to Holmes, the "root of the whole matter is the relationship of conventional inducement, each for the other, between consideration and promise." Holmes, The Common Law 230 (M. Howe ed. 1963). This "revolutionary doctrine" was then elaborated by Williston and others as the exclusive basis for enforcing promises and began to infect the entire life history of contracts. Promises on the periphery of the market, options, requirements contracts, modifications and discharges, all felt the influence of bargain and its attendant slogans, such as "mutuality of obligation." Thus, according to Gilmore, the miraculous birth and spectacular promotion of the new child as the exclusive basis for promissory liability narrowed the scope of contract, unrealistically sharpened the differences between contract and tort and left in limbo the question of liability for unbargained-for benefits voluntarily conferred (moral obligation) and for induced but not bargained-for reliance (promissory estoppel). See G. Gilmore, The Death of Contract 5–53 (1974).

Professor Gilmore's book continues to receive a great deal of critical attention. See Symposium, *Reconsidering Grant Gilmore's The Death of Contract,* 90 Nw.U.L.Rev. 1 (1995). In an early review, Speidel, *An Essay on the Reported Death and Continued Vitality of Contract,* 27 Stan.L.Rev. 1161 (1975), Professor Speidel noted: "The bargain idea has enjoyed a striking persistence in American contract law. This is partially explained, no doubt, by its strong congruence with basic human behavior. * * * [I]n retrospect, the bargain theory appears to be a very natural adaptation of prevailing economic attitudes to serve important legal needs. As an operating principle, the 'bargain' theory of consideration (1) provided a natural formality to channel human conduct and insure deliberation; (2) protected and structured the important market transaction; (3) expanded legal protection by supporting the executory exchange—a promise for a promise—and shielding the creative or idiosyncratic bargainer from later claims that the agreed exchange was disproportionate; and (4) it permitted a fuller development of remedies that protected the plaintiff's expectation interest, that is, the value to the plaintiff of the agreed exchange. * * * [I]t seems plausible to conclude that ideas about bargain were in the air in 1881 and that the winds from the frontier, if not the reported decisions, occasionally reached Boston. If bargain was everywhere, it is difficult to believe that Holmes, a perceptive student of unfolding tapestries, would miss it. * * * Viewed from this vantage point, although Holmes' leap from the English common law to the pages of The Common Law may be miraculous, a leap in 1880 from contemporary reality to the bargain theory was no leap at all. Given Holmes' perspective and the dominance of the market ideology (and giving due credit to osmosis), one might speculate that the announced bargain theory was more evolutionary than revolutionary. In fact, it might be described as an intensely practical idea somewhat behind its time but sufficiently contemporary to insure quick acceptance by student, bench, and bar." 27 Stan.L.Rev. 1161, 1168–1171 (1975).

Collateral reading: Farnsworth §§ 2.1–2.20; Calamari and Perillo §§ 4–1—4–15, 5–1—5–20; Murray §§ 52–67; C. Fried, Contract as Promise (1981); Mark B. Wessman, *Retaining the Gatekeeper: Further Reflections on the Doctrine of Consideration*, 29 Loyola(L.A.)L.Rev. 713 (1996); James Gordley, *Enforcing Promises*, 83 Cal.L.Rev. 547 (1985); Eisenberg, *The Principles of Consideration*, 67 Cornell L.Rev. 640 (1982).

Kirksey v. Kirksey

Supreme Court of Alabama, 1845.
8 Ala. 131.

Error to the Circuit Court of Talladega.

Assumpsit by the defendant, against the plaintiff in error. The question is presented in this Court, upon a case agreed, which shows the following facts:

The plaintiff was the wife of defendant's brother, but had for some time been a widow, and had several children. In 1840, the plaintiff resided on public land, under a contract of lease, she had held over, and was comfortably settled, and would have attempted to secure the land she lived on. The defendant resided in Talladega county, some sixty, or seventy miles off. On the 10th of October, 1840, he wrote to her the following letter:

"Dear sister Antillico—Much to my mortification, I heard, that brother Henry was dead, and one of his children. I know that your situation is one of grief, and difficulty. You had a bad chance before, but a great deal worse now. I should like to come and see you, but cannot with convenience at present. * * * I do not know whether you have a preference on the place you live on, or not. If you had, I would advise you to obtain your preference, and sell the land and quit the country, as I understand it is very unhealthy, and I know society is very bad. If you will come down and see me, I will let you have a place to raise your family, and I have more open land than I can tend; and on the account of your situation, and that of your family, I feel like I want you and the children to do well."

Within a month or two after the receipt of this letter, the plaintiff abandoned her possession, without disposing of it, and removed with her family, to the residence of the defendant, who put her in comfortable houses, and gave her land to cultivate for two years, at the end of which time he notified her to remove, and put her in a house, not comfortable, in the woods, which he afterwards required her to leave.

A verdict being found for the plaintiff, for two hundred dollars, the above facts were agreed, and if they will sustain the action, the judgment is to be affirmed, otherwise it is to be reversed.

■ ORMOND, J. The inclination of my mind, is, that the loss and inconvenience, which the plaintiff sustained in breaking up and moving to the defendant's, a distance of sixty miles, is a sufficient consideration to support the promise, to furnish her with a house, and land to cultivate, until she could raise her family. My brothers, however think, that the promise on the part of the defendant, was a mere gratuity, and that an action will not lie for its breach. The judgment of the Court below must therefore be reversed, pursuant to the agreement of the parties.

Langer v. Superior Steel Corp.

Superior Court of Pennsylvania, 1932.
105 Pa.Super. 579, 161 A. 571.

■ BALDRIGE, J. This in an action of assumpsit to recover damages for breach of a contract. The court below sustained questions of law raised by defendant, and entered judgment in its favor.

The plaintiff alleges that he is entitled to recover certain monthly payments provided for in the following letter:

"August 31, 1927.

"Mr. Wm. F. Langer,

"Dear Sir:

"As you are retiring from active duty with this company, as superintendent of the annealing department, on August 31st, we hope that it will give you some pleasure to receive this official letter of commendation for your long and faithful service with the Superior Steel Corporation.

"The directors have decided that you will receive a pension of $100 per month as long as you live and preserve your present attitude of loyalty to the company and its officers and are not employed in any competitive occupation. We sincerely hope that you will live long to enjoy it and that this and the other evidences of the esteem in which you are held by your fellow employees and which you will today receive with this letter, will please you as much as it does us to bestow them.

> "Cordially yours,
> "(Signed) Frank R. Frost,
> "President."

The defendant paid the sum of $100 a month for approximately four years when the plaintiff was notified that the company no longer intended to continue the payments.

The issue raised by the affidavit of defense is whether the letter created a gratuitous promise or an enforceable contract. It is frequently a matter of great difficulty to differentiate between promises creating legal obligations and mere gratuitous agreements. Each case depends to a degree upon its peculiar facts and circumstances. Was this promise supported by a sufficient consideration, or was it but a condition attached to a gift? If a contract was created, it was based on a consideration, and must have been the result of an agreement bargained for in exchange for a promise: Kirkpatrick v. Muirhead, 16 Pa. 117. It was held in Presbyterian Board of Foreign Missions v. Smith, 209 Pa. 361, 363, that "a test of good consideration is whether the promisee, at the instance of the promisor, has done, forborne or undertaken to do anything real, or whether he has suffered any detriment or whether in return for the promise he has done something that he was not bound to do or has promised to do some act or has abstained from doing something." Mr. Justice Sadler pointed out in York M. & Alloys Co. v. Cyclops S. Co., 280 Pa. 585, that a good consideration exists if one refrains from doing anything that he has a right to do, "whether there is any actual loss or detriment to him or actual benefit to the promisor or not."

* * *

The plaintiff, in his statement, which must be admitted as true in considering the statutory demurrer filed by defendant, alleges that he refrained from seeking employment with any competitive company, and that he complied with the terms of the agreement. By so doing, has he sustained any detriment? Was his forbearance sufficient to support a good consideration? Professor Williston, in his treatise on Contracts, sec. 112, states: "It is often difficult to determine whether words of condition in a promise indicate a request for consideration or state a mere condition in a gratuitous promise. An aid, though not a conclusive test in determining which construction of the promise is more reasonable is an inquiry whether the happening of the condition will be a benefit to the promisor. If so, it is a fair inference that the happening was requested as a consideration.... In case of doubt where the promisee has incurred a detriment on the faith of the promise, courts will naturally be loath to regard the promise as a mere gratuity, and the detriment incurred as merely a condition."

It is reasonable to conclude that it is to the advantage of the defendant if the plaintiff, who had been employed for a long period of time as its superintendent in the annealing department, and who, undoubtedly, had knowledge of the methods used by the employer, is not employed by a competitive company; otherwise, such a stipulation would have been unnecessary. That must have been the inducing reason for inserting that provision. There is nothing appearing of record, except the condition imposed by the defendant, that would have prevented this man of skill and experience from seeking employment elsewhere. By receiving the monthly payments, he impliedly accepted the conditions imposed and was thus restrained from doing that which he had a right to do. This was a sufficient consideration to support a contract.

The appellee refers to Kirksey v. Kirksey, 8 Ala. 131, which is also cited by Professor Williston in his work on Contracts, sec. 112, note 51, as a leading case on this subject under discussion. The defendant wrote his sister-in-law, the plaintiff: "If you will come down and see me, I will let you have a place to raise your family and I have more open land than I can tend; and on the account of your situation and that of your family, I feel like I want you and the children to do well." The plaintiff left her home and moved her family a distance of 67 miles to the residence of the defendant, who gave her the house and land, and after a period of two years, requested her to leave. The court held that the promise was a mere gratuity. In that case, as well as in Richards's Exr. v. Richards, 46 Pa. 78, there was no benefit to be derived by the promisor, as in the case at bar, and, therefore, a good consideration was lacking.

In this view, this contract is enforceable also on the theory of promissory estoppel. This principle has been stated by the American Law Institute in section 90 of the Restatement of the Law of Contracts, as follows: "A promise which the promisor should reasonably expect to induce action or forbearance of a definite and substantial character on the part of the promisee and which does induce such action or forbearance is binding if injustice can be avoided only by enforcement of the promise." As we have already observed, the plaintiff was induced by the promises made to refrain from seeking other employment. A promissory estoppel differs from the equitable estoppel, as it rests upon a promise to do something in the future, while the latter rests upon a statement of a present fact. We have an example of the former in Ricketts v. Scothorn, 57 Neb. 51, 77 N.W. 365, where a grandfather handed his granddaughter a note for $2,000 saying, "I have fixed out something that you have not got to work any more. None of my grandchildren work and you don't have to." The grandfather did not ask his granddaughter to give up her employment, but merely promised that she would not have to work unless she wanted to. She stopped working, relying upon getting $2,000. The court admitted that there was no consideration, but enforced the promise because it had misled the promisee in such a way that it would be unfair to her to do otherwise; thereby invoking the principle of promissory estoppel. We do not mean to state that in all cases where a gratuitous promise is made, and one relies upon it, the promisee can recover, but, if a detriment of a definite and substantial character has been incurred by the promisee, then the court may enforce the promise.

Judgment is reversed, and the defendant is hereby given permission to file an affidavit of defense to the merits of the plaintiff's claims.*

NOTES

(1) Does it appear from these cases that a promise, simply because it is a promise, is presumptively enforceable?

* [Upon remand, the plaintiff obtained a jury verdict. But plaintiff's judgment was reversed on appeal. Langer v. Superior Steel Corp., 318 Pa. 490, 178 A. 490 (1935). Reversal was not based on lack of consideration, however, but resulted from a finding that the president lacked authority to bind the corporation. Ed.]

(2) Assuming that the defendant's promise in *Kirksey* was, as characterized by the court, "a mere gratuity," should that, of itself, preclude relief for the plaintiff? Is it a policy of the law to discourage gratuities? Why might a court hesitate, however, to enforce a Kirksey-like promise? For example, what remedy should be given for breach of contract? See Gordley, *supra,* at 579–582 who notes that even though the case was decided before the rise of so-called promissory estoppel, Sister Antillico would not be a sympathetic figure if she "herself suspected that the promise might be indeliberate, defeasible for a host of reasons, and not intended to confer a right of action."

(3) How does the court in *Langer* purport to distinguish *Kirksey?* If the *Langer* court had decided *Kirksey* would the result likely have been the same?

(4) The "first" Restatement defined consideration in § 75(1): "Consideration for a promise is

  (a) an act other than a promise, or

  (b) a forbearance, or

  (c) the creation, modification or destruction of a legal relation, or

  (d) a return promise,

bargained for and given in exchange for the promise." How does this compare with the Restatement (Second) definition, see supra at 21?

(5) For a general perspective, see Farnsworth, *The Past of Promise: An Historical Introduction to Contract,* 69 Colum.L.Rev. 576 (1969). In this article the author quotes the following excerpt from Adam Smith's The Wealth of Nations:

> [M]an has almost constant occasion for the help of his brethren, and it is vain for him to expect it from their benevolences only. He will be more likely to prevail if he can interest their self-love in his favour, and shew them that it is for their own advantage to do for him what he requires of them. Whoever offers to another a bargain of any kind, proposes to do this. Give me that which I want, and you shall have this which you want, is the meaning of every such offer; and it is in this manner that we obtain from one another the far greater part of those good offices which we stand in need of. We address ourselves, not to their humanity but to their self-love, and never talk to them of our own necessities but of their advantages. Nobody but a beggar chooses to depend chiefly upon the benevolence of his fellow citizens.

69 Colum.L.Rev. at 576–77.

Bogigian v. Bogigian

Court of Appeals of Indiana, Second District, 1990.
551 N.E.2d 1149, rehearing denied, 559 N.E.2d 1199.

■ BUCHANAN, JUDGE.

CASE SUMMARY

Respondent-appellant David Bogigian (David) appeals from the reinstatement of a judgment in favor of Hazel Bogigian (Hazel), claiming the trial court erred when it determined Hazel's release of her judgment was not supported by consideration.

We affirm.

FACTS

The facts most favorable to the trial court's judgment reveal that on January 31, 1986, David's marriage to Hazel was dissolved, and Hazel was given the following judgment:

> "Wife shall receive a judgment on the family home in the amount of Ten Thousand Three Hundred Dollars ($10,300) ... Said judgment is to be paid when the parties' youngest child is emancipated, when Husband remarries, or if a woman is living in the residence in a married situation, *or when the Husband sells the real estate,* or if the children or the Husband cease to reside in the residence, whichever occurs first."

Record at 32 (emphasis supplied).

The residence was sold by David on February 20, 1987, and Hazel attended the closing with David. At the closing, Hazel executed several documents to effectuate the sale of the house. Among the documents executed was a quit claim deed and the release of her judgment against David. The release provided:

> "Comes now HAZEL BOGIGIAN, this 20TH day of FEBRUARY, 1987, being first duly sworn upon oath, who deposes and says:
>
> That a certain judgment rendered JANUARY 31, 1986, as Cause number # S385–126, against DAVID J. BOGIGIAN in favor of HAZEL BOGIGIAN, is hereby satisfied and released."

Record at 67.

Because David had no equity in the residence, the sale did not provide any funds from which to satisfy Hazel's judgment. Several months after the closing, David paid Hazel five dollars as her share of the sale's proceeds.

On June 30, 1988, Hazel initiated proceedings supplemental to satisfy her judgment. On January 1, 1989, David filed the release of judgment signed by Hazel during the closing. After a hearing on February 22, 1989, the trial court concluded that the release executed by Hazel was voidable for lack of consideration. The trial court reinstated Hazel's judgment on May 4, 1989.

ISSUE

David raises several issues on review which we consolidate and restate as:

Whether the trial court erred when it reinstated Hazel's judgment?

DECISION

PARTIES' CONTENTIONS—David contends that because Hazel received a benefit, as she was released from her obligations on the mortgage, her release was supported by consideration and therefore the trial court erred when it reinstated her judgment. In the alternative, David argues that Hazel should be equitably estopped from executing the judgment because he relied to his detriment on her release. Hazel responds that there was no consideration supporting her release because she did not realize the release she signed was a release of her judgment against David.

CONCLUSION—The trial court did not err when it reinstated Hazel's judgment because her release was not supported by consideration.

* * *

A release, to be valid, must be supported by consideration. Pope v. Vajen (1889), 121 Ind. 317, 22 N.E. 308; Gates v. Fauvre (1918), 74 Ind.App. 382, 119 N.E. 155. Consideration consists of *bargained-for exchange.* Tolliver v. Mathas (1989), Ind.App., 538 N.E.2d 971; Wavetek Indiana, Inc. v. K.H. Gatewood Steel Co. (1984), Ind.App., 458 N.E.2d 265, trans. denied; Burdsall v. City of Elwood (1983), Ind.App., 454 N.E.2d 434.

The evidence adequately supports the trial court's factual finding and legal conclusion that Hazel received no consideration for the release. The record demonstrates that Hazel and David did not *bargain* for the release in exchange for any benefits flowing to Hazel for detriments incurred by David. Both Hazel and David admitted that no representations concerning the release were made. *Record* at 136–37, 155. Hazel testified she thought she was signing the release of the mortgage so the house could be sold. *Record* at 165. Any benefit received by Hazel, or any detriment suffered by David, therefore, cannot be consideration for the release because David and Hazel did not *agree* the benefit or detriment would be consideration. See Colorado Nat'l Bank of Denver v. Bohm (9th Cir.,1961) 286 F.2d 494; Bank of Marion v. Robert "Chick" Fritz, Inc. (1974), 57 Ill.2d 120, 311 N.E.2d 138; 17 C.J.S. Contracts 74 (1963) pp. 762–63.

The United States Supreme Court, almost one hundred years ago, recognized:

> "The mere presence of some incident to a contract which might, under certain circumstances, be upheld as a consideration for a promise, does not necessarily make it the consideration for the promise in that contract. To give it that effect, it must have been offered by one party, and accepted by the other, as one element of the contract."

Fire Ins. Assoc., Ltd. v. Wickham (1891), 141 U.S. 564, 579, 12 S.Ct. 84, 88, 35 L.Ed. 860. That consideration must actually be bargained-for is a long recognized and fundamental common law principle, *Bohm*, supra; 1 Williston, Contracts 100 (3rd Ed.1957); Restatement, Contracts 75 Comment b (1932), a principle which frequently is seen in the cases as part of the definition of consideration: "Consideration consists of bargained-for exchange." See *Tolliver*, supra; *Wavetek*, supra; *Burdsall*, supra.

Because David and Hazel did not bargain for the release, the evidence most favorable to the trial court's judgment supports its finding and conclusion that Hazel received no consideration for the release.

As to David's estoppel claim, we observe that the elements of estoppel are: (1) a representation or concealment of material facts; (2) the representation must have been made with knowledge of the facts; (3) the party to whom it was made must have been ignorant of the matter; (4) *it must have been made with the intention that the other party should act upon it;* and (5) the other party must have been induced to act upon it to his detriment. Glaser v. Dept. of Pub. Welfare (1987), Ind.App., 512 N.E.2d 1128, trans. denied.

Because David and Hazel did not bargain for the release, and because no representations concerning the release were made, David has failed to establish that the release was made with the intent that David act upon it; thus David has failed to establish Hazel should be equitably estopped from having her judgment reinstated. *Glaser,* supra.

Judgment affirmed.

■ STATON, J. concurs.

■ SULLIVAN, J., dissents with opinion.

■ SULLIVAN, JUDGE, dissenting.

The adage that "hard cases make bad law"[1] might be applied to the case before us. But assuming that the law enunciated is not "bad," the decision nevertheless represents a dramatic change in the law of contracts—more particularly with regard to consideration.

The majority opinion states that consideration must consist of a "bargained-for exchange." In order to meet this test, it is not necessary that the benefit or detriment be negotiated, agreed upon by both parties and reflected by specific language in the instruments. It is sufficient that the detriment or benefit to the particular party flows from the bargain. The transaction of which the release was a part must be considered in its entirety. The consideration for the release need not be found in the release itself. It may be found in contemporaneous aspects of the transaction. Goeke v. Merchants National Bank and Trust Co. (1984) 1st Dist. Ind.App., 467 N.E.2d 760, trans. denied.

It is not necessary that the consideration flow between the promisor and the promisee. So long as the promisor obtains a benefit, the benefit may flow from a third party, e.g., the mortgagee here. See Timberlake v. J.R. Watkins Co. (1965) 138 Ind.App. 554, 209 N.E.2d 909, *reh. denied* 211 N.E.2d 193; 17 Am.Jur.2d, Contracts, Sec. 96.

It is clear that the benefit to Hazel was bargained for. The mortgagee's release of her upon the obligation was clearly and specifically a part of the bargain. Hazel's judgment constituted a lien against the real estate in David's name. Therefore it had to be released before the mortgage could be satisfied, taxes paid and clear title delivered. Therefore Hazel did benefit by the liability avoidance. That specific benefit was, by Hazel's own testimony,

---

1. Holmes, J. in Northern Securities Co. v. United States (1904) 193 U.S. 197, 24 S.Ct. 436, 48 L.Ed. 679.

specifically contemplated as a consequence of her execution of the documents. That this bargained-for consideration was not specifically stated as the *quid pro quo* for the unambiguous release is not determinative. As noted in 17 C.J.S., Contracts Sec. 74, p. 763, cited by the majority, consideration exists

> "if it is present anywhere in the entire transaction surrounding the agreement, regardless of whether any label has been put on it, and regardless of whether it was spelled out in the writing."

There were absolutely no representations or misrepresentations made by David nor by the mortgagee to Hazel with regard to the release. There was no hint of undue influence. The release executed was clear, unequivocal and unambiguous. That Hazel perhaps did not avail herself of the full and fair opportunity to read the release does not relieve her from the consequences of that clear and unambiguous instrument. Moore v. Bowyer (1979) 1st Dist., 180 Ind.App. 429, 388 N.E.2d 611. The release therefore must be given its full legal effect.

As stated in Robison v. Fickle (1976) 2d Dist., 167 Ind.App. 651, 340 N.E.2d 824, 829, although in a slightly different contractual context:

> "The intention of the parties to a contract is always vital to an understanding of that contract and of the relationships and rights created. However, as stated in City of Indianapolis v. Kingsbury (1884), 101 Ind. 200, 213:
>
> "'. . . the intention to which Courts give heed is not an intention hidden in the mind of the landowner, but an intention manifested by his acts. It is the intention which finds expression in conduct and not that which is secreted in the heart of the owner, that the law regards. Acts indicate the intention, and upon the intention clearly expressed by open acts and visible conduct the public and individual citizens may act.'
>
> Thus does the law hold one to the natural legal consequences of words consciously chosen and utilized in a contract. 4 Williston on Contracts (3d ed.) Sec. 606."

See also Mullen v. Tucker (1987) 4th Dist. Ind.App., 510 N.E.2d 711, 713 ("a release . . . constitutes a 'settlement' . . . *notwithstanding the motives prompting the execution of the release.*")

Though in retrospect Hazel may have made a bad bargain, such does not diminish the effect of her execution of the release. As set forth in Rutter v. Excel Industries, Inc. (1982) 3d Dist. Ind.App., 438 N.E.2d 1030, 1031:

> "The freedom to contract includes the freedom to contract improvidently, and in the absence of countervailing policy considerations, private reservations or mistake will not avoid the results of apparent consent.
>
> "If, whatever a man's real intention may be, he so conducts himself that a reasonable man would believe he was assenting to the

terms proposed by the other party, and that the other party upon that belief enters into the contract with him, the man thus conducting himself would be equally bound as if he had intended to agree to the other party's terms.' Smith v. Hughes (Eng.1871), L.R. 6 Q.B. 597.''

That the amount of Hazel's mortgage and tax liability avoidance may have been of a substantially lesser amount than the $10,300 judgment released is not a basis for the trial court's judgment. Inadequate consideration, as opposed to failure of consideration is not a basis for setting the release aside. Harrison–Floyd Farm Bureau Co–Op. v. Reed (1989) 1st Dist. Ind.App., 546 N.E.2d 855; Herrera v. Collection Service, Inc. (1982) 2d Dist. Ind.App., 441 N.E.2d 981.

A compassionate motivation to relieve Hazel from the consequences of her arguably bad bargain is understandable. Absent fraud, undue influence, incapacity or some other cognizable grounds for relief, however, I am unable to discern any legal basis for the holding today. The fact remains that Hazel signed the release which clearly stated its tenor and effect. In doing so she gave up the hope or possibility of recovering her $10,300 judgment against David, who at the time was virtually bankrupt and without any assets either in Indiana or Florida. In return she avoided having a judgment against her for an amount in excess of the $41,000 mortgage balance due at the time of closing. In light of David's relatively precarious financial position, it is not unlikely that Hazel would have felt the major impact of that mortgage liability. In this light, the bargain from Hazel's perspective may not have been all that unwise.

In any event I am constrained to dissent. I would reverse the judgment and direct the court to give full force and effect to the release.

[In denying David's petition for rehearing, Judge Buchanan added brief elaboration to his opinion that Hazel's release was not supported by consideration. See 559 N.E.2d 1199 (Ind.App.1990).]

NOTES

(1) In *Bogigian,* what was the asserted consideration for Hazel's agreement to discharge the lien? Why was this insufficient? Is this, as suggested by the dissenting judge, an instance of a hard case making bad law? If so, what, precisely, is the "bad" law that is made?

(2) To satisfy the "bargain" requirement, should it be necessary that the consideration flow from the promisee? From whom did the consideration flow to Hazel?

(3) Could you have drafted the documents in *Bogigian* so as to obviate the objections of the court majority? How much actual bargaining must occur before consideration can be found?

(4) *The Case of the Injured Mechanic.* Ray Dehn, a skilled mechanic and traveling representative of Transit Bus Sales Company of St. Louis, was sent to Knoxville to repair a bus which Ross Palmer had purchased from the company. Dehn inspected the bus and told Palmer a belt was too loose. Palmer's driver

went away and got the belt tightened. When the driver returned with the tightened belt, the three of them discussed the matter at length. Dehn then attempted to show Palmer how tight it should be when the driver started the motor cutting off two of Dehn's fingers. Dehn thought all the time that the driver was out of the bus and that no one was inside who could start the motor. Palmer immediately rushed Dehn to a local hospital. On the way, Palmer said: "I am awful sorry this happened, but don't worry a minute. I will see you are compensated for loss of your finger, take care of your expenses for the loss of your finger, and all." On these facts, what theories of liability would you expect Dehn to advance? Was there consideration for Palmer's promise? Is there any basis for promissory liability? See Palmer v. Dehn, 29 Tenn.App. 597, 198 S.W.2d 827 (1946).

(5) *The Case of the Proud Grandfather.* A baby boy was born to Mr. and Mrs. Lanfier on December 17. Two days later they named the boy "August Dwayne." He was named "August" after his maternal grandfather, August Schultz. A week later the grandfather promised the parents that if they named the baby "August" he would give them a certain painting, valued at $5,000. They agreed. Was there a binding contract? Cf. Lanfier v. Lanfier, 227 Iowa 258, 288 N.W. 104 (1939). Would all doubt concerning enforceability have been removed if, in addition, Schultz had prescribed and received a $1 payment from the Lanfiers? See materials which follow.

PROBLEM: THE CASE OF THE LESSEE'S WELL

Stone leased land to Oil Company for ten years. Oil Company was to operate a service station and had an option to purchase the land at any time for $20,000. The lease provided that Stone was to supply water to Oil Company from an existing well but "in case Lessor's well fails to supply ample water, they are not responsible, and the Lessee will be required to make their own arrangements for securing water." The well failed after 18 months and the parties, after negotiations, agreed to have a new well drilled and to split the cost. A written agreement was prepared and signed by both parties. Shortly after drilling commenced, Stone visited the site and talked with a company representative, Mr. Brinson. Stone asked "What happens to my investment in the well if you exercise the option and buy the land" and Brinson promptly answered (in front of witnesses) "Don't worry about that, you'll get your money." The well was completed at a cost of $4,000 and the parties each paid the well driller $2,000. Six months later, Oil Company exercised the option but at the closing refused to reimburse Stone for his well drilling expenses. Oil Company argued that Brinson's oral promise, if made, was unenforceable because there was no consideration. Is this argument correct? See Stonestreet v. Southern Oil Co., 226 N.C. 261, 37 S.E.2d 676 (1946).

Thomas v. Thomas

Queen's Bench, 1842.
2 Q.B. 851, 114 Eng.Rep. 330.

Assumpsit. The declaration stated an agreement between plaintiff and defendant that the defendant should, when thereto required by the plaintiff, by all necessary deeds, conveyances, assignments, or other assurances, grants, etc., or otherwise, assure a certain dwelling house and premises, in the county of Glamorgan, unto plaintiff for her life * * *.

At the trial, before Coltman, J., at the Glamorganshire Lent Assizes, 1841, it appeared that John Thomas, the deceased husband of the plaintiff, at the time of his death, in 1837, was possessed of a row of seven dwelling houses in Merthyr Tidvil, in one of which, being the dwelling house in question, he was himself residing; and that by his will he appointed his brother Samuel Thomas (since deceased) and the defendant executors thereof, to take possession of all his houses, etc., subject to certain payments in the will mentioned, among which were certain charges in money for the benefit of the plaintiff. In the evening before the day of his death he expressed orally a wish to make some further provision for his wife; and on the following morning he declared orally, in the presence of two witnesses, that it was his will that his wife should have either the house in which he lived and all that it contained, or an additional sum of £100 instead thereof.

This declaration being shortly afterward brought to the knowledge of Samuel Thomas and the defendant, the executors and residuary legatees, they consented to carry the intentions of the testator so expressed into effect; and, after the lapse of a few days, they and the plaintiff executed the agreement declared upon; which, after stating the parties, and briefly reciting the will, proceeded as follows:

"And, whereas the said testator, shortly before his death, declared in the presence of several witnesses, that he was desirous his said wife should have and enjoy during her life, or so long as she continue his widow, all and singular the dwelling house," etc., "or £100 out of his personal estate," in addition to the respective legacies and bequests given her in and by his said will; "but such declaration and desire was not reduced to writing in the lifetime of the said John Thomas and read over to him; but the said Samuel Thomas and Benjamin Thomas are fully convinced and satisfied that such was the desire of the said testator, and are willing and desirous that such intention should be carried into full effect. Now these presents witness, and it is hereby agreed and declared by and between the parties, that, in consideration of such desire and of the premises," the executors would convey the dwelling house, etc., to the plaintiff and her assigns during her life, or for so long a time as she should continue a widow and unmarried: "provided nevertheless, and it is hereby further agreed and declared, that the said Eleanor Thomas, or her assigns, shall and will, at all times during which she shall have possession of the said dwelling house, etc., pay to the said Samuel Thomas and Benjamin Thomas, their executors, etc., the sum of £1 yearly toward the ground rent payable in respect of the said dwelling house and other premises thereto adjoining, and shall keep the said dwelling house and premises in good and tenantable repair"; with other provisions not affecting the questions in this case.

The plaintiff was left in possession of the dwelling house and premises for some time; but the defendant, after the death of his coexecutor, refused to execute a conveyance tendered to him for execution pursuant to the agreement, and, shortly before the trial, brought an ejectment, under which he turned the plaintiff out of possession. It was objected for the defendant that, a part of the consideration proved being omitted in the declaration, there was a fatal variance. The learned judge overruled the objection, reserving leave to move to enter a non-suit. Ultimately a verdict was found for the plaintiff on all the issues; and, in Easter Term last, a rule nisi was obtained pursuant to the leave reserved.

* * *

■ LORD DENMAN, C.J. There is nothing in this case but a great deal of ingenuity, and a little wilful blindness to the actual terms of the instrument itself. There is nothing whatever to show that the ground rent was payable to a superior landlord; and the stipulation for the payment of it is not a mere proviso, but an express agreement. * * * This is in terms an express agreement, and shows a sufficient legal consideration quite independent of the moral feeling which disposed the executors to enter into such a contract. * * *

■ PATTESON, J. * * * Motive is not the same thing with consideration. Consideration means something which is of some value in the eye of the law, moving from the plaintiff; it may be some benefit to the plaintiff [defendant], or some detriment to the defendant [plaintiff]; but at all events it must be moving from the plaintiff. Now that which is suggested as the consideration here, a pious respect for the wishes of the testator, does not in any way move from the plaintiff; it moves from the testator; therefore, legally speaking, it forms no part of the consideration. Then it is said that, if that be so, there is no consideration at all, it is a mere voluntary gift; but when we look at the agreement we find that this is not a mere proviso that the donee shall take the gift with the burthens; but it is an express agreement to pay what seems to be a fresh apportionment of a ground rent, and which is made payable not to a superior landlord, but to the executors. So that this rent is clearly not something incident to the assignment of the house, for in that case, instead of being payable to the executors, it would have been payable to the landlord. Then as to the repairs, these houses may very possibly be held under a lease containing covenants to repair; but we know nothing about it, for anything that appears the liability to repair is first created by this instrument. The proviso certainly struck me at first * * * that the rent and repairs were merely attached to the gift by the donors; and, had the instrument been executed by the donors only, there might have been some ground for that construction; but the fact is not so. * * *

■ COLERIDGE, J. The concessions made in the course of the argument have, in fact, disposed of the case. It is conceded that mere motive need not be stated, and we are not obliged to look for the legal consideration in any particular part of the instrument, merely because the consideration is usually stated in some particular part; ut res magis valeat, we may look to any part. In this instrument, in the part where it is usual to state the consideration, nothing certainly is expressed but a wish to fulfil the intentions of the testator, but in another part we find an express agreement to pay an annual sum for a particular purpose, and also a distinct agreement to repair. If these had occurred in the first part of the instrument, it could hardly have been argued that the declaration was not well drawn and supported by the evidence. As to the suggestion of this being a voluntary conveyance, my impression is that this payment of £1 annually is more than a good consideration, it is a valuable consideration, it is clearly a thing newly created and not part of the old ground rent.

Rule discharged.

Comment: Restatement of Contracts (Second)—A Rejection of Nominal Consideration?

[The following is reprinted from the Valparaiso University Law Review.]

Restatement of Contracts § 84, illustration 1 (1932):

> A wishes to make a binding promise to his son B to convey to B Blackacre, which is worth $5000. Being advised that a gratuitous promise is not binding, A writes to B an offer to sell Blackacre for $1. B accepts. B's promise to pay $1 is sufficient consideration.

Restatement (Second) Contracts § 75,* illustration 5 (tent. draft No. 2, 1965):

> A desires to make a binding promise to give $1000 to his son B. Being advised that a gratuitous promise is not binding, A offers to buy from B for $1000 a book worth less than $1. B accepts the offer knowing that the purchase of the book is a mere pretense. There is no consideration for A's promise to pay $1000.

A generation of lawyers has been told that Blackacre may be "sold" for one dollar. Perhaps on the theory that one generation of misinformed lawyers is enough, the authors of the tentative draft of the Restatement of Contracts (Second) propose a reversal of the venerable Blackacre-for-a-dollar hypothetical. Although the factual contexts of the two above quoted illustrations vary, the Reporter has made his Committee's intention clear by stating that the "only difference" is that "instead of the promise being binding, the promise is said now to be not binding." The proposed change may not be criticized on the ground that it violates Restatement objectives by departing from rules based on existing precedents. To the contrary, the Reporter's position is that precedents are lacking to support the Blackacre illustration. Since one of the functions of a "Tentative Draft" is to invite criticism and suggestion by bar associations and the profession generally, it is appropriate to examine the academic commentary and the case law background of the doctrine of nominal consideration.

* * *

The Academic Controversy

The academic world remains divided on the question whether nominal consideration *should* be sufficient to enforce a promise. Professor Fuller

---

* [§ 71 in final draft. Ed.]

describes two main classes of objections to enforcing all promises. The first class contains objections of "substance" which relate to the nature of the promise and to its effects. The second class contains objections of "form" which relate to the manner in which the promise was made without referring to the content of the promise itself. According to Professor Fuller, the requirements of form serve three functions. These are: (1) evidentiary, (2) cautionary, and (3) channeling.[1] Applying this analysis to the doctrine of nominal consideration, Professor Fuller writes:

> The proper ground for upholding these decisions [enforcing a promise given for nominal consideration] would seem to be that the desiderata underlying the use of formalities are here satisfied by the fact that the parties have taken the trouble to cast their transaction in the form of an exchange.

According to Professor Fuller, form provides a means for a party to give a "legally effective expression of intention."

The theory that there is a close resemblance between the policies underlying form and those underlying consideration is a "misconception" according to Professor Havighurst.[2] After stating that the courts usually do not enforce a contract for nominal consideration, he argues:

> [H]owever informal the expressions and however unconscious the parties may be of their legal significance, if consideration is present as a natural element in the transaction, it suffices. Certainly this does not suggest that the reasons for the requirements of consideration and of form are similar.

It would seem that form, of any type in any situation, does emphasize to some extent the seriousness of an act to the party doing the act. But then a question which goes beyond "form" is asked by Professor Patterson:

> Even if such a red-light formality were found or invented, would we not have to ask the promisee to show some additional reason, other than his mere expectation, why the promisor's default and unwillingness to pay damages should entitle the promisee to recover damages?[3]

The above question posed by Professor Patterson brings forth the substantive issues involved in the nominal consideration question. Professor Fuller writes with regard to these issues:

> The attitude which our courts take toward private agreements rests upon a kind of tacitly accepted constitution, which has as one of its basic articles the principle of *private autonomy*. This constitution, like that which regulates the relation of the courts to statutes, is, however, a complex document, the provisions of which do not promote a single policy, but a congeries of policies. (Emphasis added.)

1. Fuller, *Consideration and Form,* 41 Colum.L.Rev. 799, 806 (1941).

2. Havighurst, *Consideration, Ethics and Administration,* 42 Colum.L.Rev. 1, 6 (1942).

3. Patterson, *An Apology for Consideration,* 58 Colum.L.Rev. 929, 943 (1958).

This principle of private autonomy views private individuals as having the power to bring about changes in their legal relations, and views the court which enforces the promise, as simply giving legal sanction to rights and duties already established by the parties.

The principle of private autonomy which allows a party to make a binding expression of his intention is rejected by Professor Patterson who states:

> To say . . . that a contract is binding upon a party because it expressed his will, is wholly inadequate because it does not explain why he may not will today the exact opposite of what he willed yesterday.

As is shown by the above statement, nominal consideration has been attacked because intent alone is believed not to be a sufficient reason to enforce a contract and that, therefore, the courts should look for something more. Professor Corbin states:

> Serious intent is not a very definite concept; and it is not identical with intention to be legally bound. . . .
>
> The chief purpose underlying the law of contract is not to carry out the will of the promisor, although that may be one of many purposes. It is believed that the chief purpose of enforcement is the avoidance of disappointment and loss to the promisee. It is the reasonable expectation of the promisee (or beneficiary) that the law chiefly takes into account. . . .[4]

One wonders what the reasonable expectation of the promisee of a nominal consideration contract, which basically is a gratuitous promise decorated by form, really is. When it seems that we are getting something for nothing, we ask "what's the catch?" It is arguable that if this skepticism is commonly experienced under circumstances similar to those above described, we really have no reasonable expectation of receiving anything of value.

Professor Cohen speaks on the root problem of the relationship between the courts and the enforcement of promises as follows:

> Contract law is commonly supposed to enforce promises. Why should promises be enforced?
>
> The simplest answer is that of the *intuitionists,* namely, that promises are sacred *per se,* that there is something inherently despicable about not keeping a promise, and that a properly organized society should not tolerate this. . . . But while this intuitionist theory contains an element of truth, it is clearly inadequate. No legal system does or can attempt to enforce all promises. Not even the canon law held all promises to be sacred and when we come to draw a distinction between those promises which should be and those which should not be enforced, the intuitionist theory, that all promises should be kept, gives us no light or guiding principle.
>
> . . . It is indeed very doubtful whether there are many who would prefer to live in an entirely rigid world in which one would be obliged

---

4. 1 Corbin, Contracts § 112, at 497 (1963) [hereinafter cited as Corbin].

to keep *all* one's promises instead of the present viable system, in which a vaguely fair proportion is sufficient.[5]

Provisions in the Uniform Written Obligations Act would authorize the enforcement of all writings containing a statement to the effect that the signer intends to be legally bound. With regard to this form and the enforcement of all promises, it has been said:

> What the Uniform Written Obligations Act proposes . . . is very close to the proposition that all promises should be enforced unless there is some reason for not doing so. The requirement of formality is a little more than mere evidence that words were uttered, for it goes beyond the writing alone. But it is hardly more than evidence that the words were intended to be a promise. . . .
>
> There is no sound *a priori* reason for assuming that all assurances intended to be promises should be enforced.

Without this sound *a priori* reason, a court, in rendering a decision on the enforceability of a promise, should advance some social interest which conforms to ethical standards of that society. Professor Havighurst answers the question "what are these standards" by saying:

> Subsequent occurrences affecting the question are the change of position by the promisee in reliance on the promise, events which affect the ability of the promisor to perform, changes in the situation which induced the promise, circumstances defeating the promisor's expectations, and the promisee's part in bringing about the circumstances.
>
> Ethical judgments with respect to the duty of performance will be the resultant of all these factors, and only in extreme instances will the presence of one of them in any specified degree be determinative. Thus an intervening event making the promisor less able to carry out the promise might be adjudged as relieving him from the moral duty to perform if little or nothing had been received in exchange for the promise, whereas the same event would not be regarded as so relieving him if he had received something of value. A man who suffers a severe financial reverse may still be regarded as morally bound to pay his grocer, but under no duty, ethically speaking, to fulfill a pledge to his alma mater.

Judicial recognition of ethical norms thus weakens, if not destroys, the desirability of nominal consideration.

As evidenced by the Blackacre illustration, the doctrine of nominal consideration is used to avoid the delivery requirement of gift law. Proponents of nominal consideration may argue, however, that the purpose of the delivery requirement is to satisfy cautionary, channeling, and evidentiary interests. Since casting a gift into the form of a bargain serves these particular interests, such formalization should be accepted as a satisfactory substitute for delivery. This argument, however, does not persuade those who contend that the gift is a sterile transaction:

5. Cohen, *The Basis of Contract,* 46 Harv.L.Rev. 553, 572–74 (1933).

When one receives a naked promise and such promise is broken, he is no worse off than he was. He gave nothing for it, he has lost nothing by it, and on its breach he has suffered no damage cognizable by courts. No benefit accrued to him who made the promise, nor did any injury flow to him who received it. Such promises are not within the scope of transactions intended to confer rights enforceable at law.

Another argument presented in support of nominal consideration states that nominal consideration is desirable since the doctrine overcomes an unintended consequence which resulted from the abolishment of the legal effect of the seal. That unintended result was the disappearance of a way to make a gratuitous promise binding. The seal was formally abolished after it had become a meaningless act due to the liberalization of the requisites of the seal from wax impressions to mere printed words. It has been also suggested that legislatures in deciding to abolish the seal requirement, may have desired to move away from medieval formalism or may have concluded that the character of the seal was inappropriate as a formality.

Professor Simpson in speaking of the Uniform Written Obligations Act states:

> Legislative refusal to adopt this Act is based fundamentally upon approval of consideration as the test of an enforceable promise, a reluctance to extend the field of substitutes therefor, and disagreement with the assumption that a gift promise where made deliberately and with intent to be bound should be legally enforceable.

There is an analogy between the "seal" and the Uniform Written Obligations Act, at least to the extent that legislatures control the effect of their respective uses. The common problem concerns whether the intent of the parties is a sufficient reason for enforcement of the promise by the state.

Professor Patterson's statement that "consideration ... includes not only a *thing* (promise or performance) that the promisor bargains for, but also the *process* of bargaining for it" would receive added support if the Restatement (Second) is adopted with the proposed revisions. Professor Patterson viewed the bargaining "process" as defined in section 75 of the Restatement. However, the "bargained-for process" is not defined in the Restatement and is weakened by section 84 which sanctions nominal consideration. With the elimination of nominal consideration from section 84, and the inclusion of a definition of "bargained for," section 75 and the "process" have become the dominant doctrine. When the process is applied to a promise to convey Blackacre for one dollar, there is no consideration. The nominal consideration of one dollar, whether delivered or not, is a pretense rather than a reality.

An inquiry into the bargaining process is not an inquiry into the adequacy of consideration. Professor Corbin states: "The smallness of the consideration may not make it insufficient to support the promise if it was in fact bargained for and given in exchange." Determining the existence of a bargain is precedent to any ruling on consideration as noted by Professor Corbin: "Courts must first determine the fact of bargain and agreed exchange before they can properly apply the rules of consideration as a bargained exchange."

Case Law Supports Proposed Revisions

Cases exist which enforce promises given for nominal consideration. However, these decisions most often occur when other elements justifying enforceability are present. . . .

* * *

Another promise for nominal consideration often enforced is that which grants an option of lease or purchase. The court may sustain such a promise since it is difficult to value a given option. What seems to be a reason worthy of more credence is that an option is simply a device for making a business offer irrevocable. Thus, the apparent disparity in the grant of a valuable option for one dollar lessens when the whole transaction is considered. Although a lease option often recites nominal consideration in return for the lease itself, more substantial benefits are usually present in the form of royalties or rentals going to the lessor. If the consideration is nominal in fact—that is, not bargained for—then no consideration has been given and the option giver has the power to revoke.

* * *

A case which possibly can be said to support the Restatement in its illustration of conveying Blackacre for one dollar is *Thomas v. Thomas.*[6] The promisee received a life estate in a dwelling house in return for 1£ yearly rent and keeping the premises in good repair. But even here Lord Denman, C.J., stated that "the obligation to repair is one which might impose charges heavier than the value of the life estate," while Justice Patterson said that "the liability to repair is first created by this instrument."

Restatement (Second) and the Bargain–Gift Promise

Although the Restatement (Second) appears to adopt the "bargained for" test for consideration, a remnant of nominal consideration still seems to remain. The remnant is found in the proposed comment *c* and illustration 6 to section 75 which would enforce a promise involving a mixture of bargain and gift even when both parties know that it is in part a bargain and in part a gift. The reason given is the time-honored rule that the court will not inquire into the adequacy of consideration. The element of bargain may furnish the consideration for the entire transaction. But when both parties know it is only in part a bargain, can it be said that the other part was bargained for? If A gives B ten dollars for a book worth only five dollars and both parties know that the extra five dollars is a gift, that five dollars is not bargained for and seemingly would not be enforced by the other requirements of the Restatement (Second). If A offered to give 5,000 dollars for the five-dollar book and there was a partial bargain shown, would there be sufficient reason to enforce the promise as to the 4,995 dollar gift?

6. 2 Q.B.Rep. 851, 114 Eng.Rep. 330 (1842).

Conclusion

The tentative draft of the Restatement (Second) in refusing to enforce a promise for nominal consideration receives at least partial support from the academic world and strong support from case law. The promise for one dollar finds case law support in a business transaction. But the business transaction involves a "bargain," other consideration than the dollar, and a necessary reliance on the promise in a fast-moving commercial world. Thus the business transaction is very easily distinguished from the conveyance of Blackacre for one dollar, which is merely a formal expression for an essentially gratuitous transfer.

It should be noted that the authors of the tentative draft have not seen fit to abolish all the legally operative effects of nominal consideration since a mixture of bargain and gift remains enforceable under provisions of the draft. However, if the Restatement (Second) is to be internally consistent, a mixture of bargain and gift should be enforced only to the extent of the bargain.

Since nominal consideration lacks case law support, the Restatement (Second) is on firm ground in omitting the Blackacre-for-a-dollar illustration. If nominal consideration is to become recognized as a desirable technique for supporting the principle of private autonomy, achieving this recognition must be the task of those who would change rather than those who restate the law. [Some footnotes omitted. Those retained have been renumbered. Ed.]

Note, *Restatement of Contracts (Second)—A Rejection of Nominal Consideration?*, 1 Val.U.L.Rev. 102 (1966).

NOTES

(1) *The Use of Form in Contracting.* Throughout history various formalities have been observed by contracting parties, either as a matter of custom or of official requirement. Thus, a libation or a handshake or the impression of a seal on a document might accompany the promise. The biblical account of God's "covenant" with Abraham describes an elaborate form: "And now God said to him, I am the Lord, who brought thee out of Ur of the Chaldees, to give thee possession of this land instead. And when he asked, Lord God, what assurance may I have that it is mine? the Lord answered, Bring me a three-year-old heifer, a three-year-old she-goat, and a three-year-old ram, and a turtle-dove, and a pigeon. All these he brought to him, and cut them in half, laying the two halves of each on opposite sides, except the dove and the pigeon; he did not divide these. . . . So the sun went down, and when the darkness of night came on, a smoking furnace was seen, a torch of fire that passed between the pieces of flesh. And the Lord, that day, made a covenant with Abram." Genesis 15:7–10, 17–18. The additional form might on occasion be the giving of something substantial to the other, akin to the pledge of collateral to secure a loan, and this might be subject to being forfeited if the promise was not performed. Indeed, at certain periods it was not uncommon for one to give over a hostage as an assurance that one would execute a promise faithfully.

A notable example of a promise cast in a formal mode, and thereby recognized as legally binding, was the famous *stipulatio* or stipulation of the Roman law. Briefly, this was a method whereby one might secure, through a process of interrogation and response, the enforceable promise of another. A would ask of B if he would promise to do such and such, and B's promise to do so would bind him in law. This formality has both ancient and modern counterparts. Today in civil law countries the promise in a notarial deed (executed before a notary, a governmental official) is binding precisely because of the method employed in making it. In the Anglo–American tradition, going back centuries, it was the seal, a wax impression placed upon a writing, which afforded a convenient method for the creation of contractual rights and duties. Recognized before consideration as the ordinary theory of contract enforcement, the seal has, particularly in recent times, lost its former efficacy. This matter will be considered further in Section 2, infra. For the moment, attention might be given to whether it would be desirable to have some "form" available for the making of binding gratuitous promises. If so, what should the form be? A writing? A writing plus nominal payment? Or what?

(2) *Professor Eisenberg on the Binding Effect of Donative Promises.* Given that unrelied-upon donative promises are normally unenforceable, the question arises whether the law should recognize some special form through which a promisor with the specific intent to be legally bound could achieve that objective. "It is something," said Williston, "that a person ought to be able . . . if he wishes to do it . . . to create a legal obligation to make a gift. Why not? . . . I don't see why a man should not be able to make himself liable if he wishes to do so."

At early common law the seal served this purpose. In modern times, most state legislatures have either abolished the distinction between sealed and unsealed promises, abolished the use of a seal in contracts, or otherwise limited the seal's effect. * * *

Should the law then recognize some new formality to play the role once played by the seal? An obvious candidate is nominal consideration—that is, the form of a bargain—because it can be safely assumed that parties who falsely cast a nonbargain promise as a bargain do so for the express purpose of making the promise legally enforceable. A rule that promises in this form were enforceable would have obvious substantive advantages, but would also involve serious difficulties of administration. As a practical matter, such a form would be primarily employed to render donative promises enforceable. Both morally and legally, however, an obligation created by a donative promise should normally be excused either by acts of the promisee amounting to ingratitude, or by personal circumstances of the promisor that render it improvident to keep the promise. If Uncle promises to give Nephew $20,000 in two years, and Nephew later wrecks Uncle's living room in an angry rage, Uncle should not remain obliged. The same result should ordinarily follow if Uncle suffers a serious financial setback and is barely able to take care of the needs of his immediate family, or if Uncle's wealth remains constant but his personal obligations significantly increase in an unexpected manner, as through illness or the birth of children.

Form alone cannot meet these problems. Thus the French and German Civil Codes, while providing special forms that enable a donative promise to be rendered legally enforceable, also provide extensive treatment of improvidence and ingratitude as defenses. For example, under article 519(1) of the German Civil Code, a promisor may refuse to keep a donative promise "insofar as, having regard to his other obligations, he is not in a position to fulfill the promise without endangering his own reasonable maintenance or the fulfillment of obligations imposed upon him by law to furnish maintenance to others." Under article 530(1), a donative promise may be revoked "if the donee, by any serious misconduct towards the donor or a close relative of the donor shows himself guilty of gross ingratitude." Similarly, under articles 960–966 of the French Civil Code, a donative promise made by a person with no living descendants is normally revoked by operation of law upon the birth of a child. Under articles 953 and 955, a donative promise can be revoked on the ground of ingratitude that involves serious cruelty, wrongs, or injuries.

As these rules suggest, the common law could not appropriately make donative promises enforceable solely on the basis of a form unless our courts were also prepared to develop and administer a body of rules dealing with the problems of improvidence and ingratitude. Certainly such an enterprise is possible. It may be questioned, however, whether the game would be worth the candle. An inquiry into improvidence involves the measurement of wealth, lifestyle, dependents' needs, and even personal utilities. An inquiry into ingratitude involves the measurement of a maelstrom, because many or most donative promises arise in an intimate context in which emotions, motives, and cues are invariably complex and highly interrelated. Perhaps the civil-law style of adjudication is suited to wrestling with these kinds of inquiries, but they have held little appeal for common-law courts, which traditionally have been oriented toward inquiry into acts rather than into personal characteristics. The question is whether the social and economic benefits of a facility for making donative promises enforceable would be worth its social and economic costs. The answer is that benefits and costs are in rough balance, so that nonrecognition of such a facility is at least as supportable as recognition would be.

Eisenberg, *The Principles of Consideration,* 67 Cornell L.Rev. 640, 659–62 (1982). [Footnotes omitted.]

(3) *Professor Barnett on Formal Consent.* For a considerable part of the history of the common law, the principal way of creating what we now think of as a contractual obligation was to cast one's agreement in the form of a sealed writing. * * * Notwithstanding their ancient history, formal commitments, such as those under seal, came to be thought of as "exceptions" to the "normal" requirement of consideration. * * * [F]ormal promises have had an uncertain place in the law of contract because they lacked a theoretical underpinning. In a climate of opinion dominated by notions of "bargain" and "induced reliance," where there is no bargain and no demonstrable reliance to support enforcement, the presence of a meaningful formality may not be enough to satisfy a court. * * * A consent theory of contract, however, provides the missing theoretical foundation of formal contracts and explains their proper place in a well-crafted law of contract. The voluntary use of a recognized formality by a promisor manifests to a promisee an intention to be legally bound in as unambiguous a manner as possible. * * * Formal contracts ought to be an "easy" case of contractual enforcement, but prevailing theories that require bargained-for consideration, induced reliance, or even economic "efficiency" would have a hard time explaining why. In a consent theory, by contrast, there need be no underlying bargain or demonstrable reliance for such a commitment to be properly enforced. The same holds true * * * for nominal

consideration and for false recitals of consideration. A consent theory acknowledges that, if properly evidenced, a recital by the parties that "consideration" exists may fulfill the channeling function of formalities, whether or not any bargained-for consideration for the commitment in fact exists. If it is widely known that the written phrase "in return for good and valuable consideration" means that one intends to make a legally binding commitment, then these words will fulfill a channeling function as well as, and perhaps better than, a seal or other formality. The current rule that the falsity of such a statement permits a court to nullify a transaction because of a lack of consideration is therefore contrary to a consent theory of contract.

Barnett, *A Consent Theory of Contract,* 86 Colum.L.Rev. 269, 310–312 (1986). [Footnotes omitted.] For more on form in contracting, see infra at Chapter 2, Section 4(A).

PROBLEM: MIXED MOTIVES AND AGREED EXCHANGE

Your client, Pauline, is a second year student at Yale Law School. Pauline's Uncle Fred, a Harvard law graduate, owns a first edition of Langdell's "Cases on Contracts", published in 1878. The value of the book is $5,000. Pauline expressed an interest in the book (to add to a growing collection) and, at Thanksgiving, Uncle Fred made a statement at the dinner table that he would give the book to her for Christmas. The next day Uncle Fred was shown Pauline's coin collection and discovered that she had two 1909s-VDB pennies, one in very fine condition (valued at $1,000) and one in fine condition (valued at $500). Fred confessed that he needed such a penny to round out his collection of Lincoln pennies and Pauline stated that she would give him the penny in "fine" condition for Christmas.

Shortly after the first of the year, Pauline visited your office and presented a writing, dated December 1, 1996, which stated: "In consideration of one penny, receipt of which is hereby acknowledged, I promise to give my niece Pauline my first edition of Langdell on Christmas day, 1996." The writing, which had been mailed to Pauline, was signed by Fred. She further said that on Christmas Day she tendered the "fine" 1909s-VDB penny to Fred and he took it. Fred, however, refused to tender the Langdell, saying he was a bit short of cash and that he had sold it to the Harvard Law Library for $7,500. He did thank Pauline for her "wonderful gift."

Advise Pauline of her rights.

(B) SUFFICIENCY OF EXCHANGE

(1) IN GENERAL

Hamer v. Sidway

Court of Appeals of New York, 1891.
124 N.Y. 538, 27 N.E. 256.
Supra at 18.

NOTES

(1) What definition of consideration did the court use, the "bargained for" concept or the "either-or" concept? If "bargained for" was used, was there

equivalency of exchange? Did the promisor gain a pecuniary advantage? Did he derive any "benefit" from the transaction at all, or is enforcement predicated solely upon "detriment" to the promisee? In what way was plaintiff's conduct detrimental? Note who the plaintiff was. Is the fact that she purchased nephew's rights under the alleged contract for value relevant to the case?

(2) *Consideration as Either Benefit to Promisor or Detriment to Promisee: An Historical Note.* "During the early phases of the development of English common law, an action on an obligation other than one embodied in a sealed instrument was maintainable only through a writ to recover on a debt. The availability of such writs, however, was limited to those narrow situations in which one of the parties withheld payment of a fixed, bargained for sum of money after the other party had performed his part of the bargain by making a loan or delivering goods or services. The underlying theory of the action was that the parties had made a bargain or had agreed upon a *quid pro quo* exchange and the promisor or debtor was now wrongfully withholding the property of the promisee by refusing to make payment after receiving that which he had bargained for. It was from this concept of a bargained for *quid pro quo* that the notion of consideration as a benefit flowing to the promisor was derived (see 1 Corbin, Contracts, § 121; Morgan, Introduction to the Study of Law [2d ed.], pp. 92–93; 1 Williston, Contracts [Jaeger 3d ed.], § 99; Holmes, Early English Equity, 1 L.Q.Rev. 162, 171).

"The action on a debt, however, proved unsatisfactory for a variety of reasons, not the least of which was its limited scope. Litigants, as a consequence, turned with increasing frequency to the vehicle of assumpsit, which was originally a simple variant of trespass on the case, the forerunner of our modern tort cause of action (see Ames, History of Assumpsit, 2 Harv.L.Rev. 1). Although assumpsit ultimately evolved into a separate and distinct form of action, its earliest uses were confined to claims based upon malfeasance or faulty performance of an assumed duty (see Williston, at p. 384). Consistent with its origins in trespass on the case, the gist of the action in assumpsit remained the injury to the promisee resulting from the promisor's misconduct in improperly performing his obligation. It was apparently not until 1588 that assumpsit was definitively expanded to encompass actions for nonfeasance or simple failure to perform a contractual duty. In that year, it was held that 'a promise against a promise will maintain an action upon the case [in assumpsit], as in consideration that you do give me £10 on such a day, I promise to give you £10 such a day after' (Strangborough and Warner's Case, 4 Leon 3, 74 Eng.Rep. 686 [QB]). With this expansion in the availability of assumpsit, the original requirement of an injury resulting from misfeasance was broadened, and an action in assumpsit could thereafter be maintained upon a showing of any detriment, loss or disadvantage to the promisee arising from the bargain (see, generally, Holdsworth, Debt, Assumpsit and Consideration, 11 Mich.L.Rev. 347).

"The final critical development in the law of assumpsit occurred in 1602 with the decision in Slade's Case (4 Coke 91a, 92b, 76 Eng.Rep. 1072, 1074 [KB]). That decision paved the way for litigants to sue in assumpsit on claims for fixed sums of money previously maintainable only in the older form of an action based on a *quid pro quo* to recover a debt (see Moses v. Macferlan, 2 Burr. 1005, 1008, 97 Eng.Rep. 676 [KB]). As a result of this development, assumpsit became the primary vehicle for litigation on contractual obligations, and the notion of 'consideration' became a term of art encompassing both a benefit to the promisor, the equivalent of the former *quid pro quo,* and a detriment to the promisee, the equivalent of the former requirement of injury in actions sounding in assumpsit (see Williston, at pp. 368–369).

"This dual notion of consideration as either a benefit to the promisor *or* a detriment to the promisee has persisted to the present day and has become an integral part of our modern approach to the enforceability of contracts. Thus, it has repeatedly been stated that ' "[a] valuable consideration may consist of some right, interest, profit or benefit accruing to one party, or some forbearance, detriment, loss or responsibility given, suffered or undertaken by the other" ' (Rector of St. Mark's Church v. Teed, 120 N.Y. 583, 586, quoting 3 Am. & Eng. Cyclopedia of Law, p. 831; accord Allegheny Coll. v. National Chautauqua County Bank of Jamestown, 246 N.Y. 369, 373, 159 N.E. 173; Walton Water Co. v. Village of Walton, 238 N.Y. 46, 50–51, 143 N.E. 786; Union Bank of Brooklyn v. Sullivan, 214 N.Y. 332, 339, 108 N.E. 558; Restatement, Contracts 2d, § 75). Indeed, we have expressly held that a promisee who has incurred a specific, bargained for legal detriment may enforce a promise against the promisor, notwithstanding the fact that the latter may have realized no concrete benefit as a result of the bargain (Melville v. Kruse, 174 N.Y. 306, 66 N.E. 965; Hamer v. Sidway, 124 N.Y. 538, 27 N.E. 256)." Holt v. Feigenbaum, 52 N.Y.2d 291, 296–299, 437 N.Y.S.2d 654, 657–58, 419 N.E.2d 332, 335–336 (1981). [Footnotes omitted.]

See also, Windeyer, **Lectures on Legal History** 106–109 (2d ed. Rev. 1967), who adds:

"With indebitatus assumpsit thus assured as an alternative remedy, the old action of debt became virtually obsolete. It was not abolished, however, until the general abolition of the forms of action in the nineteenth century. But after *Slade's Case* no plaintiff who was properly advised would sue in debt while wager of law lasted; and, as we have seen, it lasted until 1833. A plaintiff who unwisely brought an action of debt in 1824 had to abandon it when the defendant offered to wage his law.

The view that in the case of an executory contract a promise to perform it must be implied was a logical extension of indebitatus assumpsit. But it was not long before a remarkable, and by no means logical, further extension occurred. The action was held to be available for the recovery of money wrongfully received and withheld: for example money paid under a mistake of fact; money paid as the result of deceit, threats or duress; money which was the proceeds of the sale of stolen goods. These are not cases of an implied promise to perform an actual contract. Yet they were brought within the scope of indebitatus assumpsit by a fictitious promise said to be 'implied by law'. 'But the fiction was too transparent. The alleged contract by the blackmailer and the robber never was made and never could be made. The law in order to do justice, imputed to the wrongdoer a promise which alone as forms of action then existed could give the injured person a reasonable remedy.'

Out of this extension of indebitatus assumpsit grew the modern law of quasi-contract.

The history of debt and assumpsit is one instance—and we shall meet others equally striking—of a process by which old actions were abandoned, because the unyielding conservatism of the law prevented them shedding their technicalities, and other actions were modified and used to answer purposes very different from those for which they were first devised. Along with conservative loyalty to ancient rules and established forms, we find the law was, surely if clumsily, adapted to meet changing needs. The determination and ingenuity of the lawyers thus found remedies for wrongs and made the common law answer the demands of common men."

(2) In an early case, Haigh v. Brooks, 113 Eng.Rep. 119 (Q.B. 1839, Exch. Ch. 1840), Haigh sold goods to Lees on credit. Brooks, who was interested in Lee's affairs, signed a writing purporting to guaranty Lees debts to Haigh in the amount of 10,000 pounds. The problem was that the guaranty, to be enforceable under the statute of frauds, had to show in the writing that consideration was given for the promise to answer for the debt of another and the particular writing said "in consideration of your being in advance" to Lees in the sum of 10,000 pounds for the purchase of cotton "I do hereby give you my guarantee for that amount." For reasons not clear from the record, Brooks induced Haigh to surrender the writing in exchange for a promise to pay three drafts accepted by Lees in total of 9,666 pounds when they came due. Lees failed to pay at that time, Haigh sued on the promise and Lees demurred on the ground that there was no consideration.

A final judgment was entered for the plaintiff.

Lord Denman, C.J., delivered the judgment of the Queen's Bench:

"It was argued for the defendant that this guarantee is of no force, because the fact of the plaintiffs being already in advance to Lees could form no consideration for the defendant's promise to guarantee to the plaintiffs the payment of Lees's acceptances. In the first place, this is by no means clear. That 'being in advance' must necessarily mean to assert that he was in advance at the time of giving the guarantee, is an assertion open to argument. It may possibly have been intended as prospective. If the phrase had been 'in consideration of your becoming in advance,' or 'on condition of your being in advance,' such would have been the clear import. As it is, nobody can doubt that the defendant took a great interest in the affairs of Messrs. Lees, or believe that the plaintiffs had not come under the advance mentioned at the defendant's request. Here is then sufficient doubt to make it worth the defendant's while to possess himself of the guarantee; and, if that be so, we have no concern with the adequacy or inadequacy of the price paid or promised for it.

But we are by no means prepared to say that any circumstances short of the imputation of fraud in fact could entitle us to hold that a party was not bound by a promise made upon any consideration which could be valuable; while of its being so the promise by which it was obtained from the holder of it must always afford some proof.

Here, whether or not the guarantee could have been available within the doctrine of Wain v. Warlters, 5 East, 10, the plaintiffs were induced by the defendant's promise to part with something which they might have kept, and the defendant obtained what he desired by means of that promise. Both being free and able to judge for themselves, how can the defendant be justified in breaking this promise, and discovering afterwards that the thing in consideration of which he gave it did not possess that value which he supposed to belong to it? It cannot be ascertained that that value was what he most regarded. He may have had other objects and motives; and of their weight he was the only judge. We therefore think the plea bad: and the demurrer must prevail.

Judgment for the plaintiffs.''

THE JUDGMENT WAS AFFIRMED ON APPEAL TO EXCHEQUER. LORD ABINGER, C.B., delivered the judgment of the Exchequer Chamber.

''In the case of Brooks v. Haigh the judgment of the Court is to affirm the judgment of the Court of Queen's Bench.

It is the opinion of all the Court that there was in the guaranty an ambiguity that might be explained by evidence, so as to make it a valid contract; and therefore this was a sufficient consideration for the promise declared upon.

It is also the opinion of all the Court, with the exception of my brother Maule, who entertained some doubt on the question, that the words both of the declaration and the plea import that the paper on which the guaranty was written was given up; and that the actual surrender of the possession of the paper to the defendant was a sufficient consideration without reference to its contents.

Judgment affirmed.''

Which proposition in Restatement, Second 79 does this case support: ''If the requirement of consideration is met, there is no additional requirement of (a) a gain, advantage, or benefit to the promisor or a loss, disadvantage, or detriment to the promisee or (b) equivalence in the values exchanged?''

(3) SHYLOCK:

You'll ask me why I rather choose to have
A weight of carrion flesh than to receive
Three thousand ducats. I'll not answer that,
But say it is my humour—is it answer'd?
What if my house be troubled with a rat,
And I be pleas'd to give ten thousand ducats
To have it ban'd? What, are you answer'd yet?
Some men there are love not a gaping pig;
Some that are mad if they behold a cat;
And others, when the bagpipe sings i' th' nose,
Cannot contain their urine; for affection,
Mistress of passion, sways it to the mood
Of what it likes or loathes. Now, for your answer:
As there is no firm reason to be rend'red
Why he cannot abide a gaping pig;
Why he, a harmless necessary cat;
Why he, a woollen bagpipe, but of force
Must yield to such inevitable shame
As to offend, himself being offended;
So can I give no reason, nor I will not,

> More than a lodg'd hate and a certain loathing
> I bear Antonio, that I follow thus
> A losing suit against him. Are you answer'd?

Shakespeare, *The Merchant of Venice,* Act IV, Scene 1.

Apfel v. Prudential–Bache Securities, Inc.

Court of Appeals of New York, 1993.
81 N.Y.2d 470, 600 N.Y.S.2d 433, 616 N.E.2d 1095.

■ SIMONS, JUDGE.

Defendant, an investment bank, seeks to avoid an agreement to purchase plaintiffs' idea for issuing and selling municipal bonds. Its principal contention is that plaintiffs had no property right in the idea because it was not novel and, therefore, consideration for the contract was lacking. For reasons which follow, we conclude that a showing of novelty is not required to validate the contract. The decisive question is whether the idea had value, not whether it was novel.

I

In 1982, plaintiffs, an investment banker and a lawyer, approached defendant's predecessor with a proposal for issuing municipal securities through a system that eliminated paper certificates and allowed bonds to be sold, traded, and held exclusively by means of computerized "book entries". Initially, the parties signed a confidentiality agreement that allowed defendant to review the techniques as detailed in a 99–page summary. Nearly a month of negotiations followed before the parties entered into a sale agreement under which plaintiffs conveyed their rights to the techniques and certain trade names and defendant agreed to pay a stipulated rate based on its use of the techniques for a term from October 1982 to January 1988. Under the provisions of the contract, defendant's obligation to pay was to remain even if the techniques became public knowledge or standard practice in the industry and applications for patents and trademarks were denied. Plaintiffs asserted that they had not previously disclosed the techniques to anyone and they agreed to maintain them in confidence until they became public.

From 1982 until 1985, defendant implemented the contract, although the parties dispute whether amounts due were fully paid. Defendant actively encouraged bond issuers to use the computerized "book entry" system and, for at least the first year, was the sole underwriter in the industry employing such a system. However, in 1985, following a change in personnel, defendant refused to make any further payments. It maintained that the ideas conveyed by plaintiffs had been in the public domain at the time of the sale agreement and that what plaintiffs sold had never been theirs to sell. Defendant's attempts to patent the techniques proved unsuccessful. By 1985, investment banks were increasingly using computerized systems, and by 1990 such systems were handling 60% of the dollar volume of all new issues of municipal securities.

Plaintiffs commenced this litigation seeking $45 million in compensatory and punitive damages. They asserted 17 causes of action based on theories of breach of contract, breach of a fiduciary duty, fraud, various torts arising from defendant's failure to obtain patents, and unjust enrichment. Defendant's answer interposed defenses and counterclaims for breach of contract, breach of warranty, waiver, fraud, estoppel, laches, mutual mistake, rescission, and a lack of consideration. Plaintiffs then moved for partial summary judgment, defendant cross-moved for summary judgment dismissing the complaint, and plaintiffs responded with a motion seeking dismissal of the affirmative defenses.

Supreme Court concluded that triable issues existed on the questions of whether defendant breached the contract by refusing to make payments and whether plaintiffs committed a breach by allegedly disclosing the techniques to another company. The court also found defendant had raised a triable issue on whether plaintiffs had partially waived their right to payment by forgoing certain claims to compensation. The remainder of the pleadings were found to be legally insufficient. Accordingly, the court dismissed all the causes of action except the first, which alleges breach of contract, and struck all defendant's defenses and counterclaims except those relating to breach of contract and the partial defense of waiver. The Appellate Division modified the order by reinstating defendant's claim that the sale agreement lacked consideration, 183 A.D.2d 439, 583 N.Y.S.2d 386. It held that novelty was required before an idea could be valid consideration but concluded that the question was one of fact to be decided at trial. It also reinstated the cause of action for unjust enrichment, holding that the presence of an express contract did not foreclose recovery on a theory of quasi contract.

On this appeal, defendant's principal contention is that no contract existed between the parties because the sale agreement lacked consideration. Underlying that argument is its assertion that an idea cannot be legally sufficient consideration unless it is novel. Defendant supports that proposition by its reading of such cases as Downey v. General Foods Corp., 31 N.Y.2d 56, 334 N.Y.S.2d 874, 286 N.E.2d 257, Soule v. Bon Ami Co., 201 App.Div. 794, 195 N.Y.S. 574, affd. 235 N.Y. 609, 139 N.E. 754, and Murray v. National Broadcasting Co., 844 F.2d 988, cert. denied 488 U.S. 955, 109 S.Ct. 391, 102 L.Ed.2d 380. Plaintiffs insist that their system was indeed novel, but contend that, in any event, novelty is not required to validate the contract at issue here.

II

Defendant's cross motion for summary judgment insofar as it sought to dismiss the first cause of action alleging breach of contract was properly denied. Additionally, plaintiffs' motion to dismiss the lack of consideration defenses and counterclaims should be granted.

Under the traditional principles of contract law, the parties to a contract are free to make their bargain, even if the consideration exchanged is grossly unequal or of dubious value (see, Spaulding v. Benenati, 57

N.Y.2d 418, 456 N.Y.S.2d 733, 442 N.E.2d 1244; Hamer v. Sidway, 124 N.Y. 538, 27 N.E. 256; 3 Williston, Contracts § 7:21, at 390 [Lord 4th ed.]; Restatement [Second] of Contracts § 74, comment e; § 79, comment c). Absent fraud or unconscionability, the adequacy of consideration is not a proper subject for judicial scrutiny (Spaulding v. Benenati, supra, 57 N.Y.2d at 423, 456 N.Y.S.2d 733, 442 N.E.2d 1244). It is enough that something of "real value in the eye of the law" was exchanged (see, Mencher v. Weiss, 306 N.Y. 1, 8, 114 N.E.2d 177; see also, Weiner v. McGraw–Hill, Inc., 57 N.Y.2d 458, 464, 457 N.Y.S.2d 193, 443 N.E.2d 441). The fact that the sellers may not have had a property right in what they sold does not, by itself, render the contract void for lack of consideration (see, Wahl v. Barnum, 116 N.Y. 87, 95, 22 N.E. 280 [relinquishment of disputed claim is valid consideration even though claim is in fact invalid]; Spaulding v. Benenati, supra, 57 N.Y.2d at 423, 456 N.Y.S.2d 733, 442 N.E.2d 1244 ["expectancy that customers will return to the seller's former location" is legally sufficient consideration]; see also, Restatement [Second] of Contracts § 74, comment e [contract for quitclaim deed valid, even though seller has no interest in the property]; 3 Williston, Contracts § 7:21, at 391 [Lord 4th ed.]).

Manifestly, defendant received something of value here; its own conduct establishes that. After signing the confidentiality agreement, defendant thoroughly reviewed plaintiffs' system before buying it. Having done so, it was in the best position to know whether the idea had value. It decided to enter into the sale agreement and aggressively market the system to potential bond issuers. For at least a year, it was the only underwriter to use plaintiffs' "book entry" system for municipal bonds, and it handled millions of such bond transactions during that time. Having obtained full disclosure of the system, used it in advance of competitors, and received the associated benefits of precluding its disclosure to others, defendant can hardly claim now the idea had no value to its municipal securities business. Indeed, defendant acknowledges it made payments to plaintiffs under the sale agreement for more than two years, conduct that would belie any claim it might make that the idea was lacking in value or that it had actually been obtained from some other source before plaintiffs' disclosure.

Thus, defendant has failed to demonstrate on this record that the contract was void or to raise a triable issue of fact on lack of consideration.

III

Defendant's position rests on Downey v. General Foods Corp., 31 N.Y.2d 56, 334 N.Y.S.2d 874, 286 N.E.2d 257, supra and Soule v. Bon Ami Co., 235 N.Y. 609, 139 N.E. 754, affg. 201 App.Div. 794, 195 N.Y.S. 574, supra and similar decisions. It contends those cases establish an exception to traditional principles of contract law and require that the idea must be novel before it can constitute valid consideration for a contract. While our cases have discussed novelty as an element of an idea seller's claim, it is not a discrete supplemental requirement, but simply part of plaintiff's proof of either a proprietary interest in a claim based on a property theory or the validity of the consideration in a claim based on a contract theory (see generally, 3 Nimmer, Copyright, ch. 16).

In Downey, plaintiff submitted an idea for an advertising campaign. A short time later, defendant General Foods mounted a campaign that was similar to the one plaintiff had suggested and plaintiff sought damages in a complaint alleging several theories for recovery (see, 37 A.D.2d 250, 323 N.Y.S.2d 578). We ordered the dismissal of the complaint on two separate grounds: first, the lack of novelty and, second, defendant's prior possession of the idea—i.e., its lack of novelty as to defendant (Downey, 31 N.Y.2d, at 61–62, 334 N.Y.S.2d 874, 286 N.E.2d 257). To the extent plaintiff's causes of action were grounded on assertions of a property right, we found that they were untenable "if the elements of novelty and originality [were] absent, since the property right in an idea is based upon these two elements" (id., at 61, 334 N.Y.S.2d 874, 286 N.E.2d 257). Second, we concluded that the defendant possessed plaintiff's ideas prior to plaintiff's disclosure. Thus, the ideas could have no value to defendant and could not supply consideration for any agreement between the parties (see, Ferber v. Sterndent Corp., 51 N.Y.2d 782, 433 N.Y.S.2d 85, 412 N.E.2d 1311).

In Soule v. Bon Ami Co., plaintiff made an express contract with Bon Ami to disclose a way to increase profits. The idea consisted largely of a proposal to raise prices. The Appellate Division, in a frequently cited opinion, denied plaintiff any recovery, finding that the bargain lacked consideration because the idea was not novel. This Court affirmed but it did so on a different basis: it held that plaintiff had failed to show that profits resulted from the disclosure.

These decisions do not support defendant's contention that novelty is required in all cases involving disclosure of ideas. Indeed, we have explicitly held that it is not (see, Keller v. American Chain Co., 255 N.Y. 94, 174 N.E. 74). Downey, Soule and cases in that line of decisions involve a distinct factual pattern: the buyer and seller contract for disclosure of the idea with payment based on use, but no separate postdisclosure contract for use of the idea has been made. Thus, they present the issue of whether the idea the buyer was using, was, in fact, the seller's.

Such transactions pose two problems for the courts. On the one hand, how can sellers prove that the buyer obtained the idea from them, and nowhere else, and that the buyer's use of it thus constitutes misappropriation of property? Unlike tangible property, an idea lacks title and boundaries and cannot be rendered exclusive by the acts of the one who first thinks it. On the other hand, there is no equity in enforcing a seemingly valid contract when, in fact, it turns out upon disclosure that the buyer already possessed the idea. In such instances, the disclosure, though freely bargained for, is manifestly without value. A showing of novelty, at least novelty as to the buyer, addresses these two concerns. Novelty can then serve to establish both the attributes of ownership necessary for a property-based claim and the value of the consideration—the disclosure—necessary for contract-based claims.

There are no such concerns in a transaction such as the one before us. Defendant does not claim that it was aware of the idea before plaintiffs disclosed it but, rather, concedes that the idea came from them. When a seller's claim arises from a contract to use an idea entered into after the disclosure of the idea, the question is not whether the buyer misappropriated property from the seller, but whether the idea had value to the buyer and thus constitutes valid consideration. In such a case, the buyer knows what he or she is buying and has agreed that the idea has value, and the Court will not ordinarily go behind that determination. The lack of novelty, in and of itself, does not demonstrate a lack of value (see, Keller v. American Chain Co., 255 N.Y. 94, 174 N.E. 74, supra). To the contrary, the buyer may reap benefits from such a contract in a number of ways—for instance, by not having to expend resources pursuing the idea through other channels or by having a profit-making idea implemented sooner rather than later. The law of contracts would have to be substantially rewritten were we to allow buyers of fully disclosed ideas to disregard their obligation to pay simply because an idea could have been obtained from some other source or in some other way.

* * *

Accordingly, the order of the Appellate Division should be modified, without costs, in accordance with this opinion, and, as so modified, affirmed, and the certified question answered in the negative.

■ KAYE, C.J., and TITONE, HANCOCK and BELLACOSA, JJ., concur.

■ SMITH, J., taking no part.

Order modified, etc.

Comment: The Peppercorn Theory of Consideration and the Doctrine of Fair Exchange in Contract Law

[The following is reprinted from the Columbia Law Review.]

Pervading the complex field of fine-spun theories of consideration are two inconsistent ideas. On the one hand, consideration is said to be only a form; on the other, it assures a fair exchange. In substantiation of the first view and in virtually absolute negation of the second stands the age-old formula that mere inadequacy of consideration is never a bar to enforcement of a contract. Although frequently subject to evasion this general formula has gone virtually unchallenged by the courts and has met with only occasional criticism by the writers.

Justification for this purported refusal to supervise the ethics of the market place is sought in doctrines of *laissez-faire*. Aside from the somewhat anachronistic character of the argument in a period of rising recognition of the social interest in "private business," it is clear that there has been constant judicial delimitation, in the law of fraud and duress, of the permissible pressures to be used in the bargaining process. In general, the freedom from regulation postulated by *laissez-faire* adherents is demonstrably non-existent and virtually inconceivable. Bargaining power exists only because of government protection of the property rights bargained, and is properly subject to government control. Undaunted, the courts urge that their inability to compare values justifies the inadequacy rule. While the complexity of the exchange process renders a precise standard utopian, the total inability is belied in practice. Enforcement has been denied to contracts involving unfair disparity. Even more refined comparison is attempted by those jurisdictions which recognize "inadequacy" as a bar to specific performance but will decree cancellation only for "gross inadequacy." Valid logical or practical opposition to judicial enforcement of fair exchange has thus not been offered. Further, however, the weight of the mass of pronouncements supporting the rule that inadequacy is immaterial is substantially weakened by an examination of the cases. A classification of the fact situations reveals frequent unnecessary citation of the rule in cases where a fair exchange actually did exist, or where other ethical factors upheld the decision.

The non-commercial, non-bargain situation offers little difficulty. Obviously, it is not unfair to enforce a disparate promise when the promisor both knew and *desired* such disparity. As a matter of fact, it is at least arguable that there is no disparity, since the promisor has "bargained" for a psychological satisfaction not measurable in pecuniary terms. Judicial refusal to recognize such bargain equivalence is reflected in the unenforceability of executory gifts in the absence of a formal consideration. On the other hand, it is nonetheless true that enforcement of such gifts where the formal requirements are satisfied is needlessly buttressed by reference to the immateriality of inadequacy. In a similar category fall cases enforcing against a promisor's heir agreements to pay a substantial sum for a small service or for the privilege of naming a new-born child. Hardly distinguishable are transactions motivated by loyalty rather than profit, such as family settlements or payment of the debt of one member of the family by another acting under a sense of moral obligation.

The commercial bargain situation threatens greater difficulty. Men in economic transactions do not *desire* disparity; here if anywhere its disregard will conflict with the notion of fair exchange. However, in cases presenting the bargain situation and relying on the immateriality of inadequacy, difference in value is often only apparent since significant elements of the whole transaction have been overlooked. Thus, the apparent disparity in the grant of a valuable option for only one dollar diminishes in the light of the realization that the option is only preliminary to a sale. And when the inequality in the option is sufficient to render the whole transaction patently unfair, enforcement may be denied.

Frequently an element of risk renders the disparity illusory, the value of the bargain being contingent on an event the occurrence of which is independent of the will of either party. Typical instances are the promise to care for a person for life, the purchase of a going concern or of a speculative commodity, a loan for the purpose of speculative investment, compromise of an uncertain legal claim. In virtually all, reference to inadequacy is unnecessary.

Indeed, undesired disparity in a transaction would seem possible only where one party erred as to the market values of the products exchanged or where the parties were unequal in bargaining power. If the benefited party was ignorant of his advantage, the problem involves a resolution of a conflict between the enforcement of a fair exchange and the satisfaction of just expectations. Expectations based on a known error are, of course, scarcely "just," so relief is normally granted to the injured party. Disparities resulting from inequalities of bargaining power, however, can scarcely be eliminated in a capitalist economy which must enforce the inequality of property rights that produces those results. Nevertheless economic anarchy does not exist. In addition to the outlawing of fraud and duress as bargaining pressures the courts have refused enforcement of advantages gained by exercise of a power resulting from fortuitous circumstances not within the ethical range of accepted economic practice. The disadvantageous sale of a legacy by an impecunious legatee is a typical instance. Unfair exactions resulting from the creditor-debtor relationship have been subjected to a control which is facilitated by the usury analogy, but the courts have, in addition, recognized the inferior bargaining power of debtors as a class. The employer-employee relationship suggests itself as one calling for similar treatment. Legislative recognition of the individual laborer's bargaining weakness has been forced time and again. Typical judicial legalism, however, unhampered by realistic analysis, has resulted in some indications that employment at will is regarded as sufficient consideration for release by the employee of a personal injury claim against his employer. On the other hand, the rule is subject to evasion and, further, employment at will has been held an insufficient return for other exactions.

Constant reiteration of the immateriality of inadequacy has obscured the notion of fair exchange in contract law. But the rule, while prominent in dictum, is only occasionally the true basis of decision. Conscious judicial regard for the ethical norms necessarily operative in any event must dwarf, if not destroy, the peppercorn theory of consideration. [Footnotes omitted.]

Note, 35 Colum.L.Rev. 1090 (1935).

Jones v. Star Credit Corp.

Supreme Court of New York, 1969.
59 Misc.2d 189, 298 N.Y.S.2d 264.

■ WACHTLER, J. On August 31, 1965, the plaintiffs, who are welfare recipients, agreed to purchase a home freezer unit for $900 as the result of a visit from a salesman representing Your Shop At Home Service, Inc. With the addition of the time credit charges, credit life insurance, credit property insurance, and sales tax, the purchase price totaled $1,234.80. Thus far the plaintiffs have paid $619.88 toward their purchase. The defendant claims that with various added credit charges paid for an extension of time there is a balance of $819.81 still due from the plaintiffs. The uncontroverted proof at the trial established that the freezer unit, when purchased, had a maximum retail value of approximately $300. The question is whether this transaction and the resulting contract could be considered unconscionable within the meaning of § 2–302 of the Uniform Commercial Code which provides * * *:

"(1) If the court as a matter of law finds the contract or any clause of the contract to have been unconscionable at the time it was made the court may refuse to enforce the contract, or it may enforce the remainder of the contract without the unconscionable clause, or it may so limit the application of any unconscionable clause as to avoid any unconscionable result.

"(2) When it is claimed or appears to the court that the contract or any clause thereof may be unconscionable the parties shall be afforded a reasonable opportunity to present evidence as to its commercial setting, purpose and effect to aid the court in making the determination" (L.1962, chap. 553, eff. Sept. 27, 1964).

There was a time when the shield of "caveat emptor" would protect the most unscrupulous in the marketplace—a time when the law, in granting parties unbridled latitude to make their own contracts, allowed exploitive and callous practices which shocked the conscience of both legislative bodies and the courts.

The effort to eliminate these practices has continued to pose a difficult problem. On the one hand it is necessary to recognize the importance of preserving the integrity of agreements and the fundamental right of parties to deal, trade, bargain, and contract. On the other hand there is the concern for the uneducated and often illiterate individual who is the victim of gross inequality of bargaining power, usually the poorest members of the community.

Concern for the protection of these consumers against overreaching by the small but hardy breed of merchants who would prey on them is not novel. The dangers of inequality of bargaining power were vaguely recognized in the early English common law when Lord Hardwicke wrote of a fraud, "which may be apparent from the intrinsic nature and subject of the bargain itself; such as no man in his senses and not under delusion would make." The English authorities on this subject were discussed in Hume v. United States (132 U.S. 406, 10 S.Ct. 134 [1889]), where the United States Supreme Court characterized these as "cases in which one party took advantage of the other's ignorance of arithmetic to impose upon him, and the fraud was apparent from the face of the contracts."

The law is beginning to fight back against those who once took advantage of the poor and illiterate without risk of either exposure or interference. From the common law doctrine of intrinsic fraud we have, over the years, developed common and statutory law which tells not only the buyer but also the seller to beware. This body of laws recognizes the importance of a free enterprise system but at the same time will provide the legal armor to protect and safeguard the prospective victim from the harshness of an unconscionable contract.

Section 2–302 of the Uniform Commercial Code enacts the moral sense of the community into the law of commercial transactions. It authorizes the court to find, as a matter of law, that a contract or a clause of a contract was "unconscionable at the time it was made," and upon so finding the court may refuse to enforce the contract, excise the objectionable clause or limit the application of the clause to avoid an unconscionable result. "The principle," states the Official Comment to this section, "is one of the prevention of oppression and unfair surprise." It permits a court to accomplish directly what heretofore was often accomplished by construction of language, manipulations of fluid rules of contract law and determinations based upon a presumed public policy.

There is no reason to doubt, moreover, that this section is intended to encompass the price term of the agreement. In addition to the fact that it has already been so applied (State by Lefkowitz v. ITM, Inc., 52 Misc.2d 39, 275 N.Y.S.2d 303; Frostifresh Corp. v. Reynoso, 274 N.Y.S.2d 757, rev'd. 281 N.Y.S.2d 964; American Home Improvement Inc. v. MacIver, 105 N.H. 435, 201 A.2d 886), the statutory language itself makes it clear that not only a clause of the contract, but the contract in toto, may be found unconscionable as a matter of law. Indeed, no other provision of an agreement more intimately touches upon the question of unconscionability than does the term regarding prices.

Fraud, in the instant case, is not present; nor is it necessary under the statute. The question which presents itself is whether or not, under the circumstances of this case, the sale of a freezer unit having a retail value of $300 for $900 ($1,439.69 including credit charges and $18 sales tax) is unconscionable as a matter of law. The court believes it is.

Concededly, deciding the issue is substantially easier than explaining it. No doubt, the mathematical disparity between $300, which presumably includes a reasonable profit margin, and $900, which is exorbitant on its face, carries the greatest weight. Credit charges alone exceed by more than $100 the retail value of the freezer. These alone, may be sufficient to sustain the decision. Yet, a caveat is warranted lest we reduce the import of § 2–302 solely to a mathematical ratio formula. It may, at times, be that; yet it may also be much more. The very limited financial resources of the purchaser, known to the sellers at the time of the sale, is entitled to weight in the balance. Indeed, the value disparity itself leads inevitably to the felt conclusion that knowing advantage was taken of the plaintiffs. In addition, the meaningfulness of choice essential to the making of a contract can be negated by a gross inequality of bargaining power (Williams v. Walker–Thomas Furniture Co., 121 U.S.App.D.C. 315, 350 F.2d 445).

There is no question about the necessity and even the desirability of installment sales and the extension of credit. Indeed, there are many, including welfare recipients, who would be deprived of even the most basic conveniences without the use of these devices. Similarly, the retail merchant selling on installment or extending credit is expected to establish a pricing factor which will afford a degree of protection commensurate with the risk of selling to those who might be default prone. However, neither of these accepted premises can clothe the sale of this freezer with respectability.

Support for the court's conclusion will be found in a number of other cases already decided. In American Home Imp., Inc. v. MacIver (supra), the Supreme Court of New Hampshire held that a contract to install windows, a door and paint, for the price of $2,568.60, of which $809.60 constituted interest and carrying charges and $800 was a salesman's commission was unconscionable as a matter of law. In State by Lefkowitz v. ITM, Inc. (supra), a deceptive and fraudulent scheme was involved, but standing alone, the court held that the sale of a vacuum cleaner, among other things, costing the defendant $140 and sold by it for $749 cash or $920.52 on time purchase was unconscionable as a matter of law. Finally, in FrostiFresh Corp. v. Reynoso (supra), the sale of a refrigerator costing the seller $348 for $900 plus credit charges of $245.88 was unconscionable as a matter of law.

* * *

Having already [been] paid more than $600 toward the purchase of this $300 freezer unit, it is apparent that the defendant has already been amply compensated. In accordance with the statute, the application of the payment provision should be limited to amounts already paid by the plaintiffs and the contract be reformed and amended by changing the payments called for therein to equal the amount of payment actually so paid by the plaintiffs.

Submit judgment on notice.

NOTES

(1) Upon what grounds was the price term found to be unconscionable? Although the facts reveal that the plaintiff was on welfare and that the sale was probably made at home, there is no other evidence on the relative bargaining capacities (e.g., education, language skills, health, intelligence) of the parties. Does this support the "felt conclusion that knowing advantage was taken of the plaintiff?" If the contract price was disclosed and the plaintiff could have obtained a comparable freezer from another seller for $300, is judicial review of the adequacy of the exchange justified? What else do you need to know before that question can be answered?

(2) The Federal Trade Commission, by regulation, requires a "cooling off period" for door-to-door sales. In essence, the seller must inform the consumer in writing and in CONSPICUOUS type in the "same language, e.g., Spanish, as that principally used in the oral sales presentation" the following: "YOU, THE BUYER, MAY CANCEL THIS TRANSACTION AT ANY TIME PRIOR TO MIDNIGHT OF THE THIRD BUSINESS DAY AFTER THE DATE OF THIS TRANSACTION. SEE THE ATTACHED NOTICE OF CANCELLATION FORM FOR AN EXPLANATION OF THIS RIGHT." 16 C.F.R. sec. 429.1 (March 1, 1996). In addition, Section 4(c) of the Uniform Consumer Sales Practices Act provides that "in determining whether an act or practice is unconscionable, the court shall consider circumstances such as the following of which the supplier knew or had reason to know: (1) that he took advantage of the inability of the consumer reasonably to protect his interests because of his

physical infirmity, ignorance, illiteracy, inability to understand the language of an agreement or similar factors; (2) that when the consumer transaction was entered into the price grossly exceeded the price at which similar property or services were readily obtainable in similar transactions by like consumers; . . . (4) that when the consumer transaction was entered into there was no reasonable probability of payment of the obligation in full by the consumer."

(3) In California Grocers v. Bank of America, 22 Cal.App.4th 205, 27 Cal.Rptr.2d 396 (1994), defendant bank charged customers a $3 fee for certain returned deposit items (DIRs). The California Grocers Association, a trade group of retail and wholesale grocers, attacked the fee. In holding that the fee was not unconscionable ("not so high as to shock the conscience"), the court relied upon two determinations: First, there was "free" competition among banks in California and the $3 fee was at the low end of similar fees charged by other banks; and Second, the "$3 fee is not so exorbitant as to shock the conscience." Even though the cost of processing a DIR was only $1.50, the markup was "only 100 percent." "This may be a generous profit, but it is wholly within the range of commonly accepted notions of fair profitability." The court noted that price unconscionability cases "generally involve much greater price-value disparities" and cited *Jones v. Star Credit* for the proposition that a "sale of a freezer at triple its retail value" was unconscionable. Id. At 402–403. See, generally, Frank P. Darr, *Unconscionability and Price Fairness*, 30 Hous.L.Rev. 1819 (1994).

Comment: Adequacy of Consideration

To what extent, if any, should courts protect contracting parties from "bad bargains"? This is a classic policy question which must be confronted in every legal system. The standard response of the common law is that apart from instances where there is some impropriety involved (as, for example, where a promise is procured through fraud, duress, etc.) the courts take a "hands off" attitude. They insist that there be an actual bargain struck by the parties, but beyond this they will not, in traditional language, "inquire into the adequacy of the consideration." This has been regarded as a corollary of freedom of contract, buttressed by laissez-faire economics. Reflecting this approach, the first Restatement states flatly that "the relative values of a promise and the consideration for it, do not affect the sufficiency of consideration." (§ 81). Similarly, the revised Restatement provides that there is no requirement of "equivalence in the values exchanged." Restatement (Second) § 79(b). The following typifies the judicial attitude: "Appellant's argument that the contract should not be enforced because the real estate was worth much more than the purchase price named in the agreement is, likewise, without merit. * * * It is the general rule that inadequacy of consideration, exorbitance of price or improvidence in a contract will not, in the absence of fraud, constitute a defense * * *. The evidence does not show any fraud or bad faith on the part of the appellees. While appellant indicates that she was tired and ill at the time of the transaction, the nature of her illness was not disclosed, it does not appear that her mental faculties were impaired, and it is nowhere contended that she was not competent to contract. Under such circumstances, it is not inequitable or unjust to require appellant to do what she agreed to do." Hotze v. Schlanser, 410 Ill. 265, 102 N.E.2d 131, 133–4 (1951). This general respect for private autonomy, encompassing a broad recognition of the power of contracting parties to determine their own obligations, can be discerned in contemporary law. See Braucher, *Freedom of Contract and the Second Restatement,* 78 Yale L.J. 598 (1969).

At the other pole was the general medieval attitude, influenced in part by Roman law antecedents, which sought to insure equivalency of value in all exchanges. Concepts of "just price," etc. were formulated in this effort to inhibit unfair advantage in bargaining, even where the disadvantage arose from inadvertence, inexperience, carelessness, or the like. See Squillante, *The Doctrine of Just Price—Its Origin and Development,* 74 Com.L.J. 333 (1969). By the doctrine of *laesio enormis* a vendor could rescind a transaction where the price received was less than one-half its value. This was limited to real estate transactions under Roman law, but extended to others by the canonists. There are some vestiges of the lesion doctrine in civil law countries, but the trend has been in the other direction. See, e.g., Amos and Walton, Introduction to French Law 163–5 (2d ed. 1963). Interestingly, American law has moved somewhat the other way. Inadequacy, as such, is rarely an avowed reason for relief from a bargain, but it may be grounds for denying specific performance. Moreover, it may serve as a wedge whereby a very careful scrutiny will be made of the bargaining process. Thus it may be that a low price is seen as evidence of impropriety, as a "badge of fraud." Similarly, the court may be more easily persuaded to relieve because of mutual mistake or duress. The concept of duress has, in recent times, been employed in an ever-increasing variety of situations. See Dawson, *Economic Duress—An Essay in Perspective,* 45 Mich.L.Rev. 253 (1947). In addition, there is great concern over so-called "contracts of adhesion," i.e., form "contracts" drafted exclusively by one party and offered to the other on a "take-it-or-leave-it" basis. As noted in *Jones v. Star Credit Corp.,* there is an express provision in the Uniform Commercial Code (§ 2–302) which empowers a court to refuse enforcement to any contract, or clause in a contract, it deems to be "unconscionable." The official comment states that this section is intended to make it possible for the courts "to police explicitly against the contracts or clauses which they find to be unconscionable." To what extent "inadequacy" may, by judicial finding, be found to be "unconscionable" is problematical. *Jones* is representative of judicial opinion in the area. This and related aspects of the general problem are systematically developed in Chapter Four, Section 2, *Defects in Bargaining Process.*

In re Greene

United States District Court, Southern District of New York, 1930.
45 F.2d 428.

■ WOOLSEY, DISTRICT JUDGE. The petition for review is granted, and the order of the referee is reversed.

I.   The claimant, a woman, filed proof of claim in the sum of $375,700, based on an alleged contract, against this bankrupt's estate. The trustee in bankruptcy objected to the claim.

A hearing was held before the referee in bankruptcy and testimony taken.

The referee held the claim valid and dismissed the objections. The correctness of this ruling is raised by the trustee's petition to review and the referee's certificate.

II.   For several years prior to April 28, 1926, the bankrupt, a married man, had apparently lived in adultery with the claimant. He gave her substantial sums of money. He also paid $70,000 for a house on Long Island acquired by her, which she still owns.

Throughout their relations the bankrupt was a married man, and the claimant knew it. The claimant was well over thirty years of age when the connection began. She testified that the bankrupt had promised to marry her as soon as his wife should get a divorce from him; this the bankrupt denied.

The relations of intimacy between them were discontinued in April, 1926, and they then executed a written instrument under seal which is alleged to be a binding contract and which is the foundation of the claim under consideration.

In this instrument, which was made in New York, the bankrupt undertook (1) to pay to the claimant $1,000 a month during their joint lives; (2) to assign to her a $100,000 life insurance policy on his life and to keep up the premiums on it for life, the bankrupt to pay $100,000 to the claimant in case the policy should lapse for nonpayment of premiums; and (3) to pay the rent for four years on an apartment which she had leased.

It was declared in the instrument that the bankrupt had no interest in the Long Island house or in its contents, and that he should no longer be liable for mortgage interest, taxes, and other charges on this property.

The claimant on her part released the bankrupt from all claims which she had against him.

The preamble to the instrument recites as consideration the payment of $1 by the claimant to the bankrupt, "and other good and valuable considerations."

The bankrupt kept up the several payments called for by the instrument until August, 1928, but failed to make payments thereafter.

* * *

In view of my conclusion that the entire claim is void, however, the matter of damages is of no present importance.

* * *

The problem in the present case * * * is one of consideration, not of illegality, and it is clear that the past illicit intercourse is not consideration.

* * *

V.   The question, therefore, is whether there was any consideration for the bankrupt's promises, apart from the past cohabitation. It seems plain that no such consideration can be found, but I will review the following points emphasized by the claimant as showing consideration:

(1) The $1 consideration recited in the paper is nominal. It cannot seriously be urged that $1, recited but not even shown to have been paid, will support an executory promise to pay hundreds of thousands of dollars.

(2) "Other good and valuable considerations" are generalities that sound plausible, but the words cannot serve as consideration where the facts show that nothing good or valuable was actually given at the time the contract was made.

(3) It is said that the release of claims furnishes the necessary consideration. So it would if the claimant had had any claims to release. But the evidence shows no vestige of any lawful claim. Release from imaginary claims is not valuable consideration for a promise. In this connection, apparently, the claimant testified that the bankrupt had promised to marry her as soon as he was divorced. Assuming that he did—though he denies it—the illegality of any such promise, made while the bankrupt was still married, is so obvious that no claim could possibly arise from it, and the release of such claim could not possibly be lawful consideration.

(4) The claimant also urges that by the agreement the bankrupt obtained immunity from liability for taxes and other charges on the Long Island house. The fact is that he was never chargeable for these expenses. He doubtless had been in the habit of paying them, just as he had paid many other expenses for the claimant; but such payments were either gratuitous or were the contemporaneous price of the continuance of his illicit intercourse with the claimant.

It is absurd to suppose that, when a donor gives a valuable house to a donee, the fact that the donor need pay no taxes or upkeep thereafter on the property converts the gift into a contract upon consideration. The present case is even stronger, for the bankrupt had never owned the house and had never been liable for the taxes. He furnished the purchase price, but the conveyance was from the seller direct to the claimant.

(5) Finally, it is said that the parties intended to make a valid agreement. It is a non sequitur to say that therefore the agreement is valid.

A man may promise to make a gift to another, and may put the promise in the most solemn and formal document possible; but, barring exceptional cases, such, perhaps, as charitable subscriptions, the promise will not be enforced. The parties may shout consideration to the housetops, yet unless consideration is actually present, there is not a legally enforcible contract.

What the bankrupt obviously intended in this case was an agreement to make financial contribution to the claimant because of his past cohabitation with her, and, as already pointed out, such an agreement lacks consideration.

V.   The presence of the seal would have been decisive in the claimant's favor a hundred years ago. Then an instrument under seal required no consideration, or, to keep to the language of the cases, the seal was conclusive evidence of consideration. In New York, however, a seal is now only presumptive evidence of consideration on an executory instrument. Civil Practice Act, § 342; Harris v. Shorall, 230 N.Y. 343, 348, 130 N.E. 572; Alexander v. Equitable Life Assurance Society, 233 N.Y. 300, 307, 135 N.E. 509. This presumption was amply rebutted in this case, for the proof clearly shows, I think, that there was not in fact any consideration for the bankrupt's promise contained in the executory instrument signed by him and the claimant.

An order in accordance with this opinion may be submitted for settlement on two days' notice.

Fiege v. Boehm

Court of Appeals of Maryland, 1956.
210 Md. 352, 123 A.2d 316.

■ DELAPLAINE, JUDGE. This suit was brought in the Superior Court of Baltimore City by Hilda Louise Boehm against Louis Gail Fiege to recover for breach of a contract to pay the expenses incident to the birth of his bastard child and to provide for its support upon condition that she would refrain from prosecuting him for bastardy.

Plaintiff alleged in her declaration substantially as follows: (1) that early in 1951 defendant had sexual intercourse with her although she was unmarried, and as a result thereof she became pregnant, and defendant acknowledged that he was responsible for her pregnancy; (2) that on September 29, 1951, she gave birth to a female child; that defendant is the father of the child; and that he acknowledged on many occasions that he is its father; (3) that before the child was born, defendant agreed to pay all her medical and miscellaneous expenses and to compensate her for the loss of her salary caused by the child's birth, and also to pay her ten dollars per week for its support until it reached the age of 21, upon condition that she would not institute bastardy proceedings against him as long as he made the payments in accordance with the agreement; (4) that she placed the child for adoption on July 13, 1954, and she claimed the following sums: Union Memorial Hospital, $110; Florence Crittenton Home, $100; Dr. George Merrill, her physician, $50; medicines $70.35; miscellaneous expenses, $20.45; loss of earnings for 26 weeks, $1,105; support of the child, $1,440; total, $2,895.80; and (5) that defendant paid her only $480, and she demanded that he pay her the further sum of $2,415.80, the balance due under the agreement, but he failed and refused to pay the same.

Defendant demurred to the declaration on the ground that it failed to allege that in September, 1953, plaintiff instituted bastardy proceedings against him in the Criminal Court of Baltimore, but since it had been found from blood tests that he could not have been the father of the child, he was acquitted of bastardy. The Court sustained the demurrer with leave to amend.

Plaintiff then filed an amended declaration, which contained the additional allegation that, after the breach of the agreement by defendant, she filed a charge with the State's Attorney that defendant was the father of her bastard child; and that on October 8, 1953, the Criminal Court found defendant not guilty solely on a physician's testimony that "on the basis of certain blood tests made, the defendant can be excluded as the father of the said child, which testimony is not conclusive upon a jury in a trial court."

Defendant also demurred to the amended declaration, but the Court overruled that demurrer.

Plaintiff, a typist, now over 35 years old, who has been employed by the Government in Washington and Baltimore for over thirteen years, testified in the Court below that she had never been married, but that at about midnight on January 21, 1951, defendant, after taking her to a moving picture theater on York Road and then to a restaurant, had sexual intercourse with her in his automobile. She further testified that he agreed to pay all her medical and hospital expenses, to compensate her for loss of salary caused by the pregnancy and birth, and to pay her ten dollars per week for the support of the child upon condition that she would refrain from instituting bastardy proceedings against him. She further testified that between September 17, 1951, and May, 1953, defendant paid her a total of $480.

Defendant admitted that he had taken plaintiff to restaurants, had danced with her several times, had taken her to Washington, and had brought her home in the country; but he asserted that he had never had sexual intercourse with her. He also claimed that he did not enter into any agreement with her. He admitted, however, that he had paid her a total of $480. His father also testified that he stated "that he did not want his mother to know, and if it were just kept quiet, kept principally away from his mother and the public and the courts, that he would take care of it."

Defendant further testified that in May, 1953, he went to see plaintiff's physician to make inquiry about blood tests to show the paternity of the child; and that those tests were made and they indicated that it was not possible that he could have been the child's father. He then stopped making payments. Plaintiff thereupon filed a charge of bastardy with the State's Attorney.

The testimony which was given in the Criminal Court by Dr. Milton Sachs, hematologist at the University Hospital, was read to the jury in the Superior Court. In recent years the blood-grouping test has been employed in criminology, in the selection of donors for blood transfusions, and as evidence in paternity cases. The Landsteiner blood-grouping test is based on the medical theory that the red corpuscles in human blood contain two affirmative agglutinating substances, and that every individual's blood falls into one of the four classes and remains the same throughout life. According to Mendel's law of inheritance, this blood individuality is an hereditary characteristic which passes from parent to child, and no agglutinating substance can appear in the blood of a child which is not present in the blood of one of its parents. The four Landsteiner blood groups, designated as AB, A, B, and O, into which human blood is divided on the basis of the compatibility of the corpuscles and serum with the corpuscles and serum of other persons, are characterized by different combinations of two agglutinogens in the red blood cells and two agglutinins in the serum. Dr. Sachs reported that Fiege's blood group was Type O. Miss Boehm's was Type B, and the infant's was Type A. He further testified that on the basis of these tests, Fiege could not have been the father of the child, as it is impossible for a mating of Type O and Type B to result in a child of Type A.

Although defendant was acquitted by the Criminal Court, the Superior Court overruled his motion for a directed verdict. In the charge to the jury the Court instructed them that defendant's acquittal in the Criminal Court was not binding upon them. The jury found a verdict in favor of plaintiff for $2,415.80, the full amount of her claim.

Defendant filed a motion for judgment n.o.v. or a new trial. The Court overruled that motion also, and entered judgment on the verdict of the jury. Defendant appealed from that judgment.

Defendant contends that, even if he did enter into the contract as alleged, it was not enforceable, because plaintiff's forbearance to prosecute was not based on a valid claim, and hence the contract was without consideration. He, therefore, asserts that the Court erred in overruling (1) his demurrer to the amended declaration, (2) his motion for a directed verdict, and (3) his motion for judgment n.o.v. or a new trial.

It was originally held at common law that a child born out of wedlock is *filius nullius,* and a putative father is not under any legal liability to contribute to the support of his illegitimate child, and his promise to do so is unenforceable because it is based on purely a moral obligation. Some of the courts in this country have held that, in the absence of any statutory obligation on the father to aid in the support of his bastard child, his promise to the child's mother to pay her for its maintenance, resting solely on his natural affection for it and his moral obligation to provide for it, is a promise which the law cannot enforce because of lack of sufficient consideration. ... On the contrary, a few courts have stated that the natural affection of a father for his child and the moral obligation upon him to support it and to aid the woman he has wronged furnish sufficient consideration for his promise to the mother to pay for the support of the child to make the agreement enforceable at law. ...

However, where statutes are in force to compel the father of a bastard to contribute to its support, the courts have invariably held that a contract by the putative father with the mother of his bastard child to provide for the support of the child upon the agreement of the mother to refrain from invoking the bastardy statute against the father, or to abandon proceedings already commenced, is supported by sufficient consideration. . . .

In Maryland it is now provided by statute what whenever a person is found guilty of bastardy, the court shall issue an order directing such person (1) to pay for the maintenance and support of the child until it reaches the age of eighteen years, such sum as may be agreed upon, if consent proceedings be had, or in the absence of agreement, such sum as the court may fix, with due regard to the circumstances of the accused person; and (2) to give bond to the State of Maryland in such penalty as the court may fix, with good and sufficient securities, conditioned on making the payments required by the court's order, or any amendments thereof. Failure to give such bond shall be punished by commitment to the jail or the House of Correction until bond is given but not exceeding two years. Code Supp.1955, art. 12, § 8.

Prosecutions for bastardy are treated in Maryland as criminal proceedings, but they are actually civil in purpose. . . . While the prime object of the Maryland Bastardy Act is to protect the public from the burden of maintaining illegitimate children, it is so distinctly in the interest of the mother that she becomes the beneficiary of it. Accordingly a contract by the putative father of an illegitimate child to provide for its support upon condition that bastardy proceedings will not be instituted is a compromise of civil injuries resulting from a criminal act, and not a contract to compound a criminal prosecution, and if it is fair and reasonable, it is in accord with the Bastardy Act and the public policy of the State.

Of course, a contract of a putative [alleged] father to provide for the support of his illegitimate child must be based, like any other contract, upon sufficient consideration. The early English law made no distinction in regard to the sufficiency of a claim which the claimant promised to forbear to prosecute, as the consideration of a promise, other than the broad distinction between good claims and bad claims. No promise to forbear to prosecute an unfounded claim was sufficient consideration. In the early part of the Nineteenth Century, an advance was made from the criterion of the early authorities when it was held that forbearance to prosecute a suit which had already been instituted was sufficient consideration, without inquiring whether the suit would have been successful or not. . . .

In 1867 the Maryland Court of Appeals, in the opinion delivered by Judge Bartol in Hartle v. Stahl, 27 Md. 157, 172, held: (1) that forbearance to assert a claim before institution of suit, if not in fact a legal claim, is not of itself sufficient consideration to support a promise; but (2) that a compromise of a doubtful claim or a relinquishment of a pending suit is good consideration for a promise; and (3) that in order to support a compromise, it is sufficient that the parties entering into it thought at the time that there was a *bona fide* question between them, although it may eventually be found that there was in fact no such question.

We have thus adopted the rule that the surrender of, or forbearance to assert, an invalid claim by one who has not an honest and reasonable belief in its possible validity is not sufficient consideration for a contract. 1

Restatement, Contracts, sec. 76(b). We combine the subjective requisite that the claim be *bona fide* with the objective requisite that it must have a reasonable basis of support. Accordingly a promise not to prosecute a claim which is not founded in good faith does not of itself give a right of action on an agreement to pay for refraining from so acting, because a release from mere annoyance and unfounded litigation does not furnish valuable consideration.

Professor Williston was not entirely certain whether the test of reasonableness is based upon the intelligence of the claimant himself, who may be an ignorant person with no knowledge of law and little sense as to facts; but he seemed inclined to favor the view that "the claim forborne must be neither absurd in fact from the standpoint of a reasonable man in the position of the claimant, nor, obviously unfounded in law to one who has an elementary knowledge of legal principles." 1 Williston on Contracts, Rev. Ed., sec. 135. We agree that while stress is placed upon the honesty and good faith of the claimant, forbearance to prosecute a claim is insufficient consideration if the claim forborne is so lacking in foundation as to make its assertion incompatible with honesty and a reasonable degree of intelligence. Thus, if the mother of a bastard knows that there is no foundation, either in law or fact, for a charge against a certain man that he is the father of the child, but that man promises to pay her in order to prevent bastardy proceedings against him, the forbearance to institute proceedings is not sufficient consideration.

On the other hand, forbearance to sue for a lawful claim or demand is sufficient consideration for a promise to pay for the forbearance if the party forbearing had an honest intention to prosecute litigation which is not frivolous, vexatious, or unlawful, and which he believed to be well founded. . . . Thus the promise of a woman who is expecting an illegitimate child that she will not institute bastardy proceedings against a certain man is sufficient consideration for his promise to pay for the child's support, even though it may not be certain whether the man is the father or whether the prosecution would be successful, if she makes the charge in good faith. The fact that a man accused of bastardy is forced to enter into a contract to pay for the support of his bastard child from fear of exposure and the shame that might be cast upon him as a result, as well as a sense of justice to render some compensation for the injury he inflicted upon the mother, does not lessen the merit of the contract, but greatly increases it. . . .

* * *

In the case at bar there was no proof of fraud or unfairness. Assuming that the hemotologists were accurate in their laboratory tests and findings, nevertheless plaintiff gave testimony which indicated that she made the charge of bastardy against defendant in good faith. For these reasons the Court acted properly in overruling the demurrer to the amended declaration and the motion for a directed verdict.

* * *

Judgment affirmed, with costs.

NOTES

(1) In either case was there a legal obligation which the promisee agreed to relinquish? Should the existence of such a legal obligation be a necessary prerequisite to enforcement of the other's promise?

(2) Are *Greene* and *Fiege* inconsistent? In terms of the apparent rationale of consideration, should courts establish a general policy of favoring compromise agreements of the kind discussed?

(3) Should the requirement be that the claimant have both an honest *and* a reasonable belief in the validity of a claim, as in Restatement § 76, or should honest belief ("the forbearing or surrendering party believes that the claim or defense may be fairly determined to be valid") or good faith alone suffice, as under Restatement (Second) § 74(1)(b)? Can the two standards be sharply delineated? Might not the absence of a reasonable belief itself be some evidence of bad faith? See Corbin § 140. A Missouri appellate court candidly addressed the problem as follows:

In Restatement removed reasonable test

"The law favors compromise of doubtful claims, and forbearance may be a sufficient consideration for such compromise, even though the claim upon which it is based should develop to be ill-founded. The fact that, had the parties proceeded to litigate the claim, one of them would certainly have won, does not destroy the consideration for the compromise, for the consideration is said to be the settlement of the dispute.

"But there are certain essentials to the validity of such consideration. For one thing, and by all authority, the claim upon which the settlement is based must be one made in good faith. ... Secondly, the claim must have *some* foundation. As to this second consideration we find the courts using varying language. The claim cannot be 'utterly baseless.' It has been said that it must have a 'tenable ground' or a 'reasonable, tenable ground.' It must be based on a 'colorable right,' or on some 'legal foundation.' It must have at least an appearance of right sufficient to raise a 'possible doubt' in favor of the party asserting it. ...

(inconsistency btwn authorities)

"It is difficult to reconcile the antinomous rules and statements which are applied to the 'doubtful claims' and to find the words which will exactly draw the line between the compromise (on the one hand) of an honestly disputed claim which has some fair element of doubt and is therefore to be regarded as consideration and (on the other hand) a claim, though honestly made, which is so lacking in substance and virility as to be entirely baseless. The Missouri courts have struggled and not yet found apt language. We think we had best leave definitions alone, confident that, as applied to each individual case, the facts will make the thing apparent. But if we should make further effort to distinguish we would say that if the claimant, *in good faith,* makes a mountain out of a mole hill the claim is 'doubtful.' But if there is no discernible mole hill in the beginning, then the claim has no substance." Duncan v. Black, 324 S.W.2d 483, 486–8 (Mo.App.1959).

Was there a "mole hill" in *In re Greene*? In *Fiege v. Boehm?*

(2) PRE–EXISTING DUTY RULE

In our legal tradition, an agreement to discharge an existing obligation and an agreement to modify an existing contract may have consideration implications because of the so-called pre-existing duty rule. The rule is that the performance or the promise to perform a pre-existing duty does not constitute consideration. Perhaps no common law rule has been subjected to more critical evaluation than this staple of contract law. Courts have exercised considerable ingenuity in fashioning "exceptions," and there is a significant reorientation of the matter in the Uniform Commercial Code. See UCC 1–107, 2–209(1). [UCC 2–210(a)(1997)].

The rule emerged in cases involving the discharge of obligations. To illustrate: Debtor owes Creditor $1,000. The parties agree that Creditor will accept $500 in full settlement. Debtor pays the agreed $500; Creditor sues for the remaining $500. Creditor wins.

Based upon the previous cases in this chapter, is this a predictable result? Is it a good result? What additional facts might influence your judgment as to the proper outcome?

As the rule developed it was also applied to the modification of an existing contract in which one party undertook to do something additional and the other performed (or promised to perform) that which he or she had already agreed to perform. For example, Contractor agrees to build a garage, and Owner promises to pay $5,000. Contractor refuses to perform unless Owner agrees to pay an additional $1,000. Owner promises to pay the additional amount. Is this promise enforceable? The traditional answer is no. There is no consideration for Owner's promise to pay the $1,000, because Contractor did no more than that which it was already obliged to do.

Is a result favorable to Owner the logical outcome under the concept of consideration as elaborated in the preceding cases? Is it a fair result? Again, what additional factual data would be helpful?

Reflection upon these questions and a study of the materials which follow in this section will indicate that the problems in these types of cases go beyond the scope normally reached by consideration theory. Moreover, there are policy considerations which are simply not dealt with adequately under the rubric of consideration. For this reason, we return later in the book to aspects of both discharge and modification of contractual obligations. Collateral reading: Farnsworth §§ 4.21–4.25; Calamari and Perillo §§ 4–9—4–11; Murray § 64.

Levine v. Blumenthal

Supreme Court of New Jersey, 1936.
117 N.J.L. 23, 186 A. 457.

■ HEHER, J. By an indenture dated April 16th, 1931, plaintiff leased to defendants, for the retail merchandising of women's wearing apparel, store premises situate in the principal business district of the city of Paterson. The term was two years, to commence on May 1st next ensuing, with an option of renewal for the further period of three years, and the rent reserved was $2,100 for the first year, and $2,400 for the second year, payable in equal monthly installments in advance.

The state of the case settled by the District Court judge sets forth that defendants adduced evidence tending to show that, in the month of April, 1932, before the expiration of the first year of the term, they advised plaintiff that "it was absolutely impossible for them to pay any increase in rent; that their business had so fallen down that they had great difficulty in meeting the present rent of $175 per month; that if the plaintiff insisted upon the increase called for in the lease, they would be forced to remove from the premises or perhaps go out of business altogether;" and that plaintiff "agreed to allow them to remain under the same rental 'until business improved.'" While conceding that defendants informed him that "they could not pay the increase called for in the lease because of adverse business conditions," plaintiff, on the other hand, testified that he "agreed to accept the payment of $175 each month, on account." For eleven months of the second year of the term rent was paid by defendants, and accepted by plaintiff, at the rate of $175 per month. The option of renewal was not exercised; and defendants surrendered the premises at the expiration of the term leaving the last month's rent unpaid. This action was brought to recover the unpaid balance of the rent reserved by the lease for the second year—$25 per month for eleven months, and $200 for the last month.

The District Court judge found, as a fact, that "a subsequent oral agreement had been made to change and alter the terms of the written lease, with respect to the rent paid," but that it was not supported by "a lawful consideration," and therefore was wholly ineffective.

The insistence is that the current trade depression had disabled the lessees in respect of the payment of the full rent reserved, and a consideration sufficient to support the secondary agreement arose out of these special circumstances; and that, in any event, the execution of the substituted performance therein provided is a defense at law, notwithstanding the want of consideration. ... It is said also that, "in so far as the oral agreement has become executed as to the payments which had fallen due and had been paid and accepted in full as per the oral agreement," the remission of the balance of the rent is sustainable on the theory of gift, if not of accord and satisfaction. ...

It is not suggested that the primary contract under consideration was of a class which may not lawfully be modified by parol, except to the extent that the substituted performance has been actually and fully executed and accepted; and we are not therefore called upon to consider that question. ... The point made by respondent is that the subsequent oral agreement to reduce the rent is *nudum pactum,* and therefore created no binding obligation.

It is elementary that the subsequent agreement, to impose the obligation of a contract, must rest upon a new and independent consideration. The rule was laid down in very early times that even though a part of a matured liquidated debt or demand has been given and received in full satisfaction thereof, the creditor may yet recover the remainder. The payment of a part was not regarded in law as a satisfaction of the whole, unless it was in virtue of an agreement supported by a consideration. . . . The principle is firmly imbedded in our jurisprudence that a promise to do what the promisor is already legally bound to do is an unreal consideration. . . . It has been criticised, at least in some of its special applications as "mediaeval" and wholly artificial—one that operates to defeat the "reasonable bargains of business men." See Professor Ames' Treatise, tit. *"Two Theories of Consideration,"* in 12 Harvard Law Review 515, 521; . . . But these strictures are not well grounded. They reject the basic principle that a consideration, to support a contract, consists either of a benefit to the promisor or a detriment to the promisee—a doctrine that has always been fundamental in our conception of consideration. It is a principle, almost universally accepted, that an act or forbearance required by a legal duty owing to the promisor that is neither doubtful nor the subject of honest and reasonable dispute is not a sufficient consideration. Williston on Contracts (Rev.Ed.), §§ 103b, 120, 130; Contracts A.L.I., § 76; Anson on Contracts (Turck Ed.) 229, 234, et seq.

Yet any consideration for the new undertaking, however insignificant, satisfies this rule. . . . For instance, an undertaking to pay part of the debt before maturity, or at a place other than where the obligor was legally bound to pay, or to pay in property, regardless of its value, or to effect a composition with creditors by the payment of less than the sum due, has been held to constitute a consideration sufficient in law. The test is whether there is an additional consideration adequate to support an ordinary contract, and consists of something which the debtor was not legally bound to do or give. . . .

And there is authority for the view that, where there is no illegal preference, a payment of part of a debt, "accompanied by an agreement of the debtor to refrain from voluntary bankruptcy," is a sufficient consideration for the creditor's promise to remit the balance of the debt. But the mere fact that the creditor "fears that the debtor will go into bankruptcy, and that the debtor contemplates bankruptcy proceedings," is not enough; that alone does not prove that the creditor requested the debtor to refrain from such proceedings. Melroy v. Kemmerer, 218 Pa. 381; 67 Atl.Rep. 699. See Williston on Contracts (Rev.Ed.), § 120, and cases cited in footnote.

The cases to the contrary either create arbitrary exceptions to the rule, or profess to find a consideration in the form of a new undertaking which in essence was not a tangible new obligation or a duty not imposed by the lease, or, in any event, was not the price "bargained for as the exchange for the promise" (see *Coast National Bank v. Bloom,* supra), and therefore do violence to the fundamental principle. They exhibit the modern tendency, especially in the matter of rent reductions, to depart from the strictness of the basic common law rule and give effect to what has been termed a "reasonable" modification of the primary contract. . . .

So tested, the secondary agreement at issue is not supported by a valid consideration; and it therefore created no legal obligation. General economic adversity, however disastrous it may be in its individual consequences, is never a warrant for judicial abrogation of this primary principle of the law of contracts.

It remains to consider the second contention that, in so far as the agreement has been executed by the payment and acceptance of rent at the reduced rate, the substituted performance stands, regardless of the want of consideration. This is likewise untenable. Ordinarily, the actual performance of that which one is legally bound to do stands on the same footing as his promise to do that which he is legally compellable to do. Anson on Contracts (Turck Ed.) 234; Williston on Contracts (Rev.Ed.), §§ 130, 130a. This is a corollary of the basic principle. Of course, a different rule prevails where *bona fide* disputes have arisen respecting the relative rights and duties of the parties to a contract, or the debt or demand is unliquidated, or the contract is wholly executory on both sides. Anson on Contracts (Turck Ed.) 240, 241.

It is settled in this jurisdiction that, as in the case of other contracts, a consideration is essential to the validity of an accord and satisfaction. . . . On reason and principle, it could not be otherwise. This is the general rule. . . . It results that the issue was correctly determined.

Judgment affirmed, with costs.

Alaska Packers' Association v. Domenico

United States Court of Appeals, Ninth Circuit, 1902.
54 C.C.A. 485, 117 Fed. 99.

[On March 26, 1900, appellees entered into a written contract with appellant in San Francisco under which they agreed to sail on a vessel provided by appellant to Pyramid Harbor, Alaska for the 1900 fishing season and then to return. Appellant had a salmon cannery at that location in which they had invested $150,000. They agreed, as sailor and fishermen, to do "regular ship's duty, both up and down, discharging and loading: and to do any other work whatsoever when requested to do so by the captain or agent of the Alaska Packer's Association." For this work, some appellees were to be paid $50 and others $60 for the season and all were to be paid "two cents for each red salmon in the catching of which he took part."

The appellees arrived at Pyramid Harbor in April, 1900 and began to unload the ship and fit up the cannery. On May 19, however, they "stopped work in a body, and demanded of the company's superintendent there in charge $100 for services in operating the vessel to and from Pyramid Harbor, instead of the sums stipulated for in the contracts; stating that unless they were paid this additional wage they would stop work entirely, and return to San Francisco." The evidence showed that the superintendent, stated that he had no authority to modify the contract, was unable to induce the appellees to continue working and unable, because of the remoteness of the location and the shortness of the season, to obtain replacements. On May 22, the superintendent "yielded to their demands" and substituted $100 for the previously agreed seasonal rates in a document that was signed by the appellees before a shipping commissioner who had been brought in for the occasion. After completing the season and returning to San Francisco, the appellees were informed by appellant that would be paid only the amounts agreed to in March. Some of the appellees sued to enforce the agreed modification and received a judgment in the district court.]

■ ROSS, CIRCUIT JUDGE.

* * *

The real questions in the case as brought here are questions of law, and, in the view that we take of the case, it will be necessary to consider but one of those. Assuming that the appellant's superintendent at Pyramid Harbor was authorized to make the alleged contract of May 22d, and that he executed it on behalf of the appellant, was it supported by a sufficient consideration? From the foregoing statement of the case, it will have been seen that the libelants agreed in writing, for certain stated compensation, to render their services to the appellant in remote waters where the season for conducting fishing operations is extremely short, and in which enterprise the appellant had a large amount of money invested; and, after having entered upon the discharge of their contract, and at a time when it was impossible for the appellant to secure other men in their places, the libelants, without any valid cause, absolutely refused to continue the services they were under contract to perform unless the appellant would consent to pay them more money. Consent to such a demand, under such circumstances, if given, was, in our opinion, without consideration, for the reason that it was based solely upon the libelants' agreement to render the exact services, and none other, that they were already under contract to render. The case shows that they willfully and arbitrarily broke that obligation. As a matter of course, they were liable to the appellant in damages, and it is quite probable, as suggested by the court below in its opinion, that they may have been unable to respond in damages. But we are unable to agree with the conclusions there drawn, from these facts, in these words:

"Under such circumstances, it would be strange, indeed, if the law would not permit the defendant to waive the damages caused by the libelants' breach, and enter into the contract sued upon,—a contract mutually beneficial to all the parties thereto, in that it gave to the libelants reasonable compensation for their labor, and enabled the defendant to employ to advantage the large capital it had invested in its canning and fishing plant."

Certainly, it cannot be justly held, upon the record in this case, that there was any voluntary waiver on the part of the appellant of the breach of the original contract. The company itself knew nothing of such breach until the expedition returned to San Francisco, and the testimony is uncontradicted that its superintendent at Pyramid Harbor, who, it is claimed made on its behalf the contract sued on, distinctly informed the libelants that he had no power to alter the original or to make a new contract; and it would, of course, follow that if he had no power to change the original, he would have no authority to waive any rights thereunder. The circumstances of the present case bring it, we think, directly within the sound and just observations of the supreme court of Minnesota in the case of King v. Railway Co., 61 Minn. 482, 63 N.W. 1105:

"No astute reasoning can change the plain fact that the party who refuses to perform, and thereby coerces a promise from the other party to the contract to pay him an increased compensation for doing that which he is legally bound to do, takes an unjustifiable advantage of the necessities of the other party. Surely it would be a travesty on justice to hold that the party so making the promise for extra pay was estopped from asserting that the promise was without consideration. A party cannot lay the foundation of an estoppel by his own wrong, where the promise is simply a repetition of a subsisting legal promise. There can be no consideration for the promise of the other party, and there is no warrant for inferring that the parties have voluntarily rescinded or modified their contract. The promise cannot be legally enforced, although the other party has completed his contract in reliance upon it."

In Lingenfelder v. Brewing Co., 103 Mo. 578, 15 S.W. 844, the court, in holding void a contract by which the owner of a building agreed to pay its architect an additional sum because of his refusal to otherwise proceed with the contract, said:

"It is urged upon us by respondents that this was a new contract. New in what? Jungenfeld was bound by his contract to design and supervise this building. Under the new promise, he was not to do anything more or anything different. What benefit was to accrue to Wainwright? He was to receive the same service from Jungenfeld under the new, that Jungenfeld was bound to tender under the original, contract. What loss, trouble, or inconvenience could result to Jungenfeld that he had not already assumed? No amount of metaphysical reasoning can change the plain fact that Jungenfeld took advantage of Wainwright's necessities, and extorted the promise of five per cent. on the refrigerator plant as the condition of his complying with his contract already entered into. Nor had he even the flimsy pretext that Wainwright had violated any of the conditions of the contract on his part. Jungenfeld himself put it upon the simple proposition that 'if he, as an architect, put up the brewery, and another company put up the refrigerating machinery, it would be a detriment to the Empire Refrigerating Company,' of which Jungenfeld was president. To permit plaintiff to recover under such circumstances would be to offer a premium upon bad faith, and invite men to violate their most sacred contracts that they may profit by their own wrong. That a promise to pay a man for doing that which he is already under contract to do is without consideration is conceded by respondents. The rule has been so long imbedded in the common law and decisions of the highest courts of the various states that nothing but the most cogent reasons ought to shake it. [Citing a long list of authorities.] But it is 'carrying coals to Newcastle' to add authorities on a proposition so universally accepted, and so inherently just and right in itself. The learned counsel for respondents do not controvert the general proposition. Their contention is, and the circuit court agreed with them, that, when Jungenfeld declined to go further on his contract, the defendant then had the right to sue for damages, and not having elected to sue Jungenfeld, but having acceded to his demand for the additional compensation, defendant cannot now be heard to say his promise is without consideration. While it is true Jungenfeld became liable in damages for the obvious breach of his contract, we do not think it follows that defendant is estopped from showing its promise was made without consideration. * * *"

It results from the views above expressed that the judgment must be reversed, and the cause remanded, with directions to the court below to enter judgment for the respondent, with costs. It is so ordered.

NOTES

(1) Consideration is normally regarded as something which is bargained for and given in exchange for a promise. Was not the bargain requirement satisfied in *Levine?* Why, then, does the court reject the defendants' position? Would the decision have been different were it clearly established that the lessor importuned the lessees to stay on under the new arrangement?

(2) Is there a reasonable basis for distinguishing *Levine* and *Alaska Packers'* on consideration theory? Assuming the consideration argument were unavailing in *Alaska Packers,* could you argue persuasively for a similar result predicated on other grounds?

Angel v. Murray

Supreme Court of Rhode Island, 1974.
113 R.I. 482, 322 A.2d 630.

■ ROBERTS, CHIEF JUSTICE. This is a civil action brought by Alfred L. Angel and others against John E. Murray, Jr., Director of Finance of the City of Newport, the city of Newport, and James L. Maher, alleging that Maher had illegally been paid the sum of $20,000 by the Director of Finance and praying that the defendant Maher be ordered to repay the city such sum. The case was heard by a justice of the Superior Court, sitting without a jury, who entered a judgment ordering Maher to repay the sum of $20,000 to the city of Newport. Maher is now before this court prosecuting an appeal.

The record discloses that Maher has provided the city of Newport with a refuse-collection service under a series of five-year contracts beginning in 1946. On March 12, 1964, Maher and the city entered into another such contract for a period of five years commencing on July 1, 1964, and terminating on June 30, 1969. The contract provided, among other things, that Maher would receive $137,000 per year in return for collecting and removing all combustible and noncombustible waste materials generated within the city.

In June of 1967 Maher requested an additional $10,000 per year from the city council because there had been a substantial increase in the cost of collection due to an unexpected and unanticipated increase of 400 new dwelling units. Maher's testimony, which is uncontradicted, indicates the 1964 contract had been predicated on the fact that since 1946 there had been an average increase of 20 to 25 new dwelling units per year. After a public meeting of the city council where Maher explained in detail the reasons for his request and was questioned by members of the city council, the city council agreed to pay him an additional $10,000 for the year ending on June 30, 1968. Maher made a similar request again in June of 1968 for the same reasons, and the city council again agreed to pay an additional $10,000 for the year ending on June 30, 1969.

The trial justice found that each such $10,000 payment was made in violation of law. His decision, as we understand it, is premised on two independent grounds. First, he found that the additional payments were unlawful because they had not been recommended in writing to the city council by the city manager. Second, he found that Maher was not entitled to extra compensation because the original contract already required him to collect all refuse generated within the city and, therefore, included the 400 additional units. The trial justice further found that these 400 additional units were within the contemplation of the parties when they entered into the contract. It appears that he based this portion of the decision upon the rule that Maher had a preexisting duty to collect the refuse generated by the 400 additional units, and thus there was no consideration for the two additional payments.

* * *

[The court concluded that the charter provision did not preclude the city council from acting without the city manager's recommendation in altering the written contract.]

* * *

Having found that the city council had the power to modify the 1964 contract without the written recommendation of the city manager, we are still confronted with the question of whether the additional payments were illegal because they were not supported by consideration.

* * *

It is generally held that a modification of a contract is itself a contract, which is unenforceable unless supported by consideration. See Simpson, supra, § 93. In Rose v. Daniels, 8 R.I. 381 (1866), this court held that an agreement by a debtor with a creditor to discharge a debt for a sum of money less than the amount due is unenforceable because it was not supported by consideration.

Rose is a perfect example of the preexisting duty rule. Under this rule an agreement modifying a contract is not supported by consideration if one of the parties to the agreement does or promises to do something that he is legally obligated to do or refrains or promises to refrain from doing something he is not legally privileged to do. See Calamari & Perillo, Contracts § 60 (1970); 1A Corbin, Contracts §§ 171–72 (1963); 1 Williston, supra, § 130; Annot., 12 A.L.R.2d 78 (1950). In *Rose* there was no consideration for the new agreement because the debtor was already legally obligated to repay the full amount of the debt.

Although the preexisting duty rule is followed by most jurisdictions, a small minority of jurisdictions, Massachusetts, for example, find that there is consideration for a promise to perform what one is already legally obligated to do because the new promise is given in place of an action for damages to secure performance. See Swartz v. Lieberman, 323 Mass. 109, 80 N.E.2d 5 (1948); Munroe v. Perkins, 26 Mass. (9 Pick.) 298 (1830). *Swartz* is premised on the theory that a promisor's forbearance of the power to breach his original agreement and be sued in an action for damages is consideration for a subsequent agreement by the promisee to pay extra compensation. This rule, however, has been widely criticized as an anomaly. See Calamari & Perillo, supra, § 61; Annot., 12 A.L.R.2d 78, 85–90 (1950).

The primary purpose of the preexisting duty rule is to prevent what has been referred to as the "hold-up game." See 1A Corbin, supra, § 171. A classic example of the "hold-up game" is found in Alaska Packers' Ass'n v. Domenico, 117 F. 99 (9th Cir.1902). . . .

* * *

Another example of the "hold-up game" is found in the area of construction contracts. Frequently, a contractor will refuse to complete work under an unprofitable contract unless he is awarded additional compensation. The courts have generally held that a subsequent agreement to award additional compensation is unenforceable if the contractor is only performing work which would have been required of him under the original contract. See, e.g., Lingenfelder v. Wainwright Brewing Co., 103 Mo. 578, 15 S.W. 844 (1891), which is a leading case in this area. See also cases collected in Annot., 25 A.L.R. 1450 (1923), supplemented by Annot., 55 A.L.R. 1333 (1928), and Annot., 138 A.L.R. 136 (1942); cf. Ford & Denning v. Shepard Co., 36 R.I. 497, 90 A. 805 (1914).

These examples clearly illustrate that the courts will not enforce an agreement that has been procured by coercion or duress and will hold the parties to their original contract regardless of whether it is profitable or unprofitable. However, the courts have been reluctant to apply the preexisting duty rule when a party to a contract encounters unanticipated difficulties and the other party, not influenced by coercion or duress, voluntarily agrees to pay additional compensation for work already required to be performed under the contract. For example, the courts have found that the original contract was rescinded, Linz v. Schuck, 106 Md. 220, 67 A. 286 (1907); abandoned, Connelly v. Devoe, 37 Conn. 570 (1871), or waived, Michaud v. McGregor, 61 Minn. 198, 63 N.W. 479 (1895).

Although the preexisting duty rule has served a useful purpose insofar as it deters parties from using coercion and duress to obtain additional compensation, it has been widely criticized as a general rule of law. With regard to the preexisting duty rule, one legal scholar has stated: "There has been a growing doubt as to the soundness of this doctrine as a matter of social policy. * * * In certain classes of cases, this doubt has influenced courts to refuse to apply the rule, or to ignore it, in their actual decisions. Like other legal rules, this rule is in process of growth and change, the process being more active here than in most instances. The result of this is that a court should no longer accept this rule as fully established. It should never use it as the major premise of a decision, at least without giving careful thought to the circumstances of the particular case, to the moral deserts of the parties, and to the social feelings and interests that are involved. It is certain that the rule, stated in general and all-inclusive terms, is no longer so well-settled that a court must apply it though the heavens fall." 1A Corbin, supra, § 171; see also Calamari & Perillo, supra, § 61.

The modern trend appears to recognize the necessity that courts should enforce agreements modifying contracts when unexpected or unanticipated difficulties arise during the course of the performance of a contract, even though there is no consideration for the modification, as long as the parties agree voluntarily.

Under the Uniform Commercial Code, § 2–209(1), which has been adopted by 49 states, "[a]n agreement modifying a contract [for the sale of goods] needs no consideration to be binding." See G.L.1956 (1969 Reenactment) § 6A–2–209(1). Although at first blush this section appears to validate modifications obtained by coercion and duress, the comments to this section indicate that a modification under this section must meet the test of good faith imposed by the Code, and a modification obtained by extortion without a legitimate commercial reason is unenforceable.

The modern trend away from a rigid application of the preexisting duty rule is reflected by § 89D(a)* of the American Law Institute's Restatement Second of the Law of Contracts,[1] which provides: "A promise modifying a duty under a contract not fully performed on either side is binding (a) if the modification is fair and equitable in view of circumstances not anticipated by the parties when the contract was made * * *."

We believe that § 89D(a) is the proper rule of law and find it applicable to the facts of this case.[2] It not only prohibits modifications obtained by

---

* [§ 89(a) in final draft. Ed.]

1. The first nine chapters of the Restatement Second of the Law of Contracts were given tentative approval by the American Law Institute at successive meetings from 1964 to 1972. These chapters, which include §§ 1–255, were published by the Institute in 1973 in a hard-cover edition. Herbert Wechsler, Director of the Institute, in a foreword to this edition indicates that although these sections are still tentative and await final approval, it is unlikely that any further changes will be made.

2. The fact that these additional payments were made by a municipal corporation rather than a private individual does not in our opinion affect the outcome of this case. Unlike many other jurisdictions, there is no constitutional or statutory restriction in this state limiting the power of a city or town to award extra compensation to a private contractor. See, e.g., McGovern v. City of New

coercion, duress, or extortion but also fulfills society's expectation that agreements entered into voluntarily will be enforced by the courts.[3] See generally Horwitz, The Historical Foundations of Modern Contract Law, 87 Harv.L.Rev. 917 (1974). Section 89D(a), of course, does not compel a modification of an unprofitable or unfair contract; it only enforces a modification if the parties voluntarily agree and if (1) the promise modifying the original contract was made before the contract was fully performed on either side, (2) the underlying circumstances which prompted the modification were unanticipated by the parties, and (3) the modification is fair and equitable.

The evidence, which is uncontradicted, reveals that in June of 1968 Maher requested the city council to pay him an additional $10,000 for the year beginning on July 1, 1968, and ending on June 30, 1969. This request was made at a public meeting of the city council, where Maher explained in detail his reasons for making the request. Thereafter, the city council voted to authorize the Mayor to sign an amendment to the 1964 contract which provided that Maher would receive an additional $10,000 per year for the

York, 234 N.Y. 377, 138 N.E. 26 (1923); Annot., 25 A.L.R. 1450 (1923), supplemented by Annot., 55 A.L.R. 1333 (1928), and Annot., 138 A.L.R. 136 (1942). Absent such limitation, a city or town may modify an existing contract in precisely the same manner as a private individual as long as the modification is reasonable and proper. See Arnold v. Mayor of Pawtucket, 21 R.I. 15, 19, 41 A. 576, 578 (1898).

3. The drafters of § 89D(a) of the Restatement Second of the Law of Contracts use the following illustrations in comment (b) as examples of how this rule is applied to certain transactions:

"1. By a written contract A agrees to excavate a cellar for B for a stated price. Solid rock is unexpectedly encountered and A so notifies B. A and B then orally agree that A will remove the rock at a unit price which is reasonable but nine times that used in computing the original price, and A completes the job. B is bound to pay the increased amount.

"2. A contracts with B to supply for $300 a laundry chute for a building B has contracted to build for the Government for $150,000. Later A discovers that he made an error as to the type of material to be used and should have bid $1,200. A offers to supply the chute for $1,000, eliminating overhead and profit. After ascertaining that other suppliers would charge more, B agrees. The new agreement is binding.

"3. A is employed by B as a designer of coats at $90 a week for a year beginning November 1 under a written contract executed September 1. A is offered $115 a week by another employer and so informs B. A and B then agree that A will be paid $100 a week and in October execute a new written contract to that effect simultaneously tearing up the prior contract. The new contract is binding.

"4. A contracts to manufacture and sell to B 2,000 steel roofs for corn cribs at $60. Before A begins manufacture a threat of a nationwide steel strike raises the cost of steel about $10 per roof, and A and B agree orally to increase the price to $70 per roof. A thereafter manufactures and delivers 1,700 of the roofs, and B pays for 1,500 of them at the increased price without protest, increasing the selling price of the corn cribs by $10. The new agreement is binding.

"5. A contracts to manufacture and sell to B 100,000 castings for lawn mowers at 50 cents each. After partial delivery and after B has contracted to sell a substantial number of lawn mowers at a fixed price, A notifies B that increased metal costs require that the price be increased to 75 cents. Substitute castings are available at 55 cents, but only after several months delay. B protests but is forced to agree to the new price to keep its plant in operation. The modification is not binding."

duration of the contract. Under such circumstances we have no doubt that the city voluntarily agreed to modify the 1964 contract.

Having determined the voluntariness of this agreement, we turn our attention to the three criteria delineated above. First, the modification was made in June of 1968 at a time when the five-year contract which was made in 1964 had not been fully performed by either party. Second, although the 1964 contract provided that Maher collect all refuse generated within the city, it appears this contract was premised on Maher's past experience that the number of refuse-generating units would increase at a rate of 20 to 25 per year. Furthermore, the evidence is uncontradicted that the 1967–1968 increase of 400 units "went beyond any previous expectation." Clearly, the circumstances which prompted the city council to modify the 1964 contract were unanticipated.[4] Third, although the evidence does not indicate what proportion of the total this increase comprised, the evidence does indicate that it was a "substantial" increase. In light of this, we cannot say that the council's agreement to pay Maher the $10,000 increase was not fair and equitable in the circumstances.

The judgment appealed from is reversed, and the cause is remanded to the Superior Court for entry of judgment for the defendants.

NOTES

(1) Is the "unexpected or unanticipated difficulties" exception referred to in the instant case a mere technical evasion? Or is there a sound basis in policy for upholding modifications under such circumstances?

(2) *Modification under the Uniform Commercial Code.* Section 2–209(1) [UCC 2–210 (1997)] of the Code provides: "An agreement modifying a contract

---

4. The trial justice found that sec. 2(a) of the 1964 contract precluded Maher from recovering extra compensation for the 400 additional units. Section 2(a) provided: *"The Contractor, having made his proposal after his own examinations and estimates, shall take all responsibility for, and bear, any losses resulting to him in carrying out the contract;* and shall assume the defence of, and hold the City, its agents and employees harmless from all suits and claims arising from the use of any invention, patent, or patent rights, material, labor or implement, by or from any act, omission or neglect of, the Contractor, his agents or employees, in carrying out the contract." (Emphasis added). The trial justice, quoting the italicized portion of sec. 2(a), found that this section required that any losses incurred in the performance of the contract were Maher's responsibility. In our opinion, however, the trial justice overlooked the thrust of sec. 2(a) when read in its entirety.

It is clearly a contractual provision requiring the contractor to hold the city harmless and to defend it in any litigation arising out of the performance of his obligations under the contract, whether a result of affirmative action or some omission or neglect on the part of Maher or his agents or employees. We are persuaded that the portion of sec. 2(a) specifically referred to by the court refers to losses resulting to Maher from some action or omission on the part of his own agents or employees. It cannot be disputed, however, that any losses that resulted from an increase in the cost of collecting from the increased number of units generating refuse in no way resulted from any action on the part of either Maher or his employees. Rather, whatever losses he did entail by reason of the requirement of such extra collection resulted from actions completely beyond his control and thus unanticipated.

within this Article needs no consideration to be binding." The drafters append-ed the following commentary:

Subsection (1) provides that an agreement modifying a sales contract needs no consideration to be binding.

However, modifications made thereunder must meet the test of good faith imposed by this Act. The effective use of bad faith to escape perfor-mance on the original contract terms is barred, and the extortion of a 'modification' without legitimate commercial reason is ineffective as a violation of the duty of good faith. Nor can a mere technical consideration support a modification made in bad faith.

The test of "good faith" between merchants or as against merchants includes "observance of reasonable commercial standards of fair dealing in the trade" (Section 2–103), and may in some situations require an objec-tively demonstrable reason for seeking a modification. But such matters as a market shift which makes performance come to involve a loss may provide such a reason even though there is no such unforeseen difficulty as would make out a legal excuse from performance under Sections 2–615 and 2–616.

UCC 2–209(1) of the Code is obviously a departure from the common law and, as elaborated in the comments, basically reorients the subject. The emphasis is no longer upon consideration, but upon good faith. For example, it is noted that a "mere technical consideration" cannot support a "modification made in bad faith." To what extent should the Code apply in analogous transactions, as for example, construction contracts or employment contracts? Would the Code furnish a superior method of approach in these cases, or would the more traditional view(s) appear more conducive to the attainment of satisfactory results? See See James J. White & Robert S. Summers, Uniform Commercial Code 29–37 (4th ed. 1995); Kevin M. Teeven, *Development and Reform of the Pre-Existing Duty Rule and its Persistent Survival*, 47 Ala.L.Rev. 387 (1996); Brody, *Performance of a Pre–Existing Contractual Duty as Consid-eration: The Actual Criteria for the Efficacy of an Agreement Altering Contrac-tual Obligation*, 52 Den.L.J. 433 (1975); Hillman, *Policing Contract Modifica-tions Under the UCC: Good Faith and the Doctrine of Economic Duress*, 64 Iowa L.Rev. 849 (1979); Hillman, *Contract Modification in Iowa—Recker v. Gustafson and the Resurrection of the Preexisting Duty Doctrine*, 65 Iowa L.Rev. 343 (1980). See also Chapter Four, Section 2(C) and Chapter Five, Section 4(C).

PROBLEM: THE CASE OF THE DISSATISFIED ENTERTAINER

(You are a justice of a state appellate court, and the following is the beginning of an opinion which you are to complete for submission to your colleagues.)

This is an appeal from a judgment entered in the Circuit Court, after a jury trial in which the plaintiff, Oliver Ajax, received a verdict for $35,000 in a breach of contract action against the defendant, James Bond.

On February 15, Ajax and Bond entered into a written contract whereby the former, a professional entertainer, was to perform at Bond's resort hotel for the week of July 1–7 for $20,000. In late spring, Ajax had a hit record which virtually overnight made him a star who could command at least $50,000 for a one-week engagement. In early June he contacted Bond to renegotiate their contract, demanding $50,000 for the July 1–7 period. Initially, Bond refused to renegotiate, but when Ajax said he would not appear, Bond relented. After discussion Bond dictated a new contract to his stenographer, in the exact words of the first contract and running for the same period with the compensation changed to $35,000. As they signed the new contract they tore up the old one. Thereafter, Ajax kept the engagement, but Bond refused to pay more than $20,000, whereupon Ajax filed the instant suit for $35,000.

Over defendant's objection, the trial judge instructed the jury as follows: "If you find that the '$20,000 contract' was prior to or at the time of the execution of the '$35,000 contract' canceled and revoked by the parties by their mutual consent, then it is your duty to find that there was consideration for the making of the contract in suit and, in that event, the plaintiff is entitled to your verdict in the amount of $35,000." On this appeal, the defendant contends that the giving of this instruction constituted reversible error.

PROBLEM: THE CASE OF THE SUBCONTRACTOR'S ADDED INDUCEMENT

Edward Woodward is the owner of a laundry establishment in Metropolis. On August 7, Woodward entered into a written contract with Peter Rogers, a general contractor, for the construction of an additional power plant.

On August 14, Rogers entered into a written subcontract with John Newman for the erection of all structural steel work required for the power plant. For the purpose of performing his work, Newman rented certain equipment for use until the job was completed. The work continued until October 7, when Newman's employees went on strike and work was discontinued for a period of approximately nine weeks. During this time Newman was obliged to pay rent for the equipment and other sums to insure its safekeeping.

A meeting was called to adjust differences. In attendance were Newman, Rogers, Woodward and a representative of the union of the strikers. As a result of lengthy discussion the strike was called off. However, Newman refused to continue performance unless he was paid for the rentals and charges accruing during the time of the strike. Woodward then promised to pay this amount so that the work could proceed.

The work was completed under the contracts, but Woodward refused to pay the rentals and charges. Newman consults you. Advise him.

(3) MUTUALITY OF OBLIGATION

Within our legal tradition, a contractual obligation is not easily imposed upon an unwilling party. One may refuse to negotiate altogether, or explicitly state that one will not agree to any bargain unless the other party agrees to a particular term or, in the final agreement, expressly state that one will have no duty of performance unless a specified event first occurs. In the last situation, it is assumed that an enforceable contract subject to an express condition has been created. When that event is beyond the control of the promisor and, upon the failure of it to occur, he or she acts promptly to call the deal off, the courts normally will protect a privilege to withdraw without liability.

The problem becomes more complicated, however, when the final agreement of the parties or some rule of law permits one of them to withdraw sometime after performance begins for reasons totally or partially within his or her control. From one point of view, the problem is complicated by the view that consideration for a promise is a return promise, bargained for and given in exchange for the promise. Thus, if Anne promises to appear on Friday to paint Paul's house and Paul agrees to pay $1,000 when the job is completed "if I feel like it," if Anne fails to show and Paul sues for breach, Anne can defend on the ground that Paul gave no consideration for her promise. Paul's assent was illusory. Or, to put the matter more traditionally, in the attempted bilateral contract there was no mutuality of obligation ... no consideration! But suppose Anne appeared and painted the house in a proper manner. If Paul refused to pay, could Anne recover the agreed price? The reasonable value of her services? Paul will argue that he made no promise to pay and that Anne, therefore, assumed the risk. Will that argument succeed? Or will the court imply or impose some limitation upon Paul's discretion, such as a duty to act in good faith, in order to protect Anne's investment?

The following materials will touch upon these questions in several types of exchange relationships, and the subject will be developed, in a broader context, later in the book. Collateral reading: Farnsworth § 2.13–2.15; Calamari and Perillo §§ 4–12—4–13; Murray § 65.

Rehm–Zeiher Co. v. F.G. Walker Co.

Court of Appeals of Kentucky, 1913.
156 Ky. 6, 160 S.W. 777.

Appeal from Circuit Court, Jefferson County, Common Pleas Branch, Fourth Division.

Action by the Rehm–Zeiher Company against the F.G. Walker Company. Judgment for defendant, and plaintiff appeals. Affirmed.

■ CARROLL, J. The appellant, a corporation, in the years 1908, 1909, 1910, 1911, and 1912, and prior thereto, was engaged in the business of selling whisky; that is to say, it purchased from distillers certain brands and quantities of whisky, and then sold the whisky so bought to the trade. The appellee, during the years named, and prior thereto, owned and operated a distillery. In 1908 the parties entered into the following contract:

"This contract made and entered into this November 17, 1908, by and between the F.G. Walker Company, of Bardstown, Nelson county, Kentucky, a corporation, party of the first part, and the Rehm–Zeiher Company, of Louisville, Jefferson county, Kentucky, party of the second part. The party of the first part has this day sold to the party of the second part 2,000 cases of old Walker whisky put up under a private brand, to be delivered during the years 1909, 3,000 cases to be delivered during the year 1910,

4,000 cases to be delivered during the year 1911, and 5,000 cases to be delivered during the year 1912, at the following prices: Quarts bottled in bond, $6.70; pints bottled in bond, $7.20; half pints bottled in bond, $7.70. Should the party of the first part lose by fire the whisky with which this bottling is to be done or the bottling room during the life of this contract, then they are to be held excusable for not filling same. If for any unforeseen reason the party of the second part find that they cannot use the full amount of the above-named goods, the party of the first part agrees to release them from the contract for the amount desired by party of the second part.''

In 1912 the appellant brought this suit against the appellee to recover damages for its failure to furnish 2,596 cases of the 4,000 cases of whisky it was provided in the contract should be furnished in 1911. The petition averred that during the year 1911 the appellant demanded that the appellee furnish to it 4,000 cases of old Walker whisky, but that in violation of its contract the appellee only furnished 1,044 cases, and refused to furnish the remainder, to its damage in the sum of $6,798, which sum it averred was the loss it sustained by the failure of the appellee to furnish the 2,596 cases it failed and refused to furnish.

After a demurrer had been overruled, an answer was filed setting up various defenses, which were controverted by a reply, and the parties went to trial before a jury. After the evidence for the appellant had been concluded, the lower court directed a verdict in favor of the appellee, upon the ground that the contract was lacking in mutuality, and therefore could not be made the subject of an action for its breach by either party. On this appeal the only question we need concern ourselves with is the one upon which the trial judge rested his opinion that the appellant could not recover.

It appears without contradiction that in 1909 the appellant only ordered and received 786 cases of the 2,000 called for by the contract, and that in 1910 it only ordered and received 1,200 cases of the 3,000 cases called for by the contract, and that the appellee did not demand or request that it should take in either of these years the full number of cases specified in the contract or any greater number than it did take. It further appears that in the early part of 1911 whisky advanced in price, and the appellee refused to deliver to the appellant whisky it ordered. After this, however, the appellee, upon request, furnished to the appellant 1,044 cases of the 1911 whisky; but in September, 1911, it peremptorily refused to furnish any more, and thereupon this suit was brought.

* * *

There is a line of cases holding that, where, for example, A. and B. enter into a contract by which A. agrees to furnish to B. all the coal that B. will require in the operation of an established factory, the contract is not lacking in mutuality, as B. may require A. to furnish him all the coal he needs to operate his factory, and A. may insist that B. shall take from him all the coal he needs for this purpose.

An illustration of this class of cases is Crane v. Crane, 105 Fed. 869, 45 C.C.A. 96, where the court said: "It is within legal competency for one to bind himself to furnish another with such supplies as may be needed during some certain period for some certain business or manufacture, or with such commodities as the purchaser has already bound himself to furnish another. Reasonable provision in business requires that such contracts, though more or less indefinite, should be upheld. Thus a foundry may purchase all the coal needed for the season, or a furnace company its requirements in the way of iron, or a hotel its necessary supply of ice. * * * So, too, a dealer in coal in any given locality may contract for such coal as he may need to fulfill his existing contracts, regardless of whether delivery by him to his customers is to be immediate or in the future. * * * In all these cases contracts looking towards the future, and embodying subject-matter necessarily indefinite in quantity, have been upheld; but it will be observed that, although the quantity under contract is not measured by any certain standard, it is capable of an approximately accurate forecast. The capacity of the furnace, the needs of the railroad, or the requirements of the hotel are, within certain limits, ascertainable by the vendor."

* * *

If the contract had specified that the Rehm–Zeiher Company was only obliged to take so much of the whisky as it "desired to take," or as it "pleased to take," it would not any more certainly have given the company the right to exercise its pleasure as to how much whisky it would take than do the words "unforeseen reason." The unforeseen reason that would excuse the company from only taking so much of the whisky as it desired to take, if any, left the amount it should take entirely to its discretion. The contract places no limitation whatever upon the meaning of the words "unforeseen reason," so that any reason that the company might assign for not taking the whisky would relieve it of any obligation to do so. It was not necessary that the reason should be a good reason or a reasonable reason.

If the Walker Company had sought by a suit to compel the Rehm–Zeiher Company to take in any of the years the amount of whisky specified in the contract, or any part of it, it is clear that the Rehm–Zeiher Company could have defeated this suit by pleading that some unforeseen reason had arisen that justified them in not taking any of the whisky, and therefore they were not obliged to do so. If, as we think, the contract was nonenforceable by the Walker Company, either in whole or in part, it was certainly lacking in such mutuality of obligation as rendered it nonenforceable by the Rehm–Zeiher Company.

* * *

Some importance seems to be attached to the circumstance that the Walker Company furnished in 1909, 1910, and 1911 a part of the whisky mentioned in the contract, for which the Rehm–Zeiher Company paid the prices agreed upon. We do not think, however, that this circumstance is entitled to any controlling weight in determining the rights of the parties in the present litigation. The Walker Company was not obligated to furnish any whisky in the years named, nor was the Rehm–Zeiher Company obliged to take any, and the mere fact that the Walker Company voluntarily chose to furnish some of the whisky did not deny to it the privilege of refusing at its election to furnish the remainder of the whisky. In other words, its conduct in furnishing part of the whisky did not affect in any manner the rights of the parties to the contract, or amount to an election on the part of the Rehm–Zeiher Company, to accept unconditionally the terms of the contract. In short, the obstacle in the way of the Rehm–Zeiher Company in this case is that they are seeking to enforce a contract that was never at any time binding upon them. Their acceptance of a part of the whisky provided for in the contract in the years 1909 and 1910 did not oblige them to take any of it in the subsequent years.

* * *

Upon the whole case our conclusion is that the judgment of the lower court was correct, and it is affirmed.

NOTES

Frequently, parties do business for an extended period of time under an arrangement where some of the terms are agreed but neither party makes a promise to the other. Here there is no contract until one party offers to sell or to buy and the other accepts that proposal. Under these arrangements, either party can refuse to deal without risk of liability. For such a case, see Mid–South Packers v. Shoney's, Inc., 761 F.2d 1117 (5th Cir.1985). Is *Rehm–Zeiher* such a case? Suppose the market price had dropped and the seller had demanded that the buyer take and pay for the 4,000 cases. Could the buyer defend on the ground that the seller had made no promise—that seller's unexercised option to declare "unforeseen reasons" made the purported promise illusory? The answer depends upon how the phrase "unforeseen reason" is interpreted by the court. Does the phrase give the seller unfettered discretion (a "free way out") or is that discretion limited by what is foreseen and what is not? And what is unforeseen in this business context, a rise in liquor prices? Hardly. In the words of an unknown economist, "on a clear day you can foresee forever."

McMichael v. Price

Supreme Court of Oklahoma, 1936.
177 Okl. 186, 58 P.2d 549.

■ Osborn, Vice Chief Justice. This action was instituted in the district court of Tulsa county by Harley T. Price, doing business as Sooner Sand Company, hereinafter referred to as plaintiff, against W.M. McMichael, hereinafter referred to as defendant, as an action to recover damages for the breach of a contract. The cause was tried to a jury and a verdict returned in favor of plaintiff for $7,512.51. The trial court ordered a remittitur of $2,500, which was duly filed. Thereafter the trial court rendered judgment upon the verdict for $5,012.51, from which judgment defendant has appealed.

The pertinent provisions of the contract, which is the basis of this action, are as follows:

* * *

"In consideration of the mutual promises herein contained, first party agrees to purchase and accept from second party all of the sand of various grades and quality which the said first party can sell, for shipment to various and sundry points outside of the City of Tulsa, Oklahoma, provided that the sand so agreed to be furnished and loaded by the said second party shall at least be equal to in quality and comparable with the sand of various grades sold by other sand companies in the City of Tulsa, Oklahoma, or vicinity. First party agrees to pay and the second party agrees to accept as payment and compensation for said sand so furnished and loaded, a sum per ton which represents sixty percent (60%) of the current market price per ton of concrete sand at the place of destination of said shipment. It is agreed that statements are to be rendered by second party to first party every thirty days; the account is payable monthly by first party with a discount to be allowed by second party of four cents per ton for payment within ten days after shipment of any quantity of sand. * * *

"This contract and agreement shall cover a period of ten years from the date hereof, . . ."

* * *

Defendant contends that the contract between the parties was a mere revocable offer and is not a valid and binding contract of purchase and sale for want of mutuality. The general rule is that in construing a contract where the consideration on the one side is an offer or an agreement to sell, and on the other side an offer or agreement to buy, the obligation of the parties to sell and buy must be mutual, to render the contract binding on either party, or, as it is sometimes stated, if one of the parties, not having suffered any previous detriment, can escape future liability under the contract, that party may be said to have a "free way out" and the contract lacks mutuality. Consolidated Pipe Line Co. v. British American Oil Co., 163 Okl. 171, 21 P.(2d) 762. Attention is directed to the specific language used in the contract binding the defendant to "furnish all of the sand of various grades and qualities which the first party can sell" and whereby plaintiff is bound "to purchase and accept from second party all of the sand of various grades and qualities which the said first party (plaintiff) can sell." It is urged that plaintiff had no established business and was not bound to sell any sand whatever and might escape all liability under the terms of the contract by a mere failure or refusal to sell sand. In this connection it is to be noted that the contract recites that plaintiff is "engaged in the business of selling and shipping sand from Tulsa, Oklahoma, to various points." The parties based their contract on this agreed predicate.

* * *

At the time the contract involved herein was executed, plaintiff was not the owner of an established sand business. The evidence shows, however, that he was an experienced salesman of sand, which fact was well known to defendant, and that it was anticipated by both parties that on account of the experience, acquaintances, and connections of plaintiff, he would be able to sell a substantial amount of sand to the mutual profit of the contracting parties. The record discloses that for the nine months immediately following the execution of the contract plaintiff's average net profit per month was $516.88.

By the terms of the contract the price to be paid for sand was definitely fixed. Plaintiff was bound by a solemn covenant of the contract to purchase all the sand he was able to sell from defendant and for a breach of such covenant could have been made to respond in damages. The argument of defendant that the plaintiff could escape liability under the contract by going out of the sand business is without force in view of our determination, in line with the authorities hereinabove cited, that it was the intent of the parties to enter into a contract which would be mutually binding.

* * *

The judgment is affirmed.

NOTES

(1) Should any degree of limitation upon freedom of action be sufficient to insulate an agreement against a defense based on lack of mutuality? For instance, what if Price had not been an experienced sand dealer, but merely contemplated entering the business?

(2) Seller agrees with Buyer for the sale of a certain boat then owned by a third party. It was stipulated in the written contract of purchase that Seller's obligation was contingent upon his acquiring the boat from said third party. Thereafter, Seller did purchase the boat, but refuses to abide by his commitment to Buyer. He insists that the contract lacks mutuality of obligation; therefore, neither party is bound. Do you agree? Cf. Scott v. Moragues Lumber Co., 202 Ala. 312, 80 So. 394 (1918).

(3) *Requirements and Output Contracts.* As will be discussed later, infra at Chapter Five, Section 4(C), the Uniform Commercial Code is quite sympathetic to the use of "open price" terms. Section 2–305 [UCC 2–303 (1997)]. Similarly, the code promotes an additional measure of "certainty with flexibility" regarding quantity terms in its treatment of requirements and output contracts. UCC 2–306(1) provides: "A term which measures the quantity by the output of the seller or the requirements of the buyer means such actual output or requirements as may occur in good faith, except that no quantity unreasonably disproportionate to any stated estimate or in the absence of a stated estimate to any normal or otherwise comparable prior output or requirements may be tendered or demanded." Is McMichael v. Price an "output" contract? For a discussion of the commercial utility of these contract types, see Weistart, *Requirements and Output Contracts: Quantity Variations Under the UCC*, 1973 Duke L.J. 599, 607–618. See also Finch, *Output and Requirements Contracts:*

The Scope of the Duty to Remain in Business, 14 UCC L.J. 347 (1982); Axelrod, *The Requirements Contract—What is Required?*, 31 Drake L.Rev. 83 (1981–82).

Wood v. Lucy, Lady Duff–Gordon

Court of Appeals of New York, 1917.
222 N.Y. 88, 118 N.E. 214.

■ CARDOZO, J. The defendant styles herself "a creator of fashions." Her favor helps a sale. Manufacturers of dresses, millinery and like articles are glad to pay for a certificate of her approval. The things which she designs, fabrics, parasols, and what not, have a new value in the public mind when issued in her name. She employed the plaintiff to help her to turn this vogue into money. He was to have the exclusive right, subject always to her approval, to place her indorsements on the designs of others. He was also to have the exclusive right to place her own designs on sale, or to license others to market them. In return, she was to have one-half of "all profits and revenues" derived from any contracts he might make. The exclusive right was to last at least one year from April 1, 1915, and thereafter from year to year unless terminated by notice of ninety days. The plaintiff says that he kept the contract on his part, and that the defendant broke it. She placed her indorsement on fabrics, dresses and millinery without his knowledge, and withheld the profits. He sues her for the damages, and the case comes here on demurrer.

The agreement of employment is signed by both parties. It has a wealth of recitals. The defendant insists, however, that it lacks the elements of a contract. She says that the plaintiff does not bind himself to anything. It is true that he does not promise in so many words that he will use reasonable efforts to place the defendant's indorsements and market her designs. We think, however, that such a promise is fairly to be implied. The law has outgrown its primitive stage of formalism when the precise word was the sovereign talisman, and every slip was fatal. It takes a broader view to-day. A promise may be lacking, and yet the whole writing may be "instinct with an obligation," imperfectly expressed (SCOTT, J., in McCall Co. v. Wright, 133 App.Div. 62; Moran v. Standard Oil Co., 211 N.Y. 187, 198). If that is so, there is a contract.

The implication of a promise here finds support in many circumstances. The defendant gave an *exclusive* privilege. She was to have no right for at least a year to place her own indorsements or market her own designs except through the agency of the plaintiff. The acceptance of the exclusive agency was an assumption of its duties. . . . We are not to suppose that one party was to be placed at the mercy of the other. . . . Many other terms of the agreement point the same way. We are told at the outset by way of recital that "the said Otis F. Wood possesses a business organization adapted to the placing of such indorsements as the said Lucy, Lady Duff–Gordon has approved." The implication is that the plaintiff's business organization will be used for the purpose for which it is adapted. But the terms of the defendant's compensation are even more significant. Her sole compensation for the grant of an exclusive agency is to be one-half of all the profits resulting from the plaintiff's efforts. Unless he gave his efforts, she could never get anything. Without an implied promise, the transaction cannot have such business "efficacy as both parties must have intended that at all events it should have" (BOWEN, L.J., in the Moorcock, 14 P.D. 64, 68). But the contract does not stop there. The plaintiff goes on to promise that he will account monthly for all moneys received by him, and that he will take out all such patents and copyrights and trademarks as may in his judgment be necessary to protect the rights and articles affected by the agreement. It is true, of course, as the Appellate Division has said, that if he was under no duty to try to market designs or to place certificates of indorsement, his promise to account for profits or take out copyrights would be valueless. But in determining the intention of the parties, the promise *has* a value. It helps to enforce the conclusion that the plaintiff *had* some duties. His promise to pay the defendant one-half of the profits and revenues resulting from the exclusive agency and to render accounts monthly, was a promise to use reasonable efforts to bring profits and revenues into existence. For this conclusion, the authorities are ample. ...

The judgment of the Appellate Division should be reversed, and the order of the Special Term affirmed, with costs in the Appellate Division and in this court.

■ CUDDEBACK, McLAUGHLIN and ANDREWS, JJ., concur; HISCOCK, CH.J., CHASE and CRANE, JJ., dissent.

Judgment reversed, etc.

Omni Group, Inc. v. Seattle–First National Bank

Court of Appeals of Washington, 1982.
32 Wash.App. 22, 645 P.2d 727.

■ JAMES, JUDGE.

Plaintiff Omni Group, Inc. (Omni), a real estate development corporation, appeals entry of a judgment in favor of John B. Clark, individually, and as executor of the estate of his late wife, in Omni's action to enforce an earnest money agreement for the purchase of realty owned by the Clarks. We reverse.

In December 1977, Mr. and Mrs. Clark executed an exclusive agency listing agreement with the Royal Realty Company of Bellevue (Royal) for the sale of approximately 59 acres of property. The list price was $3,000 per acre.

In early May, Royal offered the Clark property to Omni. On May 17, following conversations with a Royal broker, Omni signed an earnest money agreement offering $2,000 per acre. Two Royal brokers delivered the earnest money agreement to the Clarks. The Clarks signed the agreement dated May 19, but directed the brokers to obtain further consideration in the nature of Omni's agreement to make certain improvements on adjacent land not being offered for sale. Neither broker communicated these additional terms to Omni.

In pertinent part, the earnest money agreement provides:

> This transaction is subject to purchaser receiving an engineer's and architect's feasibility report prepared by an engineer and architect of the purchaser's choice. Purchaser agrees to pay all costs of said report. If said report is satisfactory to purchaser, purchaser shall so notify seller in writing within fifteen (15) days of seller's acceptance of this offer. If no such notice is sent to seller, this transaction shall be considered null and void.

Exhibit A, ¶ 6. Omni's purpose was to determine, prior to actual purchase, if the property was suitable for development.

On June 2, an Omni employee personally delivered to the Clarks a letter advising that Omni had decided to forgo a feasibility study. They were further advised that a survey had revealed that the property consisted of only 50.3 acres. The Clarks agreed that if such were the case, they would accept Omni's offer of $2,000 per acre but with a minimum of 52 acres ($104,000). At this meeting, the Clarks' other terms (which had not been disclosed by Royal nor included in the earnest money agreement signed by the Clarks) were discussed. By a letter of June 8, Omni agreed to accept each of the Clarks' additional terms. The Clarks, however, refused to proceed with the sale after consulting an attorney.

The Clarks argued and the trial judge agreed, that by making its obligations subject to a satisfactory "engineer's and architect's feasibility report" in paragraph 6, Omni rendered its promise to buy the property illusory. Omni responds that paragraph 6 created only a condition precedent to Omni's duty to buy, and because the condition was for its benefit, Omni could waive the condition and enforce the agreement as written. We conclude Omni's promise was not illusory.

A promise for a promise is sufficient consideration to support a contract. E.g., Cook v. Johnson, 37 Wash.2d 19, 221 P.2d 525 (1950). If, however, a promise is illusory, there is no consideration and therefore no enforceable contract between the parties. Interchange Associates v. Interchange, Inc., 16 Wash.App. 359, 557 P.2d 357 (1976). Consequently, a party cannot create an enforceable contract by waiving the condition which renders his promise illusory. But that a promise given for a promise is dependent upon a condition does not necessarily render it illusory or affect its validity as consideration. In re Estate of Tveekrem, 169 Wash. 468, 14 P.2d 3 (1932); 1 A. Corbin, Contracts § 149 (1963); 3A A. Corbin, Contracts § 644 (1960). Furthermore,

> a contractor can, by the use of clear and appropriate words, make his own duty expressly conditional upon his own personal satisfaction with the quality of the performance for which he has bargained and in return for which his promise is given. Such a limitation on his own duty does not invalidate the contract as long as the limitation is not so great as to make his own promise illusory.

3A A. Corbin, Contracts § 644 at 78–79 (1960).

Paragraph 6 may be analyzed as creating two conditions precedent to Omni's duty to buy the Clarks' property. First, Omni must receive an "engineer's and architect's feasibility report." Undisputed evidence was presented to show that such "feasibility reports" are common in the real estate development field and pertain to the physical suitability of the property for development purposes. Such a condition is analogous to a requirement that a purchaser of real property obtain financing, which imposes upon the purchaser a duty to make a good faith effort to secure financing. See Highlands Plaza, Inc. v. Viking Inv. Corp., 2 Wash.App. 192, 467 P.2d 378 (1970). In essence, this initial language requires Omni to attempt, in good faith, to obtain an "engineer's and architect's feasibility report" of a type recognized in the real estate trade.

The second condition precedent to Omni's duty to buy the Clarks' property is that the feasibility report must be "satisfactory" to Omni. A condition precedent to the promisor's duty that the promisor be "satisfied" may require performance personally satisfactory to the promisor or it may require performance acceptable to a reasonable person. Whether the promisor was actually satisfied or should reasonably have been satisfied is a question of fact. In neither case is the promisor's promise rendered illusory. 3A A. Corbin, Contracts § 644 (1960).

In Mattei v. Hopper, 51 Cal.2d 119, 121, 330 P.2d 625 (1958), plaintiff real estate developer contracted to buy property for a shopping center " '[s]ubject to Coldwell Banker & Company obtaining leases satisfactory to the purchaser.' " Plaintiff had 120 days to consummate the purchase, including arrangement of satisfactory leases for shopping center buildings, before he was committed to purchase the property. The trial judge found the agreement "illusory." The California Supreme Court reversed. The court's language is apposite:

> [I]t would seem that the factors involved in determining whether a lease is satisfactory to the lessor are too numerous and varied to permit the application of a reasonable man standard as envisioned by this line of cases. Illustrative of some of the factors which would have to be considered in this case are the duration of the leases, their provisions for renewal options, if any, their covenants and restrictions, the amounts of the rentals, the financial responsibility of the lessees, and the character of the lessees' businesses.

Comparable factors doubtless determine whether an "engineer's and architect's feasibility report" is satisfactory. But

> "[t]his *multiplicity*" of factors which must be considered in evaluating a lease shows that this case more appropriately falls within the second line of authorities dealing with "satisfaction" clauses, being those involving fancy, taste, or judgment. Where the question is one of judgment, the promisor's determination that he is not satisfied, when made in good faith, has been held to be a defense to an action on the contract.... Although these decisions do not expressly discuss the

issues of mutuality of obligation or illusory promises, they necessarily imply that the promisor's duty to exercise his judgment in good faith is an adequate consideration to support the contract. None of these cases voided the contracts on the ground that they were illusory or lacking in mutuality of obligation. Defendant's attempts to distinguish these cases are unavailing, since they are predicated upon the assumption that the deposit receipt was not a contract making plaintiff's performance conditional on his satisfaction. As seen above, this was the precise nature of the agreement.

Further,

> [e]ven though the "satisfaction" clauses discussed in the above-cited cases dealt with performances to be received as parts of the agreed exchanges, the fact that the leases here which determined plaintiff's satisfaction were not part of the performance to be rendered is not material. The standard of evaluating plaintiff's satisfaction—good faith—applies with equal vigor to this type of condition and prevents it from nullifying the consideration otherwise present in the promises exchanged.

Mattei v. Hopper, supra at 123–24, 330 P.2d 625. Thus, even the fact that "[i]t was satisfaction with the leases that [the purchaser] was himself to obtain" was immaterial. 3A A. Corbin, Contracts § 644 at 84. Accord, Western Hills, Oregon, Ltd. v. Pfau, 265 Or. 137, 508 P.2d 201, 203 (1973) (purchaser was to obtain necessary permits for a development " 'satisfactory' to the parties"); Hendrix v. Sidney M. Thom & Co., 271 Ark. 378, 609 S.W.2d 98, 101 (Ct.App.1980) (loan commitment contract requiring lender's "satisfaction" with site upon which borrower's project was to be constructed). We conclude that the condition precedent to Omni's duty to buy requiring receipt of a "satisfactory" feasibility report does not render Omni's promise to buy the property illusory.

Paragraph 6 further provides, "If said report is satisfactory to purchaser, purchaser shall so notify seller in writing within fifteen (15) days of seller's acceptance of this offer"; otherwise, the transaction "shall be considered null and void." We read this language to mean that Omni is required ("shall") to notify the Clarks of its acceptance if the feasibility report was "satisfactory." As we have stated, this determination is not a matter within Omni's unfettered discretion.

Omni has, by the quoted language, reserved to itself a power to cancel or terminate the contract. See generally 1A A. Corbin Contracts § 265 (1963). Such provisions are valid and do not render the promisor's promise illusory, where the option can be exercised upon the occurrence of specified conditions. 1A A. Corbin, Contracts § 265 (1963); Benard v. Walkup, 272 Cal.App.2d 595, 77 Cal.Rptr. 544, 550 (1969) (fee agreement permitting counsel to withdraw "if 'in his opinion' " investigation of the client's claim indicated no liability of the defendant or contributory negligence of the plaintiff); Wroten v. Mobil Oil Corp., 315 A.2d 728, 730 (Del.1973) (lease permitting prospective tenant to terminate if licenses and permits "in manner and form acceptable to tenant" were not obtained). Here, Omni can cancel by failing to give notice only if the feasibility report is not "satisfactory." Otherwise, Omni is bound to give notice and purchase the property. Accordingly, we conclude paragraph 6 does not render Omni's promise illusory. The earnest money agreement was supported by consideration.

The judgment is reversed and remanded with instructions to enter a decree ordering specific performance of the earnest money agreement.

■ CALLOW and DURHAM, JJ., concur.

NOTES

(1) *You Picked a Fine Time to Leave Me, Lucile.* In *Lucy,* what did each party expressly promise? Why were not these express commitments sufficient, of themselves, to satisfy the demands of mutuality? Does the finding of implied promise do violence to the expressed understanding of the parties? See UCC 2–306(2) [UCC 2–303(b) (1997)].

(2) *Lucy, Lady Duff–Gordon: A Creator of Fashions.* "As she did with the general development of the period, Lucy personified the particular changes in the economy and in contract practice. Very much independent, Lucy renounced the traditions of her generation when she began her own business, designing women's clothing. Like many of the entrepreneurs of the period, Lucy started with little capital. Nevertheless, after overcoming early difficulties, she established herself by 1900 as one of the pre-eminent designers of fashion for women. In a manner typical of the personal style of the American economy during the Reconstruction era, Lucy at first designed only for individual women for specific grand occasions such as coronations and state funerals. Because her designs were created for one woman to wear on a particular occasion, they became known as 'personality' dresses.

"As the times changed, so did Lucy. First, she became a company, with the name 'Lucile.' Later, in 1910, she opened a branch office in New York City where she continued to embody the economic changes by depersonalizing her services. In common with much of the production in the United States, Lucy no longer personally designed each dress for each customer. Instead, she hired others to design and sew; she even began to produce more than one dress of each design. With the change in style and the concentration of population in urban areas, Lucy could now profit from marketing multiple copies of the same design. In addition, Lucy hired a manager for her branch office, further increasing the distance between herself and her customers; she would no longer be able to devote personal attention to each client for each occasion.

"Lucy also came to appreciate that something as ephemeral as her name could be of value in the emerging consumer society of the United States. As seller after seller saw production overtake demand in the last years of the nineteenth century, advertising became increasingly important both to inform buyers of products and to persuade customers to buy. To take advantage of that new demand, Lucy turned to an advertising agent, yet another intermediary between herself and her clients.

* * *

"One aspect of the agreement with Wood is especially important because it represents the most significant change in contract practice and, consequently, the critical challenge to contract doctrine at the turn of the century: The agreement did not fully define Wood's obligation; he was to do whatever his judgment directed, with the consent of Lucy's manager. In the field of advertising it was known as an 'open contract.' The agreement also contained a second type of contract provision developed in response to the economic uncertainty of the late nineteenth century—Wood's right was *exclusive.* Both aspects of the agreement were consequences of Lucy's and Wood's inability to know in advance what opportunities might exist for placing her endorsements. Like other producers who sought to develop new markets, Lucy benefited from the agreement by being freed from having to make decisions about advertising. She could concentrate on her special skill, designing, while Wood concentrated on his presumptive specialty, advertising. From Wood's perspective the agreement was beneficial because it assured him that he would have no competition in his efforts to place Lucy's endorsements. Thus, there would be one less uncertainty in the undeveloped market for her designs.

* * *

"* * * There was no disruption in the market for her endorsements. Instead, she brought Wood's lawsuit upon herself when, in one of the more innovative decisions of her career, she arranged with Sears, Roebuck and Company to sell her dresses through its catalogues. Sears published the first catalogue (which it called a 'portfolio') of Lucy's designs for the fall and winter of 1916–1917. That Lucy was once again at the forefront of commercial practice was evident from a comment in the trade journal *Printer's Ink,* which reported that the announcement of the agreement threw 'a bomb into the camp of rival mail-order houses.' The announcement, the journal further explained, was 'by far the most spectacular bid for prestige which this daring advertiser [Sears] has made since it first announced the new handy edition of the Encyclopedia Britannica.'" Pratt, *American Contract Law at the Turn of the Century,* 39 S.Car.L.Rev. 415, 429–432, 439 (1988). [Footnotes omitted.]

(3) UCC 2–306(2) [UCC 2–303(b)(1997)]: "A lawful agreement by either the seller or buyer for exclusive dealing in the kind of goods concerned imposes unless otherwise agreed an obligation by the seller to use best efforts to supply the goods and by the buyer to use best efforts to promote their sale."

(4) In *Omni,* the court observes that a "personal satisfaction" clause does not render a promise illusory, even if the satisfaction required is that of the promisor (subjective) rather than what would be acceptable to a reasonable person (objective)? But does not the subjective measure provide the promisor with, to use the *McMichael* court standard (supra at 121), a "free way out?"

(5) "When it is a condition of an obligor's duty that he be satisfied with respect to the obligee's performance or with respect to something else, and it is practicable to determine whether a reasonable person in the position of the obligor would be satisfied, an interpretation is preferred under which the condition occurs if such a reasonable person in the position of the obligor would be satisfied." Restatement (Second) § 228.

(6) *Reliance Upon Illusory Promise?* The "unfettered" or "sole" discretion cases have given the courts difficulty. On the one hand, a clear reservation of

power to act or not depending upon the unrestricted discretion of one party seems to make any promise illusory and pitches the dispute into the snakepit of mutuality. On the other hand, often the plaintiff has relied upon this illusory promise to the benefit of the possessor of unfettered discretion. Given the reservation of power, when has the plaintiff assumed the risk that it will be exercised against him or her? At what point does the plaintiff's reliance and the defendant's enrichment overcome the defendant's effort to be free from contract? To what extent should the decision turn on other factors, such as the age and experience of the plaintiff, the reasons offered for exercising discretion against the plaintiff or the impact of denying relief upon third persons? See Tilbert v. Eagle Lock Co., 116 Conn. 357, 165 A. 205 (1933) (wife of deceased employee recovers on death benefit plan even though employer reserved right to discontinue benefits "at any time without liability on our part to any employee, or any beneficiary.")

(7) *Mutuality of Obligation and UCC 2–204.* In seeking to salvage an obligation counsel must frequently press beyond the words of the written agreement. For example, in Warrick Beverage Corp. v. Miller Brewing Co., 170 Ind.App. 114, 352 N.E.2d 496 (1976), the court considered an "arrangement" between a brewery and a beer distributor. A letter from the brewery to the distributor provided, in part, as follows: "Our relationship is that of seller and buyer and in no other respect is any relationship established between us. You are not required to place orders, nor are we required to accept orders for beer. As is the custom in our industry, these sales are made on a shipment-to-shipment basis only, and either of us can terminate this relationship at any time without incurring liability to the other." Upon being "terminated" by the brewer the distributor sought the advantage of an Indiana statute which made it unlawful to "cancel or terminate an agreement or contract between a beer wholesaler and a brewer for the sale of beer, unfairly and without due regard for the equities of the other party." In rejecting the brewer's mutuality of obligation argument, the court referred to conduct after the execution of the writing which, in effect, recognized the existence of some type of contractual obligation. Principal reliance was upon UCC 2–204(1) [UCC 2–203(a) (1997)]: "A contract for sale of goods may be made in any manner sufficient to show agreement, including conduct by both parties which recognizes the existence of such a contract." Accord: Joseph Schlitz Brewing Co. v. Central Beverage Co., Inc., 172 Ind.App. 81, 359 N.E.2d 566 (1977) ($1,661 compensatory damages; $50,000 punitive damages).

(8) *The Inadequacy of Mutuality Criteria.* It is commonplace for agreements to provide a "way out" for one or both of the parties. It may be provided that performance is conditional upon the purchaser obtaining satisfactory leases, securing suitable financing, etc. Or there may be a reserved power of cancellation, exercisable by one or both of the parties. Cases of this type have traditionally been addressed in terms of mutuality of obligation. If, in the words of one court, a party is "free to perform or to withdraw from the agreement at his own unrestricted pleasure, the promise is deemed illusory and it provides no consideration." Mattei v. Hopper, 51 Cal.2d 119, 122, 330 P.2d 625, 626 (1958), cited in *Omni Group, Inc. v. Seattle–First National Bank,* supra at 125. The standard does not on its face seem difficult to apply, but cases of this type have given courts a great deal of trouble. There has been an accumulation of

confusing and conflicting precedents, few of which contain convincing reasons or any analysis of the deeper problems involved. See Corbin, Ch. 6.

There is here the same undercurrent of conflict that characterizes the cases elaborating a so-called "peppercorn" theory of consideration. For it is easy enough to locate the requisite "peppercorn" if one is intent upon doing so. One can usually find that a promisor's discretion is limited in *some* respect. Any circumscription of freedom of action would enable one to say there is no "*free* way out," to use the language of *McMichael v. Price,* supra at 121. As illustrated by *Omni,* a frequently employed technique, especially in the later cases, has been to infer an obligation of "good faith." This may be productive of satisfactory results, but then again it may not. The establishment of a minimal bargain may not remove doubts as to ultimate lack of fairness. All sorts of factors may have a bearing on the proper resolution of the case, including, most importantly, reliance by the parties. A bargain might be viewed as requiring some measure of "regulation," emanating from the courts or the legislature. The Code treatment of requirements and output contracts is one example; the implied obligation to use "best efforts" in an exclusive dealer arrangement is another. A contemporary focus is upon powers of cancellation or termination contained in franchise agreements. See, e.g., O.M. Droney Beverage Co. v. Miller Brewing Co., 365 F.Supp. 1067 (D.Minn.1973); Zapatha v. Dairy Mart, Inc., infra at 529. See, generally, Hadfield, *Problematic Relations: Franchising and the Law of Incomplete Contracts,* 42 Stan.L.Rev. 927 (1990). This general topic is developed further in Chapter 5, Section 4(E).

PROBLEM: THE CASE OF THE ILLUSORY BONUS

John was an agent for Super Life, an insurance company, and was paid a salary and commissions for writing life insurance policies. In early February, 1997, Super Life issued a bulletin addressed to all agents. The Bulletin was titled "Extra Earnings Agreement" and stated that "you will receive at the end of each 12 month period a bonus" in accordance with a formula based upon the percentage of policies that you are able to renew after lapse. The lower the lapse ratio the higher the bonus. Thus, if an agent's lapse ratio was between 0 and 10% the bonus would be 150% of the average monthly premiums in force but if the lapse ratio were, say, between 40 and 50% the bonus would only be 60% of the premiums. If the lapse ratio was over 70% there would be no bonus. In paragraph 7 (there were 12 paragraphs in all) the following term appeared in the same type size as the rest of the bulletin:

> This renewal bonus is a *voluntary* contribution on the part of Super Life. It is agreed by you and by us that it may be withheld, increased, decreased or discontinued, individually or collectively, with or without actual notice. Further, this Renewal Bonus is contingent upon you actually writing business for this Company as a licensed agent at the time such Bonus is paid.

The agents were exhorted to give their "best efforts" and requested to sign and return the "enclosed copy of this agreement." John complied.

In February, 1998 John reported that his lapse ratio over the last twelve months was between 20 and 30% and that, under the schedule, he was entitled to a bonus of 100% of the average monthly premiums in force, some $10,000.

Without giving any notice or reasons, however, Super Life discontinued the bonus plan on February 15, 1998 without paying any bonuses.

John, and other agents, sued for the bonuses. Super Life filed a motion to dismiss and argued: (1) No promise was made, since the "voluntary" contribution clause reserved complete and unfettered discretion to the company; (2) The plain and ordinary language of the clause, which the agents as "White Collar" workers should reasonably understand, should be implemented; and (3) Even if a promise was made, there was no consideration since the Agents were already obligated to sell and renew life insurance policies.

In opposing the motion to dismiss, John's attorney made the following argument. "Your honor, we think that a literal interpretation of the bonus plan language should be avoided, especially where extra efforts were expended by the agents. Super Life is subject to a duty of good faith in the performance of the contract and that duty should be imposed upon the exercise of the reserved discretion to terminate the plan unless both parties intended Super Life to have unfettered discretion. The question is whether this interpretation is within the fair contemplation of the parties and the answer is not found in the 'four corners' of the writing and the 'plain meaning' of language. If no such intention is found, the next question is whether Super Life acted in bad faith and this, at a minimum, requires an examination of Super Life's reasons for withdrawing the plan. Thus, factual questions over intention and bad faith are presented and the motion to dismiss should be dismissed." John's brief cited Nolan v. Control Data Corp., 243 N.J.Super. 420, 579 A.2d 1252 (App.Div.1990) to support this argument.

How would you rule?

SECTION 2.   MORAL OBLIGATION: PROMISE PLUS ANTECEDENT BENEFIT

Comment: Restitution and the Scope of Quasi–Contract

Return with us now to the plight of "Bascom's Folly," the ill-fated horse without an owner in *Bailey v. West,* supra at ___. It seems clear that Bailey could have recovered the reasonable value of his services if West had, by words or conduct, requested those services in exchange for a promise to pay. The benefit conferred on West's property would have been part of an agreed exchange. His promise to pay, whether express or implied, would have been supported by consideration. The general problem with which this section is concerned, however, begins with the conclusion in *Bailey v. West* that the benefit conferred was not requested—that Bailey was not justified under the circumstances in believing that he was invited to render the service and could expect compensation from West. Without an express or implied-in-fact contract, is there any way that Bailey can obtain compensation? The obvious answer is yes, *if* the conditions for an implied-in-law or quasi-contract are met. The fact that they were not met in *Bailey v. West* only stimulates a closer inquiry into quasi-contract and the claim of unjust enrichment. But first, let us take a brief look at the concept of restitution as it relates to the law of contracts.

Restitution, in general, is a broad-gauged and independent remedy designed to prevent "unjust" enrichment. A person "who receives a benefit by reason of an infringement of another person's interest or of loss suffered by the other, owes restitution to him in the manner and amount necessary to prevent unjust enrichment." Restatement (Second) Restitution § 1 (Tent.Draft No. 1, April 1983). See 1 G. Palmer, Law of Restitution § 1.1 (1978). As Professor Palmer has put it, "unjust enrichment is an indefinable idea in the same way that justice is indefinable." But the "imprecise idea" of preventing the "unjust enrichment of one person at the expense of another" has played a "creative role in the development of an important branch of modern law." Id. at 5.

The prevention of unjust enrichment is an important objective in and around the law of contracts. Section 344 of Restatement (Second), for example, states that "judicial remedies under the rules stated in this Restatement serve to protect," among other things, a promisee's "restitution interest," which is "his interest in having restored to him any benefit that he has conferred on the other party." These remedies include "requiring restoration of a specific thing," see Section 372, or "awarding a sum of money" to prevent unjust enrichment. Section 345. The sum of money awarded to protect the restitution interest "may as justice requires be measured by either (a) the reasonable value to the other party of what he received in terms of what it would have cost him to obtain it from a person in the claimant's position, or (b) the extent to which the other party's property has been increased in value or his other interests advanced." Restatement (Second) § 371. But the scope of restitution in Restatement (Second) is limited: the defendant must have made a promise, express or implied in fact, to a promisee and the claim must be asserted within clearly defined contexts. Thus, the promisee may seek restitution (1) as an alternative remedy for defendant's breach of contract, Section 373, (2) to recover a "net benefit" retained after the defendant has been fully compensated for the plaintiff's breach, Section 374, and (3) to "mop up" after a contract fails to satisfy the Statute of Frauds, Section 375; is excused for "impracticability," Section 377; is avoided for mistake or duress, Section 376; or is invalid because of illegality. Restatement (Second), however, does not deal with restitution claims when the parties, because of lack of agreement or indefiniteness, fail to conclude an enforceable contract, or where the plaintiff has conferred a benefit on the defendant where there was no request or the circumstances do not support the implication of a promise to pay. See Perillo, *Restitution in the Second Restatement of Contracts*, 81 Colum.L.Rev. 37 (1981). Thus, restitution claims marching under the label of "quasi-contract" are frequently made around the edges of contract theory in circumstances where the defendant did not request the benefit conferred or did not make a promise, express or implied, to pay.* As one court put it:

* "The object of the quasi-contractual process is so to fill the interstices of tort and contract law as to prevent unconscionable enrichment of one at the expense of anoth-

The third category is called an implied in law contract or quasi contract. However, a contract implied in law is not a contract at all, but an obligation imposed by law for the purpose of bringing about justice and equity without reference to the intent or the agreement of the parties and, in some cases, in spite of an agreement between the parties. . . . It is a non-contractual obligation that is to be treated procedurally as if it were a contract, and is often referred to as quasi contract, unjust enrichment, implied in law contract or restitution. * * * [T]he essence of a contract implied in law lies in the fact that the defendant has received a benefit which it would be inequitable for him to retain.

Continental Forest Products, Inc. v. Chandler Supply Co., 95 Idaho 739, 743, 518 P.2d 1201, 1205 (1974).

When, then, is it "inequitable" for Party B to retain a benefit conferred by Party A on Party B without Party B's request? To put the matter more concretely, why, in *Bailey v. West,* was Bailey denied recovery for the benefit conferred on West's horse? There are at least two necessary elements in this inquiry.

First, did Party A confer a measurable benefit on Party B with the expectation of compensation? In *Bailey,* the answer to the benefit question was yes and no. Bailey conferred a measurable benefit on West's horse by feeding and caring for it for over four months. But after West knew of the benefit, he refused to receive it by abandoning the horse. In cases of this sort, West was not required to make restitution unless Bailey had justifiably performed a duty imposed upon West by law, e.g., the duty of a parent to provide necessary medical care to a dependent child. See State, Division of Family Services v. Hollis, 639 S.W.2d 389 (Mo.App.1982). West clearly had no legal duty to provide necessaries to his horse, dependent or not. On

---

er." Stone, J. in Braun v. Hamack, 206 Minn. 572, 289 N.W. 553, 556 (1940).

The idea of quasi-contract as a source of legal obligation has roots in the Roman law and in later civil law development. Although early English writers spoke of quasi-contract, and there is some mention of it in early cases, its entrance into the mainstream of the common law was with Lord Mansfield's decision in Moses v. Macferlan, 2 Burr. 1005, 97 Eng. Rep. 676 (1760). The following from his opinion has been repeated numerous times as the general rationale of the doctrine:

"If the defendant be under an obligation from the ties of natural justice to refund, the law implies a debt and gives this action founded in the equity of the plaintiff's case, as it were, upon a contract ('quasi ex contractu,' as the Roman law expresses it). * * *

This kind of equitable action, to recover back money, which ought not in justice to be kept, is very beneficial, and therefore much encouraged. * * * [I]t lies for money paid by mistake; or upon a consideration which happens to fail; or for money got through imposition, (express or implied;) or extortion; or oppression; or an undue advantage taken of the plaintiff's situation, contrary to laws made for the protection of persons under those circumstances.

"In one word, the gist of this kind of action is, that the defendant, upon the circumstances of the case, is obliged by the ties of natural justice and equity to refund the money." 2 Burr. 1005, 97 Eng.Rep. 676, 678, 680–81.

For more on the history of quasi-contract, see 1 G. Palmer, Law of Restitution § 1.2 (1978).

the compensation question, the answer was yes: Bailey was in the stable business and his intention to charge for the service was apparent. But see Turner v. Unification Church, 473 F.Supp. 367, 378 (D.R.I.1978), affirmed per curiam 602 F.2d 458 (1st Cir.1979) (services performed with expectation of creating a better world).

Second, if Party B retained the benefit after knowing that it had been conferred and A expected compensation, did A give B an opportunity to decline the benefit before it was conferred? If so, and B did not object, we have taken a big step toward liability based upon a theory of consent. If not, A cannot recover in quasi-contract unless there is a reasonable excuse for failing to do so. An excuse may exist when A satisfies B's need in "circumstances of exigency." Restatement (Second) Restitution § 3 (Tent. Draft # 1, April 1983). In *Bailey v. West* those circumstances did not exist. The life or well-being of the horse was not in jeopardy, and Bailey could easily have contacted West before performing services. Thus, Bailey's intervention was "officious" and West's enrichment, to the extent it existed, was not unjust. See, e.g., Falcke v. Scottish Imperial Insurance Co., 34 Ch.D. 234, 248 (1886) (liabilities are not to be forced upon people behind their backs any more than you can confer a benefit upon a man against his will); Smith v. Recrion Corp., 91 Nev. 666, 541 P.2d 663, 665 (1975); Dawson, *The Self–Serving Intermeddler,* 87 Harv.L.Rev. 1409 (1974).

Dean John Wade has offered the following summary of when restitution is available for benefits conferred without request:

> One who, without intent to act gratuitously, confers a measurable benefit upon another, is entitled to restitution, if he affords the other an opportunity to decline the benefit or else has a reasonable excuse for failing to do so. If the other refuses to receive the benefit, he is not required to make restitution unless the actor justifiably performs for the other a duty imposed upon him by law.

Wade, *Restitution for Benefits Conferred Without Request,* 19 Vand.L.Rev. 1183, 1212 (1966). See, generally 2 G. Palmer, The Law of Restitution §§ 10.1–10.11 (1978).

Quantum Meruit. As you will have discerned, the line between genuine contract of the implied-in-fact variety and quasi-contract is not always clearly drawn or easily perceived. The confusion is compounded by instances where courts use the term *quantum meruit* which can encompass both types of transactions. A Utah court recently offered the following clarification: "Confusion surrounds the use and application of *quantum meruit,* * * * because courts have used the terms *quantum meruit,* contract implied in fact, contract implied in law, quasi-contract, unjust enrichment, and/or restitution without analytical precision. * * * *Quantum meruit* has two distinct branches. Both branches, however, are rooted in 'justice,' * * * to prevent the defendant's enrichment at the plaintiff's expense. * * * Contract implied in law, also known as quasi-contract or unjust enrichment, is one branch of *quantum meruit.* A quasi-contract is not a contract at all, but rather is a legal action in restitution. * * * The elements of a quasi-contract, or a contract implied in law, are: (1) the defendant received a benefit; (2) an appreciation or knowledge by the defendant of the benefit; (3) under circumstances that would make it unjust for the defendant to retain the benefit without paying for it. * * * The measure of recovery under quasi-contract, or contract implied in law, is the value of the benefit conferred on the defendant (the defendant's gain) and not the detriment incurred by the plaintiff, * * * or necessarily the reasonable value of the plaintiff's services. A contract implied in fact is the second branch of *quantum meruit.* A contract implied in fact is a 'contract' established by conduct. * * * The elements of a contract implied in fact are: (1) the defendant requested the plaintiff to perform work; (2) the plaintiff expected the defendant to compensate him or her for those services; and (3) the defendant knew or should have known that the plaintiff expected compensation. * * * 'Technically, recovery in contract implied in fact is the amount the parties intended as the contract price. If that amount is unexpressed, courts will infer that the parties intended the amount to be the reasonable market value of the plaintiff's services.' Kovacic, *A Proposal to Simplify Quantum Meruit Litigation,* 35 Am.U.L.Rev. 547, 556 (1986)." Davies v. Olson, 746 P.2d 264, 268–69 (Utah App.1987).

Comment: The Historical Roots of the "Moral Obligation" Doctrine

With this bit of essential background behind us, we can turn to the specific problem with which this section is concerned, moral obligation. The pattern is as follows. In the past, A has conferred a measurable benefit on B. On the one extreme, the benefit may have been intended by A to be a gift. On the other extreme, the benefit may give rise to a legal obligation to pay on the part of B, either in contract or quasi-contract. Or, the transaction may be in the fuzzy middle ground—neither clearly gift nor contract but with some elements from both extremes. Motivated by the past, B then promises to pay A for the benefit conferred. Is that promise enforceable? If so, when and why? In confronting these questions, consider first Justice Windeyer's summary of legal developments in England and the following cases and problems.

By his readiness to enlarge the scope of assumpsit and indebitatus assumpsit, Mansfield greatly assisted the development of the law of contract, which is the basis of all commercial law. But he failed to gain acceptance for a theory of consideration which, if it had been adopted, would have entirely altered the English law of contract. The established principle of English law today is that a merely gratuitous promise is not legally binding, except it be under seal. To make an enforceable agreement, otherwise than by deed, it is necessary that the promise should be given for some valuable consideration. It is not necessary that the consideration should be adequate, but it must be certain and of some value in the eye of the law. 'A valuable consideration in the sense of the law, may consist either in some right, interest, profit or benefit accruing to one party, or some forbearance, detriment, loss or responsibility given, suffered or undertaken by the other'. The

origin of the doctrine of consideration is not free from doubt. ...
Probably it owes something to the notion of *quid pro quo,* an element
in the old action of debt which, as we have seen, was superseded by
indebitatus assumpsit. Certainly it was chiefly developed as the result
of the technicalities of the action of assumpsit in which the plaintiff
was required to allege the consideration for the defendant's promise.
The canon law too may have made an indirect contribution, for it had,
by a singular adaptation of Roman law principles, reached the conclusion that promises were enforceable when supported by *causa.* The
meaning of *causa* was not indisputedly defined. 'The general meaning
on which all were agreed was the necessity of a purpose to be attained.
There was *causa,* if the promisor had in view a definite result, either
some definite legal act or something more comprehensive, such as
peace.' The Court of Chancery in the sixteenth century was working
out a theory of contract with, as its basis, the canonists' theory of
causa, which it translated as 'consideration'. Promises were enforceable if made for a sufficient consideration. A material consideration
was not necessary; a good motive, a moral obligation or natural love
and affection towards the promisee was enough.

The common law courts never accepted the Chancery Court's
doctrine of consideration. The Chancery theory ultimately perished. It
was the common law theory of contract and the common law doctrine
of valuable consideration which became the accepted principles of
English law. Some criterion of the enforceability of agreements was
considered necessary as the action of assumpsit developed. The breach
of every promise was not to be permitted to give rise to an action of
assumpsit. How then could the agreements in respect of which assumpsit would lie be determined? The common lawyers adopted the Roman
principle that *ex nudo pacto non oritur actio.* But they understood this
maxim in a sense different from that which it bore in Roman law.
Roman law had no generalised theory of consideration. For the common law, a *nudum pactum* was a promise not supported by consideration. A mere naked promise could have no assistance from the
common law; but if clothed with a consideration, however scanty, it
was received with little less respect than the covenant in its sealed
vestment.

By the eighteenth century it seemed clearly established that consideration was an essential condition of an action of assumpsit. But the
scope of the doctrine was still unsettled. Mansfield cared little for
procedural rules, but much for good faith and honest dealing. He was
eager to break down some of the barriers between law and equity and
to apply equitable principles in the administration of the common law.
He confidently asserted that any moral obligation arising from the
dictates of good conscience was a sufficient consideration to make a
promise actionable. He went even further and denied that consideration was essential to the validity of a contract. In his view consideration had only an evidentiary value. If a promise was supported by
consideration, it showed that the parties had intended their engage-

ment to be legally binding. But this might be evidenced in other ways, for example an agreement which was reduced to writing in obedience to the Statute of Frauds or as the result of commercial custom was, in Mansfield's opinion, binding without consideration. 'A *nudum pactum,*' he said 'does not exist in the usage and law of merchants.' This doctrine, which he put forward in Pillans v. Van Mierop (3 Burr. 1663), would have made all written agreements enforceable, though they were not under seal. But the traditions of the common law were here too strong even for Mansfield's great prestige. Thirteen years later the House of Lords in Rann v. Hughes (7 T.R. 350), after consulting the judges, overruled his opinion and established the need for consideration in all contracts other than those embodied in a deed. 'All contracts', the judges declared, 'are by the laws of England distinguished into agreements by specialty and agreements by parol; nor is there any such third class as . . . contracts in writing. If they be merely written and not specialties, they are parol and a consideration must be proved'.

But, although Mansfield's doctrine that no consideration at all was required to support a written agreement was soon overthrown, his opinion that a merely moral obligation was sufficient to constitute a consideration received general assent throughout the eighteenth century. It was not finally displaced until 1840, when Lord Denman pointed out in Eastwood v. Kenyon (11 Ad. & E. 438) that it would 'annihilate the necessity for any consideration at all, inasmuch as the mere fact of giving of promise creates a moral obligation to perform it.'

Windeyer, Lectures on Legal History, 237–40 (2d ed. rev. 1957). [Footnotes omitted.]

Mills v. Wyman

Supreme Judicial Court of Massachusetts, 1825.
20 Mass. (3 Pick.) 207.

This was an action of assumpsit brought to recover a compensation for the board, nursing, & c., of Levi Wyman, son of the defendant, from the 5th to the 20th of February, 1821. The plaintiff then lived at Hartford, in Connecticut; the defendant, at Shrewsbury, in this county. Levi Wyman, at the time when the services were rendered, was about 25 years of age, and had long ceased to be a member of his father's family. He was on his return from a voyage at sea, and being suddenly taken sick at Hartford, and being poor and in distress, was relieved by the plaintiff in the manner and to the extent above stated. On the 24th of February, after all the expenses had been incurred, the defendant wrote a letter to the plaintiff, promising to pay him such expenses. There was no consideration for this promise, except what grew out of the relation which subsisted between Levi Wyman and the defendant, and Howe, J., before whom the cause was tried in the Court of Common Pleas, thinking this not sufficient to support the action, directed a nonsuit. To this direction that plaintiff filed exceptions.

■ PARKER, C.J. General rules of law established for the protection and security of honest and fair-minded men, who may inconsiderately make promises without any equivalent, will sometimes screen men of a different character from engagements which they are bound in *foro conscientiae* to perform. This is a defect inherent in all human systems of legislation. The rule that a mere verbal promise, without any consideration, cannot be enforced by action, is universal in its application, and cannot be departed from to suit particular cases in which a refusal to perform such a promise may be disgraceful.

The promise declared on in this case appears to have been made without any legal consideration. The kindness and services towards the sick son of the defendant were not bestowed at his request. The son was in no respect under the care of the defendant. He was twenty-five years old, and had long left his father's family. On his return from a foreign country, he fell sick among strangers, and the plaintiff acted the part of the good Samaritan, giving him shelter and comfort until he died. The defendant, his father, on being informed of this event influenced by a transient feeling of gratitude, promises in writing to pay the plaintiff for the expenses he had incurred. But he has determined to break this promise, and is willing to have his case appear on record as a strong example of particular injustice sometimes necessarily resulting from the operation of general rules.

It is said a moral obligation is a sufficient consideration to support an express promise; and some authorities lay down the rule thus broadly; but upon examination of the cases we are satisfied that the universality of the rule cannot be supported, and that there must have been some preexisting obligation, which has become inoperative by positive law, to form a basis for an effective promise. The cases of debts barred by the statute of limitations, of debts incurred by infants, of debts of bankrupts, are generally put for illustration of the rule. Express promises founded on such preexisting equitable obligations may be enforced; there is a good consideration for them; they merely remove an impediment created by law to the recovery of debts honestly due, but which public policy protects the debtors from being compelled to pay. In all these cases there was originally a *quid pro quo;* and according to the principles of natural justice the party receiving ought to pay; but the legislature has said he shall not be coerced; then comes the promise to pay the debt that is barred, the promise of the man to pay the debt of the infant, of the discharged bankrupt to restore to his creditor what by the law he had lost. In all these cases there is a moral obligation founded upon an antecedent valuable consideration. These promises therefore have a sound legal basis. They are not promises to pay something for nothing; not naked pacts; but the voluntary revival or creation of obligation which before existed in natural law, but which had been dispensed with, not for the benefit of the party obliged solely, but principally for the public convenience. If moral obligation, in its fullest sense, is a good substratum for an express promise, it is not easy to perceive why it is not equally good to support an implied promise. What a man ought to do, generally he ought to be made to do, whether he promise or refuse. But the law of society has left most of such obligations to the *interior* forum, as the tribunal of conscience has been aptly called. Is there not a moral obligation upon every son who has become affluent by means of the education and advantages bestowed upon him by his father, to relieve that father from pecuniary embarrassment, to promote his comfort and happiness, and even to share with him his riches, if thereby he will be made happy? And yet such a son may, with impunity, leave such a father in any degree of penury above that which will expose the community in which he dwells, to the danger of being obliged to preserve him from absolute want. Is not a wealthy father under strong moral obligation to advance the interest of an obedient, well disposed son, to furnish him with the means of acquiring and maintaining a becoming rank in life, to rescue him from the horrors of debt incurred by misfortune? Yet the law will uphold him in any degree of parsimony, short of that which would reduce his son to the necessity of seeking public charity.

Without doubt there are great interests of society which justify withholding the coercive arm of the law from these duties of imperfect obligation, as they are called; imperfect, not because they are less binding upon the conscience than those which are called perfect, but because the wisdom of the social law does not impose sanctions upon them.

A deliberate promise, in writing, made freely and without any mistake, one which may lead the party to whom it is made into contracts and expenses, cannot be broken without a violation of moral duty. But if there was nothing paid or promised for it, the law, perhaps wisely, leaves the execution of it to the conscience of him who makes it. It is only when the party making the promise gains something, or he to whom it is made loses something, that the law gives the promise validity. . . .

* * *

For the foregoing reasons we are all of opinion that the nonsuit directed by the Court of Common Pleas was right, and that judgment be entered thereon for costs for the defendant.

NOTES

(1) Was there "consideration" for the promise being sued upon? On the basis of this case, would it appear that there can never be promissory obligation without consideration?

(2) Under what circumstances, if any, should a promise not supported by consideration but motivated by a past benefit conferred be enforceable as a contract? Restatement (Second) § 86 provides: "(1) A promise made in recognition of a benefit previously received by the promisor from the promisee is binding to the extent necessary to prevent injustice. (2) A promise is not binding under Subsection (1), (a) if the promisee conferred the benefit as a gift or for other reasons the promisor has not been unjustly enriched; or (b) to the extent that its value is disproportionate to the benefit." Would *Mills* be decided differently under this section? Suppose it is clear that Mills did not intend to confer a gift on Wyman's son.

(3) Are you persuaded by Judge Parker's distinction between legal and moral obligations in the making of promises? If, as Posner argues, the doctrine of consideration supports economic efficiency in exchange, what arguments can be made for enforcing promises where there is no bargain and exchange? See C. Fried, Contract as Promise 14–17 (1981).

Manwill v. Oyler

Supreme Court of Utah, 1961.
11 Utah 2d 433, 361 P.2d 177.

■ CROCKETT, JUSTICE. Defendants petitioned and obtained leave to bring this interlocutory appeal to challenge the denial of their motion to dismiss the plaintiff's complaint. The only issue presented is whether it states a cause of action against them.

Plaintiff alleged that during the years 1950, 1951, 1952 and 1953 he made payments on defendants' behalf aggregating $5,506.20 on a farm now occupied by the defendants; and that in the year 1954 he transferred to defendants a grazing permit worth $1,800 and 18 head of cattle worth $3,000. It is conceded that any action on those transactions would be barred by the statute of limitations. But the plaintiff further alleged that in July or August, 1956, the defendants orally agreed to pay said sums to him. After defendants filed a motion to dismiss, he amended to state that the oral promise to pay him $5,506.20 occurred in October, 1957. The motion to dismiss was considered as directed to the complaint as amended. It was denied and they were given 15 days in which to answer. Instead of doing so, they petitioned this court for an interlocutory appeal under Rule 72, U.R.C.P.

* * *

(interim) not a final decision

The position the plaintiff essays is that the earlier payments he claims to have made for the defendants' benefit placed them under moral obligation to repay him, and that this constitutes valid consideration to make their 1957 oral promise a binding contract. The rule quite generally recognized is that a moral obligation by itself will not do so. Although some authorities appear to be otherwise, it will usually be found that there are special circumstances bolstering what is termed the moral obligation.

The difficulty we see with the doctrine is that if a mere moral, as distinguished from a legal, obligation were recognized as valid consideration for a contract, that would practically erode to the vanishing point the necessity for finding a consideration. This is so, first because in nearly all circumstances where a promise is made there is some moral aspect of the situation which provides the motivation for making the promise even if it is to make an outright gift. And second, if we are dealing with moral concepts, the making of a promise itself creates a moral obligation to perform it. It seems obvious that if a contract to be legally enforceable need be anything other than a naked promise, something more than mere moral consideration is necessary. The principle that in order for a contract to be valid and binding, each party must be bound to give some legal consideration to the other by conferring a benefit upon him or suffering a legal detriment at his request is firmly implanted in the roots of our law.

In urging that the moral consideration here present makes a binding contract, plaintiff places reliance on what is termed the "material benefit rule" as reflecting the trend of modern authority. The substance of that rule is that where the promisors (defendants) have received something from the promisee (plaintiff) of value in the form of money or other material benefits under such circumstances as to create a moral obligation to pay for what they received, and later promise to do so there is consideration for such promise. But even the authorities standing for that rule affirm that there must be something beyond a bare promise, as of an offered gift or gratuity. The circumstances must be such that it is reasonably to be supposed that that promisee (plaintiff) expected to be compensated in some way therefor.

Accepting that proposition for the sake of argument, the plaintiff has not set forth any of the facts surrounding the original transactions to show that there was any expectation that he would be compensated in this case. This may have been done advisedly because of the difficulty which would confront him: if the circumstances were such that the parties reasonably expected he was to be paid, there may have been an implied contract, which is now outlawed. Insofar as the statements in his complaint disclose, any benefits conferred on defendants would have been donative. Therefore, at the time of the alleged 1957 promise there could have existed nothing but a bare moral obligation to support the defendants' claimed oral promise to repay him. This alone would not constitute valid consideration to make a binding contract.

The conclusion we have reached finds support in the fact that by our statute the time in which an action may be brought is extended by an acknowledgement or promise to pay the same but it "must be in writing and signed by the party to be charged thereby." This affirmative provision, which has the effect of permitting an outlawed obligation to be renewed by a promise in writing, indicates an awareness and recognition of the well-established principle that an oral promise will not revive such an obligation.

Since the plaintiff has not alleged facts sufficient to make the alleged oral promise of 1957 a binding contract, it was error to deny the defendants' motion to dismiss.

Reversed with directions to dismiss the action. Costs to defendants (appellants). [Footnotes omitted.]

NOTES

(1) *Promise to Pay Antecedent Indebtedness.* The implicit assumptions in *Manwill* unfold in two stages.

First, "a promise to pay all or part of an antecedent contractual or quasi-contractual indebtedness owed by the promisor is binding if the indebtedness is still enforceable. . . ." Restatement (Second) § 82(1). Was the plaintiff successful in establishing that there ever was any obligation by the promisor to pay? See Realty Assoc. v. Valley National Bank, 153 Ariz. 514, 738 P.2d 1121, 1124–1125 (App.1986)(written promise to pay broker after service rendered enforced).

Second, there is a "well settled" general rule "that a moral obligation arising from or connected with what was once a legal liability, which has since become suspended or barred by operation of a positive rule or law or statute, will furnish consideration for a subsequent executory promise." Orsborn v. Old National Bank of Washington, 10 Wn.App. 169, 516 P.2d 795, 797 (1973). Where the insulating event is the statute of limitations, the litigation frequently involves whether the defendant made the requisite promise, see Restatement (Second) § 82(2), and, if so, whether it met any formality requirements imposed by other legislation. Assuming, in *Manwill,* that defendant had an earlier implied contractual obligation which was barred by the statute of limitations, why was the alleged second promise not enforceable?

Assuming an antecedent contractual or quasi-contractual obligation which has not been barred, what reasons seem to justify enforcement of a second promise without new consideration to pay the earlier obligation? Professor Sullivan has suggested some historical reasons, in that enforcement was the "first step in the development of assumpsit as a functional substitute for debt. . . . [I]f a plaintiff could show a second promise to pay, subsequent to the creation of the obligation sought to be enforced, his action in assumpsit would be free of the disabling procedural impediments of debt . . . ," e.g., the wager of law requirement. The reasons for this development have long since disappeared, but, again, the melody lingers on. See Sullivan, *The Concept of Benefit in the Law of Quasi–Contract,* 64 Geo.L.J. 1, 2–4 (1975).

(2) *Promise to Pay Debt Discharged in Bankruptcy: Effect of Bankruptcy Reform Act of 1978.* Traditionally, one's promise to pay a debt discharged in bankruptcy was enforceable. This "reaffirmation" rule was altered significantly by Congress in 1978. See 11 U.S.C.A. § 524(c), (d). These sections, together with amendments enacted in 1984, place stringent restrictions upon the enforcement of such "reaffirmation" agreements. The agreement must have been made prior to the debtor's discharge, and it must contain a statement advising the debtor of a right to rescind at any time before discharge or within sixty days after the agreement is filed with the court, whichever is later. Moreover, if the debtor was not represented by an attorney during the negotiation of the "reaffirmation" agreement, court approval is required. The court must be convinced that the agreement does not impose an undue hardship on the debtor (or a dependent) and is in his or her best interest.

(3) Without an antecedent debt, barred or otherwise, would enforcement of a promise based upon prior benefit conferred require judicial enforcement of all such promises? Would, as Austin maintained, a judge be able "to enforce just whatever he pleases?" Austin, Jurisprudence 224 (3d ed. 1869). Or, as contended by Professor Fuller, could not the scope of the moral obligation principle be "tamed" by a process of judicial inclusion and exclusion? See Fuller, *Consideration and Form,* 41 Colum.L.Rev. 799, 821–22 (1941).

Webb v. McGowin

Court of Appeals of Alabama, 1935.
27 Ala.App. 82, 168 So. 196.

■ BRICKEN, PRESIDING JUDGE. This action is in assumpsit. The complaint as originally filed was amended. The demurrers to the complaint as amended were sustained, and because of this adverse ruling by the court the plaintiff took a nonsuit, and the assignment of errors on this appeal are predicated upon said action or ruling of the court.

A fair statement of the case presenting the questions for decision is set out in appellant's brief, which we adopt.

"On the 3d day of August, 1925, appellant while in the employ of W.T. Smith Lumber Company, a corporation, and acting within the scope of his employment, was engaged in clearing the upper floor of mill No. 2 of the company. While so engaged he was in the act of dropping a pine block from the upper floor of the mill to the ground below; this being the usual and ordinary way of clearing the floor, and it being the duty of the plaintiff in the course of his employment to so drop it. The block weighed about 75 pounds.

"As appellant was in the act of dropping the block to the ground below, he was on the edge of the upper floor of the mill. As he started to turn the block loose so that it would drop to the ground, he saw J. Greeley McGowin, testator of the defendants, on the ground below and directly under where the block would have fallen had appellant turned it loose. Had he turned it loose it would have struck McGowin with such force as to have caused him serious bodily harm or death. Appellant could have remained safely on the upper floor of the mill by turning the block loose and allowing it to drop, but had he done this the block would have fallen on McGowin and caused him serious injuries or death. The only safe and reasonable way to prevent this was for appellant to hold to the block and divert its direction in falling from the place where McGowin was standing and the only safe way to divert it so as to prevent its coming into contact with McGowin was for appellant to fall with it to the ground below. Appellant did this, and by holding to the block and falling with it to the ground below, he diverted the course of its fall in such way that McGowin was not injured. In thus preventing the injuries to McGowin appellant himself received serious bodily injuries, resulting in his right leg being broken, the heel of his right foot torn off and his right arm broken. He was badly crippled for life and rendered unable to do physical or mental labor.

"On September 1, 1925, in consideration of appellant having prevented him from sustaining death or serious bodily harm and in consideration of the injuries appellant had received, McGowin agreed with him to care for and maintain him for the remainder of appellant's life at the rate of $15 every two weeks from the time he sustained his injuries to and during the remainder of appellant's life; it being agreed that McGowin would pay this sum to appellant for his maintenance. Under the agreement McGowin paid or caused to be paid to appellant the sum so agreed on up until McGowin's death on January 1, 1934. After his death the payments were continued to and including January 27, 1934, at which time they were discontinued. Thereupon plaintiff brought suit to recover the unpaid installments accruing up to the time of the bringing of the suit.

* * *

1.   The averments of the complaint show that appellant saved McGowin from death or grievous bodily harm. This was a material benefit to him of infinitely more value than any financial aid he could have received. Receiving this benefit, McGowin became morally bound to compensate appellant for the services rendered. Recognizing his moral obligation, he expressly agreed to pay appellant as alleged in the complaint and complied with this agreement up to the time of his death; a period of more than 8 years.

Had McGowin been accidentally poisoned and a physician, without his knowledge or request, had administered an antidote, thus saving his life, a subsequent promise by McGowin to pay the physician would have been valid. Likewise, McGowin's agreement as disclosed by the complaint to compensate appellant for saving him from death or grievous bodily injury is valid and enforceable.

Where the promisee cares for, improves, and preserves the property of the promisor, though done without his request, it is sufficient consideration for the promisor's subsequent agreement to pay for the service, because of the material benefit received. . . .

In Boothe v. Fitzpatrick, 36 Vt. 681, the court held that a promise by defendant to pay for the past keeping of a bull which had escaped from defendant's premises and been cared for by plaintiff was valid, although there was no previous request, because the subsequent promise obviated that objection; it being equivalent to a previous request. On the same principle, had the promisee saved the promisor's life or his body from grievous harm, his subsequent promise to pay for the services rendered would have been valid. Such service would have been far more material than caring for his bull. Any holding that saving a man from death or grievous bodily harm is not a material benefit sufficient to uphold a subsequent promise to pay for the service, necessarily rests on the assumption that saving life and preservation of the body from harm have only a sentimental value. The converse of this is true. Life and preservation of the body have material, pecuniary values, measurable in dollars and cents. Because of this, physicians practice their profession charging for services rendered in saving life and curing the body of its ills, and surgeons perform operations. The same is true as to the law of negligence, authorizing the assessment of damages in personal injury cases based upon the extent of the injuries, earnings, and life expectancies of those injured.

In the business of life insurance, the value of a man's life is measured in dollars and cents according to his expectancy, the soundness of his body, and his ability to pay premiums. The same is true as to health and accident insurance.

It follows that if, as alleged in the complaint, appellant saved J. Greeley McGowin from death or grievous bodily harm, and McGowin subsequently agreed to pay him for the service rendered, it became a valid and enforceable contract.

2. It is well settled that a moral obligation is a sufficient consideration to support a subsequent promise to pay where the promisor has received a material benefit, although there was no original duty or liability resting on the promisor. Lycoming County v. Union County, 15 Pa. 166, 53 Am.Dec. 575, 579, 580; Ferguson v. Harris, 39 S.C. 323, 17 S.E. 782, 39 Am.St.Rep. 731, 734; Muir v. Kane, 55 Wash. 131, 104 P. 153, 26 L.R.A.(N.S.) 519, 19 Ann.Cas. 1180; State ex rel. Bayer v. Funk, 105 Or. 134, 199 P. 592, 209 P. 113, 25 A.L.R. 625, 634; Hawkes v. Saunders, 1 Cowp. 290; In re Sutch's Estate, 201 Pa. 305, 50 A. 943; Edson v. Poppe, 24 S.D. 466, 124 N.W. 441, 26 L.R.A.(N.S.) 534; Park Falls State Bank v. Fordyce, 206 Wis. 628, 238 N.W. 516, 79 A.L.R. 1339; Baker v. Gregory, 28 Ala. 544, 65 Am.Dec. 366. In the case of State ex rel. Bayer v. Funk, supra, the court held that a moral obligation is a sufficient consideration to support an executory promise where the promisor has received an actual pecuniary or material benefit for which he subsequently expressly promised to pay.

The case at bar is clearly distinguishable from that class of cases where the consideration is a mere moral obligation or conscientious duty unconnected with receipt by promisor of benefits of a material or pecuniary nature. Park Falls State Bank v. Fordyce, supra. Here the promisor received a material benefit constituting a valid consideration for his promise.

3. Some authorities hold that, for a moral obligation to support a subsequent promise to pay, there must have existed a prior legal or equitable obligation, which for some reason had become unenforceable, but for which the promisor was still morally bound. This rule, however, is subject to qualification in those cases where the promisor, having received a material benefit from the promisee, is morally bound to compensate him for the services rendered and in consideration of this obligation promises to pay. In such cases the subsequent promise to pay is an affirmance or ratification of the services rendered carrying with it the presumption that a previous request for the service was made. . . .

Under the decisions above cited, McGowin's express promise to pay appellant for the services rendered was an affirmance or ratification of what appellant had done raising the presumption that the services had been rendered at McGowin's request.

4. The averments of the complaint show that in saving McGowin from death or grievous bodily harm, appellant was crippled for life. This was part of the consideration of the contract declared on. McGowin was benefited. Appellant was injured. Benefit to the promisor or injury to the promisee is a sufficient legal consideration for the promisor's agreement to pay. Fisher v. Bartlett, 8 Greenl. (Me.) 122, 22 Am.Dec. 225; State ex rel. Bayer v. Funk, supra.

5. Under the averments of the complaint the services rendered by appellant were not gratuitous. The agreement of McGowin to pay and the acceptance of payment by appellant conclusively shows the contrary.

* * *

From what has been said, we are of the opinion that the court below erred in the ruling complained of; that is to say, in sustaining the demurrer, and for this error the case is reversed and remanded.

Reversed and remanded.

■ SAMFORD, JUDGE (concurring). The questions involved in this case are not free from doubt, and perhaps the strict letter of the rule, as stated by judges, though not always in accord, would bar a recovery by plaintiff, but following the principle announced by Chief Justice Marshall in Hoffman v. Porter, Fed.Cas. No. 6,577, 2 Brock. 156, 159, where he says "I do not think that law ought to be separated from justice, where it is at most doubtful," I concur in the conclusions reached by the court.*

Harrington v. Taylor

Supreme Court of North Carolina, 1945.
225 N.C. 690, 36 S.E.2d 227.

■ PER CURIAM. The plaintiff in this case sought to recover of the defendant upon a promise made by him under the following peculiar circumstances:

The defendant had assaulted his wife, who took refuge in plaintiff's house. The next day the defendant gained access to the house and began another assault upon his wife. The defendant's wife knocked him down with an axe, and was on the point of cutting his head open or decapitating him while he was laying on the floor, and the plaintiff intervened, caught the axe as it was descending, and the blow intended for defendant fell upon her hand, mutilating it badly, but saving defendant's life.

Subsequently, defendant orally promised to pay the plaintiff her damages; but after paying a small sum, failed to pay anything more. So, substantially, states the complaint.

The defendant demurred to the complaint as not stating a cause of action, and the demurrer was sustained. Plaintiff appealed.

The question presented is whether there was a consideration recognized by our law as sufficient to support the promise. The Court is of the opinion that, however much the defendant should be impelled by common gratitude to alleviate the plaintiff's misfortune, a humanitarian act of this kind, voluntarily performed, is not such consideration as would entitle her to recover at law.

The judgment sustaining the demurrer is

* [Certiorari denied by Alabama Supreme Court, 232 Ala. 374, 168 So. 199 (1936)].

Affirmed.

NOTES

(1) Is *Webb v. McGowin* an example of the old saw that "hard cases make bad law?" Can the decision be reconciled with *Mills v. Wyman,* supra at 139?

(2) Taking Dean Wade's summary of the bases for quasi-contract, supra at 136, can quasi-contract liability be found in either *Mills or Webb*? What about *Harrington*? If so, the subsequent promise would be enforceable, would it not? If not, where is the deficiency? Can it be argued that the defendant's subsequent decision to make a promise, being an exercise of choice, neutralizes the deficiency in quasi-contract and, therefore, supports enforcement?

(3) The California experience is of particular interest, since there are statutes of long standing which appear to provide alternatives to consideration. Section 1550 of the California Civil Code provides that there must be either "a sufficient cause or consideration." "Cause", or *causa,* is a concept employed in civil law countries, notably in Europe and South America. See Lorenzen, *Causa and Consideration in the Law of Contracts,* 28 Yale L.J. 621 (1919). Moreover, § 1606 of the California code states: "An existing legal obligation resting upon the promisor, *or a moral obligation originating in some benefit conferred upon the promisor, or prejudice suffered by the promisee,* is * * * good consideration for a promise, to an extent corresponding with the extent of the obligation, but no further or otherwise." (Emphasis added). For a discussion of the California decisions, set against a broad historical background, see Keyes, *Cause and Consideration in California—A Re–Appraisal,* 47 Cal.L.Rev. 74 (1959). See also Grosse, *Moral Obligation as Consideration in Contracts,* 17 Vill.L.Rev. 1 (1971).

(4) Section 5–1105 of the New York General Obligations Law provides:

A promise in writing and signed by the promisor or by his agent shall not be denied effect as a valid contractual obligation on the ground that consideration for the promise is past or executed, if the consideration is expressed in the writing and is proved to have been given or performed and would be a valid consideration but for the time when it was given or performed.

See Dick v. Dick, 167 Conn. 210, 355 A.2d 110 (1974), where it was held that the above quoted statute required proof that any consideration stated in the writing must actually be paid.

Comment: Restatement (Second) § 86 and the Future of "Moral Obligation"

The first Restatement dealt with the problem of "past" consideration or "moral" obligation under the umbrella of the bargain theory, set forth in Section 75. Provision was made for the limited enforcement of "second" promises made to pay antecedent debts, whether or not barred by the statute of limitations or discharged in bankruptcy. But beyond this, forays into the realm of *Webb v. McGowin* were met by the "bargained for and given in exchange" requirement. The revised Restatement, however, contains a new Section 86, entitled "Promise for Benefit Received":

(1) A promise made in recognition of a benefit previously received by the promisor from the promisee is binding to the extent necessary to prevent injustice.

(2) A promise is not binding under Subsection (1)

(a) if the promisee conferred the benefit as a gift or for other reasons the promisor has not been unjustly enriched; or

(b) to the extent that its value is disproportionate to the benefit.

This section eschews such terminology as "past consideration" and "moral obligation," preferring to explain it as an effort to preclude an unjust enrichment that might have occurred if the courts were limited to traditional principles of quasi-contract.

In speaking of cases such as *Webb v. McGowin*, the first Reporter, Professor Braucher, observed: "What you have, really, is a line of distinction between essentially gratuitous transactions and cases which are on the borderline of quasi-contracts, where promise removes the difficulty which otherwise would bar quasi-contractual relief." He conceded that the section "bristles with nonspecific concepts," but insisted that it captured the principle that can be sustained by the cases. 42 ALI Proceedings 273–74 (1965). Be this as it may, Professor Gilmore has noted that Section 89A, as numbered in the tentative draft, "gives overt recognition to an important principle whose existence *Restatement* ignored and, by implication denied." He suggested, wistfully perhaps, that "by the time we get to Restatement (Third) it may well be that § 89A will have flowered like Jack's bean-stalk in the same way that § 90 did between *Restatement* and *Restatement (Second)*." G. Gilmore, The Death of Contract 76 (1974). See also Henderson, *Promises Grounded in the Past: The Idea of Unjust Enrichment and the Law of Contracts*, 57 Va.L.Rev. 1115 (1971), an article that repays careful study. A search for recent cases finds nothing to suggest that this prophecy will be fulfilled. See First Nat. Bancshares of Beloit, Inc. v. Geisel, 853 F.Supp. 1333, 1336–1337 (D.Kan.1994)("material benefit" rule not applicable on facts); Steve Thel & Edward Yorio, *The Promissory Basis of Past Consideration*, 78 Va. L. Rev. 1045 (1992).

With the foregoing cases, statutes and materials in mind, how would you resolve the following problems?

PROBLEM: THE CASE OF THE BROKERAGE RENEWAL

Joe Broker, a Metropolis realtor, was contacted by Tom Owner relative to finding a buyer for certain commercial property in the city. On July 1, they executed a "listing agreement," which provided, among other things: "You [Broker] are hereby appointed exclusive agent to secure a purchaser for [here a description of the property and the price were inserted] for 90 days. In case of sale by the undersigned owner before expiration of this agreement you are to receive full cash commission." The stated commission for finding someone willing and able to buy was 7% of the selling price.

Despite strenuous efforts during the late summer and early fall, <u>Broker</u> was <u>unable to locate any real prospect</u>. He had virtually given up hope when he happened to run into Paula Purchaser at a football tailgater (November 4). He learned from Paula of her interest in finding commercial property in Metropolis. Knowing that Paula and Tom were friends, he suggested that Paula give Tom a call. Paula did so, and in a matter of days the two of them had put together a deal at the listed price. Deed and payment were exchanged on November 22.

On November 24, Broker, after learning that Owner and Purchaser had closed the deal, called Owner to his office and had Owner sign a new listing agreement, which was, in effect, a renewal of the old agreement for an additional ninety days.

A problem has come up. Owner died on December 1, and an associate in the office has warned Broker that he may not be able to collect the commission. Broker consults you. Analyze his legal position and advise him as to whether or not he has a valid claim against Owner's estate. See Realty Associates of Sedona v. Valley National Bank of Arizona, 153 Ariz. 514, 738 P.2d 1121 (App.1986).

PROBLEM: THE CASE OF THE KINDLY NEIGHBOR

Barlow, a widower aged 78, moved into a small house on Blossom Avenue next door to Anna, a married woman of 60. Shortly thereafter, Barlow fell and sprained his ankle. Anna saw the accident, took Barlow to the doctor and rendered assistance during his period of recuperation at home. Anna and her husband liked Barlow and felt sorry for him. During the next three years the three of them became fast friends. Anna did household chores for Barlow, took him shopping, fixed innumerable meals and had him for dinner at least once a week. Barlow, who lived alone and had no close relatives, was extremely appreciative. He repeatedly assured Anna that she would be well paid for her kind attention. On Christmas day almost three years after they first met, Barlow delivered to Anna a signed writing which promised to pay Anna "$25,000 from my estate upon death for services rendered." Two weeks later, Barlow was dead of a stroke, leaving an estate of $75,000 and no will. The executor refused to honor the written promise to pay $25,000, and Anna brought suit against the estate. It is stipulated that the reasonable value for services rendered by Anna over a three-year period is $4,500. What result? Cf. In re Gerke's Estate, 271 Wis. 297, 73 N.W.2d 506 (1955); In re Hatten's Estate, 233 Wis. 199, 288 N.W. 278 (1940). See also Restatement (Second) § 86, Illus. 12, 13; McMurry v. Magnusson, 849 S.W.2d 619, 622–623 (Mo.App.1993)(implied promise to pay for nursing and other services rendered in a non-family relationship).

PROBLEM: THE CASE OF THE GRATEFUL MERCHANT

[The following problem is from the February, 1982, Indiana Bar Examination.]

Marley was a wealthy merchant with a small child. Marley hired Cratchet to serve as a bodyguard for the child to reduce the threat of kidnapping for ransom. Cratchet received a reasonable salary and fringes which included a life insurance policy with a death benefit of $50,000 payable to his wife and three children.

One sad afternoon when Cratchet was picking up the Marley child after school, Moriarty attempted to kidnap the child. Cratchet responded to this threat with total disregard for his own safety. He dispatched Moriarty, but was severely wounded during the incident. Ironically, it had been Cratchet's day off, but he knew that there had been talk of a plot to kidnap the Marley child, so he cancelled his cricket match in order to safeguard the child.

As Cratchet lay dying, Marley told him: "Fear not for your family; I shall care for them." Whereupon Cratchet expired.

At Cratchet's funeral, Marley gave the bereaved widow Cratchet a signed memorandum which stated: "In consideration of the extraordinary services of your dearly departed husband, I will pay to you the sum of $500 per month for the rest of your natural life."

Damp and chilly weather prevailed at Cratchet's funeral. Marley took ill, and shortly thereafter, he died.

Mrs. Cratchet received the insurance policy proceeds, but Scrooge, as the Executor of Marley's estate, denied any liability to Mrs. Cratchet for the $500 per month payment. Mrs. Cratchet brought an action against the estate, and now has appealed the dismissal of her complaint by the trial court.

You are a law clerk for a justice on the Supreme Court of the State of Dickens, which state follows the common law of contracts, but this is a case of first impression. Your Justice has advised you that he is leaning toward Mrs. Cratchet's position. He wants an analysis of the theory or theories that he might advance to win the votes of a majority of the Supreme Court Justices. (Ignore any probate issues in your answer.)

SECTION 3. PROMISSORY ESTOPPEL: PROMISE PLUS UNBARGAINED-FOR RELIANCE

Comment: The Evolution of Promissory Estoppel

"*Nemo potest mutare consilium suum in alterius injuriam.* No one can change his purpose to the injury of another." Justinian's Digest, 50, 17, 75.

"Equitable estoppel * * * arises from the *conduct* of a party, using that word in its broadest meaning as including his spoken or written words, his positive acts, and his silence or negative omission to do anything. Its foundation is justice and good conscience. Its object is to prevent the unconscientious and inequitable assertion or enforcement of claims or rights which might have existed or been enforceable by other rules of law, unless prevented by the estoppel; and its practical effect is, from motives of equity and fair dealing, to create and vest opposing rights in the party who obtains the benefit of the estoppel."
3 Pomeroy, A Treatise on Equity Jurisprudence 180 (5th ed. 1941).

"The vital principle [of equitable estoppel] is that he who by his language or conduct leads another to do what he would not otherwise have done, shall not subject such person to loss or injury by disappointing the expectations upon which he acted."

Dickerson v. Colgrove, 100 U.S. (10 Otto) 578, 580, 25 L.Ed. 618 (1879).

"A promise which the promisor should reasonably expect to induce action or forbearance of a definite and substantial character on the part of the promisee and which does induce such action or forbearance is binding if injustice can be avoided only by enforcement of the promise."

Restatement § 90.

"A promise which the promisor should reasonably expect to induce action or forbearance on the part of the promisee or a third person and which does induce such action or forbearance is binding if injustice can be avoided only by enforcement of the promise. The remedy granted for breach may be limited as justice requires."

Restatement (Second) § 90.

Our inquiry concerning legally enforceable promises has involved mainly an extended look at the doctrine of consideration, the traditional Anglo–American theory of contract. To be sure, for centuries a promise under seal was enforceable (and still may be in a few jurisdictions), and there is still some vitality to the idea, promoted particularly by Lord Mansfield, that "moral obligation" is a sufficient basis for enforcement of a promise. Supra at 203. But in the main the common law courts have enforced bargains; something (either of benefit to the promisor or detrimental to the promisee) has to be bargained for and given in exchange for the promise. There have always, however, been discernible traces of uneasiness respecting this orthodox doctrine. (See, for example, the highly critical report on consideration of the English Law Revision Committee, Sixth Interim Report, 1937). Much of the present day dissatisfaction (and consequent activity) relates to transactions where there is substantial *unbargained-for* reliance upon the promise. For instance, if as in *Ricketts v. Scothorn,* supra at 24, one quits a job in reliance upon her grandfather's promise to pay her $2,000, is there a sound basis for binding the promisor to some sort of legal obligation? If so, what kind? Contract? Tort? The Nebraska court, in holding there was "an equitable estoppel which ought to preclude the defendant from alleging that the note in controversy is lacking in one of the essential elements of a valid contract," stated as follows: "Having intentionally influenced the plaintiff to alter her position for the worse on the faith of the note being paid when due, it would be grossly inequitable to permit the maker or his executor, to resist payment on the ground that the promise was given without consideration." Judgment for the full amount was affirmed by the Court.

That one might be "estopped" (apparently derived from the Old French *estopper,* to stop, bar) by conduct which leads another to act in reasonable reliance was hardly unprecedented. It has long been recognized that a defendant's conduct may estop or preclude one from raising an otherwise available defense or contesting the accuracy of a representation of fact. As the California Supreme Court put it:

> The doctrine of equitable estoppel is founded on concepts of equity and fair dealing. It provides that a person may not deny the existence of a state of facts if he intentionally led another to believe a particular circumstance to be true and to rely upon such belief to his detriment. The elements of the doctrine are that (1) the party to be estopped must be apprised of the facts; (2) he must intend that his conduct shall be acted upon, or must so act that the party asserting the estoppel has a right to believe it was so intended; (3) the other party must be ignorant of the true state of facts; and (4) he must rely upon the conduct to his injury.

Strong v. County of Santa Cruz, 15 Cal.3d 720, 725, 125 Cal.Rptr. 896, 898, 543 P.2d 264, 266 (1975). See Griswold v. Haven, 25 N.Y. 595 (1862). But the use of estoppel in the *Ricketts* context was unusual since there was an extreme reluctance on the part of courts to extend equitable estoppel to statements concerning "future facts." Still less was there recognition of *promissory estoppel* as an alternative or substitute for consideration. On the contrary, the first use of that term seems to have been by Professor Williston in the original edition of his treatise, published in 1920. See Boyer, *Promissory Estoppel: Requirements and Limitations of the Doctrine*, 98 U.Pa.L.Rev. 459 (1950). And the appearance of Restatement § 90, quoted above, which formulated general doctrine without using the term "promissory estoppel" undoubtedly caught many by surprise.

The cases which could be said to support the formulation were of long standing but narrow scope. They involved, primarily, gratuitous bailments, parol gifts of land and charitable subscriptions. See Boyer, *Promissory Estoppel: Principle From Precedents,* 50 Mich.L.Rev. 639, 873 (1952). The post-Restatement activity in the courts and legal periodicals has been extensive. See, e.g., Henderson, *Promissory Estoppel and Traditional Contract Doctrine,* 78 Yale L.J. 343 (1969). In fact, Professor Grant Gilmore has boldly suggested that the famous Section 90, the "unwanted stepchild of *Restatement (First),*" has, in Restatement (Second), "swallowed up the bargain principle of § 75." G. Gilmore, The Death of Contract 72 (1974). Be that as it may, the doctrine has clearly escaped the confines of its origins and may be seen at work in many contexts. We will examine further its effect in the bargain context, as well as its collision with the Statute of Frauds. At this point, we will consider its application in various settings. In each setting, the tension between consideration and promissory estoppel is evident. In addition, the reliance idea seems to serve both as a device to achieve "justice" in particular transactions and to effect a transition to principles of liability based upon policies somewhat beyond either consideration or promissory estoppel. See Shattuck, *Gratuitous Promises—A New Writ,* 35 Mich.L.Rev. 908 (1938). Finally, the question of remedy is constantly posed—should loss be measured by the value of the promised performance or the actual reliance?

Ricketts v. Scothorn

Supreme Court of Nebraska, 1898.
Supra at 24.

Allegheny College v. National Chautauqua County Bank of Jamestown

Court of Appeals of New York, 1927.
246 N.Y. 369, 159 N.E. 173.

■ CARDOZO, CH.J. The plaintiff, Allegheny College, is an institution of liberal learning at Meadville, Pennsylvania. In June 1921, a "drive" was in progress to secure for it an additional endowment of $1,250,000. An appeal to contribute to this fund was made to Mary Yates Johnston of Jamestown, New York. In response thereto, she signed and delivered on June 15, 1921, the following writing:

"Estate Pledge,

"Allegheny College Second Century Endowment

"Jamestown, N.Y., June 15, 1921.

"In consideration of my interest in Christian Education, and in consideration of others subscribing, I hereby subscribe and will pay to the order of the Treasurer of Allegheny College, Meadville, Pennsylvania, the sum of Five Thousand Dollars; $5,000.

"This obligation shall become due thirty days after my death, and I hereby instruct my Executor, or Administrator, to pay the same out of my estate. This pledge shall bear interest at the rate of _____ per cent per annum, payable annually, from _____ till paid. The proceeds of this obligation shall be added to the Endowment of said Institution, or expended in accordance with instructions on reverse side of this pledge.

"Name	MARY YATES JOHNSTON,
"Address	306 East 6th Street,
	"Jamestown N.Y.

"Dayton E. McClain	Witness
"T.R. Courtis	Witness

"to authentic signature."

On the reverse side of the writing is the following indorsement: "In loving memory this gift shall be known as the Mary Yates Johnston Memorial Fund, the proceeds from which shall be used to educate students preparing for the Ministry, either in the United States or in the Foreign Field.

"This pledge shall be valid only on the condition that the provisions of my Will, now extant, shall be first met.

"MARY YATES JOHNSTON."

The subscription was not payable by its terms until thirty days after the death of the promisor. The sum of $1,000 was paid, however, upon account in December, 1923, while the promisor was alive. The college set the money aside to be held as a scholarship fund for the benefit of students preparing for the ministry. Later, in July, 1924, the promisor gave notice to the college that she repudiated the promise. Upon the expiration of thirty days following her death, this action was brought against the executor of her will to recover the unpaid balance.

The law of charitable subscriptions has been a prolific source of controversy in this State and elsewhere. We have held that a promise of that order is unenforceable like any other if made without consideration. . . . On the other hand, though professing to apply to such subscriptions the general law of contract, we have found consideration present where the general law of contract, at least as then declared, would have said that it was absent. . . .

A classic form of statement identifies consideration with detriment to the promisee sustained by virtue of the promise (Hamer v. Sidway, 124 N.Y. 538; Anson, Contracts [Corbin's ed.], p. 116; 8 Holdsworth, History of English Law, 10). So compendious a formula is little more than a half truth. There is need of many a supplementary gloss before the outline can be so filled in as to depict the classic doctrine. "The promise and the consideration must purport to be the motive each for the other, in whole or at least in part. It is not enough that the promise induces the detriment or that the detriment induces the promise if the other half is wanting" (Wisc. & Mich. Ry. Co. v. Powers, 191 U.S. 379, 386; McGovern v. City of N.Y., 234 N.Y. 377, 389; Walton Water Co. v. Village of Walton, 238 N.Y. 46, 51; 1 Williston, Contracts, § 139; Langdell, Summary of the Law of Contracts, pp. 82–88). If A promises B to make him a gift, consideration may be lacking, though B has renounced other opportunities for betterment in the faith that the promise will be kept.

The half truths of one generation tend at times to perpetuate themselves in the law as the whole truths of another, when constant repetition brings it about that qualifications, taken once for granted, are disregarded or forgotten. The doctrine of consideration has not escaped the common lot. As far back as 1881, Judge Holmes in his lectures on the Common Law (p. 292), separated the detriment which is merely a consequence of the promise from the detriment which is in truth the motive or inducement, and yet added that the courts "have gone far in obliterating this distinction." The tendency toward effacement has not lessened with the years. On the contrary, there has grown up of recent days a doctrine that a substitute for consideration or an exception to its ordinary requirements can be found in what is styled "a promissory estoppel" (Williston, Contracts, §§ 139, 116). Whether the exception has made its way in this State to such an extent as to permit us to say that the general law of consideration has been modified accordingly, we do not now attempt to say. Cases such as Siegel v. Spear & Co. (234 N.Y. 479) and DeCicco v. Schweizer (221 N.Y. 431) may be signposts on the road. Certain, at least it is that we have adopted the doctrine of promissory estoppel as the equivalent of consideration in connection with our law of charitable subscriptions. So long as those decisions stand, the question is not merely whether the enforcement of a charitable subscription can be squared with the doctrine of consideration in all its ancient rigor. The question may also be whether it can be squared with the doctrine of consideration as qualified by the doctrine of promissory estoppel.

We have said that the cases in this State have recognized this exception, if exception it is thought to be. Thus, in Barnes v. Perine (12 N.Y. 18) the subscription was made without request, express or implied, that the church do anything on the faith of it. Later, the church did incur expense to the knowledge of the promisor, and in the reasonable belief that the promise would be kept. We held the promise binding, though consideration there was none except upon the theory of a promissory estoppel. In Presbyterian Society v. Beach (74 N.Y. 72) a situation substantially the same became the basis for a like ruling. So in Roberts v. Cobb (103 N.Y. 600) and Keuka College v. Ray (167 N.Y. 96) the moulds of consideration as fixed by the old doctrine were subjected to a like expansion. Very likely, conceptions of public policy have shaped, more or less subconsciously, the rulings thus made. Judges have been affected by the thought that "defences of that character" are "breaches of faith toward the public, and especially toward those engaged in the same enterprise, and an unwarrantable disappointment of the reasonable expectations of those interested." (W.F. Allen, J., in *Barnes v. Perine*, supra, page 24; and cf. Eastern States League v. Vail, 97 Vt. 495, 505, and cases there cited). The result speaks for itself irrespective of the motive. Decisions which have stood so long, and which are supported by so many considerations of public policy and reason, will not be overruled to save the symmetry of a concept which itself came into our law, not so much from any reasoned conviction of its justice, as from historical accidents of practice and procedure (8 Holdsworth, History of English Law, 7 et seq.). The concept survives as one of the distinctive features of our legal system. We have no thought to suggest that it is obsolete or on the way to be abandoned. As in the case of other concepts, however, the pressure of exceptions has led to irregularities of form.

It is in this background of precedent that we are to view the problem now before us. The background helps to an understanding of the implications inherent in subscription and acceptance. This is so though we may find in the end that without recourse to the innovation of promissory estoppel the transaction can be fitted within the mould of consideration as established by tradition.

The promisor wished to have a memorial to perpetuate her name. She imposed a condition that the "gift" should "be known as the Mary Yates Johnston Memorial Fund." The moment that the college accepted $1,000 as a payment on account, there was an assumption of a duty to do whatever acts were customary or reasonably necessary to maintain the memorial fairly and justly in the spirit of its creation. The college could not accept the money, and hold itself free thereafter from personal responsibility to give effect to the condition. . . . More is involved in the receipt of such a fund than a mere acceptance of money to be held to a corporate use. . . . The purpose of the founder would be unfairly thwarted or at least inadequately served if the college failed to communicate to the world, or in any event to applicants for the scholarship, the title of the memorial. By implication it undertook, when it accepted a portion of the "gift" that in its circulars of information and in other customary ways, when making announcement of this scholarship, it would couple with the announcement the name of the donor. The donor was not at liberty to gain the benefit of such an undertaking upon the payment of a part and disappoint the expectation that there would be payment of the residue. If the college had stated after receiving $1,000 upon account of the subscription that it would apply the money to the prescribed use, but that in its circulars of information and when responding to prospective applicants it would deal with the fund as an anonymous donation, there is little doubt that the subscriber would have been at liberty to treat this statement as the repudiation of a duty impliedly assumed, a repudiation justifying a refusal to make payments in the future. Obligation in such circumstances is correlative and mutual. * * * We do not need to measure the extent either of benefit to the promisor or of detriment to the promisee implicit in this duty. "If a person chooses to make an extravagant promise for an inadequate consideration it is his own affair" (8 Holdsworth, History of English Law, p. 17). It was long ago said that "when a thing is to be done by the plaintiff, be it ever so small, this is a sufficient consideration to ground an action" (Sturlyn v. Albany, 1587, Cro.Eliz. 67, quoted by Holdsworth, supra; cf. Walton Water Co. v. Village of Walton, 238 N.Y. 46, 51). The longing for posthumous remembrance is an emotion not so weak as to justify us in saying that its gratification is a negligible good.

We think the duty assumed by the plaintiff to perpetuate the name of the founder of the memorial is sufficient in itself to give validity to the subscription within the rules that define consideration for a promise of that order. When the promisee subjected itself to such a duty at the implied request of the promisor, the result was the creation of a bilateral agreement. . . . There was a promise on the one side and on the other a return promise, made it is true, by implication, but expressing an obligation that had been exacted as a condition of the payment. A bilateral agreement may exist though one of the mutual promises be a promise "implied in fact," an inference from conduct as opposed to an inference from words (Williston, Contracts, §§ 90, 22–a; Pettibone v. Moore, 75 Hun, 461, 464). We think the fair inference to be drawn from the acceptance of a payment on account of the subscription is a promise by the college to do what may be necessary on its part to make the scholarship effective. The plan conceived by the subscriber will be mutilated and distorted unless the sum to be accepted is adequate to the end in view. Moreover, the time to affix her name to the memorial will not arrive until the entire fund has been collected. The college may thus thwart the purpose of the payment on account if at liberty to reject a tender of the residue. It is no answer to say that a duty would then arise to make restitution of the money. If such a duty may be imposed, the only reason for its existence must be that there is then a failure of "consideration." To say that there is a failure of consideration is to concede that a consideration has been promised since otherwise it could not fail. No doubt there are times and situations in which limitations laid upon a promisee in connection with the use of what is paid by a subscriber lacks the quality of a consideration, and are to be classed merely as conditions (Williston, Contracts, § 112; Page, Contracts, § 523). "It is often difficult to determine whether words of condition in a promise indicate a request for consideration or state a mere condition in a gratuitous promise. An aid, though not a conclusive test in determining which construction of the promise is more reasonable is an inquiry whether the happening of the condition will be a benefit to the promisor. If so, it is a fair inference that the happening was requested as a consideration" (Williston, supra, § 112). Such must be the meaning of this transaction unless we are prepared to hold that the college may keep the payment on account, and thereafter nullify the scholarship which is to preserve the memory of the subscriber. The fair implication to be gathered from the whole transaction is assent to the condition and the assumption of a duty to go forward with performance (De Wolf Co. v. Harvey, 161 Wis. 535; Pullman Co. v. Meyer, 195 Ala. 397, 401; Braniff v. Blair, 101 Kan. 117; cf. Corbin, Offer & Acceptance, 26 Yale L.J. 169, 177, 193; McGovney, Irrevocable Offers, 27 Harv.L.R. 644; Sir Frederick Pollock, 28 L.Q.R. 100, 101). The subscriber does not say: I hand you $1,000, and you make up your mind later, after my death, whether you will undertake to commemorate my name. What she says in effect is this: I hand you $1,000, and if you are unwilling to commemorate me, the time to speak is now.

The conclusion thus reached makes it needless to consider whether, aside from the feature of a memorial, a promissory estoppel may result from the assumption of a duty to apply the fund, so far as already paid, to special purposes not mandatory under the provisions of the college charter (the support and education of students preparing for the ministry), an assumption induced by the belief that other payments sufficient in amount to make the scholarship effective would be added to the fund thereafter upon the death of the subscriber (Ladies' Collegiate Inst. v. French, 16 Gray, 196; Barnes v. Perine, 12 N.Y. 18, and cases there cited).

The judgment of the Appellate Division and that of the Trial Term should be reversed, and judgment ordered for the plaintiff as prayed for in the complaint, with costs in all courts.

■ Kellogg, J. (dissenting). The Chief Judge finds in the expression, "In loving memory this gift shall be known as the Mary Yates Johnston Memorial Fund" an offer on the part of Mary Yates Johnston to contract with Allegheny College. The expression makes no such appeal to me. Allegheny College was not requested to perform any act through which the sum offered might bear the title by which the offeror states that it shall be known. The sum offered was termed a "gift" by the offeror. Consequently, I can see no reason why we should strain ourselves to make it, not a gift, but a trade. Moreover, since the donor specified that the gift was made "In consideration of my interest in Christian education, and in consideration of others subscribing," considerations not adequate in law, I can see no excuse for asserting that it was otherwise made in consideration of an act or promise on the part of the donee, constituting a sufficient *quid quo pro* to convert the gift into a contract obligation. To me the words used merely expressed an expectation or wish on the part of the donor and failed to exact the return of an adequate consideration. But if an offer indeed was present, then clearly it was an offer to enter into a unilateral contract. The offeror was to be bound provided the offeree performed such acts as might be necessary to make the gift offered become known under the proposed name. This is evidently the thought of the Chief Judge, for he says: "She imposed a condition that the 'gift' should be known as the Mary Yates Johnston Memorial Fund." In other words, she proposed to exchange her offer of a donation in return for acts to be performed. Even so there was never any acceptance of the offer and, therefore, no contract, for the acts requested have never been performed. The gift has never been made known as demanded. Indeed, the requested acts, under the very terms of the assumed offer, could never have been performed at a time to convert the offer into a promise. This is so for the reason that the donation was not to take effect until after the death of the donor, and by her death her offer was withdrawn. (Williston on Contracts, sec. 62.) Clearly, although a promise of the college to make the gift known, as requested, may be implied, that promise was not the acceptance of an offer which gave rise to a contract. The donor stipulated for acts, not promises. "In order to make a bargain it is necessary that the acceptor shall give in return for the offer or the promise exactly the consideration which the offeror requests. If an act is requested, that very act and no other must be given. If a promise is requested, that promise must be made absolutely and unqualifiedly." (Williston on Contracts, sec. 73.) "It does not follow that an offer becomes a promise because it is accepted; it may be and frequently is, conditional, and then it does not become a promise until the conditions are satisfied; and in case of offers for a consideration, the performance of the consideration is always deemed a condition." (Langdell, Summary of the Law of Contracts, sec. 4). It seems clear to me that there was here no offer, no acceptance of an offer, and no contract. Neither do I agree with the Chief Judge that this court "found consideration present where the general law of contract, at least as then declared, would have said it was absent" in the cases of Barnes v. Perine (12 N.Y. 18), Presbyterian Society v. Beach (74 N.Y. 72) and Keuka College v. Ray (167 N.Y. 96). In the *Keuka College* case an offer to contract, in consideration of the performance of certain acts by the offeree, was converted into a promise by the actual performance of those acts. This form of contract has been known to the law from time immemorial (Langdell, sec. 46) and for at least a century longer than the other type, a bilateral contract. (Williston, sec. 13.) It may be that the basis of the decisions in *Barnes v. Perine* and *Presbyterian Society v. Beach* (supra) was the same as in the *Keuka College* case. (See Presbyterian Church of Albany v. Cooper, 112 N.Y. 517.) However, even if the basis of the decisions be a so-called "promissory estoppel," nevertheless they initiated no new doctrine. A so-called "promissory estoppel," although not so termed, was held sufficient by Lord Mansfield and his fellow judges as far back as the year

1765. (Pillans v. Van Mierop, 3 Burr. 1663.) Such a doctrine may be an anomaly; it is not a novelty. Therefore, I can see no ground for the suggestion that the ancient rule which makes consideration necessary to the formation of every contract is in danger of effacement through any decisions of this court. To me that is a cause for gratulation rather than regret. However, the discussion may be beside the mark, for I do not understand that the holding about to be made in this case is other than a holding that consideration was given to convert the offer into a promise. With that result I cannot agree and, accordingly, must dissent.

■ Pound, Crane, Lehman and O'Brien, JJ., concur with Cardozo, Ch. J.; Kellogg, J. dissents in opinion, in which Andrews, J., concurs.

Judgment accordingly.

NOTES

(1) Consider the following questions (and suggested answers) about *Ricketts*:

(a) Why was not Katie Scothorn's abandonment of employment, assuredly a "detrimental" act, sufficient as consideration for the grandfather's promise? (According to the court, it was not bargained for.)

(b) What if Katie had not quit her job? Would the grandfather's intent (or lack of it) to assume a legal obligation have been any less? (No.) Would the promise have been enforceable? (Not unless there is special legislation or you buy Professor Barnett's "consent" theory.)

(c) Suppose that in reliance on the grandfather's promise Katie had quit the job, but that shortly thereafter the promise was repudiated and she was rehired, sustaining at most a loss of $100. Should she recover anything? If so, how much? $100? $2,000? See Corbin § 205.

(2) Does Judge Cardozo in *Allegheny College* purport to find consideration for the promise being sued upon? Is the conclusion that Mrs. Johnson bargained for and received a promise by the college, implied from the conduct of accepting the $1,000 payment and putting it aside, to set up and publicize the fund when the final payment was made convincing? For a line-by-line analysis of *Allegheny College*, see Konefsky, *How to Read, Or at Least Not Misread, Cardozo in the Allegheny College Case*, 36 Buff.L.Rev. 645 (1989).

(3) "It would seem * * * that the framers of section 90 recognized the fact that there is a class of cases where gratuitous promises should be enforced for compelling reasons of justice, where the promisee incurs a substantial detriment on the faith of such promises, and this, whether the promisor intended the detriment or not. The test seems to be whether the promisor could reasonably have expected the detriment to be incurred on the strength of the promise. If the detriment is incurred, and there is no other way of avoiding injustice, the promise is enforceable. Of course, as pointed out by Judge Baldrige, in Langer v. Superior Steel Corp. . . . and also by Professor Williston in his work on 'Contracts' not every gratuitous promise and reliance thereon is enforceable. The doctrine must be limited in its application to that group of cases where the reliance on the promise brought about such a substantial,

changed condition on the part of the promisee that enforcement of the promise is the only way to avoid injustice. What constitutes injustice has not been defined; that, it would seem, must be determined from all the surrounding circumstances of each case. Professor Williston hints that injustice does not necessarily mean pecuniary loss. As he points out, the meaning is 'purposely left somewhat indefinite,' which means that the equities of each case must point the way to its solution under this doctrine of promissory estoppel." Trexler's Estate, 27 Pa.D. & C. 4, 13 (Orphans' Court of Lehigh County, Pennsylvania, 1936).

(4) *Charitable Subscriptions.* Cases enforcing promises to charities on the basis of unbargained-for reliance can be counted among the historical antecedents of modern promissory estoppel theory. See Boyer, *Promissory Estoppel: Principle From Precedents,* 50 Mich.L.Rev 639, 873 (1952). There are references to some of these decisions in *Ricketts* and *Allegheny College.* Hence, even if a court is unwilling to stretch to find consideration, as Judge Cardozo did in *Allegheny College,* there may be an alternative basis of recovery. However, this alternative basis requires a showing of reliance on the part of the promisee, and it may be impossible to establish any specific reliance. See, e.g., Mount Sinai Hospital of Greater Miami, Inc. v. Jordan, 290 So.2d 484 (Fla.1974); Congregation Kadimah Toras–Moshe v. DeLeo, 405 Mass. 365, 540 N.E.2d 691, 693 (1989) ("The inclusion of the promised $25,000 in the budget, by itself, merely reduced to writing the Congregation's expectation that it would have additional funds. A hope or expectation, even though well founded, is not equivalent to either legal detriment or reliance."). To obviate this difficulty, the drafters of Restatement (Second) dispensed with the necessity of proving reliance. Subsection (2) of Section 90 provides: "A charitable subscription * * * is binding * * * without proof that the promise induced action or forbearance." For a case adopting the Restatement position, see Salsbury v. Northwestern Bell Telephone Co., 221 N.W.2d 609 (Iowa 1974). The Iowa Supreme Court commented as follows: "We believe public policy supports this view. It is more logical to bind charitable subscriptions without requiring a showing of consideration or detrimental reliance. Charitable subscriptions often serve the public interest by making possible projects which otherwise could never come about. * * * [W]here a subscription is unequivocal the pledgor should be made to keep his word." 221 N.W.2d at 613. But see King v. Trustees of Boston University, 420 Mass. 52, 647 N.E.2d 1196, 1200 (1995), where the Restatement standard for charitable gifts was rejected.

(5) *Promissory Estoppel In New York.* The development of promissory estoppel in New York was traced in Cyberchron Corp. v. Calldata Systems Development, Inc., 47 F.3d 39, 44–46 (2d Cir.1995). According to the federal court, prior to 1980 New York courts limited promissory estoppel as a "substitute for consideration" to limited contexts, such as charitable subscriptions and bailments and to disputes over the statute of frauds. After 1980, some lower courts embraced the more general principle but imposed higher standards than those expressed in Section 90 of the Second Restatement. Thus, the promise must be "clear and unambiguous," reliance must be foreseeable to the promisor and reasonable by the promisee and the resulting injury must be "unconscionable." Some have argued that Judge Cardozo impeded the development of promissory estoppel in New York by his decision in *Allegheny College.* Do you

agree? See Phuong N. Pham (Comment), *The Waning of Promissory Estoppel,* 79 Cornell L. Rev. 1263 (1994).

Feinberg v. Pfeiffer Co.

St. Louis Court of Appeals, Missouri, 1959.
322 S.W.2d 163.

■ DOERNER, COMMISSIONER. This is a suit brought in the Circuit Court of the City of St. Louis by plaintiff a former employee of the defendant corporation on an alleged contract whereby defendant agreed to pay plaintiff the sum of $200 per month for life upon her retirement. A jury being waived, the case was tried by the court alone. Judgment below was for plaintiff for $5,100, the amount of the pension claimed to be due as of the date of the trial together with interest thereon, and defendant duly appealed.

The parties are in substantial agreement on the essential facts. Plaintiff began working for the defendant, a manufacturer of pharmaceuticals, in 1910, when she was but 17 years of age. By 1947 she had attained the position of bookkeeper, office manager, and assistant treasurer of the defendant, and owned 70 shares of its stock out of a total of 6,503 shares issued and outstanding. Twenty shares had been given to her by the defendant or its then president, she had purchased 20, and the remaining 30 she had acquired by a stock split or stock dividend. Over the years she received substantial dividends on the stock she owned, as did all of the other stockholders. Also, in addition to her salary, plaintiff from 1937 to 1949, inclusive, received each year a bonus varying in amount from $300 in the beginning to $2,000 in the later years.

On December 27, 1947, the annual meeting of the defendant's Board of Directors was held at the Company's offices in St. Louis, presided over by Max Lippman, its then president and largest individual stockholder. The other directors present were George L. Marcus, Sidney Harris, Sol Flammer, and Walter Weinstock, who, with Max Lippman, owned 5,007 of the 6,503 shares then issued and outstanding. At that meeting the Board of Directors adopted the following resolution, which, because it is the crux of the case, we quote in full:

"The Chairman thereupon pointed out that the Assistant Treasurer, Mrs. Anna Sacks Feinberg, has given the corporation many years of long and faithful service. Not only has she served the corporation devotedly, but with exceptional ability and skill. The President pointed out that although all of the officers and directors sincerely hoped and desired that Mrs. Feinberg would continue in her present position for as long as she felt able, nevertheless, in view of the length of service which she has contributed provision should be made to afford her retirement privileges and benefits which should become a firm obligation of the corporation to be available to her whenever she should see fit to retire from active duty, however many years in the future such retirement may become effective. It was, accordingly, proposed that Mrs. Feinberg's salary which is presently $350.00 per month, be increased to $400.00 per month, and that Mrs. Feinberg would be given the privilege of retiring from active duty at any time she may elect to see fit so to do upon a retirement pay of $200.00 per month for life, with the distinct understanding that the retirement plan is merely being adopted at the present time in order to afford Mrs. Feinberg security for the future and in the hope that her active services will continue with the corporation for many years to come. After due discussion and consideration, and upon motion duly made and seconded, it was—

"Resolved that the salary of Anna Sacks Feinberg be increased from $350.00 to $400.00 per month and that she be afforded the privilege of retiring from active duty in the corporation at any time she may elect to see fit so to do upon retirement pay of $200.00 per month, for the remainder of her life."

At the request of Mr. Lippman his sons-in-law, Messrs. Harris and Flammer, called upon the plaintiff at her apartment on the same day to advise her of the passage of the resolution. Plaintiff testified on cross-examination that she had no prior information that such a pension plan was contemplated, that it came as a surprise to her, and that she would have continued in her employment whether or not such a resolution had been adopted. It is clear from the evidence that there was no contract, oral or written, as to plaintiff's length of employment, and that she was free to quit, and the defendant to discharge her, at any time.

Plaintiff did continue to work for the defendant through June 30, 1949, on which date she retired. In accordance with the foregoing resolution, the defendant began paying her the sum of $200 on the first of each month. Mr. Lippman died on November 18, 1949, and was succeeded as president of the company by his widow. Because of an illness, she retired from that office and was succeeded in October, 1953, by her son-in-law, Sidney M. Harris. Mr. Harris testified that while Mrs. Lippman had been president she signed the monthly pension check paid plaintiff, but fussed about doing so, and considered the payments as gifts. After his election, he stated, a new accounting firm employed by the defendant questioned the validity of the payments to plaintiff on several occasions, and in the Spring of 1956, upon its recommendation, he consulted the Company's then attorney, Mr. Ralph Kalish. Harris testified that both Ernst and Ernst, the accounting firm, and Kalish told him there was no need of giving plaintiff the money. He also stated that he had concurred in the view that the payments to plaintiff were mere gratuities rather than amounts due under a contractual obligation, and that following his discussion with the Company's attorney plaintiff was sent a check for $100 on April 1, 1956. Plaintiff declined to accept the reduced amount, and this action followed. Additional facts will be referred to later in this opinion.

* * *

It is defendant's contention, in essence, that the resolution adopted by its Board of Directors was a mere promise to make a gift, and that no contract resulted either thereby, or when plaintiff retired, because there was no consideration given or paid by the plaintiff. It urges that a promise to make a gift is not binding unless supported by a legal consideration; that the only apparent consideration for the adoption of the foregoing resolution was the "many years of long and faithful service" expressed therein; and that past services are not a valid consideration for a promise. Defendant argues further that there is nothing in the resolution which made its effectiveness conditional upon plaintiff's continued employment, that she was not under contract to work for any length of time but was free to quit whenever she wished, and that she had no contractual right to her position and could have been discharged at any time.

Plaintiff concedes that a promise based upon past services would be without consideration, but contends that there were two other elements which supplied the required element: First, the continuation by plaintiff in the employ of the defendant for the period from December 27, 1947, the date when the resolution was adopted, until the date of her retirement on June 30, 1949. And, second, her change of position, i.e., her retirement, and the abandonment by her of her opportunity to continue in gainful employment, made in reliance on defendant's promise to pay her $200 per month for life.

We must agree with the defendant that the evidence does not support the first of these contentions. There is no language in the resolution predicating plaintiff's right to a pension upon her continued employment. She was not required to work for the defendant for any period of time as a condition to gaining such retirement benefits. She was told that she could quit the day upon which the resolution was adopted, as she herself testified, and it is clear from her own testimony that she made no promise or agreement to continue in the employ of the defendant in return for its promise to pay her a pension. Hence there was lacking that mutuality of obligation which is essential to the validity of a contract. Middleton v. Holecroft, Mo.App., 270 S.W.2d 90; Solace v. T.J. Moss Tie Co., Mo.App., 142 S.W.2d 1079; Aslin v. Stoddard County, 341 Mo. 138, 106 S.W.2d 472; Fuqua v. Lumbermen's Supply Co., 229 Mo.App. 210, 76 S.W.2d 715; Hudson v. Browning, 264 Mo. 58, 174 S.W. 393; Campbell v. American Handle Co., 117 Mo.App. 19, 94 S.W. 815.

But as to the second of these contentions we must agree with plaintiff. By the terms of the resolution defendant promised to pay plaintiff the sum of $200 a month upon her retirement. Consideration for a promise has been defined in the Restatement of the Law of Contracts, Section 75, as:

> "(1) Consideration for a promise is
>
>> (a) an act other than a promise, or
>>
>> (b) a forbearance, or
>>
>> (c) the creation, modification or destruction of a legal relation, or
>>
>> (d) a return promise,
>
> bargained for and given in exchange for the promise."

As the parties agree, the consideration sufficient to support a contract may be either a benefit to the promisor or a loss or detriment to the promisee.

Industrial Bank & Trust Co. v. Hesselberg, Mo., 195 S.W.2d 470; State ex rel. Kansas City v. State Highway Commission, 349 Mo. 865, 163 S.W.2d 948; Duvall v. Duncan, 341 Mo. 1129, 111 S.W.2d 89; Thompson v. McCune, 333 Mo. 758, 63 S.W.2d 41.

Section 90 of the Restatement of the Law of Contracts states that: "A promise which the promisor should reasonably expect to induce action or forbearance of a definite and substantial character on the part of the promisee and which does induce such action or forbearance is binding if injustice can be avoided only by enforcement of the promise." This doctrine has been described as that of "promissory estoppel," as distinguished from that of equitable estoppel or estoppel in pais, the reason for the differentiation being stated as follows:

"It is generally true that one who has led another to act in reasonable reliance on his representations of fact cannot afterwards in litigation between the two deny the truth of the representations, and some courts have sought to apply this principle to the formation of contracts, where, relying on a gratuitous promise, the promisee has suffered detriment. It is to be noticed, however, that such a case does not come within the ordinary definition of estoppel. If there is any representation of an existing fact, it is only that the promisor at the time of making the promise intends to fulfill it. As to such intention there is usually no misrepresentation and if there is, it is not that which has injured the promisee. In other words, he relies on a promise and not on a misstatement of fact; and the term 'promissory' estoppel or something equivalent should be used to make the distinction." Williston on Contracts, Rev.Ed., Sec. 139, Vol. 1.

In speaking of this doctrine, Judge Learned Hand said in Porter v. Commissioner of Internal Revenue, 2 Cir., 60 F.2d 673, 675, that "* * * 'promissory estoppel' is now a recognized species of consideration."

* * *

Was there such an act on the part of plaintiff, in reliance upon the promise contained in the resolution, as will estop the defendant, and therefore create an enforceable contract under the doctrine of promissory estoppel? We think there was. One of the illustrations cited under Section 90 of the Restatement is: "2. A promises B to pay him an annuity during B's life. B thereupon resigns a profitable employment, as A expected that he might. B receives the annuity for some years, in the meantime becoming disqualified from again obtaining good employment. A's promise is binding." This illustration is objected to by defendant as not being applicable to the case at hand. The reason advanced by it is that in the illustration B became "disqualified" from obtaining other employment *before* A discontinued the payments, whereas in this case the plaintiff did not discover that she had cancer and thereby became unemployable until *after* the defendant had discontinued the payments of $200 per month. We think the distinction is immaterial. The only reason for the reference in the illustration to the disqualification of A is in connection with that part of Section 90 regarding the prevention of injustice. The injustice would occur regardless of when the disability occurred. Would defendant contend that the contract would be enforceable if the plaintiff's illness had been discovered on March 31, 1956, the day before it discontinued the payment of the $200 a month, but not if it occurred on April 2nd, the day after? Furthermore, there are more ways to become disqualified for work, or unemployable, than as the result of illness. At the time she retired plaintiff was 57 years of age. At the time the payments were discontinued she was over 63 years of age. It is a matter of common knowledge that it is virtually impossible for a woman of that age to find satisfactory employment, much less a position comparable to that which plaintiff enjoyed at the time of her retirement.

The fact of the matter is that plaintiff's subsequent illness was not the "action or forbearance" which was induced by the promise contained in the resolution. As the trial court correctly decided, such action on plaintiff's part was her retirement from a lucrative position in reliance upon defendant's promise to pay her an annuity or pension. In a very similar case, Ricketts v. Scothorn, 57 Neb. 51, 77 N.W. 365, 367, 42 L.R.A. 794, the Supreme Court of Nebraska said:

"* * * According to the undisputed proof, as shown by the record before us, the plaintiff was a working girl, holding a position in which she earned a salary of $10 per week. Her grandfather, desiring to put her in a position of independence, gave her the note accompanying it with the remark that his other grandchildren did not work, and that she would not be obliged to work any longer. In effect, he suggested that she might abandon her employment, and rely in the future upon the bounty which he promised. He doubtless desired that she should give up her occupation, but, whether he did or not, it is entirely certain that he contemplated such action on her part as a reasonable and probable consequence of his gift. Having intentionally influenced the plaintiff to alter her position for the worse on the faith of the note being paid when due, it would be grossly inequitable to permit the maker, or his executor, to resist payment on the ground that the promise was given without consideration."

The Commissioner therefore recommends, for the reasons stated, that the judgment be affirmed.

■ PER CURIAM.

The foregoing opinion by DOERNER, C., is adopted as the opinion of the court. The judgment is, accordingly, affirmed.

NOTES

(1) Did the defendant in *Feinberg* bargain for Ms. Feinberg's early retirement? For cases finding consideration to support a promise to pay a pension or similar benefit in either the promisor's desire to induce early retirement or restrict the plaintiff's post-retirement conduct, see Osborne v. Locke Steel Chain Co., 153 Conn. 527, 218 A.2d 526 (1966) (retired officer to be available for consultation and to refrain from competition with former employer); Lowndes Cooperative Association v. Lipsey, 240 Miss. 71, 126 So.2d 276 (1961) (promise conditioned on early retirement and post-retirement cooperation);

Specht v. Eastwood–Nealley Corp., 34 N.J.Super. 156, 111 A.2d 781 (1955) (promise conditioned upon non-disclosure of trade secrets, non-competition, etc.). For cases enforcing the promise on the grounds of either consideration or promissory estoppel, see Hessler, Inc. v. Farrell, 226 A.2d 708 (Del.1967) (employee induced to forego other offers and remain with company); Wickstrom v. Vern E. Alden Co., 99 Ill.App.2d 254, 240 N.E.2d 401 (1968) (employee induced to retire early). If there was no legitimate basis for inferring a bargain in *Feinberg,* did the court stretch unduly to enforce the promise under Section 90? For a reaffirmation of *Feinberg* in Missouri, see Katz v. Danny Dare, Inc., 610 S.W.2d 121 (Mo.App.1980). Cf. Hayes v. Plantations Steel Co., 438 A.2d 1091 (R.I.1982) (*Feinberg* distinguished; court found that promise of pension in no way induced employee to retire.)

(2) *Contemporary Pension Plans.* It is common practice for employers to establish private pension plans for the benefit of their employees. Prior to the passage of The Employee Retirement Income Security Act of 1974 (ERISA), vesting provisions for many of these plans were often harsh and incapable of attainment. ERISA was enacted to improve and strengthen the protection for the majority of the participants of contemporary plans by providing statutory protection for participants in both private employee benefit plans and welfare benefit plans. ERISA's statutory protection and enforcement procedures in this area preempt state law which enforced vesting on theories of bargain contract or promissory estoppel. However, these theories still apply to unfunded plans and other types of plans exempt from ERISA coverage. For a discussion of ERISA's effect, see M. Canan, Qualified Retirement and Other Employer Benefit Plans (1990). See also, Schonholz v. Long Island Jewish Medical Center, 87 F.3d 72, 78 (2d Cir.1996)(promissory estoppel applies in ERISA cases under extraordinary circumstances).

(3) *Gratuitous Undertakings in Various Conceptual Contexts.* The problem of gratuitous promises or undertakings arises in several conceptual contexts; *viz.,* liability in tort, obligations of agents and bailees, the existence of contract and more. Some of them are unexpected. For example, in King v. Riveland, 125 Wash.2d 500, 886 P.2d 160, 168–169 (1994), prisoners convicted of sex offenses were induced to enter a state run sex offender treatment program in part by a promise that whatever was divulged in the program would be confidential. The prisoners sought an injunction against a threatened disclosure, which the court granted on a contract theory. Although there was no consideration, the promise did induce reliance and justice required its enforcement. The court relied upon Section 90.

In Abresch v. Northwestern Bell Telephone Co., 246 Minn. 408, 75 N.W.2d 206 (1956), the plaintiff sought damages he suffered when a building which he owned was destroyed by fire. Upon discovering the fire, he phoned the telephone operator, requesting her to call the fire department. The court noted that "while the telephone company is under no duty to assume responsibility of delivering messages in cases of emergency, if it does voluntarily assume such responsibility and thereby leads others to rely on such assumption of duty and to refrain from taking other and more direct action to protect themselves, the company is required to exercise reasonable care in performing the duty so assumed for a failure of which it may become liable in a tort action." 75 N.W.2d at 211–12. "It is ancient learning that one who assumes to act, even though gratuitously, may thereby become subject to the duty of acting carefully, if he acts at all." Glanzer v. Shepard, 233 N.Y. 236, 239, 135 N.E. 275, 276 (1922). Restatement (Second) of Torts § 323 provides: "One who undertakes, gratuitously or for consideration, to render services to another which he should recognize as necessary for the protection of the other's person or things, is subject to liability to the other for physical harm resulting from his failure to exercise reasonable care to perform his undertaking, if (a) his failure to exercise such care increases the risk of such harm, or (b) the harm is suffered because of the other's reliance upon the undertaking." For a recent application, see Jefferson County School District R–1 v. Justus, 725 P.2d 767 (Colo.1986) (school district undertook task of enforcing rule that students in lower grades were not eligible to ride bicycles to and from school). See, generally, Prosser and Keeton § 56.

This is a relatively undeveloped area of tort law, particularly where the act complained of is the defendant's failure to perform a promised act (nonfeasance) rather than the negligent performance of a promised act (misfeasance). Litigants have sought to enhance prospects of recovery by attempting to show that the defendant was or undertook to become an agent or bailee of the plaintiff. Certain obligations adhere to the principal-agent and bailor-bailee relationships by operation of law quite apart from the explicit agreement or understanding of the parties. See, for example, Lester v. Marshall, 143 Colo. 189, 352 P.2d 786 (1960), where a real estate broker engaged by the plaintiffs to find a home for them also gratuitously undertook to "take care of everything" prior to and after closing, assuring plaintiffs they would get title free of encumbrances. The court relied upon the revised Restatement of Agency, which in section 378 provides as follows: "One who, by a gratuitous promise or other conduct which he should realize will cause another reasonably to rely upon the performance of definite acts of service by him as the other's agent, causes the other to refrain from having such acts done by other available means is subject to a duty to use care to perform such service or, while other means are available, to give notice that he will not perform." Restatement of Agency (Second) § 378. See also Brunelle v. Nashua Building & Loan Association, 95 N.H. 391, 64 A.2d 315 (1949). Finally, cases of this type have since the emergence of promissory estoppel been analyzed in terms of contractual obligation.

Whether viewed in terms of agency, bailment, tort or contract, the misfeasance-nonfeasance dichotomy is often respected. It may be wondered if this precedented approach will or should be preserved. For it is recognized that the underlying basis of liability is the reasonable reliance, which clearly can follow a promise to perform an act as well as the negligent performance of an act already undertaken. The drafters note in comment d of Restatement (Second) of Torts § 323, supra, that "[t]he modern law has * * * witnessed a considerable weakening and blurring of the distinction [between misfeasance and nonfeasance], in situations where the plaintiff's reliance upon the defendant's promise has resulted in harm to him." The Restatement of Agency, quoted above, does not embody the distinction, nor does either the original or revised section 90 of the Restatement of Contracts.

For background reading on the overlap of tort and contract, see generally: Peter Linzer, *Law's Unity—An Essay for the Master Contortionist,* 90 Nw.

U.L.Rev. 183 (1995); Thomas C. Galligan, Jr., *Contortions Along the Boundary between Contracts and Torts,* 69 Tul.L.Rev. 457 (1994); Holmes, *Is There Life After Gilmore's Death of Contract?—Inductions from a Study of Commercial Good Faith in First Party Insurance Contracts,* 65 Cornell L.Rev. 330 (1980); Posner, *Gratuitous Promises in Economics and Law,* 6 J.Legal Stud. 411 (1977); Seavey, *Reliance upon Gratuitous Promises or Other Conduct,* 64 Harv.L.Rev. 913 (1951); Speidel, *The Borderland of Contract,* 10 N.Ky.L.Rev. 163 (1983); Wangerin, *Damages for Reliance Across the Spectrum of Law: Of Blind Men and Legal Elephants,* 72 Iowa L.Rev. 49 (1986). Corbin §§ 207–08; Prosser and Keeton § 92.

(4) *Gratuitous Promise to Procure Insurance.* Even before the American Law Institute had adopted the first Restatement, courts had imposed liability upon a party who gratuitously promised to obtain insurance for another. In Siegel v. Spear & Co., 234 N.Y. 479, 138 N.E. 414 (1923), the defendant agreed to store the plaintiff's furniture free of charge. The defendant also promised to obtain insurance on the property. The defendant never obtained the insurance, and the goods were destroyed by fire. The court noted that since the transaction between the parties was a gratuitous bailment, the defendant would normally be liable only for gross negligence. The court, however, stated: "But if in connection with taking the goods [the defendant] also voluntarily undertook to procure insurance for the plaintiff's benefit, the promise was part of the whole transaction and was linked up with the gratuitous bailment. The bailee * * * was then under as much an obligation to procure insurance as he was to take care of the goods." 138 N.E. at 415. In other words, because of the bailor-bailee relationship between the parties, the court was willing to impose liability on the promisor for failing to perform his gratuitous promise.

As discussed in the previous note, plaintiffs have sought to establish an agency or bailment relationship because the court would then impose on the defendant a higher standard of care or a duty to act. Where there is no duty to act because of a lack of a legal relationship or otherwise, courts have traditionally been reluctant to impose liability. For example, in Comfort v. McCorkle, 149 Misc. 826, 268 N.Y.S. 192 (1933), the defendant gratuitously promised to file an insurance claim on the plaintiff's behalf. After the time for filing the claim had expired, the plaintiff realized that the defendant had not filed the claim. In denying recovery, the court relied on the doctrine of Thorne v. Deas, 4 Johns. 84 (N.Y.1809), that a gratuitous promisor who wholly omits to perform the promise is not liable, notwithstanding the promisee may have sustained damage. The court stated that only where the promisor attempts to perform, but fails, can liability be imposed.

Plaintiffs have been successful in actions against insurance agents for their misfeasance in failing to procure insurance after promising to do so. For example, in Hardcastle v. Greenwood Savings & Loan Association, 9 Wash.App. 884, 516 P.2d 228 (1973), the scope of duty was put expansively: "An insurance agent who undertakes the duty of securing insurance is liable to his principal for the negligent performance of that duty. Any person undertaking to secure insurance for another becomes an insurance agent for that person; his responsibility to observe reasonable care in the performance of that duty is not lessened by the fact that such undertaking is gratuitous." 516 P.2d at 231. See also Dalrymple v. Ed Shults Chevrolet, Inc., 51 A.D.2d 884, 380 N.Y.S.2d 189

(1976), where the court concluded that a used car salesman who promised to transfer and extend insurance coverage on a car was liable for loss if he negligently failed to perform as promised. "There was no duty on the part of the salesman to secure this insurance. * * * However, once he undertook to do so, he was obliged to use reasonable care to see that plaintiff's property interests were insured in accordance with their requests." 380 N.Y.S.2d at 190.

Finally, some courts have explicitly adopted promissory estoppel as a proper theory of liability in the insurance cases. See, e.g., Verschoor v. Mountain West Farm Bureau Mutual Ins. Co., 907 P.2d 1293, 1297–1301 (Wyo.1995); East Providence Credit Union v. Geremia, 103 R.I. 597, 239 A.2d 725 (1968); Weitman v. Grange Insurance Association, 59 Wash.2d 748, 370 P.2d 587 (1962). The drafters of Restatement (Second), however, suggest that promissory estoppel should be "applied with caution" to promises to procure insurance. Restatement (Second) § 90, comment e. They elaborate: "The appropriate remedy for breach of such a promise makes the promisor an insurer, and thus may result in a liability which is very large in relation to the value of the promised service. Often the promise is properly to be construed merely as a promise to use reasonable efforts to procure the insurance, and reliance by the promisee may be unjustified or may be justified only for a short time. Or it may be doubtful whether he did in fact rely. Such difficulties may be removed if the proof of the promise and the reliance are clear, or if the promise is made with some formality, or if part performance or a commercial setting or a potential benefit to the promisor provide a substitute for formality." For a case illustrating these difficulties, see Northern Commercial Co. v. United Airmotive, 101 F.Supp. 169 (D.Alaska 1951). See also Annot., *Liability of Insurance Broker or Agent to Insured for Failure to Procure Insurance*, 64 A.L.R.3d 398 (1975); Annot., *Duty and Liability of Real–Estate Agent or Broker to Purchaser with Respect to Procurement or Transfer of Insurance Policy*, 88 A.L.R.3d 1077 (1978).

(5) *Promissory Estoppel in England.* No unitary principle of promissory estoppel has emerged in English and Commonwealth contract law. One rather suspects that the reliance interest has been (or could be) protected under the flexible definition of consideration as either a benefit to the promisor or a detriment to the promisee. The bargain rhetoric does not dominate discussions of consideration in English law. See G. Treitel, The Law of Contract 51–57, 92–93, 111–113 (5th ed.1983); P. Atiyah, Consideration in Contracts: A Fundamental Restatement (1971). Nevertheless, promises made within the framework of existing contractual or legal relations which induce the other to rely so that his or her liability under these relations would be altered have been held to justify suspension or discharge of that liability. The relief in these "variation" cases is defensive. It is generally understood that promissory estoppel will not create any new cause of action where no liability existed before. According to Professor Atiyah, English decisions suggest that the flexible doctrine of consideration rather than promissory estoppel can and should be used even in the "variation" cases. Atiyah, *Consideration and Estoppel: The Thawing of the Ice,* 38 Mod. L.Rev. 65 (1975). In any event, there is no persuasive evidence that English judges either need or want a Restatement (Second) § 90 to assist in differentiating the enforceable from the unenforceable promise. See also Cheshire, Fifoot & Furmston, Law of Contract 97–105 (12th ed. 1991).

Grouse v. Group Health Plan, Inc.

Supreme Court of Minnesota, 1981.
306 N.W.2d 114.

■ OTIS, JUSTICE.

Plaintiff John Grouse appeals from a judgment in favor of Group Health Plan, Inc., in this action for damages resulting from repudiation of an employment offer. The narrow issue raised is whether the trial court erred by concluding that Grouse's complaint fails to state a claim upon which relief can be granted. In our view, the doctrine of promissory estoppel entitles Grouse to recover and we, therefore, reverse and remand for a new trial on the issue of damages.

The facts relevant to this appeal are essentially undisputed. Grouse, a 1974 graduate of the University of Minnesota School of Pharmacy, was employed in 1975 as a retail pharmacist at Richter Drug in Minneapolis. He worked approximately 41 hours per week earning $7 per hour. Grouse desired employment in a hospital or clinical setting, however, because of the work environment and the increased compensation and benefits. In the summer of 1975 he was advised by the Health Sciences Placement office at the University that Group Health was seeking a pharmacist.

Grouse called Group Health and was told to come in and fill out an application. He did so in September and was, at that time, interviewed by Cyrus Elliott, Group Health's Chief Pharmacist. Approximately 2 weeks later Elliott contacted Grouse and asked him to come in for an interview with Donald Shoberg, Group Health's General Manager. Shoberg explained company policies and procedures as well as salary and benefits. Following this meeting Grouse again spoke with Elliott who told him to be patient, that it was necessary to interview recent graduates before making an offer.

On December 4, 1975, Elliott telephoned Grouse at Richter Drug and offered him a position as a pharmacist at Group Health's St. Louis Park Clinic. Grouse accepted but informed Elliott that 2 week's notice to Richter Drug would be necessary. That afternoon Grouse received an offer from a Veteran's Administration Hospital in Virginia which he declined because of Group Health's offer. Elliott called back to confirm that Grouse had resigned.

Sometime in the next few days Elliott mentioned to Shoberg that he had hired, or was thinking of hiring, Grouse. Shoberg told him that company hiring requirements included a favorable written reference, a background check, and approval of the general manager. Elliott contacted two faculty members at the School of Pharmacy who declined to give references. He also contacted an internship employer and several pharmacies where Grouse had done relief work. Their responses were that they had not had enough exposure to Grouse's work to form a judgment as to his capabilities. Elliott did not contact Richter because Grouse's application requested that he not be contacted. Because Elliott was unable to supply a favorable reference for Grouse, Shoberg hired another person to fill the position.

On December 15, 1975 Grouse called Group Health and reported that he was free to begin work. Elliott informed Grouse that someone else had been hired. Grouse complained to the director of Group Health who apologized but took no other action. Grouse experienced difficulty regaining full time employment and suffered wage loss as a result. He commenced this suit to recover damages; the trial judge found that he had not stated an actionable claim.

In our view the principle of contract law applicable here is promissory estoppel. Its effect is to imply a contract in law where none exists in fact. Del Hayes & Sons, Inc. v. Mitchell, 304 Minn. 275, 230 N.W.2d 588 (1975). On these facts no contract exists because due to the bilateral power of termination neither party is committed to performance and the promises are, therefore, illusory. The elements of promissory estoppel are stated in *Restatement of Contracts* § 90 (1932):

> A promise which the promisor should reasonably expect to induce action or forbearance * * * on the part of the promisee and which does induce such action or forbearance is binding if injustice can be avoided only by enforcement of the promise.

Group Health knew that to accept its offer Grouse would have to resign his employment at Richter Drug. Grouse promptly gave notice to Richter Drug and informed Group Health that he had done so when specifically asked by Elliott. Under these circumstances it would be unjust not to hold Group Health to its promise.

The parties focus their arguments on whether an employment contract which is terminable at will can give rise to an action for damages if anticipatorily repudiated. Compare Skagerberg v. Blandin Paper Co., 197 Minn. 291, 266 N.W. 872 (1936); Degen v. Investors Diversified Services, Inc., 260 Minn. 424, 110 N.W.2d 863 (1961); and Bussard v. College of St. Thomas, Inc., 294 Minn. 215, 200 N.W.2d 155 (1972) with Hackett v. Foodmaker, Inc., 69 Mich.App. 591, 245 N.W.2d 140 (1976). Group Health contends that recognition of a cause of action on these facts would result in the anomalous rule that an employee who is told not to report to work the day before he is scheduled to begin has a remedy while an employee who is discharged after the first day does not. We cannot agree since under appropriate circumstances we believe section 90 would apply even after employment has begun.

When a promise is enforced pursuant to section 90 "[t]he remedy granted for breach may be limited as justice requires." Relief may be limited to damages measured by the promisee's reliance.

The conclusion we reach does not imply that an employer will be liable whenever he discharges an employee whose term of employment is at will. What we do hold is that under the facts of this case the appellant had a right to assume he would be given a good faith opportunity to perform his duties to the satisfaction of respondent once he was on the job. He was not only denied that opportunity but resigned the position he already held in reliance on the firm offer which respondent tendered him. Since, as respondent points out, the prospective employment might have been terminated at any time, the measure of damages is not so much what he would have earned from respondent as what he lost in quitting the job he held and in declining at least one other offer of employment elsewhere.

Reversed and remanded for a new trial on the issue of damages.

NOTES

(1) In *Grouse,* the court observed that "no contract exists because due to the bilateral power of termination neither party is committed to performance and the promises are, therefore, illusory." Do you agree? Is *Grouse* an instance of one being justified in relying upon an "illusory" promise? What promise did the court enforce? See generally, Metzger and Phillips, *Promissory Estoppel and Reliance on Illusory Promises,* 44 Sw.L.J. 841 (1990). For a case in accord with *Grouse* in which liability also extended to a third person, the wife of the promisee, see Ravelo v. County of Hawaii, 66 Hawaii 194, 658 P.2d 883 (1983).

(2) How did the court measure damages in *Grouse?* Suppose Grouse had been permitted to work for a week and then terminated? Suppose Grouse worked for a year before termination? Is there any point at which the court should have measured damages by the value to Grouse of the promised employment?

(3) *The Case of the Disappointed Mortgagee.* Brad wanted to buy some land from Harold and build a new home. Harold was willing to sell 3 acres in his subdivision for $6,000. Company, in another state, was willing to sell Brad a prefabricated home for $40,000, to be delivered to the site and set up by Brad. Bank agreed to loan Brad $6,000 to pay Harold for the land and created a first mortgage on the property. Company was willing to sell the home to Brad for $3,000 down with a promise to pay the balance in installments but Company, knowing of Bank's involvement, wanted a second mortgage on the land. Company reasoned that the land with a home would be valuable and that even if Brad defaulted, the proceeds from any foreclosure sale would exceed the amount of Bank's loan. The second mortgage was executed, but before shipping the home to Brad Company obtained a written promise from Bank that if Brad was seriously in default to Bank, Bank would promptly notify Company. Company shipped the home, which Brad attempted to set up. Before the work was done, Brad was seriously in default to Bank. Bank, however, did not notify Company. Rather, Bank sold Brad's note and the first mortgage to Harold for $5,500, the amount due under the loan. Harold then foreclosed the mortgage and, at the foreclosure sale, bid on the property and purchased it for $6,000. Harold then completed construction of the home for $10,000 and sold the lot and completed home to Frank, a friend, for $30,000.

Company has been advised that it cannot upset the foreclosure sale to Frank (it had notice of the sale but did not attend) and accepts that advice. However, it wants to sue Bank for the failure to give notice of Brad's default. Is the Bank's promise enforceable? If so, what damages should Company recover? See Miles Homes Division of Insilco Corp. v. First State Bank of Joplin, 782 S.W.2d 798 (Mo.App.1990).

(4) *The Case of Friendly Ford's Loaner Vehicle.* Richard Keller purchased a new Taurus station wagon from Friendly Ford, Inc. which he returned to the dealer and for which he sought a refund "because obviously it was a lemon." Thereafter, he needed a car to drive his daughter to college in another state, and Friendly Ford's sales manager assured him on the phone that he could "have a loaner vehicle" for the journey. But when he came to pick up the "loaner," the company president refused to supply the car. At that point Keller said he had no choice but to drive the Taurus "and hope and pray it didn't break down on the trip." But break down it did, causing Keller considerable inconvenience and expense (e.g., rental of a van to complete the trip). Keller's efforts to recover for these expenses were unsuccessful. Keller v. Friendly Ford, Inc., 782 S.W.2d 170 (Mo.App.1990). The court said that while Keller might recover for the expense in driving to the dealership to pick up the car, in going ahead in the Taurus he was not acting in reliance on the promise of a free automobile. The court noted: "Had plaintiff, a week before the journey, been told by defendant's employees that no free automobile would be supplied, and had plaintiff, faced with that knowledge, commenced the journey in the Taurus instead of renting a more dependable vehicle or utilizing public transportation, it is manifest plaintiff could not have recovered from defendant the cost of the rental vehicles plaintiff was obliged to use * * * unless, of course, there was some clause in the warranty on the Taurus or some independent contractual obligation imposing such liability on defendant. No such showing was made at the trial * * *." 782 S.W.2d at 174.

(5) *Promissory Estoppel and Entertainment Contracts: The Ohio Players and "Funky Worm"; Aretha Franklin and "Mahalia."* After The Ohio Players struck it big with their hit record "Funky Worm," they sought to back out of the recording agreement they had with Westbound Records, Inc. alleging a lack of consideration. They maintained that although they were bound to record exclusively for Westbound, the latter was not, by the express terms of the agreement, obliged to make any records using the group. But the Appellate Court of Illinois found consideration in a $4,000 advance against royalties and prescinded from any inquiry into adequacy. Bonner v. Westbound Records, Inc., 76 Ill.App.3d 736, 31 Ill.Dec. 926, 394 N.E.2d 1303 (1979). Moreover, the court met an objection based on lack of mutuality of obligation by implying an obligation by Westbound to act in good faith, and, following *Wood v. Lucy, Lady Duff–Gordon,* supra at 124, a duty to use its best efforts. Finally, the court found that liability could be predicated upon promissory estoppel "as a substitute for consideration." In reliance upon the recording agreement, Westbound undertook a substantial business risk, incurring more than $80,000 in expenses which it could recoup only if the recordings were successful. The court explained: "The Ohio Players now seek to deny Westbound the sole reward of its success. Their aim is to keep for themselves the fame and money which, judging by their past experience, they could not have acquired without Westbound's aid, by asserting that Westbound did not originally promise to do what it has already actually done. This the plaintiffs are estopped to do; even if the agreements were not originally supported by consideration, they became enforceable when Westbound performed in reliance on the promises of The Ohio Players, and indeed advanced additional monies not called for by the contract, to protect its investment." 31 Ill.Dec. at 935, 394 N.E.2d at 1312.

A musical producer sought to produce a Broadway musical based on the life of Mahalia Jackson and wanted Aretha Franklin for the title role. The latter was very receptive. They negotiated over a period of several months, working out many details (including a handsome compensation package). The parties circulated drafts of a proposed agreement, but never executed a final draft. Meanwhile, the producer, on the basis of Franklin's assurance, went ahead with making arrangements, incurring substantial expense. After negotiations broke down, the producer sued. The court found that the parties were not to be bound contractually until the draft agreement was signed, but proceeded to base recovery on promissory estoppel. Elvin Associates v. Franklin, 735 F.Supp. 1177 (S.D.N.Y.1990). The court stated: "It is difficult to imagine a more fitting case for applying [promissory estoppel]. Although for her own business purposes Franklin insisted that the formal contract be with the corporate entity through which her services were to be 'furnished,' in the real world the agreement was with her, and we find that she had unequivocally and intentionally committed herself to appear in the production long before the day on which it was intended that the finished agreement with her corporation would be signed. * * * [U]nder the circumstances * * * it would be unconscionable not to compensate [plaintiff] for the losses he incurred through his entirely justified reliance on Franklin's oral promises." 735 F.Supp. at 1182–1183.

(6) *Promissory estoppel and corporate relocation.* In recent years, corporations who decided to close or move business operations have been sued by employees, a union or a local government unit on a promissory estoppel theory. The claim was that the plaintiff had relied upon a corporate promise to remain or to stay open and that injustice could be prevented only by giving an appropriate remedy, whether damages or an injunction. These claims have all foundered because a clear and definite promise by the corporation could not be proved. See, e.g., Abbington v. Dayton Malleable, Inc., 738 F.2d 438 (6th Cir.1984); Local 1330, United Steel Workers v. United States Steel Corp., 631 F.2d 1264 (6th Cir.1980); Marine Transport Lines, Inc. v. International Organization of Masters, Mates & Pilots, 636 F.Supp. 384 (S.D.N.Y.1986). See also, Charter Twp. of Ypsilanti v. General Motors Corp., 201 Mich.App. 128, 506 N.W.2d 556 (1993), appeal denied, 443 Mich. 882, 509 N.W.2d 152 (1993). The assumption in these cases is, however, that if the requisite promise and reliance were established, the court would inquire into the "injustice" question. Should a court do this? See the next case.

Cohen v. Cowles Media Co.

Supreme Court of Minnesota, 1992.
479 N.W.2d 387.

■ SIMONETT, JUSTICE. This case comes to us on remand from the United States Supreme Court. We previously held that plaintiff's verdict of $200,-000 could not be sustained on a theory of breach of contract. On remand, we now conclude the verdict is sustainable on the theory of promissory estoppel and affirm the jury's award of damages.

The facts are set out in *Cohen v. Cowles Media Co.*, 457 N.W.2d 199, 200–02 (Minn.1990), and will be only briefly restated here. On October 28, 1982, the Minneapolis Star and Tribune (now the Star Tribune) and the St.

Paul Pioneer Press each published a story on the gubernatorial election campaign, reporting that Marlene Johnson, the DFL nominee for lieutenant governor, had been charged in 1969 for three counts of unlawful assembly and in 1970 had been convicted of shoplifting. Both newspapers revealed that Dan Cohen had supplied this information to them The Star Tribune identified Cohen as a political associate of the Independent–Republican gubernatorial candidate and named the advertising firm where Cohen was employed.

Cohen then commenced this lawsuit against defendants Cowles Media Company, publisher of the Minneapolis Star Tribune, and Northwest Publications, Inc., publisher of the St. Paul Pioneer Press Dispatch. It was undisputed that Cohen had given the information about Marlene Johnson's arrests and conviction to a reporter for each of the newspapers in return for the reporters' promises that Cohen's identity be kept confidential. The newspapers' editors overruled these promises. The disparaging information about the candidate leaked in the closing days of the election campaign was such, decided the editors, that the identity of the source of the information was as important, as newsworthy, as the information itself. Put another way, the real news story was one of political intrigue, and the information about the particular candidate was only a part, an incomplete part, of that story. Moreover, not to reveal the source, felt the editors, would be misleading, as it would cast suspicion on others; and, in any event, it was likely only a matter or time before competing news media would uncover Cohen's identity. Finally, the Star Tribune had endorsed the Perpich–Johnson ticket in its opinion section, and thus to withhold Cohen's identity might be construed as an effort by the newspaper to protect its favored candidates. On the same day as the newspaper stories were published, Cohen was fired.

The case was submitted to the jury on theories of breach of contract and fraudulent misrepresentation. The jury found liability on both theories and awarded $200,000 compensatory damages against the two defendants, jointly and severally. The jury also awarded $250,000 punitive damages against each newspaper on the misrepresentation claim. The court of appeals set aside recovery on the basis of fraudulent misrepresentation (and with it the punitive damages award), but affirmed recovery of the compensatory damages on the basis of a breach of contract. *Cohen v. Cowles Media Co.*, 445 N.W.2d 248, 262 (Minn.App.1989).

We affirmed denial of recovery for fraudulent misrepresentation but also held that there could be no recovery for breach of contract.... We concluded that a contract theory, which looks only to whether there was a promise and an acceptance, does not fit a situation where the essential concern is with the intrinsic nature of the overall transaction.

We went on in *Cohen I* to consider enforcement of a confidentiality promise under the doctrine of promissory estoppel. Under this theory, the court would consider all aspects of the transaction's substance in determining whether enforcement was necessary to prevent an injustice. We found this approach, which differed from the neutral approach of the classic contract analysis, best fit the kind of confidential commitments that news media in newsgathering made. There was, however, a problem. To shed the neutrality of a contract analysis for an inquiry into the editorial process of deciding whether the identity of the news source was needed for a proper reporting of a news story constituted, we concluded, an impermissible intrusion into the newspaper's First Amendment free press rights. Consequently, we held plaintiff Cohen's verdict was not sustainable. 457 N.W.2d at 205.

The United States Supreme Court granted certiorari and held that the doctrine of promissory estoppel does not implicate the First Amendment. The doctrine is one of general application, said the Court, and its employment to enforce confidentiality promises has only "incidental effects" on news gathering and reporting, so that the First Amendment is not offended. *Cohen v. Cowles Media Co.,* 501 U.S. 663, 111 S.Ct. 2513, 2518–19, 115 L.Ed.2d 586 (1991). The Court refused to reinstate the jury verdict for $200,000 in compensatory damages, stating this was a matter for our consideration, and remanded the case.

On remand, we must address four issues: (1) Does Cohen's failure to plead promissory estoppel bar him from pursuing that theory now; (2) does our state constitutional guarantee of a free press bar use of promissory estoppel to enforce promises of confidentiality; (3) does public policy bar Cohen from enforcing the newspapers' promises of confidentiality; and (4) if Cohen may proceed under promissory estoppel, should the case be remanded for retrial or should the jury's award of compensatory damages be reinstated?

* * *

What we have here is a novel legal issue of first impression where this court has adopted an approach closely akin to the theory on which the case was originally pled and tried; under these unique circumstances we conclude it is not unfair to the defendants to allow the case to be decided under principles of promissory estoppel.

* * *

III

What, then, should be the appropriate disposition of this case? We conclude a retrial is unnecessary.

Under promissory estoppel, a promise which is expected to induce definite action by the promisee, and does induce the action, is binding if injustice can be avoided only by enforcing the promise. *Cohen I,* 457 N.W.2d at 204; Restatement (Second) of Contracts § 90(1) (1981). First of all, the promise must be clear and definite. As a matter of law, such a promise was given here. *Cohen I,* 457 N.W.2d at 204 ("[W]e have, without dispute, the reporters' unambiguous promise to treat Cohen as an anonymous source."). Secondly, the promisor must have intended to induce reliance on the part of the promisee, and such reliance must have occurred to the promisee's detriment.   Here again, these facts appear as a matter of law. In reliance on the promise of anonymity, Cohen turned over the court records and, when the promises to keep his name confidential were broken, he lost his job. *Id.*

This leads to the third step in a promissory estoppel analysis: Must the promise be enforced to prevent an injustice? As the Wisconsin Supreme Court has held, this is a legal question for the court, as it involves a policy decision. *Hoffman v. Red Owl Stores, Inc.,* 26 Wis.2d 683, 698, 133 N.W.2d 267, 275 (1965); *see also Kramer v. Alpine Valley Resort, Inc.,* 108 Wis.2d 417, 422, 321 N.W.2d 293, 296 (1982) (third element is a question of law); *Grouse v. Group Health Plan, Inc.,* 306 N.W.2d 114, 116 (Minn.1981) (this court on appeal found all three elements of promissory estoppel were present).

It is perhaps worth noting that the test is not whether the promise should be enforced to do justice, but whether enforcement is required to prevent an injustice. As has been observed elsewhere, it is easier to recognize an unjust result than a just one, particularly in a morally ambiguous situation. Cf. Edmond Cahn, *The Sense of Injustice* (1964). The newspapers argue it is unjust to be penalized for publishing the whole truth, but it is not clear this would result in an injustice in this case. For example, it would seem veiling Cohen's identity by publishing the source as someone close to the opposing gubernatorial ticket would have sufficed as a sufficient reporting of the "whole truth."

Cohen, on the other hand, argues that it would be unjust for the law to countenance, at least in this instance, the breaking of a promise. We agree that denying Cohen any recourse would be unjust. What is significant in this case is that the record shows the defendant newspapers themselves believed that they generally must keep promises of confidentiality given a news source. The reporters who actually gave the promises adamantly testified that their promises should have been honored. The editors who countermanded the promises conceded that never before or since have they reneged on a promise of confidentiality. A former Minneapolis Star managing editor testified that the newspapers had "hung Mr. Cohen out to dry because they didn't regard him very highly as a source." The Pioneer Press Dispatch editor stated nothing like this had happened in her 27 years in journalism. The Star Tribune's editor testified that protection of sources was "extremely important."   Other experts, too, stressed the ethical importance, except on rare occasions, of keeping promises of confidentiality. It was this long-standing journalistic tradition that Cohen, who has worked in journalism, relied upon in asking for and receiving a promise of anonymity.

Neither side in this case clearly holds the higher moral ground, but in view of the defendants' concurrence in the importance of honoring promises of confidentiality, and absent the showing of any compelling need in this case to break that promise, we conclude that the resultant harm to Cohen requires a remedy here to avoid an injustice. In short, defendants are liable in damages to plaintiff for their broken promise.

This leaves, then, the issue of damages. For promissory estoppel, "[t]he remedy granted for breach may be limited as justice requires." Restatement (Second) of Contracts § 90(1)(1981). *See generally Midamar Corp. v. National–Ben Franklin Ins. Co.*, 898 F.2d 1333, 1338–39 (8th Cir.1990); *Hoffman v. Red Owl Stores, Inc.*, 26 Wis.2d at 701, 133 N.W.2d at 276. In this case the jury was instructed:

> A party is entitled to recover for a breach of contract only those damages which: (a) arise directly and naturally in the usual course of things from the breach itself; or (b) are the consequences of special circumstances known to or reasonably supposed to have been contemplated by the parties when the contract was made.

This instruction, we think, provided an appropriate damages remedy for the defendants' broken promise, whether considered under a breach of contract or a promissory estoppel theory. There was evidence to support the jury's award of $200,000, and we see no reason to remand this case for a new trial on damages alone.

Our prior reversal of the verdict having been vacated, we now affirm the court of appeals' decision, but on promissory estoppel grounds. We affirm, therefore, plaintiff's verdict and judgment for $200,000 compensatory damages.

Affirmed on remand on different grounds.

NOTES

(1) If Cohen bargained for a promise of confidentiality in exchange for delivering the documents and Cowles bargained for the documents in exchange for the promise, why wasn't there consideration? Is it possible to have a bargained for exchange of a promise for a performance that is not enforceable as a contract? If so (and the promise is important), why? What can the parties do to signal that they intend to assume legal obligations?

(2) Upon remand from the Supreme Court, the court reaffirms its decision on the consideration issue and then enforces the oral promise of confidentiality on a "promissory estoppel" theory. If the parties did not intend to assume legal obligations, how can Cowles be liable for induced reliance? Does Section 90, which the court purports to apply, depend upon the intention of the parties? If not, how would you characterize the theory? Does the court's approach deviate from Section 90?

(3) *Impact of Cowles.* In an interesting empirical study, conducted after *Cowles* through extensive interviews with newspaper publishers and others, Daniel Levin and Ellen Rupert concluded that the damage award had not had any substantial effect on confidentiality policy. Of those publishers who had policies on confidentiality (e.g., the authority of reporters to promise confidentiality without prior permission or the power of publishers to override earlier promises), one-third were aware of the *Cowles* decision and roughly 50% of those had reviewed their policies within the last five years. Only one publisher had made changes in light of *Cowles* and there was no evidence of a trend toward greater supervision of reporters. In fact around 70% of the group which

was aware accepted the Cowles result as "fair and not a particularly serious infringement on editor's rights." Levin & Blumberg, *Promises of Confidentiality to News Sources After Cohen v. Cowles Media Company: A Survey of Newspaper Editors,* 24 Golden Gate Univ.L.Rev. 423, 460–461 (1994).

(4) *Recent Scholarly Opinion.* For recent studies in which the authors explore the underlying basis for promissory estoppel and in which differing theories are propounded, see Barnett and Becker, *Beyond Reliance: Promissory Estoppel, Contract Formalities, and Misrepresentations,* 15 Hofstra L.Rev. 443, 495–96 (1987) (Neither an "unfathomable conundrum nor a radical break with tradition," promissory estoppel, like traditional contract and tort doctrines, "afford[s] courts a basis for enforcing some promises intended as legally binding and for remedying some misrepresentations."); Kostritsky, *A New Theory of Assent–Based Liability Emerging Under the Guise of Promissory Estoppel: An Explanation and Defense,* 33 Wayne L.Rev. 895, 964 (1987) ("[B]oth promissory estoppel and the bargain theory share unifying elemental criteria that place them both within an assent-based theory of enforceability; both are mere doctrinal methods for evidencing a consensual exchange."); Farber and Matheson, *Beyond Promissory Estoppel: Contract Law and the "Invisible Handshake,"* 52 U.Chi.L.Rev. 903 (1985) (Noting a diminishing emphasis upon the reliance component, the authors see a new rule of promissory liability emerging; viz., any promise made in furtherance of an economic activity is enforceable); Feinman, *Promissory Estoppel and Judicial Method,* 97 Harv.L.Rev. 678, 689 (1984) ("Like the place of reliance in the greater scheme of contract, the contours of promissory estoppel doctrine remain uncertain: the doctrine's current application represents an uneasy compromise between restricting and extending the reliance principle."); Metzger and Phillips, *The Emergence of Promissory Estoppel as an Independent Theory of Recovery,* 35 Rutgers L.Rev. 472 (1983) (Promissory estoppel should continue to develop and expand as an independent theory of recovery). See also, Jay M. Feinman, *The Last Promissory Estoppel Article,* 61 Fordham L. Rev. 303 (1992); Phuong N. Pham, (Comment) *The Waning of Promissory Estoppel,* 79 Cornell L.Rev. 1263 (1994).

Comment: Promissory Estoppel and the Choice of Remedies

From one point of view, distinctly Willistonian, the full range of contract remedies should be available to enforce promises which are contracts, whether the reason for enforcement is consideration or reliance. A contract is a contract is a contract. Thus, Grandfather's promise to pay Katie Scothorn $2,000, the employer's promise to pay retirement benefits and the donor's promise to make a charitable subscription should be performed in full even though the promisee's detriment was induced rather than bargained for and, if quantified and valued, would be worth less than the value of the promised performance. Section 90 of the first Restatement was silent on this point, stating only that a promise which induces foreseeable reliance "of a definite and substantial character * * * is binding if injustice can be avoided only by enforcement of the promise." However, the total structure of the Restatement, with its definition of contract as "a promise * * * for the breach of which the law gives a remedy," (§ 1), and its expectation oriented approach to remedies (§§ 326–

384), along with the comments of its Reporter, Professor Williston, see 4 A.L.I. Proceedings 97–106 (1926), support the conclusion that expectation damages were intended to be the rule rather than the exception. See G. Gilmore, The Death of Contract 59–65 (1974).

From another and less doctrinal point of view, recovery could be limited to the amount of Plaintiff's reliance, whether this be measured in terms of "out of pocket" expenditures, foregone opportunities or both. In its historical setting, the doctrine of estoppel was defensive in that the representor was estopped to deny the accuracy of what had been stated. When the representation was by promise, *Ricketts v. Scothorn,* supra at 24, concluded that the promisor was estopped to deny the absence of consideration, and Wheeler v. White, 398 S.W.2d 93 (Tex.1965), concluded that "promissory estoppel acts defensively so as to prevent an attack upon the enforceability of a contract." The *Wheeler* court stated: "Under this theory, losses of expected profits will not be allowed even if expected profits are provable with certainty." According to Professor (now Judge) Posner, the historical limitations are consistent with the theory of economic efficiency in contract law. For example, Posner asserts that it "obscures analysis to equate reliance with consideration in circumstances where no exchange is contemplated" and suggests that a "better approach would be to treat the breach of promise likely to induce reliance as a form of actionable negligence under tort law." R. Posner, Economic Analysis of Law 70 (2d ed. 1977). The few cases on this point accord with *Wheeler v. White* even though the transaction in which the promise was made contemplated the exchange of resources. See, e.g., Hoffman v. Red Owl Stores, Inc., infra at 421; Goodman v. Dicker, 83 U.S.App.D.C. 353, 169 F.2d 684 (1948); Mooney v. Craddock, 35 Colo.App. 20, 530 P.2d 1302 (1974). Contra: Chrysler Corp. v. Quimby, 51 Del. (1 Storey) 264, 144 A.2d 885 (1958). See, generally, Comment, 37 U.Chi.L.Rev. 559 (1970).

Recognizing this other point of view, Restatement (Second) § 90 eliminates the first Restatement requirement that the reliance be "definite and substantial" and provides that the "remedy granted for breach may be limited as justice requires." Thus, the promise "is binding if injustice can be avoided only by enforcement" and the remedy may be limited "as justice requires." The assumption is that one starts from a position of full-scale enforcement, but that the "same factors which bear on whether any relief should be granted also bear on the extent and character of the remedy." This recovery might "sometimes be limited to restitution or to damages or specific relief measured by the extent of the promisee's reliance rather than by the terms of the promise." Comment d. See 1A Corbin § 205. Factors which should be relevant in the decision include policies implicit in the transaction type, (i.e., charitable subscriptions, retirement promises, family relations), the reason for the non-performance, (financial reverses might suggest a lesser while dishonest conduct might support a greater remedy), the degree of disproportion associated with enforcement of the promise, (e.g., the promise to obtain insurance), and any historical patterns of enforcement associated with the transaction type, (e.g., the bailment).

Nevertheless, Professor Melvin Eisenberg, among others, has argued that if the reason for enforcing the promise is reliance rather than bargain, then the scope of remedial protection should be limited by the reliance interest. As he put it, it is a "nice question how much difference there is between a rule that donative promises are unenforceable unless reasonably relied upon, and a rule that donative promises are enforceable but only to the extent reasonably relied upon." Eisenberg, *Donative Promises,* 47 U.Chi.L.Rev. 1, 33 (1979). This argument is part of a broader assertion that the primary reason for protecting the expectation interest in bargain contracts is to insure that "hidden" reliance, frequently in the form of hard to measure and prove opportunity costs, is fully compensated. In short, protecting the expectation interest is a surrogate for protecting reliance in the bargain contract. Thus, in a non-bargain contract, the assumption should be that the court will protect the reliance interest, with expectation damages awarded only when necessary to insure that "hidden" reliance is fully compensated. See Eisenberg, *The Bargain Principle and its Limits,* 95 Harv.L.Rev. 741, 785–98 (1982); *The Principles of Consideration,* 67 Cornell L.Rev. 640, 656–59 (1982).

A decision supporting Professor Eisenberg's thesis is Walters v. Marathon Oil Co., 642 F.2d 1098 (7th Cir. 1981). Relying on defendant's promise to supply gasoline and "continuing negotiations," plaintiff purchased and made improvements on a vacant service station site. After the negotiations were completed, however, defendant refused to sign the dealership agreement because of a newly announced moratorium on dealerships. The trial court found for plaintiff on the theory of promissory estoppel and awarded damages based upon the profits that plaintiff would have made on the sale of gasoline during the first year under the promised dealership. On appeal, defendant argued that plaintiff's damages should be measured by its reliance on the promise, namely, the investment in and improvements on the service station. As such, defendant claimed, there should be no recovery because the fair market value of the improved service station exceeded plaintiff's out-of-pocket expenditure. The court of appeals, however, affirmed the trial court. The court noted that the plaintiff had suffered "a loss of profits as a direct result of their reliance ... and the amount of the lost profits was ascertained with reasonable certainty." Moreover, "in reliance upon appellant's promise, they had foregone the opportunity to make the investment elsewhere." Characterizing promissory estoppel as "an equitable matter," the court concluded that the award of lost profits was necessary to "secure complete justice." As the court put it: "An equity court possesses some discretionary power to award damages in order to do complete justice. ... Furthermore, since it is the historic purpose of equity to secure complete justice, the courts are able to adjust the remedies so as to grant the necessary relief, ... and a district court sitting in equity may even devise a remedy which extends or exceeds the terms of a prior agreement between the parties, if it is necessary to make the injured party whole." 642 F.2d at 1000. But see Walser v. Toyota Motor Sales, U.S.A., Inc., 43 F.3d 396, 400–402 (8th Cir.1994) (damages for breach of promise to grant dealership properly limited to out of pocket expenditures).

Assuming that damage should be measured by the reliance interest, the proper measure is still a matter of some debate. See, for example, Cyberchron Corp. v. Calldata Systems Development, Inc., 47 F.3d 39 (2d Cir.1995)(plaintiff recovers expenditures incurred in part performance of proposed but never finalized contract plus "shut down" costs and overhead). See also, Gregory S. Crespi, *Recovering Pre–Contractual Expenditures as an Element of Reliance Damages*, 49 SMU L.Rev. 43 (1995); Neil G. Williams, *What to Do When There's No "I Do:" A Model For Awarding Damages Under Promissory Estoppel*, 70 Wash.L.Rev. 1019 (1995); Michael B. Kelly, *The Phantom Reliance Interest in Contract Damages*, 1992 Wis. L. Rev. 1775; Becker, *Promissory Estoppel Damages*, 16 Hofstra L.Rev. 131 (1987).

PROBLEM: THE CASE OF THE INDEPENDENT CAB DRIVER

During a lull in the proceedings of an American Legion convention a few of the participants made their way to a nearby bar for refreshments and conversation.

One of the men, Marty Lawless, began bemoaning the lot of a cab driver. Since his discharge from the Army, Marty had been driving a cab in a metropolitan area for a large company. "If I could only lay my hands on twenty thousand bucks," he remarked, "I could really make out. I could get a cab and license of my own and start working for myself, instead of the other guy."

In the group was Jim Craven, who had attended law school after his discharge and had built up a lucrative personal injury practice. After questioning Marty a bit more regarding what the latter could do with a cab of his own, Jim said to him: "I'll loan you the money. Pay it back when you want, up to ten years. And it won't cost you a thing. I owe you a lot more than that, heaven knows." (This last remark referred to the fact that Jim credits Marty with saving his life in battle.)

But Marty was hesitant. He didn't want any "charity." He answered: "I appreciate your offer, Jim. I really do. But I couldn't take it. I think a bank will loan me the money."

"Aw, Lawless, you're crazy to pass up a deal like that," said John Coburn, another member of the group.

Jim spoke up: "Now hold on. It's not charity, if that's what you're thinking. We'll make it carry one percent interest. How's that?"

This was too good to pass up, thought Marty. And, after all, Craven could afford it. So he replied: "Thanks a lot, Jim. It will sure give me a boost. And don't worry, you'll be repaid."

Jim then raised a glass and said to everyone present: "All right, everybody. Let's drink to the world's newest independent cab driver!" Everyone complied.

Upon returning home, one of Marty's first stops was to the office of his employer, where he resigned his job.

But a few days later he received a letter from Craven in which he said he had a "big deal" come up and didn't have the money to loan now. He expressed his regrets and said he hoped they "can get together real soon."

Lawless has hastened to your office and now awaits your advice. Advise him.

SECTION 4.   FORMALITIES IN CONTRACTING: THE STATUTE OF FRAUDS

(A) FORMALITIES IN CONTRACTING: PROMISE PLUS SEAL OR OTHER FORM

Seal. Formalities of an almost limitless variety have been used in the making of contracts. Both Homer and Herodotus describe a ceremonial libation which accompanied solemn agreements. Contracting parties will today, as they have presumably from time immemorial, "shake hands on it," as if the added form imported special obligation. Professor Corbin has observed that "[t]he small boys of today no doubt feel the weight of an awful sanction when they say 'I cross my heart [hope] to die.' " Thus, even though, as he puts it, "[t]he keeping of promises is in the folkways and mores of mankind" and "in the vast majority of cases they are kept and performed without the thought of breach or necessity of enforcement," not all promises are enforceable, or ever have been. And one of the factors traditionally employed in determining enforceability has been the form in which the promise is made or expressed. See Corbin § 240. That the appropriateness of form in promise-making is firmly embedded in the public consciousness is attested by Charlie Brown's trust and Lucy's riposte. Infra at 188.

At common law the form *par excellence* was the seal, at first a wax substance attached to the document. Later, writing the word "seal" or "L.S." (*locus sigilli,* place of the seal) was more common. A sealed promise was enforceable centuries before the evolution of the doctrine of consideration. Enforceability did not derive from bargain or exchange, but precisely because of the formal mode in which the promise was cast.

It has been contended that consideration itself is merely a form. This was Holmes' position: "In one sense, everything is form which the law requires in order to make a promise binding over and above the mere expression of the promisor's will. Consideration is a form as much as a seal. The only difference is, that the one form is of modern introduction, and has a foundation in good sense, or at least falls in with our common habits of thought, so that we do not notice it, whereas the other is a survival from an older condition of the law, and is less manifestly sensible, or less familiar." Holmes, The Common Law 273 (1881). Is this a valid evaluation of consideration? An excellent review, at this point, would be to take another look at the consideration materials with a view of discerning instances where consideration seems to be employed as a kind of form or formality. See Fuller, *Consideration and Form,* 41 Colum.L.Rev. 799 (1941).

There is an impressive body of learning concerning the common law seal. But most of this can be ignored for the moment. By decision and statute, the seal has lost virtually all of its former efficacy. For a table showing the status of the seal in each jurisdiction of the United States, see Williston § 219A. See also Braucher, *The Status of the Seal Today,* 9 Prac.Law. 97 (1963). The Uniform Commercial Code prescribes outright abolition: "The affixing of a seal to a writing evidencing a contract for sale or an offer to buy or sell goods does not constitute the writing a sealed instrument and the law with respect to sealed instruments does not apply to such a contract or offer." UCC 2–203. This section "makes it clear that every effect of the seal which relates to 'sealed instruments' as such is wiped out insofar as contracts for sale are concerned." UCC 2–203, comment 1. In view of this decline of the seal, one is surprised to find a Restatement (Second) provision which can be read as proposing a general revival. Section 95(1) reads: "In the absence of statute a promise is binding without consideration if (a) it is in writing and sealed; and (b) the document containing the promise is delivered; and (c) the promisor and promisee are named in the document or so described as to be capable of identification when it is delivered." For a critique of this provision, see Eisenberg, *The Principles of Consideration,* 67 Cornell L.Rev. 640, 659–60 (1982).

Model Written Obligations Act. The general abolition of the seal did not prove an unmixed blessing. Many regarded the seal as a useful legal device, if for no other reason than providing a convenient method for making binding gratuitous promises. It was inevitable that attention would be given to filling the vacuum, and it was most natural to turn to that most common of contemporary "forms," the signed writing. In 1925, largely at the instigation of Professor Williston, the National Conference of Commissioners on Uniform State Laws approved the draft of the Uniform Written Obligations Act. This recommended statute provides as follows:

"A written release or promise made and signed by the person releasing or promising shall not be invalid or unenforceable for lack of consideration, if the writing also contains an additional express statement in any form of language that the signer intends to be legally bound."

The proposal met with a singular, and somewhat surprising, lack of success. Only Pennsylvania has adopted and retained the Act, and in 1943 it was redesignated, quite appropriately, the Model Written Obligations Act. For a discussion of the Act, see Reeve, *Uniform Written Obligations Act,* 76 U.Pa.L.Rev. 580 (1928).

In addition, there are a few statutes which accord some extraordinary legal effect to a signed writing. But with the exception of New York, the practical significance of this legislation seems to have been minimal. See New York General Obligations Law §§ 5–1101—5–1115.

Uniform Commercial Code. Some resurgence of "contract form" has been ushered in by the Uniform Commercial Code. In two instances the Code uses a signed writing as a substitute for consideration. The text of these provisions is set out below:

UCC 1–107. *Waiver or Renunciation of Claim or Right After Breach.* Any claim or right arising out of an alleged breach can be discharged in whole or in part without consideration by a written waiver or renunciation signed and delivered by the aggrieved party.

UCC 2–205 [UCC 2–204(1997)]. *Firm Offers.* An offer by a merchant to buy or sell goods in a signed writing which by its terms gives assurance that it will be held open is not revocable, for lack of consideration, during the time stated or if no time is stated for a reasonable time, but in no event may such period of irrevocability exceed three months; but any such term of assurance on a form supplied by the offeree must be separately signed by the offeror.

In addition, UCC 2–209(1) [UCC 2–210(a)(1997)], relating to modification, rescission and waiver, states: "An agreement modifying a contract within this Article needs no consideration to be binding." In effect, this is added emphasis upon form, since the requirements of the Statute of Frauds section of Article 2 (UCC 2–201) must be satisfied if the contract as modified is within its provisions. UCC 2–209(3) [UCC 2–210(b)(1997)].

The reach of the foregoing sections, even if confined to the strict letter, is substantial. But there is the possibility that by analogous application the impact will be even more far-reaching, resulting in a considerable reorientation of contract theory. For example, if "firm offer" is recognized in an offer to sell goods situation, why not in an offer to perform a service? And if Sears, Roebuck and Co. makes a firm offer by the requisite assurance, why not John Sears, non-merchant? Or if a sales contract can be modified without consideration, why not a construction contract? And so on. For a good treatment of this topic, see Holohan, *Contract Formalities and the Uniform Commercial Code,* 3 Vill.L.Rev. 1 (1957).

Contract Formality à la Peanuts

© 1964 United Feature Syndicate, Inc.

Can law rescue Peanuts?

(B) THE STATUTE OF FRAUDS

(1) GENERAL SCOPE AND EFFECT

Samuel Goldwyn reportedly said that an oral contract is not worth the paper it is written on. One can hardly gainsay the desirability of reducing a contract to writing, but such has never been, in Anglo–American law, a general requisite of legal enforceability. In 1677, however, Parliament did enact legislation requiring that certain contracts be in writing, "signed by the party to be charged," and our state legislatures followed this lead. The English law, called the Statute of Frauds, was a comprehensive "Act for Prevention of Frauds and Perjuries" and applied to a wide range of transactions. Sections 4 and 17, set out below, pertained to contracts.

Section 4: [N]o action shall be brought

(1) whereby to charge any executor or administrator upon any special promise, to answer for damages out of his own estate;

(2) or whereby to charge the defendant upon any special promise to answer for the debt, default or miscarriage of another person;

(3) or to charge any person upon any agreement made upon consideration of marriage;

(4) or upon any contract or sale of lands, tenements or hereditaments, or any interest in or concerning them;

(5) or upon any agreement that is not to be performed within the space of one year from the making thereof;

(6) unless the agreement upon which such action shall be brought, or some memorandum or note thereof, shall be in writing, and signed by the party to be charged therewith or some other person thereunto by him lawfully authorized.

Section 17: And be it further enacted by the authority aforesaid, That from and after the said four and twentieth of June no contract for the sale of any goods, wares and merchandizes, for the price of ten pounds sterling or upwards, shall be allowed to be good, except the buyer shall accept part of the goods so sold, and actually receive the same, or give something in earnest to bind the bargain, or in part of payment, or that some note or memorandum in writing of the said bargain be made and signed by the parties to be charged by such contract, or their agents thereunto lawfully authorized.

Section 4 was widely followed in this country, although the language was altered in some cases and other transactions (e.g., contract to make a will or to pay a commission to a real estate agent) were sometimes added. An American counterpart of section 17 was section 4 of the Uniform Sales Act, which provided as follows:

(1) A contract to sell or a sale of any goods or choses in action of the value of five hundred dollars or upwards shall not be enforceable by action unless the buyer shall accept part of the goods or choses in action so contracted to be sold or sold, and actually receive the same, or give something in earnest to bind the contract or in part payment, or unless some note or memorandum in writing of the contract or sale be signed by the party to be charged or his agent in that behalf.

(2) The provisions of this section apply to every such contract or sale notwithstanding that the goods may be intended to be delivered at some future time or may not at the time of such contract or sale be actually made, procured, or provided, or fit, or ready for delivery, or

some act may be requisite for the making or completing thereof, or rendering the same fit for delivery; but if the goods are to be manufactured by the seller especially for the buyer and are not suitable for sale to others in the ordinary course of the seller's business, the provisions of this section shall not apply.

(3) There is an acceptance of goods within the meaning of this section when the buyer, either before or after delivery of the goods, expresses by words or conduct his assent to becoming the owner of those specific goods.

Section 4 of the Uniform Sales Act was replaced by Section 2–201 of the Uniform Commercial Code, which reads as follows:

(1) Except as otherwise provided in this section a contract for the sale of goods for the price of $500 or more is not enforceable by way of action or defense unless there is some writing sufficient to indicate that a contract for sale has been made between the parties and signed by the party against whom enforcement is sought or by his authorized agent or broker. A writing is not insufficient because it omits or incorrectly states a term agreed upon but the contract is not enforceable under this paragraph beyond the quantity of goods shown in such writing.

(2) Between merchants if within a reasonable time a writing in confirmation of the contract and sufficient against the sender is received and the party receiving it has reason to know its contents, it satisfies the requirements of subsection (1) against such party unless written notice of objection to its contents is given within ten days after it is received.

(3) A contract which does not satisfy the requirements of subsection (1) but which is valid in other respects is enforceable

(a) if the goods are to be specially manufactured for the buyer and are not suitable for sale to others in the ordinary course of the seller's business and the seller, before notice of repudiation is received and under circumstances which reasonably indicate that the goods are for the buyer, has made either a substantial beginning of their manufacture or commitments for their procurement; or

(b) if the party against whom enforcement is sought admits in his pleading, testimony or otherwise in court that a contract for sale was made, but the contract is not enforceable under this provision beyond the quantity of goods admitted; or

(c) with respect to goods for which payment has been made and accepted or which have been received and accepted (Sec. 2–606).

An enormous amount of litigation has arisen respecting the Statute of Frauds. Indicative is the fact that nearly one-sixth of Professor Corbin's major treatise is devoted to this subject. The judicial treatment has mirrored divergent convictions concerning the utility of such legislation. Controversy in this regard arose at an early date and continues unabated to this time. A commission of the Lord Chancellor gave this brief sketch of English opinion:

Lord Kenyon's verdict:—"One of the wisest laws in our Statute Book" (Chaplin v. Rogers, 1800, 1 East at 194), and, "I lament extremely that exceptions were ever introduced in construing the Statute" (Chester v. Beckett, 7 T.R. at p. 204) contrasts with that pronounced by Wilmot J., and concurred in by Lord Mansfield (in Simon v. Metivier, 1766, 1 Bl.W. at 601):—"Had the Statute of Frauds been always carried into execution according to the letter, it would have done ten times more mischief than it has done good, by protecting, rather than by preventing, frauds." The Statute, as these words imply, has not been "carried into effect according to its letter." Mitigating expedients, such as the doctrine of part performance, strained construction of its language, such as that which excluded contracts to marry from agreements in consideration of marriage, and Statutory amendments, have softened its asperities. Yet in 1851 so experienced a common lawyer as Lord Campbell could record the opinion that "the Act promotes more frauds than it prevents." Lord Nottingham (who, since the Act was his offspring, may well have felt for it some parental partiality) used to claim that "every line of it was worth a subsidy"; upon which claim a learned lawyer, nearly two centuries later, commented that "every line has cost one" (J.W. Smith, Lectures on the Law of Contract 39 (1874).

Law Revision Committee, Sixth Interim Report 6 (1937).

American opinion has also been divided. For example, Professor Llewellyn gave this salute: "That statute is an amazing product. In it de Leon might have found his secret of perpetual youth. After two centuries and a half the statute stands, in essence better adapted to our need than when it first was passed." Llewellyn, *What Price Contract?—An Essay in Perspective,* 4 Yale L.J. 104, 747 (1931). On the other hand, Professor Willis, condemning the contract clauses of the Statute of Frauds as anachronistic, insisted: "These sections * * * are no longer preventing fraud, if they ever did, but rather are a cause of fraud. They should be abolished. They should not be re-stated. The legal profession can no longer afford to stultify itself, either by enforcing their grotesque and unethical provisions, or by finding ways of escape from their unjust operation." Willis, *The Statute of Frauds—A Legal Anachronism,* 3 Ind.L.J. 427, 541 (1928). The latter's criticism is largely predicated upon the belief that conditions have changed so that the initial reasons for adoption no longer obtain. This is elaborated in the following quotation taken from his article:

The original reasons for a Statute of Frauds—to prevent men from being held by means of perjury on promises they had never made— were first the uncontrolled discretion of the jury, second, the rule as to competency of witnesses, and, third, the immaturity of contract law in the seventeenth century.

While the process of the evolution of the jury, from a tribunal where the jurors were witnesses and decided the facts in cases on their own knowledge, to a tribunal where the jurors were judges of the facts and decided cases on evidence given in open court, was just about completed, the modern control of the court over the jury, in the matter of limits and elements of injury, the rules by which compensation for pecuniary injuries shall be ascertained, and in cases of passion and prejudice, was only just beginning. It was therefore a wise precaution at this time to require certain kinds of evidence as proof of certain contracts in order to place a limitation upon the uncontrolled power of the jury, which would be exercised only in this way * * *.

At the time of the enactment of the original Statute of Frauds neither the parties to the action, nor any person who had any interest in the result of the litigation, were competent witnesses * * *. Such a state of the law of evidence was a temptation to plaintiffs to procure perjured testimony, and exposed defendants to outrageous liabilities; and it probably was in this state of the law a wise precaution to require for such liability, either writing or other adequate evidence, at least where it was feasible to do so as in the case of contracts. * * *

There was a reason for the requirement of writing to hold an executor on his promise to answer damages out of his own estate because these promises were common, due to the fact that at this time he took beneficially if there was no residuary gift and to the fact that the estate of the deceased was not liable for wrongful acts, and the idea that part of the estate should be spent in making restitution helped to exert moral pressure on the executor. There was a reason for the requirement of writing in the case of contracts of guaranty and contracts not to be performed within one year because in the then state of the law of evidence—because these were continuing contracts—it might be very difficult to find any evidence at the time they came to be enforced. There was less reason for agreements in consideration of marriage, for the sale of interests in land, and for sales of goods; but the reason for inclusion of these contracts was probably their relation to transfers of property covered by other clauses of the Statute.

Probably the true explanation for the requirements of the Statute of Frauds in contracts is that at the time of enactment thereof the modern informal contract law was in the making. The law of agreement, consideration, conditions, illegality, etc., had not been fully worked out. The Statute of Frauds was an attempt to cover a field now perhaps adequately covered by other topics.

3 Ind.L.J. at 429–31.

It has been suggested, however, that even if it be true the original reasons are no longer persuasive, there are additional grounds for insisting upon a writing in some situations. This was Professor Llewellyn's view and no doubt partly accounts for the retention of a Statute of Frauds provision, albeit in a significantly modified form, in the Uniform Commercial Code. The case for retention has been stated as follows by Professor Vold:

> The spectacle now repeatedly observed in legitimate cases, of an apparently fraudulent defendant sliding out of a genuine bargain on the merely technical defense of the lack of the statutory writing has led to much questioning as to whether the statute of frauds now serves a useful purpose. Divergent viewpoints as to the wisdom of the statute under present conditions undoubtedly account for some of the conflicting borderline decisions as to its present applications. It must not be overlooked, however, that while some of the original reasons for enacting the statute of frauds have disappeared, other reasons for continuing it in force have become apparent. The statute serves a useful purpose in so far as it contributes to the business habit of requiring a writing. The lay tradition, often encountered, that a writing signed by the party must be had to make a contract binding probably is to a certain extent derived from the statute of frauds. Not only is a writing useful to prevent fraud by deliberate overreaching regarding the terms of the bargain, but the presence of a writing prevents to a large extent otherwise possible innocent misunderstanding of what actually were the terms of the bargain. It also preserves the exact wording of the terms, rather than leaving them to the recollection of their general purport preserved in the elusive and treacherous memory of interested parties. With present day long time contracts, often negotiated for large amounts in dealings at the last moment closed in a telephone conversation or in an order given orally to a traveling salesman, it is highly important to have the written 'confirmation' in due course at the outset to ascertain that the parties have correctly understood each other, instead of finding out about the difficulty, if any, only after the lapse of weeks or months after all commitments have been made. In this viewpoint, the cases that justify the statute are not primarily the litigated cases themselves, where it often looks as if a tricky defendant slides out of an honest bargain on the mere technicality of the lack of the statutory writing. The cases that justify the statute are rather the thousands of uncontested current transactions where misunderstanding and controversy are avoided by the presence of a writing which the statute at least indirectly aided to procure. While reasons of this sort are not frequently discussed at length in the decided cases, their actual presence in this field largely explains the readiness with which the business world seems to assume that on the whole the statute of frauds as applied to sales of good is doing more good than harm, and in consequence does not press for its repeal despite the pungent criticisms occasionally in recent times directed against it. Reasons such as these, moreover, may properly claim the attention of courts when novel doubtful borderline questions of application of the statute are presented for solution....

Vold, *The Application of the Statute of Frauds Under the Uniform Sales Act,* 15 Minn.L.Rev. 391, 393–95 (1931).

Proponents of abolition scored a victory in England in 1954, when Parliament repealed all but the sections relating to promises to answer for the debts of another (suretyship clause) and contracts for the sale of land. Law Reform (Enforcement of Contracts) Act, 1954, 2 & 3 Eliz. II, c. 34. There does not seem a likelihood of general repeal in this country, at least not in the near future. Rather, as noted by one authority, "a cautious approach to the Statute of Frauds seems to be in harmony with American professional opinion." Braucher, *The Commission and the Law of Contracts,* 40 Cornell L.Q. 696, 705 (1955): It is likely that "erosion" will continue through judicial interpretations restricting statutory coverage, easing the requirements for statutory compliance, and making assertion of the statutory defense more difficult.

In a bold move, Section 2–201 of the July, 1996 Draft of revised Article 2, Sales, repeals the statute of frauds, including the "one year" clause, for contracts for the sale of goods. This follows the English repeal, discussed above, and Article 11 of the United Nations Convention on Contracts for the International Sale of Goods (CISG), which provides: "A contract for sale need not be concluded in or evidenced by writing and is not subject to any other requirement as to form." Not surprisingly, the proposal is controversial and has prompted strong objection from some quarters. See, e.g., Morris G. Shanker, *In Defense of the Sales Statute of Frauds and Parole Evidence Rule: A Fair Price of Admission to the Courts,* 100 Com.L.J. 259 (1995). As this edition goes to press, a move to restore the statute of frauds has been made and the ultimate outcome is unclear.

Collateral reading: Farnsworth §§ 6.1–6.12; Calamari and Perillo §§ 19–1—19–25; Murray §§ 68–80. See also Perillo, *The Statute of Frauds in the Light of Functions and Dysfunctions of Form,* 43 Ford. L.Rev. 39 (1974) (a thorough historical and analytical study of contractual formalities); Note, *The Statute of Frauds and the Business Community: A Re–Appraisal in Light of Prevailing Practices,* 66 Yale L.J. 1038 (1950) (an empirical study of the degree of congruence between legal supposition and business reality).

(2) "WITHIN THE STATUTE:" THE "ONE YEAR" CLAUSE

A typical statute in most states provides: "No action shall be brought . . . upon any agreement that is not to be performed within the space of one year from the making thereof . . . unless the agreement upon which such action shall be brought, or some memorandum or note thereof, shall be in writing, and signed by the party to be charged therewith or some other person thereunto by him lawfully authorized." The so-called "one year" provision will provide a focus for much of this Section.

A recurring problem involves the oral employment contract. Assume that E, a middle manager, has just been laid off in a corporate "downsizing." On March 1, 1997, E interviews with R for a job and, after negotiations, R orally agrees to employ E for two years at $35,000 per year, with the prospect of a salary increase based upon performance. E is told that he will not be eligible for health or retirement benefits until he has worked for six months. A written contract was not discussed, although E's duties were. E started work on April 1, 1997 and worked for five months before he was fired on September 1, 1997. No reason for the termination was given. E was paid for all work done and given a one month severance payment. E, who is unable to find a comparable job, sues R and alleges the above facts. R moves to dismiss on the grounds that the alleged oral contract was within the "one year" clause of the statute of frauds. Should the complaint be dismissed?

Read the following materials and answer the question.

C.R. Klewin, Inc. v. Flagship Properties, Inc.

Supreme Court of Connecticut, 1991.
220 Conn. 569, 600 A.2d 772.

■ OPINION: PETERS, J.

OPINION: The sole question before us in this certified appeal is whether the provision of the statute of frauds, General Statutes § 52–550(a)(5),[1] requiring a writing for an "agreement that is not to be performed within one year from the making thereof," renders unenforceable an oral contract that fails to specify explicitly the time for performance when performance of that contract within one year of its making is exceedingly unlikely. This case comes to this court upon our grant of an application for certification from the United States Court of Appeals for the Second Circuit pursuant to General Statutes § 51–199a.[2] C.R. Klewin, Inc. v. Flagship Properties, Inc., 936 F.2d 684 (2d Cir.1991).

The Second Circuit has provided us with the following facts. See id., 685–86. The plaintiff, C. R. Klewin, Inc. (Klewin), is a Connecticut based corporation that provides general construction contracting and construction management services. The defendants, Flagship Properties and DKM Properties (collectively Flagship), are engaged in the business of real estate development; although located outside Connecticut, they do business together in Connecticut under the trade name ConnTech.

1.   General Statutes § 52–550 provides in pertinent part: "(a) No civil action may be maintained in the following cases unless the agreement, or a memorandum of the agreement, is made in writing and signed by the party, or the agent of the party, to be charged ... (5) upon any agreement that is not to be performed within one year from the making thereof...."

2.   General Statutes § 51–199a provides in pertinent part: "(b) The supreme court may answer questions of law certified to it by the Supreme Court of the United States, a court of appeals of the United States or a United States district court when requested by the certifying court if there are involved in any proceeding before it questions of law of this state which may be determinative of the cause then pending in the certifying court and as to which it appears to the certifying court there is no controlling precedent in the decisions of the supreme court of this state.

"(c) This section may be invoked by an order of any of the courts referred to in subsection (b) of this section upon the court's own motion or upon the motion of any party to the cause.

"(d) A certification order shall set forth: (1) The questions of law to be answered; and (2) a statement of all facts relevant to the questions certified and showing fully the nature of the controversy in which the questions arose."

Flagship became the developer of a major project (ConnTech Project) in Mansfield, near the University of Connecticut's main campus. The master plan for the project included the construction of twenty industrial buildings, a 280 room hotel and convention center, and housing for 592 graduate students and professors. The estimated total cost of the project was $120 million.

In March, 1986, Flagship representatives held a dinner meeting with Klewin representatives. Flagship was considering whether to engage Klewin to serve as construction manager on the ConnTech Project. During the discussions, Klewin advised that its fee would be 4 percent of the cost of construction plus 4 percent for its overhead and profit. This fee structure was, however, subject to change depending on when different phases of the project were to be constructed. The meeting ended with Flagship's representative shaking hands with Klewin's agent and saying, "You've got the job. We've got a deal." No other specific terms or conditions were conclusively established at trial. The parties publicized the fact that an agreement had been reached and held a press conference, which was videotaped. Additionally, they ceremoniously signed, without filling in any of the blanks, an American Institute of Architects Standard Form of Agreement between Owner and Construction Manager.

Construction began May 4, 1987, on the first phase of the ConnTech Project, called Celeron Square. The parties entered into a written agreement regarding the construction of this one part of the project. Construction was fully completed by the middle of October, 1987. By that time, because Flagship had become dissatisfied with Klewin's work, it began negotiating with other contractors for the job as construction manager on the next stage of the ConnTech Project. In March, 1988, Flagship contracted with another contractor to perform the sitework for Celeron Square II, the next phase of the project.

After having been replaced as construction manager, Klewin filed suit in the United States District Court for the District of Connecticut, claiming (1) breach of an oral contract to perform as construction manager on all phases of the project; (2) quantum meruit recovery for services performed in anticipation of future stages of the project; and (3) detrimental reliance on Flagship's promise to pay for preconstruction services. Flagship moved for summary judgment, claiming, inter alia, that enforcement of the alleged oral contract was barred by the statute of frauds. The district court granted summary judgment, reasoning that (1) "the contract was not of an indefinite duration or open ended" because full performance would take place when all phases of the ConnTech Project were completed, and (2) the contract "as a matter of law" could not possibly have been performed within one year. In drawing this second conclusion, the court focused on the sheer scope of the project and Klewin's own admission that the entire project was intended to be constructed in three to ten years.

Klewin appealed to the United States Court of Appeals for the Second Circuit. The Court of Appeals held that "the issues presented involve substantial legal questions for which there is no clear precedent under the decisions of the Connecticut Supreme Court"; id., 686; and certified to this court the following questions:

"A. Whether under the Connecticut Statute of Frauds, Conn. Gen. Stat. § 52–550 (a) (5), an oral contract that fails to specify explicitly the time for performance is a contract of 'indefinite duration,' as that term has been used in the applicable Connecticut precedent, and therefore outside of the Statute's proscriptions?

"B. Whether an oral contract is unenforceable when the method of performance called for by the contract contemplates performance to be completed over a period of time that exceeds one year, yet the contract itself does not explicitly negate the possibility of performance within one year?" Id., 685.

We answer "yes" to the first question, and "no" to the second.

I

The Connecticut statute of frauds has its origins in a 1677 English statute entitled "An Act for the prevention of Fraud and Perjuries." See 6 W. Holdsworth, A History of English Law (1927) pp. 379–84. The statute appears to have been enacted in response to developments in the common law arising out of the advent of the writ of assumpsit, which changed the general rule precluding enforcement of oral promises in the King's courts. Thereafter, perjury and the subornation of perjury became a widespread and serious problem. Furthermore, because juries at that time decided cases on their own personal knowledge of the facts, rather than on the evidence introduced at trial, a requirement, in specified transactions, of "some memorandum or note . . . in writing, and signed by the party to be charged" placed a limitation on the uncontrolled discretion of the jury. See 2 A. Corbin, Contracts (1950) § 275, pp. 2–3; 6 W. Holdsworth, supra, pp. 387–89; An Act for Prevention of Fraud and Perjuries, 29 Car. 2, c. 3, § 4 (1677), quoted in J. Perillo, "The Statute of Frauds in the Light of the Functions and Dysfunctions of Form," 43 Fordham L.Rev. 39, 39 n.2 (1974). Although the British Parliament repealed most provisions of the statute, including the one-year provision, in 1954; see The Law Reform (Enforcement of Contracts) Act, 2 & 3 Eliz. 2, c. 34 (1954); the statute nonetheless remains the law virtually everywhere in the United States.

Modern scholarly commentary has found much to criticize about the continued viability of the statute of frauds. The statute has been found wanting because it serves none of its purported functions very well; see J. Perillo, supra; and because it permits or compels economically wasteful behavior; see M. Braunstein, "Remedy, Reason, and the Statute of Frauds: A Critical Economic Analysis," 1989 Utah L. Rev. 383. It is, however, the one-year provision that is at issue in this case that has caused the greatest puzzlement among commentators. As Professor Farnsworth observes, "of all the provisions of the statute, it is the most difficult to rationalize.

"If the one-year provision is based on the tendency of memory to fail and of evidence to go stale with the passage of time, it is ill-contrived because the one-year period does not run from the making of the contract to the proof of the making, but from the making of the contract to the completion of performance. If an oral contract that cannot be performed within a year is broken the day after its making, the provision applies though the terms of the contract are fresh in the minds of the parties. But if an oral contract that can be performed within a year is broken and suit is not brought until nearly six years (the usual statute of limitations for contract actions) after the breach, the provision does not apply, even though the terms of the contract are no longer fresh in the minds of the parties.

"If the one-year provision is an attempt to separate significant contracts of long duration, for which writings should be required, from less significant contracts of short duration, for which writings are unnecessary, it is equally ill-contrived because the one-year period does not run from the commencement of performance to the completion of performance, but from the making of the contract to the completion of performance. If an oral contract to work for one day, 13 months from now, is broken, the provision applies, even though the duration of performance is only one day. But if an oral contract to work for a year beginning today is broken, the provision does not apply, even though the duration of performance is a full year." 2 E. Farnsworth, Contracts (2d Ed. 1990) § 6.4, pp. 110–11; see also Goldstick v. ICM Realty, 788 F.2d 456, 464 (7th Cir.1986); D & N Boening, Inc. v. Kirsch Beverages, Inc., 63 N.Y.2d449, 454, 472 N.E.2d 992, 483 N.Y.S.2d 164 (1984); 1 Restatement (Second), Contracts (1979) § 130, comment a; J. Calamari & J. Perillo, Contracts (3d Ed. 1987) § 19–18, p. 807.[6]

Historians have had difficulty accounting for the original inclusion of the one-year provision.[7] Some years after the statute's enactment, one English judge stated that "the design of the statute was, not to trust to the memory of witnesses for a longer time than one year." Smith v. Westall, 1 Ld. Raym. 316, 317, 91 Eng. Rep. 1106, 1107 (1697). That explanation is, however, unpersuasive, since, as Farnsworth notes, the language of the statute is ill suited to this purpose. One eminent historian suggested that because such contracts are continuing contracts, it might be very difficult to give evidence of their formation, inasmuch as the rules of evidence of that time prohibited testimony by the parties to an action or any person who had an interest in the litigation. 6 W. Holdsworth, supra, p. 392. That argument, however, proves too much, since it would apply equally to all oral contracts regardless of the duration of their performance. The most extensive recent study of the history of English contract law offers plausi-

---

6. Even the statute's most notable defender chose not to mention the one-year provision when he contended that the statute is "in essence better adapted to our needs than when it was first passed." K. Llewellyn, "What Price Contract? An Essay in Perspective," 40 Yale L.J. 704, 747 (1931).

7. The language of the original English statute was nearly identical to that of the provision we are now considering, including "any agreement that is not to be performed within the space of one year from the making thereof." An Act for Prevention of Frauds and Perjuries, 29 Car. 2, c. 3, § 4(5) (1677), quoted in J. Perillo, "The Statute of Frauds in the Light of the Functions and Dysfunctions of Form," 43 Fordham L. Rev. 39, 39 n.2 (1974).

ble explanations for all of the other provisions, but acknowledges that this one is "curious." A. Simpson, A History of the Common Law of Contract (1975) p. 612. More recently, it has been suggested that the provision "may have been intended to prevent oral perjury in actions of assumpsit against customers who had forgotten the details of their purchases." P. Hamburger, "The Conveyancing Purposes of the Statute of Frauds," 27 Am. J. Leg. Hist. 354, 376 n.85 (1983).

In any case, the one-year provision no longer seems to serve any purpose very well, and today its only remaining effect is arbitrarily to forestall the adjudication of possibly meritorious claims. For this reason, the courts have for many years looked on the provision with disfavor, and have sought constructions that limited its application. See, e.g., Landes Construction Co. v. Royal Bank of Canada, 833 F.2d 1365, 1370 (9th Cir.1987) (noting policy of California courts "of restricting the application of the statute to those situations precisely covered by its language"); Cunningham v. Healthco, Inc., 824 F.2d 1448, 1455 (5th Cir.1987) (one-year provision does not apply if the contract "conceivably" can be performed within one year); Hodge v. Evans Financial Corporation, 823 F.2d 559, 561 (D.C.Cir.1987) (statute of frauds "has long been construed narrowly and literally"); Goldstick v. ICM Realty, supra, 464 ("Courts tend to take the concept of 'capable of full performance' quite literally ... because they find the one-year limitation irksome.").

II

Our case law in Connecticut, like that in other jurisdictions, has taken a narrow view of the one-year provision of the statute of frauds now codified as § 52–550 (a) (5). In Russell v. Slade, 12 Conn. 455, 460 (1838), this court held that "it has been repeatedly adjudged, that unless it appear from the agreement itself, that it is not to be performed within a year, the statute does not apply.... The statute of frauds plainly means an agreement not to be performed within the space of a year, and expressly and specifically so agreed. A contingency is not within it; nor any case that depends upon contingency. It does not extend to cases where the thing only may be performed within the year." ...

A few years later, in Clark v. Pendleton, 20 Conn. 495, 508 (1850), the statute was held not to apply to a contract that was to be performed following a voyage that both parties expected to take one and one-half years. "It is not alleged in any form, that it was made with reference to, or that its performance was to depend on the termination of a voyage which would necessarily occupy that time. It is only alleged, that it was expected by the parties, that the defendant would be absent for the period of eighteen months. But this expectation, which was only an opinion or belief of the parties, and the mental result of their private thoughts, constituted no part of the agreement itself; nor was it connected with it, so as to explain or give a construction to it, although it naturally would, and probably did, form one of the motives which induced them to make the agreement. The thing thus anticipated did not enter into the contract, as one of its terms; and according to it, as stated, the defendant, whenever he should have returned, after having embarked on the voyage, whether before or after the time during which it was thus expected to continue, would be under an obligation to perform his contract with the plaintiff. As it does not therefore appear, by its terms, as stated, that it was not to be performed within a year from the time when it was made, it is not within the statute." (Emphases added.)

In this century, in Appleby v. Noble, 101 Conn. 54, 57, 124 A. 717 (1924), this court held that " '[a] contract is not within this clause of the statute unless its terms are so drawn that it cannot by any possibility be performed fully within one year.' " (Emphasis added.) In Burkle v. Superflow Mfg. Co., 137 Conn. 488, 492–93, 78 A.2d 698 (1950), we delineated the line that separates contracts that are within the one-year provision from those that are excluded from it. "Where the time for performance is definitely fixed at more than one year, the contract is, of course, within the statute. . . . If no time is definitely fixed but full performance may occur within one year through the happening of a contingency upon which the contract depends, it is not within the statute."

More recently, in Finley v. Aetna Life & Casualty Co., 202 Conn. 190, 197, 520 A.2d 208 (1987), we stated that " '[u]nder the prevailing interpretation, the enforceability of a contract under the one-year provision does not turn on the actual course of subsequent events, nor on the expectations of the parties as to the probabilities. Contracts of uncertain duration are simply excluded; the provision covers only those contracts whose performance cannot possibly be completed within a year.' (Emphasis added.) 1 Restatement (Second), Contracts, [§ 130, comment a] . . . ."

In light of this unbroken line of authority, the legislature's decision repeatedly to reenact the provision in language virtually identical to that of the 1677 statute suggests legislative approval of the restrictive interpretation that this court has given to the one-year provision. "[T]he action of the General Assembly in re-enacting the statute, including the clause in question . . . is presumed to have been done in the light of those decisions." Turner v. Scanlon, 146 Conn. 149, 156, 148 A.2d 334 (1959); see also Ralston Purina Co. v. Board of Tax Review, 203 Conn. 425, 439–40, 525 A.2d 91 (1987).

III

Bearing this history in mind, we turn to the questions certified to us by the federal court. Our case law makes no distinction, with respect to exclusion from the statute of frauds, between contracts of uncertain or indefinite duration and contracts that contain no express terms defining the time for performance. The two certified questions therefore raise only one substantive issue. That issue can be framed as follows: in the exclusion from the statute of frauds of all contracts except those "whose performance cannot possibly be completed within a year"; (emphasis omitted) Finley v. Aetna Life & Casualty Co., supra, 197; what meaning should be attributed to the word "possibly"? One construction of "possibly" would encompass only contracts whose completion within a year would be inconsistent with the express terms of the contract. An alternate construction would include as well contracts such as the one involved in this case, in which, while no time period is expressly specified, it is (as the district court found) realistically impossible for performance to be completed within a year. We now hold that the former and not the latter is the correct interpretation. "The critical test ... is whether 'by its terms' the agreement is not to be performed within a year," so that the statute will not apply where "the alleged agreement contain[s] [no] provision which directly or indirectly regulated the time for performance." Freedman v. Chemical Construction Corporation, 43 N.Y.2d 260, 265, 372 N.E.2d 12, 401 N.Y.S.2d 176 (1977). "It is the law of this state, as it is elsewhere, that a contract is not within this clause of the statute unless its terms are so drawn that it cannot by any possibility be performed fully within one year." (Emphasis added.) Burkle v. Superflow Mfg. Co., supra, 492.

Flagship contends, to the contrary, that the possibility to which this court referred in Burkle must be a reasonable possibility rather than a theoretical possibility. It is true that in Burkle this court rejected the argument that "since all the members of a partnership [that was a party to the contract] may possibly die within a year, the contract is not within the statute." We noted that "[n]o case has come to our attention where the rule that the possibility of death within a year removes a contract from the statute has been extended to apply to the possibility of the death of more than one individual." Id., 494. In Burkle, however, we merely refused to extend further yet another of the rules by which the effect of the provision has been limited. Burkle did not purport to change the well established rule of narrow construction of the underlying one-year provision.

Most other jurisdictions follow a similar rule requiring an express contractual provision specifying that performance will extend for more than one year. * * *

Because the one-year provision "is an anachronism in modern life ... we are not disposed to expand its destructive force." Farmer v. Arabian American Oil Co., 277 F.2d 46, 51 (2d Cir.1960). When a contract contains no express terms about the time for performance, no sound reason of policy commends judicial pursuit of a collateral inquiry into whether, at the time of the making of the contract, it was realistically possible that performance of the contract would be completed within a year.[8] Such a collateral inquiry would not only expand the "destructive force" of the statute by extending it to contracts not plainly within its terms, but would also inevitably waste judicial resources on the resolution of an issue that has nothing to do with the merits of the case or the attainment of a just outcome.[9] See 2 A. Corbin,

---

8. In this case, one of the issues before the Second Circuit was whether there was a genuine issue of material fact as to whether the oral agreement could have been performed within a year.

9. We recognize, as Flagship observed at oral argument, that comment a to § 130 of the Restatement (Second) of Contracts (1979), upon which we relied in Finley v. Aetna Life & Casualty Co., 202 Conn. 190, 197, 520 A.2d 208 (1987), includes an illus-

supra, § 275, p. 14 (the statute "has been in part the cause of an immense amount of litigation as to whether a promise is within the statute or can by any remote possibility be taken out of it. This latter fact is fully evidenced by the space necessary to be devoted to the subject in this volume and by the vast number of cases to be cited").

We therefore hold that an oral contract that does not say, in express terms, that performance is to have a specific duration beyond one year is, as a matter of law, the functional equivalent of a contract of indefinite duration for the purposes of the statute of frauds. Like a contract of indefinite duration, such a contract is enforceable because it is outside the proscriptive force of the statute regardless of how long completion of performance will actually take.

The first certified question is answered "yes." The second certified question is answered "no."

No costs will be taxed in this court to either party.

North Shore Bottling Co. v. C. Schmidt & Sons, Inc.

Court of Appeals of New York, 1968.
22 N.Y.2d 171, 292 N.Y.S.2d 86, 239 N.E.2d 189.

■ FULD, CHIEF JUDGE. This appeal, here by permission of the Appellate Division on a certified question, calls upon us to determine the validity, under the one-year provision of the Statute of Frauds, of an oral agreement which entitled the defendant to terminate its contractual arrangement with the plaintiff within one year of its making.

* * *

The Statute of Frauds requires an agreement to be in writing if "[b]y its terms [it] is not to be performed within one year from the making thereof" (General Obligations Law, § 5–701, subd. 1 [formerly Personal Property Law, § 31, subd. 1]). According to the complaint before us, the

tration that is inconsistent with the result that we are reaching today. Contrary to illustration 3 (which is drawn from Warner v. Texas & Pacific R. Co., 164 U.S. 418, 17 S. Ct. 147, 41 L. Ed. 495 (1896), the facts of which are summarized in the text above), which supports our holding, illustration 4 states: "A orally promises B to sell him five crops of potatoes to be grown on a specified farm in Minnesota, and B promises to pay a stated price on delivery. The contract is within the Statute of Frauds. It is impossible in Minnesota for five crops of potatoes to mature in one year." The illustration is adapted from illustration 11 to § 198 of the Restatement (First) of Contracts (1928), which does not include case citations. The Restatement (Second) supports the illustration by citing Adams v. Big Three Industries, Inc., 549 S.W.2d 411 (Tex.Civ.App.1977). The Adams court held that "when no time for performance has been specified, a 'reasonable time' will be implied, and what is a reasonable time must be determined from all the circumstances, the situation of the parties, and the subject matter of the contract.... Where an agreement, by its terms or the nature of the performance required, cannot be performed within one year, it necessarily comes within the purview of the statute.... If, as here, the contract is not a written one and depends upon disputed facts, the determination of what constitutes a reasonable time is a question of fact." (Citations omitted.) Id., 414–15. In our view, illustration 3 more closely represents the law of this state.

plaintiff and the defendant Schmidt "entered into an agreement whereby plaintiff became the exclusive wholesale distributor in Queens County of Schmidt beer * * * for as long as Schmidt sold beer in the New York metropolitan area," and the question presented is whether the defendant's power under the agreement itself to put an end to it within the year—by discontinuing its sales of beer in the New York area—took the agreement out of the operation of the statute.

It was long ago stated, and frequently repeated, that "[i]t is not the meaning of the statute that the contract must be performed within a year. * * * if the obligation of the contract is not, by its very terms or necessary construction, to endure for a longer period than one year, it is a valid agreement, although it may be capable of an indefinite continuance." (Trustees of First Baptist Church v. Brooklyn Fire Ins. Co., 19 N.Y. 305, 307; . . .) In other words, as another court expressed the matter, "the statute only applies to agreements which are, by expressed stipulation, not to be performed within a year. It does not apply to an agreement which appears by its terms to be capable of performance within the year; nor to cases in which the performance of the agreement depends upon a contingency which may or may not happen within the year." (Dresser v. Dresser, 35 Barb. 573, 577, supra.)

* * *

Applying, these principles to the present case, it is clear that the agreement asserted by the plaintiff does not fall within the ban of the Statute of Frauds. Although the parties may have expected the agreement to last over a long period, they contemplated its possible termination by action—unquestionably within the defendant's power to take at any time—discontinuing its beer sales in the New York area. That being so, the agreement did not, by its terms, "of necessity extend beyond one year from the time of its making." (Nat Nal Serv. Stas. v. Wolf, 304 N.Y. 332, 336, 107 N.E.2d 473, 475, supra.) It is hardly necessary to say that since envisaged by its terms, such an occurrence would amount to a performance permitted by the contract. As the court declared in Blake v. Voigt (134 N.Y. 69, 72–73, 31 N.E. 256, 257, supra), it "would be executed in a way that the parties agreed that it might be executed. The contingency did not defeat the contract, but simply advanced the period of fulfillment." To state this in slightly different fashion, the parties contemplated two possibilities—a long term distributorship in the plaintiff or a termination should the defendant decide to discontinue beer sales in the New York area. The first contingency is not, in the ordinary course, performable within a year, the second is. The existence of one of two contingencies performable within a year is sufficient to take the case out of the statute. (See, e.g., 2 Corbin, Contracts [1950], § 446; 3 Williston, Contracts [3d ed., 1960], §§ 495, 498, 498B.)

* * *

Accordingly, since the present agreement was susceptible of performance within a year, it falls outside the bar of the Statute of Frauds. It follows, therefore, that the first cause of action may not be dismissed.

* * *

Mason v. Anderson

Supreme Court of Vermont, 1985.
146 Vt. 242, 499 A.2d 783.

◼ HILL, JUSTICE.

Defendant, Margery Anderson, administratrix of the estate of Earl D. Miner, Sr., appeals from an order of the Rutland Superior Court granting summary judgment in favor of the plaintiff, Clark H. Mason. We affirm.

The plaintiff alleges and proved that on or about July 14, 1980, he loaned to defendant's decedent, Earl Miner, Sr., the sum of $5,000.00. The loan was made pursuant to an oral agreement between the parties. The plaintiff also alleges that Miner agreed to pay back the loan over time at the rate of $200.00 per month.

Payments on the loan were made by Miner until the time of his death in October, 1981. Approximately $1,100.00 had been repaid. Following Miner's death, plaintiff submitted to the defendant a claim for the remainder of the loan amount. This claim was denied and plaintiff then filed a complaint in superior court for the balance due on the loan.

Defendant moved for summary judgment on the grounds that the Statute of Frauds prohibited the enforcement of the alleged loan agreement, because the agreement could not be completed within a year, and was not evidenced by any writing. The trial court denied defendant's motion and granted summary judgment in favor of the plaintiff. The sole issue on appeal is whether the court erred in determining that the defendant is precluded from raising the Statute of Frauds, 12 V.S.A. § 181, as a defense in this action.

Under the Statute of Frauds, 12 V.S.A. § 181(4), "[a]n agreement not to be performed within one year from the making thereof" must be evidenced by a writing signed by the party to be charged. An exception to this provision of the Statute of Frauds which is followed by a majority of jurisdictions is that complete performance by one of the parties to an alleged oral agreement takes the agreement out of the one-year provision of the Statute of Frauds. E.G., Ortega v. Kimbell Foods, Inc., 462 F.2d 421 (10th Cir.1972); Emerson v. Universal Products Co., 35 Del. 277, 162 A. 779 (1932); Aldape v. State, 98 Idaho 912, 575 P.2d 891 (1978); Coker v. Richtex Corp., 261 S.C. 402, 200 S.E.2d 231 (1973); 2 Corbin on Contracts § 457 (1950); Restatement (Second) of Contracts § 130 and comment d (1981). But see Montgomery v. Futuristic Foods, Inc., 66 A.D.2d 64, 411 N.Y.S.2d 371 (1978) (only full performance by both sides will take contract out of the one year provision of the Statute of Frauds). Defendant argues that Vermont does not follow the majority rule. She relies on the case of Parks v. Franciss' Admr., 50 Vt. 626 (1878), in which the plaintiff named his son after an individual in exchange for that person's oral promise to make four yearly deposits in a bank account for the benefit of the son. After making two deposits, the individual died and no further deposits were made. The Vermont Supreme Court reversed a judgment for the plaintiff and held that the agreement was unenforceable because, by operation of the Statute of Frauds, the plaintiff was unable to submit parol evidence to prove the agreement. We decline to follow Parks and, to the extent it conflicts with our holding today, it is overruled.

The purpose of the Statute of Frauds is to prevent a party from being compelled, by oral and perhaps false testimony, to be held responsible for an agreement he or she claims was never made. First National Bank v. Laperle, 117 Vt. 144, 149, 86 A.2d 635, 638 (1952). Application of the Statute in the present case would operate to perpetrate a fraud rather than prevent one. The plaintiff fully performed his obligations under the agreement. He acted in reliance on the agreement in lending Miner $5,000.00 and thereby changed his position in a manner which prejudiced himself. In such a situation, to insist on a strict and mechanical operation of the Statute would defeat its purpose. We therefore join with those jurisdictions which follow the majority rule and hold that because the plaintiff had fully performed his obligations under the alleged agreement, the one-year provision of the Statute of Frauds does not prevent the plaintiff from proving the existence of the contract by parol evidence.

Affirmed.

NOTES

(1) "It is pointed out in Corbin on Contracts, that the provision of the statute of frauds relating to agreements which are 'not to be performed within the space of one year from the making thereof' has been narrowly interpreted. They (the courts) have observed the exact words of this provision and have interpreted them literally and very narrowly. The words are 'agreement that is not to be performed.' They are not 'agreement that is not in fact performed' or 'agreement that may not be performed' or 'agreement that is not at all likely to be performed.' To fall within the words of the provision, therefore, the agreement must be one of which it can truly be said at the very moment that it is made, 'This agreement is not to be performed within one year'; in general, the cases indicate that there must not be the slightest possibility that it can be fully performed within one year." 2 Corbin on Contracts 535, § 444." Goodwin v. Southtex Land Sales, 243 S.W.2d 721, 725 (Tex.Civ.App.1951.)

Are the decisions in *North Shore* and *C.R. Klewin* consistent with Corbin's analysis?

(2) Suppose that E and R orally agreed that if E terminated their employment contract at any time, E would not compete with R within a 20-mile radius for five years but if E did compete E would pay R a liquidated damage sum of $10,000 per year until the five-year period expired. After two years, E started to complete with R. Six months later E was killed by lightning on a golf course.

Alleging the oral agreement, R sued E's estate for $25,000, the liquidated amount due for the balance of the five-year period. E's executor moved to dismiss, arguing that the alleged oral agreement was within the "one year" provision. R then argued that death fully performed a contract not to compete, citing *Young v. Ward*, 917 S.W.2d 506 (Tex.App.1996), and since death could have occurred within one year of the alleged agreement the "one year" provision did not apply. Moreover, the agreement to pay liquidated damages could not possibly be performed within one year. E's executor responded that R's argument failed to distinguish between performance of the contract and an excuse for non-performance. Death fell into the latter category. E's executor cited Frantz v. Parke, 111 Idaho 1005, 729 P.2d 1068, 1071 (1986), where the court stated: "[T]he great weight of authority holds that a contract not to compete would be 'terminated,' not fully performed, by death of the promisor.... Indeed, if the unstated but omnipresent possibility of death could take an agreement for a definite time outside the statute of frauds, it would eviscerate the statute in virtually all contracts for definite terms between mortals." Assuming that the covenant not to compete and the liquidated damage provision are otherwise enforceable, how should the statute of frauds defense be decided?

(3) *One Side Rule.* Restatement § 198: "Where any of the promises in a bilateral contract cannot be fully performed within a year from the time of the formation of the contract, all promises in the contract are within [the one-year clause of the Statute of Frauds], unless and until one party to such a contract completely performs what he has promised. When there has been such complete performance, none of the promises in the contract is [within such provision]." Restatement (Second) § 130 is in accord. As one court put it: "Why, in the present case, should not a plaintiff be entitled to recover upon a contract which he has completely performed? The defendant has received the full benefit—not of an implied contract, but of an express one. He has received everything that the express contract stipulated that he should receive and nothing remains to be done on his part but the payment of money. Nor do we see any substance in the minority rule. In almost every case where a recovery on the contract has been refused it has been suggested that a recovery could be had under quantum meruit or quantum valebant counts." Emerson v. Universal Products Co., 35 Del. 277, 162 A. 779, 781 (1932).

(4) *Cumulative Effect of Statute of Frauds Provisions.* In Freedman v. Chemical Construction Corporation, 43 N.Y.2d 260, 401 N.Y.S.2d 176, 372 N.E.2d 12 (1977), the plaintiff, "a self-described retired industrialist," sued on an alleged oral agreement to pay him a 5% fee ($2,500,000) for his participation in the obtaining by the defendant of a $41,000,000 contract to build a plant in Saudi Arabia. Payment was to be made upon completion of the plant. Plaintiff's services extended over a three-year period, and it took another six years to build the plant. Nonetheless, the alleged contract was not within the "one year" clause, for "[i]t matters not * * * that it was unlikely or improbable that a $41 million plant would be constructed within one year." 372 N.E.2d at 15. However, the court held that the action was barred by another Statute of Frauds provision covering "a contract to pay compensation for services rendered in negotiating a loan, or in negotiating the purchase, sale, exchange, renting or leasing of any real estate or interest therein, *or of a business opportunity*, business, its good will, inventory, fixtures or an interest therein.

* * *'' (Emphasis added) Statute of Frauds provisions are "cumulative." It takes but one provision to bar enforcement. For a consideration of the possibility of restitutionary relief for one who performs pursuant to an alleged oral agreement within the Statute of Frauds, see infra at 745. There is, however, support for the view that if an oral contract for the sale of goods meets the requirements of UCC 2–201 it is enforceable despite the fact that it might be unenforceable under another general statute of frauds provision. See, e.g., Roth Steel Products v. Sharon Steel Corp., 705 F.2d 134 (6th Cir.1983); H & W Industries, Inc. v. Formosa Plastics Corp., USA, 860 F.2d 172 (5th Cir.1988).

PROBLEM: THE CASE OF JANE FONDA'S ATTORNEY

In 1968, Jane Fonda retained the services of a New York law firm to represent her in general business matters, orally agreeing to pay five percent of her earnings as compensation for the firm's services. Richard Rosenthal, a member of the firm, assumed responsibility for a large share of the firm's activities on Fonda's behalf.

In 1971, the law firm dissolved and in 1972, Rosenthal began to represent Fonda as an independent private practitioner. In April of 1972, he and Fonda entered into an oral contract whereby he agreed to continue performing a variety of services for her and she, in turn, agreed to pay him ten percent of all gross professional income derived from the projects that were initiated during his tenure.

Rosenthal continued to represent Fonda from his New York office. But in 1978, he and his family moved to California, at Fonda's request, so that he could represent her more effectively.

Approximately two years later, on May 30, 1980, Fonda discharged Rosenthal. Rosenthal sued to recover commissions on projects that were initiated during his tenure and produced or continued to produce income after his termination. What result? See Rosenthal v. Fonda, 862 F.2d 1398 (9th Cir. 1988).

Comment: Statutes of Frauds in the Uniform Commercial Code

The 1995 Official Text of the UCC contains several statutes of frauds. To illustrate, suppose that (1) Lessor and Lessee enter an oral lease for four years and (2) Seller and Buyer enter an oral contract for sale of goods with a three-year duration. In both, Lessor and Seller reserve power to terminate the contract "at will" upon giving reasonable notice.

As noted above, these oral agreements are not within the scope of the "one year" clause, since they can be properly terminated within one year from the making of the contract. Both, however, may be within the scope of a UCC statute of frauds, the oral lease under UCC 2A–201(1) and the oral sale under UCC 2–201(1). If the dollar amount of the lease contract and the contract for sale are high enough ($1,000 for the lease and $500 for the sale), the statute of frauds defense may be available. Moreover, there is a residual statute of frauds for the sale of personal property "beyond five thousand dollars in amount or value" that is not within the definition of a contract for sale of goods. UCC 1–206(1). This reinforces the warning that statute of frauds provisions are cumulative and there may be more than one provision lurking in the bushes.

What are "goods" within the phrase "contract for the sale of goods" in UCC 2–201(1)? Problems of classification have arisen most often in differentiating goods and land (e.g., what of the sale of standing timber?) and goods and services (e.g., what of the sale of false teeth made specially for the buyer?). The Code provides specific guidance.

Section 2–105(1) defines goods as follows:

"Goods" means all things (including specially manufactured goods) which are movable at the time of identification to the contract for sale other than the money in which the price is to be paid, investment securities (Article 8) and things in action. "Goods" also includes the unborn young of animals and growing crops and other identified things attached to realty as described in the section on goods to be severed from realty (Section 2–107).

UCC 2–107(1) and (2) treat of goods to be severed from realty as follows:

(1) A contract for the sale of minerals or the like (including oil and gas) or a structure or its materials to be removed from realty is a contract for the sale of goods within this Article if they are to be severed by the seller but until severance a purported present sale thereof which is not effective as a transfer of an interest in land is effective only as a contract to sell.

(2) A contract for the sale apart from the land of growing crops or other things attached to realty and capable of severance without material harm thereto but not described in subsection (1) or of timber to be cut is a contract for the sale of goods within this Article whether the subject matter is to be severed by the buyer or by the seller even though it forms part of the realty at the time of contracting, and the parties can by identification effect a present sale before severance.

As indicated in the extensive interpretive case law, the basic character of the performance due will determine whether the contract is for goods or services. A leading case on the Code's applicability to "mixed" contracts which involve both goods and services is Bonebrake v. Cox, 499 F.2d 951 (8th Cir.1974). The court held that a contract for the sale and installation of bowling equipment was a contract for the sale of goods under the UCC. "The test for inclusion or exclusion is not whether they are mixed, but, granting that they are mixed, whether their predominant factor, their thrust, their purpose, reasonably stated, is the rendition of service, with goods incidentally involved (e.g., contract with artist for painting) or is a transaction of sale, with labor incidentally involved (e.g., installation of a water heater in a bathroom)." 499 F.2d at 960. Accord: Colorado Carpet Installation, Inc. v. Palermo, 668 P.2d 1384 (Colo.1983) (sale and installation of carpeting and other flooring materials).

The UCC offers additional guidance in determining Statute of Frauds coverage where specially manufactured or custom made goods are involved.

See UCC 2–201(3)(a). Goods specially manufactured *for* the buyer (even if not manufactured *by* the seller) are *not* within UCC 2–201 if (1) they are not suitable for sale to others in the ordinary course of the seller's business and (2) the seller, before notice of repudiation is received and under circumstances which indicate that the goods are for the buyer, has made either a substantial beginning of their manufacture or commitments for their procurement. A contract for the sale of standard white shirts would be covered by the goods section of the Statute of Frauds. Not so if the seller, under the contract, added the buyer's business name and logo to the shirts. See, e.g., Smith–Scharff Paper Co. v. P. N. Hirsch & Co. Stores, Inc., 754 S.W.2d 928 (Mo.App.1988) (paper bags imprinted with buyer's logo); Flowers Baking Co. of Lynchburg, Inc. v. R–P Packaging, Inc., 229 Va. 370, 329 S.E.2d 462 (1985) (cellophane wrapping material manufactured to size required by buyer's containers and imprinted with buyer's name and unique artwork). Cf. Mel–Tex Valve, Inc. v. Rio Supply Co., 710 S.W.2d 184 (Tex.App.1986). What if the seller is in the business of manufacturing custom designed goods, and the goods, with some alteration, could be marketed? Should the seller be able to claim the advantage of the specially manufactured goods exception? See Impossible Electronic Techniques, Inc. v. Wackenhut Protective Systems, Inc., 669 F.2d 1026 (5th Cir.1982) (sale of electronic closed-circuit cameras). See generally, Annot., *Sales: "Specially Manufactured Goods" Statute of Frauds Exception in UCC § 2–201(3)(a)*, 45 A.L.R.4th 1126 (1986).

Sections 2–201, 2A–201 and 1–206 are not the only Statute of Frauds provisions in the Code. UCC 8–319 governs contracts for the sale of investment securities. In addition, there are sections which, although not ordinarily referred to as Statute of Frauds provisions, do prescribe a writing as a formal requisite of liability. Examples are negotiable instruments (UCC 3–104(a)), letters of credit (UCC 5–103), and security agreements (UCC 9–203). Beyond this there are numerous statutory provisions of a regulatory nature which not only insist upon a signed writing as a *sine qua non* of legal obligation, but prescribe, often in considerable detail, the content of the writing. Examples are statutes dealing with insurance, small loans and retail installment sales.

Note again that the July 1996 Draft of UCC 2–201(a) purported to repeal the Statute of Frauds as it applied to contracts for the sale of goods, including the "one year" provision. Some version of the Statute of Frauds, however, was restored in the January, 1997 draft of UCC 2–201.

(3) COMPLIANCE WITH THE STATUTE: THE "ONE YEAR" CLAUSE

Once an oral agreement is found to be "within" an applicable provision of the statute of frauds, the fun begins. Have the requirements of the statute been satisfied? If so, there are no formal barriers to enforcement. If not, the agreement is not enforceable (even though other requisites have been satisfied) unless other grounds, e.g., waiver, an admission or estoppel, can be established. See subsection (4), infra.

What, then, does it take to comply with the statute?

Crabtree v. Elizabeth Arden Sales Corp.

Court of Appeals of New York, 1953.
305 N.Y. 48, 110 N.E.2d 551.

■ FULD, JUDGE. In September of 1947, Nate Crabtree entered into preliminary negotiations with Elizabeth Arden Sales Corporation, manufacturers and sellers of cosmetics, looking toward his employment as sales manager. Interviewed on September 26th, by Robert P. Johns, executive vice-president and general manager of the corporation, who had apprised him of the possible opening, Crabtree requested a three-year contract at $25,000 a year. Explaining that he would be giving up a secure well-paying job to take a position in an entirely new field of endeavor—which he believed would take him some years to master—he insisted upon an agreement for a definite term. And he repeated his desire for a contract for three years to Miss Elizabeth Arden, the corporation's president. When Miss Arden finally indicated that she was prepared to offer a two-year contract, based on an annual salary of $20,000 for the first six months, $25,000 for the second six months and $30,000 for the second year, plus expenses of $5,000 a year for each of those years, Crabtree replied that that offer was "interesting." Miss Arden thereupon had her personal secretary make this memorandum on a telephone order blank that happened to be at hand:

"EMPLOYMENT AGREEMENT WITH

NATE CRABTREE At 681—5th Ave	Date Sept. 26–1947 6:PM

* * *

Begin 6 months 6 "	10000. 25000. 30000.

5000.—per year
Expense Money
[2 years to make good]

Arrangement with Mr. Crabtree

By Miss Arden

Present

    Miss Arden

    Mr. John

    Mr. Crabtree

    Miss O'Leary"

A few days later, Crabtree phoned Mr. Johns and telegraphed Miss Arden; he accepted the "invitation to join the Arden organization", and Miss Arden wired back her "welcome". When he reported for work, a "payroll change" card was made up and initialed by Mr. Johns, and then forwarded to the payroll department. Reciting that it was prepared on September 30, 1947, and was to be effective as of October 22d, it specified the names of the parties, Crabtree's "Job Classification" and, in addition, contained the notation that "This employee is to paid as follows:

"First six months of employment	$20,000.	per annum
Next six months of employment	25,000.	" "
After one year of employment	30,000.	" "

Approved by,   RPJ   [initialed]"

After six months of employment, Crabtree received the scheduled increase from $20,000 to $25,000, but the further specified increase at the end of the year was not paid. Both Mr. Johns and the comptroller of the corporation, Mr. Carstens, told Crabtree that they would attempt to straighten out the matter with Miss Arden, and, with that in mind, the comptroller prepared another "pay-roll change" card, to which his signature is appended, noting that there was to be a "Salary increase" from $25,000 to $30,000 a year, "per contractual arrangements with Miss Arden". The latter, however, refused to approve the increase and, after further fruitless discussion, plaintiff left defendant's employ and commenced this action for breach of contract.

At the ensuing trial, defendant denied the existence of any agreement to employ plaintiff for two years, and further contended, that, even if one had been made, the statute of frauds barred its enforcement. The trial court found against defendant on both issues and awarded plaintiff damages of about $14,000, and the Appellate Division, two justices dissenting, affirmed. Since the contract relied upon was not to be performed within a year, the primary question for decision is whether there was a memorandum of its terms, subscribed by defendant, to satisfy the statute of frauds, Personal Property Law, § 31.

Each of the two payroll cards—the one initialed by defendant's general manager, the other signed by its comptroller—unquestionably constitutes a memorandum under the statute. That they were not prepared or signed with the intention of evidencing the contract, or that they came into existence subsequent to its execution, is of no consequence, see Marks v. Cowdin, 226 N.Y. 138, 145, 123 N.E 139, 141; Spiegel v. Lowenstein, 162 App.Div. 443, 448–449, 147 N.Y.S. 655, 658; see, also, Restatement, Contracts, §§ 209, 210, 214; it is enough, to meet the statute's demands, that they were signed with intent to authenticate the information contained therein, and that such information does evidence the terms of the contract. ... Those two writing contain all of the essential terms of the contract— the parties to it, the position that plaintiff was to assume, the salary that he was to receive—except that relating to the duration of plaintiff's employment. Accordingly, we must consider whether that item, the length of the contract, may be supplied by reference to the earlier unsigned office memorandum, and, if so, whether its notation, "2 years to make good", sufficiently designates a period of employment.

The statute of frauds does not require the "memorandum * * * to be in one document. It may be pieced together out of separate writings, connected with one another either expressly or by the internal evidence of subject-matter and occasion." Marks v. Cowdin, supra, 226 N.Y. 138, 145, 123 N.E. 139, 141, see, also, 2 Williston, op. ct., p. 1671; Restatement, Contracts, § 208, subd. [a]. Where each of the separate writings has been subscribed by the party to be charged, little if any difficulty is encountered. See, e.g., Marks v. Cowdin, supra, 226 N.Y. 138, 144–145, 123 N.E. 139, 141. Where, however, some writings have been signed, and others have not—as in the case before us—there is basic disagreement as to what constitutes a sufficient connection permitting the unsigned papers to be considered as part of the statutory memorandum. The courts of some jurisdictions insist that there be a reference, of varying degrees of specificity, in the signed writing to that unsigned, and, if there is no such reference, they refuse to permit consideration of the latter in determining whether the memorandum satisfies the statute. See, e.g., Osborn v. Phelps, 19 Conn. 63; Hewett Grain & Provision Co. v. Spear, 222 Mich. 608, 193 N.W. 291. That conclusion is based upon a construction of the statute which requires that the connection between the writings and defendant's acknowledgment of the one not subscribed, appear from examination of the papers alone, without the aid of parol evidence. The other position—which has gained increasing support over the years—is that a sufficient connection between the papers is established simply by a reference in them to the same subject matter or transaction. See, e.g., Frost v. Alward, 176 Cal. 691, 169 P. 379; Lerned v. Wannemacher, 9 Allen, 412, 91 Mass. 412. The statute is not pressed "to the extreme of a literal and rigid logic", Marks v. Cowdin, supra, 226 N.Y. 138, 144, 123 N.E. 139, 141, and oral testimony is admitted to show the connection between the documents and to establish the acquiescence, of the party to be charged, to the contents of the one unsigned. . . .

The view last expressed impresses us as the more sound, and, indeed—although several of our cases appear to have gone the other way, see, e.g., Newbery v. Wall, 65 N.Y. 484; Wilson v. Lewiston Mill Co., 150 N.Y. 314, 44 N.E. 959—this court has on a number of occasions approved the rule, and we now definitively adopt it, permitting the signed and unsigned writings to be read together, provided that they clearly refer to the same subject matter or transaction. . . .

The language of the statute—"Every agreement * * * is void, unless * * * some note or memorandum thereof be in writing, and subscribed by the party to be charged", Personal Property Law, § 31—does not impose the requirement that the signed acknowledgment of the contract must appear from the writings alone, unaided by oral testimony. The danger of fraud and perjury, generally attendant upon the admission of parol evidence, is at a minimum in a case such as this. None of the terms of the contract are supplied by parol. All of them must be set out in the various writings presented to the court, and at least one writing, the one establishing a contractual relationship between the parties, must bear the signature of the party to be charged, while the unsigned document must on its face refer to the same transaction as that set forth in the one that was signed. Parol evidence—to portray the circumstances surrounding the making of the memorandum—serves only to connect the separate documents and to show that there was assent, by the party to be charged, to the contents of the one unsigned. If that testimony does not convincingly connect the papers, or does not show assent to the unsigned paper, it is within the province of the judge to conclude, as a matter of law, that the statute has not been satisfied. True, the possibility still remains that, by fraud or perjury, an agreement never in fact made may occasionally be enforced under the subject matter or transaction test. It is better to run that risk, though, than to deny enforcement to all agreements, merely because the signed document made nonspecific mention of the unsigned writing. As the United States Supreme Court declared, in sanctioning the admission of parol evidence to establish the connection between the signed and unsigned writings, "There may be cases in which it would be a violation of reason and common sense to ignore a reference which derives its significance from such [parol] proof. If there is ground for any doubt in the matter, the general rule should be enforced. But where there is no ground for doubt, its enforcement would aid, instead of discouraging, fraud." * * *

Turning to the writings in the case before us—the unsigned office memo, the payroll change form initialed by the general manager Johns, and the paper signed by the comptroller Carstens—it is apparent, and most patently, that all three refer on their face to the same transaction. The parties, the position to be filled by plaintiff, the salary to be paid him, are all identically set forth; it is hardly possible that such detailed information could refer to another or a different agreement. Even more, the card signed by Carstens notes that it was prepared for the purpose of a "Salary increase per contractual arrangements with Miss Arden". That certainly constitutes a reference of sorts to a more comprehensive "arrangement," and parol is permissible to furnish the explanation.

The corroborative evidence of defendant's assent to the contents of the unsigned office memorandum is also convincing. Prepared by defendant's agent, Miss Arden's personal secretary, there is little likelihood that that paper was fraudulently manufactured or that defendant had not assented to its contents. Furthermore, the evidence as to the conduct of the parties at the time it was prepared persuasively demonstrates defendant's assent to its terms. Under such circumstances, the courts below were fully justified in finding that the three papers constituted the "memorandum" of their agreement within the meaning of the statute.

Nor can there by any doubt that the memorandum contains all of the essential terms of the contract. See N.E.D. Holding Co. v. McKinley, 246 N.Y. 40, 157 N.E. 923; Friedman & Co. v. Newman, 255 N.Y. 340, 174 N.E. 703, 73 A.L.R. 95. Only one term, the length of the employment, is in dispute. The September 26th office memorandum contains the notation, "2 years to make good". What purpose, other than to denote the length of the contract term, such a notation could have, is hard to imagine. Without it, the employment would be at will, see Martin v. New York Life Ins. Co., 148 N.Y. 117, 121, 42 N.E. 416, 417, and its inclusion may not be treated as meaningless or purposeless. Quite obviously, as the courts below decided, the phrase signifies that the parties agreed to a term, a certain and definite term, of two years, after which, if plaintiff did not "make good", he would be subject to discharge. And examination of other parts of the memorandum supports that construction. Throughout the writings, a scale of wages, increasing plaintiff's salary periodically, is set out; that type of arrangement is hardly consistent with the hypothesis that the employment was meant to be at will. The most that may be argued from defendant's standpoint is that "2 years to make good", is a cryptic and ambiguous statement. But, in such a case, parol evidence is admissible to explain its meaning. See Martocci v. Greater New York Brewery, 301 N.Y. 57, 63, 92 N.E.2d 887, 889; Marks v. Cowdin, supra, 226 N.Y. 138, 143–144, 123 N.E. 139, 140, 141; 2 Williston, op. cit., § 576; 2 Corbin, op. cit., § 527. Having in mind the relations of the parties, the course of the negotiations and plaintiff's insistence upon security of employment, the purpose of the phrase—or so the trier of the facts was warranted in finding—was to grant plaintiff the tenure he desired.

The judgment should be affirmed, with costs.

[Footnotes omitted.]

NOTES

(1) What writings constituted the requisite memorandum? To what extent was parol evidence needed to show actual connection?

(2) The first Restatement, § 208, stated: "The memorandum may consist of several writings, (a) if each writing is signed by the party to be charged and the writings indicate that they relate to the same transaction, or (b) though one writing only is signed if (i) the signed writing is physically annexed to the other writing by the party to be charged, or (ii) the signed writing refers to the unsigned writing, or (iii) it appears from examination of all the writings that the signed writing was signed with reference to the unsigned writings." Did *Crabtree* go beyond the limits set in the Restatement? Should it have? See Corbin §§ 512–518. Restatement (Second) § 132, influenced by *Crabtree*, provides: "The memorandum may consist of several writings if one of the writings is signed and the writings in the circumstances clearly indicate that they relate to the same transaction."

(3) UCC 2–201(1) [UCC 2–201(a) (1997)] requires "some writing sufficient to indicate that a contract for sale has been made between the parties and signed by the party against whom enforcement is sought or his authorized agent or broker." Further: "A writing is not insufficient because it omits or incorrectly states a term agreed upon but the contract is not enforceable under this paragraph beyond the quantity of goods shown in such writing." The drafters added the following commentary: "The required writing need not contain all the material terms of the contract and such material terms as are stated need not be precisely stated. All that is required is that the writing afford a basis for believing that the offered oral evidence rests on a real transaction.... It need not indicate which party is buyer and which the seller. The only term which must appear is the quantity term which need not be accurately stated. The price, time and place of payment or delivery, the general quality of the goods, or any particular warranty may all be omitted." UCC 2–

201, comment 1. Courts have tended to be strict respecting the need for a statement of quantity in the writing. See, e.g., Thomas J. Kline, Inc. v. Lorillard, Inc., 878 F.2d 791 (4th Cir.1989). For a powerful critique, see Bruckel, *The Weed and the Web: Section 2–201's Corruption of the UCC's Substantive Provisions—the Quantity Problem*, U.Ill.L.Rev. 811 (1983). What would be the effect of a statutory revision that deleted all reference to quantity in UCC 2–201?

(4) *Tape Recording Sufficient as a Signed Writing?* Seller and Buyer negotiate a contract for the sale of goods via telephone. Assume that one party, with knowledge of the other, tape records the conversation. Will the tape recording meet the "writing" and "signing" requirements of UCC 2–201? For an argument that it should, see Misner, *Tape Recordings, Business Transactions via Telephone, and the Statute of Frauds,* 61 Iowa L.Rev. 941 (1976). For cases upholding a tape recording as a sufficient writing for Statute of Frauds purposes, see Ellis Canning Co. v. Bernstein, 348 F.Supp. 1212 (D.Colo.1972) (Colorado law; sale of securities); Londono v. City of Gainesville, 768 F.2d 1223 (11th Cir.1985) (Florida law; sale of land). But see Sonders v. Roosevelt, 64 N.Y.2d 869, 487 N.Y.S.2d 551, 476 N.E.2d 996 (1985); Swink & Company, Inc. v. Carroll McEntee & McGinley, Inc., 266 Ark. 279, 584 S.W.2d 393 (1979) (Writing? Maybe. Signature? No.). See also *Comment, Electronic "Writings" and the Statute of Frauds*, infra.

PROBLEM: THE CASE OF THE UNANSWERED PURCHASE ORDER

Karen Fedorko, representing Mast Industries, and Tuvia Feldman, representing Bazak International, negotiated an oral agreement for the sale by Mast of certain textiles to Bazak for $103,330. One week later Feldman sent a "purchase order" to the Mast office. It contained a description of the goods, the price and other essential terms. It also contained the handwritten words: "As presented by Karen Fedorko," and was signed by an authorized representative of Bazak.

→ subsection 2 of 2-201

Mast received the order and made no objections to its content. However, it refuses to deliver the goods, and Bazak contemplates suit. If litigation ensues, how would you expect a court to rule? See Bazak International Corp. v. Mast Industries, Inc., 73 N.Y.2d 113, 538 N.Y.S.2d 503, 535 N.E.2d 633 (1989).

Comment: Electronic "Writings" and the Statute of Frauds

Various provisions of Article 2 of the Uniform Commercial Code require a writing for transactional recognition or enforcement; notably, Section 2–201. A "writing" or "written agreement" includes "printing, typewriting or any other intentional reduction to tangible form." UCC 1–201(46). A computer printout, like other documents produced by electronic technology (e.g., telegrams, telexes and telecopies) should satisfy the "writing" requirement of Section 2–201.

The case for such recognition has been put as follows:

Telegrams, telexes, telecopies, and EDI [electronic data interchange], therefore, are inherently similar; all involve the transmission of a message by a series of electronic impulses. The message on which the transmission is based may, but need not, be in writing. Telegrams, telexes, and telecopies do differ from EDI in that their transmissions always result in a writing, whereas whether an EDI transmission results in a printout depends upon whether the receiver desires one. The important point, from the Statute of Frauds perspective, is that EDI has the capacity to produce the writing on request. Telegrams, telexes, and telecopies differ from EDI documents in that the end result of their electronic transmission is designed to be a paper-based writing. An EDI document transmission is more versatile. It may result in a paper-based writing (a printout) or may be stored in magnetic or other non-paper media at the option of the receiver. Telegrams, telexes, and telecopies have all been accepted as offering circumstantial guarantees of trustworthiness which are equivalent to those which a writing (in the more conventional pencil-and-paper sense) provide. A similar result with respect to EDI (assuming reliable record retention procedures are in place) should not be unexpected.

The Commercial Use of Electronic Data Interchange—A Report and Model Trading Partner Agreement, 45 Bus.Law. 1645, 1686 (1990). See also Dziewit, Graziano and Daley, *The Quest for the Paperless Office Electronic Contracting: State of the Art Possibility But Legal Impossibility?*, 5 Santa Clara Computer & High Tech. L.J. 75, 79, 80 (1989) ("The Uniform Commercial Code (UCC) provides an interpretation of what constitutes a writing. Under the UCC, a writing includes 'printing, typewriting or any other intentional reduction to tangible form.' The 'intentional' limitation in the definition 'relates only to the intending that there be a tangible representation of the intelligence or information' that comprises the subject matter of a contract. Computer storage media, such as floppy or hard discs, are a tangible form that comprise 'intelligence' or 'information.' The data is expressed in machine readable form that can be translated to human readable form, such as a printout. This printout constitutes a tangible representation of the intelligence or information, i.e., contract terms and conditions.").

Even assuming courts can be persuaded to accept EDI printouts as a writing for Statute of Frauds purposes, questions remain. One arises in the context of UCC 2–201(2) which pertains to receipt of "a writing in confirmation of the contract" and "written notice of objection to its contents." Unless the parties transmit printouts to each other, which would be unusual, it is doubtful that they have made written communication. For the printout would not come into existence until after communication had already been made. In the report cited above, the authors suggest that parties may be able to obviate this difficulty by agreeing in advance to expand the definition of "writing" to include the electronically transmitted messages themselves. See 45 Bus.Law. at 1690.

Another objection to Statute of Frauds compliance by electronic message transmission is the "signature" requirement of UCC 2–201; *viz.*, "signed by the party against whom enforcement is sought or by his authorized agent or broker." UCC 1–201(39) defines "signed" to include "any symbol executed or adopted by a party with present intention to authenticate a writing." The drafters note: "No catalog of possible authentications can be complete and the court must use common sense and commercial experience in passing upon these matters. The question always is whether the symbol was executed or adopted by the party with present intention to authenticate the writing." UCC 1–201(39), comment 39. In the typical EDI transmission, is there the requisite signature? The authors of the foregoing report insist that there is: "[T]he electronic transmission will undoubtedly include a name, access code, or other identifier which not only documents the source of the transmission, but also evidences an intention on the part of the sender to authenticate the transmission ..." 45 Bus.Law. at 1688 n. 177. But to be on the safe side, they recommend that parties agree in advance to adopt as signatures some electronic identification, consisting of a symbol or a code, to be affixed to or contained in each document transmitted. 45 Bus.Law. at 1731.

(4) EFFECT OF NONCOMPLIANCE

An oral contract which is within and does not satisfy the Statute of Frauds is not a complete nullity. Rather, the vast majority of the cases have held that such a contract is "not void in the strict sense that no contract has come into being at all, but [is] merely unenforceable at the option of the party against whom enforcement is sought." Borchardt v. Kulick, 234 Minn. 308, 319, 48 N.W.2d 318, 325 (1951). For example, "a contract that cannot be performed within one year, though described as 'void' by the statute and by courts on occasion ... is actually voidable or unenforceable." Keenan v. Artintype, Inc., 145 Misc.2d 90, 546 N.Y.S.2d 741, 743 (1989). This means that the defense may be waived. In addition, if there has been complete performance there is no cause to "undo" the transaction.

Although waivable, the defense has traditionally been relatively easy to raise. One has been able, for example, to admit *arguendo* the existence of an oral agreement while insisting upon its nonenforceability. One has not been obliged to deny the existence of the alleged oral contract before being permitted to assert the statutory defense. The ethical propriety of this procedure has been questioned. See, e.g., Stevens, *Ethics and the Statute of Frauds*, 37 Cornell L.Rev. 355 (1952). Moreover, the issue has become more prominent, particularly with respect to contracts for the sale of goods, by reason of UCC 2–201(3)(b), which provides that a contract not satisfying the requirements of subsection (1) but valid in other respects *is* enforceable "if the party against whom enforcement is sought admits in his pleading, testimony or otherwise in court that a contract for sale was made, but the contract is not enforceable under this provision beyond the quantity of goods admitted."

Judicial opinion and scholarly comment would indicate that this provision is likely to have a significant impact, perhaps, as one writer put it, eventually removing "all remaining vestiges of the bar of the statute of frauds where a valid oral contract existed, save for the party willing to commit perjury by denying the existence of the contract in his pleading, testimony, or otherwise in court." Cunningham, *A Proposal to Repeal Section 2–201: The Statute of Frauds Section of Article 2*, 85 Com.L.J. 361, 363 (1980). Although the judicial returns are not all in, and there are conflicting precedents, the clear direction is toward permitting full discovery and a trial on the merits in order to afford the plaintiff an opportunity to elicit an admission from the defendant. See, generally, Annot., *Construction and Application of UCC § 2–201(3)(b) Rendering Contract of Sale Enforceable Notwithstanding Statute of Frauds, to Extent it is Admitted in Pleading, Testimony, or Otherwise in Court*, 88 A.L.R.3d 416 (1978); Kreisman and Weisz, *The UCC Judicial Admissions Exception to the Statute of Frauds*, 77 Ill.B.J. 276 (1989); Shedd, *Statute of Frauds: Judicial Admission Exception—Where Has it Gone? Is it Coming Back?*, 6 Whittier L.Rev. 1 (1984) (discussion of non-UCC cases); Gaines, *The Application of the Oral Admissions Exception to the Uniform Commercial Code's Statute of Frauds*, 32 U.Fla.L.Rev. 487 (1980); Yonge, *The Unheralded Demise of the Statute of Frauds Welsher in Oral Contracts for the Sale of Goods and Investment Securities*, 33 Wash. & Lee L.Rev. 1 (1976); Parker, *The Evidential Scope of the Admissions Exception to the U.C.C. Statute of Frauds: Proving an Unwritten Contract under Section 2–201(3)(b) and 8–319(d)*, 56 Tex.L.Rev. 915 (1978); Duesenberg, *The Statute of Frauds in the 300th Year: The Challenge of Admissions and Estoppel*, 33 Bus.Law. 1859 (1978).

These are issues which are being litigated:

First, may the defendant demur or move to dismiss on the ground that the agreement as alleged is unenforceable?

Second, may the defendant move for summary judgment on the basis that the pleadings and supporting affidavits show an unenforceable oral agreement?

Third, when may the plaintiff "compel" admissions, either in a deposition or by cross-examination in open court, and thereby render the contract enforceable?

Fourth, must the admission conclusively prove the existence of the contract? Or is it sufficient if it merely evidences the contract?

Fifth, to what extent can the defense be avoided on grounds of estoppel, either equitable or promissory?

Finally, a plaintiff who is unsuccessful in removing the bar of the statute as such may seek restitution for benefits conferred. This is treated in the concluding problem, infra at 225.

DF Activities Corporation v. Brown

United States Court of Appeals, Seventh Circuit, 1988.
851 F.2d 920.

■ POSNER, CIRCUIT JUDGE.

This appeal in a diversity breach of contract case raises an interesting question concerning the statute of frauds, in the context of a dispute over a chair of more than ordinary value. The plaintiff, DF Activities Corporation (owner of the Domino's pizza chain), is controlled by a passionate enthusiast for the work of Frank Lloyd Wright. The defendant, Dorothy Brown, a resident of Lake Forest (a suburb of Chicago) lived for many years in a house designed by Frank Lloyd Wright—the Willits House—and became the owner of a chair that Wright had designed, the Willits Chair. This is a stark, high-backed, uncomfortable-looking chair of distinguished design that DF wanted to add to its art collection. In September and October 1986, Sarah–Ann Briggs, DF's art director, negotiated with Dorothy Brown to buy the Willits Chair. DF contends—and Mrs. Brown denies—that she agreed in a phone conversation with Briggs on November 26 to sell the chair to DF for $60,000, payable in two equal installments, the first due on December 31 and the second on March 26. On December 3 Briggs wrote Brown a letter confirming the agreement, followed shortly by a check for $30,000. Two weeks later Brown returned the letter and the check with the following handwritten note at the bottom of the letter: "Since I did not hear from you until December and I spoke with you the middle of November, I have made other arrangements for the chair. It is no longer available for sale to you." Sometime later Brown sold the chair for $198,000, precipitating this suit for the difference between the price at which the chair was sold and the contract price of $60,000. Brown moved under Fed.R.Civ.P. 12(b)(6) to dismiss the suit as barred by the statute of frauds in the Uniform Commercial Code. See UCC § 2–201. (The Code is, of course, in force in Illinois, and the substantive issues in this case are, all agree, governed by Illinois law.) Attached to the motion was Brown's affidavit that she had never agreed to sell the chair to DF or its representative, Briggs. The affidavit also denied any recollection of a conversation with Briggs on November 26, and was accompanied by both a letter from Brown to Briggs dated September 20 withdrawing an offer to sell the chair and a letter from Briggs to Brown dated October 29 withdrawing DF's offer to buy the chair.

The district judge granted the motion to dismiss and dismissed the suit. DF appeals, contending that although a contract for a sale of goods at a price of $500 or more is subject to the statute of frauds, the (alleged) oral contract made on November 26 may be within the statutory exception for cases where "the party against whom enforcement is sought admits in his pleading, testimony or otherwise in court that a contract for sale was made." UCC § 2–201(3)(b). DF does not argue that Brown's handwritten note at the bottom of Briggs' letter is sufficient acknowledgment of a contract to bring the case within the exemption in section 2–201(1).

At first glance DF's case may seem quite hopeless. Far from admitting in her pleading, testimony, or otherwise in court that a contract for sale was made, Mrs. Brown denied under oath that a contract had been made. DF argues, however, that if it could depose her, maybe she would admit in her deposition that the affidavit was in error, that she had talked to Briggs on November 26, and that they had agreed to the sale of the chair on the terms contained in Briggs' letter of confirmation to her.

There is remarkably little authority on the precise question raised by this appeal—whether a sworn denial ends the case or the plaintiff may press on, and insist on discovery. In fact we have found no authority at the appellate level, state or federal. Many cases hold, it is true, that the defendant in a suit on an oral contract apparently made unenforceable by the statute of frauds cannot block discovery aimed at extracting an admission that the contract was made, simply by moving to dismiss the suit on the basis of the statute of frauds or by denying in the answer to the complaint that a contract had been made. See, e.g., M & W Farm Service v. Callison, 285 N.W.2d 271, 275–76 (Iowa 1979). There is also contrary authority, illustrated by Boylan v. G.L. Morrow Co., 63 N.Y.2d 616, 618, 479 N.Y.S.2d 499, 500, 468 N.E.2d 681, 682 (1984). The clash of views is well discussed in Triangle Marketing, Inc. v. Action Industries, Inc., 630 F.Supp. 1578, 1581–83 (N.D.Ill.1986), which, in default of any guidance from Illinois courts, adopted the Boylan position. We need not take sides on the conflict. When there is a bare motion to dismiss, or an answer, with no evidentiary materials, the possibility remains a live one that, if asked under oath whether a contract had been made, the defendant would admit it had been. The only way to test the proposition is for the plaintiff to take the defendant's deposition, or, if there is no discovery, to call the defendant as an adverse witness at trial. But where as in this case the defendant swears in an affidavit that there was no contract, we see no point in keeping the lawsuit alive. Of course the defendant may blurt out an admission in a deposition, but this is hardly likely, especially since by doing so he may be admitting to having perjured himself in his affidavit. Stranger things have happened, but remote possibilities do not warrant subjecting the parties and the judiciary to proceedings almost certain to be futile.

A plaintiff cannot withstand summary judgment by arguing that although in pretrial discovery he has gathered no evidence of the defendant's liability, his luck may improve at trial. See Anderson v. Liberty Lobby, Inc., 477 U.S. 242, 106 S.Ct. 2505, 91 L.Ed.2d 202 (1986); Barker v. Henderson, Franklin, Starnes & Holt, 797 F.2d 490, 496 (7th Cir.1986); Spellman v. Commissioner, 845 F.2d 148, 151 (7th Cir.1988). The statement in a leading commercial law text that a defense based on the statute of fraud must always be determined at trial because the defendant might in cross-examination admit the making of the contract, see White & Summers, Handbook of the Law Under the Uniform Commercial Code 67 (1980), reflects a misunderstanding of the role of summary judgment; for the statement implies, contrary to modern practice, that a party unable to generate a genuine issue of fact at the summary judgment stage, because he has no evidence with which to contest an affidavit of his adversary, see Fed.R.Civ.P. 56(e), may nevertheless obtain a trial of the issue. He may not. By the same token, a plaintiff in a suit on a contract within the statute of frauds should not be allowed to resist a motion to dismiss, backed by an affidavit that the defendant denies the contract was made, by arguing that his luck may improve in discovery. Just as summary judgment proceedings differ from trials, so the conditions of a deposition differ from the conditions in which an affidavit is prepared; affidavits in litigation are prepared by lawyers, and merely signed by affiants. Yet to allow an affiant to be deposed by opposing counsel would be to invite the unedifying form of discovery in which the examining lawyer tries to put words in the witness's mouth and construe them as admissions.

The history of the judicial-admission exception to the statute of frauds, well told in Stevens, *Ethics and the Statute of Frauds,* 37 Cornell L.Q. 355 (1952), reinforces our conclusion. The exception began with common-sense recognition that if the defendant admitted in a pleading that he had made a contract with the plaintiff, the purpose of the statute of frauds—protection against fraudulent or otherwise false contractual claims—was fulfilled. (The situation would be quite otherwise, of course, with an oral admission, for a plaintiff willing to testify falsely to the existence of a contract would be equally willing to testify falsely to the defendant's having admitted the existence of the contract.) Toward the end of the eighteenth century the courts began to reject the exception, fearing that it was an invitation to the defendant to perjure himself. Later the pendulum swung again, and the exception is now firmly established. The concern with perjury that caused the courts in the middle period to reject the exception supports the position taken by Mrs. Brown in this case. She has sworn under oath that she did not agree to sell the Willits Chair to DF. DF wants an opportunity to depose her in the hope that she can be induced to change her testimony. But if she changes her testimony this will be virtually an admission that she perjured herself in her affidavit (for it is hardly likely that her denial was based simply on a faulty recollection). She is not likely to do this. What is possible is that her testimony will be sufficiently ambiguous to enable DF to argue that there should be still further factual investigation—perhaps a full-fledged trial at which Mrs. Brown will be questioned again about the existence of the contract.

With such possibilities for protraction, the statute of frauds becomes a defense of meager value. And yet it seems to us as it did to the framers of the Uniform Commercial Code that the statute of frauds serves an important purpose in a system such as ours that does not require that all contracts be in writing in order to be enforceable and that allows juries of lay persons to decide commercial cases. The methods of judicial factfinding do not distinguish unerringly between true and false testimony, and are in any event very expensive. People deserve some protection against the risks and costs of being hauled into court and accused of owing money on the basis of an unacknowledged promise. And being deposed is scarcely less unpleasant than being cross-examined—indeed, often it is more unpleasant, because the examining lawyer is not inhibited by the presence of a judge or jury who might resent hectoring tactics. The transcripts of depositions are often very ugly documents.

Some courts still allow the judicial-admission exception to be defeated by the defendant's simple denial, in a pleading, that there was a contract; this is the position well articulated in Judge Shadur's opinion in the

Triangle Marketing case. To make the defendant repeat the denial under oath is already to erode the exception (as well as to create the invitation to perjury that so concerned the courts that rejected the judicial-admission exception altogether), for there is always the possibility, though a very small one, that the defendant might be charged with perjury. But, in any event, once the defendant has denied the contract under oath, the safety valve of section 2–201(3)(b) is closed. The chance that at a deposition the defendant might be badgered into withdrawing his denial is too remote to justify prolonging an effort to enforce an oral contract in the teeth of the statute of frauds. If Dorothy Brown did agree on November 27 to sell the chair to DF at a bargain price, it behooved Briggs to get Brown's signature on the dotted line, posthaste.

AFFIRMED.

■ FLAUM, CIRCUIT JUDGE, dissenting.

Because I disagree with the majority's holding that additional discovery is prohibited whenever a defendant raises a statute of frauds defense and submits a sworn denial that he or she formed an oral contract with the plaintiff, I respectfully dissent. Neither would I hold, however, that a plaintiff is automatically entitled to additional discovery in the face of a defendant's sworn denial that an agreement was reached. Rather, in my view district courts should have the authority to exercise their discretion to determine the limits of permissible discovery in these cases. This flexibility is particularly important where, as here, the defendant's affidavit does not contain a conclusive denial of contract formation. While district courts have broad discretion in discovery matters, I believe the district court abused that discretion in the present case.

* * *

Because in my view the district court abused its discretion when it prohibited further discovery, I would remand this case to the district court with instructions to permit discovery to continue at least to the point where DF is given an opportunity to depose Brown. If Brown then denies under oath during her deposition that any oral contract was made, summary judgment might well be appropriate at that time.

NOTES

(1) *To Demur or Not to Demur?* Judge Posner notes that the court did not have to take sides as to whether a defendant in a suit on an oral contract can block discovery aimed at extracting an admission by moving to dismiss. But (alas), you do, at least for classroom purposes. Before deciding, consider these examples of the "clash of views" to which Judge Posner alludes:

(a) "The admission exception now included in the Statute of Frauds governing sales would be meaningless were the defendant permitted by the simple expedient of a motion to dismiss to deprive plaintiff of the opportunity to obtain from defendant either an admission 'in his pleading, testimony or otherwise in court' or a sworn denial of the existence of a contract.... If a prepleading motion to dismiss is permitted to defeat a cause of action on an oral sales contract before plaintiff has had an opportunity to elicit from defendant a statement in court of any kind, only malpractice by defendant's attorney would subject the defendant to the statute's ameliorative purpose. The Legislature in adopting the Uniform Commercial Code and the drafters of the Code cannot reasonably be thought to have intended that the exception have such limited application." Meyer, J., dissenting in Boylan v. G.L. Morrow Co., 63 N.Y.2d 616, 623, 479 N.Y.S.2d 499, 503, 468 N.E.2d 681, 684–85 (1984).

(b) "But those 'admissions' are not really admissions in the factual sense at all. Parties who move to dismiss do not truly say: 'I admit the things you allege are true fact, but I am entitled to judgment on the law.' They rather say something more like: 'Even if your allegations were true, I am entitled to judgment on the law.' Thus a motion to dismiss 'admits' the complaint's allegations only in a 'technical' sense inadequate to meet Section 2–201(3)(b)'s admission requirement...." Shadur, J. in Triangle Marketing, Inc. v. Action Industries, Inc., 630 F.Supp. 1578, 1583–1584 (N.D.Ill.1986).

(2) If the defense is provided by statute, should there not be a convenient procedure by which to raise the defense? If so, what should it be?

Comment: The Statute of Frauds and Estoppel

Assume that Farmer and Dealer made an oral contract in March to sell 5,000 bushels of #1 Yellow Corn for $2.80 per bushel, delivery in October. Relying on Farmer's oral promise, Dealer promptly resold the corn to a third person for $3.50 per bushel. Farmer, based upon their prior course of dealing, knew that this resale would probably occur. When the market price rose to $5.00 per bushel in September, Farmer refused to deliver. Dealer, alleging the oral contract and the resale, claims damages. Farmer moves to dismiss on the ground of the statute of frauds. UCC 2–201. Dealer argues that the statute of frauds should be avoided because of reliance upon Farmer's oral promise to deliver. Should this argument be accepted?

The question has created difficulty because an affirmative answer appears to be in direct conflict with the purpose and policy of the statute. There are no misrepresentations of fact by Farmer here or no representation that Farmer will not insist upon a writing. Rather, it is the oral promise that should have been in writing that induced the reliance by Dealer. According to one Court: "[T]he moral wrong of refusing to be bound by an agreement because it does not comply with the Statute of Frauds, does not of itself authorize the application of the doctrine of estoppel, for the breach of a promise which the law does not regard as binding is not a fraud.... To hold otherwise would be to render the statute entirely nugatory." Ozier v. Haines, 411 Ill. 160, 103 N.E.2d 485 (1952).

Reflecting the sparsity of case law in which a plaintiff has successfully employed estoppel in a Statute of Frauds case, the drafters of the first Restatement did not include a specific section on the subject. They did, however, append the following comment: "Though there has been no satisfaction of the Statute, an estoppel may preclude objection on that ground in the same way that objection to the non-existence of other facts essential for the establishment of a right or a defense may be precluded. A misrepresentation that there has been such satisfaction if substantial action is taken in reliance on the representation, precludes proof by the party who made the representation that it was false; and a promise to make a memorandum, if similarly relied on, may give rise to an effective promissory estoppel if the Statute would otherwise operate to defraud." Restatement § 178, comment f.

By contrast, the revised Restatement includes a separate section on "enforcement by virtue of action in reliance." Restatement (Second) § 139. It provides as follows:

(1) A promise which the promisor should reasonably expect to induce action or forbearance on the part of the promisee or a third person and which does induce the action or forbearance is enforceable notwithstanding the Statute of Frauds if injustice can be avoided only by enforcement of the promise. The remedy granted for breach is to be limited as justice requires.

(2) In determining whether injustice can be avoided only by enforcement of the promise, the following circumstances are significant: (a) the availability and adequacy of other remedies, particularly cancellation and restitution; (b) the definite and substantial character of the action or forbearance in relation to the remedy sought; (c) the extent to which the action or forbearance corroborates evidence of the making and terms of the promise, or the making and terms are otherwise established by clear and convincing evidence; (d) the reasonableness of the action or forbearance; (e) the extent to which the action or forbearance was foreseeable by the promisor.

Section 139 complements Section 90 of the revised Restatement, and, like that section, states a "flexible" principle. However, it is acknowledged that "the requirement of consideration is more easily displaced than the requirement of a writing." Restatement (Second) § 139, Comment b.

Section 139 should give Dealer hope, especially if subsection 2(c) can be satisfied. Despite this embrace of the general principal, there is disagreement over whether promissory estoppel is available to save an oral contract for sale under UCC 2–201. In his treatment of promissory estoppel and UCC 2–201, part of a major study of the relationship of estoppel to Article 2 of the Code, Professor Michael Gibson insists that the legislative history, the language, and the structure of Section 2–201 show that promissory estoppel was not to be used to evade the rather simple requirements of the section. Gibson, *Promissory Estoppel, Article 2 of the U.C.C., and the Restatement (Third) of Contracts,* 73 Iowa L.Rev. 659, 695 (1988). He recounts the apparent opposition of Karl Llewellyn to using reliance other than that specified (*viz.,* subsection 3(a) dealing with specially manufactured goods and subsection 3(c) dealing with acceptance and receipt or payment) as a reason to avoid statutory requirements. Given that the opening words of UCC 2–201 are that "[e]xcept as otherwise provided in this section" an oral contract for $500 or more is not enforceable, there is no warrant for engrafting an additional promissory estoppel "exception" to UCC 2–201.

Professor Gibson documents the split of authority. Some courts refuse to use promissory estoppel in this area; some apply it whenever fraud or unconscionability is present; still others, like the Seventh Circuit in R.S. Bennett & Co. v. Economy Mechanical Industries, Inc., 606 F.2d 182 (7th Cir.1979), will evidently apply it whenever the ordinary elements of promissory estoppel are present. For competing views, see Lige Dickson Co. v. Union Oil Co. of California, 96 Wn.2d 291, 635 P.2d 103 (1981) ("If we were to adopt [promissory estoppel] in the context of the sale of goods, we would allow parties to circumvent the U.C.C." 635 P.2d at 107); C.G. Campbell & Son, Inc. v. Comdeq Corp., 586 S.W.2d 40 (Ky.App.1979) ("[A]ny attempt by the courts to judicially amend the statute which is plain on its face would contravene the separation of powers mandated by the Constitution." 586 S.W.2d at 40); Warder & Lee Elevator, Inc. v. Britten, 274 N.W.2d 339 (Iowa 1979) ("If [UCC 2–201] were construed as displacing principles otherwise preserved in [UCC 1–103], it would mean that an oral contract coming within its terms would be [enforceable] despite fraud, deceit, misrepresentation, dishonesty or any other form of unconscionable conduct by the party relying on the statute." 274 N.W.2d at 342); Potter v. Hatter Farms, Inc., 56 Or.App. 254, 641 P.2d 628 (1982) ("Because it is not mentioned in the statute, the only arguable means of displacement is the legislature's silence. We do not believe that silence constitutes displacement of estoppel from the Statute of Frauds. In light of [UCC 1–103], we hold that if the legislature did not want estoppel to apply to application of the Statute of Frauds, it would have stated that intent expressly." 641 P.2d at 632). A quick perusal of recent cases will reveal that the disagreement has not been resolved. See James J. White & Robert S. Summers, Uniform Commercial Code § 2–6 (4th ed. 1995).

Thesis: In view of the erosion of UCC 2–201, through "admissions" and "estoppel" exceptions, the provision no longer serves a useful purpose and should be repealed. Agree or disagree?

PROBLEM: THE CASE OF THE LAKE WOBEGON LOT PURCHASE

For years Paula Purchaser has sought to buy a lot on Lake Wobegon owned by Vincent Vendor. Last week Paula made yet another attempt to purchase the land, a one acre lot with lake frontage and the only property owned by Vince, and this time the latter was agreeable. While discussing the matter at Vince's house, they agreed upon all of the essential terms, including the cash price of $10,000. After "shaking on it," Paula wrote a check for $1,000, down payment on the purchase. The check was made out to Vincent Vendor and contained the following legend: "$1,000 down on lot on Lake Wobegon, balance due $9,000." The following week, however, Vince changed his mind about selling and tendered the check back to Paula. Does Paula have legal recourse? What if Paula, in the meantime, had made a commitment to a bank to borrow funds to complete the purchase?

Assume, instead, that after agreeing upon the essential terms, including the cash price of $10,000, Paula wrote out the $1,000 check as down payment (but without the legend, as above) and gave it to Vince. Vince immediately cashed the check. Thereafter, Paula determined not to go through with the deal and wants her down payment returned. Vince, however, is willing to complete the transaction whenever agreeable to Paula. Is Paula entitled to a return of the $1,000?

CHAPTER THREE

THE BARGAIN RELATIONSHIP

SECTION 1. THE AGREEMENT PROCESS: MANIFESTATION OF MUTUAL ASSENT

In the bargain relationship, the two primary objectives of the parties are to reach agreement on a proposed exchange of economic or other resources and then satisfactorily to complete the exchange. Depending upon the situation of the parties, the transaction and other market or legal constraints, a certain amount of negotiation over terms may precede the final expression of agreement. Put another way, whenever the options of the parties are subject to their own choice rather than predetermined by law or circumstances, negotiation (or bargaining) is likely to occur. See J. Cross, The Economics of Bargaining 3–15 (1969). Thus, in any given transaction the parties may negotiate over such items as willingness to deal one with the other, the description, quality and quantity of what it is that one party is proposing to provide, the price and method of payment, the time and method of performance, which party bears what risks, the duration of the relationship and so forth. An assumption here is that individual bargainers will define their wants in a rational way and seek to satisfy them through a process of voluntary exchange. Similarly, if there is adequate information and sufficient choice, another assumption is that both parties will gain from the completed exchange, that is, that both parties will conclude that the transaction has increased if not maximized their satisfactions.

The two objectives of the bargain relationship (agreement and performance) are consistent with the concept of consideration, examined in the previous chapter, and an exchange completed to the satisfaction of both parties satisfies a standard of efficiency. Further, to the extent that our legal system permits these transactions to occur and supports them through adequate remedies whenever disputes erupt, it promotes the exercise of individual freedom through private ordering, supports the development of a market economy and encourages a system of decentralized power which Professor Harry W. Jones has called the "institution of contract." Jones, *The Jurisprudence of Contract*, 44 U.Cin.L.Rev. 43, 50–54 (1975).

Against this general background, the purpose of this section is to explore the legal consequences of breakdowns in the first objective of the bargain relationship, the effort to reach agreement on the proposed exchange. In a typical dispute, after negotiations have commenced and sometimes before any performance of the proposed exchange has occurred, one party will withdraw from the relationship. The other will assert that agreement had reached a point where a contract was formed and that the withdrawal is a breach of contract. How the withdrawing party responds to this and the extent to which the law of contracts supports these responses at various stages of the agreement process is the central problem to be considered. At stake is the general issue of freedom "from" contract. In most situations an individual in our society can refuse to deal or to negotiate with another without liability. But once negotiations have commenced, to what extent is one party privileged to withdraw for any reason without liability? What is the scope of mobility once the bargaining begins? Collateral reading: Farnsworth §§ 3.1–3.30; Calamari and Perillo §§ 2–1—2–26; Murray §§ 28–51.

(A) ASCERTAINMENT OF ASSENT: THE "OBJECTIVE" TEST

What is the overall approach that a court should take to ascertaining whether the parties have assented to a bargain and what their relevant intentions were in the process? The traditional answer and some of the problems associated with it are suggested in the following two cases and notes.

Embry v. Hargadine, McKittrick Dry Goods Co.

St. Louis Court of Appeals, Missouri, 1907.
127 Mo.App. 383, 105 S.W. 777.

[Appellant's written employment contract with Appellee expired on December 15, 1903. He had been unsuccessful in obtaining a meeting with Appellee's president before the expiration date. On December 23, during peak season, Appellant met with the president, Mr. McKittrick, and, according to his testimony, stated that unless he had another contract for the next year he would "quit" then and there. According to Appellant, the president replied: "Go ahead, you're all right; get your men out and don't let that worry you." Appellant thought that the contract had been renewed and made no further effort to find employment. When his employment was terminated on March 1, 1904, Appellant sued for breach of contract. At the trial, the president denied making the "you're all right statement" and testified that he was pressed to prepare for a board meeting, did not intend at that point to renew the contract and had deferred the renewal issue until a later date.]

■ GOODE, J.

* * *

It is assigned for error that the court required the jury, in order to return a verdict for appellant, not only to find the conversation occurred as appellant swore, but that both parties intended by such conversation to contract with each other for plaintiff's employment for the year from December, 1903, at a salary of $2,000. * * * [I]t remains to determine whether or not this part of the instruction was a correct statement of the law in regard to what was necessary to constitute a contract between the parties; that is to say, whether the formation of a contract by what, according to Embry, was said, depended on the intention of both Embry and McKittrick. Or, to put the question more precisely, did what was said constitute a contract of re-employment on the previous terms irrespective of the intention or purpose of McKittrick?

Judicial opinion and elementary treatises abound in statements of the rule that to constitute a contract there must be a meeting of the minds of the parties, and both must agree to the same thing in the same sense. Generally speaking, this may be true; but it is not literally or universally true. That is to say, the inner intention of parties to a conversation subsequently alleged to create a contract cannot either make a contract of what transpired, or prevent one from arising, if the words used were sufficient to constitute a contract. In so far as their intention is an influential element, it is only such intention as the words or acts of the parties indicate; not one secretly cherished which is inconsistent with those words or acts. The rule is thus stated by a text-writer, and many decisions are cited in support of his text: "The primary object of construction in contract law is to discover the intention of the parties. This intention in express contracts is, in the first instance, embodied in the words which the parties have used and is to be deduced therefrom. This rule applies to oral contracts, as well as to contracts in writing, and is the rule recognized by courts of equity." 2 Page, Contracts, § 1104. So it is said in another work: "Now this measure of the contents of the promise will be found to coincide, in the usual dealings of men of good faith and ordinary competence, both with the actual intention of the promisor and with the actual expectation of the promisee. But this is not a constant or a necessary coincidence. In exceptional cases, a promisor may be bound to perform something which he did not intend to promise, or a promisee may not be entitled to require that performance which he understood to be promised to him." Walds–Pollock, Contracts (3d Ed.) 309. In Brewington v. Mesker, 51 Mo.App. 348, 356, it is said that the meeting of minds, which is essential to the formation of a contract, is not determined by the secret intention of the parties, but by their expressed intention, which may be wholly at variance with the former. * * *

In view of those authorities, we hold that, though McKittrick may not have intended to employ Embry by what transpired between them according to the latter's testimony, yet if what McKittrick said would have been taken by a reasonable man to be an employment, and Embry so understood it, it constituted a valid contract of employment for the ensuing year.

The next question is whether or not the language used was of that character, namely, was such that Embry, as a reasonable man, might consider he was re-employed for the ensuing year on the previous terms, and act accordingly. * * * Embry was demanding a renewal of his contract, saying he had been put off from time to time, and that he had only a few days before the end of the year in which to seek employment from other houses, and that he would quit then and there unless he was re-employed.

McKittrick inquired how he was getting along with the department, and Embry said they (i.e., the employees of the department) were very busy getting out salesmen; whereupon McKittrick said: "Go ahead, you are all right; get your men out and do not let that worry you." We think no reasonable man would construe that answer to Embry's demand that he be employed for another year, otherwise than as an assent to the demand, and that Embry had the right to rely on it as an assent. The natural inference is, though we do not find it testified to, that Embry was at work getting samples ready for the salesmen to use during the ensuing season. Now, when he was complaining of the worry and mental distress he was under because of his uncertainty about the future, and his urgent need, either of an immediate contract with respondent, or a refusal by it to make one, leaving him free to seek employment elsewhere, McKittrick must have answered as he did for the purpose of assuring appellant that any apprehension was needless, as appellant's services would be retained by the respondent. The answer was unambiguous, and we rule that if the conversation was according to appellant's version, and he understood he was employed, it constituted in law a valid contract of re-employment, and the court erred in making the formation of a contract depend on a finding that both parties intended to make one. It was only necessary that Embry, as a reasonable man, had a right to and did so understand.

Some other rulings are assigned for error by the appellant, but we will not discuss them because we think they are devoid of merit.

The judgment is reversed, and the cause remanded. All concur.

Lucy v. Zehmer

Supreme Court of Appeals of Virginia, 1954.
196 Va. 493, 84 S.E.2d 516.

■ BUCHANAN, JUSTICE. This suit was instituted by W.O. Lucy and J.C. Lucy, complainants, against A.H. Zehmer and Ida S. Zehmer, his wife, defendants, to have specific performance of a contract by which it was alleged the Zehmers had sold to W.O. Lucy a tract of land owned by A.H. Zehmer in Dinwiddie county containing 471.6 acres, more or less, known as the Ferguson farm, for $50,000. J.C. Lucy, the other complainant, is a brother of W.O. Lucy, to whom W.O. Lucy transferred a half interest in his alleged purchase.

The instrument sought to be enforced was written by A.H. Zehmer on December 20, 1952, in these words: "We hereby agree to sell to W.O. Lucy the Ferguson Farm complete for $50,000.00, title satisfactory to buyer," and signed by the defendants, A.H. Zehmer and Ida S. Zehmer.

The answer of A.H. Zehmer admitted that at the time mentioned W.O. Lucy offered him $50,000 cash for the farm, but that he, Zehmer, considered that the offer was made in jest; that so thinking, and both he and Lucy having had several drinks, he wrote out "the memorandum" quoted above and induced his wife to sign it; that he did not deliver the memorandum to Lucy, but that Lucy picked it up, read it, put it in his pocket, attempted to offer Zehmer $5 to bind the bargain, which Zehmer refused to accept, and realizing for the first time that Lucy was serious, Zehmer assured him that he had no intention of selling the farm and that the whole matter was a joke. Lucy left the premises insisting that he had purchased the farm.

Depositions were taken and the decree appealed from was entered holding that the complainants had failed to establish their right to specific performance, and dismissing their bill. The assignment of error is to this action of the court.

[At the trial, Lucy testified that he was a farmer and had known Zehmer for 15 to 20 years. He stated that he knew the farm well and, seven years earlier, Zehmer had rejected his offer to purchase it for $20,000. Lucy claimed that he wanted to try again to buy the farm and said to Zehmer, "bet you won't take $50,000." Zehmer responded, "yes, but you wouldn't give it" and expressed doubt that Lucy could raise the money. Lucy then told Zehmer to write an agreement and, after 30–40 minutes of discussion and modification, all of the parties, including Mrs. Zehmer, signed. Zehmer then refused Lucy's tender of $5 to seal the bargain. Lucy conceded that there was a bottle on the table between them and that they had had a "couple of drinks." He also testified that the next day, in order to raise the $50,000, he persuaded his brother to put up half of the money. He also had the title examined. Upon stating that he was ready to proceed, Zehmer told him that there was no contract.

Zehmer's testimony was that he had purchased the farm eleven years ago for $11,000 and had refused many offers to buy it. It was just before Christmas, there was "lots of drinking," and he was "high as a Georgia pine." When Lucy approached him about selling the farm, Zehmer doubted that Lucy had $50,000. He claimed he was just "needling" and stated that after the writing was signed he told Lucy that it was just "liquor talking" and that he would not sell. Zehmer's wife testified that she would not sign the writing until told it was a joke, that both men were "tight" and that the husband told Lucy before he left that there was no sale. This latter fact was corroborated by a waitress, who witnessed the transaction.]

* * *

The defendants insist that the evidence was ample to support their contention that the writing sought to be enforced was prepared as a bluff or dare to force Lucy to admit that he did not have $50,000; that the whole matter was a joke; that the writing was not delivered to Lucy and no binding contract was ever made between the parties.

It is an unusual, if not bizarre, defense. When made to the writing admittedly prepared by one of the defendants and signed by both, clear evidence is required to sustain it.

In his testimony Zehmer claimed that he "was high as a Georgia pine," and that the transaction "was just a bunch of two doggoned drunks bluffing to see who could talk the biggest and say the most." That claim is inconsistent with his attempt to testify in great detail as to what was said and what was done. It is contradicted by other evidence as to the condition of both parties, and rendered of no weight by the testimony of his wife that when Lucy left the restaurant she suggested that Zehmer drive him home. The record is convincing that Zehmer was not intoxicated to the extent of being unable to comprehend the nature and consequences of the instrument he executed, and hence that instrument is not to be invalidated on that ground. C.J.S. Contracts § 133, b., p. 483; Taliaferro v. Emery, 124 Va. 674, 98 S.E. 627. It was in fact conceded by defendants' counsel in oral argument that under the evidence Zehmer was not too drunk to make a valid contract.

The evidence is convincing also that Zehmer wrote two agreements, the first one beginning "I hereby agree to sell." Zehmer first said he could not remember about that, then that "I don't think I wrote but one out." Mrs. Zehmer said that what he wrote was "I hereby agree," but that the "I" was changed to "We" after that night. The agreement that was written and signed is in the record and indicates no such change. Neither are the mistakes in spelling that Zehmer sought to point out readily apparent.

The appearance of the contract, the fact that it was under discussion for forty minutes or more before it was signed; Lucy's objection to the first draft because it was written in the singular, and he wanted Mrs. Zehmer to sign it also; the rewriting to meet that objection and the signing by Mrs. Zehmer; the discussion of what was to be included in the sale, the provision for the examination of the title, the completeness of the instrument that was executed, the taking possession of it by Lucy with no request or suggestion by either of the defendants that he give it back, are facts which furnish persuasive evidence that the execution of the contract was a serious business transaction rather than a casual, jesting matter as defendants now contend.

* * *

If it be assumed, contrary to what we think the evidence shows, that Zehmer was jesting about selling his farm to Lucy and that the transaction was intended by him to be a joke, nevertheless the evidence shows that Lucy did not so understand it but considered it to be a serious business transaction and the contract to be binding on the Zehmers as well as on himself. The very next day he arranged with his brother to put up half the money and take a half interest in the land. The day after that he employed an attorney to examine the title. The next night, Tuesday, he was back at Zehmer's place and there Zehmer told him for the first time, Lucy said, that he wasn't going to sell and he told Zehmer, "You know you sold that place fair and square." After receiving the report from his attorney that the title was good he wrote to Zehmer that he was ready to close the deal.

Not only did Lucy actually believe, but the evidence shows he was warranted in believing, that the contract represented a serious business transaction and a good faith sale and purchase of the farm.

In the field of contracts, as generally elsewhere, "We must look to the outward expression of a person as manifesting his intention rather than to his secret and unexpressed intention. 'The law imputes to a person an intention corresponding to the reasonable meaning of his words and acts.'" First Nat. Exchange Bank of Roanoke v. Roanoke Oil Co., 169 Va. 99, 114, 192 S.E. 764, 770.

* * *

The mental assent of the parties is not requisite for the formation of a contract. If the words or other acts of one of the parties have but one reasonable meaning, his undisclosed intention is immaterial except when an unreasonable meaning which he attaches to his manifestations is known to the other party. Restatement of the Law of Contracts, Vol. I, § 71, p. 74.

"* * * The law, therefore, judges of an agreement between two persons exclusively from those expressions of their intentions which are communicated between them. * * *." Clark on Contracts, 4 ed., § 3, p. 4.

An agreement or mutual assent is of course essential to a valid contract but the law imputes to a person an intention corresponding to the reasonable meaning of his words and acts. If his words and acts, judged by a reasonable standard, manifest an intention to agree, it is immaterial what may be the real but unexpressed state of his mind. 17 C.J.S. Contracts § 32, p. 361; 12 Am.Jur., Contracts, § 19, p. 515.

So a person cannot set up that he was merely jesting when his conduct and words would warrant a reasonable person in believing that he intended a real agreement. 17 C.J.S. Contracts § 47, p. 390; Clark on Contracts, 4 ed., § 27, at p. 54.

Whether the writing signed by the defendants and now sought to be enforced by the complainants was the result of a serious offer by Lucy and a serious acceptance by the defendants, or was a serious offer by Lucy and an acceptance in secret jest by the defendants, in either event it constituted a binding contract of sale between the parties.

* * *

The complainants are entitled to have specific performance of the contract sued on. The decree appealed from is therefore reversed and the cause is remanded for the entry of a proper decree requiring the defendants to perform the contract in accordance with the prayer of the bill.

Reversed and remanded.

NOTES

(1) *Objective Theory of Contracts.* A bargain contract is a consensual transaction, in that each party must give unqualified approval or assent to the terms of the bargain. But by what standard is this requisite assent to be determined? Must the parties be in subjective agreement; i.e., must there be an actual "meeting of minds"? Or can there be a binding contract if by their

manifestations the parties *appear* to agree; i.e., is the outward manifestation, rather than the inner intention, the decisive factor?

To be sure, in the vast majority of cases it would not matter whether a court followed the so-called subjective theory of contracts ("meeting of minds") or the objective theory (manifestation of mutual assent). In most instances our outward expression corresponds with our inner intention; we say what we mean. But this is not always true, and the courts must sometimes choose between alternative theories. Additionally, there are other problems, such as whether the revocation of an offer must be communicated to the offeree, which force this choice upon the courts.

At one time common law judges, along with their counterparts in civil law countries, strictly adhered to the subjective theory, requiring, as they were fond of saying, a "meeting of minds." For example, if A made an offer to B, allowing the offeree until later in the afternoon to accept or reject, B's assent to the proposal within that period would be ineffective if A could establish he or she was not then of a mind to contract. An offeror need not communicate a withdrawal (revocation) of the offer; one need only prove one no longer intended to contract when the other party undertook to accept. See Cook v. Oxley, 3 Term.R. 653, 100 Eng.Rep. 785 (1790). Secret, unmanifested intention could defeat what outwardly was an expression of assent. For if actual assent was the decisive factor, the outward manifestation was not controlling. It must not be supposed, however, that even under the subjective theory the outward expression is of no consequence. One would obviously have some explaining to do if it were maintained in court that when one said "I promise to pay $5,000," one actually meant to say "I promise to pay $4,000." Just as in other fields of law where the central inquiry is the ascertainment of actual intent, circumstances may be very persuasive.

There has been a notable shift in the common law decisions, especially since the turn of the century, toward a greater acceptance of the objective theory. The avowed reason has been to protect the stability of contractual relationships by enabling one to act upon reasonable appearance. There is then no assumption of the risk that what was said was different from what was meant. The break with the subjective theory was cautious at first, but eventually courts began to express themselves in this uncompromising fashion: "While ordinarily present, it is not the meeting of minds of the parties, but the expression of their mutual assent that * * * is the culmination of the contract-making process * * *. It is not the subjective thing known as meeting of the minds, but the objective thing, manifestation of mutual assent, which is essential." Field–Martin Company v. Fruen Milling Company, 210 Minn. 388, 298 N.W. 574, 575 (1941).

The following by Justice Learned Hand is recognized as a classic statement of the objective theory of contracts:

A contract has, strictly speaking, nothing to do with the personal, or individual, intent of the parties. A contract is an obligation attached by mere force of law to certain acts of the parties, usually words, which ordinarily accompany and represent a known intent. If, however, it were proved by twenty bishops that either party, when he used the words, intended something else than the usual meaning which the law imposes upon them, he would still be held, unless there were some mutual mistake or something else of the sort.

Hotchkiss v. National City Bank of New York, 200 Fed. 287, 293 (S.D.N.Y. 1911).

A contemporary judge puts it this way: "* * * Walters stoutly maintains that he subjectively intended to be bound and he wants to invite a jury to infer the same about Telstar. * * * Yet 'intent' does not invite a tour through Walters's cranium, with Walters as the guide. * * * 'The intent of the parties [to be bound] must necessarily be derived from a consideration of their words, written and oral, and their actions.' * * * Secret hopes and wishes count for nothing. The status of a document as a contract depends on what the parties express to each other and to the world, not on what they keep to themselves. * * * The objective approach is an essential ingredient to allowing the parties jointly to control the effect of their document. If unilateral or secret intentions could bind, parties would become wary, and the written word would lose some of its power. The ability to fix the consequences with certainty is especially important in commercial transactions that are planned with care in advance." Easterbrook, J., in Skycom Corporation v. Telstar Corporation, 813 F.2d 810, 814–5 (7th Cir.1987).

This is not to say that even today courts do not speak of "meeting of minds" as a requisite of contract. But when they do, it is simply a case of the music having stopped but the melody lingering on.

There is, however, as one prominent writer observed, "a 'subjective' as well as an 'objective' side" to the law of contracts, and "although the 'objective' theory has now become fashionable," it is "erroneous to regard it as a complete statement of the law." Williams, *Mistake as to Party in the Law of Contract,* 23 Can.B.Rev. 271, 380, 387 (1945). We will return to this later when specific attention is given to the effect of mistake upon contract formation. See infra, Chapter Four, Section 2(A). In addition, when dealing with a so-called "adhesion" contract, or standardized agreements characterized by fine print clauses favoring the party with superior bargaining power who drafts the writing and submits it to the other on a "take-it-or-leave-it" basis, a court may be persuaded to look beyond the manifested intent. See, e.g., Weaver v. American Oil Co., 257 Ind. 458, 276 N.E.2d 144 (1971), infra at 525, involving a gas station lease obligating the lessee (Weaver) to indemnify the lessor (American Oil Company) if anyone was injured by the lessor's negligence and holding the latter harmless for injuries to the lessee. The court spoke as follows: "The party seeking to enforce such a contract has the burden of showing that the provisions were explained to the other party and *came to his knowledge* and there was in fact *a real and voluntary meeting of the minds and not merely an objective meeting.*" (276 N.E.2d at 148) (emphasis in original).

(2) *Consequences of "Objective" Approach.* What is at stake in the choice between a "subjective" and an "objective" approach to contract? One consequence is revealed in the two cases just considered. If Mr. McKittrick did not intend to renew Mr. Embry's contract and Mr. Zehmer did not intend to sell the land to Mr. Lucy and both acted honestly, the objective test excludes as irrelevant what they actually intended. It protects the plaintiff's reasonable understanding based upon what was said and done rather than what was thought. Put another way, if the court and jury find that the plaintiff's

expectations based upon what was said or done were reasonable and the other requisites for contract formation are present, those expectations are protected. Thus, in *Embry*, Mr. Embry reasonably thought that his contract had been renewed. He remained on the job, thereby foregoing other opportunities, and was not informed about Mr. McKittrick's real intention until over two months later. But are the facts so compelling in *Lucy?* At what point was Mr. Lucy first clearly informed that Mr. Zehmer did not intend to sell? Had Mr. Lucy changed his position in any substantial way at that time? Should that make any difference? See Sharp, "Contracts" in *Mr. Justice Holmes: Some Modern Views,* 31 U.Chi.L.Rev. 268, 272–74 (1964), where it is argued that in light of the costs to individual freedom, the objective test should be employed only where the defendant has carelessly used language which induced actual and justified reliance by the plaintiff.

A broader consequence is that the "objective" test affords the courts an opportunity to control or regulate individual exchange behavior through use of that great "collectivist," the "reasonable" person. As Professor J. Willard Hurst has put it, the test satisfied a "particular need" in a market society "to create and maintain a framework of reasonably well defined and assured expectations as to the likely official and nonofficial consequences of private venture and decision." J.W. Hurst, Law and the Conditions of Freedom in Nineteenth Century America 21–22 (1956). Professor Gilmore, a bit more critical, has noted that the objective test represents a move toward absolute liability and, under the guidance of O.W. Holmes, Jr. and Williston, it became the "great metaphysical solvent—the critical test for distinguishing between the false and the true." G. Gilmore, The Death of Contract 42–43 (1974). And, finally, Professor Horwitz has suggested that the development in the nineteenth century of an objective approach based on the external manifestation of mutual assent was a pro-commercial market attack on the theory of intrinsic value which lay at the base of the eighteenth century equity idea of contract. It expressed a market ideology, downplayed justice and gave courts an opportunity to prefer certain groups and interests as more reasonable than others. Horwitz, *The Historical Foundations of Modern Contract Law,* 87 Harv.L.Rev. 917 (1974).

A final and more practical consequence concerns the problem of proof. As we shall see in the following materials, the focus is upon what was said and done rather than what was thought, and the question is what the plaintiff could reasonably understand or, in some cases, what the defendant knew or should have known that the plaintiff understood. Throughout, a question concerning the range of "objective" evidence relevant to the question of what the parties knew or should have known becomes critical. Also, who should make the critical determination of reasonableness, the court or the jury? Would you conclude, for example, that it would be sounder to limit extrinsic evidence to the words, written or spoken, of the parties and let the court decide who is reasonable or have a more expansive concept of relevance with the jury as the ultimate arbiter of reasonableness? Consider the following statement and then return to *Lucy v. Zehmer* with a more critical eye:

> Whether the parties are merely negotiating a contract or entering into a present contract is purely a question of intention. ... [I]n construing contracts, courts must look not only to the specific language employed but

also to the subject matter contracted about, the relationship of the parties, the circumstances surrounding the transaction, or in other words place themselves in the same position the parties occupied when the contract was entered into and view the terms and intent of the agreement in the same light in which the parties did when the same was formulated and accepted.

Cohen v. Johnson, 91 F.Supp. 231, 235 (M.D.Pa.1950).

Did the Virginia Supreme Court of Appeals unduly narrow the scope of relevance and improperly substitute its judgment for the trier of fact? How should a court draw the line between evidence that goes to what one party actually intended and evidence from surrounding circumstances that is relevant to what one party should have known about the other party's actual intention?

(3) *Alice in Wonderland.* The Hatter opened his eyes very wide on hearing this; but all he *said* was "Why is a raven like a writing-desk?"

"Come, we shall have some fun now!" thought Alice. "I'm glad they've begun asking riddles—I believe I can guess that," she added aloud.

"Do you mean that you think you can find out the answer to it?" said the March Hare.

"Exactly so," said Alice.

"Then you should say what you mean," the March Hare went on.

"I do," Alice hastily replied; "at least—at least I mean what I say—that's the same thing, you know."

"Not the same thing a bit!" said the Hatter. "Why, you might just as well say that 'I see what I eat' is the same thing as 'I eat what I see!' "

"You might just as well say," added the March Hare, "that 'I like what I get' is the same thing as 'I get what I like!' "

"You might just as well say," added the Dormouse, which seemed to be talking in its sleep, "that 'I breathe when I sleep' is the same thing as 'I sleep when I breathe!' "

"It *is* the same thing with you," said the Hatter, and here the conversation dropped, and the party sat silent for a minute, while Alice thought over all she could remember about ravens and writing-desks, which wasn't much.

Lewis Carroll, *Alice's Adventures in Wonderland.*

(5) *A Lawyer's Alice.* At that moment Alice's attention was distracted by the entry of a fluffy white figure. It was the White Rabbit, and a hum of conversation broke out from the gathering as he entered. He was dressed in immaculate morning dress, with a white camellia in the buttonhole, and immediately went up to where the little Lizard was sitting.

Alice suddenly realised the reason for the whole proceeding. The White Rabbit was to be married to the Lizard. That was why he had been so agitated about the time. "Of course," Alice said aloud to herself when she made this discovery.

"My dear, then I am so happy," said the Tortoise.

"Happy about what?" asked Alice.

"Happy that you will marry me," said the Tortoise.

"I will do nothing of the kind," replied Alice with dignity.

"But you just said so. I asked you to marry me and you replied 'Of course.' "

"I didn't hear you asking me to marry you, and I was talking to myself."

"Oh, Oh," cried the Tortoise, weeping bitterly. "I didn't know that. You couldn't expect me to." He sighed gustily, and looked up at Alice with a face all smeary with tears.

"Still," he added, brightening, "you have promised to marry me, you know."

"I have done nothing of the sort," said Alice.

"Yes you have," replied the Tortoise. "I thought you promised, therefore you did promise."

"How could I make you a promise," asked Alice, "when I was not speaking to you?"

"Anyway," said the Tortoise, "promise or not, I thought you were promising, and it was quite natural that I should think so. So you really ought to marry me."

Alice had never before considered marrying a Tortoise, but she had once kept one in her garden and had thought it quite a nice creature.

She did not feel at all certain what was the right thing to do in the circumstances, but the easiest thing seemed to be to do as the Tortoise wanted, and to see what would happen. Accordingly she replied, "Oh, all right," which made the Tortoise look contented.

Williams, *A Lawyer's Alice,* 9 Camb.L.J. 171, 172 (1945).

PROBLEM: THE CASE OF THE HOLE–IN–ONE

Amos Cobaugh was playing in the East End Open Golf Tournament on the Fairview Golf Course in Cornwall, Pennsylvania. When he arrived at the ninth tee he saw a new Chevrolet Beretta with signs posted reading as follows: "HOLE–IN–ONE Wins this 1988 Chevrolet Beretta GT Courtesy of KLICK–LEWIS Buick Chevy Pontiac $49 OVER FACTORY INVOICE in Palmyra." Cobaugh aced the hole and claimed the automobile as his prize. Klick–Lewis refused. It had offered the car as a prize for a charity golf tournament sponsored by the Hershey–Palmyra Sertoma Club two days earlier and had neglected to remove the car and signs. Cobaugh sues. What result? See Cobaugh v. Klick–Lewis, Inc., 385 Pa.Super. 587, 561 A.2d 1248 (1989).

Cohen v. Cowles Media Company

Supreme Court of Minnesota, 1990.
457 N.W.2d 199, *reversed,* 501 U.S. 663, 111 S.Ct. 2513, 115 L.Ed.2d 586 (1991), opinion on remand, 479 N.W.2d 387 (1992).

[The facts are stated *supra* at 176, where the Supreme Court of Minnesota, after remand from the United States Supreme Court, affirmed its earlier conclusion that the promise of confidentiality was not enforce-able on a bargain theory but, nevertheless, enforced the promise on a reliance theory.]

■ SIMONETT, JUSTICE.

* * *

I.

First of all, we agree with the court of appeals that the trial court erred in not granting defendants' post-trial motions for judgment notwithstand-ing the verdict on the misrepresentation claim.

For fraud there must be a misrepresentation of a past or present fact. A representation as to future acts does not support an action for fraud merely because the represented act did not happen, unless the promisor did not intend to perform at the time the promise was made. *Vandeputte v. Soderholm,* 298 Minn. 505, 508, 216 N.W.2d 144, 147 (1974). Cohen admits that the reporters intended to keep their promises, as, indeed, they testified and as their conduct confirmed. Moreover, the record shows that the editors had no intention to reveal Cohen's identity until later when more information was received and the matter was discussed with other editors. These facts do not support a fraud claim. For this reason and for the other reasons cited by the court of appeals, we affirm the court of appeals' ruling. Because the punitive damages award hinges on the tort claim of misrepre-sentation, it, too, must be set aside as the court of appeals ruled.

II.

A contract, it is said, consists of an offer, an acceptance, and consider-ation. Here, we seemingly have all three, plus a breach. We think, however, the matter is not this simple.

Unquestionably, the promises given in this case were intended by the promisors to be kept. The record is replete with the unanimous testimony of reporters, editors, and journalism experts that protecting a confidential source of a news story is a sacred trust, a matter of "honor," of "morality," and required by professional ethics. Only in dire circumstances might a promise of confidentiality possibly be ethically broken, and instances were cited where a reporter has gone to jail rather than reveal a source. The keeping of promises is professionally important for at least two reasons. First, to break a promise of confidentiality which has induced a source to give information is dishonorable. Secondly, if it is known that promises will not be kept, sources may dry up. The media depend on confidential sources for much of their news; significantly, at least up to now, it appears that journalistic ethics have adequately protected confidential sources.

The question before us, however, is not whether keeping a confidential promise is ethically required but whether it is legally enforceable; whether, in other words, the law should superimpose a legal obligation on a moral and ethical obligation. The two obligations are not always coextensive.

The newspapers argue that the reporter's promise should not be contractually binding because these promises are usually given clandestinely and orally, hence they are often vague, subject to misunderstanding, and a fertile breeding ground for lawsuits. See Ruzicka v. Conde Nast Publications, Inc., 733 F.Supp. 1289, 1300–01 (D.Minn.1990) (a promise not to make a source identifiable found too vague to be enforceable). Perhaps so, and this may be a factor to weigh in the balance; but this objection goes only to problems of proof, rather than to the merits of having such a cause of action at all. Moreover, in this case at least, we have a clear-cut promise.

The law, however, does not create a contract where the parties intended none. Linne v. Ronkainen, 228 Minn. 316, 320, 37 N.W.2d 237, 239 (1949). Nor does the law consider binding every exchange of promises. See, e.g., Minn.Stat. ch. 553 (1988) (abolishing breaches of contract to marry); see also Restatement (Second) of Contracts §§ 189–91 (1981) (promises impairing family relations are unenforceable). We are not persuaded that in the special milieu of media newsgathering a source and a reporter ordinarily believe they are engaged in making a legally binding contract. They are not thinking in terms of offers and acceptances in any commercial or business sense. * * *

In other words, contract law seems here an ill fit for a promise of news source confidentiality. To impose a contract theory on this arrangement puts an unwarranted legal rigidity on a special ethical relationship, precluding necessary consideration of factors underlying that ethical relationship. We conclude that a contract cause of action is inappropriate for these particular circumstances. * * *

[The dissents of Justices Yetka and Kelly are omitted.]

NOTES

(1) The court recognizes that there was, seemingly, an offer, an acceptance, and consideration. Why, then, was there not a contract?

(2) *Intention to Be Bound as a Requisite of Contractual Obligation.* Refusing to superimpose "a legal obligation on a moral and ethical obligation," the court insists that the law "does not create a contract where the parties intended none." Based upon your studies to this point, do you agree? Is it necessary that there be an intent to assume a legal obligation (subjective) or a manifestation of intent to assume such an obligation (objective)? See Restatement (Second) § 21: "Neither the real nor apparent intention that a promise be legally binding is essential to the formation of a contract...." In the typical contract, it may be wondered whether the parties ever consciously consider the legal consequences of their agreement. The question evidently did not come up during the negotiations here. If they had thought about the matter, do you believe the parties would have considered their agreement to be legally binding? See generally, Murray § 31. For an elaboration of a general theory of contract which relies heavily upon determining whether there is "a manifestation of intention to be legally bound," see Barnett, *A Consent Theory of Contract*, 86 Colum.L.Rev. 269 (1986). See also Barnett, *Contract Remedies and*

Inalienable Rights, 4 Soc.Phil. & Pol. 179, 184 (1986) (''A consent theory of contract specifies that an enforceable contract requires the satisfaction of at least two conditions. First, the *subject* of the contract must be a morally cognizable right possessed by the transferor that is interpersonally transferable, or 'alienable.' Second, the holder of the right must *consent* to its transfer. Thus, commitments will generally be enforced only if they manifest to the promisee the promisor's assent to transfer rights.'').

(3) *Manifested Intention Not to Be Bound.* The objective theory, by considering the impression on the hearer rather than the intent of the speaker, obviously makes it possible for one to be held to a contract without any real intention to assume a legal obligation. For no protest of intention differing from the outward manifestation is recognized. Should the converse be true as well? That is, if the outward expression clearly negates contractual intent, should that manifestation be controlling? In Rose and Frank Company v. J.R. Crompton and Brothers, Ltd., a 1923 decision of the English Court of Appeal ([1923] 2 K.B. 261), there was an elaborate document executed by the parties pertaining to the sale of paper by British companies to an American corporation, appointing the latter exclusive selling agent in the United States for a three-year period. One clause of the document read as follows:

> This agreement is not entered into, nor is this memorandum written, as a formal or legal agreement, and shall not be subject to legal jurisdiction in the Law Courts either of the United States or England, but it is only a definite expression and record of the purpose and intention of the three parties concerned to which they each honourably pledge themselves with the fullest confidence, based on past business with each other, that it will be carried through by each of the three parties with mutual loyalty and friendly cooperation.

The court refused to recognize the document as evidencing a contract. In his opinion, Lord Justice Scrutton observed:

> Now it is quite possible for parties to come to an agreement by accepting a proposal with the result that the agreement concluded does not give rise to legal relations. The reason for this is that the parties do not intend that their agreement shall give rise to legal relations. This intention may be implied from the subject matter of the agreement, but it may also be expressed by the parties. In social and family relations such an intention is readily implied, while in business matters the opposite result would ordinarily follow. But I see no reason why, even in business matters, the parties should not intend to rely on each other's good faith and honour, and to exclude all idea of settling disputes by any outside intervention, with the accompanying necessity of expressing themselves so precisely that outsiders may have no difficulty in understanding what they mean. If they clearly express such an intention I can see no reason in public policy why effect should not be given to their intention.

For other cases in accord, see Kind v. Clark, 161 F.2d 36, 46 (2d Cir.1947); I.H. Rubenstein & Son, Inc. v. Sperry & Hutchinson Co., 222 So.2d 329 (La.App. 1969); Smith v. MacDonald, 37 Cal.App. 503, 174 P. 80 (1918). See also Pappas v. Hauser, 197 N.W.2d 607 (Iowa 1972) (explicit agreement that charitable pledge was not intended to be binding).

(4) *Social Engagements*. Ordinarily, social engagements are not thought to be legally binding, and cases of this type rarely reach the courts. That there are exceptions is attested by the following *New York Times* article of May 23, 1973, dateline San Francisco:

It had to happen in this litigious nation. A San Francisco woman has been sued in Small Claims Court here by a San Jose area man for breaking a date.

Tom Horsley of Campbell is asking Alyn Chesselet for $38 as a matter of principle, because she broke an "oral contract" to have dinner and see a show with him early this year.

Miss Chesselet said Mr. Horsley is "nuts" to think she will pay.

Mr. Horsley wants to be paid for two hours spent driving to and from San Francisco at his minimum rate as a certified public accountant of $8.50 an hour and 17 cents a mile in auto expenses for the 100–mile distance. His claim is for $34 plus $2 filing fee and $2 to serve court papers.

"She had 10 days to call me and cancel the date," Mr. Horsley said in a telephone interview. "And she promised to pay."

Miss Chesselet said that she had had to cancel her date with Mr. Horsley at the last moment because of a sudden change in her work schedule as a waitress and that she had made every attempt to let him know. "So I told him I'd pay his expenses or to sue me, but I was just kidding," she said.

The case is tentatively scheduled to be heard in July. In the words of his lawyer in one letter, Mr. Horsley is "not the type of man to take standing up lying down."

Judge Wapner, call your answering service!

Were Tom to press the matter in court, how might Alyn respond? She might argue that although there was some sort of bargain, the context suggests to a reasonable person that she did not intend to assume legal obligations. The social setting is as effective to convey this intention as the explicit "not legally binding" clause in a commercial agreement. See *Rose and Frank Company v. J.R. Compton & Brothers, Ltd.*, supra note 3. As Professor Corbin put it: "If the subject matter and terms are not such as customarily have affected legal relations, the transaction is not legally operative unless the expressions of the party indicate an intention to make it so." Corbin § 34. The following statement of the late Professor Grismore is apposite:

The fact is that, in most cases, when people make offers and acceptances they give no thought whatever to the question as to whether the undertakings shall be legally obligatory. When agreements are made it is normally assumed that they will be performed without regard to the law. The thought of legal sanction does not enter in, since serious agreements are made to be performed not to be broken. Of course, we might say the intent to contract will be presumed in the absence of affirmative evidence of a contrary intent, on the assumption that if the parties had thought about the matter at all they would have intended that their agreement should be legally obligatory. However, if we do say this we are in reality saying that no such intent is essential. Unless we take some such view as this, it would be almost impossible to find the existence of contract in most cases; since, as has already been indicated, when parties make agreements they seldom address their minds to the question of legal obligation, and seldom have any intent in regard to it. It is believed that the views here set forth are in accord with what is actually decided by the courts. The cases which have been thought to go counter to this view are those involving social engagements and family agreements. Thus, it said that, if A invites B to dinner and B accepts, no binding obligations exist. This is probably true. But it is true, not because an intent to have a contract is essential to contractual obligation, and no such intent can be shown here; but because in such a case it is fair to say that had the parties thought about the matter at all, it is quite clear they would have regarded such an engagement as binding only in honor.

Grismore, Contracts § 19 (1st ed. 1947).

Alyn might further maintain that even if the circumstances remove the usual assumptions about social agreements, there are strong policy arguments against enforcement. First, it would be wrong for the court to regulate these transactions through the imposition of liability. These agreements are on the periphery of the market where "talk is cheap," mobility is important and certain non-legal sanctions, such as social stigma, are more effective than contract remedies. Second, unless the parties have clearly indicated the importance to them of a non-economic transaction, the cost to society of enforcing these promises far outweighs any conceivable benefits. Third, the losses to Tom are insignificant. Alyn has not been unjustly enriched, and Tom's reliance has not produced any substantial losses. Intervention here would create a dangerous precedent.

(5) *Noncommercial Bargains and Public Policy.* Even if there is a clear expression of intention by the parties to be legally bound, the court may refuse to enforce the agreement on grounds of public policy. The court alluded to this in *Sullivan v. O'Connor,* supra at 32, in connection with a physician's promise to effect a cure. Clearly, considerations of public policy influenced the court majority in the instant case. There is today an increasing use of contracts to establish the terms of personal relationships (e.g., cohabitation agreements), and courts are called upon to judge their validity. See generally, Amy H. Kastely, *Cogs or Cyborgs?: Blasphemy and Irony in Contract Theories,* 90 Nw.U.L.Rev. 132 (1995); Temple, *Freedom of Contract and Intimate Relationships,* 8 Harv.J.Law & Pub.Pol. 121 (1985). We examine these issues in Chapter Four, Section 3.

(B) OFFER: CREATION OF POWER OF ACCEPTANCE

Lonergan v. Scolnick

Court of Appeals of California, 1954.
129 Cal.App.2d 179, 276 P.2d 8.

■ BARNARD, PRESIDING JUSTICE. This is an action for specific performance or for damages in the event specific performance was impossible.

The complaint alleged that on April 15, 1952, the parties entered into a contract whereby the defendant agreed to sell, and plaintiff agreed to buy a 40–acre tract of land for $2,500; that this was a fair, just and reasonable value of the property; that on April 28, 1952, the defendant repudiated the contract and refused to deliver a deed; that on April 28, 1952, the property was worth $6,081; and that plaintiff has been damaged in the amount of $3,581. The answer denied that any contract had been entered into, or that anything was due to the plaintiff.

By stipulation, the issue of whether or not a contract was entered into between the parties was first tried, reserving the other issues for a further trial if that became necessary. The issue as to the existence of a contract was submitted upon an agreed statement, including certain letters between the parties, without the introduction of other evidence.

The stipulated facts are as follows: During March, 1952, the defendant placed an ad in a Los Angeles paper reading, so far as material here, "Joshua Tree vic. 40 acres, * * * need cash, will sacrifice." In response to an inquiry resulting from this ad the defendant, who lived in New York, wrote a letter to the plaintiff dated March 26, briefly describing the property, giving directions as to how to get there, stating that his rock-bottom price was $2,500 cash, and further stating that "This is a form letter." On April 7, the plaintiff wrote a letter to the defendant saying that he was not sure he had found the property, asking for its legal description, asking whether the land was all level or whether it included certain jutting rock hills, and suggesting a certain bank as escrow agent "should I desire to purchase the land." On April 8, the defendant wrote to the plaintiff saying "From your description you have found the property"; that this bank "is O.K. for escrow agent"; that the land was fairly level; giving the legal description; and then saying, "If you are really interested, you will have to decide fast, as I expect to have a buyer in the next week or so." On April 12, the defendant sold the property to a third party for $2,500. The plaintiff received defendant's letter of April 8, on April 14. On April 15 he wrote to the defendant thanking him for his letter "confirming that I was on the right land", stating that he would immediately proceed to have the escrow opened and would deposit $2,500 therein "in conformity with your offer", and asking the defendant to forward a deed with his instructions to the escrow agent. On April 17, 1952, the plaintiff started an escrow and placed in the hands of the escrow agent $100, agreeing to furnish an additional $2,400 at an unspecified time, with the provision that if the escrow was not closed by May 15, 1952, it should be completed as soon thereafter as possible unless a written demand for a return of the money or instruments was made by either party after that date. It was further stipulated that the plaintiff was ready and willing at all times to deposit the $2,400.

The matter was submitted on June 11, 1953. On July 10, 1953, the judge filed a memorandum opinion stating that it was his opinion that the letter of April 8, 1952, when considered with the previous correspondence, constituted an offer of sale which offer was, however, qualified and conditioned upon prompt acceptance by the plaintiff; that in spite of the condition thus imposed, the plaintiff delayed more than a week before notifying the defendant of his acceptance; and that since the plaintiff was aware of the necessity of promptly communicating his acceptance to the defendant his delay was not the prompt action required by the terms of the offer. Findings of fact were filed on October 2, 1953, finding that each and all of the statements in the agreed statement are true, and that all allegations to the contrary in the complaint are untrue. As conclusions of law, it was found that the plaintiff and defendant did not enter into a contract as alleged in the complaint or otherwise, and that the defendant is entitled to judgment against the plaintiff. Judgment was entered accordingly, from which the plaintiff has appealed.

The appellant contends that the judgment is contrary to the evidence and to the law since the facts, as found, do not support the conclusions of law upon which the judgment is based. It is argued that there is no conflict in the evidence, and this court is not bound by the trial court's construction of the written instruments involved; that the evidence conclusively shows that an offer was made to the plaintiff by the defendant, which offer was accepted by the mailing of plaintiff's letter of April 15; that upon receipt of defendant's letter of April 8th plaintiff had a reasonable time within which to accept the offer that had been made; that by his letter of April 15 and his starting of an escrow the plaintiff accepted said offer; and that the agreed statement of facts establishes that a valid contract was entered into between the parties. In his briefs the appellant assumes that an offer was made by the defendant, and confined his argument to contending that the evidence shows that he accepted that offer within a reasonable time.

There can be no contract unless the minds of the parties have met and mutually agreed upon some specific thing. This is usually evidenced by one party making an offer which is accepted by the other party. Section 25 of the Restatement of the Law on Contracts reads:

"If from a promise, or manifestation of intention, or from the circumstances existing at the time, the person to whom the promise or manifestation is addressed knows or has reason to know that the person making it does not intend it as an expression of his fixed purpose until he has given a further expression of assent, he has not made an offer."

The language used in Niles v. Hancock, 140 Cal. 157, 73 P. 840, 842, "It is also clear from the correspondence that it was the intention of the defendant that the negotiations between him and the plaintiff were to be purely preliminary," is applicable here. The correspondence here indicates an intention on the part of the defendant to find out whether the plaintiff was interested, rather than an intention to make a definite offer to the plaintiff. The language used by the defendant in his letters of March 26 and April 8 rather clearly discloses that they were not intended as an expression of fixed purpose to make a definite offer, and was sufficient to advise the plaintiff that some further expression of assent on the part of the defendant was necessary.

The advertisement in the paper was a mere request for an offer. The letter of March 26 contains no definite offer, and clearly states that it is a form letter. It merely gives further particulars, in clarification of the advertisement, and tells the plaintiff how to locate the property if he was interested in looking into the matter. The letter of April 8 added nothing in the way of a definite offer. It merely answered some questions asked by the plaintiff, and stated that if the plaintiff was really interested he would have to act fast. The statement that he expected to have a buyer in the next week or so indicated that the defendant intended to sell to the first-comer, and was reserving the right to do so. From this statement, alone, the plaintiff knew or should have known that he was not being given time in which to accept an offer that was being made, but that some further assent on the part of the defendant was required. Under the language used the plaintiff was not being given a right to act within a reasonable time after receiving the letter; he was plainly told that the defendant intended to sell to another, if possible, and warned that he would have to act fast if he was interested in buying the land.

Regardless of any opinion previously expressed, the court found that no contract had been entered into between these parties, and we are in accord with the court's conclusion on that controlling issue. The court's construction of the letters involved was a reasonable one, and we think the most reasonable one, even if it be assumed that another construction was possible.

The judgment is affirmed.

NOTES

(1) How does the analysis of the appellate court differ from that of the trial court?

(2) Would the result likely have been different if the March 26th letter had not contained the sentence "This is a form letter"? Or, if the concluding sentence of the April 8th letter ("If you are really interested . . .") had been omitted?*

* A tradition of legal education is the use of the hypothetical question or problem. The following is a description of practice in the Inns of Court: "Students were given topics in advance on which to prepare a pleading: two men, sometimes one of them younger, one further along, were set to argue an issue, and their arguments were then criticized by older men, by Readers and Benchers, perhaps a Serjeant-at-law, or by a great Judge who happened to be in residence. In other moots men had to plead ex tempore; in others, the student was required to recite the pleadings from memory; in still others the pleadings were given in law French, which the student had to turn at once into English. Putting a case was a less formal procedure. As men were at dinner or supper one of the older men might put a case and draw out all those at the table as to what action should be taken and what pleadings used. Young men walking about the quadrangles were encouraged to put cases to one another, and those who were skillful became known as put-case men. Law, said Serjeant Maynard, was a babblative art; men should study all morning and talk all afternoon. A plan for a new building in one of the Inns was opposed because it would cut down the walking space and so interfere with the put-case men." Notestein, The English

(3) Section 25 of the First Restatement, quoted in *Lonergan,* formulates what may be called the "fixed purpose" test. Is the focus upon the intention of the one who makes the manifestation, or is it upon the reasonable impression created in the mind of the other? The corresponding provision of Restatement (Second) § 26 reads as follows: "A manifestation of willingness to enter into a bargain is not an offer if the person to whom it is addressed knows or has reason to know that the person making it does not intend to conclude a bargain until he has made a further manifestation of assent." More affirmatively, Section 24 of the Restatement defines an offer as "the manifestation of willingness to enter into a bargain, so made as to justify another person in understanding that his assent to that bargain is invited and will conclude it."

(4) An offer has an immediate and significant legal effect. It enables or empowers the offeree to accept and thereby place the parties in a contractual relationship. Thus, an offer is said to confer upon the offeree a "power of acceptance." See Corbin § 11. Cases and other materials in this section consider the existence and attributes of this power; that is, how it is created (Subsection B), how it is exercised (Subsection C), how it is terminated (Subsection D), and how it may be made indestructible (Subsection E).

Lefkowitz v. Great Minneapolis Surplus Store

Supreme Court of Minnesota, 1957.
251 Minn. 188, 86 N.W.2d 689.

■ MURPHY, JUSTICE. This is an appeal from an order of the Municipal Court of Minneapolis denying the motion of the defendant for amended findings of fact, or, in the alternative, for a new trial. The order for judgment awarded the plaintiff the sum of $138.50 as damages for breach of contract.

This case grows out of the alleged refusal of the defendant to sell to the plaintiff a certain fur piece which it had offered for sale in a newspaper advertisement. It appears from the record that on April 6, 1956, the defendant published the following advertisement in a Minneapolis newspaper:

"Saturday 9 A.M. Sharp
3 Brand New
Fur
Coats
Worth to $100.00
First Come
First Served
$1 Each"

On April 13, the defendant again published an advertisement in the same newspaper as follows:

"Saturday 9 A.M.
2 Brand New Pastel

People on the Eve of Colonization 88–89 (1954).

> Mink 3–Skin Scarfs
> Selling for $89.50
> Out they go
> Saturday. Each ... $1.00
> 1 Black Lapin Stole
> Beautiful,
> worth $139.50 ... $1.00
> First Come
> First Served"

The record supports the findings of the court that on each of the Saturdays following the publication of the above-described ads the plaintiff was the first to present himself at the appropriate counter in the defendant's store and on each occasion demanded the coat and the stole so advertised and indicated his readiness to pay the sale price of $1. On both occasions, the defendant refused to sell the merchandise to the plaintiff, stating on the first occasion that by a "house rule" the offer was intended for women only and sales would not be made to men, and on the second visit that plaintiff knew defendant's house rules.

The trial court properly disallowed plaintiff's claim for the value of the fur coats since the value of these articles was speculative and uncertain. The only evidence of value was the advertisement itself to the effect that the coats were "Worth to $100.00," how much less being speculative especially in view of the price for which they were offered for sale. With reference to the offer of the defendant on April 13, 1956, to sell the "1 Black Lapin Stole * * * worth $139.50 * * *" the trial court held that the value of this article was established and granted judgment in favor of the plaintiff for that amount less the $1 quoted purchase price.

1.   The defendant contends that a newspaper advertisement offering items of merchandise for sale at a named price is a "unilateral offer" which may be withdrawn without notice. He relies upon authorities which hold that, where an advertiser publishes in a newspaper that he has a certain quantity or quality of goods which he wants to dispose of at certain prices and on certain terms, such advertisements are not offers which become contracts as soon as any person to whose notice they may come signifies his acceptance by notifying the other that he will take a certain quantity of them. Such advertisements have been construed as an invitation for an offer of sale on the terms stated, which offer, when received, may be accepted or rejected and which therefore does not become a contract of sale until accepted by the seller; and until a contract has been so made, the seller may modify or revoke such prices or terms. ... Craft v. Elder & Johnston Co., 38 N.E.2d 416, 34 Ohio L.A. 603; Annotation, 157 A.L.R. 746.

The defendant relies principally on Craft v. Elder & Johnston Co. supra. In that case, the court discussed the legal effect of an advertisement offering for sale, as a one-day special, an electric sewing machine at a named price. The view was expressed that the advertisement was (38 N.E.2d 417, 34 Ohio L.A. 605) "not an offer made to any specific person but was made to the public generally. Thereby it would be properly designated as a unilateral offer and not being supported by any consideration could be withdrawn at will and without notice." It is true that such an offer may be withdrawn before acceptance. Since all offers are by their nature unilateral because they are necessarily made by one party or on one side in the negotiation of a contract, the distinction made in that decision between a unilateral offer and a unilateral contract is not clear. On the facts before us we are concerned with whether the advertisement constituted an offer, and, if so, whether the plaintiff's conduct constituted an acceptance.

There are numerous authorities which hold that a particular advertisement in a newspaper or circular letter relating to a sale of articles may be construed by the court as constituting an offer, acceptance of which would complete a contract. . . .

The test of whether a binding obligation may originate in advertisements addressed to the general public is "whether the facts show that some performance was promised in positive terms in return for something requested." 1 Williston Contracts (Rev. ed.) § 27.

The authorities above cited emphasize that, where the offer is clear, definite, and explicit, and leaves nothing open for negotiation, it constitutes an offer, acceptance of which will complete the contract. The most recent case on the subject is Johnson v. Capital City Ford Co., La.App., 85 So.2d 75, in which the court pointed out that a newspaper advertisement relating to the purchase and sale of automobiles may constitute an offer, acceptance of which will consummate a contract and create an obligation in the offeror to perform according to the terms of the published offer.

Whether in any individual instance a newspaper advertisement is an offer rather than an invitation to make an offer depends on the legal intention of the parties and the surrounding circumstances. Annotation, 157 A.L.R. 744, 751; 77 C.J.S. Sales § 25b; 17 C.J.S. Contracts § 389. We are of the view on the facts before us that the offer by the defendant of the sale of the Lapin fur was clear, definite, and explicit, and left nothing open for negotiation. The plaintiff having successfully managed to be the first one to appear at the seller's place of business to be served, as requested by the advertisement, and having offered the stated purchase price of the article, he was entitled to performance on the part of the defendant. We think the trial court was correct in holding that there was in the conduct of the parties a sufficient mutuality of obligation to constitute a contract of sale.

2.   The defendant contends that the offer was modified by a "house rule" to the effect that only women were qualified to receive the bargains advertised. The advertisement contained no such restriction. This objection may be disposed of briefly by stating that, while an advertiser has the right at any time before acceptance to modify his offer, he does not have the right, after acceptance, to impose new or arbitrary conditions not contained in the published offer. . . .

Affirmed.

NOTES

(1) *Advertisement: Making an Offer or Inviting an Offer?* Does the ordinary advertisement indicate a "fixed purpose" by the advertiser to be bound without a further expression of assent? In the view of most courts, the answer is no unless there are exceptional circumstances and the words are "plain and clear." Thus, in O'Keefe v. Lee Calan Imports, Inc., 128 Ill.App.2d 410, 262 N.E.2d 758, 43 A.L.R.3d 1097 (1970), the court held that the presumption against an offer was not overcome where a dealer's newspaper ad to sell a used car contained an error in the price (the intended price was $1,795; the advertised price was $1,095), the error was not the fault of the dealer, and there was "no reference to several material matters relating to the purchase of an automobile, such as equipment to be furnished or warranties to be offered by defendant. Indeed the terms were so incomplete and so indefinite that they could not be regarded as a valid offer." But see Chang v. First Colonial Savings Bank, 242 Va. 388, 410 S.E.2d 928 (1991)(bank's advertisement regarding interest account was an offer). Did the advertisement in *Lefkowitz* overcome these objections?

(2) Did the fact that the plaintiff had been told of the "house" rule have any bearing on the outcome of *Lefkowitz?* Should it have? Did the court regard the advertisement as legally objectionable? In the *O'Keefe* case, supra note 1, *Lefkowitz* was distinguished on the ground that the defendant "deliberately used misleading advertising." States have statutes, modeled generally upon Section 5 of the Federal Trade Commission Act, prohibiting "unfair" and "deceptive" trade practices or acts. A few outlaw false advertising in general terms, while others specify types of prohibited advertising in a "laundry list" of per se violations. See, generally, J. Sheldon, Unfair and Deceptive Acts and Practices (3d ed.1991, Supp.).

(3) *Bait and Switch.* If, in *Lefkowitz,* the advertisement was not used as a bona fide device to make or solicit offers but, rather, as a means of obtaining leads, we have an illustration of so-called "bait advertising." This practice can also be evidenced by a seller's refusal to show the advertised product, a demonstration of a defective product, a failure to have available for sale a sufficient quantity of the advertised product to meet reasonably anticipated demands, or a sales or compensation plan which has the effect of discouraging sales personnel from selling the advertised product. The Federal Trade Commission's Guides Against Bait Advertising, 16 C.F.R. § 238, define the practice as follows: "Bait advertising is an alluring but insincere offer to sell a product or service which the advertiser in truth does not intend or want to sell. Its purpose is to switch consumers from buying the advertised merchandise, in order to sell something else, usually at a higher price or on a basis more advantageous to the advertiser. The primary aim of a bait advertisement is to obtain leads as to persons interested in buying merchandise of the type so advertised." Neither the law of contracts nor ordinary judicial remedies have been of great help to the unwary consumer who is persuaded to make the switch. Some state legislatures have declared bait advertising to be a misdemeanor, subjecting the violator to criminal sanctions. Others have defined the practice as within their consumer protection statutes and thus made relief available to private parties harmed by the proscribed activity. The Federal

Trade Commission, however, has been responsible for most of the litigation and activity in this area. It issues cease and desist orders and frequently seeks injunctive relief. See J. Sheldon, Unfair and Deceptive Acts and Practices § 4.6.1 (3d ed.1991, Supp.); Annot., *Validity, Construction, and Effect of State Legislation Regulating or Controlling "Bait-and-Switch" or Disparagement Advertising or Sales Practices*, 50 A.L.R.3d 1008 (1973).

PROBLEM: THE CASE OF THE MINIMUM TRADE–IN ALLOWANCE

Gus Machado Ford placed the following advertisement in the *Miami Herald:*

Ahmad Izadi read the ad and thereafter sought to purchase a 1988 Ford Ranger Pick–Up by tendering $3,595 in cash and an unspecified trade-in. Machado refused, insisting that the minimum trade-in allowance, as indicated by the small print, applied only toward the purchase of "any New '88 Eddie Bauer Aerostar or Turbo T–Bird in stock."

Action at Restatement (secret) violation of Florida's Deceptive Trade Practice law

What legal recourse, if any, does Izadi have? See Izadi v. Machado Ford, Inc., 550 So.2d 1135 (Fla.App.1989).

PROBLEM: THE CASE OF THE STATUE OF LIBERTY COMMEMORATIVE COINS

In 1985, Congress authorized the sale of a limited number of specially-minted commemorative coins "to restore and renovate the Statue of Liberty and the facilities used for immigration at Ellis Island." Pursuant to this authorization, the U.S. Mint mailed certain advertising materials to previous customers/coin collectors. The materials, which included an order form, represented that if the Mint received "your reservation by December 31, 1985, you will enjoy a favorable Pre–Issue Discount saving you up to 16% on your coins." Payment could be made either by check, money order, or credit card.

Demand for the five-dollar gold coins far exceeded the 500,000 supply. News of the sell-out caused keen disappointment to would-be purchasers, especially in view of the fact that the gold coins had increased in value by approximately 200% within the first few months of 1986.

Mary and Anthony Mesaros were among the many disappointed parties. They had forwarded an order to the Mint on November 26, 1985, but the order was not filled, ostensibly because of an inability to process their credit card but really because of the deluge of orders. Mr. and Mrs. Mesaros filed a class action lawsuit against the government. Based on *Lefkowitz*, what are the prospects of recovery? See Mesaros v. United States, 845 F.2d 1576 (Fed.Cir.1988).

Comment: When Is a Public Solicitation From a Commercial Party an Offer?

In cases where a seller advertises or solicits bids from the public, the questions is not what is offered for sale but at what price and to whom. Since the seller is trying to obtain the best price, the usual assumption is that the seller is soliciting offers which may be accepted or rejected. Under what circumstances will that assumption be reversed?

The Courteen Seed Case. On September 21, 1927, Defendant, a grain dealer in Oregon, mailed a sample of clover seed to numerous parties, including Plaintiff, a grain wholesaler in Wisconsin. The following language appeared on the face of the envelope containing the seed: "Red clover. 50,000 lbs. like sample. I am asking 24 cents per, f.o.b. Amity, Oregon." Plaintiff acknowledged receipt of the sample and advised Defendant that it had accumulated quite a stock of clover seed and preferred to wait a while before "operating further."

After rains created unfavorable hulling conditions, Defendant, on October 4, contacted Plaintiff again and Plaintiff responded: "Special delivery sample received. Your price is too high. Wire firm offer, naming absolutely lowest f.o.b." On October 8, Defendant telegraphed Plaintiff as follows: "I am asking 23 cents per pound for the car of red clover seed from which your sample was taken. No. 1 seed, practically no plantain whatever. Have an offer 22¾ per pound, f.o.b. Amity." Plaintiff promptly telegraphed "We accept your offer" and gave shipment instructions. Plaintiff also resold the clover seed at a profit. Defendant, however, sold the carload to another buyer and refused to deliver.

Plaintiff sued Defendant for damages. The court held that Defendant had made no offer and entered a nonsuit. In essence, the court concluded that from the language "am asking" in the telegram of October 8 Defendant should have known that Plaintiff was still soliciting offers to buy rather than making an offer to sell. Even though all other material terms were stated, the implication was that Defendant must say "I will sell to you" before any offer to sell was made. Courteen Seed Co. v. Abraham, 129 Or. 427, 275 P. 684 (1929).

The decision is somewhat rigid. From a more contemporary perspective, the issue was whether the buyer, on October 8, 1927, was justified in believing that the seller had manifested willingness to sell the car of clover to him for 23 cents per pound and that his assent to the proposed bargain was invited and when given would conclude the deal. The conclusion of the court that no offer was made rests upon the assumption that the meaning to a reasonable buyer of the words "am asking" did not change from the first communication on September 21 to the last telegram on October 8.

Perhaps the conclusion is not that pat. The reasonable interpretation of the same language by the buyer and the seller's knowledge of what the buyer's understanding will be may change as the negotiations proceed. Thus, while many cases hold that a quotation of prices standing alone is not an offer, it seems clear that the context may indicate a contrary intention. In Fairmount Glass Works v. Grunden–Martin Woodenware Co., 106 Ky. 659, 51 S.W. 196, 197–98 (1899), the appellee-buyer asked the appellant-seller to "advise us the lowest price you can make" on certain goods. The latter obliged with a price quotation which was stated to be "for immediate acceptance." The court held this to be an offer and gave the following reasons:

[E]ach case must turn largely upon the language used. In this case we think there was more than a quotation of prices, although appellant's letter uses the word "quote" in stating the prices given. The true meaning of the correspondence must be determined by reading it as a whole. Appellee's letter ... which began the transaction, did not ask for a quotation of prices. It reads: "Please advise us the lowest price you can make us on our order for ten carloads of Mason green jars. ... State terms and cash discount." From this appellant could not fail to understand that appellee wanted to know at what price it would sell ten car loads of these jars; so when, in answer, it wrote: "We quote you Mason fruit jars ... pints $4.50, quarts $5.00, half gallons $6.50, per gross, ..."—it must be deemed as intending to give appellee the information it asked for. We can hardly understand what is meant by the words "for immediate acceptance," unless the latter was intended as a proposition to sell at these prices if accepted immediately. In construing every contract, the aim of the court is to arrive at the intention of the parties. ... The expression in appellant's letter, "for immediate acceptance," taken in connection with appellee's letter, in effect, at what price it would sell it the goods, is, it seems to us, much stronger evidence of a present offer, which, when accepted immediately, closed the contract. Appellee's letter was plainly an inquiry for the price and terms on which appellant would sell it the goods, and appellant's answer to it was not a quotation of prices, but a definite offer to sell on the terms indicated, and could not be withdrawn after the terms had been accepted.

Professor Malcolm P. Sharp has commented on a similar case in his classic article on "Promissory Liability."

> It is the offer which may start the trouble. * * * After negotiations in which the word "quote" appears, together with a price list for flour and bran "subject to change without notice" and a boast that the prospective seller will "meet all competition in prices," the buyer inquires about a price for bran. He names a price at which he can buy at his place of business, and adds "If you will sell us at the same price wire us this A.M. as we have an order to fill." The same day the seller replies by letter, "cannot sell bran for less than" a named price. There is no reference to quantity. The next day, on receipt of the letter, the buyer wires ordering fifty tons, a not unreasonable quantity. It has been held that there is an offer, which has been accepted, and so a contract. [College Mill Co. v. Fidler, 58 S.W. 382 (Tenn.App.1899).] * * *
>
> What is it that a sensible business man is looking for in such a series of communications? We say an offer, as distinguished from a mere statement of intention or invitation to deal, and we find that when we examine the matter further, we begin to talk naturally about promises. The offer which may be significant in these situations is also a promise.
>
> What then is a promise? * * * As a matter of everyday experience and common usage, a promise has something reliable about it. In the bran case, in spite of the ambiguity of the words used and vagueness about the terms, a striking circumstance is that the buyer has told the seller that he has an order to fill. He has almost, if not quite, said he is going to count on the reply to his inquiry. The reply must be read in relation to the inquiry. The seller seems to be saying you can rely on this proposal, first in your thinking and then in the conduct of your affairs. * * *
>
> It may be suggested that a promise is the maker's statement about his future conduct so made that the maker should expect the person to whom it is made mentally to rely on it as dependable. [Compare Section 2(1) of the Restatement, Second of Contracts. Ed.]

Sharp, *Promissory Liability,* 7 U.Chi.L.Rev. 1, 3–4 (1939). In light of this, *Courteen* was, arguably, wrongly decided.

Interpretation Against the Party Soliciting Offers. Another approach to the same result, i.e., a reversal of *Courteen Seed Co.,* may be found in Jenkins Towel Service, Inc. v. Fidelity–Philadelphia Trust Co., 400 Pa. 98,

161 A.2d 334 (1960). Because of an acute cash shortage, the defendant trustees decided to sell certain real estate which was part of the trust. After an initial offering at a public auction was withdrawn because of low bids, the trustees negotiated with several parties, including the plaintiff, without success for the next three years. At the end of this period, Defendant offered to sell the property to Plaintiff for $85,000, but Plaintiff's counter-offer of $82,500 was declined. Defendant then decided to cease negotiations and to sell the property to the party who submitted the highest acceptable cash bid in excess of $92,000. A letter was mailed to Plaintiff and others, which read as follows:

"June 18, 1959

"Jenkins Towel Service, Inc.

"Attention: Mr. James E. Mitchell Vice President

"Dear Mr. Mitchell:

"We wish to acknowledge your letter of recent date submitting an offer for the purchase of the group of properties situate and known as '241–47 North 11th Street, 1030–32 Vine Street, and 1018–22 Vine Street', Philadelphia, Pa.

"As you already know, several offers have been submitted for the purchase of these properties which offers are approximately of the same amount and on the same terms and conditions. The Fidelity–Philadelphia Trust Company is acting in a fiduciary capacity in the management of these properties and is, of course, obligated to recommend the offer which it believes most advantageous to its Estate.

"In order to give each and every prospect a fair and equal chance and in order to secure the highest and best price for the Estate which it represents it has been decided to ask for sealed bids from all interested parties. It is suggested, therefore, that you forward to this office on or before Wednesday, June 24, 1959, your highest offer for the properties. At that time the bids will be opened and an Agreement of Sale tendered to the highest acceptable bidder provided the offer is in excess of $92,000. cash, free and clear of any and all brokerage commissions. All offers must be on an all cash basis and must be accompanied by a check to the order of the Fidelity–Philadelphia Trust Company, Trustee, in the amount of at least 10% of the offer. The Agreement of Sale will provide for the equal division of all Realty Transfer Taxes between buyer and seller. The Agreement of sale shall also contain a provision that the Vendee or purchaser has not been interested in the property through any real estate broker or attorney and that no commission is therefore due by the Vendor to anyone. Further, that if any claim is filed for a commission by any broker or attorney, the Vendee or purchaser is to assume full responsibility therefor. The Trustees, of course, reserve the right to approve or disapprove of any and all offers, or to withdraw the properties from the market.

"In submitting your bid please note on the envelope containing the bid and check 'Sealed bid—June 24, 1959' and direct the bid to the undersigned.

"If you desire any further information or if we can be of any assistance please do not hesitate to call upon us.

> "Very truly yours,
> "George Butterworth, Jr.
> "Assistant Vice President."

Plaintiff's response manifested unequivocal assent to Defendant's letter, and the only other "bidder" submitted a conditional response. Defendant, however, asserted that its letter of June 18 merely solicited offers and refused to convey the property to Plaintiff. Over a strong dissent, the court found Defendant's letter of June 18 to be ambiguous and, therefore, to be interpreted "most strongly against the Fidelity, which drew it." It held that the lower court erred in sustaining Defendant's preliminary objections and dismissing Plaintiff's amended complaint.

If, as defendants contend, Fidelity's letter of June 18 was merely an invitation to prospective purchasers who had been negotiating unsuccessfully for several years to submit a higher bid or offer which it could accept or reject in its sole and arbitrary discretion, why did Fidelity ask for "sealed bids" from all interested parties on or before June 24, 1959, and further state "at that time the bids will be opened and an Agreement of Sale tendered to the highest acceptable bidder, provided the offer is in excess of $92,000.00 cash, free and clear of all brokerage commissions," and then specify in detail the other provisions which were to be incorporated in the agreement of sale? On its face, and especially in the light of the prior negotiations, the surrounding circumstances and the objects which the parties apparently had in view, the contention of defendants that this was merely an invitation to bid, which Fidelity could reject in its unfettered discretion, is unreasonable.

In an attempt to support Fidelity's construction and position, defendants have overlooked not only the law as to the interpretation of a contract which must be considered in its entirety, but also the most important provision, viz. that after the bids are opened it will tender to the highest acceptable bidder an agreement of sale, the details of which are set forth in Fidelity's letter of June 18.

Defendants rely upon the statement in Fidelity's letter that "it was acting as fiduciary and was obligated to recommend the offer which it believed most advantageous to its estate." This contention is devoid of merit. Plaintiff unconditionally and unqualifiedly accepted all the terms and conditions of Fidelity's offer, and no other party did; and there was no higher or more advantageous offer. Defendants also rely upon the following sentence—"The Trustees, of course, reserve the right to approve or disapprove of any and all offers, or to withdraw the properties from the market." This sentence standing alone is what creates a possible ambiguity. This sentence must be interpreted, we repeat, by considering the surrounding circumstances, the objects Fidelity apparently had in view, and the contract in its entirety, and if there is any ambiguity which is reasonably susceptible of two interpretations, the ambiguity must be resolved against the Fidelity which drew the letter-offer. So interpreted, we believe the sentence means that Fidelity can withdraw the properties from the market at any time before the opening of the sealed bids, and can approve or disapprove any offer which does not fully comply with all the conditions set forth by the Fidelity, or which complies but adds unsatisfactory terms.

Although a reversal of *Courteen* on the "interpretation against the drafter" theory is plausible, what little authority there is seems to be most reluctant to apply the *Jenkins* rule to determine the *existence* rather than the *meaning* of a contract.

"Because of strict rules governing offer and acceptance, which require that an acceptance be in terms of the offer, we are reluctant to follow by analogy rules laid down with respect to contracts already formed. In passing upon questions of offer and acceptance, courts may wisely require greater exactitude than when they are trying to salvage an existing contract. Where no contract has been completed and neither party has acted to his detriment, there is no compulsion on a court to guess at what the parties intended." Henry Simons Lumber Co. v. Simons, 232 Minn. 187, 44 N.W.2d 726, 730 (1950). See also United States v. Braunstein, 75 F.Supp. 137 (S.D.N.Y.1947), appeal dismissed, 168 F.2d 749 (2d Cir.1948).

See also Fenstermacher v. Philadelphia National Bank, 493 F.2d 333, 341–43 (3d Cir.1974) (absence of special circumstances and ambiguity in writing supports application of ordinary rule that notices soliciting competitive bids for the sale of stock invite offers not acceptances); La Salle National Bank v. Vega, 167 Ill.App.3d 154, 117 Ill.Dec. 778, 520 N.E.2d 1129 (1988), infra at 306.

Offers Under Article 2 of the UCC. How would *Courteen Seed* be decided under Article Two of the UCC? Since the clover seed was goods as defined in UCC 2–105(1) [2–102(a)(19)(1997)], the transaction was within the general scope of Article 2. UCC 2–102 [2–103(a)(1997)]. Also, the definition of "agreement" in UCC 1–201(3) and the underlying purposes and policies of the Code, as expressed in UCC 1–102(1), seem consistent with a more flexible approach to the issue than was exhibited by *Courteen*. But if the issue is whether the seller made an offer in the telegram of October 8, 1927, there is no provision in Part 2 of Article 2, dealing generally with "form, formation and readjustment of contract," that provides very much assistance. Although the word "offer" is used in three sections, UCC 2–205, 2–206 and 2–207 [2–203, 2–204 and 2–205(1997)], it is not explicitly defined and is given implicit meaning only in the context of a buyer's "order or other offer to buy goods for prompt or current shipment." UCC 2–206(1)(b) [2–205(a)(1997)]. Further, the precise issue in

Courteen is not covered by the general formation principles in UCC 2–204 [2–203(1997)]. Thus, one can argue with some persuasion that since a definition of offer is not provided by any particular provision of Article 2, the court should turn to other law in the state to resolve the question. See UCC 1–103.

This argument finds support in Cannavino & Shea, Inc. v. Water Works Supply Corp., 361 Mass. 363, 280 N.E.2d 147 (1972), where the court turned to sources other than the UCC to decide that an alleged offer to sell goods "was not an offer but a quotation of prices, a request or suggestion that an offer be made to the defendant." An authoritative definition is that of Restatement (Second) § 24: "An offer is the manifestation of willingness to enter into a bargain, so made as to justify another person in understanding that his assent to that bargain is invited and will conclude it." Accord: Architectural Metal Systems, Inc. v. Consolidated Systems, Inc., 58 F.3d 1227 (7th Cir.1995)(Illinois law).

If it seems strange that a court is required to deal with both the Code and the common law to determine whether an offer to sell goods has been made, keep in mind the following comment by Professor Grant Gilmore:

> The Uniform Commercial Code . . . derives from the common law, not the civil law tradition. We shall do better to think of it as a big statute—or a collection of statutes bound together in the same book—which goes as far as it goes and no further. It assumes the continuing existence of a large body of pre-Code and non-Code law on which it rests for support, which it displaces to the least possible extent, and without which it could not survive.

Gilmore, *Article 9: What It Does for the Past,* 26 La.L.Rev. 285, 286 (1966).

(4) If a case like *Courteen* came before the Oregon Supreme Court today, would you expect a different result? Consider the case which follows.

Southworth v. Oliver

Supreme Court of Oregon, 1978.
284 Or. 361, 587 P.2d 994.

■ TONGUE, JUSTICE.

This is a suit in equity for a declaratory judgment that defendants "are obligated to sell" to plaintiff 2,933 acres of ranch lands in Grant County. Defendants appeal from a decree of specific performance in favor of plaintiff. We affirm.

Defendants contend on this appeal that a certain "writing" mailed by them to plaintiff was not an offer to sell such lands; that if it was an offer there was no proper acceptance of that offer and that any such offer and acceptance did not constitute a binding contract, at least so as to be specifically enforceable. Defendants also filed a demurrer in this court upon the ground that it appears from the face of plaintiff's complaint that the alleged agreement to sell such lands was void as in violation of the statute of frauds.

The parties and the property.

Defendants are ranchers in Grant County and owned ranches in both the Bear Valley area and also in the John Day valley. In 1976 defendants came to the conclusion that they should "cut the operation down" and sell some of the Bear Valley property, as well as some of their Forest Service grazing permits. Defendant Joseph Oliver discussed this matter with his wife, defendant Arlene Oliver, and also with his son, and the three of them "jointly arrived" at a decision to sell a portion of the Bear Valley property. Joseph Oliver also conferred with his accountant and attorney and, as a result, it was decided that the sale "had to be on terms" rather than cash, for income tax reasons. Defendant Joseph Oliver then had "a discussion with Mr. Southworth [the plaintiff] about the possibility of * * * selling this Bear Valley property." Plaintiff Southworth was also a cattle rancher in Bear Valley. The land which defendants had decided to sell was adjacent to land owned by him and was property that he had always wanted.

The initial meeting between the parties on May 20, 1976.

According to plaintiff, defendant Joseph Oliver stopped by his ranch on May 20, 1976, and said that he [Oliver] was interested in "selling the ranch" and asked "would I be interested in buying it, and I said 'yes'." Mr. Southworth also testified that "he thought I would be interested in the land and that Clyde [Holliday, also a neighbor] would be interested in the permits" and that "I told him that I was very interested in the land * * *."

Plaintiff Southworth also testified that at that time defendant Oliver showed him a map, showing land that he "understood them to offer for sale"; that there was no discussion at that time of price or terms of sale, or whether the sale of the land was contingent on sale of any of the permits, but that the conversation terminated with the understanding:

> "That he would develop and determine value and price and I would make an investigation to determine whether or not I could find the money and get everything arranged for a purchase. In other words, he was going to do A and then I would B."

According to plaintiff Southworth, defendant Oliver said that when he determined the value of the property he would send that information to Southworth so as to give him "notice" of "what he wanted for the land," but did not say that he was also going to give that same information to Mr. Holliday, although he did say that "he planned to talk to Clyde [Holliday] about permits," with the result that plaintiff knew that Oliver "might very well be * * * talking to Clyde about the same thing he talked to you [plaintiff] about" and "give that information to Clyde Holliday as well as yourself."

According to defendant Joseph Oliver, the substance of that initial conversation with plaintiff was as follows:

"* * * I told him we were going to condense our ranch down and sell some property and that we were in the process of trying to get some figures from the Assessor on it to determine what we wanted to sell and what we might want to do. Whenever we got this information together we were going to send it to him and some of my neighbors and give them first chance at it. * * *"

Mr. Oliver also testified that plaintiff said that "he was interested"; that he had a map with him; that he mentioned to plaintiff that he "was going to sell some permits," but that there was no discussion "about the permits going with the land at that time" and that he [Oliver] "talked along the lines that Clyde [Holliday] would probably be interested in those permits." On cross-examination Mr. Oliver also answered in the affirmative a question to the effect that the property which he and Mr. Southworth "delineated on the map" during that conversation "was the property" that he "finally decided to sell and made the general offering to the four neighbors."

Plaintiff also testified that on May 26, 1976, he called Clyde Holliday to ask if he was interested in buying the land and Mr. Holliday said "no," that he was interested only in the permits, but would be interested in trading some other land for some of the land plaintiff was buying from defendants.

The telephone call of June 13, 1976.

Plaintiff testified that on June 13, 1976, he called defendant Oliver by telephone to "ask him if his plans for selling * * * continued to be in force, and he said 'yes'," that "he was progressing and there had been some delay in acquiring information from the Assessor, but they expected soon to have the information needed to establish the value on the land." Defendant Oliver's testimony was to the same effect, but he also recalled that at that time Mr. Southworth "said everything was in order and that I didn't have to worry, he had the money available and that everything was ready to go."

The letters of June 17, June 21, and June 24, 1976.

Several days later plaintiff received from defendants a letter dated June 17, 1976, as follows:

"Enclosed please find the information about the ranch sales that I had discussed with you previously.

"These prices are the market value according to the records of the Grant County Assessor.

"Please contact me if there are any questions."

There were two enclosures with that letter. The first was as follows:

"JOSEPH C. and ARLENE G. OLIVER

200 Ford Road

John Day, OR 97845

"Selling approximately 2933 Acres in Grant County in T. 16 S., R. 31 E., W.M. near Seneca, Oregon at the assessed market value of:

LAND	$306,409
IMPROVEMENTS	18,010
Total	$324,419

"Terms available—29% down—balance over 5 years at 8% interest. Negotiate sale date for December 1, 1976 or January 1, 1977.

"Available after hay is harvested and arrangements made for removal of hay, equipment and supplies.

"ALSO: Selling

"Little Bear Creek allotment permit ___ 100 head @ $225

"Big Bear Creek allotment permit ___ 200 head @ $250"

The second enclosure related to "selling approximately 6365 acres" in Grant County near John Day—another ranch owned by the Oliver family.

Defendant Joseph Oliver testified that this letter and enclosures were "drafted" by his wife, defendant Arlene Oliver; that he then read and signed it; that he sent it not only to plaintiff, but also to Clyde Holliday and two other neighbors; that it was sent because "I told them I would send them all this information and we would go from there," that it was not made as an offer, and that it was his intention that the "property" and "permits" be transferred "together."

Upon receiving that letter and enclosures, plaintiff immediately responded by letter addressed to both defendants, dated June 21, 1976, as follows:

"Re the land in Bear Valley near Seneca, Oregon that you have offered to sell; I accept your offer."

Plaintiff testified that on June 23, 1976, Clyde Holliday called and said he needed to acquire a portion of the land "that I had agreed to buy from Joe [Oliver], and I said I have bought the land," and that we would "work out an exchange in accord with what we have previously mentioned," but that "[h]e said he needed more land."

Defendant Joseph Oliver testified that after receiving plaintiff's letter dated June 21, 1976, Clyde Holliday told him that "they [Holliday and plaintiff] were having a little difficulty getting this thing worked out," apparently referring to the "exchange" previously discussed between plaintiff and Holliday, and that he (Oliver) then told plaintiff that:

"* * * [T]here seemed to be some discrepancies between what I was getting the two parties and that I didn't exactly want to be an arbitrator or say you are right or you are wrong with my neighbors. I wished they would straighten the thing out, and if they didn't, I really didn't have to sell it, that I would pull it off the market, because I didn't want to get in trouble. I would have to live with my neighbors."

Finally, on June 24, 1976, defendants mailed the following letter to plaintiff:

"We received your letter of June 21, 1976. You have misconstrued our prior negotiations and written summaries of the lands which we and J.C. wish to sell. That was not made as or intended to be a firm offer of sale, and especially was not an offer of sale of any portion of the lands and permits described to any one person separately from the rest of the lands and permits described.

"The memorandum of ours was for informational purposes only and as a starting point for further negotiation between us and you and the others also interested in the properties.

"It is also impossible to tell from the attachment to our letter of June 17, 1976, as to the legal description of the lands to be sold, and would not in any event constitute an enforceable contract.

"We are open to further negotiation with you and other interested parties, but do not consider that we at this point have any binding enforceable contract with you."

This lawsuit then followed.

Defendants' letter of June 19 [17], 1976, was an "offer to sell" the ranch lands.

Defendants first contend that defendants' letter of June 17, 1976, to plaintiff was "not an offer, both as a matter of law and under the facts of this case." In support of that contention defendants say that their testimony that the letter was not intended as an offer was uncontradicted and that similar writings have been held not to constitute offers.[1] Defendants also say that there is "authority for the proposition that all the evidence of surrounding circumstances may be taken into consideration in making that determination"[2] and that the circumstances in this case were such as to require the conclusion that defendants did not intend the letter as an offer and that plaintiff knew or reasonably should have known that it was not intended as an offer because:

"1. Defendants obviously did not intend it as an offer.

"2. The wording of the 'offer' made it clear that this was 'information' that plaintiff had previously expressed an interest in receiving.

---

1. Citing Courteen Seed Co. v. Abraham, 129 Or. 427, 275 P. 684 (1929); Klimek v. Perisich, 231 Or. 71, 371 P.2d 956 (1962); Nebraska Seed Co. v. Harsh, 98 Neb. 89, 152 N.W. 310 (1915); Mellen v. Johnson, 322 Mass. 236, 76 N.E.2d 658 (1948); Owen v. Tunison, 131 Me. 42, 158 A. 926 (1932); and Richards v. Flower, 193 Cal.App.2d 233, 14 Cal.Rptr. 228 (1961).

2. Citing Metropolitan Life Ins. Co. v. Kimball, 163 Or. 31, 94 P.2d 1101 (1939); Nebraska Seed Co. v. Harsh, supra n. 1; Klimek v. Perisich, supra n. 1; Mellen v. Johnson, supra n. 1; and 1 Restatement of Contracts § 25 (1932).

"3. It did not use the term offer, but only formally advised plaintiff that defendants are selling certain lands and permits and set forth generally the terms upon which they would consider selling.

"4. The plaintiff knew of the custom of transferring permits with land and had no knowledge from the writing or previous talk that defendants were selling any cattle.

"5. Plaintiff knew and expected this same information to go to others."

Defendants conclude that

"Considering the factors determined important by the authorities cited, these factors preponderate heavily that this was not an offer to sell the land only, or to sell at all, and should not reasonably have been so construed by the plaintiff."

In Kitzke v. Turnidge, 209 Or. 563, 573, 307 P.2d 522, 527 (1957), this court quoted with approval the following rule as stated in 1 Williston on Contracts 49–50, § 22A (1957):

" '* * * In the early law of assumpsit stress was laid on the necessity of a promise in terms, but the modern law rightly construes both acts and words as having the meaning which a reasonable person present would put upon them in view of the surrounding circumstances. Even where words are used, "a contract includes not only what the parties said, but also what is necessarily to be implied from what they said." And it may be said broadly that any conduct of one party, from which the other may reasonably draw the inference of a promise, is effective in law as such.' "

To the same effect, see Kabil Developments Corp. v. Mignot, 279 Or. 151, 158, 566 P.2d 505 (1977); Klimek v. Perisich, 231 Or. 71, 78, 371 P.2d 956 (1962); Restatement of Contracts 2d § 24 (1973); and Murray on Contracts 36, § 22 (1974). See also Harty v. Bye, 258 Or. 398, 404, 483 P.2d 458 (1971).

As also stated in 1 Restatement of Contracts § 25, Comment (a) (1932) as quoted by this court with approval in Metropolitan Life Ins. Co. v. Kimball, 163 Or. 31, 58, 94 P.2d 1101, 1111 (1939):

"It is often difficult to draw an exact line between offers and negotiations preliminary thereto. It is common for one who wishes to make a bargain to try to induce the other party to the intended transaction to make the definite offer, he himself suggesting with more or less definiteness the nature of the contract he is willing to enter into. Besides any direct language indicating an intent to defer the formation of a contract, the definiteness or indefiniteness of the words used in opening the negotiation must be considered, as well as the usages of business, and indeed all accompanying circumstances."

The difficulty in determining whether an offer has been made is particularly acute in cases involving price quotations, as in this case. It is recognized that although a price quotation, standing alone, is not an offer,[3] there may be circumstances under which a price quotation, when considered together with facts and circumstances, may constitute an offer which, if accepted, will result in a binding contract.[4] It is also recognized that such an offer may be made to more than one person.[5] Thus, the fact that a price quotation is sent to more than one person does not, of itself, require a holding that such a price quotation is not an offer.

We agree with the analysis of this problem as stated in Murray on Contracts 37–40, § 24 (1977), as follows:

> "If A says to B, 'I am going to sell my car for $500,' and B replies, 'All right, here is $500, I will take it,' no contract results, assuming that A's statement is taken at its face value. A's statement does not involve any promise, commitment or undertaking; it is at most a statement of A's *present intention.* * * *

> "* * *

> "* * * However, a price quotation or advertisement may contain sufficient indication of willingness to enter a bargain so that the party to whom it is addressed would be justified in believing that his assent would conclude the bargain. * * *

> "* * *

> "* * * The basic problem is found in the expressions of the parties. People very seldom express themselves either accurately or in complete detail. Thus, difficulty is encountered in determining the correct interpretation of the expression in question. Over the years, some more or less trustworthy guides to interpretation have been developed.

> "The first and strongest guide is that the particular expression is to be judged on the basis of what a reasonable man in the position of the offeree has been led to believe. This requires an analysis of what the offeree should have understood under all of the surrounding circumstances, with all of his opportunities for comprehending the intention of the offeror, rather than what the offeror, in fact, intended. This guide may be regarded as simply another manifestation of the objective test. Beyond this universally accepted guide to interpretation, there are other guides which are found in the case law involving factors that tend to recur. The most important of the remaining guides is the language used. If there are no words of promise, undertaking or commitment, the tendency is to construe the expression to be an invitation for an offer or mere preliminary negotiations in the absence of strong, countervailing circumstances. Another guide which has been widely accepted is the determination of the party or parties to whom

3. See 1 Corbin on Contracts 77–78, § 26 (1963).

4. See 1 Williston on Contracts 65, § 221 (1957); Murray on Contracts 37–40,

§ 24 (1974), and Calimari and Perillo, Contracts 39, § 2–10 (1977).

5. 1 Restatement of Contracts 36, § 28 (1932).

the purported offer has been addressed. If the expression definitely names a party or parties, it is more likely to be construed as an offer. If the addressee is an indefinite group, it is less likely to be an offer. The fact that this is simply a guide rather than a definite rule is illustrated by the exceptional cases which must be noted. The guide operates effectively in relation to such expressions as advertisements or circular letters. The addressee is indefinite, and, therefore, the expression is probably not an offer. However, in reward cases, the addressee is equally indefinite and, yet, the expression is an offer. Finally, the definiteness of the proposal itself may have a bearing on whether it constitutes an offer. In general, the more definite the proposal, the more reasonable it is to treat the proposal as involving a commitment. * * *'' (Footnotes omitted)

Upon application of these tests to the facts of this case we are of of the opinion that defendants' letter to plaintiff dated June 17, 1976, was an offer to sell the ranch lands. We believe that the "surrounding circumstances" under which this letter was prepared by defendants and sent by them to plaintiff were such as to have led a reasonable person to believe that defendants were making an offer to sell to plaintiff the lands described in the letter's enclosure and upon the terms as there stated.

That letter did not come to plaintiff "out of the blue," as in some of the cases involving advertisements or price quotations. Neither was this a price quotation resulting from an inquiry by plaintiff. According to what we believe to be the most credible testimony, defendants decided to sell the lands in question and defendant Joseph Oliver then sought out the plaintiff who owned adjacent lands. Defendant Oliver told plaintiff that defendants were interested in selling that land, inquired whether plaintiff was interested, and was told by plaintiff that he was "very interested in the land," after which they discussed the particular lands to be sold. That conversation was terminated with the understanding that Mr. Oliver would "determine" the value and price of that land, i.e., "what he wanted for the land," and that plaintiff would undertake to arrange financing for the purchase of that land. In addition to that initial conversation, there was a further telephone conversation in which plaintiff called Mr. Oliver "to ask him if his plans for selling * * * continued to be in force" and was told "yes"; that there had been some delay in getting information from the assessor, as needed to establish the value of the land; and that plaintiff then told Mr. Oliver that "everything was in order" and that "he had the money available and everything was ready to go."

Under these facts and circumstances, we agree with the finding and conclusion by the trial court, in its written opinion, that when plaintiff received the letter of June 17th, with enclosures, which stated a price of $324,419 for the 2,933 acres in T 16 S, R 31 E., W.M., as previously identified by the parties with reference to a map, and stating "terms" of 29 percent down—balance over five years at eight percent interest—with a "sale date" of either December 1, 1976, or January 1, 1977, a reasonable person in the position of the plaintiff would have believed that defendants were making an offer to sell those lands to him.

This conclusion is further strengthened by "the definiteness of the proposal," not only with respect to price, but terms, and by the fact that "the addressee was not an indefinite group." *See* Murray, supra at 40.

As previously noted, defendants contend that they "obviously did not intend [the letter] as an offer." While it may be proper to consider evidence of defendants' subjective intent under the "objective test" to which this court is committed, it is the manifestation of a previous intention that is controlling, rather than a "person's actual intent."[6] We do not agree with defendants' contention that it was "obvious" to a reasonable person, under the facts and circumstances of this case that the letter of January 17th was not intended to be an offer to sell the ranch lands to plaintiff.

We recognize, as contended by defendants, that the failure to use the word "offer," the fact that the letter included the "information" previously discussed between the parties, and the fact that plaintiff knew that the same information was to be sent to others, were important facts to be considered in deciding whether plaintiff, as a reasonable person, would have been led to believe that this letter was an "offer." See also Murray, supra, at 40. We disagree, however, with defendants' contention that these and other factors relied upon by defendants "preponderate" so as to require a holding that the letter of January 17th was not an offer.

The failure to add the word "offer" and the use of the word "information" are also not controlling, and, as previously noted, an offer may be made to more than one person. The question is whether, under all of the facts and circumstances existing at the time that this letter was received, a reasonable person in the position of the plaintiff would have understood the letter to be an offer by defendants to sell the land to him.

Defendants also contend that "plaintiff knew of the custom of transferring [Forest Service grazing] permits with the land and had no knowledge from the writing or previous talk that defendants were selling any cattle" (so as to provide such a basis for a transfer of the permits).[7] Plaintiff testified, however, that at the time of the initial conversation, Mr. Oliver told plaintiff that he thought plaintiff "would be interested in the land and that Clyde would be interested in the permits." In addition, defendant Joseph Oliver, in response to questions by the trial judge, although denying that at that time he told plaintiff that he was "going to offer the permits to Mr. Holliday," admitted that he "knew Mr. Holliday was interested in the

---

6. See Kabil Developments Corp. v. Mignot, 279 Or. 151, 158, 566 P.2d 505 (1977).

7. Defendants offered testimony that Forest Service grazing permits could only be transferred with a sale of "commensurate land" sufficient to support the cattle subject to such permits or with a sale of such cattle to another party and that defendants did not desire to sell such cattle and had a policy against doing so. Defendants contend that, as a result, the value of these permits would be lost to them unless the permits were sold with the land and at a price to be added to the price for the land. Defendants also contend that plaintiff was aware of these facts.

permits" and "could have" told plaintiff that he was "going to talk to Mr. Holliday about him purchasing the permits."

On this record we believe that plaintiff's knowledge of the facts noted by defendants relating to the transfer of such permits did not require a holding that, as a reasonable man, he did not understand or should not have understood that defendants' letter of June 17th was an offer to sell the ranch lands to him.

* * *

[The Court concluded that the plaintiff's letter of June 21, 1976, was an acceptance of defendants' offer to sell the ranch lands; that the resulting agreement was sufficiently definite for enforcement by specific performance; and that the Statute of Frauds was no bar to the action.]

For all of these reasons, the decree of the trial court is affirmed.

PROBLEM: THE CASE OF SAM THE COIN DEALER

Sam, a coin dealer, wrote Joe that he had a rare dollar and asked Joe if he wanted it. Joe wrote Sam that if it was uncirculated he would pay $3,000.00. Sam wrote Joe the dollar was in extra fine condition but he only wanted $2,700.00. Joe wrote Sam that he would pay no more than $2,000.00 for the coin. Sam wrote Joe that he wouldn't take less than $2,400.00 for the coin. Joe and his sister each wrote a letter to Sam on the same day and the letters were delivered to Sam on the same day. Joe wrote he would pay $2,400.00. Joe's sister wrote that she would accept the offer Sam made to sell the dollar to his brother for $2,700.00 and enclosed a certified check in that amount. Sam comes to you for advice. What do you advise Sam? Why?

Comment: Auctions and Other Forms of Competitive Bidding

An auction is a contracting technique invoked most frequently by sellers of goods or land to stimulate price competition. The seller, by soliciting bids from a group of prospective buyers, seeks to develop a market whose prices are determined by on-the-spot competitive bidding. Auctions dispose of real estate, livestock, household goods, antiques and works of art. In addition to owners, they are used by repossessing creditors, public officials, such as the sheriff, and executors of decedents' estates. The terms and procedures of an auction are usually determined by the advertisement, trade usage or practice and statutes. The terms of the sale are normally set out in advertisements and other writings before the auction is conducted. See, e.g., Dulman v. Martin Fein & Co., Inc., 66 A.D.2d 809, 411 N.Y.S.2d 358 (1978); Restatement (Second) § 28(2). Often, auction disputes involve a combination of advertisement, trade usage and statutory controls and raise issues of agency law (the auctioneer is agent for a principal who may be undisclosed) and property ownership (sometimes stolen goods are sold by auction).

In most auctions the only important term left for agreement is price. The prospective buyer should understand that the function of an auction is to generate price competition and that there is, therefore, some risk that the property will be withdrawn before being sold. The law supports the seller: the consistent legal conclusion has been that, in the absence of agreement to the contrary, an advertisement that described property will be sold to the highest bidder at a stated time and place is not an offer, even though the power to withdraw the goods is *not* expressly reserved. The advertisement merely solicits offers which the seller is privileged to accept or reject. See UCC 2–328(3); Restatement (Second) § 28(1)(a); Weinstein v. Green, 347 Mass. 580, 199 N.E.2d 310 (1964); Drew v. John Deere Company of Syracuse, Inc., 19 A.D.2d 308, 241 N.Y.S.2d 267 (1963); Annot., 37 A.L.R.2d 1049 (1954). Unless otherwise agreed, the offer is accepted when the auctioneer "so announces by the fall of the hammer or in other customary manner." UCC 2–328(2).

On the other hand, if the sale is announced to be "without reserve" then the sale must be made to the highest bidder. In the language of UCC 2–328(3): "In an auction without reserve, after the auctioneer calls for bids on an article or lot, that article or lot cannot be withdrawn unless no bid is made within a reasonable time." Accord: Pitchfork Ranch Co. v. Bar TL, 615 P.2d 541 (Wyo.1980); Zuhak v. Rose, 264 Wis. 286, 58 N.W.2d 693 (1953) (high bidder gets specific performance after dissatisfied owner of land discharges auctioneer). Moreover, in an auction without reserve the seller cannot bid. See Pyles v. Goller, 109 Md.App. 71, 674 A.2d 35 (1996).

Does this mean that the advertisement is converted into an offer which is accepted by the bidder, subject to discharge if a higher bid is made? Or, has the high bidder simply made an offer which the auctioneer has a legal duty to accept? One court has stated that the best explanation is "that the owner, by making such an announcement, enters into a collateral contract with all persons bidding at the auction that he will not withdraw the property for sale, regardless of how low the highest bid may be." Drew v. John Deere Company of Syracuse, supra, 241 N.Y.S.2d at 269. But to further complicate matters, UCC 2–328(3) provides that the high bidder "may retract this bid until the auctioneer's announcement of completion of the sale" and that the retraction does not revive any previous bids which have lapsed upon the making of a higher bid. Accord: Restatement (Second) § 28(1)(c). Thus, if it is a "collateral" contract it binds the auctioneer but not the high bidder—at least until the hammer falls.

At first blush these rules appear to be anomalous deviations from normal contract formation procedures. But they serve a useful purpose in auctions. The "without reserve" language informs prospective bidders that the owner is dispensing with a broad power to withdraw goods once they are put up for sale—that he or she is willing to take the highest bid produced by competition. This information may induce greater reliance on the part of individual bidders in attending the auction. The bidder's withdrawal privilege affords some measure of protection from a hasty bid made in the heat of competition. There is some time to reflect and repent before the hammer falls. In view of this, is the fact that bidders have more mobility than sellers in "without reserve" auctions disturbing? Anomalous? For additional discussion, see Corbin § 108; Williston §§ 29–30.

A bid in a sealed auction of "*X* dollars over the highest bid" is commonly referred to as a "sharp" bid, and the practice has been soundly condemned. Such a bid is said to be unfair to other bidders, by allowing the "sharp" bidder to appropriate the judgment of the other bidders, as well as unfair to the seller, in that, if allowed, it would discourage and drive off sum-certain bidders. Webster v. French, 11 Ill. 254 (1849) (contrary to public policy and void); Casey v. Independence County, 109 Ark. 11, 159 S.W. 24 (1913) ("no bid at all," being both unfair and incomplete). Sharp bidding is clearly a fraudulent practice, and with respect to a public sale, such a bid is void from its inception. It is illegal *per se*. In case of a private sale, it has been held that while concealed sharp bidding taints a resulting contract with fraud, it is not void but voidable at the election of the defrauded parties. Ordinarily, the defrauded parties would be the seller and the highest sum-certain bidder. See Short v. Sun Newspapers, Inc., 300 N.W.2d 781 (Minn.1980).

Public contracting. Government entities at all levels employ competitive procedures in procuring supplies and services. The Competition in Contracting Act, enacted by Congress in 1984, is designed to further encourage competitive practice by the federal government. Title VII of Division B of the Deficit Reduction Act of 1984, P.L. 98–369, 98 Stat. 494. Under the Act, "sealed bidding" must be utilized if (1) time permits the solicitation, submission, and evaluation of sealed bids, (2) the award will be made on the basis of price and other price-related factors, (3) it is not necessary to conduct discussion with the responding sources about their bids, and (4) there is a reasonable expectation of receiving more than one sealed bid. Otherwise, the contract is negotiated through the solicitation of competitive proposals from private contractors.

A variation of the auction technique, sealed bidding unfolds in a series of distinct steps. First, contracting officials prepare an invitation for bids (IFB) which describes the government's needs, states the basic terms and conditions (quantity, time and place of delivery, method of payments, etc.), and incorporates by reference applicable standard forms of the government. Second, the IFB is distributed or otherwise publicized to a sufficient number of prospects so as to insure adequate competition. Third, bidders prepare and submit their bids. This bid is the offer. To be eligible for acceptance, it must be submitted on time and conform in every material respect to the IFB. That is, the bidder must submit a responsive bid. Fourth, the bids are opened and evaluated by the government. After bid opening, the bidder cannot change the bid or withdraw the offer unless a mistake has been made and some rather rigid conditions are satisfied. Unlike the private auction, the offeror may not withdraw after bids are opened, but the offeree may reject all bids if there is a "compelling" reason for doing so; e.g., supplies or services contracted for are no longer required; bids indicate that the needs of the government can be satisfied by a less expensive article differing from that for which the bids were invited. Federal Acquisitions Regulation 14.404. Fifth, if everything is in order, an award is made, either by written notice of award or by furnishing the successful bidder with an executed award document. FAR 14.407. The award is, of course, the acceptance, a matter to be examined a "little bid later."

Sealed bidding minimizes the questions as to whether an offer was made and, if so, by whom. This highly structured process is designed to produce full and complete agreement on all material terms without negotiation and clearly designates the bidder as offeror. Litigation over traditional questions of offer and acceptance in government contracts is rare.

(C) ACCEPTANCE: EXERCISE OF POWER OF ACCEPTANCE

(1) METHOD AND COMMUNICATION OF ACCEPTANCE

La Salle National Bank v. Vega

Appellate Court of Illinois, Second District, 1988.
167 Ill.App.3d 154, 117 Ill.Dec. 778, 520 N.E.2d 1129.

■ PRESIDING JUSTICE LINDBERG delivered the opinion of the court:

* * *

Plaintiff's first amended complaint alleged the existence of a contract for the sale of real estate between it and Mel [Vega] and sought specific performance of the alleged contract and damages from defendants for willfully and intentionally breaching it. Borg was permitted to intervene and filed a counterclaim naming plaintiff and defendants as counterdefendants. As finally amended, the counterclaim sought specific performance of a different contract for sale of the same real estate to Borg; a judgment declaring the alleged contract between Mel and plaintiff void and holding it for naught; and, if the alleged contract with plaintiff was "held to be a valid and enforceable contract," damages from defendants for fraud for failure to disclose the contract with plaintiff to Borg.

Borg moved for partial summary judgment (Ill.Rev.Stat.1985, ch. 110, par. 2–1005(d)) requesting a determination by the court that the alleged contract between plaintiff and Mel was unenforceable because it was not "signed in accordance with its terms and provisions" and because plaintiff abandoned it. The trial court granted partial summary judgment on the basis of the first ground argued by Borg.

In its verified first amended complaint, plaintiff alleged, *inter alia:*

"The Defendant, MEL VEGA, on March 12, 1985, in his own behalf and in behalf of all the owners of record, entered into a Real Estate Sale Contract (herein 'Contract') with the Plaintiff, a true and correct copy of said Contract is attached hereto and incorporated herein as Exhibit A."

Exhibit A is a document, drafted by counsel for plaintiff, entitled "Real Estate Sale Contract." On the first page of this document appears the date March 12, 1985, and the statement that "Attached Rider is part of this Contract." One of the Rider's provisions states:

"This contract has been executed and presented by an authorized agent for the purchaser, the beneficiaries of the La Salle National Bank, under Trust No. 109529, as Trustee aforesaid for the benefit of the Trust only and not personally. Upon execution of this contract by the Seller, this contract shall be presented to the trust for full execution. Upon the trust's execution, this contract will then be in full force and a copy of a fully executed contract along with evidence of the earnest money deposit will be delivered back to Seller."

The document was signed by Bernard Ruekberg as the purchaser's purchasing agent and by Mel Vega (on March 19, 1985, according to the date by his signature on the Rider) as the seller but not by the trustee for the purchaser.

* * *

It has long been settled that a contract is " 'an agreement between competent parties, upon a consideration sufficient in law, to do or not to do a particular thing.' " (Steinberg v. Chicago Medical School (1977), 69 Ill.2d 320, 329, 13 Ill.Dec. 699, 704, 371 N.E.2d 634, 639, quoting People v. Dummer (1916), 274 Ill. 637, 640, 113 N.E. 934, 935.) The formation of a contract requires an offer, an acceptance, and consideration. (Steinberg v. Chicago Medical School (1977), 69 Ill.2d 320, 329–30, 13 Ill.Dec. 699, 704, 371 N.E.2d 634, 639; Milanko v. Jensen (1949), 404 Ill. 261, 266–67, 88 N.E.2d 857, 859.) The trial court held that there was no genuine issue of material fact that no contract was formed because the offer was made by Mel, the offer could only be accepted by execution of the document at issue by the trust, and the document was not executed by the trust. * * *

* * *

Whether a contract was formed without execution of the document by the trust may now be considered. This requires first an analysis of the events which occurred with respect to the document in terms of offer and acceptance.

The pertinent provision of the document stated: [The court quoted the attached rider, supra.] Thus, a specific order of events was contemplated, after which the contract would be in full force. Ruekberg (the purchasing agent) was to execute the document and present it to Mel (the seller). Then Mel was to execute it. After Mel executed it, the document was to be presented to the trust for execution. Finally, "upon the trust's execution," the contract would be in full force.

An offer is an act on the part of one person giving another person the legal power of creating the obligation called a contract. (McCarty v. Verson Allsteel Press Co. (1980), 89 Ill.App.3d 498, 507, 44 Ill.Dec. 570, 576, 411 N.E.2d 936, 942.) Where "the so-called offer is not intended to give the so-called offeree the power to make a contract there is no offer." (McCarty v. Verson Allsteel Press Co. (1980), 89 Ill.App.3d 498, 508, 44 Ill.Dec. 570, 577, 411 N.E.2d 936, 943.) From the provisions contained in the document at bar, particularly the language quoted, it is apparent that there was to be no contract (i.e., the "contract" was not to be in full force) until it was executed by the trust. Thus, Ruekberg's presentation of the document he had executed to Mel was not an offer because it did not give Mel the power to make a contract by accepting it. On the other hand, when Mel executed the document and gave it back to Ruekberg he made an offer which could be accepted by execution of the document by the trust.

An offeror has complete control over an offer and may condition acceptance to the terms of the offer. (McCarty v. Verson Allsteel Press Co. (1980), 89 Ill.App.3d 498, 509, 44 Ill.Dec. 570, 578, 411 N.E.2d 936, 944.) The language of an offer may moreover govern the mode of acceptance required, and, where an offer requires a written acceptance, no other mode may be used. (Zeller v. First National Bank & Trust Co. (1979), 79 Ill.App.3d 170, 172, 34 Ill.Dec. 473, 475, 398 N.E.2d 148, 150; Nationwide Commercial Co. v. Knox (1973), 10 Ill.App.3d 13, 15, 293 N.E.2d 638, 640; Brophy v. City of Joliet (1957), 14 Ill.App.2d 443, 453–56, 144 N.E.2d 816, 821–23.) In the case at bar, the document at issue stated clearly that the contract would be in full force upon the trust's execution. This indicates that the only mode by which Mel's offer could be accepted was execution of the document by the trust. The trust not having executed the document, there was no acceptance of the offer, and so there was no contract. E.g., Zeller v. First National Bank & Trust Co. (1979), 79 Ill.App.3d 170, 172, 34 Ill.Dec. 473, 474, 398 N.E.2d 148, 149 ("It is elementary that for a contract to exist, there must be an offer and acceptance. [Citations.]"); Moore v. Lewis (1977), 51 Ill.App.3d 388, 392, 9 Ill.Dec. 337, 342, 366 N.E.2d 594, 599 ("[A]n offer does not ripen into a contract until it is accepted").

* * *

The judgment of the circuit court of Du Page County is accordingly affirmed.

Affirmed.

Hendricks v. Behee

Missouri Court of Appeals, Southern District, 1990.
786 S.W.2d 610.

■ FLANIGAN, PRESIDING JUDGE.

Plaintiff Steve L. Hendricks, d/b/a Hendricks Abstract & Title Co., instituted this interpleader action, Rule 52.07, V.A.M.R., against defendants Eugene Behee, Artice Smith, and Pearl Smith. Plaintiff was the escrowee of $5,000 which had been paid by defendant Behee as a deposit accompanying Behee's offer to purchase real estate owned by defendants Artice Smith and Pearl Smith, husband and wife, in Stockton, Missouri. A dispute between Behee and the Smiths as to whether their dealings resulted in a binding contract prompted the interpleader action. Behee filed a cross-claim against the Smiths.

After a nonjury trial, the trial court awarded plaintiff $997.50 to be paid out of the $5,000 deposit. None of the parties challenges that award. The trial court awarded the balance of $4,002.50 to defendant Behee. Defendants Smith appeal.

In essence the Smiths contend that the dealings between them and Behee ripened into a contract and entitled the Smiths to the balance of $4,002.50, and that the trial court erred in ruling otherwise.

After Behee, as prospective buyer, and the Smiths, as prospective sellers, had engaged in unproductive negotiations, Behee, on March 2, 1987, made a written offer of $42,500 for the real estate and $250 for a dinner bell and flower pots. On March 3 that offer was mailed to the Smiths, who lived in Mississippi, by their real estate agent. There were two real estate agents involved. The trial court found that both were the agents of the Smiths, and that finding has not been disputed by the Smiths in this appeal. For simplicity, the two agents will be considered in this opinion as one agent who acted on behalf of the Smiths.

On March 4 the Smiths signed the proposed agreement in Mississippi. Before Behee was notified that the Smiths had accepted the offer, Behee withdrew the offer by notifying the real estate agent of the withdrawal. That paramount fact is conceded by this statement in the Smiths' brief: "On either March 5, 6 or 7, 1987, Behee contacted [the Smiths' real estate agent] and advised her that he desired to withdraw his offer to purchase the real estate. Prior to this communication, Behee had received no notice that his offer had been accepted by the Smiths."

There is no contract until acceptance of an offer is communicated to the offeror. ACF Ind., Inc. v. Ind. Comm., 320 S.W.2d 484, 492[10] (Mo. banc 1959); Robinson v. St. Louis, Kansas City & Northern Railway Company, 75 Mo. 494, 498 (1882); Londoff v. Conrad, 749 S.W.2d 463, 465[1] (Mo.App.1988); Tri–State Motor Tr. Co. v. Ind. Comm., 509 S.W.2d 217, 226[11] (Mo.App.1974); Lynch v. Webb City School District No. 92, 418 S.W.2d 608, 615 (Mo.App.1967); Sokol v. Hill, 310 S.W.2d 19, 20 (Mo.App.1958); 17 Am.Jur.2d Contracts § 43, p. 380; 17 C.J.S. Contracts § 45, p. 690.

An uncommunicated intention to accept an offer is not an acceptance. Thacker v. Massman Const. Co., 247 S.W.2d 623, 629–30 (Mo.1952); Medicine Shoppe Intern., Inc. v. J–Pral Corp., 662 S.W.2d 263, 269[3, 4] (Mo.App.1983). When an offer calls for a promise, as distinguished from an act, on the part of the offeree, notice of acceptance is always essential. Thacker v. Massman Const. Co., supra, at 629; Daggett v. Kansas City Structural Steel Co., 334 Mo. 207, 65 S.W.2d 1036, 1039 (1933). A mere private act of the offeree does not constitute an acceptance. Lynch v. Webb City School District No. 92, supra, at 615[6]; Hunt v. Jeffries, 236 Mo.App. 476, 484, 156 S.W.2d 23, 27[3] (Mo.App.1941); 17 Am.Jur.2d Contracts § 44, p. 382. Communication of acceptance of a contract to an agent of the offeree is not sufficient and does not bind the offeror. Horton v. N.Y. Life Ins. Co., 151 Mo. 604, 620, 52 S.W. 356, 360 (1899); *Sokol v. Hill*, supra, at 20[1].

Unless the offer is supported by consideration, Coffman Industries, Inc. v. Gorman–Taber Co., 521 S.W.2d 763, 772 (Mo.App.1975), an offeror may withdraw his offer at any time "before acceptance and communication of that fact to him." *Sokol v. Hill,* supra, at 20[2]. To similar effect see National Advertising Co. v. Herold, 735 S.W.2d 74, 77 (Mo.App.1987). To be effective, revocation of an offer must be communicated to the offeree before he has accepted. Medicine Shoppe Intern., Inc. v. J–Pral Corp., supra, at 269; Rodgers v. Rodgers, 505 S.W.2d 138, 144 (Mo.App.1974); Lynch v. Webb City School District No. 92, supra, at 617; 17 Am.Jur.2d Contracts § 35, p. 374; 17 C.J.S. Contracts § 50(d), p. 712.

Notice to the agent, within the scope of the agent's authority, is notice to the principal, and the agent's knowledge is binding on the principal. Hunter v. Hunter, 327 Mo. 817, 39 S.W.2d 359, 364[10] (1931); Dace v. John Hancock Mut. Life Ins. Co., 148 S.W.2d 93, 95[1] (Mo.App.1941). See also Luker v. Moffett, 327 Mo. 929, 38 S.W.2d 1037, 1041[6] (1931); 3 C.J.S. Agency § 432, p. 295.

Before Behee was notified that the Smiths had accepted his offer, Behee notified the agent of the Smiths that Behee was withdrawing the offer. The notice to the agent, being within the scope of her authority, was binding upon the Smiths. Behee's offer was not supported by consideration and his withdrawal of it was proper. Cases involving facts similar to those at bar include National Advertising Co. v. Herold, supra, and *Sokol v. Hill,* supra.

The judgment is affirmed.

NOTES

(1) *Offeror's Mastery of Offer.* The offeror is master of the offer. It is recognized that the offeror may stipulate the terms upon which he or she is willing to bargain, and, also, prescribe the method by which the offeree may accept. The offeror fashions the power of acceptance which is conferred upon the offeree and can expressly limit the ways in which that power may be exercised. Hence, it follows that an examination of the terms of the offer is a first step in determining the validity of an alleged acceptance.

Consider the *La Salle Bank* and the *Hendricks* cases and answer the following questions: (a) What did the offeror indicate as to the permissible manner of acceptance? Was that manner invited or required? (b) Did the offeree accept in either case? Why not? (c) Suppose in *La Salle Bank* that the bank had executed the written offer by signature before Vega revoked it. Would there then be a contract or would, as in *Hendricks*, notice to Vega of the signature be required?

(2) A signature, if invited or required as a method of acceptance, constitutes assent to the proposed bargain, including a promise to perform the agreement. A signature is not part performance of the proposed exchange. But is the signature alone enough? Consider this quote from an earlier treatise on contracts. See also, Restatement (Second) of Contracts §§ 50–56.

"If we are to proceed on an objective theory of mutual assent, it would seem to be too clear for argument that the offeree's assent should be communicated or manifested to the offeror before a contract can come into being. This is so because, it is what the one party has caused the other to believe he intends, that is important, rather than what he actually intends or what he has caused the world at large to believe he intends. Moreover, where the offer is one that calls for the making of a promise as the requested return, there is an additional reason for reaching this conclusion. The very idea of promise involves communication. In other words, a promise is a communicated undertaking." Grismore, Contracts § 45 (1st ed. 1947).

Ever–Tite Roofing Corp. v. Green

Court of Appeal of Louisiana, 1955.
83 So.2d 449.

■ AYRES, JUDGE. This is an action for damages allegedly sustained by plaintiff as the result of the breach by the defendants of a written contract for the re-roofing of defendants' residence. Defendants denied that their written proposal or offer was ever accepted by plaintiff in the manner stipulated therein for its acceptance, and hence contended no contract was ever entered into. The trial court sustained defendants' defense and rejected plaintiff's demands and dismissed its suit at its costs. From the judgment thus rendered and signed, plaintiff appealed.

Defendants executed and signed an instrument June 10, 1953, for the purpose of obtaining the services of plaintiff in re-roofing their residence situated in Webster Parish, Louisiana. The document set out in detail the work to be done and the price therefor to be paid in monthly installments. This instrument was likewise signed by plaintiff's sale representative, who, however, was without authority to accept the contract for and on behalf of the plaintiff. This alleged contract contained these provisions:

"This agreement shall become binding only upon written acceptance hereof, by the principal or authorized officer of the Contractor, *or upon commencing performance of the work*. This contract is Not Subject to Cancellation. . . ." (Emphasis supplied.)

Inasmuch as this work was to be performed entirely on credit, it was necessary for plaintiff to obtain credit reports and approval from the lending institution which was to finance said contract. With this procedure defendants were more or less familiar and knew their credit rating would have to be checked and a report made. On receipt of the proposed contract in plaintiff's office on the day following its execution, plaintiff requested a credit report, which was made after investigation and which was received in due course and submitted by plaintiff to the lending agency. Additional information was requested by this institution, which was likewise in due course transmitted to the institution, which then gave its approval.

The day immediately following this approval, which was either June 18 or 19, 1953, plaintiff engaged its workmen and two trucks, loaded the trucks with the necessary roofing materials and proceeded from Shreveport to defendants' residence for the purpose of doing the work and performing the services allegedly contracted for the defendants. Upon their arrival at defendants' residence, the workmen found others in the performance of the work which plaintiff had contracted to do. Defendants notified plaintiff's workmen that the work had been contracted to other parties two days before and forbade them to do the work.

Formal acceptance of the contract was not made under the signature and approval of an agent of plaintiff. It was, however, the intention of plaintiff to accept the contract by commencing the work, which was one of the ways provided for in the instrument for acceptance, as will be shown by reference to the extract from the contract quoted hereinabove. Prior to this time, however, defendants had determined on a course of abrogating the agreement and engaged other workmen without notice thereof to plaintiff.

The basis of the judgment appealed was that defendants had timely notified plaintiff before "commencing performance of work". The trial court held that notice to plaintiff's workmen upon their arrival with the materials that defendants did not desire them to commence the actual work was sufficient and timely to signify their intention to withdraw from the contract. With this conclusion we find ourselves unable to agree.

Defendants' attempt to justify their delay in thus notifying plaintiff for the reason they did not know where or how to contact plaintiff is without merit. The contract itself, a copy of which was left with them, conspicuously displayed plaintiff's name, address and telephone number. Be that as it may, defendants at no time, from June 10, 1953, until plaintiff's workmen arrived for the purpose of commencing the work, notified or attempted to notify plaintiff of their intention to abrogate, terminate or cancel the contract.

Defendants evidently knew this work was to be processed through plaintiff's Shreveport office. The record discloses no unreasonable delay on plaintiff's part in receiving, processing or accepting the contract or in commencing the work contracted to be done. No time limit was specified in the contract within which it was to be accepted or within which the work was to be begun. It was nevertheless understood between the parties that some delay would ensue before the acceptance of the contract and the commencement of the work, due to the necessity of compliance with the requirements relative to financing the job through a lending agency. The evidence as referred to hereinabove shows that plaintiff proceeded with due diligence.

The general rule of law is that an offer proposed may be withdrawn before its acceptance and that no obligation is incurred thereby. This is, however, not without exceptions. For instance, Restatement of the Law of Contracts stated:

"(1) The power to create a contract by acceptance of an offer terminates at the time specified in the offer, or, if no time is specified, at the end of a reasonable time.

"What is a reasonable time is a question of fact depending on the nature of the contract proposed, the usages of business and other circumstances of the case which the offeree at the time of his acceptance either knows or has reason to know."

* * *

Therefore, since the contract did not specify the time within which it was to be accepted or within which the work was to have been commenced, a reasonable time must be allowed therefor in accordance with the facts and circumstances and the evident intention of the parties. A reasonable time is contemplated where no time is expressed. What is a reasonable time depends more or less upon the circumstances surrounding each particular case. The delays to process defendants' application were not unusual. The contract was accepted by plaintiff by commencement of the performance of the work contracted to be done. This commencement began with the loading of the trucks with the necessary materials in Shreveport and transporting such materials and the workmen to defendants' residence. Actual commencement or performance of the work therefore began before any notice of dissent by defendants was given plaintiff. The proposition and its acceptance thus became a completed contract.

By their aforesaid acts defendants breached the contract. They employed others to do the work contracted to be done by plaintiff and forbade plaintiff's workmen to engage upon that undertaking. By this breach defendants are legally bound to respond to plaintiff in damages. . . .

* * *

Plaintiff expended the sum of $85.37 in loading the trucks in Shreveport with materials and in transporting them to the site of defendants' residence in Webster Parish and in unloading them on their return, and for wages for the workmen for the time consumed. Plaintiff's Shreveport manager testified that the expected profit on this job was $226. None of this evidence is controverted or contradicted in any manner.

* * *

For the reasons assigned, the judgment appealed is annulled, avoided, reversed and set aside and there is now judgment in favor of plaintiff, Ever–Tite Roofing Corporation, against the defendants, G.T. Green and Mrs. Jessie Fay Green, for the full sum of $311.37, with 5 per cent per annum interest thereon from judicial demand until paid, and for all costs.

Reversed and rendered.

NOTES

(1) In legal contemplation what did "commencement of performance" signify in *Ever-Tite*? Was it a promise to perform the work? If so, should it have been communicated to the offeror before the contract was concluded? See Restatement (Second) of Contracts §§ 53, 54; Corbin § 62.

(2) Granted that an acceptance by "commencement of performance" was invited in *Ever-Tite,* was there, on the facts stated, such a commencement? At what point could one say the work commenced? With the loading of the trucks? When the trip to Webster Parish began? Or when? Note that the offer (by the homeowner) was made on a form prepared by the offeree. How should this fact affect the analysis?

(3) Homeowner submitted an order to Manufacturer on a form prepared by Manufacturers for the purchase of aluminum storm doors and windows. The order contained the following stipulation: "This contract is not binding on manufacturer until accepted by signature of authorized agent at the home office. It shall then be a binding contract as to all parties, and is not, thereafter, subject to cancellation." When the order was received at the home office, Manufacturer checked Homeowner's credit and found it satisfactory. Whereupon, it began fabricating the doors and windows. At no time, however, was the order signed by Manufacturer, nor did the latter notify Homeowner that work had commenced. Homeowner telephoned Manufacturer that he had changed his mind and wanted to cancel the order. Was his revocation timely? See Venters v. Stewart, 261 S.W.2d 444 (Ky.1953). Would your answer be the same if Homeowner had been aware that work had begun?

Corinthian Pharmaceutical Systems, Inc. v. Lederle Laboratories

United States District Court, Southern District, Indiana, 1989.
724 F.Supp. 605.

■ McKINNEY, DISTRICT JUDGE.

* * *

Defendant Lederle Laboratories is a pharmaceutical manufacturer and distributor that makes a number of drugs, including the DTP vaccine. Plaintiff Corinthian Pharmaceutical is a distributor of drugs that purchases supplies from manufacturers such as Lederle Labs and then resells the product to physicians and other providers. One of the products that Corinthian buys and distributes with some regularity is the DTP vaccine.

In 1984, Corinthian and Lederle became entangled in litigation when Corinthian ordered more than 6,000 vials of DTP and Lederle refused to fill the order. That lawsuit was settled by written agreement whereby Lederle agreed to sell a specified amount of vaccine to Corinthian at specified times. Lederle fully performed under the 1984 settlement agreement, and that prior dispute is not at issue. One of the conditions of the settlement was that Corinthian "may order additional vials of [vaccine] from Lederle at the market price and under the terms and conditions of sale in effect as of the date of the order."

After that litigation was settled Lederle continued to manufacture and sell the vaccine, and Corinthian continued to buy it from Lederle and other sources. Lederle periodically issued a price list to its customers for all of its products. Each price list stated that all orders were subject to acceptance by

Lederle at its home office, and indicated that the prices shown "were in effect at the time of publication but are submitted without offer and are subject to change without notice." The price list further stated that changes in price "take immediate effect and unfilled current orders and back orders will be invoiced at the price in effect at the time shipment is made."

From 1985 through early 1986, Corinthian made a number of purchases of the vaccine from Lederle Labs. During this period of time, the largest single order ever placed by Corinthian with Lederle was for 100 vials. When Lederle Labs filled an order it sent an invoice to Corinthian.
* * *

* * *

During this period of time, product liability lawsuits concerning DTP increased, and insurance became more difficult to procure. As a result, Lederle decided in early 1986 to self-insure against such risks. In order to cover the costs of self-insurance, Lederle concluded that a substantial increase in the price of the vaccine would be necessary.

In order to communicate the price change to its own sales people, Lederle's Price Manager prepared "PRICE LETTER NO. E–48." This document was dated May 19, 1986, and indicated that effective May 20, 1986, the price of the DTP vaccine would be raised from $51.00 to $171.00 per vial. Price letters such as these were routinely sent to Lederle's sales force, but did not go to customers. Corinthian Pharmaceutical did not know of the existence of this internal price letter until a Lederle representative presented it to Corinthian several weeks after May 20, 1986.

Additionally, Lederle Labs also wrote a letter dated May 20, 1986, to its customers announcing the price increase and explaining the liability and insurance problems that brought about the change. Corinthian somehow gained knowledge of this letter on May 19, 1986, the date before the price increase was to take effect. In response to the knowledge of the impending price increase, Corinthian immediately ordered 1000 vials of DTP vaccine from Lederle. Corinthian placed its order on May 19, 1986, by calling Lederle's "Telgo" system. The Telgo system is a telephone computer ordering system that allows customers to place orders over the phone by communicating with a computer. After Corinthian placed its order with the Telgo system, the computer gave Corinthian a tracking number for its order. On the same date, Corinthian sent Lederle two written confirmations of its order. On each form Corinthian stated that this "order is to receive the $64.32 per vial price."

On June 3, 1986, Lederle sent invoice 1771 to Corinthian for 50 vials of DTP vaccine priced at $64.32 per vial. The invoice contained the standard Lederle conditions noted above. The 50 vials were sent to Corinthian and were accepted. At the same time, Lederle sent its customers, including Corinthian, a letter regarding DTP vaccine pricing and orders. This letter stated that the "enclosed represents a partial shipment of the order for DTP vaccine, which you placed with Lederle on May 19, 1986." The letter stated that under Lederle's standard terms and conditions of sale the normal policy would be to invoice the order at the price when shipment was made. However, in light of the magnitude of the price increase, Lederle had decided to make an exception to its terms and conditions and ship a portion of the order at the lower price. The letter further stated that the balance would be priced at $171.00, and that shipment would be made during the week of June 16. The letter closed, "If for any reason you wish to cancel the balance of your order, please contact [us] . . . on or before June 13."

Based on these facts, plaintiff Corinthian Pharmaceutical brings this action seeking specific performance for the 950 vials of DTP vaccine that Lederle Labs chose not to deliver. In support of its summary judgment motion, Lederle urges a number of alternative grounds for disposing of this claim, including that no contract for the sale of 1000 vials was formed, that if one was formed, it was governed by Lederle's terms and conditions, and that the 50 vials sent to Corinthian were merely an accommodation.

* * *

[T]his is a straightforward sale of goods problem resembling those found in a contracts or sales casebook. The fundamental question is whether Lederle Labs agreed to sell Corinthian Pharmaceuticals 1,000 vials of DTP vaccine at $64.32 per vial. As shown below, the undisputed material facts mandate the conclusion as a matter of law that no such agreement was ever formed.

* * *

Initially, it should be noted that this is a sale of goods covered by the Uniform Commercial Code, and that both parties are merchants under the Code. The parties do not discuss which state's laws are to apply to action, but because the Code is substantially the same in all states having any connection to this dispute, the Court will, for ease of reference, refer in general to the U.C.C. with relevant interpretations from Indiana and other states.[8]

The starting point in this analysis is where did the first offer originate. An offer is "the manifestation of willingness to enter into a bargain, so made as to justify another person in understanding that his assent to that bargain is invited and will conclude it." H. Greenberg, *Rights and Remedies Under U.C.C. Article 2* § 5.2 at 50 (1987) [*hereinafter* "Greenberg, *U.C.C. Article 2* "], (*quoting 1 Restatement (Second), Contracts* § 4 (1981)). The only possible conclusion in this case is that Corinthian's "order" of May 19, 1986, for 1,000 vials at $64.32 was the first offer. Nothing that the seller had done prior to this point can be interpreted as an offer.

First, the price lists distributed by Lederle to its customers did not constitute offers. It is well settled that quotations are mere invitations to

---

8. The Court notes that Lederle's standard terms state that any contract is to be construed under New Jersey law. For purposes of this motion, because it is not estab-lished that there is any difference between New Jersey's and Indiana's interpretation of the Code, the Court will use Indiana U.C.C. decisions for simplicity.

make an offer, Greenberg, *U.C.C. Article 2* § 5.2 at 51; *Corbin on Contracts* §§ 26, 28 (1982), particularly where, as here, the price lists specifically stated that prices were subject to change without notice and that all orders were subject to acceptance by Lederle. Greenberg, *U.C.C. Article 2* § 5.2 at 51; Quaker State Mushroom v. Dominick's Finer Foods, 635 F.Supp. 1281, 1284 (N.D.Ill.1986) (No offer where price quotation is subject to change and orders are subject to seller's confirmation); Interstate Industries, Inc. v. Barclay Industries, Inc., 540 F.2d 868, 873 (7th Cir.1976) (price quotation not an offer).

Second, neither Lederle's internal price memorandum nor its letter to customers dated May 20, 1986, can be construed as an offer to sell 1,000 vials at the lower price. There is no evidence that Lederle intended Corinthian to receive the internal price memorandum, nor is there anything in the record to support the conclusion that the May 20, 1986, letter was an offer to sell 1,000 vials to Corinthian at the lower price. If anything, the evidence shows that Corinthian was not supposed to receive this letter until after the price increase had taken place. Moreover, the letter, just like the price lists, was a mere quotation (i.e., an invitation to submit an offer) sent to all customers. As such, it did not bestow on Corinthian nor other customers the power to form a binding contract for the sale of one thousand, or, for that matter, one million vials of vaccine.[9]

Thus, as a matter of law, the first offer was made by Corinthian when it phoned in and subsequently confirmed its order for 1,000 vials at the lower price. The next question, then, is whether Lederle ever accepted that offer.

Under the Code, an acceptance need not be the mirror-image of the offer. U.C.C. § 2–207. However, the offeree must still do some act that manifests the intention to accept the offer and make a contract. Under § 2–206, an offer to make a contract shall be construed as inviting acceptance in any manner and by any medium reasonable in the circumstances. The first question regarding acceptance, therefore, is whether Lederle accepted the offer prior to sending the 50 vials of vaccine.

The record is clear that Lederle did not communicate or do any act prior to shipping the 50 vials that could support the finding of an acceptance. When Corinthian placed its order, it merely received a tracking number from the Telgo computer. Such an automated, ministerial act cannot constitute an acceptance. See, e.g., Foremost Pro Color, Inc. v. Eastman Kodak Co., 703 F.2d 534, 539 (9th Cir.1983) (logging purchase orders as received did not manifest acceptance); Southern Spindle & Flyer Co. v. Milliken & Co., 53 N.C.App. 785, 281 S.E.2d 734, 736 (1981) (seller's acknowledgement of receipt of purchase order did not constitute assent to its terms). Thus, there was no acceptance of Corinthian's offer prior to the deliver of 50 vials.

9. Nor is there any course of dealing that can support the existence of an offer by   Lederle to Corinthian.

The next question, then, is what is to be made of the shipment of 50 vials and the accompanying letter. Section 2–206(b) of the Code speaks to this issue:

> [A]n order or other offer to buy goods for prompt or current shipment shall be construed as inviting acceptance either by a prompt promise to ship or by the prompt or current shipment of conforming or non-conforming goods, *but such a shipment of non-conforming goods does not constitute an acceptance if the seller seasonably notifies the buyer that the shipment is offered only as an accommodation to the buyer.*

§ 2–206 (emphasis added). Thus, under the Code a seller accepts the offer by shipping goods, whether they are conforming or not, but if the seller ships non-conforming goods and seasonably notifies the buyer that the shipment is a mere accommodation, then the seller has not, in fact, accepted the buyer's offer. See Greenberg, *U.C.C. Article 2* § 5.5 at 53.

In this case, the offer made by Corinthian was for 1,000 vials at $64.32. In response, Lederle Labs shipped only 50 vials at $64.32 per vial, and wrote Corinthian indicating that the balance of the order would be priced at $171.00 per vial and would be shipped during the week of June 16. The letter further indicated that the buyer could cancel its order by calling Lederle Labs. Clearly, Lederle's shipment was non-conforming, for it was for only 1/20th of the quantity desired by the buyer. See § 2–106(2) (goods or conduct are conforming when they are in accordance with the obligations under the contract); Michiana Mack, Inc. v. Allendale Rural Fire Protection, 428 N.E.2d 1367, 1370 (Ind.App.1981) (non-conformity describes goods and conduct). The narrow issue, then, is whether Lederle's response to the offer was a shipment of non-conforming goods not constituting an acceptance because it was offered only as an accommodation under § 2–206.

An accommodation is an arrangement or engagement made as a favor to another. *Black's Law Dictionary* (5th ed. 1979). The term implies no consideration. *Id.* In this case, then, even taking all inferences favorably for the buyer, the only possible conclusion is that Lederle Labs' shipment of 50 vials was offered merely as an accommodation; that is to say, Lederle had no obligation to make the partial shipment, and did so only as a favor to the buyer. The accommodation letter, which Corinthian is sure it received, clearly stated that the 50 vials were being sent at the lower price as an exception to Lederle's general policy, and that the balance of the offer would be invoiced at the higher price. The letter further indicated that Lederle's proposal to ship the balance of the order at the higher price could be rejected by the buyer. Moreover, the standard terms of Lederle's invoice stated that acceptance of the order was expressly conditioned upon buyer's assent to the seller's terms.

Under these undisputed facts, § 2–206(1)(b) was satisfied. Where, as here, the notification is properly made, the shipment of nonconforming goods is treated as a counteroffer just as at common law, and the buyer may accept or reject the counteroffer under normal contract rules. 2 W. Hawkland, *Uniform Commercial Code Series* § 2–206:04 (1987).

Thus, the end result of this analysis is that Lederle Lab's price quotations were mere invitations to make an offer, that by placing its order Corinthian made an offer to buy 1,000 vials at the low price, that by shipping 50 vials at the low price Lederle's response was non-conforming, but the non-conforming response was a mere accommodation and thus constituted a counteroffer. Accordingly, there being no genuine issues of material fact on these issues and the law being in favor of the seller, summary judgment must be granted for Lederle Labs.

* * *

For all these reasons, the defendant's motion for summary judgment is granted.

IT IS SO ORDERED.

[Some footnotes omitted.]

NOTES

(1) UCC 2–206(1)[UCC 2–205 (1997)]: "Unless otherwise unambiguously indicated by the language or circumstances

  (a) an offer to make a contract shall be construed as inviting acceptance in any manner and by any medium reasonable in the circumstances;

  (b) an order or other offer to buy goods for prompt or current shipment shall be construed as inviting acceptance either by a prompt promise to ship or by the prompt or current shipment of conforming or non-conforming goods, but such a shipment of non-conforming goods does not constitute an acceptance if the seller seasonably notifies the buyer that the shipment is offered only as an accommodation to the buyer."

Section 2–205(a)(1997) makes no substantive changes except that the following phrase is added after the phrase "reasonable in the circumstances": "including a definite expression of acceptance containing terms that vary the terms of the offer."

(2) The past three cases have concerned the mode by which an offeree may or must indicate a return commitment or promise. As it bears on cases of this type, UCC 2–206 reflects a belief that in the ordinary transaction the offeror is relatively indifferent as to whether acceptance is indicated by "promissory language" or a "promissory act." Conduct, such as commencement of performance, might serve equally as well as the signing of a document to manifest the offeree's assent to the offer.

(3) Had Lederle Labs not given notice to Corinthian that the 50 vials were shipped as an accommodation, what would have been the legal effect of such shipment? Is it possible, under UCC 2–206, to have an "acceptance" which is also a "breach"?

(4) If the offeror specifies that "the signed acceptance of this proposal shall constitute a contract," the requisite signature would seem to conclude a

contract whether or not the offeror knew the action had been taken and despite the lack of any attempt by the offeree to so inform the offeror. For the offeror's mastery of the offer enables one to prescribe how the power of acceptance can be exercised, and one may, if one sees fit, agree to be bound at the moment of signing. By necessary inference the offeror appears to dispense with the necessity of communication of the offeree's assent, and one can be placed in a contractual relationship without knowing it. But what if the offeror does not expressly indicate when the acceptance is to become operative? Are we to assume, then, that there must be a communication, just as there would seem to be no operative offer until it is communicated? Cases which follow deal with these questions as they arise in varying contexts.

PROBLEM: THE CASE OF THE BROAD INDEMNITY

Ford ordered machinery and equipment which was to be delivered and installed by Allied under a purchase order which provided that "the signing and returning to Buyer by Seller of the Acknowledgment Copy shall constitute acceptance." The printed purchase order, prepared by Ford, also provided that if work was done on Ford's premises Allied would be responsible for any and all damages and personal injuries caused by the fault or negligence of Allied employees. A broader indemnity clause, attached to the form, was marked VOID and did not become part of the contract. Ford then deleted the requirement that Allied install the goods and the agreement was fully performed.

Eleven months later Ford submitted a second purchase order for additional goods to be installed by Allied. (Amendment No. 2). The written order provided: "This purchase order agreement is not binding until accepted. Acceptance should be executed on acknowledgment copy which should be returned to buyer." This time, however, the broader indemnity clause was included in the form, under which Allied was responsible for the acts of its employees and Ford's. (Form 3618). The indemnity form was not marked VOID as it had been in the first contract and the printed form clearly stated that terms in the second contract which were inconsistent with the first controlled. On September 5, 1956, after Allied had commenced work on Ford premises, an employee of Allied was injured by the negligence of a Ford employee. The acknowledgment was duly executed by Allied on November 10, 1956 and received by Ford on November 12. Later, the injured employee sued Ford which brought in Allied as a third-party defendant liable to Ford under the indemnity clause. The jury returned a verdict in favor of the employee against Ford, and Ford against Allied under the indemnity clause. Allied appealed from the judgment against it. What result? See Allied Steel and Conveyors, Inc. v. Ford Motor Co., 277 F.2d 907 (6th Cir.1960).

Carlill v. Carbolic Smoke Ball Co.

Court of Appeal, 1893.
[1893] 1 Q.B. 256.

The defendants, who were the proprietors and vendors of a medical preparation called "The Carbolic Smoke Ball," inserted in the *Pall Mall Gazette* of November 13, 1891, and in other newspapers, the following advertisement: "100£. reward will be paid by the Carbolic Smoke Ball

Company to any person who contracts the increasing epidemic influenza, colds, or any disease caused by taking cold, after having used the ball three times daily for two weeks according to the printed directions supplied with each ball. 1000£. is deposited with the Alliance Bank, Regent Street, shewing our sincerity in the matter.

JAN. 23, 1892.   THE ILLUSTRATED LONDON NEWS   113

CARBOLIC SMOKE BALL

WILL POSITIVELY CURE

COUGHS	CATARRH	HOARSENESS	THROAT DEAFNESS	INFLUENZA	CROUP
Cured in 1 week	Cured in 1 to 3 months.	Cured in 12 hours.	Cured in 1 to 3 months.	Cured in 24 hours.	Relieved in 5 minutes.
COLD IN THE HEAD	ASTHMA	LOSS OF VOICE	SNORING	HAY FEVER	WHOOPING COUGH
Cured in 12 hours.	Relieved in 10 minutes.	Fully restored.	Cured in 1 week	Cured in every case.	Relieved the first application.
COLD ON THE CHEST	BRONCHITIS	SORE THROAT	SORE EYES	HEADACHE	NEURALGIA
Cured in 12 hours.	Cured in every case.	Cured in 12 hours.	Cured in 2 weeks.	Cured in 10 minutes.	Cured in 10 minutes.

As all the Diseases mentioned above proceed from one cause, they can be Cured by this Remedy

£100 REWARD

WILL BE PAID BY THE

CARBOLIC SMOKE BALL CO.

to any Person who contracts the Increasing Epidemic

INFLUENZA,

Colds, or any Diseases caused by taking Cold, after having used the **CARBOLIC SMOKE BALL** according to the printed directions supplied with each Ball.

£1000 IS DEPOSITED

with the ALLIANCE BANK, Regent Street, showing our sincerity in the matter.

During the last epidemic of **INFLUENZA** many thousand **CARBOLIC SMOKE BALLS** were sold as preventives against this disease, and in no ascertained case was the disease contracted by those using the **CARBOLIC SMOKE BALL**.

THE CARBOLIC SMOKE BALL,

TESTIMONIALS.

The DUKE OF PORTLAND writes: "I am much obliged for the Carbolic Smoke Ball which you have sent me, and which I find most efficacious."

SIR FREDERICK MILNER, Bart., M.P., writes from Nice, March ?, 1890: "Lady Milner and my children have derived much benefit from the Carbolic Smoke Ball."

Lady MOSTYN writes from Carshalton, Cary Crescent, Torquay, Jan. 10, 1890: "Lady Mostyn believes the Carbolic Smoke Ball to be a certain check and a cure for a cold, and will have great pleasure in recommending it to her friends. Lady Mostyn hopes the Carbolic Smoke Ball will have all the success its merits deserve."

Lady ERSKINE writes from Sprotton Hall Northampton, Jan. 1, 1890: "Lady Erskine is pleased to say that the Carbolic Smoke Ball has given every satisfaction; she considers it a very good invention."

Mrs GLADSTONE writes: "She finds the Carbolic Smoke Ball has done her a great deal of good."

Madame ADELINA PATTI writes: "Madame Patti has found the Carbolic Smoke Ball very beneficial, and the only thing that would enable her to rest well at night when having a severe cold."

AS PRESCRIBED BY
SIR MORELL MACKENZIE, M.D.,
HAS BEEN SUPPLIED TO
H.I.M. THE GERMAN EMPRESS.

H.R.H. The Duke of Edinburgh, K.G.
H.R.H. The Duke of Connaught, K.G.
The Duke of Fife, K.T.
The Marquis of Salisbury, K.G.
The Duke of Argyll, K.T.
The Duke of Westminster, K.G.
The Duke of Richmond and Gordon, K.G.
The Duke of Manchester.
The Duke of Newcastle.
The Duke of Norfolk.
The Duke of Rutland, K.G.
The Duke of Wellington
The Marquis of Ripon, K.G.
The Earl of Derby, K.G
Earl Spencer, K.G.
The Lord Chancellor.
The Lord Chief Justice.
Lord Tennyson.

TESTIMONIALS.

The BISHOP OF LONDON writes: "The Carbolic Smoke Ball has benefited me greatly."

The MARCHIONESS DE SALIS writes from Padworth House, Reading, Jan. 13, 1890: "The Marchioness de Salis has daily used the Smoke Ball since the commencement of the epidemic of Influenza, and has not taken the Influenza, although surrounded by those suffering from it."

Dr. J. RUSSELL GARNER, M.D. writes from 5, Adam Street, Adelphi, Sept. 24, 1891: "Many obstinate cases of post-nasal catarrh, which have resisted other treatment, have yielded to your Carbolic Smoke Ball."

A. GIBBONS, Esq., Editor of the *Lady's Pictorial*, writes from 172, Strand, W.C., Feb. 14, 1890: "During a recent sharp attack of the prevailing epidemic I had none of the unpleasant and dangerous catarrh and bronchial symptoms. I attribute this entirely to the use of the Carbolic Smoke Ball."

The Rev. Dr. CHICHESTER A. W. RYADE, LL.D., D.C.L., writes from Banstead Downs, Surrey, May 1890: "My duties in a large public institution have brought me daily during the recent epidemic of influenza, in close contact with the disease. I have been perfectly free from any symptom by having the Smoke Ball always handy. It has also wonderfully improved my voice for speaking and singing."

The Originals of these Testimonials may be seen at our Consulting Rooms, with hundreds of others.

One **CARBOLIC SMOKE BALL** will last a family several months, making it the cheapest remedy in the world at the price 10s., post free.

The **CARBOLIC SMOKE BALL** can be refilled, when empty, at a cost of 5s., post free. Address:

CARBOLIC SMOKE BALL CO., 27, PRINCES ST., HANOVER SQ., LONDON, W.

[B4345]

"During the last epidemic of influenza many thousand carbolic smoke balls were sold as preventives against this disease, and in no ascertained case was the disease contracted by those using the carbolic smoke ball.

"One carbolic smoke ball will last a family several months, making it the cheapest remedy in the world at the price, 10*s.*, post free. The ball can be refilled at a cost of 5*s.* Address, Carbolic Smoke Ball Company, 27 Princes Street, Hanover Square, London."

The plaintiff [Lilli Carlill], a lady, on the faith of this advertisement, bought one of the balls at a chemist's, and used it as directed, three times a day, from November 20, 1891, to January 17, 1892, when she was attacked by influenza. Hawkins, J., held that she was entitled to recover the 100£. The defendants appealed.

■ LINDLEY, L.J.

* * * The first observation I will make is that we are not dealing with any inference of fact. We are dealing with an express promise to pay 100£. in certain events. Read the advertisement how you will, and twist it about as you will, here is a distinct promise expressed in language which is perfectly unmistakable—"100£. reward will be paid by the Carbolic Smoke Ball Company to any person who contracts the influenza after having used the ball three times daily for two weeks according to the printed directions supplied with each ball."

We must first consider whether this was intended to be a promise at all, or whether it was a mere puff which meant nothing. Was it a mere puff? My answer to that question is No, and I base my answer upon this passage: "1000£. is deposited with the Alliance Bank, shewing our sincerity in the matter." Now, for what was that money deposited or that statement made except to negative the suggestion that this was a mere puff and meant nothing at all? The deposit is called in aid by the advertiser as proof of his sincerity in the matter—that is, the sincerity of his promise to pay this 100£. in the event which he has specified. I say this for the purpose of giving point to the observation that we are not inferring a promise; there is the promise, as plain as words can make it.

Then it is contended that it is not binding. In the first place, it is said that it is not made with anybody in particular. Now that point is common to the words of this advertisement and to the words of all other advertisements offering rewards. They are offers to anybody who performs the conditions named in the advertisement, and anybody who does perform the condition accepts the offer. In point of law this advertisement is an offer to pay 100£. to anybody who will perform these conditions, and the performance of the conditions is the acceptance of the offer.

* * *

We, therefore, find here all the elements which are necessary to form a binding contract enforceable in point of law, subject to two observations. First of all it is said that this advertisement is so vague that you cannot really construe it as a promise—that the vagueness of the language shews that a legal promise was never intended or contemplated. The language is vague and uncertain in some respects, and particularly in this, that the 100£. is to be paid to any person who contracts the increasing epidemic after having used the balls three times daily for two weeks. It is said, When are they to be used? According to the language of the advertisement no time is fixed, and, construing the offer most strongly against the person who has made it, one might infer that any time was meant. I do not think that was meant, and to hold the contrary would be pushing too far the doctrine of taking language most strongly against the person using it. I do not think that business people or reasonable people would understand the words as meaning that if you took a smoke ball and used it three times daily for two weeks you were to be guaranteed against influenza for the rest of your life, and I think it would be pushing the language of the advertisement too far to construe it as meaning that. But if it does not mean that, what does it mean? It is for the defendants to shew what it does mean; and it strikes me that there are two, and possibly three, reasonable constructions to be put on this advertisement, any one of which will answer the purpose of the plaintiff. Possibly it may be limited to persons catching the "increasing epidemic" (that is, the then prevailing epidemic), or any colds or diseases caused by taking cold, during the prevalence of the increasing epidemic. That is one suggestion; but it does not commend itself to me. Another suggested meaning is that you are warranted free from catching this epidemic, or colds or other diseases caused by taking cold, whilst you are using this remedy after using it for two weeks. If that is the meaning, the plaintiff is right, for she used the remedy for two weeks and went on using it till she got the epidemic. Another meaning, and the one which I rather prefer, is that the reward is offered to any person who contracts the epidemic or other disease within a reasonable time after having used the smoke ball. Then it is asked, What is a reasonable time? It has been suggested that there is no standard of reasonableness; that it depends upon the reasonable time for a germ to develop! I do not feel pressed by that. It strikes me that a reasonable time may be ascertained in a business sense and in a sense satisfactory to a lawyer, in this way; find out from a chemist what the ingredients are; find out from a skilled physician how long the effect of such ingredients on the system could be reasonably expected to endure so as to protect a person from an epidemic or cold, and in that way you will get a standard to be laid before a jury, or a judge without a jury, by which they might exercise their judgment as to what a reasonable time would be. It strikes me, I confess, that the true construction of this advertisement is that 100£. will be paid to anybody who uses this smoke ball three times daily for two weeks according to the printed directions, and who gets the influenza or cold or other diseases caused by taking cold within a reasonable time after so using it; and if that is the true construction, it is enough for the plaintiff. . . .

It appears to me, therefore, that the defendants must perform their promise, and, if they have been so unwary as to expose themselves to a great many actions, so much the worse for them.

■ BOWEN, L.J. I am of the same opinion.

* * * One cannot doubt that, as an ordinary rule of law, an acceptance of an offer made ought to be notified to the person who makes the offer, in order that the two minds may come together. Unless this is done the two minds may be apart, and there is not that consensus which is necessary according to the English law—I say nothing about the laws of other countries—to make a contract. But there is this clear gloss to be made upon the doctrine, that as notification of acceptance is required for the benefit of the person who makes the offer, the person who makes the offer may dispense with notice to himself if he thinks it desirable to do so and I suppose there can be no doubt that where a person in an offer made by him to another person, expressly or impliedly intimates a particular mode of acceptance as sufficient to make the bargain binding, it is only necessary for the other person to whom such offer is made to follow the indicated method of acceptance; and if the person making the offer, expressly or impliedly intimates in his offer that it will be sufficient to act on the proposal without communicating acceptance of it to himself, performance of the condition is a sufficient acceptance without notification.

* * *

Now, if that is the law, how are we to find out whether the person who makes the offer does intimate that notification of acceptance will not be necessary in order to constitute a binding bargain? In many cases you look to the offer itself. In many cases you extract from the character of the transaction that notification is not required, and in the advertisement cases it seems to me to follow as an inference to be drawn from the transaction itself that a person is not to notify his acceptance of the offer before he performs the condition, but that if he performs the condition notification is dispensed with. It seems to me that from the point of view of common sense no other idea could be entertained. If I advertise to the world that my dog is lost, and that anybody who brings the dog to a particular place will be paid some money, are all the police or other persons whose business it is to find lost dogs to be expected to sit down and write me a note saying that they have accepted my proposal? Why, of course, they at once look after the dog, and as soon as they find the dog they have performed the condition. The essence of the transaction is that the dog should be found, and it is not necessary under such circumstances, as it seems to me, that in order to make the contract binding there should be any notification of acceptance. It follows from the nature of the thing that the performance of the condition is sufficient acceptance without the notification of it, and a person who makes an offer in an advertisement of that kind makes an offer which must be read by the light of that common sense reflection. He does, therefore, in his offer impliedly indicate that he does not require notification of the acceptance of the offer.

A further argument for the defendants was that this was a nudum pactum—that there was no consideration for the promise—that taking the influenza was only a condition, and that the using the smoke ball was only a condition, and that there was no consideration at all; in fact that there was no request, express or implied, to use the smoke ball. * * * Can it be said here that if the person who reads this advertisement applies thrice daily, for such time as may seem to him tolerable, the carbolic smoke ball to his nostrils for a whole fortnight, he is doing nothing at all—that it is a mere act which is not to count towards consideration to support a promise (for the law does not require us to measure the adequacy of the consideration). Inconvenience sustained by one party at the request of the other is enough to create a consideration. I think, therefore, that it is consideration enough that the plaintiff took the trouble of using the smoke ball. But I think also that the defendants received a benefit from this user, for the use of the smoke ball was contemplated by the defendants as being indirectly a benefit to them, because the use of the smoke balls would promote their sale.

* * *

I cannot picture to myself the view of the law on which the contrary could be held when you have once found who are the contracting parties. If I say to a person, "If you use such and such a medicine for a week I will give you 5£.," and he uses it, there is ample consideration for the promise.

■ A.L. SMITH, L.J.

* * *

[I]t was argued, that if the advertisement constituted an offer which might culminate in a contract if it was accepted, and its conditions performed, yet it was not accepted by the plaintiff in the manner contemplated, and that the offer contemplated was such that notice of the acceptance had to be given by the party using the carbolic ball to the defendants before user, so that the defendants might be at liberty to superintend the experiment. All I can say is, that there is no such clause in the advertisement, and that, in my judgment, no such clause can be read into it; and I entirely agree with what has fallen from my Brothers, that this is one of those cases in which a performance of the condition by using these smoke balls for two weeks three times a day is an acceptance of the offer.

* * *

Lastly, it was said that there was no consideration, and that it was nudum pactum. There are two considerations here. One is the consideration of the inconvenience of having to use this carbolic smoke ball for two weeks three times a day; and the other more important consideration is the money gain likely to accrue to the defendants by the enhanced sale of the smoke balls, by reason of the plaintiff's user of them. There is ample consideration to support this promise. I have only to add that as regards the policy and the wagering points, in my judgment, there is nothing in either of them.

Appeal dismissed.

NOTES

What manner of acceptance was invited by the offer? At what point did a contract come into existence? Was notification of the offeror a requisite of contractual obligation?

Glover v. Jewish War Veterans of United States

Municipal Court of Appeals for the District of Columbia, 1949.
68 A.2d 233.

■ CLAGETT, ASSOCIATE JUDGE. The issue determinative of this appeal is whether a person giving information leading to the arrest of a murderer without any knowledge that a reward has been offered for such information by a non-governmental organization is entitled to collect the reward. The trial court decided the question in the negative and instructed the jury to return a verdict for defendant. Claimant appeals from the judgment on such instructed verdict.

The controversy grows out of the murder on June 5, 1946, of Maurice L. Bernstein, a local pharmacist. The following day, June 6, Post No. 58, Jewish War Veterans of the United States, communicated to the newspapers an offer of a reward of $500 "to the person or persons furnishing information resulting in the apprehension and conviction of the persons guilty of the murder of Maurice L. Bernstein." Notice of the reward was published in the newspaper June 7. A day or so later Jesse James Patton, one of the men suspected of the crime, was arrested and the police received information that the other murderer was Reginald Wheeler and that Wheeler was the "boy friend" of a daughter of Mary Glover, plaintiff and claimant in the present case. On the evening of June 11 the police visited Mary Glover, who in answer to questions informed them that her daughter and Wheeler had left the city on June 5. She told the officers she didn't know exactly where the couple had gone, whereupon the officers asked for names of relatives whom the daughter might be visiting. In response to such questions she gave the names and addresses of several relatives, including one at Ridge Spring, South Carolina, which was the first place visited by the officers and where Wheeler was arrested in company with plaintiff's daughter on June 13. Wheeler and Patton were subsequently convicted of the crime.

Claimant's most significant testimony, in the view that we take of the case, was that she first learned that a reward had been offered on June 12, the day after she had given the police officers the information which enabled them to find Wheeler. Claimant's husband, who was present during the interview with the police officers, also testified that at the time of the interview he didn't know that any reward had been offered for Wheeler's arrest, that nothing was said by the police officers about a reward and that he didn't know about it "until we looked into the paper about two or three days after that."

We have concluded that the trial court correctly instructed the jury to return a verdict for defendant. While there is some conflict in the decided cases on the subject of rewards, most of such conflict has to do with rewards offered by governmental officers and agencies. So far as rewards offered by private individuals and organizations are concerned, there is little conflict on the rule that questions regarding such rewards are to be based upon the law of contracts.

Since it is clear that the question is one of contract law, it follows that, at least so far as private rewards are concerned, there can be no contract unless the claimant when giving the desired information knew of the offer of the reward and acted with the intention of accepting such offer; otherwise the claimant gives the information not in the expectation of receiving a reward but rather out of a sense of public duty or other motive unconnected with the reward. "In the nature of the case," according to Professor Williston, "it is impossible for an offeree actually to assent to an offer unless he knows of its existence." After stating that courts in some jurisdictions have decided to the contrary, Williston adds, "It is impossible, however, to find in such a case [that is, in a case holding to the contrary] the elements generally held in England and America necessary for the formation of a contract. If it is clear the offeror intended to pay for the service, it is equally certain that the person rendering the service performed it voluntarily and not in return for a promise to pay. If one person expects to buy, and the other to give, there can hardly be found mutual assent. These views are supported by the great weight of authority, and in most jurisdictions a plaintiff in the sort of case under discussion is denied recovery."

The American Law Institute in its Restatement of the Law of Contracts follows the same rule, thus: "It is impossible that there should be an acceptance unless the offeree knows of the existence of the offer." The Restatement gives the following illustration of the rule just stated: "A offers a reward for information leading to the arrest and conviction of a criminal. B, in ignorance of the offer, gives information leading to his arrest and later, with knowledge of the offer and intent to accept it, gives other information necessary for conviction. There is no contract."

We have considered the reasoning in state decisions following the contrary rule. Mostly, as we have said, they involve rewards offered by governmental bodies and in general are based upon the theory that the government is benefited equally whether or not the claimant gives the information with knowledge of the reward and that therefore the government should pay in any event. We believe that the rule adopted by Professor Williston and the Restatement and in the majority of the cases is the better reasoned rule and therefore we adopt it. We believe furthermore that this rule is particularly applicable in the present case since the claimant did not herself contact the authorities and volunteer information but gave the information only upon questioning by the police officers and did not claim any knowledge of the guilt or innocence of the criminal but only knew where he probably could be located.

Affirmed.

[Footnotes omitted.]

NOTES

(1) "The liability for a reward of this kind must be created, if at all, by contract. There is no rule of law which imposes it except that which enforces contracts voluntarily entered into. A mere offer or promise to pay does not give rise to a contract. That requires the assent or meeting of two minds, and therefore is not complete until the offer is accepted. Such an offer as that alleged may be accepted by any one who performs the service called for when the acceptor knows that it has been made and acts in performance of it, but not otherwise. He may do such things as are specified in the offer, but, in so doing, does not act in performance of it, and therefore does not accept it, when he is ignorant of its having been made. There is no such mutual agreement of minds as is essential to a contract. The offer is made to any one who will accept it by performing the specified acts, and it only becomes binding when another mind has embraced and accepted it. The mere doing of the specified things without reference to the offer is not the consideration for which it calls. This is the theory of the authorities which we regard as sound." Broadnax v. Ledbetter, 100 Tex. 375, 99 S.W. 1111–12 (1907).

(2) "If the offer was made in good faith, why should the defendant inquire whether the plaintiff knew that it had been made? Would the benefit to him be diminished by the discovery that the plaintiff, instead of acting from mercenary motives, has been impelled solely by the desire to prevent the larceny from being profitable to the person who had committed it?" Dawkins v. Sappington, 26 Ind. 199, 201 (1866).

(3) Do you think the result would have been different in *Glover* if the reward had been offered by a public authority, as, for example, the District of Columbia? This problem came before the court two years later. See Glover v. District of Columbia, 77 A.2d 788 (Mun.Ct.D.C.1951).

(4) Assume Mary Glover knew of the reward, but when she furnished the information she did so reluctantly and with no desire to assist apprehension. Would she be entitled to the reward?

(5) Again, assuming Mary Glover knew of the reward, but it was her information combined with information from another person that led to the apprehension. What, if anything, should she recover? See Reynolds v. Charbeneau, 744 S.W.2d 365 (Tex.App.1988).

(6) Assume that the reward claimant was a District police officer, who furnished the information in the course of his usual employment. Would he be eligible for the reward? Would your answer be the same if it were established that he had not been assigned to the Bernstein murder case, nor had he participated in the official investigation thereof, but had worked on the matter, with the hope of obtaining the reward, during off-duty hours? See Maryland Casualty Co. v. Mathews, 209 F.Supp. 822 (S.D.W.Va.1962). *Cf.* Denney v. Reppert, 432 S.W.2d 647 (Ky.1968) (Deputy sheriff who assisted in arrest outside of his jurisdiction held entitled to reward.)

(7) *A Unilateral Contract Sampler.* Although not used in the Restatement (Second), the phrase "unilateral contract" refers to an offer which invites acceptance by performance of the bargained for exchange and does not invite acceptance by a promise. See Section 53(3). Unilateral contract analysis has been utilized in resolving an important employment contract issue. See, e.g., Pine River State Bank v. Mettille, 333 N.W.2d 622 (Minn.1983) (whether terms of employee handbook become part of contract). But even if a unilateral contract case lacks real importance, it is seldom lacking in human interest. E.g.:

Barnes v. Treece, 15 Wn.App. 437, 549 P.2d 1152 (1976) (Offer by punch board distributor to pay $100,000 to anyone who found a "crooked" punchboard.)

Las Vegas Hacienda, Inc. v. Gibson, 77 Nev. 25, 359 P.2d 85 (1961) (Offer by owner of golf course to pay $5,000 to anyone shooting a hole-in-one.)

James v. Turilli, 473 S.W.2d 757 (Mo.App.1971) (Offer by owner of "Jesse James Museum" in Stanton, Missouri, to pay $10,000 to anyone who could disprove his claim that the man shot and buried in 1882 as Jesse James was an impostor, and that the real Jesse James, under the name of J. Frank Dalton, lived at the offeror's museum for many years.)

Newman v. Schiff, 778 F.2d 460 (8th Cir.1985) (Offer on CBS nightwatch program to pay $100,000 to anyone who called the show and cited any section of the Internal Revenue Code "that says an individual is required to file a tax return.")

All of this and Carbolic Smoke Balls too!

Industrial America, Inc. v. Fulton Industries, Inc.

Supreme Court of Delaware, 1971.
285 A.2d 412.

[The plaintiff, "Industrial America," Inc., was a broker specializing in the sale or merger of businesses. Bush Hog, Inc. (B–H) was a farm machinery company which had informed several brokers, including the plaintiff, of its desire to consummate a merger. With B–H's authorization, and armed with documentary data furnished by it, the plaintiff's president, Millard B. Deutsch, first approached the Borg Warner Corporation with the B–H merger possibility; but nothing came of that effort. Next, again with B–H's authorization and up-dated material, Deutsch attempted to interest the Wickes Corporation in the merger possibility. After negotiations were carried on for several months between the two corporations, Deutsch participating actively therein, the talks ceased in early 1965. During the Wickes discussions, Deutsch outlined to B–H the commission arrangement he would expect if the merger were consummated. After the Wickes negotiations ended, according to B–H, it decided not to deal further with Deutsch or any other broker; but this decision was never communicated to Deutsch.

In the fall of 1965, while eating lunch with an accountant friend, Deutsch learned that Fulton Industries, Inc., (and its successor, Allied

Products Corporation), the defendant herein, was an "acquisition minded" company. Deutsch forthwith took from his own office files a copy of the following ad in the *Wall Street Journal:*

> WANTED—PRODUCT LINES! Heavy or Medium Machinery of Industrial Products. One of Fulton Industries' divisions desires additional products to manufacture. Its modern manufacturing facility of more than 250,000 sq. ft. includes: grey iron foundry, heavy and light machining, sheet metal forming, and capable engineering, sales and service staffs.

> Fulton will buy outright, or acquire by merger, active product line with annual sales of $2 million or more. Will take over manufacture, sales, service and key people. Brokers fully protected.

On October 7, 1965, Deutsch wrote to Fulton, describing but not naming B–H as a prospective acquisition; the response, dated October 14, was a request for financial data. On October 19, Deutsch replied by naming B–H as the prospect and transmitting financial data supplied to him by B–H. By letter dated October 22, Fulton stated it was "very much interested," and requested Deutsch to arrange a visit by the Fulton people to the B–H plant. By letter of October 26, with copy to Fulton, Deutsch advised B–H of Fulton's interest and suggestion for a visit. At some time after October 26 and prior to November 2, Fulton's executive vice president telephoned B–H's president directly and arranged a meeting for November 4. Deutsch first learned of this when, on November 3, he inquired of B–H regarding its failure to reply to his letter of October 26. Despite his repeated efforts and offers to assist, neither B–H nor Fulton dealt further with Deutsch; they both ignored his inquiries except for B–H's promise to keep him informed. Negotiations between B–H and Fulton continued until March 11, 1966, when a merger agreement between them was consummated.

After a series of hearings and appeals, the plaintiff was successful in getting a judgment for his broker's commission against B–H ($125,000) on the grounds that it was the procuring cause. The plaintiff, however, was unsuccessful in recovering judgment against Fulton; through special interrogatories, the trial court found that the plaintiff had never accepted Fulton's "offer."]

■ HERRMANN, JUSTICE.

It was handwritten in right margin: B·H liable for broker fees / never communicated revocation to chalot America

* * *

The basic question for decision in this appeal, in our view, is whether the plaintiff had the burden of proving a subjective intent on the part of Deutsch to accept the offer of guaranty which had been made in the advertisement by Fulton under the jury's findings.

We are of the opinion that Deutsch's subjective intent was not a relevant issue; that, rather, the relevant issues were (1) whether Fulton's offer of guaranty invited acceptance by performance; (2) whether Deutsch knew of the offer; and (3) whether Deutsch's course of action constituted a performance amounting to an acceptance.

It is basic that overt manifestation of assent—not subjective intent—controls the formation of a contract; that the "only intent of the parties to a contract which is essential is an intent to say the words or do the acts which constitute their manifestation of assent"; that "the intention to accept is unimportant except as manifested." Restatement of Contracts, § 20; 1 Williston on Contracts (3d Ed.) § 21, p. 39, § 66, p. 213; compare Western Natural Gas v. Cities Service Gas Co., Del.Supr., 223 A.2d 379, 383 (1966); Canister Co. v. National Can Corp. (D.Del.) 63 F.Supp. 361, 365 (1945).

Where an offeror requests an act in return for his promise and the act is performed, the act performed becomes the requisite overt manifestation of assent if the act is done intentionally; i.e., if there is a "conscious will" to do it. Restatement of Contracts, § 20; 1 Williston on Contracts (3d Ed.) § 68. But "it is not material what induces the will," Restatement of the Law of Contracts, § 20, Comment (a). Otherwise stated, motive in the manifestation of assent is immaterial. There may be primary and secondary reasons or motives for a performance constituting manifestation of assent to an offer inviting acceptance by performance; and the "chief reason" or the prevailing motive need not necessarily be the offer itself. A unilateral contract may be enforceable when the promisor has received the desired service even though the service was primarily motivated by a reason other than the offer. The "motivating causes of human action are always complex and are frequently not clearly thought out or expressed by the actor himself. This being true, it is desirable that not much weight should be given to the motives of an offeree and that no dogmatic requirement should be embodied in a stated rule of law." 1 Corbin on Contracts, § 58, p. 244, § 59, p. 246. It follows that a unilateral contract may arise even though at the time of performance the offeree did not "rely" subjectively upon, i.e., was not primarily motivated by, the offer. See Simmons v. United States (4 Cir.) 308 F.2d 160 (1962); Eagle v. Smith (Del.) 4 Houst. 293 (1871); Carlill v. Carbolic Smoke Ball Co. [1893] Q.B. 256; Restatement of Contracts, § 55, Comment b (1932): "* * * contracts may exist where if the offer is in any sense a cause of the acceptor's action it is so slight a factor that a statement that the acceptance is caused by the offer is misleading."

The clear trend and development of the law in this connection is demonstrated by a proposed change in the status of Section 55 of the Restatement of Contracts (1932).[2] The development of this facet of the law of contracts became apparent in Section 55 of the 1964 Tentative Draft of Restatement of Contracts (Second).[3] A comparison of the 1932 and the 1964

2.   Section 55 provided:

"*ACCEPTANCE OF OFFER FOR UNI-LATERAL CONTRACT; NECESSITY OF INTENT TO ACCEPT*

"If an act or forbearance is requested by the offeror as the consideration for a unilateral contract, the act or forbear-

ance must be given with the intent of accepting the offer."

3.   The Draft contains the following:

"*ACCEPTANCE BY PERFORMANCE; MANIFESTATION OF INTENTION NOT TO ACCEPT*

"(1) An offer may be accepted by the rendering of a performance only if the

versions of Section 55 indicates that under the currently developing rule of law, an offer that invites an acceptance by performance will be deemed accepted by such performance unless there is a manifestation of intention to the contrary. See 1 Williston on Contracts (3d Ed.) § 67. Thus, in the establishment of a contractual obligation, the favored rule shifts the emphasis away from a manifestation of intent to accept to a manifestation of intent not to accept; thereby establishing, it would appear, a rebuttable presumption of acceptance arising from performance when the offer invites acceptance by performance. See Braucher, Offer and Acceptance in Second Restatement, 74 Yale L.J. 302, 308 (1964). The law thus rightfully imputes to a person an intention corresponding to the reasonable meaning of his words and deeds.

The defendants contend that, because an offer of guaranty is here involved, the issue is whether the plaintiff gave to Fulton the necessary notice of acceptance of the offer, citing 1 Williston on Contracts (3d Ed.) § 69AA, p. 223. The position is untenable in the light of the following portion of the *Williston* statement upon which the defendants rely:

> "Ordinarily there is no occasion to notify the offeror of the acceptance of such an offer, if the doing of the act is sufficient acceptance, and the promisor knows that he is bound when he sees that action has been taken on the faith of his offer. * * *."

See also Restatement of Contracts, § 56 (1932); 1 Corbin on Contracts, § 68, f. n. 91. The facts of this case meet the test. In this connection, the Trial Judge ruled that Fulton's knowledge of the plaintiff's submission of B–H's name to it was notice to Fulton of an act constituting acceptance of its offer. We concur in that ruling.

Applying the law we find applicable to the facts of this case: we conclude that the Trial Court erred in submitting the issue of subjective reliance to the jury under Interrogatory No. 4. We hold that there was no relevant issue of fact as to the plaintiff's subjective reliance upon Fulton's offer. As a matter of law, it appears unquestionable that Fulton's offer invited acceptance by performance; it is uncontroverted that Deutsch knew of the offer at the time of performance; by the jury's finding of procuring cause, it has been established that the plaintiff did in fact and in law perform. It follows as a matter of law, in the absence of any manifestation of intention to the contrary, that the plaintiff's performance constituted an acceptance of the offer of Fulton which was found by the jury to be an offer of guaranty outstanding and viable at the time of the performance.

The necessary result of the foregoing chain is that the plaintiff is entitled to judgments against Fulton and Allied as a matter of law upon the

offer invites such an acceptance. (2) Except as stated in § 72, the rendering of a performance does not constitute an acceptance if within a reasonable time the offeree exercises reasonable diligence to notify the offeror of nonacceptance. (3) Where an offer of a promise invites acceptance by performance and does not invite a promissory acceptance, the rendering of the invited performance does not constitute an acceptance if before the offeror performs his promise the offeree manifests an intention not to accept." [This is § 53 in the final draft. Ed.]

basis of the judgment against B–H, unless there is validity in any of the grounds of the defendants' appeals herein.

* * *

Accordingly, upon the bases of the jury's answers to the special interrogatories and of the conclusions we have reached herein, we conclude that as a matter of law the plaintiff is entitled to judgments against Fulton and Allied as well as against B–H upon the verdict of $125,000. The cause is remanded for further proceedings consistent herewith. [Some footnotes omitted.]

PROBLEM: THE CASE OF THE LITTLE LEAGUE SPONSORS

Charley, a public spirited citizen, placed an advertisement in the *Suburbia Press,* stating that he would give $1,000 to anyone who sponsored a little league baseball club in the area for the ensuing season.

Baker, unaware of the advertisement, sponsored a little league club that year in Suburbia. He did not learn of the ad until the season was over, but at the instigation of his son, a first-year law student, brought suit against Charley for the $1,000. Any recovery? Assume, instead, that Baker had seen the advertisement before the season began but did not give it another thought until the season was concluded. Would he then be entitled to claim the $1,000?

Abel, owner of a Suburbia restaurant, sponsored a local club that season, the same as he had in previous years. He did not learn of the advertisement until midseason, at which time he determined to claim the $1,000. At the end of the season he filed suit against Charley. What result? See Richard D. Price, Jr. & Assoc., Ltd. v. City of East Peoria, 154 Ill.App.3d 725, 107 Ill.Dec. 564, 507 N.E.2d 228 (1987); Restatement (Second) Contracts § 51; Corbin § 60.

Comment: Acceptance by Performance Under Restatement (Second)

In the first Restatement, a sharp dichotomy between bilateral and unilateral contracts was maintained. Although Section 31 established a presumption in favor of the bilateral contract, it was supposed that every offer invited acceptance by either a promise or by full performance. This view was criticized by Karl Llewellyn, see Llewellyn, *Our Case Law of Contract—Offer and Acceptance,* 48 Yale L.J. 779, 786 (1939), and was explicitly rejected by UCC 2–206(1)(a), which provides that "unless otherwise unambiguously indicated," an offer "shall be construed as inviting acceptance in any manner and by any medium reasonable in the circumstances." [See UCC 2–205(a)(1)(1997)] Thus, if a buyer offers to purchase goods for "prompt or current shipment," and the language or circumstances do not unambiguously indicate that acceptance by shipment is required, the offer "shall be construed as inviting acceptance either by a prompt promise to ship or by the prompt or current shipment" of goods. UCC 2–206(1)(b). [UCC 2–205(a)(2)] The rule of construction operates to give an offeree a choice among reasonable methods of acceptance and by expanding the power to create a contract protects the offeree's reasonable reliance.

Restatement (Second) has followed this lead by abolishing the labels "bilateral" and "unilateral" and by charting a middle ground for acceptance between assent expressed by words of promise and assent expressed by completing a performance that the offeror required exclusively for acceptance. For a critical view of this development, see Pettit, *Modern Unilateral Contracts,* 63 B.U.L.Rev. 551 (1983). This middle ground emerges in a case where acceptance by "rendering a performance" is invited or required by the offer but where the offeree also has power to accept by making a promise. To accept the offer, the offeree must at least perform or tender part of the performance invited. Section 50(2). More importantly, this tender or beginning of performance is an acceptance which "operates as a promise to render complete performance." Section 62(2). It does not create an option contract, à la Section 45. Rather, it creates a full-blown reciprocal commitment, which used to be called a "bilateral" contract. Finally, "no notification is necessary to make such an acceptance effective unless the offer requests" it. Section 54(1). The contractual duties may be discharged if the offeree "has reason to know that the offeror has no adequate means of learning of the performance with reasonable promptness" and fails to exercise "reasonable diligence to notify the offeror of acceptance." Section 54(2)(a). But the contract, under these circumstances, is formed by the conduct of part performance or tender, not the giving or the effort to give notice to the offeror.

The intricate Restatement (Second) maze can be illustrated by three examples.

1. A, who lives in the city, owns 100 acres of farm land some 100 miles away. In the past, B, a farmer, has plowed the field for A in the Spring. On Monday, A telephoned B and said: "If you will agree by 4 PM tomorrow to plow my field, I will pay you $500 when the job is done." B said he would "consider it." The next day, B started to plow the field at 3 PM but had not notified A by 4 PM and, in fact, did not inform A until the next morning. There is no contract if the court accepts the following version of the case. The offer invited or required B's acceptance to be made "by an affirmative answer in words" and did not invite acceptance by performance. Section 30. Put another way, the language and circumstances clearly limited the manner of acceptance to an affirmative promise in words. See Section 32. As such, B did not "complete every act essential to the making of the promise," Section 50(3), or exercise "reasonable diligence to notify the offeror of acceptance," Section 56, before the offer lapsed at 4 PM. What about B's reliance (and A's enrichment, to the extent the field was plowed)? In theory, at least, if B knew that the only way to accept was to "say yes" before 4 PM and failed to do so, he plowed at his own peril.

2. Suppose, in Example # 1, that A had telephoned B and said: "When and only when you plow my 100 acres by 4 PM next Monday, I will pay you $500." B replied: "I'll do it. You can count on it." A

responded: "I want a plowed field not a promise. Plow it or we have no deal." B started to plow the field on Friday, completing 20% by sunset. The next day, A telephoned before 7 AM and revoked the offer. B ignored A and completed the plowing before 4 PM on Monday. There is a contract if the court accepts the following version of the case. A's offer required acceptance by rendering a completed performance but did not invite acceptance by promise. These limitations were clear and unambiguous. As such, B's commencing performance does not operate as a "promise to render complete performance." See Section 62. But it did create an option contract under Section 45 when B began the invited performance. And, under Section 45(2), B properly completed the performance "in accordance with the terms of the offer," thus imposing on A the duty to pay $500. Note that Section 45 applies only where the offer "invites an offeree to accept by rendering a performance and does *not* invite a promissory acceptance."

3. Suppose, in Example # 1, that A had telephoned B and said: "If you will plow my field by 4 PM next Monday I will pay you $500." B replied: "I'll consider it." The next day, B started to plow the field and was 20% completed when, in the evening, A called to revoke the offer. There is a contract if the court accepts the following version of the case. The offer empowered B to make a choice between acceptance by promise (he could have said yes over the telephone) and acceptance by performance. Section 30. There are no language or circumstances clearly to the contrary and Section 32 provides that "in case of doubt an offer is interpreted as inviting the offeree to accept either by promising to perform what the offer requests or by rendering the performance, as the offeree chooses." Thus, the offer was accepted when part-performance occurred, Section 50(2), and the acceptance by performance operated as a promise to complete the plowing. Section 62(2). Notice of acceptance to A was not required, Section 54(1), and, anyway, A learned of the performance when he telephoned to revoke the offer. Note that where the offer invites a choice between a performance and a promise, the reliance in part performance creates a promise to complete (yes, a "bilateral" contract) rather than an option under Section 45.

PROBLEM: THE CASE OF THE LASER SALE

Swift Ray is a manufacturer of industrial lasers. After extended negotiations with Swift Ray, Brice Electronics mailed, on October 7, a written detailed offer to Swift Ray which concluded as follows: "If you will agree to manufacture the lasers according to the above stated terms, we will pay the stipulated contract price upon delivery next January." When Swift Ray received the offer on October 9, the president told his purchasing agent: "It's a good deal. Buy the necessary materials to fill the order." The order to suppliers was placed the next day. Similarly, the sales manager prepared and signed an acknowledgment. However, on October 12, before the acknowledgment was mailed, the purchasing agent from Brice Electronics telephoned Swift Ray and cancelled the order. An unexpected cutback in business was given as the justification.

Swift Ray sued Brice for damages whereupon Brice filed a motion to dismiss the complaint for failure to state a cause of action. At the hearing on the motion, Brice argued that the written offer clearly invited acceptance by a promise to perform. As such, the offeree failed to complete every act essential to the making of the promise before the revocation was received, i.e., the offeree did not actually notify or exercise reasonable diligence to notify the offeror of his agreement. Swift Ray argued that the written offer did not unambiguously narrow the method and manner of acceptance to that asserted by Brice. Rather, the offer should be interpreted as inviting the offeree to accept either by promise or by rendering part of the performance. Since the offer did not request notification, no notification of acceptance by performance was required unless the offeree had reason to know that the offeror had no adequate way of learning of the acceptance and then failed to exercise due diligence in notification.

1.   What result under UCC 2–206? [UCC 2–205].

2.   Suppose that Swift Ray mailed the acknowledgment on October 9. Thereafter but before the acknowledgment arrived, Brice telephoned Swift Ray and canceled the deal. Is there a contract? See UCC 2–206(1) [UCC 2–205(a)(1)] and the case which follows.

Adams v. Lindsell

Court of King's Bench, 1818.
1 Barn. & Ald. 681, 106 Eng.Rep. 250.

Action for non-delivery of wool according to agreement. At the trial at the last Lent Assizes for the county of Worcester, before Burrough, J., it appeared that the defendants, who were dealers in wool, at St. Ives, in the county of Huntingdon, had, on Tuesday the 2d of September 1817, written the following letter to the plaintiffs, who were woolen manufacturers residing in Bromsgrove, Worcestershire. "We now offer you eight hundred tods of wether fleeces, of a good fair quality of our country wool, at 35s. 6d. per tod, to be delivered at Leicester, and to be paid for by two months' bill in two months, and to be weighed up by your agent within fourteen days, receiving your answer in course of post."

This letter was misdirected by the defendants, to Bromsgrove, Leicestershire, in consequence of which it was not received by the plaintiffs in Worcestershire till 7 P.M. on Friday, September 5th. On that evening the plaintiffs wrote an answer, agreeing to accept the wool on the terms proposed. The course of the post between St. Ives and Bromsgrove is through London, and consequently this answer was not received by the defendants till Tuesday, September 9th. On the Monday September 8th, the defendants not having, as they expected, received an answer on Sunday September 7th, (which in case their letter had not been misdirected, would have been in the usual course of post,) sold the wool in question to another person. Under these circumstances, the learned Judge held, that the delay having been occasioned by the neglect of the defendants, the jury must take it, that the answer did come back in due course of post; and that then the defendants were liable for the loss that had been sustained; and the plaintiffs accordingly recovered a verdict.

Jervis having in Easter term obtained a rule nisi for a new trial, on the ground that there was no binding contract between the parties.

Dauncey, Puller, and Richardson, showed cause. They contended, that at the moment of the acceptance of the offer of the defendants by the plaintiffs, the former became bound. And that was on the Friday evening, when there had been no change of circumstances. They were then stopped by the Court, who called upon Jervis and Campbell in support of the rule. They relied on Payne v. Cave (3 T.R. 148), and more particularly on Cooke v. Oxley (Ibid. 653). In that case, Oxley, who had proposed to sell goods to Cooke, and given him a certain time at his request, to determine whether he would buy them or not, was held not liable to the performance of the contract, even though Cooke, within the specified time, had determined to buy them, and given Oxley notice to that effect. So here the defendants who have proposed by letter to sell this wool, are not to be held liable, even though it be now admitted that the answer did come back in due course of post. Till the plaintiffs' answer was actually received, there could be no binding contract between the parties; and before then, the defendants had retracted their offer, by selling the wool to other persons. But—

The Court said, that if that were so, no contract could ever be completed by the post. For if the defendants were not bound by their offer when accepted by the plaintiffs till the answer was received, then the plaintiffs ought not to be bound till after they had received notification that the defendants had received their answer and assented to it. And so it might go on ad infinitum. The defendants must be considered in law as making, during every instant of the time their letter was travelling, the same identical offer to the plaintiffs; and then the contract is completed by the acceptance of it by the latter. Then as to the delay in notifying the acceptance, that arises entirely from the mistake of the defendants, and it therefore must be taken as against them, that the plaintiffs' answer was received in course of post.

Rule discharged.

NOTES

(1) *The Mailbox Rule.* The so-called "mailbox" rule, derived from the landmark case of *Adams v. Lindsell* and others which followed, has gained almost universal acceptance in common law jurisdictions. Restatement (Second) § 63(a) provides: "Unless the offer provides otherwise, (a) an acceptance made in a manner and by a medium invited by an offer is operative and completes the manifestation of mutual assent as soon as put out of the offeree's possession, without regard to whether it ever reaches the offeror; * * *." An exception to the prevailing view is Guardian National Bank v. Huntington County State Bank, 206 Ind. 185, 187 N.E. 388 (1933) (court relied upon change in postal regulations in 1913, permitting withdrawal of letter from the mail). A frontal attack upon the rule by the Court of Claims has apparently

failed. In Rhode Island Tool Co. v. United States, 130 Ct.Cl. 698, 128 F.Supp. 417 (1955), the offeror, who had made a mistake in bid, communicated a withdrawal of the offer to the contracting officer after written notice of award was mailed but before it was received. The court, in holding that no contract was created, relied substantially upon revised postal regulations which gave the sender control over a letter up to delivery: "The acceptance, therefore, is not final until the letter reaches destination, since the sender has the absolute right of withdrawal from the post office, and even the right to have the postmaster at the delivery point return the letter at any time before actual delivery." Is this reasoning persuasive?

(2) "There is no doubt that the implication of a complete, final, and absolutely binding contract being formed, as soon as the acceptance of an offer is posted, may in some cases lead to inconvenience and hardship. But such there must be at times in every view of the law. It is impossible in transactions which pass between parties at a distance, and have to be carried on through the medium of correspondence, to adjust conflicting rights between innocent parties, so as to make the consequences of mistake on the part of a mutual agent fall equally upon the shoulders of both. At the same time I am not prepared to admit that the implication in question will lead to any great or general inconvenience or hardship. An offeror, if he chooses, may always make the formation of the contract which he proposes dependent upon the actual communication to himself of the acceptance. If he trusts to the post he trusts to a means of communication which, as a rule, does not fail, and if no answer to his offer is received by him, and the matter is of importance to him, he can make inquiries of the person to whom his offer was addressed. On the other hand, if the contract is not finally concluded, except in the event of the acceptance actually reaching the offerer, the door would be opened to the perpetration of much fraud, and, putting aside this consideration, considerable delay in commercial transactions, in which despatch, is as a rule, of the greatest consequence, would be occasioned; for the acceptor would never be entirely safe in acting upon his acceptance until he had received notice that his letter of acceptance had reached its destination." Household Fire & Carriage Accident Insurance Co., Ltd. v. Grant (1879) 4 Ex.D. 216, 223–24. For a recent example of stipulation in offer for receipt of acceptance, precluding application of "mailbox" rule, see Crane v. Timberbrook Village, Ltd., 774 P.2d 3 (Utah App.1989).

The foregoing explanation, of course, will not assist private contractors who neglect clearly to specify when the acceptance becomes a contract. Similarly, the emotional appeal of a mistake in bids, found in the *Rhode Island* case, will not often be present. What, then, is the justification for ever holding an offeror to a bilateral contract before he or she knows of the acceptance? If there is some justification, to what methods of communication and to what kind of facts should the "mailbox" rule be limited? For example, if an offer is sent by telegraph is a contract formed when an acceptance is mailed? Sent by carrier pigeon? Spoken into a telephone receiver? See UCC 2–206(1) [UCC 2–205(a)(1)]. Similarly, should the "mailbox" rule apply to all of the following fact situations: offeree mails acceptance; offeror communicates revocation of offer before acceptance received; offeree mails acceptance which is lost and never received by offeror; offeree mails acceptance, changes mind and communicates rejection before offeror receives acceptance; offeree, in State A, mails an acceptance which is received by offeror in State B—offeree claims that law of State A governs because that is where the contract was formed? These problems are well discussed in Macneil, *Time of Acceptance: Too Many Problems for a Single Rule,* 112 U.Pa.L.Rev. 947 (1964).

(4) *Electronic Communication and the Demise of the "Mailbox" Rule?* As time goes on, more and more contracting will be by electronic transmission where communication is virtually instantaneous. See *Comment: Electronic Data Interchange and Contract Formation,* infra at 215. Under such circumstances, there is good reason for holding that an acceptance is effective when received, not when transmitted. The authors of a recent study observe that an important premise upon which the "mailbox" rule is predicated is the notion that delayed media, such as mailed writings, do not provide either party the ability to verify in a timely fashion that receipt of a message has occurred and that the message as received is without error. Hence, they maintain that electronic transmission should be governed by the same rules that apply when parties are in the presence of each other and the acceptance should be deemed effective when received. See *The Commercial Use of Electronic Data Interchange—A Report and Model Trading Partner Agreement,* 45 Bus.Law. 1645, 1666–67 (1990). The new Article 2B of the UCC on Licenses is in accord: See UCC 2B–206(a)(January, 1997 Draft).

(5) *Civil Law and International Law Treatment.* While generalization is risky, it seems that other legal systems—particularly the civil law—are more willing to enforce an offeror's statement that the offer is "irrevocable" without the presence of formality, bargain or reliance than the common law. See 1 Schlesinger, Formation of Contracts: A Study of the Common Core of Legal Systems 109–11, 747–91 (1968). There is clearly some correlation between the irrevocability of an offer and the willingness of a particular legal system to hold that a contract is created when the acceptance is mailed. Thus, in Austria and Germany where offers are normally irrevocable, a contract is not formed until the acceptance is received by the offeror since there is "no necessity for fixing an earlier moment for the acceptance in order to protect the offeree against possible speculations of the offeror." Schlesinger, supra at 159. As we shall see, the common law starts from the premise that an offer stated to be "irrevocable" is nevertheless revocable unless accompanied by authorized formality, consideration or reliance. Could it be that the "mailbox" rule evolved as a common law substitute for the civil law doctrine of irrevocability? Put another way, does the "mailbox" rule make the most sense when employed to protect the offeree's opportunity to make a sound decision against an unexpected revocation? If so, should it be extended to fact patterns where no threat of revocation is involved? If, as we shall see, the doctrine of promissory estoppel is increasingly invoked to protect the relying offeree against precipitous revocation, is there any real need for a "mailbox" rule?

See Articles 16(2) and 18(2) of the Convention on Contracts for the International Sale of Goods (CISG), which make it harder for an offeror to revoke an offer which states a fixed time for acceptance or that it is irrevocable but requires an acceptance to be received before it is effective. The UNIDROIT Principles of International Commercial Contracts are in accord. See Articles 2.4(2) and 2.6(2).

(6) Assume that upon receipt of a written "Offer and Acceptance" signed by Purchaser, Vendor signed as seller and deposited the writing in the mail, properly addressed to Purchaser. Before the letter arrived Vendor telephoned Purchaser that he had decided not to sell. Was there a binding contract? Cf. Morrison v. Thoelke, 155 So.2d 889 (Fla.App.1963); Corbin § 94.

Russell v. Texas Co.

United States Court of Appeals, Ninth Circuit, 1956.
238 F.2d 636.

■ HALBERT, DISTRICT JUDGE. Plaintiff-appellant, Russell, claims title to certain real property, which will be referred to in this opinion as section 23. Russell's predecessors in interest acquired their interest in this property from the Northern Pacific Railway Company, defendant-appellee herein, through a contract followed by a warranty deed executed in 1918. In both the contract and the deed was a reservation of mineral rights by the grantor. The Texas Company, defendant-appellee and cross-appellant herein, has been conducting extensive operations on section 23 since 1952 under an oil and gas lease granted by Northern Pacific Railway Company. The Texas Company has also made use of the surface of section 23 in connection with operations carried on by it on lands other than section 23.

Russell, as plaintiff, instituted this action seeking relief under three causes of action. * * * By the second and third causes of action, Russell seeks to recover damages from The Texas Company for its use of the surface of section 23 in connection with its operations on section 23 and on adjacent lands.

* * *

Second and Third Causes of Action. The damages which Russell seeks to recover from The Texas Company in his second and third causes of action are based on the following:

* * *

(B) The sums alleged to be due under a revocable license commencing on October 30, 1952, which obligated The Texas Company to pay Russell $150.00 a day for the continued use of section 23 in connection with its operations on adjacent lands, a use admittedly in excess of the easement flowing from the mineral reservation in the original deed.

The evidence shows that The Texas Company received on October 30, 1952, an offer from Russell for a revocable license to cover the use of section 23 in connection with operations on adjacent lands for the sum of $150.00 a day, which offer contained the express proviso that, "your continued use of the roadway, water and/or materials will constitute your acceptance of this revocable permit." The evidence further shows that The Texas Company did so continue to use section 23 until November 22, 1952, and it was not until sometime in December of that year that Russell finally received a communication from the Company to the effect that the offer was rejected. Neither party depends in any material respect on this purported rejection.

* * *

Judgment was entered in favor of Russell and against The Texas Company in the amount of $3,837.60, which consisted of $3,600.00 due under the revocable license and $237.60 due for the use of the land under the terms of the mineral reservation.

The Texas Company appeals from that portion of the judgment which awarded Russell $3,600.00 as the amount due under the terms of the revocable license, contending that the court erred as a matter of law in finding that the offer for the said license was accepted.

Russell appeals from that portion of the judgment against The Texas Company which awarded him $237.60, claiming that the court, in arriving at the measure of compensation, applied the wrong rule of damages. * * *

The Texas Company argues that the revocable license, which Russell offered to it in connection with its wrongful use of section 23, was never accepted, because the Company had no intention of accepting it. Appellant presents for our consideration numerous passages from the Restatement of Contracts and Williston on Contracts dealing with the necessity of the offeree's intent to accept where an ambiguous act is selected by the offeror to signify acceptance, or where silence and inaction can be considered an acceptance. None of these citations deal with the precise question that we are confronted with in this case. The question here is whether an offeree may vitiate a contract by a claim of lack of intention to accept an offer when he accepts and retains the benefits offered to him by the offeror, with a positive and affirmative proviso by the offeror that such acceptance of the benefits will, in and of itself, be deemed by the offeror to be an acceptance. To put the problem in homely terms, may an offeree accept all of the benefits of a contract and then declare that he cannot be held liable for the burdens because he secretly had said, "King's Ex"? We think not. A rule with such effect would be unconscionable and is not in line with either fairness or justice. The correct rule, we believe, is found in § 72(2) of the Restatement of Contracts, wherein it is stated:

"Where the offeree exercises dominion over things which are offered to him, such exercise of dominion in the absence of other circumstances showing a contrary intention is an acceptance. *If circumstances indicate that the exercise of dominion is tortious the offeror may at his option treat it as an acceptance, though the offeree manifests an intention not to accept.*" (Emphasis added).

Russell's offer of the license in clear and unambiguous terms stated that the continued use of section 23 in connection with activities and operations on other lands would constitute an acceptance of the offer of the license. The trial court found on the evidence that The Texas Company did so continue to use section 23, and hence unequivocally came within the terms specified for acceptance. It is a well established principle of property law that the right to use the surface of land as an incident of the ownership of mineral rights in the land, does not carry with it the right to use the surface in aid of mining or drilling operations on other lands. (See 36 Am.Jur., Mines and Minerals, § 177, § 180 and § 181; anno.: 48 A.L.R. 1406, 1407). That such use by The Texas Company was tortious admits of no doubt. But even in the absence of a tortious use, the true test would be whether or not the offeror was reasonably led to believe that the act of the offeree was an acceptance, and upon the facts of this case it seems evident that even this test is met.

* * *

The conclusion reached by the trial court on this phase of the case was correct.

* * *

The judgment is affirmed as to both appellants. [The Court's discussion of issues raised by Russell's appeal is omitted. Footnotes omitted.]

NOTES

(1) The court refers to authority dealing with "the necessity of the offeree's intent to accept where an ambiguous act is selected by the offeror to signify acceptance." Is the decision in *"Industrial America"*, *supra* at 294, inconsistent with this view?

(2) Was there a "meeting of minds" in *Russell?* Was there a manifestation of mutual assent?

(3) *Waiver of Tort and Suit in Assumpsit.* Offeror offers goods to Offeree upon specified terms. Offeree, without responding expressly to the offer, proceeds to exercise dominion over the goods, as, for example, by using them. What legal recourse is available to Offeror? Offeror might sue Offeree for the tort of conversion and recover damages. Might Offeror, however, sue for breach of contract? Prevailing authority indicates that this option might be available. Restatement (Second) § 69 provides: "An offeree who does any act inconsistent with the offeror's ownership of offered property is bound in accordance with the offered terms unless they are manifestly unreasonable. But if the act is wrongful as against the offeror it is an acceptance only if ratified by him." The use of the goods, albeit a wrongful use, can be construed as an implied acceptance of the offer. In effect, Offeror can treat Offeree as either a tortfeasor or a contract breaker.

The foregoing option grew out of a common law procedural alternative called "waiver of tort and suit in assumpsit." This process encompassed not only "implied acceptance" situations, but also those in which there was no outstanding offer. For instance, *A* steals goods belonging to *B* and sells them to *C*. It came to be recognized that *B* could "waive" the tort and sue in "assumpsit" under the fictitious assumption that *A* promised to restore to *B* benefits received from *C*. The remedy was essentially restitutionary in nature, designed to prevent *A*'s unjust enrichment. Since the objective was the disgorgement of *A*'s benefit, the amount of recovery might, if *A* made an advantageous sale to *C,* exceed the market value of the goods, the tort measure of recovery. Problems in this area are taken up in other law school courses.

(4) "We have not been cited to a case in this state involving the liability of a person who, though not having subscribed for a newspaper, continues to accept it by receiving it through the mail. There are, however, certain well-understood principles in the law of contracts that ought to solve the question. It is certain that one cannot be forced into contractual relations with another and that therefore he cannot, against his will, be made the debtor of a newspaper publisher. But it is equally certain that he may cause contractual relations to arise by necessary implication from his conduct. The law in respect of contractual indebtedness for a newspaper is not different from that relating to other things which have not been made the subject of an express agreement. Thus one may not have ordered supplies for his table, or other household necessities, yet if he continue to receive and use them, under circumstances where he had no right to suppose they were a gratuity, he will be held to have agreed, by implication, to pay their value. In this case defendant admits that, notwithstanding he ordered the paper discontinued at the time when he paid a bill for it, yet plaintiff continued to send it, and he continued to take it from the post office to his home. This was an acceptance and use of the property, and, there being no pretense that a gratuity was intended, an obligation arose to pay for it." Austin v. Burge, 156 Mo.App. 286, 137 S.W. 618 (1911).

(5) *The Problem of Unordered Merchandise.* The widespread practice of sending unordered merchandise to prospective purchasers has elicited legislative responses at both the state and federal levels. As with the problem of "bait advertising," discussed supra at 247, general contract law has not operated as an effective control of the abusive practice. The Federal Trade Commission has become increasingly active in the area through issuance of cease and desist orders. These are based on findings that the methods employed constitute unfair and deceptive acts and practices in violation of Section 5 of the Federal Trade Commission Act. In addition, there is now a federal statute covering the shipment of unsolicited merchandise through the mails. It provides as follows:

(a) Except for (1) free samples clearly and conspicuously marked as such, and (2) merchandise mailed by a charitable organization soliciting contributions, the mailing of unordered merchandise or of communications prohibited by subsection (c) of this section constitutes an unfair method of competition and an unfair trade practice in violation of section 45(a)(1) of title 15 [§ 5 of Federal Trade Commission Act].

(b) Any merchandise mailed in violation of subsection (a) of this section, or within the exceptions contained therein, may be treated as a gift by the recipient, who shall have the right to retain, use, discard, or dispose of it in any manner he sees fit without any obligation whatsoever to the sender. All such merchandise shall have attached to it a clear and conspicuous statement informing the recipient that he may treat the merchandise as a gift to him and has the right to retain, use, discard, or dispose of it in any manner he sees fit without any obligation whatsoever to the sender.

(c) No mailer of any merchandise mailed in violation of subsection (a) of this section, or within the exceptions contained therein, shall mail to any recipient of such merchandise a bill for such merchandise or any dunning communications.

(d) For the purposes of this section, "unordered merchandise" means merchandise mailed without the prior expressed request or consent of the recipient.

39 U.S.C.A. § 3009. See Annot., *Validity, Construction, and Application of 39 U.S.C.A. § 3009, Making It an Unfair Trade Practice to Mail Unordered Merchandise*, 39 A.L.R.Fed. 674 (1978).

State authorities have also been responsive to this problem. An Illinois statute, for instance, reads as follows: "Unless otherwise agreed, where unsolicited goods are delivered to a person, he has a right to refuse to accept delivery of the goods and is not bound to return such goods to the sender. If such unsolicited goods are either addressed to or intended for the recipient, they shall be deemed a gift to the recipient, who may use them or dispose of them in any manner without any obligation to the sender." Smith–Hurd Ill.Ann.Stat. ch. 121½, § 351. See generally, Comment, *Unsolicited Merchandise: State and Federal Remedies for a Consumer Problem*, 1970 Duke L.J. 991; J. Sheldon, Unfair and Deceptive Acts and Practices § 5.8.4 (3d ed.1991, Supp.).

(6) *The "Shrink Wrap" License.* Customer buys from Dealer a computer program produced by Producer on a CD–ROM disk contained in a cellophane wrapped package. Conspicuous language on the package states: "Important license terms contained herein." Customer pays for the disk, returns home and installs the program on the computer. Both the written license agreement in the package and the computer program provide clear limitations upon the uses to which put, i.e., personal and household but not commercial use, and state that use of the program constitutes agreement to all of the terms in the license. With knowledge of the terms, Customer uses the program and subsequently violates the license. When sued by Producer, who produced the program, Customer argued that the contract was formed when Customer paid for and took possession of the program, not when the program was actually used. Thus, unless the restrictions on use were communicated at the time of payment they could be ignored later on. In effect, Customer argues, they are simply proposals to modify the contract which Customer, although using the program, did not intend to accept. Producer, on the other hand, argues that Customer was alerted at the time of payment that there were license terms in the box and was given a choice after reading the terms to return the program and get a refund or use the program and be bound by the restrictions. Customer exercised the choice to use the program and was, therefore, bound by the license restriction. What result under Article 2 of the UCC. See ProCD, Inc. v. Zeidenberg, 86 F.3d 1447, 1452–1453 (7th Cir.1996)(contract formed on producer's terms).

Ammons v. Wilson & Co.

Supreme Court of Mississippi, 1936.
176 Miss. 645, 170 So. 227.

■ ANDERSON, JUSTICE. Appellant brought this action in the circuit court of Bolivar county against appellee, a Delaware corporation engaged in the meat packing business with its principal office at Kansas City, Kansas, to recover the sum of six hundred and fifty-eight dollars and seventy-four cents—damages claimed by appellant and alleged to have been caused by appellee's breach of contract to ship appellant nine hundred and forty-two cases of shortening. Appellant testified in his own behalf, and was the only witness who testified in the case. At the conclusion of the evidence, on appellee's motion, the court excluded it and directed a verdict and judgment for appellee which were accordingly entered. From that judgment appellant prosecutes this appeal.

Appellant was engaged in the wholesale grocery business at Beulah in Bolivar county. Appellee, as stated, was engaged in the business of meat packing, part of which was the manufacture and sale of shortening. Appellant made the following case by his evidence: Appellee had one Tweedy as its traveling salesman in the territory including Bolivar county. On or about the 9th, 10th or 11th of August, 1934 (appellant could not make it more definite in his testimony), Tweedy "booked" him for sixty thousand pounds of shortening at seven and one-half cents per pound tierce basis. The booking meant nothing more than the appellee was willing to receive orders from appellant for shortening up to that amount at seven and one-half cents per pound tierce basis, such orders subject to acceptance by appellee, and that by the booking appellant was not bound to order all or any part of the sixty thousand pounds, nor was appellee bound to accept orders for all or any part thereof. In other words, the evidence showed that the booking neither constituted a contract nor an absolute offer to contract—it was merely tentative. On the 23rd and 24th of August appellant, through appellee's traveling salesman Tweedy, ordered for prompt shipment nine hundred and forty-two cases of shortening, aggregating forty-three thousand, nine hundred and sixteen pounds. These orders were sent in by Tweedy. Appellant heard nothing from them until the 4th of September following, when he was advised by appellee, in response to his inquiry as to when the shipment would be made, that the orders had been declined. At that time the price of shortening was nine cents instead of seven and one-half cents a pound. In other words, appellee waited twelve days from the time the orders were given before declining to accept them. Tweedy had represented appellee in that territory for six or eight months and during that time he had taken several orders from appellant for certain of appellee's products, which orders in every case had been accepted and shipped not later than one week from the time they were given.

The orders here involved, as well as prior ones, were in writing and contained this provision: "This order taken subject to acceptance by seller's authorized agent at point of shipment." Under this stipulation the orders constituted mere offers to purchase on appellant's part and were not binding on appellee until received and accepted. It is also true, as contended by appellee, that its traveling salesman Tweedy was without authority to make a binding contract for it. The extent of his authority was to solicit and transmit orders to his principal for approval. Becker Co. v. Clardy, 96 Miss. 301, 51 So. 211, Ann.Cas.1912B, 355; Cape County Savings Bank v. Grocery Co., 123 Miss. 443, 86 So. 275; Fairbanks Morse & Co. v. Dale & Co., 172 Miss. 271, 159 So. 859.

The question in the case is whether or not, under the law, appellee should be charged with an implied acceptance of the orders by its silence. As above stated, all of appellant's previous orders had been accepted and the goods shipped not later than a week from the giving of such orders, while appellee was silent for twelve days after the giving of the orders here involved, and then refused to accept them in response to appellant's request for shipment. We think the sound governing principles are laid down in Restatement, Contracts, subsection 1(c) of section 72, the applicable part of which is as follows:

"(1) Where an offeree fails to reply to an offer, his silence and inaction operate as an acceptance in the following cases and in no others: * * *

"(c) Where because of previous dealings or otherwise, the offeree has given the offeror reason to understand that the silence of [or] inaction is intended by the offeree as a manifestation of assent, and the offeror does so understand."

"Illustration of Subsection (1, c): 5. A, through salesmen, has frequently solicited orders for goods from B, the orders to be subject to A's personal approval. In every case A has shipped the goods ordered within a week and without other notification to B than billing the goods to him. A's salesman solicits and receives another order from B. A receives the order and remains silent. B relies on the order and forbears to buy elsewhere for a week. A is bound to fill the order."

We are not aware of any decisions of our court in conflict with these principles; certainly those relied on by appellee are not.

We are of the opinion that it was a question for the jury whether or not appellee's delay of twelve days before rejecting the orders, in view of the past history of such transactions between the parties, including the booking, constituted an implied acceptance. The evidence was rather uncertain as to the damages suffered by appellant on account of the alleged breach of contract. If there was a breach, appellant was entitled to at least nominal damages. If there were actual damages, it devolves on appellant to trace them directly to the breach of the contract and make them definite enough to comply with the governing rules of law.

Reversed and remanded.

NOTES

(1) *Silence as Assent.* If A offers to sell B a certain book for $5, and the latter remains silent, is the silence indicative of assent? Not necessarily. B may be weighing the proposal, mentally determining whether to accept or reject, or may be thinking about something else altogether. Hence, there is the general refusal of courts to regard silence, standing alone, as constituting acceptance. But what if A adds: "If you say nothing I will know you accept." What objection is there then to holding B to a contract? Should the offeree be obliged to reply in order to prevent a contract? Finally, would there be any reason for objection to contract if B, taking A at his or her word, remained silent with the intention of accepting the offer?

(2) If it be conceded that an offeror, acting reasonably, should not ordinarily interpret silence to mean assent, what additional factors might alter the reasonable impression?

(3) Would the result in *Ammons* have been the same even if there had been no previous dealings? Compare Hendrickson v. International Harvester Co., 100 Vt. 161, 135 A. 702 (1927) with Sell v. General Electric Supply Corp., 227 Wis. 242, 278 N.W. 442 (1938). Most likely there would have been no contract. What, then, was the effect of the prior course of dealing? The court in *Ammons* held that the jury should decide whether there was an implied acceptance. How does the Restatement (Second) change that analysis? See Section 69, note (4) infra.

(4) Restatement (Second) § 69, pertaining to acceptance by silence or exercise of dominion, provides as follows:

(1) Where an offeree fails to reply to an offer, his silence and inaction operate as an acceptance in the following cases only:

(a) Where an offeree takes the benefit of offered services with reasonable opportunity to reject them and reason to know that they were offered with the expectation of compensation.

(b) Where the offeror has stated or given the offeree reason to understand that assent may be manifested by silence or inaction, and the offeree in remaining silent and inactive intends to accept the offer.

(c) Where because of previous dealings or otherwise, it is reasonable that the offeree should notify the offeror if he does not intend to accept.

(2) An offeree who does any act inconsistent with the offeror's ownership of offered property is bound in accordance with the offered terms unless they are manifestly unreasonable. But if the act is wrongful as against the offeror it is an acceptance only if ratified by him.

(5) What is the difference between an express contract and a so-called implied-in-fact contract? In what sense might all contracts be regarded as "express"? Is there a sense in which all contracts are "implied"?

(6) *An Agent's Authority.* In *Ammons*, Tweedy, the traveling salesman, was an agent of Wilson & Co., but did not have the authority to bind the latter contractually. When does an agent have such authority? In brief, when the principal confers the authority (actual) or holds the agent out as having the authority (apparent).

As defined by the Restatement of Agency, authority is "the power of the agent to affect the legal relations of the principal by acts done in accordance with the principal's manifestations of consent to him." Restatement (Second) of Agency § 7 (1958). This actual authority may be express (i.e., spelled out by the principal in directions to the agent) or implied (i.e., inferred from directions to the agent, customs of trade, etc.)

Whereas actual authority, express or implied, derives from what the principal tells the agent, apparent authority results from the principal's manifestations to third persons. "To bind the principal * * * the one dealing with the agent must prove that the principal was responsible for the appearance of authority by doing something or permitting the agent to do something which reasonably led others, including the plaintiff, to believe that the agent had the authority he purported to have. If this is proved, the principal should have realized that his conduct would cause others to believe that the agent was authorized, and the principal and the other party are bound by the ordinary rules of contract, unless the other has notice that the agent was unauthorized." Seavey, Handbook of the Law of Agency 13 (1964). Obviously, the objective theory of contracts and the agency doctrine of apparent authority are compatible ideas.

Comment: The Role of Conduct in UCC Article 2.

UCC 1–201(3) defines "agreement" as the "bargain of the parties in fact as found in their language or by implication from other circumstances including course of dealing or usage of trade or course of performance as provided in this Act (Sections 1–205, 2–208, ...)." "Contract" is defined as the "total legal obligation which results from the parties' agreement as affected by this Act and any other applicable rules of law." UCC 1–201(11). Where a claimed sale of goods or a lease of goods are involved, whether an agreement as defined in Article 1 is a contract depends upon the application of Article 2 or Article 2A of the UCC. In answering the formation question in a "code covered" transaction, e.g., an alleged sale of goods, Article 1 and Article 2 may be read together.

Consider again the facts in *Ammons v. Wilson & Co.*, supra. The seller's agent, Tweedy, solicited an order of a specific quantity of goods at a fixed price from Ammons for "prompt shipment." This order was treated as an offer.

Under UCC 2–206(1)(a) [2–205(a)(1)(1997)], the offer could be accepted by a "prompt promise to ship" or by the "prompt or current shipment of conforming goods ..." Thus, an invited method of acceptance is the conduct of shipment. Moreover, the "beginning of a requested performance", if reasonable, may also create a contract. UCC 2–206(2) [2–205(b)(1997)]. This, however, is not the *Ammons* case.

To vary the facts a bit more, suppose the offer was for 942 cases of shortening and the seller responded by telephone that it could ship only 800 cases. At this point there is no contract but the seller has made a counteroffer to ship 800 cases which the seller can accept or reject. Suppose the buyer initially says no to the counteroffer but the seller, nevertheless, ships 800 cases and the buyer accepts them without objection. Is there a contract? See UCC 2–204(1) [2–203(a)(1997)]. If so, what are the terms? More pointedly, what is the agreement upon which the contract rests? Clearly, it is at a minimum an agreement to buy 800 cases.

Return to Ammons where the offer was to buy 942 cases at 7½ cents per pound. Since Wilson neither shipped nor promised to ship (and in fact ultimately rejected the offer), is the failure to reject within a reasonable time an acceptance under Article 2? The answer depends on whether the seller has agreed to the buyer's proposed bargain and this turns on how one uses the prior course of dealing between the parties. Read UCC 1–205(1) & (3). Is that course of dealing "other circumstances" from which the seller's agreement to accept orders by silence unless a prompt rejection is given can be implied? If not, may the buyer turn to the protective arm of Section 69(1)(c) of the Restatement (Second)? We think that the answer to the first question is "probably not" but that the answer to the second question is yes.

In light of this analysis, what do you think of the next case?

Smith–Scharff Paper Company v. P. N. Hirsch & Co. Stores, Inc.

Missouri Court of Appeals, Eastern District, 1988.
754 S.W.2d 928.

■ STEPHAN, PRESIDING JUDGE.

This is an appeal from a jury tried case in the circuit court of St. Louis County. Plaintiff, Smith–Scharff Paper Company ("Smith–Scharff") filed suit alleging breach of contract. Defendant, P.N. Hirsch & Co. Stores, Inc. ("P.N. Hirsch") denied the existence of such a contract, but, asserted that if there were a contract, Smith–Scharff breached first. The jury found for Smith–Scharff and awarded damages. P.N. Hirsch appeals; we affirm.

Smith–Scharff is a Missouri corporation, engaged in business as a distributor of paper products. At all relevant times herein after 1964, P.N. Hirsch was a division of INTERCO INCORPORATED, a Delaware corporation. Prior to 1964, P.N. Hirsch was a privately held company.

Smith–Scharff began selling paper products to P.N. Hirsch in 1947. Their business relationship was very nearly continuous until 1983, except for a one year interruption sometime in the 1950's or 1960's. During this one year period, P.N. Hirsch bought its paper bags from another company. At the time this interruption occurred, P.N. Hirsch bought all the bags with the P.N. Hirsch logo that Smith–Scharff had in its possession.

The paper bags that Smith–Scharff sold to P.N. Hirsch were imprinted by the manufacturer with the P.N. Hirsch logo. Smith–Scharff kept a supply of these bags in stock so that, when a purchase order was received from P.N. Hirsch, Smith–Scharff could fill it in a timely fashion. Smith–Scharff ordered these bags from the manufacturer based on its own historical sales record to P.N. Hirsch. P.N. Hirsch was aware of this arrangement and would provide a generalized profile of its business forecasts to Smith–Scharff.

P.N. Hirsch was liquidated and its retail outlets sold to Dollar General. When Smith–Scharff discovered this, its president, Arthur L. Scharff, wrote a letter to the president of P.N. Hirsch, Bernard Mayer. Subsequently, Mr. Scharff spoke with Mr. Mayer. Smith–Scharff was looking for assurance that the P.N. Hirsch bags they had in stock would be bought. Mayer told Scharff that P.N. Hirsch would honor all commitments, and, that the integrity of P.N. Hirsch should not be questioned.

Thereafter, Smith–Scharff sent P.N. Hirsch a bill for $65,000, representing the amount of all the P.N. Hirsch bags in stock. Between October

1983 and May 1984, P.N. Hirsch purchased approximately $45,000 worth of these bags. Smith–Scharff was left with an inventory totaling $20,679.46.

The jury found for Smith–Scharff and awarded damages of $27,000 (the inventory plus interest). P.N. Hirsch filed a motion for a new trial, which was denied, and this appeal followed.

P.N. Hirsch raises two points on appeal. They are: 1) The trial court erred in failing to direct a verdict for P.N. Hirsch because there was no evidence of an agreement between the parties regarding disposition of inventory upon termination; and, 2) The trial court erred in failing to direct a verdict for P.N. Hirsch because Smith–Scharff breached the agreement first.

P.N. Hirsch argues that a written agreement was necessary under the Statute of Frauds, § 400.2–201, RSMo 1978. We disagree. The goods herein are specially made and are generally not suitable for sale to others in the ordinary course of business. These goods, therefore, come within an exception to the statute, § 400.2–201(3)(a), RSMo 1978.

customized

This means that an implied contract can be found even though it was not reduced to writing. In order to find such an agreement, we must look to the parties' "bargain . . . in fact as found in their language or by implication from other circumstances including course of dealing . . ." § 400.1–201(3), RSMo 1978. Course of dealing is defined as:

> . . . a sequence of previous conduct between the parties to a particular transaction which is fairly to be regarded as establishing a common basis of understanding for interpreting their expressions and other conduct. § 400.1–205(1).

2-204 gives more "wiggle room" may be a better argument

After reviewing the record, we find that there was sufficient evidence to support the existence of a contract. Smith–Scharff and P.N. Hirsch had been engaged in business together for thirty-six years. In that time, Smith–Scharff discovered that the best way to service P.N. Hirsch and stay competitive in the market was to keep a supply of bags with the P.N. Hirsch logo in stock. P.N. Hirsch was aware of the way its account was handled by Smith–Scharff. While it is true that P.N. Hirsch did not specifically request Smith–Scharff to conduct business in this fashion, P.N. Hirsch accepted the benefits of the practice which avoided the delays involved in ordering the bags from the manufacturer. P.N. Hirsch could have told Smith–Scharff to stop stockpiling bags, but, chose not to because the situation, as it stood, suited its business purposes. Under the Uniform Commercial Code, P.N. Hirsch is under an obligation of good faith. § 400.1–203, RSMo 1978. It is, therefore, estopped from denying the existence of a contract.

Having found that there was an agreement, we now look to whether it included disposition of merchandise upon termination of the relation. This contingency was never discussed by the parties, but there was a previous termination of relations which lasted approximately one year. At that time, P.N. Hirsch bought the remaining bags left in the possession of Smith–Scharff. It was, therefore, not unreasonable for Smith–Scharff to expect the same treatment again. It makes no difference that this time the termination was permanent because P.N. Hirsch was going out of business under that name.

It is clear that the bags were made specially for the benefit of P.N. Hirsch. P.N. Hirsch was aware of Smith–Scharff's business practice of pre-ordering bags, therefore, Hirsch is estopped from denying its responsibility to pay for them. It was reasonable for Smith–Scharff to expect P.N. Hirsch to purchase the remaining inventory. We, therefore, deny Point I on all grounds.

[The court held that Smith–Scharff was not unreasonable in demanding that the inventory be taken and paid for and did not breach the contract.]

* * *

The judgment of the trial court is affirmed.

NOTES

(1) What's going on here? Was there "offer and acceptance"? Was there "agreement"? How does Article 2 affect the outcome here? See also UCC 2–204(1) [UCC 2–203(a)(1997)]. For a discussion of how Code emphasis upon agreement in fact and corresponding deemphasis of traditional rules governing mutual assent has the potential for a basic restructuring of the law governing the agreement process, see Murray, *The Article 2 Prism: The Underlying Philosophy of Article 2 of the Uniform Commercial Code,* 21 Washburn L.J. 1 (1981); Murray, *A New Design for the Agreement Process,* 53 Cornell L.Rev. 785 (1968); King, *The New Conceptualism of the Uniform Commercial Code,* 10 St. Louis U.L.J. 30 (1965); Mooney, *Old Kontract Principles and Karl's New Kode: An Essay on the Jurisprudence of Our New Commercial Law,* 11 Vill.L.Rev. 213 (1966).

(2) A concern expressed in many quarters today is that rules formulated for governing "one shot" deals may be inappropriate for resolving controversies between parties who have or contemplate long-term relationships. Pioneering work in this area has been done by Professor Ian Macneil. See, e.g., Macneil, *Restatement (Second) of Contracts and Presentiation,* 60 Va.L.Rev. 589 (1974); Macneil, *The Many Futures of Contract,* 47 S.Cal.L.Rev. 691 (1974); Macneil, *Economic Analysis of Contract Relations: Its Shortfalls and the Need for a Rich Classificatory Apparatus,* 75 Nw.U.L.Rev. 1018 (1981).

(3) *Technical Validity, But Time Slips Away.* Are you ready for some review? The next case provides an opportunity to review some of the old learning and to consider much else besides. Should you be concerned about the trifling amount involved here, have patience. We will consider shortly a lawsuit that netted Pennzoil a $10.53 billion judgment against Texaco. For now, the tale of a public interest attorney's battle with Time, Inc.

Harris v. Time, Inc.

Court of Appeals of California, 1987.
191 Cal.App.3d 449, 237 Cal.Rptr. 584.

■ KING, ASSOCIATE JUSTICE.

In this action where plaintiffs suffered no damage or loss other than having been enticed by the external wording of a piece of bulk rate mail to open the envelope, believing that doing so would result in the receipt of a free plastic calculator watch, we hold that the maxim "the law disregards trifles" applies and dismissal of the action was proper on this ground.

Mark Harris, Joshua Gnaizda and Richard Baker appeal from a judgment of dismissal of this class action lawsuit arising from their receipt of a direct mail advertisement from Time, Inc. They contend the court erred when it sustained Time's demurrer as to a cause of action for breach of contract and granted summary judgment as to causes of action for unfair advertising. We affirm.

It all began one day when Joshua Gnaizda, the three-year-old son of a prominent Bay Area public interest attorney, received what he (or his mother) thought was a tantalizing offer in the mail from Time. The front of the envelope contained two see-through windows partially revealing the envelope's contents. One window showed Joshua's name and address. The other revealed the following statement: "JOSHUA A GNAIZDA, I'LL GIVE YOU THIS VERSATILE NEW CALCULATOR WATCH FREE Just for Opening this Envelope Before Feb. 15, 1985." Beneath the offer was a picture of the calculator watch itself. Joshua's mother opened the envelope and apparently realized she had been deceived by a ploy to get her to open a piece of junk mail. The see-through window had not revealed the full text of Time's offer. Printed below the picture of the calculator watch, and not viewable through the see-through window, were the following additional words: "AND MAILING THIS CERTIFICATE TODAY!" The certificate itself clearly required that Joshua purchase a subscription to Fortune magazine in order to receive the free calculator watch.

As is so often true in life situations these days, the certificate contained both good news and bad news. The good news was that Joshua could save up to 66 percent on the subscription, which might even be tax deductible.[1] Even more important to the bargain hunter, prices might never be this low again. The bad news was that Time obviously had no intention of giving Joshua the versatile new calculator watch just for opening the envelope.

Although most of us, while murmuring an appropriate expletive, would have simply thrown away the mailer, and some might have stood on principle and filed an action in small claims court to obtain the calculator watch, Joshua's father did something a little different: he launched a $15,000,000 lawsuit in San Francisco Superior Court.

The action was prosecuted by Joshua, through his father, and by Mark Harris and Richard Baker, who had also received the same mailer. We are not informed of the ages of Harris and Baker. The complaint alleged one cause of action for breach of contract, three causes of action for statutory

---

1. The record does not disclose whether Joshua could take advantage of the tax deductibility feature.

unfair advertising, and four causes of action for promissory estoppel and fraud.

The complaint sought the following relief: (1) a declaration that all recipients of the mailer were entitled to receive the promised item or to rescind subscriptions they had purchased,[2] (2) an injunction against future similar mailings, (3) compensatory damages in an amount equal to the value of the item, and (4) $15,000,000 punitive damages to be awarded to a consumer fund "to be used for education and advocacy on behalf of consumer protection and enforcement of laws against unfair business practices."

The complaint also alleged that before commencing litigation, Joshua's father demanded that Time give Joshua a calculator watch without requiring a subscription. Time not only refused to give a watch, it did not even give Joshua or his father the time of day. There was no allegation that Harris or Baker made such a demand on Time.

Time demurred to the entire complaint for failure to state facts sufficient to constitute a cause of action. The court sustained the demurrer as to the causes of action for breach of contract, promissory estoppel and fraud, but overruled the demurrer as to the causes of action for unfair advertising.

However, Time subsequently obtained summary judgment on the causes of action for unfair advertising. Based on the orders sustaining the demurrer and granting summary judgment, the court rendered a judgment of dismissal.

Plaintiffs filed a notice of appeal after the court granted summary judgment, but two days before rendition of the judgment itself. We treat the notice of appeal as filed immediately after entry of judgment. (Cal.Rules of Court, rule 2(c).)

The appeal challenges the dismissal only as to the causes of action for breach of contract and unfair advertising. Plaintiffs state in their opening brief that they abandon the causes of action for promissory estoppel and fraud.

* * *

BREACH OF CONTRACT

In sustaining the demurrer as to the cause of action for breach of contract, the court stated no specific grounds for its ruling. Time had argued the complaint did not allege an offer, did not allege adequate consideration, and did not allege notice of performance by the plaintiffs. On appeal, plaintiffs challenge each of these points as a basis for dismissal.

A.   Offer.

2.   No claim is made that Time did not provide a free calculator watch to each person who subscribed to Fortune magazine.

On the first point, Time argues there was no contract because the text of the unopened mailer amounted to a mere advertisement rather than an offer.

It is true that advertisements are not typically treated as offers, but merely as invitations to bargain. (1 Corbin on Contracts (1963) § 25, pp. 74–75; Rest.2d, Contracts, § 26, com. b, at p. 76.) There is, however, a fundamental exception to this rule: an advertisement can constitute an offer, and form the basis of a unilateral contract, if it calls for performance of a specific act without further communication and leaves nothing for further negotiation. (Lefkowitz v. Great Minneapolis Surplus Store (1957) 251 Minn. 188, 86 N.W.2d 689, 691; 1 Corbin on Contracts (1963) §§ 25, 64, pp. 75–76, 264–270; Rest.2d, Contracts, § 26, com. b, at p. 76.) This is a basic rule of contract law, contained in the Restatement Second of Contracts and normally encountered within the first few weeks of law school in cases such as *Lefkowitz* (furs advertised for sale at a specified date and time for "$1.00 First Come First Served") and Carlill v. Carbolic Smoke Ball Co. (1893) 1 Q.B. 256 (advertisement of reward to anyone who caught influenza after using seller's medicine). (See, e.g., Murphy & Speidel, Studies in Contract Law (3d ed. 1984) pp. 112, 154.)

The text of Time's unopened mailer was, technically, an offer to enter into a unilateral contract: the promisor made a promise to do something (give the recipient a calculator watch) in exchange for the performance of an act by the promisee (opening the envelope). Time was not in the same position as a seller merely advertising price; the proper analogy is to a seller promising to give something to a customer in exchange for the customer's act of coming to the store at a specified time. (*Lefkowitz v. Great Minneapolis Surplus Store*, supra.)

B.   Consideration.

Time also argues that there was no contract because the mere act of opening the envelope was valueless and therefore did not constitute adequate consideration. Technically, this is incorrect. It is basic modern contract law that, with certain exceptions not applicable here (such as illegality or preexisting legal duty), *any* bargained-for act or forbearance will constitute adequate consideration for a unilateral contract. (Rest.2d, Contracts, § 71; see 1 Witkin, Summary of Cal.Law (8th ed. 1973) Contracts, §§ 162–169, pp. 153–162.) Courts will not require equivalence in the values exchanged or otherwise question the adequacy of the consideration. (Schumm v. Berg (1951) 37 Cal.2d 174, 185, 231 P.2d 39; Rest.2d, Contracts, § 79.) If a performance is bargained for, there is no further requirement of benefit to the promisor or detriment to the promisee. (Rest.2d, Contracts, § 79, coms. a & b, at pp. 200–201.)

Moreover, the act at issue here—the opening of the envelope, with consequent exposure to Time's sales pitch—may have been relatively insignificant to the plaintiffs, but it was of great value to Time. At a time when our homes are bombarded daily by direct mail advertisements and solicitations, the name of the game for the advertiser or solicitor is to *get the recipient to open the envelope*. Some advertisers, like Time in the present case, will resort to ruse or trick to achieve this goal. From Time's perspective, the opening of the envelope was "valuable consideration" in every sense of that phrase.

Thus, assuming (as we must at this juncture) that the allegations of the complaint are true, Time made an offer proposing a unilateral contract, and plaintiffs supplied adequate consideration for that contract when they performed the act of opening the envelope and exposing themselves to the sales pitch within.

C.   Notice of Performance.

Although there was an offer with technical consideration, Time had no means of learning of the acceptance by performance. Thus the recipients of the offer were required to provide Time with notice of their performance within a reasonable period of time. Absent such notice, Time could treat the offer as having lapsed before acceptance. (Com.Code, § 2206, subd. (2); Rest.2d, Contracts, § 54, com. b, p. 137.)[4] The complaint alleged Joshua Gnaizda gave Time notice of his performance before commencing litigation, but contained no such allegation as to co-plaintiffs Harris and Baker. Thus, as Time correctly contends, the complaint failed to state a cause of action for breach of contract as to Joshua's co-plaintiffs.[5]

[The court rejected the claim that Time, by repudiating the promise to deliver a calculator, breached the contract and thereby discharged any condition of notice.]

* * *

III

CONCLUSION

As a final argument, Time claims the judgment of dismissal was correct based on the legal maxim "de minimis non curat lex," or "the law disregards trifles." (Civ.Code, § 3533.) In this age of the consumer class action this maxim usually has little value. However, the present action is "de minimus" in the extreme. This lawsuit is an absurd waste of the resources of this court, the superior court, the public interest law firm handling the case and the citizens of California whose taxes fund our judicial system. It is not a use for which our legal system is designed.

As a practical matter, plaintiffs' real complaint is that they were tricked into opening a piece of junk mail, *not* that they were misled into buying anything or expending more than the effort necessary to open an envelope. If Joshua's mother lost the initial skirmish in the battle of direct mail advertising by opening the envelope, she could have won the war by simply throwing the thing away. If she were angry she might even have

---

4. The Uniform Commercial Code permits the offeror to treat the offer as "having lapsed before acceptance" (Com.Code, § 2206, subd. (2)), while the Restatement Second of Contracts states that "the contractual duty of the offeror is discharged" (Rest.2d, Contracts, § 54, subd. (2)).

5. Plaintiffs Harris and Baker argue their complaint gave notice of the performance. Filing a lawsuit against one making an offer is certainly a peculiar method of accepting the offer.

returned Time's business reply envelope empty, requiring Time to pay the return postage. If she felt particularly hostile, she might have inserted a nasty note or other evidence of her displeasure in the reply envelope. A $15,000,000 lawsuit, filed in a superior court underfunded and already overburdened with serious felony prosecutions and complex civil litigation involving catastrophic injury from asbestos, prescription drugs and intra-uterine devices, is a vast overreaction. The law may permit junk mail to be delivered for a lower cost than the individual citizen must pay. It does not require that the public subsidize junk litigation.

For many, an unpleasant aspect of contemporary American life is returning to the sanctity of one's home each day and emptying the mailbox, only to be inundated with advertisements and solicitations. Some days, among all of the junk mail, one is fortunate to be able to locate a bill, let alone a letter from a friend or loved one. Insult is added to injury when one realizes that individual citizens must pay first class postage rates to send their mail, while junk mail, for reasons apparent only to Congress and the United States Postal Service, is sent at less than one-half of that rate. The irritation level soars to new heights when, succumbing to the cleverness or ruse of the sender of junk mail and believing one is being offered something for nothing, one actually opens an envelope and examines its contents, both of which would otherwise been deposited unopened in their rightful place, the garbage can. Snake oil salesmen have been replaced by bulk rate advertisers whose wares must be causing our postal carriers' backs to be nearing the breaking point under the weight of such mail.

As much as one might decry this intrusion into our lives and our homes and sympathize with Joshua's plight, eliminating it lies with Congress, not the courts. The courts cannot solve every complaint or right every technical wrong, particularly one which causes no actual damage beyond the loss of the few seconds it takes to open an envelope and examine its contents. Our courts are too heavily overburdened to be used as a vehicle to punish by one whose only real damage is feeling foolish for having opened what obviously was junk mail.

We therefore affirm despite the partial technical validity of the action, because the judgment is correct based on the "de minimus" theory. A judgment that is correct on any theory will be affirmed even if the reasons stated by the trial court in support of the judgment were wrong. (Davey v. Southern Pacific Co., supra, 116 Cal. at p. 329, 48 P. 117.)

The judgment is affirmed. The parties shall bear their own costs on appeal.

(2) NATURE AND EFFECT OF COUNTER–OFFER

Minneapolis & St. Louis Railway Co. v. Columbus Rolling–Mill Co.

Supreme Court of the United States, 1886.
119 U.S. 149, 7 S.Ct. 168, 30 L.Ed. 376.

This was an action by a railroad corporation established at Minneapolis in the State of Minnesota against a manufacturing corporation established at Columbus in the State of Ohio. The petition alleged that on December 19, 1879, the parties made a contract by which the plaintiff agreed to buy of the defendant, and the defendant sold to the plaintiff, two thousand tons of iron rails of the weight of fifty pounds per yard, at the price of fifty-four dollars per ton gross, to be delivered free on board cars at the defendant's rolling mill in the month of March, 1880, and to be paid for by the plaintiff in cash when so delivered. The answer denied the making of the contract. It was admitted at the trial that the following letters and telegrams were sent at their dates, and were received in due course, by the parties, through their agents.

December 5, 1879. Letter from plaintiff to defendant: "Please quote me prices for 500 to 3000 tons 50 lb. steel rails, and for 2000 to 5000 tons 50 lb. iron rails, March 1880 delivery."

December 8, 1879. Letter from defendant to plaintiff: "Your favor of the 5th inst. at hand. We do not make steel rails. For iron rails, we will sell 2000 to 5000 tons of 50 lb. rails for fifty-four ($54.00) dollars per gross ton for spot cash, F.O.B. cars at our mill, March delivery, subject as follows: In case of strike among our workmen, destruction of or serious damage to our works by fire or the elements, or any causes of delay beyond our control, we shall not be held accountable in damages. If our offer is accepted, shall expect to be notified of same prior to Dec. 20th, 1879."

December 16, 1879. Telegram from plaintiff to defendant: "Please enter our order for twelve hundred tons rails, March delivery, as per your favor of the eighth. Please reply."

December 16, 1879. Letter from plaintiff to defendant: "Yours of the 8th came duly to hand. I telegraphed you to-day to enter our order for twelve hundred (1200) tons 50 lb. iron rails for next March delivery, at fifty-four dollars ($54.00) F.O.B. cars at your mill. Please send contract. Also please send me templet of your 50 lb. rail. Do you make splices? If so, give me prices for splices for this lot of iron."

December 18, 1879. Telegram from defendant to plaintiff received same day: "We cannot book your order at present at that price."

December 19, 1879. Telegram from plaintiff to defendant: "Please enter an order for two thousand tons rails, as per your letter of the sixth. Please forward written contract. Reply." (The word "sixth" was admitted to be a mistake for "eighth.")

December 22, 1879. Telegram from plaintiff to defendant: "Did you enter my order for two thousand tons rails, as per my telegram of December nineteenth? Answer."

After repeated similar inquiries by the plaintiff, the defendant, on January 19, 1880, denied the existence of any contract between the parties.

The jury returned a verdict for the defendant, under instructions which need not be particularly stated; and the plaintiff alleged exceptions, and sued out this writ of error.

Mr. Justice Gray, after making the foregoing statement of the case, delivered the opinion of the court.

The rules of law which govern this case are well settled. As no contract is complete without the mutual assent of the parties, an offer to sell imposes no obligation until it is accepted according to its terms. So long as the offer has been neither accepted nor rejected, the negotiation remains open, and imposes no obligation upon either party; the one may decline to accept, or the other may withdraw his offer; and either rejection or withdrawal leaves the matter as if no offer had ever been made. A proposal to accept, or an acceptance, upon terms varying from those offered, is a rejection of the offer, and puts an end to the negotiation, unless the party who made the original offer renews it, or assents to the modification suggested. The other party, having once rejected the offer, cannot afterwards revive it by tendering an acceptance of it. . . . If the offer does not limit the time for its acceptance, it must be accepted within a reasonable time. If it does, it may, at any time within the limit and so long as it remains open, be accepted or rejected by the party to whom, or be withdrawn by the party by whom, it was made. . . .

The defendant, by the letter of December 8, offered to sell to the plaintiff two thousand to five thousand tons of iron rails on certain terms specified, and added that if the offer was accepted the defendant would expect to be notified prior to December 20. This offer, while it remained open, without having been rejected by the plaintiff or revoked by the defendant, would authorize the plaintiff to take at his election any number of tons not less than two thousand nor more than five thousand, on the terms specified. The offer, while unrevoked, might be accepted, or rejected by the plaintiff at any time before December 20. Instead of accepting the offer made, the plaintiff, on December 16, by telegram and letter, referring to the defendant's letter of December 8, directed the defendant to enter an order for twelve hundred tons on the same terms. The mention, in both telegram and letter, of the date and the terms of the defendant's original offer, shows that the plaintiff's order was not an independent proposal, but an answer to the defendant's offer, a qualified acceptance of that offer, varying the number of tons, and therefore in law a rejection of the offer. On December 18, the defendant by telegram declined to fulfil the plaintiff's order. The negotiation between the parties was thus closed, and the plaintiff could not afterwards fall back on the defendant's original offer. The plaintiff's attempt to do so, by the telegram of December 19, was therefore ineffectual and created no rights against the defendant.

Such being the legal effect of what passed in writing between the parties, it is unnecessary to consider whether, upon a fair interpretation of the instructions of the court, the question whether the plaintiff's telegram and letter of December 16 constituted a rejection of the defendant's offer of December 8 was ruled in favor of the defendant as a matter of law, or was submitted to the jury as a question of fact. The submission of a question of law to the jury is no ground of exception if they decide it aright. Pence v. Langdon, 99 U.S. 578, 25 L.Ed. 420.

Judgment affirmed.

NOTES

(1) *Common Law Mirror Image Rule.* "When the plaintiffs submitted an offer in their letter of April 4th to the defendant, only one of two courses of action was open to the defendant. It could accept the offer made and thus manifest that assent which was essential to the creation of a contract, or it could reject the offer. There was no middle course. * * * A proposal to accept the offer it modified or an acceptance subject to other terms and conditions was equivalent to an absolute rejection of the offer made by the plaintiffs." Poel v. Brunswick–Balke–Collender Co., 216 N.Y. 310, 110 N.E. 619, 622 (1915). In so speaking the New York Court of Appeals was simply reaffirming settled doctrine that for a valid bargain contract there must be an offer and an acceptance, with the acceptance expressing unconditional assent to the terms of the offer. An offeree cannot pick and choose from among the terms, agreeing here and disagreeing there, and then assert the existence of an operative acceptance. If the terms are varied or changed, there is a counter-offer. No contract can arise until agreement is reached as to those changes; i.e., until the counter-offer has itself been accepted. Traditionally, courts have insisted upon total congruence between offer and acceptance, the latter required to be the "mirror image" of the former. Even a non-material variation is fatal. But see City of Roslyn v. Paul E. Hughes Construction Co., Inc., 19 Wn.App. 59, 573 P.2d 385 (1978) (dictum to the effect that the additional term must be a *material* modification).

Although a reply which purports to be an acceptance but which adds qualifications or requires performance of conditions is not an acceptance, but a counter-offer, Restatement (Second) § 59, an acceptance which *requests* a change or addition to the terms of the offer is not invalidated unless the acceptance is made to depend on an assent to the changed or added terms. Restatement (Second) § 61. There is a considerable body of law differentiating a so-called "conditional" acceptance, which is really no acceptance at all, from a genuine acceptance accompanied by mere "inquiries," "requests," or "suggestions" of the offeree. See, e.g., Valashinas v. Koniuto, 308 N.Y. 233, 124 N.E.2d 300 (1954). Finally, it must be borne in mind that an added term or qualifier in the acceptance may be no more than a repetition of what is already contained, expressly or impliedly, in the offer. United States v. National Optical Stores Co., 407 F.2d 759, 761 (7th Cir.1969) is illustrative. The federal government's notice of acceptance was made subject to approval of credit and antitrust clearance by the Department of Justice. But these two conditions were found to be incorporated in the bid itself. The court concluded: "Since defendant's bid promise included the credit data and antitrust conditions and was accepted by the Government, both parties then became bound in accordance with the mutual assent they had expressed * * * The Government's letter * * * imposed no additional or different terms from those offered and was therefore not a counter-offer."

(2) *The "Grumbling" Acceptance.* In Panhandle Eastern Pipe Line Co. v. Smith, 637 P.2d 1020 (Wyo.1981), an employer (Panhandle) fired an employee (Smith). The latter, following the grievance procedure of a collective bargaining

agreement, unsuccessfully challenged the dismissal. However, Mr. Smith's union representative requested Panhandle to reconsider, and the latter responded with a letter to Smith in which it offered to withdraw the discharge if he would comply with certain terms and conditions. Smith signed under the typewritten words, "Understood, Agreed to and Accepted," added some handwritten notations, and again signed his name. The notations contained a request by Smith to see his personnel file and to contest any mistakes he found there. Panhandle contended that Smith, by adding the request to see his personnel file and to contest mistakes, made a counter-offer. The Wyoming Supreme Court disagreed. There was testimony that all Panhandle employees had a right to see their personnel files, and while the court acknowledged that the acceptance was what Corbin once referred to as a "grumbling" acceptance, it was an acceptance nonetheless.

(3) *The Battle of Forms, Mirror Image and UCC 2–207.* In the preceding case, the parties, who were at a distance, exchanged letters and telegrams. The terms of these writings were read and responded to. But the contract failed because of a disagreement over a material, negotiated term, the quantity of steel to be sold.

In many transactions, the writings of the parties may be a bit more complex. The buyer's purchase order and the seller's acknowledgment may be standard forms that contain terms that are not read or negotiated over by the other party. Put differently, these terms are in the pre-printed "boiler plate" and are drafted by one party in their own interest. Sometimes these terms add to terms in the offer of the other party or to an agreement previously reached. Sometimes these terms contradict other terms. In all cases, however, the party drafting the terms will claim that they are part of the agreement.

In resolving disputes of this sort, keep your eye on three questions: (1) Was any contract formed between the parties; (2) If so, what are its terms; and (3) What commercial policies explain (or should explain) UCC 2–207?

Leonard Pevar Company v. Evans Products Co.

United States District Court, D. Delaware, 1981.
524 F.Supp. 546.

■ LATCHUM, CHIEF JUDGE.

This is a diversity action by the Leonard Pevar Company ("Pevar") against the Evans Products Company ("Evans") for an alleged breach of express and implied warranties in Evans' sale to Pevar of medium density overlay plywood. Defendant denies liability, claiming that it expressly disclaimed warranties and limited its liability in its contract with Pevar. The parties agree that their respective rights and liabilities in this action are governed by the Uniform Commercial Code. The parties have filed cross motions for summary judgment pursuant to Rule 56, F.R.Civ.P. This Court will deny both motions because it finds material facts that are in genuine dispute.

* * *

In the fall of 1977, Pevar began obtaining price quotations for the purchase of medium density overlay plywood to be used in the construction of certain buildings for the State of Pennsylvania. As part of this process, Pevar's contract administrator, Marc Pevar, contacted various manufacturers of this product. Evans was one of the manufacturers contacted and was the supplier that quoted the lowest price for this material.

On October 12, 1977, Marc Pevar had a telephone conversation with Kenneth Kruger of Evans to obtain this price quotation. It is at this juncture that a material fact appears in dispute that precludes this Court from granting summary judgment. Pevar claims that on October 14 it again called Evans, ordered plywood, and entered into an oral contract of sale. Evans admits that Pevar called Evans, but denies that Evans accepted that order.

After the October 14th telephone conversation, Pevar sent a written purchase order to Evans for the plywood. In the purchase order, Pevar did not make any reference to warranties or remedies, but simply ordered the lumber specifying the price, quantity and shipping instructions. On October 19, 1979, Evans sent an acknowledgment to Pevar stating, on the reverse side of the acknowledgment and in boilerplate fashion, that the contract of sale would be expressly contingent upon Pevar's acceptance of all terms contained in the document.[12] One of these terms disclaimed most warranties and another limited the "buyer's remedy" by restricting liability if the plywood proved to be defective.[13]

* * *

Turning now to Section 2–207, it provides:

(1) A definite and seasonable expression of acceptance or a written confirmation which is sent within a reasonable time operates as an acceptance even though it states terms additional to or different from those offered or agreed upon, unless acceptance is expressly made conditional on assent to the additional or different terms.

(2) The additional terms are to be construed as proposals for addition to the contract. Between merchants such terms become part of the contract unless:

12. Paragraph 1 of the Acknowledgment provided:

> Any acceptance by Seller contained herein is expressly made conditional on Buyer's assent to the additional or different terms contained herein. Any acceptance by Buyer contained herein is expressly limited to the terms herein.

See D.I. 4, Exhibit B.

13. Both of these terms were in boldface type:

> 9. Unless seller delivers to buyer a separate written warranty with respect to goods, to the extent legally permissible the sale of all goods is "as is" and there is hereby excluded and seller hereby disclaims any express or implied warranty, including, without limiting the generality of the foregoing, any implied warranty of merchantability or any implied warranty of fitness for any particular use or purpose; provided, however, there is not hereby excluded or disclaimed any implied warranty that seller owns goods or any implied warranty that goods are free from any security interest or other lien or encumbrance of which buyer has no knowledge at the time of contracting to buy such goods.

(a) the offer expressly limits acceptance to the terms of the offer;

(b) they materially alter it; or

(c) notification of objection to them has already been given or is given within a reasonable time after notice of them is received.

(3) Conduct by both parties which recognizes the existence of a contract is sufficient to establish a contract for sale although the writings of the parties do not otherwise establish a contract. In such case the terms of the particular contract consists of those terms on which the writings of the parties agree, together with any supplementary terms incorporated under any other provisions of this Act.

Section 2–207 was intended to eliminate the "ribbon matching" or "mirror" rule of common law, under which the terms of an acceptance or confirmation were required to be identical to the terms of the offer or oral agreement, respectively. Dorton v. Collins & Aikman Corp., 453 F.2d 1161 (C.A.6, 1972). The drafters of the Code intended to preserve an agreement, as it was originally conceived by the parties, in the face of additional material terms included in standard forms exchanged by merchants in the normal course of dealings. Alan Wood Steel Co. v. Capital Equipment Enterprises Inc., 39 Ill.App.3d 48, 349 N.E.2d 627 (1976). Section 2–207 recognizes that a buyer and seller can enter into a contract by one of three methods. First, the parties may agree orally and thereafter send confirmatory memoranda. § 2–207(1). Second, the parties, without oral agreement, may exchange writings which do not contain identical terms, but nevertheless constitute a seasonable acceptance. § 2–207(1). Third, the conduct of the parties may recognize the existence of a contract, despite the previous failure to agree orally or in writing. § 2–207(3).

A. *Oral agreement followed by confirmation.*

Section 2–207(1) applies to those situations where an "oral agreement has been reached ... followed by one or both of the parties sending formal memoranda embodying the terms so far as agreed upon and adding terms not discussed." Uniform Commercial Code, Comment 1 to § 2–207. These additional terms are treated as proposals under 2–207(2) and will become part of the agreement unless they materially alter it. *Dorton, supra,* 453 F.2d at 1169–70.[17]

---

17. The "unless" proviso in § 2–207(1) does not apply to confirmatory memoranda because the parties have already entered into an agreement and one party does not have the power pursuant to § 2–207 to terminate it unilaterally:

Confirmation connotes that the parties reached an agreement before exchange of the forms in question. The purpose of the Code drafters here must have been to make clear that confirmations need not

mirror each other in order to find contract. Simply stated, then, under this first clause of section 2–207(1) it is reasonable to assume that the parties have a deal, that there is a contract even though terms of the writing exchanged do not match. All of the language following the comma in subsection (1) simply preserves for the offeree his right to make a counter-offer if he does so expressly. This phrase cannot possibly effect the deal

In the present case, paragraphs 9 and 12 of Evans' acknowledgment, which disclaimed warranties and limited liability,[18] may include terms not in the original agreement. Generally, these types of clauses "materially alter" the agreement. Uniform Commercial Code, Comment 4 to § 2–207. Nevertheless, the question of a material alteration rests upon the facts of each case.[19] *See Dorton,* supra, 453 F.2d at 1169 n. 8; *Medical Development Corp. v. Industrial Molding Corp.,* 479 F.2d 345, 348 (C.A.10, 1973); *Ebasco Services Inc. v. Pennsylvania Power & Light Co.,* 402 F.Supp. 421, 442 (E.D.Pa.1975). If the trier of fact determines that the acknowledgment includes additional terms which do not materially alter the oral agreement, then the terms will be incorporated into the agreement. If they materially alter it, however, the terms will not be included in the agreement, and the standardized "gap filler" provisions of Article Two will provide the terms of the contract. If the facts reveal that no oral agreement was created, then § 2–207(1) may still apply, but in a different manner.

B. *Written documents not containing identical terms.*

The second situation in which § 2–207(1) may apply is where the parties have not entered into an oral agreement but have exchanged writings which do not contain identical terms. If the Court determines that Pevar and Evans did not orally agree prior to the exchange of documents, then this second situation may apply. In such a case, both Pevar and Evans agree that Pevar's purchase order constituted an offer to purchase. The parties, however, disagree with the characterization of Evans' acknowledgment and Pevar's acceptance of and payment for the shipped goods. Evans contends that the terms disclaiming warranties and limiting liability in the acknowledgment should control because the acknowledgment constituted a counteroffer which Pevar accepted by receiving and paying for the goods. Evans argues that by inserting the "unless" proviso[20] in the terms and conditions of acceptance of the acknowledgment, it effectively rejected and terminated Pevar's offer, and initiated a counteroffer; and when Pevar received and paid for the goods, it accepted the terms of the counteroffer.

Evans relies upon *Roto–Lith, Ltd. v. F.P. Bartlett & Co.,* 297 F.2d 497 (C.A.1, 1962) for the proposition that a buyer accepts the terms of the seller's counteroffer merely by receiving and paying for shipped goods. In *Roto–Lith,* the buyer of goods sent a written purchase order to the seller.

between parties that have reached an agreement and then exchanged confirmations. In that situation it is too late for a counter-offer and subsection (2) must be applied to determine what becomes of the non-matching terms of the confirmations.

Air Products & Chemicals, Inc. v. Fairbanks Morse, Inc., 58 Wis.2d 193, 206 N.W.2d 414, 422–23 (1973), *quoting Section 2–207 of the Uniform Commercial Code—New Rules for the "Battle of the Forms",* 32 U.Pitt.L.Rev. 209, 210 (1971).

18. *See* note 13 *supra.*

19. Therefore, even if there were no dispute that the oral agreement existed, the question of materiality would preclude the Court from granting summary judgment.

20. Section 2–207(1) "unless" proviso provides: "unless acceptance is expressly made conditional on assent to the additional or different terms." Evans followed this language in its acknowledgment.

The seller thereafter sent an acknowledgment, accepting the purchase order in part, but also added terms which disclaimed warranties and limited liabilities. The buyer received the goods but did not object to the seller's terms. The court found that the seller's acceptance (acknowledgment) was expressly conditional on assent to the additional terms and, therefore, a counteroffer. It held that the buyer accepted the terms of the counteroffer when it received and paid for the goods.

Roto–Lith has been widely criticized because it does not reflect the underlying principles of the Code. Rather, it reflects the orthodox common law reasoning—that the terms of the counteroffer control if the goods are accepted unless the counterofferee specifically objects to those terms. The drafters of the Code, however, intended to change the common law in an attempt to conform contract law to modern day business transactions. They believed that businessmen rarely read the terms on the back of standardized forms and that the common law, therefore, unduly rewarded the party who sent the last form prior to the shipping of the goods. The Code disfavors any attempt by one party to impose unilaterally conditions that would create hardship on another party. Thus, before a counteroffer is accepted, the counterofferee must expressly assent to the new terms.

This Court joins those courts that have rejected the *Roto–Lith* analysis. *Itoh, supra,* 552 F.2d at 1235; *Dorton, supra,* 453 F.2d at 1166; *Uniroyal, Inc. v. Chambers Gasket & Manufacturing Co.,* 380 N.E.2d 571, 577–78 (C.A.Ind.1978); *Falcon Tankers Inc. v. Litton Systems, Inc.,* 355 A.2d 898, 906 (Del.Super.1976). *See also Construction Aggregates Corp. v. Hewitt-Robins Corp.,* 404 F.2d 505 (C.A.7), *cert. denied,* 395 U.S. 921, 89 S.Ct. 1774, 23 L.Ed.2d 238 (1969). "It finds that [t]he consequence of a clause conditioning acceptance on assent to the additional or different terms is that *as of the exchanged writings there is no contract.* Either party may at this point in their dealing walk away from the transaction" or reach an express assent. *Itoh,* at 1236, *quoting Duesenberg & King, Sales & Bulk Transfer* (Bender) § 3.06(3) at 73. Without the express assent by the parties no contract is created pursuant to § 2–207(1).[21] Nevertheless, the parties' conduct may create a contract pursuant to § 2–207(3).

C. *Conduct establishing the existence of a contract.*

Section 2–207(3) is the third method by which parties may enter into a contract. This section applies when the parties have not entered into an oral or written contract. Section 2–207(3) provides that "[c]onduct by both

---

21. Pevar and Evans had conversations subsequent to the shipping of the goods where Pevar did not object to the terms of Evans' acknowledgment. Evans, relying upon *Construction Aggregates, supra,* contends that Pevar's failure to object to the acknowledgment during these subsequent conversations constitutes an implicit acceptance of those terms. The facts in *Construction Aggregates* are readily distinguishable from the facts in this case. In that case, the buyer specifically objected to some terms of the acknowledgment, while remaining silent on the others. The court found that the purchaser thereby agreed to those terms in which it remained silent. Contrasting *Construction Aggregates,* Pevar and Evans did not specifically discuss Evans' acknowledgment. Thus, there is no basis to hold that Pevar consented to those terms.

parties which recognizes the existence of a contract is sufficient to establish a contract for sale although the writing of the parties do not otherwise establish a contract." As *Dorton,* supra, 453 F.2d at 1166 noted:

> When no contract is recognized under Subsection 2–207(1) . . . the entire transaction aborts at this point. If, however, the subsequent conduct of the parties—particularly, performance by both parties under what they apparently believe to be a contract—recognizes the existence of a contract, under Subsection 2–207(3), such conduct by both parties is sufficient to establish a contract, notwithstanding the fact that no contract would have been recognized on the basis of their writings alone.

> Section 2–207(3) also provides that where a contract has been consummated by the conduct of the parties, "the terms of the particular contract consist of those terms in which the writings of the parties agree, together with any supplementary terms incorporated under any other provisions of this Act."

In this case, the parties' conduct indicates that they recognized the existence of a contract. If this Court finds after trial that Pevar and Evans did not enter into an oral agreement, Section 2–207(3) will apply. The terms of the contract will include those terms in which Pevar's purchase order and Evans' acknowledgment agree. For those terms where the writings do not agree, the standardized "gap filler" provisions of Article Two will provide the terms of the contract. *Itoh,* supra, 552 F.2d at 1237.[22]

An Order will be entered in accordance with this Memorandum Opinion.

[Some footnotes omitted.]

NOTES

(1) *On Saying Too Much and Agreeing Upon Too Little.* "The problem underlying any 'battle of the forms' is that parties engaged in commerce have failed to incorporate into one formal, signed contract the terms of their contractual relationship. Instead, each has been content to rely upon standard terms which each has included in its purchase orders or acknowledgments, terms which often conflict with those in the other party's documents. Usually, these standard terms mean little, for a contract looks to its fulfillment and rarely anticipates its breach. Hope springs eternal in the commercial world and expectations are usually, but not always, realized. It is only when the good faith expectations of the parties are frustrated that the legal obligations and rights of the parties must be precisely determined. This case presents a situation typical in any battle of the forms: it is not that the parties' forms have said too little, but rather that they have said too much yet have expressly agreed upon too little." McJunkin Corporation v. Mechanicals, Inc., 888 F.2d 481, 482 (6th Cir.1989).

22. See e.g., §§ 2–314, 315 & 715.

(2) How might a binding contract be found under UCC 2–207? How does the analysis differ from that traditionally employed by common law courts?

(3) Under what circumstances might a form's variant terms automatically become a part of the contract?

(4) It has been said that UCC 2–207(1) is "unusually poorly drafted as it applies to written confirmations." Utz, *More on the Battle of the Forms: The Treatment of 'Different' Terms Under the Uniform Commercial Code,* 16 U.C.C.L.J. 103, 105, n. 5 (1983). The written confirmation is said to operate as an acceptance even though it states terms at variance with those agreed upon. But if the parties reached a prior agreement, was there not a prior acceptance?

(5) What is the rationale for concluding that a seller's acknowledgment might operate as an acceptance even if it contains variant terms; e.g., disclaimer of warranty? How might a seller make certain that the response is not so interpreted? Should language such as that contained in Evans' acknowledgment suffice? On the need for explicit language of condition, see Idaho Power Co. v. Westinghouse Electric Corp., 596 F.2d 924 (9th Cir.1979); Dorton v. Collins & Aikman Corp., 453 F.2d 1161 (6th Cir.1972). See generally, Annot., *What Constitutes Acceptance "Expressly Made Conditional" Converting It to Rejection and Counteroffer Under UCC § 2–207(1),* 22 A.L.R.4th 939 (1983).

(6) It is to be noted that UCC 2–207(1) uses the phrase "terms additional to or different from" but that subsection (2) refers only to "additional" terms. It is generally assumed that both types of variant terms should be disposed of in accordance with the rules of subsection (2). For an excellent treatment of this issue, see Utz, note 4 supra. But see James J. White & Robert S. Summers, Uniform Commercial Code 8–13 (4th ed. 1995)(disagreement over treatment of "different" terms). However, the omission of "different" from subsection (2) has influenced some courts to apply a so-called "knock out" doctrine, whereby even if a contract is formed under subsection (1), the terms of the contract are not those contained in the "offer" plus whatever terms are added by reason of subsection (2), but those upon which the "forms" agree. That is, the differing terms cancel each other. See, e.g., Northrop Corp. v. Litronic Industries, 29 F.3d 1173 (7th Cir.1994); Daitom, Inc. v. Pennwalt Corp., 741 F.2d 1569 (10th Cir.1984); Ionics, Inc. v. Elmwood Sensors, Inc., 896 F.Supp. 66 (D.Mass.1995); St. Paul Structural Steel Company v. ABI Contracting, Inc., 364 N.W.2d 83 (N.D.1985). Where is the statutory basis for this? If the "different" terms in the "acceptance" are not handled under subsection (2), they should drop out altogether. See UCC 2–207(3).

(7) The *Pevar* court says that even if an oral agreement existed, the question of materiality would preclude the court from granting summary judgment. Why? Because of doubt as to whether the terms were material? There has been extensive litigation as to whether particular terms (e.g., disclaimer of warranty, arbitration clauses) constitute a material alteration, resulting in a bewildering array of precedent. See Annot., *What Are Additional Terms Materially Altering Contract Within Meaning of UCC § 2–207(2)(b),* 72 A.L.R.3d 479 (1976).

(8) Commentary upon UCC 2–207 is voluminous, much of it critical. What do you think? For more, see Symposium, *Ending the Battle of the Forms,* 49 Bus. Law. 1019 (1994); Alexander M. Meiklejohn, *Castles in the Air: Blanket*

Assent and the Revision of Article 2, 51 Wash. & Lee L. Rev. 599 (1994); John Murray, *The Chaos of the Battle of the Forms,* 39 Vand. L. Rev. 1307 (1986); Barron and Dunfee, *Two Decades of 2–207: Review, Reflection and Revision,* 24 Clev.St.L.Rev. 171 (1975).

Comment: Standard Forms, Standard Terms and Revised Article 2.

Under revised UCC 2–207, problems of contract formation are separated from questions of whether additional or different terms become part of the agreement. The contract formation questions are answered under UCC 2–203 and 2–205(1997) and the inclusion questions are answered under UCC 2–207. The revision clarifies the analysis without changing the results in most cases.

Unlike the 1990 Official Text, the November, 1996 Draft of revised Article 2, dealt specifically with problems created by the use of standard forms and standard terms in contract formation in two ways.

First, if all or part of the agreement is contained in a standard form, defined in UCC 2–102(a)(Nov. 1996), and the other party has signed the form or appeared to assent to it by conduct, that party is not bound to terms in the form if there was no manifestation of assent to it. "Manifested assent" is a term of art defined in UCC 2–103(Nov. 1996). At a minimum, a party manifesting assent must have had an opportunity to review the form as that is defined in UCC 2–103(b)(Nov. 1996). UCC 2–206(a)(Nov. 1996). If one party manifests assent to the form, he or she is bound by terms included therein unless the terms are unconscionable. UCC 2–206(a)(Nov.1996). A higher standard of assent is required for consumers. See UCC 2–206(b)(Nov. 1996). The objective here is to reduce the risk of unfair surprise by increasing the odds that the party not preparing the form will have information about its contents before agreeing to it.

Second, if only part of the agreement is contained in a standard form, there is a risk that other records containing varying terms will be exchanged by parties dealing at a distance. In cases to which UCC 2–206(Nov. 1996) does not apply, how is the risk that one party will be unfairly surprised by standard terms in a record or a standard form which are not read or understood? In the classic "battle of the forms" setting, where the parties focus on the negotiated terms such as price, quantity, payment, time and delivery rather than the boiler plate, the risk of unfair surprise and strategic game playing is the highest.

The solution in revised UCC 2–207(Nov. 1996) was to isolate terms in standard forms (they are likely to be standard terms, as defined) and impose an even higher standard for assent. The judgment was that the concept of "manifest assent" would not work in the unstructured, "battle of the forms" setting. Thus, UCC 2–207(a)(Nov. 1996) required express agreement to those varying terms before they are included in the agreement.

In January, 1997, however, the Article Drafting Committee: (1) withdrew UCC 2–206(a)(Nov. 1996) dealing with standard form commercial contracts; (2) withdrew UCC 2–103 (Nov. 1996) dealing with the concept of "manifest assent"; and (3) eliminated all references to standard forms and standard terms in UCC 2–203, 2–205 and 2–207.

The latest version (January, 1997) of UCC 2–207 provides:

Section 2–207. Terms

(a) Subject to subsection (b) and Section 2–202, if a contract is formed as provided in Sections 2–203 and 2–205, the terms are:

(1) those terms on which the records of the parties substantially agree;

(2) those terms to which the parties have, through language or other conduct, otherwise agreed;

(3) those terms supplied by usage of trade, course of dealing or course of performance; and

(4) any supplementary terms incorporated under any other provision of this Act.

(b) If a contract is formed under Section 2–205(a)(1) and the acceptance contains terms that vary the contract, the following terms are not part of the contract:

(1) terms in the acceptance that materially vary the contract; and

(2) conflicting terms.

Comment: Electronic Data Interchange and Contract Formation

[The following, published in The Business Lawyer, is from a report prepared by the Electronic Messaging Services Task Force and submitted to the Committee on the Uniform Commercial Code, Section of Business Law of the American Bar Association.]

Electronic data interchange ("EDI") is the method by which business data may be communicated electronically between computers in standardized formats (such as purchase orders, invoices, shipping notices, and remittance advices) in substitution for conventional paper documents. The integration of EDI into ongoing business activities has occurred, and is expected to continue, at a considerable rate. Over time, EDI will likely become the predominant method of sales contracting. * * *

* * *

An example best illustrates the manner in which EDI frequently is implemented to effect commercial sales transactions.

ABC and XYZ have a long-standing purchase and sale relationship. Recognizing the economic and administrative benefits attributed to EDI, ABC announces to its vendors, including XYZ, that ABC will require, or provide incentives for, the use of EDI in future transactions. ABC engages a third party service provider (referred to in the Model Agreement as a

"Provider"*) to receive, transmit, and sort the various EDI transmissions of ABC. In addition, ABC determines which paper-based documents will be replaced by EDI formats, as well as which industry standards will be adopted around which all transmissions will be structured, and implements certain security procedures for assuring the authenticity and integrity of the electronic communications. All of this information is communicated to ABC's vendors, one of which is XYZ, who must implement EDI accordingly to keep ABC's business (or obtain the available incentives, as the case may be).

A sales transaction is initiated by the electronic transmission from ABC (as buyer) of a purchase order which sets forth, in the sequence specified by the selected standard, the elements of information typically included in any purchase order (such as ABC's name, shipping information, quantity, style, color, price, freight, taxes, and required date of delivery). The purchase order is included within an electronic "envelope" which may contain other messages to XYZ relating to other transactions. The purchase order is initially sent to ABC's Provider, who, in turn, stores and subsequently transmits the purchase order, together with any other electronic "documents" within the envelope, to XYZ. Upon receipt of the purchase order, XYZ transmits a message in return (called a functional acknowledgement), which verifies that no syntactical errors have occurred in the transmission of the purchase order (i.e., the data was complete and in the correct format). Upon reviewing the terms set forth in the purchase order and determining their acceptability, XYZ electronically transmits an additional transmission to ABC, which confirms acceptance of those terms; such transmission may be, for example, a purchase order acknowledgement or a shipping notice. Upon receipt of XYZ's purchase order acknowledgement, ABC in turn sends a functional acknowledgement back to XYZ. All transmissions from XYZ are sent to the Provider designated by ABC (with whom XYZ also has contracted), which stores and transmits XYZ's messages to ABC at pre-arranged times (or permits ABC to access electronically the Provider's appropriate files and have such messages transferred to ABC's computer).

Following formation of the contract, additional commercial messages may be communicated electronically between ABC and XYZ. These documents may include change orders, invoices, remittance advices, and similar types of communications. Generally, a Provider will enter into written agreements with ABC and XYZ which may also provide for certain value-added services, in addition to the transmission, storage, and receipt of EDI documents.

In a fully automated EDI environment, trading partners have developed applications software programs which eliminate human decision making with respect to particular transactions. For example, in the event that reported inventory reaches a certain level, ABC's computer might automat-

---

* [The authors of the report also furnish a Model Trading Partner Agreement, with Commentary, "designed as a framework which counsel may adapt to the needs of clients establishing trading relationships in an electronic setting." Preface to Report. Ed.]

ically generate an appropriate purchase order, including terms as to price, quantity, and similar items pre-defined to be within the parameters of the business relationship with XYZ. Similarly, XYZ's computer may be programmed to automatically accept any purchase order whose terms fall within predefined parameters. This process may be sufficient, if fully established, to permit ordering, shipping, invoicing, and payment to occur electronically, with human review and intervention, if it occurs at all, limited to supervisory summaries of daily activity.

* * *

Electronic commerce creates opportunities for more rapid and precise understandings between the parties. The Task Force was impressed by the potential of EDI technology, when effectively implemented, to introduce increased accuracy, as well as increased speed, in the communication of business data. The significant functional feature of EDI is that it provides the ability for businesses to immediately confirm, by return message, that a receiving party has received the original message, and to confirm that no errors or omissions occurred in the transmissions. In this manner, ambiguities or misunderstandings, as well as errors in the communication process, can be promptly resolved. In addition, since messages which are inconsistent with past arrangements or established contractual limits can potentially be detected and investigated electronically, trading partners encouraged by the functions of the technology to establish procedures which better match the moment at which a legal obligation arises from a message with the time at which the parties may mutually verify the content of the message.

* * *

The drafters of Article 2 of the Code specifically did not address the question of when a contract is effectively formed.[76] That process occurs under applicable principles of common law.[77] The Task Force considered that, for the purpose of its analysis, the Restatement (Second) of Contracts provided an effective structure for analyzing the treatment of the role of the medium of communication in the contract formation process.[78]

---

76. The Code provides that a contract may be formed in any manner, including through the conduct of the parties, and has limited provisions dealing with acceptance of offers by shipment. See, e.g., U.C.C. §§ 2–204, 2–206. The Code is silent, however, on rules pertaining to the timing of contract formation, except to the extent it provides that a contract may be formed even though the time of its making is uncertain. Id. § 2–206. Consequently, common law principles of contract formation continue to apply. Id. § 1–103.

77. See id. § 1–103. The Code more specifically addresses the effectiveness of additional commercial communications relating to contracts and their validity and enforceability. See, e.g., id. § 2–207 (the "battle of the forms" provision).

78. See, e.g., Restatement (Second) of Contracts §§ 64–65 (1981). See also 1 A. Corbin, Corbin on Contracts §§ 39–41, 62–66, 72–81 (1963 & Supp.1989) [hereinafter 1 Corbin]; 1 S. Williston, Williston on Contracts §§ 81–89 (3d ed. 1957) [hereinafter 1 Williston].

The Restatement allocates between contracting parties the risks relating to the method of communication chosen by each party, and identifies the relative priority of contradictory or simultaneous communications (particularly when the means of communication utilized, such as mailed writings, do not provide for instantaneous, direct interaction between the parties). The Restatement distinguishes between two situations. In the first, the parties are in each other's presence and are able to communicate without any substantial lapse of time. In the second, the parties are not in each other's presence and the means of communication utilized to transmit offers, acceptances, modifications, revocations, and other messages result in a delay between the dispatch and receipt of those communications. In the latter situation, the common law provides, for example, the "mailbox rule," pursuant to which the dispatch of a message is effective without regard to whether the message ever reaches the other party. An important premise upon which those rules are predicated is the notion that delayed media, such as mailed writings, do not provide either party the ability to verify in a timely fashion that receipt of a message has occurred and that the message as received is without errors. However, section 64 of the Restatement specifically acknowledges the use of technology in communication, in the form of "telephone or other medium of substantially instantaneous two-way communication," and sets forth the principle that communications using those technologies are governed by the same principles that apply when the parties are in the presence of each other.

As discussed, EDI has the capability to permit prompt, reliable verification that a message has been received, and that it has been received intact and without communication errors. This verification can occur immediately, and several EDI industry standards require such verification to be sent in a commercially prompt manner. If there are ambiguities or misunderstandings perceived by either party, the problems can be corrected by additional, immediate communication. If there is a failure in the communication, EDI permits one or both parties to know or have reason to know of the failure by virtue of the capability of the technology to provide timely verifications. Of course, a distinguishing characteristic of EDI is that the communication is transmitted and received in an essentially "written" format; to review the message, users "read" the data, either electronically or by human review (presented either as a screen display or a printout on paper). The Task Force concluded that the "written" characteristic was not important to its analysis; the applicable legal principles focus on the immediacy of communication, and not the format. Accordingly, the use of EDI to communicate was determined to satisfy the criteria of section 64 of the Restatement. As a result, the Model Agreement incorporates rules that parallel those provided by common law for other types of technology which facilitate instantaneous communication.

The Model Agreement constructs an environment in which receipt, and not transmission, determines the legal effect of any message transmitted by EDI, and in which verification of the transmission is a mandatory element (with certain negotiated exceptions) of conducting business with EDI. The functionality of the technology permits a more fair allocation of the benefits and burdens, and resulting legal consequences, of the choice of a communication medium. Existing rules proceed from the proposition that the originating party controls the selection of the means of communication (and absorbs its risk). With EDI, however, the choice of an electronic means of communication is essentially mutual and different rules reflecting that mutuality seem appropriate. * * *

* * *

Offers are treated by the Model Agreement like any other Document. An offer does not give rise to any obligation until properly received. Irrespective of whether the receiving party wishes to accept the offer, the receiving party should transmit a functional acknowledgement in return. Of course, at common law, an offer creates no contract until accepted. With respect to acceptance, the Model Agreement unambiguously requires that, for each type of Document, the parties are to specify in the Appendix whether acceptance is required and, if so, the corresponding Acceptance Document that will evidence such acceptance. If acceptance is required by the Model Agreement, no obligation will arise from any Document unless and until an appropriate Acceptance Document has been properly received in return. By preserving the ability of the parties to define by negotiation what constitutes an appropriate Acceptance Document, the Model Agreement permits the parties to define the level of certainty and agreement to be achieved with respect to the terms of any Document. For example, the parties may provide that before a purchase order gives rise to an enforceable contract, the recipient of the purchase order must accept by the issuance of a purchase order acknowledgement. In contrast to a functional acknowledgement, an Acceptance Document responds to the substance of the original transmission and signifies that the substantive terms are acceptable. An Acceptance Document may be a computer generated response, or it may require human evaluation at the receiving end before the response can be transmitted.[121]

As drafted, the concept of acceptance under the Model Agreement is not limited to the contract formation process. An Acceptance Document might be specified for a variety of communications to better assure the

---

121. The more human intervention required before the transmission of any Document, including an Acceptance Document, the slower the resulting communication and the less significant the operational benefits of EDI. The needs of a particular business may well warrant human intervention. The elimination of human intervention, however, does not mean the elimination of any review of the substantive message. It is possible to program the Receipt Computer to review the incoming message against certain pre-defined variables, and to issue an Acceptance Document only if the message falls within certain parameters. The Receipt Computer, for example, can be programmed to review an incoming purchase order and determine such matters as: (i) whether the quantity and quality of the requested goods was in stock; (ii) whether the quantity order is within the limits pre-established by the trading parties or is within the normal limits ordered by the trading party; (iii) whether the price or other specified terms are current and acceptable; (iv) whether the delivery point is one which has been agreed upon or used in the past; and (v) whether the time for delivery can be accommodated. Once all these factors are reviewed, and found within pre-defined limits, the computer can then generate the required Acceptance Document.

absence of misunderstanding. A shipping notice may require "acceptance" by means of a confirmation of shipment date, in order to assure the buyer may accommodate delivery at the proposed time. Of course, for certain Documents (for example, a notice of rejection of goods from a buyer), no Acceptance Document would be appropriate. If, for any Document, no Acceptance Document is specified, such Document will only be given legal effect upon proper receipt; what that legal effect will be will depend upon the type of communication and its treatment under applicable law. Some Documents, such as a notice of rejection, should have legal effect upon proper receipt, with nothing more. In no event, however, does the Model Agreement eliminate the need for acceptance of an offer. In the absence of an Acceptance Document being specified for a Document from which an offer is made, no obligation may arise before the Document has been properly received. Then, even if no functional acknowledgement is issued, the conduct of the receiving party, if it acts to accept or otherwise justifiably relies upon the original Document, may be sufficient to create a binding obligation.[125] *The Commercial Use of Electronic Data Interchange— A Report and Model Trading Partner Agreement,* 45 Bus.Law. 1645, 1649, 1655–1657, 1665, 1666–1668, 1674–1675 (1990). Some footnotes omitted. Reprinted by permission of the American Bar Association.

(D) TERMINATION OF OFFER: DESTRUCTION OF POWER OF ACCEPTANCE

By now a few patterns should be apparent. In the bargaining relationship, an offer, however defined, must be communicated to be effective. Once communicated, the offer creates in the offeree a power of acceptance, the duration of which may be limited by either the terms of the offer or some concept of reasonable time. Up to now, we have examined the efforts by offerees to accept the offer before the power of acceptance was terminated. The focus has been upon what an acceptance is and by what method or manner assent should be manifested. And we have seen that when something called a counter-offer is actually communicated to the offeror, the power of acceptance is terminated, much like a specific rejection, by conduct of the offeree. See *Minneapolis & St. Louis Railway Co. v. Columbus Rolling–Mill Co.,* supra at 358. But in the fuzzy background of these cases, it is apparent that there is a race between the proper exercise of the power of acceptance by the offeree and, perhaps, lapse of time, a change of mind by the offeror or some other terminating event. This "race" is vividly demonstrated in the so-called "mailbox" rule, where the contract is created if the letter of acceptance is posted before the offeror's revocation is actually received by the offeree.

---

125. See generally U.C.C. §§ 2–204(1), 2–206(1): Restatement (Second) of Contracts § 90 (1981). In addition, if the parties establish a course of performance involving the transmission of a purchase order, for which no Acceptance Document is provided but the contract is nevertheless routinely performed, the absence of an Acceptance Document will not interfere with the existence of a valid contract. See U.C.C. § 2–208 * * *.

In this subsection, we will briefly explore some other aspects of this "race," emphasizing the overlaps with problems previously discussed and the underlying policies. In the next subsection, we will survey the basic varieties of option contracts, with emphasis upon the methods of creation, effect upon the power of acceptance and overlap with materials previously covered.

Hendricks v. Behee

Missouri Court of Appeals, Southern District, 1990.
Supra at 273.

Dickinson v. Dodds

Court of Appeal, Chancery Division, 1876.
2 Ch.D. 463.

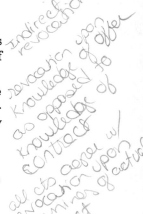

On Wednesday, the 10th of June, 1874, the Defendant John Dodds signed and delivered to the Plaintiff, George Dickinson, a memorandum, of which the material part was as follows:—

"I hereby agree to sell to Mr. George Dickinson the whole of the dwelling-houses, garden ground, stabling, and outbuildings thereto belonging, situate at Croft, belonging to me, for the sum of 800. As witness my hand this tenth day of June, 1874.

"£800.(Signed) John Dodds."

"P.S.—This offer to be left over until Friday, 9 o'clock, A.M. J.D. (the twelfth), 12th June, 1874.

"(Signed) J. Dodds."

The bill alleged that Dodds understood and intended that the Plaintiff should have until Friday 9 A.M. within which to determine whether he would or would not purchase, and that he should absolutely have until that time the refusal of the property at the price of £800, and that the Plaintiff in fact determined to accept the offer on the morning of Thursday, the 11th of June, but did not at once signify his acceptance to Dodds, believing that he had the power to accept it until 9 A.M. on the Friday.

In the afternoon of the Thursday the Plaintiff was informed by a Mr. Berry that Dodds had been offering or agreeing to sell the property to Thomas Allan, the other Defendant. Thereupon the Plaintiff, at about half-past seven in the evening, went to the house of Mrs. Burgess, the mother-in-law of Dodds, where he was then staying, and left with her a formal acceptance in writing of the offer to sell the property. According to the evidence of Mrs. Burgess this document never in fact reached Dodds, she having forgotten to give it to him.

On the following (Friday) morning, at about seven o'clock, Berry, who was acting as agent for Dickinson, found Dodds at the Darlington railway station, and handed to him a duplicate of the acceptance by Dickinson, and explained to Dodds its purport. He replied that it was too late, as he had sold the property. A few minutes later Dickinson himself found Dodds entering a railway carriage, and handed him another duplicate of the notice of acceptance, but Dodds declined to receive it, saying, "You are too late. I have sold the property."

It appeared that on the day before, Thursday, the 11th of June, Dodds had signed a formal contract for the sale of the property to the Defendant Allan for £800, and had received from him a deposit of £40.

The bill in this suit prayed that the Defendant Dodds might be decreed specifically to perform the contract of the 10th of June, 1874; that he might be restrained from conveying the property to Allan; that Allan might be restrained from taking any such conveyance; that, if any such conveyance had been or should be made, Allan might be declared a trustee of the property for, and might be directed to convey the property to, the Plaintiff; and for damages.

The cause came on for hearing before Vice–Chancellor Bacon on the 25th of January, 1876.

[A decree for specific performance was entered, and the Defendants appealed.]

■ JAMES, L.J., after referring to the document of the 10th of June, 1874, continued:—

The document, though beginning "I hereby agree to sell," was nothing but an offer, and was only intended to be an offer, for the Plaintiff himself tells us that he required time to consider whether he would enter into an agreement or not. Unless both parties had then agreed there was no concluded agreement then made; it was in effect and substance only an offer to sell. The Plaintiff, being minded not to complete the bargain at that time, added this memorandum—"This offer to be left over until Friday, 9 o'clock A.M., 12th June, 1874." That shews it was only an offer. There was no consideration given for the undertaking or promise, to whatever extent it may be considered binding, to keep the property unsold until 9 o'clock on Friday morning; but apparently Dickinson was of opinion, and probably Dodds was of the same opinion, that he (Dodds) was bound by that promise, and could not in any way withdraw from it, or retract it, until 9 o'clock on Friday morning, and this probably explains a good deal of what afterwards took place. But it is clear settled law, on one of the clearest principles of law, that this promise, being a mere nudum pactum, was not binding, and that at any moment before a complete acceptance by Dickinson of the offer, Dodds was as free as Dickinson himself. Well, that being the state of things, it is said that the only mode in which Dodds could assert that freedom was by actually and distinctly saying to Dickinson, "Now I withdraw my offer." It appears to me that there is neither principle nor authority for the proposition that there must be an express and actual withdrawal of the offer, or what is called a retraction. It must, to constitute a contract, appear that the two minds were at one, at the same moment of time, that is, that there was an offer continuing up to the time of the acceptance. If there was not such a continuing offer, then the acceptance comes to nothing. Of course it may well be that the one man is bound in some way or other to let the other man know that his mind with regard to the offer has been changed; but in this case, beyond all question, the Plaintiff knew that Dodds was no longer minded to sell the property to him as plainly and clearly as if Dodds had told him in so many words, "I withdraw the offer." This is evident from the Plaintiff's own statements in the bill.

The Plaintiff says in effect that, having heard and knowing that Dodds was no longer minded to sell to him, and that he was selling or had sold to some one else, thinking that he could not in point of law withdraw his offer, meaning to fix him to it, and endeavouring to bind him, "I went to the house where he was lodging, and saw his mother-in-law, and left with her an acceptance of the offer, knowing all the while that he had entirely changed his mind. I got an agent to watch for him at 7 o'clock the next morning, and I went to the train just before 9 o'clock, in order that I might catch him and give him my notice of acceptance just before 9 o'clock, and when that occurred he told my agent, and he told me, you are too late, and he then threw back the paper." It is to my mind quite clear that before there was any attempt at acceptance by the Plaintiff, he was perfectly well aware that Dodds had changed his mind, and that he had in fact agreed to sell the property to Allan. It is impossible, therefore, to say there was ever that existence of the same mind between the two parties which is essential in point of law to the making of an agreement. I am of opinion, therefore, that the Plaintiff has failed to prove that there was any binding contract between Dodds and himself.

■ MELLISH, L.J.:—

I am of the same opinion. The first question is, whether this document of the 10th of June, 1874, which was signed by Dodds, was an agreement to sell, or only an offer to sell, the property therein mentioned to Dickinson; and I am clearly of opinion that it was only an offer, although it is in the first part of it, independently of the postscript, worded as an agreement. I apprehend that, until acceptance, so that both parties are bound, even though an instrument is so worded as to express that both parties agree, it is in point of law only an offer, and, until both parties are bound, neither party is bound. It is not necessary that both parties should be bound within the Statute of Frauds, for, if one party makes an offer in writing, and the other accepts it verbally, that will be sufficient to bind the person who has signed the written document. But, if there be no agreement, either verbally or in writing, then, until acceptance, it is in point of law an offer only, although worded as if it were an agreement. But it is hardly necessary to resort to that doctrine in the present case, because the postscript calls it an offer, and says, "This offer to be left over until Friday, 9 o'clock A.M." Well, then, this being only an offer, the law says—and it is a perfectly clear rule of law—that, although it is said that the offer is to be left open until Friday morning at 9 o'clock, that did not bind Dodds. He was not in point of law bound to hold the offer over until 9 o'clock on Friday morning. He was not so bound either in law or in equity. Well, that being so, when on the next day he made an agreement with Allan to sell the property to him, I am not aware of any ground on which it can be said that that contract with Allan was not as good and binding a contract as ever was made. Assuming Allan to have known (there is some dispute about it, and Allan does not admit that he knew of it, but I will assume that he did) that Dodds had made the offer to Dickinson, and had given him till Friday morning at 9 o'clock to accept it, still in point of law that could not prevent Allan from making a more favourable offer than Dickinson, and entering at once into a binding agreement with Dodds.

Then Dickinson is informed by Berry that the property has been sold by Dodds to Allan. Berry does not tell us from whom he heard it, but he says that he did hear it, that he knew it, and that he informed Dickinson of it. Now, stopping there, the question which arises is this—If an offer has been made for the sale of property, and before that offer is accepted, the person who has made the offer enters into a binding agreement to sell the property to somebody else, and the person to whom the offer was first made receives notice in some way that the property has been sold to another person, can he after that make a binding contract by the acceptance of the offer? I am of opinion that he cannot. The law may be right or wrong in saying that a person who has given to another a certain time within which to accept an offer is not bound by his promise to give that time; but, if he is not bound by that promise, and may still sell the property to some one else, and if it be the law that, in order to make a contract, the two minds must be in agreement at some one time, that is, at the time of the acceptance, how is it possible that when the person to whom the offer has been made knows that the person who has made the offer has sold the property to someone else, and that, in fact, he has not remained in the same mind to sell it to him, he can be at liberty to accept the offer and thereby make a binding contract? It seems to me that would be simply absurd. If a man makes an offer to sell a particular horse in his stable, and says, "I will give you until the day after to-morrow to accept the offer," and the next day goes and sells the horse to somebody else, and receives the purchase-money from him, can the person to whom the offer was originally made then come and say, "I accept," so as to make a binding contract, and so as to be entitled to recover damages for the non-delivery of the horse? If the rule of law is that a mere offer to sell property, which can be withdrawn at any time, and which is made dependent on the acceptance of the person to whom it is made, is a mere nudum pactum, how is it possible that the person to whom the offer has been made can by acceptance make a binding contract after he knows that the person who has made the offer has sold the property to some one else? It is admitted law that, if a man who makes an offer dies, the offer cannot be accepted after he is dead, and parting with the property has very much the same effect as the death of the owner, for it makes the performance of the offer impossible. I am clearly of opinion that, just as when a man who has made an offer dies before it is accepted it is impossible that it can then be accepted, so when once the person to whom the offer was made knows that the property has been sold to some one else, it is too late for him to accept the offer, and on that ground I am clearly of opinion that there was no binding contract for the sale of this property by Dodds to Dickinson, and even if there had been, it seems to me that the sale of the property to Allan was first in point of time. However, it is not necessary to consider, if there had been two binding contracts, which of them would be entitled to priority in equity, because there is no binding contract between Dodds and Dickinson.

NOTES

(1) Restatement (Second) § 36: "(1) An offeree's power of acceptance may be terminated by (a) rejection or counter-offer by the offeree, or (b) lapse of time, or (c) revocation by the offeror, or (d) death or incapacity of the offeror or offeree. (2) In addition, an offeree's power of acceptance is terminated by the non-occurrence of any condition of acceptance under the terms of the offer."

(2) Since under the doctrine of *Adams v. Lindsell* an acceptance may be effective upon dispatch, a decided advantage to the offeree, would it not be fair to accord a similar benefit to the offeror by making a revocation effective upon the sending of the message?

(3) "It seems to us a reasonable requirement that, to disable the plaintiffs from accepting their offer, the defendants should bring home to them actual notice that it has been revoked. By their choice and act they brought about a relation between themselves and the plaintiffs, which the plaintiffs could turn into a contract by an act on their part, and authorized the plaintiffs to understand and to assume that that relation existed. When the plaintiffs acted in good faith on the assumption, the defendants could not complain. Knowingly to lead a person reasonably to suppose that you offer, and to offer, are the same thing. ... The offer must be made before the acceptance, and it does not matter whether it is made a longer or shorter time before, if, by its express or implied terms, it is outstanding at the time of the acceptance. Whether much or little time has intervened, it reaches forward to the moment of the acceptance, and speaks then. It would be monstrous to allow an inconsistent act of the offeror, not known or brought to the notice of the offeree, to affect the making of the contract; for instance, a sale by an agent elsewhere one minute after the principal personally has offered goods which are accepted within five minutes by the person to whom he is speaking. The principle is the same when the time is longer, and the act relied on a step looking to, but not yet giving notice." Holmes J., in Brauer v. Shaw, 168 Mass. 198, 46 N.E. 617, 618 (1897).

(4) Why was not the offer, in *Dickinson,* irrevocable in view of the postscript that "this offer to be left over until Friday ... 12th June, 1874"?

(5) Do the opinions clearly disclose whether Berry told Dickinson that Dodds had actually contracted to sell to another or had merely made an offer to sell? Would the result likely be the same in either case?

(6) Is *Dickinson* consistent with the objective theory of contracts? See G. Gilmore, The Death of Contract 28–34 (1974).

(7) Restatement § 42, following *Dickinson,* states: "Where an offer is for the sale of an interest in land or in other things, if the offeror, after making the offer, sells or contracts to sell the interest to another person, and the offeree

acquires reliable information of that fact, before he has exercised his power of creating a contract by acceptance of the offer, the offer is revoked." Should this rule of "indirect revocation" be limited to cases involving "the sale of an interest in land or in other things"? The drafters of the revised Restatement have extended the scope of this section as follows: "An offeree's power of acceptance is terminated when the offeror takes definite action inconsistent with an intention to enter into the proposed contract and the offeree acquires reliable information to that effect." Restatement (Second) § 43.

(8) Suppose, in *Dickinson,* that Dodds learned from a reliable third person that Dickinson was no longer interested in the offer and had agreed to purchase other property instead. Could Dickinson, assuming he had not spoken with Dodds about the matter, change his mind and accept the offer of Dodds?

(9) Additional considerations are involved in determining how a general offer may be revoked. If, for example, the offeror in *Glover v. Jewish War Veterans* (supra at 291) had decided to withdraw its offer, how could it have done so? It would scarcely be feasible to notify directly all offerees, nor would "indirect revocation" reach the vast majority of those who had read the advertisements. The authorities favor a practical rule which, in general, obliges the offeror to give the notice of revocation publicity equal to that given the offer. See Restatement (Second) § 46; Corbin § 41; Williston §§ 59–59A.

(10) *Lapse of Offer.* An offer "lapses" of its own terms after the expiration of the time stipulated in the offer or upon the occurrence of a stipulated event, or if there is no such stipulation, after a reasonable period of time. See Restatement (Second) § 41. What is reasonable will depend upon the circumstances. For example, one would expect an offer to sell securities which are subject to rapid price fluctuations to lapse after a shorter period of time than an offer to sell unimproved real estate. Where the offer stipulates that it will be open for a stated period (e.g., ten days), generally the period will begin when the offer is received, not when it is dispatched. Caldwell v. Cline, 109 W.Va. 553, 156 S.E. 55 (1930). Finally, an offer made by one to another in face to face conversation is ordinarily deemed to continue only to the close of their conversation, and cannot be accepted thereafter. Akers v. J.B. Sedberry, Inc., 39 Tenn.App. 633, 286 S.W.2d 617 (1955). See also Newman v. Schiff, 778 F.2d 460 (8th Cir.1985) (Schiff's statement on the live CBS Nightwatch program that he would pay $100,000 to anyone who called the show and cited any section of the Internal Revenue Code "that says an individual is required to file a tax return" constituted an offer, but it did not extend beyond the time of the program).

PROBLEM: THE CASE OF THE REJECTION, REVOCATION AND ACCEPTANCE RACE

On July 4, 1997, A mailed to B a written offer to sell ten shares of an unlisted stock at $60.00 per share. B was given four days from the date of the letter to accept. The offer was received on July 6, at 2 PM. At 3 PM on July 6, B mailed a letter to A which stated, in part: "will purchase ten shares at $55.00 per share. ..." At 11 AM on July 6, however, A had sold the ten shares to C for $65.00 and at 1 PM of the same day had mailed a letter to B revoking the offer. B, who was blissfully unaware of A's activity, learned at 4 PM on July 6 that the market price of the shares might increase and, at 5 PM on the same day, telegraphed A to "disregard letter . . . will take offered stock for $60.00 per share." B's telegram of July 6 was received by A at 9 AM on July 7. B's letter of July 6 was received by A at 2 PM on July 8. A's letter of July 6 was received by B at 2 PM on July 8.

(1) B claims that he has a contract with A for the purchase of the stock. Is this contention correct?

(2) Suppose at 3 PM on July 6 that B mailed a letter to A which "accepted your offer." Shortly thereafter the market for the shares of stock dropped sharply and, at 5 PM, B telegraphed A to "disregard" my prior letter, I have "decided not to buy." The telegram was received by A on July 7 at 9 AM, whereupon A sold the shares to C. B's letter of acceptance was received on July 8 at 2 PM. Is there a contract? What are A's options?

PROBLEM: THE CASE OF THE DEAD GUARANTOR

You are an Associate Justice of the Supreme Court of Nowhere. The case of *Millcreek Corporation v. Simmons, Executor,* is now under advisement. Set out below are draft opinions by our colleagues. You are the "swing" vote in the case. Prepare a short opinion in which you either affirm or reverse the courts below and give reasons for your decision.

The facts of the case are simple. Beginning in 1989 the plaintiff, a wholesaler of building supplies, sold a number of items to Bishop, a house painter. The sales were on credit, and although all of the bills were finally paid, Bishop was slow in paying and appeared to be in some financial difficulty. Early in 1990, Millcreek refused to sell paint and other supplies to Bishop unless he paid cash or provided suitable security. Bishop then contacted his father, a retired building contractor of some wealth who lived some 300 miles away, and the father agreed to "guarantee" Bishop's debts to Millcreek. Later, Bishop presented for Millcreek's approval a written guaranty agreement, dated February 1, 1990, in which his father promised that if, in the next six months, Millcreek extended credit to Bishop in an amount not to exceed $8,000, he (the father) would pay Bishop's obligation to Millcreek if Bishop failed to do so when the obligation was due. After calling the elder Bishop's attorney to verify the signature, Millcreek accepted the guaranty as appropriate security.

From February 5 through March 13, Millcreek made five separate credit sales to Bishop. Three of these sales occurred after March 8, when, unknown to Millcreek (but clearly known to Bishop), the elder Bishop had died. The amount involved in these three transactions was $5,000. On March 13, Millcreek received a letter from the elder Bishop's executor, informing it of the death and requesting a surrender of the guaranty. Later, after Bishop failed to pay the $5,000 obligations due to insolvency, Millcreek brought suit against Simmons, the executor, to recover on the guaranty contract. The trial court, at the conclusion of the evidence, granted Simmons' motion for a judgment on the ground that the guaranty constituted an offer for a series of separate contracts and that the death of the offeror on March 8 automatically terminated the offer with regard to sales made thereafter. This judgment was affirmed in the appellate court and the plaintiff, Millcreek, has appealed.

Altman, J. I am of the opinion that the judgment below should be affirmed. The law is clear. An offer is terminated by the death of the offeror before an acceptance occurs, even if the offeree is unaware of that death. This rule finds consistent support in the precedents of this and other states and in the Restatement of Contracts of the American Law Institute. See, e.g., Restatement (First) § 48; Jordan v. Dobbins, 122 Mass. 168 (1877); New Headley Tobacco Warehouse Co. v. Gentry's Ex'r, 307 Ky. 857, 212 S.W.2d 325 (1948). As one court put it: "This rule has been criticized on the ground that under the modern view of the formation of contracts, it is not the actual meeting of minds of the contracting parties that is the determining fact, but rather the apparent state of mind of the parties embodied in an expression of mutual consent; so that the acceptance by an offeree of an offer, which is apparently still open, should result in an enforceable contract notwithstanding the prior death of the offeror unknown to the offeree. On the other hand, it has been forcibly suggested that ordinarily the condition is implied in an offer that the offeror will survive to supervise the performance if his offer is accepted, and therefore an acceptance after death is ineffective even though the acceptor be ignorant of the offeror's death. ... These conflicting views, however, were given consideration in the preparation of the Restatement, and the rule announced was adopted as representing the weight of authority and professional opinion." Chain v. Wilhelm, 84 F.2d 138, 140 (4th Cir.1936). Accord: Restatement (Second) § 48: A. Farnsworth, Contracts § 3.18 (2d ed.1990). See also Biggins v. Shore, 523 Pa. 148, 565 A.2d 737 (1989).

The guaranty, properly interpreted, was an offer looking forward to a series of separate acceptances. No contract was formed until Millcreek had actually extended credit to Bishop within the limits of the guaranty. Although the decedent agreed that the guaranty should last for six months, Millcreek gave no consideration to support this promise. As such, the agreement to keep the offer of guaranty open for six months was not enforceable.

From these rules it logically follows that the offer to guarantee Bishop's debts was terminated by the offeror's death on March 8, and the judgment below is affirmed.

Oliver, J., concurring. I concur in the majority opinion written by Justice Altman, but for different reasons. Surely we can agree that a sound judicial decision cannot be made from logic and logic alone. As Justice Holmes said, "the life of the law has been experience, not logic." I feel strongly that law in general and contract law in particular exists to serve human needs and that the rules of contract must constantly be adjusted and adapted to the human conditions which produce the disputes. But there is no evidence of those "human conditions" in this case and the court has no way of knowing what impact the rather clear rule that death terminates an unaccepted offer has had upon the planning and other relevant behavior of contracting parties. Do the parties take this rule into account when they negotiate guaranty contracts? What would be the impact upon business practices if the rule were overturned? There are no answers to these questions contained in the record before us. Since the rule has a long history of acceptance in the law and since the effect of its alteration by this court is uncertain, I am hesitant to intervene at this time and change the law. The risk of death is well known to all and surely the plaintiff in this case is just as capable as the decedent to make provision in the agreement or otherwise against the risk of death. If change is needed it should come from the legislature, not the court.

Roscoe J., dissenting. I dissent. It is obviously unfair to leave the risk of death upon the plaintiff in this case. The plaintiff relied in good faith upon a written promise of guaranty without actual knowledge that the guarantor had died. The plaintiff had no reason to know of the death—the guarantor lived 300 miles away and no method of quick notice was available. A basic policy of the law of contracts is to protect the reasonable expectations of parties to whom promises have been made. See Corbin § 54. Application of the old rule in this case would impair this policy and produce an unfair result in this case. Neither result would, in my mind, be sound.

But we do not have to change the law in this case. A realistic construction of the writing signed by the decedent persuades me that an offer looking forward to a bilateral contract accepted by the first extension of credit was made. Thus, when the plaintiff made the first extension of credit on February 5, he impliedly promised that during the life of the guaranty he would extend credit up to the $8,000 limit to Bishop. See Restatement (Second) §§ 53(1), 54(1) and 62. Thus, the decedent died during the performance of an existing bilateral contract, not before an outstanding offer had been accepted. Or, if the bilateral contract analysis is unsound, the court should, after the first extension of credit is made, imply a promise to hold the guaranty open for six months. Restatement (Second) § 87(2). See § 88. In either case, thus, the question is whether obligations to pay money incurred after death but when the plaintiff had no knowledge of the death are enforceable against the Estate. The answer is "yes." See Restatement (Second) § 262. Although death of one contracting party may discharge some contracts, when the other party has fully performed and the obligation is to pay money alone, the obligation will not be discharged. In my view, the court below erroneously construed the guaranty writing and committed other material errors of law. The judgment below should be reversed and a final judgment entered for the plaintiff.

Earl, J., dissenting. The rule of law in dispute here is of ancient vintage and, presumably, served some legitimate purpose in a time when contracts were more personal and a "subjective" theory of relationships seemed to dominate. But in this day of impersonal, complicated and widespread commerce, the old rule is anachronistic. It is but another example of "slow moving" law getting out of joint with ever changing life. At the same time, the rule seems to provide a rather arbitrary protection to promisors who die without considering the interests of promisees—those who rely on promises. Assuming that both parties have legitimate interests to protect, if they have not provided for the risk of death clearly in the agreement, the question is whether the current rule provides a fair allocation of risk in the circumstances.

The question is not without difficulty. If we limit, as we must, the problem to contracts of guaranty (and not try to over-generalize), we find almost no evidence in the record about business practices and methods of risk allocation in this particular setting. Perhaps it is enough to say that the burden is on the plaintiff to show clearly that the old rule produces disruptive and unfair results when applied to guaranty contracts, especially when the decedent was not compensated for the risk he assumed. As the defendant Executor forcefully argued, why should the estate make payments to the detriment of lawful heirs for credit extensions which occurred after death and for which the estate received no valuable exchange? This makes the point of Justice Oliver in a slightly different manner.

Even so, it seems clear that in the absence of clear agreement by the parties allocating the risk and other compelling social policies, the general purpose to be achieved by these rules of offer and acceptance should be to facilitate and promote on-going commercial transactions. Without a strained construction of the writing, the parties contemplated a six-month period where the plaintiff probably would be extending credit to Bishop. They were at a distance, and it is unrealistic to expect the plaintiff to telephone the decedent or check the obituary column in the newspaper before every extension of credit. The plaintiff honestly and without reason to know of death, did precisely what the written guaranty permitted—extended credit to Bishop in reliance upon the decedent's promise. In this context, at least, where both parties were equally capable of providing against the risk in the contract, there seems to be no reason for the arbitrary preference given to the decedent. The broader policy concern for smooth, dependable commercial activity supports the plaintiff's contention that the rule should be changed, and we would so hold. In guaranty contracts, at least, where death occurs before the extension of credit but the promisee acts in good faith and without reason to know, the estate must pay these obligations. This rule is realistically attuned to the needs and problems of the parties. It rejects mechanical applications of the old and strained constructions in order to put the law more solidly into the life around it. The result is not clearly inefficient unless the plaintiff was the "least cost" risk avoider.

(E) IRREVOCABLE OFFER: NONDESTRUCTIBLE POWER OF ACCEPTANCE

Humble Oil & Refining Co. v. Westside Investment Corp.

Supreme Court of Texas, 1968.
428 S.W.2d 92.

■ SMITH, JUSTICE. Petitioner, Humble Oil & Refining Company, filed this suit on February 10, 1965, against Westside Investment Corporation seeking a judgment commanding specific performance based on a written option and contract for the sale of real estate. Petitioner, Marvin H. Mann, a realtor, as a third-party plaintiff, filed a plea in intervention, seeking a judgment for $1260.00 against Westside as brokerage charges in connection with the transaction. Westside, Humble and Mann each filed a motion for summary judgment. The court granted Westside's motion, and overruled the motions of Humble and Mann. The court of civil appeals affirmed. 419 S.W.2d 448. We reverse the judgments of the courts below. We hold that Humble is entitled to specific performance of the option contract and render judgment for Humble. We hold that a material issue of fact exists as to whether Mann is entitled to a brokerage commission and remand that portion of the case to the district court for trial.

The facts, most of which are either stipulated or established by affidavits, are these:

On April 5, 1963, Westside as seller and Humble as buyer agreed and entered into a written contract whereby Westside gave and granted to Humble an exclusive and irrevocable option to purchase for a consideration of $35,000.00 a tract of land situated outside of the city limits of San Antonio, Bexar County, Texas, being all of lots 19, 20, 21, 22 and 23 of Block 2, Lackland Heights Subdivision.

The option contract was supported by a consideration. The contract provided that Humble might exercise the option by giving notice at any time prior to 9:00 p.m. on the 4th day of June, 1963, and by paying to Westside at the time of such notice or within ten (10) days following such notice the sum of $1750.00 as earnest money. This sum of money, together with the sum of Fifty Dollars ($50.00) as consideration paid at the time of the execution of the option contract, made a total of $1800.00 paid by Humble, leaving a balance of $33,200.00 yet to be paid as purchase money in accordance with the option contract.

On May 14, 1963, within the time period provided for in the option contract, Humble paid the above mentioned sum of $1750.00 to the designated escrow agent, Commercial Abstract & Title Company.

Westside admits in its pleadings that it entered into the option contract with Humble, but contends that the option agreement was "rejected, repudiated, and terminated by Humble." Westside contends that summary judgment proof of rejection of the option contract is contained in letters written by Humble to Westside on May 2, 1963, and May 14, 1963. The pertinent portion of the May 2nd letter reads:

"Humble Oil & Refining Company hereby exercises its option to purchase Lots 19, 20, 21, 22 and 23, Block 2, Lackland Heights Subdivision, in or near the City of San Antonio, Bexar County, Texas, granted in Option and Purchase Contract dated April 5, 1963. As additional inducement for Humble to exercise its option to purchase, you have agreed that all utilities (gas, water, sewer and electricity) will be extended to the property prior to the closing of the transaction. The contract of sale is hereby amended to provide that Seller shall extend all utility lines to the property before the date of closing.

"Please sign and return one copy of this letter in the space indicated below to signify your agreement to the amendment to the purchase contract."

The May 14th communication provided, in part, as follows:

"Humble * * * hereby notifies you of its intention to exercise the option granted in option and purchase contract dated April 5, 1963, covering Lots 19, 20, 21, 22 and 23, Block 2, Lackland Heights Subdivision in or near the City of San Antonio, Bexar County, Texas. *The exercise of said option is not qualified and you may disregard the proposed amendment to the contract suggested in letter of May 2, 1963.* * * *" (Emphasis added.)

We conclude from this record that the parties are in agreement that Humble's letter of May 14, 1963, and the payment of earnest money within 10 days thereof was in law a timely exercise of the option to purchase *unless* Humble's letter of May 2, 1963, terminated and rendered unenforceable the option contract. The narrow question to be determined is whether or not the letter of May 2, 1963, constitutes a rejection of the option contract. If it does, the trial court properly granted Westside's motion for summary judgment and the court of civil appeals correctly affirmed such judgment.

Westside contends that Humble's letter of May 2nd was a conditional acceptance which amounted in law to a rejection of the option contract. Westside argues that the letter of May 2nd "clearly evidences Humble's intent to accept the offer *only if* Westside would agree to an amendment to the terms of its original offer." (Emphasis added.) It further argues that Humble's letter of May 14, 1963, reflects that Humble itself understood that its letter of May 2, 1963, contained a qualified acceptance, and did not form a contract. The basis for this conclusion is the sentence in the May 14 letter which reads: "The exercise of said option is not qualified and you may disregard the proposed amendment to the contract suggested in letter dated May 2, 1963, from the undersigned. * * *" We cannot agree with Westside's contentions.

The mere fact that the parties may choose to negotiate before accepting an option does not mean that the option contract is repudiated. As stated in James on Option Contracts § 838:

"It is laid down in the law of offers that a qualified or conditional acceptance is a rejection of the offer. It is clearly established by the decisions that a qualified or conditional acceptance of an offer does not raise a contract because the minds of the parties do not meet in agreement upon the same terms. It is said that such an acceptance is a counter-proposal for a new contract, to give legal life to which requires the assent or acceptance of the other party. It is in this sense that a qualified or conditional acceptance is a rejection of the offer first made because the original negotiations are dropped and negotiations for a new and different contract begun.

"An option is a contract, the negotiations for the making of which are concluded by the execution and delivery of the option. The minds of the parties have met in agreement, the distinctive feature of which is that the optionor, for a consideration, binds himself to keep the option open for election by the optionee, for and during the time stipulated, or implied by law.

"Under an option, the act necessary to raise a binding promise to sell, is not, therefore, an acceptance of the offer, but rather the performance of the condition of the option contract. If this is true, then the rule peculiar to offers to the effect that a conditional acceptance is, in itself, in every case, a rejection of the offer, is not applicable to an option contract, supported by a consideration and fixing a time limit for election."

* * *

We hold that Humble's letter of May 2, 1963, did not terminate the option contract. Humble, for a valuable consideration, purchased the right to keep the option contract open for the time specified, and the right to create a contract of purchase. Although Humble did have the right to *accept* or *reject* the option in the sense that it was free to take the action required to close the transaction, Humble was not foreclosed from negotiating relative to the contract of sale as distinguished from the option. The option, considered as an independent completed agreement, gave the optionee the right to purchase the property within the time specified. The option contract bound Humble to do nothing but granted it the right to accept or reject the option in accordance with its terms within the time and in the manner specified in the option. Westside was bound to keep the option open and could not act in derogation of the terms of the option. By the letter of May 2, 1963, Humble did not surrender or reject the option. The option to purchase was still a binding obligation between the parties when Humble exercised it on May 14, 1963. . . .

Our holding falls within the rule stated in 1 Corbin on Contracts § 91. According to Corbin:

"If the original offer is an irrevocable offer, creating in the offeree a 'binding option,' the rule that a counter offer terminates the power of acceptance does not apply. Even if it is reasonable to hold that it terminates a revocable power, it should not be held to terminate rights and powers created by a contract. A 'binding option' is such a contract (usually unilateral); and an offer in writing, that allows a time for acceptance (either definite or reasonable) and that is irrevocable by virtue of a statute, is itself a unilateral contract. A counter offer by such an offeree, or other negotiation not resulting in a contract, does not terminate the power of acceptance."

* * *

[Footnotes omitted.]

NOTES

(1) Critically evaluate the following statement from Langdell, Law of Contracts § 178 (2d ed. 1880): "An offer is merely one of the elements of a contract; and it is indispensable to the making of a contract that the wills of the contracting parties do, in legal contemplation, concur at the moment of making it. An offer, therefore, which the party making it has no power to revoke, is a legal impossibility."

(2) "While it may seem at first blush a legal paradox that a contract for the sale of land, mutual and enforceable, can be made when at the time it is claimed to have been made one party to it is openly protesting that he will make no such contract, and while reasons may be advanced to support the proposition that the option holder should be in such a case remitted to an action for damages for refusal to hold the offer open for the stipulated time, there is reason and precedent for holding that the offer to sell, if paid for, may not be withdrawn during the stipulated time, being, in law, a continuing offer to sell." Ostrander, J., concurring in Solomon Mier Co. v. Hadden, 148 Mich. 488, 111 N.W. 1040, 1043 (1907).

(3) *Effect of Rejection by Optionee.* "Where an offer is supported by a binding contract that the offeree's power of acceptance shall continue for a stated time, will a communicated rejection terminate the offeree's power to accept within the time? On principle, there is no reason why it should. The offeree has a contract right to accept within the time. At most rejection is a waiver of this right, but waiver not supported by consideration or an estoppel by change of position can have no effect upon subsequent assertion of the right. So an option holder may complete a contract by communicating his acceptance despite the fact that he has previously rejected the offer. Where, however, before the acceptance the offeror has materially changed his position in reliance on the communicated rejection, as by selling or contracting to sell the subject matter of the offer elsewhere, the subsequent acceptance will be inoperative. Here the rejection is a waiver of the offeree's contract right to accept the offer, binding the offeree by estoppel, so his power to accept is gone." Simpson on Contracts, 2d ed., § 23, quoted in Ryder v. Wescoat, 535 S.W.2d 269, 270 (Mo.App.1976). See also Restatement (Second) § 37: "[T]he power of acceptance under an option contract is not terminated by rejection or counter-offer, by revocation, or by death or incapacity of the offeror, unless the requirements are met for the discharge of a contractual duty." For a criticism of the majority view that rejection or counter-offer by offeree-optionee should not, of itself, terminate the latter's power of acceptance, see Cozzillio, *The Option Contract: Irrevocable Not Irrejectable,* 39 Cath.U.L.Rev. 491 (1990).

(4) *Option Varieties.* Restatement (Second) § 25 defines an "option contract" as follows: "An option contract is a promise which meets the requirements for the formation of a contract and limits the promisor's power to revoke an offer." This may take the form of a collateral contract not to revoke an existing offer. ("In consideration of $1, I promise not to revoke for thirty days my offer to sell Blackacre for $10,000. . . .") Another method is a contract between the parties whereby, for a consideration (usually a nominal payment), the owner promises to sell and convey the property for a stated price on condition of either notice of acceptance or actual payment within a specified time. ("In consideration of $1, I promise to convey Blackacre, if within thirty days you pay me $10,000. . . .") This type of "option contract" is actually a conditional contract to sell; it does not take the form of an offer accompanied by an enforceable promise not to revoke. By prevailing law the practical effect is the same in both cases; *viz.,* the offeror has no power to revoke, and any attempt to do so is ineffectual. See Corbin § 262. An option may also appear as part of a larger transaction, as, for example, a renewal option in a lease. See, e.g., 1020 Park Ave., Inc. v. Raynor, 97 Misc.2d 288, 411 N.Y.S.2d 172 (1978).

(5) *Recital of Consideration as Implied Promise to Pay.* "The majority of cases from other jurisdictions hold that the offeror may prove that the consideration had not been paid and that no other consideration had taken its place. Bard v. Kent, 19 Cal.2d 449, 122 P.2d 8, 139 A.L.R. 1032 (1942); Calamari & Perillo, Law of Contracts, § 58 (1970). However, the minority rule, and what we consider to be the best view, is that even if it is shown that the dollar was not paid it does not void the contract. We have held many times that the recital of the one dollar consideration gives rise to an implied promise to pay which can be enforced by the other party." Smith v. Wheeler, 233 Ga. 166, 210 S.E.2d 702, 703–4 (1974). Contra: Board of Control of Eastern Michigan University v.

Burgess, 45 Mich.App. 183, 206 N.W.2d 256 (1973)(recited consideration of $1 must be paid or tendered).

Restatement (Second) § 87(1)(a) provides: "An offer is binding as an option contract if it (a) is in writing and signed by the offeror, recites a purported consideration for the making of the offer, and proposes an exchange on fair terms within a reasonable time. . . ."

(6) *Irrevocability by Statute.* Certain offers are made irrevocable by statute. For example, UCC 2–205 provides: "An offer by a merchant to buy or sell goods in a signed writing which by its terms gives assurance that it will be held open is not revocable, for lack of consideration, during the time stated or if no time is stated for a reasonable time, but in no event may such period of irrevocability exceed three months; but any such term of assurance on a form supplied by the offeree must be separately signed by the offeror." See also Article 16 of the United Nations Convention on Contracts for the International Sale of Goods: "(1) Until a contract is concluded an offer may be revoked if the revocation reaches the offeree before he has dispatched an acceptance. (2) However, an offer cannot be revoked: (a) if it indicates, whether by stating a fixed time limit or otherwise, that it is irrevocable; or (b) if it was reasonable for the offeree to rely on the offer as being irrevocable and the offeree has acted in reliance on the offer."

(7) *The "Mailbox" Rule and Acceptance under an Option Contract.* As you will recall, under the "mailbox" rule, supra at 301, a dispatched but uncommunicated acceptance may preclude revocation of the offer, for the acceptance is effective upon dispatch. Should the rule apply as well in the option contract context, as, for example, where optionee must "notify" optionor before a stipulated date? Most courts have said no, the position adopted by the Restatement of Contracts. See Restatement (Second) § 63. In the view of the drafters, since the option contract provides for irrevocability of the offer, the primary reason for the rule of *Adams v. Lindsell* and its progeny is absent. Professor Corbin has commented: "If in an option contract the duty of the promisor is conditional on notice within 30 days, does this mean notice received or notice properly mailed? It is believed that, in the absence of an expression of contrary intention, it should be held that the notice must be received. As above explained, the notice is in one respect a notice of acceptance of an offer; but in another aspect it is a condition of the promisor's already existing conditional duty. It is more likely to be regarded in this latter aspect by the parties themselves. The rule that an acceptance by post is operative on mailing was itself subjected to severe criticism; and, even though it may now be regarded as settled, it should not be extended to notice of acceptance in already binding option contracts." Corbin § 264. See Romain v. A. Howard Wholesale Co., 506 N.E.2d 1124 (Ind.App.1987). Not all courts follow this powerful tandem, however. See, e.g., Worms v. Burgess, 620 P.2d 455 (Okl.App.1980); Palo Alto Town and Country Village, Inc. v. BBTC Company, 11 Cal.3d 494, 113 Cal. Rptr. 705, 521 P.2d 1097 (1974). See also Jameson v. Foster, 646 P.2d 955 (Colo.App.1982) (Exercise of option effective upon mailing where the option clause provided: "The lessees have an option to purchase said property * * * should the option be exercised on or before Jan. 1, 1980."); APC Operating Partnership v. Mackey, 841 F.2d 1031 (10th Cir.1988) (option to renew lease properly exercised).

(8) *Problem: Effect of "First Refusal."* Defendant owned a tract of land containing three lots, all of which were zoned commercial. In June, 1989, Defendant sold two of the lots to Plaintiff for $400,000. As part of the transaction, Defendant granted Plaintiff a "first refusal" on the third lot for a period to end on July 1, 1991. In June, 1991, Defendant, without informing Plaintiff, solicited offers on the third lot from third parties. A written offer to buy for $175,000 cash was made by a third party. Plaintiff learned of the offer and, on June 25, 1991, informed Defendant that it intended to exercise the right of "first refusal" and tendered a certified check for $175,000. Defendant rejected both the third party offer and Plaintiff's tender and did not sell the property.

It is now July 10, 1991. The property has not been sold. Plaintiff claims that it exercised its right of "first refusal" before July 1, 1991 and that it is entitled to specific performance for the third lot. As authority, it cites *Humble Oil*, supra, and other authorities on option contracts. What result? See LIN Broadcasting Corp. v. Metromedia, Inc., 74 N.Y.2d 54, 544 N.Y.S.2d 316, 542 N.E.2d 629 (1989); Cestone v. Brown, 163 A.D.2d 563, 558 N.Y.S.2d 622 (1990).

Petterson v. Pattberg

Court of Appeals of New York, 1928.
248 N.Y. 86, 161 N.E. 428.

Appeal from a judgment of the Appellate Division of the Supreme Court in the second judicial department, entered November 18, 1927, affirming a judgment in favor of plaintiff entered upon a verdict directed by the court.

■ KELLOGG, J. The evidence given upon the trial sanctions the following statement of facts: John Petterson, of whose last will and testament the plaintiff is the executrix, was the owner of a parcel of real estate in Brooklyn, known as 5301 Sixth avenue. The defendant was the owner of a bond executed by Petterson, which was secured by a third mortgage upon the parcel. On April 4th, 1924, there remained unpaid upon the principal the sum of $5,450. This amount was payable in installments of $250 on April 25th, 1924, and upon a like monthly date every three months thereafter. Thus the bond and mortgage had more than five years to run before the entire sum became due. Under date of the 4th of April, 1924, the defendant wrote Petterson as follows: "I hereby agree to accept cash for the mortgage which I hold against premises 5301 6th Ave., Brooklyn, N.Y. It is understood and agreed as a consideration I will allow you $780 providing said mortgage is paid on or before May 31, 1924, and the regular quarterly payment due April 25, 1924, is paid when due." On April 25, 1924, Petterson paid the defendant the installment of principal due on that date. Subsequently, on a day in the latter part of May, 1924, Petterson presented himself at the defendant's home, and knocked at the door. The defendant demanded the name of his caller. Petterson replied: "It is Mr. Petterson. I have come to pay off the mortgage." The defendant answered that he had sold the mortgage. Petterson stated that he would like to talk with the defendant, so the defendant partly opened the door. Thereupon Petterson exhibited the cash and said he was ready to pay off the mortgage according to the agreement. The defendant refused to take the money. Prior to this conversation Petterson had made a contract to sell the land to a third person free and clear of the mortgage to the defendant. Meanwhile, also, the defendant had sold the bond and mortgage to a third party. It, therefore, became necessary for Petterson to pay to such person the full amount of the bond and mortgage. It is claimed that he thereby sustained a loss of $780, the sum which the defendant agreed to allow upon the bond and mortgage if payment in full of principal, less that sum, was made on or before May 31st, 1924. The plaintiff has had a recovery for the sum thus claimed, with interest.

Clearly the defendant's letter proposed to Petterson the making of a unilateral contract, the gift of a promise in exchange for the performance of an act. The thing conditionally promised by the defendant was the reduction of the mortgage debt. The act requested to be done, in consideration of the offered promise, was payment in full of the reduced principal of the debt prior to the due date thereof. "If an act is requested, that very act and no other must be given." (Williston on Contracts, sec. 73.) "In case of offers for a consideration, the performance of the consideration is always deemed a condition." (Langdell's Summary of the Law of Contracts, sec. 4.) It is elementary that any offer to enter into a unilateral contract may be withdrawn before the act requested to be done has been performed. (Williston on Contracts, sec. 60; Langdell's Summary, sec. 4; Offord v. Davies, 12 C.B. [N.S.] 748.) A bidder at a sheriff's sale may revoke his bid at any time before the property is struck down to him. (Fisher v. Seltzer, 23 Penn.St. 308.) The offer of a reward in consideration of an act to be performed is revocable before the very act requested has been done. (Shuey v. United States, 92 U.S. 73; Biggers v. Owen, 79 Ga. 658; Fitch v. Snedaker, 38 N.Y. 248.) So, also, an offer to pay a broker commissions, upon a sale of land for the offeror, is revocable at any time before the land is sold, although prior to revocation the broker performs services in an effort to effectuate a sale. (Stensgaard v. Smith, 43 Minn. 11; Smith v. Cauthen, 98 Miss. 746.) An interesting question arises when, as here, the offeree approaches the offeror with the intention of proffering performance and, before actual tender is made, the offer is withdrawn. Of such a case Williston says: "The offeror may see the approach of the offeree and know that an acceptance is contemplated. If the offeror can say 'I revoke' before the offeree accepts, however brief the interval of time between the two acts, there is no escape from the conclusion that the offer is terminated." (Williston on Contracts, sec. 60–b.) In this instance Petterson, standing at the door of the defendant's house, stated to the defendant that he had come to pay off the mortgage. Before a tender of the necessary moneys had been made the defendant informed Petterson that he had sold the mortgage. That was a definite notice to Petterson that the defendant could not perform his offered promise and that a tender to the defendant, who was no longer the creditor, would be ineffective to satisfy the debt. "An offer to sell property may be withdrawn before acceptance without any formal notice to the person to whom the offer is made. It is sufficient if that person has actual knowledge that the person who made the offer has done some act inconsistent with the continuance of the offer, such as selling the property to a third person." (Dickinson v. Dodds, 2 Ch.Div. 463, headnote.) To the same effect is Coleman v. Applegarth (68 Md. 21). Thus, it clearly appears that the defendant's offer was withdrawn before its acceptance had been tendered. It is unnecessary to determine, therefore, what the legal situation might have been had tender been made before withdrawal. It is the individual view of the writer that the same result would follow. This would be so, for the act requested to be performed was the completed act of payment, a thing incapable of performance unless assented to by the person to be paid. (Williston on Contracts, sec. 60–b.) Clearly an offering party has the right to name the precise act performance of which would convert his offer into a binding promise. Whatever the act may be until it is performed the offer must be revocable. However, the supposed case is not before us for decision. We think that in this particular instance the offer of the defendant was withdrawn before it became a binding promise, and, therefore, that no contract was ever made for the breach of which the plaintiff may claim damages.

The judgment of the Appellate Division and that of the Trial Term should be reversed and the complaint dismissed, with costs in all courts.

■ LEHMAN, J. (dissenting).

* * *

I recognize that in this case only an offer of payment, and not a formal tender of payment, was made before the defendant withdrew his offer to accept payment. Even the plaintiff's part in the act of payment was then not technically complete. Even so, under a fair construction of the words of the letter I think the plaintiff had done the act which the defendant requested as consideration for his promise. The plaintiff offered to pay with present intention and ability to make that payment. A formal tender is seldom made in business transactions, except to lay the foundation for subsequent assertion in a court of justice of rights which spring from refusal of the tender. If the defendant acted in good faith in making his offer to accept payment, he could not well have intended to draw a distinction in the act requested of the plaintiff in return, between an offer which unless refused would ripen into completed payment, and a formal tender. Certainly the defendant could not have expected or intended that the plaintiff would make a formal tender of payment without first stating that he had come to make payment. We should not read into the language of the defendant's offer a meaning which would prevent enforcement of the defendant's promise after it had been accepted by the plaintiff in the very way which the defendant must have intended it should be accepted, if he acted in good faith.

The judgment should be affirmed.

■ CARDOZO, CH. J., POUND, CRANE and O'BRIEN, JJ., concur with KELLOGG, J., LEHMAN, J., dissents in opinion, in which ANDREWS, J., concurs.

Judgments reversed, etc.

Marchiondo v. Scheck

Supreme Court of New Mexico, 1967.
78 N.M. 440, 432 P.2d 405.

■ WOOD, JUDGE, Court of Appeals.

The issue is whether the offeror had a right to revoke his offer to enter a unilateral contract.

Defendant, in writing, offered to sell real estate to a specified prospective buyer and agreed to pay a percentage of the sales price as a commission to the broker. The offer fixed a six-day time limit for acceptance. Defendant, in writing, revoked the offer. The revocation was received by the broker on the morning of the sixth day. Later that day, the broker obtained the offeree's acceptance.

Plaintiff, the broker, claiming breach of contract, sued defendant for the commission stated in the offer. On the above facts, the trial court dismissed the complaint.

We are not concerned with the revocation of the offer as between the offeror and the prospective purchaser. With certain exceptions (see 12 C.J.S. Brokers § 95(2), pp. 223–224), the right of a broker to the agreed compensation, or damages measured thereby, is not defeated by the refusal of the principal to complete or consummate a transaction. Southwest Motel Brokers, Inc. v. Alamo Hotels, Inc., 72 N.M. 227, 382 P.2d 707 (1963).

Plaintiff's appeal concerns the revocation of his agency. As to that revocation, the issue between the offeror and his agent is not whether defendant had the power to revoke; rather, it is whether he had the right to revoke. 1 Mechem on Agency, § 568 at 405 (2d ed. 1914).

When defendant made his offer to pay a commission upon sale of the property, he offered to enter a unilateral contract; the offer was for an act to be performed, a sale. 1 Williston on Contracts, § 13 at 23 (3rd ed. 1957); Hutchinson v. Dobson–Bainbridge Realty Co., 31 Tenn.App. 490, 217 S.W.2d 6 (1946).

Many courts hold that the principal has the right to revoke the broker's agency at any time before the broker has actually procured a purchaser. See Hutchinson v. Dobson–Bainbridge Realty Co., supra, and cases therein cited. The reason given is that until there is performance, the offeror has not received that contemplated by his offer, and there is no contract. Further, the offeror may never receive the requested performance because the offeree is not obligated to perform. Until the offeror receives the requested performance, no consideration has passed from the offeree to the offeror. Thus, until the performance is received, the offeror may withdraw the offer. Williston, supra, § 60; Hutchinson v. Dobson–Bainbridge Realty Co., supra.

Defendant asserts that the trial court was correct in applying this rule. However, plaintiff contends that the rule is not applicable where there has been part performance of the offer.

Hutchinson v. Dobson–Bainbridge Realty Co., supra, states:

"A greater number of courts, however, hold that part performance of the consideration may make such an offer irrevocable and that where the offeree or broker manifests his assent to the offer by entering upon performance and spending time and money in his efforts to perform, then the offer becomes irrevocable during the time stated and binding upon the principal according to its terms. * * *"

Defendant contends that the decisions giving effect to a part performance are distinguishable. He asserts that in these cases the offer was of an exclusive right to sell or of an exclusive agency. Because neither factor is present here, he asserts that the "part performance" decisions are not applicable.

Many of the decisions do seem to emphasize the exclusive aspects of the offer. . . .

Such emphasis reaches its extreme conclusion in Tetrick v. Sloan, 170 Cal.App.2d 540, 339 P.2d 613 (1959), where no effect was given to the part performance because there was neither an exclusive agency, nor an exclusive right to sell.

Defendant's offer did not specifically state that it was exclusive. Under § 70–1–43, N.M.S.A.1953, it was not an exclusive agreement. It is not the exclusiveness of the offer that deprives the offeror of the right to revoke. It is the action taken by the offeree which deprives the offeror of that right. Until there is action by the offeree—a partial performance pursuant to the offer—the offeror may revoke even if his offer is of an exclusive agency or an exclusive right to sell. Levander v. Johnson, 181 Wis. 68, 193 N.W. 970 (1923).

Once partial performance is begun pursuant to the offer made, a contract results. This contract has been termed a contract with conditions or an option contract. This terminology is illustrated as follows:

"If an offer for a unilateral contract is made, and part of the consideration requested in the offer is given or tendered by the offeree in response thereto, the offeror is bound by a contract, the duty of immediate performance of which is conditional on the full consideration being given or tendered within the time stated in the offer, or, if no time is stated therein, within a reasonable time." Restatement of Contracts, § 45 (1932).

Restatement (Second) Contracts § 45, Tent.Draft No. 1, (approved 1964, Tent.Draft No. 2, p. vii) states:

"(1) Where an offer invites an offeree to accept by rendering a performance and does not invite a promissory acceptance, an option contract is created when the offeree begins the invited performance or tenders part of it.*

* [The final draft replaces the final three words, "part of it," with "a beginning of it." Ed.]

"(2) The offeror's duty of performance under any option contract so created is conditional on completion or tender of the invited performance in accordance with the terms of the offer."

Restatement (Second) Contracts § 45, Tent.Draft No. 1, comment (g), says:

"This Section frequently applies to agency arrangements, particularly offers made to real estate brokers. * * *"

See Restatement (Second) Agency § 446, comment (b).

The reason for finding such a contract is stated in Hutchinson v. Dobson–Bainbridge Realty Co., supra, as follows:

"This rule avoids hardship to the offeree, and yet does not hold the offeror beyond the terms of his promise. It is true by such terms he was to be bound only if the requested act was done; but this implies that he will let it be done, that he will keep his offer open till the offeree who has begun can finish doing it. At least this is so where the doing of it will necessarily require time and expense. In such a case it is but just to hold that the offeree's part performance furnishes the 'acceptance' and the 'consideration' for a binding subsidiary promise not to revoke the offer, or turns the offer into a presently binding contract conditional upon the offeree's full performance."

We hold that part performance by the offeree of an offer of a unilateral contract results in a contract with a condition. The condition is full performance by the offeree. Here, if plaintiff-offeree partially performed prior to receipt of defendant's revocation, such a contract was formed. Thereafter, upon performance being completed by plaintiff, upon defendant's failure to recognize the contract, liability for breach of contract would arise. Thus, defendant's right to revoke his offer depends upon whether plaintiff had partially performed before he received defendant's revocation. In re Ward's Estate, 47 N.M. 55, 134 P.2d 539, 146 A.L.R. 826 (1943), does not conflict with this result. Ward is clearly distinguishable because there the prospective purchaser did not complete or tender performance in accordance with the terms of the offer.

What constitutes partial performance will vary from case to case since what can be done toward performance is limited by what is authorized to be done. Whether plaintiff partially performed is a question of fact to be determined by the trial court.

The trial court denied plaintiff's requested finding concerning his partial performance. It did so on the theory that partial performance was not material. In this the trial court erred.

Because of the failure to find on the issue of partial performance, the case must be remanded to the trial court. State ex rel. Reynolds v. Board of County Comm'rs., 71 N.M. 194, 376 P.2d 976 (1962). We have not considered, and express no opinion on the question of whether there is or is not substantial evidence in the record which would support a finding one way or the other on this vital issue. Compare Geeslin v. Goodno, Inc., 75 N.M. 174, 402 P.2d 156 (1965).

The cause is remanded for findings on the issue of plaintiff's partial performance of the offer prior to its revocation, and for further proceedings consistent with this opinion and the findings so made.

It is so ordered.

NOTES

(1) If Pattberg agreed to hold the offer open until May 31st, why was he not bound to do so? At what point short of actually tendering the cash should he have been bound?

(2) If Pattberg knew that Petterson had come to accept the offer, did he act in "bad faith"? Would it, or should it, matter if he did?

(3) In both *Petterson* and *Marchiondo* the offer looked forward to a performance (tendering the cash; finding a ready, able and willing buyer) as the only method of acceptance. Would the rationale adopted in *Marchiondo* have yielded a different result in *Petterson?* Was "a part of the consideration requested in the offer" given in either case? Cf. Knight v. Seattle First National Bank, 22 Wash.App. 493, 589 P.2d 1279 (1979).

(4) It will be noted the first Restatement does not state that the offer becomes irrevocable after part performance, but that the offeror is "bound by a contract," etc. The formulation of the rule in this manner by Professor Williston, principal author of the Restatement, was challenged at a discussion of the tentative draft. The following colloquy took place:

> JUDGE CARDOZO: Are there any suggestions as to * * * Section 45? * * *

> MR. WILLIS: I wonder if there is not an inaccuracy in Section 45 in lines 22, 23 and 24 as follows: "the offeror is bound by a contract, liability upon which is conditional on the completion by the offeree of the requested performance within the time stated in the offer, etc." Under such circumstances as we find in Section 45, we do not have a contract of course. The statement in line 23 does not say that we have a contract, and yet it says the offeror is bound by a contract. I wonder if that is not misleading. The actual fact is that in our most recent cases and the modern development of the law the power of revocation on the part of the offeror is destroyed, and therefore the offeree has the power to go on if he wants to and complete his acceptance. If he does we finally get a contract, but if he does not go on and perform the rest of the work of course there is no contract. * * *

> MR. WILLISTON: I call an irrevocable offer a contract. The offeror has promised to do something and he is liable if he does not do it.

> MR. WILLIS: I beg your pardon, you do not want to call this an irrevocable offer, do you?

> MR. WILLISTON: That is what you called it, did you not?

> MR. WILLIS: Oh, no.

> MR. WILLISTON: You stated the power to revoke is destroyed.

> MR. WILLIS: It becomes irrevocable—

MR. WILLISTON: All right. When it becomes irrevocable it is an irrevocable offer.

MR. WILLIS: But it does not seem to me that that is so; it seems to me that a contract is one thing and an irrevocable offer is another.

MR. WILLISTON: We are apart on that. An irrevocable [offer] is not *the* contract which the offer proposes, but being a binding promise, it is a contract.

3 ALI Proceedings 204–5 (1925).

(5) The drafters of the first Restatement appended the following commentary to § 45: "The main offer includes as a subsidiary promise, necessarily implied, that if part of the requested performance is given, the offeror will not revoke his offer, and that if tender is made it will be accepted. Part performance or tender may thus furnish consideration for the subsidiary promises. Moreover, merely acting in justifiable reliance on an offer may in some cases serve as sufficient reason for making a promise binding (see § 90)." Is this comment consistent with the "black letter" of Section 45? Is *Petterson v. Pattberg* one of those cases where Section 90 should be applied? What about Section 45 or Section 87(2) in the Restatement (Second)?

PROBLEM: THE CASE OF PROFESSOR FUZZY'S WELL

The well of Professor Fuzzy's suburban homesite ran dry during an extended drought period. He hastened to make arrangements for the drilling of a new one, contacting among others the Retaw Drilling Company. He told of his plight, but a company representative said they were so committed they could not assist him. Fuzzy countered by saying he was desperate and would give them $1,000 if they would drill a well for him, a sum about double the estimated cost. The drilling company agent said, "Well, we can't guarantee you anything, but if we can pull a rig off another job, we'll try to help you out."

It happened the following day that a rig did become available, and the company, at considerable expense, moved drilling equipment onto Professor Fuzzy's property.

Meanwhile, however, the professor's neighbor informed him that a connection could be made to the municipal water supply system and it was a waste of money to drill a new well. Fuzzy verified the fact that he was eligible to so purchase water from the city and decided this was his best course. Accordingly, he told the company not to drill. The company transferred its equipment to another location, but sent him a bill. The latter asserted he "did not owe a cent." The Retaw Drilling Company sues for damages. Any recovery?

Assume, instead, that after transfer of the equipment to Fuzzy's property, circumstances arose which prompted the drilling company to claim the absence of obligation to proceed. (E.g., a more profitable job came along.) Would Fuzzy have any legal recourse?

James Baird Co. v. Gimbel Brothers, Inc.

United States Court of Appeals, Second Circuit, 1933.
64 F.2d 344.

■ L. HAND, CIRCUIT JUDGE. The plaintiff sued the defendant for breach of a contract to deliver linoleum under a contract of sale; the defendant denied the making of the contract; the parties tried the case to the judge under a written stipulation and he directed judgment for the defendant. The facts as found, bearing on the making of the contract, the only issue necessary to discuss, were as follows: The defendant, a New York merchant, knew that the Department of Highways in Pennsylvania had asked for bids for the construction of a public building. It sent an employee to the office of a contractor in Philadelphia, who had possession of the specifications, and the employee there computed the amount of the linoleum which would be required on the job, underestimating the total yardage by about one-half the proper amount. In ignorance of this mistake, on December twenty-fourth the defendant sent to some twenty or thirty contractors, likely to bid on the job, an offer to supply all the linoleum required by the specifications at two different lump sums, depending upon the quality used. These offers concluded as follows: "If successful in being awarded this contract, it will be absolutely guaranteed, * * * and * * * we are offering these prices for reasonable" (sic), "prompt acceptance after the general contract has been awarded." The plaintiff, a contractor in Washington, got one of these on the twenty-eighth, and on the same day the defendant learned its mistake and telegraphed all the contractors to whom it had sent the offer, that it withdrew it and would substitute a new one at about double the amount of the old. This withdrawal reached the plaintiff at Washington on the afternoon of the same day, but not until after it had put in a bid at Harrisburg at a lump sum, based as to linoleum upon the prices quoted by the defendant. The public authorities accepted the plaintiff's bid on December thirtieth, the defendant having meanwhile written a letter of confirmation of its withdrawal, received on the thirty-first. The plaintiff formally accepted the offer on January second, and, as the defendant persisted in declining to recognize the existence of a contract, sued it for damages on a breach.

Unless there are circumstances to take it out of the ordinary doctrine, since the offer was withdrawn before it was accepted, the acceptance was too late. Restatement of Contracts, § 35. To meet this the plaintiff argues as follows: It was a reasonable implication from the defendant's offer that it should be irrevocable in case the plaintiff acted upon it, that is to say, used the prices quoted in making its bid, thus putting itself in a position from which it could not withdraw without great loss. While it might have withdrawn its bid after receiving the revocation, the time had passed to submit another, and as the item of linoleum was a very trifling part of the cost of the whole building, it would have been an unreasonable hardship to expect it to lose the contract on that account, and probably forfeit its deposit. While it is true that the plaintiff might in advance have secured a contract conditional upon the success of its bid, this was not what the defendant suggested. It understood that the contractors would use its offer in their bids, and would thus in fact commit themselves to supplying the linoleum at the proposed prices. The inevitable implication from all this was that when the contractors acted upon it, they accepted the offer and promised to pay for the linoleum, in case their bid were accepted.

It was of course possible for the parties to make such a contract, and the question is merely as to what they meant; that is, what is to be imputed to the words they used. Whatever plausibility there is in the argument, is in the fact that the defendant must have known the predicament in which the contractors would be put if it withdrew its offer after the bids went in. However, it seems entirely clear that the contractors did not suppose that they accepted the offer merely by putting in their bids. If, for example, the successful one had repudiated the contract with the public authorities after it had been awarded to him, certainly the defendant could not have sued him for a breach. If he had become bankrupt, the defendant could not prove against his estate. It seems plain therefore that there was no contract between them. And if there be any doubt as to this, the language of the offer sets it at rest. The phrase, "if successful in being awarded this contract," is scarcely met by the mere use of the prices in the bids. Surely such a use was not an "award" of the contract to the defendant. Again the phrase, "we are offering these prices for * * * prompt acceptance after the general contract has been awarded," looks to the usual communication of an acceptance, and precludes the idea that the use of the offer in the bidding shall be the equivalent. It may indeed be argued that this last language contemplated no more than an early notice that the offer had been accepted, the actual acceptance being the bid, but that would wrench its natural meaning too far, especially in the light of the preceding phrase. The contractors had a ready escape from their difficulty by insisting upon a contract before they used the figures; and in commercial transactions it does not in the end promote justice to seek strained interpretations in aid of those who do not protect themselves.

But the plaintiff says that even though no bilateral contract was made, the defendant should be held under the doctrine of "promissory estoppel." This is to be chiefly found in those cases where persons subscribe to a venture, usually charitable, and are held to their promises after it has been completed. It has been applied much more broadly, however, and has now been generalized in section 90, of the Restatement of Contracts. We may arguendo accept it as it there reads, for it does not apply to the case at bar. Offers are ordinarily made in exchange for a consideration, either a counter-promise or some other act which the promisor wishes to secure. In such cases they propose bargains; they presuppose that each promise or performance is an inducement to the other. Wisconsin, etc., Ry. v. Powers, 191 U.S. 379, 386, 387, 24 S.Ct. 107, 48 L.Ed. 229; Banning Co. v. California, 240 U.S. 142, 152, 153, 36 S.Ct. 338, 60 L.Ed. 569. But a man may make a promise without expecting an equivalent; a donative promise, conditional or absolute. The common law provided for such by sealed instruments, and it is unfortunate that these are no longer generally available. The doctrine of "promissory estoppel" is to avoid harsh results of allowing the promisor in such a case to repudiate, when the promisee has acted in reliance upon the promise. Siegel v. Spear & Co., 234 N.Y. 479, 138 N.E. 414, 26 A.L.R. 1205. Cf. Allegheny College v. National Bank, 246 N.Y. 369, 159 N.E. 173, 57 A.L.R. 980. But an offer for an exchange is not meant to become a promise until a consideration has been received, either a counterpromise or whatever else is stipulated. To extend it would be to hold the offeror regardless of the stipulated condition of his offer. In the case at bar the defendant offered to deliver the linoleum in exchange for the plaintiff's acceptance, not for its bid, which was a matter of indifference to it. That offer could become a promise to deliver only when the equivalent was received; that is, when the plaintiff promised to take and pay for it. There is no room in such a situation for the doctrine of "promissory estoppel."

Nor can the offer be regarded as of an option, giving the plaintiff the right seasonably to accept the linoleum at the quoted prices if its bid was accepted, but not binding it to take and pay, if it could get a better bargain elsewhere. There is not the least reason to suppose that the defendant meant to subject itself to such a one-sided obligation. True, if so construed, the doctrine of "promissory estoppel" might apply, the plaintiff having acted in reliance upon it, though, so far as we have found, the decisions are otherwise. Ganss v. Guffey Petroleum Co., 125 App.Div. 760, 110 N.Y.S. 176; Comstock v. North, 88 Miss. 754, 41 So. 374. As to that, however, we need not declare ourselves.

Judgment affirmed.

Drennan v. Star Paving Co.

Supreme Court of California, 1958.
51 Cal.2d 409, 333 P.2d 757.

■ TRAYNOR, JUSTICE. Defendant appeals from a judgment for plaintiff in an action to recover damages caused by defendant's refusal to perform certain paving work according to a bid it submitted to plaintiff.

On July 28, 1955, plaintiff, a licensed general contractor, was preparing a bid on the "Monte Vista School Job" in the Lancaster school district. Bids had to be submitted before 8:00 p.m. Plaintiff testified that it was customary in that area for general contractors to receive the bids of subcontractors by telephone on the day set for bidding and to rely on them in computing their own bids. Thus on that day plaintiff's secretary, Mrs. Johnson, received by telephone between fifty and seventy-five subcontractors' bids for various parts of the school job. As each bid came in, she wrote it on a special form, which she brought into plaintiff's office. He then posted it on a master cost sheet setting forth the names and bids of all subcontractors. His own bid had to include the names of subcontractors who were to perform one-half of one percent or more of the construction work, and he had also to provide a bidder's bond of ten percent of his total bid of $317,385 as a guarantee that he would enter the contract if awarded the work.

Late in the afternoon, Mrs. Johnson had a telephone conversation with Kenneth R. Hoon, an estimator for defendant. He gave his name and telephone number and stated that he was bidding for defendant for the paving work at the Monte Vista School according to plans and specifications and that his bid was $7,131.60. At Mrs. Johnson's request he repeated his bid. Plaintiff listened to the bid over an extension telephone in his office and posted it on the master sheet after receiving the bid form from Mrs. Johnson. Defendant's was the lowest bid for the paving. Plaintiff computed his own bid accordingly and submitted it with the name of defendant as the subcontractor for the paving. When the bids were opened on July 28th, plaintiff's proved to be the lowest, and he was awarded the contract.

On his way to Los Angeles the next morning plaintiff stopped at defendant's office. The first person he met was defendant's construction engineer, Mr. Oppenheimer. Plaintiff testified: "I introduced myself and he immediately told me that they had made a mistake in their bid to me the night before, they couldn't do it for the price they had bid, and I told him I would expect him to carry through with their original bid because I had used it in compiling my bid and the job was being awarded them. And I would have to go and do the job according to my bid and I would expect them to do the same."

Defendant refused to do the paving work for less than $15,000. Plaintiff testified that he "got figures from other people" and after trying for several months to get as low a bid as possible engaged L & H Paving Company, a firm in Lancaster, to do the work for $10,948.60.

The trial court found on substantial evidence that defendant made a definite offer to do the paving on the Monte Vista job according to the plans and specifications for $7,131.60, and that plaintiff relied on defendant's bid in computing his own bid for the school job and naming defendant therein as the subcontractor for the paving work. Accordingly, it entered judgment for plaintiff in the amount of $3,817.00 (the difference between defendant's bid and the cost of the paving to plaintiff) plus costs.

Defendant contends that there was no enforceable contract between the parties on the ground that it made a revocable offer and revoked it before plaintiff communicated his acceptance to defendant.

There is no evidence that defendant offered to make its bid irrevocable in exchange for plaintiff's use of its figures in computing his bid. Nor is there evidence that would warrant interpreting plaintiff's use of defendant's bid as the acceptance thereof, binding plaintiff, on condition he received the main contract, to award the subcontract to defendant. In sum, there was neither an option supported by consideration nor a bilateral contract binding on both parties.

Plaintiff contends, however, that he relied to his detriment on defendant's offer and that defendant must therefore answer in damages for its refusal to perform. Thus the question is squarely presented: Did plaintiff's reliance make defendant's offer irrevocable?

Section 90 of the Restatement of Contracts states: "A promise which the promisor should reasonably expect to induce action or forbearance of a definite and substantial character on the part of the promisee and which does induce such action or forbearance is binding if injustice can be avoided only by enforcement of the promise." This rule applies in this state. . . .

Defendant's offer constituted a promise to perform on such conditions as were stated expressly or by implication therein or annexed thereto by operation of law. (See 1 Williston, Contracts [3rd ed.], § 24A, p. 56, § 61, p. 196.) Defendant had reason to expect that if its bid proved the lowest it would be used by plaintiff. It induced "action * * * of a definite and substantial character on the part of the promisee."

Had defendant's bid expressly stated or clearly implied that it was revocable at any time before acceptance we would treat it accordingly. It was silent on revocation, however, and we must therefore determine whether there are conditions to the right of revocation imposed by law or reasonably inferable in fact. In the analogous problem of an offer for a unilateral contract, the theory is now obsolete that the offer is revocable at any time before complete performance. Thus section 45 of the Restatement of Contracts provides: "If an offer for a unilateral contract is made, and part of the consideration requested in the offer is given or tendered by the offeree in response thereto, the offeror is bound by a contract, the duty of immediate performance of which is conditional on the full consideration being given or tendered within the time stated in the offer, or, if no time is stated therein, within a reasonable time." In explanation, comment *b* states that the "main offer includes as a subsidiary promise, necessarily implied, that if part of the requested performance is given, the offeror will not revoke his offer, and that if tender is made it will be accepted. Part performance or tender may thus furnish consideration for the subsidiary promise. Moreover, merely acting in justifiable reliance on an offer may in some cases serve as sufficient reason for making a promise binding (see § 90)."

Whether implied in fact or law, the subsidiary promise serves to preclude the injustice that would result if the offer could be revoked after the offeree had acted in detrimental reliance thereon. Reasonable reliance resulting in a foreseeable prejudicial change in position affords a compelling basis also for implying a subsidiary promise not to revoke an offer for a bilateral contract.

The absence of consideration is not fatal to the enforcement of such a promise. It is true that in the case of unilateral contracts the Restatement finds consideration for the implied subsidiary promise in the part performance of the bargained-for exchange, but its reference to section 90 makes clear that consideration for such a promise is not always necessary. The very purpose of section 90 is to make a promise binding even though there was no consideration "in the sense of something that is bargained for and given in exchange." (See 1 Corbin, Contracts 634 et seq.) Reasonable reliance serves to hold the offeror in lieu of the consideration ordinarily required to make the offer binding. In a case involving similar facts the Supreme Court of South Dakota stated that "we believe that reason and justice demand that the doctrine [of section 90] be applied to the present facts. We cannot believe that by accepting this doctrine as controlling in the state of facts before us we will abolish the requirement of a consideration in contract cases, in any different sense than an ordinary estoppel abolishes some legal requirement in its application. We are of the opinion, therefore, that the defendants in executing the agreement [which was not supported by consideration] made a promise which they should have reasonably expected would induce the plaintiff to submit a bid based thereon to the Government, that such promise did induce this action, and that injustice can be avoided only by enforcement of the promise." Northwestern Engineering Co. v. Ellerman, 69 S.D. 397, 408, 10 N.W.2d 879, 884; see also, Robert Gordon, Inc. v. Ingersoll–Rand Co., 7 Cir., 117 F.2d 654, 661; cf. James Baird Co. v. Gimbel Bros., 2 Cir., 64 F.2d 344.

When plaintiff used defendant's offer in computing his own bid, he bound himself to perform in reliance on defendant's terms. Though defendant did not bargain for this use of its bid neither did defendant make it idly, indifferent to whether it would be used or not. On the contrary it is reasonable to suppose that defendant submitted its bid to obtain the subcontract. It was bound to realize the substantial possibility that its bid would be the lowest, and that it would be included by plaintiff in his bid. It was to its own interest that the contractor be awarded the general contract; the lower the subcontract bid, the lower the general contractor's bid was likely to be and the greater its chance of acceptance and hence the greater defendant's chance of getting the paving subcontract. Defendant had reason not only to expect plaintiff to rely on its bid but to want him to. Clearly defendant had a stake in plaintiff's reliance on its bid. Given this interest and the fact that plaintiff is bound by his own bid, it is only fair that plaintiff should have at least an opportunity to accept defendant's bid after the general contract has been awarded to him.

It bears noting that a general contractor is not free to delay acceptance after he has been awarded the general contract in the hope of getting a better price. Nor can he reopen bargaining with the subcontractor and at the same time claim a continuing right to accept the original offer. See R.J. Daum Const. Co. v. Child, Utah, 247 P.2d 817, 823. In the present case plaintiff promptly informed defendant that plaintiff was being awarded the job and that the subcontract was being awarded to defendant.

Defendant contends, however, that its bid was the result of mistake and that it was therefore entitled to revoke it. * * * Plaintiff, however, had no reason to know that defendant had made a mistake in submitting its bid, since there was usually a variance of 160 per cent between the highest and lowest bids for paving in the desert around Lancaster. He committed himself to performing the main contract in reliance on defendant's figures. Under these circumstances defendant's mistake, far from relieving it of its obligation, constitutes an additional reason for enforcing it, for it misled plaintiff as to the cost of doing the paving. Even had it been clearly understood that defendant's offer was revocable until accepted, it would not necessarily follow that defendant had no duty to exercise reasonable care in preparing its bid. It presented its bid with knowledge of the substantial possibility that it would be used by plaintiff; it could foresee the harm that would ensue from an erroneous underestimate of the cost. Moreover, it was motivated by its own business interest. Whether or not these considerations alone would justify recovery for negligence had the case been tried on that theory (see Biakanja v. Irving, 49 Cal.2d 647, 650, 320 P.2d 16), they are persuasive that defendant's mistake should not defeat recovery under the rule of section 90 of the Restatement of Contracts. As between the subcontractor who made the bid and the general contractor who reasonably relied on it, the loss resulting from the mistake should fall on the party who caused it.

* * *

The judgment is affirmed.

NOTES

(1) In Pavel Enterprises, Inc. v. A.S. Johnson, 342 Md. 143, 674 A.2d 521 (1996), the Court of Appeals of Maryland did an inciteful analysis of *James Baird* and *Drennan* with a unexpected twist.

Pavel, preparing to bid on an NIH renovation project, solicited bids from Johnson and others for the mechanical work. Johnson bid $898,000 and Pavel, using that bid, submitted an overall bid to NIH of $1,585,000. Pavel's bid was the second lowest, but the low bidder was disqualified by NIH on August 5, 1993 and Pavel was notified in mid-August that its bid would be accepted later. Pavel met with Johnson on August 26 to discuss the situation, but Johnson's bid was not accepted. Rather, Pavel resolicited the prospective mechanical subcontractors, informed them of NIH's intention, and asked for a revised price quotation. On August 30, Pavel informed NIH that Johnson was to be the mechanical subcontractor and on September 1, Pavel mailed and faxed a letter of intent to accept Johnson's August 5 offer to do the work for $898,000. The letter informed Pavel "of our intent to award a subcontract" at the quoted price of $898,000 and that "this subcontract will be forwarded upon receipt of our contract from the NIH, which we expect any day." Johnson immediately attempted to withdraw the offer due to a mistake which had not been communicated to Pavel because Johnson believed that Pavel had not been awarded the NIH contract. After receiving the NIH contract on September 28, Pavel contracted with another subcontractor at a cost of $930,000 and sued Johnson for the difference, some $32,000. The trial court held for Johnson, concluding that there was no contract under "traditional contract theory" or under "detrimental reliance theory." After a direct appeal to the Court of Appeals of Maryland the judgment was affirmed.

After describing the construction bidding process, the court discussed *James Baird* and *Drennan*. According to the court, *James Baird* was unfair to the general contractor because the "subcontractors are not bound, and are free to withdraw." *Drennan*, on the other hand, partially rectified the situation by using Sections 45 and 90 of the First Restatement to imply in the subcontractor's bid a "subsidiary promise not to revoke the bid." The court stated, correctly we believe, that *Drennan* did not use promissory estoppel "as a substitute for the entire contract" but, rather, used "promissory estoppel as consideration for an implied promise to kept the bid open for a reasonable time." 674 A. 2d at 527. The court then noted the criticism of *Drennan*'s lack of symmetry in that "subcontractors are bound to the general, but the general is not bound to the subcontractors." 674 A.2d at 528. The general is free to "bid shop, bid chop, and to encourage bid peddling, to the detriment of the subcontractor" who may have made a mistake in bids and is usually in a weaker negotiating position. The court then discussed other theories designed to rectify this bargaining imbalance. See the next case and notes following.

In the midst of this description of bidding dynamics, the court stated: "Recovery [in *Drennan*] was then predicated on traditional bilateral contract, with the sub-bid as the offer and *promissory estoppel serving to replace acceptance.*" (Emphasis added). This, of course, is a misreading of *Drennan*, since the subcontractor's offer was accepted in the traditional manner after the attempt to revoke. Reliance was invoked to protect the prime contractor against revocation before acceptance and this principle is now expressed, as the court recognized, in Section 87(2) of the Restatement (Second).

In *Pavel Enterprises*, however, the prime contractor attempted to accept the sub-bid *before* Johnson's revocation. There was no need for reliance theory to hold the offer open and, arguably, everything the court said about reliance options was dictum. Moreover, the purported acceptance was made more than three weeks after the offer and, in the interim, there was confusion over who would get the prime contract and Pavel actively solicited new bids (bid shopping) from the subcontractors. Assuming that the September 1 letter was an acceptance, the court could plausibly conclude that Johnson's offer had lapsed and, therefore, could not be accepted.

But no. After penning an unneeded treatise on reliance options, the court endorsed the complex and somewhat dubious reasoning of the trial court leading the same result.

First, the trial court concluded that there was no "traditional bilateral contract." Why? Johnson's sub-bid was an offer of a contingent contract which Pavel accepted on September 1 "subject to the condition precedent" of Pavel's receipt of the award from NIH. Prior to the occurrence of the condition precedent (on September 28), Johnson was free to withdraw and did in fact withdraw on September 2 before the "valid final acceptance." But the facts do not clearly support this so-called "condition precedent" and the court never explored the possibility that the parties created a contingent bilateral contract, the duty to perform of which was conditioned upon NIH awarding Pavel the contract. Under that interpretation, Johnson's attempt to withdraw would have been a breach of contract unless relief from the mistake was available.

Second, the trial court attempted to apply Section 90 of the Restatement (Second) of Contracts to determine whether Pavel's reliance (use of the bid) "binds Johnson to its bid." Concluding that Johnson's bid was an offer, the court applied Section 90 on the assumption that Pavel's reliance in using the bid might bind Johnson to its offer even though that offer invited acceptance in a different manner and bargained for a promised performance in exchange. The court held, however, that the requirements of Section 90 were not satisfied, primarily because Pavel's conduct demonstrated that it was no longer relying on Johnson's offer. 674 A.2d at 533. But in pursuing this analysis, the court seemingly broke new ground and repudiated Judge Learned Hand's wisdom in *Baird* that there is "no room" for promissory estoppel in cases like this. Do you agree with *Pavel*?

Could the court conclude that use of Johnson's bid was an invited method of acceptance and, by implication, constituted a promise to perform contingent upon award of the NIH contract? Compare *Drennan* and see the next case.

Electrical Construction & Maintenance Company, Inc. v. Maeda Pacific Corporation

United States Court of Appeals, Ninth Circuit, 1985.
764 F.2d 619.

■ PREGERSON, CIRCUIT JUDGE.

Appellant subcontractor seeks damages based on breach of contract and promissory estoppel against appellee general contractor. Appellant appeals from the District Court of Guam's order of dismissal for failure to state a claim upon which relief could be granted. For the reasons stated below, we reverse and remand for further proceedings.

FACTS

Appellant Electrical Construction & Maintenance Company, Inc. (ECM), and appellee Maeda Pacific Corporation (Maeda) are construction contractors.

The government of Guam awarded appellee Maeda the prime contract on the Container Yard Expansion Project, a Guamanian government construction project designed to expand and modernize its port facilities. Prior to bidding on the project, Maeda solicited proposals from various subcontractors to perform the electrical work. ECM was one of the subcontractors Maeda contacted. ECM alleges that when Maeda solicited ECM's bid, Maeda was told by ECM that it was unwilling to bid unless Maeda agreed to award ECM the subcontract if it were the lowest bidder on the subcontract and Maeda were the successful bidder on the prime contract. ECM further alleges that Maeda accepted ECM's proposal. The alleged agreement was oral. Maeda disputes that it made such a promise to ECM and that ECM was the lowest bidder. Although Maeda was awarded the prime contract, it chose not to hire ECM for the electrical subcontract.

DISCUSSION

* * *

Appellant contends that the district court erred in concluding that appellant's amended complaint failed to state a claim for relief. We agree. The district court concluded that because a subcontractor is bound not to revoke a bid once relied upon by a prime contractor, there was no consideration in this case for ECM's promise to submit a bid on condition that Maeda accept the bid if it were the low bid and if Maeda were awarded the prime contract.

Generally, the mere use of a subcontractor's bid by a general contractor bidding on a prime contract does not constitute acceptance of the subcontractor's bid and imposes no obligation upon the prime contractor to accept the subcontractor's bid. See Merritt–Chapman & Scott Corp. v. Gunderson Bros. Engineering Corp., 305 F.2d 659 (9th Cir.), cert. denied, 371 U.S. 935, 83 S.Ct. 307, 9 L.Ed.2d 271 (1962); Southern Cal. Acoustics Co. v. C.V. Holder, Inc., 71 Cal.2d 719, 456 P.2d 975, 79 Cal.Rptr. 319 (1969); Williams v. Favret, 161 F.2d 822 (5th Cir.1947). Moreover, ECM concedes that the mere solicitation of bids by a general contractor is not an offer and does not impose any obligations upon the general contractor. But ECM points out that even if it were obligated not to revoke its bid, it was not obligated to bid in the first place. ECM alleged in its complaint that it initially refused Maeda's solicitation to bid and only subsequently bid because Maeda promised that if ECM undertook the time and expense to prepare and submit an electrical subcontractor's bid, Maeda would award ECM the subcontract if its bid were the lowest. While this is an issue of first impression, we believe that where a subcontractor allegedly agreed to bid only after receiving the general contractor's promise to accept the bid if it were the low bid and if the general contractor were awarded the prime contract, there is consideration for the general contractor's promise. The consideration for Maeda's promise was ECM's submission of a bid—an act for which Maeda bargained and that ECM was not under a legal duty to perform. See Restatement (Second) of Contracts §§ 71–73 (any bargained for performance other than the performance of a legal duty owed to the promisor is consideration for a promise). See also A. Corbin, *Corbin on Contracts* § 123 (1963); J. Calamari & J. Perillo, *Contracts* 136–39 (2d ed. 1977).

While this does seem to be a case of first impression, at least one scholar has implied that an agreement such as that involved in the present case may be enforceable:

> A final point of interest is whether the prime and the sub could [create a binding contract requiring the prime to use the sub's services] by agreeing between themselves in advance that the sub would always get the subcontract from the prime bidder in a case where the prime used his bid to get the prime contract. Initially, the prime is not under any obligation to use the sub's bid (and the sub is under no obligation to make any bid), but if the prime should decide to use the sub's bid, then he is obligated to accept no other sub's bid for the same work, should he get the contract. *The chief problem here is finding consideration for the prime's promise to award the subcontract. Note that the subcontractor does not promise to make any bids for the prime to use.... The prime will be bound by his promise as to any bids submitted by the sub in reliance on it,* but ... he can revoke that promise as to future bids at any time without liability.

A. Corbin, *Corbin on Contracts,* § 24 at 50–51 (C. Kaufman Supp.1984) (emphasis added).

The Appellate Division overlooked ECM's contention that ECM submitted its bid in the first place because of Maeda's conditional promise, and the court erroneously assumed that ECM's promise not to revoke its bid was the sole consideration alleged in the present case. Specifically, the Appellate Division found that ECM provided insufficient consideration because once it submitted its bid to Maeda and Maeda relied upon that bid, ECM was precluded from withdrawing the bid under Drennan v. Star Paving Co., 51 Cal.2d 409, 333 P.2d 757 (1958).

In *Drennan,* a subcontractor discovered a mistake in the preparation of a bid submitted to a prime contractor and then sought to revoke the bid after the prime contractor had used the sub's bid in submitting its own bid. The subcontractor had not reserved the right to revoke the bid. The California Supreme Court found the subcontractor liable under a theory of an implied promise not to revoke the bid. The present case is distinguishable from Drennan. ECM does not allege that it promised not to revoke its bid in consideration for Maeda's conditional promise to accept ECM's bid. Rather, ECM contends that it obtained a commitment from Maeda, before bidding on Maeda's project, that if ECM were to bid, Maeda would award ECM the subcontract if its bid were the lowest and if Maeda's prime bid were successful. Drennan did not involve the question whether submission of a bid in the first place, in contrast to a promise not to revoke a bid, can be adequate consideration for a conditional promise to accept the bid.

We find no authority for the proposition that ECM's submission of its electrical subcontractor's bid constituted insufficient consideration for Maeda's bargained for conditional promise to accept ECM's bid. ECM was under no legal obligation to submit its bid. To uphold a dismissal for failure to state a claim, it must appear to a certainty that the law would not entitle a plaintiff to relief under any set of facts that could be proved. *Halet,* 672 F.2d at 1309 (citations omitted). Because the Appellate Division based its dismissal of ECM's complaint upon the untenable theory that the only consideration alleged by ECM was its implied promise not to revoke its bid, the Appellate Division's decision cannot be upheld on the grounds of absence of consideration.

* * *

[After pointing out that the basis for the promissory estoppel claim arose out of the same facts as the breach of contract claim, the court held that since the amended complaint requested breach of contract damages and "all such relief as may be just," the appellant should have been permitted to assert a promissory estoppel claim at the time of trial, even if not specifically alleged in the complaint.]

For these reasons, we reverse the District Court of Guam's order of dismissal for failure to state a claim, and remand to the district court with instructions that it remand to the Superior Court of Guam so that the superior court can hear appellant's claim for damages based on breach of contract and promissory estoppel on the merits.

REVERSED and REMANDED for further proceedings consistent with this opinion.

NOTES

(1) In *Drennan,* Judge Traynor observes that "there was neither an option supported by consideration nor a bilateral contract binding on both parties."

He then proceeds to create an option under promissory estoppel doctrine. How does he avoid Judge Hand's reasoning in *Baird*? For what reasons and by what methodology is the option created? What is the scope of the protection afforded the general contractor by the option?

(2) Did the general contractor, in *Drennan*, know or have reason to know that a mistake had been made? Would such knowledge affect the outcome? See Chapter 4, Section 1(A).

(3) The position adopted by Judge Traynor has come to predominate. See Pavel v. A.S. Johnson, 342 Md. 143, 674 A.2d 521, 526–530 (1996); Bishop, *The Subcontractor's Bid: An Option Contract Arising through Promissory Estoppel*, 34 Emory L.J. 42 (1985). The revised Restatement appears not only to follow *Drennan*, but to extend it. Section 87(2) provides: "An offer which the offeror should reasonably expect to induce action or forbearance of a substantial character by the offeree before acceptance and which does induce such action or forbearance is binding as an option contract to the extent necessary to avoid injustice." But what is the likely impact of limiting the binding effect of the option "to the extent necessary to avoid injustice"? Cf. Loranger Construction Corp. v. E.F. Hauserman Co., 376 Mass. 757, 384 N.E.2d 176 (1978). In an opinion by Judge Braucher, first Reporter of Restatement (Second), the court eschews promissory estoppel analysis ("it tends to confusion rather than clarity"), preferring to base liability on a "typical bargain." See generally, Colsen and Weiland, *The Construction Industry Bidding Cases: Application of Traditional Contract, Promissory Estoppel and Other Theories to the Relations between General Contractors and Subcontractors*, 13 J.Mar.L.Rev. 565 (1980).

(4) Oil Lease Owner offered to enter a "farmout agreement" with Oil Driller. The offer stated that it was irrevocable for a period of 120 days, plus a 30 day extension. Driller, who was to accept the offer by drilling on a designated parcel, paid nothing for the option. Before acceptance, Driller in reliance on the option drilled a test well on another parcel. Data from this drilling would help to evaluate whether to accept the offer. Before acceptance, however, Owner attempted to change the terms of the offer. Held: Under Section 90 of the Restatement (Second), Driller's reliance upon the written option promise made the offer irrevocable and Driller could create a contract on the original terms of the offer. Strata Production v. Mercury Exploration, 121 N.M. 622, 916 P.2d 822, 827–830 (1996).

(5) *Protection for the Subcontractor?* Under *Drennan*, a general contractor, armed with an award of the overall project, can solicit a new round of subcontractor bids. Subcontractors thus anxious about the prospect of obtaining certain subcontracts for the project are susceptible to pressures to lower their bids. Since the overall project contract has already been awarded at this point, only the general contractor, not the project owner, will profit from this "bid shopping." How did the subcontractor, in *Electrical Construction*, protect itself from bid shopping by the general contractor? By what other method(s) might this result be achieved? Would a promise by ECM not to revoke its bid in consideration of Maeda's promise to award ECM the subcontract providing Maeda obtains the prime contract suffice?

Recognizing a potential for abuse, in 1963 the California legislature adopted the Subletting and Subcontracting Fair Practices Act, West's Ann.Cal. Gov.Code §§ 4100–08. This statute provides that a general contractor bidding on "any public work or improvement" must disclose in its bid the name of any subcontractor whose bid is incorporated into and exceeds ½ of 1% of the price of the general contractor's bid. The statute further provides that a general contractor whose bid on a public project is accepted shall not replace a subcontractor listed in his bid with another subcontractor, except where a listed subcontractor refuses to execute or perform a written contract for the work, becomes insolvent, or fails to satisfy bonding requirements. In addition, replacement of a listed subcontractor under any of these circumstances requires the awarding authority's consent. In Southern California Acoustics Co. v. C.V. Holder, Inc., 71 Cal.2d 719, 79 Cal.Rptr. 319, 456 P.2d 975 (1969), the California Supreme Court held that public authorities have a duty to listed subcontractors under the Act not to consent to wrongful substitutions. See also W.J. Lewis Corp. v. C. Harper Construction Co., Inc., 116 Cal.App.3d 27, 171 Cal.Rptr. 806 (1981). Florida has enacted similar legislation. See West's Fla. Stat.Ann. § 286.27. See E.M. Watkins Co. v. Board of Regents, 414 So.2d 583 (Fla.Dist.Ct.App.1982).

(5) *Some more analysis.* In this recurring fact pattern, at what point are the subcontractor and the prime bound by an enforceable contract?

As the *Electrical Construction* case demonstrates, they could create such a contract by an exchange of promises made before the subcontractor's bid was made. The contract would be conditional upon the prime using the sub's low bid and receiving the prime contract from the owner. At this point, both parties are bound, subject to possible relief from mistake by the sub [See Chapter 4, Section 2(A) infra] and to any subsequent bargaining over terms left open or not yet agreed. [See next subsection.] In a competitive market, however, how many subcontractors will have the bargaining power to strike such a deal?

At the other extreme, suppose that the sub's bid was not an offer. Here there would be no contract until the prime, after receiving the prime contract, made an offer which the sub accepted. Neither party would be bound until the last possible minute, thereby protecting the sub from mistakes and permitting the prime to "bid shop" or "bid chop." Put differently, the reliance of neither party is protected until the sub accepts the prime's offer.

If an offer is made by the sub, the *Drennan* case held that although the offer was not accepted by the prime's use of the bid and that promissory estoppel could not be used as a substitute for the invited acceptance, the prime's reliance in using the bid could create an option contract. This result, born from Judge Traynor's marriage of Sections 45 and 90 in the First Restatement, is now enshrined, in Section 87(2) of the Second Restatement.

But is this constructed option a satisfactory solution? Under this approach the sub's pre-contractual reliance is not protected and its freedom to withdraw if a mistake is discovered may be foreclosed if the prime accepts first. The prime contractor, on the other hand, can accept the offer or not, depending upon its assessment of the situation after receiving the prime contract.

In light of this, should the prime's use of the bid be treated either as an acceptance of the offer or as reliance that supports the enforcement of the sub's offer rather than as the basis for an option contract? What doctrinal problems are posed by this move? Would it be a perversion of intention? Would it provide disincentives to reliance that, in many cases, would be beneficial to both parties? For interesting discussions of these and other formation problems from the standpoint of economic analysis, see Richard Craswell, *Offer, Acceptance and Efficient Reliance,* 48 Stan. L. Rev. 481, 531–536 (1996)(arguing that courts will find a way to protect the prime where its reliance would increase the expected value of the deal so that even the sub would want to be committed) and Avery Katz, *When Should an Offer Stick: The Economics of Promissory Estoppel in Preliminary Negotiations,* 105 Yale L. J. 1249, 1259–1263, 1302 (1996)(arguing that courts will hold large, informed, wealthy repeat players to their pre-contractual offers and excuse the small, uniformed, liquidity constrained novices from theirs to create appropriate incentives for the weak to make reliance investments).

PROBLEM: THE CASE OF THE BID–SHOPPING CONTRACTOR

School Corporation decided to build an annex to its senior high school. Plans and specifications were prepared, and various building firms were invited to submit bids. Among those contacted was Contractor. The latter, in turn, determined to submit a bid and proceeded to contact potential subcontractors relative to various components of the project.

Subcontractor *A* telephoned a bid for the excavating work. Since this was the low bid of the responding excavating subcontractors, Contractor used *A*'s figure in computing his bid to School Corporation. Subcontractor *B* submitted a bid in writing for the electrical work, which Contractor also used in computing the general bid since *B*'s price was the lowest of the electrical subcontractors. Subcontractor *C*'s bid was low for the plumbing component, and it, too, was used by Contractor in preparing the prime bid.

At the bid opening on March 18, Contractor was found to be low bidder, and two days later was awarded the contract. Armed with this award, Contractor immediately sought out other excavating subcontractors in an effort to get a lower figure, but he was unsuccessful. On March 22 he wired an acceptance to *A*. He fared better, however, with respect to the electrical work. He secured, on March 23, the agreement of subcontractor *D* to do the work for $15,000 less than specified by *B*. He took no further action regarding *B*'s bid.

At the bid opening Contractor mentioned to another general contractor that he thought *C*'s bid on the plumbing work was too high and that he could do much better elsewhere. Two days later the other contractor told *C* of this conversation, and the latter, thinking Contractor would not want him to do the work, accepted an outstanding offer from another. However, Contractor did not seek out other plumbing subcontractors, and on March 24 undertook to accept *C*'s offer.

Contractor is now beset with problems. *A* and *C* refuse to perform; *B* insists he has a binding contract for the electrical work. Contractor consults you. Advise him both as to his present difficulties and as to how he should proceed in future post-award negotiations. See generally, Comment, *Bid Shopping and Peddling in the Subcontract Construction Industry,* 18 U.C.L.A.L.Rev. 389 (1970); Comment, *Construction Bidding Problem: Is There a Solution Fair to Both the General Contractor and Subcontractor?,* 19 St.L.U.L.J. 552 (1975).

SECTION 2.   INSUFFICIENT OR DEFECTIVE FORMULATION OF AGREEMENT: INDEFINITE, INCOMPLETE, AND DEFERRED TERMS

In the foregoing materials on the agreement process, we have considered the nature and effect of "offer" and "acceptance" and the circumstances under which negotiations can be terminated without liability to either party. We now turn to a closely related problem. If, after the negotiations have produced some agreement on the proposed exchange, one party withdraws because certain material terms were not agreed, or were agreed in an indefinite way or were explicitly left for future agreement, when, if ever, will that withdrawal result in liability for damages caused? If the withdrawing party has explicitly conditioned a willingness to deal upon the other party's clear agreement to material terms and the other has failed or refused to agree, no liability should attach. See Fairway Center Corp. v. U.I.P. Corp., 502 F.2d 1135 (8th Cir.1974). But suppose there is no explicit condition. Should contract law provide that there can be no contract until clear and complete agreement to all material terms is reached? If so, why? Or, should contract law permit the parties, if they so intend, to conclude bargains without clear agreement on all material terms? If so, why? How should lack of complete agreement or indefiniteness affect the enforcement of these bargains? What if the parties "agree to agree" on a term and do not? Are there any duties to negotiate or to bargain in good faith? These are some of the questions to be considered in this section.

Before seeking answers to these questions, it should be noted that you will observe a shift from a strict view that no contract can be formed until clear and complete agreement is reached on material terms to more flexible standards, such as those announced in UCC 2–204 and Sections 33 and 34 of Restatement (Second). There are several explanations for this shift from "rules to standards." See Speidel, *Restatement Second: Omitted Terms and Contract Method,* 67 Cornell L.Rev. 785, 786–92 (1982). According to Professor Ian Macneil, a possible reason is a different perception of the nature of contractual relationships. The assumption underlying the so-called "strict" view was that the parties could and should "presentiate," that is, express all of the material elements of the future exchange in the present agreement. In its extreme form, the transaction model was the "one shot deal" involving the sale of Dobbin or Blackacre. See Macneil, *Restatement (Second) of Contracts and Presentiation,* 60 Va.L.Rev. 589, 592–94 (1974). But the assumptions underlying the traditional theory of mutual assent are hardly consistent with such long-term relationships that exist between professor and university, husband and wife, union and corporation, supplier and middleman, government and aircraft manufacturer, franchisor and franchisee, or, even, two state-owned enterprises in a socialist economy. These parties may wish to have the protection of contract but be unwilling or unable to articulate all terms of the future exchange in an initial agreement. But if that protection is extended to them, new techniques must be developed to manage the inevitable disputes that will arise as the parties attempt to perform and to adjust these open-ended relationships. See also Macneil, *The Many Futures of Contracts,* 47 S.Cal.L.Rev. 691 (1974); Macneil, *A Primer of Contract Planning,* 48 S.Cal.L.Rev. 627 (1975).

(A) DEFECTIVE FORMULATION AND EXPRESSION OF AGREEMENT

We now consider a series of problems associated with attempts to withdraw from the bargaining relationship. These problems derive from the "objective" test, introduced in Chapter Two, Section 1(A), and focus upon one party's assertion that certain "defects" in the process of either formulating or expressing an agreement justify withdrawal or avoidance without liability, even though that agreement otherwise satisfies the requisites for a contract.

Your task in this section will be to develop a feel for the conditions that must exist before relief will be granted, the nature of that relief, and the policies implicit in the undertaking. Also, you should be aware that although these problems appear to be analytically distinct, there are clear overlaps with other areas. For example, although the theory of avoidance is not fraud or misrepresentation by one party (we will consider this infra Chapter Four, Section 2), a relevant factor may be whether one party has taken unfair advantage of a mistake by the other. Similarly, although the law of torts is not explicitly involved, an underlying purpose of the objective test is to protect the reasonable expectations or reliance of one party against the careless or negligent errors of another. Look carefully for themes premised upon fault in these materials. Further, even though the manifested agreement is supported by consideration, the defect in the process of formulation or expression may produce such disproportion as to make enforcement of the agreement unfair.

Raffles v. Wichelhaus

Court of Exchequer, 1864.
2 H. & C. 906, 159 Eng.Rep. 375.

Declaration. For that it was agreed between the plaintiff and the defendants, to wit, at Liverpool, that the plaintiff should sell to the defendants, and the defendants buy of the plaintiff, certain goods, to wit, 125 bales of Surat cotton, guaranteed middling fair merchant's Dhollorah, to arrive ex "Peerless" from Bombay; and that the cotton should be taken from the quay, and that the defendants would pay the plaintiff for the same at a certain rate, to wit, at the rate of 17¼d. per pound, within a certain time then agreed upon after the arrival of said goods in England. Averments: that the said goods did arrive by the said ship from Bombay in England, to wit, at Liverpool, and the plaintiff was then and there ready and willing and offered to deliver the said goods to the defendants, &c. Breach: that the defendants refused to accept the said goods or pay the plaintiff for them.

Plea. That the said ship mentioned in the said agreement was meant and intended by the defendants to be the ship called the "Peerless," which sailed from Bombay, to wit, in October; and that the plaintiff was not ready and willing, and did not offer to deliver to the defendants any bales of cotton which arrived by the last-mentioned ship, but instead thereof was only ready and willing, and offered to deliver to the defendants 125 bales of Surat cotton which arrived by another and different ship, which was also called the "Peerless," and which sailed from Bombay, to wit, in December.

Demurrer, and joinder therein.

Milward, in support of the demurrer. The contract was for the sale of a number of bales of cotton of a particular description, which the plaintiff was ready to deliver. It is immaterial by what ship the cotton was to arrive, so that it was a ship called the "Peerless." The words "to arrive ex 'Peerless,'" only mean that if the vessel is lost on the voyage, the contract is to be at an end. [Pollock, C.B. It would be a question for the jury whether both parties meant the same ship called the "Peerless."] That would be so if the contract was for the sale of a ship called the "Peerless"; but it is for the sale of cotton on board a ship of that name. [Pollock, C.B. The defendant only bought that cotton which was to arrive by a particular ship. It may as well be said, that if there is a contract for the purchase of certain goods in warehouse A., that is satisfied by the delivery of goods of the same description in warehouse B.] In that case there would be goods in both warehouses; here it does not appear that the plaintiff had any goods on board the other "Peerless." [Martin, B. It is imposing on the defendant a contract different from that which he entered into. Pollock, C.B. It is like a contract for the purchase of wine coming from a particular estate in France or Spain, where there are two estates of that name.] The defendant has no right to contradict by parol evidence a written contract good upon the face of it. He does not impute misrepresentation or fraud, but only says that he fancied the ship was a different one. Intention is of no avail, unless stated at the time of the contract. [Pollock, C.B. One vessel sailed in October and the other in December.] The time of sailing is no part of the contract.

Mellish (Cohen with him), in support of the plea. There is nothing on the face of the contract to shew that any particular ship called the "Peerless" was meant; but the moment it appears that two ships called the "Peerless" were about to sail from Bombay there is a latent ambiguity, and parol evidence may be given for the purpose of shewing that the defendant meant one "Peerless," and the plaintiff another. That being so, there was no consensus ad idem, and therefore no binding contract. He was then stopped by the Court.

■ PER CURIAM. There must be judgment for the defendants.

Judgment for the defendants.

NOTES

(1) Professor Corbin states that the subject of mistake is "one of the most difficult in the law * * * because men make so many mistakes, of so many

different kinds, with so many varying effects." Corbin § 103. Was *Raffles v. Wichelhaus,* commonly referred to as the *Peerless Case,* a mistake case? If so, what kind of mistake was involved? If both parties manifested assent to "Peerless" (and this term was to determine the time for delivery), why did not the court apply the objective test and enforce the contract?

(2) *Gilmore on the Peerless Case.* Professor Grant Gilmore, in the course of tracing the development of the objective test, suggests that a break in the price of cotton on the Liverpool market between the arrival dates of the two ships Peerless may explain why the buyer rejected the goods and that the court, despite the probing of plaintiff's counsel Milward, remained unshaken in its conclusion that "Peerless" was a material term in the bargain in that it manifested the time for delivery of the goods.

> In any event it does not necessarily follow that a ship sailing from Bombay in October would have made port in Liverpool before a ship sailing in December. Either Peerless may have been a sailing vessel, subject to the vagaries of wind and weather—or both of them may have been—and either one (or both) may have called at intermediate ports. Since the buyer did not in his plea raise any issue about the time of the seller's tender in Liverpool, we may, I think, safely assume that there was no such issue to be raised. Furthermore, as Milward * * * correctly pointed out, there was no provision in the contract relating to the time of sailing from Bombay. * * * None of the judges thought of asking Mellish what would seem to be obvious questions. Would a reasonably well-informed cotton merchant in Liverpool have known that there were two ships called Peerless? Ought this buyer to have known? If in fact the October Peerless had arrived in Liverpool first, had the buyer protested the seller's failure to tender the cotton?

The failure to probe Mellish with the same zeal exhibited toward Milward suggests to Gilmore that the court was "entirely content to let the case go off on the purely subjective failure of the minds to meet at the time the contract was entered into." G. Gilmore, The Death of Contract 35–39 (1974).

(3) *Holmes on the Peerless Case.*

> "It is commonly said that such a contract is void, because of mutual mistake as to the subject matter, and because therefore the parties did not consent to the same thing. But this way of putting it seems to me misleading. The law has nothing to do with the actual state of the parties' minds. In contract, as elsewhere, it must go by externals, and judge parties by their conduct. If there had been but one 'Peerless,' and the defendant had said 'Peerless' by mistake, meaning 'Peri,' he would have been bound. The true ground of the decision was not that each party meant a different thing from the other, as is implied by the explanation which has been mentioned, but that each said a different thing. The plaintiff offered one thing, the defendant expressed his assent to another."

O. Holmes, The Common Law 242 (Howe ed. 1963).

(4) *Gilmore on Holmes on the Peerless Case.*

> "Even for Holmes this was an extraordinary tour de force * * * The magician who could 'objectify' *Raffles v. Wichelhaus* could, the need arising, objectify anything."

G. Gilmore, The Death of Contract 41 (1974). See Birmingham, *Holmes on "Peerless"*: Raffles v. Wichelhaus *and the Objective Theory of Contract*, 47 U.Pitt.L.Rev. 183 (1985).

(5) *Simpson on Gilmore on the Peerless Case.*

What of Grant Gilmore's discussion of the case in *The Death of Contract* ? His speculations as to the background are inevitably misconceived, being unrelated to evidence. But his principal point was that the judges in the case foolishly failed to grasp, in spite of Clement Milward's attempts to put the point to them, that in terms of commercial understanding the identity of the carrying ship was immaterial. Its only relevance was to the risk of loss. He backs this claim up with a classic statement of the ahistorical attitude to legal sources: "In commercial understanding, that is exactly what the terms mean today and there is no reason to believe that they meant anything else a hundred years ago." And to be sure, Gilmore is correct in saying that there is no reason if we pay no attention whatever to the historical context in which the dispute arose. But from what I have said, it is perfectly plain that in arrival contracts where ship and port were named, the identity of the carrying vessel was of central importance. It was the identity of the carrying vessel that fixed the time of arrival and delivery. In the volatile cotton market, that time was critical to the success or failure of the speculation. The reason why time was not specified directly was technological, and as the technology changed, "shipments" were to be superseded by a new form of contract, "deliveries," which did directly specify time. Out of transactions involving this newer form of arrival contract was to develop the practice of futures trading, but that is another story.

Simpson, *Contracts for Cotton to Arrive: The Case of the Two Ships Peerless*, 11 Cardozo L.Rev. 287, 324 (1989).

(6) *Restatement (Second) on the Peerless Case.*

Effect of Misunderstanding.

(1) There is no manifestation of mutual assent to an exchange if the parties attach materially different meanings to their manifestations and (a) neither party knows or has reason to know the meaning attached by the other; or (b) each party knows or each party has reason to know the meaning attached by the other.

(2) The manifestations of the parties are operative in accordance with the meaning attached to them by one of the parties if (a) that party does not know of any different meaning attached by the other, and the other knows the meaning attached by the first party; or (b) that party has no reason to know of any different meaning attached by the other, and the other has reason to know the meaning attached by the first party.

Restatement (Second) § 20.

Translation, please! See also, Young, *Equivocation in the Making of Agreements*, 64 Colum.L.Rev. 619 (1964); Palmer, *The Effect of Misunderstanding on Contract Formation and Reformation under the Restatement of Contracts, Second*, 65 Mich.L.Rev. 33, 33–51, 56–58 (1966); Farnsworth, *"Meaning" in the Law of Contracts*, 76 Yale L.J. 939 (1967).

Konic International Corporation v. Spokane Computer Services, Inc.

Court of Appeals of Idaho, 1985.
109 Idaho 527, 708 P.2d 932.

■ WALTERS, CHIEF JUDGE.

Konic International Corporation sued Spokane Computer Services, Inc., to collect the price of an electrical device allegedly sold by Konic to Spokane Computer. The suit was tried before a magistrate sitting without a jury. The magistrate entered judgment for Spokane Computer, concluding there was no contract between the parties because of lack of apparent authority of an employee of Spokane Computer to purchase the device from Konic. The district court, on appeal, upheld the magistrate's judgment. On further appeal by Konic, we also affirm the magistrate's judgment but base our result on reasoning different from that of the lower court.

The magistrate found the following facts. David Young, an employee of Spokane Computer, was instructed by his employer to investigate the possibility of purchasing a surge protector, a device which protects computers from damaging surges of electrical current. Young's investigation turned up several units priced from $50 to $200, none of which, however, were appropriate for his employer's needs. Young then contacted Konic. After discussing Spokane Computer's needs with a Konic engineer, Young was referred to one of Konic's salesmen. Later, after deciding on a certain unit, Young inquired as to the price of the selected item. The salesman responded, "fifty-six twenty." The salesman meant $5,620. Young in turn thought $56.20.

The salesman for Konic asked about Young's authority to order the equipment and was told that Young would have to get approval from one of his superiors. Young in turn prepared a purchase order for $56.20 and had it approved by the appropriate authority. Young telephoned the order and purchase order number to Konic who then shipped the equipment to Spokane Computer. However, because of internal processing procedures of both parties the discrepancy in prices was not discovered immediately. Spokane Computer received the surge protector and installed it in its office. The receipt and installation of the equipment occurred while the president of Spokane Computer was on vacation. Although the president's father, who was also chairman of the board of Spokane Computer, knew of the installation, he only inquired as to what the item was and who had ordered it. The president came back from vacation the day after the surge protector had been installed and placed in operation and was told of the purchase. He immediately ordered that power to the equipment be turned off because he realized that the equipment contained parts which alone were worth more than $56 in value. Although the president then told Young to verify the price of the surge protector, Young failed to do so. Two weeks later, when Spokane Computer was processing its purchase order and Konic's invoice, the discrepancy between the amount on the invoice and the amount on the purchase order was discovered. The president of Spokane Computer then contacted Konic, told Konic that Young had no authority to order such equipment, that Spokane Computer did not want the equipment, and that Konic should remove it. Konic responded that Spokane Computer now owned the equipment and if the equipment was not paid for, Konic would sue for the price. Spokane Computer refused to pay and this litigation ensued.

Following trial, the magistrate found that Young had no actual, implied, or apparent authority to enter into the transaction and, therefore, Spokane Computer did not owe Konic for the equipment.[1] In reaching its decision, the magistrate also noted that when Spokane Computer acquired full knowledge of the facts, it took prompt action to disaffirm Young's purchase.

We agree with the magistrate's result. However, rather than base our decision on the agency principle of apparent authority, as did the trial court, we believe that more basic principles of contract are determinative in this case. "When the result reached by the trial court is correct, but entered on a different theory, we will affirm it on the correct theory." Goodwin v. Nationwide Insurance Co., 104 Idaho 74, 83, 656 P.2d 135, 144 (Ct.App.1982).

Basically what is involved here is a failure of communication between the parties. A similar failure to communicate arose over 100 years ago in the celebrated case of Raffles v. Wichelhaus, 2 Hurl. 906, 159 Eng.Rep. 375 (1864) which has become better known as the case of the good ship "Peerless". In *Peerless,* the parties agreed on a sale of cotton which was to be delivered from Bombay by the ship "Peerless". In fact, there were two ships named "Peerless" and each party, in agreeing to the sale, was referring to a different ship. Because the sailing time of the two ships was materially different, neither party was willing to agree to shipment by the "other" Peerless. The court ruled that, because each party had a different ship in mind at the time of the contract, there was in fact no binding contract. The *Peerless* rule later was incorporated into section 71 of the RESTATEMENT OF CONTRACTS and has now evolved into section 20 of RESTATEMENT (SECOND) OF CONTRACTS (1981). Section 20 states in part:

> (1) There is no manifestation of mutual assent to an exchange if the parties attach materially different meanings to their manifestations and
>
> (a) neither knows or has reason to know the meaning attached by the other.

Comment (c) to section 20 further explains that "even though the parties manifest mutual assent to the same words of agreement, there may be no contract because of a material difference of understanding as to the terms of the exchange." Another authority, Williston, discussing situations where

---

1. Although the trial court's decision was not explicit about possession of the equipment, the district court, on appeal, determined that Konic was entitled to possession of the equipment.

a mistake will prevent formation of a contract, agrees that "where a phrase of contract ... is reasonably capable of different interpretations ... there is no contract." 1 S. WILLISTON, CONTRACTS § 95 (3d ed. 1957).

One commentator on the *Peerless* case, maintaining that the doctrine should be cautiously applied, indicates three principles about the case doctrine that are generally in agreement: (1) "the doctrine applies only when the parties have different understandings of their expression of agreement"; (2) the doctrine does not apply when one party's understanding, because of that party's fault, is less reasonable than the other party's understanding; and (3) parol evidence is admissible to establish the facts necessary to apply the rule. Young, *Equivocation in the Making of Agreements,* 64 COLUM.L.REV. 619 (1964).

The second principle indicates that the doctrine may be applicable to this case because, arguably, both parties' understandings were reasonable. Also, as pointed out by the district court, both parties were equally at fault in contributing to the resulting problems. The third principle is not relevant to the present case.

* * *

In the present case, both parties attributed different meanings to the same term, "fifty-six twenty." Thus, there was no meeting of the minds of the parties. With a hundred fold difference in the two prices, obviously price was a material term. Because the "fifty-six twenty" designation was a material term expressed in an ambiguous form to which two meanings were obviously applied, we conclude that no contract between the parties was ever formed. Accordingly, we do not reach the issue of whether Young had authority to order the equipment.

* * *

[Judgment affirmed.]

NOTES

(1) The key question: when the parties to a bargain assert materially different understandings of the same words or conduct, how is the court to determine which understanding to prefer? The *"Peerless"* result, as reflected in *Konic,* means that no contract was formed and that any reliance by either party on the arrangement will be protected only if the other party has received and retained a measurable benefit. The risk of unreimbursed reliance and the fortuity of which party is left with the difficult burden of proving the existence of a contract has led some courts to express a preference for avoiding the *Peerless* result "if there is any reasonable means to giving effect to the contract at issue." Consumers Ice Company v. United States, 201 Ct.Cl. 116, 475 F.2d 1161, 1165 (1973). One such reasonable means is through expansive principles of contract interpretation, which deem a wide range of context evidence relevant to the question of which party's understanding is the more reasonable. See, e.g., Frigaliment Importing Co. v. B.N.S. International Sales Corp., 190 F.Supp. 116 (S.D.N.Y.1960) (What is "chicken?" Does the term include "stew-

ing" chickens as well as broilers?), *infra* at 617. See also *Shrum v. Zeltwanger*, 559 P.2d 1384 (Wyo.1977) (What is a "cow"? Does the term include a "heifer" which has not had a calf?) If this process of interpretation is inconclusive, the court may, as a last resort, prefer the understanding "which operates against the party who supplies the words or from whom a writing otherwise proceeds." Restatement (Second) § 206. In effect, the basis for preference here is the failure of one party responsible for supplying key language to be clear enough. But if the process of interpretation fully extended is inconclusive, it may be possible to show that one party, from particularized information, knew or had reason to know that the other party had a materially different understanding. Put another way, although a reasonable person placed in the negotiations would not from objective factors in language or circumstances know that the seller had the "December" Peerless in mind, the particular buyer, from a prior course of dealing or even from a luncheon conversation, might know what the seller intended. If the buyer fails to clarify the situation, does this mean that there is a contract on the seller's understanding? If so, on what theory? See Restatement (Second) §§ 20, 201. On the basis of the foregoing, was *Konic* decided correctly?

(2) *The Case of the "Ambiguous" Legal Description.* Vendor owned land containing three contiguous tracts. Vendor listed the middle and northern tracts with a broker. Purchaser offered to buy these tracts, but Vendor made a counter-offer. In this proposal, which Purchaser accepted, the land to be sold was identified by detailed legal description alone and described the middle and *southern* tracts. After Vendor's refusal to perform, Purchaser seeks specific performance. Assuming that extrinsic evidence shows that Vendor intended to sell the middle and northern tracts and the Purchaser intended to buy the middle and southern tracts, what result? See *Hill–Shafer Partnership v. Chilson Family Trust*, 165 Ariz. 469, 799 P.2d 810 (1990).

(B) INDEFINITE AGREEMENTS

Varney v. Ditmars

Court of Appeals of New York, 1916.
217 N.Y. 223, 111 N.E. 822.

■ CHASE J. This is an action brought for an alleged wrongful discharge of an employé. The defendant is an architect employing engineers, draftsmen, and other assistants. The plaintiff is an architect and draftsman. In October, 1910, he applied to the defendant for employment and when asked what wages he wanted, replied that he would start for $40 per week. He was employed at $35 per week. A short time thereafter he informed the defendant that he had another position offered to him, and the defendant said that if he would remain with him and help him through the work in his office he thought he could offer him a better future than anybody else. He continued in the employ of the defendant and became acquainted with a designer in the office, and said designer and the plaintiff from time to time prior to the 1st of February, 1911, talked with the defendant about the work in his office. On that day by arrangement the two remained with the defendant after the regular office hours, and the defendant said: "I am going to give you $5 more a week; if you boys will go on and continue the way you have been and get me out of this trouble and get these jobs started that were in the office three years, on the 1st of next January I will close my books and give you a fair share of my profits." That was the result of the conversation. That was all of that conversation.

The plaintiff was given charge of the drafting. Thereafter suggestions were made by the plaintiff and said designer about discharging many of the defendant's employés and employing new men, and such suggestions were carried out and the two worked in the defendant's office overtime and many Sundays and holidays. At least one piece of work that the defendant said had been in his office for three years was completed. The plaintiff on his cross-examination told the story of the employment of himself and said designer as follows: "And he says at that time, 'I am going to give you $5 more a week starting this week.' This was about Thursday. He says, 'You boys go on and continue the work you are doing and the first of January next year I will close my books and give you a fair share of my profits.' Those were his exact words."

Thereafter the plaintiff was paid $40 a week. On November 6, 1911, the night before the general election in this state, the defendant requested that all of his employés that could do so, should work on election day. The plaintiff told the defendant that he wanted to remain at home to attend an election in the village where he lived. About 4 o'clock in the afternoon of election day he was taken ill and remained at his house ill until a time that as nearly as can be stated from the evidence was subsequent to December 1, 1911. On Saturday, November 11th, the defendant caused to be delivered to the plaintiff a letter in which he said: "I am sending you herewith your pay for one day's work of seven hours, performed on Monday, the 6th inst. On Monday night, I made it my special duty to inform you that the office would be open all day Election Day and that I expected you and all the men to report for work. Much to my surprise and indignation, on Tuesday you made no appearance and all of the men remained away, in obedience of your instructions to them of the previous evening. An act of this kind I consider one of extreme disloyalty and insubordination and I therefore am obliged to dispense with your services."

After the plaintiff had recovered from his illness and was able to do so he went to the defendant's office (the date does not appear) and told him that he was ready, willing, and able to continue his services under the agreement. The defendant denied that he had any agreement with him, and refused to permit him to continue in his service. Thereafter and prior to January 1, 1912, the plaintiff received for special work about $50.

The plaintiff seeks to recover in this action for services from November 7, 1911, to December 31, 1911, inclusive, at $40 per week and for a fair and reasonable percentage of the net profits of the defendant's business from February 1, 1911, to January 1, 1912, and demands judgment for $1,680.

At the trial he was the only witness sworn as to the alleged contract, and at the close of his case the complaint was dismissed.

The statement alleged to have been made by the defendant about giving the plaintiff and said designer a fair share of his profits is vague, indefinite, and uncertain, and the amount cannot be computed from anything that was said by the parties or by reference to any document, paper, or other transaction. The minds of the parties never met upon any particular share of the defendant's profits to be given the employés or upon any plan by which such share could be computed or determined. The contract so far as it related to the special promise or inducement was never consummated. It was left subject to the will of the defendant or for further negotiation. It is urged that the defendant by use of the word "fair," in referring to a share of his profits, was as certain and definite as people are in the purchase and sale of a chattel when the price is not expressly agreed upon, and that if the agreement in question is declared to be too indefinite and uncertain to be enforced, a similar conclusion must be reached in every case where a chattel is sold without expressly fixing the price therefor.

The question whether the words "fair" and "reasonable" have a definite and enforceable meaning when used in business transactions is dependent upon the intention of the parties in the use of such words and upon the subject-matter to which they refer. In cases of merchandising and in the purchase and sale of chattels the parties may use the words "fair and reasonable value" as synonymous with "market value." A promise to pay the fair market value of goods may be inferred from what is expressly agreed by the parties. The fair, reasonable, or market value of goods can be shown by direct testimony of those competent to give such testimony. The competency to speak grows out of experience and knowledge. The testimony of such witnesses does not rest upon conjecture. The opinion of this court in United Press v. N.Y. Press Co., 164 N.Y. 406, 58 N.E. 527, 53 L.R.A. 288, was not intended to assert that a contract of sale is unenforceable, unless the price is expressly mentioned and determined.

In the case of a contract for the sale of goods or for hire without a fixed price or consideration being named it will be presumed that a reasonable price or consideration is intended, and the person who enters into such a contract for goods or service is liable therefor as on an implied contract. Such contracts are common, and when there is nothing therein to limit or prevent an implication as to the price they are, so far as the terms of the contract are concerned, binding obligations.

The contract in question, so far as it relates to a share of the defendant's profits, is not only uncertain, but it is necessarily affected by so many other facts that are in themselves indefinite and uncertain that the intention of the parties is pure conjecture. A fair share of the defendant's profits may be any amount from a nominal sum to a material part according to the particular views of the person whose guess is considered. Such an executory contract must rest for performance upon the honor and good faith of the parties making it. The courts cannot aid parties in such a case when they are unable or unwilling to agree upon the terms of their own proposed contract.

It is elementary in the law that, for the validity of a contract, the promise, or the agreement, of the parties to it must be certain and explicit, and that their full intention may be ascertained to a reasonable degree of certainty. Their agreement must be neither vague nor indefinite, and, if thus defective, parol proof cannot be resorted to. *United Press v. N.Y. Press Co.*, supra, and cases cited; Ruling Case Law, vol. 6, 644.

The courts in this state, in reliance upon and approval of the rule as stated in the United Press Case, have decided many cases involving the same rule. Thus, in Mackintosh v. Thompson, 58 App.Div. 25, 68 N.Y.Supp. 492, and again in Mackintosh v. Kimball, 101 App.Div. 494, 92 N.Y.Supp. 132, the plaintiff sought to recover compensation in addition to a stated salary which he had received and which additional amount rested upon a claim by him that while he was employed by the defendants he informed them that he intended to leave their employ, unless he was given an increase in salary, and that one of the defendants said to him that they would make it worth his while if he would stay on, and would increase his salary, and that his idea was to give him an interest in the profits on certain buildings that they were then erecting. The plaintiff further alleges that he asked what would be the amount of the increase and was told, "You can depend upon me; I will see that you get a satisfactory amount." The court held that the arrangement was too indefinite to form the basis of any obligation on the part of the defendant.

* * *

The rule stated from the United Press Case does not prevent a recovery upon quantum meruit in case one party to an alleged contract has performed in reliance upon the terms thereof, vague, indefinite, and uncertain though they are. In such case the law will presume a promise to pay the reasonable value of the services. Judge Gray, who wrote the opinion in the United Press Case, said therein: "I entertain no doubt that, where work has been done, or articles have been furnished, a recovery may be based upon quantum meruit, or quantum valebant; but, where a contract is of an executory character and requires performance over a future period of time, as here, and it is silent as to the price which is to be paid to the plaintiff during its term, I do not think that it possesses binding force. As the parties had omitted to make the price a subject of covenant, in the nature of things, it would have to be the subject of future agreement, or stipulation." Page 412 of 164 N.Y., page 529 of 58 N.E. (53 L.R.A. 288).

In Petze v. Morse Dry Dock & Repair Co., 125 App.Div. 267, 109 N.Y.S. 328, 331, the court said: "There is no contract so long as any essential element is open to negotiation."

In that case a contract was made by which an employé in addition to certain specified compensation was to receive 5 per cent. of the net distributable profits of a business, and it was further provided: "That 'the method of accounting to determine the net distributable profits is to be agreed upon later when the company's accounts have developed for a better understanding.' "

The parties never agreed as to the method of determining the net profits and the plaintiff was discharged before the expiration of the term. The court in the opinion say: "That 'the plaintiff could recover for what he had done on a quantum meruit, and the employment must be deemed to have commenced with a full understanding on the part of both parties that that was the situation.'"

The judgment of the Appellate Division was unanimously affirmed without opinion in this court. 195 N.Y. 584, 89 N.E. 1110.

So, in this case, while I do not think that the plaintiff can recover anything as extra work, yet if the work actually performed as stated was worth more than $40 per week he, having performed until November 7, 1910, could, on a proper complaint, recover its value less the amount received. See Bluemner v. Garvin, supra; s.c., 124 App.Div. 491, 108 N.Y.Supp. 791; King v. Broadhurst, 164 App.Div. 689, 150 N.Y.Supp. 376.

* * *

The judgment should be affirmed, with costs.

 CARDOZO, J., (dissenting). I do not think it is true that a promise is always and of necessity too vague to be enforced. . . . The promise must, of course, appear to have been made with contractual intent. . . . But if that intent is present, it cannot be said from the mere form of the promise that the estimate of the reward is inherently impossible. The data essential to measurement may be lacking in the particular instance, and yet they may conceivably be supplied. It is possible, for example, that in some occupations an employé would be able to prove a percentage regulated by custom. The difficulty in this case is not so much in the contract as in the evidence. Even if the data required for computation might conceivably have been supplied, the plaintiff did not supply them. He would not have supplied them if all the evidence which he offered and which the court excluded had been received. He has not failed because the nature of the contract is such that damages are of necessity incapable of proof. He has failed because he did not prove them.

There is nothing inconsistent with this view in United Press v. N.Y. Press Co., 164 N.Y. 406, 58 N.E. 527, 53 L.R.A. 288. The case is often cited as authority for the proposition that an agreement to buy merchandise at a fair and reasonable price is so indefinite that an action may not be maintained for its breach in so far as it is still executory. Nothing of the kind was decided, or with reason could have been. What the court did was to construe a particular agreement, and to hold that the parties intended to reserve the price for future adjustment. If instead of reserving the price for future adjustment, they had manifested an intent on the one hand to pay and on the other to accept a fair price, the case is far from holding that a jury could not determine what such a price would be and assess the damages accordingly. Such an intent, moreover, might be manifested not only through express words, but also through reasonable implication. It was because there was neither an express statement nor a reasonable implication of such an intent that the court held the agreement void to the extent that it had not been executed.

On the ground that the plaintiff failed to supply the data essential to computation, I concur in the conclusion that profits were not to be included as an element of damages. I do not concur, however, in the conclusion that he failed to make out a case of damage to the extent of his loss of salary. The amount may be small, but none the less it belongs to him. The hiring was not at will. . . . The plain implication was that it should continue until the end of the year when the books were to be closed. The evidence would permit the jury to find that the plaintiff was discharged without cause, and he is entitled to damages measured by his salary for the unexpired term.

The judgment should be reversed, and a new trial granted, with costs to abide the event.

Judgment affirmed.

Lefkowitz v. Great Minneapolis Surplus Store

Supreme Court of Minnesota, 1957.
Supra at 247.

NOTES

(1) If the majority opinion in *Varney* represents the traditional approach to judging definiteness in contracting, how would you characterize that approach? What is the difference between the majority and the dissent of Judge Cardozo?

(2) In Community Design Corporation v. Antonell, 459 So.2d 343 (Fla.App. 1984), an employer promised a specific bonus if an architect completed an indefinite amount of work. The court held the contract to be sufficiently definite to allow jury to give reasonable meaning to ambiguous terms. The court in *Community* distinguished *Varney* because a particular amount was offered. Is this a sufficient reason for enforcement?

(3) Should a different rule govern indefinite offers than covers indefinite contracts? Consider Ian Ayres and Robert Gertner, *Filling Gaps in Incomplete Contracts: An Economic Theory of Default Rules*, 99 Yale L.J. 87, 106 (1989):

> In applying the common-law standard that indefinite contracts are unenforceable, the [Lefkowitz] court ignored the likely market response to the non-enforceability default. [N]on-enforceability can be viewed as a penalty default that encourages both parties to come forward and fill in the gap; that is, refusing to enforce indefinite contracts drives out indefinite contracts. In Lefkowitz, however, the court's refusal to enforce the indefinite offer leads to exactly the opposite result. Ask yourself the simple question: What kind of ad is the Great Minneapolis Surplus Store going to run the week following the court's decision? By lending its imprimatur to the indefinite ad, the court allows retailers to induce inefficient consumer reliance with impunity. The Lefkowitz case dramatically illustrates that only by enforcing indefinite offers against the offeror can one drive out indefinite offers.

(4) In Schade v. Diethrich, 158 Ariz. 1, 760 P.2d 1050 (1988), an employer offered, in consideration of the employee's resignation, "a very generous and fair separation agreement that reflects the contributions that you have made to this organization, to the Institute, and to me over this 10 year period." Reluctant to resign, and doubtful of the employer's ability to be fair under the circumstances, the employee voiced his doubts to the employer's attorney. The latter proposed the appointment of a committee to recommend an appropriate severance package. The employee agreed to this. The committee recommended the payment of one year's salary as separation pay, plus compensation for untaken vacation time over the past two years. After the employer refused to abide by this recommendation, the employee sued. The Supreme Court of Arizona upheld the employee's claim. Finding that the parties clearly manifested an intention to be bound, any requirement of "reasonable certainty" is satisfied if the agreement provides "a basis for determining the existence of a breach and for giving an appropriate remedy." Restatement (Second) § 33(2). The court noted that the task here was made easier because it had the opinion of experts mutually selected by the parties.

(5) If a court is convinced that the parties have manifested an intention to be bound, should it, despite indefiniteness of expression, strive to resolve all questions of doubt on the basis of what seems fair and reasonable? Or would this amount to the court "making the contract for the parties"? Influenced by the Uniform Commercial Code and reflecting some modern precedent, Restatement (Second) § 33 sets forth the following standards for judging the impact of indefiniteness and open terms:

"(1) Even though a manifestation of intention is intended to be understood as an offer, it cannot be accepted so as to form a contract unless the terms of the contract are reasonably certain. (2) The terms of a contract are reasonably certain if they provide a basis for determining the existence of a breach and for giving an appropriate remedy. (3) The fact that one or more terms of a proposed bargain are left open or uncertain may show that a manifestation of intention is not intended to be understood as an offer or as an acceptance."

(6) *Varieties of Indefiniteness.* There is never a shortage of litigation contesting contractual validity on the basis of alleged indefiniteness of terms. Each term must, of course, be considered contextually, as Judge Cardozo insisted in *Varney.* But even when so considered, many fail to pass muster. For a sampling of contemporary litigation, see Union State Bank v. Woell, 434 N.W.2d 712 (N.D.1989) (promise of bank to provide future financing if borrower could market a particular product nationally); Roy v. Danis, 553 A.2d 663 (Me.1989) (promise of purchaser of transmission business to employ the seller for life to do "anything [purchaser] asked," such as "putting [seller] on the road * * * running errands"; promise of purchaser to seller that if latter started another shop, purchaser would "send him some work"); Trimmer v. Van Bomel, 107 Misc.2d 201, 434 N.Y.S.2d 82 (1980) (promise of wealthy widow to her former companion and paid escort to pay latter an amount sufficient to cover "costs and expenses for sumptuous living and maintenance for the remainder of his life"); Champaign National Bank v. Landers Seed Co., Inc., 165 Ill.App.3d 1090, 116 Ill.Dec. 742, 519 N.E.2d 957 (1988) (promise of bank not to collect on note "as long as [debtor] make[s] progress toward profitabili-

ty"); University National Bank v. Ernst & Whinney, 773 S.W.2d 707 (Tex.App. 1989) (promise of accounting firm to provide "loan supervision information" for bank); Cobble Hill Nursing Home, Inc. v. Henry and Warren, 74 N.Y.2d 475, 548 N.Y.S.2d 920, 548 N.E.2d 203 (1989) (promise of nursing home owner to sell property to New York Department of Health "at a price to be determined by the Department in accordance with the Public Health Law and all applicable rules and regulations of the Department"); Kane v. McDermott, 191 Ill.App.3d 212, 138 Ill.Dec. 541, 547 N.E.2d 708 (1989) (promise in option to sell property "at the appraised bid as established by three disinterested persons").

(7) In Hall v. Busst, a 1960 decision of the High Court of Australia (34 A.L.J.R. 332), the court considered the following "price term" of an option contained in a contract for the sale of an island off the coast of Queensland:

"The purchase price relating to such option shall be [13,157 4s.] to which shall be added the value of all additions and improvements to the said property since date of purchase by the Grantor (such value to be taken as at date of exercise of this option) and from which shall be subtracted the value of all deficiencies of chattel property and a reasonable sum to cover depreciation of all buildings and other property on the land." The majority found this to be too uncertain to be the basis of an enforceable contract. Dixon, C.J., observed:

"There could be no external standard of value of additions and improvements to the island: no standard yielding a figure reasonably fixed or ascertainable. Still less would it be possible to find an external standard for the reasonable sum to cover depreciation even if one knew what 'other property' is referred to. And indeed the value of deficiencies is another uncertain element in the ascertainment of the price. It is said that 'value' or 'fair value' is to be found objectively by a jury. But here we are dealing with substantive rights, not the procedure by which they are to be enforced. Can it be supposed that men contract to pay a price if and when fixed by a jury in a law suit?" (34 A.L.J.R. at 334–35).

WINDEYER, J., dissenting, disagreed:

"An offer to sell at a fair value might, of course, be no more than an offer to negotiate as to a price. But, if parties, intending to make a concluded contract of sale, agree that the sale shall be at a fair valuation of the property sold, they have fixed the price by reference to an ascertainable fact—the fair value. The value of any property, except commodities commonly bought and sold and having a current market price, may, in one sense, be always a matter of opinion unless there be some fixed or standard price; so that subjective considerations necessarily intrude into questions of value. Yet the law regards value as an ascertainable fact, and land no less than other forms of property as susceptible of valuation. The valuation of land and improvements upon land is, in fact, commonly undertaken for a variety of purposes, for example, for rating, or to determine compensation on a compulsory acquisition, or for trustees proposing to invest funds upon mortgage. I do not find any logical difficulty in the idea of a reasonable price for land in a system of law that by statute asserts that there is a reasonable price for goods of all kinds—for a picture, a racehorse, or an ancient vase, for examples, just as much as for a loaf of bread or a pound of tea."   34 A.L.J.R. at 344.

For a thorough and critical study of English and Commonwealth materials, see Ellinghaus, *Agreements Which Defer "Essential" Terms,* 45 Austr.L.J. 4–20, 72–82 (1971).

(C) INCOMPLETE AND DEFERRED AGREEMENT

Metro–Goldwyn–Mayer, Inc. v. Scheider

Court of Appeals of New York, 1976.
40 N.Y.2d 1069, 392 N.Y.S.2d 252, 360 N.E.2d 930.

■ PER CURIAM.

Following a nonjury trial and confronted with sometimes conflicting evidence, the court found that the parties had entered into an oral contract by which appellant had agreed to be principal actor in a pilot film and in the television series which might develop therefrom. After performing in the pilot and being fully compensated therefor, appellant refused to perform in the subsequent television series.

The core issue on this appeal is whether the determination that there was a complete contract between the parties is to be upheld. The negotiations of the parties extended over many weeks. Initially the broad outlines of the contract and its financial dimensions were agreed to in September, 1971, with explicit expectations that further agreements were to follow. Additional important provisions were negotiated over the following weeks. It was during this period that appellant went to Europe for the filming of the pilot. All culminated in supplemental agreements concluded in February, 1972. The only essential term as to which there was no finding of articulated understanding was the starting date for filming the television series. This term was supplied by a finding of the trial court based on proof of established custom and practice in the industry, of which both parties were found to be aware, set in the context of the other understandings reached by them. As Mr. Justice Arnold L. Fein wrote at Trial Term (75 Misc.2d 418, 422, 347 N.Y.S.2d 755, 761): "[W]here the parties have completed their negotiations of what they regard as essential elements, and performance has begun on the good faith understanding that agreement on the unsettled matters will follow, the court will find and enforce a contract even though the parties have expressly left these other elements for future negotiation and agreement, if some objective method of determination is available, independent of either party's mere wish or desire. Such objective criteria may be found in the agreement itself, commercial practice or other usage and custom. If the contract can be rendered certain and complete, by reference to something certain, the court will fill in the gaps" (see Restatement 2d, Contracts, § 230, esp. Comment *d*; § 247; Corbin, Contracts, § 95, pp. 401–404; cf. May Metropolitan Corp. v. May Oil Burner Corp., 290 N.Y. 260, 49 N.E.2d 13).

The findings of fact by the trial court were expressly approved and adopted at the Appellate Division. In this procedural posture such findings, supported as they are by evidence in this record, are now beyond the scope of our review.

Noting that the defense predicated in the courts below on the Statute of Frauds has been abandoned on the appeal to us, we have examined appellant's objection to the Appellate Division's remand for a second trial on the issue of damages and his other contentions and find them to be without merit.

Accordingly, the judgment of Supreme Court should be affirmed.

Joseph Martin, Jr., Delicatessen, Inc. v. Schumacher

Court of Appeals of New York, 1981.
52 N.Y.2d 105, 436 N.Y.S.2d 247, 417 N.E.2d 541.

■ FUCHSBERG, JUDGE.

This case raises an issue fundamental to the law of contracts. It calls upon us to review a decision of the Appellate Division, 70 A.D.2d 1, 419 N.Y.S.2d 558 which held that a realty lease's provision that the rent for a renewal period was "to be agreed upon" may be enforceable.

holdings - Appellate

The pertinent factual and procedural contexts in which the case reaches this court are uncomplicated. In 1973, the appellant, as landlord, leased a retail store to the respondent for a five-year term at a rent graduated upwards from $500 per month for the first year to $650 for the fifth. The renewal clause stated that "[t]he Tenant may renew this lease for an additional period of five years at annual rentals to be agreed upon; Tenant shall give Landlord thirty (30) days written notice, to be mailed certified mail, return receipt requested, of the intention to exercise such right". It is not disputed that the tenant gave timely notice of its desire to renew or that, once the landlord made it clear that he would do so only at a rental starting at $900 a month, the tenant engaged an appraiser who opined that a fair market rental value would be $545.41.

The tenant thereupon commenced an action for specific performance in Supreme Court, Suffolk County, to compel the landlord to extend the lease for the additional term at the appraiser's figure or such other sum as the court would decide was reasonable. For his part, the landlord in due course brought a holdover proceeding in the local District Court to evict the tenant. On the landlord's motion for summary judgment, the Supreme Court, holding that a bald agreement to agree on a future rental was unenforceable for uncertainty as a matter of law, dismissed the tenant's complaint. Concordantly, it denied as moot the tenant's motion to remove the District Court case to the Supreme Court and to consolidate the two suits.

It was on appeal by the tenant from these orders that the Appellate Division, expressly overruling an established line of cases in the process, reinstated the tenant's complaint and granted consolidation. In so doing, it reasoned that "a renewal clause in a lease providing for future agreement on the rent to be paid during the renewal term is enforceable if it is established that the parties' intent was not to terminate in the event of a failure to agree". It went on to provide that, if the tenant met that burden, the trial court could proceed to set a "reasonable rent". One of the Justices, concurring, would have eliminated the first step and required the trial court to proceed directly to the fixation of the rent. Each party now appeals by leave of the Appellate Division pursuant to CPLR 5602 (subd. [b], par. 1). The tenant seeks only a modification adopting the concurrer's position. The question formally certified to us by the Appellate Division is simply whether its order was properly made. Since we conclude that the disposition at the Supreme Court was the correct one, our answer must be in the negative.

We begin our analysis with the basic observation that, unless otherwise mandated by law (e.g., residential emergency rent control statutes), a contract is a private "ordering" in which a party binds himself to do, or not to do, a particular thing (Fletcher v. Peck, 6 Cranch [10 U.S.] 87, 136; 3 L.Ed. 162. Hart and Sachs, Legal Process, 147–148 [1958]). This liberty is no right at all if it is not accompanied by freedom not to contract. The corollary is that, before one may secure redress in our courts because another has failed to honor a promise, it must appear that the promisee assented to the obligation in question.

It also follows that, before the power of law can be invoked to enforce a promise, it must be sufficiently certain and specific so that what was promised can be ascertained. Otherwise, a court, in intervening, would be imposing its own conception of what the parties should or might have undertaken, rather than confining itself to the implementation of a bargain to which they have mutually committed themselves. Thus, definiteness as to material matters is of the very essence in contract law. Impenetrable vagueness and uncertainty will not do * * *.

Dictated by these principles, it is rightfully well settled in the common law of contracts in this State that a mere agreement to agree, in which a material term is left for future negotiations, is unenforceable (Willmott v. Giarraputo, 5 N.Y.2d 250, 253, 184 N.Y.S.2d 97, 157 N.E.2d 282; Sourwine v. Truscott, 17 Hun. 432, 434).* This is especially true of the amount to be paid for the sale or lease of real property * * *. The rule applies all the more, and not the less, when, as here, the extraordinary remedy of specific performance is sought * * *.

This is not to say that the requirement for definiteness in the case before us now could only have been met by explicit expression of the rent to be paid. The concern is with substance, not form. It certainly would have sufficed, for instance, if a methodology for determining the rent was to be

---

* Other States which are in accord include: Arkansas (Lutterloh v. Patterson, 211 Ark. 814, 202 S.W.2d 767); Maine (Metcalf Auto Co. v. Norton, 119 Me. 103, 109 A. 384); Missouri (State ex rel. Johnson v. Blair, 351 Mo. 1072, 174 S.W.2d 851); North Carolina (Young v. Sweet, 266 N.C. 623, 146 S.E.2d 669); Oregon (Karamanos v. Hamm, 267 Or. 1, 513 P.2d 761); and Rhode Island (Vartabe- dian v. Peerless Wrench Co., 46 R.I. 472, 129 A. 239). But see: Alaska (Hammond v. Ringstad, 10 Alaska 543); Arizona (Hall v. Weatherford, 32 Ariz. 370, 259 P. 282); California (Chaney v. Schneider, 92 Cal.App.2d 88, 206 P.2d 669); Ohio (Moss v. Olson, 148 Ohio St. 625, 76 N.E.2d 875); and Tennessee (Playmate Club v. Country Clubs, 62 Tenn.App. 383, 462 S.W.2d 890).

found within the four corners of the lease, for a rent so arrived at would have been the end product of agreement between the parties themselves. Nor would the agreement have failed for indefiniteness because it invited recourse to an objective extrinsic event, condition or standard on which the amount was made to depend. All of these, *inter alia,* would have come within the embrace of the maxim that what can be made certain is certain (9 Coke, 47a). * * *

But the renewal clause here in fact contains no such ingredients. Its unrevealing, unamplified language speaks to no more than "annual rentals to be agreed upon". Its simple words leave no room for legal construction or resolution of ambiguity. Neither tenant nor landlord is bound to any formula. There is not so much as a hint at a commitment to be bound by the "fair market rental value" which the tenant's expert reported or the "reasonable rent" the Appellate Division would impose, much less any definition of either. Nowhere is there an inkling that either of the parties directly or indirectly assented, upon accepting the clause, to subordinate the figure on which it ultimately would insist, to one fixed judicially, as the Appellate Division decreed be done, or, for that matter, by an arbitrator or other third party.

Finally in this context, we note that the tenant's reliance on May Metropolitan Corp. v. May Oil Burner Corp., 290 N.Y. 260, 49 N.E.2d 13 is misplaced. There the parties had executed a franchise agreement for the sale of oil burners. The contract provided for annual renewal, at which time each year's sales quota was "to be mutually agreed upon". In holding that the defendant's motion for summary judgment should have been denied, the court indicated that the plaintiff should be given an opportunity to establish that a series of annual renewals had ripened into a course of dealing from which it might be possible to give meaning to an otherwise uncertain term. This decision, in the more fluid sales setting in which it occurred, may be seen as a precursor to the subsequently enacted Uniform Commercial Code's treatment of open terms in contracts for the sale of goods (see Uniform Commercial Code, § 1–205, subd. [1]; § 2–204, subd. [3]; see, also, Restatement, Contracts 2d, § 249). As the tenant candidly concedes, the code, by its very terms, is limited to the sale of goods. The *May* case is therefore not applicable to real estate contracts. Stability is a hallmark of the law controlling such transactions * * *.

For all these reasons, the order of the Appellate Division should be reversed, with costs, and the orders of the Supreme Court, Suffolk County, reinstated. The certified question, therefore, should be answered in the negative. As to the plaintiff's appeal, since that party was not aggrieved by the order of the Appellate Division, the appeal should be dismissed (CPLR 5511), without costs.

■ MEYER, JUDGE (concurring).

While I concur in the result because the facts of this case do not fit the rule of May Metropolitan Corp. v. May Oil Burner Corp., 290 N.Y. 260, 49 N.E.2d 13, I cannot concur in the majority's rejection of that case as necessarily inapplicable to litigation concerning leases. That the setting of that case was commercial and that its principle is now incorporated in a statute (the Uniform Commercial Code) which by its terms is not applicable to real estate is irrelevant to the question whether the principle can be applied in real estate cases.

As we recognized in Farrell Lines v. City of New York, 30 N.Y.2d 76, 82, 330 N.Y.S.2d 358, 281 N.E.2d 162, quoting from A.Z.A. Realty Corp. v. Harrigan's Cafe, 113 Misc. 141, 147, 185 N.Y.S. 212: "An agreement of lease possesses no peculiar sanctity requiring the application of rules of construction different from those applicable to an ordinary contract." To the extent that the majority opinion can be read as holding that no course of dealing between the parties to a lease could make a clause providing for renewal at a rental "to be agreed upon" enforceable I do not concur.

■ JASEN, JUDGE (dissenting in part).

While I recognize that the traditional rule is that a provision for renewal of a lease must be "certain" in order to render it binding and enforceable, in my view the better rule would be that if the tenant can establish its entitlement to renewal under the lease, the mere presence of a provision calling for renewal at "rentals to be agreed upon" should not prevent judicial intervention to fix rent at a reasonable rate in order to avoid a forfeiture. Therefore, I would affirm the order of the Appellate Division for the reasons stated in the opinion of Justice Leon D. Lazer at the Appellate Division.

On defendant's appeal: Order reversed, with costs, the orders of Supreme Court, Suffolk County, reinstated and the question certified answered in the negative.

On plaintiff's appeal: Appeal dismissed, without costs.

NOTES

(1) *Agreement to Negotiate in Good Faith.* In Channel Home Centers, Division of Grace Retail Corporation v. Grossman, 795 F.2d 291 (3d Cir.1986), a retailer negotiated with a mall developer for a lease. The parties executed a detailed "letter of intent," containing a commitment by the developer "to withdraw the Store from the rental market, and only negotiate the above described leasing transaction to completion." The letter of intent specified, however, that execution of the lease was expressly subject to approval by the retailer's parent corporation. Negotiations were cut off after the developer made a deal with a competitor of the retailer at a substantially higher rental than that contemplated in the letter of intent. In concluding that there was sufficient evidence to support a finding that the parties intended to enter into "a binding agreement to negotiate in good faith," the court stated:

> It is hornbook law that evidence of preliminary negotiations or an agreement to enter into a binding contract in the future does not alone constitute a contract. * * * [Developer believes] that this doctrine settles this case, but, in so arguing, [developer misconstrues retailer's] contract claim. [Retailer] does not contend that the letter of intent is binding as a lease or an agreement to enter into a lease. Rather, it is [retailer's] position

that this document is enforceable as a mutually binding obligation *to negotiate in good faith.* By unilaterally terminating negotiations with [retailer] and precipitously entering into a lease agreement with Mr. Good Buys, [retailer] argues, [developer] acted in bad faith and breached his promise to "withdraw the Store from the rental market and only negotiate the above-described leasing transaction to completion." * * *

Under Pennsylvania law, the test for enforceability of an agreement is whether both parties have manifested an intention to be bound by its terms and whether the terms are sufficiently definite to be specifically enforced. * * * Additionally, of course, there must be consideration on both sides. * * *

Although no Pennsylvania court has considered whether an agreement to negotiate in good faith may meet these conditions, the jurisdictions that have considered the issue have held that such an agreement, if otherwise meeting the requisites of a contract is an enforceable contract. See, e.g., *Thompson v. Liquichimica of America, Inc.,* 481 F.Supp. 365, 366 (S.D.N.Y. 1979); ("Unlike an agreement to agree, which does not constitute a closed proposition, an agreement to use best efforts [or to negotiate in good faith] is a closed proposition, discrete and actionable."); *accord Reprosystem, B.V. v. SCM Corp.,* 727 F.2d 257, 264 (2d Cir.1984); *Chase v. Consolidated Foods Corp.,* 744 F.2d 566, 571 (7th Cir.1984); *Arnold Palmer Golf Co. v. Fuqua Industries, Inc.,* 541 F.2d 584 (6th Cir.1976); *Itek Corp. v. Chicago Aerial Industries, Inc.,* 248 A.2d 625 (Del.1968); Restatement (Second) of Contracts § 205 comment (c) (1979) ("Good faith in negotiation"); see generally Kessler and Fine, *Culpa in Contrahendo, Bargaining in Good Faith, and Freedom of Contract, a Comparative Study,* 77 Harv.L.Rev. 401 (1984). We are satisfied that Pennsylvania would follow this rule.

795 F.2d at 298, 291 (footnotes omitted). See also Arcadian Phosphates, Inc. v. Arcadian Corporation, 884 F.2d 69 (2d Cir.1989) (even if preliminary agreement not binding may be able to base promissory estoppel claim on promise to negotiate in good faith).

(2) *Contract to Bargain.* In an excellent article, Professor Charles Knapp has analyzed transactions where final agreement has been delayed either to await the occurrence of future events which control future agreement (agreement to agree). He argues that in cases like these where the parties have reached agreement to such a degree that they regard themselves as bound to each other, neither can withdraw for an "unjustified" reason yet neither can be compelled to perform if, after good faith bargaining, actual agreement cannot be reached. Thus is created a "contract to bargain" which stresses that unjustified withdrawals will give rise to appropriate contract remedies but that essential obligations are met by bargaining in good faith for as long as may reasonably be required under the circumstances. See Knapp, *Enforcing the Contract to Bargain,* 44 N.Y.U.L.Rev. 673 (1969).

(3) *Written Contract Intended.* Suppose it is clear that both parties to a negotiation contemplate that their final agreement will be reduced to writing and signed by both of them. Suppose, further, that the parties reach sufficient agreement to conclude a contract but that one of them withdraws from the relationship before the writing is signed. Is there a contract? If the parties have explicitly stated that they do not intend to be bound until the writing is signed,

the answer is no. The writing clearly is a condition precedent to liability. Even without an explicit condition, the question is still whether parties who contemplate a written memorial of the agreement intend that event to occur before a contract is formed. See, e.g., Asbestos Products, Inc. v. Healy Mechanical Contractors, 306 Minn. 74, 235 N.W.2d 807 (1975); Pennsylvania Co. v. Wilmington Trust Co., 39 Del.Ch. 453, 166 A.2d 726 (1960); Smith v. Onyx Oil and Chemical Co., 218 F.2d 104 (3d Cir.1955); Knapp, *Enforcing the Contract to Bargain*, 44 N.Y.U.L.Rev. 673, 716–719 (1969). But how is this intention to be ascertained? A Second Circuit case, applying New York law, gives the following criteria: "We have articulated several factors that help determine whether the parties intended to be bound in the absence of a document executed by both sides. The court is to consider (1) whether there has been an express reservation of the right not to be bound in the absence of a writing; (2) whether there has been partial performance of the contract; (3) whether all of the terms of the alleged contract have been agreed upon; and (4) whether the agreement at issue is the type of contract that is usually committed to writing." Winston v. Mediafare Entertainment Corporation, 777 F.2d 78, 80 (2d Cir.1985).

Oglebay Norton Company v. Armco, Inc.

Supreme Court of Ohio, 1990.
52 Ohio St.3d 232, 556 N.E.2d 515.

On January 9, 1957, Armco Steel Corporation, n.k.a. Armco, Inc., appellant, entered into a long-term contract with Columbia Transportation Company, which later became a division of Oglebay Norton Company, appellee. The principal term of this contract required Oglebay to have adequate shipping capacity available and Armco to utilize such shipping capacity if Armco wished to transport iron ore on the Great Lakes from mines in the Lake Superior district to Armco's plants in the lower Great Lakes region.

In the 1957 contract, Armco and Oglebay established a primary and a secondary price rate mechanism which stated:

"*Armco agrees to pay* * * * for all iron ore transported hereunder *the regular net contract rates for the season* in which the ore is transported, *as recognized by the leading iron ore shippers* in such season for the transportation of iron ore * * *. If, in any season of navigation hereunder, *there is no regular net contract rate recognized by the leading iron ore shippers* for such transportation, *the parties shall mutually agree upon a rate* for such transportation, *taking into consideration the contract rate being charged for similar transportation* by the leading independent vessel operators engaged in transportation of iron ore from The Lake Superior District." (Emphasis added.)

During the next twenty-three years, Armco and Oglebay modified the 1957 contract four times. With each modification Armco agreed to extend the time span of the contracts beyond the original date. Both parties acknowledged that the ever-increasing requirements capacity Armco sought from Oglebay would require a substantial capital investment from Oglebay to maintain, upgrade, and purchase iron ore carrier vessels.

The fourth amendment, signed in 1980, required Oglebay to modify and upgrade its fleet to give each Oglebay vessel that Armco utilized a self-unloading capability.[1] It is undisputed that Oglebay began a $95 million capital improvement program at least in part to accommodate Armco's new shipping needs. For its part, Armco agreed to pay an additional twenty-five cents per ton for ore shipped in Oglebay's self-unloading vessels[2] and agreed to extend the running of the contract until December 31, 2010.

During trial, the court recognized Armco's and Oglebay's close and long-standing business relationship, which included a seat for Armco on Oglebay's Board of Directors, Armco's owning Oglebay Norton stock, and a partnership in another venture. In fact, one of Oglebay's vessels was named "The Armco."

This relationship is perhaps best characterized by the language contained in the 1962 amendment, wherein the parties provided:

"* * * Armco has a vital and unique interest in the continued dedication of * * * [Oglebay's] bulk vessel fleet * * * since such service is a necessary prerequisite to Armco's operation as a major steel producer. * * * Armco's right to require the dedication of * * * [Oglebay's] bulk vessels to Armco's service * * * is the essence of this Agreement[.] * * *." The amendment also granted to Armco the right to seek a court order for specific performance of the terms of the contract.

From 1957 through 1983 the parties established the contract shipping rate that Oglebay charged Armco by referring to a specified rate published in "Skillings Mining Review," in accordance with the 1957 contract's primary price mechanism. The published rate usually represented the price that Innerlake Steamship Company, a leading independent iron ore shipper, charged its customers for a similar service. Oglebay would quote this rate to Armco, which would then pay it to Oglebay.

Unfortunately, in 1983 the iron and steel industry suffered a serious downturn in business. Thus, in late 1983, when Oglebay quoted Armco the shipping rate for the 1984 season, Armco challenged that rate. Due to its weakened economic position, Armco requested that Oglebay reduce the rate Oglebay was going to charge Armco. The parties then negotiated a mutually satisfactory rate for the 1984 season.

In late 1984 the parties were unable to establish a mutually satisfactory shipping rate for the 1985 season. Oglebay billed Armco $7.66 ($.25 self-unloading vessel surcharge included) per gross ton, and Armco reduced the invoice amount to $5 per gross ton. Armco then paid the $5 per ton figure, indicating payment in full language on the check to Oglebay, and explaining its position in an accompanying letter. In late 1985, the parties again

---

1. A self-unloading vessel has the capability to unload without the assistance of cranes and crews standing by on dockside. This capability somewhat lessens cargo capacity but allows the vessel more freedom from docking restraints.

2. The twenty-five cents per gross ton differential was a standard rate charged by Columbia and Oglebay Norton to its shipping customers for use of its self-unloading vessels.

attempted to negotiate a rate, this time for the 1986 season. Again they failed to reach a mutually satisfactory rate.

On April 11, 1986, Oglebay filed a declaratory judgment action requesting the court to declare the rate set forth in the contract to be the correct rate, or in the absence of such a rate, to declare a reasonable rate for Oglebay's services. Armco's answer denied that the $7.41 rate sought by Oglebay was the "contract rate," and denied that the trial court had jurisdiction to declare this rate of its own accord, as a "reasonable rate" or otherwise.

During the 1986 season, Oglebay continued to ship iron ore for Armco. Armco paid Oglebay $4.22 per gross ton for ore shipped prior to August 1, 1986 and $3.85 per gross ton for ore shipped after August 1, 1986.

On August 12, 1987, Armco filed a supplemental counterclaim[3] seeking a declaration that the contract was no longer enforceable, because the contract had failed of its purpose due to the complete breakdown of the rate pricing mechanisms.

After a lengthy bench trial, the trial court on November 20, 1987 issued its declaratory judgment, which made four basic findings of fact and law. First, the court held that it was apparent from the evidence presented that Oglebay and Armco intended to be bound by the 1957 contract, even though the rate or price provisions in the contract were not settled.

Second, the court held that where the parties intended to be bound, but where a service contract pricing mechanism based upon the mutual agreement of the parties fails, "* * * then the price shall be the price that is 'reasonable' under all the circumstances at the time the service is rendered."

Third, the trial court held that the parties must continue to comply with the alternative pricing provision contained within paragraph two of the 1957 contract. That alternative pricing provision mandates that the parties consider rates charged for similar services by leading independent iron ore vessel operators.

Fourth, the trial court held that if the parties were unable to agree upon a rate for the upcoming seasons, then the parties must notify the court immediately. Upon such notification, the court, through its equitable jurisdiction, would appoint a mediator and require the parties' chief executive officers "* * * to meet for the purpose of mediating and determining the rate for such season, i.e., that they 'mutually agree upon a rate.'"

The court of appeals affirmed the judgment of the trial court.

The cause is now before the court upon the allowance of a motion to certify the record.

■ PER CURIAM.

3. According to the trial court, Armco withdrew its first counterclaim in open court at trial.

This case presents three mixed questions of fact and law. First, did the parties intend to be bound by the terms of this contract despite the failure of its primary and secondary pricing mechanisms? Second, if the parties did intend to be bound, may the trial court establish $6.25 per gross ton as a reasonable rate for Armco to pay Oglebay for shipping Armco ore during the 1986 shipping season? Third, may the trial court continue to exercise its equitable jurisdiction over the parties, and may it order the parties to utilize a mediator if they are unable to mutually agree on a shipping rate for each annual shipping season? We answer each of these questions in the affirmative and for the reasons set forth below affirm the decision of the court of appeals.

I

Appellant Armco argues that the complete breakdown of the primary and secondary contract pricing mechanisms renders the 1957 contract unenforceable, because the parties never manifested an intent to be bound in the event of the breakdown of the primary and secondary pricing mechanisms. Armco asserts that it became impossible after 1985 to utilize the first pricing mechanism in the 1957 contract, i.e., examining the published rate for a leading shipper in the "Skillings Mining Review," because after 1985 a new rate was no longer published. Armco asserts as well that it also became impossible to obtain the information necessary to determine and take into consideration the rates charged by leading independent vessel operators in accordance with the secondary pricing mechanism. This is because that information was no longer publicly available after 1985 and because the trial court granted the motions to quash of nonparties, who were subpoenaed to obtain this specific information.[4] Armco argues that since the parties never consented to be bound by a contract whose specific pricing mechanisms had failed, the trial court should have declared the contract to be void and unenforceable.

The trial court recognized the failure of the 1957 contract pricing mechanisms. Yet the trial court had competent, credible evidence before it to conclude that the parties intended to be bound despite the failure of the pricing mechanisms. The evidence demonstrated the long-standing and close business relationship of the parties, including joint ventures, interlocking directorates and Armco's ownership of Oglebay stock. As the trial court pointed out, the parties themselves contractually recognized Armco's vital and unique interest in the combined dedication of Oglebay's bulk

---

4. Oglebay Norton sought subpoenas from independent vessel operators and captive fleets to obtain information about rates those carriers were charging for the transportation of iron ore to lower lake ports. The other carriers resisted the subpoenas, requesting that the court quash the subpoenas or issue a protective order. The subpoenas were quashed prior to trial. The trial court's reasons for sustaining the motion to quash rather than issuing a protective order are unclear. It would appear that such information taken pursuant to a protective order under Civ.R. 26(C) might have been appropriate, given the dearth of reliable information concerning past and future controversies regarding rates.

vessel fleet, and the parties recognized that Oglebay could be required to ship up to 7.1 million gross tons of Armco iron ore per year.

Whether the parties intended to be bound, even upon the failure of the pricing mechanisms, is a question of fact properly resolved by the trier of fact. Normandy Place Assoc. v. Beyer (1982), 2 Ohio St.3d 102, 106, 2 OBR 653, 656, 443 N.E.2d 161, 164. Since the trial court had ample evidence before it to conclude that the parties did so intend, the court of appeals correctly affirmed the trial court regarding the parties' intent. We thus affirm the court of appeals on this question.

II

Armco also argues that the trial court lacked jurisdiction to impose a shipping rate of $6.25 per gross ton when that rate did not conform to the 1957 contract pricing mechanisms. The trial court held that it had the authority to determine a reasonable rate for Oglebay's services, even though the price mechanism of the contract had failed, since the parties intended to be bound by the contract. The court cited 1 Restatement of the Law 2d, Contracts (1981) 92, Section 33, and its relevant comments to support this proposition. Comment *e* to Section 33 explains in part:

"* * * Where * * * [the parties] * * * intend to conclude a contract for the sale of goods * * * and the price is not settled, the price is a reasonable price at the time of delivery if * * * (c) the price is to be fixed in terms of some agreed market or other standard as set or recorded by a third person or agency and it is not so set or recorded. Uniform Commercial Code § 2–305(1)." Id. at 94–95.

As the trial court noted, Section 33 was cited with approval by the Court of Appeals for Cuyahoga County in Mr. Mark Corp. v. Rush, Inc. (1983), 11 Ohio App.3d 167, 11 OBR 259, 464 N.E.2d 586, and in North Coast Cookies, Inc. v. Sweet Temptations, Inc. (1984), 16 Ohio App.3d 342, 16 OBR 391, 476 N.E.2d 388. Restatement Section 33, Comment *e* follows virtually identical language contained in Section 2–305(1) of the Uniform Commercial Code, which was adopted in Ohio as R.C. 1302.18(A). Moreover the Court of Appeals for Cuyahoga County applied R.C. 1302.18 by analogy to a contract for services involving an open price term in Winning Sheet Metal Mfg. Co. v. Heat Sealing Equip. Mfg. Co. (Sept. 30, 1982), Cuyahoga App. No. 44365, unreported, at 3–4, 1982 WL 5944.

The court therefore determined that a reasonable rate for Armco to pay to Oglebay for transporting Armco's iron ore during the 1986 shipping season was $6.00 per gross ton with an additional rate of twenty-five cents per gross ton when self-unloading vessels were used. The court based this determination upon the parties' extensive course of dealing, "* * * the detriment to the parties respectively, and valid comparisons of market price which reflect [the] economic reality of current depressed conditions in the American steel industry."

The court of appeals concluded that the trial court was justified in setting $6.25 per gross ton as a "reasonable rate" for Armco to pay Oglebay for the 1986 season, given the evidence presented to the trial court concerning various rates charged in the industry and given the intent of the parties to be bound by the agreement.

The court of appeals also held that an open price term could be filled by a trial court, which has the authority to review evidence and establish a "reasonable price," when the parties clearly intended to be bound by the contract. To support this holding, the court cited Restatement of the Law 2d, Contracts, supra, at 92, Section 33, and its comments, and 179, Section 362, and its comments.

Section 33, Comment *a* provides in part:

"* * * [T]he actions of the parties may show conclusively that they have intended to conclude a binding agreement, even though one or more terms are missing or are left to be agreed upon. In such cases courts endeavor, if possible, to attach a sufficiently definite meaning to the bargain.

"An offer which appears to be indefinite may be given precision by usage of trade or by course of dealing between the parties. Terms may be supplied by factual implication, and in recurring situations the law often supplies a term in the absence of agreement to the contrary. * * *" Id. at 92.

As the court of appeals noted, we have held that "agreements to agree," such as the pricing mechanisms in the 1957 contract, are enforceable when the parties have manifested an intention to be bound by their terms and when these intentions are sufficiently definite to be specifically enforced. Normandy Place Assoc., supra, 2 Ohio St.3d at 105–106, 2 OBR at 656, 443 N.E.2d at 164. We have also held that "[i]f it is found that the parties intended to be bound, the court should not frustrate this intention, if it is reasonably possible to fill in some gaps that the parties have left, and reach a fair and just result." Litsinger Sign Co. v. American Sign Co. (1967), 11 Ohio St.2d 1, 14, 40 O.O.2d 30, 37, 227 N.E.2d 609, 619.

The court of appeals conducted an extensive review of the evidence presented to the trial court and concluded that the $6.25 per gross ton figure was a "reasonable rate" in this situation. The court of appeals noted that Oglebay presented evidence from Jesse J. Friedman, an economic and financial expert, who testified that $7.44 per gross ton was a reasonable rate for such services. Further evidence showed that Armco paid $5.00 per gross ton to Oglebay for the 1985 season, even though the published rate for that season was $7.41 per gross ton.

There was also testimony that Oglebay quoted Armco $5.66 per gross ton as the rate for the 1987 season. The evidence also showed that LTV Steel, prior to its bankruptcy renegotiations with Oglebay, had paid Oglebay the published rate of $7.41 per gross ton. Evidence also indicated that American Steamship Co. had quoted Armco a $5.90 per gross ton rate for the 1986 season.

The court of appeals concluded that the $6.25 per gross ton figure fell acceptably between the rate range extremes proven at trial. The court found this to be a reasonable figure. We find there was competent, credible evidence in the record to support this holding and affirm the court of appeals on this question.

III

Armco also argues that the trial court lacks equitable jurisdiction to order the parties to negotiate or in the failure of negotiations, to mediate, during each annual shipping season through the year 2010. The court of appeals ruled that the trial court did not exceed its jurisdiction in issuing such an order.

3 Restatement of the Law 2d, Contracts (1981) 179, Section 362, entitled "Effect of Uncertainty of Terms," is similar in effect to Section 33 and states:

"Specific performance or an injunction will not be granted unless the terms of the contract are sufficiently certain to provide a basis for an appropriate order."

Comment *b* to Section 362 explains:

"* * * Before concluding that the required certainty is lacking, however, a court will avail itself of all of the usual aids in determining the scope of the agreement. * * * Expressions that at first appear incomplete may not appear so after resort to usage * * * or the addition of a term supplied by law * * *." Id. at 179.

Ordering specific performance of this contract was necessary, since, as the court of appeals pointed out, "* * * the undisputed dramatic changes in the market prices of great lakes shipping rates and the length of the contract would make it impossible for a court to award Oglebay accurate damages due to Armco's breach of the contract." We agree with the court of appeals that the appointment of a mediator upon the breakdown of court-ordered contract negotiations neither added to nor detracted from the parties' significant obligations under the contract.

It is well-settled that a trial court may exercise its equitable jurisdiction and order specific performance if the parties intend to be bound by a contract, where determination of long-term damages would be too speculative. See 3 Restatement of the Law 2d, Contracts, supra, at 171–172, Section 360(a), Comment *b*; Columbus Packing Co. v. State, ex rel. Schlesinger (1919), 100 Ohio St. 285, 294, 126 N.E. 291, 293–294. Indeed, the court of appeals pointed out that under the 1962 amendment, Armco itself had the contractual right to seek a court order compelling Oglebay to specifically perform its contractual duties.

The court of appeals was correct in concluding that ordering the parties to negotiate and mediate during each shipping season for the duration of the contract was proper, given the unique and long-lasting business relationship between the parties, and given their intent to be bound and the difficulty of properly ascertaining damages in this case. The court of appeals was also correct in concluding that ordering the parties to negotiate and mediate with each shipping season would neither add to nor detract from the parties' significant contractual obligations. This is because the order would merely facilitate in the most practical manner the parties' own ability to interact under the contract. Thus we affirm the court of appeals on this question.

The court of appeals had before it competent, credible evidence from which to conclude that the parties intended to be bound by the terms of the contract, to conclude that the $6.25 per gross ton figure was a "reasonable rate" under the circumstances, and to conclude that the trial court's exercise of continuing equitable jurisdiction was proper in this situation. Accordingly, we affirm the decision of the court of appeals.

Judgment affirmed.

NOTES

(1) *A UCC Perspective on Indefiniteness and Open Terms.* The traditional common law approach to questions of indefiniteness is epitomized in the recurring statement that the courts will not make a contract for the parties. Courts have been disinclined to fill gaps in the manifestations of the parties by enforcing some judicially approved standard (reasonable price, etc.). Similarly, despite evident intention to be bound, so-called agreements to agree have generally been held to be unenforceable.

In the business context, various types of escalator clauses (e.g., rent geared to gross receipts, wages scaled to cost of living index, price tied to specified market quotation) have been utilized to protect against invalidation of an agreement on account of open terms. Critics have insisted that the traditional approach does not comport with commercial expectations and is inadequate to satisfy legitimate commercial needs. One writer has commented as follows: "This pre-Code view was troublesome, particularly as it applied to business transactions. Indefiniteness in such transactions may occur in one of several ways. Frequently, parties arrive at an agreement in a piecemeal fashion and after a lengthy series of negotiations. Although the parties intend to be bound, they inadvertently fail to specify all terms. In addition, it is not unusual for parties not to specify essential terms, such as price, at the time the agreement is made because performance is to occur in the distant future. Under these circumstances, they do not want to be bound in the future by terms established at the time of contracting. It is also common in some industries that the parties are not able at the time of entering into an agreement to set all the terms. It is understood by them that the terms will be established according to prevailing industry standards during the performance of the agreement." Edwards, *Contract Formation Under Article 2 of the Uniform Commercial Code*, 61 Marq. L.Rev. 215, 219 (1977). *Oglebay* is illustrative.

The Uniform Commercial Code breaks decisively with the traditional approach. UCC 2–204(3) [UCC 2–203(c)(1997)], which states the basic principle as to open terms agreements underlying other sections, reads as follows: "Even though one or more terms are left open a contract for sale does not fail for indefiniteness if the parties have intended to make a contract and there is a reasonably certain basis for giving an appropriate remedy."

Subsection (3) establishes two standards: viz. (1) the parties must have intended to make a contract; (2) there must be a reasonably certain basis for giving an appropriate remedy. Compliance with the first standard is judged primarily with reference to other Code provisions dealing with intent to contract; viz., UCC 2–204(1), UCC 2–206 and UCC 2–207 [UCC 2–203(a), 2–205 and 2–207 (1997)]. Enforcement hinges upon whether the parties completed their preliminary negotiations or intended that agreement on the open terms was to be a condition of contractual obligation. The second test, as elaborated in the Code comments, is not one of certainty as to what the parties were to do nor as to the exact amount of damages due the plaintiff. The fact that one or more terms are left to be agreed is not enough of itself to defeat an otherwise adequate agreement. Commercial standards on the point of indefiniteness are to be applied. For an indication of the importance of commercial context in judging requisite definiteness, see Riegel Fiber Corp. v. Anderson Gin Co., 512 F.2d 784 (5th Cir.1975) ("We think [the evidence] clearly makes out a prima facie case that the quantity terms . . . conform to acceptable practice in the cotton trade." 512 F.2d at 792); Bornstein v. Somerson, 341 So.2d 1043 (Fla.App.1977) ("Despite its common use, this 'Purchase Agreement and Contract' could, in another factual context, be held void for indefiniteness. . . . We would suggest that the nature of the citrus industry requires many factors to be left open in sales contracts for future crops." 341 So.2d at 1048, n. 10); Allied Disposal, Inc. v. Bob's Home Service, Inc., 595 S.W.2d 417 (Mo.App.1980) ("The distinctive nature of some contracts has caused courts to uphold them even where there is no more than an agreement to agree on price. . . . Here it is apparent from the allegations that the parties intended to contract. They operated under that contract for several months and the petition does not reflect that the allegedly vague term has been a subject of controversy. The nature of the business [use of waste disposal site] is unusual and is subject to extensive state regulation." 595 S.W.2d at 420, 421). Other sections of the Code provide useful "gap fillers" for missing terms. See infra at 409.

Obviously, liability and remedy issues are often intertwined in disputes over indefiniteness. The agreement may be too indefinite to warrant specific performance but not money damages, or, as in *Oglebay,* the court may, in the exercise of its equitable jurisdiction, appoint a mediator and order the parties to negotiate. Similarly, damages measured by lost expectations may be unwarranted, but not damages measured by costs reasonably incurred in reliance upon the other's promise. Finally, the plaintiff should have a restitutionary remedy for the value of benefits conferred on the defendant through part performance.

(2) *The Effect of an "Agreement To Agree" under the UCC and Restatement (Second).* Suppose, in an agreement for the sale of goods, the parties apparently concluded their negotiations but explicitly left the quantity and the price of the described goods "to be agreed." Later, the seller refused to negotiate over the terms and the deal fell through. Did the seller breach a "contract" for the sale of goods? With regard to the *quantity* term, the general standard of UCC 2–204(3) [UCC 2–203(c) (1997)] applies: "Even though one or more terms are left open a contract for sale does not fail for indefiniteness if the parties have intended to make a contract and there is a reasonably certain basis for giving an appropriate remedy." It is possible that the parties may have intended to contract on these facts, but such sturdy stuff as trade usage, or a prior course of dealing or performance by both parties under the contract would

be required to support the inference of intent. Even so, if the parties have not agreed, from what source shall the court derive a quantity term to supply in the agreement? As interpreted, the Statute of Frauds, Section 2–201(1) [UCC 2–201(a)(1997)], limits enforcement to the quantity of goods shown in the writing (what is "shown" by an agreement to agree?), and the problems of determining a reasonable quantity term in the absence of some agreement are virtually insuperable. Thus, even with an intent to contract, lack of agreement on the quantity term should support a conclusion that the contract failed "for indefiniteness." In short, there was no "reasonably certain basis for giving an appropriate remedy."

With regard to the *price* term, the particular standard is supplied by Section 2–305 [UCC 2–303 (1997)]. If the parties intend "not to be bound unless the price be fixed or agreed and it is not fixed or agreed there is no contract." UCC 2–305(4). If the requisite intent is present and the "price is left to be agreed by the parties and they fail to agree," the "price is a reasonable price at the time for delivery." UCC 2–305(1)(b). At this point, Section 2–305 is not concerned with why the parties failed to agree or with whether either or both of them negotiated in good faith. The fact of a failure to agree coupled with the requisite intent to contract justifies the court's intervention to fill the "gap" with a "reasonable price." Although it is easier for a court to ascertain reasonable price than reasonable quantity, success is not guaranteed. Thus, in North Central Airlines, Inc. v. Continental Oil Co., 574 F.2d 582 (D.C.Cir. 1978), a contract for the sale of oil failed for indefiniteness when the agreed pricing standard became inoperable and there was no reasonable basis for determining a substitute price. But see D.R. Curtis, Co. v. Mathews, 103 Idaho 776, 653 P.2d 1188 (App.1982), where the court upheld the trial court's substitute price, determined after the parties failed to agree, as not unreasonable. See also Vigano v. Wylain, Inc., 633 F.2d 522, 526–27 (8th Cir.1980) (enforcing a contract where the seller agreed "to sell and deliver to Distributor at their current prices, and upon such terms as may be agreed between the parties"); Schmieder v. Standard Oil Co. of Indiana, 69 Wis.2d 419, 230 N.W.2d 732 (1975) (enforcing option to purchase goods at "agent's cost" less "such depreciation as may be mutually agreed upon"); H.C. Schmieding Produce Co. v. Cagle, 529 So.2d 243 (Ala.1988) ("market price at time of delivery" not too indefinite in contract for the sale of seed potatoes).

Restatement (Second) contains rules and standards intended to cover all exchange transactions, not just contracts for the sale of goods. Further, Restatement (Second) does not explicitly provide different rules for different transactions. Thus, unlike the opinion of Judge Fuchsberg in the *Schumacher* case, *supra,* there is no attempt to suggest that the need for security in real estate transactions dictates a different approach to the "agreement to agree" issue than in the more "fluid" sale of goods situation. How, then, might a case like *Schumacher* be decided under Restatement (Second)? Again, the first question would be whether leaving the rent on renewal "to be agreed" precluded contract formation. Section 33(3) states that leaving such a term "open or uncertain may show that a manifestation of intention is not intended to be understood as an offer or as an acceptance." Although the agreement to agree may "strongly indicate that the parties do not intend to be bound," see Illustration 8 to Section 33, the course of performance of the parties and the lessee's not unreasonable reliance under the first lease clearly answer that question in the affirmative. If, then, the parties intended to be bound and failed to agree, Restatement (Second), like the UCC, directs the court to enforce the renewal lease if the terms are "reasonably certain." See Sections 33(1) & (2) and 34. The terms of a contract are "reasonably certain if they provide a basis for determining the existence of a breach and for giving an appropriate remedy." Section 33(2). Part performance under an agreement "may remove uncertainty," Section 34(2), or, because it is reliance on the contract, part performance or other action "may make a contractual remedy appropriate even though uncertainty is not removed." Section 34(2). Finally, Section 204 provides:

> When the parties to a bargain sufficiently defined to be a contract have not agreed with respect to a term which is essential to a determination of their rights and duties, a term which is reasonable in the circumstances is supplied by the court.

It is clear, is it not, that Restatement (Second) would dictate a different result than that reached by the court in *Schumacher*? The parties intended to contract. Although the performance of the parties did not provide a basis for agreement on the renewal price, the lessee's reliance on the option to renew was reasonable. A fair market value for the leasehold interest could be determined with reasonable certainty. Finally, the lessor, by insisting upon a rental some $300 over the fair rental value, may be negotiating in bad faith. Cumulatively, don't these factors support the intervention of the court to supply a reasonable term over the "freedom from contract" argument advanced by Judge Fuchsberg?

(3) Questions of indefiniteness frequently arise in contracts to lease, see Annot., 85 A.L.R.3d 414 (1978), the exercise of an option to renew a lease, see Annot., 58 A.L.R.3d 500 (1974), and in the interpretation of rent adjustment clauses contained in the lease, see Annot., 87 A.L.R.3d 986 (1978). See also George Backer Management Corp. v. Acme Quilting Co., 46 N.Y.2d 211, 413 N.Y.S.2d 135, 385 N.E.2d 1062 (1978). The tension here, as in other cases of indefiniteness, is between asserted "rules" that require full and complete agreement on all material terms before the agreement is enforceable and the standards, announced by the UCC and Restatement (Second), that turn the question of enforceability upon both the intention of the parties and the ability of the court to supply a "reasonable" term to fill the gap. What are the advantages and disadvantages of the competing approaches? What values are at stake? Should the UCC approach be extended to all exchange transactions? Professor Speidel, in discussing the UCC approach, has stated:

> A more complete triumph of standards over rules is hard to imagine. Furthermore, such standards as 'intention to conclude a contract,' 'reasonable price,' and 'reasonably certain basis' for enforcement require particularization within the commercial circumstances made relevant by the definition of agreement. * * * [T]his method reflects Llewellyn's view that the law of the transaction is imbedded in the total situation and that the task of the 'law authority' is to discover it. Law is 'immanent' in existing patterns of conduct or relationships and, when discovered, provides a more reliable source of certainty than does the rigid, external system of classical contract law. The problem with standards is that they may lead the court to water without explaining how to drink. * * * [T]he drafters of the Code

left off at critical points, leaving the judge to fill in from what the parties could extract from the commercial context. * * * [T]he method pointed to the commercial context without clarifying how the diverse data were to be assembled and used. (Footnotes omitted.)

Speidel, *Restatement Second: Omitted Terms and Contract Method,* 67 Cornell L.Rev. 785, 791–92 (1982).

Comment: Open Terms Other Than Price

[The following is reprinted from Nordstrom, Handbook of the Law of Sales 105–10 (1970).]

There are a number of Code sections, other than the one dealing with open price contracts, which supply content to incomplete agreements. Many of these sections are discussed later in this text. Some, however, can be conveniently grouped under two hypothetical cases.

Case # 1. Seller manufactures men's shoes; buyer owns and operates a large chain of retail stores which sells men's shoes. Two weeks ago buyer and seller agreed as follows: seller promised to sell to buyer 10,000 pairs of shoes and buyer promised to pay to seller $55,000 for the shoes. The two parties signed a writing which was sufficient to satisfy the statute of frauds but which contained only the terms set out above. This is the first time that this buyer and seller have dealt with each other, and there are no trade customs which affect any portion of this transaction.

It is readily admitted that Case # 1 is, indeed, "hypothetical." The more normal case would involve a writing (or writings) which would fill out many terms of the basic agreement reached in Case # 1. Such a writing would probably contain terms on whether the goods are to be delivered at one time or in installments, the time and place of delivery, credit terms (if any), as well as other details applicable to this transaction. However, Case # 1—with its skeletal agreement—was chosen as a basis for presenting several Code sections which give content to the parties' agreement.

Most of the sections applicable to Case # 1 begin with the familiar "unless otherwise agreed," the following rules are to apply. The Code, therefore, leaves the parties free to work out their own agreement. This agreement need not be entirely in writing; to the extent that the parol evidence rule is not violated, evidence of oral agreements is admissible to supplement the writing. Also, usage of trade can give content to language used by the parties. It is only when a term is left open that the Code steps in to supply a meaning for the parties. This is the type of situation imagined in Case # 1: the parties have worked out only the minimum elements of the entire sale. The solutions for the open terms, unless otherwise agreed, are:

1.   All of the goods are to be delivered at one time, not in several lots.[98]

---

98.   UCC § 2–307.

2. The buyer has the option of selecting the assortment of the goods; the seller has the option of determining the specifications or arrangements relating to shipment.[99]

3. The seller has a reasonable time to make delivery.[1] Indeed, when the contract calls for any act without specifying a time for its performance, the Code provides that act must be performed within a reasonable time.

4. The place for delivery of goods in a noncommercial sale and for those occasional commercial sales where no means or place of delivery was agreed upon is determined by the following rules: Rule # 1, if the contract is for the sale of identified goods and if the parties know the location of those goods, that location is the place of delivery; and Rule # 2, if Rule # 1 is not applicable, the seller's place of business (or, if he has no place of business, his residence) is the place of delivery.[2] These rules would not be applicable to Case # 1 if the agreement can be interpreted as requiring or authorizing the seller to ship the goods to the buyer.

5. If the agreement authorizes the seller to send the goods to the buyer (and the location of buyer and seller in distant cities could amount to this authorization), the seller may use documents of title and ship under reservation.[3]

6. Payment of the price is due on receipt of the goods,[4] subject to the buyer's right to inspect and this inspection may be after the goods have arrived if they are shipped to the buyer,[5] "but where the circumstances give either party the right to make or demand delivery in lots the price if it can be apportioned may be demanded for each lot."[6]

Applying these rules to Case # 1, the seller is obligated to deliver the 10,000 pairs of shoes at one time; he may ship them to the buyer under reservation; and the buyer is obligated to pay for them after they have been inspected or the right to inspection has been waived. Payment may be by check unless the seller demands cash.[7] The Code has filled these terms into the skeletal agreement which the parties entered into concerning the sale and purchase of shoes.

Case # 2. Assume the same basic factual pattern as in Case # 1: a contract for the sale and purchase of 10,000 pairs of shoes at a total price of $55,000. Assume further that the agreement between the parties gave the buyer the option of choosing sizes and colors.

---

99. UCC § 2–311(2).

1. UCC § 2–309(1).

2. UCC § 2–308.

3. UCC § 2–310(b).

4. UCC §§ 2–301, 2–310(a), 2–507. "Tender" is defined in UCC § 2–503(1). The seller's tender must be at a reasonable hour and kept available reasonably long enough for the buyer to take possession. UCC § 2–503(1)(a).

5. UCC § 2–513. See also UCC § 2–310(b). Inspection may be waived in the contract. UCC §§ 2–512, 2–513(3).

6. UCC § 2–307.

7. UCC § 2–511. If cash is demanded by the seller, the buyer has a reasonable time to procure the cash. UCC § 2–511(2); § 112 infra.

In addition to the terms filled out by the prior discussion, the Code gives content to the term which allows one of the parties to fill in the particulars of the agreement.[8] The specifications by that party (the buyer in Case # 2) "must be made in good faith and within limits set by commercial reasonableness."[9] Further, where the specifications are not seasonably made and materially affect the other party's performance (as they possibly would when the buyer fails to select the sizes and colors of the shoes he wants), the other party may have any remedies given by the Code and (a) is excused for the resulting delay in his performance and (b) may perform in some reasonable manner or treat the failure to specify as a breach.[10]

The result of these rules can be summarized thus: The parties are free to work out the terms of their own contract. As long as those terms fall within the boundaries of conscionability and fair dealing, the courts will enforce those terms. However, failure to agree on each and every term will not result in an unenforceable agreement. The Code fleshes out the skeletal contract by providing terms which the drafters thought would most probably be in the minds of the parties. Most agreements will contain more terms than the ones imagined in this section of the text; for these, only one or two terms will be added by the Code. Nevertheless, even with agreements as abbreviated as those contained in Cases # 1 and # 2, the Code provides sufficient certainty so that standards are available against which performance can be measured.

Comment: Open Terms and "Default" Rules

The preceding cases and problems barely scratch the surface of a problem that has challenged contract scholars. If the parties have intended to contract but the agreement is incomplete, what "default" rules should be inserted to fill the gaps? To illustrate, suppose the open term is price. Should the "default" rule be the price that the parties would have wanted if they had agreed (a particularized rule) or should it be the price that a majority of contracting parties would have wanted? *Oglebay,* by upholding evidence of a "reasonable" price, clearly adopts the latter approach.

Ayres and Gertner have challenged the application of the "would have wanted" approach, whether objective or subjective, in all cases. Ayres & Gertner, *Filling Gaps in Incomplete Contracts: An Economic Theory of Default Rules,* 99 Yale L.J. 87 (1989). That approach makes more sense to them if the reason for the incomplete agreement is the high transaction costs of negotiating detailed terms and conditions. But suppose the reason for the incomplete agreement is strategic. One party, with superior information, refuses to contract around a particular default rule to avoid the disclosure that would inevitably follow. The objective is to "get a larger piece of the smaller contractual pie." Id. at 127. In these cases, Ayres and

---

8. "An agreement for sale which is otherwise sufficiently definite (subsection (3) of Section 2–204) to be a contract is not made invalid by the fact that it leaves particulars of performance to be specified by one of the parties." UCC § 2–311(1)).

9. UCC § 2–311(1).

10. UCC § 2–311(3).

Gertner argue for what they call a "penalty" default rule. In essence, the "penalty" default rule is a rule that neither party would have wanted. Its presence in the right case will provide "an incentive to contract around the default rule and therefore to choose affirmatively the contract provision they prefer. In contrast to the received wisdom, penalty defaults are purposely set at what the parties would not want—in order to encourage the parties to reveal information to each other or to third parties (especially the courts)." Id. at 91.

The complexity of this argument and its application in particular settings will not be explored here. Suffice it to say, that a primary objective is to achieve higher efficiency in the contracting process. As the authors put it, "When strategic considerations cause a more knowledgeable party not to raise issues that could improve contractual efficiency, a default that penalizes the more informed party may encourage the revelation of information." Id. at 128.

For other articles discussing the same set of complex problems, see Gillette, *Commercial Relationships and the Selection of Default Rules for Remote Risks*, 19 J.Legal Stud. 535 (1990); Scott, *A Relational Theory of Default Rules for Commercial Contracts*, 19 J.Legal Stud. 597 (1990); Hadfield, *Problematic Relations: Franchising and Incomplete Contracts*, 42 Stan.L.Rev. 927 (1990); Craswell, *Contract Law, Default Rules, and the Philosophy of Promising*, 88 Mich.L.Rev. 489 (1989); Coleman, Heckathorn, & Maser, *A Bargaining Theory Approach to Default Provisions and Disclosure Rules in Contract Law*, 12 Harv.J.L. & Pub.Pol'y 639 (1989).

Empro Manufacturing Co., Inc. v. Ball–Co Manufacturing, Inc.

United States Court of Appeals, Seventh Circuit, 1989.
870 F.2d 423.

■ EASTERBROOK, CIRCUIT JUDGE.

We have a pattern common in commercial life. Two firms reach concord on the general terms of their transaction. They sign a document, captioned "agreement in principle" or "letter of intent," memorializing these terms but anticipating further negotiations and decisions—an appraisal of the assets, the clearing of a title, the list is endless. One of these terms proves divisive, and the deal collapses. The party that perceives itself the loser then claims that the preliminary document has legal force independent of the definitive contract. Ours is such a dispute.

Ball–Co Manufacturing, a maker of specialty valve components, floated its assets on the market. Empro Manufacturing showed interest. After some preliminary negotiations, Empro sent Ball–Co a three-page "letter of intent" to purchase the assets of Ball–Co and S.B. Leasing, a partnership holding title to the land under Ball–Co's plant. Empro proposed a price of $2.4 million, with $650,000 to be paid on closing and a 10–year promissory note for the remainder, the note to be secured by the "inventory and equipment of Ball–Co." The letter stated "[t]he general terms and conditions of such proposal (which will be subject to and incorporated in a formal, definitive Asset Purchase Agreement signed by both parties)." Just in case Ball–Co might suppose that Empro had committed itself to buy the assets, paragraph four of the letter stated that "Empro's purchase shall be subject to the satisfaction of certain conditions precedent to closing including, but not limited to" the definitive Asset Purchase Agreement and, among five other conditions, "[t]he approval of the shareholders and board of directors of Empro."

Although Empro left itself escape hatches, as things turned out Ball–Co was the one who balked. The parties signed the letter of intent in November 1987 and negotiated through March 1988 about many terms. Security for the note proved to be the sticking point. Ball–Co wanted a security interest in the land under the plant; Empro refused to yield.

When Empro learned that Ball–Co was negotiating with someone else, it filed this diversity suit. Contending that the letter of intent obliges Ball–Co to sell only to it, Empro asked for a temporary restraining order. The district judge set the case for a prompt hearing and, after getting a look at the letter of intent, dismissed the complaint under Fed.R.Civ.P. 12(b)(6) for failure to state a claim on which relief may be granted. Relying on Interway, Inc. v. Alagna, 85 Ill.App.3d 1094, 41 Ill.Dec. 117, 407 N.E.2d 615 (1st Dist.1980), the district judge concluded that the statement, appearing twice in the letter, that the agreement is "subject to" the execution of a definitive contract meant that the letter has no independent force.

Empro insists on appeal that the binding effect of a document depends on the parties' intent, which means that the case may not be dismissed— for Empro says that the parties intended to be bound, a factual issue. Empro treats "intent to be bound" as a matter of the parties' states of mind, but if intent were wholly subjective there would be no parol evidence rule, no contract case could be decided without a jury trial, and no one could know the effect of a commercial transaction until years after the documents were inked. That would be a devastating blow to business. Contract law gives effect to the parties' wishes, but they must express these openly. Put differently, "intent" in contract law is objective rather than subjective—a point *Interway* makes by holding that as a matter of law parties who make their pact "subject to" a later definitive agreement have manifested an (objective) intent not to be bound, which under the parol evidence rule becomes the definitive intent even if one party later says that the true intent was different. As the Supreme Court of Illinois said in Schek v. Chicago Transit Authority, 42 Ill.2d 362, 364, 247 N.E.2d 886, 888 (1969), "intent must be determined solely from the language used when no ambiguity in its terms exists." See also Feldman v. Allegheny International, Inc., 850 F.2d 1217 (7th Cir.1988) (Illinois law); Skycom Corp. v. Telstar Corp., 813 F.2d 810, 814–17 (7th Cir.1987) (New York and Wisconsin law). Parties may decide for themselves whether the results of preliminary negotiations bind them, Chicago Investment Corp. v. Dolins, 107 Ill.2d 120,

89 Ill.Dec. 869, 871, 481 N.E.2d 712, 715 (1985), but they do this through their words.

Because letters of intent are written without the care that will be lavished on the definitive agreement, it may be a bit much to put dispositive weight on "subject to" in every case, and we do not read *Interway* as giving these the status of magic words. They might have been used carelessly, and if the full agreement showed that the formal contract was to be nothing but a memorial of an agreement already reached, the letter of intent would be enforceable. Borg–Warner Corp. v. Anchor Coupling Co., 16 Ill.2d 234, 156 N.E.2d 513 (1958). Conversely, Empro cannot claim comfort from the fact that the letter of intent does not contain a flat disclaimer, such as the one in *Feldman* pronouncing that the letter creates no obligations at all. The text and structure of the letter—the objective manifestations of intent—might show that the parties agreed to bind themselves to some extent immediately. *Borg–Warner* is such a case. One party issued an option, which called itself "firm and binding"; the other party accepted; the court found this a binding contract even though some terms remained open. After all, an option to purchase is nothing if not binding in advance of the definitive contract. The parties to *Borg–Warner* conceded that the option and acceptance usually would bind; the only argument in the case concerned whether the open terms were so important that a contract could not arise even if the parties wished to be bound, a subject that divided the court. See 156 N.E.2d at 930–36 (Schaefer, J., dissenting).

A canvass of the terms of the letter Empro sent does not assist it, however. "Subject to" a definitive agreement appears twice. The letter also recites, twice, that it contains the "general terms and conditions," implying that each side retained the right to make (and stand on) additional demands. Empro insulated itself from binding effect by listing, among the conditions to which the deal was "subject", the "approval of the shareholders and board of directors of Empro." The board could veto a deal negotiated by the firm's agents for a reason such as the belief that Ball–Co had been offered too much (otherwise the officers, not the board, would be the firm's final decisionmakers, yet state law vests major decisions in the board). The shareholders could decline to give their assent for any reason (such as distrust of new business ventures) and could not even be required to look at the documents, let alone consider the merits of the deal. See Earl Sneed, *The Shareholder May Vote As He Pleases: Theory and Fact*, 22 U.Pittsburgh L.Rev. 23, 31–36, 40–42 (1960) (collecting cases). Empro even took care to require the return of its $5,000 in earnest money "without set off, in the event this transaction is not closed," although the seller usually gets to keep the earnest money if the buyer changes its mind. So Empro made clear that it was free to walk.

Neither the text nor the structure of the letter suggests that it was to be a one-sided commitment, an option in Empro's favor binding only Ball–Co. From the beginning Ball–Co assumed that it could negotiate terms in addition to, or different from, those in the letter of intent. The cover letter from Ball–Co's lawyer returning the signed letter of intent to Empro stated that the "terms and conditions are generally acceptable" but that "some clarifications are needed in Paragraph 3(c) (last sentence)," the provision concerning Ball–Co's security interest. "Some clarifications are needed" is an ominous noise in a negotiation, foreboding many a stalemate. Although we do not know what "clarifications" counsel had in mind, the specifics are not important. It is enough that even on signing the letter of intent Ball–Co proposed to change the bargain, conduct consistent with the purport of the letter's text and structure.

The shoals that wrecked this deal are common hazards in business negotiations. Letters of intent and agreements in principle often, and here, do no more than set the stage for negotiations on details. Sometimes the details can be ironed out; sometimes they can't. Illinois, as *Chicago Investment, Interway,* and *Feldman* show, allows parties to approach agreement in stages, without fear that by reaching a preliminary understanding they have bargained away their privilege to disagree on the specifics. Approaching agreement by stages is a valuable method of doing business. So long as Illinois preserves the availability of this device, a federal court in a diversity case must send the disappointed party home empty-handed. Empro claims that it is entitled at least to recover its "reliance expenditures," but the only expenditures it has identified are those normally associated with pre-contractual efforts: its complaint mentions the expenses "in negotiating with defendants, in investigating and reviewing defendants' business, and in preparing to acquire defendants' business." Outlays of this sort cannot bind the other side any more than paying an expert to tell you whether the painting at the auction is a genuine Rembrandt compels the auctioneer to accept your bid.

AFFIRMED.

NOTES

(1) *Contract to Bargain.* In an excellent article, Professor Charles Knapp has analyzed transactions where final agreement has been delayed either to await the occurrence of future events which control future agreement (agreement to agree) or to permit negotiations which will settle the details of a transaction already fully agreed upon in its essential terms (formal contract is contemplated). *Borg-Warner,* a case distinguished by the court in *Empro,* is thought to be a case in the first category. He argues that in cases like these where the parties have reached agreement to such a degree that they regard themselves as bound to each other, neither can withdraw for an "unjustified" reason yet neither can be compelled to perform if, after good faith bargaining, actual agreement cannot be reached. Thus is created a "contract to bargain" which stresses that unjustified withdrawals will give rise to appropriate contract remedies but that essential obligations are met by bargaining in good faith for as long as may reasonably be required under the circumstances. He has this to say about the *Borg-Warner* case:

> A better case could hardly be imagined to demonstrate the dilemma created by the common law for the judge concerned both with justice to the

parties and with well-structured legal reasoning. While a majority of the court was persuaded by the parties' intention to make a binding agreement at the time they exchanged the letters, they were forced to take the position either that the contract was complete and binding in the absence of provisions for continued employment of personnel, *including the second-largest stock-holder,* or that the whole agreement was binding and enforceable—even specifically enforceable—despite the failure of buyer and seller to reach final agreement on the terms of continued employment. As Justice Schaefer points out, the selling company must have been concerned with the welfare of those personnel, and indeed Conroy himself must have been vitally concerned over the prospects for his continued employment. Justice Schaefer, arguing against the imposition of liability, was forced to take the position that the plaintiff should not even get to the jury, despite the allegation that the parties believed they were concluding a binding contract, acted as though they believed it, and—with only one apparent exception—still believed it.

By contrast, applying the contract to bargain framework to such a situation would permit the court to take notice of, and give effect to, the parties' intention to create a relation which was, at least to some extent, legally binding. Second, it would save the court from inserting "reasonable" terms in the agreement where the terms are of such importance that they should only be decided by the parties. Third, it would direct the attention of the court to another important fact in the case: *Why has the defendant refused to go through with the sale?* If he has simply changed his mind, or now thinks a better price can be found elsewhere, then he should be liable to the plaintiff for breach of contract. If, however, he has withdrawn because negotiations have broken down on the terms of his employment contract, and he has bargained in good faith, then he should be subject to no liability.

Of course, the court may have properly characterized the agreement as a complete and fully binding contract. The common law, however, forces the court to choose one extreme or the other, and, by directing the court's attention to the completeness of the agreement, the law diverts attention from the good faith of the non-performing party, which should be the most important question of all.

Knapp, *Enforcing the Contract to Bargain,* 44 N.Y.U.L.Rev. 673, 715–16 (1969). [Reprinted by permission of the New York University Law Review.]

(2) How did Empro make clear it was "free to walk"? How else might this objective have been achieved? Does it appear that Ball–Co withdrew from the negotiations "in bad faith"? Should it make any difference if they did? For a comprehensive discussion of problems in this area, see Farnsworth, *Precontractual Liability and Preliminary Agreements: Fair Dealing and Failed Negotiations,* 87 Colum.L.Rev. 217 (1987).

PROBLEM: THE CASE OF THE DON KING/"BUSTER" DOUGLAS LEGAL BOUT

James "Buster" Douglas and his manager John Johnson, entered into a boxing promotion agreement on December 31, 1988 (the "Promotional Agreement" or "Agreement"), with Don King Productions, Inc. (DKP). The Promotional Agreement provided for payment of $25,000 to Douglas in return for his granting DKP the exclusive right to promote his professional boxing bouts for three years. The Agreement also stated that this term would be automatically extended in the event Douglas was recognized as world champion, "to cover the entire period you are world champion and a period of two years following" loss of the title. Compensation for the individual bouts contemplated by the Promotional Agreement was to be made subject to further negotiation and agreement, with the agreed-to terms to be set forth in the individually-negotiated bout agreements. The Promotional Agreement specified a floor level of compensation of $50,000, plus $10,000 in training expenses, for Douglas' fights, except that in the case of a title bout or defense, no floor was provided, but such a purse was to be "negotiated and mutually agreed upon."

During the first year of the agreement, Douglas participated in three bouts arranged by DKP, the last of which was the heavyweight championship bout held in Tokyo on February 10, 1990, in which Douglas "shocked the world" by defeating then-heavyweight champion, Mike Tyson. In accordance with the Promotional Agreement, which called for monetary terms of each bout to be negotiated and set forth in a separate bout agreement, Douglas and Johnson had entered into a bout agreement on August 14, 1989 (the "Bout Agreement") pursuant to which Douglas was to be paid $1.3 million. This Bout Agreement granted DKP an "exclusive option to promote [Douglas'] next three bouts following the Tokyo bout, such option to be exercised by giving notice to Douglas no later than 30 days after the Tokyo bout." The Bout Agreement provided that Douglas would receive $1 million for each of these bouts, except that in the event Douglas was the winner of the Tokyo bout, subsequent bouts would be subject to negotiation of a higher purse.

DKP sought to exercise its option and hold a rematch between Douglas and Tyson in June, 1990 at Trump Plaza in Atlantic City. However, on February 21, 1990, Douglas and Johnson executed a contract with Golden Nugget, Inc. and The Mirage Casino–Hotel (collectively, "Mirage") to stage Douglas' next two fights at the Mirage in Las Vegas, with a guaranteed minimum purse of $25 million dollars for the first bout and $25 million for a second heavyweight championship bout. This contract was made contingent upon Douglas obtaining a release from any obligation to DKP or a judicial declaration that DKP's exclusive Promotional and Bout Agreements were void and unenforceable.

In seeking such a declaration, Douglas and Johnson contend that they are not bound by the foregoing "Promotional and Bout Agreements" with DKP because these "are indefinite as to the essential term of consideration." Assuming New York law controls, how would you expect a court to rule? See Don King Productions, Inc. v. Douglas (James "Buster"), 742 F.Supp. 741 (S.D.N.Y.1990).

Comment: Texaco, Pennzoil and Outposts of Contract Law

The celebrated litigation between Pennzoil and Texaco, which generated the largest civil judgment in history ($10.53 billion), represents an outpost in contract law on several fronts. Texaco, Inc. v. Pennzoil, Co., 729 S.W.2d 768 (Tex.App.1987), cert. denied 485 U.S. 994, 108 S.Ct. 1305, 99 L.Ed.2d 686 (1988). First, it underscores the viability of the tort claim of interference with contractual relations and thereby illustrates a potent intersection between contract and tort law. Second, the case effectively evokes the specter of precontractual liability, which, combined with the tort claim, raises difficult (and frightening) possibilities for the corporate lawyer. Third, the question of what remedy to apply (i.e., whether tort or contract) and on what basis received a debatable answer. Finally, a fourth concern not addressed by the court, but subsequently of great concern to lawyers, is how to avoid the dangers of this "pre-contract" liability while maintaining the board of director's fiduciary responsibility to the shareholders.

The following is Professor Epstein's succinct description of the facts:

[Pennzoil] saw in the demoralization at Getty Oil an opportunity to become a major player in the oil industry by gaining control of Getty Oil's extensive reserves.

The two companies reached a deal, the gist of which was that Pennzoil and the Getty Trust [owner of 40.2% of Getty Oil stock] were to establish a new corporate vehicle to purchase the Getty shares from the [Getty] museum [owner of 10.8% of Getty Oil stock] and the public at large for a price set at $110 per share, plus $5 in deferred compensation. Pennzoil would wind up with about a 43 percent stake, and the Trust with a 57 percent stake. In essence Pennzoil and the Getty Trust engineered a squeeze play meant to displace present management while providing a handsome profit for the museum and the public shareholders.

Champagne glasses tinkled in celebration, press releases were duly issued, and on January 4, 1984, the deal was reported in the newspapers. Much detailed drafting of complex corporate documents remained to be done, but that was never to come to pass. Within hours of the original announcement Texaco stepped in with an offer to purchase all shares of Getty at $125 per share (later raised to $128), for a total price of just over $10 billion. That offer was accepted with great alacrity by * * * the museum on January 5, but only after Texaco agreed to indemnify the Getty interests for any liability they might have had to Pennzoil. * * * Pennzoil then * * * su[ed] Texaco for the common law tort of inducement of breach of contract. The rest is history.

Epstein, *The Pirates of Pennzoil, A Comic Opera Made Possible by a Grant from the Texaco Corporation,* 9 Regulation (November–December, 1985) p. 18. The case inspired another famous line attributed to Mr. Berra. "When Texaco's Chairman, John K. McKinley, asked Getty Oil's Chairman Sidney Peterson whether Getty might still be available even though an 'agreement in principle' had been entered into with Pennzoil, Peterson responded that 'the fat lady had not yet sung.'" Temkin, *When Does the Fat Lady Sing?: An Analysis of "Agreements in Principle" in Corporate Acquisitions,* 55 Ford.L.Rev. 125, n. 1 (1986).

Pennzoil brought suit in Delaware against Getty for specific enforcement of the merger contract. The Delaware Chancery Court denied specific performance, stating that as it was a remedy of last resort Pennzoil should pursue its damage remedy under contract law.[1]

Unfortunately for Texaco, with the failure of the Delaware action, Pennzoil was left to try its tort claim in Texas. Now tort damages, both expectation and punitive, could be sought.

There has been considerable criticism of the award of damages in the case, which took into account Pennzoil's expectations of acquiring the oil reserves rather than, as some have suggested, the value of the company it was acquiring in terms of the price of its stock. The different measures produce vastly different results.[2]

It appears most corporate lawyers have looked at *Pennzoil* as an aberration. However, though the lesson may not be that one is liable under a "letter of intent" (or some such instrument) for contract damages for breach, it still may have something of value to teach. Practitioners may be somewhat lulled into a false sense of security by "practices of the trade" where the "gentleman's agreement" is that there is no contract until the formal writing. Lawyers must take into account that at some point a jury not privy to the "gentleman's agreement" might look over their shoulders. Aware of this, they should be careful to draft any letters, notes or memorandums of agreement so as to make clear at what point the client manifests assent and that prior to that time there is (emphatically) no contract. See generally, Farnsworth, *Precontractual Liability and Preliminary Agreements: Fair Dealing and Failed Negotiations,* 87 Colum. L.Rev. 217 (1987); Temkin, *When Does the Fat Lady Sing?: An Analysis of "Agreements in Principle" in Corporate Acquisitions,* 55 Ford.L.Rev. 125 (1986); Note, *The $10.53 Billion Question—When are the Parties Bound?: Pennzoil and the Use of Agreements in Principle in Mergers and Acquisitions,* 40 Vand.L.Rev. 1367 (1987).

1. Several commentators have seized on this issue to call for a more liberal use of specific performance in the corporate acquisitions area. Dean Yudof and John Jeffers wrote: "[T]he Chancellor's decision indicates how foolish the ancient rules are about specific performance in the modern context. Specific performance should have been the remedy of choice, not the remedy of last resort, applicable only if damages were inadequate. The dissolution of the Getty/Texaco deal and adherence to the original Getty/Pennzoil contract would have obviated the necessity of valuing the huge assets in dispute. And that valuation process is more complex for the courts than specific performance would have been." Yudof & Jeffer, *Pennzoil v. Texaco,* 27 Alberta L.Rev. 77, 79 (1988).

2. "With respect to damages, Pennzoil presented an attractive formula premised on a substitution of assets (an equivalent of 1 billion barrels of oil) for stock (3/7 of Getty stock) with the difference between the purchase price and Pennzoil's historical development cost being $7.53 billion. The logic of Pennzoil's theory flows nicely; however, it lacks authoritative support for the substitution of assets for stock. Furthermore, it contradicts the recognized rules which set the measure of damages in such cases at the difference between the market value of the property (stock price) at the time of the breach and the contract price." Baron and Baron, *The Pennzoil–Texaco Dispute: An Independent Analysis,* 38 Baylor L.Rev. 253 (1986).

Another complication is encountered when the company has agreed to be bought through a merger or some other type of transfer of control. Under Delaware law (most Fortune 500 companies are chartered in Delaware and are subject to Delaware law concerning duties to shareholders), when a corporation places itself for sale, the board owes a duty to its shareholders to maximize shareholder value. See Revlon, Inc. v. MacAndrews & Forbes Holdings, Inc. Corp., Inc., 506 A.2d 173 (Del.1985). Essentially, the board must auction off the corporation to the highest bidder. If the board of directors were to enter into a contractual arrangement with another company to acquire their company without seeking competing bids, the board of directors might be held in breach of their fiduciary duty to the shareholders. This duty may override their ability to bind the corporation to a contract under agency law, in that the directors might not have the authority to bind the corporation in such a situation. In which case, the corporation might not be bound to the contract, and the directors might be held liable for breach for the company's failure to perform. Under agency law, the directors' breach is described as a breach of their warranty of authority. Though this complex area of the law is covered in several other law school courses, a brief exposure to the types of problems presented serves to illustrate the grey, outer fringe of contract law. See also Ansaldi, *Texaco, Pennzoil and the Revolt of the Masses: A Contracts Postmortem,* 27 Hous.L.Rev. 733 (1990).

(D) REMEDIES WHERE AGREEMENT INCOMPLETE OR INDEFINITE

In disputes over indefiniteness, liability and remedy issues are intertwined. For example, even though the agreement is presumptively *enforceable* because the parties "intended" to contract, the contract will fail for indefiniteness if the court is unable to determine whether there has been a breach or find a "reasonably certain basis for giving an appropriate remedy." UCC 2–204(3); Restatement (Second) § 33(1). Depending upon the nature and the extent of the indefiniteness, however, there will be a sliding scale of remedial protection. Thus, indefiniteness in some terms of the agreement may preclude specific performance but not interfere with the plaintiff's ability to prove damages measured by lost expectations. Similarly, an open term may foreclose proof of lost profits with reasonable certainty but not interfere with proof of costs reasonably incurred in reliance upon the defendant's promise or the value of benefits conferred on the defendant through part performance. The point is this: If the incomplete or indefinite agreement is enforceable by whatever test, the plaintiff may seek to protect the expectation interest through specific performance or damages. If these remedies are not available because of indefiniteness in the agreement, alternative remedies protect the reliance and, if all else fails, the restitution interests. We will return to this sliding scale of remedial protection for breach of an enforceable agreement in Chapter Six.

What is the remedial situation where the agreement is found to be unenforceable due to indefinite or incomplete terms? In a theory of contract rooted in such concepts as "consideration" and protecting "reasonable expectations," the plaintiff is not entitled to either specific performance or damages measured by lost profits. Protection of the expectation interest depends upon an enforceable bargain. Similarly, one could argue that a plaintiff assumes the risk of any reliance in preparation for or performance of an unenforceable bargain, whether or not the defendant is benefited. Notable exceptions to this argument exist when the plaintiff's part performance is under a severable rather than an entire contract or when the plaintiff has made a down payment which the defendant, in all fairness, ought not retain. Here, more general principles of restitution to avoid unjust enrichment begin to operate and are softened even more when the part performance is under an agreement that both parties intended and thought to be enforceable. See Arrowsmith, *Ineffective Transactions and Unjust Enrichment: A Framework for Analysis,* 9 Legal Stud. 121 (1989).

With this general background in mind, consider the following famous case and the notes.

Hoffman v. Red Owl Stores, Inc.

Supreme Court of Wisconsin, 1965.
26 Wis.2d 683, 133 N.W.2d 267.

The complaint alleged that Lukowitz, as agent for Red Owl, represented to and agreed with plaintiffs that Red Owl would build a store building in Chilton and stock it with merchandise for Hoffman to operate in return for which plaintiffs were to put up and invest a total sum of $18,000; that in reliance upon the above mentioned agreement and representations plaintiffs sold their bakery building and business and their grocery store and business; also in reliance on the agreement and representations Hoffman purchased the building site in Chilton and rented a residence for himself and his family in Chilton; plaintiffs' action in reliance on the representations and agreement disrupted their personal and business life; plaintiffs lost substantial amounts of income and expended large sums of money as expenses. Plaintiffs demanded recovery of damages for the breach of defendants' representations and agreements.

The action was tried to a court and jury. The facts hereafter stated are taken from the evidence adduced at the trial. Where there was a conflict in the evidence the version favorable to plaintiffs has been accepted since the verdict rendered was in favor of plaintiffs.

Hoffman assisted by his wife operated a bakery at Wautoma from 1956 until sale of the building late in 1961. The building was owned in joint tenancy by him and his wife. Red Owl is a Minnesota corporation having its home office at Hopkins, Minnesota. It owns and operates a number of grocery supermarket stores and also extends franchises to agency stores which are owned by individuals, partnerships and corporations. Lukowitz resides at Green Bay and since September, 1960, has been divisional manager for Red Owl in a territory comprising Upper Michigan and most of Wisconsin in charge of 84 stores. Prior to September, 1960, he was district manager having charge of approximately 20 stores.

In November, 1959, Hoffman was desirous of expanding his operations by establishing a grocery store and contacted a Red Owl representative by the name of Jansen, now deceased. Numerous conversations were had in 1960 with the idea of establishing a Red Owl franchise store in Wautoma. In September, 1960, Lukowitz succeeded Jansen as Red Owl's representative in the negotiations. Hoffman mentioned that $18,000 was all the capital he had available to invest and he was repeatedly assured that this would be sufficient to set him up in business as a Red Owl store. About Christmastime, 1960, Hoffman thought it would be a good idea if he bought a small grocery store in Wautoma and operated it in order that he gain experience in the grocery business prior to operating a Red Owl store in some larger community. On February 6, 1961, on the advice of Lukowitz and Sykes, who had succeeded Lukowitz as Red Owl's district manager, Hoffman bought the inventory and fixtures of a small grocery store in Wautoma and leased the building in which it was operated.

After three months of operating this Wautoma store, the Red Owl representatives came in and took inventory and checked the operations and found the store was operating at a profit. Lukowitz advised Hoffman to sell the store to his manager, and assured him that Red Owl would find a larger store for him elsewhere. Acting on this advice and assurance, Hoffman sold the fixtures and inventory to his manager on June 6, 1961. Hoffman was reluctant to sell at that time because it meant losing the summer tourist business, but he sold on the assurance that he would be operating in a new location by fall and that he must sell this store if he wanted a bigger one. Before selling, Hoffman told the Red Owl representatives that he had $18,000 for "getting set up in business" and they assured him that there would be no problems in establishing him in a bigger operation. The makeup of the $18,000 was not discussed; it was understood plaintiff's father-in-law would furnish part of it. By June, 1961, the towns for the new grocery store had been narrowed down to two, Kewaunee and Chilton. In Kewaunee, Red Owl had an option on a building site. In Chilton, Red Owl had nothing under option, but it did select a site to which plaintiff obtained an option at Red Owl's suggestion. The option stipulated a purchase price of $6,000 with $1,000 to be paid on election to purchase and the balance to be paid within 30 days. On Lukowitz's assurance that everything was all set plaintiff paid $1,000 down on the lot on September 15th.

On September 27, 1961, plaintiff met at Chilton with Lukowitz and Mr. Reymund and Mr. Carlson from the home office who prepared a projected financial statement. Part of the funds plaintiffs were to supply as their investment in the venture were to be obtained by sale of their Wautoma bakery building.

On the basis of this meeting Lukowitz assured Hoffman: "* * * [E]verything is ready to go. Get your money together and we are set." Shortly after this meeting Lukowitz told plaintiffs that they would have to sell their bakery business and bakery building, and that their retaining this property was the only "hitch" in the entire plan. On November 6, 1961, plaintiffs sold their bakery building for $10,000. Hoffman was to retain the bakery equipment as he contemplated using it to operate a bakery in connection with his Red Owl store. After sale of the bakery Hoffman obtained employment on the night shift at an Appleton bakery.

The record contains different exhibits which were prepared in September and October, some of which were projections of the fiscal operation of the business and others were proposed building and floor plans. Red Owl was to procure some third party to buy the Chilton lot from Hoffman, construct the building, and then lease it to Hoffman. No final plans were ever made, nor were bids let or a construction contract entered. Some time prior to November 20, 1961, certain of the terms of the lease under which the building was to be rented by Hoffman were understood between him and Lukowitz. The lease was to be for 10 years with a rental approximating $550 a month calculated on the basis of 1 percent per month on the building cost, plus 6 percent of the land cost divided on a monthly basis. At the end of the 10–year term he was to have an option to renew the lease for an additional 10–year period or to buy the property at cost on an instalment basis. There was no discussion as to what the instalments would be or with respect to repairs and maintenance.

On November 22nd or 23rd, Lukowitz and plaintiffs met in Minneapolis with Red Owl's credit manager to confer on Hoffman's financial standing and on financing the agency. Another projected financial statement was there drawn up entitled, "Proposed Financing For An Agency Store." This showed Hoffman contributing $24,100 of cash capital of which only $4,600 was to be cash possessed by plaintiffs. Eight thousand was to be procured as a loan from a Chilton bank secured by a mortgage on the bakery fixtures, $7,500 was to be obtained on a 5 percent loan from the father-in-law, and $4,000 was to be obtained by sale of the lot to the lessor at a profit.

A week or two after the Minneapolis meeting Lukowitz showed Hoffman a telegram from the home office to the effect that if plaintiff could get another $2,000 for promotional purposes the deal could go through for $26,000. Hoffman stated he would have to find out if he could get another $2,000. He met with his father-in-law, who agreed to put $13,000 into the business provided he could come into the business as a partner. Lukowitz told Hoffman the partnership arrangement "sounds fine" and that Hoffman should not go into the partnership arrangement with the "front office." On January 16, 1962, the Red Owl credit manager teletyped Lukowitz that the father-in-law would have to sign an agreement that the $13,000 was either a gift or a loan subordinate to all general creditors and that he would prepare the agreement. On January 31, 1962, Lukowitz teletyped the home office that the father-in-law would sign one or other of the agreements. However, Hoffman testified that it was not until the final meeting some time between January 26th and February 2nd, 1962, that he was told that his father-in-law was expected to sign an agreement that the $13,000 he was advancing was to be an outright gift. No mention was then made by the Red Owl representatives of the alternative of the father-in-law signing a subordination agreement. At this meeting the Red Owl agents presented Hoffman with the following projected financial statement:

"Capital required in operation:

"Cash	$ 5,000.00	
"Merchandise	20,000.00	
"Bakery	18,000.00	
"Fixtures	17,500.00	
"Promotional Funds	1,500.00	
"TOTAL:		$62,000.00

"Source of funds:

"Red Owl 7–day terms	$5,000.00	
"Red Owl Fixture contract (Term 5 years)	14,000.00	
"Bank loans (Term 9 years Union State Bank of Chilton	8,000.00	
"(Secured by Bakery Equipment)		
"Other loans (Term No-pay) No interest Father-in-law	13,000.00	
"(Secured by None)		
"(Secured by Mortgage on	2,000.00	
"Wautoma Bakery Bldg.)		
"Resale of land	6,000.00	
"Equity Capital:	$5,000.00-Cash	
"Amount owner has	17,500.00-Bakery	
Equip. to invest:	22,500.00	
"TOTAL:		$70,500.00"

Hoffman interpreted the above statement to require of plaintiffs a total of $34,000 cash made up of $13,000 gift from his father-in-law, $2,000 on mortgage, $8,000 on Chilton bank loan, $5,000 in cash from plaintiff, and $6,000 on the resale of the Chilton lot. Red Owl claims $18,000 is the total of the unborrowed or unencumbered cash, that is, $13,000 from the father-in-law and $5,000 cash from Hoffman himself. Hoffman informed Red Owl he could not go along with this proposal, and particularly objected to the requirement that his father-in-law sign an agreement that his $13,000 advancement was an absolute gift. This terminated the negotiations between the parties.

[At the conclusion of the trial, the trial court determined that P and D engaged in negotiations looking toward the establishment of a franchise and that they had not reached final agreement on all details at the time P withdrew from negotiations. The jury, in response to specific questions, found that D represented that if P met certain conditions he would get a franchise, that P reasonably relied upon these representations and that P had fulfilled all conditions required at the time negotiations terminated. The jury also determined that $3,265 would reasonably compensate P for the sale of the bakery building, taking up the Chilton option and various moving and rental expenses and that $16,735 should be awarded for the sale of the Wautoma store fixtures and inventory. After appropriate motions, the trial court vacated the finding concerning the Wautoma store, affirmed the other findings and ordered a new trial on the Wautoma damage issue. D appealed the awarding of any compensation and P appealed the order for a new trial. After stating the issues to be, 1) whether the facts support a cause of action for promissory estoppel, and 2) whether the jury's findings with respect to damages were sustained by the evidence, the court, speaking through Chief Justice Currie, endorsed and adopted for Wisconsin "the doctrine of promissory estoppel . . . which supplies a needed tool which courts may employ in a proper case to prevent injustice."]

* * *

Applicability of Doctrine to Facts of this Case

The record here discloses a number of promises and assurances given to Hoffman by Lukowitz in behalf of Red Owl upon which plaintiffs relied and acted upon to their detriment.

Foremost were the promises that for the sum of $18,000 Red Owl would establish Hoffman in a store. After Hoffman had sold his grocery store and paid the $1,000 on the Chilton lot, the $18,000 figure was changed to $24,100. Then in November, 1961, Hoffman was assured that if the $24,100 figure were increased by $2,000 the deal would go through. Hoffman was induced to sell his grocery store fixtures and inventory in June, 1961, on the promise that he would be in his new store by fall. In November, plaintiffs sold their bakery building on the urging of defendants and on the assurance that this was the last step necessary to have the deal with Red Owl go through.

We determine that there was ample evidence to sustain the answers of the jury to the questions of the verdict with respect to the promissory representations made by Red Owl, Hoffman's reliance thereon in the exercise of ordinary care, and his fulfillment of the conditions required of him by the terms of the negotiations had with Red Owl.

There remains for consideration the question of law raised by defendants that agreement was never reached on essential factors necessary to establish a contract between Hoffman and Red Owl. Among these were the size, cost, design, and layout of the store building; and the terms of the lease with respect to rent, maintenance, renewal, and purchase options. This poses the question of whether the promise necessary to sustain a cause of action for promissory estoppel must embrace all essential details of a proposed transaction between promisor and promisee so as to be the equivalent of an offer that would result in a binding contract between the parties if the promisee were to accept the same.

Originally the doctrine of promissory estoppel was invoked as a substitute for consideration rendering a gratuitous promise enforceable as a contract. See Williston, Contracts (1st ed.), p. 307, sec. 139. In other words, the acts of reliance by the promisee to his detriment provided a substitute for consideration. If promissory estoppel were to be limited to only those situations where the promise giving rise to the cause of action must be so definite with respect to all details that a contract would result were the promise supported by consideration, then the defendants' instant promises to Hoffman would not meet this test. However, sec. 90 of Restatement, 1 Contracts, does not impose the requirement that the promise giving rise to the cause of action must be so comprehensive in scope as to meet the requirements of an offer that would ripen into a contract if accepted by the promisee. Rather the conditions imposed are:

(1) Was the promise one which the promisor should reasonably expect to induce action or forbearance of a definite and substantial character on the part of the promisee?

(2) Did the promise induce such action or forbearance?

(3) Can injustice be avoided only by enforcement of the promise?

We deem it would be a mistake to regard an action grounded on promissory estoppel as the equivalent of a breach of contract action. As Dean Boyer points out, it is desirable that fluidity in the application of the concept be maintained. 98 University of Pennsylvania Law Review (1950), 459, at page 497. While the first two of the above listed three requirements of promissory estoppel present issues of fact which ordinarily will be resolved by a jury, the third requirement, that the remedy can only be invoked where necessary to avoid injustice, is one that involves a policy decision by the court. Such a policy decision necessarily embraces an element of discretion.

We conclude that injustice would result here if plaintiffs were not granted some relief because of the failure of defendants to keep their promises which induced plaintiffs to act to their detriment.

Damages

Defendants attack all the items of damages awarded by the jury. [The court affirmed the trial court's decision to uphold the jury's award of reliance damages in the amount of $3,265.]

* * *

We turn now to the damage item with respect to which the trial court granted a new trial, i.e., that arising from the sale of the Wautoma grocery store fixtures and inventory for which the jury awarded $16,735. The trial court ruled that Hoffman could not recover for any loss of future profits for the summer months following the sale on June 6, 1961, but that damages would be limited to the difference between the sales price received and the fair market value of the assets sold, giving consideration to any goodwill attaching thereto by reason of the transfer of a going business. There was no direct evidence presented as to what this fair market value was on June 6, 1961. The evidence did disclose that Hoffman paid $9,000 for the inventory, added $1,500 to it and sold it for $10,000 or a loss of $500. His 1961 federal income tax return showed that the grocery equipment had been purchased for $7,000 and sold for $7,955.96. Plaintiffs introduced evidence of the buyer that during the first eleven weeks of operation of the grocery store his gross sales were $44,000 and his profit was $6,000 or roughly 15 percent. On cross-examination he admitted that this was gross and not net profit. Plaintiffs contend that in a breach of contract action damages may include loss of profits. However, this is not a breach of contract action.

The only relevancy of evidence relating to profits would be with respect to proving the element of goodwill in establishing the fair market value of the grocery inventory and fixtures sold. Therefore, evidence of profits would be admissible to afford a foundation for expert opinion as to fair market value.

Where damages are awarded in promissory estoppel instead of specifically enforcing the promisor's promise, they should be only such as in the opinion of the court are necessary to prevent injustice. Mechanical or rule of thumb approaches to the damage problem should be avoided. In discussing remedies to be applied by courts in promissory estoppel we quote the following views of writers on the subject:

"Enforcement of a promise does not necessarily mean Specific Performance. It does not necessarily mean Damages for breach. Moreover the amount allowed as Damages may be determined by the plaintiff's expenditures or change of position in reliance as well as by the value to him of the promised performance. Restitution is also an 'enforcing' remedy, although it is often said to be based upon some kind of a rescission. In determining what justice requires, the court must remember all of its powers, derived from equity, law merchant, and other sources, as well as the common law. Its decree should be molded accordingly." 1A Corbin, Contracts, p. 221, sec. 200.

"The wrong is not primarily in depriving the plaintiff of the promised reward but in causing the plaintiff to change position to his detriment. It would follow that the damages should not exceed the loss caused by the change of position, which would never be more in amount, but might be less, than the promised reward." Seavey, Reliance on Gratuitous Promises or Other Conduct, 64 Harvard Law Review (1951), 913, 926.

"There likewise seems to be no positive legal requirement, and certainly no legal policy, which dictates the allowance of contract damages in every case where the defendant's duty is consensual." Shattuck, Gratuitous Promises—A New Writ?, 35 Michigan Law Review (1936), 908, 912.

At the time Hoffman bought the equipment and inventory of the small grocery store at Wautoma he did so in order to gain experience in the grocery store business. At that time discussion had already been had with Red Owl representatives that Wautoma might be too small for a Red Owl operation and that a larger city might be more desirable. Thus Hoffman made this purchase more or less as a temporary experiment. Justice does not require that the damages awarded him, because of selling these assets at the behest of defendants, should exceed any actual loss sustained measured by the difference between the sales price and the fair market value.

Since the evidence does not sustain the large award of damages arising from the sale of the Wautoma grocery business, the trial court properly ordered a new trial on this issue.

Order affirmed. Because of the cross-appeal, plaintiffs shall be limited to taxing but two-thirds of their costs.

[Footnotes omitted.]

NOTES

(1) In Earhart v. William Low Co., 25 Cal.3d 503, 158 Cal.Rptr. 887, 600 P.2d 1344 (1979), there was a completed agreement for construction subject to an express condition precedent; viz., the obtaining of adequate financing. Before the condition was satisfied, Defendant requested Plaintiff to commence performance of the conditional bargain but did not expressly promise to pay. The plaintiff's performance did not confer a direct benefit on the defendant and the express condition was never satisfied. Nevertheless, the court concluded that "compensation for a party's performance should be paid by the person whose request induced the performance." According to the court, it was a "pure fiction" to base recovery on a restitution theory. Rather, either the party requesting performance had a moral obligation to "restore to his original position a party who has acted to his detriment in reliance on a representation" or that recovery should be based upon "promissory estoppel" under Section 90. Under either approach, where there is an "urgent" request by the defendant and reasonable reliance by the plaintiff, the defendant is liable for the reasonable value of the plaintiff's part performance. Accord: Cyberchron Corp. v. Calldata Systems Development, Inc., 47 F.3d 39, 46–47 (2d Cir.1995)(plaintiff recovered actual expenditures in preparing to perform and performing work requested under a failed agreement to produce computer equipment, including overhead).

(2) The *Red Owl* case, which might be called the "high water mark" in the development of promissory estoppel, has received considerable attention in the literature. See, e.g., Henderson, *Promissory Estoppel and Traditional Contract Law*, 78 Yale L.J. 343, 376–87 (1969); Summers, *"Good Faith" in General Contract Law and the Sales Provisions of the Uniform Commercial Code*, 54 Va.L.Rev. 195, 216–27, 256–58 (1968). See also, Barnett & Becker, *Promissory Estoppel, Contract Formalities, and Misrepresentation*, 15 Hofstra L.Rev. 443, 485–495 (1987); Feinman, *Critical Approaches to Contract Law*, 30 U.C.L.A.L.Rev. 829, 852–57 (1983). The case represents the farthest advance of contract, i.e., promise-based theory, into policing conduct in pre-contract negotiations. Neither UCC 1–203 nor Restatement (Second) § 205 impose a duty of good faith in the negotiation of a contract, although protection may be achieved through such doctrines as unconscionability and through remedies in restitution or tort. See Restatement (Second) § 205, Comment c. The contract remedy under *Red Owl* and similar cases has usually been limited to protection of the reliance interest. Profits that would have been earned if the contract had been formed have not been allowed. See, e.g., Wheeler v. White, 398 S.W.2d 93 (Tex.1965); Restatement (Second) § 90, Comment d. But for a case awarding lost profits where liability was based upon promissory estoppel, see Walters v. Marathon Oil Co., 642 F.2d 1098 (7th Cir.1981).

CHAPTER FOUR

AVOIDANCE OF CONTRACT

This chapter explores a variety of ways that parties can avoid legal obligation for promises that seem to satisfy the requirements for contract (e.g., bargained for consideration) that we have explored in the last two chapters. Courts at times will refuse to enforce contracts because of (a) impermissible parties to the agreement, (b) impermissible defects in the bargaining process, or (c) impermissible terms in the agreement.

While it is possible to contract around many of the rules of agreement (e.g., the mail box rule), performance (e.g., payment of a reasonable price), and liability (e.g., expectation damages), the rules in this chapter are for the most part "immutable"—in that the contracting parties do not have the freedom to waive these defenses.[1]

Our focus here is on defenses to contract that arise at the time the contract is formed. In the next chapter on performance, we will turn our attention to events occurring after formation—such as events which render performance impossible—that may also void contractual obligation.

SECTION 1. CAPACITY TO CONTRACT: INFANCY; MENTAL INCOMPETENCE

A person must have legal capacity to contract. In the words of Restatement (Second) § 12(1), "No one can be bound by contract who has not legal capacity to incur at least voidable contractual duties. * * *" Several questions must be considered:

(1) Under what circumstances is a person so incapacitated that either no contract can arise from the bargain (contract "void") or a contract which does arise can be rescinded or avoided (contract "voidable")?

(2) What must be done to effectively rescind a "voidable" contract?

(3) What are the appropriate remedies available to both parties involved in the transaction?

A broader consideration is the extent to which the "capacity" cases relate both to the objective of achieving fairness in the exchange and to the

---

1. Immutable rules are sprinkled throughout the book. For example, "consideration" has to varying degrees been an immutable prerequisite for forming a legal obli-gation. And the next chapter will show that the duty of "good faith" immutably governs how parties must perform their contractual obligations.

processes of change in the society, such as the legislative trend lowering the age of majority from twenty-one to eighteen[2] and changes in the understanding and treatment of mental illness and drug addiction.[3] Collateral reading: Farnsworth §§ 4.2–4.8; Calamari and Perillo §§ 8–1—8–15; Murray §§ 21–27; Dobbs § 13.4.

(A) INFANCY

We recognize what seems to be an injustice to the defendant to permit the minor-plaintiff to possess and enjoy the use of the automobile for almost a year, drive it into a telephone pole and wreck it, then haul it into a yard and elect to rescind the whole transaction. However, this is not an equitable proceeding and is controlled entirely by legal principles under which a minor has the right as to contracts made during minority to affirm or disaffirm his contracts other than those for necessaries. Those who deal with a minor must do so charged with the knowledge of the controlling principle of law which, as here, may work some injustice in individual cases but affords, in general, the protection of minors against their own improvidence at a time when they are presumed to be incapable of protecting themselves.

Thus did the Court of Appeals of Ohio, Madison County, reaffirm orthodox common law doctrine in Davis v. Clelland, 92 N.E.2d 827, 829 (Ohio App.1950). The minor (or infant, the term frequently used in the legal literature) has long been accorded special contractual immunity. The extent of protection has diminished somewhat in recent years, either by decision or statute, but nowhere today is the minor recognized as possessing full legal capacity to contract. In general, a minor's contracts are voidable; obligation may be avoided by timely and appropriate disaffirmance. The other party, if an adult, is bound, reflecting the risk of contracting with one who is under age.

Bowling v. Sperry

Appellate Court of Indiana, Division No. 1, 1962.
133 Ind.App. 692, 184 N.E.2d 901.

■ MYERS, JUDGE.

This is an appeal from a judgment of the Noble Circuit Court in a civil action brought by appellant, Larry Bowling, by Norma Lemley as next friend, hereinafter referred to as Larry, against appellee, Max E. Sperry,

2. Exceptions to 18 as age of majority: Mississippi (21); Alabama (19); Nebraska (19); Wyoming (19). In Iowa, all minors attain their majority by marriage.

3. Article 19 of the Louisiana Civil Code provides: "All persons have capacity to contract, except unemancipated minors, interdicts, and persons deprived of reason at the time of contracting." For an analysis of this provision in the light of civil law antecedents, see Dugas, *The Contractual Capacity of Minors: A Survey of the Prior Law and the New Articles,* 62 Tul.L.Rev. 745 (1988).

d/b/a Sperry Ford Sales, to disaffirm and set aside a contract for the purchase of an automobile on the grounds of infancy.

Larry was a minor, sixteen years of age. On June 29, 1957, he purchased from appellee a 1947 Plymouth automobile for the sum of $140 cash. He paid $50 down on that day and returned on July 1, 1957, to pay the balance of $90 and take possession of the car. Appellee delivered to him a certificate of title and a written receipt. This receipt stated that as of June 29, 1957, Max Sperry Ford Sales sold to Larry Bowling a 1947 Plymouth for the amount of $140, cash, paid in full.

Larry drove the car several times during the following week and discovered that the main bearing was burned out. He had the car brought back to appellee's place of business where he was informed that it would cost him from $45 to $95 to make repairs. He declined to pay this amount and left the car on appellee's lot. Subsequently, he mailed a letter to appellee to the effect that he disaffirmed the contract of purchase and demanded the return of his money. Upon appellee's refusal to pay back the $140, this lawsuit followed.

Larry's complaint is based upon the fact that appellee sold him a car knowing that he was a minor; that he tendered back the car, rescinded the contract, and demanded the sum of $140. Appellee's answer was in two paragraphs, the first being in the nature of a general denial, pursuant to the provisions of Supreme Court Rule 1–3, and the second being an allegation that Larry was accompanied by his grandmother and aunt at the time of the purchase, and that the aunt paid appellee the sum of $90 of the purchase price. Upon trial of the case by the court, judgment was rendered in favor of appellee and against Larry.

It has been the rule in Indiana for many years that the contracts of minors are voidable and may be disaffirmed. It is not necessary that the other party be placed in *statu quo,* nor is it necessary that the minor tender back the money or property he has received before suing for the value or possession of the money or property given by him to the adult. All such voidable contracts by a minor in regard to personal property may be avoided at any time during his minority or upon his arrival at full age. Shipley v. Smith (1904), 162 Ind. 526, 70 N.E. 803; McKee v. Harwood Automotive Co. (1932), 204 Ind. 233, 183 N.E. 646; Wooldridge, by Next Friend v. Hill (1953), 124 Ind.App. 11, 114 N.E.2d 646.

The evidence showed that Larry's grandmother and aunt accompanied him to appellee's used car lot on June 29, 1957, when he selected the automobile, and that his aunt drove the car around the lot at that time. Furthermore, it was revealed that his aunt had loaned him $90 in order to make final payment on the car and that he had commenced to pay this back at $10 a week thereafter.

These facts, however, do not change the general rule. In so far as the agreement and sale is concerned, there was sufficient evidence to show that it was made between appellee and Larry, and no one else. It is of no consequence that his aunt and grandmother accompanied him at the time of purchase; and the fact that his aunt made payment of the $90 balance due could have no effect upon Larry's right to take advantage of his minority in an action to recover such payment. Story, etc., Piano Co. v. Davy (1918), 68 Ind.App. 150, 119 N.E. 177. Appellee was fully aware of Larry's age when the sale was negotiated. The written receipt was in Larry's name alone. This contract was squarely between an adult and a minor and falls within the rule pronounced above. Larry had every right to disaffirm it and set it aside.

Appellee claims there is doubt as to whether Larry received a certificate of title from appellee with his name on it. It is contended that the certificate was delivered in blank. As was said in the case of Wooldridge, by Next Friend, v. Hill, supra (at page 14 of 124 Ind.App., at page 648 of 114 N.E.2d): "It is of little consequence whether title to the property involved had passed to the infant or not." The certificate of title is only evidence of ownership, and in this case it would make no difference whether Larry had received a certificate in blank or with his name on it. Automobile Underwriters v. Tite (1949), 119 Ind.App. 251, 85 N.E.2d 365.

Appellee argues that an inference may be drawn from the evidence to show that the burned-out bearing was caused by Larry's operation of the car and his failure to put oil in the crankcase. Even if this were true, it is no defense to this action. There is no requirement in Indiana that before a disaffirmance is effected the parties must be placed in *statu quo*. Story, etc., Piano Co. v. Davy, supra.

The question of whether or not the automobile was a necessary was injected into the trial of the case although appellee did not plead it as a defense. Some argument on this subject was made by the parties in the briefs. Section 58–102, Burns' Ind.Stat., 1961 Replacement, reads as follows:

> "Capacity to buy and sell is regulated by the general law concerning capacity to contract, and to transfer and acquire property.

> "Where necessaries are sold and delivered to an infant, or to a person who by reason of mental incapacity or drunkenness is incompetent to contract, he must pay a reasonable price therefor.

> "Necessaries in this section means goods suitable to the condition in life of such infant or other person, and to his actual requirements at the time of delivery."

In the case of Price et al. v. Sanders et al. (1878), 60 Ind. 310, 314, the following is stated:

> " 'Necessaries,' in the technical sense, mean such things as are necessary to the support, use or comfort of the person of the minor, as food, raiment, lodging, medical attendance, and such personal comforts as comport with his condition and circumstances in life, including a common school education; but it has been pithily and happily said, that necessaries do not include 'horses, saddles, bridles, liquors, pistols, powder, whips and fiddles.' "

Whether the goods are necessaries is a question of law, and if they are deemed as such, their quantity, quality and reasonable value are matters of fact. Garr et al. v. Haskett et al. (1882), 86 Ind. 373.

It has been stated in 27 Am.Jur., Infants, § 17, pp. 760, 761, as follows:

"Aside from such things as are obviously for maintenance of existence, what are or what are not necessaries for an infant depends on what is reasonably necessary for the proper and suitable maintenance of the infant in view of his social position and situation in life, the customs of the social circle in which he moves or is likely to move, and the fortune possessed by him and by his parents. It has been said that articles of mere luxury or adornment cannot be included, but that useful articles, although of an expensive and luxurious character, may be included if they are reasonable in view of the infant's circumstances. The necessities to be procured by the contract must be personal necessities, that is, for the living or personal well-being of the infant. * * *

"What is furnished to the infant must be suitable, not only to his condition in life, but also to his actual requirements at the time—in other words, the infant must not have at the time of delivery an adequate supply from other sources. To be liable for articles as necessaries, an infant must be in actual need of them, and obliged to procure them for himself."

The evidence revealed that at the time of this transaction, Larry was living with his grandmother in Cromwell, Indiana, where he had lived for the past fifteen years; that his mother was dead and his father resided in Fort Wayne; that he was a student at Cromwell High School, but was on vacation; that he had a summer job working at a restaurant in the town of Syracuse, Indiana, which was eight or nine miles away from his home; that his usual means of transportation back and forth was with the cook; that on occasion he could "bum" rides with other people.

The acting manager for appellee, who had dealt with Larry, testified that when Larry's aunt and grandmother came to the sales lot on June 29, 1957, "they" said Larry needed something for him to get back and forth to work. He said it was his "understanding" that the car was needed for that purpose. Larry stated that during the short period of time he had possession of it, he only used it for pleasure, and did not drive it to work.

We are well aware of the overwhelming increase in the use and number of automobiles in this country since World War II. What once was a great luxury for only the wealthy has become a matter of common necessity for the ordinary workingman, farmer and businessman. The automobile is as important to the modern household as food, clothing and shelter. The problem here is whether the car in question was so needed by Larry, in view of his situation in life, his social status and his financial position, that he could not be maintained properly or suitably without it. The burden of showing this was upon appellee. Robertson v. King (1955), 225 Ark. 276, 280 S.W.2d 402, 52 A.L.R.2d 1108. From the evidence presented, we do not think appellee met this burden. While every high school boy today wants a car of his own, and many of them own automobiles which under given circumstances may be considered as necessaries, we do not consider the car in this case so vital to Larry's existence that it could be classified as a necessary.

Judgment reversed, and cause remanded with instructions that the trial court sustain appellant's motion for a new trial on the ground that the judgment is contrary to law.

NOTES

(1) After this brief excursion into the world of minors' contracts, what are your reactions? Are just results being achieved? What reform(s), if any, are in order?

(2) What do you advise an adult client who proposes to contract with a minor? In *Bowling*, for example, would Sperry have been protected if Larry's grandmother had agreed to become jointly liable with him?

(3) In what respect might contractual immunity be legally disadvantageous for the minor?

(4) *Legal Responsibility of Emancipated Minor.* "The law governing agreements made during infancy reaches back over many centuries. The general rule is that '* * * the contract of a minor, other than for necessaries, is either void or voidable at his option.' The only other exceptions to the rule permitting disaffirmance are statutory or involve contracts which deal with duties imposed by law such as a contract of marriage or an agreement to support an illegitimate child. The general rule is not affected by the minor's status as emancipated or unemancipated.

"Appellant does not advance any argument that would put this case within one of the exceptions to the general rule, but rather urges that this court, as a matter of public policy, adopt a rule that an emancipated minor over eighteen years of age be made legally responsible for his contracts.

"The underpinnings of the general rule allowing the minor to disaffirm his contracts were undoubtedly the protection of the minor. It was thought that the minor was immature in both mind and experience and that, therefore, he should be protected from his own bad judgments as well as from adults who would take advantage of him. The doctrine of the voidability of minors' contracts often seems commendable and just. If the beans that the young naive Jack purchased from the crafty old man in the fairy tale 'Jack and the Bean Stalk' had been worthless rather than magical, it would have been only fair to allow Jack to disaffirm the bargain and reclaim his cow. However, in today's modern and sophisticated society the 'infancy doctrine' seems to lose some of its gloss.

"Paradoxically, we declare the infant mature enough to shoulder arms in the military, but not mature enough to vote; mature enough to marry and be responsible for his torts and crimes, but not mature enough to assume the burden of his own contractual indiscretions. In Wisconsin, the infant is deemed mature enough to use a dangerous instrumentality—a motor vehicle—at sixteen, but not mature enough to purchase it without protection until he is twenty-one.

"No one really questions that a line as to age must be drawn somewhere below which a legally defined minor must be able to disaffirm his contracts for nonnecessities. The law over the centuries has considered this age to be twenty-one. Legislatures in other states have lowered the age. We suggest that the appellant might better seek the change it proposes in the legislative halls rather than this court. A recent law review article in the Indiana Law Journal explores the problem of contractual disabilities of minors and points to three different legislative solutions leading to greater freedom to contract. The first approach is one gleaned from the statutes of California and New York, which would allow parties to submit a proposed contract to a court which would remove the infant's right of disaffirmance upon a finding that the particular contract is fair. This suggested approach appears to be extremely impractical in light of the expense and delay that would necessarily accompany the procedure. A second approach would be to establish a rebuttable presumption of incapacity to replace the strict rule. This alternative would be an open invitation to litigation. The third suggestion is a statutory procedure that would allow a minor to petition a court for the removal of disabilities. Under this procedure a minor would only have to go to court once, rather than once for each contract as in the first suggestion.

"Undoubtedly, the infancy doctrine is an obstacle when a major purchase is involved. However, we believe that the reasons for allowing that obstacle to remain viable at this point outweigh those for casting it aside. Minors require some protection from the pitfalls of the market place. Reasonable minds will always differ on the extent of the protection that should be afforded. For this court to adopt a rule that the appellant suggests and remove the contractual disabilities from a minor simply because he becomes emancipated, which in most cases would be the result of marriage, would be to suggest that the married minor is somehow vested with more wisdom and maturity than his single counterpart. However, logic would not seem to dictate this result especially when today a youthful marriage is oftentimes indicative of a lack of wisdom and maturity." Kiefer v. Fred Howe Motors, Inc., 39 Wis.2d 20, 158 N.W.2d 288, 290–291 (1968) (footnotes omitted).

(5) *Restoration or Restitution? Bowling* adheres to the prevailing view as to the degree of restitution required of a minor upon disaffirmance. The minor is obliged to return what he or she still has; i.e., in specie. There is no obligation to account for use or depreciation or to return an equivalent of what was received. Thus, the requirement is one of restoration, not restitution. See, e.g., Star Chevrolet Co. v. Green, 473 So.2d 157 (Miss.1985) (minor who wrecked vehicle not obliged to account for proceeds received from insurance company); Halbman v. Lemke, 99 Wis.2d 241, 298 N.W.2d 562 (1980); Quality Motors v. Hays, 216 Ark. 264, 225 S.W.2d 326 (1949); Utterstrom v. Myron D. Kidder, Inc., 124 Me. 10, 124 A. 725 (1924). Contra: Valencia v. White, 134 Ariz. 139, 654 P.2d 287 (App.1982) (discussion of various departures from the majority rule in cases from New Hampshire, Minnesota, Pennsylvania, New York and New Jersey). See generally, Annot., *Infant's Liability for Use or Depreciation of Subject Matter in Action to Recover Purchase Price Upon His Disaffirmance of Contract to Purchase Goods,* 12 A.L.R.3d 1174 (1967).

(6) *Disaffirmance and Ratification.* "An infant cannot affirmatively ratify until he comes of age. After that date any manifestation by him of an intent to regard the bargain as binding will deprive him of the power to avoid the contract.... Mere silence or inaction by a former infant after attaining majority does not amount to ratification.... However, an infant should be required to disaffirm within a reasonable time after coming of age.... Disavowal of a contract by an infant need not be by any prescribed form or ceremony; the filing of an answer by him or in his behalf disaffirming the contract is sufficient in itself to accomplish the result." Mechanics Finance Co. v. Paolino, 29 N.J.Super. 449, 455–56, 102 A.2d 784, 787 (1954).

In Bobby Floars Toyota, Inc. v. Smith, 48 N.C.App. 580, 269 S.E.2d 320 (1980), a minor made eleven monthly payments on the purchase of an automobile, ten of them after his eighteenth birthday. Did he thereby impliedly ratify the contract and lose his right to disaffirm? After noting that a reasonable time for disaffirmance depends upon the circumstances of each case, no hard-and-fast rule regarding time limits being capable of definition, the court concluded that ten months was enough time within which to elect between disaffirmance and ratification with respect to an item of personal property which is constantly depreciating in value. Cf. Keser v. Chagnon, 159 Colo. 209, 410 P.2d 637 (1966) (court upheld lower court's conclusion that the minor did not ratify by using the car (an Edsel) for sixty days after reaching his majority before disaffirming and returning the car ten days after that). Continued use of the automobile is not a ratification where the contract was promptly disaffirmed, the defendant refused a tender back of the car, and the plaintiff continued to use it pending litigation. Adams v. Barcomb, 125 Vt. 380, 216 A.2d 648 (1966); Loomis v. Imperial Motors, Inc., 88 Idaho 74, 396 P.2d 467 (1964) (minor becomes bailee of the car; may use free of rent subject to duty of ordinary care).

(7) *Recovery for Necessaries Furnished.* The law is replete with instances where the effect of a strict rule is mitigated by successful assertion of a claim of unjust enrichment. For example, a contract may be within the Statute of Frauds, and for that reason unenforceable, but the plaintiff may be able to proceed on a theory of quasi-contract. Granting relief on this basis does not, in the ordinary situation, thwart statutory purposes. In much the same way, a recovery for necessaries furnished to a minor is not viewed as inconsistent with the policy of contractual immunity. The suit is not on the contract. Rather, as one court put it, the minor "is held on a promise implied by law, and not, strictly speaking, on his actual promise.... [H]e is liable to pay only what the necessaries were reasonably worth, and not what he may improvidently have agreed to pay for them." Trainer v. Trumbull, 141 Mass. 527, 530, 6 N.E. 761, 762 (1886). Even if necessaries are involved, recovery is limited to unjust enrichment.

Given the foregoing rationale, it is surprising that the courts have been unwilling to expand the category of necessaries. One would think, for example, that adult parties would have had little difficulty in establishing the necessitous character of an automobile. But such has not been the situation, as the instant case attests. Accord: Warwick Municipal Employees Credit Union v. McAllister, 110 R.I. 399, 293 A.2d 516 (1972); Harvey v. Hadfield, 13 Utah 2d 258, 372 P.2d 985 (1962) (house trailer); Robertson v. King, 225 Ark. 276, 280 S.W.2d 402 (1955) (farm truck); Raymond v. General Motorcycle Co., 230 Mass. 54, 119

N.E. 359 (1918) (motorcycle); Schoenung v. Gallet, 206 Wis. 52, 238 N.W. 852 (1931). Contra: Bancredit, Inc. v. Bethea, 65 N.J.Super. 538, 168 A.2d 250 (1961); Rose v. Sheehan Buick, 204 So.2d 903 (Fla.App.1967). See generally, Annot., *Automobile or Motorcycle as Necessary for Infant*, 56 A.L.R.3d 1335 (1974).

Finally, if recovery for necessaries furnished is based on quasi-contract, designed to preclude an unjust enrichment, then why limit recovery to necessary items? See Wolfe, *A Reevaluation of the Contractual Rights of Minors*, 57 UMKC L.Rev. 145 (1988).

(8) *Effect of Misrepresentation of Age: Tort; Estoppel.* There are a number of approaches to the effect of a misrepresentation of age. At one extreme is the Massachusetts rule which states that minors are "not liable in tort for deceit arising from false representations as to . . . age or for damages to the machines while in their possession and used by them." Raymond v. General Motorcycle Co., 230 Mass. 54, 119 N.E. 359 (1918). In the middle are the cases which hold that misrepresentation will not estop the minor from disaffirming but will justify damages in tort. See Mestetzko v. Elf Motor Co., 119 Ohio St. 575, 165 N.E. 93 (1929); Creer v. Active Automobile Exchange, 99 Conn. 266, 121 A. 888 (1923); Annot., *Liability for an Infant in Tort for Inducing Contract by Misrepresenting His Age*, 67 A.L.R. 1264 (1930). At the other extreme is estoppel: "When a minor has reached that stage of maturity which indicates that he is of full age, and enters into a contract falsely representing himself to be of age, accepting the benefits of the contract, he will be estopped to deny that he is not of age when the obligation of the contract is sought to be enforced against him." Johnson v. McAdory, 228 Miss. 453, 88 So.2d 106, 107 (1956). See Miller, *Fraudulent Misrepresentation of Age as Affecting the Infant's Contract—A Comparative Study*, 15 U.Pitt.L.Rev. 73 (1953); Annot., *Infant's Misrepresentation as to His Age as Estopping Him from Disaffirming His Voidable Transactions*, 29 A.L.R.3d 1270 (1970).

The estoppel approach has been codified by statute in Indiana: "When, in case of any loan or sale made by seller, creditor or secured party, the borrower, or any other person furnishing security on behalf of the borrower, shall, as an inducement to the seller, creditor or secured party to make the loan or sale, represent to it, in writing, that he or she is eighteen (18) years of age or older, whereas in fact such person or persons are under the age of eighteen (18) years, or shall otherwise make any false statement or representation to the seller, creditor or secured party and the seller, creditor or secured party is thereby deceived, and the loan or sale is made in reliance upon such representation, neither the person so representing, nor any one in his or her behalf, nor any person otherwise legally liable to pay such loan or sale, shall afterwards be allowed, as against such seller, creditor or secured party, to take advantage of the fact that the person making the representation was under eighteen (18) years of age, but each such person shall be estopped by such representation." Ind.Code 28–1–26.5–1.

PROBLEM: THE CASE OF THE BOLD GRADUATES

After receiving their high school diplomas, Matt and Pat, age seventeen, determined to strike out on their own. They decided to rent an apartment together, find jobs, and see if they could make it in the "real world." Their parents were pleased, but somewhat dubious. They assured the boys that "they would always be welcome at home."

On June 15, the boys signed a one-year lease with Landlord, Inc., calling for a $250 monthly rental, payable in advance, plus a security deposit of $250. They paid the first month's rent and the security deposit. However, they vacated the premises on July 15 and demanded a return of all monies paid. Were they entitled to repayment? Cf. Webster Street Partnership, Ltd. v. Sheridan, 220 Neb. 9, 368 N.W.2d 439 (1985).

Tiring of life in the real world, the boys took off in the fall for State U. They again executed a one-year lease (monthly rental of $400 plus $400 security deposit). But, alas, their educational careers were short-lived, and they again decided to strike out for other parts. They confronted the landlord with a demand for the return of all payments. The landlord refused. He conceded that they were paid up for the period of their stay, but he insisted they were breaching the lease and were accountable for damages that would be sustained. How should the matter be resolved?

(B) MENTAL INCOMPETENCE

Restatement (Second) § 15 provides:

Mental Illness or Defect

(1) A person incurs only voidable contractual duties by entering into a transaction if by reason of mental illness or defect (a) he is unable to understand in a reasonable manner the nature and consequences of the transaction, or (b) he is unable to act in a reasonable manner in relation to the transaction and the other party has reason to know of his condition.

(2) Where the contract is made on fair terms and the other party is without knowledge of the mental illness or defect, the power of avoidance under Subsection (1) terminates to the extent that the contract has been so performed in whole or in part or the circumstances have so changed that avoidance would be unjust. In such a case a court may grant relief as justice requires.

The rationale of this section is explained as an effort to reconcile "two conflicting policies: the protection of justifiable expectations and of the security of transactions, and the protection of persons unable to protect themselves against imposition." Comment a. If a guardian is appointed, the problem is resolved: "A person has no capacity to incur contractual duties if his property is under guardianship * * *." Restatement (Second) § 13. But without a guardian, the search for a mediating principle is complicated by the "wide variety of types and degrees of mental incompetency." This means that a "person may be able to understand almost nothing, or only simple or routine transactions, or he may be incompetent only with respect to a particular type of transaction." Also, even if his "understanding is complete, he may lack capacity to control his acts in the way that the normal individual can and does control them; in such cases the incapacity makes the contract voidable only if the other person has reason to know of his condition." Comment b.

Professor Dobbs has this to say:

> Mental incompetency is, of course, a widespread phenomenon in one degree or another, so widespread that courts have usually insisted that not just any mental weakness will relieve an incompetent of his contract or conveyance. Once it is decided, however, that the mental weakness in question is significant as a matter of substantive law, the incompetent may or may not be allowed to avoid his contract or conveyance.

According to Dobbs, a few courts take the position that a contract with an incompetent will be enforced if the exchange is fair, unless the other party "recognizes the other's incapacity." If so, the other party is "guilty of a fraud." The more common rule is that the incompetent should be able to avoid the contract provided that he can restore the other party to his pre-contract position. This rule depends upon whether the other party acted in "good faith" and was unaware of the incapacity and stands "in stark contrast to the rule usually applied in cases of avoidance by minors, who are permitted to rescind a contract upon returning whatever depreciated value remains in their hands." He concludes by suggesting that the "real concern in the cases is to avoid unfair treatment or—and it is not necessarily the same thing—disparate exchange of values working a hardship on the incompetent." Dobbs § 13.4. For a comprehensive analysis, see Meiklejohn, *Contractual and Donative Capacity*, 39 Case Wes.Res.L.Rev. 307 (1988–89).

Heights Realty, Ltd. v. Phillips

Supreme Court of New Mexico, 1988.
106 N.M. 692, 749 P.2d 77.

■ STOWERS, JUSTICE.

This case involves an exclusive listing contract between plaintiff-appellant, Heights Realty, Ltd. (Heights Realty), and Johnye Mary Gholson (Mrs. Gholson), the original named defendant. Heights Realty filed an amended complaint seeking its commission for having performed under the terms of the contract by having provided a buyer to purchase Mrs. Gholson's property. During the pendency of this action, Mrs. Gholson was adjudicated incompetent and E.A. Phillips (Phillips), the present defendant-appellee, was appointed conservator of her estate. Following a bench trial, the district court found Mrs. Gholson lacked the mental capacity to have validly executed the listing contract and entered judgment in favor of Phillips. On appeal, Heights Realty argues that the presumption of competency was not overcome by clear and convincing evidence. We disagree and affirm the judgment of the district court.

In 1984, Mrs. Gholson was interested in selling her North Valley property. She telephoned Heights Realty and spoke with Pat Eichenberg, a real estate broker and owner of Heights Realty and also an acquaintance of hers, who brought Mrs. Gholson an exclusive listing agreement. Mrs. Gholson was approximately eighty-four years old when she signed the contract on September 26, 1984, listing the property for one year in the amount of $250,000 with a cash down payment of $75,000. No other terms were included in the agreement. Subsequently, Mrs. Gholson changed her mind about the amount of the down payment and on October 10, 1984, signed an addendum increasing it to $100,000. In November 1984 an offer was made to purchase the property for $255,000. Mrs. Gholson did not accept that offer.

The question to be determined is whether substantial evidence was presented from which the trial court could properly conclude that the presumption of competency was overcome by clear and convincing evidence.

On appeal, this court reviews the record to determine whether there is substantial evidence to support the trial court's findings of fact. State ex rel. Goodmans Office Furnishings, Inc. v. Page & Wirtz Constr. Co., 102 N.M. 22, 24, 690 P.2d 1016, 1018 (1984). If such substantial evidence appears in the record, we will not disturb those findings. Phelps Dodge Corp. v. New Mexico Employment Sec. Dept., 100 N.M. 246, 247, 669 P.2d 255, 256 (1983).

The test of mental capacity is whether a person is capable of understanding in a reasonable manner the nature and effect of the act in which the person is engaged. In re Estate of Head, 94 N.M. 656, 659, 615 P.2d 271, 274 (Ct.App.), cert. denied sub nom. Taute v. Poppe, 94 N.M. 675, 615 P.2d 992 (1980). The law presumes that every person is competent. To show the contrary, the burden of proof rests on the person asserting lack of capacity to establish the same by clear and convincing proof. Roybal v. Morris, 100 N.M. 305, 309, 669 P.2d 1100, 1104 (Ct.App.1983); In re Estate of Taggart, 95 N.M. 117, 120, 619 P.2d 562, 565 (Ct.App.1980); Estate of Head, 94 N.M. at 659, 615 P.2d at 274. The burden remains on those alleging incompetency unless the case is brought within the exception in which previous incompetency is admitted or sufficiently shown and thus changes that burden. If incompetency of a general permanent nature has been shown to once exist for a period of time prior to the execution of the instrument under attack, it is presumed to continue until there is a showing by the person relying on the validity of that instrument that proves the existence of a lucid interval at the time of its execution. Willis v. James, 284 Ala. 673, 676–77, 227 So.2d 573, 576–77 (1969); In re Peter's Estate, 43 Wash.2d 846, 862, 264 P.2d 1109, 1118 (1953); In re Ingram's Estate, 384 P.2d 1020, 1021 (Wyo.1963).

Although the test of mental capacity is applied as of the date that the attacked instrument is executed, evidence of a person's prior or subsequent condition is admissible to show the condition at the time in issue. Harrison v. City Nat'l Bank of Clinton, Iowa, 210 F.Supp. 362, 371 (S.D.Iowa 1962). The combined weight of all the evidence in each case determines the result. The court is entitled to take into consideration the individual's physical condition; the adequacy of consideration; whether or not the transaction was improvident; the relation of trust and confidence between the parties to the transaction and the weakness of the mind of the alleged incompetent person as judged by all other acts within a reasonable time prior and subsequent to the act in question. Harrison, 210 F.Supp. at 371; see also Turner v. Cole, 116 N.J.Eq. 368, 380, 173 A. 613, 619 (Ch.1934). Cf. In re Meyers, 410 Pa. 455, 476–77, 189 A.2d 852, 862 (1963) (the testimony of those who observed the speech and conduct of the person on the date the instrument is executed outranks the testimony as to observations made prior to and subsequent to that date).

Only Mrs. Eichenberg and Mrs. Gholson were present at the time of the signing of the exclusive listing agreement on September 26, 1984, and its addendum on October 10, 1984. Mrs. Eichenberg testified that Mrs. Gholson was "just as sharp as a tack" when the agreement was executed. She further testified that on the date the addendum was signed, Mrs. Eichenberg read the contents of it to Mrs. Gholson who had been lying down on the couch because she had injured her foot and that Mrs. Gholson appeared to have no problems understanding the addendum since she even corrected a misspelling in her name.

Testimony was presented that Mrs. Gholson owned approximately twelve acres with a residence in Albuquerque's North Valley at the time she decided to sell the property for financial reasons. Mrs. Gholson stated that she set the asking price of $250,000 by guessing at the value of the property and left open all other terms vital to the contract. Mrs. Gholson also testified that she had no recollection of signing the addendum because she "couldn't think of anything in sequence at that time." Evidence showed that no family or lawyer assisted her in executing the agreements. It appears from the record that the trial court discounted Mrs. Eichenberg's testimony.

Additional testimony as to Mrs. Gholson's mental capacity was elicited from her son-in-law, Phillips, and granddaughter, Louise Loomis, both of whom had for many years observed Mrs. Gholson's speech and conduct. Phillips testified that he first noticed behavior evidencing her gradual mental decline in 1959, after the death of her husband. He recounted a number of incidents: for example, beginning in May 1983, Mrs. Gholson began to mismanage the payment of her bills, confusing credit with debit balances; she set off her burglar alarm and left it running; she locked herself out of her automobile while the engine was still on; and she failed to recall the death of her younger brother, with whom she had been extremely close, on September 19, 1984. Phillips characterized her as being constantly confused.

Louise Loomis testified that she always maintained a close and intimate relationship with her grandmother. She described the degeneration of Mrs. Gholson's mind over a period of years. In particular, she stated that around 1979 or 1980, her grandmother began to have problems comprehending matters. Mrs. Loomis testified that by the summer of 1984 on a trip to Utah, her grandmother was unable to communicate with people or dial a telephone number for room service and that shortly thereafter, Mrs. Gholson could not carry on her personal affairs nor make appointments with the hairdresser. She also developed erratic eating habits and was incapable of dealing with restaurant bills. Continuing, Mrs. Loomis testified that her grandmother became much more confused after she broke her foot in September of 1984. She opined that her grandmother did not have the mental capacity to understand a listing agreement.

Two psychiatrists testified, Dr. Farber for Heights Realty, and Dr. Muldawer on behalf of Mrs. Gholson. Dr. Farber neither met with nor examined Mrs. Gholson and only reviewed documents about her. Dr. Farber indicated that primarily he relied on Dr. Muldawer's handwritten notes and his deposition. Dr. Farber averred that he neither had sufficient evidence nor had he made a timely examination of her to enable him to say that she was incompetent, and therefore the presumption of competency had to prevail.

Dr. Muldawer testified that he examined Mrs. Gholson on January 11, 1985, reviewed relevant documents, and thereafter conferred with her relatives. He found that Mrs. Gholson showed a general decline in her cognitive skills about 1979 or 1980 involving her judgment, reasoning and memory. He further stated that this decline was slow and subtle and was evidenced by increasing forgetfulness and the general inability to take care of her own needs. He concluded that when she signed the listing agreement "she certainly didn't fully understand the terms" even though "in a broader sense she knew she was disposing of property." He then stated he could not use the word "conclusively" to describe Mrs. Gholson's lack of contractual capacity on September 26, 1984, but he could state that she was incompetent on that date within "reasonable medical probability."

A review of the trial record indicates, as properly found by the court below, that "on September 26, 1984 and thereafter Mrs. Gholson was suffering from a progressive, deteriorating mental disease which prevented her from understanding the nature and consequences of the * * * agreement and the Addendum thereto"; and that "on September 26, 1984 and thereafter, Mrs. Gholson was without lucid intervals."

There was a conflict in the general medical testimony adduced from Dr. Muldawer, who observed Mrs. Gholson, and Dr. Farber, who never observed her but relied on observations of another party. This type of medical testimony therefore, in and of itself, is not sufficient to overcome the presumption of competency. See In re Estate of Head, 94 N.M. at 659, 615 P.2d at 273; see also In re Estate of Taggart, 95 N.M. at 120, 619 P.2d at 565. The opinions expressed by Phillips and Mrs. Loomis were predicated on their many experiences with Mrs. Gholson tending to afford them opportunities to observe her mental capacity. Thus, there was substantial evidence presented from those who were in a position to observe Mrs. Gholson's conduct before and after the day the instrument in question was executed.

Even though some of the evidence adduced was conflicting, this goes to the question of credibility, a question solely for resolution by the trier of fact, who after hearing the testimony resolved the question in favor of Mrs. Gholson. This court will not resolve conflicts or substitute its judgment where the record as a whole substantially supports the trial court's findings of fact. Sternloff v. Hughes, 91 N.M. 604, 608, 577 P.2d 1250, 1254 (1978). The fact that there may have been some evidence upon which the court might have found facts other than what it did is not sufficient for reversal. Dibble v. Garcia, 98 N.M. 21, 25, 644 P.2d 535, 539 (Ct.App.), cert. denied, 98 N.M. 50, 644 P.2d 1039 (1982).

Although the trial court did not specifically state in its findings that the presumption of competency was overcome by clear and convincing evidence, it is implicit in those findings when the evidence is viewed in its entirety that this burden of proof had been sustained. We hold that substantial evidence was presented from which the trial court could properly conclude that the presumption of competency was overcome by clear and convincing evidence; consequently, Mrs. Gholson lacked mental capacity to enter into the exclusive listing agreement and its addendum. The judgment of the district court is affirmed.

IT IS ORDERED.

NOTES

(1) Is adequacy of consideration relevant to the issue of mental capacity? See Restatement (Second) § 15, comment b: "Where a person has some understanding of a particular transaction which is affected by mental illness or defect, the controlling consideration is whether the transaction in its result is one which a reasonably competent person might have made." See also Green, *Proof of Mental Incompetence and the Unexpressed Major Premise*, 53 Yale L.J. 271, 304–5 (1944); Alexander and Szasz, *From Contract to Status via Psychiatry*, 13 Santa Clara L.Rev. 537, 557–8 (1973). What evidence was there here that the listing agreement was improvident or unfair?

(2) *Inadequacy of Consideration Plus Something Else.* "[I]nadequacy of price *within itself,* and disconnected from all other facts, cannot be a ground for setting aside a contract, or affording relief against it. There must be something else besides the mere inadequacy of consideration or inequality in the bargain, to justify a court in granting relief by setting aside the contract. *What this something else besides the inadequacy* should be, perhaps no court ought to say, lest the wary and cunning, by employing other means than those named, should escape with their fraudulent gains. I, however, will venture to say, that it ought, in connection with the inadequacy of consideration, to superinduce the belief that there had been either a suppression of the truth, the suggestion of falsehood, abuse of confidence, a violation of duty arising out of some fiduciary relation between the parties, the exercise of undue influence, or the taking of an unjust and inequitable advantage of one whose peculiar situation at the time would be calculated to render him an easy prey to the cunning and the artful. But if no one of these appears, or if no fact is proved that will lead the mind to the conclusion, that the party against whom relief is sought has suppressed some fact that he ought to have disclosed, or that he has suggested some falsehood, or abused in some manner the confidence reposed in him, or that some fiduciary relation existed between the parties, or that the party complaining was under his influence, or at the time of the trade was in a condition, *from*

any cause, that would render him an easy victim to the unconscientious, then relief cannot be afforded; for inadequacy of consideration, *standing alone and unsupported by any thing else, can authorize no court, governed by the rules of the English law, to set aside a contract....*" Judge v. Wilkins, 19 Ala. 765, 772 (1851), quoted in Williamson v. Matthews, 379 So.2d 1245, 1247 (Ala.1980) (emphasis in original).

(3) What result if the conservator, pleased with the offer procured by Heights Realty, had proceeded to sell to the offeror? Would this rule out the incompetency defense? Would there be a basis for recovery by the realty company?

(4) *The Case of the Adjudged Incompetent.* Manzelle Johnson was declared incompetent, and her nephew, Obbie Neal, was appointed her guardian. Obbie persuaded Mrs. Johnson to deed real property to him in his individual capacity, and he, in turn, conveyed the property to Charles Weatherly, a bona fide purchaser. Obbie was later removed as guardian, and the new guardian sued to cancel the deeds and to collect profits from the land which accrued to Weatherly. Weatherly counterclaimed for the amount of consideration paid for the land and the value of improvements which he had made. What result? See Beavers v. Weatherly, 250 Ga. 546, 299 S.E.2d 730 (1983).

(5) *Incapacity Due to Intoxication.* "Our rule regarding intoxication is much the same. The drunkenness of a party at the time of making a contract may render the contract voidable, but it does not render it void; and to render the contract voidable, it must be made to appear that the party was intoxicated to such a degree that he was, at the time of the contracting, incapable of exercising judgment, understanding the proposed engagement, and of knowing what he was about when he entered into the contract sought to be avoided.... Proof merely that the party was drunk on the day the sale was executed does not per se, show that he was without contractual capacity; there must be some evidence of a resultant condition indicative of that extreme impairment of the faculties which amounts to contract incapacity." Williamson v. Matthews, 379 So.2d 1245, 1247–48 (Ala.1980). See Restatement (Second) § 16; Annot., *Intoxication as Ground for Avoiding Contract,* 36 A.L.R. 619 (1925).

PROBLEM: THE CASE OF THE DRUG INFLUENCED SELLER

Alvin, a graduate student, age 25, owned a gold and silver belt which was given to his grandfather when he was welterweight champion of the world. The belt was worth about $500, but had great sentimental value to Alvin. On the evening of October 20, Alvin, alone in his apartment, took an LSD tablet. Shortly thereafter, he began to hallucinate and, soon, a "voice" told him that he must sell the belt and donate the proceeds to charity. Alvin went promptly to Bart's Pawnshop and sold the belt for $475. When the effects of the drug had gone, Alvin realized what had happened. Bart, however, refused to return the belt, claiming that he "bought it fair and square."

Alvin brought suit to rescind the contract for sale and to recover the belt. At the trial, Plaintiff's expert testified that LSD, like other hallucinogens, can produce a range of mental states, including hallucinations, delusions, and partial amnesia. He also stated that the effects of the drug may range from a loss of time and space perception to panic, paranoid delusions and reactions very similar to schizophrenia. He then concluded that at the time of the sale, Plaintiff was under the influence of the drug and "was not aware of the quality and nature of his act." On cross-examination, it was brought out that Plaintiff had no mental disease or defect and that he had used LSD on previous occasions. Defendant's testimony, corroborated by another witness, was that Plaintiff entered his store, offered to sell the belt for $600 and after about ten minutes of bargaining, agreed to take $475. Defendant testified that Plaintiff acted a "little strange" but that he was lucid and bargained very well. At the close of the evidence, Defendant made a motion for a directed verdict which the trial court granted. In an oral opinion from the bench, the judge stated that he was relying on Restatement (Second) § 16 on "intoxicated persons" and that although he believed that Plaintiff was, at the time of the sale, unable to understand in a reasonable manner the nature and consequences of the transaction, he found that Defendant had no reason to know about the lessened capacity. Also, he opined that Plaintiff must bear some of the responsibility, since he elected to take LSD. Accordingly, the motion was granted and a judgment was entered for Defendant.

On appeal, what result?

SECTION 2.   DEFECTS IN BARGAINING PROCESS

In Chapters Two and Three, you studied the ordinary requisites of promissory liability. By and large, an assumption has been indulged that the negotiating parties have roughly equal intelligence, information and economic resources and that one party has not abused any superiority in bargaining power or ability. When these traditional conditions have been met and the indulged assumptions not shaken, courts have been perfectly willing to enforce what the parties have agreed is a "fair exchange," refusing, as they say, to inquire into "adequacy." Put another way, in the absence of mistake or misunderstanding, a breach of contract after the parties have complied with the paradigm of "offer-acceptance" and "consideration" is likely to trigger remedies designed to protect the value of the bargain.

In this section, the focus is upon acts or omissions by one party which seriously disrupt the bargaining process. This conduct varies in type and is placed under such labels as mistake, fraud, constructive fraud, misrepresentation, undue influence, duress, bad faith and unconscionability. See, e.g., Germantown Manufacturing Co. v. Rawlinson, 341 Pa.Super. 42, 491 A.2d 138 (1985) (combination of fraud and misrepresentation, duress, unconscionability, and bad faith). When these are present, a court may be persuaded to give relief from the bargain even though the traditional conditions of promissory liability have been met. The grounds for this relief, available remedies, and the significance for a general theory about contracts will be the subject of the materials in this section. There is considerable overlap with other law school courses; notably, torts, specialized consumer and commercial law courses, and trade regulation.

(A) UNILATERAL AND MUTUAL MISTAKE

Failure of the parties to possess sufficient or accurate information about a "basic assumption on which the contract was made" undermines our confidence that the bargaining process will produce an equitable or efficient outcome. The discovery of a mistake, that is, "a belief that is not in accord with the facts," Restatement (Second) § 151, by one (unilateral) or both (mutual) parties can provide a basis for rescinding a contract.

The Restatement (Second) of Contract §§ 152 and 153 summarize the conditions under which "mistake" will lead courts to void contractual obligations:

§ 152   When Mistake of Both Parties Makes a Contract Voidable

(1) Where a mistake of both parties at the time a contract was made as to a basic assumption on which the contract was made has a material effect on the agreed exchange of performances, the contract is voidable by the adversely affected party unless he bears the risk of the mistake. . . .

§ 153   When Mistake of One Party Makes a Contract Voidable

Where a mistake of one party at the time a contract was made as to a basic assumption on which he made the contract has a material effect on the agreed exchange of performances that is adverse to him, the contract is voidable by him if he does not bear the risk of the mistake . . ., and

(a) the effect of the mistake is such that enforcement of the contract would be unconscionable, or (b) the other party had reason to know of the mistake or his fault caused the mistake.

Is it clear whether unilateral or mutual mistake will be easier to prove in practice? While the Restatement might seem to crisply describe the preconditions for voiding the contract, as an empirical matter courts only rarely (and somewhat erratically) void contracts because of mistake. This may be because (unlike the intentional abuses of fraud, duress and unconscionability) the mistaken beliefs at issue in "mistake" cases may not be the defendant's fault.

Even though excuse for mistake concerns mistaken assumptions about reality at the time of contracting, the mere fortuity that the mistake concerned events occurring after the contract was formed will transform the issue into one of "impossibility of performance" or frustration of purpose, see infra, Chapter Five. Collateral reading: Fuller, *Mistake and Error in the Law of Contracts*, 33 Emory L.Rev. 41 (1984); Farnsworth §§ 7.9, 9.2–9.4; Calamari and Perillo §§ 9–25—9–36; Dobbs §§ 11.1–11.6; Murray § 91.

Boise Junior College District v. Mattefs Construction Co.

Supreme Court of Idaho, 1969.
92 Idaho 757, 450 P.2d 604.

■ SPEAR, JUSTICE. The issue presented is whether, under the circumstances of this case, a contractor is entitled to the equitable relief of rescission when it has submitted a bid which contains a material clerical mistake. We conclude that such relief is available.

Mattefs Construction Company (hereinafter termed respondent) was one of ten bidders on a construction contract to be let by Boise Junior College District (hereinafter referred to as appellant). Along with its bid respondent submitted the customary bid bond containing a promise to pay the difference between its bid and the next higher bid actually accepted if respondent refused to enter into a contract with appellant. Contract specifications also provided that the bid could be not withdrawn for 45 days after it was opened.

The architect's estimate of costs on the building project was $150,000, but when the bids were opened seven of them ran in excess of $155,000 while three of them were less than $150,000. Fulton Construction Company bid $134,896. The respondent bid $141,048. The third bid by Cain and Hardy, Inc., was $148,915. When Fulton refused to sign a contract it was tendered to respondent who likewise refused to sign it. Ultimately the contract was awarded to Cain and Hardy, Inc., the third lowest bidder and appellant proceeded to attempt collection on respondent's bid bond.

One who errs in preparing a bid for a public works contract is entitled to the equitable relief of rescission if he can establish the following conditions: (1) the mistake is material; (2) enforcement of a contract pursuant to the terms of the erroneous bid would be unconscionable; (3) the mistake did not result from violation of a positive legal duty or from culpable negligence; (4) the party to whom the bid is submitted will not be prejudiced except by the loss of his bargain; and (5) prompt notice of the error is given. These principles are established by substantial authority, i.e., Annot., 52 A.L.R.2d 792, § III; . . . . That appellant recognizes these principles is evident, because it has raised questions as to the existence of each one of these elements by its assignments of error. Therefore, we shall consider each of these conditions necessary for equitable relief, in the context of the objections raised.

I

Appellant contends that the trial court erred in determining that omission of the glass bid was a material mistake. The trial court found:

"This was the second largest sub bid item in the whole contract, only the mechanical sub bid being larger. It amounted to about 14% of the contract and was thus a material item."

Thus, the issue is whether, as a matter of law, a 14% error in bid is a material error. We have no difficulty in reaching the conclusion that omission of an item representing 14% of the total bid submitted is substantial and material. Appellant cites a number of cases wherein courts have directly or indirectly determined that material error was not involved, in spite of mistakes which ranged up to 50%, i.e., Modany v. State Public School Building Authority, 417 Pa. 39, 208 A.2d 276 (1965); . . . . However, we are persuaded we should adopt a rule which is not so harsh and turn instead to authority such as Elsinore Union Elementary School Dist. v. Kastorff, 54 Cal.2d 380, 6 Cal.Rptr. 1, 353 P.2d 713 (1960), in which the court stated:

"Plaintiff suggests that in any event the amount of the plumbing bid omitted from the total was immaterial. The bid as submitted was in the sum of $89,994, and whether the sum for the omitted plumbing was $6,500 or $9,285 (the two sub bids), the omission of such a sum is plainly material to the total. In Lemoge (Lemoge Electric v. County of San Mateo (1956), supra, 46 Cal.2d 659, 661–662, 297 P.2d 638) the error which it was declared would have entitled plaintiff to rescind was the listing of the cost of certain materials as $104.52, rather than $10,452, in a total bid of $172,421. Thus the percentage of error here was larger than in Lemoge, and was plainly material."

II

An error in the computation of a bid may be material, representing a large percentage of the total bid submitted, and yet requiring compliance with the bid may not be unconscionable. Thus, omission of a $25,000 item in a $100,000 bid would be material, but if the $100,000 bid included $50,000 in profit, no hardship would be created by requiring the contractor to comply with the terms of his bid.

This does not represent the case at bar. Here the record reveals that if respondent were forced to comply with the terms of its bid it would lose at least $10,000. Respondent's costs, including the omitted item, would be roughly $151,000 while the total amount of its bid was only $141,000. Enforcement of the bid is deemed unconscionable as working a substantial hardship on the bidder where it appears he would incur a substantial pecuniary loss. Donaldson v. Abraham, 68 Wash. 208, 122 P. 1003 (1912). This is particularly so where, as here, no injury is caused by withdrawal of the bid. (See sec. IV, infra.)

III

One who seeks equitable relief from error must establish that such error does not result from violation of a positive legal duty or from culpable negligence.

"* * * [This] generally means carelessness or lack of good faith in calculation which violates a positive duty in making up a bid, so as to amount to gross negligence, or wilful negligence, when it takes on a sinister meaning and will furnish cause, if established, for holding a mistake of the offending bidder to be one not remediable in equity. *It is thus distinguished from a clerical or inadvertent error in handling items of a bid either through setting them down or transcription.*" (emphasis added) Annot., 52 A.L.R.2d 792, 794.

In several of its assignments appellant contends that the trial court erred in not finding that respondent was negligent to the point of being grossly negligent. . . .

* * *

On the basis of these facts the trial court concluded:

"There was no willful or even negligent act by plaintiff's agents which prevented knowledge of the error from reaching Mr. Mattefs prior to the opening. In preparing the bid Mattefs Construction Company proceeded in the usual way and under the same last minute pressures that are experienced by all general contractors bidding on bids of this kind. Under the evidence I conclude that it was using ordinary care in its methods of bid preparation; that is, the same care that other contractors in the area use in making bids of the kind here involved. There was no evidence of any gross negligence or fraudulent or willful intent to omit this item for the purpose of obtaining any advantage in the bidding."

It is appellant's contention that the trial court erred in making these findings. It has long been the rule of this court that:

"Where the findings of the trial court are supported by substantial and competent, though conflicting, evidence, such findings will not be disturbed on appeal."

Riley v. Larson, 91 Idaho 831, 432 P.2d 775 (1967); Meridian Bowling Lanes, Inc. v. Brown, 90 Idaho 403, 412 P.2d 586 (1966). Additionally, the trial judge is the arbiter of conflicting evidence; his determination of the weight, credibility, inference and implications thereof is not to be supplanted by this court's impressions or conclusions from the written record. *Meridian Bowling Lanes, Inc. v. Brown,* supra. Also findings of fact shall not be set aside unless clearly erroneous. I.R.C.P. 52(a).

Thus, the finding of the trial court that the mistake of respondent was not due to the required type of negligence must be affirmed. As was held in the *Kemper* case:

"The type of error here involved is one which will sometimes occur in the conduct of reasonable and cautious businessmen, and, under all the circumstances, we cannot say as a matter of law that it constituted a neglect of legal duty such as would bar the right to equitable relief." 235 P.2d at p. 11.

IV

It is well settled by the authorities that a bid may not be withdrawn if such withdrawal would work a substantial hardship on the offeree. Many situations can be hypothesized where such a hardship would result. However, none appears here, nor has appellant attempted to prove any hardship. Appellant expected to pay $150,000 for the work it solicited. Its actual cost will be $149,000. It complains because it cannot have the work done for $141,000. Thus, appellant's injury consists of a failure to save $9,000 on its construction rather than saving $1,000.

"* * * [T]he city will not be heard to complain that it cannot be placed in statu quo because it will not have the benefit of an inequitable bargain. [citations]" * * * *Kemper Const. Co.,* supra, at page 11. See also Kutsche v. Ford, 222 Mich. 442, 192 N.W. 714, 717 (Mich.1923).

The most appellant can argue is that its damage is presumed by the requirement of a bid bond and that release of a bid bond and that release of a bidder whenever he makes a mistake will impair the purposes for which a bid bond is required. . . .

* * *

The proper purpose of a provision against withdrawal of a bid was fully explained by the Maryland Court of Appeals, quoting from Geremia v. Boyarsky, 107 Conn. 387, 140 A. 749 (1928):

" 'It is objected that the rule should be different where, as here, there is a proviso forbidding the withdrawal of bids. To be sure, this puts a bidder on notice that there is a certain finality about bidding for a government contract. But this by no means should enable a governmental agency to take an unconscionable advantage of its special status as a government body. * * * The proper effect of the requirement that bids remain unrevoked is to assure the State that a bidder will be relieved of his obligation only when it is legally justifiable. That means that the State is in the same position as any acceptor when there is a question of rectifying an error. * * * Of course, it is obvious, as the State contends, that the system of public bidding, developed by experience and usual in public contracts, should not be broken down by lightly permitting bidders to withdraw because of change of mind. Such a course would be unfair to other straightforward bidders, as well as disruptive of public business. But it can hardly be a substantial impairment of such system to grant the relief—which would clearly be given as between private citizens—in a case where a bona fide mistake is proven and was known to the State before acceptance or any loss to it.' " City of Baltimore v. De Luca–Davis Construction Co., 124 A.2d at p. 565.

V

The final element of the right to equitable relief raised by appellant is actually an adjunct of the previous question of whether the offeree will be damaged by withdrawal of the bid. The requirement of prompt notice is separately stated here because appellant earnestly argues that it was not given such prompt notice. This contention is not supported by the evidence.

* * *

Relief from mistaken bids is consistently allowed where the acceptor has actual notice of the error prior to its attempted acceptance and the other elements necessary for equitable relief are present. M.F. Kemper Const. Co., 235 P.2d at page 10. We see no reason to deviate from this rule where, as here, the party opposing the grant of equitable relief can show no damage other than loss of benefit of an inequitable bargain. We conclude that appellant's position is no better here than it was when similar arguments were presented to the U.S. Supreme Court nearly 70 years ago. In quoting from the circuit court opinion, the court held:

" '* * * If the defendants [appellants] are correct in their contention there is absolutely no redress for a bidder for public work, no matter how aggravated or palpable his blunder. The moment his proposal is opened by the executive board he is held as in a grasp of steel. There is no remedy, no escape. If, through an error of his clerk, he has agreed to do work worth $1,000,000 for $10, he must be held to the strict letter of his contract, while equity stands by with folded hands and sees him driven into bankruptcy. The defendants' [appellants'] position admits of no compromise, no exception, no middle ground.' " Moffett, Hodgkins & Clarke Co. v. City of Rochester, 178 U.S. 373, 386, 20 S.Ct. 957, 961, 44 L.Ed. 1108 (1900). This reasoning is equally applicable to the cause at bar.

Judgment affirmed. Costs to respondent.

NOTES

(1) Since the offeree appeared to have actual notice of the error prior to acceptance, why was not this knowledge sufficient to terminate the power of acceptance? Under the court's analysis in *Boise,* would the result have been the same if the offer had been accepted before the offeree knew of the error? Restatement (Second) § 153 takes the position that a material mistake by one party as to a "basic assumption on which he made the contract" makes the contract "voidable by him if * * * the effect of the mistake is such that enforcement of the contract would be unconscionable, or * * * the other party had reason to know of the mistake or his fault caused the mistake." For a recent application, see First Baptist Church of Moultrie v. Barber Contracting Company, 189 Ga.App. 804, 377 S.E.2d 717 (1989).

The offeree's actual or constructive knowledge of a mistake is often an important factor in judicial opinions granting relief to the mistaken party. Relief typically takes the form of rescission, an equitable remedy invalidating the contract. Thus, it is evidently conceded that a contract of some sort has been formed. Yet if the offeree knew or should have known about the mistake it is arguable that he or she had no power to accept the offer at all. In Rushlight Automatic Sprinkler Co. v. City of Portland, 189 Or. 194, 219 P.2d 732 (1950), the plaintiff's bid was substantially below the others because the cost of steel was mistakenly omitted. In allowing rescission, the court observed: "We believe that in this State an offer and acceptance are deemed to effect a meeting of the minds, even though the offeror made a material mistake in compiling his offer, provided the acceptor was not aware of the mistake and had no reason to suspect it. But if the offeree knew of the mistake, and it was basic, or if the circumstances were such that he, a reasonable man, should have inferred that a basic mistake was made, a meeting of the minds does not occur. The circumstances which should arouse the suspicions of the fair-minded offeree are many, as stated in § 94 of Williston on Contracts, Rev.Ed.: '. . . And the same principle is applicable in any case where the offeree should know that the terms of the offer are unintended or misunderstood by the offeror. The offeree will not be permitted to snap up an offer that is too good to be true; no contract based on such an offer can then be enforced by the acceptor.' " 219 P.2d at 752–53.

Where the remedy of rescission is sought, it may make little difference whether the court concludes that there was no mutual assent or that the contract was voidable. But are there cases where this would not be true? Is *Boise* such a case? See *Problem: The Case of the Four Million Labels*, infra. See also Wil–Fred's Inc. v. Metropolitan Sanitary District of Greater Chicago, 57 Ill.App.3d 16, 14 Ill.Dec. 667, 372 N.E.2d 946 (1978), where the court considered the distinction traditionally made between a clerical or mathematical error and an error in business judgment. The court observed: "Generally, relief is refused for errors in judgment and allowed for clerical or mathematical mistakes. ... Nonetheless, we believe, in fairness to the individual bidder, that the facts surrounding the error, not the label, i.e. 'mistake of fact' or 'mistake of judgment,' should determine whether relief is granted." 14 Ill.Dec. at 674, 372 N.E.2d at 953. The court pointed out that the plaintiff's error in judgment derived, at least in part, from misleading specifications furnished by the defendant. But the court went on to state: "Furthermore, it was established that Wil–Fred's quotation was $233,775 lower than the next lowest bid. It is apparent that such a sizable discrepancy should have placed the Sanitary District on notice that plaintiff's bid contained a material error. ... Accordingly equity will not allow the District to take advantage of Wil–Fred's low offer." 14 Ill.Dec. at 674, 372 N.E.2d at 953. There is a hint here that a "palpable" error, however derived, may be sufficient to warrant relief. For a thorough treatment of the mistaken bid problem, see Jones, *The Law of Mistaken Bids*, 48 U.Cin.L.Rev. 43 (1979).

(2) *Effect of Bidder Negligence.* "The very term 'mistake' connotes some degree of negligent conduct. * * * In most circumstances it would be illogical, if not impossible, to require a bidder who made a mistake in calculating a bid to establish that the mistake was one most reasonable bidders would make under the same or substantially similar circumstances. Requiring proof of freedom from negligence focuses substantial attention on the cause of the mistake; the question of the availability of equitable relief from a mistaken bid should focus primarily on the consequences of the mistake. * * * Numerous courts and commentators have concluded that in public construction contract cases in which a bidder seeks equitable relief from bond forfeiture provisions because of a mistaken bid, the fundamental issue is whether the bidder made an honest or good faith mistake and any question of gross or extreme negligence of the bidder should be considered only as evidence of the bidder's lack of good faith. * * * This approach recognizes that a bidder should not be allowed to rescind a mistaken bid if the bid were made in bad faith and emphasizes the desirability of ensuring that public projects proceed on the basis of accurate cost estimates. A contrary rule would encourage manipulative bidding practices and undermine the stability of the bidding process. Furthermore, evenhanded application of a good faith standard ensures fair treatment of all parties involved in dealings with municipal authorities, thereby enhancing the integrity of the bidding process." Powder Horn Constructors, Inc. v. City of Florence, 754 P.2d 356, 362 (Colo.1988).

(3) *Mistakes in Bids and Federal Government Contracting.* Applicable regulations oblige a contracting officer to examine all bids for mistakes. Federal Acquisition Regulation 14.406–1. In cases of apparent mistakes and in cases where the contracting officer has reason to believe that a mistake may have been made, the contracting officer shall request from the bidder a verification

of the bid, calling attention to the suspected mistake. Id. Any clerical mistake, apparent on the face of the bid, may be corrected by the contracting officer before the award. FAR 14.406–2. If a bidder requests permission to correct a mistake and clear and convincing evidence establishes both the existence of the mistake and the bid actually intended, the agency head may make a determination permitting the bidder to correct the mistake; provided, that if this correction would result in displacing one or more lower bids, such a determination shall not be made unless the existence of the mistake and the bid actually intended are ascertainable substantially from the invitation and the bid itself. FAR 14.406–3. Relief from the mistake is, of course, more difficult to obtain after the award of the contract. Here one is, in general, obliged to show by clear and convincing evidence either mutual mistake or a unilateral mistake of which the contracting officer had actual or constructive knowledge; i.e., knew or should have known of the error. FAR 14.406–4. For such mistakes, agencies are authorized to (1) rescind the contract or (2) reform the contract so as to delete the items involved in the mistake, or to increase the price if the contract price, as corrected, does not exceed that of the next lowest acceptable bid under the original invitation for bids. Id. The United States Claims Court recently denied relief from an accepted bid on a latrine repair project, where the 13% price disparity was quite close to the government's own estimate and where the government's representative neither knew nor had reason to know of the mistake. Fadeley v. United States, 15 Cl.Ct. 706 (1988). The court observed: "The granting of equitable relief is based upon a concern with the overreaching of a contractor by a contracting officer who suspects a mistake in the bid and is willing to accept it nevertheless. This is not the situation here. Therefore, Federal Acquisition Regulation 14.406–4 (1986), which allows for the reformation of a contract to reflect the correction of a prior, unilateral bid mistake when the contracting officer is charged with knowledge of that mistake is not applicable in the instant case." 15 Cl.Ct. at 712.

(4) *Mistaken Admissions.*

"Two of the 9,691 envelopes that were mailed last month to applicants to next year's freshman class contained the wrong letter, and two high school seniors who were supposed to be sent rejection notices received acceptances. 'Somebody must have pulled the form letter off the wrong pile,' explained Spencer J. Reynolds '61, associate director of admission. To his knowledge, he said, this was the first such error in his nine years at Princeton, during which time some 76,000 applications have been processed.

"In one of the cases, the mistake was discovered when the recipient visited the campus and noticed that his name was not included in the list of admitted students posted in the admissions office. The other case came to light when the student called because his envelope had not contained a reply card. Since legally a letter of admission may be considered a binding contract, the university decided to honor the acceptances. One of the students is viewed as academically unqualified and has been advised that he probably could not handle the workload, while the other has been informed that he is thought capable of doing the work. As of Memorial Day, neither had yet notified the university of his decision." *Princeton Alumni Weekly,* May 27, 1975, p. 8.

PROBLEM: THE CASE OF THE FOUR MILLION LABELS

Reed, operator of a small photography store, had need of adhesive pricing labels. He began to prepare a purchase order for five different types of labels. In handwriting he filled in the blank spaces for four different types and in the quantity column noted opposite each "2M." At that point he was interrupted by a customer, and it was not until later that he finished writing the order. He described the fifth label as "Label as Attached," attached a copy of the desired label, and in the quantity column wrote "4MM." He then mailed the completed order to Monarch, a nationwide manufacturer and supplier of pricing and product identification labels.

The designation "M" is understood in the label industry to mean one thousand. "MM" stands for one million. Reed intended to order 4,000 of the fifth type; his use of "MM" was a mistake.

In previous transactions the largest order Monarch had received from Reed for any one item was 4,000. Indeed, the largest order Monarch ever received previously from any source was for one million labels. Without checking further, Monarch proceeded to fill the order. The first four items were in stock and were mailed to Reed. The fifth required a special printing. Reed did not become aware of any problem until a truck drove up to his store with seven cartons of labels weighing 622 pounds!

Reed refused to receive the merchandise; Monarch sued for the $2,680 purchase price. What result? Consider the matter pro and con before consulting Reed's Photo Mart v. Monarch Marking System Co., 475 S.W.2d 356 (Tex.Civ. App.1971), reversed 485 S.W.2d 905 (Tex.1972).

Beachcomber Coins, Inc. v. Boskett

Superior Court of New Jersey, Appellate Division, 1979.
166 N.J.Super. 442, 400 A.2d 78.

■ CONFORD, P.J.A.D. (retired and temporarily assigned).

Plaintiff, a retail dealer in coins, brought an action for rescission of a purchase by it from defendant for $500 of a dime purportedly minted in 1916 at Denver. Defendant is a part-time coin dealer. Plaintiff asserts a mutual mistake of fact as to the genuineness of the coin as Denver-minted, such a coin being a rarity and therefore having a market value greatly in excess of its normal monetary worth. Plaintiff's evidence at trial that the "D" on the coin signifying Denver mintage was counterfeited is not disputed by defendant. Although at trial defendant disputed that the coin tendered back to him by plaintiff was the one he sold, the implicit trial finding is to the contrary, and that issue is not raised on appeal.

The trial judge, sitting without a jury, held for defendant on the ground that the customary "coin dealing procedures" were for a dealer purchasing a coin to make his own investigation of the genuineness of the coin and to "assume the risk" of his purchase if his investigation is faulty. The judge conceded that the evidence demonstrated satisfaction of the ordinary requisites of the rule of rescission for mutual mistake of fact that both parties act under a mistake of fact and that the fact be "central" [material] to the making of the contract. The proofs were that the seller had himself acquired this coin and two others of minor value for a total of $450 and that his representative had told the purchaser that he would not sell the dime for less than $500. The principal of plaintiff firm spent from 15 to 45 minutes in close examination of the coin before purchasing it. Soon thereafter he received an offer of $700 for the coin subject to certification of its genuineness by the American Numismatic Society. That organization labelled it a counterfeit, and as a result plaintiff instituted the present action.

The evidence and trial judge's findings establish this as a classic case of rescission for mutual mistake of fact. As a general rule,

> * * * where parties on entering into a transaction that affects their contractual relations are both under a mistake regarding a fact assumed by them as the basis on which they entered into the transaction, it is voidable by either party if enforcement of it would be materially more onerous to him than it would have been had the fact been as the parties believed it to be. [Restatement, Contracts, § 502 at 961 (1932);* 13 Williston on Contracts (3 ed. 1970), § 1543, 74–75]

By way of example, the *Restatement* posits the following:

> A contracts to sell to B a specific bar of silver before them. The parties supposed that the bar is sterling. It has, however, a much larger admixture of base metal. The contract is voidable by B. [Op. cit. at 964].

Moreover, "negligent failure of a party to know or to discover the facts as to which both parties are under a mistake does not preclude rescission or reformation on account thereof." Restatement, op. cit., § 502 at 977. The law of New Jersey is in accord. See Riviere v. Berla, 89 N.J.Eq. 596, 597, 106 A. 455 (E. & A. 1918); Dencer v. Erb, 142 N.J.Eq. 422, 429, 60 A.2d 282 (Ch.1948). In the *Riviere* case relief was denied only because the parties could not be restored to the *status quo ante*. In the present case they can be. It is undisputed that both parties believed that the coin was a genuine Denver-minted one. The mistake was mutual in that both parties were laboring under the same misapprehension as to this particular, essential fact. The price asked and paid was directly based on that assumption. That plaintiff may have been negligent in his inspection of the coin (a point not expressly found but implied by the trial judge) does not, as noted above, bar its claim for rescission. Cf. Smith v. Zimbalist, 2 Cal.App.2d 324, 38 P.2d 170 (D.Ct.App.1934).

[handwritten margin note: both believed it was genuine @ time of contract]

---

* No substantial change in the rule was effected by Restatement, Contracts 2d, § 294(1), Tent.Dr. No. 10 (1975) at 10. This provides:

> (1) Where a mistake of both parties at the time a contract was made as to a basic assumption on which the contract was made has a material effect on the agreed exchange of performances, the contract is voidable by the adversely affected party unless he bears the risk of the mistake under the rule stated in § 296.

The exceptions in § 296 are not here applicable [§ 294(1) is § 152(1) in the final draft. Ed.]

Defendant's contention that plaintiff assumed the risk that the coin might be of greater or lesser value than that paid is not supported by the evidence. It is well established that a party to a contract can assume the risk of being mistaken as to the value of the thing sold. 13 Williston, Contracts, op. cit., § 1543A at 85. The *Restatement* states the rule this way:

> Where the parties know that there is doubt in regard to a certain matter and contract on that assumption, the contract is not rendered voidable because one is disappointed in the hope that the facts accord with his wishes. The risk of the existence of the doubtful fact is then assumed as one of the elements of the bargain. [Restatement, op. cit., § 502, Comment f at 964. See also Restatement, Contracts 2d, op. cit., § 296(b), Comment c at 4.]

However, for the stated rule to apply, the parties must be conscious that the pertinent fact may not be true and make their agreement at the risk of that possibility. 17 Am.Jur.2d, Contracts, § 145 at 492. In this case both parties were certain that the coin was genuine. They so testified. Plaintiff's principal thought so after his inspection, and defendant would not have paid nearly $450 for it otherwise. A different case would be presented if the seller were uncertain either of the genuineness of the coin or of its value [if] genuine, and had accepted the expert buyer's judgment on these matters.

The trial judge's rationale of custom of the trade is not supported by the evidence. It depended upon the testimony of plaintiff's expert witness who on cross-examination as to the "procedure" on the purchase by a dealer of a rare coin, stated that the dealer would check it with magnification and then "normally send it to the American Numismatic Certification Service for certification." This testimony does not in our opinion establish that practice as a usage of trade "having such regularity of observance in a * * * trade as to justify an expectation that it will be observed with respect to the transaction in question," within the intent of the Uniform Commercial Code, N.J.S.A. 12A:1–205(2).**

The cited code provision contemplates that the trade usage is so prevalent as to warrant the conclusion that the parties contracted with reference to, and intended their agreement to be governed by it. Cf. Manhattan Overseas Co. v. Camden Co. Beverage Co., 125 N.J.L. 239, 244, 15 A.2d 217 (Sup.Ct.1940), aff'd 126 N.J.L. 421, 19 A.2d 828 (E. & A. 1941). Our reading of the testimony does not indicate any basis for findings either that this was a trade usage within the Code definition at all or that these parties in fact accepted it as such to the extent that they were agreeing that because of it the sale was an "as is" transaction. Indeed, the same witness testified there was a "normal policy" among coin dealers throughout the United States of a "return privilege" for altered coins.

** Note, also, that evidence of a trade usage is not admissible unless the offering party gives the other party advance notice to prevent unfair surprise. N.J.S.A. 12A:1–105(6). Plaintiff received no notice that the judge intended to decide this case on the basis of the alleged trade usage.

The foregoing conclusions make it unnecessary for us to discuss plaintiff's alternative contention that the contract was "unenforceable" because it constituted an illegal contract to purchase a counterfeit coin. We regard that position as devoid of merit.

Reversed.

Lenawee County Board of Health v. Messerly

Supreme Court of Michigan, 1982.
417 Mich. 17, 331 N.W.2d 203.

■ RYAN, JUSTICE.

In March of 1977, Carl and Nancy Pickles, appellees, purchased from appellants, William and Martha Messerly, a 600–square-foot tract of land upon which is located a three-unit apartment building. Shortly after the transaction was closed, the Lenawee County Board of Health condemned the property and obtained a permanent injunction which prohibits human habitation on the premises until the defective sewage system is brought into conformance with the Lenawee County sanitation code.

We are required to determine whether appellees should prevail in their attempt to avoid this land contract on the basis of mutual mistake and failure of consideration. We conclude that the parties did entertain a mutual misapprehension of fact, but that the circumstances of this case do not warrant rescission.

I

The facts of the case are not seriously in dispute. In 1971, the Messerlys acquired approximately one acre plus 600 square feet of land. A three-unit apartment building was situated upon the 600–square-foot portion. The trial court found that, prior to this transfer, the Messerlys' predecessor in title, Mr. Bloom, had installed a septic tank on the property without a permit and in violation of the applicable health code. The Messerlys used the building as an income investment property until 1973 when they sold it, upon land contract, to James Barnes who likewise used it primarily as an income-producing investment.

Mr. and Mrs. Barnes, with the permission of the Messerlys, sold approximately one acre of the property in 1976, and the remaining 600 square feet and building were offered for sale soon thereafter when Mr. and Mrs. Barnes defaulted on their land contract. Mr. and Mrs. Pickles evidenced an interest in the property, but were dissatisfied with the terms of the Barnes–Messerly land contract. Consequently, to accommodate the Pickleses' preference to enter into a land contract directly with the Messerlys, Mr. and Mrs. Barnes executed a quit-claim deed which conveyed their interest in the property back to the Messerlys. After inspecting the property, Mr. and Mrs. Pickles executed a new land contract with the Messerlys on March 21, 1977. It provided for a purchase price of $25,500. A clause was added to the end of the land contract form which provides:

"17. Purchaser has examined this property and agrees to accept same in its present condition. There are no other or additional written or oral understandings."

Five or six days later, when the Pickleses went to introduce themselves to the tenants, they discovered raw sewage seeping out of the ground. Tests conducted by a sanitation expert indicated the inadequacy of the sewage system. The Lenawee County Board of Health subsequently condemned the property and initiated this lawsuit in the Lenawee Circuit Court against the Messerlys as land contract vendors, and the Pickleses, as vendees, to obtain a permanent injunction proscribing human habitation of the premises until the property was brought into conformance with the Lenawee County sanitation code. The injunction was granted, and the Lenawee County Board of Health was permitted to withdraw from the lawsuit by stipulation of the parties.

When no payments were made on the land contract, the Messerlys filed a cross-complaint against the Pickleses seeking foreclosure, sale of the property, and a deficiency judgment. Mr. and Mrs. Pickles then counterclaimed for rescission against the Messerlys, and filed a third-party complaint against the Barneses, which incorporated, by reference, the allegations of the counterclaim against the Messerlys. In count one, Mr. and Mrs. Pickles alleged failure of consideration. Count two charged Mr. and Mrs. Barnes with willful concealment and misrepresentation as a result of their failure to disclose the condition of the sanitation system. Additionally, Mr. and Mrs. Pickles sought to hold the Messerlys liable in equity for the Barneses' alleged misrepresentation. The Pickleses prayed that the land contract be rescinded.

After a bench trial, the court concluded that the Pickleses had no cause of action against either the Messerlys or the Barneses as there was no fraud or misrepresentation. This ruling was predicated on the trial judge's conclusion that none of the parties knew of Mr. Bloom's earlier transgression or of the resultant problem with the septic system until it was discovered by the Pickleses, and that the sanitation problem was not caused by any of the parties. The trial court held that the property was purchased "as is," after inspection and, accordingly, its "negative * * * value cannot be blamed upon an innocent seller." Foreclosure was ordered against the Pickleses, together with a judgment against them in the amount of $25,943.09.

Mr. and Mrs. Pickles appealed from the adverse judgment. The Court of Appeals unanimously affirmed the trial court's ruling with respect to Mr. and Mrs. Barnes but, in a two-to-one decision, reversed the finding of no cause of action on the Pickleses' claims against the Messerlys. Lenawee County Board of Health v. Messerly, 98 Mich.App. 478, 295 N.W.2d 903 (1980). It concluded that the mutual mistake between the Messerlys and the Pickleses went to a basic, as opposed to a collateral, element of the contract, and that the parties intended to transfer income-producing rental property but, in actuality, the vendees paid $25,500 for an asset without value.[1]

We granted the Messerlys' application for leave to appeal. 411 Mich. 900 (1981).

II

We must decide initially whether there was a mistaken belief entertained by one or both parties to the contract in dispute and, if so, the resultant legal significance.

A contractual mistake "is a belief that is not in accord with the facts." 1 Restatement Contracts, 2d, § 151, p. 383. The erroneous belief of one or both of the parties must relate to a fact in existence at the time the contract is executed. Richardson Lumber Co. v. Hoey, 219 Mich. 643, 189 N.W. 923 (1922); Sherwood v. Walker, 66 Mich. 568, 580, 33 N.W. 919 (1887) (Sherwood, J., dissenting). That is to say, the belief which is found to be in error may not be, in substance, a prediction as to a future occurrence or non-occurrence. . . .

The Court of Appeals concluded, after a *de novo* review of the record, that the parties were mistaken as to the income-producing capacity of the property in question. 98 Mich.App. 487–488, 295 N.W.2d 903. We agree. The vendors and the vendees each believed that the property transferred could be utilized as income-generating rental property. All of the parties subsequently learned that, in fact, the property was unsuitable for any residential use.

* * *

Having determined that when these parties entered into the land contract they were laboring under a mutual mistake of fact, we now direct our attention to a determination of the legal significance of that finding.

A contract may be rescinded because of a mutual misapprehension of the parties, but this remedy is granted only in the sound discretion of the court. Harris v. Axline, 323 Mich. 585, 36 N.W.2d 154 (1949). Appellants argue that the parties' mistake relates only to the quality or value of the real estate transferred, and that such mistakes are collateral to the agreement and do not justify rescission, citing A & M Land Development Co. v. Miller, 354 Mich. 681, 94 N.W.2d 197 (1959).

In that case, the plaintiff was the purchaser of 91 lots of real property. It sought partial rescission of the land contract when it was frustrated in its attempts to develop 42 of the lots because it could not obtain permits from the county health department to install septic tanks on these lots.

---

1. The trial court found that the only way that the property could be put to residential use would be to pump and haul the sewage, a method which is economically unfeasible, as the cost of such a disposal system amounts to double the income generated by the property. There was speculation by the trial court that the adjoining land might be utilized to make the property suitable for residential use, but in the absence of testimony directed at that point, the court refused to draw any conclusions. The trial court and the Court of Appeals both found that the property was valueless, or had a negative value.

This Court refused to allow rescission because the mistake, whether mutual or unilateral, related only to the value of the property.

"There was here no mistake as to the form or substance of the contract between the parties, or the description of the property constituting the subject matter. The situation involved is not at all analogous to that presented in Scott v. Grow, 301 Mich. 226; 3 N.W.2d 254; 141 ALR 819 (1942). There the plaintiff sought relief by way of reformation of a deed on the ground that the instrument of conveyance had not been drawn in accordance with the intention and agreement of the parties. It was held that the bill of complaint stated a case for the granting of equitable relief by way of reformation. In the case at bar plaintiff received the property for which it contracted. The fact that it may be of less value than the purchaser expected at the time of the transaction is not a sufficient basis for the granting of equitable relief, neither fraud nor reliance on misrepresentation of material facts having been established." 354 Mich. 693–694, 94 N.W.2d 197.

Appellees contend, on the other hand, that in this case the parties were mistaken as to the very nature of the character of the consideration and claim that the pervasive and essential quality of this mistake renders rescission appropriate. They cite in support of that view Sherwood v. Walker, 66 Mich. 568, 33 N.W. 919 (1887), the famous "barren cow" case. In that case, the parties agreed to the sale and purchase of a cow which was thought to be barren, but which was, in reality, with calf. When the seller discovered the fertile condition of his cow, he refused to deliver her. In permitting rescission, the Court stated:

"It seems to me, however, in the case made by this record, that the mistake or misapprehension of the parties went to the whole substance of the agreement. If the cow was a breeder, she was worth at least $750; if barren, she was worth not over $80. The parties would not have made the contract of sale except upon the understanding and belief that she was incapable of breeding, and of no use as a cow. It is true she is now the identical animal that they thought her to be when the contract was made; there is no mistake as to the identity of the creature. Yet the mistake was not of the mere quality of the animal, but went to the very nature of the thing. A barren cow is substantially a different creature than a breeding one. There is as much difference between them for all purposes of use as there is between an ox and a cow that is capable of breeding and giving milk. If the mutual mistake had simply related to the fact whether she was with calf or not for one season, then it might have been a good sale; but the mistake affected the character of the animal for all time, and for her present and ultimate use. She was not in fact the animal, or the kind of animal, the defendants intended to sell or the plaintiff to buy. She was not a barren cow, and, if this fact had been known, there would have been no contract. The mistake affected the substance of the whole consideration, and it must be considered that there was no contract to sell or sale of the cow as she actually was. The thing sold and bought had in fact no existence. She was sold as a beef creature would be sold; she is in fact a breeding cow, and a valuable one.

"The court should have instructed the jury that if they found that the cow was sold, or contracted to be sold, upon the understanding of both parties that she was barren, and useless for the purpose of breeding, and that in fact she was not barren, but capable of breeding, then the defendants had a right to rescind, and to refuse to deliver, and the verdict should be in their favor." 66 Mich. 577–578, 33 N.W. 919.

As the parties suggest, the foregoing precedent arguably distinguishes mistakes affecting the essence of the consideration from those which go to its quality or value, affording relief on a per se basis for the former but not the latter. See, e.g., Lenawee County Board of Health v. Messerly, 98 Mich.App. 478, 492, 295 N.W.2d 903 (1980) (Mackenzie, J., concurring in part).

However, the distinctions which may be drawn from *Sherwood* and *A & M Land Development Co.* do not provide a satisfactory analysis of the nature of a mistake sufficient to invalidate a contract. Often, a mistake relates to an underlying factual assumption which, when discovered, directly affects value, but simultaneously and materially affects the essence of the contractual consideration. It is disingenuous to label such a mistake collateral. McKay v. Coleman, 85 Mich. 60, 48 N.W. 203 (1891). Corbin, Contracts (One Vol. ed.), § 605, p. 551.

Appellant and appellee both mistakenly believed that the property which was the subject of their land contract would generate income as rental property. The fact that it could not be used for human habitation deprived the property of its income-earning potential and rendered it less valuable. However, this mistake, while directly and dramatically affecting the property's value, cannot accurately be characterized as collateral because it also affects the very essence of the consideration. "The thing sold and bought [income generating rental property] had in fact no existence." Sherwood v. Walker, 66 Mich. 568, 33 N.W. 919.

We find that the inexact and confusing distinction between contractual mistakes running to value and those touching the substance of the consideration serves only as an impediment to a clear and helpful analysis for the equitable resolution of cases in which mistake is alleged and proven. Accordingly, the holdings of *A & M Land Development Co.* and *Sherwood* with respect to the material or collateral nature of a mistake are limited to the facts of those cases.

Instead, we think the better-reasoned approach is a case-by-case analysis whereby rescission is indicated when the mistaken belief relates to a basic assumption of the parties upon which the contract is made, and which materially affects the agreed performances of the parties. Denton v. Utley, 350 Mich. 332, 86 N.W.2d 537 (1957); Farhat v. Rassey, 295 Mich. 349, 294 N.W. 707 (1940); Richardson Lumber Co. v. Hoey, 219 Mich. 643, 189 N.W.

923 (1922). 1 Restatement Contracts, 2d, § 152, pp. 385–386.[2] Rescission is not available, however, to relieve a party who has assumed the risk of loss in connection with the mistake. Denton v. Utley, 350 Mich. 344–345, 86 N.W.2d 537; Farhat v. Rassey, 295 Mich. 349, 294 N.W. 707; Corbin, Contracts (One Vol. ed.), § 605, p. 552; 1 Restatement Contracts, 2d, §§ 152, 154, pp. 385–386, 402–406.[3]

All of the parties to this contract erroneously assumed that the property transferred by the vendors to the vendees was suitable for human habitation and could be utilized to generate rental income. The fundamental nature of these assumptions is indicated by the fact that their invalidity changed the character of the property transferred, thereby frustrating, indeed precluding, Mr. and Mrs. Pickles' intended use of the real estate. Although the Pickleses are disadvantaged by enforcement of the contract, performance is advantageous to the Messerlys, as the property at issue is less valuable absent its income-earning potential. Nothing short of rescission can remedy the mistake. Thus, the parties' mistake as to a basic assumption materially affects the agreed performances of the parties.

Despite the significance of the mistake made by the parties, we reverse the Court of Appeals because we conclude that equity does not justify the remedy sought by Mr. and Mrs. Pickles.

Rescission is an equitable remedy which is granted only in the sound discretion of the court. Harris v. Axline, 323 Mich. 585, 36 N.W.2d 154 (1949); Hathaway v. Hudson, 256 Mich. 694, 239 N.W. 859 (1932). A court need not grant rescission in every case in which the mutual mistake relates to a basic assumption and materially affects the agreed performance of the parties.

2. The parties have invited our attention to the first edition of the Restatement of Contracts in their briefs, and the Court of Appeals cites to that edition in its opinion. However, the second edition was published subsequent to the issuance of the lower court opinion and the filing of the briefs with this Court. Thus, we take it upon ourselves to refer to the latest edition to aid us in our resolution of this case.

Section 152 delineates the legal significance of a mistake.

"§ 152. When Mistake of Both Parties Makes a Contract Voidable

"(1) Where a mistake of both parties at the time a contract was made as to a basic assumption on which the contract was made has a material effect on the agreed exchange of performances, the contract is voidable by the adversely affected party unless he bears the risk of the mistake under the rule stated in § 154.

"(2) In determining whether the mistake has a material effect on the agreed exchange of performances, account is taken of any relief by way of reformation, restitution, or otherwise."

3. "§ 154. When a Party Bears the Risk of a Mistake

"A party bears the risk of a mistake when

"(a) the risk is allocated to him by agreement of the parties, or

"(b) he is aware, at the time the contract is made, that he has only limited knowledge with respect to the facts to which the mistake relates but treats his limited knowledge as sufficient, or

"(c) the risk is allocated to him by the court on the ground that it is reasonable in the circumstances to do so."

In cases of mistake by two equally innocent parties, we are required, in the exercise of our equitable powers, to determine which blameless party should assume the loss resulting from the misapprehension they shared.[4] Normally that can only be done by drawing upon our "own notions of what is reasonable and just under all the surrounding circumstances."[5]

Equity suggests that, in this case, the risk should be allocated to the purchasers. We are guided to that conclusion, in part, by the standards announced in § 154 of the Restatements of Contracts 2d, for determining when a party bears the risk of mistake. See fn. 12. Section 154(a) suggests that the court should look first to whether the parties have agreed to the allocation of the risk between themselves. While there is no express assumption in the contract by either party of the risk of the property becoming uninhabitable, there was indeed some agreed allocation of the risk to the vendees by the incorporation of an "as is" clause into the contract which, we repeat, provided:

> "Purchaser has examined this property and agrees to accept same in its present condition. There are no other or additional written or oral understandings."

That is a persuasive indication that the parties considered that, as between them, such risk as related to the "present condition" of the property should lie with the purchaser. If the "as is" clause is to have any meaning at all, it must be interpreted to refer to those defects which were unknown at the time that the contract was executed. Thus, the parties themselves assigned the risk of loss to Mr. and Mrs. Pickles.

We conclude that Mr. and Mrs. Pickles are not entitled to the equitable remedy of rescission and, accordingly, reverse the decision of the Court of Appeals. [Some footnotes omitted.]

NOTES

(1) *Sherwood v. Walker and Restatement (Second) of Contracts. Sherwood v. Walker,* discussed in *Lenawee,* concerned the sale of a presumed barren cow named "Rose the Second of Aberlone." It is the classic mutual mistake case, renowned in prose and poetry. See Birmingham, *A Rose by Any Other Word: Mutual Mistake in Sherwood v. Walker,* 21 U.C.D.L.Rev. 197 (1987). Professor Brainerd Currie's poem "Aberlone, Rose Of," is one of the delights of legal literature. See 10 The Student Lawyer 4 (1965). For your enjoyment and edification, the beginning and the ending are reprinted below.

4. This risk-of-loss analysis is absent in both *A & M Land Development Co.* and *Sherwood,* and this omission helps to explain, in part, the disparate treatment in the two cases. Had such an inquiry been undertaken in *Sherwood,* we believe that the result might have been different. Moreover, a determination as to which party assumed the risk in *A & M Land Development Co.* would have alleviated the need to characterize the mistake as collateral so as to justify the result denying rescission. Despite the absence of any inquiry as to the assumption of risk in those two leading cases, we find that there exists sufficient precedent to warrant such an analysis in future cases of mistake.

5. Hathaway v. Hudson, 256 Mich. 694, 239 N.W. 859, quoting 9 C.J., p. 1161.

The court, in *Sherwood v. Walker,* noted that the mistake was not of the "mere quality of the animal, but went to the very nature of the thing." Moreover, "the thing sold and bought had in fact no existence." What was the point of making these distinctions? What are the competing policy considerations in cases of this type? What does *Lenawee,* the later Michigan case, add to *Sherwood v. Walker*?

What requirements are prescribed by Restatement (Second) for avoiding a contract on the grounds of mutual mistake? Can *Beachcomber* and *Lenawee* be reconciled on the basis of Restatement prescriptions?

(2) *Aberlone, Rose Of.*

'Tis the middle of night on the Greenfield farm
And the creatures are huddled to keep them from harm.

Ah me!—Ah moo!

Respectively their quidsome balm
How mournfully they chew!
And one there is who stands apart
With hanging head and heavy heart,
Have pity on her sore distress,
This norm of bovine loveliness,
Her gentle limbs, her hornless brow
Proclaim no ordinary cow:
Fair as a pasture sweet with hay
Mown in the very month of May!
Nay, fairer yet! And yet more fair!
She stands alone, the short black hair
Heaving sometimes on her breast,
Shunned and despised by all the rest.
If one should ask her why she doth grieve
She would answer sadly, "I can't conceive."
Her shame is a weary weight like stone
For Rose the Second of Aberlone.
Her sire is of a noble line
Of most aristocratic kine:
Angus of Aberdeen, black and polled;
Their name is proud and their get pure gold.
Their procreation hath won renown,
But Rose the Second hath let them down.
Her forbears have labored for bitter meed,
For Rose is barren and will not breed.
Now the gate that is strait and the way that is narrow
Call for a cow to forgo being farrow.
In a cow one condones a trifle of loose
Morality if she will just reproduce,
The stars in their courses deliver us
From the cow that is non-frugiferous!
If a heifer aspires to a niche on high
She must certainly plan to fructify,
And when she reaches puberty

Must concentrate on uberty.
No honor is there for the boss of that ilk
That produceth no young and giveth no milk;
And this is the reason her kith make moan
For Rose the Second of Aberlone.

* * *

'Tis the middle of night before the exam,
And there's nothing to eat but a cold bit of ham,

Ah me!—Ah moo!

Mark how the eager students cram,
What coffee black they brew!
A dismal specter haunts this wake—
The law of mutual mistake;
And even the reluctant drone
Must cope with Rose of Aberlone.
She rules the cases, she stalks the page
Even in this atomic age.
In radioactive tracts of land,
In hardly collectible notes of hand,
In fiddles of dubious pedigree,
In releases of liability,
In zoning rules unknown to lessors,
In weird conceits of law professors,
In printers' bids and ailing kings,
In all mutations and sorts of things,
In many a hypothetical
With characters alphabetical,
In many a subtle and sly disguise
There lurks the ghost of her sad brown eyes.
That she will turn up in some set of facts is
Almost as certain as death and taxes:
For students of law must still atone
For the shame of Rose of Aberlone.

(3) *An Anomalous Situation.* In a case which the court said presents an "anomalous" situation, the *vendors* sought to rescind a contract for the sale of land based on a defect (leaking underground gasoline storage tanks) discovered after the agreement. The transaction involved the sale for $320,000 of a gas station and automobile parts store in East Lansing for use as a 7–Eleven store. The agreement contained an "as is" clause. The vendors sought to rescind because state environmental statutes make previous owners of sites liable for environmental contamination and responsible for cleanup. The court upheld the vendor's right to rescind based on mutual mistake. Garb–Ko, Inc. v. Lansing–Lewis Services, Inc., 167 Mich.App. 779, 423 N.W.2d 355 (1988). Asserting that the "as is" clause held no significance since the purchaser was not the adversely affected party, the court noted: "[Vendors] have a continuing obligation and responsibility for the contaminated property. One expert estimated that the cost of cleanup could be anywhere from $100,000 to $1,000,000. In order to contain further cleanup costs and third-party claims arising from

use of the contaminated land, [Vendors] need control over the use of the property. Sale to plaintiff would not give them such control." 423 N.W.2d at 358.

(4) *The Treasure in the Dunghill: A Rabbinical Account.* Alexander of Macedon visited King Kazia beyond the dark mountains. He came forth, offering him golden bread on a golden tray. 'Do I then need your gold?' he demanded. 'Had you then nothing to eat in your own country that you have come here?' he retorted. 'I came only because I wished to see how you dispense justice,' was the reply. As he sat with him a man came with a complaint against his neighbour. 'This man,' he stated, 'sold me a dunghill and I found a treasure in it.' The buyer argued, 'I bought a dunghill only,' while the vendor maintained, 'I sold the dunghill and all it contained.' Said he [the king] to one: 'Have you a son?' 'Yes,' replied he. 'And have you a daughter?' he asked the other, 'Yes,' was the answer. 'Then marry them and let the treasure belong to both.' He noticed him [Alexander] sitting astonished, and asked him, 'Have I then not judged well?' 'Yes,' he replied. 'Had this happened among you, how would you have judged?' 'I would have slain both and kept the treasure for myself'. 1 Midrash Rabbah, ch. XXXIII (H. Freedman trans. 3d ed. 1983). Can you suggest other alternatives?

PROBLEMS: THE CASES OF THE UNKNOWN OIL DEPOSITS, MESTROVIC'S DRAWINGS, AND A BARREN COW

(a) Vendor, a farmer, agreed in writing to sell forty acres of land to Purchaser, a neighbor, for $40,000 ($1,000 per acre). Before closing it was discovered that the land contained valuable oil deposits, which fact if known at the time of contracting, would have justified a price of $400,000 ($10,000 per acre). Does Vendor have a case for rescission? Cf. Tetenman v. Epstein, 66 Cal.App. 745, 226 P. 966 (1924).

(b) The 1st Source Bank, as executor of the estate of Olga Mestrovic, deceased widow of renowned Yugoslavian sculptor Ivan Mestrovic, entered into a contract to sell the family home to Terrence and Antoinette Wilkin. No mention was made of any works of art. After closing, the Wilkins complained that the premises were left in a cluttered condition and needed extensive cleaning. The Bank proposed that they would arrange to have the cleaning done by a rubbish removal service, or that the Wilkins could clean the house themselves and retain any items of personal property which remained. The Wilkins opted to do the work themselves, and in so doing found eight drawings and a sculpture apparently created by Ivan Mestrovic. Neither the Bank nor the Wilkins suspected that any works of art remained on the premises. In a contest of ownership between the Bank and the Wilkins, who wins? See Wilkin v. 1st Source Bank, 548 N.E.2d 170 (Ind.App.1990).

(c) Forest Sherwood and Hiram Walker are cattlemen, living on adjacent farms. Each breeds and sells livestock. On May 1, Sherwood agreed in writing to sell Walker a certain cow ("Rose") which each assumed to be "with calf." The price was $2,000, a price five times the market price for a comparable non-pregnant, barren cow. It was discovered shortly thereafter that "Rose" was barren. Could Walker rescind? Could he, in the alternative, secure reformation? See the comment that follows.

Comment: Reformation for Mistake in Expression

Reformation, like rescission, is an equitable remedy. Unlike rescission, however, reformation is designed to restore the efficacy of a writing which does not reflect the earlier agreement of the parties, frequently oral, which they apparently intended to be reflected in the writing. It has been described as a "way station" to some other remedy, in that the ultimate objective of the plaintiff is to enforce the writing as reformed. See Dobbs §§ 9.5, 11.5. In the classic case for reformation, the plaintiff must show by clear and convincing evidence that the parties had actually reached agreement over the term at issue, that both intended the term to be included in a subsequent writing, and because of "mutual mistake" in expression, the term was not included. See Wellman Savings Bank v. Adams, 454 N.W.2d 852 (Iowa 1990); Novak v. Smith, 197 Ill.App.3d 390, 143 Ill.Dec. 717, 554 N.E.2d 652 (1990); United Bank of Ariz. v. Ashland Dev. Corp., 164 Ariz. 312, 792 P.2d 775 (App.1990) (reformation granted); Frantl Industries, Inc. v. Maier Construction, Inc., 68 Wis.2d 590, 229 N.W.2d 610 (1975); Housing Authority of College Park v. Macro Housing, Inc., 275 Md. 281, 340 A.2d 216 (1975). Since the defendant will invariably deny that he intended the term to be included in the writing, the plaintiff must shoulder an uphill burden in establishing the mistake. The "fault" of the plaintiff in not carefully reading the writing before signing or of an agent selected to reduce the agreement to writing, however, will not bar reformation if the plaintiff can otherwise demonstrate that both parties believed that the writing expressed their true agreement. See Treadaway v. Camellia Convalescent Hospitals, Inc., 43 Cal.App.3d 189, 118 Cal.Rptr. 341 (1974). On the other hand, if the "mutual" mistake is in the formulation rather than the expression of the agreement, the proper remedy is rescission rather than reformation of the contract. See Restatement (Second) §§ 153–155; National Resort Communities v. Cain, 526 S.W.2d 510 (Tex.1975) (mutual mistake in formulation).

As time passes, a broader basis for reformation may be emerging in the cases. Under the traditional view, reformation is granted only where there is a mutual mistake in expression. See, e.g., Hoffman v. Chapman, 182 Md. 208, 34 A.2d 438 (1943) (rescission is proper remedy for unilateral mistake, fraud, duress or other inequitable conduct). A slightly broader basis is found in New York, where the "classic" case for reformation is said to include mutual mistake in expression or a "mistake on plaintiff's part and a fraud by defendant." Brandwein v. Provident Mutual Life Insurance Co., 3 N.Y.2d 491, 168 N.Y.S.2d 964, 146 N.E.2d 693 (1957). See Barash v. Pennsylvania Terminal Real Estate Corp., 26 N.Y.2d 77, 308 N.Y.S.2d 649, 256 N.E.2d 707 (1970). An even broader basis for reformation is stated in Kufer v. Carson, 230 N.W.2d 500, 504 (Iowa 1975), where the court stated:

> Ultimately equity will grant relief if an instrument as written fails to express the true agreement between the parties without regard to the cause of the failure to express the agreement as actually made, whether it is due to fraud, mistake in the use of language, or anything else

which prevented the instrument from expressing the true intention of the parties.

Finally, some courts have "reformed" contracts to purge them of defects in the formulation process, such as illegality and unconscionability. See Karpinski v. Ingrasci, 28 N.Y.2d 45, 320 N.Y.S.2d 1, 268 N.E.2d 751 (1971) (illegality) and Jones v. Star Credit Corp., infra at 146. See also UCC 2–302(1); 2–719(2) & (3). At least one court has "reformed" a contract to relieve a party whose duty of performance was excused due to commercial impracticability. See Aluminum Co. of America v. Essex Group, Inc., 499 F.Supp. 53 (W.D.Pa.1980). These developments purport to grant "reformation" to remedy problems other than mistake in the expression of the agreement and, as you can plainly see, have little to do with the intention of the parties.

Ayer v. Western Union Telegraph Co.

Supreme Judicial Court of Maine, 1887.
79 Me. 493, 10 A. 495.

■ EMERY, J. On report. The defendant telegraph company was engaged in the business of transmitting messages by telegraph between Bangor and Philadelphia, and other points. The plaintiff, a lumber dealer in Bangor, delivered to the defendant company in Bangor, to be transmitted to his correspondent in Philadelphia, the following message: "Will sell 800 M laths, delivered at your wharf, two ten net cash. July shipment. Answer quick." The regular tariff rate was prepaid by the plaintiff for such transmission. The message delivered by the defendant company to the Philadelphia correspondent was as follows: "Will sell 800 M laths, delivered at your wharf, two net cash. July shipment. Answer quick." It will be seen that the important word "ten" in the statement of price was omitted. The Philadelphia party immediately returned by telegraph the following answer: "Accept your telegraphic offer on laths. Cannot increase price spruce." Letters afterwards passed between the parties, which disclosed the error in the transmission of the plaintiff's message. About two weeks after the discovery of the error, the plaintiff shipped the laths, as per the message received by his correspondent, to-wit, at two dollars per M. He testified that his correspondent insisted he was entitled to the laths at that price, and they were shipped accordingly.

The defendant telegraph company offered no evidence whatever, and did not undertake to account for or explain the mistake in the transmission of the message. The presumption therefore is that the mistake resulted from the fault of the telegraph company. * * *

The fault and consequent liability of the defendant company being thus established, the only remaining question is the extent of that liability in this case. The plaintiff claims it extends to the difference between the market price of laths and the price at which they were shipped. The defendant claims its liability is limited to the amount paid for the transmission of the message. * * *

The defendant company ... claims that the plaintiff was not in fact damaged to a greater extent than the price paid by him for the transmission. It contends that the plaintiff was not bound by the erroneous message delivered by the company to the Philadelphia party, and hence need not have shipped the laths at the lesser price. This raises the question whether the message written by the sender, and intrusted to the telegraph company for transmission, or the message written out and delivered by the company to the receiver at the other end of the line, as and for the message intended to be sent, is the better evidence of the rights of the receiver against the sender. The question is important and not easy of solution. It would be hard that the negligence of the telegraph company, or an error in transmission resulting from uncontrollable causes, should impose upon the innocent sender of a message a liability he never authorized nor contemplated. It would be equally hard that the innocent receiver, acting in good faith upon the message as received by him, should through such error lose all claim upon the sender. If one, owning merchandise, write a message offering to sell at a certain price, it would seem unjust that the telegraph company could bind him to sell at a less price, by making that error in the transmission. On the other hand, the receiver of the offer may in good faith, upon the strength of the telegram as received by him, have sold all the merchandise to arrive, perhaps at the same rate. It would seem unjust that he should have no claim for the merchandise. If an agent receives instructions by telegraph from his principal, and in good faith acts upon them as expressed in the message delivered him by the company, it would seem he ought to be held justified, though there were an error in the transmission.

It is evident that in case of an error in the transmission of a telegram either the sender or receiver must often suffer loss. As between the two, upon whom should the loss finally fall? We think the safer and more equitable rule, and the rule the public can most easily adapt itself to, is that, as between the sender and receiver, the party who selects the telegraph as the means of communication shall bear the loss caused by the errors of the telegraph. The first proposer can select one of many modes of communication, both for the proposal and the answer. The receiver has no such choice, except as to his answer. If he cannot safely act upon the message he received through the agency selected by the proposer, business must be seriously hampered and delayed. The use of the telegraph has become so general, and so many transactions are based on the words of the telegram received, that any other rule would now be impracticable.

Of course, the rule above stated presupposes the innocence of the receiver, and that there is nothing to cause him to suspect an error. If there be anything in the message, or in the attendant circumstances, or in the prior dealings of the parties, or in anything else, indicating a probable error in the transmission, good faith on the part of the receiver may require him to investigate before acting. Neither does the rule include forged messages, for in such case the supposed sender did not make any use of the telegraph.
* * *

It follows that the plaintiff in this case is entitled to recover the difference between the two dollars and the market price, as to laths. The evidence shows that the difference was 10 cents per M. Judgment for plaintiff for $80, with interest from the date of the writ.

NOTES

(1) How is it that the existence of a contract between the sender and the recipient of the message is put in issue in this case versus the telegraph company?

(2) Was Ayer in any way responsible for the mistake? How, then, is there justification for holding him to a contract on the altered terms? Do reasons of business policy support the decision? Does the case accord with the objective theory of contractual assent? What about economic efficiency?

PROBLEM: MISTAKES IN TRANSMISSION—THE OUTER FRINGES OF THE OBJECTIVE TEST

Sam, a breeder of race horses, owned Flasher and Dasher, who, as two-year olds, had shown great promise. Brenda, a sportsperson, was interested in buying one or both. She visited Sam's farm and, after some discussion, offered to buy Dasher for $5,000 and Flasher for $6,000. Sam replied that "under no circumstances" would he sell Flasher, who was promised to his daughter on her next birthday, but that he would sell Dasher to Brenda for $7,000. Brenda replied that the price on Dasher was "too high" but that if Sam could lower it a bit, please contact her at home some 500 miles away.

(1) The next day, Sam decided to sell Dasher to Brenda for $6,000. Accordingly, he typed out an offer to sell and placed it in a properly addressed, stamped envelope. On his way to the mail box, Sam had a change of mind. Before he could return to his office, however, Sam was struck by a bicycle and knocked unconscious. A stranger, seeing the letter on the sidewalk, mailed it. Upon receipt the next day, Brenda promptly telegraphed an acceptance and resold Dasher to Thad, a friend, for $8,000. Later, the fully conscious Sam telephoned to say that he did not intend to sell Dasher. Is there a contract to sell Dasher?

(2) Suppose that Sam had indicated an offer to sell Dasher for $6,000 but his secretary typed Flasher instead and Sam signed the letter without reading. Upon receipt, Brenda promptly telegraphed "accept your offer to sell Flasher" and resold Flasher to Thad for $8,000. Is there a contract to sell Flasher? How about Dasher?

(3) Suppose that Sam went to a telegraph office and upon a standard form clearly wrote the following: "Will sell Dasher to you for $6,000." The form contained a limitation of liability approved by the Federal Communications Commission that the company would not be liable for mistakes or delays in transmission beyond the sum of $500, unless the message was sent at repeated message rates or was specially valued. The outer limit of liability for a repeated message was $5,000. Sam read the limitation and chose not to pay the extra charge for a repeated or specially valued message. Due to a mistake of the telegraph company, the telegram as sent offered to sell Dasher for $5,000.

Brenda promptly telegraphed her acceptance and resold Dasher to Thad for $8,000. Is there a contract to sell Dasher for $5,000? Assuming that the telegraph company was negligent, what is its liability, if any, to Sam? To Brenda? To Thad?

(B) FRAUD AND THE DUTY TO DISCLOSE

Morta v. Korea Insurance Corp.

United States Court of Appeals, Ninth Circuit, 1988.
840 F.2d 1452.

■ KOZINSKI, CIRCUIT JUDGE:

We consider whether, under Guam law, a release signed as part of a settlement of claims arising from an automobile accident bars recovery for after-discovered injuries.

Facts

On November 26, 1982, appellee Vicente Morta suffered a collision that damaged his 1976 Mazda station wagon and caused him bodily injury. According to Morta, the car was "a total loss." 1 Reporter's Transcript (RT) at 39. Morta himself was knocked unconscious and taken by ambulance to the emergency room at Guam Memorial Hospital. After treating Morta, the attending physician assured him that he was fine and could go home. Afterwards, Morta continued to have pain in his muscles, chin and chest. He was treated three days later by a second physician at the Seventh Day Adventist Clinic, who also told him he was fine and the pain would eventually subside.

Morta sought compensation for his losses from appellant Korea Insurance Corporation (KIC), which insured the driver who had caused the accident. Morta was directed to Bernabe Santa Maria, a claims adjuster. Morta and Santa Maria happened to be from the same area of the Philippines and conversed in their native tongues, Tagalog and Ilocano. Morta testified that he had no problem understanding Santa Maria.

Santa Maria helped Morta complete the claim form, received from Morta his medical reports, examined the damaged Mazda and, acknowledging the liability of his insured, offered Morta $900. Morta testified that the settlement offer had several components: "Three Hundred Dollars for my car; $250 from loss of compensation of work, like that; and Two Hundred some for sufferings and injury that I suffered, you know. So, they told me, included also the medical bill from SDA and the towing expenses, that item." 1 RT at 70–71; id. at 44.[1]

Morta was not satisfied with that amount, claiming that the car alone

---

1. Santa Maria testified that the settlement broke down into $500 for Morta's car and $400 for personal injuries.

had a blue-book value of $2300.[2] Santa Maria told him that $900 was all he could pay. Morta did not jump at the offer; he thought it over and went to see a lawyer. He showed the lawyer the medical and police reports. The lawyer evaluated Morta's claim and advised him that he would be unlikely to recover much more than the $900 KIC had offered and that any attempt to do so would delay payment. Morta returned to Santa Maria's office and accepted the $900. Because the settlement check covered damages for the car as well as for personal injuries—in short, all of Morta's claims—Morta signed a standard release.

About a week after the settlement, Morta began to feel ill and dizzy. He was given medication by his doctor but soon thereafter he collapsed unconscious, awaking in a Honolulu hospital after undergoing emergency surgery for a blood clot in his brain. The medical bills amounted to approximately $11,000, all paid for by Morta's insurer, FHP, Inc.

Morta filed suit to recover damages resulting from this injury, disavowing the release on the ground that Santa Maria fraudulently misrepresented its contents. . . . The jury returned a general verdict holding the release invalid, and the superior court entered judgment to that effect. The parties then stipulated, subject to KIC's right to appeal, to entry of judgment against KIC for $14,600, which, together with the $900 settlement, constituted the limits of the insurance policy.

The Appellate Division of the District Court for the District of Guam affirmed the judgment and KIC appealed to us under 48 U.S.C. § 1424–3(c) (Supp. III 1985).

Contentions of the Parties

KIC argues that Morta signed the release with eyes open and for valuable consideration. By its terms, the release covers all claims arising out of the accident, whether known or unknown.

[Morta] argues the release is subject to rescission because it was obtained by fraud, undue influence, mistake or deceit. * * *

A directed verdict will be granted only if, examining the evidence in the light most favorable to the nonmoving party and drawing all reasonable inferences in its favor, "there is no substantial evidence to support a verdict for that party." Fabrica Inc. v. El Dorado Corp., 697 F.2d 890, 892 (9th Cir.1983); see Peterson v. Kennedy, 771 F.2d 1244, 1256 (9th Cir. 1985), cert. denied, 475 U.S. 1122, 106 S.Ct. 1642, 90 L.Ed.2d 187 (1986) (directed verdict proper where "the evidence permits only one reasonable conclusion as to the verdict"). We apply the same standard as the trial court in reviewing its decision. Walker v. KFC Corp., 728 F.2d 1215, 1223 (9th Cir.1984); Fabrica, 697 F.2d at 892.

---

2. He also admitted, however, that the 1976 Mazda station wagon was not in mint condition: "the body got some rusty spots which are in the hood." 1 RT at 77–78.

I

The jury was properly instructed that the release could be set aside if induced by fraud, undue influence, mistake or deceit.[3] We therefore examine the record to see whether there is any substantial evidence to support rescission on any of these theories.[4]

A. *Fraud.* Morta's original complaint did not attack the release at all. He later amended the complaint to add two counts disavowing the release and alleging that KIC "falsely and fraudulently and with intent to deceive and defraud the plaintiff represented to plaintiff that the Release of All Claims form was not a complete settlement of damages plaintiff was requesting for injuries sustained in an auto accident." Excerpt of Record at 4; see Guam Civ.Code § 1572 (1970) (defining actual fraud). The proof at trial does not bear out this allegation.

The evidence presented to the jury consisted largely of testimony from Morta and Santa Maria, each giving his account of the negotiations between them. Those accounts do not differ all that much. Significantly, Morta did not testify that Santa Maria misrepresented the content or effect of the release in any way, only that Santa Maria never said anything about it at all. According to Morta, Santa Maria handed him the release, stating, "This is for your claim." 1 RT at 38. This statement, standing alone, certainly does not amount to fraud or anything close to it.

Morta argues, however, that Santa Maria committed fraud when he told Morta that $900 was "the only amount the insurance could give [him]." 1 RT at 70. Morta testified that when he asked, "Is that all I can get?," Santa Maria responded, "Well, I'm not the one who decide [sic] this. They decide it in there. I'm just working for them, so, I can't do nothing." Id. at 71. According to Morta, this "led [him] to believe that $900.00 was the only amount available to compensate him." Appellees' Brief at 12. This is not a reasonable construction of Santa Maria's statement, and the evidence conclusively establishes that Morta did not interpret it in this fashion. After reviewing the offer, Morta consulted a lawyer about the possibility of recovering more. The lawyer advised him that he could in fact get more—perhaps $1500—but cautioned that it would take time. Santa Maria's representation that he could pay no more—the type of statement frequently made by parties during negotiations—simply does not amount to

---

3. Although the superior court gave a separate instruction on deceit, it was all but identical to the instruction on actual fraud. Moreover, there is no separate provision concerning deceit in the Guam Civil Code. We therefore consider deceit as merely a species of fraud.

4. Morta did not plead mistake in his complaint, even though mistake must be averred with particularity. See Guam R.Civ.P. 9(b) ("[i]n all averments of fraud or mistake, the circumstances constituting fraud or mistake shall be stated with particularity"). Nor did he attempt to amend his com-

plaint to plead mistake. Furthermore, under Guam Civ.Code § 1691(2) (1970), Morta was obligated to tender return of the $900 consideration he received for signing the release as a prerequisite to rescission on any ground other than fraud. See Graham v. Atchison, T. & S.F. Ry., 176 F.2d 819, 826 (9th Cir.1949). The record is unclear about whether those procedural requirements were satisfied or waived. To conserve judicial resources, however, we assume they were satisfied and proceed to address these issues on the merits.

fraud. Neither does anything else presented at trial. We therefore are unable to find any support for the jury's verdict on a theory of actual fraud.

The jury was also instructed on constructive fraud, which consists of *"any breach of duty* which, without an actually fraudulent intent, gains an advantage to the person in fault, or anyone claiming under him, by misleading another to his prejudice, or to the prejudice of anyone claiming under him." Guam Civ.Code § 1573(1) (1970) (emphasis added). As the language of the statute suggests, a finding of constructive fraud requires a confidential or trust relationship. Guthrie v. Times–Mirror Co., 51 Cal. App.3d 879, 889, 124 Cal.Rptr. 577, 584 (1975).[5] KIC had no duty to Morta, however: As Morta was well aware, KIC was not his insurer, but that of an adverse party, the driver who caused the accident. Santa Maria and Morta dealt openly and at arm's length. There was no basis for a finding of constructive fraud. See Sanger v. Yellow Cab Co., 486 S.W.2d 477, 481 (Mo.1972) ("[t]he releasee does not stand in a fiduciary relation to the releasor").

B.   *Undue influence.* Under Guam law, undue influence may be established under any of the following circumstances: (1) "the use, by one in whom a confidence is reposed by another, ... of such confidence ... for the purpose of obtaining an unfair advantage over him"; or (2) "taking an unfair advantage of another's weakness of mind"; or (3) "taking a grossly oppressive and unfair advantage of another's necessities or distress." Guam Civ.Code § 1575 (1970). We find no evidence that Morta signed the release as a result of any of these circumstances.

Morta points to nothing in the record suggesting that he reposed any confidence in Santa Maria. To the contrary, all the available evidence suggests that Morta and Santa Maria negotiated at arm's length. Morta did not rely on Santa Maria to take care of him: He carefully checked the bluebook value of his car, obtained treatment from two physicians of his own choosing and consulted a lawyer. He complained to Santa Maria about the amount of the offered settlement and tried to get him to pay more. On the basis of the lawyer's advice, Morta finally decided to take the money offered to him and be done with the business.

DuBois v. Sparrow, 92 Cal.App.3d 290, 154 Cal.Rptr. 717 (1979), cited below, is not on point. There, the insurance agent and plaintiff "were not dealing at arms length"; the agent at first represented the plaintiff but then, without telling her, switched to an adversarial position, which " 'furnished the opportunity for overreaching.' " Id. at 300, 154 Cal.Rptr. at 723 (citation omitted). Morta and Santa Maria always maintained a purely adversarial relationship. Morta did not testify otherwise.

Nor is there any evidence that Morta suffered from mental weakness of which Santa Maria could have taken advantage. Morta was not incapacitated by his injury; he was neither hospitalized, drugged, in serious pain nor

---

5.   Section 1573, like most of the Guam Codes, was borrowed from the California Codes, and we consider California decisions in construing identical provisions of Guam law. See, e.g., Smith v. Lujan, 588 F.2d 1304, 1306 (9th Cir.1979).

otherwise prevented from bargaining effectively.[6] Morta testified that he did not begin to suffer from headaches and dizziness until several days after he received the settlement check. Indeed, the unknown, and unknowable, nature of Morta's latent symptoms forms the basis of his alternative argument. See p. 1458 infra.

Finally, nothing in the record suggests that Santa Maria knew or suspected Morta had any continuing vulnerability, or that Santa Maria did anything to take advantage of the situation. There was no reason for Santa Maria to believe Morta was in dire straits; Morta was not hospitalized, he was working and did not disclose any particularly pressing need for the settlement money. Like anyone else involved in an accident, Morta was anxious to get the unpleasant business behind him, advising Santa Maria that " 'I'm getting tired of borrowing my daughter's car.' " 1 RT at 41; see id. at 77. That hardly amounts to the type of pressing need that would provide a basis for a claim of undue influence or overreaching. See Sanger, 486 S.W.2d at 478 (upholding release as to unknown injuries where plaintiff quickly settled, being "anxious to get his car fixed because he was going on vacation in two weeks").

In any event, Santa Maria did nothing to pressure Morta into accepting the settlement in full or in part. Santa Maria did not intimate that the settlement would be withdrawn if not accepted on the spot, or that settlement on the car would be held hostage to a release of the personal injury claim; nor did Santa Maria delay making an offer in order to push Morta to the wall, or refuse a request for an advance payment or a rental car; nor was the offer shockingly low in light of what the parties knew at the time. No reasonable jury fairly applying the law could reach a verdict of invalidity on the basis of undue influence.

C. *Mistake.* The jury was instructed that it could set aside the release if it found that Morta's consent was vitiated by mistake. Under Guam law, "[m]istake of fact is a mistake, *not caused by the neglect of a legal duty on the part of the person making the mistake,* and consisting in ... [a]n unconscious ignorance or forgetfulness of a fact past or present, material to the contract." Guam Civ.Code § 1577(1) (1970) (emphasis added).

Morta alleges that he did not read the release and was mistaken about is contents. That mistake is inadequate to justify rescinding the release, however, because it was "caused by the neglect of a legal duty on the part of the person making the mistake." Morta spoke English; he was able to

---

6. Cf. Backus v. Sessions, 17 Cal.2d 380, 384, 110 P.2d 51, 53 (1941) (plaintiff still hospitalized in drugged, semiconscious state); Wetzstein v. Thomasson, 34 Cal. App.2d 554, 558–59, 93 P.2d 1028, 1030–31 (1939) (adjuster repeatedly visited plaintiff at her bedside for hours despite her stated wish not to discuss settlement); Weger v. Rocha, 138 Cal.App. 109, 114–15, 32 P.2d 417, 420 (1934) (plaintiff was "confined in a cast flat on her back, in a highly nervous and hysteri-cal condition, suffering much pain, ... importuned and importuned by the agent"); Raynale v. Yellow Cab Co., 115 Cal.App. 90, 92, 300 P. 991, 991 (1931) (defendants discussed minor property damage with plaintiff while she was still dazed and "in such agony that she could not and did not read the paper she signed," and then, "without explaining its effect, plac[ed] before her a release covering matters not discussed").

identify and read the release on the witness stand. Had he bothered to read the release before signing it, he would no doubt have understood its meaning and purpose.[7] Under established law, Morta may not rely on his failure to read the release as a basis for disavowing it, "particularly where he is given an opportunity to have it read and explained to him by some competent and reliable person," such as an attorney. 66 Am.Jur.2d Release § 15, at 690 (1973); see, e.g., Casey v. Proctor, 59 Cal.2d 97, 105, 378 P.2d 579, 583, 28 Cal.Rptr. 307, 311 (1963); Izzi v. Mesquite Country Club, 186 Cal.App.3d 1309, 1319, 231 Cal.Rptr. 315, 319 (1986); accord Dobler v. Story, 268 F.2d 274, 277 (9th Cir.1959) (applying California law); Sanger, 486 S.W.2d at 481 (upholding release even though plaintiff "thought he was signing a receipt").

> [A] person who, without coercion or undue persuasion, executes a solemn release cannot subsequently impeach it on the ground of his own carelessness, if at the time of its execution he might have advised himself fully as to the nature and legal effect of the act done. *He cannot then complain that an imposition has been practiced upon him, and if he knows or by inquiry might know the exact nature of the act done, cannot subsequently invoke his own heedlessness to impeach his release by calling such heedlessness someone else's fraud.* He has no right to act as one who understands what he is doing, unless he intends to lead those with whom he is dealing to believe that he understands the act done.

66 Am.Jur.2d at 691 (emphasis added).

In short, nothing on this record supports rescission of the settlement agreement and release under the theories presented to the jury.[8] * * *

The judgment of the district court is REVERSED, and the case is REMANDED to the superior court for entry of a directed verdict in favor of KIC.

---

7. There is nothing ambiguous, unclear or tricky about the release. It is less than a page long. At the top, in characters a quarter-inch tall, is the word "RELEASE"; immediately beneath, in slightly smaller letters, are the words "OF ALL CLAIMS." A few concise sentences follow, clearly and unequivocally stating that Morta releases KIC from all claims "growing out of any and all known and unknown, foreseen and unforeseen bodily and personal injuries and property damage" arising out of the accident in question. Morta also acknowledges that "the injuries sustained are or may be permanent and progressive and that recovery therefrom is uncertain and indefinite...." In capital letters near the bottom is a certification that the signer has read and understands the terms of the release; immediately above the signature line, also in capitals, is a "caution" instruct-ing the signer to read the release before signing it.

8. The dissent suggests six factors that might lead a reasonable jury to conclude that Santa Maria's conduct was "objectionable enough to excuse the plaintiff from his failure to read and understand the release that he signed and the waiver that it contained." Dissent at 1461. With all due respect, "objectionable enough" is not a legal standard. Morta cannot avoid the release on the basis of general unease the jury might feel about the fairness of the settlement; there must be substantial evidence justifying rescission on one of the specific grounds provided by Guam law. The dissent does not analyze the six factors in terms of any particular legal theory, and with good reason: None of them, alone or in combination, amounts to fraud, undue influence or mistake.

■ GRAY, DISTRICT JUDGE, dissenting:

* * *

Based upon my own examination of the record, I am convinced that a reasonable jury could have concluded that:

(a) Morta's comparatively limited education was a disadvantage to him in his dealings with the much more sophisticated and experienced Santa Maria, and that the latter took undue advantage of this circumstance.

(b) The recent nature of Morta's personal injuries and the serious illness that they later and suddenly precipitated may have been indicative of a reduced physical condition and competence at the time the release was signed.

(c) Santa Maria knew that Morta was in immediate need of settlement money and was in no position to challenge whatever proposal that KIC might offer.

(d) Santa Maria did not encourage Morta to read the proposed release or otherwise cause him to understand that it provided for a waiver of liability for any injuries that might later develop from the accident.

(e) When Morta went to an attorney, he had not read the proposed release, nor had he obtained a copy from Santa Maria. The conversation with the attorney did not in any manner alert Morta to the consequences of a release.

(f) When Morta returned to Santa Maria's office, he signed the four papers that were put before him, including the release, without having read them, in order that he might get his much needed $900, and without any awareness of the extent of the release.

Under such circumstances, I believe that a reasonable jury readily could have concluded that Santa Maria's conduct was objectionable enough to excuse the plaintiff from his failure to read and understand the release that he signed and the waiver that it contained.

There is a further reason why I believe that the decision below must be affirmed, Section 1542 of the Civil Code of Guam (which is quoted at page 1458 of the majority opinion) was taken word for word from Section 1542 of the California Civil Code. In the California Supreme Court case of Casey v. Proctor, 59 Cal.2d 97, 109, 28 Cal.Rptr. 307, 314, 378 P.2d 579, 586 (1963), Justice Peters, in writing the carefully reasoned opinion of the court, ruled that:

> "It therefore appears beyond reasonable doubt that Civil Code, section 1542 was intended by its drafters to preclude the application of a release to unknown claims in the absence of a showing, *apart from the words of the release* of an intent to include such claims.

* * *

Accordingly, I would affirm the decision of the United States District Court for the District of Guam.

NOTES

(1) Does it matter that the release is of "unknown" personal injury rather than commercial loss? Should it? See Murray § 91K.

(2) For *review* purposes, consider the following questions about the *Morta* case:

> (a) Should the plaintiff be able to reform the contract so as to delete the reference to "all claims" and "unknown" injuries?

> (b) Should the plaintiff be able to rescind because of a mistake as to the character of the writing (he did not think it was a release) or the content of the writing (he did not know it contained an "all claims" release)?

> (c) Should the court hold that no contract was formed because each party had a materially different understanding as to the effect of the release?

Laidlaw v. Organ

United States Supreme Court, 1817.
15 U.S. (2 Wheat.) 178, 4 L.Ed. 214.

[Error to the district court for the Louisiana district. The plaintiff/buyer (defendant in error), Organ, filed suit against Laidlaw, the defendant/seller (plaintiff in error), seeking to recover possession of 111 hogsheads of tobacco that defendant took from plaintiff's possession. Defendant initially delivered the tobacco to plaintiff under a contract for $7,544.69, but later the defendant/seller "by force, and of their own wrong, took possession of the same." The defendant/seller alleged, however, that fraud in the inception nullified its duty to sell: "[O]n the night of the 18th of February, 1815, [messengers] brought from the British fleet news that a treaty of peace had been signed at Ghent by the American and British commissioners"... [ending the war of 1812 and consequently the British blockade of New Orleans]. This news was "made public in a handbill on Sunday morning, 8 o'clock, the 19th of February, 1815." Plaintiff call defendant "(with whom he had been bargaining for the tobacco mentioned in the petition, the evening previous,) ... soon after sunrise on the morning of Sunday, the 19th of February, 1815, before [defendant] had heard said news. [Defendant] asked if there was any news which was calculated to enhance the price or value of the article about to be purchased." The plaintiff apparently remained silent; "the purchase was then and there made ... and in consequence of said news the value of said article had risen from 30 to 50 per cent." The lower court found for the plaintiff.]

C. J. Ingersoll, for the plaintiffs in error. The first question is, whether the sale, under the circumstances of the case, was a valid sale; whether fraud, which vitiates every contract, must be proved by the communication of positive misinformation, or by withholding information when asked. Suppression of material circumstances within the knowledge of the vendee, and not accessible to the vendor, is equivalent to fraud, and vitiates the contract. Pothier, in discussing this subject, adopts the distinction of the forum of conscience, and the forum of law; but he admits that *fides est servanda.* The parties treated on an unequal footing, as the one party had received intelligence of the peace of Ghent, at the time of the contract, and the other had not. This news was unexpected, even at Washington, much more at New–Orleans, the recent scene of the most sanguinary operations of the war. In answer to the question, whether there was any news calculated to enhance the price of the article, the vendee was silent. This reserve, when such a question was asked, was equivalent to a false answer, and as much calculated to deceive as the communication of the most fabulous intelligence. Though the plaintiffs in error, after they heard the news of peace, still went on, in ignorance of their legal rights, to complete the contract, equity will protect them. . . .

Key, contra. . . . The only real question in the cause is, whether the sale was invalid because the vendee did not communicate information which he received precisely as the vendor might have got it had he been equally diligent or equally fortunate? And, surely, on this question there can be no doubt. Even if the vendor had been entitled to the disclosure, he waived it by not insisting on an answer to his question; and the silence of the vendee might as well have been interpreted into an affirmative as a negative answer. But, on principle, he was not bound to disclose. Even admitting that his conduct was unlawful, in foro conscientiae, does that prove that it was so in the civil forum? Human laws are imperfect in this respect, and the sphere of morality is more extensive than the limits of civil jurisdiction. The maxim of caveat emptor could never have crept into the law, if the province of ethics had been co-extensive with it. There was, in the present case, no circumvention or manaeuvre practised by the vendee, unless rising earlier in the morning, and obtaining by superior diligence and alertness that intelligence by which the price of commodities was regulated, be such. It is a romantic equality that is contended for on the other side. Parties never can be precisely equal in knowledge, either of facts or of the inferences from such facts, and both must concur in order to satisfy the rule contended for. The absence of all authority in England and the United States, both great commercial countries, speaks volumes against the reasonableness and practicability of such a rule.

C.J. Ingersoll, in reply. Though the record may not show that any thing tending to mislead by positive assertion was said by the vendee, in answer to the question proposed by Mr. Girault, yet it is a case of manaeuvre; of mental reservation; of circumvention. The information was monopolized by the messengers from the British fleet, and not imparted to the public at large until it was too late for the vendor to save himself. The rule of law and of ethics is the same. It is not a romantic, but a practical and legal rule of equality and good faith that is proposed to be applied.

Marshall, Ch. J. The question in this case is, whether the intelligence of extrinsic circumstances, which might influence the price of the commodity, and which was exclusively within the knowledge of the vendee, ought to have been communicated by him to the vendor? The court is of opinion that he was not bound to communicate it. It would be difficult to circumscribe the contrary doctrine within proper limits, where the means of intelligence are equally accessible to both parties. But at the same time, each party must take care not to say or do any thing tending to impose upon the other. The court thinks that the absolute instruction of the judge was erroneous, and that the question, whether any imposition was practised by the vendee upon the vendor ought to have been submitted to the jury. For these reasons the judgment must be reversed, and the cause remanded to the district court of Louisiana, with directions to award a venire facias de novo.

Venire de novo awarded.

NOTES

(1) Anthony Kronman in *Mistake, Disclosure, Information and the Law of Contracts*, 7 J. Legal Stud. 1 (1978) distinguishes between deliberately-acquired and casually-acquired information. Kronman argues that the law should not require contractual parties to disclose deliberately-acquired information so that private parties can profit from this type of private information and hence be encouraged to create it.

(2) Robert Cooter and Tom Ulen in Law and Economics 258–61 (1988), however, have drawn a second useful distinction between "productive facts" ("information that can be used to increase wealth") and "redistributive facts" ("information creating a bargaining advantage that can be used to redistribute wealth in favor of the knowledgeable party but that does not lead to the creation of new wealth"). Which type of information is at stake in *Laidlaw*? See Steven Shavell, *Acquisition and Disclosure of Information Prior to Sale*, 25 Rand J. Econ. 20 (1994) (using this distinction to argue sellers should be required to disclose so that they do not have unduly high incentives to acquire information, but that buyers be allowed to conceal their information).

Vokes v. Arthur Murray, Inc.

District Court of Appeal of Florida, Second District, 1968.
212 So.2d 906.

■ PIERCE, JUDGE.

This is an appeal by Audrey E. Vokes, plaintiff below, from a final order dismissing with prejudice, for failure to state a cause of action, her fourth amended complaint, hereinafter referred to as plaintiff's complaint.

Defendant Arthur Murray, Inc., a corporation, authorizes the operation throughout the nation of dancing schools under the name of "Arthur Murray School of Dancing" through local franchised operators, one of whom was defendant J.P. Davenport whose dancing establishment was in Clearwater.

Plaintiff Mrs. Audrey E. Vokes, a widow of 51 years and without family, had a yen to be "an accomplished dancer" with the hopes of finding "new interest in life". So, on February 10, 1961, a dubious fate, with the assist of a motivated acquaintance, procured her to attend a "dance party" at Davenport's "School of Dancing" where she whiled away the pleasant hours, sometimes in a private room, absorbing his accomplished sales technique, during which her grace and poise were elaborated upon and her rosy future as "an excellent dancer" was painted for her in vivid and glowing colors. As an incident to this interlude, he sold her eight ½-hour dance lessons to be utilized within one calendar month therefrom, for the sum of $14.50 cash in hand paid, obviously a baited "come-on".

Thus she embarked upon an almost endless pursuit of the terpsichorean art during which, over a period of less than sixteen months, she was sold fourteen "dance courses" totalling in the aggregate 2302 hours of dancing lessons for a total cash outlay of $31,090.45, all at Davenport's dance emporium. All of these fourteen courses were evidenced by execution of a written "Enrollment Agreement—Arthur Murray's School of Dancing" with the addendum in heavy black print, "No one will be informed that you are taking dancing lessons. Your relations with us are held in strict confidence", setting forth the number of "dancing lessons" and the "lessons in rhythm sessions" currently sold to her from time to time, and always of course accompanied by payment of cash of the realm.

These dance lesson contracts and the monetary consideration therefor of over $31,000 were procured from her by means and methods of Davenport and his associates which went beyond the unsavory, yet legally permissible, perimeter of "sales puffing" and intruded well into the forbidden area of undue influence, the suggestion of falsehood, the suppression of truth, and the free exercise of rational judgment, if what plaintiff alleged in her complaint was true. From the time of her first contract with the dancing school in February, 1961, she was influenced unwittingly by a constant and continuous barrage of flattery, false praise, excessive compliments, and panegyric encomiums, to such extent that it would be not only inequitable, but unconscionable, for a Court exercising inherent chancery power to allow such contracts to stand.

She was incessantly subjected to overreaching blandishment and cajolery. She was assured she had "grace and poise"; that she was "rapidly improving and developing in her dancing skill"; that the additional lessons would "make her a beautiful dancer, capable of dancing with the most accomplished dancers"; that she was "rapidly progressing in the development of her dancing skill and gracefulness", etc., etc. She was given "dance aptitude tests" for the ostensible purpose of "determining" the number of remaining hours of instructions needed by her from time to time.

At one point she was sold 545 additional hours of dancing lessons to be entitled to award of the "Bronze Medal" signifying that she had reached "the Bronze Standard", a supposed designation of dance achievement by students of Arthur Murray, Inc.

Later she was sold an additional 926 hours in order to gain the "Silver Medal", indicating she had reached "the Silver Standard", at a cost of $12,501.35.

At one point, while she still had to her credit about 900 unused hours of instructions, she was induced to purchase an additional 24 hours of lessons to participate in a trip to Miami at her own expense, where she would be "given the opportunity to dance with members of the Miami Studio".

She was induced at another point to purchase an additional 126 hours of lessons in order to be not only eligible for the Miami trip but also to become "a life member of the Arthur Murray Studio", carrying with it certain dubious emoluments, at a further cost of $1,752.30.

At another point, while she still had over 1,000 unused hours of instruction she was induced to buy 151 additional hours at a cost of $2,049.00 to be eligible for a "Student Trip to Trinidad", at her own expense as she later learned.

Also, when she still had 1100 unused hours to her credit, she was prevailed upon to purchase an additional 347 hours at a cost of $4,235.74, to qualify her to receive a "Gold Medal" for achievement, indicating she had advanced to "the Gold Standard".

On another occasion, while she still had over 1200 unused hours, she was induced to buy an additional 175 hours of instruction at a cost of $2,472.75 to be eligible "to take a trip to Mexico".

Finally, sandwiched in between other lesser sales promotions, she was influenced to buy an additional 481 hours of instruction at a cost of $6,523.81 in order to "be classified as a Gold Bar Member, the ultimate achievement of the dancing studio".

All the foregoing sales promotions, illustrative of the entire fourteen separate contracts, were procured by defendant Davenport and Arthur Murray, Inc., by false representations to her that she was improving in her dancing ability, that she had excellent potential, that she was responding to instructions in dancing grace, and that they were developing her into a beautiful dancer, whereas in truth and in fact she did not develop in her dancing ability, she had no "dance aptitude", and in fact had difficulty in "hearing the musical beat". The complaint alleged that such representations to her "were in fact false and known by the defendant to be false and contrary to the plaintiff's true ability, the truth of plaintiff's ability being fully known to the defendants, but withheld from the plaintiff for the sole and specific intent to deceive and defraud the plaintiff and to induce her in the purchasing of additional hours of dance lessons". It was averred that the lessons were sold to her "in total disregard to the true physical, rhythm, and mental ability of the plaintiff". In other words, while she first exulted that she was entering the "spring of her life", she finally was awakened to the fact there was "spring" neither in her life nor in her feet.

The complaint prayed that the Court decree the dance contracts to be null and void and to be cancelled, that an accounting be had, and judgment entered against the defendants "for that portion of the $31,090.45 not charged against specific hours of instruction given to the plaintiff". The

Court held the complaint not to state a cause of action and dismissed it with prejudice. We disagree and reverse.

The material allegations of the complaint must, of course, be accepted as true for the purpose of testing its legal sufficiency. Defendants contend that contracts can only be rescinded for fraud or misrepresentation when the alleged misrepresentation is as to a material fact, rather than an opinion, prediction or expectation, and that the statements and representations set forth at length in the complaint were in the category of "trade puffing", within its legal orbit.

It is true that "generally a misrepresentation, to be actionable, must be one of fact rather than of opinion". Tonkovich v. South Florida Citrus Industries, Inc., Fla.App.1966, 185 So.2d 710; Kutner v. Kalish, Fla.App. 1965, 173 So.2d 763. But this rule has significant qualifications, applicable here. It does not apply where there is a fiduciary relationship between the parties, or where there has been some artifice or trick employed by the representor, or where the parties do not in general deal at "arm's length" as we understand the phrase, or where the representee does not have equal opportunity to become apprised of the truth or falsity of the fact represented. 14 Fla.Jur. Fraud and Deceit, § 28; Kitchen v. Long, 1914, 67 Fla. 72, 64 So. 429. As stated by Judge Allen of this Court in Ramel v. Chasebrook Construction Company, Fla.App.1961, 135 So.2d 876:

"* * * A statement of a party having * * * superior knowledge may be regarded as a statement of fact although it would be considered as opinion if the parties were dealing on equal terms."

It could be reasonably supposed here that defendants had "superior knowledge" as to whether plaintiff had "dance potential" and as to whether she was noticeably improving in the art of terpsichore. And it would be a reasonable inference from the undenied averments of the complaint that the flowery eulogiums heaped upon her by defendants as a prelude to her contracting for 1944 additional hours of instruction in order to attain the rank of the Bronze Standard, thence to the bracket of the Silver Standard, thence to the class of the Gold Bar Standard, and finally to the crowning plateau of a Life Member of the Studio, proceeded as much or more from the urge to "ring the cash register" as from any honest or realistic appraisal of her dancing prowess or a factual representation of her progress.

Even in contractual situations where a party to a transaction owes no duty to disclose facts within his knowledge or to answer inquiries respecting such facts, the law is if he undertakes to do so he must disclose the *whole truth*. Ramel v. Chasebrook Construction Company, supra; Beagle v. Bagwell, Fla.App.1964, 169 So.2d 43. From the face of the complaint, it should have been reasonably apparent to defendants that her vast outlay of cash for the many hundreds of additional hours of instruction was not justified by her slow and awkward progress, which she would have been made well aware of if they had spoken the "whole truth".

In Hirschman v. Hodges, etc., 1910, 59 Fla. 517, 51 So. 550, it was said that—

"* * * what is plainly injurious to good faith ought to be considered as a fraud sufficient to impeach a contract",

and that an improvident agreement may be avoided—

"* * * because of surprise, or mistake, *want of freedom, undue influence, the suggestion of falsehood, or the suppression of truth*". (Emphasis supplied.)

We repeat that where parties are dealing on a contractual basis at arm's length with no inequities or inherently unfair practices employed, the Courts will in general "leave the parties where they find themselves". But in the case sub judice, from the allegations of the unanswered complaint, we cannot say that enough of the accompanying ingredients, as mentioned in the foregoing authorities, were not present which otherwise would have barred the equitable arm of the Court to her. In our view, from the showing made in her complaint, plaintiff is entitled to her day in Court.

It accordingly follows that the order dismissing plaintiff's last amended complaint with prejudice should be and is reversed.

Reversed.

NOTES

(1) *Fraud: Kaleidoscopic and Infinite.* "Fraud is kaleidoscopic, infinite. Fraud being infinite and taking on protean form at will, were courts to cramp themselves by defining it with a hard and fast definition, their jurisdiction would be cunningly circumvented at once by new schemes beyond the definition. Messieurs, the fraud-feasors, would like nothing half so well as for courts to say they would go thus far, and no further in its pursuit. * * * Accordingly definitions of fraud are of set purpose left general and flexible, and thereto courts match their astuteness against the versatile inventions of fraud-doers." Stonemets v. Head, 248 Mo. 243, 263, 154 S.W. 108, 114 (1913).

(2) *Statutory Protection.* Not only is fraud "kaleidoscopic," so also are the judicial attempts to reach the varieties of deceptive practices. The court in *Vokes* drew upon a tradition of case law under which the agreement might be rescinded. In a similar case, a Texas court awarded treble damages and attorney's fees, pursuant to a statute entitled "Deceptive Trade Practices—Consumer Protection Act." Bennett v. Bailey, 597 S.W.2d 532 (Tex.Civ.App. 1980). Statutes of this type figure prominently in contemporary litigation, granting additional rights not only to consumers but in some instances to commercial parties as well.

(3) Collateral Reading: Restatement (Second) §§ 159–173; Farnsworth §§ 4.10–4.15; Dobbs §§ 9.1–9.6; Calamari & Perillo §§ 9–13—9–24; Murray § 95; Prosser (5th ed.) §§ 105–110.

Comment: Misrepresentation, Rescission and Restitution

A misrepresentation is "an assertion that is not in accord with the facts." Restatement (Second) § 159. The effect of such an assertion by one party inducing another to enter into a contract may be to provide the latter with a tort claim for damages, or alternatively, the aggrieved party may sue to rescind the contract because of the other's deceptive language or conduct. In general, the misrepresentation must be an assertion or affirmation of an existing fact (not an expression of opinion, a promise to do something in the future, or a prediction of future events) upon which the other party justifiably relies in entering the contract. The misrepresentation may be fraudulent or innocent. Moreover, the misrepresentation may be the assertion of a "half truth" or consist of the concealment of a fact (e.g., covering over the evidence of termite infestation to mislead prospective purchaser) or even the failure to disclose. Finally, the usual effect of wrongful misrepresentation is to render the contract "voidable," but courts have identified a kind of fraud in the "execution" (as distinguished from the ordinary fraud in the "inducement") which precludes the formation of any contract at all (or, as is sometimes said, a "void" contract). An example is where a party secures another's signature by misrepresenting the character of the document. See Restatement (Second) § 163.

A good statement of the law of "innocent misrepresentation" is found in Norton v. Poplos, 443 A.2d 1 (Del. 1982).

"Essentially, the equitable remedy of rescission results in abrogation or 'unmaking' of an agreement, and attempts to return the parties to the *status quo*. Common grounds for rescission of a contract for the sale of real property include fraud, misrepresentation and mistake.... But in addition to rescission for fraudulent misrepresentation, rescission also may be granted under certain circumstances for innocent misrepresentations made by a seller. Thus, as stated by Professor Williston:

> 'It is not necessary, in order that a contract may be rescinded for fraud or misrepresentation, that the party making the misrepresentation should have known that it was false. Innocent misrepresentation is sufficient for though the representation may have been made innocently, it would be unjust and inequitable to permit a person who has made false representations, even innocently, to retain the fruits of a bargain induced by such representations.'

Williston, supra, at § 1500, pp. 400, 401. Similarly, the recently promulgated Restatement 2d of Contracts, § 164, states that,

> 'If a party's manifestation of assent is induced by either a fraudulent *or material* misrepresentation by the other party upon which the recipient is justified in relying, the contract is voidable by the recipient.' (Emphasis added.)

See also Restatement 1st of Contracts, § 476 (1932). Most American jurisdictions which have addressed this issue appear to recognize that an innocent material misrepresentation by a vendor which induces the sale of the property is ground for rescission of the contract. In addition to ordering rescission, a court will generally direct that a down payment by a buyer be returned on a theory of restitution....

A misrepresentation need not be in the form of written or spoken words. Stated simply, a misrepresentation is merely an 'assertion not in accordance with the facts,' Restatement 2d of Contracts, § 159, and such an assertion may be made by conduct as well as words. Id. Comment a. And although a statement or assertion may be facially true, it may constitute an actionable misrepresentation if it causes a false impression as to the true state of affairs, and the actor fails to provide qualifying information to cure the mistaken belief. . . . Stated another way,

> '[a] statement may be true with respect to the facts stated, but may fail to include qualifying matters necessary to prevent the implication of an assertion that is false with respect to other facts. For example a true statement that an event has recently occurred may carry the false implication that the situation has not changed since its occurrence. Such half-truth may be as misleading as an assertion that is wholly false.'

Restatement 2d of Contracts, § 159, comment b."

One remedy for misrepresentation is to rescind the contract.

The purpose of rescission, whether through a legal or equitable action, is "restitutionary;" i.e., there is a dissolution or "undoing" of the contract and a restoration of the parties to their pre-contract position (*status quo ante*). Originally, rescission was exclusively an equitable remedy, but eventually law courts recognized the right to utilize rescission as a way of securing appropriate restitutionary relief. Whether equitable or legal rescission, an "adjustment of the equities" of the parties is a matter of major concern. For example, "when a party elects to rescind the contract, he is only entitled to a return to the status quo. This usually requires a plaintiff to restore *any benefit* he received under the contract, *including a return in specie of any property received and a reasonable rental value for the use of the property*, plus damages for waste if any. Likewise, *the defendant must restore any money paid by the plaintiff under the contract plus interest*, monetary reimbursement for reasonable repairs, expenditures and improvements made on the property by the plaintiff, and, where a business has been sold, a reasonable amount of compensation for the value of the plaintiff's labor and services rendered during the period of time which he operated and possessed the property. . . ." Smeekens v. Bertrand, 262 Ind. 50, 58, 311 N.E.2d 431, 436 (1974) (emphasis in original).

According to Professor Dan Dobbs: "The most common way in which fraud litigation reaches the courts is in the direct action for damages—the action that once would have been called the deceit action. However, fraud is also grounds for rescission of a transaction fraudulently induced. Where, as a result of one party's fraud, the other party is induced to sign an instrument that does not express their true agreement, the reformation remedy is the appropriate one.

"The constructive trust is quite suited to fraud cases and often furnishes a useful remedy as does the equitable lien.

"At other times, the fraud is not the basis of an action or claim at all, but is merely operable as a defense or as an estoppel.

"In any kind of case the remedy available should carry out the substantive policy in question. In fraud cases perhaps more than others the relation between substance and remedy is an especially close one. If the plaintiff demands a relatively mild remedy—rescission—he may be given relief even if he does not show actual intent to deceive by the defendant. On the other hand, if he seeks a harsher damages measure, many courts will require him to show such an intent. It is for this reason quite impossible to separate completely the substantive and remedial rules in fraud cases." Dobbs § 9.1.

Hill v. Jones

Court of Appeals of Arizona, 1986.
151 Ariz. 81, 725 P.2d 1115.

■ MEYERSON, JUDGE.

Must the seller of a residence disclose to the buyer facts pertaining to past termite infestation? This is the primary question presented in this appeal. Plaintiffs Warren G. Hill and Gloria R. Hill (buyers) filed suit to rescind an agreement to purchase a residence. Buyers alleged that Ora G. Jones and Barbara R. Jones (sellers) had made misrepresentations concerning termite damage in the residence and had failed to disclose to them the existence of the damage and history of termite infestation in the residence. The trial court dismissed the claim for misrepresentation based upon a so-called integration clause in the parties' agreement.

Sellers then sought summary judgment on the "concealment" claim arguing that they had no duty to disclose information pertaining to termite infestation and that even if they did, the record failed to show all of the elements necessary for fraudulent concealment. The trial court granted summary judgment, finding that there was "no genuinely disputed issue of material fact and that the law favors the ... defendants." The trial court awarded sellers $1,000.00 in attorney's fees. Buyers have appealed from the judgment and sellers have cross-appealed from the trial court's ruling on attorney's fees.

I. FACTS

In 1982, buyers entered into an agreement to purchase sellers' residence for $72,000. The agreement was entered after buyers made several visits to the home. The purchase agreement provided that sellers were to pay for and place in escrow a termite inspection report stating that the property was free from evidence of termite infestation. Escrow was scheduled to close two months later.

One of the central features of the house is a parquet teak floor covering the sunken living room, the dining room, the entryway and portions of the halls. On a subsequent visit to the house, and when sellers were present, buyers noticed a small "ripple" in the wood floor on the step leading up to the dining room from the sunken living room. Mr. Hill asked if the ripple could be termite damage. Mrs. Jones answered that it was water damage. A few years previously, a broken water heater in the house had in fact caused water damage in the area of the dining room and steps which necessitated that some repairs be made to the floor. No further discussion on the subject, however, took place between the parties at that time or afterwards.

Mr. Hill, through his job as maintenance supervisor at a school district, had seen similar "ripples" in wood which had turned out to be termite damage. Mr. Hill was not totally satisfied with Mrs. Jones's explanation, but he felt that the termite inspection report would reveal whether the ripple was due to termites or some other cause.

The termite inspection report stated that there was no visible evidence of infestation. The report failed to note the existence of physical damage or evidence of previous treatment. The realtor notified the parties that the property had passed the termite inspection. Apparently, neither party actually saw the report prior to close of escrow.

After moving into the house, buyers found a pamphlet left in one of the drawers entitled "Termites, the Silent Saboteurs." They learned from a neighbor that the house had some termite infestation in the past. Shortly after the close of escrow, Mrs. Hill noticed that the wood on the steps leading down to the sunken living room was crumbling. She called an exterminator who confirmed the existence of termite damage to the floor and steps and to wood columns in the house. The estimated cost of repairing the wood floor alone was approximately $5,000.

Through discovery after their lawsuit was filed, buyers learned the following. When sellers purchased the residence in 1974, they received two termite guarantees that had been given to the previous owner by Truly Nolen, as well as a diagram showing termite treatment at the residence that had taken place in 1963. The guarantees provided for semi-annual inspections and annual termite booster treatments. The accompanying diagram stated that the existing damage had not been repaired. The second guarantee, dated 1965, reinstated the earlier contract for inspection and treatment. Mr. Jones admitted that he read the guarantees when he received them. Sellers renewed the guarantees when they purchased the residence in 1974. They also paid the annual fee each year until they sold the home.

On two occasions during sellers' ownership of the house but while they were at their other residence in Minnesota, a neighbor noticed "streamers" evidencing live termites in the wood tile floor near the entryway. On both occasions, Truly Nolen gave a booster treatment for termites. On the second incident, Truly Nolen drilled through one of the wood tiles to treat for termites. The neighbor showed Mr. Jones the area where the damage and treatment had occurred. Sellers had also seen termites on the back fence and had replaced and treated portions of the fence.

Sellers did not mention any of this information to buyers prior to close of escrow. They did not mention the past termite infestation and treatment to the realtor or to the termite inspector. There was evidence of holes on the patio that had been drilled years previously to treat for termites. The inspector returned to the residence to determine why he had not found evidence of prior treatment and termite damage. He indicated that he had not seen the holes in the patio because of boxes stacked there. It is unclear whether the boxes had been placed there by buyers or sellers. He had not found the damage inside the house because a large plant, which buyers had purchased from sellers, covered the area. After investigating the second time, the inspector found the damage and evidence of past treatment. He acknowledged that this information should have appeared in the report. He complained, however, that he should have been told of any history of termite infestation and treatment before he performed his inspection and that it was customary for the inspector to be given such information.

Other evidence presented to the trial court was that during their numerous visits to the residence before close of escrow, buyers had unrestricted access to view and inspect the entire house. Both Mr. and Mrs. Hill had seen termite damage and were therefore familiar with what it might look like. Mr. Hill had seen termite damage on the fence at this property. Mrs. Hill had noticed the holes on the patio but claimed not to realize at the time what they were for. Buyers asked no questions about termites except when they asked if the "ripple" on the stairs was termite damage. Mrs. Hill admitted she was not "trying" to find problems with the house because she really wanted it.

II. CONTRACT INTEGRATION CLAUSE

We first turn to the trial court's ruling that the agreement of the parties did not give buyers the right to rely on the statement made by Mrs. Jones that the "ripple" in the floor was water damage. We find this ruling to be in error. The contract provision upon which the trial court based its ruling reads as follows:

> That the Purchaser has investigated the said premises, and the Broker and the Seller are hereby released from all responsibility regarding the valuation thereof, and neither Purchaser, Seller, nor Broker shall be bound by any understanding, agreement, promise, representation or stipulation expressed or implied, not specified herein.

In Lutfy v. R.D. Roper & Sons Motor Co., 57 Ariz. 495, 506, 115 P.2d 161, 166 (1941), the Arizona Supreme Court considered a similar clause in an agreement and concluded that "any provision in a contract making it possible for a party thereto to free himself from the consequences of his own fraud in procuring its execution is invalid and necessarily constitutes no defense." The court went on to hold that "parol evidence is always admissible to show fraud, and this is true, even though it has the effect of varying the terms of a writing between the parties." 57 Ariz. at 506–507, 115 P.2d at 166; Barnes v. Lopez, 25 Ariz.App. 477, 480, 544 P.2d 694, 697 (1976). In this case, the claimed misrepresentation occurred after the parties executed the contract.[1] Assuming, for the purposes of this decision, that the integration clause would extend to statements made subsequent to the execution of the contract, the clause could not shield sellers from liability should buyers be able to prove fraud.

III.   DUTY TO DISCLOSE

The principal legal question presented in this appeal is whether a seller has a duty to disclose to the buyer the existence of termite damage in a residential dwelling known to the seller, but not to the buyer, which materially affects the value of the property. For the reasons stated herein, we hold that such a duty exists.

This is not the place to trace the history of the doctrine of caveat emptor. Suffice it to say that its vitality has waned during the latter half of the 20th century. E.g., Richards v. Powercraft Homes, Inc., 139 Ariz. 242, 678 P.2d 427 (1984) (implied warranty of workmanship and habitability extends to subsequent buyers of homes); see generally Quashnock v. Frost, 299 Pa.Super. 9, 445 A.2d 121 (1982); Ollerman v. O'Rourke Co., 94 Wis.2d 17, 288 N.W.2d 95 (1980). The modern view is that a vendor has an affirmative duty to disclose material facts where:

> 1.   Disclosure is necessary to prevent a previous assertion from being a misrepresentation or from being fraudulent or material;
>
> 2.   Disclosure would correct a mistake of the other party as to a basic assumption on which that party is making the contract and if nondisclosure amounts to a failure to act in good faith and in accordance with reasonable standards of fair dealing;
>
> 3.   Disclosure would correct a mistake of the other party as to the contents or effect of a writing, evidencing or embodying an agreement in whole or in part;
>
> 4.   The other person is entitled to know the fact because of a relationship of trust and confidence between them.

Restatement (Second) of Contracts § 161 (1981) (Restatement); see Restatement (Second) of Torts § 551 (1977).

Arizona courts have long recognized that under certain circumstances there may be a "duty to speak." Van Buren v. Pima Community College Dist. Bd., 113 Ariz. 85, 87, 546 P.2d 821, 823 (1976); Batty v. Arizona State Dental Bd., 57 Ariz. 239, 254, 112 P.2d 870, 877 (1941). As the supreme court noted in the context of a confidential relationship, "[s]uppression of a material fact which a party is bound in good faith to disclose is equivalent to a false representation." Leigh v. Loyd, 74 Ariz. 84, 87, 244 P.2d 356, 358 (1952); National Housing Indus. Inc. v. E.L. Jones Dev. Co., 118 Ariz. 374, 379, 576 P.2d 1374, 1379 (1978).

Thus, the important question we must answer is whether under the facts of this case, buyers should have been permitted to present to the jury

---

1. Buyers' fraud theory is apparently based on the premise that they were not bound under the contract until a satisfactory termite inspection report was submitted.

their claim that sellers were under a duty to disclose their (sellers') knowledge of termite infestation in the residence. This broader question involves two inquiries. First, must a seller of residential property advise the buyer of material facts within his knowledge pertaining to the value of the property? Second, may termite damage and the existence of past infestation constitute such material facts?

The doctrine imposing a duty to disclose is akin to the well-established contractual rules pertaining to relief from contracts based upon mistake. Although the law of contracts supports the finality of transactions, over the years courts have recognized that under certain limited circumstances it is unjust to strictly enforce the policy favoring finality. Thus, for example, even a unilateral mistake of one party to a transaction may justify rescission. Restatement § 153.

There is also a judicial policy promoting honesty and fair dealing in business relationships. This policy is expressed in the law of fraudulent and negligent misrepresentations. Where a misrepresentation is fraudulent or where a negligent misrepresentation is one of material fact, the policy of finality rightly gives way to the policy of promoting honest dealings between the parties. See Restatement § 164(1).

Under certain circumstances nondisclosure of a fact known to one party may be equivalent to the assertion that the fact does not exist. For example "[w]hen one conveys a false impression by the disclosure of some facts and the concealment of others, such concealment is in effect a false representation that what is disclosed is the whole truth." State v. Coddington, 135 Ariz. 480, 481, 662 P.2d 155, 156 (App.1983). Thus, nondisclosure may be equated with and given the same legal effect as fraud and misrepresentation. One category of cases where this has been done involves the area of nondisclosure of material facts affecting the value of property, known to the seller but not reasonably capable of being known to the buyer.

Courts have formulated this "duty to disclose" in slightly different ways. For example, the Florida Supreme Court recently declared that "where the seller of a home knows of facts materially affecting the value of the property which are not readily observable and are not known to the buyer, the seller is under a duty to disclose them to the buyer." Johnson v. Davis, 480 So.2d 625, 629 (Fla.1985) (defective roof in three-year old home). In California, the rule has been stated this way:

> [W]here the seller knows of facts materially affecting the value or desirability of the property which are known or accessible only to him and also knows that such facts are not known to, or within the reach of the diligent attention and observation of the buyer, the seller is under a duty to disclose them to the buyer.

Lingsch v. Savage, 213 Cal.App.2d 729, 735, 29 Cal.Rptr. 201, 204 (1963); contra Ray v. Montgomery, 399 So.2d 230 (Ala.1980); see generally W. Prosser & W. Keeton, The Law of Torts § 106 (5th ed. 1984).[2] We find that

---

2. There are variations on this same theme. For example, Pennsylvania has limited the obligation of disclosure to cases of dangerous defects. Glanski v. Ervine, 269 Pa.Super. 182, 191, 409 A.2d 425, 430 (1979).

the Florida formulation of the disclosure rule properly balances the legitimate interests of the parties in a transaction for the sale of a private residence and accordingly adopt it for such cases.

As can be seen, the rule requiring disclosure is invoked in the case of material facts.[3] Thus, we are led to the second inquiry—whether the existence of termite damage in a residential dwelling is the type of material fact which gives rise to the duty to disclose. The existence of termite damage and past termite infestation has been considered by other courts to be sufficiently material to warrant disclosure. See generally Annot., 22 A.L.R.3d 972 (1968).

In Lynn v. Taylor, 7 Kan.App.2d 369, 642 P.2d 131 (1982), the purchaser of a termite-damaged residence brought suit against the seller and realtor for fraud and against the termite inspector for negligence. An initial termite report found evidence of prior termite infestation and recommended treatment. A second report indicated that the house was termite free. The first report was not given to the buyer. The seller contended that because treatment would not have repaired the existing damage, the first report was not material. The buyer testified that he would not have purchased the house had he known of the first report. Under these circumstances, the court concluded that the facts contained in the first report were material. See Hunt v. Walker, 483 S.W.2d 732 (Tenn.App.1971) (severe damage to the residence by past termite infestation); Mercer v. Woodard, 166 Ga.App. 119, 123, 303 S.E.2d 475, 481–82 (1983) (duty of disclosure extends to fact of past termite damage).

Although sellers have attempted to draw a distinction between live termites[4] and past infestation, the concept of materiality is an elastic one which is not limited by the termites' health. "A matter is material if it is one to which a reasonable person would attach importance in determining his choice of action in the transaction in question." Lynn v. Taylor, 7 Kan.App.2d at 371, 642 P.2d at 134–35. For example, termite damage substantially affecting the structural soundness of the residence may be material even if there is no evidence of present infestation. Unless reasonable minds could not differ, materiality is a factual matter which must be determined by the trier of fact. The termite damage in this case may or may not be material. Accordingly, we conclude that buyers should be allowed to present their case to a jury.

Sellers argue that even assuming the existence of a duty to disclose, summary judgment was proper because the record shows that their "si-

---

3. Arizona has recognized that a duty to disclose may arise where the buyer makes an inquiry of the seller, regardless of whether or not the fact is material. Universal Inv. Co. v. Sahara Motor Inn, Inc., 127 Ariz. 213, 215, 619 P.2d 485, 487 (1980). The inquiry by buyers whether the ripple was termite damage imposed a duty upon sellers to disclose what information they knew concerning the existence of termite infestation in the residence.

4. Sellers acknowledge that a duty of disclosure would exist if live termites were present. Obde v. Schlemeyer, 56 Wash.2d 449, 353 P.2d 672 (1960).

lence ... did not induce or influence" the buyers. This is so, sellers contend, because Mr. Hill stated in his deposition that he intended to rely on the termite inspection report. But this argument begs the question. If sellers were fully aware of the extent of termite damage and if such information had been disclosed to buyers, a jury could accept Mr. Hill's testimony that had he known of the termite damage he would not have purchased the house.

Sellers further contend that buyers were put on notice of the possible existence of termite infestation and were therefore "chargeable with the knowledge which [an] inquiry, if made, would have revealed." Godfrey v. Navratil, 3 Ariz.App. 47, 51, 411 P.2d 470 (1966) (quoting Luke v. Smith, 13 Ariz. 155, 162, 108 P. 494, 496 (1910)). It is also true that "a party may ... reasonably expect the other to take normal steps to inform himself and to draw his own conclusions." Restatement § 161 comment d. Under the facts of this case, the question of buyers' knowledge of the termite problem (or their diligence in attempting to inform themselves about the termite problem) should be left to the jury.[5]

By virtue of our holding, sellers' cross-appeal is moot. Reversed and remanded.

NOTES

(1) *Duty of Disclosure in Contract Negotiations.* What is the scope of the duty to disclose material facts during contract negotiations? See *Laidlaw v. Organ*, supra.

The existing guidelines are succinctly stated in Simpson Timber Co. v. Palmberg Construction Co., 377 F.2d 380, 385 (9th Cir.1967): "It is well settled that in the absence of a duty to speak, silence as to a material fact does not of itself constitute fraud. ... On the other hand, once a duty to disclose has arisen, suppression of a material fact is tantamount to an affirmative misrepresentation. ... However, businessmen dealing at arm's length are rarely under a duty to speak." As another court observed with disquieting candor, in the absence of rather special circumstances the standards of conduct rise "no higher than the morals of the market place." Rader v. Boyd, 252 F.2d 585, 587 (10th Cir.1957).

The presence of a fiduciary or confidential relationship is a traditional reason for augmenting a party's duty to disclose. As stated by one court, the presence of a confidential relationship "imposes a duty on the party in whom the confidence is reposed to exercise the utmost good faith and to refrain from obtaining any advantage at the expense of the confiding party." Hyde v. Hyde, 78 S.D. 176, 99 N.W.2d 788, 793 (1959). This status is open-ended and arises from special relationships of trust or confidence or an agreement, express or implied. Its existence is a question of fact, the proof of which may be aided by presumptions which the party in a position of superior knowledge must rebut.

---

5. Sellers also contend that they had no knowledge of any existing termite damage in the house. An extended discussion of the facts on this point is unnecessary. Simply stated, the facts are in conflict on this issue.

Its presence gives rise to a duty to speak and more. For example, in Vai v. Bank of America National Trust & Savings Association, 56 Cal.2d 329, 15 Cal.Rptr. 71, 364 P.2d 247 (1961), a community property settlement was invalidated where the husband failed to disclose property value information to his wife. Even more striking is Jackson v. Seymour, 193 Va. 735, 71 S.E.2d 181 (1952), where the court ordered a deed from sister to brother cancelled and the status quo restored when it appeared that the brother, after the deed was recorded, had cut and marketed timber worth at least ten times the agreed price for the land. The court stated:

"This is not the ordinary case in which the parties dealt at arm's length and the shrewd trader was entitled to the fruits of his bargain. The parties were brother and sister. He was a successful business man and she a widow in need of money and forced by circumstances * * * to sell a part of the lands which she had inherited. Because of their friendly and intimate relations she entrusted to him and he assumed the management and renting of a portion of this very land. He engaged tenants for such of the land as could be cultivated and collected the rents. She accepted his settlements without question.

"Moreover, it is undisputed that neither of the parties knew of the timber on the land and we have from the defendant's own lips the admission that as it turned out 'afterwards' he had paid a grossly inadequate price for the property and that he would not have bought it from her for the small amount paid if he had then known of the true situation.

"To hold that under these circumstances the plaintiff is without remedy would be a reproach to the law. Nor do we think that a court of equity is so impotent." 71 S.E.2d at 184. See also First National Bank in Lenox v. Brown, 181 N.W.2d 178 (Iowa 1970), where the bank made a loan knowing that the proceeds would be used to purchase an interest in personal property in which the bank held a perfected security interest. The court concluded that the bank and the plaintiff were in a relationship of "trust and confidence," that the "trusted party" had "superior knowledge of the facts" and therefore, "a duty to disclose all material facts of which he is aware, or at least those favorable to his own position and adverse to the other." 181 N.W.2d at 182. The mere recording of the security interest by the bank was an insufficient disclosure and, on these facts, "silence qualified as a misrepresentation."

Another traditional case involving a duty to "speak up" is where such disclosure is necessary to correct a previous statement or false impression. Beyond this, courts have been reluctant to recognize a disclosure obligation in an ordinary arm's length transaction. *Hill* is exceptional, but is a likely precursor of more to come. Consider, again, the potential impact of the following Restatement formulation which influenced the Arizona court: "A person's non-disclosure of a fact known to him is equivalent to an assertion that the fact does not exist in the following cases only: * * * (b) where he knows that disclosure of the fact would correct a mistake of the other party as to a basic assumption on which that party is making the contract and if non-disclosure of the fact amounts to a failure to act in good faith and in accordance with reasonable standards of fair dealing. * * *" Restatement (Second) § 161(b). For a discussion of developing doctrine requiring the vendor of a house to disclose its defects to prospective purchasers, see Curnes, *Protecting the Virginia Homebuyer: A Duty to Disclose Defects*, 73 Va.L.Rev. 459 (1987).

Finally, some have urged the imposition of a general obligation to exercise "good faith" in the *formation* of contracts, as is now prescribed by the Uniform Commercial Code for *performance* and *enforcement*. ("Every contract or duty within this Act imposes an obligation of good faith in its performance and enforcement." UCC 1–203.) What would be the relative advantages and disadvantages of such an approach? For a thoughtful treatment, set in the context of insurance litigation, see Holmes, *A Contextual Study of Commercial Good Faith: Good–Faith Disclosure in Contract Formation,* 39 U.Pitt.L.Rev. 381, 450–51 (1978) ("Although the concept is not precise, detailed, or rigid as compared with others generally used in formulations of contract law, it is suggested that 'good faith' has a sufficiently common core of meaning, over a considerable range of applications, to make it functional in practical affairs. Properly perceived, 'good faith' is a single mode of analysis comprising a spectrum of related, factual considerations. The context of its use is critically important. In the context of disclosures required in contracting, for example, the following factual elements should be considered: the nature of the undisclosed fact, accessibility of knowledge, the nature of the contract, trade customs and prior course of dealing, conduct of the party in obtaining knowledge, and the status and relationship of the parties."). See also Kessler and Fine, *Culpa in Contrahendo, Bargaining in Good Faith, and Freedom of Contract: A Comparative Study,* 77 Harv.L.Rev. 401 (1964).

(2) *From Common Law "Fraud" to Statutory "Unfairness" and "Deception."* Every state has legislation, modeled generally upon Section 5 of the Federal Trade Commission Act, prohibiting "unfair" or "deceptive" trade practices or acts. See, generally J. Sheldon, Unfair and Deceptive Acts and Practices [3d ed. 1991, 1996 Supp.], published by the National Consumer Law Center and containing extensive annotation and commentary. As originally enacted, these laws were designed to protect consumers, but in nearly half of the jurisdictions the protective mantle now extends to business entities as well. See Gilleran and Standfeld, *Little FTC Acts Emerge in Business Litigation,* 72 A.B.A.J. 58 (May, 1986). For a thorough study of this trend, see Shell, *Substituting Ethical Standards for Common Law Rules in Commercial Cases: An Emerging Statutory Trend,* 82 Nw.U.L.Rev. 1198 (1988). Professor Shell examines these laws in the context of a general movement away from specific rules and toward open-ended standards, resulting in the dramatic expansion of business liability under such concepts as promissory estoppel, unconscionability, and good faith.

Although these "unfair and deceptive acts or practices" laws (UDAP) vary from state to state, one can identify some common features; notably, (1) vague criteria; (2) private remedy.

First, the proscribed actions are described in general terms; e.g., "deceptive"; "unfair"; "unconscionable." Some statutes also enumerate specific prohibitions, violation of which is a *per se* violation of the statute. Some of these are specific in character; others are not. For example, in the Texas "laundry list" the following is a deceptive trade practice: "disconnecting, turning back, or resetting the odometer of any motor vehicle so as to reduce the number of miles indicated on the odometer gauge." But so is the following: "the failure to disclose information concerning goods or services which was known at the time of the transaction if such failure to disclose such information was intended to induce the consumer into a transaction into which the consumer would not have entered had the information been disclosed."

Second, a private remedy is provided. Unlike the FTC Act, these Little FTC acts provide a right of action to the aggrieved party. At a minimum, actual damages may be recovered, and this includes, in appropriate situations, consequential damages. In addition, provision is made in many of the statutes for a recovery of multiple damages, double or triple. Finally, most of the laws permit the recovery of attorney's fees and costs. In a case brought under the Massachusetts Unfair and Deceptive Trade Practice Act, a buyer of a computer system was awarded compensatory damages of $2.3 million, which the court doubled to $4.6 million, and attorney's fees of $270,000. Computer Systems Engineering, Inc. v. Qantel Corp., 571 F.Supp. 1365 (D.Mass.1983), affirmed 740 F.2d 59 (1st Cir.1984).

There is always tension between "rule" and "discretion." A specific rule provides certainty and predictability, whereas the exercise of discretion pursuant to general standards provides flexibility and adaptability. Is one a clearly superior method of governance in the commercial area? For a thoughtful weighing of competing arguments, see Shell, supra. Professor Shell reaches the following conclusion: "This article has concluded that state legislatures should reform state FTC Acts to balance this impulse toward doing justice with restrictions that will curb the potential for abuse inherent in this regulatory scheme. This conclusion does not rest on a finding that ethical standards are improper vehicles for regulation, but rather derives from a recognition that such open-ended standards, when combined with liberal awards of treble damages and attorneys' fees, create incentives for litigation that are inappropriate in the commercial setting." 82 Nw.U.L.Rev. at 1253–4.

(3) *RICO: Panacea or Nightmare?* On October 15, 1970, Congress enacted the Racketeer Influenced and Corrupt Organizations Act (RICO), which one writer has characterized as "perhaps the most powerful federal criminal enactment in American law." McIntosh, *Racketeer Influenced and Corrupt Organizations Act: Powerful New Tool of the Defrauded Securities Plaintiff,* 31 Kan.L.Rev. 7, 8 (1982). The statutory purpose is "to seek the eradication of organized crime in the United States by strengthening the legal tools in the evidence-gathering process, by establishing new penal prohibitions, and by providing enhanced sanctions and new remedies to deal with the unlawful activities of those engaged in organized crime." Pub.L. No. 91–452, 84 Stat. 922, 923 (Congressional Statement of Findings and Purpose).

Among the key provisions is that which allows a private litigant to recover treble damages, costs and attorney fees if it is established that the form of fraud constitutes a "pattern of racketeering activity" cognizable under the statute. There has been a growing realization that RICO remedies may be available in situations where no direct link to "organized crime" is proven. Hence, the potential of the statute in more ordinary commercial litigation is enormous and affords a defrauded party a civil remedy far more effective than that traditionally provided by, for example, federal securities law.

The widespread use of RICO by civil plaintiffs, particularly when using state and federal fraud statutes to satisfy the statute's predicate acts requirement, has generated heated controversy. Critics insist that the application of RICO to ordinary commercial disputes far exceeds Congressional intent. They maintain that RICO was intended to be used against the infiltration of legitimate business by organized crime, not ordinary commercial fraud. Further, it is argued that the statute's use in fraud suits has resulted in the unnecessary and unwise federalization of an area of law that should be left to the states. Finally, critics argue that the prospect of treble damages intimidates many defendants, causing them to settle frivolous claims out of court. In sum, the general thrust of the criticism is that RICO's broad language and draconian penalties help increase uncertainty in the marketplace and tend to discourage legitimate business activity.

Proponents, on the other hand, contend that Congress clearly intended the statute to be used against any criminal "enterprise," not just organized crime. Further, they maintain that RICO is expressly designed to supplement those federal and state fraud laws which were perceived to be inadequate. To the defenders of the statute, out of court settlements indicate the success of RICO by providing plaintiffs a statutory weapon which fills gaps left in existing legislation and the common law.

To date RICO has survived efforts to weaken or remove its fraud provisions. And while these provisions remain, RICO is certain to become more popular with civil plaintiffs. See Blakey and Perry, *An Analysis of the Myths that Bolster Efforts to Rewrite RICO and the Various Proposals for Reform: "Mother of God—Is This the End of RICO?"*, 43 Vand.L.Rev. 851 (1990).

PROBLEMS: UNCOMMUNICATIVE PARTIES AND THE DUTY TO DISCLOSE

(a) Mr. Mc, prospective purchaser, enters into negotiations to purchase a house belonging to Ms. M. Mc inquires of M's agent as to whether the house has ever had termites. Her agent answers that it has been inspected for termites and is due for another inspection shortly. The agent does not disclose that the prior inspection indicated termite infestation. Should the parties enter into a contract for the sale of the property, could the purchaser rescind? See Murphy v. McIntosh, 199 Va. 254, 99 S.E.2d 585 (1957).

(b) A Jewish congregation seeks to employ a rabbi to serve the congregation. Chaim W applies for the position. Neither in his resume nor during the employment negotiations does he disclose that he had previously been convicted of mail fraud and disbarred as an attorney. After he is hired and enters upon his duties, these facts of his past life come to light. Does the congregation have a right to rescind the contract? See Jewish Center of Sussex County v. Whale, 86 N.J. 619, 432 A.2d 521 (1981).

(c) Nurse N and Doctor K, employees of a local hospital, date each other frequently. The latter has genital herpes, but does not disclose this fact to Nurse N. They engage in sexual intercourse at a time when Dr. K knows the disease is active and would be transmitted. Nurse N contracts the disease. Does she have a cause of action for fraud? See B.N. v. K.K., 312 Md. 135, 538 A.2d 1175 (1988).

(d) D, an elderly person living alone, purchases a house from K. Neither K nor his agent tells D that a woman and her four children were murdered there ten years earlier. D learns of the gruesome episode from a neighbor after the sale. Can she rescind? See Reed v. King, 145 Cal.App.3d 261, 193 Cal.Rptr. 130 (1983).

(e) Driller learns through an independent investigation that Owner's land contains valuable oil deposits. Knowing that Owner is not aware of this, Driller persuades him to enter into a contract to sell the land at a price much less than Owner would have insisted upon had he been aware of the oil potential. Should Owner be entitled to rescind? Would your answer be different if Driller obtained the information from trespassing upon Owner's land? Or if Driller had received "inside" information from a relative at a State agency? See Restatement (Second) § 161, Illus. 10.

(f) While looking through used books at a "flea market," Adam comes upon a Dickens first edition which carries a price tag of $5. Adam knows that the book will fetch several thousand dollars on the market and that Barbara, the proprietor, is unaware of this fact. Any duty to disclose?

(g) Employee interviews for a position in the accounting department of Employer. During the negotiations no mention is made to the prospective employee that plans are already in place for a sale of the company. Employee is hired on an "at will" basis, and shortly thereafter the sale is announced and new management takes over. Employee is among those let go. Did Employer have a duty to disclose information regarding the pending sale to Employee? Cf. Stowman v. Carlson Companies, Inc., 430 N.W.2d 490 (Minn.App.1988). Assume, instead, that Employee intends to work only until he can enter law school, but makes no mention of this to Employer. Should he be obliged to disclose this information?

(h) During an interview for summer employment, Jake, first-year law student, is questioned extensively about prior educational background and other personal matters. Jake knows that his chances for the job will be significantly reduced if he discloses that during his sophomore year in high school he was suspended from the basketball team for disciplinary reasons. Should he have a duty to volunteer this information? Should he be obliged to disclose that in college he was found guilty of plagiarism and placed on probation?

(C) DURESS

In the fraud materials just considered, the aggrieved party assented to the bargain without complete or accurate information. He or she justifiably relied upon false representations of material facts by the defendant. In the materials to follow, the aggrieved party, who is accurately informed and primed to resist a proposed deal, is told by the defendant "unless you agree to this bargain, I will see that X happens." Because X is presumably less pleasant than contracting, the aggrieved party, in the typical case, agrees to the bargain (which, by the way, may be perfectly fair) and later claims that the "apparent" assent was coerced. Put another way, it is claimed that one's "free will" was overcome by the threat and, therefore, the bargain is not enforceable. Although the factors in the analysis tend to be both complicated and infused with a bias against the duress defense, we will try in this short subsection to determine when the defense that choice was impaired by threat is likely to succeed.

Austin Instrument, Inc. v. Loral Corp.

Court of Appeals of New York, 1971.
29 N.Y.2d 124, 324 N.Y.S.2d 22, 272 N.E.2d 533.

■ FULD, CHIEF JUDGE. The defendant, Loral Corporation, seeks to recover payment for goods delivered under a contract which it had with the plaintiff Austin Instrument, Inc., on the ground that the evidence establishes, as a matter of law, that it was forced to agree to an increase in price on the items in question under circumstances amounting to economic duress.

In July of 1965, Loral was awarded a $6,000,000 contract by the Navy for the production of radar sets. The contract contained a schedule of deliveries, a liquidated damages clause applying to late deliveries and a cancellation clause in case of default by Loral. The latter thereupon solicited bids for some 40 precision gear components needed to produce the radar sets, and awarded Austin a subcontract to supply 23 such parts. That party commenced delivery in early 1966.

In May, 1966, Loral was awarded a second Navy contract for the production of more radar sets and again went about soliciting bids. Austin bid on all 40 gear components but, on July 15, a representative from Loral informed Austin's president, Mr. Krauss, that his company would be awarded the subcontract only for those items on which it was low bidder. The Austin officer refused to accept an order for less than all 40 of the gear parts and on the next day he told Loral that Austin would cease deliveries of the parts due under the existing subcontract unless Loral consented to substantial increases in the prices provided for by that agreement—both retroactively for parts already delivered and prospectively on those not yet shipped—and placed with Austin the order for all 40 parts needed under Loral's second Navy contract. Shortly thereafter, Austin did, indeed, stop delivery. After contacting 10 manufacturers of precision gears and finding none who could produce the parts in time to meet its commitments to the Navy,[*] Loral acceded to Austin's demands; in a letter dated July 22, Loral wrote to Austin that "We have feverishly surveyed other sources of supply and find that because of the prevailing military exigencies, were they to start from scratch as would have to be the case, they could not even remotely begin to deliver on time to meet the delivery requirements established by the Government. * * * Accordingly, we are left with no choice or alternative but to meet your conditions."

Loral thereupon consented to the price increases insisted upon by Austin under the first subcontract and the latter was awarded a second subcontract making it the supplier of all 40 gear parts for Loral's second contract with the Navy. Although Austin was granted until September to resume deliveries, Loral did, in fact, receive parts in August and was able to produce the radar sets in time to meet its commitments to the Navy on

---

[*] The best reply Loral received was from a vendor who stated he could commence deliveries sometime in October.

both contracts. After Austin's last delivery under the second subcontract in July, 1967, Loral notified it of its intention to seek recovery of the price increases.

On September 15, 1967, Austin instituted this action against Loral to recover an amount in excess of $17,750 which was still due on the second subcontract. On the same day, Loral commenced an action against Austin claiming damages of some $22,250—the aggregate of the price increases under the first subcontract—on the ground of economic duress. The two actions were consolidated and, following a trial, Austin was awarded the sum it requested and Loral's complaint against Austin was dismissed on the ground that it was not shown that "it could not have obtained the items in question from other sources in time to meet its commitment to the Navy under the first contract." A closely divided Appellate Division affirmed (35 A.D.2d 387, 316 N.Y.S.2d 528, 532). There was no material disagreement concerning the facts; as Justice Steuer stated in the course of his dissent below, "[t]he facts are virtually undisputed, nor is there any serious question of law. The difficulty lies in the application of the law to these facts." (35 A.D.2d 392, 316 N.Y.S.2d 534.)

The applicable law is clear and, indeed, is not disputed by the parties. A contract is voidable on the ground of duress when it is established that the party making the claim was forced to agree to it by means of a wrongful threat precluding the exercise of his free will. . . . The existence of economic duress or business compulsion is demonstrated by proof that "immediate possession of needful goods is threatened" . . . more or, more particularly, in cases such as the one before us, by proof that one party to a contract has threatened to breach the agreement by withholding goods unless the other party agrees to some further demand. . . . However, a mere threat by one party to breach the contract by not delivering the required items, though wrongful, does not in itself constitute economic duress. It must also appear that the threatened party could not obtain the goods from another source of supply and that the ordinary remedy of an action for breach of contract would not be adequate.

We find without any support in the record the conclusion reached by the courts below that Loral failed to establish that it was the victim of economic duress. On the contrary, the evidence makes out a classic case, as a matter of law, of such duress.

It is manifest that Austin's threat—to stop deliveries unless the prices were increased—deprived Loral of its free will. As bearing on this, Loral's relationship with the Government is most significant. As mentioned above, its contract called for staggered monthly deliveries of the radar sets, with clauses calling for liquidated damages and possible cancellation on default. Because of its production schedule, Loral was, in July, 1966, concerned with meeting its delivery requirements in September, October and November, and it was for the sets to be delivered in those months that the withheld gears were needed. Loral had to plan ahead, and the substantial liquidated damages for which it would be liable, plus the threat of default, were genuine possibilities. Moreover, Loral did a substantial portion of its business with the Government, and it feared that a failure to deliver as agreed upon would jeopardize its chances for future contracts. These genuine concerns do not merit the label " 'self-imposed, undisclosed and subjective' " which the Appellate Division majority placed upon them. It was perfectly reasonable for Loral, or any other party similarly placed, to consider itself in an emergency, duress situation.

Austin, however, claims that the fact that Loral extended its time to resume deliveries until September negates its alleged dire need for the parts. A Loral official testified on this point that Austin's president told him he could deliver some parts in August and that the extension of deliveries was a formality. In any event, the parts necessary for production of the radar sets to be delivered in September were delivered to Loral on September 1, and the parts needed for the October schedule were delivered in late August and early September. Even so, Loral had to "work * * * around the clock" to meet its commitments. Considering that the best offer Loral received from the other vendors it contacted was commencement of delivery sometime in October, which, as the record shows, would have made it late in its deliveries to the Navy in both September and October, Loral's claim that it had no choice but to accede to Austin's demands is conclusively demonstrated.

We find unconvincing Austin's contention that Loral, in order to meet its burden, should have contacted the Government and asked for an extension of its delivery dates so as to enable it to purchase the parts from another vendor. Aside from the consideration that Loral was anxious to perform well in the Government's eyes, it could not be sure when it would obtain enough parts from a substitute vendor to meet its commitments. The only promise which it received from the companies it contacted was for *commencement* of deliveries, not full supply, and, with vendor delay common in this field, it would have been nearly impossible to know the length of the extension it should request. It must be remembered that Loral was producing a needed item of military hardware. Moreover, there is authority for Loral's position that nonperformance by a subcontractor is not an excuse for default in the main contract. (See, e.g., McBride & Wachtel, Government Contracts, § 35.10, [11].) In light of all this, Loral's claim should not be held insufficiently supported because it did not request an extension from the Government.

Loral, as indicated above, also had the burden of demonstrating that it could not obtain the parts elsewhere within a reasonable time, and there can be no doubt that it met this burden. The 10 manufacturers whom Loral contacted comprised its entire list of "approved vendors" for precision gears, and none was able to commence delivery soon enough. As Loral was producing a highly sophisticated item of military machinery requiring parts made to the strictest engineering standards, it would be unreasonable to hold that Loral should have gone to other vendors, with whom it was either unfamiliar or dissatisfied, to procure the needed parts. As Justice Steuer noted in his dissent, Loral "contacted all the manufacturers whom it believed capable of making these parts" (35 A.D.2d at p. 393, 316 N.Y.S.2d at p. 534), and this was all the law requires.

It is hardly necessary to add that Loral's normal legal remedy of accepting Austin's breach of the contract and then suing for damages would have been inadequate under the circumstances, as Loral would still have had to obtain the gears elsewhere with all the concomitant consequences mentioned above. In other words, Loral actually had no choice, when the prices were raised by Austin, except to take the gears at the "coerced" prices and then sue to get the excess back.

* * *

In sum, the record before us demonstrates that Loral agreed to the price increases in consequence of the economic duress employed by Austin. Accordingly, the matter should be remanded to the trial court for a computation of its damages.

The order appealed from should be modified, with costs, by reversing so much thereof as affirms the dismissal of defendant Loral Corporation's claim and, except as so modified, affirmed.

■ BERGAN, JUDGE (dissenting).

Whether acts charged as constituting economic duress produce or do not produce the damaging effect attributed to them is normally a routine type of factual issue.

Here the fact question was resolved against Loral both by the Special Term and by the affirmance at the Appellate Division. It should not be open for different resolution here.

* * *

[Some footnotes omitted.]

Machinery Hauling, Inc. v. Steel of West Virginia

Supreme Court of Appeals of West Virginia, 1989.
181 W.Va. 694, 384 S.E.2d 139.

■ MILLER, JUSTICE:

In this case, the Cabell County Circuit Court certifies questions concerning the effect of threats made by one party for the purpose of inducing contract concessions from the other. We consider today whether, and under what circumstances, such threats are actionable.

We restate the facts of the case as they appear in the complaint. Machinery Hauling, Inc., the plaintiff below, is a West Virginia corporation whose principal business is the transport of freight. In January, 1988, the defendant, Steel of West Virginia (Steel), contracted with the plaintiff to transport seventeen loads of steel product to Shelby Steel, Inc. (Shelby), a firm located in Louisville, Kentucky. When delivery was nearly completed, Steel informed the plaintiff that the product was not of merchantable quality and that Shelby had rejected it.

Steel orally directed the plaintiff to return the last three loads of the product to Steel's plant in Huntington, West Virginia. Shortly thereafter, Robert Bunting, an agent and employee of Steel, instructed the plaintiff to pay to Steel the sum of $31,000, the price of the undelivered loads, "or else [Steel] would cease to do business with the [p]laintiff." In its complaint, the plaintiff avers that Steel and Bunting "negligently attempted to extort money from the [p]laintiff" by their joint threat to sever business relations unless payment for the defective product was made. Loss of business that resulted from this threat was claimed to have been in excess of $1,000,000 per year.

The plaintiff filed suit in the Circuit Court of Cabell County against Steel and Bunting, seeking monetary damages for their "extortionate demands." The circuit court concluded that threats against business interests may in some circumstances be actionable, but that the threats made by the defendants were not.

We are initially confronted with the parties' disagreement over the legal theory that applies to this situation. The plaintiff argues that there is a cause of action under our criminal extortion statute, W.Va.Code, 61–2–13.[1] Particular reliance is placed on Hurley v. Allied Chemical Corp., 164 W.Va. 268, 262 S.E.2d 757 (1980), where we formulated a general rule with regard to permitting a private cause of action for the violation of a statute.[2] Reliance is also placed on W.Va.Code, 55–7–9, which provides: "Any person injured by the violation of a statute may recover from the offender such

---

1. W.Va.Code, 61–2–13, provides:

"If any person threaten injury to the character, person or property of another person, or to the character, person or property of his wife or child, or to accuse him or them of any offense, and thereby extort money, pecuniary benefit, or any bond, note or other evidence of debt, he shall be guilty of a felony, and, upon conviction, shall be confined in the penitentiary not less than one nor more than five years. And if any person make such threat of injury or accusation of an offense as herein set forth, but fail thereby to extort money, pecuniary benefit, or any bond, note or other evidence of debt, he shall be guilty of a misdemeanor, and, upon conviction, shall be confined in jail not less than two nor more than twelve

months and fined not less than fifty nor more than five hundred dollars."

2. Syllabus Point 1 of *Hurley* states:

"The following is the appropriate test to determine when a State statute gives rise by implication to a private cause of action: (1) the plaintiff must be a member of the class for whose benefit the statute was enacted; (2) consideration must be given to legislative intent, express or implied, to determine whether a private cause of action was intended; (3) an analysis must be made of whether a private cause of action is consistent with the underlying purpose of the legislative scheme; and (4) such private cause of action must not intrude into an area delegated exclusively to the federal government."

damages as he may sustain by reason of the violation. . . ."[3] See Jenkins v. J.C. Penney Casualty Ins. Co., 167 W.Va. 597, 280 S.E.2d 252 (1981).

* * *

We find few cases that analyze recovery in this type of situation from the perspective of an implied civil cause of action arising from a criminal extortion statute.[4] Furthermore, since there was no threat in the legal sense, the facts would not appear to come within the statutory language of a threatened injury to the "character, person or property of another person." W.Va.Code, 61–2–13. * * * As we discuss in more detail later, the plaintiff had no continuing contract with Steel. As a consequence, Steel was free to place its haulage business wherever it chose. Its statement to the plaintiff did not constitute an unlawful act.

The more common analysis proceeds under a theory of business or economic loss. In the early common law, duress per minas, i.e., by threats, was available to void a contract where the threat involved imprisonment, mayhem, or loss of life or limb. Restatement (Second) of Torts § 871, comment f (1979); 25 Am.Jur.2d Duress & Undue Influence § 11 (1966). Through the years, there has been a steady expansion of duress principle such that direct dire harm is no longer essential, the focus instead being on whether the threat overbears the exercise of free will. Professor Williston, in discussing the status of business compulsion, has identified two basic elements: (1) the party who asserts business compulsion "must show that he has been the victim of a wrongful or unlawful act or threat," and (2) "[s]uch act or threat must be one which deprives the victim of his unfettered will." 13 Williston on Contracts § 1617 at 704 (1970).[5]

Recently, courts have tended to avoid the term "free will" as applied to the victim, but instead have utilized the concept that the victim had "no reasonable alternative." This is found in Section 175(1) of the Restatement (Second) of Contracts (1981): "If a party's manifestation of assent is induced by an improper threat by the other party that leaves the victim no reasonable alternative, the contract is voidable by the victim." A more difficult issue is determining what type of threat is sufficient to invoke the rule. Courts tend to use as a shorthand summary, words such as "wrong-

---

3. The full text of W.Va.Code, 55–7–9, is: "Any person injured by the violation of any statute may recover from the offender such damages as he may sustain by reason of the violation, although a penalty or forfeiture for such violation be thereby imposed, unless the same be expressly mentioned to be in lieu of such damages."

4. See Printers II, Inc. v. Professionals Publishing, Inc., 784 F.2d 141 (2d Cir.1986) (assuming if implied cause of action possible under New York's extortion statute, conduct did not constitute extortion); Battlefield Builders, Inc. v. Swango, 743 F.2d 1060 (4th Cir.1984) (applying civil RICO action to de-

fendant's claimed extortion activities on a building lease); Iden v. Adrian Buckhannon Bank, 661 F.Supp. 234 (N.D.W.Va.1987), modified, 841 F.2d 1122 (4th Cir.1988) (no extortion on bank's requiring additional collateral on refinancing of existing loan).

5. As to commentators' views on economic duress, see, e.g., Dawson, Economic Duress—An Essay in Perspective, 45 Mich. L.Rev. 253 (1947); Dalzell, Duress by Economic Pressure I, 20 N.C.L.Rev. 237 (1942); Dalzell, Duress by Economic Pressure II, 20 N.C.L.Rev. 341 (1942).

ful," "oppressive," or "unconscionable" to describe conduct, but the complexity of the term "threat" is demonstrated in Section 176 of the Restatement.[6] The concept of "economic or business duress" may be generally stated as follows: Where the plaintiff is forced into a transaction as a result of unlawful threats or wrongful, oppressive, or unconscionable conduct on the part of the defendant which leaves the plaintiff no reasonable alternative but to acquiesce, the plaintiff may void the transaction and recover any economic loss.[7] . . .

Furthermore, while economic duress principles are more prevalent in contract cases, they are not limited solely to this area.[8] Some courts have proceeded to analyze economic duress cases in terms of a tort theory. Under this theory, the duty is deemed to be the reasonable use of the superior economic power of the defendant. The breach is using such power unlawfully or unreasonably. The proximate cause is shown by the fact that the victim had no reasonable recourse but to acquiesce in the unlawful conduct of the defendant and is damaged thereby. E.g., Pecos Constr. Co. v. Mortgage Inv. Co. of El Paso, 80 N.M. 680, 459 P.2d 842 (1969); Housing Auth. of City of Dallas v. Hubbell, 325 S.W.2d 880 (Tex.Civ.App.1959); Wurtz v. Fleischman, 89 Wis.2d 291, 278 N.W.2d 266 (1979), rev'd on other grounds, 97 Wis.2d 100, 293 N.W.2d 155 (1980). See also Note, Economic Duress After the Demise of Free Will Theory: A Proposed Tort Analysis, 53 Iowa L.Rev. 892 (1968). It is apparent that this tort theory is not substantially different from the economic duress theory under a contract analysis.

In several cases, we have utilized what amounts to a "business compulsion" analysis, although we characterized it only as "duress." Our earliest

6. Section 176 of the Restatement (Second) of Contracts provides:

"(1) A threat is improper if

"(a) what is threatened is a crime or a tort, or the threat itself would be a crime or a tort if it resulted in obtaining property,

"(b) what is threatened is a criminal prosecution,

"(c) what is threatened is the use of civil process and the threat is made in bad faith, or

"(d) the threat is a breach of the duty of good faith and fair dealing under a contract with the recipient.

"(2) A threat is improper if the resulting exchange is not on fair terms, and

"(a) the threatened act would harm the recipient and would not significantly benefit the party making the threat,

"(b) the effectiveness of the threat in inducing the manifestation of assent is significantly increased by prior unfair

dealing by the party making the threat, or

"(c) what is threatened is otherwise a use of power for illegitimate ends."

7. Section 70 of the Restatement of Restitution (1937) provides:

"A person who has conferred a benefit upon another as the result of a transaction which is void or voidable because of duress or undue influence, is entitled to restitution under the same conditions as if the benefit had been conferred as the result of fraud."

8. E.g., Reiver v. Murdoch & Walsh, P.A., 625 F.Supp. 998 (D.C.Del.1985) (threats of termination of at-will employee to obtain release of already accrued benefits could form basis of economic duress); Housing Auth. of City of Dallas v. Hubbell, 325 S.W.2d 880 (Tex.Civ.App.1959) (subcontractor having no contract with housing authority could recover for economic coercion for being required to apply two coats of paint at no extra cost instead of one coat as required in specifications).

case is West Virginia Transp. Co. v. Sweetzer, 25 W.Va. 434 (1885), where the defendant purchased quantities of oil in northern West Virginia and attempted to transport the same to market. The sole outlet for the oil was the plaintiff's railroad. Even though the freight charges made by the plaintiff were in excess of that authorized by statute, the defendant paid the charges so as to ensure delivery of the oil. When the plaintiff sued to recover the unpaid freight charges, the defendant counterclaimed to recover the excess charges. We summarized the cases from other jurisdictions, and found that the overpayments were made by the defendant under duress:

> "[W]hen the shipper was one whose business could not be successfully carried on without frequent use of this identical railroad for transportation purposes, then, . . . in making over-payments for freight on the demand of the railroad company he should be regarded as making them under a species of moral duress, and such payments should be regarded as involuntary, and he should in an action of assumpsit for money had and received be allowed to recover back of the railroad company what he had paid in excess of legal charges[.]" 25 W.Va. at 461.

Much the same principles were applied in Central Acceptance Corp. v. Nash Bluefield Motor Co., 104 W.Va. 174, 139 S.E. 654 (1927). There, the plaintiff sought to collect on several notes executed by the motor company and personally indorsed by the defendant, Speiden. Speiden claimed he had been coerced into signing the notes because an agent of the plaintiff had advised him that the manager of the car company had illegally "double financed" some cars and had threatened Speiden with criminal prosecution if he did not indorse the notes. In finding duress in Central Acceptance Corp., 104 W.Va. at 177–78, 139 S.E. at 656, we quoted from 13 C.J. § 319 at 402 (1917):

> " '[T]he question of duress is one of fact in the particular case, to be determined on consideration of the surrounding circumstances, such as age, sex, capacity, situation, and relation of the parties; and that duress may exist whether or not the threat is sufficient to overcome the mind of a man of ordinary courage, it being sufficient to constitute duress that one party to the transaction is prevented from exercising his free will by reason of threats made by the other, and that the contract is obtained by reason of such fact. Unless these elements are present, however, duress does not exist. The test is not so much the means by which the party was compelled to execute the contract as it is the state of mind induced by the means employed—the fear of which made it impossible for him to exercise his own free will.' "

See also First Nat'l Bank of Peterstown v. Hansbarger, 129 W.Va. 418, 40 S.E.2d 822 (1946) (no duress found in procurement of accommodation endorsements); Bank of Clinchburg v. Carter, 101 W.Va. 669, 133 S.E. 370 (1926) (duress found as to accommodation endorser).[9]

---

9. In a noncontractual setting, Boggs v. Greenbrier Grocery Co., 53 W.Va. 536, 44 S.E. 777 (1903), we appeared to recognize a duress theory where the plaintiff was forced

While we recognize the concept of business or economic duress, we do not find it exists in this case. There was no continuing contract between the plaintiff and the defendants. Thus, the demand by the defendants that the plaintiff pay $31,000 for the defective steel was not coupled with a threat to terminate an existing contract. Furthermore, the plaintiff did not accede to the defendants' demand and pay over the money.

The plaintiff's claim, stripped to its essentials, is that it has been deprived of its future prospects of doing business with the defendants. However, this future expectancy is not a legal right on which the plaintiff can anchor a claim of economic duress. The claim here is similar to that in Oregon Bank v. Nautilus Crane & Equip. Corp., supra, where an equipment dealer contended that its dealer agreement had been coerced. This was based on the premise that if the dealer had not obtained the equipment, it would have gone out of business. The court disposed of this argument as follows:

> "Here, defendant has alleged only that NCI threatened to cease doing business with it if Gordon did not sign the agreement and that defendant would have gone out of business but for NCI's supply of cranes. It is well established, however, that threats to do what the threatening person had a legal right to do does not constitute duress. Wurtz v. Fleischman, 97 Wis.2d 100, 293 N.W.2d 155, 160 (1980)." 68 Or.App. at 143, 683 P.2d at 103.

[handwritten margin note: cases don't support]

See 805 Third Avenue Co. v. M.W. Realty Associates, 58 N.Y.2d at 453, 461 N.Y.S.2d at 781, 448 N.E.2d at 448 ("[A] party cannot be guilty of economic duress for refusing to do that which it is not legally required to do.").

Finally, there appears to be general acknowledgement that duress is not shown because one party to the contract has driven a hard bargain or that market or other conditions now make the contract more difficult to perform by one of the parties or that financial circumstances may have caused one party to make concessions.[10] E.g., Continental Bank of Pennsylvania v. Barclay Riding Academy, Inc., supra; Production Credit Ass'n of Minot v. Geving, 218 N.W.2d 185 (N.D.1974); 13 Williston, supra at § 1617 at 708.

---

to release a lien in favor of the defendant's subordinate lien by the defendant's threat to have the plaintiff's son arrested on a felony. See also Carroll v. Fetty, 121 W.Va. 215, 2 S.E.2d 521, cert. denied, 308 U.S. 571, 60 S.Ct. 85, 84 L.Ed. 479 (1939) (duress might be shown to void release of wrongful death action).

10. We do not imply from this statement that the decision of the Supreme Court of Alaska in Totem Marine Tug & Barge, Inc. v. Alyeska Pipeline Serv. Co., supra, is incor-

rect. There, Alyeska owed between $260,000 to $300,000 to Totem, a small delivery company. Alyeska delayed payment on this obligation until Totem became severely impaired financially. To avoid bankruptcy, Totem accepted a $97,500 settlement. Totem then sued to obtain the balance due, claiming that the settlement had been coerced through economic duress. The case was dismissed on summary judgment, but the Supreme Court reversed, holding that there were genuine issues of fact on the economic duress issue.

The questions certified to us by the Cabell County Circuit Court are, therefore, answered, and this case is dismissed from the docket.

Certified questions answered and dismissed.

NOTES

(1) *Duress: Wrongful Coercion.* Duress as such is seldom recognized as an independent tort. The victim does not usually maintain an action for damages. *Machinery Hauling* is exceptional in this respect. In the usual case, duress is pleaded as a defense or as a basis for avoiding a transaction and securing restitutionary relief. Moreover, the issue seldom arises in connection with initial contract formation; most often there is an attempt to bar enforcement of a contract modification or a settlement agreement. More on this later. See infra, Chapter Five, Section 4(C).

Normally, duress by physical compulsion prevents formation of a contract, Restatement (Second) § 174, whereas duress by threats makes a contract voidable. Restatement (Second) § 175 provides: "If a party's manifestation of assent is induced by an improper threat by the other party that leaves the victim no reasonable alternative, the contract is voidable by the victim." Collateral reading: Restatement (Second) §§ 174–176; Farnsworth §§ 4.16–4.19; Dobbs § 10.2; Calamari & Perillo §§ 9–2—9–8; Murray § 93.

(2) In *Austin Instruments,* Loral insisted that it was "left with no choice or alternative but to meet your [Austin's] conditions." What, precisely, were its alternatives? Was there a "reasonable" alternative? For an extensive discussion of duress in connection with federal government contracts, see Harley, *Economic Duress and Unconscionability: How Fair Must the Government Be?*, 18 Pub.Cont.L.J. 76 (1988).

(3) Can it ever be unlawful to threaten to do what one has a legal right to do? Quoting from an Oregon case, the court in *Machinery Hauling* states: "It is well established, however, that threats to do what the threatening person had a legal right to do does not constitute duress." This is misleading. The Oklahoma Supreme Court recently offered this clarification: "Ordinarily a party may threaten to do what is lawful; however, a coercer's threats may be wrongful even though the threatened action would have been legal. The key factor, therefore, must be the fact that the threatened action is an unreasonable alternative to an injurious contractual demand in a bargaining situation. The wrongfulness of the coercer's conduct must be related to the unreasonableness of the alternatives which he presents to the weaker party, and the inherent wrongfulness of either alternative is relevant only insofar as it shows the unreasonableness of the alternatives. 'Unlawful' when applied to promises, agreements, contracts and considerations, means that the agreements are legally ineffective because they were obtained by bad faith coercion or compulsion, even though the acts may not be illegal per se." Centric Corporation v. Morrison–Knudsen Company, 731 P.2d 411, 419 (Okl.1986). A common example, and one referred to in *Machinery Hauling,* is the threat of criminal prosecution as an "improper means of inducing the recipient to make a contract . . . a misuse, for personal gain, of power given for other legitimate ends." Restatement (Second) § 176, Comment c. Even a threat of civil process may, under exceptional circumstances, be abusive "if the threat is shown to

have been made in bad faith." Id. Comment d. For other examples of wrongful threats to do what one has a legal right to do, see Berger v. Berger, 466 So.2d 1149 (Fla.App.1985) (husband threatens to inform Internal Revenue Service of wife's tax evasion if she does not sign settlement agreement); Wolf v. Marlton Corporation, 57 N.J.Super. 278, 154 A.2d 625 (1959) (purchaser under land contract threatens to sell to an "undesirable" in order to force vendor-developer to return deposit). Does *Machinery Hauling* fit here?

(4) *Morta v. Korea Insurance Corp. Revisited.* Return now to the plight of Vincente Morta (supra at 471). Under which, if any, of the following situations would a duress argument be successful? In each, assume that Vincente was fully informed about the "all claims" release.

A.   Vincente agreed only because he was desperately short of cash to meet emergency expenses.

B.   Vincente agreed after being informed that the company would go to his employer and "tell how unreasonable you are being."

C.   Vincente agreed after being informed that he either signed or the company would break off all negotiations.

(5) *Undue Influence.* "While law courts developed the idea of duress, equity courts developed the parallel, but distinct, idea of undue influence." Dobbs § 10.3. Undue influence is characterized by "unfair" persuasion that may fall short of constituting actual duress. "The hallmark of such persuasion is high pressure, a pressure which works on mental, moral, or emotional weakness to such an extent that it approaches the boundaries of coercion." Odorizzi v. Bloomfield School District, 246 Cal.App.2d 123, 130, 54 Cal.Rptr. 533, 539 (1966). Moreover, it is ordinarily limited to situations where there is a relationship of trust and confidence (e.g., parent and child; husband and wife; attorney and client), and one party is particularly susceptible to pressure by the other. However, undue influence has been found where a confidential relationship in the usual sense does not exist. The *Odorizzi* case, supra, is illustrative. In that case a school teacher was arrested on criminal charges of homosexual activity and after conferring with school officials submitted a letter of resignation the following day. A month later the charges were dismissed, and the teacher sued for rescission of the resignation and other appropriate relief. In upholding the teacher's position, the court observed that the pattern of "over-persuasion" usually involves several of the following elements: "(1) discussion of the transaction at an unusual or inappropriate time, (2) consummation of the transaction in an unusual place, (3) insistent demand that the business be finished at once, (4) extreme emphasis on untoward consequences of delay, (5) the use of multiple persuaders by the dominant side against a single servient party, (6) absence of third-party advisers to the servient party, (7) statements that there is no time to consult financial advisers or attorneys." 246 Cal.2d at 133, 54 Cal.Rptr. at 541. See Farnsworth § 4.20; Calamari & Perillo §§ 9–9—9–12; Murray § 94; Note, *Duress and Undue Influence—A Comparative Analysis,* 22 Baylor L.Rev. 572 (1970).

(D) UNCONSCIONABILITY

Section 2–302 of the Uniform Commercial Code [UCC 2–105 (1997)] provides:

(1) If the court as a matter of law finds the contract or any clause of the contract to have been unconscionable at the time it was made the court may refuse to enforce the contract, or it may enforce the remainder of the contract without the unconscionable clause, or it may so limit the application of any unconscionable clause as to avoid any unconscionable result.

(2) When it is claimed or appears to the court that the contract or any clause thereof may be unconscionable the parties shall be afforded a reasonable opportunity to present evidence as to its commercial setting, purpose and effect to aid the court in making the determination.

Comment 1, in an effort to explain, contains the following language:

This section is intended to make it possible for the courts to police explicitly against the contracts or clauses which they find to be unconscionable. In the past such policing has been accomplished by adverse construction of language, by manipulation of the rules of offer and acceptance or by determinations that the clause is contrary to public policy or to the dominant purpose of the contract. This section is intended to allow the court to pass directly on the unconscionability of the contract or particular clause therein and to make a conclusion of law as to its unconscionability. The basic test is whether, in the light of the general commercial background and the commercial needs of the particular trade or case, the clauses involved are so one-sided as to be unconscionable under the circumstances existing at the time of the making of the contract. Subsection (2) makes it clear that it is proper for the court to hear evidence upon these questions. The principle is one of the prevention of oppression and unfair surprise * * * and not of disturbance of allocation of risks because of superior bargaining power.*

The mandate "to police explicitly against the contracts or clauses which [the courts] find to be unconscionable" has generated intense interest and controversy across the land. For able statements of opposing views, see Leff, *Unconscionability and the Code—The Emperor's New Clause*, 115 U.Pa.L.Rev. 485 (1967) and Ellinghaus, *In Defense of Unconscionability*, 78 Yale L.J. 757 (1969). The following is a representative sample of the extensive "unconscionability" literature: Murray, *Unconscionability: Unconscionability*, 31 U.Pitt.L.Rev. 1 (1969); Spanogle, *Analyzing Unconscionability Problems*, 117 U.Pa.L.Rev. 931 (1969); Schwartz, *A Reexamination*

---

* "The comments are Delphic. On the one hand they state that 'the basic test is whether, in the light of the general commercial background and the commercial needs of the particular trade, or case, the clauses involved are so one-sided as to be unconscionable under the circumstances existing at the time of the making of the contract.' But rest assured—the comment continues—UCC 2– 302 does not have as one of its purposes 'disturbance of allocation of risks because of superior bargaining power.' How one can overturn an important clause as unconscionable and not thereby 'disturb the allocation of risks' is hard to imagine." Speidel, Summers and White, Commercial Transactions, Teaching Materials 241 (1st ed. 1969).

of Nonsubstantive Unconscionability, 63 Va.L.Rev. 1053 (1977); Fort, *Understanding Unconscionability: Defining the Principle,* 9 Loy.U.L.J. 765 (1978); Hillman, *Debunking Some Myths about Unconscionability: A New Framework for U.C.C. Section 2–302,* 67 Cornell L.Rev. 1 (1981).

There are some historical antecedents to UCC 2–302 reflected, for example, in the equitable maxim that "Equity will not enforce unconscionable bargains." Moreover, there has evidently been a significant strain of American case law wherein courts have "limited and sometimes denied contractual obligation by reference to the fairness of the underlying exchange." Horwitz, *The Historical Foundations of Modern Contract Law,* 87 Harv.L.Rev. 917, 123 (1974). But it was only with the advent of UCC 2–302, limited to transactions in goods but extended by analogy to other types of transactions, that courts began in earnest to grapple with the ramifications of unconscionability doctrine and to spell out specific content.

A key question in the controversy concerns the extent that the prevention of "oppression and unfair surprise" adds to the evolving doctrines of fraud and duress and the expanding category of agreements or terms violative of public policy (infra at 539).

The principal task is to identify the transaction types and the critical factors that increase the chances that a court will, at the very least, insist that there be a hearing on the unconscionability issue. This may turn on the attitude of the judge or court as well. For example, a judge who agrees with Professor Richard Epstein that it is improper for courts to "act as roving commissions to set aside those agreements whose substantive terms they find objectionable" and that the proper function of unconscionability is only to "police the process whereby private agreements are formed, and in that connection, only to facilitate the setting aside of agreements that are as a matter of probabilities likely to be vitiated by the classical defenses of duress, fraud or incompetence" is likely to have little receptivity to the unconscionability defense. See Epstein, *Unconscionability: A Critical Reappraisal,* 18 J.Law & Econ. 293, 294–95 (1975). Also, remember that the unconscionability doctrine is likely to be a transitional device in the movement, in a particular problem area, from lesser to greater legal control. Use by a court of the doctrine signals the breakdown of more traditional contract doctrine, such as the "duty to read" and, in many cases, heralds the coming of more comprehensive legislative and administrative regulation, some of which was discussed in the preceding section. Like promissory estoppel, unconscionability operates in the interstices to achieve particularized fairness. But unlike promissory estoppel, fairness is achieved by restricting rather than expanding the scope of contractual liability. In short, its development and use are symptomatic of important changes in the society and, therefore, is worth some serious consideration.

(1) CONSUMER TRANSACTIONS

The notion that an unconscionable bargain should not be enforced is not foreign to the common law. See, e.g., the oft-quoted definition of an unconscionable bargain as one "such as no man in his senses and not under delusion would make on the one hand, and as no honest and fair man would accept on the other." Earl of Chesterfield v. Janssen, 2 Ves.Sr. 125, 28 Eng.Rpt. 82 (1750), quoted in Hume v. United States, 132 U.S. 406, 411, 10 S.Ct. 134, 136, 33 L.Ed. 393, 396 (1889). But this occasional language belies the normal assumption that "people should be entitled to contract on their own terms without the indulgence of paternalism by courts in the alleviation of one side or another from the effects of a bad bargain * * * [and] should be permitted to enter into contracts that actually may be unreasonable or which may lead to hardship on one side." Carlson v. Hamilton, 8 Utah 2d 272, 332 P.2d 989, 990–91 (1958). At the risk of oversimplification, it is suggested that two developments have changed the perception of, if not the underlying assumptions about, unconscionability. The first was a tremendous expansion after World War II of the demand for and availability of consumer credit. One result was that more transactions between individuals who purchased or borrowed for personal, family or household purposes and professional sellers or lenders took place. The second was the perfection of the so-called "contract of adhesion," that is, a standard form contract drafted by one party and offered on a "take-it-or-leave-it" basis. We begin our examination of unconscionability with an "early" classic.

Cutler Corp. v. Latshaw

Supreme Court of Pennsylvania, 1953.
374 Pa. 1, 97 A.2d 234.

■ MUSMANNO, JUSTICE. On November 20, 1951, Jennie M. Latshaw contracted in writing to pay the Cutler Corporation the sum of $6,456 for certain work to be done and material to be furnished in repairing her premises at 914 S. 49th Street, Philadelphia. Dissatisfied with the manner in which the work was being performed, Miss Latshaw ordered the employees of the plaintiff corporation to cease operation until defects in the work were corrected.

On July 23, 1952, the Cutler Corporation confessed judgment against Miss Latshaw in the sum of $5,238.56 under an alleged warrant of attorney contained in the contract. The defendant petitioned for a rule to show cause why the judgment should not be stricken from the record; the lower Court made the rule absolute; and the plaintiff appealed.

The contract consisted of five form sheets carrying certain printed matter. The face of each sheet began with a standardized identification of the parties and the designating of the plaintiff and defendant, respectively, as "Contractor" and "buyer."

Then followed in small type the wording:

"Upon your acceptance below, you are hereby requested by the undersigned owner of the installation premises, hereinafter called 'Buyer,' to furnish and install the materials shown in the following specifications at the installation premises mentioned below (subject to conditions on reverse side.)"

In the middle of the sheet, in large type, appeared the single word: SPECIFICATIONS. Beneath this word, *in handwriting,* followed a list of the various items of work to be done and materials to be supplied by the plaintiff.

The reverse side of each sheet carried in very small type eight paragraphs, No. 6 of which spelled out a warrant of attorney with confession of judgment. Although each reverse sheet also carried the word, SPECIFICATIONS, with "Continued" in parentheses, no specifications were listed. This, in spite of the fact that the entire list of the specifications could not be contained on the first sheet and had to go over to other sheets. In fact, with the exception of the printing indicated, the reverse sides of the sheets were blank.

Did Miss Latshaw authorize a warrant of attorney and confession of judgment? In the case of Griffin Oil Co. v. Toms, 170 Pa.Super. 203, 85 A.2d 595, the plaintiff entered a judgment against the defendant on a warrant of attorney contained in an "Equipment Agreement." This document was not signed by the defendant but it was attached to an "Owner's Consent" bearing the defendant's signature. The "Owner's Consent" acknowledged notice of the agreement and contained an assent to its terms and conditions. In affirming the lower Court's striking off the judgment, the Superior Court said:

"In a proceeding to strike off a judgment, only matters apparent on the face of the record will be considered. Peerless Soda Fountain Service Co. v. Lipschutz, 101 Pa.Super. 568, 571. On the present record it conclusively appears that defendant did not sign the agreement containing the warrant of attorney. An authority to confess judgment must be clear and explicit. Solazo v. Boyle, 365 Pa. 586, 76 A.2d 179. There was no authority for entering a judgment by confession against defendant who had not signed the warrant of attorney; a judgment by confession must be self-sustaining on the record."

Equally in the case at bar the defendant did not sign the warrant of attorney-confession of judgment. The reference on the face side of the contract to the "conditions" on the reverse side, among which was buried the supposed authority for a warrant of attorney, can hardly be accepted in a court of law as an acknowledgment of a confession of judgment. While the word "condition" may conceivably embrace almost any circumstance, upon which, or, because of which, a right is created or a liability attaches, it cannot be used to mean surrender of fundamental personal and property absolutes unless the word appears within a setting which warns of the potency of the capitulation being made.

A warrant of attorney authorizing judgment is perhaps the most powerful and drastic document known to civil law. The signer deprives himself of every defense and every delay of execution, he waives exemption of personal property from levy and sale under the exemption laws, he places his cause in the hands of a hostile defender. The signing of a warrant of attorney is equivalent to a warrior of old entering a combat by discarding his shield and breaking his sword. For that reason the law jealously insists on proof that this helplessness and impoverishment was voluntarily accepted and consciously assumed.

The case at bar falls far short of producing evidence that Miss Latshaw was even aware that a warrant of attorney was remotely contemplated. The physical characteristics of the five-page document demonstrate that the reverse sides were entirely ignored. Although the sizeable blank spaces on the reverse pages could have been utilized for the continuing enumeration of specifications, the parties adopted additional sheets, writing only on the faces thereof, for that list. In the absence of any explanation as to why five pages were used when three would have sufficed (employing the reverse sides), the conclusion is inescapable that the parties purposely intended not to make the reverse sides of the sheets any part of the contract.

The mere physical inclusion of the warrant of attorney in a mass of fine type verbiage on each reverse sheet does not of itself make it part of the contract. * * *

In the case of Sturtevant Co. v. Fireproof Film Co., 216 N.Y. 199, 110 N.E. 440, 441, L.R.A.1916D, 1069, the defendant there sought to avoid liability on a contract because at the bottom of the plaintiff's letterhead, upon which the agreement was written, appeared the words: "All prices are subject to change without notice, and all contracts and orders taken are subject to the approval of the executive office at Hyde Park, Mass.," and there was no proof that the executive office at Hyde Park had approved the contract. The Court of Appeals of New York rejected this contention:

"In view of the manner in which this provision is printed upon the stationery of the plaintiff, it cannot be held, as a matter of law, that it was incorporated in and a part of the proposal. The language of the proposal is clear and explicit, and this provision, which is printed in small type, cannot be allowed to change, alter, or modify it, unless it was a part of the proposal. It was not incorporated in the body of the proposal or referred to in it. * * *

"When an offer, proposal, or contract is expressed in clear and explicit terms, matter printed in small type at the top or bottom of the office stationery of the writer, where it is not easily seen, which is not in the body of the instrument or referred to therein, is not necessarily to be considered as a part of such offer, proposal, or contract."

One of the most hateful acts of the ill-famed Roman tyrant Caligula was that of having the laws inscribed upon pillars so high that the people could not read them. Although the warrant of attorney in the numerous sheets of the contract at bar was within the vision of the defendant, it was so placed as to be completely beyond her contemplation of its purport. An inconspicuously printed legend on a contract form or letterhead which is obviously fortuitous, irrelevant or superfluous is no more part of the agreement entered into than the advertisements on the walls of the room in which the contract is signed.

Diminutive type grossly disproportionate to that used in the face body of a contract cannot be ignored; it has its place in law, and, where space is at a premium, it allows for instruction, guidance and protection which might otherwise be lost, but where it is used as an ambush to conceal legalistic spears to strike down other rights agreed upon, it will receive rigorous scrutinization by the courts for the ascertainment of the true meaning which may go beyond the literal import. As early as 1858 this Court denounced subterfuge of fine print in Verner v. Sweitzer, 32 Pa. 208, where a common carrier sought to limit his implied liability by certain restrictions on the baggage check:

"... it has been adjudged, that proof of general notice of limitation of liability, must be such as amounts to actual notice, or shown to have been so conspicuous, that the party sought to be affected by it could not have failed to discover it without gross negligence, the affirmative of which is upon the carrier. And that emblazoning the general object on a check, ticket, or notice, like the one used here, in large letters, but stating the restriction in small ones is insufficient."

* * *

Although these cases have to do with limitation on the liability of common carriers, their reasoning applies with equal force to the facts in the case at bar. When a party to a contract seeks to bind the other party with the unyielding thongs of a warrant of attorney-confession of judgment, a device not ordinarily expected by a homeowner in a simple agreement for alterations and repairs, the inclusion of such a self-abnegating provision must appear in the body of the contract and cannot be incorporated by a casual reference with a designation not its own.

Order affirmed.

NOTES

(1) Did the court regard the "confession of judgment" clause as *per se* unenforceable?

(2) Why was Miss Latshaw excused from the "duty" to read and understand the terms in the writing before assenting to it?

(3) How might one articulate a workable test to determine when a consumer is "unfairly surprised" by a contract provision? Consider the words of Karl Llewellyn:

The answer, I suggest, is this: Instead of thinking about "assent" to boilerplate clauses, we can recognize so far as concerns the specific, there is no assent at all. What has in fact been assented to, specifically, are the few dickered terms, and the broad type of the transaction, and but one thing more. That one thing more is a blanket assent (not a specific assent) to any not unreasonable or indecent terms the seller may have on his form, which do not alter or eviscerate the reasonable meaning of the dickered terms.

The fine print which has not been read has no business to cut under the reasonable meaning of those dickered terms which constitute the dominant and only real expression of agreement, but much of it commonly belongs in. * * * [A]ny contract with boiler-plate results in two several contracts: the *dickered* deal, and the collateral one of *supplementary* boiler plate. Rooted in sense, history, and simplicity, it is an answer which could occur to anyone.

Llewellyn, The Common Law Tradition: Deciding Appeals 370–71 (1960).

(4) If Miss Latshaw had read and fully understood the clause at stake and the clause was not *per se* unenforceable, is there any other basis for declaring it unconscionable? What does oppression mean in this context?

(5) Collateral reading: Farnsworth §§ 4.27–4.28; Calamari & Perillo §§ 9–37—9–40; Murray § 96; White & Summers, Uniform Commercial Code §§ 4–1—4–9 (2d ed. 1980); Restatement (Second) § 208 (In applying the concept to all contracts, the drafters state in Comment a: "The determination that a contract or term is or is not unconscionable is made in the light of its setting, purpose and effect. Relevant factors include weakness in the contracting process like those involved in more specific rules as to contractual capacity, fraud, and other invalidating causes; the policy also overlaps with rules which render particular bargains or terms unenforceable on grounds of public policy.").

Williams v. Walker–Thomas Furniture Co.

United States Court of Appeals, District of Columbia, 1965.
Supra at 27, 29.

NOTES

(1) Is the contract in *Williams* inherently unfair? Assume that a contract similar to that in *Williams* was signed, after a careful reading, by a bright, sophisticated first-year law student. Clearly, there would be no "unfair surprise." (Right?) Would the "cross-collateral" clause still be so "oppressive" as to warrant a finding of unconscionability?

(2) *Procedural and Substantive Unconscionability.* Courts and commentators frequently distinguish between "procedural" unconscionability (some kind of deception or overreaching that constitutes an abuse in the process of bargaining) and "substantive" unconscionability (some sort of objectionable or oppressive clause that may have been knowingly and voluntarily assented to). In one case the focus is upon the *process;* in the other it is upon the *result.* To justify a finding of unconscionability should it be necessary to establish elements of each; i.e., some kind of mix of "procedural" and "substantive" unconscionability? In a case in the District of Columbia subsequent to *Williams* and involving Walker–Thomas Furniture Co., the court emphasized that unconscionability required both the absence of meaningful choice and a commercially unreasonable term. Patterson v. Walker–Thomas Furniture Co., 277 A.2d 111 (D.C.App.1971).

(3) "Unconscionability has been defined as 'an absence of meaningful choice on the part of one of the parties, together with contract terms which are unreasonably favorable to the other party.' ... To show that a provision is conscionable, the party seeking to uphold the provision must show that the provision bears some reasonable relationship to the risks and needs of the business. ... The indicators of procedural unconscionability generally fall into two areas: (1) lack of knowledge, and (2) lack of voluntariness. A lack of knowledge is demonstrated by a lack of understanding of the contract terms arising from inconspicuous print or the use of complex, legalistic language, ... disparity in sophistication of parties, ... and lack of opportunity to study the contract and inquire about contract terms.... A lack of voluntariness is demonstrated in contracts of adhesion when there is a great imbalance in the parties' relative bargaining power, the stronger party's terms are unnegotiable, and the weaker party is prevented by market factors, timing or other pressures from being able to contract with another party on more favorable terms or to refrain from contracting at all. ...

"Substantive unconscionability is found when the terms of the contract are of such an oppressive character as to be unconscionable. It is present when there is a one-sided agreement whereby one party is deprived of all the benefits of the agreement or left without a remedy for another party's nonperformance or breach, ... a large disparity between the cost and price or a price far in excess of that prevailing in the market [place], ... or terms which bear no reasonable relationship to business risks assumed by the parties...." Bank of Indiana, National Association v. Holyfield, 476 F.Supp. 104, 109–10 (S.D.Miss. 1979).

(4) *Posner on "Meaningful Choice."* "There can be no objection to using the one-sidedness of a transaction as evidence of deception, lack of agreement, or compulsion, none of which is shown here. The problem with unconscionability as a legal doctrine comes in making sense out of lack of 'meaningful choice' in a situation where the promisor was not deceived or compelled and really did agree to the provision that he contends was unconscionable. Suppose that for reasons unrelated to any conduct of the promisee the promisor has very restricted opportunities. Maybe he is so poor that he can be induced to sell the clothes off his back for a pittance, or is such a poor credit risk that he can be made (in the absence of usury laws) to pay an extraordinarily high interest rate to borrow money that he wants desperately. Does he have a 'meaningful choice' in such circumstances? If not he may actually be made worse off by a rule of nonenforcement of hard bargains; for, knowing that a contract with him will not be enforced, merchants may be unwilling to buy his clothes or lend him money. Since the law of contracts cannot compel the making of contracts on terms favorable to one party, but can only refuse to enforce contracts with unfavorable terms, it is not an institution well designed to rectify inequalities in wealth." Posner, J. in Amoco Oil Company v. Ashcraft, 791 F.2d 519, 522 (7th Cir.1986).

Comment: Renting–To–Own As A Modern Method to "Profit on Poverty"

[Retailers can often avoid consumer credit regulation by restructuring the transaction as "renting-to-own" where the consumer has the option to stop renting before attaining ownership of the chattel. Unlike traditional credit contracts, rent-to-own customers do not unconditionally promise to pay off a loan and therefore the transaction falls outside the definition of most consumer credit statutes. The following article describes the business practices of Rent–A–Center, a chain of stores that controls 25% of the $2.8 billion U.S. market.]

For low-income customers, Rent–A–Center has tremendous appeal. The chain gives them immediate use of brand-name merchandise, and the weekly payments are usually less than $20. But while in theory customers can eventually own the goods outright, the company says three out of every four are unable to meet all their payments.

Their failure is partially responsible for Thorn's success. The company earns considerably more by renting, repossessing and then re-renting the same goods than it does if the first customer makes all the payments. Derrick–Myers, who was fired as manager of the Rent–A–Center store in Victorville, California, recalls one particular Philco VCR, for example, that he says retailed for about $119—but that brought in more than $5,000 in a five-year period.

That means the most profitable customers are people like Minneapolis welfare mother Angela Adams, who says Rent–A–Center salespeople cajoled her into renting more than a dozen items at a monthly cost that reached about $325. Though the salespeople knew how little she earned, "they pushed it on me," she says. When she fell behind in her payments in late 1991, Rent–A–Center sued her and repossessed the goods, ranging from a bedroom set to two VCRs. Ms. Adams is now a named plaintiff in one of the two class-action suits, this one pending in federal court in Minneapolis. Rent–A–Center declines comment.

"Even if a customer can't afford it and you know it and they know it, we'll rent to them anyway," says Rod Comeaux, a former store manager from Onley, VA., who was fired a year ago for unrelated reasons. "We can always get it back" and re-rent it to others, he says.

Rent–A–Center's Mr. Gates denies that salespeople put excessive pressure on customers or intentionally overload them with goods. On average, customers rent 2.85 items a month, at a total monthly cost of $99.07, and they are able to cancel rentals at any time without a penalty, he points out. Store managers—who are required to obtain income and other financial information from customers—ideally should act as "financial planners" for customers, he says, adding that the "worst thing" employees can do is to rent to customers whose "eyes are bigger than their stomachs."

Rent–A–Center says its customer base is 25% to 30% black and 10% to 15% Hispanic, and just 15% are on welfare or government subsidies. But former store managers consistently maintain that the total on government assistance is more than 25%, with some claiming up to 70%. Indeed, they unanimously report that sales always spiked on "Mother's Day," as they call the day when welfare mothers get their checks. * * *

According to a thick training manual, salespeople are supposed to quote the weekly and monthly rental rates. The manual doesn't instruct employees to quote the total cost, and former store managers say they made sure they never did. In fact, in 40 states, the total isn't even on the price tag. (Ten states require that it be listed on price tags, a rule Rent–A–Center says it will honor in all 50 states by next month.) Instead, the manual instructs employees to focus on "features and benefits," such as Rent–A–Center's free delivery and repair, and most of all, the low weekly price.

But the advertised weekly price is designed to yield each store about 3½ times its cost of purchasing the merchandise from Rent–A–Center headquarters. The total is jacked up further by a one-time processing fee (typically $7.50) and late fees (typically $5). The total price is usually revealed only in the rental agreement that customers sign at the end of the sales process, former store managers say.

To boost Rent–A–Center's profits, employees also push a "customer protection" plan that offers minimal benefits but that 95% of customers end up subscribing to. "It's better than insurance," saleswoman Laura Daupino of the Bloomfield, N.J. store was overheard telling an unemployed welfare mother recently. Yet, unlike insurance, it doesn't replace stolen or destroyed items, or reimburse customers for their loss. It offers customers basically one benefit: It prevents Rent–A–Center from suing customers if goods are stolen or destroyed.

For Rent–A–Center, however, the benefit is considerably larger: The protection plan is a $29 million annual revenue booster, much of which drops to the bottom line, as does most of the $27 million racked up from the other fees, according to internal company financial documents.

Rent–A–Center has long justified his high prices by citing customer defaults and the costs associated with its free repairs. But part of Rent–A–Center's secret of success is that those costs are minimal. Internal documents show its service expenses ran 3.3% of rental revenue in fiscal 1993, though Rent–A–Center says the actual figure is closer to 10%. And its total inventory losses—from junked merchandise and "skips and stolens" (as in customers who skip town)—run a bit over 2% of revenue. * * *

Thorn executives say there is nothing insidious about Rent-A-Center's strategy of courting customers who are of limited means, and of treating them well. Customers receive "fantastic" service, say Sir Colin, who professes to be "always puzzled" why the rent-to-own industry is "badly regarded." Rent–A–Center, he adds, "treats them like kings and queens."

Customers like Carol Baker, a waitress at a resort hotel in Bolton Landing, N.Y., are appreciative. "The prices could be cheaper," says Ms. Baker, whose home is almost completely furnished by Rent–A–Center, "but they treat me like I'm a somebody."

Former employees and other customers see things differently. "The Rent–A–Center philosophy," says Mr. Comeaux, the former store manager in Virginia, "is that if you treat the customer like they're royalty, you can bleed them through the nose." * * *

Inevitably, some customers take on more than they can handle. So it is that behind every Rent–A–Center salesman lurks his doppelganger: Repo man.

Repossessions are never pretty, and the pre-Thorn era was no exception. But because of the ambitious targets, people who have worked under both regimes say, employees now push harder than ever. Customers typically make their payments every Saturday and, throughout the morning, store employees work the phones exacting promises from the tardy. In these conversations, former customers say, they have been harassed, intimidated and even threatened with violence. Robert Keeling, a former manager in Gadsden, Ala., who was fired in March in part for carrying a gun, says that a "favorite ploy is falsely informing customers or their relatives that a warrant for arrest has been issued for the theft of rental property. * * *

On Halloween night in 1991, three Rent–A–Center employees in Utica, N.Y., dressed up, respectively, as the Cookie Monster, a gorilla and an alien life form and knocked on a customer's door. Once inside, they successfully repossessed a home-entertainment system on which payments hadn't been made in almost three months. Gary Gerhardt, the store manager who blessed this plan, calls the ruse "a last-ditch effort," adding, "it was the only way we could think to get someone in the door."

At the crack of dawn one Sunday, Mr. Myers, the store manager in Victorville, Calif., until March 1992, pulled off a particularly tough repossession by enlisting three burly Hell's Angles. He adds that in other instances he vented his spleen on delinquent customers who wouldn't come to the door by slathering superglue all over their deadbolts and doorknobs. (Messrs. Gerhardt and Myers both were fired, but over unrelated matters.)

The grueling routine grates on some Rent–A–Center employees. Mr. Baker, the former Maryland store manager, quite in disgust in 1991 after one of his employees repossessed a refrigerator from a welfare mother with an infant, plunking her meat and milk on the kitchen table. * * *

Yet another tactic in Rent–A–Center's repo repertoire is the "couch payment"—sexual favors exacted by employees in lieu of cash. Of 28 former store managers interviewed, six said the practice had occurred in their areas. [S]ome store employees have boasted that they "have gone out to the customers' homes, had sex with them, and then repoed the merchandise anyway." * * *

In its new ventures, Rent–A–Center will surely be able to count on its current customers, a loyal lot: Most feel they can't get quality goods any other way.

Nancy Thornley, an Ogden, Utah, housewife, for example, was diligently handing over about $261 a month in rental payments to Rent–A–Center in 1991 when she lost a leg to diabetes. Faced with a $1,000 bill for a prosthetic limb, she arranged to defer part of her rental tab, she says. But shortly after she returned home from the hospital, she was shocked when two store employees showed up without notice on a Saturday afternoon, accused her of being three months behind in payments and carted away all the goods, primarily basics such as a refrigerator and a couch.

"It was total humiliation," she says. "All my neighbors were watching."

A year later, though, Ms. Thornley was back, having been inundated by Rent–A–Center letters and "We Want You Back" coupons. She was reluctant to return, she says. But "I needed the item," a microwave oven, and couldn't afford to buy it. Says Ms. Thornley: "I felt like there was nowhere else to go."

Alix M. Freedman, *A Marketing Giant Uses Its Sales Prowess To Profit on Poverty*, Wall Street Journal, Sept. 22, 1993, p. A12. [Reprinted by permission of Wall Street Journal, © 1993 Dow Jones & Company, Inc. All Rights Reserved Worldwide.]

Jones v. Star Credit Corporation

Supreme Court of New York, 1969.
Supra at 90.

NOTES

(1) Was the result based upon price excessiveness alone? Would a reasonably prudent law student (or law professor!) be able to successfully assert unconscionability in a case of this type? Cf. *Comment: The Peppercorn Theory of Consideration and the Doctrine of Fair Exchange in Contract Law*, supra at 88.

(2) *Price Unconscionability.* Buyers have not been notably successful in pressing a UCC 2–302 unconscionability argument without showing, as in *Jones,* an admixture of so-called procedural and substantive unconscionability. For a review of the cases, see Horowitz, *Reviving the Law of Substantive Unconscionability: Applying the Implied Covenant of Good Faith and Fair Dealing to Excessively Priced Consumer Credit Contracts,* 33 U.C.L.A.L.Rev. 940 (1986) (because of this judicial reluctance, the author urges a shift to "good faith" analysis). Litigants have fared better under other statutes; e.g. McRaild v. Shepard Lincoln Mercury, 141 Mich.App. 406, 367 N.W.2d 404 (1985) (Michigan Consumer Protection Act; trade of an automobile valued at $17,000 and $11,000 in cash for a house determined to have a minimum value of $43,000); Town East Ford Sales, Inc. v. Gray, 730 S.W.2d 796 (Tex.App.1987) (gross disparity between automobile and price paid); People by Abrams v. Two Wheel Corp., 71 N.Y.2d 693, 530 N.Y.S.2d 46, 525 N.E.2d 692 (1988) (New York "price gouging" statute which prohibits merchants from charging unconscionably excessive prices for essential consumer goods during disruptions in the market caused by such forces as strikes, power failures, weather conditions and other emergencies; sale of 100 generators at inflated prices ranging from 4% to 67% over the base prices); Ramirez–Eames v. Hover, 108 N.M. 520, 775 P.2d 722 (1989) (Uniform Owner–Resident Relations Act; agreement to pay $850 monthly rental for apartment, where market value was $725).

(3) *Procedural Aspects.* UCC 2–302 provides that if "the court as a matter of law" finds the contract to have been unconscionable "at the time it was made," it may refuse to enforce it. Thus, unconscionability is an issue of law to be decided by the court. Moreover, the focus is upon the situation as it existed at the time of the contract.

Ordinarily, a party will plead unconscionability as an affirmative defense. Although in some cases the pleadings may be sufficient to permit a court to resolve the issue on a motion for summary judgment, in the usual case there will be a hearing at which the parties present evidence for the trial judge's consideration. What kind of evidence? The Uniform Commercial Code does not say, other than that it should pertain to the contract's "commercial setting, purpose and effect," so as "to aid the court in making the determination." This is sufficient to indicate, however, that the scope of inquiry is broad. An Arizona court has commented as follows: "It was the obvious intention of the drafters and our Legislature that the court have the widest latitude in hearing evidence on the issue of commercial setting in cases where unconscionability was claimed, either in whole or in part. * * * In this context, while serious questions can be raised, and have indeed been raised here, concerning the admissibility of some of the evidence under general contract law terms (the parole evidence rule), the trial court was obviously correct in allowing the widest latitude in receiving evidence on the issue of commercial setting and unconscionability." Raybond Electronics, Inc. v. Glen–Mar Door Manufacturing Co., 22 Ariz.App. 409, 528 P.2d 160, 167 (1974). For helpful discussion of this and other procedural aspects of unconscionability litigation, see R. Duesenberg & L. King, Sales and Bulk Transfers § 4.08[2][b].

Subsection (2) of UCC 2–302 guarantees the right of the parties to present evidence of the contract's commercial setting, purpose, and effect. This may be of particular importance to one who seeks to defend against unconscionability, for evidence of commercial context may demonstrate that a contract or clause which superficially seems to be one-sided in character is actually quite reasonable when viewed in the totality of the circumstances. See, e.g., In re Elkins–Dell Manufacturing Co., 253 F.Supp. 864 (E.D.Pa.1966).

The burden of proof is said to be upon the one who claims the unconscionability. See, e.g., *Zapatha v. Dairy Mart, Inc.,* infra at 529. This means, in practice, that one claiming an unconscionability defense must come forward with the evidence showing a prima facie case. The burden would then seem to shift to the other party to persuade the court that the contract or clause was conscionable. See note 4, infra.

Finally, if there is a judicial finding of unconscionability, what are the remedial consequences? The Code states that the court "may refuse to enforce the contract, or it may enforce the remainder of the contract without the unconscionable clause, or it may so limit the application of any unconscionable clause as to avoid any unconscionable result." Essentially, the aggrieved party is limited to defensive weapons. As illustrated in *Jones,* however, the court may do more than simply refuse to enforce the contract or clause. There the court, in effect, reformed the contract by holding that the amount due was to be equal to the amount already paid. See also Vockner v. Erickson, 712 P.2d 379 (Alaska 1986) (land purchase agreement deemed unconscionable under section 208 of the revised Restatement; amount of installment payment changed).

There is, evidently, no right to recover damages under UCC 2–302. See, e.g., Cowin Equipment Co. v. General Motors Corporation, 734 F.2d 1581 (11th Cir.1984); Best v. United States National Bank, 78 Or.App. 1, 714 P.2d 1049 (1986) (court acknowledged that relief might possibly be predicated upon breach of an implied covenant of good faith and fair dealing). Although UCC 2–302 does not specifically authorize money damages, it does authorize a court to "enforce the contract without the unconscionable clause." Thus, after striking an unconscionable clause, a court may then award damages for breach of the contract without that clause. Langemeier v. National Oats, Inc., 775 F.2d 975 (8th Cir.1985). Finally, damages may be recovered under a state's deceptive trade practice statute, twelve of which specifically prohibit unconscionable practices. See J. Sheldon, Unfair and Deceptive Acts and Practices 112 (3d ed. 1991, 1996 Supp.) (Alabama; District of Columbia; Kansas; Kentucky; Michigan; Nebraska; New Jersey; New Mexico; New York; Ohio; Texas; Utah).

(4) *Burden of Proof in Unconscionability Litigation.* "First, the party raising the defense should have the burden of persuading the court that the contract or clause 'appears' to be unconscionable. Put another way, the consumer must establish a *prima facie* case. In most cases this can be done by showing a substantial disparity between the value of the bargain as measured by the price agreed for the described goods or services and the value of the bargain when the seller invokes a particular contract term against the consumer. Thus, if the consumer pays $350 for a described new freezer which contains a latent defect not discovered until 15 days after delivery and the seller invokes a contract term requiring notice of defects within 10 days of delivery, material disparity would seem to exist. If a particular term is disclosed, the consumer may establish a *prima facie* case by showing a substantial disparity between the value of the bargain agreed to and a competitive opportunity in the relevant market area. Thus, if Mrs. Williams knew about the 'add-on' clause and still assented, the contract would be *prima facie* unconscionable if the same stereo were available to her on credit without the clause in a relevant market area. In most cases, however, material disparity will turn upon the impact of the assented clause upon the consumer's bargain as measured by the agreed price for described goods or services. In this determination, whether the consumer should have understood that impact or could have comparatively shopped is irrelevant. These tests, as previously discussed, are unreliable and cannot dispel lingering doubts whether the consumer did in fact understand or could have realistically shopped comparatively.

"Second, if a *prima facie* case is established to the satisfaction of the court, the burden shifts to the professional to persuade the court that the contract or term was conscionable at the time of contracting. To use Professor Leff's word, the professional will be given an opportunity to 'resuscitate' a term or contract which is *prima facie* unconscionable from evidence of its 'commercial setting, purpose and effect.' The burden will be on him to show that, regardless of *real* or *apparent assent,* the term is commercially reasonable. Placing the risk of non-persuasion on the professional is supported by analogy to UCC 2–719(3), which provides that 'limitation of consequential damages for injury to the person in the case of consumer goods is *prima facie* unconscionable,' the implicit allocation in UCC 2–302(2), a general policy favoring consumer protection, and the plain fact that he is in the best position to know and to prove the commercial setting, purpose and effect. Under this approach, failure of the professional to justify its behavior as commercially reasonable would result in a judgment for the consumer." Speidel, *Unconscionability, Assent and Consumer Protection,* 31 U.Pitt.L.Rev. 359, 368–69 (1970). See also Lawrence, *Toward a More Efficient and Just Economy: An Argument for Limited Enforcement of Consumer Promises,* 48 Ohio St.L.J. 815 (1987).

PROBLEM: THE CASE OF THE LIFE–CARE CONTRACT

Kathleen MacKay, age 79, visited a number of retirement facilities in the Santa Fe and Albuquerque area. She liked La Vida Llena the best. She took several weeks to study the Residence Agreement which this facility used. She discussed the proposed agreement with her friends, but not with an attorney. On March 2, 1983 she signed the agreement and made a deposit toward the entry fee; on June 16, upon payment of the remainder of the $36,950 entry fee, she moved in. She became sick on December 29th of that year, and two days later she died.

Under the Residence Agreement, the entry fee entitled Mrs. MacKay to occupy a one-bedroom unit for the rest of her life, and guaranteed her admission to the La Vida Llena Nursing Care Center whenever required. She was also obliged to pay a monthly service fee of $537.00 to cover meals, laundry, etc. She had the right to terminate the agreement upon 30–days notice if she were unable to live alone and if monthly payments were current. La Vida Llena would then refund the entrance fee less "10% plus 1% for each month of residency." There was no refund of entry fee upon a resident's death.

Mrs. MacKay's personal representative sought a refund of the entrance fee on the ground that the agreement was an unconscionable adhesion contract. What result? See Guthmann v. LaVida Llena, 103 N.M. 506, 709 P.2d 675 (1985).

(2) COMMERCIAL TRANSACTIONS

Should the defense of unconscionability be limited to consumer cases? Or might it be used as well in commercial transactions? To date the "merchant" has not been notably successful in raising the defense. See, e.g., W.L. May Co., Inc. v. Philco–Ford Corp., 273 Or. 701, 543 P.2d 283 (1975) ("It may also be noted that both parties to the contract were sophisticated business people. This is clearly not the case of an innocent consumer who has unsuspectingly signed an adhesion contract." 543 P.2d at 287); Gillman v. Chase Manhattan Bank, 73 N.Y.2d 1, 537 N.Y.S.2d 787, 534 N.E.2d 824 (1988) (security agreement provision for issuance of letter of credit not unconscionable; a type of routine commercial transaction with which parties were necessarily familiar); County Asphalt, Inc. v. Lewis Welding & Engineering Corp., 323 F.Supp. 1300 (S.D.N.Y.1970) ("[I]t is the exceptional commercial setting where a claim of unconscionability will be allowed * * *." 323 F.Supp. at 1308); Stanley A. Klopp, Inc. v. John Deere Co., 510 F.Supp. 807 (E.D.Pa.1981) ("Although commercial contracts can be unenforceable in whole or in part for unconscionability, it would be improper to borrow, without differentiation, concepts developed to protect consumers and employ them in favor of one commercial party over another." 510 F.Supp. at 810). Nevertheless, neither the Code nor case law specifically limits UCC 2–302 and the principles underlying it to consumer transactions, and, as illustrated in the materials to follow, commercial entities can sometimes derive protection from unconscionability theory. Arguments based upon unconscionability appear regularly in commercial litigation, and courts are being called upon to examine the issue in a wide variety of contexts. See, generally Mallor, *Unconscionability in Contracts Between Merchants,* 40 Sw.L.J. 1065 (1986).

Weaver v. American Oil Co.

Supreme Court of Indiana, 1971.
257 Ind. 458, 276 N.E.2d 144.

■ ARTERBURN, CHIEF JUSTICE.

In this case the appellee oil company presented to the appellant-defendant leasee, a filling station operator, a printed form contract as a lease to be signed, by the defendant, which contained, in addition to the normal leasing provisions, a "hold harmless" clause which provided in substance that the leasee operator would hold harmless and also indemnify the oil company for any negligence of the oil company occurring on the leased premises. The litigation arises as a result of the oil company's own employee spraying gasoline over Weaver and his assistant and causing them to be burned and injured on the leased premises. This action was initiated by American Oil and Hoffer (Appellees) for a declaratory judgment to determine the liability of appellant Weaver, under the clause in the lease. The trial court entered judgment holding Weaver liable under the lease.

Clause three [3] of the lease reads as follows:

"Lessor, its agents and employees shall not be liable for any loss, damage, injuries, or other casualty of whatsoever kind or by whomsoever caused to the person or property of anyone (including Lessee) on or off the premises, arising out of or resulting from Lessee's use, possession or operation thereof, or from defects in the premises whether apparent or hidden, or from the installation existence, use, maintenance, condition, repair, alteration, removal or replacement of any equipment thereon, whether due in whole or in part to negligent acts or omissions of Lessor, its agents or employees; and Lessee for himself, his heirs, executors, administrators, successors and assigns, hereby agrees to indemnify and hold Lessor, its agents and employees, harmless from and against all claims, demands, liabilities, suits or actions (including all reasonable expenses and attorneys' fees incurred by or imposed on the Lessor in connection therewith) for such loss, damage, injury or other casualty. Lessee also agrees to pay all reasonable expenses and attorneys' fees incurred by Lessor in the event that Lessee shall default under the provisions of this paragraph."

It will be noted that this lease clause not only exculpated the leasor oil company from its liability for its negligence, but also compelled Weaver to indemnify them for any damages or loss incurred as a result of its negligence. The appellate court held the exculpatory clause invalid, 261 N.E.2d 99, but the indemnifying clause valid, 262 N.E.2d 663. In our opinion, both these provisions must be read together since one may be used to effectuate the result obtained through the other. We find no ground for any distinction and we therefore grant the petition to transfer the appeal to this court.

This is a contract, which was submitted (already in printed form) to a party with lesser bargaining power. As in this case, it may contain unconscionable or unknown provisions which are in fine print. Such is the case now before this court.

The facts reveal that Weaver had left high school after one and a half years and spent his time, prior to leasing the service station, working at various skilled and unskilled labor oriented jobs. He was not one who should be expected to know the law or understand the meaning of technical terms. The ceremonious activity of signing the lease consisted of nothing more than the agent of American Oil placing the lease in front of Mr. Weaver and saying "sign," which Mr. Weaver did. There is nothing in the record to indicate that Weaver read the lease; that the agent asked Weaver to read it; or that the agent, in any manner, attempted to call Weaver's attention to the "hold harmless" clause in the lease. Each year following, the procedure was the same. A salesman, from American Oil, would bring the lease to Weaver, at the station, and Weaver would sign it. The evidence showed that Weaver had never read the lease prior to signing and that the clauses in the lease were never explained to him in a manner from which he could grasp their legal significance. The leases were prepared by the attorneys of American Oil Company, for the American Oil Company, and the agents of the American Oil Company never attempted to explain the conditions of the lease nor did they advise Weaver that he should consult legal counsel, before signing the lease. The superior bargaining power of American Oil is patently obvious and the significance of Weaver's signature upon the legal document amounted to nothing more than a mere formality to Weaver for the substantial protection of American Oil.

Had this case involved the sale of goods it would have been termed an "unconscionable contract" under sec. 2–302 of the Uniform Commercial Code as found in Burns' Ind.Stat. sec. 19–2–302, IC 1971, 26–1–2–302.
* * *

According to the Comment to Official Text, the basic test of unconscionability is whether, in light of the general commercial background and the commercial needs of the particular trade or case, the clauses involved are so one-sided as to be unconscionable under the circumstances existing at the time of the making of the contract. Subsection two makes it clear that it is proper for the court to hear evidence upon these questions.

"An 'unconscionable contract' has been defined to be such as no sensible man not under delusion, duress or in distress would make, and such as no honest and fair man would accept. There exists here an 'inequality so strong, gross and manifest that it is impossible to state it to a man of common sense without producing an exclamation at the inequality of it.' 'Where the inadequacy of the price is so great that the mind revolts at it the court will lay hold on the slightest circumstances of oppression or advantage to rescind the contract.' "

"It is not the policy of the law to restrict business dealings or to relieve a party of his own mistakes of judgment, but where one party has taken advantage of another's necessities and distress to obtain an unfair advantage over him, and the latter, owing to his condition, has encumbered himself with a heavy liability or an onerous obligation for the sake of a small or inadequate present gain, there will be relief granted." Stiefler v. McCullough (1931), 97 Ind.App. 123, 174 N.E. 823.

The facts of this case reveal that in exchange for a contract which, if the clause in question is enforceable, may cost Mr. Weaver potentially thousands of dollars in damages for negligence of which he was not the cause, Weaver must operate the service station seven days a week for long hours, at a total yearly income of $5,000–$6,000. The evidence also reveals that *the clause was in fine print* and *contained no title heading* which would have identified it as an indemnity clause. It seems a deplorable abuse of justice to hold a man of poor education, to a contract prepared by the attorneys of American Oil, for the benefit of American Oil which was presented to Weaver on a "take it or leave it basis."

Justice Frankfurter of the United States Supreme Court spoke on the question of inequality of bargaining power in his dissenting opinion in United States v. Bethlehem Steel Corp. (1942), 315 U.S. 289, 326, 62 S.Ct. 581, 599, 86 L.Ed. 855, 876.

"(I)t is said that familiar principles would be outraged if Bethlehem were denied recovery on these contracts. But is there any principle which is more familiar or more firmly embedded in the history of Anglo–American law than the basic doctrine that the courts will not permit themselves to be used as instruments of inequity and injustice? Does any principle in our law have more universal application than the doctrine that courts will not enforce transactions in which the relative positions of the parties are such that one has unconscionably taken advantage of the necessities of the other?"

"These principles are not foreign to the law of contracts. Fraud and physical duress are not the only grounds upon which courts refuse to enforce contracts. The law is not so primitive that it sanctions every injustice except brute force and downright fraud. More specifically, the courts generally refuse to lend themselves to the enforcement of a 'bargain' in which one party has unjustly taken advantage of the economic necessities of the other. * * *"

The traditional contract is the result of free bargaining of parties who are brought together by the play of the market, and who meet each other on a footing of approximate economic equality. In such a society there is no danger that freedom of contract will be a threat to the social order as a whole. But in present-day commercial life the standardized mass contract has appeared. It is used primarily by enterprises with strong bargaining power and position. The weaker party, in need of the good or services, is frequently not in a position to shop around for better terms, either because the author of the standard contract has a monopoly (natural or artificial) or because all competitors use the same clauses.

Judge Frankfurter's dissent was written nearly twenty years ago. It represents a direction and philosophy which the law, at that time was taking and is now compelled to accept in our modern society over the old principle known as the *parole evidence rule*. The parole evidence rule states that an agreement or contract, signed by the parties, is *conclusively presumed* to represent an integration or meeting of the minds of the parties. This is an archaic rule from the old common law. The objectivity of the rule has as its only merit its simplicity of application which is far outweighed by its failure in many cases to represent the actual agreement, particularly where a printed form prepared by one party contains hidden clauses unknown to the other party is submitted and signed. The law should seek the truth or the subjective understanding of the parties in this more enlightened age. The burden should be on the party submitting such "a package" in printed form to show that the other party had knowledge of any unusual or unconscionable terms contained therein. The principle should be the same as that applicable to implied warranties, namely that a package of goods sold to a purchaser is fit for the purposes intended and contains no harmful materials other than that represented. Caveat lessee is no more the current law than caveat emptor. Only in this way can justice be served and the true meaning of freedom of contract preserved. The analogy is rational. We have previously pointed out a similar situation in the Uniform Commercial Code, which prohibits unconscionable contract clauses in sales agreements.

When a party can show that the contract, which is sought to be enforced, was in fact an unconscionable one, due to a prodigious amount of bargaining power on behalf of the stronger party, which is used to the stronger party's advantage and is unknown to the lesser party, causing a great hardship and risk on the lesser party, the contract provision, or the contract as a whole, if the provision is not separable, should not be enforceable on the grounds that the provision is contrary to public policy. The party seeking to enforce such a contract has the burden of showing that the provisions were explained to the other party and *came to his knowledge* and there was in fact *a real and voluntary meeting of the minds and not merely an objective meeting.*

Unjust contract provisions have been found unenforceable, in the past, on the grounds of being contrary to public policy, where a party has a greater superior bargaining position. In Pennsylvania Railroad Co. v. Kent (1964), 136 Ind.App. 551, 198 N.E.2d 615, Judge Hunter, speaking for the court said that although the proposition that "parties may enter into such contractual arrangement as they may desire may be conceded in the general sense; when, however, such special agreement may result in affecting the public interest and thereby contravene public policy, the abrogation of the rules governing common carriers must be zealously guarded against.''

We do not mean to say or infer that parties may not make contracts exculpating one of his negligence and providing for indemnification, but it must be done *knowingly* and *willingly* as in insurance contracts made for that very purpose.

It is the duty of the courts to administer justice and that role is not performed, in this case, by enforcing a written instrument, not really an agreement of the parties as shown by the evidence here, although signed by the parties. The parole evidence rule must yield to the equities of the case. The appeal is transferred to this court and the judgment of the trial court is reversed with direction to enter judgment for the appellant.

[Dissenting opinion of Judge Prentice is omitted.]

NOTES

(1) Would the exculpatory/indemnification clause have escaped condemnation if Weaver had read the lease? To what extent was his ''poor education'' a factor in the case? What if commercial loss alone and not personal injury had been involved? Cf. UCC 2–719(3).

(2) As counsel for the American Oil Company, what evidence of ''commercial context'' would you have liked the court to consider? What would you advise the client as to future lease negotiations? For a thorough treatment of *Weaver* and related cases, see Jordan, *Unconscionability at the Gas Station*, 62 Minn.L.Rev. 813 (1978).

Zapatha v. Dairy Mart, Inc.

Supreme Judicial Court of Massachusetts, 1980.
381 Mass. 284, 408 N.E.2d 1370.

■ WILKINS, JUSTICE.

We are concerned here with the question whether Dairy Mart, Inc. (Dairy Mart), lawfully undertook to terminate a franchise agreement under which the Zapathas operated a Dairy Mart store on Wilbraham Road in Springfield. The Zapathas brought this action seeking to enjoin the termination of the agreement, alleging that the contract provision purporting to authorize the termination of the franchise agreement without cause was unconscionable and that Dairy Mart's conduct was an unfair and deceptive act or practice in violation of G.L. c. 93A. The judge ruled that Dairy Mart did not act in good faith, that the termination provision was unconscionable, and that Dairy Mart's termination of the agreement without cause was an unfair and deceptive act. We granted Dairy Mart's application for direct appellate review of a judgment that stated that Dairy Mart could terminate the agreement only for good cause and that the attempted termination was null and void. We reverse the judgments.

Mr. Zapatha is a high school graduate who had attended college for one year and had also taken college evening courses in business administration and business law. From 1952 to May, 1973, he was employed by a company engaged in the business of electroplating. He rose through the ranks to foreman and then to the position of operations manager, at one time being in charge of all metal finishing in the plant with 150 people working under him. In May, 1973, he was discharged and began looking for other opportunities, in particular a business of his own. Several months later he met with a representative of Dairy Mart. Dairy Mart operates a chain of franchised "convenience" stores. The Dairy Mart representative told Mr. Zapatha that working for Dairy Mart was being in business for one's self and that such a business was very stable and secure. Mr. Zapatha signed an application to be considered for a franchise. In addition, he was presented with a brochure entitled "Here's a Chance," which made certain representations concerning the status of a franchise holder.[1]

Dairy Mart approved Mr. Zapatha's application and offered him a store in Agawam. On November 8, 1973, a representative of Dairy Mart showed him a form of franchise agreement, entitled Limited Franchise and License Agreement, asked him to read it, and explained that his wife would have to sign the agreement as well.

Under the terms of the agreement, Dairy Mart would license the Zapathas to operate a Dairy Mart store, using the Dairy Mart trademark and associated insignia, and utilizing Dairy Mart's "confidential" merchandising methods. Dairy Mart would furnish the store and the equipment and would pay rent and gas and electric bills as well as certain other costs of doing business. In return Dairy Mart would receive a franchise fee, computed as a percentage of the store's gross sales. The Zapathas would have to pay for the starting inventory, and maintain a minimum stock of saleable merchandise thereafter. They were also responsible for wages of employees, related taxes, and any sales taxes. The termination provision, which is set forth in full in the margin,[2] allowed either party, after twelve months, to

---

1. It included the following statements: "... you'll have the opportunity to own and run your own business ..."; "We want to be sure we're hooking up with the right person. A person who sees the opportunity in owning his own business ... who requires the security that a multi-million dollar parent company can offer him ... who has the good judgment and business sense to take advantage of the unique independence that Dairy Mart offers its franchisees ... We're looking for a partner ... who can take the tools we offer and build a life of security and comfort ..."

2. "(9) The term of this Limited Franchise and License Agreement shall be for a period of Twelve (12) months from date hereof, and shall continue uninterrupted thereafter. If DEALER desires to terminate after 12

months from date hereof, he shall do so by giving COMPANY a ninety (90) day written notice by Registered Mail of his intention to terminate. If COMPANY desires to terminate, it likewise shall give a ninety (90) day notice, except for the following reasons which shall not require any written notice and shall terminate the Franchise immediately:

"(a) Failure to pay bills to suppliers for inventory or other products when due.

"(b) Failure to pay Franchise Fees to COMPANY.

"(c) Failure to pay city, state or federal taxes as said taxes shall become due and payable.

"(d) Breach of any condition of this Agreement."

terminate the agreement without cause on ninety days' written notice. In the event of termination initiated by it without cause, Dairy Mart agreed to repurchase the saleable merchandise inventory at retail prices, less 20%.

The Dairy Mart representative read and explained the termination provision to Mr. Zapatha. Mr. Zapatha later testified that, while he understood every word in the provision, he had interpreted it to mean that Dairy Mart could terminate the agreement only for cause. The Dairy Mart representative advised Mr. Zapatha to take the agreement to an attorney and said "I would prefer that you did." However, he also told Mr. Zapatha that the terms of the contract were not negotiable. The Zapathas signed the agreement without consulting an attorney. When the Zapathas took charge of the Agawam store, a representative of Dairy Mart worked with them to train them in Dairy Mart's methods of operation.

In 1974, another store became available on Wilbraham Road in Springfield, and the Zapathas elected to surrender the Agawam store. They executed a new franchise agreement, on an identical printed form, relating to the new location.

In November, 1977, Dairy Mart presented a new and more detailed form of "Independent Operator's Agreement" to the Zapathas for execution. Some of the terms were less favorable to the store operator than those of the earlier form of agreement.[3] Mr. Zapatha told representatives of Dairy Mart that he was content with the existing contract and had decided not to sign the new agreement. On January 20, 1978, Dairy Mart gave written notice to the Zapathas that their contract was being terminated effective in ninety days. The termination notice stated that Dairy Mart "remains available to enter into discussions with you with respect to entering into a new Independent Operator's Agreement; however, there is no assurance that Dairy Mart will enter into a new Agreement with you, or even if entered into, what terms such Agreement will contain." The notice also indicated that Dairy Mart was prepared to purchase the Zapathas' saleable inventory.

The judge found that Dairy Mart terminated the agreement solely because the Zapathas refused to sign the new agreement. He further found that, but for this one act, Dairy Mart did not behave in an unconscionable manner, in bad faith, or in disregard of its representations. * * *

[Because the franchise agreement involves mostly transactions in services, the court is disinclined to find that the transaction is a "sale of goods" exclusively covered by the U.C.C. However, the court applies the U.C.C.'s

---

3. In his testimony, Mr. Zapatha said that he objected to a new provision under which Dairy Mart reserved the option to relocate an operator to a new location and to a requirement that the store be open from 7 A.M. to 11 P.M. every day. Previously the Zapathas' store had been open from 8 A.M. to 10 P.M.

There were other provisions, such as an obligation to pay future increases in the cost of heat and electricity, that were more burdensome to a franchisee. A few changes may have been to the advantage of the franchisee.

statement of policy concerning good faith and unconscionability together with their common law counterparts.]

2. We consider first the plaintiffs' argument that the termination clause of the franchise agreement, authorizing Dairy Mart to terminate the agreement without cause, on ninety days' notice, was unconscionable by the standards expressed in G.L. c. 106, § 2–302. The same standards are set forth in Restatement (Second) of Contracts § 234 (Tent. Drafts Nos. 1–7, 1973). The issue is one of law for the court, and the test is to be made as of the time the contract was made. * * * In measuring the unconscionability of the termination provision, the fact that the law imposes an obligation of good faith on Dairy Mart in its performance under the agreement should be weighed. * * *

The official comment to § 2–302 states that "[t]he basic test is whether, in the light of the general commercial background and the commercial needs of the particular trade or case, the clauses involved are so one-sided as to be unconscionable under the circumstances existing at the time of the making of the contract. . . . The principle is one of prevention of oppression and unfair surprise . . . and not of disturbance of allocation of risks because of superior bargaining power." Official Comment 1 to U.C.C. § 2–302.[4] Unconscionability is not defined in the Code, nor do the views expressed in the official comment provide a precise definition. The annotation prepared by the Massachusetts Advisory Committee on the Code states that "[t]he section appears to be intended to carry equity practice into the sales field." See 1 R. Anderson, Uniform Commercial Code § 2–302:7 (1970) to the same effect. This court has not had occasion to consider in any detail the meaning of the word "unconscionable" in § 2–302. Because there is no clear, all-purpose definition of "unconscionable," nor could there be, unconscionability must be determined on a case by case basis (* * *), giving particular attention to whether, at the time of the execution of the agreement, the contract provision could result in unfair surprise and was oppressive to the allegedly disadvantaged party.

We start with a recognition that the Uniform Commercial Code itself implies that a contract provision allowing termination without cause is not per se unconscionable. See Corenswet, Inc. v. Amana Refrigeration, Inc., 594 F.2d 129, 138 (5th Cir.1979) ("We seriously doubt, however, that public policy frowns on any and all contract clauses permitting termination without cause."); Division of Triple T Serv., Inc. v. Mobil Oil Corp., 60 Misc.2d 720, 730, 304 N.Y.S.2d 191 (1969), aff'd 34 App.Div.2d 618, 311 N.Y.S.2d 961 (N.Y.1970). Section 2–309(3) provides that "[t]ermination of a contract by one party except on the happening of an agreed event requires that reasonable notification be received by the other party and an agree-

---

4. The comment has been criticized as useless and at best ambiguous (J. White & R. Summers, The Uniform Commercial Code, 116 [1972]), and § 2–302 has been characterized as devoid of any specific content. Leff, Unconscionability and the Code—(The Em- peror's New Clause, 115 U.Pa.L.Rev. 485, 487–489 [1967]). On the other hand, it has been said that the strength of the unconscionability concept is its abstraction, permitting judicial creativity. See Ellinghaus, In Defense of Unconscionability, 78 Yale L.J. 757 (1969).

ment dispensing with notification is invalid if its operation would be unconscionable." G.L. c. 106, § 2–309, as appearing in St.1957, c. 765, § 1. This language implies that termination of a sales contract without agreed "cause" is authorized by the Code, provided reasonable notice is given. * * * There is no suggestion that the ninety days' notice provided in the Dairy Mart franchise agreement was unreasonable.

We find no potential for unfair surprise to the Zapathas in the provision allowing termination without cause. We view the question of unfair surprise as focused on the circumstances under which the agreement was entered into.[5] The termination provision was neither obscurely worded, nor buried in fine print in the contract. Contrast Williams v. Walker–Thomas Furniture Co., 350 F.2d 445, 449 (D.C.Cir.1965). The provision was specifically pointed out to Mr. Zapatha before it was signed; Mr. Zapatha testified that he thought the provision was "straightforward," and he declined the opportunity to take the agreement to a lawyer for advice. The Zapathas had ample opportunity to consider the agreement before they signed it. Significantly, the subject of loss of employment was paramount in Mr. Zapatha's mind. He testified that he had held responsible jobs in one company from 1952 to 1973, that he had lost his employment, and that he "was looking for something that had a certain amount of security; something that was stable and something I could call my own." We conclude that a person of Mr. Zapatha's business experience and education should not have been surprised by the termination provision and, if in fact he was, there was no element of unfairness in the inclusion of that provision in the agreement. * * *

We further conclude that there was no oppression in the inclusion of a termination clause in the franchise agreement. We view the question of oppression as directed to the substantive fairness to the parties of permitting the termination provisions to operate as written. The Zapathas took over a going business on premises provided by Dairy Mart, using equipment furnished by Dairy Mart. As an investment, the Zapathas had only to purchase the inventory of goods to be sold but, as Dairy Mart concedes, on termination by it without cause Dairy Mart was obliged to repurchase all the Zapathas' saleable merchandise inventory, including items not purchased from Dairy Mart, at 80% of its retail value. There was no potential for forfeiture or loss of investment. * * *

3. We see no basis on the record for concluding that Dairy Mart did not act in good faith, as that term is defined in the sales article ("honesty in fact and the observance of reasonable commercial standards of fair

5. As we shall note subsequently, the concept of oppression deals with the substantive unfairness of the contract term. This two-part test for unconscionability involves determining whether there was "an absence of meaningful choice on the part of one of the parties, together with contract terms which are unreasonably favorable to the other party." Williams v. Walker–Thomas Furniture Co., 350 F.2d 445, 449 (D.C.Cir.1965). See Corenswet, Inc. v. Amana Refrigeration, Inc., 594 F.2d 129, 139 (5th Cir.1979). The inquiry involves a search for components of "procedural" and "substantive" unconscionability. See generally Leff, Unconscionability and the Code—The Emperor's New Clause, 115 Pa. L.Rev. 485 (1967). * * *

dealing in the trade"). G.L. c. 106, § 2–103(1)(b). There was no evidence that Dairy Mart failed to observe reasonable commercial standards of fair dealing in the trade in terminating the agreement. If there were such standards, there was no evidence of what they were.

The question then is whether there was evidence warranting a finding that Dairy Mart was not honest "in fact." The judge concluded that the absence of any commercial purpose for the termination other than the Zapathas' refusal to sign a new franchise agreement violated Dairy Mart's obligation of good faith. Dairy Mart's right to terminate was clear, and it exercised that right for a reason it openly disclosed. The sole test of "honesty in fact" is whether the person was honest. * * * We think that, whether or not termination according to the terms of the franchise agreement may have been arbitrary, it was not dishonest.[6] * * *

4. Although what we have said disposes of arguments based on application by analogy of provisions of the sales article of the Uniform Commercial Code, there remains the question whether the judge's conclusions may be supported by some general principle of law. The provisions of the Uniform Commercial Code with which we have dealt by analogy in this opinion may not have sufficient breadth to provide protection from conduct that has produced an unfair and burdensome result, contrary to the spirit of the bargain, against which the law reasonably should provide protection. See Restatement (Second) of Contracts § 231 (Tent. Drafts Nos. 1–7 1973); Corbin, Contracts § 654A (C.K. Kaufman 1980 Supp.).[7]

The law of the Commonwealth recognizes that under some circumstances a party to a contract is not free to terminate it according to its terms. In Fortune v. National Cash Register Co., 373 Mass. 96, 104–105,

---

6. Under G.L. c. 106, § 1–203, "[e]very contract ... imposes an obligation of good faith *in its performance or enforcement*" (emphasis supplied). We shall assume that an act of termination falls within the "performance" of the agreement. See Baker v. Ratzlaff, 1 Kan.App.2d 285, 288, 564 P.2d 153 (1977). But see Summers, "Good Faith" in General Contract Law and the Sales Provisions of the Uniform Commercial Code, 54 Va.L.Rev. 195, 252 (1968). * * *

It has been suggested that, despite the limited definition of good faith in the Code, in some contexts the general obligation of good faith in § 1–203 can be used to import an objective standard of "decency, fairness or reasonableness in performance or enforcement" into a contract to which it applies. Farnsworth, Good Faith Performance and Commercial Reasonableness Under the Uniform Commercial Code, 30 U.Chi.L.Rev. 666, 668 (1963). Good faith in this sense can be regarded as an "excluder," barring varied forms of unreasonable conduct in different circumstances. See Summers, "Good Faith" in General Contract Law and the Sales Provisions of the Uniform Commercial Code, 54 Va.L.Rev. 195, 196 (1968). Rather than stretch the Code definition of good faith beyond the plain meaning of the words used to define good faith, we prefer, as we are about to do, to analyze the question of fairness and reasonableness independently of the Code.

7. The unconscionability provision of G.L. c. 106, § 2–302, concerns circumstances determined at the time of the making of the agreement and relates only to the unconscionability of a term or terms of the contract. The "good faith" obligation of G.L. c. 106, § 1–203, deals with "honesty in fact," a question of the state of mind of the merchant or of his adherence to whatever reasonable commercial standards there may be in his trade. A merchant's conduct might not be dishonest and might adhere to reasonable standards, if any, in his trade and thus might be in good faith under § 1–203, and yet be unfair and unreasonably burdensome.

364 N.E.2d 1251 (1977), we held that where an employer terminated an at will employment contract in order to deprive its employee of a portion of a commission due to him, the employer acted in bad faith. There, the employer correctly argued that termination of the employee was expressly permitted by the contract, and that all amounts payable under the terms of the contract at the time of termination had been paid. We concluded, however, that the law imposed an obligation of good faith on the employer and that the employer violated that obligation in terminating the relationship in order to avoid the payment of amounts earned, but not yet payable. The Legislature has limited the right of certain franchisors to terminate franchise agreements without cause.[8] On the other hand, the Legislature has not adopted limitations on the right to terminate all franchise agreements in general, and its failure to do so is understandable because of the varied nature of franchise arrangements, where such varying factors exist as the relative bargaining power of the parties, the extent of investment by franchisees, and the degree to which the franchisee's goodwill, as opposed to that of the franchisor, is involved in the business operation. * * *

We are most concerned, as was the judge below, with the introductory circular that Dairy Mart furnished Mr. Zapatha. The judge ruled that the introductory circular contained misleading information concerning the Zapathas' status as franchisees. However, we cannot find in that document any deception or unfairness that has a bearing on the right of Dairy Mart to terminate the agreement as it did. A representative read the termination clause to Mr. Zapatha before the Zapathas signed the agreement. Mr. Zapatha declined an invitation to take the agreement to a lawyer. He understood individually every word of the termination clause. Moreover, when Dairy Mart terminated the agreement, it offered to negotiate further, and the Zapathas did not take the opportunity to do so. * * *

Dairy Mart lawfully terminated the agreement because there was no showing that in terminating it Dairy Mart engaged in any unfair, deceptive, or bad faith conduct.

Judgments reversed.

NOTES

(1) Section 208 of Restatement (Second) provides:

If a contract or term thereof is unconscionable at the time the contract is made a court may refuse to enforce the contract, or may enforce the remainder of the contract without the unconscionable term, or may so limit

---

8. See G.L. c. 93B, § 4(3)(e), (4) concerning the cancellation or nonrenewal of a motor vehicle dealer's franchise and requiring good cause for manufacturer's or distributor's action; G.L. c. 93E, §§ 5, 5A, requiring cause for a supplier's termination or nonrenewal of a gasoline station dealer's agreement and imposing an obligation on the supplier to repurchase merchantable products sold to the dealer. * * *

The special status of service station operators has prompted some courts to adopt common law rules requiring good cause for termination in spite of contract language that seemed to allow termination without cause. [citations omitted]

the application of any unconscionable terms as to avoid any unconscionable result.

For a general discussion, see Hillman, *Debunking Some Myths About Unconscionability: A New Framework for U.C.C. Section 2–302,* 67 Cornell L.Rev. 1 (1981).

(2) Section 205 of Restatement (Second) provides:

Every contract imposes upon each party a duty of good faith and fair dealing in its performance and its enforcement.

For a general discussion, see Summers, *The General Duty of Good Faith—Its Recognition and Conceptualization,* 67 Cornell L.Rev. 810 (1982). The problem of what legal controls should govern the exercise of discretion reserved to terminate a contract is discussed in Goetz and Scott, *Principles of Relational Contracts,* 67 Va.L.Rev. 1089, 1130–49 (1981).

(3) How do the business relationships in *Weaver* and *Zapatha* differ?

(4) Was there "cause" for termination in *Zapatha*? Did the franchisor act in bad faith? Would you support legislation barring franchise termination except for cause?

(5) In 1987, the National Conference of Commissioners on Uniform State Laws approved and recommended the Uniform Franchise and Business Opportunities Act. 7A U.L.A. 77 (Supp.1990). Section 201 imposes on the parties a duty of good faith in performance and enforcement, and good faith is defined as "honesty in fact and the observance of reasonable commercial standards of fair dealing in the trade." As explained by the drafters, the basic purpose of the section is as follows: "The section is intended to prevent arbitrary, malicious, or abusive conduct, or conduct that deprives the other contracting party of the benefit of the bargain, and to preserve the justifiable expectations of the parties to a franchise or business opportunity relationship. It does not apply in the give and take of bargaining preceding the formation of the agreement. It is not intended to eliminate risk." § 201, comment. The section does not establish a "good cause" rule. Id. The duty of good faith prescribed by the act may not be waived or excluded by agreement of the parties. § 103.

(6) *Beyond Commercial Transactions: Separation Agreements.* After fifteen years of marriage and the birth of three children, Charles and Kathleen Williams experienced marital difficulties and decided to separate. Kathleen's lawyer prepared a separation agreement which Charles signed without the advice of counsel, evidently with the hope that his signing might help lead to a resolution of their problems and bring about a reconciliation. Under the agreement, Charles was required to transfer his interest in their home to Kathleen, together with the contents of the house and their automobile. In addition, Charles agreed to pay the mortgage on the house, the car loan, and all other marital obligations. In sum, under the agreement the wife was to receive property valued at approximately $131,000, while the husband was to retain property valued at about $1,100. Indeed, his total weekly financial obligations under the agreement exceeded his weekly net salary.

In a later divorce action, Charles sought to have the separation agreement set aside; Kathleen asked that it be incorporated into the divorce decree. The trial court found the agreement to be unconscionable, and this was upheld on appeal, the court citing Restatement (Second) § 208: "If a contract or term thereof is unconscionable at the time the contract is made a court may refuse to enforce the contract, or may enforce the remainder of the contract without the unconscionable term, or may so limit the application of any unconscionable term as to avoid any unconscionable result." Williams v. Williams, 306 Md. 332, 508 A.2d 985 (1986).

"In separation agreements particularly," a Virginia court has observed, "unconscionability may be of heightened importance." Derby v. Derby, 8 Va.App. 19, 378 S.E.2d 74, 79 (1989). The court elaborated:

> While no fiduciary duty exists between the parties, marriage and divorce create a relationship which is particularly susceptible to over-reaching and oppression. * * * Professor Homer Clark suggests three reasons for this special emphasis. First, the relationship between husband and wife is not the usual relationship that exists between parties to ordinary commercial contracts. Particularly when the negotiation is be-tween the parties rather than between their lawyers, the relationship creates a situation ripe for subtle overreaching and misrepresentation. Behavior that might not constitute fraud or duress in an arm's length context may suffice to invalidate a grossly inequitable agreement where the relationship is utilized to overreach or take advantage of a situation in order to achieve an oppressive result. Second, Clark notes that unlike commercial contracts, the state itself has an interest in the terms and enforceability of separation agreements. If either spouse is left in necessi-tous circumstances by a separation agreement, that spouse and any chil-dren might become public charges. Finally, Clark notes that courts have recognized that the law should encourage the resolution of property issues through the process of negotiation rather than through litigation. "These processes are more likely to succeed if the parties and their lawyers know in advance that ... fairness will be insisted upon by the courts when they are called upon to approve the agreement." Clark, supra [The Law of Domestic Relations in the United States, 1987] § 19.2.

PROBLEM: THE CASE OF BISKO'S COMPUTER

As a result of your firm's superb handling of *The Case of the Recalcitrant Manufacturer,* the president of Bisko, Inc., John Baker, has returned for more legal advice. It seems that with the addition of the two new ovens the business prospered and the company's old accounting system was suffering from the strain. The company management decided it was time to enter the mysterious world of modern data processing. Caraway Co. had installed a computer system, and while the Bisko people did not really know all the advantages of computeri-zation, they were determined to keep up with the competition. Baker contacted several computer companies, who responded by flooding them with literature and sending representatives to call.

Bisko was a family business, and no one knew very much about computers. One of Bisko's customers, who operated a chain of supermarkets, had told Baker that their Computron computer system had done extremely well and that they "would hate to think of going back to the old ways." After discussing the matter among themselves, the Bisko management decided to "go with" the Computron Company, if they could work out a satisfactory deal.

Computron sales representatives, after making a study of Bisko's needs, recommended the Ajax 0–500 plus the "software" that would perform five basic functions: (1) accounts receivable; (2) payroll; (3) inventory control; (4) invoicing; and (5) state taxes. The salesman said the whole system would be "up and running" within a few weeks and would be the equivalent of a "turn key" operation. (A turn key system is one that is ready to operate as soon as it is turned on.) Computron, he said, would train the Bisko personnel, and thereafter the system would require only minimal maintenance. He assured them that they would be amazed at the difference the system would make in business efficiency and that they would, of course, have Computron "behind them all the way."

On April 5, the parties executed a written contract for the purchase of the "hardware" (the Ajax 0–500), the "software" (the programs) and related services, all for a total price of $35,000. Five thousand was paid down, and the balance plus interest was to be paid in monthly installments stretching over a three year period. On the first page of the form, prepared by Computron and styled "Computron Computer Package Contract," appeared the basic information regarding names of parties, description of goods and services, price and payment terms, etc. The following clause also appeared on this page:

EXCEPT AS SPECIFICALLY PROVIDED IN THIS AGREEMENT, THERE ARE NO OTHER WARRANTIES, EXPRESS OR IMPLIED, INCLUDING BUT NOT LIMITED TO ANY IMPLIED WARRANTIES OF MERCHANTABILITY OR FITNESS FOR A PARTICULAR PURPOSE.

IN NO EVENT SHALL COMPUTRON COMPANY BE LIABLE FOR LOSS OF PROFITS OR OTHER ECONOMIC LOSS, INDIRECT, SPECIAL, CONSEQUENTIAL, OR SIMILAR DAMAGES ARISING OUT OF ANY BREACH OF THE AGREEMENTS OR OBLIGATIONS UNDER THIS AGREEMENT.

COMPUTRON COMPANY SHALL NOT BE LIABLE FOR ANY DAMAGES CAUSED BY DELAY IN DELIVERY, INSTALLATION OR FURNISHING OF EQUIPMENT OR SERVICES UNDER THIS AGREEMENT BEYOND WHAT IS PROVIDED HEREIN.

On the second and last page was a provision that Computron warranted its product for "one (1) year after delivery against defects in material, workmanship and operational failure from ordinary use" and that "services would be performed in a skillful and workmanlike manner." It further provided that the "sole and exclusive remedy for breach of this express warranty is repair or replacement of the defective parts." The concluding paragraph was as follows: "This contract states the entire obligation of seller in connection with this transaction."

Computron delivered the Ajax 0–500 to Bisko on May 17 of last year, and the system was brought on line later that month. From the very beginning Bisko encountered problems with the Computron system. The figures on the first batch of invoices were all wrong. Computron personnel, murmuring reassurances, threw out this first run and produced a second which, when sent out to Bisko's customers, produced a wave of complaints about billing inaccuracies. Since then, Baker reports, things have gone from bad to worse. In one case a hardware defect caused the computer to destroy data stored in the memory.

Bisko then had to hire an accounting firm at great expense to reconstruct the data. Computron has responded to each call for help, but they are seemingly unable to get the "bugs" out of the system. In desperation, Baker comes to you. "I've had it!" he tells you. "You've got to help me. It's too bad, I suppose, I didn't contact you before we got into this computer business."

Senior partner calls you in, relates the foregoing, and asks your evaluation of three UCC-related aspects; *viz.,* 2–302; effectiveness of exclusive or limited remedy; availability of consequential damages. Oblige her.

SECTION 3.   ILLEGALITY: AGREEMENTS UNENFORCEABLE ON GROUNDS OF PUBLIC POLICY

Another control upon promissory liability is imposed by the world around the bargain: the promise or term of the agreement may not be enforceable on grounds of "public policy." In these cases, the bargain will probably satisfy the conditions established by the general law of contracts. There will be an offer and acceptance, consideration will be present, the agreement will satisfy the Statute of Frauds, and there will be no issues of fraud, duress or unconscionability. But one of the parties or the court may assert that the bargain itself, its performance or the objectives to be achieved are "illegal" or against "public policy" and ought not be enforced. At the same time, the defendant will argue that if the promise is not enforceable the plaintiff should be denied restitution of any benefits conferred on the defendant by performance or part performance. If these arguments are successful, the defendant will have avoided contractual liability and may be permitted to retain any benefits received on the ground that the contract in which he or she was involved was against public policy. When and why this result is justified will be the subject of this subsection.

Some of the analytical difficulties are illustrated by a simple and clear example. Suppose that Abner and Boscoe agree that Boscoe will murder Clyde for $5,000, with $2,500 down and the balance when the job is done. Without more, this is a simple, enforceable bilateral contract. But the performance by Boscoe and the bargain itself are felonies, the former being murder and the latter being a conspiracy to commit murder. What is the effect of this on enforceability? The first Restatement took a firm position with a predictable result: "A bargain is illegal * * * if either its formation or its performance is criminal, tortious, or otherwise opposed to public policy." Section 512. Similarly, where both parties are equally involved in the illegality, the effect is that neither can "recover damages for breach thereof nor, by rescinding the bargain, recover the performance that he has rendered thereunder or its value." Section 598. But note that it was the Restatement rather than the criminal law statutes that declared the contract unenforceable and denied restitution. The statute, regulation or other source of public policy may say nothing about contracts and their enforceability. Thus, the jump from the conclusion that the bargain or its performance is a crime or a tort or "otherwise opposed to public policy" to the conclusion that it should not be enforced and restitution should be denied is not without difficulty. Suppose, for example, that the performance of the bargain is a crime but its making is not. Or *vice versa*. What if one party is ignorant of the illegality? Suppose the crime is a misdemeanor rather than a felony. Suppose that the court concludes that the public policy is strong enough to deny enforcement of the bargain but not to deny restitution. The problems are varied, complex, and difficult.

The drafters of Restatement (Second) propose an interest balancing approach. Section 178(1) provides, first, that a "promise or other term of an agreement is unenforceable on grounds of public policy if legislation provides that it is unenforceable. * * *" Thus, if a constitution, statute, administrative regulation or local ordinance preempts the enforceability question by clear language, the court's job is to implement that legislative decision. See Comment a. But if there is no clear legislative mandate, the promise or term is still unenforceable if the "interest in its enforcement is clearly outweighed in the circumstances by a public policy against the enforcement of such terms." Section 178(1). What are the factors to be weighed in the balance? Section 178(2) provides that in "weighing the interest in the enforcement of a term, account is taken of (a) the parties' justified expectations, (b) any forfeiture that would result if enforcement were denied, and (c) any special public interest in the enforcement of the particular term." Section 178(3) provides that in "weighing a public policy against enforcement of a term, account is taken of (a) the strength of that policy as manifested by legislation or judicial decisions, (b) the likelihood that a refusal to enforce the term will further that policy, (c) the seriousness of any misconduct involved and the extent to which it was deliberate, and (d) the directness of the connection between that misconduct and the term." Obviously, the outcome in our Abner–Boscoe "contract" will be the same under both Restatements, even though the court may balance interests under either Restatement approach. The virtue of the Restatement (Second) test is that it would seem to provide more flexibility in cases that are not so clear cut. Similarly, there is more discretion for a court to grant restitution to the plaintiff even though the bargain itself is unenforceable. See Sections 197–199.

For a recent application of the Restatement (Second) "balancing" test in a case involving the machinations of the "erstwhile president of Old Court Savings & Loan Association," see Springlake Corporation v. Symmarron Limited Partnership, 81 Md.App. 694, 569 A.2d 715 (1990). Observing that the "bent" of the Restatement seems to favor enforcement in the doubtful cases, the court summed up the competing factors as follows: "In weighing the interest favoring enforcement, account is to be taken of the parties' 'justified expectations,' any forfeiture that would result if enforcement were denied, and 'any special public interest in the enforcement of the particular term.' Weighing against enforcement are the strength of the public policy, the likelihood that a refusal to enforce the promise will further that policy, the seriousness of the misconduct involved and the extent to which it was deliberate, and the directness of the connection between the misconduct and the promise." 569 A.2d at 702–3.

All of this analysis and balancing is relevant to a fundamental policy question: what is the purpose to be served in denying enforcement and restitution when the contract is against public policy? A principal reason advanced for denying judicial relief is that it will discourage illegal bargaining.

Opportunistic behavior tends to drive out contracting and different doctrines of contract law (such as the duty of good faith) can be seen as an attempt to constrain contractual opportunism. The refusal to enforce illegal contracts or order restitution has the socially valuable effect of *encouraging opportunism* with regard to substantively illegal agreements. Allowing Boscoe to abscond with the downpayment dampens Abner's interest in contracting. For an excellent study of this deterrence rationale, see Kostritsky, *Illegal Contracts and Efficient Deterrence: A Study in Modern Contract Theory,* 74 Ia.L.Rev. 115 (1988). An alternative explanation is that courts withhold judicial access to unworthy claimants to preserve their institutional integrity—or phrased in the more florid prose of Corbin, "in pious fear that the 'judicial ermine' might otherwise be spoiled."

Collateral reading: Farnsworth §§ 5.1–5.9; Calamari and Perillo §§ 22–1—22–9; Murray § 98; Havighurst, Book Review, 61 Yale L.J. 1138, 1144–45 (1952).

Sinnar v. Le Roy

Supreme Court of Washington, Department 2, 1954.
44 Wn.2d 728, 270 P.2d 800.

■ WEAVER, J.—Plaintiff brings this action to recover four hundred fifty dollars which he delivered to defendant upon the latter's promise either to get a beer license for plaintiff or return the money. Defendant appeals from a judgment against him.

Respondent owns and operates a grocery store on Jackson street, in Seattle. Prior to the transaction involved, he made application to the Washington state liquor control board for a license to sell beer, and paid sixty dollars license fee; the license was denied and the license fee returned.

Appellant, a customer, neighbor, and friend of respondent, is a business machine operator at Boeing Airplane Company. When the license was denied, the parties discussed the matter. Appellant testified:

"Well, I talked to—I told John [respondent] that I knew a fellow that worked for the—well, at that time I didn't know that the license come from the state, I thought beer licenses like these come from the city, and I knew this Mr. Lewis worked for the city in this County–City Building here for a number of years, and so then I talked to Mr. Lewis and he said that—(interrupted). ... after I told him I thought I could get the license, I told him I'd see about it, and then I called about it, and I called him, after telephone conversations back and forth to me, and then I called John [respondent] ... and I told him that it would cost him $450.00, and that's all I said and then I went on to work."

Both parties knew that a third party was to be involved. Appellant testified that he gave respondent's four hundred fifty dollars cash to a Mr. Lewis, who is not identified except as reference was made to him in appellant's testimony, herein quoted. Respondent did not receive a beer license.

He testified:

"Well, I told him to be careful who he gives the money to. I found out that this was just a sucker game, and knowing him as well as I did, I thought he'd do me some good. Q. What, if any, conditions were attached to the delivery of the money? A. Well, he told me the license or the money back. He said it was good as in the bank. ... I didn't care how. He was to get my license or the money back. I didn't care what he done with it, whether he bought a retired license or what."

Respondent testified several times that he told appellant to be "careful who he gave the money to." There is no indication in the evidence that the money was paid for professional services.

Appellant's assignments of error are presented upon the theory that this was an illegal transaction. The defense of illegality not having been pleaded, respondent argues that appellant is foreclosed from raising the question. We cannot agree with this conclusion.

"Illegality, if of a serious nature, need not be pleaded. If it appears in evidence the court of its own motion will deny relief to the plaintiff. The defendant cannot waive the defense if he wishes to do so. Indeed, if the court suspects illegality, it may examine witnesses and develop facts not brought out by the parties, and thereby establish illegality that precludes recovery by the plaintiff. If, however, the illegality is not serious, and neither public policy nor statute clearly requires denial of relief, courts refuse to give effect to facts showing illegality unless those facts are essential to establish a prima facie right of recovery or are pleaded by defendant." Restatement, Contracts, § 600, Comment a.

The only place such a license might have been secured was from the Washington state liquor control board. Laws of 1937, chapter 217, § 1, § 23–U, p. 1066 (Rem.Rev.Stat. (Sup.), § 7306–23U [cf. RCW 66.24.010]), provides:

"The holder of one or more licenses may assign and transfer the same to any qualified person under such rules and regulations as the board may prescribe: *Provided, however,* That no such assignment and transfer shall be made which will result in both a change of licensee and change of location; the fee for such assignment and transfer shall be ten dollars ($10.00)."

The illegality, which is claimed and argued in the instant case, is of a serious nature. The situation involves a beer license, which can be secured only from an agency of the state; it purports to deal with a matter which is exclusively within the realm of public policy. A party to such a situation cannot waive his right to set up the defense of illegality, and, if the evidence produced in support of the cause of action also establishes the illegality of the transaction, it should be considered by the trier of the facts, even though illegality has not been pleaded as a defense. Rathke v. Yakima Valley Grape Growers Ass'n, 30 Wn.(2d) 486, 496 to 501, 192 P.(2d) 349 (1948), and cases cited.

* * *

In principle, we cannot distinguish the instant case from Goodier v. Hamilton, 172 Wash. 60, 63, 19 P.(2d) 392 (1933), wherein we said:

"It is within the realm of contemplation that a contract of this nature would readily suggest to one desirous of securing a highly compensatory result, to employ means which the law, good morals and public policy do not sanction. To anticipate and prevent a subversion of a proper administration of justice, the law should make it impossible for any such temptation to be carried into fruition by condemning a contract that contains the germ of possible corruption."

The record not only discloses that this transaction "contains the germ of possible corruption," but the evidence, and all inferences which may be drawn, lead us to conclude that the parties contemplated the use of means other than legal to accomplish the end desired.

A court will not knowingly aid in the furtherance of an illegal transaction, but will leave the parties where it finds them.

The judgment is reversed, with instructions to dismiss the action. Since the parties are in *pari delicto,* it is consistent with our decision that each bear his own costs.

NOTES

(1) Exactly where was the "illegality" in *Sinnar*—in the making of the contract, its performance, the objective to be achieved or what? Would the court come out differently on the enforceability issue using the Restatement (Second) balancing test, supra at 540? Restatement (Second) clearly supports the power of a court to raise the public policy issue *sua sponte*:

Even if neither party's pleading or proof reveals the contravention, the court may ordinarily inquire into it and decide the case on the basis of it if it finds it just to do so, subject to any relevant rules of pleading or proof by which it is bound.

Restatement (Second), Chapter 8, Topic 1, Introductory Note.

(2) *Restitutionary Exceptions.* The result in *Sinnar v. Le Roy* is that the defendant (or some unknown third person) is permitted to keep the plaintiff's $450. Yet both were equally involved in the wrongdoing. What policy justifies this result? This result—no restitution—is supported by Section 197 of Restatement (Second) as a general rule with some exceptions; e.g., (1) The denial of restitution causes "disproportionate forfeiture," Section 197; (2) The plaintiff was excusably ignorant of facts or of legislation "of a minor character, in the absence of which the promise would be enforceable," Section 198(a); (3) The plaintiff was "not equally in the wrong with the promisor," Section 198(b); and (4) The plaintiff did not "engage in serious misconduct and * * * he withdraws

from the transaction before the improper purpose has been achieved." Section 199(a). See Section 199(b), stating that restitution will also be allowed where the plaintiff did "not engage in serious misconduct and * * * allowance of the claim would put an end to a continuing situation that is contrary to the public interest."

(3) *Lord Mansfield Justifies.* The following statement of Lord Mansfield in Holman v. Johnson, [1775] 1 Cowp. 341, is most frequently advanced to justify disallowance of recovery where both parties are *in pari delicto*:

"The objection that a contract is immoral or illegal as between plaintiff and defendant, sounds at all times very ill in the mouth of the defendant. It is not for his sake, however, that the objection is ever allowed; but it is founded in general principles of policy, which the defendant has the advantage of, contrary to the real justice as between him and the plaintiff, by accident, if I may so say. The principle of public policy is this: Ex dolo malo non oritur actio. No court will lend its aid to a man who founds his cause of action upon an immoral or an illegal act. If, from the plaintiff's own stating or otherwise, the cause of action appears to arise ex turpi causa, or the transgression of a positive law of this country, there the court says he has no right to be assisted. It is upon that ground the court goes; not for the sake of defendant, but because they will not lend their aid to such a plaintiff. So if the plaintiff and defendant were to change sides, and the defendant was to bring his action against the plaintiff, the latter would then have the advantage of it; for where both parties are equally in fault, potior est conditio defendentis."

What judicial alternatives are available? Can you suggest a more acceptable approach? Cf. Wade, *Restitution of Benefits Acquired Through Illegal Transactions,* 95 U.Pa.L.Rev. 261 (1947); Grodecki, *In Pari Delicto Potior Est Conditio Defendentis,* 71 L.Q.Rev. 254 (1955). Both authors point out that Mansfield recognized that the *in pari delicto* maxim should not be applied rigidly and mechanically. For example, in Clarke v. Shee, [1774] 1 Cowp. 197, 200, he wrote:

"There are two sorts of prohibitions enacted by positive law, in respect of contracts. 1st. To protect weak or necessitous men from being overreached, defrauded or oppressed. There the rule in pari delicto, potior est conditio defendentis, does not hold; and an action will lie; because where the defendant imposes upon the plaintiff it is not par delictum. * * * The next sort of prohibition is founded upon general reasons of policy and public expedience. There both parties offending are equally guilty; par est delictum, et potior est conditio defendentis."

(4) *Dean Wigmore Dissents.* "The real theory of *pari delicto* seems to be that the plaintiff loses his right by partaking in wrong-doing. * * * But the whole notion is radically wrong in principle and produces extreme injustice. If A owes B $5,000 why should he not pay it whether B has violated a statute or not? Where the issue is as to the rights of two litigants, it is unscientific to impose a penalty incidentally by depriving one of the litigants of his admitted right. It is unjust, also, for two reasons: first, one guilty party suffers, while another of equal guilt is rewarded; secondly, the penalty is usually utterly disproportionate to the offense. If there is one part of criminal jurisprudence which needs even more careful attention than it now receives it is the apportionment of penalty to offense. Yet the doctrine now under consideration

requires, with monstrous injustice and blind haphazard, that the plaintiff shall be mulcted in the amount of his right, whatever that may be. Take for example the case of Cambrioso v. Maffet (2 Wash.C.C. 98), in which plaintiff and defendant were joint owners of a vessel. To avoid paying the tax on alien owners, the vessel was registered in the name of the defendant. For this illegality the plaintiff is denied the help of the courts in making the defendant account for the vessel's profits. In this way, and in a hundred similar ways, a fine of thousands of dollars may be imposed for petty violations of law. One cannot imagine why we have so long allowed such an unworthy principle to remain.

"The expedient that naturally suggests itself is merely to order the sum due to be paid into court and to deduct from it such a portion as may be named by the proper tribunal as the penalty for the violation of the law." Wigmore, *A Summary of Quasi–Contracts,* 25 Am.L.Rev. 695, 712–13 (1891).

(5) *Public Policy: An Elusive Concept.* "From the dawn of the common law tradition in England, courts have refused to implement those private contractual undertakings which, when measured against the prevailing mores and moods of society, contravene judicial perceptions of so-called 'public policy.' See 1 E. Coke, *Institutes of the Laws of England: A Commentary upon Littleton* *19 (Thomas ed. 1827) ('*nihil quod est inconveniens est licitum*'); Winfield, *Public Policy in the English Common Law,* 42 Harv.L.Rev. 76, 79 et seq. (1928). This Court stated early on that considerations of public policy are deemed paramount to private rights and where conflict between the two exists, private interests must yield to the public good. Wildey v. Collier, 7 Md. 273, 278–79, 61 Am.Dec. 346 (1854).

"Nearly 150 years ago Lord Truro set forth what has become the classical formulation of the public policy doctrine—that to which we adhere in Maryland:

'Public policy is that principle of the law which holds that no subject can lawfully do that which has a tendency to be injurious to the public, or against the public good, which may be termed, as it sometimes has been, the policy of the law, or public policy in relation to the administration of the law.' Egerton v. Earl Brownlow, 4 H.L.Cas. 1, 196 (1853).

"... But beyond this relatively indeterminate description of the doctrine, jurists to this day have been unable to fashion a truly workable definition of public policy. Not being restricted to the conventional sources of positive law (constitutions, statutes and judicial decisions), judges are frequently called upon to discern the dictates of sound social policy and human welfare based on nothing more than their own personal experience and intellectual capacity. See 6A A. Corbin, *Contracts* § 1375, at 10 and 18 (1962). Inevitably, conceptions of public policy tend to ebb and flow with the tides of public opinion, making it difficult for courts to apply the principle with any degree of certainty. 1 W. Story, *A Treatise on the Law of Contracts* § 675 (5th ed. 1874).

'[P]ublic policy ... is but a shifting and variable notion appealed to only when no other argument is available, and which, if relied upon today, may be utterly repudiated tomorrow.' Kenneweg v. Allegany County, 102 Md. 119, 125, 62 A. 249, 251 (1905).

"Fearing the disruptive effect that invocation of the highly elusive public policy principle would likely exert on the stability of commercial and contractual relations, Maryland courts have been hesitant to strike down voluntary bargains on public policy grounds, doing so only in those cases where the challenged agreement is patently offensive to the public good, that is, where 'the common sense of the entire community would ... pronounce it' invalid. Estate of Woods, Weeks & Co., 52 Md. 520, 536 (1879); Trupp v. Wolff, 24 Md.App. 588, 616, 335 A.2d 171, cert. denied, 275 Md. 757 (1975); see Aged Men's Home v. Pierce, 100 Md. 520, 526, 60 A. 277, 70 L.R.A. 485 (1905). This reluctance on the part of the judiciary to nullify contractual arrangements on public policy grounds also serves to protect the public interest in having individuals exercise broad powers to structure their own affairs by making legally enforceable promises, a concept which lies at the heart of the freedom of contract principle. Restatement (Second) of Contracts, Introductory Note to Ch. 14, at 46 (Tent. Draft No. 12, 1977); see Baltimore & Ohio etc. Railway v. Voigt, 176 U.S. 498, 505–06, 20 S.Ct. 385, 44 L.Ed. 560 (1900); Miller v. Continental Ins. Co., 40 N.Y.2d 675, 389 N.Y.S.2d 565, 358 N.E.2d 258, 261 (1976); Printing & Numerical Reg. Co. v. Sampson, L.R., 19 Eq. 462, 465 (Ch.1875).

"In the final analysis, it is the function of a court to balance the public and private interests in securing enforcement of the disputed promise against those policies which would be advanced were the contractual term held invalid. Enforcement will be denied only where the factors that argue against implementing the particular provision clearly and unequivocally outweigh 'the law's traditional interest in protecting the expectations of the parties, its abhorrence of any unjust enrichment, and any public interest in the enforcement' of the contested term. Restatement (Second) of Contracts § 320, Comment b (Tent. Draft No. 12, 1977)." Maryland–National, etc. v. Washington National Arena, 282 Md. 588, 386 A.2d 1216, 1227–28 (1978).

PROBLEM: THE CASE OF THE GREEN DOOR TAVERN

Patricia Myers operated the Green Door tavern in Granby, Missouri. Mrs. Myers had a three-year lease with option to purchase the premises from the owner John Hurn, Jr. and a beer by-the-drink license issued by the Missouri Division of Liquor Control.

Todd Clouse was a patron of the tavern. During one of his visits, Patricia's husband Jerry asked Clouse if he would be interested in purchasing an interest in the business. Negotiations followed which resulted in the signing of an "Employment/Management Contract" under which the Myers, as "Employers," agreed to hire Clouse to manage the business for a four-year period and pay him sixty percent of the net profit of the business as salary. In addition, Clouse was to receive, at the termination of the agreement or upon the exercise of the lease option to purchase, whichever came first, a 60 percent interest in the Green Door, with the Myers agreeing to exercise the option to purchase the property from Hurn within the lease period. Upon purchase of the property from Hurn, the Myers and Clouse were each to pay 50 percent of the purchase price. Finally, Clouse agreed to pay the Myers $15,000, $7,500 at the time of signing.

After executing the contract, Clouse paid the $7,500 and began operating the tavern. Two weeks later, however, the parties were summoned to the office of Larry Fuhr of the Missouri Liquor Commission. Fuhr questioned the agreement because an agreement with a licensed person (Patricia Myers) to operate a tavern, is in violation of Missouri law. Fuhr also objected to Jerry Myers' name on the contract because the latter, evidently a convicted felon, could have nothing to do with the operation of the tavern. The upshot was that Patricia surrendered her license to Fuhr.

Clouse later applied for and received a liquor license to operate the tavern in his own name, and he negotiated a new lease with Hurn. Clouse then requested that the Myers return his $7,500. They refused. He sued. What result? See Clouse v. Myers, 753 S.W.2d 316 (Mo.App.1988).

Homami v. Iranzadi

California Court of Appeal, Sixth District, 1989.
211 Cal.App.3d 1104, 260 Cal.Rptr. 6.

■ BRAUER, ASSOCIATE JUSTICE.

Ahmad Homami sued Mansoor Iranzadi to collect the balance due on a promissory note. Iranzadi claimed he had paid down the principal balance by approximately $40,000. Homami acknowledged receiving that amount but claimed the payments represented interest only. The note expressly provided: "This note shall bear no interest." But Homami testified at trial that the parties nonetheless had an oral agreement for the payment of 12 percent interest per annum. According to Homami the no interest provision on the note was only so that he could avoid reporting the income for state and federal income tax purposes.

The trial court granted judgment in favor of Homami. We reverse on the basis that Homami's claim is dependent upon an agreement for the express purpose of violating the law and defrauding state and federal governments.

FACTS

Homami and Iranzadi were brothers-in-law. At the time of this transaction, they had been involved in various business dealings together both in Iran and in the United States.

On January 9, 1984, Homami wrote a check for $250,000 to California Land Title in order to fund a real estate transaction on behalf of Iranzadi. The close of escrow was delayed until March 22, 1984. In the interim Homami kept the money available to make the loan.

The $250,000 loan was evidenced by two identical promissory notes dated March 22, 1984, in the amount of $125,000 each. Each note provided that it was all due and payable in two years and each recited that it would bear no interest. One note was secured by property known as the "Pinehill" property, and the other by property known as the "Outlook" property.

Iranzadi, who was not fluent in English, had granted Homami a power of attorney. Pursuant to this power Homami routinely wrote checks for his brother-in-law.

On March 25, 1984, three days after the loan was funded, Homami signed a check to himself for $2,104.68 on Iranzadi's account. The check bore a notation in Persian that it was for interest to March. According to Homami, this amount represented interest lost to him by virtue of the fact that he had kept the $250,000 accessible for two and a half months. He testified that Iranzadi had agreed to pay him the difference between the interest he was earning in his regular bank account and the 12 percent he would be receiving from Iranzadi.

Thereafter, checks were drawn to Homami on Iranzadi's account more or less on a monthly basis for approximately a year. For the first few months Homami signed the checks. The last six checks were signed by Iranzadi's son. With the exception of two payments, all of the checks were for $2,500. That would be the exact amount of monthly interest on a debt for $250,000 bearing a rate of 12 percent per annum. The total amount paid to Homami from Iranzadi, including the initial payment of $2,104.68, was $39,324.68.

On March 18, 1985, Homami and Iranzadi signed a document entitled "Modification Agreement" for each of the promissory notes. The modification agreements were identical except for their reference to the respective notes and deeds of trust. Each provided for the following modification of terms:

"1. The note shall be all due and payable on or before September 22, 1985.

2. The note shall bear no interest until June 22, 1985.

3. On June 22, 1985, interest shall commence at the rate of eighteen percent per annum; said interest shall be payable monthly commencing on July 22, 1985 and continue monthly thereafter until the maturity date expressed herein."

Thereafter, two more payments of $2,500 were made, on May 22, 1985 and June 23, 1985. No further payments of any amount were made.

On August 14, 1985, Homami filed notices of default on the ground that Iranzadi had failed to pay the monthly installment of interest due July 22, 1985. Foreclosures were commenced on both properties. Iranzadi found a buyer for the Pinehill property and escrow closed at the end of January, 1986. Homami was paid through that escrow the full principal balance of $125,000 on the one note, plus interest at 18 percent from June 22, 1985, as per the modification agreement, and foreclosure fees; however, Iranzadi expressly reserved the right to claim a credit for approximately $40,000, plus fees and costs, against the second note.

The Outlook property sold in June 1986. Homami submitted a demand for the full $125,000 plus interest on that amount from June 22, 1985, and foreclosure fees. Iranzadi, maintaining he had paid $39,324.68 on the principal balance between March 1984 and June 1985, claimed a credit in that amount. Escrow closed but the sum of $43,500 was held out of the proceeds and delivered to Albert Ham, a stakeholder, pending resolution of the dispute.

Homami filed suit October 15, 1986, alleging breach of a written contract. Attached to the complaint were the two promissory notes and modification agreements. Iranzadi filed a cross-complaint for declaratory relief, alleging that he had paid $39,324.68 towards reducing the principal, and seeking a determination of rights as to the monies held in trust. He also pleaded a cause of action for conversion of the $39,324.68 and prayed for compensatory relief and punitive damages against Homami.

At trial Homami testified that he and Iranzadi had orally agreed on an interest rate of 12 percent, and had also agreed that Iranzadi would not report interest paid and Homami would not have to report receiving the income. He testified that this arrangement was discussed and reiterated at a family meeting March 15, 1985. And he specifically stated that the reason the loan documents did not reflect any interest was so that he could avoid reporting income to the IRS.

Iranzadi, on the other hand, claimed that he and Homami had never discussed interest on the loan. He testified that in family dealings interest was never charged and that he had often loaned money to Homami without interest. He stated that he had authorized Homami to take $2,000 to $3,000 from his account every month to reduce the principal balance.

The trial court found that the payments made by Iranzadi to Homami totalling $39,324.68 represented interest only, and no principal reduction. Therefore Iranzadi still owed Homami that amount on the loan. The court rendered judgment in favor of Homami for $39,324.68 plus interest at 18 percent from June 30, 1986, the close of escrow, plus attorneys fees and costs. The judgment ordered that Albert Ham, the stakeholder, be awarded $588.11 for his costs and that he distribute the balance in the trust account to Homami in partial payment of the judgment.

DISCUSSION

[Iranzadi argues] that a contract which has as its object an illegal purpose is contrary to public policy and void. Since we find the last point to be dispositive, we need not address the remaining issues.

The Civil Code provides a starting place. A contract must have a lawful object. (Civ.Code, § 1550.) Any contract which has as its object the violation of an express provision of law is unlawful. (Civ.Code, § 1667, subd. (1).) The object of a contract is the thing which it is agreed, on the part of the party receiving the consideration, to do or not to do. (Civ.Code, § 1595.) The object must be lawful when the contract is made. (Civ.Code, § 1596.) And that part of the contract which is unlawful is void. (Civ.Code, § 1599.)

Courts have interpreted these statutes liberally. " 'The general principle is well established that a contract founded on an illegal consideration, or which is made for the purpose of furthering any matter or thing prohibited by statute, or to aid or assist any party therein, is void. This rule applies to every contract which is founded on a transaction *malum in se,* or which is prohibited by a statute on the ground of public policy.' " (C.I.T. Corp. v. Breckenridge (1944) 63 Cal.App.2d 198, 200, 146 P.2d 271.)

It makes no difference whether the contract has been partially or wholly performed. Rather, the test is " ' "whether the plaintiff requires the aid of the illegal transaction to establish his case. If the plaintiff cannot open his case without showing that he has broken the law, the court will not assist him, whatever his claim in justice may be upon the defendant." ' " (C.I.T. Corp. v. Breckenridge, supra, 63 Cal.App.2d 198, 200, 146 P.2d 271.)

Nor does it matter that the illegality has not been pleaded. "[I]f the question of illegality develops during the course of a trial, a court must consider it whether pleaded or not.... 'Whenever the evidence discloses the relations of the parties to the transaction to be illegal and against public policy, it becomes the duty of the court to refuse to entertain the action.' " (Russell v. Soldinger (1976) 59 Cal.App.3d 633, 642, 131 Cal.Rptr. 145.)

Cases which have applied these principles fall into several broad categories. A common situation involves the unlicensed contractor, or other unlicensed professional, who seeks to collect money for services rendered. Courts have routinely refused to grant relief in such cases on the ground that the failure to comply with licensing requirements violates a law designed to protect and benefit the public. Therefore a party who has violated the law and entered into an agreement to perform services while unlicensed cannot obtain the aid of courts to enforce the agreement. (Loving & Evans v. Blick (1949) 33 Cal.2d 603, 607, 204 P.2d 23; Franklin v. Nat. C. Goldstone Agency (1949) 33 Cal.2d 628, 204 P.2d 37; Harrison v. Butte Steel Buildings, Inc. (1957) 150 Cal.App.2d 296, 310 P.2d 126; Mansfield v. Hyde (1952) 112 Cal.App.2d 133, 138–139, 245 P.2d 577.)

In another factual context, courts have refused to grant relief to parties seeking to collect monies arising from illegal gambling activities. (Lee On v. Long (1951) 37 Cal.2d 499, 234 P.2d 9; Fong v. Miller (1951) 105 Cal. App.2d 411, 233 P.2d 606.)

A third group of cases closer to our facts involves plaintiffs who have attempted to circumvent federal law. Generally these cases arise where nonveterans seek to obtain government benefits and entitlements available to veterans only, either by setting up a strawman veteran or otherwise by falsifying documents.

For example, in May v. Herron (1954) 127 Cal.App.2d 707, 274 P.2d 484, the Newmans transferred property to a veteran for the sole purpose of obtaining a Veteran's Priority under Federal Priorities Regulation No. 33. That regulation provided that veterans who wished to build houses for their own occupancy would receive preferential treatment in obtaining construction materials. The Newmans had been advised to obtain the illegal veteran's priority by their building contractor, who then entered into a contract with the veteran to build a house which he knew the Newmans intended to occupy. When the builder sued to recover a balance due on the construction contract, the court refused to come to his aid, finding that he had "initiated, suggested and directed a conspiracy to violate and circumvent a federal regulation which had the force of law." (Id. at p. 711, 274

P.2d 484.) The court concluded in this vein: "To permit a recovery here on any theory would permit plaintiff to benefit from his wilful and deliberate flouting of a law designed to promote the general public welfare." (Id. at p. 712, 274 P.2d 484.)

In a similar case, Lala v. Maiorana (1959) 166 Cal.App.2d 724, 333 P.2d 862, plaintiffs conveyed real property to defendant without consideration or a change of possession. Defendant, by virtue of his status as a serviceman, obtained a loan on the property. He continued to hold title although plaintiffs occupied the property and made all the loan payments. Eventually creditors of defendant filed liens on the property. Plaintiffs sought to be relieved of those liens, claiming that the property was rightfully theirs. But in order to prove their claim, plaintiffs had to disclose the illegal purpose behind the conveyance to defendant. Because of that, the court refused to grant them relief.

Young v. Hampton (1951) 36 Cal.2d 799, 228 P.2d 1, also involved an agreement for the purpose of circumventing federal legislation. In that case Helen Young, a contractor, agreed to build a house for Hampton, a veteran. She gave him a bid for $8,500 and he applied for a veteran's loan. The Veteran's Administration appraised the project at $8,283 and agreed to make a loan limited to that amount. Hampton and Young then executed a contract to build the house for $8,283 and also signed a side agreement by which Hampton was to pay Young cost plus 10 percent, not to exceed $9,000. When Young was not fully paid, she filed a mechanic's lien based upon the cost plus contract and sued for the balance due. The Supreme Court found that "the entire transaction was designed to evade the provisions of the act (the Servicemen's Readjustment Act) and also to obtain its benefits." (Id. at pp. 805–806, 228 P.2d 1.) The secret agreement between Young and Hampton to pay more than the value insured by the VA violated public policy and was therefore unenforceable.

The message from these cases couldn't be clearer. As the Supreme Court has expressed it: " 'No principle of law is better settled than that a party to an illegal contract cannot come into a court of law and ask to have his illegal objects carried out; nor can he set up a case in which he must necessarily disclose an illegal purpose as the groundwork of his claim.' " (Lee On v. Long, supra, 37 Cal.2d 499, 502, 234 P.2d 9.)

We do not perceive any meaningful difference between the unlawful agreements described in the above example and the tax evasion scheme perpetrated by Homami and Iranzadi in our case. Here Homami entered into a written agreement which specifically provided that he would be paid no interest. The purpose of the provision was to enable him to avoid compliance with state and federal income tax regulations. He then secretly collected interest income which he had no intention of reporting. And when a dispute developed, he sought the aid of the court to enforce the secret agreement so that he could keep the money he had collected.

[E]ven though a written contract is legal on its face, evidence may be introduced to establish its illegal character. (May v. Herron, supra, 127 Cal.App.2d 707, 710–711, 274 P.2d 484.) And if the substance of the transaction is illegal, it matters not when or how the illegality is raised in the course of the lawsuit. Whether the evidence comes from one side or the other, the disclosure is fatal to the case ... The fact is that Homami, in order to state his claim to the funds held out of the escrow proceeds, was obliged to testify and did testify that he collected interest secretly in order to circumvent income tax laws. As the cases have repeatedly pointed out, "the test ... is whether the plaintiff can establish his case otherwise than through the medium of an illegal transaction to which he himself was a party." (Schur v. Johnson (1934) 2 Cal.App.2d 680, 683–684, 38 P.2d 844.) It is clear that Homami could not do so.

Because his agreement violated the law, Homami is not entitled to the $39,624.86 he collected as unreported interest. That amount is to be credited to Iranzadi from the escrow proceeds. Distribution of the balance of the funds held in the trust account is to be determined by the court on remand.

NOTES

(1) In *Homami*, what is the public policy said to be violated? To what extent, if any, would the denial of judicial remedy promote this policy?

(2) The court in *Homami* refers to "the importance of deterring illegal conduct." Appraise the deterrent effect of the opinion. See generally Kostritsky, *Illegal Contracts and Efficient Deterrence: A Study in Modern Contract Theory*, 74 Ia.L.Rev. 115 (1988).

(3) Illegality may not prevent the enforcement of a contract if the court construes the illegality not to be "serious." For example, in Town Planning and Engineering Assoc. v. Amesbury Specialty Co., 369 Mass. 737, 342 N.E.2d 706 (1976), an uncredentialed engineer was hired but subsequently not paid for engineering work. Even though a Massachusetts statute provides that engineering is to be performed only by registered engineers, the court found that the illegal behavior contracted for was *de minimus*.

(4) *Public Policy and the Role of the Judiciary.* If a constitutionally valid statute provides explicitly that a particular contract is "illegal" or otherwise opposed to public policy, the task of the court is relatively easy. The court responds, in appropriate ways, to the declared will of the legislature. Most contract illegality cases are not of this type, however. More likely the statute does not address the precise issue; there is, at most, merely an indication of general legislative policy. This means that the question of what sound policy requires regarding the allegedly illegal bargain is plainly a "judicial" question. Corbin § 1375. The court may state that it will be "guided" by a legislative declaration of policy, but it cannot escape the responsibility of doing justice in the particular case. In short, it is the court which must perform the task of elaborating the public policy of the jurisdiction, and this, of course, is frequently a difficult undertaking. See, generally, Gellhorn, *Contracts and Public Policy*, 35 Colum.L.Rev. 679 (1935).

(5) *A Cautionary Note.* In an English case, St. John Shipping Corp. v. Joseph Rauk, Ltd., [1966] 3 All E.R. 683, the plaintiff sued for the balance of freight charges due for transporting wheat from Mobile, Alabama to Liverpool.

The defendant insisted that it was not obliged to pay because the freighter had been overloaded in violation of a statute making it a criminal offense to load a ship so that the load line was submerged. In holding for the plaintiff, the court said that the question was "whether the statute is meant to prohibit the contract being sued upon." It is significant, however, that the court was influenced by practical considerations. Speaking for the court, Lord Devlin said: "If a contract has as its whole object the doing of the very act which the statute prohibits, it can be argued that you can hardly make sense of a statute which forbids an act and yet permits to be made a contract to do it; that is a clear implication. But unless you get a clear implication of that sort, I think that a court ought to be very slow to hold that a statute intends to interfere with the rights and remedies given by the ordinary law of contract. Caution in this respect is, I think, especially necessary in these times when so much of commercial life is governed by regulations of one sort or another which may easily be broken without wicked intent. Persons who deliberately set out to break the law cannot expect to be aided in a court of justice, but it is a different matter when the law is unwittingly broken. To nullify a bargain in such circumstances frequently means that in a case—perhaps of such triviality that no authority would have felt it worth while to prosecute—a seller, because he cannot enforce his civil rights, may forfeit a sum vastly in excess of any penalty that a criminal court would impose; and the sum forfeited will not go into the public purse but into the pockets of someone who is lucky enough to pick up the windfall or astute enough to have contrived to get it. It is questionable how far this contributes to public morality * * *. It may be questionable also whether public policy is well served by driving from the seat of judgment anyone who has been guilty of a minor transgression. Commercial men who have unwittingly offended against one of a multiplicity of regulations may nevertheless feel that they have not thereby forfeited all right to justice, and may go elsewhere for it if courts of law will not give it to them. In the last resort they will, if necessary, set up their own machinery for dealing with their own disputes in the way that those whom the law puts beyond the pale, such as gamblers, have done." 3 All E.R. at 690–691. See Note, *The Doctrine of Illegality and Petty Offenders: Can Quasi–Contract Bring Justice?,* 42 Notre Dame Law. 46 (1966).

(6) *Problems: Impact upon Contract Enforcement of Statutory Violation.* (a) *The Case of the Unregistered Apartment.* Tenant signed a one-year lease with Landlord, but decided not to occupy the premises. Landlord sues for damages. Tenants argues that the lease is void because the apartment was not registered as a residential unit, nor did the Landlord secure an occupancy permit, as required by city code. What result? See Noble v. Alis, 474 N.E.2d 109 (Ind.App. 1985).

(b) *The Case of the Umetered Fuel Oil Deliveries.* Buyer owned two homes to which Seller delivered fuel oil on several occasions. Not all of the deliveries were metered as required by law, and for which Seller was subject to fine and/or imprisonment. Seller sues for $5,000 worth of oil delivered but not metered. What result? See Rupert's Oil Service v. Leslie, 40 Conn.Sup. 295, 493 A.2d 926 (1985).

(c) *The Case of the Excessive Interest Charge.* Plaintiff, an investment company licensed by the Small Business Administration, loaned defendant

$64,000. The loan was secured by a mortgage on defendant's residence. When the defendant defaulted on the loan, plaintiff sought to foreclose on the mortgage. The defendant argued that the plaintiff had charged interest above that allowed by regulations of the Small Business Administration, and this made the contract unenforceable. The trial court agreed. What result on appeal? See Lloyd Capital Corp. v. Pat Henchar, Inc., 152 A.D.2d 725, 544 N.Y.S.2d 178 (1989).

(d) *The Case of the Uncertified Carrier.* On four occasions Carrier transported Owner's horses in interstate commerce, but without having obtained a "certificate of public convenience and necessity" as required by the Interstate Commerce Commission Act. Can Owner interpose this statutory violation as a legal justification for not paying the Carrier? See Hull and Smith Horse Vans, Inc. v. Carras, 144 Mich.App. 712, 376 N.W.2d 392 (1985). See also Northern Indiana Public Service Company v. Carbon County Coal Company, 799 F.2d 265 (7th Cir.1986) (good commentary on "balancing" by Judge Posner in case involving violation of "anachronistic" provision of Mineral Lands Leasing Act of 1920).

(e) *The Case of the "No Bid" Contract.* Seller contacted Buyer, a community hospital, concerning the sale of radiator covers needed by the hospital for accreditation purposes. The county commissioners negotiated the contract with Seller but without going through the formal bidding process mandated by law. Seller sues for the $56,600 price. The county treasurer refuses to pay. Who wins? See Majestic Radiator Enclosure Company, Inc. v. County Commissioners of Middlesex, 397 Mass. 1002, 490 N.E.2d 1186 (1986).

(f) *The Case of the Delayed Title Delivery.* Buyer bought a boat from Seller, but after having experienced several problems with the boat sought to avoid the sale. Buyer argued that Seller's failure to deliver a certificate of title within 20 days, as mandated by state law, made the contract unenforceable. Is Buyer correct? See Saulny v. RDY, Inc., 760 S.W.2d 813 (Tex.App.1988).

(g) *The Case of the Missing Repair Estimate.* Owner brought his Jaguar in for service and orally agreed to pay $187 for certain repairs. When he returned to pick up the car he agreed to pay $200 for further work which the mechanic recommended. Later the car was delivered to his home, accompanied by a repair bill for $500. Owner refused to pay, insisting that the contract was void because the service station failed to provide a written estimate as required by statute. Does Owner make a convincing argument? See Bennett v. Hayes, 53 Cal.App.3d 700, 125 Cal.Rptr. 825 (1975).

(h) *The Case of the Unlicensed Employment Agency.* Employer contracted with Employment Agency to find a computer programmer. The Agency found a qualified applicant, whom the employer later hired. However, Employer refused to pay the agreed upon fee, based upon Employment Agency's lack of license required by statute. What, if anything, should the Agency be able to recover? See T.E.C. & Associates, Inc. v. Alberto–Culver Company, 131 Ill.App.3d 1085, 87 Ill.Dec. 220, 476 N.E.2d 1212 (1985). See also Design Development, Inc. v. Brignole, 20 Conn.App. 685, 570 A.2d 221 (1990) (architect); Hoffman v. Dunn, 496 N.E.2d 818 (Ind.App.1986) (realtor); Haberman v. Elledge, 42 Wn.App. 744, 713 P.2d 746 (1986) (well driller).

Patterson v. McLean Credit Union

United State Supreme Court, 1989.
491 U.S. 164, 109 S.Ct. 2363, 105 L.Ed.2d 132.

[Petitioner Brenda Patterson, a black woman, was employed by respondent McLean Credit Union as a teller and a file coordinator, commencing in May 1972. In July 1982, she was laid off. After the termination, petitioner commenced this action alleging that respondent, in violation of 14 Stat. 27, 42 U. S. C. § 1981, had harassed her and then discharged her, because of her race. The District Court ruled in favor of respondent and the Court of Appeals affirmed]

■ KENNEDY, J. In this case, we consider important issues respecting the meaning and coverage of one of our oldest civil rights statutes, 42 U.S.C. § 1981. . . .

We granted certiorari to decide whether petitioner's claim of racial harassment in her employment is actionable under § 1981. [After oral argument], we requested the parties to brief and argue an additional question: "Whether or not the interpretation of 42 U.S.C. § 1981 adopted by this Court in Runyon v. McCrary, 427 U.S. 160 (1976), should be reconsidered." [Because of stare decisis, the Court declined to overturn Runyon v. McCrary.]

Our conclusion that we should adhere to our decision in Runyon that § 1981 applies to private conduct is not enough to decide this case. We must decide also whether the conduct of which petitioner complains falls within one of the enumerated rights protected by § 1981.

Section 1981 reads as follows:

"All persons within the jurisdiction of the United States shall have the same right in every State and Territory to make and enforce contracts, to sue, be parties, give evidence, and to the full and equal benefit of all laws and proceedings for the security of persons and property as is enjoyed by white citizens, and shall be subject to like punishment, pains, penalties, taxes, licenses, and exactions of every kind, and to no other." Rev. Stat. § 1977.

The most obvious feature of the provision is the restriction of its scope to forbidding discrimination in the "mak[ing] and enforce[ment]" of contracts alone. Where an alleged act of discrimination does not involve the impairment of one of these specific rights, § 1981 provides no relief. Section 1981 cannot be construed as a general proscription of racial discrimination in all aspects of contract relations, for it expressly prohibits discrimination only in the making and enforcement of contracts. See also Jones v. Alfred H. Mayer Co., 392 U.S. 409, 436 (1968) (§ 1982, the companion statute to § 1981, was designed "to prohibit all racial discrimination, whether or not under color of law, with respect to the rights enumerated therein") (emphasis added); Georgia v. Rachel, 384 U.S. 780, 791 (1966) ("The legislative history of the 1866 Act clearly indicates that Congress intended to protect a limited category of rights").

By its plain terms, the relevant provision in § 1981 protects two rights: "the same right ... to make ... contracts" and "the same right ... to ... enforce contracts." The first of these protections extends only to the formation of a contract, but not to problems that may arise later from the conditions of continuing employment. The statute prohibits, when based on race, the refusal to enter into a contract with someone, as well as the offer to make a contract only on discriminatory terms. But the right to make contracts does not extend, as a matter of either logic or semantics, to conduct by the employer after the contract relation has been established, including breach of the terms of the contract or imposition of discriminatory working conditions. Such postformation conduct does not involve the right to make a contract, but rather implicates the performance of established contract obligations and the conditions of continuing employment, matters more naturally governed by state contract law and Title VII. * * *

Applying these principles to the case before us, we agree with the Court of Appeals that petitioner's racial harassment claim is not actionable under § 1981. Petitioner has alleged that during her employment with respondent, she was subjected to various forms of racial harassment from her supervisor. As summarized by the Court of Appeals, petitioner testified that "[her supervisor] periodically stared at her for several minutes at a time; that he gave her too many tasks, causing her to complain that she was under too much pressure; that among the tasks given her were sweeping and dusting, jobs not given to white employees. On one occasion, she testified, [her supervisor] told [her] that blacks are known to work slower than whites. According to [petitioner, her supervisor] also criticized her in staff meetings while not similarly criticizing white employees." 805 F. 2d, at 1145.

[N]one of the conduct which petitioner alleges as part of the racial harassment against her involves either a refusal to make a contract with her or the impairment of her ability to enforce her established contract rights. * * *

The Solicitor General argues that the language of § 1981, especially the words "the same right," requires us to look outside § 1981 to the terms of particular contracts and to state law for the obligations and covenants to be protected by the federal statute. Under this view, § 1981 has no actual substantive content, but instead mirrors only the specific protections that are afforded under the law of contracts of each State. Under this view, racial harassment in the conditions of employment is actionable when, and only when, it amounts to a breach of contract under state law. We disagree. For one thing, to the extent that it assumes that prohibitions contained in § 1981 incorporate only those protections afforded by the States, this theory is directly inconsistent with Runyon, which we today decline to overrule. A more fundamental failing in the Solicitor's argument is that racial harassment amounting to breach of contract, like racial harassment alone, impairs neither the right to make nor the right to enforce a contract. It is plain that the former right is not implicated directly by an employer's breach in the performance of obligations under a contract already formed.

Nor is it correct to say that racial harassment amounting to a breach of contract impairs an employee's right to enforce his contract. To the contrary, conduct amounting to a breach of contract under state law is precisely what the language of § 1981 does not cover. That is because, in such a case, provided that plaintiff's access to state court or any other dispute resolution process has not been impaired by either the State or a private actor, see Goodman v. Lukens Steel Co., 482 U.S. 656 (1987), the plaintiff is free to enforce the terms of the contract in state court, and cannot possibly assert, by reason of the breach alone, that he has been deprived of the same right to enforce contracts as is enjoyed by white citizens.

In addition, interpreting § 1981 to cover racial harassment amounting to a breach of contract would federalize all state-law claims for breach of contract where racial animus is alleged, since § 1981 covers all types of contracts, not just employment contracts. Although we must do so when Congress plainly directs, as a rule we should be and are "reluctant to federalize" matters traditionally covered by state common law. Santa Fe Industries, Inc. v. Green, 430 U.S. 462, 479 (1977); see also Sedima, S. P. R. L. v. Imrex Co., 473 U.S. 479, 507 (1985) (Marshall, J., dissenting). By confining § 1981 to the impairment of the specific rights to make and enforce contracts, Congress cannot be said to have intended such a result with respect to breach of contract claims. It would be no small paradox, moreover, that under the interpretation of § 1981 offered by the Solicitor General, the more a State extends its own contract law to protect employees in general and minorities in particular, the greater would be the potential displacement of state law by § 1981. We do not think § 1981 need be read to produce such a peculiar result.

NOTES

(1) Is the court correct in assuming that racial harassment "amounts to a breach of contract under state law"? Is the employer's implicit covenant not to harass merely a default rule? Would contracting around this covenant violate public policy?

(2) How does one distinguish pre- and post-formation discrimination with regard to employment-at-will contracts?

Comment: Validity of a Contract Limiting Liability for Negligence

Should one be able to contract so as to gain immunity from suit for any future wrong committed? For example, suppose A and B agree that the latter may not sue for damages growing out of a future assault committed by A upon B. Obviously, such an agreement would be violative of public policy. However, would an agreement absolving A from damages for negligent injury to B also be illegal? In most cases, it would not. See Williston § 1749A; Corbin § 1472. For a discussion of recent precedent and statutory regulation, see Cava and Wiesner, *Rationalizing a Decade of Judicial Responses to Exculpatory Clauses*, 28 Santa Clara L. Rev. 611 (1988).*

There is widespread recognition of the ability of parties whose bargaining power is not substantially unequal to contract against liability for negligence. Such arrangements are usually regarded as realistic efforts to allocate perceived risks. Thus, the drafters of Restatement (Second) observe that "a party to a contract can ordinarily exempt himself from liability for harm caused by his failure to observe the standard of reasonable care imposed by the law of negligence." Restatement (Second) § 195, Comment a. But they stipulate major exceptions. Section 195 reads as follows:

(1) A term exempting a party from tort liability for harm caused intentionally or recklessly is unenforceable on grounds of public policy.

(2) A term exempting a party from tort liability for harm caused negligently is unenforceable on grounds of public policy if

(a) the term exempts an employer from liability to an employee for injury in the course of his employment;

(b) the term exempts one charged with a duty of public service from liability to one to whom that duty is owed for compensation for breach of that duty; or

(c) the other party is similarly a member of a class protected against the class to which the first party belongs.

(3) A term exempting a seller of a product from his special tort liability for physical harm to a user or consumer is unenforceable on grounds of public policy unless the term is fairly bargained for and is consistent with the policy underlying that liability.**

The courts' delineation of a "public service" exception is imprecise. What, for example, of an exculpatory clause in a contract for advertising in the "yellow pages"? See Annot., *Liability of Telephone Company for Mistakes in or Omissions from its Directory*, 47 A.L.R.4th 883 (1986). Compare Richard A. Berjian, D.O., Inc. v. Ohio Bell Telephone Company, 54 Ohio

---

* A related question concerns the validity of indemnification or "hold harmless" provisions, whereby one secures another's promise to indemnify one against one's own negligence. "An indemnity clause purports to shift responsibility for the payment of damages from one party to another. * * * As such, an indemnity clause allocates the risk of loss or injury resulting from a particular venture between the parties to the agreement. An exculpatory clause relieves one party from the consequences of its own negligence. * * * Such clause relieves one party from responsibility for injuries incurred by the other party from a particular transaction or occurrence." Whitson v. Goodbodys, Inc., 773 S.W.2d 381 (Tex.App.1989) (upheld exculpatory clause in plaintiff's agreement with health club).

** Several states have legislated against particular types of exculpatory clauses; e.g., Illinois (real property leases); New York (comprehensive statutory scheme affecting lessors of real property, caterers, construction contractors, building service or maintenance contractors, architects, engineers, surveyors, garages and parking places, pools, gymnasiums, and public amusement places). In addition, many states have enacted some form of anti-indemnification statute applicable to construction contracts. See Smith, *Combatting Adhesion Contracts: Where Does the Buck Stop?*, 9 Construction Lawyer § 3, p. 3 (1989).

St.2d 147, 375 N.E.2d 410 (1978) ("In the overwhelming majority of jurisdictions confronting the issue of whether the classified advertising service is a service within the scope of the duties owed by the telephone company to the public, courts have found such service to be a matter of private concern only, and, therefore, have held that telephone companies through use of exculpatory clauses in their service contracts can limit their liability for negligently failing to place a customer's order for advertising in the yellow pages." 375 N.E.2d at 415) with Morgan v. South Central Bell Telephone Co., 466 So.2d 107 (Ala.1985) ("We are satisfied that the plaintiffs did not have a meaningful choice relative to the inclusion of an exculpatory clause * * * and that the defendant had the bargaining power in a gross and unbalanced manner in determining the terms and conditions in the directory advertisement." 466 So.2d at 118).***

Moreover, it is clear that exculpatory agreements are not favorites of the law. "The law expresses this disfavor either by indulging in a presumption against the parties' intention to contract for immunity against the consequences of their own negligence by requiring that such a provision for immunity in a contract must be expressed in clear and unequivocal language to be valid and effective." Williston § 1749A. *Colgan* is an example of this heightened scrutiny. See also Scott & Fetzer Company v. Montgomery Ward & Company, 112 Ill.2d 378, 98 Ill.Dec. 1, 493 N.E.2d 1022 (1986) (Exculpatory clauses "are not favored * * * and are to be strictly construed against the party they benefit * * * especially when that party was also the draftsman * * *. Such clauses must spell out the intention of the parties with great particularity and will not be construed to defeat a claim which is not explicitly covered by their terms." 98 Ill.Dec. at 8–9, 493 N.E.2d at 1029–30).

Where the agreement is of an adhesion type between parties with disproportionate bargaining power, there may be a conceptual overlap of "illegality" and "unconscionability." See *Weaver v. American Oil Company,*

*** In making this determination, the Alabama court referred to criteria stated in an influential California decision, Tunkl v. Regents of the University of California, 60 Cal.2d 92, 32 Cal.Rptr. 33, 383 P.2d 441 (1963). In invalidating an exculpatory clause in a contract between a charitable research hospital and a patient, the court offered the following guidelines: "It concerns a business of the type generally thought suitable for public regulation. The party seeking exculpation is engaged in performing a service of great importance to the public, which is often a matter of practical necessity for some members of the public. The party holds himself out as willing to perform this service for any member of the public who seeks it, or at least for any member coming within certain established standards. As a result of the essential nature of the service, in the economic setting of the transaction, the party invoking exculpation possesses a decisive advantage of bargaining strength against any member of the public who seeks his services. In exercising a superior bargaining power the party confronts the public with a standardized adhesion contract of exculpation and makes no provision whereby a purchaser may pay additional reasonable fees and obtain protection against negligence. Finally, as a result of the transaction, the person or property of the purchaser is placed under the control of the seller, subject to risk of carelessness by the seller or his agents." 60 Cal.2d at 98–101, 32 Cal.Rptr. at 37–38, 383 P.2d at 445–446. For a recent application of the *Tunkl* criteria, see Wagenblast v. Odessa School District, 110 Wn.2d 845, 758 P.2d 968 (1988). For a critique of *Wagenblast,* see Recent Cases, 102 Harv.L.Rev. 729 (1989).

supra at 525, involving a gas station lease with a fine print clause requiring lessee (Weaver) to indemnify lessor (American Oil Company) if anyone was injured by the lessor's negligence and holding the latter harmless for injuries to lessee. An American Oil Company employee spilled gasoline on Weaver and one of his employees. Both were injured when the gasoline ignited. The court reasoned, by analogy to UCC 2–302, that this disparity in bargaining power, the lack of awareness of the fine print clause by the lessee, and the hardship it imposed upon him, rendered the clause unconscionable. The court noted: "We do not mean to say or infer that parties may not make contracts exculpating one of his negligence and providing for indemnification, but it must be done *knowingly* and *willingly* as in insurance contracts made for that very purpose." 276 N.E.2d at 148. See also Lloyd v. Service Corporation of Alabama, Inc., 453 So.2d 735 (Ala.1984) (use of UCC 2–302 to invalidate exculpatory clause in residential lease). Cf. LaFrenz v. Lake County Fair Board, 172 Ind.App. 389, 360 N.E.2d 605 (1977) (written release, whereby fair board relieved of any liability resulting from wife being with her husband in pit area during a demolition derby, upheld; *Weaver* distinguished).

Under Section 402A of Restatement (Second) of Torts, a manufacturer's or seller's attempt to disclaim or limit liability for damages to person or property caused by a dangerously defective product is against public policy. See Comment m. This policy is endorsed in Section 195(3) of Restatement (Second) for a "term exempting seller of a product from his special tort liability for physical harm to a user or consumer * * * unless the term is fairly bargained for and is consistent with the policy underlying that liability." Comment c states that the exception is for the "rare situation in which the term is consistent with the policy underlying the liability." Where a seller's breach of warranty causes economic loss rather than damage to person or property, "disclaimers" of warranty and limitations upon remedy are enforceable if not unconscionable. See UCC 2–302, 2–316(2) and 2–719(3). Put another way, there is no public policy against these risk allocation devices but, at the very least, they must be fairly bargained for. For a decision holding that these clauses were unconscionable in a commercial setting, see A & M Produce Co. v. FMC Corp., 135 Cal.App.3d 473, 186 Cal.Rptr. 114 (1982).

Data Management, Inc. v. Greene

Supreme Court of Alaska, 1988.
757 P.2d 62.

■ MATTHEWS, CHIEF JUSTICE.

FACTS

Data Management, Inc. employed James H. Greene and Richard Van Camp. The parties signed a contract containing a covenant not to compete.

The covenant provides that the employees will not compete with Data Management in Alaska for five years after termination.[1]

Shortly after the employees' termination from Data Management, the company filed suit against them for breach of the covenant not to compete. Data Management sought a preliminary injunction enjoining Greene and Van Camp from rendering computing services to twenty-one named individuals.[2] The preliminary injunction was granted.

Subsequently, the court granted summary judgment to Greene and Van Camp. The court found that the anti-competition covenant was not severable and was wholly unenforceable. Data Management appeals.

DISCUSSION

We have not yet decided whether an overly broad covenant not to compete can be altered to render it legal. A survey of other jurisdictions reveals three different approaches.

The first approach is to hold that a covenant which is overbroad, and hence unconscionable, will not be enforced. This strict view was adopted by Arkansas in Rector–Phillips–Morse, Inc. v. Vroman, 253 Ark. 750, 489 S.W.2d 1 (1973). In that case, the court held that a three year covenant not to compete was too long. The court rejected the employer's request to alter the covenant from three years to six months. The court held, "our rule is that when a restriction such as this one is too far-reaching to be valid, the court will not make a new contract for the parties by reducing the restriction to a shorter time or to a smaller area." Id. 489 S.W.2d 1 at 4. Georgia has also adopted this position. See, Rollins Protective Serv. Co. v. Palermo, 249 Ga. 138, 287 S.E.2d 546, 549 (1982).

We do not favor this approach. The parties' contract is a bargain. One of the elements of that bargain is the covenant not to compete. As a general rule, courts should respect the rights of parties to enter into contracts, and

---

1. The covenant not to compete stated:

Inasmuch as the Employee will acquire or have access to information which is of a highly confidential and secret nature, it is agreed that for the terms of this agreement and for a period of 5 years after the termination of this agreement, Eployee [sic] will not, within the State of Alaska, directly or indirectly, perform any similar services for any other person or firm located within the State of Alaska, without first obtaining the written consent and approval of the Employer, and that Employee will not own, manage, operate or control, be employed by, participate in, or be connected in any manner with the ownership, management, operation or control of any business similar to the type of business conducted by the Employer at the time of the termination of this contract or in competition with, directly or indi-

rectly, the business of the Employer. In the event of an actual or threatened breach by the Employee of the provisions of this paragraph, the Employer shall be entitled to an injunction restraining the Employee from owning, managing, operating, controling, [sic] being employed by, participating in, or being in any way so connected with any business similar to the type of business engaged in by the Employer. Nothing herein stated shall be construed as prohibiting the Employer from pursuing any other remedies available for such breach or threatened breach, including the recovery of damages from the Employee.

2. Data Management argues that this is a reasonable modification of the covenant not to compete, and that the trial court erred in not so modifying the covenant.

should not interfere with their contractual relationships. There is a need to strike a balance between protecting the rights of parties to enter into contracts, and the need to protect parties from illegal contracts. Obliterating all overbroad covenants not to compete, regardless of their factual settings, is too mechanistic and may produce unduly harsh results. In response to objections like these, a second approach was developed.

The second approach is to hold that if words in an overbroad covenant not to compete can be deleted in such a way as to render it enforceable then the court may do so. This is the so-called "blue pencil" rule. See Restatement of Contracts § 518 (1932). This position was adopted by Indiana in Licocci v. Cardinal Associates, Inc., 432 N.E.2d 446, 452 (Ind. App.1982), vacated on other grounds, 445 N.E.2d 556 (Ind.1983) where the court stated, "if the covenant is clearly separated into parts and some parts are reasonable and others are not, the contract may be held divisible. The reasonable restrictions may then be enforced." See also Capital Bakers v. Leahy, 20 Del.Ch. 407, 178 A. 648, 650 (1935); General Bronze Corp. v. Schmeling, 208 Wis. 565, 243 N.W. 469, 472 (1932).

This rule has been criticized as being too mechanical, in that it values the wording of the contract over its substance. For example, if a seller promised not to compete "anywhere in England," the whole provision would be void because the quoted clause cannot be narrowed by deleting any words. On the other hand, if the seller promised not to compete "in London or elsewhere in England," the covenant would be enforceable as to London because "elsewhere in England" could be "blue pencilled." The difference is merely semantic and we reject it.

The third approach, and the one we adopt, is to hold that if an overbroad covenant not to compete can be reasonably altered to render it enforceable, then the court shall do so unless it determines the covenant was not drafted in good faith. The burden of proving that the covenant was drafted in good faith is on the employer. This is the position taken in most United States jurisdictions[3] and by the Restatement (Second) of Contracts § 184(2) (1981).[4]

Ohio explained this approach in Raimonde v. Van Vlerah, 42 Ohio St.2d 21, 325 N.E.2d 544 (1975).

[M]any courts have abandoned the "blue pencil" test in favor of a rule of "reasonableness" which permits courts to determine, on the basis of all available evidence, what restrictions would be reasonable between the parties. Essentially, this test differs from the "blue pencil" test only in the

---

3. See Bess v. Bothman, 257 N.W.2d 791 (Minn.1977).

4. Restatement (Second) of Contracts § 184(2) (1981) states:

A court may treat only part of a term as unenforceable ... if the party who seeks to enforce the term obtained it in good faith and in accordance with reasonable standards of fair dealing.

The Restatement (Second) goes on to say, "this Section rejects the so-called 'blue pencil rule' of former § 518.... This rule is rejected because it is now contrary to the weight of authority and has been strongly criticized by scholarly writers." Id. at reporter's note (citations omitted).

manner of modification allowed. It permits courts to fashion a contract reasonable between the parties, in accord with their intention at the time of contracting, and enables them to evaluate all the factors comprising "reasonableness" in the context of employee covenants.

Among the factors properly to be considered are: "[t]he absence or presence of limitations as to time and space, * * * whether the employee represents the sole contact with the customer; whether the employee is possessed with confidential information or trade secrets; whether the covenant seeks to eliminate competition which would be unfair to the employer or merely seeks to eliminate ordinary competition; whether the covenant seeks to stifle the inherent skill and experience of the employee; whether the benefit to the employer is disproportional to the detriment to the employee; whether the covenant operates as a bar to the employee's sole means of support; whether the employee's talent which the employer seeks to suppress was actually developed during the period of employment; and whether the forbidden employment is merely incidental to the main employment."

Id. at 546–47 (citations and footnote omitted).

This approach is consistent with U.C.C. § 2–302, as codified in Alaska under AS 45.02.302, which states:

(a) If the court as a matter of law finds the contract or a clause of the contract unconscionable at the time it was made, the court may refuse to enforce the contract, enforce the remainder of the contract without the unconscionable clause, or so limit the application of an unconscionable clause as to avoid an unconscionable result.

(b) If it is claimed or appears to the court that the contract or any clause of the contract may be unconscionable, the parties shall be given a reasonable opportunity to present evidence as to its commercial setting, purpose, and effect to aid the court in making the determination.

One criticism of this position is that employers are encouraged to overreach; if the covenant they draft is overbroad then the court redrafts it for them. While we recognize that the problem of overreaching exists, we think it can be overcome by stressing the good faith element of the test. The trial court must determine whether an employer has overreached willfully and, if so, the court should refuse to alter the covenant.

Accordingly, we REMAND this case to the trial court so it can determine whether Data Management acted in good faith, and if so, whether the covenant not to compete can be reasonably altered.[5]

---

5. Because it found the overbroad covenant not to compete was unenforceable, the trial court denied Data Management's request for the liquidated damages provided for in the contract. If, on remand, the trial court finds it appropriate to alter the covenant not to compete to render it enforceable, it should also address the issue of liquidated damages.

NOTES

(1) *Covenant Not To Compete and the Concept of Partial Illegality.* A prolific source of "illegality" litigation has been the covenant not to compete, involving either the promise of a vendor of a business not to compete with the purchaser or the promise of an employee not to compete with his or her employer after termination of the employment. There are numerous decisions and a wealth of critical commentary treating various aspects of the matter. See generally, Farnsworth § 5.3; Calamari and Perillo §§ 16–19—16–22; Murray § 98.

In an opinion which must surely rank among the most exhaustive (and exhausting!) on record, the court began as follows:

"When the defendant, Clifford Witter, a dance instructor, waltzed out of the employment of the plaintiff, the Arthur Murray Dance Studios of Cleveland, Inc., into the employment of the Fred Astaire Dancing Studios, the plaintiff waltzed Witter into court. For brevity, the two studios are called 'Arthur Murray' and 'Fred Astaire.' At the time Witter took his contentious step, Arthur Murray had a string attached to him—a certain contract prohibiting Witter, after working for Arthur Murray no more, from working for a competitor. That Arthur Murray and Fred Astaire are rivals in dispensing Terpsichorean erudition is not disputed. Now Arthur Murray wants the court to pull that string and yank Witter out of Fred Astaire's pedagogical pavilion.

"No layman could realize the legal complication involved in Witter's uncomplicated act. That is not one of those questions on which the legal researcher cannot find enough to quench his thirst. To the contrary there is so much authority it drowns him. It is a sea—vast and vacillating, overlapping and bewildering. One can fish out of it any kind of strange support for anything, if he lives so long. This deep and unsettled sea pertaining to an employee's covenant not to compete with his employer after termination of employment is really Seven Seas; and now that the court has sailed them, perhaps it should record those seas so that the next weary traveler may be saved the terrifying time it takes just to find them." Arthur Murray Dance Studios of Cleveland v. Witter, 105 N.E.2d 685 (Ohio Com.Pl.1952).

In general, the courts focus upon two aspects of the covenant: (1) whether it protects some legitimate interest of the promisee; (2) whether it is reasonable in scope. Moreover, courts tend to be more favorably disposed to those covenants which are ancillary to the sale of a business than to those which restrict an employee's competitive activities. See Blake, *Employee Agreements Not to Compete*, 73 Harv. L.Rev. 625 (1960). For a criticism of this judicial inclination, see Callahan, *Post–Employment Restraint Agreements: A Reassessment*, 52 U.Chi.L.Rev. 703 (1985) (argument that treating employee covenants in an exceptional way, vis., presuming invalidity, may actually have an anti-competitive impact and work to employee's disadvantage).

A covenant ancillary to the sale of a business is usually seen as protective of the good will being sold. With respect to the employee covenant, where the party does not have a special or unique skill, the usual attempt is to protect by precluding the use of trade secrets, confidential information, customer lists and the like. For "[a]s a general rule, an employer is not entitled to protection from an employee's use of his knowledge, skill, or general information acquired or increased through experience or instruction while in the employment." Century Personnel, Inc. v. Brummett, 499 N.E.2d 1160, 1161 (Ind.App.1986). Compare Field v. Alexander & Alexander of Indiana, Inc., 503 N.E.2d 627 (Ind.App.1987) (uphold covenant not to compete by insurance salesman whereby latter obliged for a period of two years following termination to not solicit customers with whom employee had personal contact during previous two-year period) with American Shippers Supply Co. v. Campbell, 456 N.E.2d 1040 (Ind.App.1983) (employer did not have a protectible interest in customer lists which could have been easily obtained from a telephone book or trade publication).

The reasonableness criterion deals primarily with the area covered and the duration. And it is here that efforts are frequently made, as in the instant case, to convince a court that the excessive parts should be excised, leaving intact that which is reasonable both as to space and time. Efforts are thus made to sever or divide the legal portion from that which is illegal. The court here discusses three judicial responses. Which do you prefer? Why? For recent cases in accord with the Alaska decision, see Ellis v. James V. Hurson Associates, 565 A.2d 615 (D.C.App.1989); Durapin, Inc. v. American Products, Inc., 559 A.2d 1051 (R.I.1989). For examples of this mitigating technique in other contexts, see International Paper Company v. Corporex Constructors, Inc., 96 N.C.App. 312, 385 S.E.2d 553 (1989) (invalid indemnification clause severable from remainder of provision); Turnpike Motors, Inc. v. Newbury Group, Inc., 403 Mass. 291, 528 N.E.2d 1176 (1988) (unlicensed realtor able to recover agreed-upon commission for sale of personal property, even though not entitled to commission on sale of real estate); Lund v. Bruflat, 159 Wash. 89, 292 P. 112 (1930) (unlicensed plumber unable to recover for services rendered, but entitled to recover for materials furnished).

(2) *Mitigation of Strict Rule by Allowance of Restitution.* Courts recognize that rigorous application of the *in pari delicto* maxim may at times lead to results which are hardly consonant with sound public policy. Hence, the appearance of ameliorative doctrines, such as "partial illegality" discussed above, which permits enforcement of the legal portion. To quote Judge Cardozo, speaking of an unrelated matter but in a way which is apropos, courts are hesitant "to visit venial fault with oppressive retribution." *Jacob & Youngs v. Kent,* infra at 645. An effective method of avoiding application of the strict rule is to establish that the parties are not equally at fault; i.e., they are not in *pari delicto.* An illustration is Webb v. Fulchire, 25 N.C. (3 Ired.) 485 (1843), where the victim of a "shell game" successfully sued to recover his losses, the court observing: "Surely, the artless fool, who seems to have been alike bereft of his senses and his money, is not to be deemed a partaker in the same crime, in *pari delicto,* with the juggling knave, who gulled and fleeced him." One may be able to establish a lack of parity of blame by showing one's ignorance of the illegality, the other party's fraud or deception, or membership in a class the public policy is designed to protect. Finally, one may avoid strict application by withdrawing from the contract before its illegal purpose has been attained. This is known as the doctrine of *locus poenitentiae.* See, generally Dobbs § 13.5.

(3) *The Illegality Spectrum.* A thorough study of illegality in contracting could involve no less than a complete study of law and the sources from which it derives. As noted, a bargain is "illegal" if it contravenes "public policy." The term "public policy" is, of course, broad and comprehensive. In its ordinary signification, it encompasses, first of all, the declared law—constitutions, statutes, ordinances, regulations, judicial decisions, etc. But beyond this it includes conceptions and attitudes which order society itself and thereby shape its laws. Hence, in the present context public policy may be viewed as a framework or structure within which freedom of contract may be exercised. The following materials in this subsection, which pertain to still other aspects of the pervasive problem of "freedom and policy," oblige one to identify and evaluate certain basic policies which are largely presuppositional in character. These policies are among the basic premises, the fundamentals, of the legal and social systems. *Go for it!*

Watts v. Watts

Supreme Court of Wisconsin, 1987.
137 Wis.2d 506, 405 N.W.2d 303.

■ SHIRLEY S. ABRAHAMSON, JUSTICE.

This is an appeal from a judgment of the circuit court for Dane County, William D. Byrne, Judge, dismissing Sue Ann Watts' amended complaint, pursuant to sec. 802.06(2)(f), Stats.1985–86, for failure to state a claim upon which relief may be granted. This court took jurisdiction of the appeal upon certification by the court of appeals under sec. (Rule) 809.61, Stats. 1985–86. * * *

The case involves a dispute between Sue Ann Evans Watts, the plaintiff, and James Watts, the defendant, over their respective interests in property accumulated during their nonmarital cohabitation relationship which spanned 12 years and produced two children. The case presents an issue of first impression and comes to this court at the pleading stage of the case, before trial and before the facts have been determined.

The plaintiff asked the circuit court to order an accounting of the defendant's personal and business assets accumulated between June 1969 through December 1981 (the duration of the parties' cohabitation) and to determine plaintiff's share of this property. * * *

The circuit court dismissed the amended complaint, concluding that sec. 767.255, Stats. 1985–86, authorizing a court to divide property, does not apply to the division of property between unmarried persons. * * *

We agree with the circuit court that the legislature did not intend sec. 767.255 to apply to an unmarried couple. We disagree with the circuit court's implicit conclusion that courts cannot or should not, without express authorization from the legislature, divide property between persons who have engaged in nonmarital cohabitation. Courts traditionally have settled contract and property disputes between unmarried persons, some of whom have cohabited. Nonmarital cohabitation does not render every agreement between the cohabiting parties illegal and does not automatically preclude one of the parties from seeking judicial relief, such as statutory or common law partition, damages for breach of express or implied contract, constructive trust and quantum meruit where the party alleges, and later proves, facts supporting the legal theory. The issue for the court in each case is whether the complaining party has set forth any legally cognizable claim.

* * *

We test the sufficiency of the plaintiff's amended complaint by first setting forth the facts asserted in the complaint and then analyzing each of the five legal theories upon which the plaintiff rests her claim for relief.

I.

The plaintiff commenced this action in 1982. The plaintiff's amended complaint alleges the following facts, which for purposes of this appeal must be accepted as true. The plaintiff and the defendant met in 1967, when she was 19 years old, was living with her parents and was working full time as a nurse's aide in preparation for a nursing career. Shortly after the parties met, the defendant persuaded the plaintiff to move into an apartment paid for by him and to quit her job. According to the amended complaint, the defendant "indicated" to the plaintiff that he would provide for her.

Early in 1969, the parties began living together in a "marriage-like" relationship, holding themselves out to the public as husband and wife. The plaintiff assumed the defendant's surname as her own. Subsequently, she gave birth to two children who were also given the defendant's surname. The parties filed joint income tax returns and maintained joint bank accounts asserting that they were husband and wife. The defendant insured the plaintiff as his wife on his medical insurance policy. He also took out a life insurance policy on her as his wife, naming himself as the beneficiary. The parties purchased real and personal property as husband and wife. The plaintiff executed documents and obligated herself on promissory notes to lending institutions as the defendant's wife.

During their relationship, the plaintiff contributed childcare and home-making services, including cleaning, cooking, laundering, shopping, running errands, and maintaining the grounds surrounding the parties' home. Additionally, the plaintiff contributed personal property to the relationship which she owned at the beginning of the relationship or acquired through gifts or purchases during the relationship. She served as hostess for the defendant for social and business-related events. The amended complaint further asserts that periodically, between 1969 and 1975, the plaintiff cooked and cleaned for the defendant and his employees while his business, a landscaping service, was building and landscaping a golf course.

From 1973 to 1976, the plaintiff worked 20–25 hours per week at the defendant's office, performing duties as a receptionist, typist, and assistant bookkeeper. From 1976 to 1981, the plaintiff worked 40–60 hours per week at a business she started with the defendant's sister-in-law, then continued and managed the business herself after the dissolution of that partnership. The plaintiff further alleges that in 1981 defendant made their relationship so intolerable that she was forced to move from their home and their relationship was irretrievably broken. Subsequently, the defendant barred the plaintiff from returning to her business.

The plaintiff alleges that during the parties' relationship, and because of her domestic and business contributions, the business and personal wealth of the couple increased. Furthermore, the plaintiff alleges that she never received any compensation for these contributions to the relationship and that the defendant indicated to the plaintiff both orally and through his conduct that he considered her to be his wife and that she would share equally in the increased wealth.

The plaintiff asserts that since the breakdown of the relationship the defendant has refused to share equally with her the wealth accumulated through their joint efforts or to compensate her in any way for her contributions to the relationship.

[The court rejects plaintiff's contentions that (1) she is entitled to an equitable division of property under Wisconsin's Family Code and (2) defendant should be estopped from asserting lack of legal marriage.]

IV.

The plaintiff's third legal theory on which her claim rests is that she and the defendant had a contract to share equally the property accumulated during their relationship. The essence of the complaint is that the parties had a contract, either an express or implied in fact contract, which the defendant breached.

Wisconsin courts have long recognized the importance of freedom of contract and have endeavored to protect the right to contract. A contract will not be enforced, however, if it violates public policy. A declaration that the contract is against public policy should be made only after a careful balancing, in the light of all the circumstances, of the interest in enforcing a particular promise against the policy against enforcement. Courts should be reluctant to frustrate a party's reasonable expectations without a corresponding benefit to be gained in deterring "misconduct" or avoiding inappropriate use of the judicial system. . . .

The defendant appears to attack the plaintiff's contract theory on three grounds. First, the defendant apparently asserts that the court's recognition of plaintiff's contract claim for a share of the parties' property contravenes the Wisconsin Family Code. Second, the defendant asserts that the legislature, not the courts, should determine the property and contract rights of unmarried cohabiting parties. Third, the defendant intimates that the parties' relationship was immoral and illegal and that any recognition of a contract between the parties or plaintiff's claim for a share of the property accumulated during the cohabitation contravenes public policy.

The defendant rests his argument that judicial recognition of a contract between unmarried cohabitants for property division violates the

Wisconsin Family Code on Hewitt v. Hewitt, 77 Ill.2d 49, 31 Ill.Dec. 827, 394 N.E.2d 1204, 3 A.L.R.4th 1 (1979). In Hewitt the Illinois Supreme Court concluded that judicial recognition of mutual property rights between unmarried cohabitants would violate the policy of the Illinois Marriage and Dissolution Act because enhancing the attractiveness of a private arrangement contravenes the Act's policy of strengthening and preserving the integrity of marriage. The Illinois court concluded that allowing such a contract claim would weaken the sanctity of marriage, put in doubt the rights of inheritance, and open the door to false pretenses of marriage. Hewitt, 77 Ill.2d at 65, 31 Ill.Dec. at 834, 394 N.E.2d at 1211.

We agree with Professor Prince and other commentators that the *Hewitt* court made an unsupportable inferential leap when it found that cohabitation agreements run contrary to statutory policy and that the *Hewitt* court's approach is patently inconsistent with the principle that public policy limits are to be narrowly and exactly applied.[14]

Furthermore, the Illinois statutes upon which the Illinois supreme court rested its decision are distinguishable from the Wisconsin statutes. The Illinois supreme court relied on the fact that Illinois still retained "fault" divorce and that cohabitation was unlawful. By contrast, Wisconsin abolished "fault" in divorce in 1977 and abolished criminal sanctions for nonmarital cohabitation in 1983.[15]

The defendant has failed to persuade this court that enforcing an express or implied in fact contract between these parties would in fact violate the Wisconsin Family Code. The Family Code, chs. 765–768 Stats. 1985–86, is intended to promote the institution of marriage and the family. We find no indication, however, that the Wisconsin legislature intended the Family Code to restrict in any way a court's resolution of property or contract disputes between unmarried cohabitants.

The defendant also urges that if the court is not willing to say that the Family Code proscribes contracts between unmarried cohabiting parties, then the court should refuse to resolve the contract and property rights of unmarried cohabitants without legislative guidance. The defendant asserts that this court should conclude, as the *Hewitt* court did, that the task of determining the rights of cohabiting parties is too complex and difficult for the court and should be left to the legislature. We are not persuaded by the defendant's argument. Courts have traditionally developed principles of

---

14. Prince, *Public Policy Limitations in Cohabitation Agreements: Unruly Horse or Circus Pony,* 70 Minn.L.Rev. 163, 189–205 (1985).

15. Both Illinois and Wisconsin have abolished common law marriages. In our view this abolition does not invalidate a private cohabitation contract. Cohabitation agreements differ in effect from common law marriage. There is a significant difference between the consequences of achieving common law marriage status and of having an enforceable cohabitation agreement.

In Latham v. Latham, 274 Or. 421, 426–27, 547 P.2d 144, 147 (1976), the Oregon supreme court found that the Legislature's decriminalization of cohabitation represented strong evidence that enforcing agreements made by parties during cohabitation relationships would not be contrary to Oregon public policy.

contract and property law through the case-by-case method of the common law. While ultimately the legislature may resolve the problems raised by unmarried cohabiting parties, we are not persuaded that the court should refrain from resolving such disputes until the legislature gives us direction.[16] Our survey of the cases in other jurisdictions reveals that *Hewitt* is not widely followed.

We turn to the defendant's third point, namely, that any contract between the parties regarding property division contravenes public policy because the contract is based on immoral or illegal sexual activity. * * *

Courts have generally refused to enforce contracts for which the sole consideration is sexual relations, sometimes referred to as "meretricious" relationships. See In Matter of Estate of Steffes, 95 Wis.2d 490, 514, 290 N.W.2d 697 (1980), citing Restatement of Contracts Section 589 (1932). Courts distinguish, however, between contracts that are explicitly and inseparably founded on sexual services and those that are not. This court, and numerous other courts,[17] have concluded that "a bargain between two people is not illegal merely because there is an illicit relationship between the two so long as the bargain is independent of the illicit relationship and the illicit relationship does not constitute any part of the consideration bargained for and is not a condition of the bargain." Steffes, supra, 95 Wis.2d at 514, 290 N.W.2d 697.

While not condoning the illicit sexual relationship of the parties, many courts have recognized that the result of a court's refusal to enforce contract and property rights between unmarried cohabitants is that one party keeps all or most of the assets accumulated during the relationship, while the other party, no more or less "guilty," is deprived of property which he or she has helped to accumulate. See e.g., Glasgo v. Glasgo, 410 N.E.2d 1325, 1330 (Ind.App.1980); Latham v. Latham, 274 Or. 421, 426, 547 P.2d 144 (1976); Marvin v. Marvin, supra, 18 Cal.3d at 682, 134 Cal.Rptr. at 830, 557 P.2d at 121; West v. Knowles, 50 Wash.2d 311, 315–16, 311 P.2d 689 (1957).

* * *

Having reviewed the complaint and surveyed the law in this and other jurisdictions, we hold that the Family Code does not preclude an unmarried cohabitant from asserting contract and property claims against the other

---

16. We have previously acted in the absence of express legislative direction. See Estate of Fox, 178 Wis. 369, 190 N.W. 90 (1922), in which the court allowed relief under the doctrine of unjust enrichment to a woman who in good faith believed that she was married when she actually was not, discussed infra. See also Smith v. Smith, 255 Wis. 96, 38 N.W.2d 12 (1949), in which the court refused equitable property division to

one party to an illegal common law marriage, discussed infra; and *Steffes.*

17. See, e.g., Glasgo v. Glasgo, 410 N.E.2d 1325, 1331 (Ind.App.1980); Tyranski v. Piggins, 44 Mich.App. 570, 573–74, 205 N.W.2d 595, 598–99 (1973); Kozlowski v. Kozlowski, 80 N.J. 378, 387, 403 A.2d 902, 907 (1979); Latham v. Latham, 274 Or. 421, 426–27, 547 P.2d 144, 147 (1976); Marvin v.

party to the cohabitation. We further conclude that public policy does not necessarily preclude an unmarried cohabitant from asserting a contract claim against the other party to the cohabitation so long as the claim exists independently of the sexual relationship and is supported by separate consideration. Accordingly, we conclude that the plaintiff in this case has pleaded the facts necessary to state a claim for damages resulting from the defendant's breach of an express or an implied in fact contract to share with the plaintiff the property accumulated through the efforts of both parties during their relationship. Once again, we do not judge the merits of the plaintiff's claim; we merely hold that she be given her day in court to prove her claim.

V.

The plaintiff's fourth theory of recovery involves unjust enrichment. Essentially, she alleges that the defendant accepted and retained the benefit of services she provided knowing that she expected to share equally in the wealth accumulated during their relationship. She argues that it is unfair for the defendant to retain all the assets they accumulated under these circumstances and that a constructive trust should be imposed on the property as a result of the defendant's unjust enrichment. In his brief, the defendant does not attack specifically either the legal theory or the factual allegations made by the plaintiff.

Unlike claims for breach of an express or implied in fact contract, a claim of unjust enrichment does not arise out of an agreement entered into by the parties. Rather, an action for recovery based upon unjust enrichment is grounded on the moral principle that one who has received a benefit has a duty to make restitution where retaining such a benefit would be unjust. Puttkammer v. Minth, 83 Wis.2d 686, 689, 266 N.W.2d 361, 363 (1978).

Because no express or implied in fact agreement exists between the parties, recovery based upon unjust enrichment is sometimes referred to as "quasi contract," or contract "implied in law" rather than "implied in fact." Quasi contracts are obligations created by law to prevent injustice. Shulse v. City of Mayville, 223 Wis. 624, 632, 271 N.W. 643 (1937).[20]

In Wisconsin, an action for unjust enrichment, or quasi contract, is based upon proof of three elements: (1) a benefit conferred on the defendant by the plaintiff, (2) appreciation or knowledge by the defendant of the benefit, and (3) acceptance or retention of the benefit by the defendant under circumstances making it inequitable for the defendant to retain the benefit. Puttkammer, supra, 83 Wis.2d at 689, 266 N.W.2d 361; Wis.J.I.Civil No. 3028 (1981).

The plaintiff has cited no cases directly supporting actions in unjust enrichment by unmarried cohabitants, and the defendant provides no authority against it. * * *

Marvin, 18 Cal.3d 660, 670–71, 134 Cal.Rptr. 815, 822, 557 P.2d 106, 113 (1976).

20. For a discussion regarding the relationship between express, implied-in-fact, and implied-in-law contracts, see *Steffes,* supra, 95 Wis.2d at 497 & n. 4, 290 N.W.2d 697.

As we have discussed previously, allowing no relief at all to one party in a so-called "illicit" relationship effectively provides total relief to the other, by leaving that party owner of all the assets acquired through the efforts of both. Yet it cannot seriously be argued that the party retaining all the assets is less "guilty" than the other. Such a result is contrary to the principles of equity. Many courts have held, and we now so hold, that unmarried cohabitants may raise claims based upon unjust enrichment following the termination of their relationships where one of the parties attempts to retain an unreasonable amount of the property acquired through the efforts of both.[21]

In this case, the plaintiff alleges that she contributed both property and services to the parties' relationship. She claims that because of these contributions the parties' assets increased, but that she was never compensated for her contributions. She further alleges that the defendant, knowing that the plaintiff expected to share in the property accumulated, "accepted the services rendered to him by the plaintiff" and that it would be unfair under the circumstances to allow him to retain everything while she receives nothing. We conclude that the facts alleged are sufficient to state a claim for recovery based upon unjust enrichment.

As part of the plaintiff's unjust enrichment claim, she has asked that a constructive trust be imposed on the assets that the defendant acquired during their relationship. A constructive trust is an equitable device created by law to prevent unjust enrichment. Wilharms v. Wilharms, 93 Wis.2d 671, 678, 287 N.W.2d 779, 783 (1980). To state a claim on the theory of constructive trust the complaint must state facts sufficient to show (1) unjust enrichment and (2) abuse of a confidential relationship or some other form of unconscionable conduct. The latter element can be inferred from allegations in the complaint which show, for example, a family relationship, a close personal relationship, or the parties' mutual trust. These facts are alleged in this complaint or may be inferred. Gorski v. Gorski, 82 Wis.2d 248, 254–55, 262 N.W.2d 120 (1978). Therefore, we hold that if the plaintiff can prove the elements of unjust enrichment to the satisfaction of the circuit court, she will be entitled to demonstrate further that a constructive trust should be imposed as a remedy.

NOTES

Hewitt v. Hewitt: The Other Side. The Wisconsin court is highly critical of *Hewitt v. Hewitt,* an opinion of the Illinois Supreme Court which espouses the traditional view respecting the enforcement of cohabitation agreements. The following is from that opinion:

21. See, e.g., Harman v. Rogers, 147 Vt. 11, 510 A.2d 161, 164–65 (1986); Collins v. Davis, 68 N.C.App. 588, 315 S.E.2d 759, 761–62 (1984), aff'd, 312 N.C. 324, 321 S.E.2d 892; Mason v. Rostad, 476 A.2d 662 (D.C. 1984); Coney v. Coney, 207 N.J.Super. 63, 503 A.2d 912, 918 (1985); In re Estate of Eriksen, 337 N.W.2d 671 (Minn.1983).

The issue of whether property rights accrue to unmarried cohabitants can not, however, be regarded realistically as merely a problem in the law of express contracts.

* * *

* * * There are major public policy questions involved in determining whether, under what circumstances, and to what extent it is desirable to accord some type of legal status to claims arising from such relationships. Of substantially greater importance than the rights of the immediate parties is the impact of such recognition upon our society and the institution of marriage. Will the fact that legal rights closely resembling those arising from conventional marriages can be acquired by those who deliberately choose to enter into what have heretofore been commonly referred to as "illicit" or "meretricious" relationships encourage formation of such relationships and weaken marriage as the foundation of our family-based society? In the event of death shall the survivor have the status of a surviving spouse for purposes of inheritance, wrongful death actions, workmen's compensation, etc.? And still more importantly: what of the children born of such relationships? What are their support and inheritance rights and by what standards are custody questions resolved? What of the sociological and psychological effects upon them of that type of environment? Does not the recognition of legally enforceable property and custody rights emanating from nonmarital cohabitation in practical effect equate with the legalization of common law marriage—at least in the circumstances of this case? And, in summary, have the increasing numbers of unmarried cohabitants and changing mores of our society (Bruch, *Property Rights of De Facto Spouses Including Thoughts on the Value of Homemakers' Services,* 10 Fam.L.Q. 101, 102–03 (1976); Nielson, *In re Cary: A Judicial Recognition of Illicit Cohabitation,* 25 Hastings L.J. 1226 (1974)) reached the point at which the general welfare of the citizens of this State is best served by a return to something resembling the judicially created common law marriage our legislature outlawed in 1905?

* * *

The real thrust of plaintiff's argument here is that we should abandon the rule of illegality because of certain changes in societal norms and attitudes. It is urged that social mores have changed radically in recent years, rendering this principle of law archaic. It is said that because there are so many unmarried cohabitants today the courts must confer a legal status on such relationships. This, of course, is the rationale underlying some of the decisions and commentaries. (See, e.g., Marvin v. Marvin (1976), 18 Cal.3d 660, 683, 134 Cal.Rptr. 815, 831, 557 P.2d 106, 122; Beal v. Beal (1978), 282 Or. 115, 577 P.2d 507; Kay & Amyx, *Marvin v. Marvin: Preserving the Options,* 65 Cal.L.Rev. 937 (1977).) If this is to be the result, however, it would seem more candid to acknowledge the return of varying forms of common law marriage than to continue displaying the naivete we believe involved in the assertion that there are involved in these relationships contracts separate and independent from the sexual activity, and the assumption that those contracts would have been entered into or would continue without that activity.

Even if we were to assume some modification of the rule of illegality is appropriate, we return to the fundamental question earlier alluded to: If resolution of this issue rests ultimately on grounds of public policy, by what body should that policy be determined? *Marvin*, viewing the issue as governed solely by contract law, found judicial policy-making appropriate. Its decision was facilitated by California precedent and that State's no-fault divorce law. In our view, however, the situation alleged here was not the kind of arm's length bargain envisioned by traditional contract principles, but an intimate arrangement of a fundamentally different kind. The issue, realistically, is whether it is appropriate for this court to grant a legal status to a private arrangement substituting for the institution of marriage sanctioned by the State. The question whether change is needed in the law governing the rights of parties in this delicate area of marriage-like relationships involves evaluations of sociological data and alternatives we believe best suited to the superior investigative and fact-finding facilities of the legislative branch in the exercise of its traditional authority to declare public policy in the domestic relations field.

Hewitt v. Hewitt, 77 Ill.2d 49, 31 Ill.Dec. 827, 830–832, 394 N.E.2d 1204, 1207–1209 (1979). For a comparative law perspective, see M. Glendon, The Transformation of Family Law (1989); Stenger, *Cohabitants and Constructive Trusts—Comparative Approaches*, 27 J.Fam.Law 373 (1988–89).

Comment: Baby M—Are There Some Things Money Can't Buy?

In March of 1984, Mary Beth Whitehead responded to an advertisement in the Asbury Park Press asking for women willing to help infertile couples bear children. She was sent an "application," which she completed and returned. Being told that she had been "accepted," she was directed to the Manhattan law office of Noel Keane, a specialist in surrogate parenting law. He explained to Mrs. Whitehead that for each deal arranged he received $10,000, and the mother received $10,000, but only if she gave birth to, and surrendered, a healthy baby. If the baby was deformed, retarded, or damaged in any way, the couple could call the deal off, keep most of the $10,000, and return the baby to her.[1]

On February 6, 1985, Mrs. Whitehead entered into a written surrogacy contract with William Stern. The contract provided that through artificial insemination using Mr. Stern's sperm, Mrs. Whitehead would become pregnant, carry the child to term, bear it, deliver it to Mr. Stern and his wife, and thereafter do whatever was necessary to terminate her maternal rights so that Mrs. Stern could adopt the child. Mrs. Whitehead's husband, Richard, was also a party to the contract; Mrs. Stern was not. Mr. Stern agreed to pay Mrs. Whitehead $10,000 for her services, and in a separate contract, agreed to pay the Infertility Center of New York the sum of $7,000. Mrs. Whitehead agreed that she would "not abort the child once conceived except, if in the professional medical opinion of the inseminating physician, such action is necessary for the physical health of Mary Beth Whitehead or the child has been determined by said physician to be physically abnormal," and Mrs. Whitehead further agreed that "upon the request of said physician to undergo amniocentesis . . . or similar tests to

---

1. According to Mrs. Whitehead, Noel Keane claimed he had arranged three hundred births in the year Mrs. Whitehead was pregnant with Baby M. The facts in this paragraph are taken from Mary Beth White-head's account. See M. Whitehead, A Mother's Story (1989). The remaining facts are taken from the opinion of the Supreme Court of New Jersey, 109 N.J. 396, 537 A.2d 1227 (1988).

detect genetic and congenital defects." If such defects were detected, Mrs. Whitehead agreed to abort the fetus upon demand of Mr. Stern. 109 N.J. 396, 473, 537 A.2d 1227, 1268.

After several artificial inseminations over a period of months, Mrs. Whitehead finally became pregnant. On March 27, 1986, she gave birth to a baby girl whom she named Sara Elizabeth. Mrs. Whitehead realized almost at once that she could not part with the child. But she did surrender the baby to the Sterns on March 30 at the Whitehead home. The Sterns, who were childless and who feared that pregnancy was a health risk for Mrs. Stern, were overjoyed. They took the baby, whom they renamed Melissa, to their home.

There then followed a series of bitter conflicts and confrontations, culminating in a trial before Judge Sorkow of the Superior Court of New Jersey. See Matter of Baby M, 217 N.J.Super. 313, 525 A.2d 1128 (1987). After a thirty-two day trial over a period of two months, the court upheld the surrogate contract, ordering that Mrs. Whitehead's parental rights be terminated and that sole custody of the child be granted to Mr. Stern, and, after hearing brief testimony from Mrs. Stern, immediately entered an order allowing the adoption of Melissa by Mrs. Stern, all in accordance with the surrogacy contract. On appeal, the Supreme Court of New Jersey affirmed in part and reversed in part, remanding for further proceedings. It invalidated the contract and refused to terminate Mrs. Whitehead's parental rights. But it agreed that custody should be awarded to Mr. Stern, with visitation rights to Mrs. Whitehead. Matter of Baby M, 109 N.J. 396, 537 A.2d 1227 (1988).

In voiding the contract, Chief Justice Willentz, speaking for the court, stated emphatically: "This is the sale of a child, or at the very least, the sale of a mother's right to her child, the only mitigating factor being that one of the purchasers is the father. Almost every evil that prompted the prohibition on the payment of money in connection with adoptions exist here." 109 N.J. at 438, 537 A.2d at 1248.

Responding to the argument that Mrs. Whitehead had agreed to the surrogacy arrangement, supposedly fully understanding the consequences, the court noted:

> Putting aside the issue of how compelling her need for money may have been, and how significant her understanding of the consequences, we suggest that her consent is irrelevant. There are, in a civilized society, some things that money cannot buy. In America, we decided long ago that merely because conduct purchased by money was "voluntary" did not mean it was good or beyond regulation or prohibition. * * * There are in short, values that society deems more important than granting to wealth whatever it can buy, be it labor, love, or life. 109 N.J. at 440, 537 A.2d at 1249.

The court then alluded to potential long-term effects of surrogacy:

> The long-term effect of surrogacy contracts are not known, but feared—the impact on the child who learns her life was bought, that she is the offspring of someone who gave birth to her only to obtain money; the impact on the natural mother as the full weight of her

isolation is felt along with the full reality of the sale of her body and her child; the impact on the natural father and the adoptive mother once they realize the consequences of their conduct. 109 N.J. at 441, 537 A.2d at 1250.

The court concluded this analysis as follows:

The surrogate contract is based on principles that are directly contrary to the objective of our laws. It guarantees the separation of a child from its mother; it looks to adoption regardless of suitability; it totally ignores the child; it takes the child from the mother regardless of her wishes and maternal fitness; and it does all of this, it accomplishes all of its goals, through the use of money.

Beyond that is the potential degradation of some women that may result from this arrangement. In many cases, of course, surrogacy may bring satisfaction, not only to the infertile couple, but to the surrogate mother herself. The fact, however, that many women may not perceive surrogacy negatively but rather see it as an opportunity does not diminish its potential for devastation to other women.

In sum, the harmful consequences of the surrogacy arrangement appear to us all too palpable. In New Jersey the surrogate mother's agreement to sell her child is void. Its irrevocability infects the entire contract, as does the money that purports to buy it. 109 N.S. at 441–444, 537 A.2d at 1250.

The Baby M case has generated an enormous amount of commentary. For a sampling of competing views, see *Colloquy: In Re Baby M,* 76 Geo.L.J. 1717–1844 (1988). See also Annot., *Validity and Construction of Surrogate Parenting Agreement,* 77 A.L.R. 4th 70 (1990).

PROBLEM: THE CASE OF DONNIS AND BENJAMIN'S COHABITATION AGREEMENT

At the time Donnis G. Whorton and Benjamin F. Dillingham, III, began dating and entered into a homosexual relationship, Donnis was a college student pursuing a Bachelor of Arts degree. When they began living together, they orally agreed that Whorton's full-time occupation was to be Dillingham's chauffeur, bodyguard, social and business secretary, and partner and counselor in real estate investments. Additionally, Whorton was to be Dillingham's constant companion, confidant, traveling and social companion, and lover. In return, Dillingham agreed to financially support Whorton for life, and to open bank accounts, grant Whorton invasionary powers to savings accounts held in Dillingham's name, and permit Whorton to charge on Dillingham's personal accounts. Dillingham was also to engage in a homosexual relationship with Whorton. (They specifically agreed that if any portion of the agreement was found to be legally unenforceable, it was severable and the balance of the provisions were to remain in full force and effect.).

Whorton allegedly complied with all of the terms of the agreement for seven years, at which point Dillingham barred him from his premises. Dillingham refuses to perform his part of the contract, and Whorton sues. What result? See Whorton v. Dillingham, 202 Cal.App.3d 447, 248 Cal.Rptr. 405 (1988).

CHAPTER FIVE

PERFORMANCE OF THE CONTRACT

SECTION 1. DETERMINING THE SCOPE AND CONTENT OF OBLIGATION

There is no general requirement that an agreement or promise be in writing to be enforceable as a contract. As we have seen, the Statute of Frauds imposes that requirement in particular cases, and the parties may, if they desire, condition liability upon the reducing of their agreement to a complete writing. Similarly, statutes occasionally give legal effect to written promises which comply with a stated form. See UCC 2–205 [UCC 2–204 (1997)]. On the whole, however, the modern trend is toward informality in the formation of contracts. Indeed, UCC 1–201(3) defines agreement as the "bargain of the parties in fact as found in their language or by implication from other circumstances including course of dealing or usage of trade or course of performance * * *."

Nevertheless, many contracts are written in whole or in part. These written agreements may be the product of intensive and thorough bargaining between equal parties assisted by counsel or a standard form drafted exclusively by one party and offered to the other on a take-it-or-leave-it basis. They may contain all of the agreed terms or just part. They may be clear or ambiguous. Or, they may be the product of amateurs operating with little experience and without the advice of counsel. In short, the only sure thing is that the problems will be varied and the disputes plentiful.

In this section we are not primarily concerned with whether a contract has been formed, whether there has been a misunderstanding *à la Peerless*, or whether the parties have made a mistake in reducing their oral agreement to writing. Assuming that there is some written expression of the agreement, the basic questions are whether one party may prove prior or contemporaneously agreed terms or conditions which alter or add to the writing and how a court determines the meaning of language in dispute which is admittedly part of the bargain. The first issue involves the "parol evidence rule" which determines the provability of a prior or contemporaneous oral agreement when the parties have assented to a written agreement. The second issue involves "interpretation," the ascertainment of the meaning to be given contract language. ("Interpretation of a promise or agreement or a term thereof is the ascertainment of its meaning." Restatement (Second) § 200.) As the selected materials will indicate, there is often a confusing overlap of these issues. Collateral reading: Farnsworth §§ 7.2–7.6 (parol evidence rule), 7.7–7.14 (interpretation); Murray §§ 82–85 (parol evidence rule), 87–90 (interpretation); Calamari and Perillo §§ 3–2—3–8 (parol evidence rule), 3–9—3–18 (interpretation).

(A) INTEGRATED WRITINGS AND THE PAROL EVIDENCE RULE

Mitchill v. Lath

Court of Appeals of New York, 1928.
247 N.Y. 377, 160 N.E. 646.

■ ANDREWS, J. In the fall of 1923 the Laths owned a farm. This they wished to sell. Across the road, on land belonging to Lieutenant–Governor Lunn, they had an ice house which they might remove. Mrs. Mitchill looked over the land with a view to its purchase. She found the ice house objectionable. Thereupon "the defendants orally promised and agreed, for and in consideration of the purchase of their farm by the plaintiff, to remove the said ice house in the spring of 1924." Relying upon this promise, she made a written contract to buy the property for $8,400, for cash and a mortgage and containing various provisions usual in such papers. Later receiving a deed, she entered into possession and has spent considerable sums in improving the property for use as a summer residence. The defendants have not fulfilled their promise as to the ice house and do not intend to do so. We are not dealing, however, with their moral delinquencies. The question before us is whether their oral agreement may be enforced in a court of equity.

This requires a discussion of the parol evidence rule—a rule of law which defines the limits of the contract to be construed. (Glackin v. Bennett, 226 Mass. 316.) It is more than a rule of evidence, and oral testimony, even if admitted, will not control the written contract (O'Malley v. Grady, 222 Mass. 202), unless admitted without objection. (Brady v. Nally, 151 N.Y. 258.) It applies, however, to attempts to modify such a contract by parol. It does not affect a parol collateral contract distinct from and independent of the written agreement. It is, at times, troublesome to draw the line. Williston, in his work on Contracts (sec. 637) points out the difficulty. "Two entirely distinct contracts," he says, "each for a separate consideration may be made at the same time and will be distinct legally. Where, however, one agreement is entered into wholly or partly in consideration of the simultaneous agreement to enter into another, the transactions are necessarily bound together. * * * Then if one of the agreements is oral and the other is written, the problem arises whether the bond is sufficiently close to prevent proof of the oral agreement." That is the situation here. It is claimed that the defendants are called upon to do more than is required by their written contract in connection with the sale as to which it deals.

The principle may be clear, but it can be given effect by no mechanical rule. As so often happens, it is a matter of degree, for, as Professor Williston also says, where a contract contains several promises on each side it is not difficult to put any one of them in the form of a collateral agreement. If this were enough, written contracts might always be modified by parol. Not form, but substance, is the test.

In applying this test the policy of our courts is to be considered. We have believed that the purpose behind the rule was a wise one not easily to be abandoned. Notwithstanding injustice here and there, on the whole it works for good. Old precedents and principles are not to be lightly cast aside unless it is certain that they are an obstruction under present conditions. New York has been less open to arguments that would modify this particular rule, than some jurisdictions elsewhere. Thus in Eighmie v. Taylor (98 N.Y. 288) it was held that a parol warranty might not be shown although no warranties were contained in the writing.

Under our decisions before such an oral agreement as the present is received to vary the written contract at least three conditions must exist, (1) the agreement must in form be a collateral one; (2) it must not contradict express or implied provisions of the written contract; (3) it must be one that parties would not ordinarily be expected to embody in the writing; or put in another way, an inspection of the written contract, read in the light of surrounding circumstances must not indicate that the writing appears "to contain the engagements of the parties, and to define the object and measure the extent of such engagement." Or again, it must not be so clearly connected with the principal transaction as to be part and parcel of it.

The respondent does not satisfy the third of these requirements. It may be, not the second. We have a written contract for the purchase and sale of land. The buyer is to pay $8,400 in the way described. She is also to pay her portion of any rents, interest on mortgages, insurance premiums and water meter charges. She may have a survey made of the premises. On their part the sellers are to give a full covenant deed of the premises as described, or as they may be described by the surveyor if the survey is had, executed and acknowledged at their own expense; they sell the personal property on the farm and represent they own it; they agree that all amounts paid them on the contract and the expense of examining the title shall be a lien on the property; they assume the risk of loss or damage by fire until the deed is delivered; and they agree to pay the broker his commissions. Are they to do more? Or is such a claim inconsistent with these precise provisions? It could not be shown that the plaintiff was to pay $500 additional. Is it also implied that the defendants are not to do anything unexpressed in the writing?

That we need not decide. At least, however, an inspection of this contract shows a full and complete agreement, setting forth in detail the obligations of each party. On reading it, one would conclude that the reciprocal obligations of the parties were fully detailed. Nor would his opinion alter if he knew the surrounding circumstances. The presence of the ice house, even the knowledge that Mrs. Mitchill thought it objectionable, would not lead to the belief that a separate agreement existed with regard to it. Were such an agreement made it would seem most natural that the inquirer should find it in the contract. Collateral in form it is found to be, but it is closely related to the subject dealt with in the written agreement—so closely that we hold it may not be proved.

Where the line between the competent and the incompetent is narrow the citation of authorities is of slight use. Each represents the judgment of the court on the precise facts before it. How closely bound to the contract is the supposed collateral agreement is the decisive factor in each case. * * *

We do not ignore the fact that authorities may be found that would seem to support the contention of the appellant. Such are Erskine v. Adeane (L.R. 8 Ch.App. 756) and Morgan v. Griffith (L.R. 6 Exch. 70), where although there was a written lease a collateral agreement of the landlord to reduce the game was admitted. In this State *Wilson v. Deen* might lead to the contrary result. Neither are they approved in New Jersey (Naumberg v. Young, 15 Vroom, 331). Nor in view of later cases in this court can Batterman v. Pierce (3 Hill, 171) be considered an authority. A line of cases in Massachusetts, of which Durkin v. Cobleigh (156 Mass. 108) is an example, have to do with collateral contracts made before a deed is given. But the fixed form of a deed makes it inappropriate to insert collateral agreements, however closely connected with the sale. This may be cause for an exception. Here we deal with the contract on the basis of which the deed to Mrs. Mitchill was given subsequently, and we confine ourselves to the question whether its terms may be modified.

* * *

Our conclusion is that the judgment of the Appellate Division and that of the Special Term should be reversed and the complaint dismissed, with costs in all courts.

■ LEHMAN, J. (dissenting). I accept the general rule as formulated by Judge ANDREWS. I differ with him only as to its application to the facts shown in the record. * * *

Judge Andrews has formulated a standard to measure the closeness of the bond. Three conditions, at least, must exist before an oral agreement may be proven to increase the obligation imposed by the written agreement. I think we agree that the first condition that the agreement "must in form be a collateral one" is met by the evidence. I concede that this condition is met in most cases where the courts have nevertheless excluded evidence of the collateral oral agreement. The difficulty here, as in most cases, arises in connection with the two other conditions.

The second condition is that the "parol agreement must not contradict express or implied provisions of the written contract." Judge Andrews voices doubt whether this condition is satisfied. The written contract has been carried out. The purchase price has been paid; conveyance has been made; title has passed in accordance with the terms of the written contract. The mutual obligations expressed in the written contract are left unchanged by the alleged oral contract. When performance was required of the written contract, the obligations of the parties were measured solely by its terms. By the oral agreement the plaintiff seeks to hold the defendants to other obligations to be performed by them thereafter upon land which was not conveyed to the plaintiff. The assertion of such further obligation is not inconsistent with the written contract unless the written contract contains a provision, express or implied, that the defendants are not to do anything not expressed in the writing. Concededly there is no such express provision in the contract, and such a provision may be implied, if at all, only if the asserted additional obligation is "so clearly connected with the principal transaction as to be part and parcel of it," and is not "one that the parties would not ordinarily be expected to embody in the writing." The hypothesis so formulated for a conclusion that the asserted additional obligation is inconsistent with an implied term of the contract is that the alleged oral agreement does not comply with the third condition as formulated by Judge Andrews. In this case, therefore, the problem reduces itself to the one question whether or not the oral agreement meets the third condition.

I have conceded that upon inspection the contract is complete. "It appears to contain the engagements of the parties, and to define the object and measure the extent of such engagement;" it constitutes the contract between them and is presumed to contain the whole of that contract. (Eighmie v. Taylor, 98 N.Y. 288.) That engagement was on the one side to convey land; on the other to pay the price. The plaintiff asserts further agreement based on the same consideration to be performed by the defendants after the conveyance was complete, and directly affecting only other land. It is true, as Judge Andrews points out, that "the presence of the ice house, even the knowledge that Mrs. Mitchill thought it objectionable, would not lead to the belief that a separate agreement existed with regard to it;" but the question we must decide is whether or not, *assuming* an agreement was made for the removal of an unsightly ice house from one parcel of land as an inducement for the purchase of another parcel, the parties would ordinarily or naturally be expected to embody the agreement for the removal of the ice house from one parcel in the written agreement to convey the other parcel. Exclusion of proof of the oral agreement on the ground that it varies the contract embodied in the writing may be based only upon a finding or presumption that the written contract was intended to cover the oral negotiations for the removal of the ice house which lead up to the contract of purchase and sale. To determine what the writing was intended to cover "the document alone will not suffice. What it was intended to cover cannot be known till we know what there was to cover. The question being whether certain subjects of negotiation were intended to be covered, we must compare the writing and the negotiations before we can determine whether they were in fact covered." (Wigmore on Evidence [2d ed.], section 2430.)

The subject-matter of the written contract was the conveyance of land. The contract was so complete on its face that the conclusion is inevitable that the parties intended to embody in the writing all the negotiations covering at least the conveyance. The promise by the defendants to remove the ice house from other land was not connected with their obligation to convey, except that one agreement would not have been made unless the other was also made. The plaintiff's assertion of a parol agreement by the defendants to remove the ice house was completely established by the great weight of evidence. It must prevail unless that agreement was part of the agreement to convey and the entire agreement was embodied in the writing.

* * *

The rule of integration undoubtedly frequently prevents the assertion of fraudulent claims. Parties who take the precaution of embodying their oral agreements in a writing should be protected against the assertion that other terms of the same agreement were not integrated in the writing. The limits of the integration are determined by the writing, read in the light of the surrounding circumstances. A written contract, however complete, yet covers only a limited field. I do not think that in the written contract for the conveyance of land here under consideration we can find an intention to cover a field so broad as to include prior agreements, if any such were made, to do other acts on other property after the stipulated conveyance was made.

In each case where such a problem is presented, varying factors enter into its solution. Citation of authority in this or other jurisdictions is useless, at least without minute analysis of the facts. The analysis I have made of the decisions in this State leads me to the view that the decision of the courts below is in accordance with our own authorities and should be affirmed.

■ CARDOZO, CH. J., POUND, KELLOGG and O'BRIEN, JJ., concur with ANDREWS, J.; LEHMAN, J., dissents in opinion in which CRANE, J., concurs.

Judgment accordingly.

Masterson v. Sine

Supreme Court of California, 1968.
68 Cal.2d 222, 65 Cal.Rptr. 545, 436 P.2d 561.

■ TRAYNOR, CHIEF JUSTICE. Dallas Masterson and his wife Rebecca owned a ranch as tenants in common. On February 25, 1958, they conveyed it to Medora and Lu Sine by a grant deed "Reserving unto the Grantors herein an option to purchase the above described property on or before February 25, 1968" for the "same consideration as being paid heretofore plus their depreciation value of any improvements Grantees may add to the property from and after two and a half years from this date." Medora is Dallas' sister and Lu's wife. Since the conveyance Dallas has been adjudged bankrupt. His trustee in bankruptcy and Rebecca brought this declaratory relief action to establish their right to enforce the option.

The case was tried without a jury. Over defendants' objection the trial court admitted extrinsic evidence that by "the same consideration as being paid heretofore" both the grantors and the grantees meant the sum of $50,000 and by "depreciation value of any improvements" they meant the depreciation value of improvements to be computed by deducting from the total amount of any capital expenditures made by defendants grantees the amount of depreciation allowable to them under United States income tax regulations as of the time of the exercise of the option.

The court also determined that the parol evidence rule precluded admission of extrinsic evidence offered by defendants to show that the parties wanted the property kept in the Masterson family and that the option was therefore personal to the grantors and could not be exercised by the trustee in bankruptcy.

The court entered judgment for plaintiffs, declaring their right to exercise the option, specifying in some detail how it could be exercised, and reserving jurisdiction to supervise the manner of its exercise and to determine the amount that plaintiffs will be required to pay defendants for their capital expenditures if plaintiffs decide to exercise the option.

Defendants appeal. They contend that the option provision is too uncertain to be enforced and that extrinsic evidence as to its meaning should not have been admitted. The trial court properly refused to frustrate the obviously declared intention of the grantors to reserve an option to repurchase by an overly meticulous insistence on completeness and clarity of written expression. . . . It properly admitted extrinsic evidence to explain the language of the deed . . . to the end that the consideration for the option would appear with sufficient certainty to permit specific enforcement. . . . The trial court erred, however, in excluding the extrinsic evidence that the option was personal to the grantors and therefore nonassignable.

When the parties to a written contract have agreed to it as an "integration"—a complete and final embodiment of the terms of an agreement—parol evidence cannot be used to add to or vary its terms. When only part of the agreement is integrated, the same rule applies to that part, but parol evidence may be used to prove elements of the agreement not reduced to writing. . . .

The crucial issue in determining whether there has been an integration is whether the parties intended their writing to serve as the exclusive embodiment of their agreement. The instrument itself may help to resolve that issue. It may state, for example, that "there are no previous understandings or agreements not contained in the writing," and thus express the parties' "intention to nullify antecedent understandings or agreements." (See 3 Corbin, Contracts (1960) § 578, p. 411.) Any such collateral agreement itself must be examined, however, to determine whether the parties intended the subjects of negotiation it deals with to be included in, excluded from, or otherwise affected by the writing. Circumstances at the time of the writing may also aid in the determination of such integration. (See 3 Corbin, Contracts (1960) §§ 582–584; McCormick, Evidence (1954) § 216, p. 441; 9 Wigmore, Evidence (3d ed. 1940) § 2430, p. 98, § 2431, pp. 102–103; Witkin, Cal.Evidence (2d ed. 1966) § 721; Schwartz v. Shapiro, supra, 229 Cal.App.2d 238, 251, fn. 8, 40 Cal.Rptr. 189; contra, 4 Williston, Contracts (3d ed. 1961) § 633, pp. 1014–1016.)

California cases have stated that whether there was an integration is to be determined solely from the face of the instrument ... and that the question for the court is whether it "appears to be a complete * * * agreement * * *." (See Ferguson v. Koch (1928) 204 Cal. 342, 346, 268 P. 342, 344, 58 A.L.R. 1176; ...) Neither of these strict formulations of the rule, however, has been consistently applied. The requirement that the writing must appear incomplete on its face has been repudiated in many cases where parol evidence was admitted "to prove the existence of a separate oral agreement as to any matter on which the document is silent and which is not inconsistent with its terms"—even though the instrument appeared to state a complete agreement. ... Even under the rule that the writing alone is to be consulted, it was found necessary to examine the alleged collateral agreement before concluding that proof of it was precluded by the writing alone. (See 3 Corbin, Contracts (1960) § 582, pp. 444–446.) It is therefore evident that "The conception of a writing as wholly and intrinsically self-determinative of the parties' intent to make it a sole memorial of one or seven or twenty-seven subjects of negotiation is an impossible one." (9 Wigmore, Evidence (3d ed. 1940) § 2431, p. 103.) For example, a promissory note given by a debtor to his creditor may integrate all their present contractual rights and obligations, or it may be only a minor part of an underlying executory contract that would never be discovered by examining the face of the note.

In formulating the rule governing parol evidence, several policies must be accommodated. One policy is based on the assumption that written evidence is more accurate than human memory. (Germain Fruit Co. v. J.K. Armsby Co. (1908) 153 Cal. 585, 595, 96 P. 319.) This policy, however, can be adequately served by excluding parol evidence of agreements that directly contradict the writing. Another policy is based on the fear that fraud or unintentional invention by witnesses interested in the outcome of the litigation will mislead the finder of facts. (Germain Fruit Co. v. J.K. Armsby Co., supra, 153 Cal. 585, 596, 96 P. 319; Mitchill v. Lath (1928) 247 N.Y. 377, 388, 160 N.E. 646, 68 A.L.R. 239 [dissenting opinion by Lehman, J.]; see 9 Wigmore, Evidence (3d ed. 1940) § 2431, p. 102; Murray, The Parol Evidence Rule: A Clarification (1966) 4 Duquesne L.Rev. 337, 338–339.) McCormick has suggested that the party urging the spoken as against the written word is most often the economic underdog, threatened by severe hardship if the writing is enforced. In his view the parol evidence rule arose to allow the court to control the tendency of the jury to find through sympathy and without a dispassionate assessment of the probability of fraud or faulty memory that the parties made an oral agreement collateral to the written contract, or that preliminary tentative agreements were not abandoned when omitted from the writing. (See McCormick, Evidence (1954) § 210.) He recognizes, however, that if this theory were adopted in disregard of all other considerations, it would lead to the exclusion of testimony concerning oral agreements whenever there is a writing and thereby often defeat the true intent of the parties. See McCormick, op. cit. supra, § 216, p. 441.

Evidence of oral collateral agreements should be excluded only when the fact finder is likely to be misled. The rule must therefore be based on the credibility of the evidence. One such standard, adopted by section 240(1)(b) of the Restatement of Contracts, permits proof of a collateral agreement if it "is such an agreement as might *naturally* be made as a separate agreement by parties situated as were the parties to the written contract." (Italics added; see McCormick, Evidence (1954) § 216, p. 441; see also 3 Corbin, Contracts (1960), § 583, p. 475, § 594, pp. 568–569; 4 Williston, Contracts (3d ed. 1961) § 638, pp. 1039–1045.) The draftsmen of the Uniform Commercial Code would exclude the evidence in still fewer instances: "If the additional terms are such that, if agreed upon, they would *certainly* have been included in the document in the view of the court, then evidence of their alleged making must be kept from the trier of fact." (Com. 3, § 2–202, italics added.)[1]

The option clause in the deed in the present case does not explicitly provide that it contains the complete agreement, and the deed is silent on the question of assignability. Moreover, the difficulty of accommodating the formalized structure of a deed to the insertion of collateral agreements makes it less likely that all the terms of such an agreement were included. ... The statement of the reservation of the option might well have been placed in the recorded deed solely to preserve the grantors' rights against any possible future purchasers and this function could well be served without any mention of the parties' agreement that the option was personal. There is nothing in the record to indicate that the parties to this family transaction, through experience in land transactions or otherwise, had any warning of the disadvantages of failing to put the whole agreement in the deed. This case is one, therefore, in which it can be said that a collateral agreement such as that alleged "might naturally be made as a separate agreement." *A fortiori,* the case is not one in which the parties "would certainly" have included the collateral agreement in the deed.

It is contended, however, that an option agreement is ordinarily presumed to be assignable if it contains no provisions forbidding its transfer or indicating that its performance involves elements personal to the parties. ... The fact that there is a written memorandum, however, does not necessarily preclude parol evidence rebutting a term that the law would otherwise presume. * * *

In the present case defendants offered evidence that the parties agreed that the option was not assignable in order to keep the property in the Masterson family. The trial court erred in excluding that evidence.

---

1. Corbin suggests that, even in situations where the court concludes that it would not have been natural for the parties to make the alleged collateral oral agreement, parol evidence of such an agreement should nevertheless be permitted if the court is convinced that the unnatural actually happened in the case being adjudicated. (3 Corbin, Contracts, § 485, pp. 478, 480; cf. Murray, The Parol Evidence Rule: A Clarification (1966) 4 Duquesne L.Rev. 337, 341–342.) This suggestion may be based on a belief that judges are not likely to be misled by their sympathies. If the court believes that the parties intended a collateral agreement to be effective, there is no reason to keep the evidence from the jury.

The judgment is reversed.

■ PETERS, TOBRINER, MOSK, and SULLIVAN, JJ., concur.

[In a dissenting opinion, Justice Burke, with whom Justice McComb concurred, insisted that the majority opinion, 1) undermined the parol evidence rule as it has been known in California since 1872, 2) rendered suspect instruments of conveyance absolute on their face, 3) materially lessened the reliance which might be placed upon written instruments affecting title to real estate, and 4) opened the door, albeit unintentionally, to a new technique for the defrauding of creditors.]

NOTES

(1) "When two parties have made a contract and have expressed it in a writing to which they have both assented as the complete and accurate integration of that contract, evidence, whether parol or otherwise, of antecedent understandings and negotiations will not be admitted for the purpose of varying or contradicting the writing." Corbin § 573.

(2) "Unfortunately the name by which it is known is misleading. * * * It is not a rule of evidence, nor does it necessarily have anything to do with 'parol'. Neither is it a rule of interpretation. It is in reality a rule of the substantive law which, whenever it is applicable, determines * * * what utterances are to be regarded as the source of the intentions of the parties in relation to the matter in hand. When the rule applies to a contract, it, rather than the rules of evidence, determines what manifestations of intention are to be taken as embodying the contract." Grismore, Contracts § 94 (1st ed. 1947).

(3) What policy reasons support the parol evidence rule? To what extent are they similar to those advanced in favor of the Statute of Frauds? How do the Statute of Frauds and the parol evidence rule differ? See Corbin § 575.

(4) Of what significance was the form of the documentation in the instant cases? Would the result in *Mitchill* have been the same if the writing had been a deed?

(5) What would have been the effect of a showing that the promise to remove the ice house was made for a separate consideration?

(6) For an analysis of the varying approaches of Williston and Corbin, see Calamari and Perillo, *A Plea for a Uniform Parol Evidence Rule and Principles of Contract Interpretation*, 42 Ind.L.J. 333 (1967).

(7) Critics of the parol evidence rule have insisted that it ought not be regarded as a "rule of form." E.g., Sweet, *Contract Making and Parol Evidence: Diagnosis and Treatment of a Sick Rule*, 53 Cornell L.Rev. 1036, 1060 (1968). An emphasis upon the "formal aspects" of the rule tends to restrict the use of parol evidence and to protect the exclusivity of the written terms. The avowed goal is the maintenance of the security of transactions as the "four corners" of the writing is looked to as defining the scope of obligation. Interested parties may thereby gain some assurance that evidence of informal expression may not be introduced to alter the apparent obligation. Note how the dissenting judge in *Masterson* is fearful of the majority opinion's effect in lessening the reliance which may be placed upon written instruments. But the cost of this protection may be too high. Does it not bespeak disinterest in determining the real agreement of the parties? If, as in *Mitchill*, the defendants for the same

consideration promised to remove the ice house, why should they not be legally obliged to do so? It must be borne in mind that the admission of the proffered evidence would not have conclusively established the fact. The vendors could, of course, have offered evidence disputing the existence of such an oral promise, and the resultant credibility issue would have been decided in the usual way. Cf. *Comment: Formal Aspects of Rules of Interpretation,* infra at 600.

(8) *Does the Parol Evidence Rule Give Preference to Written Evidence of Contract Terms?* "The law should give effect to the contract. In an important kind of trouble case, the parties dispute over contract terms. The contract might be entirely oral, or it might be partly oral and partly in writing. If the contract is not unenforceable under the statute of frauds, a court will have to ascertain its terms. Partly to guard against the uncertainties of litigation over oral contract terms, parties frequently undertake to put their contracts in writing. But there can be no magic in this. One party may later contend that the writing does not embody the terms agreed on; a writing cannot prevent disputes over terms. Moreover, a writing cannot by itself tell us what any of the terms really were. A writing is only potential evidence to be introduced in court, should the parties go to court to resolve a dispute over terms.

"Courts are frequently called on to resolve disputes over terms. The novice might expect that the process of adjudication here would be the same as in any other type of case in which facts are disputed: the parties would introduce all relevant evidence as to terms, including any writing, and the trier of fact would then determine what terms the parties actually contracted for. Also there would be the usual division of labor between judge and jury. Judges would, for example, rule on relevancy and admissibility, and they would be empowered to grant a motion for a non-suit, for a directed verdict, or for a judgment *n.o.v.* Thus, the usual protections against unreasonable jury determinations would be available to help assure that in the end, the court gives effect to the contract of the parties as actually agreed.

"But Anglo–American law does not handle all disputes over contract terms in this way. Our courts apply a so-called 'parol evidence rule' when some of the evidence of terms is embodied in a writing. The usual effect of this is to give preference to the written version of terms. Writings are more reliable than memories to show contract terms, and forgery is supposedly easier to detect than is lying on the witness stand. These are the principal premises of a parol evidence rule. Early critics of the rule challenged these premises and emphasized that the rule is inconsistent with our usual processes of proof. If juries are to be 'trusted' in disputes over contract terms not involving writings, then why should they not hear all the evidence, even where writings are involved, and decide accordingly? The debate still rages." White and Summers, Uniform Commercial Code 94–95 (3d ed. 1988). [Footnotes omitted.] [This text is slightly revised in White and Summers, Uniform Commercial Code 67 (4th ed. 1995.]

Alaska Northern Development, Inc. v. Alyeska Pipeline Service Co.

Supreme Court of Alaska, 1983.
666 P.2d 33, cert. denied 464 U.S. 1041, 104 S.Ct. 706, 79 L.Ed.2d 170 (1984).

Opinion

■ COMPTON, JUSTICE.

Alaska Northern Development, Inc. ("AND") appeals a judgment in favor of Alyeska Pipeline Service Co. ("Alyeska") in a dispute involving contract formation and interpretation. For the reasons stated below, we affirm.

I. FACTUAL AND PROCEDURAL BACKGROUND

In late October or early November 1976, David Reed, a shareholder and corporate president of AND, initiated discussion with Alyeska personnel in Fairbanks regarding the purchase of surplus parts. The Alyeska employees with whom Reed dealt were Juel Tyson, Clarence Terwilleger and Donald Bruce.

After a series of discussions, Terwilleger indicated that Reed's proposal should be put in writing so it could be submitted to management. With the assistance of AND's legal counsel, Reed prepared a letter of intent dated December 10, 1976. In this letter, AND proposed to purchase "the entire Alyeska inventory of Caterpillar parts." The place for the purchase price was left blank.

Alyeska responded with its own letter of intent dated December 11, 1976. The letter was drafted by Bruce and Tyson in consultation with William Rickett, Alyeska's manager of Contracts and Material Management. Again, the price term was absent. The letter contained the following language, which is the focus of this lawsuit: "Please consider this as said letter of intent, *subject to the final approval of the owner committee*." (Emphasis added.)

Reed was given an unsigned draft of the December 11 letter, which was reviewed by AND's legal counsel. Reed then met with Rickett, and they agreed on sixty-five percent of Alyeska's price as the price term to be filled in the blank on the December 11 letter. Rickett filled in the blank as agreed and signed the letter. In March 1977, the owner committee rejected the proposal embodied in the December 11 letter of intent.

AND contends that the parties understood the subject to approval language to mean that the Alyeska owner committee would review the proposed agreement only to determine whether the price was fair and reasonable. Alyeska contends that Reed was never advised of any such limitation on the authority of the owner committee. In April 1977, AND filed a complaint alleging that there was a contract between AND and Alyeska, which Alyeska breached. The complaint was later amended to include counts for reformation and punitive damages.

Alyeska moved for summary judgment on the punitive damages and breach of contract counts. The superior court granted summary judgment in favor of Alyeska on the punitive damages count. The court initially denied Alyeska's motion for summary judgment on the breach of contract claim; however, based on a review of the case after discovery had closed, the court announced at a hearing on September 26, 1980, that it would reverse its earlier ruling and grant Alyeska's motion. The court confirmed this ruling at a hearing on November 5, 1980, after consideration of AND's Motion for Clarification.

* * *

II. APPLICATION OF THE PAROL EVIDENCE RULE

The superior court held that the parol evidence rule of the Uniform Commercial Code, section 2–202, codified as AS 45.02–202,[3] applied to the December 11 letter and therefore no extrinsic evidence could be presented to a jury which limited the owner committee's right of approval. AND contends that the court erred in applying the parol evidence rule. We disagree.

In order to exclude parol evidence concerning the inclusion of additional terms to a writing, a court must make the following determinations. First, the court must determine whether the writing under scrutiny was integrated, i.e., intended by the parties as a final expression of their agreement with respect to some or all of the terms included in the writing. Second, the court must determine whether evidence of a prior or contemporaneous agreement contradicts or is inconsistent with the integrated portion. If the evidence is contradictory or inconsistent, it is inadmissible. If it is consistent, it may nevertheless be excluded if the court concludes that the consistent term would necessarily have been included in the writing by the parties if they had intended it to be part of their agreement. AS 45.02.202; Braund, Inc. v. White, 486 P.2d 50, 56 (Alaska 1971); U.C.C. § 2–202 comment 3 (1977).

A. *Was the December 11 Letter a Partial Integration?*

An integrated writing exists where the parties intend that the writing be a final expression of one or more terms of their agreement. Kupka v. Morey, 541 P.2d 740, 747 n. 8 (Alaska 1975); Restatement (Second) of Contracts § 209(a) (1979). Whether a writing is integrated is a question of fact to be determined by the court in accordance with all relevant evidence. Restatement (Second) of Contracts § 209 comment c (1979).

In granting summary judgment on the breach of contract claim, the superior court stated that it had carefully considered all relevant evidence, including oral and written records of all facets of the business deal in question, to arrive at its finding that the agreement was partially integrat-

---

3. AS 45.02.202 provides:

Final written expression; parol or extrinsic evidence. Terms with respect to which the confirmatory memoranda of the parties agree, or which are otherwise set out in a writing intended by the parties as a final expression of their agreement with respect to the terms included in the writing, may not be contradicted by evidence of a prior agreement or of a contemporaneous oral agreement, but may be explained or supplemented

(1) by course of dealing or usage of trade (AS 45.01.205) or by course of performance (AS 45.02.208); and

(2) by evidence of consistent additional terms unless the court finds the writing was intended also as a complete and exclusive statement of the terms of the agreement.

ed.[4] After the six-week trial on the reformation issue, the superior court reaffirmed this finding:

35.   The plaintiff initially contends that the letter of December 11, 1976 (the letter) was not integrated or partially integrated and therefore the court was in error in granting summary judgment in favor of defendant on the contract counts of the plaintiff's complaint on September 26, 1980.

36.   After considering the evidence submitted at trial, the court reaffirms its prior conclusion that the letter was integrated as to the Owners Committee's approval clause.

37.   The parties intended to write down their discussions in a comprehensive form which allowed Reed to seek financing and allow the primary actors (Tyson, Bruce, Terwilleger, Rickett) to submit the concept embodied by the letter to higher management....

38.   There are three subjects upon which plaintiff seeks reformation.... As to the first, [limiting the Owner Committee to a consideration of price] which has been plaintiff's primary focus, the court finds that such reference was integrated such that the parole [sic] evidence rule would bar any inconsistent testimony. Testimony that the owners were limited to "price" in their review is inconsistent.

* * *

41.   With respect to the Owners Committee's approval clause, according to the plaintiff's contention the owners were entitled to review the transaction, on whatever basis, only one time. This was testified to by both Mr. Reed and argued by plaintiff in closing.... It was also conceded in closing that the review by the owners, on whatever standard, would occur prior to any formal contract being negotiated and executed.... This is also consistent with the testimony of each of the participants.

42.   In addition, Mr. Reed, in consultation with Ed Merdes and Henry Camarot, his attorneys, tendered the letter of March 4, 1977, as a document which could serve as "the contract".... The March 4 letter contains no further reference to the Owners Committee's approval function.... Therefore, I find that as to the Owners Committee's approval ... the letter of December 11 constitutes an integration

---

4.   At the hearing on AND's Motion for Clarification, the superior court stated:

   [I]t seems to me absolutely conclusive on this evidence, and I'm making this as a finding of fact, that this agreement is partially integrated, and I'm not making it by reference only to the four corners of the—of the writings but reference to all the extrinsic evidence that has been proffered to me, read everybody's deposition, considered in detail all the processes of negotiations, everything that was said and done by everybody as related by them up till the time that Rickett included the language in the letter and turned it over to Reed. So we're not here talking about the for [sic] corners or ambiguity or anything like that. We're talking about all the extrinsic evidence, meaning on balance to a conclusion more probable than not that this is a partially integrated agreement.

or partial integration. . . . This having been established, the analysis outlined by the court on September 26, 1980, when granting defendant's motion for summary judgment on the contract claims is applicable. [Citations omitted.]

After reviewing the record, we cannot say that this finding of a partial integration was clearly erroneous.

* * *

B.   *Does the Excluded Evidence Contradict the Integrated Terms?*

Having found a partial integration, the next determination is whether the excluded evidence contradicts the integrated portion of the writing. Comment b to section 215 of the Restatement (Second) of Contracts is helpful in resolving this issue.[5] Comment b states:

> An earlier agreement may help the interpretation of a later one, but it may not contradict a binding later integrated agreement. Whether there is a contradiction depends . . . on whether the two are consistent or inconsistent. This is a question which often cannot be determined from the face of the writing; the writing must first be applied to its subject matter and placed in context. The question is then decided by the court as part of a question of interpretation. Where reasonable people could differ as to the credibility of the evidence offered and the evidence if believed could lead a reasonable person to interpret the writing as claimed by the proponent of the evidence, the question of credibility and the choice among reasonable inferences should be treated as questions of fact. But the asserted meaning must be one to which the language of the writing, read in context, is reasonably susceptible. If no other meaning is reasonable, the court should rule as a matter of law that the meaning is established.

According to comment b, therefore, a question of interpretation may arise before the contradiction issue can be resolved. If the evidence conflicts, the choice between competing inferences is for the trier of fact to resolve. Alyeska Pipeline Service Co. v. O'Kelley, 645 P.2d 767, 771 n. 2 (Alaska 1982). The meaning is determined as a matter of law, however, if "the asserted meaning [is not] one to which the language of the writing, read in context, is reasonably susceptible." Restatement (Second) of Contracts § 215 comment b (1979). *See also* J. Calamari & J. Perillo, The Law of Contracts §§ 3–12, 3–13 (2d ed. 1977).

AND contends that the superior court erred in granting summary judgment because the evidence conflicted as to the meaning of the owner committee approval clause. It concludes that under *Alyeska* it was entitled to a jury trial on the interpretation issue. Alyeska contends, and the

---

5. Restatement (Second) of Contracts § 215, which parallels the rule stated in U.C.C. § 2–202, reads: "Except as stated in the preceding Section, where there is a binding agreement, either completely or partially integrated, evidence of prior or contemporaneous agreements or negotiations is not admissible in evidence to contradict a term of the writing."

superior court ruled, that a jury trial was inappropriate because, as a matter of law, AND's asserted meaning of the clause at issue was not reasonably susceptible to the language of the writing. The superior court stated:

> The Court is making the . . . ruling that the offer of evidence to show that Rickett's letter really meant to limit owner committee approval to the price term alone . . . is not reasonably susceptible—or the writing is not reasonably susceptible to that purpose. And therefore, that extrinsic evidence operates to contradict the writing, not specific words in the writing, but the words in the context of the totality of the writing and the totality of the extrinsic evidence.

We agree that the words used in the December 11 letter are not reasonably susceptible to the interpretation advanced by AND. Therefore, we find no merit to AND's contention that it was entitled to a jury trial on the interpretation issue.

After rejecting the extrinsic evidence for purposes of interpretation, the superior court found AND's offered testimony, that the owner committee's approval power was limited to approval of the price, to be inconsistent with and contradictory to the language used by the negotiators in the December 11 letter. AND contends that the offered testimony did not contradict, but rather explained or supplemented the writing with consistent additional terms. For this contention, AND relies on the standard articulated in Hunt Foods & Industries, Inc. v. Doliner, 26 A.D.2d 41, 270 N.Y.S.2d 937 (N.Y.App.1966). In Hunt Foods, the defendant signed an option agreement under which he agreed to sell stock to Hunt Foods at a given price per share. When Hunt Foods attempted to exercise the option, the defendant contended that the option could only be exercised if the defendant had received offers from a third party. The court held that section 2–202 did not bar this evidence from being admitted because it held that the proposed oral condition to the option agreement was not "inconsistent" within the meaning of section 2–202; to be inconsistent, "the term must contradict or negate a term of the writing. A term or condition which has a lesser effect is provable." Id. 270 N.Y.S.2d at 940.

The narrow view of consistency expressed in Hunt Foods has been criticized. In Snyder v. Herbert Greenbaum & Associates, Inc., 38 Md.App. 144, 380 A.2d 618 (Md.App.1977), the court held that the parol evidence of a contractual right to unilateral rescission was inconsistent with a written agreement for the sale and installation of carpeting. The court defined "inconsistency" as used in section 2–202(b) as "the absence of reasonable harmony in terms of the language and respective obligations of the parties." Id. 380 A.2d at 623 (emphasis in original) (citing U.C.C. § 1–205(4)). Accord: Luria Brothers & Co. v. Pielet Brothers Scrap Iron & Metal, Inc., 600 F.2d 103, 111 (7th Cir.1979); Southern Concrete Services, Inc. v. Mableton Contractors, Inc., 407 F.Supp. 581 (N.D.Ga.1975), aff'd mem., 569 F.2d 1154 (5th Cir.1978).

We agree with this view of inconsistency and reject the view expressed in *Hunt Foods*.[6] Under this definition of inconsistency, it is clear that the proffered parol evidence limiting the owner committee's right of final approval to price is inconsistent with the integrated term that unconditionally gives the committee the right to approval. Therefore, the superior court was correct in refusing to admit parol evidence on this issue.[7]

* * *

Affirmed.

NOTES

(1) What are the legal consequences of a finding that a writing is, under UCC 2–202, a "final" expression of an agreement? What if a court finds, in addition, that a writing is a "complete and exclusive" statement of the terms of an agreement? How does the Code test for determining completeness or exclusivity (i.e., complete or total integration) differ from that used in *Mitchill v. Lath,* supra at 578? Would application of the Code rule to the facts of *Mitchill* produce a different result? See J. White & R. Summers, Uniform Commercial Code § 2–10 (4th ed. 1995).

(2) Restatement (Second) § 216(2) provides: "An agreement is not completely integrated if the writing omits a consistent additional agreed term which is * * * (b) such a term as in the circumstances might naturally be omitted from the writing." For a critical analysis of *Restatement Second's* treatment of the parol evidence rule, see Murray, *The Parol Evidence Process and Standardized Agreements under the Restatement (Second) of Contracts,* 123 U.Pa.L.Rev. 1342 (1975).

(3) In A. Kemp Fisheries, Inc. v. Castle & Cooke, Inc., 852 F.2d 493, 495 (9th Cir.1988), the court, applying California law, held that a Charter Agreement between the parties was an integrated writing, even though it did not contain a "merger" clause. In making this determination, the court considered:

> [T]he language and completeness of the written agreement and whether it contains an integration clause, the terms of the alleged . . . agreement and whether they contradict those in the writing, whether the . . . agreement might naturally be made as a separate agreement, and whether the jury might be misled by the introduction of the parol testimony. A court also considers the circumstances surrounding the transaction and its subject matter, nature and object. 852 F.2d at 495.

6. Hunt Foods was implicitly rejected in Johnson v. Curran, 633 P.2d 994, 996–97 (Alaska 1981) (parol evidence concerning an early termination right based on nightclub owner's dissatisfaction with the band's performance was inconsistent with parties' written contract specifying definite time without mention of any right of early termination and thus inadmissible).

7. Our affirmance of the superior court's holding that the proposed version is inconsistent with the integrated clause obviates discussion of whether the addition, if consistent, would have been included in the December 11 letter. Furthermore, we decline to reach AND's contentions regarding the applicability of U.C.C. § 2–207 because AND never raised the § 2–207 argument at the superior court level. See, e.g., Jeffries v. Glacier State Telephone Co., 604 P.2d 4, 11 (Alaska 1979).

Luther Williams, Jr., Inc. v. Johnson

District of Columbia Court of Appeals, 1967.
229 A.2d 163.

■ QUINN, JUDGE. Appellant (plaintiff below) sought to recover $670 as liquidated damages under a contract for improvements on appellees' home. Appellees' defense was that the contract never came into existence because of an unfulfilled condition precedent. This appeal raises the sole question of whether the parol evidence rule required exclusion of all testimony regarding the alleged condition.

At the trial, Luther Williams, Jr., president of appellant corporation, testified that prior to the signing of the contract, he offered to arrange any necessary financing for appellees, but was advised that they had their own. He was further informed that the down payment would be made in a few days when they received their funds. After drawing plans and contacting appellees several times, he was told that their financing had not been obtained and that they had procured another contractor to make certain improvements on the property.

Appellees testified that they signed the contract thinking it was merely an estimate; that they told Mr. Williams the improvements would depend upon approval of their financing by their bank; and that it was their understanding with him that they would not become obligated until they had procured the funds. Appellant objected to the introduction of all testimony concerning a parol agreement regarding financing, and later objected to jury instructions on that subject. The objections were overruled, and the jury returned a verdict for appellees.

As previously stated, the issue here is a narrow one, namely, whether the admission of testimony concerning the oral condition precedent violated the parol evidence rule. Briefly stated, that rule provides that when the parties to a contract reduce their agreement to writing, that writing is presumed to be the final repository of all prior negotiations, and testimony concerning prior or contemporaneous oral agreements which tends to vary, modify or contradict the terms of the writing is inadmissible. See 3 Corbin, Contracts § 573 (1960); 4 Williston, Contracts, § 631 (3d ed. 1961).

In this jurisdiction, however, it is well settled that a written contract may be conditioned on an oral agreement that the contract shall not become binding until some condition precedent resting in parol shall have been performed. ... Furthermore, parol testimony to prove such a condition is admissible when the contract is silent on the matter, the testimony does not contradict nor is it inconsistent with the writing, and if under the circumstances it may properly be inferred that the parties did not intend the writing to be a complete statement of their transaction. ...

The contract in question contained the following clause:

"This contract embodies the entire understanding between the parties, and there are no verbal agreements or representations in connection therewith." Two problems thus arise when applying the above rules to the instant case. First, in the light of an "integration clause," can evidence be admitted to show that the parties did not intend the writing to be a complete statement of their transaction? Second, can it be said that the testimony regarding the condition precedent does not contradict the writing when the contract states there are no agreements other than those contained in the writing?

As to the first question, it has always been presumed that a written contract is the final repository of the agreement of the parties. 4 Williston, op. cit. supra § 631 at 953–954. In this regard, an integration clause merely strengthens this presumption. However, intent is a question of fact, and to determine the intent of the parties, it is necessary to look not only to the written instrument, but to the circumstances surrounding its execution.

In Mitchell v. David, supra, we quoted with approval from 9 Wigmore, Evidence § 2430 (3d ed. 1940) as follows:

"Whether a particular subject of negotiation is embodied by the writing *depends wholly upon the intent of the parties* thereto. In this respect the contrast is between voluntary integration and integration by law. Here the parties are not obliged to embody their transaction in a single document; yet they may, if they choose. Hence it becomes merely a question whether they have intended to do so."

"This intent must be sought where always intent must be sought, namely, in the *conduct* and *language* of the parties and the *surrounding circumstances*. The document alone will not suffice. What it was intended to cover cannot be known till we know what there was to cover. The question being whether certain subjects of negotiation were intended to be covered, we must compare the writing and the negotiations before we can determine whether they were in fact covered. Thus the apparent paradox is committed of receiving proof of certain negotiations in order to determine whether to exclude them; and this doubtless has sometimes seemed to lower the rule to a quibble. But the paradox is apparent only. The explanation is that these alleged negotiations are received only provisionally. Although in form the witnesses may be allowed to recite the facts, yet in truth the facts will be afterwards treated as immaterial and legally void, if the rule is held applicable. There is a preliminary question for the judge to decide as to the intent of the parties, and upon this he hears evidence on both sides; his decision here, *pro* or *con,* concerns merely this question preliminary to the ruling of law. If he decides that the transaction was covered by the writing, he does not decide that the excluded negotiations did not take place, but merely that *if* they did take place they are nevertheless legally immaterial. If he decides that the transaction was not intended to be covered by the writing, he does not decide that the negotiations did take place, but merely that *if* they did, they are legally effective, and he then leaves to the jury the determination of fact whether they did take place." 51 A.2d at 378. See also, Giotis v. Lampkin, D.C.Mun. App., 145 A.2d 779 (1958); 3 Corbin, op. cit. supra § 582. We are still of the opinion that this expresses the better practice.

As to the second question, we are aware that some courts have answered it in the negative. See, e.g., Rowe v. Shehyn, 192 F.Supp. 428

(D.D.C.1961); J & J Construction Co. v. Mayernik, 241 Or. 537, 407 P.2d 625 (1965). We believe, however, that this is an erroneous interpretation of Restatement, Contracts § 241 (1932) which provides as follows:

"Where parties to a writing which purports to be an integration of a contract between them orally agree, before or contemporaneously with the making of the writing, that it shall not become binding until a future day or until the happening of a future event, the oral agreement is operative *if there is nothing in the writing inconsistent therewith*." (Emphasis added.)

To explain this section, the following illustration is given:

"A and B make and sign a writing in which A promises to sell and B promises to buy goods of a certain description at a stated price. The parties at the same time orally agree that the writing shall not take effect unless within ten days their local railroad has cars available for shipping the goods. The oral agreement is operative according to its terms. If, however, the writing provides 'delivery shall be made within thirty days' from the date of the writing, the oral agreement is inoperative." In our opinion, it is clear from the example that what is intended is not the exclusion of evidence because of the existence of an "integration clause," 3 Corbin, op. cit. supra § 578 at 405–407, but an exclusion only if the alleged parol condition contradicts some other specific term of the written agreement. See Fadex Foreign Trad. Corp. v. Crown Steel Corp., 272 App.Div. 273, 70 N.Y.S.2d 892, aff'd 297 N.Y. 903, 79 N.E.2d 739 (1948); 3 Corbin, op. cit. supra § 577 example (5). In the instant case, no provision was made regarding financing. Therefore, the parol condition would not contradict the terms of the writing.

For the above-stated reasons, we hold that it was not error to admit testimony tending to show that the writing was not intended to be a complete statement of the agreement of the parties and to instruct the jury to find for appellees if they determined that the negotiations regarding the condition precedent had taken place and that the contract was not to become binding unless the financing was first obtained.

Affirmed.

NOTES

(1) These writings contain an added element not present in preceding cases of this section; *viz.,* a provision usually referred to as a "merger" or "integration" clause. What is its significance relative to ascertaining whether the writing is a complete or only a partial integration?

(2) Why would not the parol evidence rule apply even if the alleged agreement was made subsequent to the writing? As to the consideration requirement, recall the dispensation in UCC 2–209(1) [UCC 2–210(a)(1997)].

(3) *Evidence of Nonexistence or Invalidity of Agreement.* The parol evidence rule contemplates the protection of a writing embodying the terms of a contract. If there is no contract the Rule's protective shield is obviously unavailable. Thus, evidence establishing invalidity of the purported agreement,

such as lack of consideration, fraud, mistake, duress or illegality, is readily admitted. A difficulty is encountered, however, where there is a valid contract in the ordinary sense, but a party asserts an oral "condition" to the assumed duty. Evidence of this condition does not establish the non-existence of the underlying contract; rather, it establishes a condition or qualification of the duty to perform. (See infra, Section 2). If the evidence of an oral condition is to be admitted, and the authorities are conflicting, it should be upon a ground other than that of showing the non-existence of a contract. See Corbin §§ 589, 592. How is this type of problem resolved under UCC 2–202? See also Restatement (Second) § 217: "Where the parties to a written agreement agree orally that performance of the agreement is subject to the occurrence of a stated condition, the agreement is not integrated with respect to the oral condition."

(4) *Effect of Merger Clause in Commercial Sales.* In a commercial transaction, is the presence of a "merger" clause conclusive on the intention of the parties to have a total integration of the writing? In ARB, Inc. v. E–Systems, Inc., 663 F.2d 189, 198–99 (D.C.Cir.1980), the answer, under Maryland law at least, was no. Integration clauses are not "absolutely conclusive." Rather, they are "indicative of the intention of the parties to finalize their complete understanding in the written contract ... that there was no other prior or contemporaneous agreement not included in the written contract." Thus, the court should consider "the circumstances surrounding the making of the contract ... to discover whether the integration clause in question does, in fact, express the genuine intention of the parties to make the written contract the complete and exclusive statement of their agreement." These circumstances include the length and detail of the contract, the length and nature of the negotiations preceding execution and the absence of "persuasive evidence supporting a determination that the parties intended, at the time of contracting, that non-written terms be part of the overall agreement." See White and Summers, Uniform Commercial Code 82–88 (4th ed. 1995).

(5) *Effect of Merger Clause in Consumer Sales.* According to Professor Justin Sweet, the exclusive purpose of the parol evidence rule is to protect "truly integrated writings." Sweet, *Contract Making and Parol Evidence: Diagnosis and Treatment of a Sick Rule,* 53 Cornell L.Rev. 1036, 1060 (1967). In most cases a merger clause contained in a writing which has objectively been assented to by both parties is the best evidence of an intention to integrate. In a wide range of retail sales to consumers, however, the merger clause buried in the boiler plate of a written contract can be a potent weapon in the hands of the seller. For example, in the pre-sale "dickering" the seller may make an oral, express warranty which becomes part of the basis of the buyer's bargain. UCC 2–313(1). Later, the buyer signs a written contract for sale containing the merger clause which, of course, was not read, not called to his or her attention and, even if read, would not clearly indicate that a material, inducing term of the sale was being excluded. If the merger clause is viewed as an attempt to "disclaim" the express warranty, the warranty prevails under UCC 2–316(1). If the merger clause is viewed as an attempt totally to integrate the writing, UCC 2–202 applies and would appear to protect the seller. Is the use by a professional seller of a merger clause in consumer transactions without full disclosure of its presence and meaning unconscionable? See Comment, *Warranties, Disclaimers and the Parol Evidence Rule,* infra; White and Summers, Uniform Commercial Code § 2–12 (4th ed. 1995); Broude, *The Consumer and the Parol Evidence*

Rule: Section 2–202 of the Uniform Commercial Code, 1970 Duke L.J. 881; Murray, *The Parol Evidence Process and Standardized Agreements under the Restatement (Second) of Contracts,* 123 U.Pa.L.Rev. 1342, 1372–89 (1975).

Restatement (Second) § 211(3) provides: "Where the other party has reason to believe that the party manifesting such assent would not do so if he knew that the writing contained a particular term, the term is not part of the agreement." The drafters appended the following comment: "[A] party who adheres to the other party's standard terms does not assent to a term if the other party has reason to believe that the adhering party would not have accepted the agreement if he had known that the agreement contained the particular term. Such a belief or assumption may be shown by the prior negotiations or inferred from the circumstances. Reason to believe may be inferred from the fact that the term is bizarre or oppressive, from the fact that it eviscerates the non-standard terms explicitly agreed to, or from the fact that it eliminates the dominant purpose of the transaction. The inference is reinforced if the adhering party never had an opportunity to read the term, or if it is illegible or otherwise hidden from view. This rule is closely related to the policy against unconscionable terms and the rule of interpretation against the draftsman. See §§ 206 and 208." Restatement (Second) § 211, Comment f. See also Birnbaum, Stahl & West, *Standardized Agreements and the Parol Evidence Rule: Defining and Applying the Expectations Principle,* 26 Ariz.L.Rev. 793 (1984).

Comment: Warranties, Disclaimers and the Parol Evidence Rule

In contracts for the sale of goods, the seller may make four warranties of quality: express warranties, UCC 2–313; an implied warranty of merchantability, UCC 2–314; an implied warranty of fitness for particular purpose, UCC 2–315; and a warranty of good title, UCC 2–312(1). These warranties, when made, are clearly terms of the agreement. The Code also regulates efforts by the seller to exclude or modify warranties made. For example, "to exclude or modify the implied warranty of merchantability or any part of it the language must mention merchantability and in case of a writing must be conspicuous * * *." UCC 2–316(2). Similarly, a warranty that "title shall be good and its transfer rightful" can be excluded or modified "only by specific language" or by special circumstances defined in UCC 2–312(2). In short, a warranty made may be very difficult to take away by a disclaimer. In the case of express warranties it is impossible: if words or conduct creating an express warranty and words or conduct "tending to negate or limit warranty" cannot be construed as consistent with each other, "negation or limitation is inoperative to the extent that such construction is unreasonable." UCC 2–316(1).

How does the parol evidence rule, UCC 2–202, mesh with the giving and taking of warranties? *First,* if a disclaimer is effective, the parol evidence rule is irrelevant. The warranty has been excluded from the agreement by other means. *Second,* suppose the seller has made an implied warranty of merchantability and it has not been disclaimed. Since the warranty is a term of the agreement, one could argue that it is subject to exclusion under UCC 2–202 if the parties intended the writing to be a "complete and exclusive statement of the terms of the agreement." UCC 2–202(b). The problem is that this implied warranty emerges from the very roots of the bargain and UCC 2–316(2) sets a high standard for its exclusion. A good court, therefore, might be hesitant to exclude an implied warranty of merchantability by virtue of a general "merger" clause, even though that clause was conspicuous. In short, to protect this particular warranty, the court should insist upon the same level of detail and conspicuousness in the manifestation of intention to integrate the writing as UCC 2–316(2) requires for a disclaimer. *Third,* UCC 2–316(1), which makes it impossible to disclaim an express warranty, states that the matter is "subject to the provisions of this Article on parol or extrinsic evidence (Section 2–202)." Suppose, then, this situation. The used car salesman has made "affirmations of fact" about the condition of a particular used car and they become "part of the basis" of the buyer's bargain. UCC 2–313(1). Later, the buyer signs a writing that attempts to disclaim all express warranties except a promise to share 50–50 in all repairs needed during the first 30 days and contains a general merger clause that provides: THIS WRITING IS THE FINAL AND EXCLUSIVE STATEMENT AND EXPRESSION OF ALL OF THE TERMS OF THE AGREEMENT. Buyer signs the agreement but, 60 days later, discovers a major defect that is inconsistent with the salesman's oral representation. Is the seller protected? The answer is no if the court concludes that the writing was not intended as a total integration and the oral representations can be admitted as "consistent additional terms." Similarly, the parol evidence rule does not apply at all if the representations were fraudulent. Further, there is a hint in some cases that even if a total integration was intended, the oral representation may not be excluded if the buyer was surprised by an "unexpected and unbargained for" exclusion. See Jordan v. Doonan Truck & Equipment, Inc., 220 Kan. 431, 552 P.2d 881 (1976). At least one court has concluded that an inconspicuous and broadly worded merger clause is unconscionable to the extent it is asserted to exclude oral express warranties. See Seibel v. Layne & Bowler, Inc., 56 Or.App. 387, 641 P.2d 668 (1982) review denied 293 Or. 190, 648 P.2d 852 (1982). The court endorsed the merger clause proposed by White and Summers, Uniform Commercial Code 111–112 (3d ed. 1988) [compare the "merger clause" in the fourth edition at 82–83]:

> THIS AGREEMENT SIGNED BY BOTH PARTIES AND SO INITIALED BY BOTH PARTIES IN THE MARGIN OPPOSITE THIS PARAGRAPH CONSTITUTES A FINAL WRITTEN EXPRESSION OF ALL THE TERMS OF THIS AGREEMENT AND IS A COMPLETE AND EXCLUSIVE STATEMENT OF THOSE TERMS. ANY AND ALL REPRESENTATIONS, PROMISES, WARRANTIES OR STATEMENTS BY SELLER'S AGENT THAT DIFFER IN ANY WAY FROM THE TERMS OF THIS WRITTEN AGREEMENT SHALL BE GIVEN NO FORCE OR EFFECT.

Would this "merger" clause exclude implied warranties? [In revised Article 2, the warranty sections discussed above are renumbered and put in a separate Part 4 entitled "Warranties." The substance of the discussion above, however, remains essentially the same.] See also chapter 5, § 2(C), infra.

PROBLEM: THE CASE OF THE UNEXPECTED SPOUSE

After ten years of marriage, Ira Soper deserted his wife in Ohio under circumstances contrived to persuade that he had committed suicide. Later, he surfaced in Minneapolis under the name of John Young and became established in business and in a social way. Two years later he married a widow, but she died three years later. Two years later he married another widow and they lived together as husband and wife for five years until Soper died, this time for real, by his own hand. Prior to his death, however, he had entered into a stock insurance plan with his business partner. Under this plan, upon the death of either partner the survivor could acquire the other's business interest from the estate and the surviving "wife" was to be compensated by life insurance to be taken out by each partner on his life, premiums to be paid by the company. The resulting written insurance "trust" provided that upon the death of the Depositor the "trust company shall deliver the stock certificates of the deceased Depositor to the surviving Depositor and it shall deliver the proceeds of the insurance on the life of the deceased Depositor to the wife of the deceased Depositor if living ..." The insurance proceeds were duly paid by the trust officer to Gertrude Young, the woman with whom the deceased had been living as husband and wife. Shortly thereafter, Adeline, the first Mrs. Soper appeared and established that she was the legal spouse of the deceased. Mrs. Soper had an administrator appointed for the estate of the deceased and brought suit against Mrs. Young to recover the insurance proceeds.

Based upon the preceding materials and the materials to come in Chapter 5:

(1) What are the strongest arguments in favor of Adeline Soper?

(2) What are the strongest arguments in favor of Gertrude Young?

(3) How should the Court rule? See In re Soper's Estate, 196 Minn. 60, 264 N.W. 427 (1935).

(B) INTERPRETATION

Comment: Formal Aspects of Rules of Interpretation

[The following is reprinted from the Northwestern University Law Review.]

The Anglo–American rules for interpreting written documents are many and variable. Some are verbose, some pithy; some are specific, some general; some are statutory, some judge-made. For our purposes, we will single out one formal variable: whether the rule is *mandatory* or *discretionary*. Some rules are so phrased that they seem to allow no leeway to the interpreter (the court). Among these are the familiar "conclusive presumptions." A classic example of this type was the Rule in Shelley's case. If a devise or gift by deed is made to A for life, remainder to the heirs (or heirs of the body) of A, A takes an estate in fee simple. The heirs of A have no interest in the property, no "remainder" at all. The rule was said to be not a rule of construction but a rule of law. This meant that the court was not supposed to ask what the man who wrote the deed or will meant; once the court discovered the magic words which brought the deed or will within the rule, the fee simple to A automatically resulted. The rule recognized no discretionary power in the judge to "construe" the instrument which contained the phrase. Of course, the judges invented the rule, and could (as they later did in some jurisdictions) disinvent it. But as formulated, the classic rule in Shelley's case left no room for the exercise of discretion by the judge; he was not supposed to vary the application of the rule according to the circumstances of the case. The rule was absolute. Such rules are here called *mandatory* rules.

Other rules are less stringent. They leave the judge greater scope to vary application of the rule according to circumstances. For example, consider the problem of a will which makes gifts to each "child" of A. Suppose that A has an adopted child B. Does B qualify as a "child"? Two mandatory rules are theoretically possible: (a) that the word "child" can never mean an adopted child; and (b) that the word "child" must always cover adopted as well as natural children. But there are other possibilities. A court might lay down a rule that "child" may mean an adopted child if that interpretation proved to be the fairest one in the light of all relevant circumstances. Or the court might claim that the true meaning of the word must be sought in the "intention of the testator." Both of these are rules of a type we here call *discretionary*. The judge has the power to weigh the facts and tailor his decision to the particular case. He is not bound (even theoretically) to react mechanically to the mere presence of the word "child" in a will. Of course, few rules are completely discretionary—few rules are phrased in such a way that the judge seems to have completely free reign in making up his mind one way or another. He may have this power in fact, but the formal rules usually suggest some sort of guide-line. "Presumptions" are examples of such guide-lines. A court (or statute) can lay down a rule that the word "child" in a will shall be "presumed" to include adopted children, or, conversely, that the word shall be "presumed" to mean only blood children. There are other ways of phrasing presumptions. One way is to use a stop-gap rule—for example, that the word "child" in a will does (or does not) include an adopted child, unless the contrary is clearly expressed by the testator. There are weak presumptions and strong presumptions. In short, rules of legal interpretation run along a continuum from completely mandatory to completely discretionary, with many stages in between.

* * *

So far, we have spoken only of two classes of legal decision-makers—judges and legislators. There are other decision-makers who are profoundly affected by the form of rules of interpretation—for example, the general public. A man who wants to leave some money to an adopted child is very much concerned with whether there is a mandatory or a discretionary rule covering the subject. Provided he knows about the rules, his job is simplified if the rules are mandatory; at the very least, it takes less time and paper to accomplish his purposes. Often the effect of mandatory rules is to enhance a particular quality of written documents, which we will here call their *autonomy*. Consider the case of the negotiable instrument. A check, bill, or note can be made payable to bearer, which means that the instrument can then be transferred as a negotiable instrument without endorsement. Under the Negotiable Instruments Law payable to "bearer" or to "John Smith or bearer" *is* bearer paper. The rule is mandatory. The word "bearer" always has this effect and there are no exceptions worth taking into account. The mandatory quality of the rule on the meaning of "bearer" on a note means that the note can stand on its own two feet; it can be used without consulting or channeling one's actions through a court or any other discretion-bearing legal agency. Thus the hard-and-fast "bearer" rule is really an expression of the distribution of power over the subject matter within the legal system; in this case, courts are told that they may not look into the "circumstances," but are bound by the legal import of the word "bearer." At the same time, the power of private citizens to produce predictable consequences in the framing of private transactions is much enhanced. In general, mandatory rules make for autonomous instruments, with standard meanings, usable for business purposes without the intervention of legal agencies.

* * *

In modern law the term "contract" covers business agreements (and some non-business ones) of almost infinite variety. It is not possible to "cover" contracts with a network of mandatory rules of interpretation. In a sense, the free form of the "contract" is its essence; the growth of contract law in the last two centuries is the growth of the area of the free market, the area of dealings not subject to mandatory rules of interpretation and phraseology. In a sense then, a single basic principle underlies the Anglo–American law of contract: that courts will enforce contracts as written, without imposing set rules of interpretation or requiring the use of ritual phrases. Contracts law was private law; the courts did not in general try to exercise their power to prescribe and enforce formality. This state of affairs was a natural one. Forms of economic bargain were developing so rapidly and so diversely that any attempt to channel draftsmanship into prescribed formalities would be pointless. Of course, contract law entered the modern economic world with some inherited doctrines of formality—the effect of the seal, the Statute of Frauds, and the parol evidence rule are examples. The seal quickly became "obsolete." The typical user of contract law (and by 1800 millions could "use" the law of contract) did not know about the effect of the seal, or for that matter, own a seal. Consequently, the old doctrines were no longer useful or usable; they were nuisances. Vague popular understanding about the efficacy of writing has probably kept the Statute of Frauds alive, or half alive. In any event, memory is so frail that most planned, large-scale contracts *must* be in writing so that the Statute has only marginal impact. The parol evidence rule was a rule to foster autonomy, analogous to the "four corners" rule in wills. It reminds us that the goal of documentary autonomy touched this field of law, too. Other rules of contract law tended in this direction. For example, the law heavily favored definiteness in phrasing—open-price contracts, contracts missing essential terms, out-put and requirements contracts, were of dubious enforceability in the 19th century. Every beginning law student knows that an offer must be accepted without variation; otherwise it is nothing but a "counteroffer." This rule suggests that the law wants a series of documents from which an objective third party could determine, with complete precision, whether or not a "contract" had been reached.

Just as Gray gave classic expression to "mathematical" precision in the law of perpetuities, so the ideal of autonomy in contract law reached its classic expression late in life (and naturally in a weaker form). Gray's role was played by Williston and the "objective theory" of contracts. For Williston, an enforceable contract could be formed though the "contract" was "in accordance with the intention of neither party." He was speaking of a contract whose text suffered from "mutual mistake": "Where each party is mistaken, but as to a different matter, that will not affect the formation of a valid contract. ... The Court will give the language [of a contract] its natural and appropriate meaning; and, if the words are unambiguous, will not even admit evidence of what the parties may have thought the meaning to be."[8] Learned Hand made a similar point in a well-known passage: "A contract has, strictly speaking, nothing to do with the personal, or individual intent of the parties." In the ordinary case, the objective meaning of the words had to prevail, even though "twenty bishops" testified that "either party, when he used the words, intended something else than the usual meaning which the law imposes upon them." It is no greater paradox to think of a phrase in a contract which neither of two people meant to say, than to think of carrying out a clause in a will which says something that the testator clearly never meant to say. And to speak of meanings which the law "imposes" on words is to imply that the courts are accomplishing some purpose in "imposing" meanings, unless courts impose for imposing's sake, which is not generally a tenable position.

Very generally, the purpose of objectivity in the law of contracts is similar to the purpose of formal purity in the law of negotiable instruments. Although contracts are not transferred from hand to hand like currency, they are often documents setting forth the agreed framework within which business transactions are to be carried out. It was at least not farfetched for a court to imagine that precision and certainty of interpretation aided business rationality. Quite apart from this, objectivity and autonomy were attractive ideals to the scholars of the late 19th and early 20th centuries. Legal thought of the time tended to perceive law as a "science": a "body of rules all rationally related to and connected with one another in such a way that any given rule can be deduced by a process of logic from other rules already known."[9] The rules we are discussing were basically logical, all-inclusive, and symmetrical; they tended toward certi-

---

8. Williston, Contracts § 95 (rev. ed. 1936).

9. Dickinson, *The Problem of the Unprovided Case*, 81 U.Pa.L.Rev. 115, 116 (1932).

tude. They had the clean, scientific lines so appealing to the intellectual predilections of Williston's generation.

Some fifty years later, precisely those parts of the law of contracts in which autonomy was a strong influence have undergone change. Requirements contracts are freely enforced, for example. Much less objective certainty is demanded of contractual instruments. American law is increasingly generous in permitting the exercise of wide discretion by courts, administrative bodies, and private persons (trustees, agents, and parties to contracts) operating under written documents. The courts themselves have increasingly exercised their discretion by replacing hard-and-fast rules with rules appealing to "reasonableness" and "fairness"—vague standards which vary from case to case.

As a result, a certain looseness and decay of doctrine seem to have crept into the law of contract. But on closer look, we find that the process has been really quite selective. We distort the picture if we look only at the classical boundaries of the law of contracts, and only at the courts. Legal change takes place in many ways. Those changes which are internal to a legal agency or a "field" of law are easiest to see for an observer whose eyes are fixed on the agency or field. But law also changes by shifting subject matters from field to field, and by shifting jurisdiction from agency to agency; and these changes, while they may be equally great, can escape the observer whose eyes are rigid. The history of contract law is particularly full of pitfalls (and lessons). Classical contract law labored to set up conditions under which business transactions could be smoothly carried on. It attempted to preserve stability and maintain order by laying down fixed precepts and applying them in a reasonably uniform manner. At the same time, it allowed room for economic change and business development by taking a general hands-off attitude toward the form and content of business agreements. These policies determined the general shape of contract law: on the negative side, an avoidance of mandatory rules and "magic" words; on the positive side, rules which fostered precise and objective interpretation of freely-bargained contracts.

The looseness in modern contract law does not mean that the legal system has abandoned entirely its former values. But certain functions have been transferred from the judge-made law of contracts to other agencies and fields of law. The courts now play a quite limited role in laying down basic business ground rules. Within the limited, peripheral jurisdiction left to the courts, judges are freer to adopt a case-by-case approach; the residual controversies in court tend to be non-recurrent, rare, or marginal. Naturally the courts feel less need to create or confirm mandatory rules, or rules of "objective" interpretation. This change is well illustrated by the history of insurance law. All states now heavily regulate insurance. Insurance commissions supervise the companies; in some states there are even "standard" policies—pre-packaged, mandatory statutory policies. In the occasional insurance case, an appellate court can take this regulatory background for granted and turn its attention to details of the particular case. In 19th century insurance case-law the legal demands of the insurance companies conflicted with the demands of the insurance consumer. The companies might have operated either under a system of autonomous rules (provided the ultimate source of these rules was business practice) or under a system which validated without qualification whatever appeared in a company's printed form-contracts. Either system contemplated in effect a cession of power to the companies. The consumer litigant preferred a case-by-case approach, in which full discretionary decision-making power was retained by the courts; or a system which ceded power to the consuming public indirectly by throwing as many cases as possible to the jury. The case-law, faced by these conflicts, wobbled and vacillated. "Sympathy" for litigants pulled the court one way, "principle" the other. The pull of "principle" was strong because the courts felt that they had a duty to lay down general rules of a kind that a growing and mighty business could work with. Now that the general principles are legislative and administrative, the court no longer sees itself building a legal framework for a billion-dollar industry, brick by brick; and it can therefore more readily picture itself as concerned only with "justice" between Mr. A and Company B.

Even within traditional contract law, there was no uniform movement from mandatory to discretionary rules. Particularly where the consumers of a given rule were members of the "public" (or at least a very large group), the court was under some pressure to reject the classical approach which merely validated professionally drafted documents and allowed parties to "make their own law." In labor contracts, contracts of common carriers, and insurance contracts, the courts began with such rules. A rule that all contracts of type A are enforceable as written is a mandatory rule, just as the Rule in Shelley's case was. But the courts came to reject this mandatory rule where they saw "inequality of bargaining power" or some danger to the general society. Take the case of contracting-out of negligence. The result of a mandatory rule enforcing contracts as written struck the courts as dangerous here. As a practical matter, "inequality of bargaining power" meant inequality of drafting skill and inequality of workable knowledge of the existing rules of law * * *. The courts tended to redress the balance by "presumptions" and high-handed interpretation rules (recall the rule that construed drafted documents against the draftsman). But where the imbalance of drafting skills was greatest, the courts were sometimes forced by tighter and tighter drafting to abandon their presumptive rules and bring in a new mandatory rule, e.g., that contracting-out of negligence was always "void." Ultimately, many of these areas of high public concern passed to other branches of government, and the courts were left with cases which could not be or need not be standardized. [Some footnotes omitted.]

Friedman, *Law, Rules and Interpretation of Written Documents,* 59 Nw.L.Rev. 751, 753–55, 774–79 (1965). Reprinted by special permission from the Northwestern University Law Review, Northwestern University School of Law, Copyright © 1965. [Some footnotes omitted. Those retained have been renumbered.]

Pacific Gas and Electric Co. v. G. W. Thomas Drayage & Rigging Co.

Supreme Court of California, 1968.
69 Cal.2d 33, 69 Cal.Rptr. 561, 442 P.2d 641.

■ TRAYNOR, CHIEF JUSTICE. Defendant appeals from a judgment for plaintiff in an action for damages for injury to property under an indemnity clause of a contract.

In 1960 defendant entered into a contract with plaintiff to furnish the labor and equipment necessary to remove and replace the upper metal cover of plaintiff's steam turbine. Defendant agreed to perform the work "at [its] own risk and expense" and to "indemnify" plaintiff "against all loss, damage, expense and liability resulting from * * * injury to property, arising out of or in any way connected with the performance of this contract." Defendant also agreed to procure not less than $50,000 insurance to cover liability for injury to property. Plaintiff was to be an additional named insured, but the policy was to contain a cross-liability clause extending the coverage to plaintiff's property.

During the work the cover fell and injured the exposed rotor of the turbine. Plaintiff brought this action to recover $25,144.51, the amount it subsequently spent on repairs. During the trial it dismissed a count based on negligence and thereafter secured judgment on the theory that the indemnity provision covered injury to all property regardless of ownership.

Defendant offered to prove by admissions of plaintiff's agents, by defendant's conduct under similar contracts entered into with plaintiff, and by other proof that in the indemnity clause the parties meant to cover injury to property of third parties only and not to plaintiff's property. Although the trial court observed that the language used was "the classic language for a third party indemnity provision" and that "one could very easily conclude that * * * its whole intendment is to indemnify third parties," it nevertheless held that the "plain language" of the agreement also required defendant to indemnify plaintiff for injuries to plaintiff's property. Having determined that the contract had a plain meaning, the court refused to admit any extrinsic evidence that would contradict its interpretation.

When a court interprets a contract on this basis, it determines the meaning of the instrument in accordance with the "* * * extrinsic evidence of the judge's own linguistic education and experience." (3 Corbin on Contracts (1960 ed.) [1964 Supp. § 579, p. 225, fn. 56].) The exclusion of testimony that might contradict the linguistic background of the judge reflects a judicial belief in the possibility of perfect verbal expression. (9 Wigmore on Evidence (3d ed. 1940) § 2461, p. 187.) This belief is a remnant of a primitive faith in the inherent potency and inherent meaning of words.

The test of admissibility of extrinsic evidence to explain the meaning of a written instrument is not whether it appears to the court to be plain and unambiguous on its face, but whether the offered evidence is relevant to prove a meaning to which the language of the instrument is reasonably susceptible. . . .

A rule that would limit the determination of the meaning of a written instrument to its four-corners merely because it seems to the court to be clear and unambiguous, would either deny the relevance of the intention of the parties or presuppose a degree of verbal precision and stability our language has not attained.

Some courts have expressed the opinion that contractual obligations are created by the mere use of certain words, whether or not there was any intention to incur such obligations. Under this view, contractual obligations flow, not from the intention of the parties but from the fact that they used certain magic words. Evidence of the parties' intention therefore becomes irrelevant.

In this state, however, the intention of the parties as expressed in the contract is the source of contractual rights and duties. A court must ascertain and give effect to this intention by determining what the parties meant by the words they used. Accordingly, the exclusion of relevant, extrinsic evidence to explain the meaning of a written instrument could be justified only if it were feasible to determine the meaning the parties gave to the words from the instrument alone.

If words had absolute and constant referents, it might be possible to discover contractual intention in the words themselves and in the manner in which they were arranged. Words, however, do not have absolute and constant referents. "A word is a symbol of thought but has no arbitrary and fixed meaning like a symbol of algebra or chemistry, * * *." (Pearson v. State Social Welfare Board (1960) 54 Cal.2d 184, 195, 5 Cal.Rptr. 553, 559, 353 P.2d 33, 39.) The meaning of particular words or groups of words varies with the "* * * verbal context and surrounding circumstances and purposes in view of the linguistic education and experience of their users and their hearers or readers (not excluding judges). * * * A word has no meaning apart from these factors; much less does it have an objective meaning, one true meaning." (Corbin, The Interpretation of Words and the Parol Evidence Rule (1965) 50 Cornell L.Q. 161, 187.) Accordingly, the meaning of a writing "* * * can only be found by interpretation in the light of all the circumstances that reveal the sense in which the writer used the words. The exclusion of parol evidence regarding such circumstances merely because the words do not appear ambiguous to the reader can easily lead to the attribution to a written instrument of a meaning that was never intended. [Citations omitted.]"

* * *

Although extrinsic evidence is not admissible to add to, detract from, or vary the terms of a written contract, these terms must first be determined before it can be decided whether or not extrinsic evidence is being offered for a prohibited purpose. The fact that the terms of an instrument appear clear to a judge does not preclude the possibility that the parties chose the language of the instrument to express different terms. That possibility is not limited to contracts whose terms have acquired a particular meaning by trade usage, but exists whenever the parties' understanding of the words used may have differed from the judge's understanding.

Accordingly, rational interpretation requires at least a preliminary consideration of all credible evidence offered to prove the intention of the parties. (Civ.Code, § 1647; Code Civ.Proc. § 1860; see also 9 Wigmore on Evidence, op. cit. supra, § 2470, fn. 11, p. 227.) Such evidence includes testimony as to the "circumstances surrounding the making of the agreement * * * including the object, nature and subject matter of the writing * * *" so that the court can "place itself in the same situation in which the parties found themselves at the time of contracting." (Universal Sales Corp. v. Cal. Press Mfg. Co., supra, 20 Cal.2d 751, 761, 128 P.2d 665, 671; . . .) If the court decides, after considering this evidence, that the language of a contract, in the light of all the circumstances, is "fairly susceptible of either one of the two interpretations contended for * * *." (Balfour v. Fresno C. & I. Co. (1895) 109 Cal. 221, 225, 41 P. 876, 877 . . .) extrinsic evidence relevant to prove either of such meanings is admissible.

In the present case the court erroneously refused to consider extrinsic evidence offered to show that the indemnity clause in the contract was not intended to cover injuries to plaintiff's property. Although that evidence was not necessary to show that the indemnity clause was reasonably susceptible of the meaning contended for by defendant, it was nevertheless relevant and admissible on that issue. Moreover, since that clause was reasonably susceptible of that meaning, the offered evidence was also admissible to prove that the clause had that meaning and did not cover injuries to plaintiff's property. Accordingly, the judgment must be reversed.

A. Kemp Fisheries, Inc. v. Castle & Cooke, Inc.

United States Court of Appeals, Ninth Circuit, 1988.
852 F.2d 493.

■ EUGENE A. WRIGHT, CIRCUIT JUDGE.

In this case we consider whether the court properly admitted parol evidence to determine the terms of the Charter Agreement between A. Kemp Fisheries, Inc. and Bumble Bee Samoa, Inc., a subsidiary of Castle & Cooke, Inc. We conclude that the court applied the parol evidence rule incorrectly and reverse its judgment.

BACKGROUND

A. Kemp Fisheries Inc. and Bumble Bee Samoa, Inc., a fully owned subsidiary of Castle & Cooke, Inc., agreed that Kemp would charter, with an option to purchase, the M/V CITY OF SAN DIEGO. Kemp needed the vessel to fish for herring and salmon in Alaska from April to August 1983. In February of that year they signed a letter of intent that incorporated certain telexes exchanged in their negotiations. This letter served as their agreement "[p]ending preparation and execution of final documentation required for the bareboat charter and option to purchase." To compensate

Bumble Bee for removing the vessel from the market Kemp paid a nonrefundable deposit of $50,000.

After reviewing drafts of the agreement with Kemp's attorney, Bumble Bee sent the final bare boat Charter Agreement late in March. Louis Kemp, the charterer's president, found that the agreement differed from his understanding of the arrangement. Specifically, he understood that Bumble Bee had agreed that the engines would be in good working order and had represented orally that the freezing system would meet Kemp's specific needs. The agreement contained no such provisions and in fact, disclaimed all warranties, express or implied. Despite his reservations, Kemp signed it without voicing his concerns to Bumble Bee. He took the vessel in early April and sailed to Alaska for the May herring season.

In the midst of herring season, two of the three auxiliary engines that powered the SAN DIEGO's freezing system broke down. After repairing one engine, Kemp switched from freezing to curing the herring because it lacked confidence that the engine would last. Kemp sold the cured herring for a price below that for frozen herring.

In preparation for salmon season at the end of June, Kemp repaired the auxilliary engines and rented an additional engine. Although the engines were operating at full power and suffered no breakdowns, the salmon froze in a block and the flesh was "honey combed." Kemp's buyer rejected most of it. Kemp took it to a shore-based freezing plant in Bellingham where it was thawed and refrozen. It sold the salmon for 75¢ a pound, 50¢ less than the price it would have received for properly frozen salmon.

Kemp sued Bumble Bee and Castle & Cooke in admiralty for breach of the Charter Agreement, intentional and negligent misrepresentation, estoppel, and rescission. It claimed that Bumble Bee agreed to provide engines in good working order and represented that the freezing system would meet its specific needs.

The trial judge found that the Charter Agreement signed in March was ambiguous and admitted parol evidence to clarify the parties' intent. She concluded that the letter of intent and referenced telexes reflected the parties' final intent and indicated that no other negotiations would occur. From evidence of their negotiations, she found that Bumble Bee warranted the vessel to be seaworthy and the engines to be in good working condition, and represented orally that the vessel's freezing system could meet Kemp's specific requirements. She held Bumble Bee liable for all of Kemp's damages because the "inability of the M/V CITY OF SAN DIEGO to freeze herring and salmon within the parameters specified by Bumble Bee is solely the result of Bumble Bee's breach of warranties." Bumble Bee appeals.

ANALYSIS

* * *

[The court held that the Charter Agreement was an integrated writing.]

A. *Integration*

The Charter Agreement is an integrated contract. The agreement itself is complete and comprehensive. It covers in great detail the various rights and responsibilities of the parties. Although the Charter does not contain an integration clause, the letter of intent shows clearly that the parties intended that the Charter would be the "final documentation" of their agreement.

The alleged agreements regarding the warranties of the vessel's seaworthiness, engines, and freezing system are not collateral agreements that would normally be made in a separate contract. These alleged understandings directly contradict the Charter's waiver of all warranties. In addition, the agreement specifies Bumble Bee's responsibility for testing and repairing the freezing system and preparing the vessel for Kemp. If Bumble Bee warranted the freezing system and the engines, the Charter Agreement would typically provide that.

The circumstances surrounding this transaction also support our conclusion that the contract is integrated. Kemp and Bumble Bee are corporations familiar with business transactions. Kemp's attorney reviewed the Charter with Bumble Bee in the month before it signed. Bumble Bee incorporated some of Kemp's changes into the final Charter presented in March. Kemp had ample opportunity to express its understanding of the deal. Nothing suggests that this agreement was not recognized by both parties as final and complete.

B. *Ambiguity*

The judge admitted parol evidence to resolve ambiguities and contradictions within sub-paragraphs 3B, E and F. Sub-paragraph 3B provides:

> B.   Prior to delivery of the Vessel, Owner shall maintain the Vessel in good condition and shall cause the Vessel to be surveyed, on its own account, by a competent surveyor chosen by Owner, which survey shall show that the Vessel meets TA 2003 insurance requirements and is in all respects tight, staunch, strong and seaworthy.

Sub-paragraphs 3E and F provide:

> E.   Delivery to Charterer shall constitute full performance by Owner of all of Owner's obligations hereunder, and thereafter Charterer shall not be entitled to make or assert any claim against Owner on account of any representations or warranties, express or implied, with respect to the Vessel.

> F.   Charterer's acceptance of delivery of the Vessel, its equipment, gear and nonconsumable stores shall constitute conclusive evidence that the same have been inspected by Charterer and are accepted by Charterer as suitable for the intended use hereunder and, as between the parties, the seaworthiness and suitability of the Vessel, its equipment, gear and nonconsumable stores are deemed admitted.

The judge construed sub-paragraph 3B as an express warranty of seaworthiness and sub-paragraphs 3E and F as a waiver of that warranty. To resolve this conflict, she turned to parol evidence.

The court erred. The parol evidence rule requires that courts consider extrinsic evidence to determine whether the contract is ambiguous. Drayage, 69 Cal.Rptr. at 565–66, 442 P.2d at 645–46 ("[R]ational interpretation requires at least a preliminary consideration of all credible evidence offered to prove the intention of the parties."); Trident Center v. Connecticut General Life Ins. Co., 847 F.2d 564, 569 (9th Cir.1988). But if the extrinsic evidence advances an interpretation to which the language of the contract is not reasonably susceptible, the evidence is not admissible. Drayage, 69 Cal.Rptr. at 564, 442 P.2d at 644: "The test of admissibility of extrinsic evidence to explain the meaning of a written instrument is . . . whether the offered evidence is relevant to prove a meaning to which the language of the instrument is reasonably susceptible." Cf. *Trident*, at 570 n. 6.[2] The Charter Agreement is not "reasonably susceptible" to the court's interpretation that it warrants the seaworthiness of the vessel, the condition of the engines, and the capacity of the freezing system.

Sub-paragraph 3B concerns the condition of the vessel prior to delivery. It imposes on Bumble Bee an obligation to maintain the vessel in "good," not seaworthy condition, and to see that a "competent surveyor" surveys it to show that it is "tight, staunch, strong and seaworthy" for insurance purposes. It guarantees neither the accuracy of the survey nor the seaworthiness of the vessel.

Sub-paragraphs 3E and F address Bumble Bee's obligations after delivery. They provide that once Kemp accepts delivery, Bumble Bee's responsibility for the condition of the vessel ceases. They make clear that Kemp's acceptance of delivery releases Bumble Bee from responsibility for the vessel's condition and cannot be interpreted reasonably to warrant seaworthiness.

Nor should the court similarly have admitted evidence that Bumble Bee warranted the condition of the engines and the capacity of the freezing system. Paragraphs 3B, E and F do not even mention the engines or the freezing system and are not "reasonably susceptible" to that interpretation.

The court erred in admitting parol evidence and in enforcing warranties of seaworthiness, the engines, and freezing capacity. The Charter Agreement contains none of these warranties.

* * *

2. The broad language in *Trident* suggests that under California law courts must always admit extrinsic evidence to determine the meaning of disputed contract language. *Trident* held only that courts may not dismiss on the pleadings when one party claims that extrinsic evidence renders the contract ambiguous. The case must proceed beyond the pleadings so that the court may consider the evidence. If, after considering the evidence, the court determines that the contract is not reasonably susceptible to the interpretation advanced, the parol evidence rule operates to exclude the evidence. The court may then decide the case on a motion for summary judgment. See *Trident* at 570 n. 6. The court decided this case on a fully developed record.

CONCLUSION

The judgment is REVERSED and is rendered for the defendant. The Charter Agreement is an integrated contract and contained all the parties' agreements. It is not ambiguous and the court erred in admitting parol evidence on the warranty of seaworthiness, the capacity of the freezing system, and the engines. Bumble Bee effectively waived the implied warranty of seaworthiness and all other warranties. Bumble Bee is not liable for Kemp's losses.

[Some footnotes omitted.]

NOTES

(1) Restatement (Second) § 212, Comment b: "It is sometimes said that extrinsic evidence cannot change the plain meaning of a writing, but meaning can almost never be plain except in a context. Accordingly, the rule stated in Subsection (1) [pertaining to interpretation of integrated agreements] is not limited to cases where it is determined that the language used is ambiguous. Any determination of meaning or ambiguity should only be made in the light of the relevant evidence of the situation and relations of the parties, the subject matter of the transaction, preliminary negotiations and statements made therein, usages of trade, and the course of dealing between the parties."

(2) *The Interpretation Process.* The standard criterion for determining the existence of requisite assent in a contract is not subjective ("meeting of minds"), but objective. One is bound by the reasonable impression created in the mind of the other party. When a court is considering the existence of an offer, as in *Lucy v. Zehmer* (supra at 230), ostensibly it is attempting to ascertain the "intention" of the parties, but more accurately, it is appraising external conduct. Did the parties appear to agree? Not: did the parties actually agree? Of course, appearance and actuality will usually coincide, but the courts do not "read the mind." ("It is trite learning that the thought of man is not triable, for the devil himself knows not the thought of man." Brian, C.J. in Y.B., 17 Edw. IV, 1). The judiciary's task is more modest, albeit difficult: determination of the legal effect of manifestations. When a court acts in this way it is often said to be engaged in "interpretation." And indeed it is. But the common meaning of the word may not suggest the full scope of the judicial effort or adequately indicate precisely what is being done. It is submitted that the court is not merely describing a fact; it is ascribing legal effects to conduct. In a word, it is law making. The effort is not purely scientific, as in analyzing the chemical composition of a mixture. Rather, it is normative, indicating what ought to be the legal consequences of doing a particular thing.

Hence, while the avowed purpose of interpretation is the ascertainment of the contracting parties' intention, it is not actual subjective intention which is sought, but expressed or apparent intent. Primarily this involves consideration of the language used, be it oral or written, taken in the context in which it is found. Initially courts will inquire into the "plain meaning" of the words used. What is the ordinary signification of the language employed? Hundreds of decisions have been predicated upon a finding that the words used were clear and unambiguous, their meaning easily ascertained without resort to "extrinsic facts," leaving no room for "interpretation." Yet as Judge Traynor persuasively argues in *Pacific Gas,* in a sense every contract needs "interpretation." See also Williston § 609; Corbin § 535. "A word is not a crystal, transparent and unchanged; it is the skin of a living thought and may vary greatly in color and content according to the circumstances and the times in which it is used." Holmes, J. in Towne v. Eisner, 245 U.S. 418, 425, 38 S.Ct. 158, 159, 62 L.Ed. 372 (1918). For this reason, no sooner do courts advance a general rule of strict construction than are exceptions made. For many additional reasons words may have more than one meaning.

> Words are the conduits by which thoughts are communicated, yet scarcely any of them have such a fixed and single meaning that they are incapable of denoting more than one thought. In addition to the multiplicity in meaning of words set forth in the dictionaries there are the meanings imparted to them by trade customs, local uses, dialects, telegraphic codes, etc. One meaning crowds a word full of significance, while another almost empties the utterance of any import. The various groups above indicated are constantly amplifying our language; in fact, they are developing what may be called languages of their own. Thus one is justified in saying that the language of the dictionaries is not the only language spoken in America. For instance, the word 'thousand' as commonly used has a very specific meaning; it denotes ten hundreds or fifty scores, but the language of the various trades and localities has assigned to it meanings quite different from that just mentioned. Thus in the bricklaying trade a contract which fixes the bricklayer's compensation at '$5.25 a thousand' does not contemplate that he need lay actually 1,000 bricks in order to earn $5.25, but that he should build a wall of a certain size. . . . And, where the custom of a locality considers 100 dozen as constituting a thousand, one who has 19,200 rabbits upon a warren under an agreement for their sale at the price of 60 pounds for each thousand rabbits will be paid for only 16,000 rabbits. . . . Numerous other instances could readily be cited showing the manner in which the meaning of words has been contracted, expanded or otherwise altered by local usage, trade custom, dialect influence, code agreement, etc.

Hurst v. Lake & Co., Inc., 141 Or. 306, 16 P.2d 627, 629 (1932).

(3) *Interpretation Under the UCC.* Under the UCC, one must distinguish rules for construing the statute itself and rules for interpreting agreements of the parties otherwise within the scope of the statute. With regard to the former, UCC 1–102(1) provides that this "Act shall be liberally construed and applied to promote" the underlying purposes and policies set forth in UCC 1–102(2), e.g., "to permit the continued expansion of commercial practices through custom, usage and agreement of the parties." UCC 1–102(2)(b). In addition, Comment 1 to UCC 1–102 states that the text of each section should be read in the light of the purpose and policy of the rule or principle in question, as also of the Act as a whole, and the application of the language should be construed narrowly or broadly, as the case may be, in conformity with the purposes and policies involved. With regard to the latter, the UCC provides no comprehensive approach to the interpretation of agreements. However, Subsection (a) of UCC 2–202 [UCC 2–202 (1997)] provides that terms which are not to be *contradicted* because of the finality of the writing may be

explained or *supplemented* "by course of dealing or usage of trade (Section 1–205) or by course of performance (Section 2–208)." The Code thereby explicitly encourages the use of these important extrinsic aids in the interpretation process. See Kastely, *Stock Equipment for the Bargain in Fact: Trade Usage, "Express Terms," and Consistency Under Section 1–205 of the UCC,* 64 N.C.L.Rev. 777 (1986).

The "course of performance" provision, UCC 2–208(1) [UCC 2–209 (1997)], reads as follows:

"Where the contract for sale involves repeated occasions for performance by either party with knowledge of the nature of the performance and opportunity for objection to it by the other, any course of performance accepted or acquiesced in without objection shall be relevant to determine the meaning of the agreement."

The significant Code provision relative to course of dealing and usage of trade is UCC 1–205, which provides:

"(1) A course of dealing is a sequence of previous conduct between the parties to a particular transaction which is fairly to be regarded as establishing a common basis of understanding for interpreting their expressions and other conduct.

"(2) A usage of trade is any practice or method of dealing having such regularity of observance in a place, vocation or trade as to justify an expectation that it will be observed with respect to the transaction in question. The existence and scope of such a usage are to be proved as facts. If it is established that such a usage is embodied in a written trade code or similar writing the interpretation of the writing is for the court.

"(3) A course of dealing between parties and any usage of trade in the vocation or trade in which they are engaged or of which they are or should be aware give particular meaning to and supplement or qualify terms of an agreement.

"(4) The express terms of an agreement and an applicable course of dealing or usage of trade shall be construed wherever reasonable as consistent with each other; but when such construction is unreasonable express terms control both course of dealing and usage of trade and course of dealing controls usage of trade.

"(5) An applicable usage of trade in the place where any part of performance is to occur shall be used in interpreting the agreement as to that part of the performance.

"(6) Evidence of a relevant usage of trade offered by one party is not admissible unless and until he has given the other party such notice as the court finds sufficient to prevent unfair surprise to the latter."

(4) Assuming that the parol evidence rule and judicial utterances about the "plain meaning" of language will not be unduly restrictive upon the production of relevant evidence, the next problem is to understand how the court goes about the interpretation process. The following comment and case deal with this process. As you analyze the opinion, consider the following factors: (1) the nature of the negotiation process leading up to the agreement—were lawyers involved, did both parties participate, was it careful and thorough, etc.; (2) the

type of evidence which the court admits as relevant—trade usage, conduct of the parties, statements in the course of negotiations, prior course of dealing, etc.; (3) the various "maxims," if any, employed by the court to assist in ascertaining meaning; (4) the "test," if any, employed by the court to determine whether the plaintiff's or the defendant's understanding of what the language meant is to be preferred and the role of the jury in this process.

Comment: Judge Traynor v. Judge Kozinski: A Return to the "Plain Meaning" Rule?

In Trident Center v. Connecticut General Life Ins., 847 F.2d 564 (9th Cir.1988), discussed in *A. Kemp Fisheries,* supra at 608, sophisticated parties, with the assistance of counsel, negotiated a commercial loan for more than $56,000,000. The contract, which was lengthy and detailed, provided for a secured loan at 12.25% interest for 15 years. The promissory note provided that the maker "shall not have the right to prepay the principal amount hereof in whole or in part" for the first 12 years. After 12 years, prepayment was permitted subject to a sliding scale prepayment fee. The note also provided that in case of default during the first two years, the defendant could accelerate the note and add a 10% prepayment fee. Interest rates dropped, however, and in 1987, some four years after the contract was signed, the plaintiff claimed that it was entitled to prepay the loan, subject to only a 10% prepayment fee. When the defendant objected, the plaintiff sought a declaratory judgment that it was entitled to prepay. The district court dismissed the complaint on the ground that the loan documents "clearly and unambiguously precluded prepayment during the first 12 years." On appeal, the decision was reversed and remanded for the court to hear extrinsic evidence on the parties' intention in drafting the agreement.

In the course of his opinion, Judge Kozinski had this to say about Judge Traynor's opinion in *Pacific Gas & Electric Co.,* supra:

* * *

B.   Extrinsic Evidence

Trident argues in the alternative that, even if the language of the contract appears to be unambiguous, the deal the parties actually struck is in fact quite different. It wishes to offer extrinsic evidence that the parties had agreed Trident could prepay at any time within the first 12 years by tendering the full amount plus a 10 percent prepayment fee. As discussed above, this is an interpretation to which the contract, as written, is not reasonably susceptible. Under traditional contract principles, extrinsic evidence is inadmissible to interpret, vary or add to the terms of an unambiguous integrated written instrument. See 4 S. Williston, supra p. 5, § 631, at 948–49; 2 B. Witkin, California Evidence § 981, at 926 (3d ed. 1986).

Trident points out, however, that California does not follow the traditional rule. Two decades ago the California Supreme Court in Pacific Gas & Electric Co. v. G.W. Thomas Drayage & Rigging Co., 69 Cal.2d 33, 69 Cal.Rptr. 561, 442 P.2d 641 (1968), turned its back on the notion that a contract can ever have a plain meaning discernible by a court without resort to extrinsic evidence. The court reasoned that contractual obligations flow not from the words of the contract, but from the intention of the parties. "Accordingly," the court stated, "the exclusion of relevant, extrinsic, evidence to explain the meaning of a written instrument could be justified only if it were feasible to determine the meaning the parties gave to the words from the instrument alone." 69 Cal.2d at 38, 69 Cal.Rptr. 561, 442 P.2d 641. This, the California Supreme Court concluded, is impossible: "If words had absolute and constant referents, it might be possible to discover contractual intention in the words themselves and in the manner in which they were arranged. Words, however, do not have absolute and constant referents." Id. In the same vein, the court noted that "[t]he exclusion of testimony that might contradict the linguistic background of the judge reflects a judicial belief in the possibility of perfect verbal expression. This belief is a remnant of a primitive faith in the inherent potency and inherent meaning of words." Id. at 37, 69 Cal.Rptr. 561, 442 P.2d 641 (citation and footnotes omitted).[5]

Under *Pacific Gas*, it matters not how clearly a contract is written, nor how completely it is integrated, nor how carefully it is negotiated, nor how squarely it addresses the issue before the court: the contract cannot be rendered impervious to attack by parol evidence. If one side is willing to claim that the parties intended one thing but the agreement provides for another, the court must consider extrinsic evidence of possible ambiguity. If that evidence raises the specter of ambiguity where there was none before, the contract language is displaced and the intention of the parties must be divined from self-serving testimony offered by partisan witnesses whose recollection is hazy from passage of time and colored by their conflicting interests. See Delta Dynamics, Inc. v. Arioto, 69 Cal.2d 525, 532, 446 P.2d 785, 72 Cal.Rptr. 785 (1968) (Mosk, J., dissenting). We question whether this approach is more likely to divulge the original intention of the parties than reliance on the seemingly clear words they agreed upon at the time. See generally Morta v. Korea Ins. Corp., 840 F.2d 1452, 1460 (9th Cir. 1988).

Pacific Gas casts a long shadow of uncertainty over all transactions negotiated and executed under the law of California. As this case illustrates, even when the transaction is very sizeable, even if it involves only sophisticated parties, even if it was negotiated with the aid of counsel, even if it results in contract language that is devoid of ambiguity, costly and protracted litigation cannot be avoided if one party has a strong enough motive for challenging the contract. While this rule creates much business for lawyers and an occasional windfall to some clients, it leads only to

---

5. In an unusual footnote, the court compared the belief in the immutable meaning of words with " '[t]he elaborate system of taboo and verbal prohibitions in primitive groups ... [such as] the Swedish peasant custom of curing sick cattle smitten by witchcraft, by making them swallow a page torn out of the psalter and put in dough....' " Id. n. 2 (quoting Ullman, The Principles of Semantics 43 (1963)).

frustration and delay for most litigants and clogs already overburdened courts.

It also chips away at the foundation of our legal system. By giving credence to the idea that words are inadequate to express concepts, *Pacific Gas* undermines the basic principle that language provides a meaningful constraint on public and private conduct. If we are unwilling to say that parties, dealing face to face, can come up with language that binds them, how can we send anyone to jail for violating statutes consisting of mere words lacking "absolute and constant referents"? How can courts ever enforce decrees, not written in language understandable to all, but encoded in a dialect reflecting only the "linguistic background of the judge"? Can lower courts ever be faulted for failing to carry out the mandate of higher courts when "perfect verbal expression" is impossible? Are all attempts to develop the law in a reasoned and principled fashion doomed to failure as "remnant[s] of a primitive faith in the inherent potency and inherent meaning of words"?

847 F.2d at 568–69.

Frigaliment Importing Co. v. B.N.S. International Sales Corp.

United States District Court, S.D. New York, 1960.
190 F.Supp. 116.

■ FRIENDLY, CIRCUIT JUDGE. The issue is, what is chicken? Plaintiff says "chicken" means a young chicken, suitable for broiling and frying. Defendant says "chicken" means any bird of that genus that meets contract specifications on weight and quality, including what it calls "stewing chicken" and plaintiff pejoratively terms "fowl." Dictionaries give both meanings, as well as some others not relevant here. To support its, plaintiff sends a number of volleys over the net; defendant essays to return them and adds a few serves of its own. Assuming that both parties were acting in good faith, the case nicely illustrates Holmes' remark "that the making of a contract depends not on the agreement of two minds in one intention, but on the agreement of two sets of external signs—not on the parties' having *meant* the same thing but on their having *said* the same thing." The Path of the Law, in Collected Legal Papers, p. 178. I have concluded that plaintiff has not sustained its burden of persuasion that the contract used "chicken" in the narrower sense.

The action is for breach of the warranty that goods sold shall correspond to the description, New York Personal Property Law, McKinney's Consol.Laws, c. 41 § 95. Two contracts are in suit. In the first, dated May 2, 1957, defendant, a New York sales corporation, confirmed the sale to plaintiff, a Swiss corporation, of

"US Fresh Frozen Chicken, Grade A, Government Inspected, Eviscerated

2½–3 lbs. and 1½–2 lbs. each

all chicken individually wrapped in cryovac, packed in secured fiber cartons or wooden boxes, suitable for export

75,000 lbs. 2½-3 lbs. .... @ $33.00
25,000 lbs. 1½-2 lbs. .... @ $36.50

per 100 lbs. FAS New York

scheduled May 10, 1957 pursuant to instructions from Penson & Co., New York."

The second contract, also dated May 2, 1957, was identical save that only 50,000 lbs. of the heavier "chicken" were called for, the price of the smaller birds was $37 per 100 lbs., and shipment was scheduled for May 30. The initial shipment under the first contract was short but the balance was shipped on May 17. When the initial shipment arrived in Switzerland, plaintiff found, on May 28, that the 2½-3 lbs. birds were not young chicken suitable for broiling and frying but stewing chicken or "fowl"; indeed, many of the cartons and bags plainly so indicated. Protests ensued. Nevertheless, shipment under the second contract was made on May 29, the 2½-3 lbs. birds again being stewing chicken. Defendant stopped the transportation of these at Rotterdam.

This action followed. Plaintiff says that, notwithstanding that its acceptance was in Switzerland, New York law controls under the principle of Rubin v. Irving Trust Co., 1953, 305 N.Y. 288, 305, 113 N.E.2d 424, 431; defendant does not dispute this, and relies on New York decisions. I shall follow the apparent agreement of the parties as to the applicable law.

Since the word "chicken" standing alone is ambiguous, I turn first to see whether the contract itself offers any aid to its interpretation. Plaintiff says the 1½-2 lbs. birds necessarily had to be young chicken since the older birds do not come in that size, hence the 2½-3 lbs. birds must likewise be young. This is unpersuasive—a contract for "apples" of two different sizes could be filled with different kinds of apples even though only one species came in both sizes. Defendant notes that the contract called not simply for chicken but for "US Fresh Frozen Chicken, Grade A, Government Inspected." It says the contract thereby incorporated by reference the Department of Agriculture's regulations, which favor its interpretation; I shall return to this after reviewing plaintiff's other contentions.

The first hinges on an exchange of cablegrams which preceded execution of the formal contracts. The negotiations leading up to the contracts were conducted in New York between defendant's secretary, Ernest R. Bauer, and a Mr. Stovicek, who was in New York for the Czechoslovak government at the World Trade Fair. A few days after meeting Bauer at the fair, Stovicek telephoned and inquired whether defendant would be interested in exporting poultry to Switzerland. Bauer then met with Stovicek, who showed him a cable from plaintiff dated April 26, 1957, announcing that they "are buyer" of 25,000 lbs. of chicken 2½-3 lbs. weight, Cryovac packed, grade A Government inspected, at a price up to 33¢ per pound, for shipment on May 10, to be confirmed by the following morning, and were interested in further offerings. After testing the market for price Bauer accepted, and Stovicek sent a confirmation that evening. Plaintiff stresses that, although these and subsequent cables between plaintiff and defendant, which laid the basis for the additional quantities under the first and for all of the second contract, were predominantly in German, they used the English word "chicken"; it claims this was done because it understood "chicken" meant young chicken whereas the German word, "Huhn," included both "Brathuhn" (broilers) and "Suppenhuhn" (stewing chicken), and that defendant, whose officers were thoroughly conversant with German, should have realized this. Whatever force this argument might otherwise have is largely drained away by Bauer's testimony that he asked Stovicek what kind of chickens were wanted, received the answer "any kind of chickens," and then, in German, asked whether the cable meant "Huhn" and received an affirmative response. Plaintiff attacks this as contrary to what Bauer testified on his deposition in March, 1959, and also on the ground that Stovicek had no authority to interpret the meaning of the cable. The first contention would be persuasive if sustained by the record, since Bauer was free at the trial from the threat of contradiction by Stovicek as he was not at the time of the deposition; however, review of the deposition does not convince me of the claimed inconsistency. As to the second contention, it may well be that Stovicek lacked authority to commit plaintiff for prices or delivery dates other than those specified in the cable; but plaintiff cannot at the same time rely on its cable to Stovicek as its dictionary to the meaning of the contract and repudiate the interpretation given the dictionary by the man in whose hands it was put. See Restatement of the Law of Agency, 2d, § 145; 2 Mecham, Agency § 1781 (2d ed. 1914); Park v. Moorman Mfg. Co., 1952, 121 Utah 339, 241 P.2d 914, 919, 40 A.L.R.2d 273; Henderson v. Jimmerson, Tex.Civ.App.1950, 234 S.W.2d 710, 717–718. Plaintiff's reliance on the fact that the contract forms contain the words "through the intermediary of: _____", with the blank not filled, as negating agency, is wholly unpersuasive; the purpose of this clause was to permit filling in the name of an intermediary to whom a commission would be payable, not to blot out what had been the fact.

Plaintiff's next contention is that there was a definite trade usage that "chicken" meant "young chicken." Defendant showed that it was only beginning in the poultry trade in 1957, thereby bringing itself within the principle that "when one of the parties is not a member of the trade or other circle, his acceptance of the standard must be made to appear" by proving either that he had actual knowledge of the usage or that the usage is "so generally known in the community that his actual individual knowledge of it may be inferred." 9 Wigmore, Evidence (3d ed. 1940) § 2464. Here there was no proof of actual knowledge of the alleged usage; indeed, it is quite plain that defendant's belief was to the contrary. In order to meet the alternative requirement, the law of New York demands a showing that "the usage is of so long continuance, so well established, so notorious, so universal and so reasonable in itself, as that the presumption is violent that the parties contracted with reference to it, and made it a part of their agreement." Walls v. Bailey, 1872, 49 N.Y. 464, 472–473.

Plaintiff endeavored to establish such a usage by the testimony of three witnesses and certain other evidence. Strasser, resident buyer in New York for a large chain of Swiss cooperatives, testified that "on chicken I would definitely understand a broiler." However, the force of this testimony was considerably weakened by the fact that in his own transactions the witness, a careful businessman, protected himself by using "broiler" when that was what he wanted and "fowl" when he wished older birds. Indeed, there are some indications, dating back to a remark of Lord Mansfield, Edie v. East India Co., 2 Burr. 1216, 1222 (1761), that no credit should be given "witnesses to usage, who could not adduce instances in verification." 7 Wigmore, Evidence (3d ed.1940), § 1954; see McDonald v. Acker, Merrall & Condit Co., 2d Dept.1920, 192 App.Div. 123, 126, 182 N.Y.S. 607. While Wigmore thinks this goes too far, a witness' consistent failure to rely on the alleged usage deprives his opinion testimony of much of its effect. Niesielowski, an officer of one of the companies that had furnished the stewing chicken to defendant, testified that "chicken" meant "the male species of the poultry industry. That could be a broiler, a fryer or a roaster," but not a stewing chicken; however, he also testified that upon receiving defendant's inquiry for "chickens," he asked whether the desire was for "fowl or frying chickens" and, in fact, supplied fowl, although taking the precaution of asking defendant, a day or two after plaintiff's acceptance of the contracts in suit, to change its confirmation of its order from "chickens," as defendant had originally prepared it, to "stewing chickens." Dates, an employee of Urner–Barry Company, which publishes a daily market report on the poultry trade, gave it as his view that the trade meaning of "chicken" was "broilers and fryers." In addition to this opinion testimony, plaintiff relied on the fact that the Urner–Barry service, the Journal of Commerce, and Weinberg Bros. & Co. of Chicago, a large supplier of poultry, published quotations in a manner which, in one way or another, distinguish between "chicken," comprising broilers, fryers and certain other categories, and "fowl," which, Bauer acknowledged, included stewing chickens. This material would be impressive if there were nothing to the contrary. However, there was, as will now be seen.

Defendant's witness Weininger, who operates a chicken eviscerating plant in New Jersey, testified "Chicken is everything except a goose, a duck, and a turkey. Everything is a chicken, but then you have to say, you have to specify which category you want or that you are talking about." Its witness Fox said that in the trade "chicken" would encompass all the various classifications. Sadina, who conducts a food inspection service, testified that he would consider any bird coming within the classes of "chicken" in the Department of Agriculture's regulations to be a chicken. The specifications approved by the General Services Administration include fowl as well as broilers and fryers under the classification "chickens." Statistics of the Institute of American Poultry Industries use the phrases "Young chickens" and "Mature chickens," under the general heading

"Total chickens." and the Department of Agriculture's daily and weekly price reports avoid use of the word "chicken" without specification.

Defendant advances several other points which it claims affirmatively support its construction. Primary among these is the regulation of the Department of Agriculture, 7 C.F.R. §§ 70.300–70.370, entitled, "Grading and Inspection of Poultry and Edible Products Thereof." and in particular § 70.301 which recited:

"Chickens. The following are the various classes of chickens:

(a) Broiler or fryer . . .

(b) Roaster . . .

(c) Capon . . .

(d) Stag . . .

(e) Hen or stewing chicken or fowl . . .

(f) Cock or old rooster . . ."

Defendant argues, as previously noted, that the contract incorporated these regulations by reference. Plaintiff answers that the contract provision related simply to grade and Government inspection and did not incorporate the Government definition of "chicken," and also that the definition in the Regulations is ignored in the trade. However, the latter contention was contradicted by Weininger and Sadina; and there is force in defendant's argument that the contract made the regulations a dictionary, particularly since the reference to Government grading was already in plaintiff's initial cable to Stovicek.

Defendant makes a further argument based on the impossibility of its obtaining broilers and fryers at the 33 price offered by plaintiff for the 2½–3 lbs. birds. There is no substantial dispute that, in late April, 1957, the price for 2½–3 lbs. broilers was between 35 and 37 per pound, and that when defendant entered into the contracts, it was well aware of this and intended to fill them by supplying fowl in these weights. It claims that plaintiff must likewise have known the market since plaintiff had reserved shipping space on April 23, three days before plaintiff's cable to Stovicek, or, at least, that Stovicek was chargeable with such knowledge. It is scarcely an answer to say, as plaintiff does in its brief, that the 33 price offered by the 2½–3 lbs. "chickens" was closer to the prevailing 35 price for broilers than to the 30 at which defendant procured fowl. Plaintiff must have expected defendant to make some profit—certainly it could not have expected defendant deliberately to incur a loss.

Finally, defendant relies on conduct by the plaintiff after the first shipment had been received. On May 28 plaintiff sent two cables complaining that the larger birds in the first shipment constituted "fowl." Defendant answered with a cable refusing to recognize plaintiff's objection and announcing "We have today ready for shipment 50,000 lbs. chicken 2½–3 lbs. 25,000 lbs. broilers 1½–2 lbs.," these being the goods procured for shipment under the second contract, and asked immediate answer "whether we are to ship this merchandise to you and whether you will accept the merchandise." After several other cable exchanges, plaintiff replied on May 29, "Confirm again that merchandise is to be shipped since resold by us if not enough pursuant to contract chickens are shipped the missing quantity is to be shipped within ten days stop we resold to our customers pursuant to your contract chickens grade A you have to deliver us said merchandise we again state that we shall make you fully responsible for all resulting costs."* Defendant argues that if plaintiff was sincere in thinking it was entitled to young chickens, plaintiff would not have allowed the shipment under the second contract to go forward, since the distinction between broilers and chickens drawn in defendant's cablegram must have made it clear that the larger birds would not be broilers. However, plaintiff answers that the cables show plaintiff was insisting on delivery of young chickens and that defendant shipped old ones at its peril. Defendant's point would be highly relevant on another disputed issue—whether if liability were established, the measure of damages should be the difference in market value of broilers and stewing chicken in New York or the larger difference in Europe, but I cannot give it weight on the issue of interpretation. Defendant points out also that plaintiff proceeded to deliver some of the larger birds in Europe, describing them as "poulets"; defendant argues that it was only when plaintiff's customers complained about this that plaintiff developed the idea that "chicken" meant "young chicken." There is little force in this in view of plaintiff's immediate and consistent protests.

When all the evidence is reviewed, it is clear that defendant believed it could comply with the contracts by delivering stewing chicken in the 2½–3 lbs. size. Defendant's subjective intent would not be significant if this did not coincide with an objective meaning of "chicken." Here it did coincide with one of the dictionary meanings, with the definition in the Department of Agriculture Regulations to which the contract made at least oblique reference, with at least some usage in the trade, with the realities of the market, and with what plaintiff's spokesman had said. Plaintiff asserts it to be equally plain that plaintiff's own subjective intent was to obtain broilers and fryers; the only evidence against this is the material as to market prices and this may not have been sufficiently brought home. In any event it is unnecessary to determine that issue. For plaintiff has the burden of showing that "chicken" was used in the narrower rather than in the broader sense, and this it has not sustained.

This opinion constitutes the Court's findings of fact and conclusions of law. Judgment shall be entered dismissing the complaint with costs.

NOTES

(1) Judge Friendly concluded in *Frigaliment* that the seller should win because its understanding coincided with an "objective" meaning of "chicken," and the buyer failed to show that the word was "used in the narrower rather

---

* These cables were in German; "chicken," "broilers" and, on some occasions, "fowl," were in English.

than in the broader sense." Professor Corbin applauded this result, adding that the buyer also failed to prove that the seller "knew or had reason to know that plaintiff intended to buy broilers only." Corbin, *The Interpretation of Words and the Parol Evidence Rule,* 50 Cornell L.Q. 161, 169–70 (1964). Thus, extrinsic evidence both demonstrated that the word "chicken" was ambiguous and that the seller's understanding of "chicken" was, apparently, reasonable and the buyer's was not. Judge Friendly, however, had second thoughts about *Frigaliment.* Dissenting in Dadourian Export Corp. v. United States, 291 F.2d 178, 187 n. 4 (2d Cir.1961), he suggested that the "chicken" case should have been resolved under the *Peerless* doctrine (no contract unless both parties have same meaning in mind) "with the loss still left on the plaintiff because of the defendant's not unjustifiable reliance." Does this make sense? Professor Young has argued that *Peerless* should be limited to cases of "true equivocation," i.e., where a full exposure to objective evidence in context fails to establish that one party's understanding is more reasonable than the other's. Young, *Equivocation in the Making of Agreements,* 64 Colum.L.Rev. 619 (1964). Is the "chicken" case within this category? In Shrum v. Zeltwanger, 559 P.2d 1384 (Wyo.1977), the court addressed the equally momentous question: "What is a cow?" The parties disagreed as to whether the term included a "heifer" which had never had a calf. The court overturned a summary judgment award for the buyer. Concluding that the word "cow" had "within the corral of this case, no plain and ordinary meaning," the matter should go to trial, presumably in order to determine which party offered the better interpretation. See also A.J. Cunningham Packing Corp. v. Florence Beef Co., 785 F.2d 348 (1st Cir.1986) (seller's interpretation of "75% chemically lean beef" preferred).

(2) *Chickens, Contract Interpretation and Restatement (Second).* In the interpretation of a promise or agreement, the key test under Restatement (Second) of whose meaning prevails is found in Section 201(2):

> Where the parties have attached different meanings to a promise or agreement or a term thereof, it is interpreted in accordance with the meaning attached by one of them if at the time the agreement was made
>
> (a) that party did not know of any different meaning attached by the other, and the other knew the meaning attached by the first party; or
>
> (b) that party had no reason to know of any different meaning attached by the other, and the other had reason to know the meaning attached by the first party.

Subsection 3 provides that except as provided "in this section, neither party is bound by the meaning attached by the other, even though the result may be a failure of mutual assent." Comment d states that Subsection (2) follows the terminology of § 20, referring to the understanding of each party as the meaning "attached" by him to a term of a promise of agreement, and provides the following illustration:

> 4. A agrees to sell and B to buy a quantity of eviscerated "chicken." A tenders "stewing chicken" or "fowl;" B rejects on the ground that the contract calls for "broilers" or "fryers." Each party makes a claim for damages against the other. It is found that each acted in good faith and that neither had reason to know of the difference in meaning. Both claims fail.

Does this illustration correctly summarize the conclusion of Judge Friendly in the *Frigaliment* case?

Sections 202 and 203 of Restatement (Second) provide some general rules and standards of preference to be followed in the process of interpretation. Section 202 provides:

§ 202.   Rules in Aid of Interpretation

(1) Words and other conduct are interpreted in the light of all the circumstances, and if the principal purpose of the parties is ascertainable it is given great weight.

(2) A writing is interpreted as a whole, and all writings that are part of the same transaction are interpreted together.

(3) Unless a different intention is manifested,

> (a) where language has a generally prevailing meaning, it is interpreted in accordance with that meaning;

> (b) technical terms and words of art are given their technical meaning when used in a transaction within their technical field.

(4) Where an agreement involves repeated occasions for performance by either party with knowledge of the nature of the performance and opportunity for objection to it by the other, any course of performance accepted or acquiesced in without objection is given great weight in the interpretation of the agreement.

(5) Wherever reasonable, the manifestations of intention of the parties to a promise or agreement are interpreted as consistent with each other.

Finally, in Section 206, entitled "Interpretation Against the Draftsman," we have the Restatement (Second) version of the much used *contra proferentum* rule: "In choosing among the reasonable meanings of a promise or agreement or a term thereof, that meaning is generally preferred which operates against the party who supplies the words or from whom a writing otherwise proceeds."

With the option of the *Peerless* result on the one extreme and the rule of construction against the drafter on the other, does Restatement (Second) provide much help in the middle for a judge with a "chicken" case? Using the Restatement (Second) approach to contract interpretation, can you improve upon the reasoning and result in *Frigaliment?* See generally Braucher, *Interpretation and Legal Effect in the Second Restatement of Contracts,* 81 Colum.L.Rev. 13 (1981).

(3) *A Contra Proferentum Sampler.* Mastrobuono v. Shearson Lehman Hutton, Inc., 514 U.S. 52, ___, 115 S.Ct. 1212, 1219, 131 L.Ed.2d 76 (1995)(broker who drafted an ambiguous document on choice of law governing arbitration "cannot now claim the benefit of the doubt" because the party who did not choose the language must be protected "from an unintended or unfair result"); E.I. du Pont de Nemours and Co. v. Shell Oil Co., 498 A.2d 1108 (Del.1985) ("Where all parties to a contract are knowledgeable, there is no reason for imposing sanctions against the party who drafted the final provision." 498 A.2d at 1114); Matter of Estate of Orris, 622 P.2d 337 (Utah 1980) ("Where the draftsman is an attorney, as well as a party, strict construction is particularly apt." 622 P.2d at 339–40); Neal v. State Farm Insurance Co., 188 Cal.App.2d

690, 10 Cal.Rptr. 781 (1961) ("The rule that any ambiguities caused by the draftsman of the contract must be resolved against the party * * * applies with peculiar force in the case of a contract of adhesion." 188 Cal.App.2d at 695, 10 Cal.Rptr. at 784); Franklin Life Insurance Co. v. Commonwealth Edison Co., 451 F.Supp. 602 (S.D.Ill.1978) ("[T]he idea of construing a contract against the drafter is not a result oriented rule but rather a rule which provides an answer when all other methods of construction and interpretation still leave the contract ambiguous." 451 F.Supp. at 616); Wilner's, Inc. v. Fine, 153 Ga.App. 591, 266 S.E.2d 278 (1980) ("It is also a well established rule that ambiguities in writings are to be construed most strongly against the author or the party for whose benefit the writing was prepared, which, in this case, is the land-lord." 266 S.E.2d at 280); Gaunt v. John Hancock Mutual Life Insurance Co., 160 F.2d 599 (2d Cir.1947) ("[T]he canon contra proferentum is more rigorous-ly applied in insurance than in other contracts, in recognition of the difference between the parties in their acquaintance with the subject matter." 160 F.2d at 602).

Gray v. Zurich Insurance Co.

Supreme Court of California, 1966.
65 Cal.2d 263, 54 Cal.Rptr. 104, 419 P.2d 168.

■ TOBRINER, JUSTICE. This is an action by an insured against his insurer for failure to defend an action filed against him which stemmed from a complaint alleging that he had committed an assault. The main issue turns on the argument of the insurer that an exclusionary clause of the policy excuses its defense of an action in which a plaintiff alleges that the insured intentionally caused the bodily injury. Yet the language of the policy does not clearly define the application of the exclusionary clause to the duty to defend. Since in that event we test the meaning of the policy according to the insured's reasonable expectation of coverage and since the language of the policy would lead the insured here to expect defense of the third party suit, we cannot exonerate the carrier from the rendition of such protection.

Plaintiff, Dr. Vernon D. Gray, is the named insured under an insur-ance policy issued by defendant. A "Comprehensive Personal Liability Endorsement" in the policy states, under a paragraph designated "Cover-age L," that the insurer agrees "[T]o pay on behalf of the insured all sums which the insured shall become legally obligated to pay as damages because of bodily injury or property damage, and the company shall defend any suit against the insured alleging such bodily injury or property damage and seeking damages which are payable under the terms of this endorsement, even if any of the allegations are groundless, false or fraudulent; but the company may make such investigation and settlement of any claim or suit as it deems expedient." The policy contains a provision that "[T]his endorsement does not apply" to a series of specified exclusions set forth under separate headings, including a paragraph (c) which reads, "under coverages L and M, to bodily injury or property damages caused intention-ally by or at the direction of the insured."

The suit which Dr. Gray contends Zurich should have defended arose out of an altercation between him and a Mr. John R. Jones.[1] Jones filed a complaint in Missouri alleging that Dr. Gray "wilfully, maliciously, brutally and intentionally assaulted" him; he prayed for actual damages of $50,000 and punitive damages of $50,000. Dr. Gray notified defendant of the suit, stating that he had acted in self-defense, and requested that the company defend. Defendant refused on the ground that the complaint alleged an intentional tort which fell outside the coverage of the policy. Dr. Gray thereafter unsuccessfully defended on the theory of self-defense; he suffered a judgment of $6,000 actual damages although the jury refused to award punitive damages.

Dr. Gray then filed the instant action charging defendant with breach of its duty to defend. Defendant answered, admitting the execution of the policy but denying any such obligation. The record on appeal has been augmented to include an offer of proof, presented by plaintiff and rejected by the trial court, which detailed the circumstances surrounding the altercation. The augmented record also includes exhibits introduced at the trial, consisting of copies of the pleadings and verdict in the Missouri suit and a copy of the subject insurance policy. The parties waived written findings of fact and conclusions of law; the court rendered judgment in favor of defendant. We must decide whether or not defendant bore the obligation to defend plaintiff in the Missouri action.

Defendant argues that it need not defend an action in which the complaint reveals on its face that the claimed bodily injury does not fall within the indemnification coverage; that here the Jones complaint alleged that the insured committed an assault, which fell outside such coverage. Defendant urges, as a second answer to plaintiff's contention, that the contract, if construed to require defense of the insured, would violate the public policy of the state and that, indeed, the judgment in the third party suit upholding the claim of an intentional bodily injury operates to estop the insured from recovery. Defendant thirdly contends that any requirement that it defend the Jones suit would embroil it in a hopeless conflict of interest. Finally it submits that, even if it should have defended the third party suit, the damages against it should encompass only the insured's expenses of defense and not the judgment against him.

We shall explain our reasons for concluding that defendant was obligated to defend the Jones suit, and our grounds for rejecting defendant's remaining propositions. Since the policy sets forth the duty to defend as a primary one and since the insurer attempts to avoid it only by an unclear exclusionary clause, the insured would reasonably expect, and is legally entitled to, such protection. * * *

---

1. Immediately preceding the altercation Dr. Gray had been driving an automobile on a residential street when another automobile narrowly missed colliding with his car. Jones, the driver of the other car, left his vehicle, approached Dr. Gray's car in a menacing manner and jerked open the door. At that point Dr. Gray, fearing physical harm to himself and his passengers, rose from his seat and struck Jones.

In interpreting an insurance policy we apply the general principle that doubts as to meaning must be resolved against the insurer and that any exception to the performance of the basic underlying obligation must be so stated as clearly to apprise the insured of its effect.

These principles of interpretation of insurance contracts have found new and vivid restatement in the doctrine of the adhesion contract. As this court has held, a contract entered into between two parties of unequal bargaining strength, expressed in the language of a standardized contract, written by the more powerful bargainer to meet its own needs, and offered to the weaker party on a "take it or leave it basis" carries some consequences that extend beyond orthodox implications. Obligations arising from such a contract inure not alone from the consensual transaction but from the relationship of the parties.

Although courts have long followed the basic precept that they would look to the words of the contract to find the meaning which the parties expected from them, they have also applied the doctrine of the adhesion contract to insurance policies, holding that in view of the disparate bargaining status of the parties[6] we must ascertain that meaning of the contract which the insured would reasonably expect. Thus as Kessler stated in his classic article on adhesion contracts: "In dealing with standardized contracts courts have to determine what the weaker contracting party could legitimately expect by way of services according to the enterpriser's 'calling', and to what extent the stronger party disappointed reasonable expectations based on the typical life situation." (Kessler, Contracts of Adhesion (1943) 43 Colum.L.Rev. 629, 637.)

Professor Patterson, in describing one characteristic consequence of "the conception of adhesion, whether that term is used or not," writes: "The court interprets the form contract to mean what a reasonable buyer would expect it to mean, and thus protects the weaker party's expectation at the expense of the stronger's. This process of interpretation was used many many years ago in interpreting (or construing) insurance contracts. * * *" (Fn. omitted; Patterson, The Interpretation and Construction of Contracts (1964) 64 Colum.L.Rev. 833, 858).

Thus we held in Steven v. Fidelity & Casualty Co., supra, 58 Cal.2d 862, 27 Cal.Rptr. 172, 377 P.2d 284, that we would not enforce an exclusionary clause in an insurance contract which was unclear, saying: "If [the insurer] deals with the public upon a mass basis, the notice of non-coverage of the policy, in a situation in which the public may reasonably expect coverage, must be conspicuous, plain and clear." P. 878, 27 Cal.Rptr. p. 182, 377 P.2d p. 294.

When we test the instant policy by these principles we find that its provisions as to the obligation to defend are uncertain and undefined; in the light of the reasonable expectation of the insured, they require the

---

6. Isaacs, The Standardizing of Contracts (1917) 27 Yale L.J. 34, in an early analysis, suggests the basis for the adhesion contract, pointing out that standardized contracts create "status" relationships as opposed to individualized relationships. * * *

performance of that duty. At the threshold we note that the nature of the obligation to defend is itself necessarily uncertain. Although insurers have often insisted that the duty arises only if the insurer is bound to indemnify the insured, this very contention creates a dilemma. No one can determine whether the third party suit does or does not fall within the indemnification coverage of the policy until that suit is resolved; in the instant case, the determination of whether the insured engaged in intentional, negligent or even wrongful conduct depended upon the judgment in the Jones suit, and, indeed, even after that judgment, no one could be positive whether it rested upon a finding of plaintiff's negligent or his intentional conduct. The carrier's obligation to indemnify inevitably will not be defined until the adjudication of the very action which it should have defended. Hence the policy contains its own seeds of uncertainty; the insurer has held out a promise that by its very nature is ambiguous.

Although this uncertainty in the performance of the duty to defend could have been clarified by the language of the policy we find no such specificity here. An examination of the policy discloses that the broadly stated promise to defend is not conspicuously or clearly conditioned solely on a nonintentional bodily injury; instead, the insured could reasonably expect such protection.

The policy is a "comprehensive personal liability" contract; the designation in itself connotes general protection for alleged bodily injury caused by the insured. The insurer makes two wide promises: "[1.] To pay on behalf of the insured all sums which the insured shall become legally obligated to pay as damages because of bodily injury or property damage, and [2.] the company shall defend any suit against the insured alleging such bodily injury or property damage and seeking damages which are payable under the terms of this endorsement, even if any of the allegations of the suit are groundless, false, or fraudulent": clearly these promises, without further clarification, would lead the insured reasonably to expect the insurer to defend him against suits seeking damages for bodily injury, whatever the alleged cause of the injury, whether intentional or inadvertent.

But the insurer argues that the third party suit must seek "damages which are *payable* under the terms of this endorsement"; it contends that this limitation *modifies* the general duty to defend by confining the duty only to actions seeking damages within the primary coverage of the policy. Under "Exclusions" the policy provides that it "does not apply * * * under coverage L and M to bodily injury * * * caused intentionally by * * * the insured."

The very first paragraph as to coverage, however, provides that "the company shall defend any such suit against the insured alleging such bodily injury" although the allegations of the suit are groundless, false or fraudulent. This language, in its broad sweep, would lead the insured reasonably to expect defense of *any* suit regardless of merit or cause. The relation of the exclusionary clause to this basic promise is anything but clear. The basic promise would support the insured's reasonable expectation that he had bought the rendition of legal services to defend against a suit for bodily injury which alleged he had caused it, negligently, nonintentionally, intentionally or in any other manner. The doctrines and cases we have set forth tell us that the exclusionary clause must be "conspicuous, plain and clear." (Steven v. Fidelity & Casualty Co., supra, 58 Cal.2d 862, 878, 27 Cal.Rptr. 172, 377 P.2d 284.) This clause is not "conspicuous" since it appears only after a long and complicated page of fine print, and is itself in fine print; its relation to the remaining clauses of the policy and its effect is surely not "plain and clear."

A further uncertainty lurks in the exclusionary clause itself. It alludes to damage caused "intentionally by or at the direction of the insured." Yet an act of the insured may carry out his "intention" and also cause unintended harm. When set next to the words "at the direction of the insured" the word "intentionally" might mean to the layman collusive, wilful or planned action beyond the classical notion of intentional tort. This built-in ambiguity has caused debate and refined definition in many courts; in any event, the word surely cannot be "plain and clear" to the layman.

The insured is unhappily surrounded by concentric circles of uncertainty: the first, the unascertainable nature of the insurer's duty to defend; the second, the unknown effect of the provision that the insurer must defend even a groundless, false or fraudulent claim; the third, the uncertain extent of the indemnification coverage. Since we must resolve uncertainties in favor of the insured and interpret the policy provisions according to the layman's reasonable expectations, and since the effect of the exclusionary clause is neither conspicuous, plain nor clear, we hold that in the present case the policy provides for an obligation to defend and that such obligation is independent of the indemnification coverage.

* * *

In summary, the individual consumer in the highly organized and integrated society of today must necessarily rely upon institutions devoted to the public service to perform the basic functions which they undertake. At the same time the consumer does not occupy a sufficiently strong economic position to bargain with such institutions as to specific clauses of their contracts of performance, and, in any event, piecemeal negotiation would sacrifice the advantage of uniformity. Hence the courts in the field of insurance contracts have tended to require that the insurer render the basic insurance protection which it has held out to the insured. This obligation becomes especially manifest in the case in which the insurer has attempted to limit the principal coverage by an unclear exclusionary clause. We test the alleged limitation in the light of the insured's reasonable expectation of coverage; that test compels the indicated outcome of the present litigation.

The judgment is reversed and the trial court instructed to take evidence solely on the issue of damages alleged in plaintiff's complaint including the amount of the judgment in the Jones suit, and the costs, expenses and attorney's fees incurred in defending such suit.

■ TRAYNOR, C.J., and PETERS, PEEK, MOSK and BURKE, JJ., concur.

DISSENTING OPINION

■ McCOMB, JUSTICE.

I dissent. I would affirm the judgment for the reasons expressed by Mr. Justice Fox in the opinion prepared by him for the District Court of Appeal in Gray v. Zurich Ins. Co. (Cal.App.) 49 Cal.Rptr. 271.

[Some footnotes omitted.]

NOTES

(1) The typical insurance policy is an "adhesion" contract, a standard form offered on a take-it-or-leave-it basis by the party with superior bargaining power. The "mass produced" character of these agreements results in cost savings but raises contractual assent questions where, as is usual, the insured does not read the policy and is not otherwise adequately informed of the terms. *Gray* is illustrative of a growing number of cases which have provided a measure of protection for the insurance consumer by not interpreting the policy according to strict letter but in light of overall "reasonable expectations." The Supreme Court of New Jersey formulated the doctrine of reasonable expectations in insurance contracts as follows: "When members of the public purchase policies of insurance they are entitled to the broad measure of protection necessary to fulfill their reasonable expectations." Kievit v. Loyal Protective Life Insurance Co., 34 N.J. 475, 482, 170 A.2d 22, 26 (1961). See R. Keeton & A. Widiss, Insurance Law § 6.3 (1988). For helpful update and elaboration, see Abraham, *Judge-Made Law and Judge–Made Insurance: Honoring the Reasonable Expectations of the Insured,* 67 Va.L.Rev. 1151 (1981); Note, 57 N.Y.U.L.Rev. 1175 (1982). See also Comment, *Insurance as Contract: The Argument for Abandoning the Ambiguity Doctrine,* 88 Colum.L.Rev. 1849 (1988).

(2) The November, 1996 Draft of UCC 2–206(b) provided: "If a consumer manifests assent to a standard form, a term contained in the form which the consumer could not reasonably have expected is not part of the contract unless the consumer expressly agrees to it."

PROBLEM: THE CASE OF THE MISSING FERTILIZER

Plaintiff, a businessman, obtained from Defendant insurance company a Broad Form Storekeepers Policy and a Mercantile Burglary and Robbery Policy. These policies promised to "pay for loss by burglary or by robbery of a watchman, while the premises are not opened for business, of merchandise, furniture, fixtures and equipment within the premises." Both policies specifically excluded any "loss due to any fraudulent, dishonest or criminal act by any Insured, a partner therein, or an officer, employee, director, trustee or authorized representative thereof." On page 3 of both policies in fine print, "burglary" was defined as meaning:

> ... the felonious abstraction of insured property (1) from within the premises by a person making felonious entry therein by actual force and violence, of which force and violence there are visible marks made by tools,

explosive, electricity or chemicals upon, or physical damage to, the exterior of the premises at the place of such entry.

Before the policies were issued, Plaintiff's president, a 37–year-old farmer with a high school education, and Defendant's agent negotiated over the insurance. The agent ascertained that Plaintiff would be storing farm chemicals and made suggestions concerning additional security. He pointed out to Plaintiff that under the proposed policy there must be visible evidence of burglary. But there was no indication that Plaintiff was informed about the definition of burglary or that he ever read that definition in the policy.

Shortly after the policies were issued, Plaintiff reported a weekend loss of chemicals worth $9,582 and shop equipment worth $400 from the insured building. When the theft was discovered early on Monday morning, all exterior doors were locked but the interior door to the storage area had been forced open and carried visible marks made by tools. There were tire treads in a driveway leading to an exterior, locked Plexiglas door entrance to the warehouse. There were, however, no visible marks on this door, which could be forced open without leaving visible marks or physical damage, on the exterior of the building. Relying on the definition of "burglary" in the policy, Defendant refused to pay. At the trial, Plaintiff argued that, considering all of the evidence, a burglary rather than an "inside job" had taken place and Defendant's agent conceded under cross-examination that from what he saw "the thought didn't enter my mind that it wasn't covered." Nevertheless, the trial court found for Defendant, concluding that there was no evidence upon which to base a finding "that the door to plaintiff's place of business was entered feloniously, by actual force and violence" and that the "evidence in this case is just as consistent with a theory that an employee entered the building with a key as it is to a theory that the building was entered by force and violence." Thus, Plaintiff had failed to satisfy the definition of burglary contained in the policy.

Plaintiff appealed and made the following arguments to the state supreme court. If you were a justice on that court, which, if any, of these arguments would you accept?

1. This is a standard form contract of insurance offered to Plaintiff on a take-it-or-leave-it basis. Defendant prepared all of the clauses without participation by Plaintiff. For this reason alone, the "fine print" limitation upon the promise to pay if a burglary took place is not enforceable.

2. Since Plaintiff was not informed of the limitation at the time of contracting, his reasonable expectations regarding coverage should be protected. Here those reasonable expectations were that if covered goods were taken and there was no "hard evidence" that the theft was an inside job, recovery should be allowed.

3. Upon delivery of the policy for value, Defendant made an implied warranty that the coverage of the policy was reasonably fit for its intended purpose. The limitation clause altered and impaired the fair meaning of the bargain these parties made for Plaintiff's insurance protection.

4. This is a perfect case for applying the doctrine of *contra proferentum*— construing all ambiguities in a writing where both parties are equally careless or equally reasonable against the drafter.

5.   This is a classic case of "unfair surprise" associated with a contract of adhesion. There was no "meaningful choice" and the limitation clause, therefore, is unconscionable.

SECTION 2.   ALLOCATION OF RISK: CONDITIONS AND WARRANTIES

A working principle is that freedom of contract allows the parties to a bargain to allocate or to adjust performance risks by agreement. A corollary is that when an allocation agreement exists, the court will normally enforce it. In this section, we will test these principles and their limitations in cases where risk is allocated by: (1) express or constructive conditions and (2) express or implied warranties.

The failure (or non-occurrence) of a condition relieves at least one party of her obligations to perform the contract. The failure of a warranty, by contrast, gives the non-breaching party a right to recover damages. A party to a contract can thus assure itself of the other side's performance by contracting for affirmative protection of a warranty or the defensive protection of a condition (that is, making the other side's performance a condition of your own duty to perform).

While the affirmative protection of warranty might seem to provide a stronger assurance than conditions, the failure of a conditions can work great forfeiture. For example, if a condition to a buyer's duty to pay is that the seller tender goods that perfectly comply with the terms of the agreement, then a slight deviations in performance could potentially relieve the buyer from any contractual obligation to pay for goods in its possession (although non-contractual or quasi-contractual basis such as restitution or quantum meruit may pertain). We will see that common law courts have developed a number of ways to avoid such forfeitures.

As you confront these materials on conditions and warranties, consider what mixture of protections are likely to maximize the gains from trade.

(A) EXPRESS CONDITIONS

(1) NATURE AND EFFECT

A rational person making commitments for the future is likely to take at least two things into account: first, what must one receive from the other party in exchange for one's promise or performance, and second, assuming that the return performance is satisfactory, what events could occur that would impair the incentive to complete the exchange and what can be done about them? Naturally, if the other party refuses to commit in a satisfactory way or, after making the promise, fails to perform, our rational person has protection. This protection is explained in terms of "no contract was ever formed" or "the defendant has breached the contract." But if a contract has been created and the defendant is not in breach, what protection is available when an event occurs which impairs the value of the bargain to the other?

A general answer is that if the agreement does not provide for this event, i.e., there is a "gap" in the agreement after legitimate processes of ascertaining and interpreting the agreement have been exhausted, the disappointed party faces an uphill battle. Here, as we shall see, the battle to escape from the contract is waged under such labels as "mutual mistake," "constructive conditions of exchange," and "impossibility or frustration of performance." The court is asked to fill this gap in the agreement and to protect the aggrieved party from severe disruptions, the risk of which he or she should not, under the circumstances, be made to assume.

But suppose the risk is foreseen by one party and expressly provided for in the agreement. For example, suppose that Uncle, a noted historian, has a nephew in law school and that Nephew has absolutely no interest in "cultural" courses, such as legal history or jurisprudence. After an appropriate bit of bargaining, Uncle induces Nephew to promise to take Professor Holmes' course in Common Law Miracles by promising to pay him $500, "provided that he take the course for a grade and earn a grade of B or better." Nephew takes the course and earns a grade of C+. What is the legal position of the parties at this point? Can Uncle, if he chooses, refuse to pay the $500 without liability for breach of contract?

The argument on both sides might run something like this. Uncle will argue that the "B or better" requirement was an express condition to his duty to pay $500. In Restatement (Second) parlance, it was "an event, not certain to occur, which must occur, unless its non-occurrence is excused, before performance under a contract becomes due." Section 224. See generally Corbin, *Conditions in the Law of Contracts,* 28 Yale L.J. 739 (1919). Moreover, the event was made a condition "by agreement of the parties." Section 226. Since the event did *not* occur (Nephew earned a C plus), two legal consequences follow: First, Uncle's unconditional duty to pay $500 never arose; and Second, the duty (and, thus, the contract) is discharged "when the condition can no longer occur." Section 225(1) & (2). Uncle's legal position is purely defensive—he avoids the duty to pay because the condition failed. As a consequence, Nephew bears the risk of the investment to earn a "B or better" in a situation where Uncle has received no tangible benefit from that effort.

Nephew's counterarguments, most of which will emerge more clearly in the materials to follow, might take these forms: (1) The event was not a condition at all. Rather, it was a matter of convenience that did not affect the rights and duties of the parties. (2) The event was promised by Nephew as a part of the agreed exchange. Although Uncle's duty to pay is "constructively" conditioned upon performance of the promise, the "constructive" condition is satisfied by substantial rather than literal compliance. In short, C plus is close enough. (3) The condition was excused, i.e., deleted from the agreement, either because Uncle "waived it" or because its excuse is necessary to avoid forfeiture.

With these arguments in mind, consider the following materials. After due consideration, who has the better of it, Uncle or Nephew? For collateral reading, see Farnsworth §§ 8.1–8.7; Calamari and Perillo §§ 11–1—11–10; Murray §§ 99–111.

Dove v. Rose Acre Farms, Inc.

Court of Appeals of Indiana, First District, 1982.
434 N.E.2d 931.

■ NEAL, JUDGE.

Plaintiff-appellant Mark Dove (Dove) appeals a negative judgment of the Decatur Circuit Court in favor of defendant-appellee Rose Acre Farms, Inc. in a trial before the court without the intervention of a jury.

We affirm.

STATEMENT OF THE FACTS

The evidence most favorable to support the judgment and the facts found specially by the trial court are as follows. Dove had been employed by Rose Acre Farms, operated by David Rust (Rust), its president and principal owner, in the summers and other times from 1972 to 1979. The business of Rose Acre was the production of eggs, and, stocked with 4,000,000 hens and staffed with 300 employees, it produced approximately 256,000 dozen eggs per day. Rust had instituted and maintained extensive bonus programs, some of which were for one day only, or one event or activity only. For example, one bonus was the white car bonus; if an employee would buy a new white car, keep it clean and undamaged, place a Rose Acre sign on it, commit no tardiness or absenteeism, and attend one management meeting per month, Rose Acre would pay $100 per month for 36 months as a bonus above and beyond the employee's regular salary, to apply on payments. Any slight violation, such as being a minute late for work, driving a dirty or damaged car, or missing work for any cause, would work a forfeiture of the bonus. Other bonuses consisted of egg production bonuses, deed conversion bonuses, house management bonuses, and a silver feather bonus. This last bonus program required the participant to wear a silver feather, and a system of rewards and penalties existed for employees who participated. While the conditions of the bonuses varied, one condition existed in all bonus programs: during the period of the bonus, the employee must not be tardy for even a minute, and must not miss work any day for any cause whatever, even illness. If the employee missed any days during the week, he was sometimes permitted to make them up on Saturday and/or Sunday. Any missed work not made up within the same week worked a forfeiture of the bonus. These rules were explained to the employees and were stated in a written policy. The bonus programs were voluntary, and all the employees did not choose to participate in them. When a bonus was offered a card was issued to the participant stating his name and the terms and amount of the bonus. Upon completion of the required tasks, the card was attached to the pay sheet, and the bonus was added to the paycheck. Rust was strict about tardiness and absenteeism, whether an employee was on a bonus program or not. If an employee was tardy, his pay would be docked to the minimum wage, or he would be sent home and lose an entire day. A minute's tardiness would also deprive the employee of a day for purposes of seniority. As was stated in the evidence, bonuses were given for the "extra mile" or actions "above and beyond the call of duty." The purpose of the bonus programs and penalties was to discourage absenteeism and tardiness, and to promote motivation and dependability.

In June 1979, Rust called in Dove and other construction crew leaders and offered a bonus of $6,000 each if certain detailed construction work was completed in 12 weeks. As Dove conceded in his own testimony, the bonus card indicated that in addition to completing the work, he would be required to work at least five full days a week for 12 weeks to qualify for the bonus. On the same day Dove's bonus agreement, by mutual consent, was amended to ten weeks with a bonus of $5,000 to enable him to return to law school by September 1. Dove testified that there was no ambiguity in the agreement, and he understood that to qualify for the bonus he would have to work ten weeks, five days a week, commencing at starting time and quitting only at quitting time. Dove testified that he was aware of the provisions concerning absenteeism and tardiness as they affected bonuses, and that if he missed any work, for any reason, including illness, he would forfeit the bonus. The evidence disclosed that no exception had ever been made except as may have occurred by clerical error or inadvertence.

In the tenth week Dove came down with strep throat. On Thursday of that week he reported to work with a temperature of 104°, and told Rust that he was unable to work. Rust told him, in effect, that if he went home, he would forfeit the bonus. Rust offered him the opportunity to stay there and lay on a couch, or make up his lost days on Saturday and/or Sunday. Rust told him he could sleep and still qualify for the bonus. Dove left to seek medical treatment and missed two days in the tenth week of the bonus program.

Rust refused Dove the bonus based solely upon his missing the two days of work. While there was some question of whether the construction job was finished, Rust does not seem to have made that issue the basis of his refusal. Bonuses to other crew leaders were paid. The trial court denied Dove's recovery and, in the conclusions of law, stated that Dove had not shown that all of the conditions of the bonus contract had been met. Specifically, Dove failed to work five full days a week for ten weeks.

* * *

Dove argues that the bonus agreement was implemented to (1) insure his presence on the construction site, and (2) cut the cost of construction through maximum production by workers. He next contends that Rose Acre got what it bargained for, that is the completion of the project. He argues that he was present on the job, including the hours he worked late, at least 750 hours during the ten weeks, while regular working hours would amount to only 500 hours. Therefore, he concludes, there was substantial compliance with the agreement, and he should not be penalized because he failed to appear on the last two days because of illness. * * *

* * *

We are constrained to observe, in the case before us, that the bonus rules at Rose Acre were well known to Dove when he agreed to the disputed bonus contract. He certainly knew Rust's strict policies and knew that any absence for any cause whatever worked a forfeiture of the bonus. With this knowledge he willingly entered into this bonus arrangement, as he had done in the past, * * *; he must be held to have agreed to all of the terms upon which the bonus was conditioned. If the conditions were unnecessarily harsh or eccentric, and the terms odious, he could have shown his disdain by simply declining to participate, for participation in the bonus program was not obligatory or job dependent.

Contrary to Dove's assertion that completion of a task was the central element of the bonus program, we are of the opinion that the rules regarding tardiness and absenteeism were a central theme. Rust stated that the purpose of the bonus program was to discourage tardiness and absenteeism and to promote motivation and dependability. Indeed, some of the bonus programs such as the white car bonus and the silver feather bonus were apparently an effort on the part of Rust to establish among the employees an identity with Rose Acre and to create an *esprit de corps*. The direct tangible benefits to Rose Acre would be unmeasurable, and the burden upon the employees would be equally unmeasurable. Yet, Rust was willing to pay substantial bonuses in the implementation of his program, and the employees, including Dove, were quite as willing to take the money.

No fraud or bad faith has been shown on the part of Rose Acre, and no public policy arguments have been advanced to demonstrate why the bonus contract should not be enforced as agreed between the parties. * * *

Dove argues that he should be relieved of strict performance because his illness rendered his performance impossible. He cites Gregg School Township v. Hinshaw, (1921) 76 Ind.App. 503, 132 N.E. 586. That case states that where the performance of a contract becomes impossible, non-performance is excused, and no damages can be recovered. The rule was applied in denying a teacher wages for lost time where a school was closed by health authorities because of an epidemic. He cites also In re Traubs's Estate, (1958) 354 Mich. 263, 92 N.W.2d 480; Bracken v. Wagner (1956) 3 Ohio Opin.2d 25, 134 N.E.2d 382; and Leonard v. Autocar Sales & Service Co., (1945) 392 Ill. 182, 64 N.E.2d 477, for the proposition that contracts to perform personal services are considered to have been made on the implied condition that the party shall be alive and capable of performing the contract; hence, death or disability, including sickness, will operate as a discharge or termination of the contract or an excuse for non-performance.

None of these cases involved a contract for personal services, though dicta contained general language applicable to such contracts. Generally, impossibility of performance is a defense to an action for damages. See

Gregg School Township, supra. Dove has not demonstrated how the doctrine is applicable here. Certainly a plaintiff cannot, upon failing to perform his part of the contract, sue his adversary for damages alleging that his own non-performance was because of impossibility. Suppose Dove, because of illness, could not work at all. Could he sue for wages? * * *

For the reasons given above, we hold that Dove failed to perform all of the conditions of the contract and is not entitled to recover any portion of the bonus. The judgment is affirmed.

Affirmed.

NOTES

(1) What is the "condition" in *Dove?* What was the legal effect of its non-occurrence? Is it relevant that the "condition" was a performance by Dove that was necessary to create a contract?

(2) "An obligor will often qualify his duty by providing that performance will not become due unless a stated event, which is not certain to occur, does occur. Such an event is called a condition. An obligor may make an event a condition of his duty in order to shift to the obligee the risk of its nonoccurrence. In this case the event may be within the control of the obligee (e.g., his furnishing security), or of the obligor (e.g., his satisfaction with the obligee's performance), or of neither (e.g., the accidental destruction of the subject matter)." Restatement (Second), Chapter 9, Topic 5, Introductory Note.

(3) *Condition Precedent and Condition Subsequent.* A standard classification is based on the distinction between conditions which are "precedent" and those which are "subsequent." The reference point is the accrual of the cause of action; i.e., the point in time when the obligor is under a duty to render an immediate performance. Conditions precedent must be satisfied before a contractual duty of this type comes into existence; the effect of the occurrence of a condition subsequent is to extinguish or discharge such a duty. For example, in Abolin v. Farmers' American Mutual Fire Insurance Co., 100 Pa.Super. 433 (1931), a fire insurance policy provided that "no suit or action on this policy for the recovery of any claim shall be sustainable in any court of law or equity * * * unless commenced within twelve months next after the fire * * * for which claim is made." After a fire occurred and proof of loss was made, both conditions precedent, the company was under a duty to make payment. But payment was not made, and the insured did not bring suit to collect within twelve months of the fire. Applying the foregoing provision, the court denied recovery. The company's duty was discharged by the failure to bring suit within the stipulated period. Such failure, in traditional usage, amounts to the occurrence of a condition subsequent in the contract.

Conditions subsequent are comparatively rare in contracts, and at times those which are treated in the cases as "subsequent" are clearly "precedent." See, e.g., Gray v. Gardner, 17 Mass. 188 (1821); Capitol Land Co. v. Zorn, 134 Ind.App. 431, 184 N.E.2d 152 (1962). Noting the relationship of the traditional condition subsequent to the discharge of obligation, the drafters of Restatement (Second) do not use the term and confine their use of "condition" to those of the precedent variety. See Restatement (Second) § 224, Comment e, § 230, Comment a.

Actually, the need for distinguishing between events which are "precedent" and "subsequent" in the above sense derives from procedural requirements. Under Rule 9(c) of the Federal Rules of Civil Procedure it is sufficient that the plaintiff allege generally in the complaint that all conditions precedent have been performed or have occurred. The defendant, on the other hand, is obliged to deny specifically and with particularity that they have not. A failure to plead accordingly will prevent using it as a defense in the federal courts. See, e.g., Ginsburg v. Insurance Company of North America, 427 F.2d 1318, 1321–22 (6th Cir.1970); Lumbermens Mutual Insurance Co. v. Bowman, 313 F.2d 381, 387 (10th Cir.1963). Federal courts take a similar approach on conditions subsequent. Thus, if a party fails in a required responsive pleading to raise an issue regarding the existence of a condition subsequent, that party may not later rely on the condition subsequent as a defense. Title Guaranty & Surety Co. v. Nichols, 224 U.S. 346, 32 S.Ct. 475, 56 L.Ed. 795 (1912). See, generally, F. James & G. Hazard, Civil Procedure § 3.19 (1985). Since several States have promulgated pleading requirements based on the Federal Rules or have comparable provisions relative to the pleading of conditions, similar alertness is demanded in other jurisdictions. See, e.g., Travers v. Travelers Insurance Co., 385 Mass. 811, 434 N.E.2d 208 (1982).

Wal–Noon Corp. v. Hill

Court of Appeals of California, 1975.
45 Cal.App.3d 605, 119 Cal.Rptr. 646.

■ PUGLIA, PRESIDING JUSTICE.

* * *

In August of 1957, the parties entered into a lease agreement for the construction and occupancy of a building. The major portion of the building was to be occupied and used by plaintiffs for a market and the remainder was to be sublet by plaintiffs for various satellite enterprises. Construction was completed in 1959.

In 1967 or 1968 the roof started to leak over the market portion of the building. Shortly thereafter complaints were made to plaintiffs by other tenants of similar leaky conditions. On several occasions, repairs were made to the roof at plaintiffs' expense. After approximately 12 to 15 repairs, plaintiffs were advised by roofers whom they consulted that repair was no longer practicable and that a new roof should be installed. Plaintiffs sought and obtained competitive bids for replacing the roof and awarded the job to the lowest bidders. Replacement was accomplished in two stages, the satellite portion being done by one company in September 1968 at a cost of $4,800, and the market portion by another in August 1969 at a cost of $4,000.

The lease in part provided as follows: "MAINTENANCE AND REPAIRS. The Lessors agree, at their own cost and expense, to make all repairs to the roof and exterior walls (except glazing and painting replacements and/or repairs which Lessees agree to do) of the new building, provided, however, that the Lessors shall have no obligation to make any repairs to the new building made necessary by the negligence or improper use thereof by the Lessees, their sub-lessees, agents or employees. Except as herein qualified, Lessees shall keep the leased premises in good order and condition at their own expense and surrender the same in good order and condition upon the expiration or sooner termination of this lease, reasonable wear from proper use thereof and damage from the elements excepted.

"...

"WRITTEN COMMUNICATIONS. All notices, demands, consents and denials hereunder by either party to the other shall be in writing and shall be sufficiently given and served if either personally served, or if sent by United States registered mail, return receipt requested, postage prepaid, in a sealed envelope addressed as follows:

"If sent by mail to Lessors, the same shall be addressed to the Lessors at 4920 15th Avenue, Sacramento, California;

"If sent by mail to Lessees, the same shall be addressed to the Lessees at the leased premises.

"Either the Lessors or the Lessees may change such address by notice in writing to the other party of such new address as the Lessors or the Lessees may desire used for such purpose. All rent or other sums payable hereunder may be paid to Lessors at the above listed address for notices.

"...

"INTERPRETATION. The various headings and numbers herein and the groupings of the provisions of this lease into separate articles and paragraphs shall not be construed to limit or restrict either the meaning or application of any provision hereof, and are for the purpose of convenience only."

Prior to the repairs to and later replacement of the roof, plaintiffs did not review the lease to determine upon which party the obligation for such work was placed. However, in 1971, the plaintiffs finally became aware of the lease provision which allocated the responsibility for such repair and replacement to defendant lessors. Thereafter plaintiffs requested that defendants reimburse them for the sums expended to replace the roof. Defendants refused and this action was thereafter instituted.

The complaint filed by plaintiffs was phrased purely in terms of contract, as was defendants' answer. The action proceeded to trial on that theory, plaintiffs seeking to establish the provisions of the lease and the circumstances surrounding repair and replacement of the roof. Defendants sought to show that they were prejudiced by plaintiffs' failure to notify them of the defective condition of the roof at a time when they could exercise their contractual right to control repair or replacement.

The contractor who replaced the roof over the market testified that he was asked by plaintiffs to estimate cost of replacement but did not recall if he was asked to estimate cost of repair. He also stated that some of the roof damage possibly could have been caused in servicing the air conditioning equipment placed on the roof by plaintiffs and further, that some of the roof damage was attributable to water overflow from this equipment. The roof that he installed had a 15–year life expectancy. He testified that for an additional $1,200 to $1,300 a roof with a 20–year life expectancy could have been installed. He also testified that roofs can always be repaired, although in some cases it may not be economically feasible to do so.

The contractor who re-roofed the satellite area testified that plaintiffs did not ask him the cost of repair but only for an estimate of replacement cost. He also was of the opinion that some of the damage to the roof could have been caused in servicing the air conditioning equipment. The roof which he installed had a two-year warranty but this could have been extended to 20 years by the purchase at the time of installation of a bond for approximately $600.

Defendant Hill testified that he had no knowledge of leaks in the roof, the need for repairs, or that the roof had been replaced until he was so advised by plaintiffs in February 1971. He was of the opinion that the original roof on the building had a 20–year life expectancy, and that recourse might have been available against the installing contractor had he been timely notified. He testified that as a contractor himself, he might have been able to obtain more advantageous terms for required repairs or replacement. Hill further testified that an examination of the damage to the old roof might have disclosed the cause thereof and that if caused by plaintiffs' activities relating to the air conditioning system, he would not be liable under the lease for repairs or replacement.

The trial court prepared its own findings of fact and conclusions of law. It found that the lease required defendants to repair the roof except for repairs necessitated by plaintiffs' negligent or improper use; that repairs become necessary for which plaintiffs spent $8,941; and that defendants had neither notice from plaintiffs nor knowledge of the need for repairs prior to completion of the work.

From those facts the court concluded that plaintiffs breached the contract by failing to give notice; that they were, however, entitled to restitution because defendants had been unjustly enriched; that an offset equal to one-third of the replacement cost was equitable; and that plaintiffs were therefore entitled to judgment against defendants for $5,867 plus legal interest from the date demand was made for reimbursement under the lease. The court further concluded that plaintiffs were not entitled to attorney's fees "Inasmuch as this action was not predicated on the lease, and plaintiffs in any event had breached the lease, . . ."

Plaintiffs take the position on appeal that the judgment as rendered by the trial court "is outside the scope of the pleadings and the theory of the case as presented at the trial" and that the "case should stand or fall upon the contractual provisions of the lease." Plaintiffs then argue that the trial court erred in finding them in breach of the lease for failure to give notice and in denying them full recovery thereunder. The argument is made that the lease provision governing the form and manner of giving notice cannot be expanded into a condition precedent that notice to repair in fact be given.

The plaintiffs are, of course, correct that the lease does not contain an express provision that defendants be given notice to repair. However, it is impossible to conceive of how the intentions of the parties as expressed in the covenant to repair could be implemented if notice were not required. Defendants' duty to repair was not unconditional. It did not extend to repairs made necessary by the negligence or improper use of the premises by the lessees, their agents or employees. Such repairs were by necessary implication the responsibility of lessees who were by the lease obligated to keep the premises "in good order and condition at their own expense. . . ." Clearly the parties did not intend that when repairs became necessary the lessees could unilaterally and conclusively determine the responsibility therefor and allocate the burden thereof as between lessor and lessee. If the interpretation of the lease urged by plaintiffs were accepted, however, it would permit plaintiffs to alter conditions without the lessors' knowledge and to their disadvantage, at the same time eliminating any real opportunity for the lessors to dispute their liability under the lease.

As an actual consequence of plaintiffs' unilateral action herein, defendants were irreparably handicapped in presenting a defense. Confronted with a *fait accompli,* defendants, in an effort to prove plaintiffs' responsibility for the roof damage or alternatively, to contest the necessity for repairs of the extent accomplished, were necessarily consigned to reliance upon evidence of a conjectural quality.

Moreover, it is necessarily implied in the covenant to repair at lessors' "own cost and expense" that the right to determine and control the nature, quality, course and manner, as well as the cost of repairs, is a concomitant of the burden so to do. The unilateral action of plaintiffs herein deprived defendants of this important right.

That which is necessarily implied in the language of a contract is as much a part of it as that which is expressed. (Bliss v. California Cooperative Producers (1947) 30 Cal.2d 240, 249, 181 P.2d 369.) Unexpressed provisions of a contract may be inferred from the writing. (Cal. Lettuce Growers v. Union Sugar Co. (1955) 45 Cal.2d 474, 482, 289 P.2d 785; Addiego v. Hill (1965) 238 Cal.App.2d 842, 846, 48 Cal.Rptr. 240.) In the case at bench, notice as a condition precedent to the lessors' obligation to repair is not only clearly apparent from the terms of the written lease, it is indispensable to effectuate the intentions of the parties. (See Addiego v. Hill, supra, 238 Cal.App.2d at p. 847, 48 Cal.Rptr. 240.) It has been held that unless explicitly excluded therein, performance under an express covenant to repair is conditional upon notice from the tenant. (Sieber v. Blanc (1888) 76 Cal. 173, 174, 18 P. 260; McNally v. Ward (1961) 192 Cal.App.2d 871, 884, 14 Cal.Rptr. 260.) Accordingly, we hold that notice is an indispensable condition precedent to defendants' duty to perform under the covenant to repair.

In the sense that the implied condition precedent of notice to repair does not in itself constitute a promise or covenant, plaintiffs are correct that the trial court erred in concluding that they breached the lease. (See 3A Corbin on Contracts (1960) § 634, p. 33.) However, the "error" is one of semantics, not substance. It is a minor departure from strict legal parlance and avails plaintiffs nothing, because their recovery upon the lease-contract is dependent upon alleging and proving performance of all conditions precedent to defendants' duty to repair. (Sosin v. Richardson (1962) 210 Cal.App.2d 258, 264, 26 Cal.Rptr. 210; Civ.Code, § 1439.) It is conceded by plaintiffs, and the trial court so found, that no notice was given defendants prior to completion of the repairs. Accordingly, the trial court was correct in denying recovery to plaintiffs under the lease.

* * *

[The court rejected Plaintiffs' claim, in the alternative, that their expenditures for the new roof should be granted on the quasi-contractual theory of money paid by mistake. The court concluded that there "cannot be a valid, express contract and an implied contract, each embracing the same subject matter, existing at the same time." The reason was that "where the parties have freely, fairly and voluntarily bargained for certain benefits in exchange for undertaking certain obligations, it would be inequitable to imply a different liability and to withdraw from one party benefits for which he has bargained and to which he is entitled," i.e., the "right of control over repairs for which they are therein held responsible."]

NOTES

(1) How did the condition in *Wal–Noon* differ from that in *Dove?* Was the defendant in either case unjustly enriched by being allowed to keep benefits conferred by the plaintiff before the condition failed? See Suburban Transfer Serv., Inc. v. Beech Holdings, Inc., 716 F.2d 220, 222–227 (3d Cir.1983) (quasi-contract claim rejected where subject within scope of failed express condition).

(2) In *Wal–Noon*, the trial court held that the lessee "breached" the contract by failing to give notice. Was this holding correct? How does a court decide whether an event within the control of one party was promised as part of the agreed exchange? See the next two cases. See also Willis, *Promissory and Non–Promissory Conditions*, 16 Ind.L.J. 349 (1941).

Jacob & Youngs v. Kent

Court of Appeals of New York, 1921.
230 N.Y. 239, 129 N.E. 889.

■ CARDOZO, J. The plaintiff built a country residence for the defendant at a cost of upwards of $77,000, and now sues to recover a balance of $3,483.46, remaining unpaid. The work of construction ceased in June, 1914, and the defendant then began to occupy the dwelling. There was no complaint of defective performance until March, 1915. One of the specifications for the plumbing work provides that "all wrought iron pipe must be well galvanized, lap welded pipe of the grade known as 'standard pipe' of Reading manufacture." The defendant learned in March, 1915, that some of the pipe, instead of being made in Reading, was the product of other factories. The plaintiff was accordingly directed by the architect to do the work anew. The plumbing was then encased within the walls except in a few places where it had to be exposed. Obedience to the order meant more than the substitution of other pipe. It meant the demolition at great expense of substantial parts of the completed structure. The plaintiff left the work untouched, and asked for a certificate that the final payment was due. Refusal of the certificate was followed by this suit.

The evidence sustains a finding that the omission of the prescribed brand of pipe was neither fraudulent nor willful. It was the result of the oversight and inattention of the plaintiff's subcontractor. Reading pipe is distinguished from Cohoes pipe and other brands only by the name of the manufacturer stamped upon it at intervals of between six and seven feet. Even the defendant's architect, though he inspected the pipe upon arrival, failed to notice the discrepancy. The plaintiff tried to show that the brands installed, though made by other manufacturers, were the same in quality, in appearance, in market value and in cost as the brand stated in the contract—that they were, indeed, the same thing, though manufactured in another place. The evidence was excluded, and a verdict directed for the defendant. The Appellate Division reversed, and granted a new trial.

We think the evidence, if admitted, would have supplied some basis for the inference that the defect was insignificant in its relation to the project. The courts never say that one who makes a contract fills the measure of his duty by less than full performance. They do say, however, that an omission, both trivial and innocent, will sometimes be atoned for by allowance of the resulting damage, and will not always be the breach of a condition to be followed by a forfeiture (Spence v. Ham, 163 N.Y. 220; Woodward v. Fuller, 80 N.Y. 312; Glacius v. Black, 67 N.Y. 563, 566; Bowen v. Kimbell, 203 Mass. 364, 370). The distinction is akin to that between dependent and independent promises, or between promises and conditions (Anson on Contracts [Corbin's ed.], sec. 367; 2 Williston on Contracts, sec. 842). Some promises are so plainly independent that they can never by fair construction be conditions of one another. (Rosenthal Paper Co. v. Nat. Folding Box & Paper Co., 226 N.Y. 313; Bogardus v. N.Y. Life Ins. Co., 101 N.Y. 328). Others are so plainly dependent that they must always be conditions. Others, though dependent and thus conditions when there is departure in point of substance, will be viewed as independent and collateral when the departure is insignificant (2 Williston on Contracts, secs. 841, 842; Eastern Forge Co. v. Corbin, 182 Mass. 590, 592; Robinson v. Mollett, L.R., 7 Eng. & Ir.App. 802, 814; Miller v. Benjamin, 142 N.Y. 613). Considerations partly of justice and partly of presumable intention are to tell us whether this or that promise shall be placed in one class or in another. The simple and the uniform will call for different remedies from the multifarious and the intricate. The margin of departure within the range of normal expectation upon a sale of common chattels will vary from the margin to be expected upon a contract for the construction of a mansion or a "skyscraper." There will be harshness sometimes and oppression in the implication of a condition when the thing upon which labor has been expended is incapable of surrender because united to the land, and equity and reason in the implication of a like condition when the subject-matter, if defective, is in shape to be returned. From the conclusion that promises may not be treated as dependent to the extent of their uttermost minutiae without a sacrifice of justice, the progress is a short one to the conclusion that they may not be so treated without a perversion of intention. Intention not otherwise revealed may be presumed to hold in contemplation the reasonable and probable. If something else is in view, it must not be left to implication. There will be no assumption of a purpose to visit venial faults with oppressive retribution.

Those who think more of symmetry and logic in the development of legal rules than of practical adaptation to the attainment of a just result will be troubled by a classification where the lines of division are so wavering and blurred. Something, doubtless, may be said on the score of consistency and certainty in favor of a stricter standard. The courts have balanced such considerations against those of equity and fairness, and found the latter to be the weightier. The decisions in this state commit us to the liberal view, which is making its way, nowadays, in jurisdictions slow to welcome it (Dakin & Co. v. Lee, 1916, 1 K.B. 566, 579). Where the line is to be drawn between the important and the trivial cannot be settled by a formula. "In the nature of the case precise boundaries are impossible" (2 Williston on Contracts, sec. 841). The same omission may take on one aspect or another according to its setting. Substitution of equivalents may not have the same significance in fields of art on the one side and in those of mere utility on the other. Nowhere will change be tolerated, however, if it is so dominant or pervasive as in any real or substantial measure to frustrate the purpose of the contract (Crouch v. Gutman, 134 N.Y. 45, 51). There is no general license to install whatever, in the builder's judgment, may be regarded as "just as good" (Easthampton L. & C. Co., Ltd., v. Worthington, 186 N.Y. 407, 412). The question is one of degree, to be answered, if there is doubt, by the triers of the facts (Crouch v. Gutmann; Woodward v. Fuller, supra), and, if the inferences are certain, by the judges of the law (Easthampton L. & C. Co., Ltd., v. Worthington, supra). We must weigh the purpose to be served, the desire to be gratified, the excuse for deviation from the letter, the cruelty of enforced adherence. Then only can we tell whether literal fulfilment is to be implied by law as a condition. This is not to say that the parties are not free by apt and certain words to effectuate a purpose that performance of every term shall be a condition of recovery. That question is not here. This is merely to say that the law will be slow to impute the purpose, in the silence of the parties, where the significance of the default is grievously out of proportion to the oppression of the forfeiture. The willful transgressor must accept the penalty of his transgression (Schultze v. Goodstein, 180 N.Y. 248, 251; Desmond–Dunne Co. v. Friedman–Doscher Co., 162 N.Y. 486, 490). For him there is no occasion to mitigate the rigor of implied conditions. The transgressor whose default is unintentional and trivial may hope for mercy if he will offer atonement for his wrong (Spence v. Ham, supra).

In the circumstances of this case, we think the measure of the allowance is not the cost of replacement, which would be great, but the difference in value, which would be either nominal or nothing. Some of the exposed sections might perhaps have been replaced at moderate expense. The defendant did not limit his demand to them, but treated the plumbing as a unit to be corrected from cellar to roof. In point of fact, the plaintiff never reached the stage at which evidence of the extent of the allowance became necessary. The trial court had excluded evidence that the defect was unsubstantial, and in view of that ruling there was no occasion for the plaintiff to go farther with an offer of proof. We think, however, that the offer, if it had been made, would not of necessity have been defective because directed to difference in value. It is true that in most cases the cost of replacement is the measure (Spence v. Ham, supra). The owner is entitled to the money which will permit him to complete, unless the cost of completion is grossly and unfairly out of proportion to the good to be attained. When that is true, the measure is the difference in value. Specifications call, let us say, for a foundation built of granite quarried in Vermont. On the completion of the building, the owner learns that through the blunder of a subcontractor part of the foundation has been built of granite of the same quality quarried in New Hampshire. The measure of allowance is not the cost of reconstruction. "There may be omissions of that which could not afterwards be supplied exactly as called for by the contract without taking down the building to its foundations, and at the same time the omission may not affect the value of the building for use or otherwise, except so slightly as to be hardly appreciable" (Handy v. Bliss, 204 Mass. 513, 519. Cf. Foeller v. Heintz, 137 Wis. 169, 178; Oberlies v. Bullinger, 132 N.Y. 598, 601; 2 Williston on Contracts, sec. 805, p. 1541). The rule that gives a remedy in cases of substantial performance with compensation for defects of trivial or inappreciable importance, has been developed by the courts as an instrument of justice. The measure of the allowance must be shaped to the same end.

The order should be affirmed, and judgment absolute directed in favor of the plaintiff upon the stipulation, with costs in all courts.

■ McLAUGHLIN, J. (dissenting). I dissent. The plaintiff did not perform its contract. Its failure to do so was either intentional or due to gross neglect which, under the uncontradicted facts, amounted to the same thing, nor did it make any proof of the cost of compliance, where compliance was possible.

Under its contract it obligated itself to use in the plumbing, only pipe (between 2,000 and 2,500 feet) made by the Reading Manufacturing Company. The first pipe delivered was about 1,000 feet and the plaintiff's superintendent then called the attention of the foreman of the subcontractor, who was doing the plumbing, to the fact that the specifications annexed to the contract required all pipe used in the plumbing to be of the Reading Manufacturing Company. They then examined it for the purpose of ascertaining whether this delivery was of that manufacture and found it was. Thereafter, as pipe was required in the progress of the work, the foreman of the subcontractor would leave word at its shop that he wanted a specified number of feet of pipe, without in any way indicating of what manufacture. Pipe would thereafter be delivered and installed in the building, without any examination whatever. Indeed, no examination, so far as appears, was made by the plaintiff, the subcontractor, defendant's architect, or any one else, of any of the pipe except the first delivery, until after the building had been completed. Plaintiff's architect then refused to give the certificate of completion, upon which the final payment depended, because all of the pipe used in the plumbing was not of the kind called for by the contract. After such refusal, the subcontractor removed the covering or insulation from about 900 feet of pipe which was exposed in the basement, cellar and attic, and all but 70 feet was found to have been manufactured, not by the Reading Company, but by other manufacturers, some by the Cohoes Rolling Mill Company, some by the National Steel Works, some by the South Chester Tubing Company, and some which bore no manufacturer's mark at all. The balance of the pipe had been so installed in the building that an inspection of it could not be had without demolishing, in part at least, the building itself.

I am of the opinion the trial court was right in directing a verdict for the defendant. The plaintiff agreed that all the pipe used should be of the Reading Manufacturing Company. Only about two-fifths of it, so far as appears, was of that kind. If more were used, then the burden of proving that fact was upon the plaintiff, which it could easily have done, since it knew where the pipe was obtained. The question of substantial performance of a contract of the character of the one under consideration depends in no small degree upon the good faith of the contractor. If the plaintiff had intended to, and had complied with the terms of the contract except as to minor omissions, due to inadvertence, then he might be allowed to recover the contract price, less the amount necessary to fully compensate the defendant for damages caused by such omissions. (Woodward v. Fuller, 80 N.Y. 312; Nolan v. Whitney, 88 N.Y. 648.) But that is not this case. It installed between 2,000 and 2,500 feet of pipe, of which only 1,000 feet at most complied with the contract. No explanation was given why pipe called for by the contract was not used, nor was any effort made to show what it would cost to remove the pipe of other manufacturers and install that of the Reading Manufacturing Company. The defendant had a right to contract for what he wanted. He had a right before making payment to get what the contract called for. It is no answer to this suggestion to say that the pipe put in was just as good as that made by the Reading Manufacturing Company, or that the difference in value between such pipe and the pipe made by the Reading Manufacturing Company would be either "nominal or nothing." Defendant contracted for pipe made by the Reading Manufacturing Company. What his reason was for requiring this kind of pipe is of no importance. He wanted that and was entitled to it. It may have been a mere whim on his part, but even so, he had a right to this kind of pipe, regardless of whether some other kind, according to the opinion of the contractor or experts, would have been "just as good, better, or done just as well." He agreed to pay only upon condition that the pipe installed were made by that company and he ought not to be compelled to pay unless that condition be performed. . . . The rule, therefore, of substantial performance, with damages for unsubstantial omissions, has no application.

* * *

I am of the opinion the trial court did not err in ruling on the admission of evidence or in directing a verdict for the defendant.

For the foregoing reasons I think the judgment of the Appellate Division should be reversed and the judgment of the Trial Term affirmed.

Order affirmed, etc.

NOTES

(1) The dissenting judge insists that "[t]he plaintiff did not perform its contract." Does Judge Cardozo disagree? If not, where is the express condition in this case? Arguably, the plaintiff satisfied a "constructive" condition of substantial performance that was precedent to the defendant's duty to pay the last installment.

(2) Is the issue here one of liability, remedy, or both?

(3) Could the contract have been drafted so as to preclude any recovery if Reading pipe was not installed? How would you draft a clause that ensures the protection of Kent's idiosyncratic preference?

(4) Does the character of the breach have an effect upon availability of remedy? Should it?

(5) If damages are to be allowed, how should they be measured? For more on damages for breach of a construction contract, see Chapter Six, Section 2(B).

(6) In Internatio–Rotterdam v. River Brand Rice Mills, 259 F.2d 137 (2d Cir.1958), cert. denied 358 U.S. 946, 79 S.Ct. 352, 3 L.Ed.2d 352 (1959), a buyer who had contracted to buy rice failed by twelve hours to give seller two-weeks notice (where to ship). Because the price of rice was rising, the seller terminated the contract. The court, examining conditions at the time the contract was made in July rather than the time of performance in December, held that the notice requirement was "the essence of the contract" and found that the defendant's refusal to sell was not a breach. Professor Childres concluded that the "question should have been whether the delivery period was material; or more precisely, whether it was sufficiently material to justify seller's canceling the deal." Further, "if this had been the question, it seems clear that the buyer would have won, that the seller could not have established any material prejudice from the buyer's less than twelve-hour delay." Childres, *Conditions in the Law of Contracts*, 45 N.Y.U.L.Rev. 33, 57 (1970). Do you agree with this analysis? See Continental Grain Co. v. Simpson Feed Co., 102 F.Supp. 354 (E.D.Ark.1951), affirmed 199 F.2d 284 (8th Cir.1952), where the issue was whether the buyer's 48–hour delay in furnishing shipping instructions "was sufficiently material" to justify the seller in attempting to cancel the contract. In holding that it was not, the court stated that whether undisputed facts

amounted to a material breach was a question of law to be decided by the court. After reviewing the facts and identifying the factors listed in first Restatement § 275 which were relevant to materiality, the court concluded: (1) While installment deliveries were contemplated, time was not of the essence except to the extent that the defendant was obligated to complete its deliveries by the end of the agreed period; (2) Plaintiff's delay was not accompanied by any repudiation or manifested inability to perform; (3) Defendant suffered no substantial damage from the delay, nor did it run the risk of future damage—the market was rising and any loss from demurrage was outweighed by plaintiff's loss of bargain; (4) Plaintiff's delay was neither willful nor negligent; (5) "In truth, the defendant entered into a contract with the plaintiff which became disadvantageous when the soybean market rose, and from all of the facts and circumstances in the case we can not escape the conclusion that the defendant simply seized upon what was at most an inconsequential breach on the part of the plaintiff as an excuse for release from that contract."

(7) *Promise or Condition?* It is, of course, possible in a case like *River Brand Rice* for the parties explicitly to make a timely call or prompt sailing a condition precedent to the obligor's duty. But if there is doubt about whether this has been done and the event is within the other party's control, Restatement (Second) § 227(2) prefers an interpretation that "a duty is imposed on an obligee that an event occur" rather than that the "event is made a condition of the obligor's duty." According to Comment d, the "preferred interpretation avoids the harsh results that might otherwise result from the nonoccurrence of a condition and still gives adequate protection to the obligor under the rules * * * relating to promises for an exchange of performances * * * [where] the obligee's failure to perform his duty has, if it is material, the effect of the nonoccurrence of a condition of the obligor's duty."

This preference, however, does not apply to contracts "of a type under which only the obligor generally undertakes duties." Restatement (Second) § 227, Comment d. Insurance is regarded as a contract of this type, where the usual interpretation is that the insured has no enforceable duty to pay premiums. Rather, if the risk insured against occurs, the insurance company's duty to pay under the policy is expressly conditioned upon the payment of premiums. Unless special arrangements with third parties have been made, however, the insured's failure to pay is a failure of condition rather than a breach of contract. See General Credit Corp. v. Imperial Casualty & Indemnity Co., 167 Neb. 833, 95 N.W.2d 145 (1959).

(8) North American Graphite Corp. v. Allan, 184 F.2d 387 (D.C.Cir.1950), concerned an employment contract under which the bulk of the plaintiff's compensation was not payable until completion of a project. Following completion of most of the plaintiff's services, defendant fined him and abandoned the project. The court in *Allan* conceded that the parties could have made payment for services contingent upon successful operation of the mine, but did not clearly do so. The case thus turns upon the court's interpretation of the contract—upon "the intention of the parties" as "gathered from the language used, the situation of the parties, and the subject matter of the contract, as presented by the evidence." It should not be surprising, therefore, that in situations of this type decisions may at times be difficult to reconcile, at least on the basis of the rather meager data ordinarily appearing in an appellate

court opinion. For example, in Mascioni v. Miller, Inc., 261 N.Y. 1, 184 N.E. 473 (1933), a prime contractor's promise to a subcontractor of "[p]ayment to be made as received from the owner" was held to condition liability. However, the vast majority of decisions are in accord with Dancy v. William J. Howard, Inc., 297 F.2d 686 (7th Cir.1961), where the promise of a prime contractor to make final payment after he "has received final payment for construction" was said not to make such receipt of final payment a condition precedent, "but rather fixed it as a convenient time for payment." See also Mularz v. Greater Park City Co., 623 F.2d 139, 142–144 (10th Cir.1980). Like problems of interpretation have arisen from promises to pay out of earnings or profits, or "when able," etc. See Corbin §§ 639, 641. How clear must the language be to avoid the presumption against conditions?

In re Carter

Supreme Court of Pennsylvania, 1957.
390 Pa. 365, 134 A.2d 908.

■ Opinion by MR. JUSTICE BENJAMIN R. JONES.

This is an appeal from a judgment entered upon an arbitrator's award in a proceeding under the Act of 1927.

In June 1954 the Edwin J. Schoettle Co., a Pennsylvania corporation, and its six subsidiaries were available for purchase. Lester L. Kardon, interested in purchasing the company and five of its subsidiaries, opened negotiations for that purpose. The negotiations extended from June 24, 1954 to September 17, 1954, on which latter date the parties entered into a written agreement under the terms of which Kardon (hereinafter called the buyer) purchased all the issued and outstanding capital stock of Schoettle Co. and all its subsidiaries (hereinafter called sellers). The total purchase price set forth in the agreement of sale (excluding certain real estate) was $2,100,000 of which amount $187,863.60 was set aside under paragraph 11 of the agreement to be held by the Provident Trust Company of Philadelphia as escrow agent to indemnify the buyer against "the liabilities of sellers by reason of any and all provisions of this agreement."

The present litigation arises from the fact that the buyer has presented a claim against the escrow fund for $69,998.42 as a "liability" of the seller under the agreement. Payment of this claim having been disputed by the sellers, both parties, under the provisions of the agreement, submitted to arbitration and Judge Gerald F. Flood was selected as arbitrator. On October 26, 1956 Judge Flood, as arbitrator, and after hearing, awarded to the buyer $3,182.88. Buyer's motion to correct the arbitrator's award was dismissed by the Court of Common Pleas No. 6 of Philadelphia County and judgment was entered in the amount of $3,182.88 in conformity with the arbitrator's award. From that judgment this appeal ensued.

The resolution of this controversy depends upon the interpretation of certain portions of the 25-page written agreement of September 17, 1954. The pertinent portions of this agreement are paragraphs 5(g), 9(a), 9(b), 9(c), 10(d) and 15, which read as follows: "5. *Representations and warran-*

ties. Sellers *represent* and *warrant* as follows: [emphasis supplied] ... (g) *Absence of certain changes.* Since June 30, 1954, there have not been (i) any changes in Company's or its subsidiaries' financial condition, assets, liabilities, or businesses, other than changes in the ordinary course of business, none of which have been materially adverse, and changes required or permitted hereunder; (ii) any damage, destruction, or loss, whether or not covered by insurance, materially and adversely affecting the properties or businesses of Company and its subsidiaries as an entirety; (iii) any declaration, or setting aside, or payment of any dividend or other distribution in respect of Company's capital stock or that of any subsidiary (except that prior to the date hereof, Company has declared and paid a dividend of Sixteen and Two Thirds Cents ($.16⅔) per share on all issued and outstanding shares of its said capital stock), or any direct or indirect redemption, purchase, or other acquisition of any such stock; or (iv) any increase in the compensation payable or to become payable by Company or any subsidiary to any of their officers, employees, or agents, or any bonus payment or arrangement made to or with any of them.

* * *

"9. *Conditions precedent.* All obligations of Buyer under this agreement are subject to the fulfillment, prior to or at the closing of each of the following *conditions:* [emphasis supplied]. (a) *Financial condition at closing.* As of the time of closing the financial condition of the Company and its subsidiaries in the aggregate shall be no less favorable than the financial condition shown on the statements of said corporations dated June 30, 1954 and warranted to be true and complete in paragraph 5(e) hereof. (b) *Representations and warranties true at closing.* Sellers' representations and warranties contained in this agreement shall be true at the time of closing as though such representations and warranties were made at such time. (c) *Performance.* Sellers shall have performed and complied with all agreements and conditions required by this agreement to be performed or complied with by them prior to or at the closing.

* * *

"10. *Indemnification.* Sellers shall indemnify and hold harmless Buyer, subject to the limitations of paragraph 11 hereof, against and in respect of: * * * (d) any damage or deficiency resulting from any misrepresentation, breach of warranty, or nonfulfillment of any agreement on the part of Sellers, or any of them, under this agreement, or from any misrepresentation in or omission from any certificate or other instrument furnished or to be furnished to Buyer hereunder;

"15. *Survival of representations.* All representations, warranties and agreements made by Sellers and Buyer in this agreement or pursuant hereto shall survive closing, subject to the provisions of paragraph 11 hereof."

The buyer (appellant) contends that the financial condition on the date of purchase—September 17, 1954—was less favorable than that reflected in the company's financial statement of June 30, 1954 and, therefore, he is entitled to reimbursement out of the escrow fund for the amount of the deficiency. Sellers (appellees) deny any reduction in the financial condition and further argue that, even if there were any reduction, buyer has no right to reimbursement under the agreement unless such reduction resulted from occurrences outside the ordinary course of business or which caused a materially adverse change in the company's financial condition. Actually the buyer's position is that paragraph 9(a), supra, constituted a "warranty" on the sellers' part that the financial condition of the company and its subsidiaries was not less favorable than demonstrated by the financial statement of June 30, 1954 and, therefore, sellers having breached the warranty the buyer is entitled to claim the difference between the net worth on June 30, 1954 and September 17, 1954. On the other hand, sellers take the position that their engagement under paragraph 9(a) constituted a "condition" and not a warranty and the buyer had simply the right to refuse a consummation of the sale if the "condition" was not fulfilled; when the buyer elected to consummate the sale it waived the "condition."

* * *

This written agreement was carefully and meticulously prepared by able and competent counsel after long and thorough negotiations. Each general paragraph of the agreement is headed by a title descriptive of the contents of each paragraph. Paragraph 5, entitled "Representations and Warranties," expressly states that the sellers "represented and warranted" fifteen separate and carefully spelled out factual situations. Paragraph 9, entitled "Conditions precedent" expressly states that "All obligations of buyer under this agreement are subject to the fulfillment, prior to or at the closing, of each of the following *conditions*." It is to be noted that included among the "*conditions*" was the financial condition of the company and its subsidiaries at the time of closing, that the fulfillment of the "conditions" was to take place not subsequent to but "prior to or at the closing" and that the buyer's obligations, not the sellers', were made subject to the fulfillment of the condition. This agreement, in distinct and indubitable language, distinguishes between such engagements on the sellers' part as constitute "Warranties" and such engagements as constitute "Conditions."

Assuming, arguendo, that the company and its subsidiaries' financial condition was less favorable on September 17, 1954 than the financial condition shown on the statement dated June 30, 1954, what under this agreement was the buyer's remedy? The buyer claims that such fact constituted a breach of warranty which gave to him the right to recover the amount of the reduced net worth, while the sellers claim that the buyer had the choice on September 17, 1954 either to accept the situation or to refuse to proceed under the agreement.

The buyer argues that it was impossible to ascertain at the date of closing whether or not the net worth of the company and its subsidiaries had been reduced, and that only by an examination after date of closing could this fact be ascertained and, therefore, both parties must have intended that the buyer have a reasonable time after the date of closing to ascertain this fact. Such an argument not only finds no support in the wording of the agreement but, on the contrary, is in direct conflict with the express terms of the agreement. Such a contention would require that we read into the agreement that which is in direct variance with the clear and unambiguous language employed to express the parties' intent.

* * *

The arbitrator concluded that to construe paragraph 9(a) as creative of a promise for the breach of which the buyer could recover damages—i.e., a warranty—would be inconsistent with paragraph 5(g). With this conclusion we are in full agreement. The sellers in paragraph 5(g) represented and warranted, inter alia, that there had not been any changes in the financial condition of the company or its subsidiaries other than changes in the ordinary course of business, none of which had been materially adverse and were changes required or permitted under the agreement. Paragraph 9(a) covers an entirely different situation in that it referred to such changes in the financial condition of the company and its subsidiaries in the ordinary course of business which were materially adverse and not permitted under the agreement; if this situation arose the agreement specifically provided that the buyer was under no obligation to complete the purchase. A comparison of paragraph 5(g) with paragraph 9(a) clearly leads to this conclusion; to place upon paragraph 9(a) any other construction than that placed upon it by the arbitrator would amount to a redundancy.

A resolution of the instant controversy depends entirely upon an interpretation of the language of this agreement. The language employed by the parties is manifestly indicative of that which was intended and the meaning of the agreement—free as it is of ambiguity and doubt—is to be determined by what the agreement states. The parties carefully and scrupulously delineated between the sellers' undertakings which were intended to be "warranties" and those which were intended to be "conditions." It is crystal clear that the undertaking under paragraph 9(a) was simply a "condition" and not a "warranty" and once the buyer elected to accept this agreement the provisions of paragraph 9(a) ceased to be operative and the buyer had no right to recover any damages.

The judgment of the Court below is affirmed. Costs to be paid by appellant.

[Footnotes omitted.]

NOTES

(1) Why was it important to differentiate warranties and conditions precedent in *In re Carter?* Note that the court appears to use the "plain meaning rule" of contract interpretation. Was that justified on these facts?

(2) It is sometimes said that failure of an express condition precedent gives the promisor a "shield" but not a "sword"; he or she can avoid the contract but has no claim for damages. Why was this defensive protection denied to the buyer in *In re Carter?*

PROBLEM: THE CASE OF THE INSOLVENT OWNER

S entered a subcontract with P for excavation work to be performed on land owned by O. P had the prime contract with O for the overall project, the development of a shopping center. The contract between S and P provided in part:

Article 5: Material and work invoices submitted before the 25th of the current month will be paid by the 28th of the following month, provided the material so delivered is acceptable, and if payment for invoiced material has been received by [P] under its general contract.

Article 18: ... [I]f the work has been satisfactorily performed and invoice as rendered is approved and if payment for such labor and material so invoiced has been received by [P] under its general contract, the subcontractor will be paid 85% of invoice as approved, less any payments previously made on account for previous periods. No payments made shall be considered as evidence of acceptance of the work either in whole or in part until the work is completed and accepted, whereupon final payment will be made within thirty (30) days of such acceptance upon receipt of all or any bonds, guarantees required.

O became insolvent and the project was terminated before S was paid in full for work done. S filed a mechanic's lien on O's property. The trustee in the insolvency proceeding found that S was owed $84,000 for work done, but ruled that the claim against O and its land was subordinated to other creditors of O. S then sued P under the subcontract. P alleged that it had not been paid in full by O before the insolvency and argued that under the subcontract payment by O was a condition precedent to its duty to pay S. What result? See A.A. Conte, Inc. v. Campbell–Lowrie–Lautermilch, 132 Ill.App.3d 325, 87 Ill.Dec. 429, 477 N.E.2d 30 (1985).

(2) EXCUSE OF CONDITIONS

On the one hand, the law of conditions fosters a policy favoring freedom *from* contract. If an express condition precedent has failed, the promisor has a defense and may be discharged from the contract without any obligation to compensate the promisee for part-performance. Whether the promisor was in fact prejudiced by the failure is immaterial. On the other hand, a strict application of the law of conditions can produce a perceived forfeiture, especially where the promisor is not actually prejudiced by the failure of condition and the promisee has engaged in extensive preparation to perform or part-performance. Put differently, if the condition turns out to be immaterial to the promisor and the promisee has relied or conferred a benefit on the promisor, discharging the promisor may provide a severe test for the "freedom from" contract policy.

A good example of this "severe test" is Inman v. Clyde Hall Drilling Co., 369 P.2d 498 (Alaska 1962), where the court discharged an employer from a claim by a terminated employee because the employee failed to satisfy a 30–day condition of notice, even though the lawsuit was filed and service was made within the 30–day period and there was no evidence that the promisor was prejudiced by the delay. The court stated:

Service of the complaint probably gave the Company actual knowledge of the claim. But that does not serve as an excuse for not giving the kind of written notice called for by the contract. Inman agreed that no suit would be instituted "prior to six (6) months *after the filing of the written notice of claim.*" (emphasis ours) If this means what it says (and we have no reason to believe it does not), it is clear that the commencement of an action and service of the complaint was not an effective substitute for the kind of notice called for by the agreement. To hold otherwise would be to simply ignore an explicit provision of the contract and say that it had no meaning. We are not justified in doing that.

As we have seen, one way to deal with the forfeiture problem is to argue that a condition precedent was not intended. But this will not work if the contract was clearly drafted. Another way to temper forfeiture is to excuse the condition on some other ground. Some possible grounds for excuse include: (1) An agreement by both parties modifying the contract to discharge the condition; (2) Conduct by the party for whose benefit the condition was made that "waives" the condition; (3) Changed circumstances that make compliance by the promisee with the condition impracticable; and (4) Discharge by the court. In this subsection, we will explore when these grounds for excuse of condition are available.

Clark v. West

Court of Appeals of New York, 1908.
193 N.Y. 349, 86 N.E. 1.

On February 12th, 1900, the plaintiff and defendant entered into a written contract under which the former was to write and prepare for publication for the latter a series of law books the compensation for which was provided in the contract. After the plaintiff had completed a three-volume work known as "Clark & Marshall on Corporations," the parties disagreed. The plaintiff claimed that the defendant had broken the contract by causing the book to be copyrighted in the name of a corporation, which was not a party to the contract, and he brought this action to recover what he claims to be due him, for an accounting and other relief. The defendant demurred to the complaint on the ground that it did not state facts sufficient to constitute a cause of action. The Special Term overruled the demurrer, but upon appeal to the Appellate Division, that decision was reversed and the demurrer sustained.

Those portions of the contract which are germane to the present stage of the controversy are as follows: The plaintiff agreed to write a series of books relating to specified legal subjects; the manuscript furnished by him was to be satisfactory to the defendant; the plaintiff was not to write or edit anything that would interfere with the sale of books to be written by him under the contract and he was not to write any other books unless requested so to do by the defendant, in which latter event he was to be paid $3,000 a year. The contract contained a clause which provided that "The first party (the plaintiff) agrees to totally abstain from the use of intoxicating liquors during the continuance of this contract, and that the payment to him in accordance with the terms of this contract of any money in excess of $2 per page is dependent on the faithful performance of this as well as the other conditions of this contract. * * *"

In a later paragraph it further recited that, "In consideration of the above promises of the first party (the plaintiff), the second party (the defendant) agrees to pay to the first party $2 per page, * * * on each book prepared by the first party under this contract and accepted by the second party, and if said first party abstains from the use of intoxicating liquor and otherwise fulfills his agreements as hereinbefore set forth, he shall be paid an additional $4 per page in manner hereinbefore stated." * * *

The plaintiff in his complaint alleges completion of the work on corporations and publication thereof by the defendant; the sale of many copies thereof from which the defendant received large net receipts; the number of pages it contained (3,469), for which he had been paid at the rate of $2 per page, amounting to $6,938; and that defendant has refused to pay him any sum over and above that amount, or any sum in excess of $2 per page. Full performance of the agreement on plaintiff's part is alleged, except that he "did not totally abstain from the use of intoxicating liquor during the continuation of said contract, but such use by the plaintiff was not excessive and did not prevent or interfere with the due and full performance by the plaintiff of all the other stipulations in said contract." The complaint further alleges a waiver on the part of the defendant of the plaintiff's stipulation to totally abstain from the use of intoxicating liquors * * *.

The defendant's breach of the contract is then alleged which is claimed to consist in his having taken out a copyright upon the plaintiff's work on corporations in the name of a publishing company which had no relation to the contract, and the relief asked for is that the defendant be compelled to account, and that the copyright be transferred to the plaintiff or that he recover its value.

The appeal is by permission of the Appellate Division and the following questions have been certified to us: 1. Does the complaint herein state facts sufficient to constitute a cause of action? 2. Under the terms of the contract alleged in the complaint, is the plaintiff's total abstinence from the use of intoxicating liquors a condition precedent which can be waived so as to render defendant liable upon the contract notwithstanding plaintiff's use of intoxicating liquors? 3. Does the complaint herein allege facts constituting a valid and effective waiver of plaintiff's non-performance of such condition precedent?

■ WERNER, J. * * * Briefly stated, the defendant's position is that the stipulation as to plaintiff's total abstinence is the consideration for the payment of the difference between $2 and $6 per page and therefore could not be waived except by a new agreement to that effect based upon a good consideration; that the so-called waiver alleged by the plaintiff is not a waiver but a modification of the contract in respect to its consideration.

The plaintiff on the other hand argues that the stipulation for his total abstinence was merely a condition precedent intended to work a forfeiture of the additional compensation in case of a breach and that it could be waived without any formal agreement to that effect based upon a new consideration.

The subject-matter of the contract was the writing of books by the plaintiff for the defendant. The duration of the contract was the time necessary to complete them all. The work was to be done to the satisfaction of the defendant, and the plaintiff was not to write any other books except those covered by the contract unless requested so to do by the defendant, in which latter event he was to be paid for that particular work by the year. The compensation for the work specified in the contract was to be $6 per page, unless the plaintiff failed to totally abstain from the use of intoxicating liquors during the continuance of the contract, in which event he was to receive only $2 per page. That is the obvious import of the contract construed in the light of the purpose for which it was made, and in accordance with the ordinary meaning of plain language. It is not a contract to write books in order that the plaintiff shall keep sober, but a contract containing a stipulation that he shall keep sober so that he may write satisfactory books. When we view the contract from this standpoint it will readily be perceived that the particular stipulation is not the consideration for the contract, but simply one of its conditions which fits in with those relating to time and method of delivery of manuscript, revision of proof, citation of cases, assignment of copyrights, keeping track of new cases and citations for new editions, and other details which might be waived by the defendant, if he saw fit to do so. This is made clear, it seems to us, by the provision that, "In consideration of the above promises," the defendant agrees to pay the plaintiff $2 per page on each book prepared by him, and if he "abstains from the use of intoxicating liquor and otherwise fulfills his agreements as hereinbefore set forth, he shall be paid an additional $4 per page in manner hereinbefore stated." The compensation of $2 per page, not to exceed $250 per month, was an advance or partial payment of the whole price of $6 per page, and the payment of the two-thirds, which was to be withheld pending the performance of the contract, was simply made contingent upon the plaintiff's total abstention from the use of intoxicants during the life of the contract. * * * It is obvious that the parties thought that the plaintiff's normal work was worth $6 per page. That was the sum to be paid for the work done by the plaintiff and not for total abstinence. If the plaintiff did not keep to the condition as to total abstinence, he was to lose part of that sum. * * * This, we think, is the fair interpretation of the contract, and it follows that the stipulation as to the plaintiff's total abstinence was nothing more nor less than a condition precedent. If that conclusion is well founded there can be no escape from the corollary that this condition could be waived; and if it was waived the defendant is clearly not in a position to insist upon the forfeiture which his waiver was intended to annihilate. The forfeiture must stand or fall with the condition. If the latter was waived, the former is no longer a part of the contract. Defendant still has the right to counterclaim for any damages which he may have sustained in consequence of the plaintiff's breach, but he cannot insist upon strict performance. Dunn v. Steubing, 120 N.Y. 232, 24 N.E. 315; Parke v. Franco–American Trading Co., 120 N.Y. 51, 56, 23 N.E. 996; Brady v. Cassidy, 145 N.Y. 171, 39 N.E. 814.

This whole discussion is predicated of course upon the theory of an express waiver. We assume that no waiver could be implied from the defendant's mere acceptance of the books and his payment of the sum of $2 per page without objection. It was the defendant's duty to pay that amount in any event after acceptance of the work. The plaintiff must stand upon his allegation of an express waiver and if he fails to establish that he cannot maintain his action.

The theory upon which the defendant's attitude seems to be based is that even if he has represented to the plaintiff that he would not insist upon the condition that the latter should observe total abstinence from intoxicants, he can still refuse to pay the full contract price for his work. The inequity of this position becomes apparent when we consider that this contract was to run for a period of years, during a large portion of which the plaintiff was to be entitled only to the advance payment of $2 per page, the balance being contingent, among other things, upon publication of the books and returns from sales. Upon this theory the defendant might have waived the condition while the first book was in process of production, and yet, when the whole work was completed, he would still be a position to insist upon the forfeiture because there had not been strict performance. Such a situation is possible in a case where the subject of the waiver is the very consideration of a contract, Organ v. Stewart, 60 N.Y. 413, 420, but not where the waiver relates to something that can be waived. In the case at bar, as we have seen, the waiver is not of the consideration or subject-matter, but of an incident to the method of performance. The consideration remains the same. The defendant has had the work he bargained for, and it is alleged that he has waived one of the conditions as to the manner in which it was to have been done. He might have insisted upon literal performance and then he could have stood upon the letter of his contract. If, however, he has waived that incidental condition, he has created a situation to which the doctrine of waiver very precisely applies.

The cases which present the most familiar phases of the doctrine of waiver are those which have arisen out of litigation over insurance policies where the defendants have claimed a forfeiture because of the breach of some condition in the contract, Insurance Co. v. Norton, 96 U.S. 234; Titus v. Glens Falls Ins. Co., 81 N.Y. 410; Kiernan v. Dutchess Co. Mut. Insurance Co., 150 N.Y. 190, 44 N.E. 698, but it is a doctrine of general application which is confined to no particular class of cases. A waiver has been defined to be the intentional relinquishment of a known right. It is voluntary and implies an election to dispense with something of value, or forego some advantage which the party waiving it might at its option have demanded or insisted upon, Herman on Estoppel & Res Adjudicata, vol. 2, p. 954; Cowenhoven v. Ball, 118 N.Y. 231, 23 N.E. 470, and this definition is supported by many cases in this and other states. In the recent case of

Draper v. Oswego Co. Fire R. Ass'n, 190 N.Y. 12, 16, 82 N.E. 755, Chief Judge Cullen, in speaking for the court upon this subject, said: "While that doctrine and the doctrine of equitable estoppel are often confused in insurance litigation, there is a clear distinction between the two. A waiver is the voluntary abandonment or relinquishment by a party of some right or advantage. As said by my Brother Vann in the Kiernan Case, 150 N.Y. 190, 44 N.E. 698: 'The law of waiver seems to be a technical doctrine, introduced and applied by the court for the purpose of defeating forfeitures. * * * While the principle may not be easily classified, it is well established that, if the words and acts of the insurer reasonably justify the conclusion that with full knowledge of all the facts it intended to abandon or not to insist upon the particular defense afterwards relied upon, a verdict or finding to that effect establishes a waiver, which, if it once exists, can never be revoked.' The doctrine of equitable estoppel, or estoppel *in pais,* is that a party may be precluded by his acts and conduct from asserting a right to the detriment of another party who, entitled to rely on such conduct, has acted upon it. * * * As already said, the doctrine of waiver is to relieve against forfeiture; it requires no consideration for a waiver, nor any prejudice or injury to the other party." To the same effect, see Knarston v. Manhattan Life Ins. Co., 140 Cal. 57, 73 P. 740.

It remains to be determined whether the plaintiff has alleged facts which, if proven, will be sufficient to establish his claim of an express waiver by the defendant of the plaintiff's breach of the condition to observe total abstinence. In the 12th paragraph of the complaint, the plaintiff alleges facts and circumstances which we think, if established, would prove defendant's waiver of plaintiff's performance of that contract stipulation. These facts and circumstances are that long before the plaintiff had completed the manuscript of the first book undertaken under the contract, the defendant had full knowledge of the plaintiff's non-observance of that stipulation, and that with such knowledge he not only accepted the completed manuscript without objection, but "repeatedly avowed and represented to the plaintiff that he was entitled to and would receive said royalty payments (i.e., the additional $4 per page), and plaintiff believed and relied upon such representations, * * * and at all times during the writing of said treatise on corporations, and after as well as before publication thereof as aforesaid, it was mutually understood, agreed, and intended by the parties hereto that, notwithstanding plaintiff's said use of intoxicating liquors, he was nevertheless entitled to receive and would receive said royalty as the same accrued under said contract." * * *

The three questions certified should be answered in the affirmative, the order of the Appellate Division reversed, the interlocutory judgment of the Special Term affirmed, with costs in both courts, and the defendant be permitted to answer the complaint within twenty days upon payment of costs.

NOTES

(1) *Excuse of Conditions by "Waiver."* Since a condition is a term of the contract, it can be deleted or modified by a subsequent agreement between the

parties. If, however, the condition, to use Restatement (Second) language, is a "material part of the agreed exchange," see Section 84(1)(a), the agreement must satisfy the usual requirements for an enforceable modification, including, upon occasion, consideration. See UCC 2–209(1) [UCC 2–210(a)(1997)]; Restatement (Second) § 89. It is frequently asserted, however, that a condition can be excused by conduct by one party to the contract which falls short of an agreed modification. An umbrella covering some of these situations is the word "waiver," which has been defined generally as the "voluntary relinquishment of a known right." Analysis reveals that where express conditions are involved, "waiver" is associated with three recurring fact patterns, aptly illustrated by insurance contracts: (1) Plaintiff-insured has not satisfied an express condition that notice be given within 30 days after a covered accident, but Defendant-insurer, with full knowledge, elects to process the claim rather than to deny payment. Because of the "election" after the condition has failed, the insurer cannot thereafter insist upon the condition. See, e.g., Lee v. Casualty Co. of America, 90 Conn. 202, 96 A. 952 (1916); Restatement (Second) § 84(1) (conduct of insurer is a "promise to perform all * * * of a conditional duty under an antecedent contract in spite of the non-occurrence of the condition * * *"). (2) Immediately after the accident, Defendant-insurer tells Plaintiff-insured not to worry about the 30–day notice condition. Relying on this, Plaintiff submitted notice within 45 days of the accident and defendant refused to process the claim. The condition is waived because Plaintiff has materially changed his or her position in reliance upon Defendant's representation. See UCC 2–209(5); Restatement (Second) §§ 84(2), 89(c). (3) After Plaintiff has substantially performed the contract, Defendant states that it will not insist upon a non-material condition. The condition is waived without "election" or "estoppel." Imperator Realty Co. v. Tull, 228 N.Y. 447, 127 N.E. 263 (1920). More broadly, when one party has promised or represented that he or she will not insist upon express conditions, "waiver" becomes a judicial device to avoid forfeiture in particular cases where an agreed modification cannot be found. See L. Friedman, Contract Law in America 122–24 (1965); Morris, *Waiver and Estoppel in Insurance Policy Litigation,* 105 U.Pa.L.Rev. 925 (1957). See also Rubin, *Toward a General Theory of Waiver,* 28 U.C.L.A.L.Rev. 478 (1981).

(2) *Effect of Term Requiring Written Modification.* A contract term that prohibits a non-written modification can be waived without a writing at common law. See First Nat. Bank of Pa. v. Lincoln Nat. Life Ins. Co., 824 F.2d 277, 280 (3d Cir.1987); Udevco, Inc. v. Wagner, 100 Nev. 185, 678 P.2d 679, 682 (1984); Universal Builders, Inc. v. Moon Motor Lodge, Inc., 430 Pa. 550, 244 A.2d 10 (1968). UCC 2–209(2), however, provides that "A signed agreement which excludes modification or rescission except by a signed writing cannot be otherwise modified or rescinded ..." Does this foreclose a non-written waiver? In Wisconsin Knife Works v. National Metal Crafters, 781 F.2d 1280 (7th Cir.1986), the court, relying on UCC 2–209(4), held it did not. An "attempt at modification or rescission [which] does not satisfy the requirements of subsection (2) ... can operate as a waiver." The court, however, disagreed on the type of waiver required. The majority, speaking through Judge Posner, concluded that the waiver conduct must induce reliance by the other party. See UCC 2–209(5). Judge Easterbrook, in dissent, found that UCC 2–209 incorporated a broader concept of waiver. In short, proof of reliance was not required if the promisor, with knowledge of the failed condition, elected not to insist on it and

proceeded with performance. For a critical evaluation of both UCC 2–209 and the majority opinion in *Wisconsin Knife,* see Murray, *The Modification Mystery: Section 2–209 of the Uniform Commercial Code,* 32 Vill.L.Rev. 1 (1987).

Revised UCC 2–210 (1997) adopts Judge Posner's interpretation in *Wisconsin Knife.* Subsection (c) permits a term "prohibiting modification or rescission except by a signed record" and then provides: "However, a party whose language or conduct in modifying or rescinding a contract is inconsistent with a term requiring a signed record to modify or rescind the contract may not assert the term if the language or conduct induced the other party to change its position reasonably and in good faith."

(3) *Effect of Anti–Waiver Clause.* In M.J.G. Properties, Inc. v. Hurley, 27 Mass.App.Ct. 250, 537 N.E.2d 165 (1989), the lessee covenanted that it would use the property consistent with applicable zoning ordinances. The lease also provided that upon any breach of covenant, the lessor could repossess the premises "at any time" notwithstanding any waiver. After three breaches, the lessor sought to repossess the property. The lessee argued and the trial court agreed that the lessor, despite the "anti-waiver" clause, had waived its power to repossess. On appeal, the judgment was affirmed. The court stated:

> On the record before us, the trial judge was presented with the following evidence: two breaches occurring in 1985 had been ignored by the lessor, and no mention of them had been made to the lessee; nothing was said about a third breach for seven months, after which time the lessor attempted to terminate the lease; in the meantime two actions in small claims court were brought against the lessee on other grounds (one for increased rent); rent was accepted without reservation throughout the period prior to notice of termination; notice of termination came only after the lessee had exercised the option to extend. On this evidence, considering the antiwaiver clause as relevant but not dispositive, we cannot say, especially in view of the incomplete record before us ... that the judge erred in finding a waiver by the lessor. Id. at 167.

[Footnotes omitted.]

Aetna Casualty and Surety Co. v. Murphy

Supreme Court of Connecticut, 1988.
206 Conn. 409, 538 A.2d 219.

■ PETERS, CHIEF JUSTICE.

The sole issue in this appeal is whether an insured who belatedly gives notice of an insurable claim can nonetheless recover on the insurance contract by rebutting the presumption that his delay has been prejudicial to the insurance carrier. The plaintiff, Aetna Casualty and Surety Company, brought an action against the defendant, George A. Murphy III, to recover for damage he allegedly caused to a building it had insured. The defendant then filed a third party complaint impleading his comprehensive liability insurer, Federal Insurance Company, Chubb Group of Insurance Companies (hereinafter Chubb), as third party defendant. Chubb successfully moved for summary judgment on the ground that Murphy, the defendant and third party plaintiff, had inexcusably and unreasonably delayed in complying with the notice provisions of the insurance contract. The defendant appeals from this judgment. We find no error.

The underlying facts are undisputed. The defendant, George A. Murphy III, a dentist, terminated a lease with Hopmeadow Professional Center Associates on or about November 30, 1982. The manner in which he had dismantled his office gave rise to a claim for damages to which the plaintiff, Aetna Casualty and Surety Company, became subrogated. Although served with the plaintiff's complaint on November 21, 1983, the defendant gave no notice of the existence of this claim to Chubb until January 10, 1986. The motion to implead Chubb as third party defendant was filed on May 14, 1986, and granted on June 2, 1986.

Chubb moved for summary judgment on its three special defenses, alleging Murphy's noncompliance with the terms of his insurance policy. Its first claim was that it was entitled to judgment because Murphy had ignored two provisions in the Chubb policy imposing notice requirements on its policyholders. The first of these provisions states: "In the event of an occurrence, written notice ... shall be given by or for the insured to the company ... as soon as practicable." The other states: "If claim is made or suit is brought against the insured, the insured shall immediately forward to the company every demand, notice, summons, or other process received by him or his representative." In his answer to Chubb's special defenses, Murphy admitted his failure to comply with these provisions. Accordingly, his affidavit opposing summary judgment raised no question of fact but relied on his argument that, as a matter of law, an insurer may not deny coverage because of late notice without a showing, on its part, that it has been prejudiced by its insured's delay.

The trial court granted Chubb's motion for summary judgment on its first special defense. It found that Murphy's two year delay in giving notice to Chubb was inexcusable and unreasonable, and concluded that such a delay "voids coverage and insurer's duties under the contract [of insurance]...."

On appeal, Murphy challenges only the trial court's conclusion of law. Despite his inexcusable and unreasonable delay in giving notice, he maintains that he is entitled to insurance coverage because Chubb has failed to allege or to show prejudice because of his late notice.

As Murphy concedes, the trial court's decision accurately reflects numerous holdings of this court that, absent waiver, an unexcused, unreasonable delay in notification constitutes a failure of condition that entirely discharges an insurance carrier from any further liability on its insurance contract....

In our appraisal of the continued vitality of this line of cases, it is noteworthy that they do not reflect a searching analysis of what role prejudice, or its absence, should play in the enforcement of such standard clauses in insurance policies. That issue was put on the table, but not resolved, by a vigorous dissent in Plasticrete Corporation v. American

Policyholders Ins. Co., 184 Conn. 231, 240–44, 439 A.2d 968 (1981) (*Bogdanski, J.,* dissenting). The time has come for us to address it squarely.

We are confronted, in this case, by a conflict between two competing principles in the law of contracts. On the one hand, the law of contracts supports the principle that contracts should be enforced as written, and that contracting parties are bound by the contractual provisions to which they have given their assent. Among the provisions for which the parties may bargain are clauses that impose conditions upon contractual liability. "If the occurrence of a condition is required by the agreement of the parties, rather than as a matter of law, a rule of strict compliance traditionally applies." E. Farnsworth, Contracts (1982) § 8.3, p. 544; ... On the other hand, the rigor of this traditional principle of strict compliance has increasingly been tempered by the recognition that the occurrence of a condition may, in appropriate circumstances, be excused in order to avoid a "disproportionate forfeiture." See, e.g., 2 Restatement (Second), Contracts (1981) § 229;[2] Johnson Controls, Inc. v. Bowes, 381 Mass. 278, 280, 409 N.E.2d 185 (1980); 3A A. Corbin, Contracts (1960 & Sup.1984) § 754; E. Farnsworth, supra, § 8.7, pp. 570–71; 5 S. Williston, Contracts (3d Ed. Jaeger 1961) §§ 769 through 811.

In numerous cases, this court has held that, especially in the absence of conduct that is "wilful," a contracting party may, despite his own departure from the specifications of his contract, enforce the obligations of the other party with whom he has dealt in good faith. In construction contracts, a builder's deviation from contract specifications, even if such a departure is conscious and intentional, will not totally defeat the right to recover in an action against the owner on the contract ... In contracts for the sale of real property, the fact that a contract states a date for performance does not necessarily make time of the essence ... A purchaser of real property does not, despite his knowing default, forfeit the right to seek restitution of sums of money earlier paid under the contract of sale, even when such payments are therein characterized as liquidated damages ... Finally, despite a failure to deliver contract goods, a seller need not pay

2. The Restatement (Second) of Contracts (1981) § 229, entitled "Excuse of a Condition to Avoid Forfeiture," provides: "To the extent that the non-occurrence of a condition would cause disproportionate forfeiture, a court may excuse the non-occurrence of that condition unless its occurrence was a material part of the agreed exchange."

Comment b elaborates on the concept of "disproportionate forfeiture" as follows: "The rule stated in the present Section is, of necessity, a flexible one, and its application is within the sound discretion of the court. Here, as in § 227(1), 'forfeiture' is used to refer to the denial of compensation that results when the obligee loses his right to the agreed exchange after he has relied substan-tially, as by preparation or performance on the expectation of that exchange. See Comment b to § 227. The extent of the forfeiture in any particular case will depend on the extent of that denial of compensation. In determining whether the forfeiture is 'disproportionate,' a court must weigh the extent of the forfeiture by the obligee against the importance to the obligor of the risk from which he sought to be protected and the degree to which that protection will be lost if the non-occurrence of the condition is excused to the extent required to prevent forfeiture. *The character of the agreement may, as in the case of insurance agreements, affect the rigor with which the requirement is applied.*" (Emphasis added.)

an amount contractually designated as liquidated damages to a buyer who has suffered no damages attributable to the seller's breach....

This case law demonstrates that, in appropriate circumstances, a contracting party, despite his own default, may be entitled to relief from the rigorous enforcement of contract provisions that would otherwise amount to a forfeiture. On the question of what circumstances warrant such relief, no better guidelines have ever been proffered than those articulated by Judge Benjamin Cardozo in the celebrated case of Jacob & Youngs, Inc. v. Kent, 230 N.Y. 239, 129 N.E. 889 (1921). * * *

In the setting of this case, three considerations are central. First, the contractual provisions presently at issue are contained in an insurance policy that is a "contract of adhesion," the parties to this form contract having had no occasion to bargain about the consequences of delayed notice. Second, enforcement of these notice provisions will operate as a forfeiture because the insured will lose his insurance coverage without regard to his dutiful payment of insurance premiums. Third, the insurer's legitimate purpose of guaranteeing itself a fair opportunity to investigate accidents and claims can be protected without the forfeiture that results from presuming, irrebuttably, that late notice invariably prejudices the insurer.

There can be no question that the insurance policy in this case is a "contract of adhesion." That term was first introduced into American legal vocabulary by Professor Edwin Patterson, who noted that life insurance contracts are contracts of adhesion because "[t]he contract is drawn up by the insurer and the insured, who merely 'adheres' to it, has little choice as to its terms." E. Patterson, "The Delivery of a Life–Insurance Policy," 33 Harv.L.Rev. 198, 222 (1919). Standardized contracts of insurance continue to be prime examples of contracts of adhesion, whose most salient feature is that they are not subject to the normal bargaining processes of ordinary contracts.... F. Kessler, "Contracts of Adhesion—Some Thoughts about Freedom of Contract," 43 Colum.L.Rev. 629, 631–32 (1943). The fact that the notice provisions in the Chubb insurance policy were an inconspicuous part of a printed form; cf. General Statutes §§ 42a–1–201(10) and 42a–2–316(2); supports the characterization of these clauses as a "contract of adhesion." Nothing in the record suggests that they were brought to Murphy's attention or that, if they had been, their terms would have been subject to negotiation.

It is equally clear that literal enforcement of the notice provisions in this case will discharge Chubb from any further liability to Murphy with regard to the present claims for insurance coverage. That indeed is the necessary purport of Chubb's special defense and the consequence of the trial court's ruling on its motion for summary judgment. The operative effect of noncompliance with the notice provisions is a forfeiture of the interests of the insured that is, in all likelihood, disproportionate....

In determining whether an insured is entitled to relief from such a disproportionate forfeiture, loss of coverage must be weighed against an insurer's legitimate interest in protection from stale claims. "The purpose of a policy provision requiring the insured to give the company prompt notice of an accident or claim is to give the insurer an opportunity to make a timely and adequate investigation of all the circumstances.... And further, if the insurer is thus given the opportunity for a timely investigation, reasonable compromises and settlements may be made, thereby avoiding prolonged and unnecessary litigation." 8 J. Appleman, Insurance Law and Practice (Rev.Ed.1981) § 4731, pp. 2–5. If this legitimate purpose can be protected by something short of automatic enforcement of the notice provisions, then their strict enforcement is unwarranted.

In our judgment, a proper balance between the interests of the insurer and the insured requires a factual inquiry into whether, in the circumstances of a particular case, an insurer has been prejudiced by its insured's delay in giving notice of an event triggering insurance coverage. If it can be shown that the insurer suffered no material prejudice from the delay, the nonoccurrence of the condition of timely notice may be excused because it is not, in Restatement terms, "a material part of the agreed exchange." Literal enforcement of notice provisions when there is no prejudice is no more appropriate than literal enforcement of liquidated damages clauses when there are no damages....

A significant number of cases in other jurisdictions lend support to our conclusion that, absent a showing of material prejudice, an insured's failure to give timely notice does not discharge the insurer's continuing duty to provide insurance coverage. Most of these decisions place the burden of proof on the issue of prejudice on the insurer.... In a few jurisdictions, although prejudice from delay is presumed, that presumption is rebuttable if the insured can demonstrate an actual lack of material prejudice.... By contrast to these cases which afford some latitude for factual inquiry into prejudice, some jurisdictions continue to enforce delayed notice provisions literally....

In light of existing related precedents in this jurisdiction, although we are persuaded that the existence or nonexistence of prejudice from delayed notice should be determined on a factual basis, the burden of establishing lack of prejudice must be borne by the insured. It is the insured who is seeking to be excused from the consequences of a contract provision with which he has concededly failed to comply. His position is akin to that of the defaulting purchaser of real property in Vines v. Orchard Hills, Inc., supra, 181 Conn. at 510, 435 A.2d 1022, where we held that, "[t]o prove unjust enrichment, in the ordinary case, the purchaser, because he is the party in breach, must prove that the damages suffered by his seller are less than moneys received from the purchaser.... It may not be easy for the purchaser to prove the extent of the seller's damages, it may even be strategically advantageous for the seller to come forward with relevant evidence of the losses he has incurred and may expect to incur on account of the buyer's breach. Nonetheless, only if the breaching party satisfies his burden of proof that the innocent party has sustained a net gain may a claim for unjust enrichment be sustained." Principles of unjust enrichment and restitution bear a family resemblance to those involved in considerations of forfeiture. Under both sets of principles, the law has come to permit a complainant to seek a fair allocation of profit and loss despite the complainant's own failure to comply fully with his contract obligations. The determination of what is fair, as a factual matter, must however depend upon a proper showing by the complainant who seeks this extraordinary relief.

Applying these principles to the present case, we conclude that the trial court was correct in granting summary judgment, although not for the reason upon which it relied. . . . Chubb, the third party defendant, was not automatically discharged because of the delay of Murphy, the third party plaintiff, in giving notice of an insured occurrence. Chubb was, however, entitled to summary judgment because Murphy's affidavit opposing summary judgment contained no factual basis for a claim that Chubb had not been materially prejudiced by Murphy's delay.

There is no error.

NOTES

(1) Although notice conditions are within the control of the promisee and are part of the agreed exchange, the promisee does not promise to give notice that a claim has arisen. A failure to give notice, therefore, is not a breach. Rather, the failure is simply a defense to the promisor unless the condition has been waived or otherwise excused. Was there a waiver in *Murphy?* If not, how might the court justify the excuse of condition? To what extent can the court justifiably rely upon cases where there was a failure of a promised performance, e.g., *Jacob & Youngs v. Kent,* to excuse the condition?

(2) Restatement (Second) § 229 provides: "To the extent that the non-occurrence of a condition would cause disproportionate forfeiture, a court may excuse the non-occurrence of that condition unless its occurrence was a material *part* of the agreed exchange." (Emphasis added). Does this principle justify the result in *Murphy?*

(3) *Limitations on Waiver Doctrine.* P, a consultant, was retained by D, a manufacturer, to give advice on how utility rates might be reduced by increased efficiency at D's plants. Compensation depended, in part upon the degree of increased efficiency resulting from the advice. P was to advise D about the plant at St. Joseph as well as others but St. Joseph, because of evaluations already under way, was excluded by the contract from the compensation base. P made recommendations about St. Joseph and increased efficiency resulted. Relying upon an exchange of letters after the contract was formed but before the evaluation was completed, P claimed that D, by stating that compensation would be paid for St. Joseph, had waived the limitation in the contract. There was no evidence of new consideration or that P had relied upon D's letter. The court affirmed a directed verdict for the defendant.

> The theory of "waiver" upon which appellant now bases its right to recover compensation has no application to this case. A party may waive performance of a condition inserted for his benefit and thereby make unconditional the other party's duty under an agreement, but he cannot by waiver of a condition precedent to his own liability create obligation in

himself where none previously existed. To create such an obligation requires a new contract and new consideration.... "One cannot 'waive' himself into a duty to make a gift of money...."

National Utility Service, Inc. v. Whirlpool Corp., 325 F.2d 779, 781 (2d Cir.1963).

PROBLEM: THE CASE OF THE MISSING INSURED

Cicero's life was insured by Magnanimous Indemnity Co. for $20,000. The policy also covered accidents. A critical clause provided: "Notice in writing of every accident, for or on account of which a claim may be made, shall be given immediately to the Secretary with full particulars of the accident and injury; failure to give such immediate notice shall invalidate all claims under this contract which may be made on account of such accident, and unless affirmative and positive proof of the death or injury and that the same resulted from causes covered by the contract shall be furnished within six months of the happening of such accident, then all claims based thereon shall be forfeited. * * * Notice of death for which a claim may be made shall be given in writing to the Secretary within ten days from the date of such death, and failure to give such notice within said ten days shall invalidate any claim for loss by death." Cicero disappeared on January 1, 1987. His wife promptly notified the Company of that fact. Diligent efforts failed to locate Cicero. On March 1, 1989, police located Cicero's body in his car at the bottom of the Mississippi River, some 30 miles from home. Experts found evidence of brake failure, and it was surmised that he had an accident. There was also an empty bourbon bottle in the car, but experts could not tell whether Cicero had been drinking. The policy contained an "exclusion" clause protecting the Company if any accident or death was proximately caused by drinking. Cicero's wife presented a notice of death and a claim under the policy to the Secretary on March 10, 1989. The company, on advice of counsel, refused to pay the claim on the grounds that the notice of death was too late.

Cicero's widow has retained you as counsel. After some research, you have reached the following conclusions about the law in your state: (1) The Insured may allege generally in the petition that all conditions precedent have been met. The Insurer then has the burden to raise specifically those conditions which have not been satisfied. Subject to one exception, to be noted below, the Insured has the ultimate risk of persuading the court that the condition was either satisfied or excused. (2) Notice requirements in insurance contracts are treated as express conditions rather than promises. This state recognizes that notice conditions can be "waived" by election or estoppel. But there are no decisions consistent with the view that to avoid extreme forfeiture the court should either construe the contract against the drafter or simply excuse the condition. Nevertheless, Restatement (Second) § 229 states that "to the extent that the non-occurrence of a condition would cause disproportionate forfeiture, a court may excuse the non-occurrence of that condition unless its occurrence was a material part of the agreed exchange." See, in accord, *Aetna Casualty & Surety Co. v. Murphy,* supra at 660; Burger King Corp. v. Family Dining, Inc., 426 F.Supp. 485, 492–94 (E.D.Pa.1977), affirmed without opinion 566 F.2d 1168 (3d Cir.1977). (3) The aversion to forfeiture, however, appears in one case where a condition of notice was excused due to the insanity of the insured. In that case, all of the premiums were paid, the loss was clearly within the scope of the policy and neither the insured nor any third person was in a position to give notice. The court, citing Restatement (Second) § 271 and Corbin § 1362, concluded that the existence of the condition was "no material part" of the agreed exchange and that discharge of the Insurer would operate as a forfeiture especially since the policy did not insure against insanity. There are decisions in other states where the same result was reached where the insured died rather than became insane. In either case, the condition is excused due to "impracticability." (4) Even if the notice condition were excused, the Insured must still prove that the risk insured against, whether it be accident or death, actually occurred and was within the scope of the policy. These are treated as conditions precedent. In this state, however, a big exception exists with regard to "exclusion" clauses. For example, if the policy protects against death in general but contains a clause excluding death where caused by specific events, such as intoxication, then the burden is on the Insurer to plead and prove the exception. One or two early cases treated "exclusion" as a condition subsequent for purposes of proof, but a more recent decision allocated the burden to the Insurer because the company had better resources to ascertain the facts and for considerations of fairness. You have been unable to find any case, however, where the Insurer failed to prove the exclusion *and* the Insured's failure to give prompt notice was excused.

Assuming that this is an accurate statement of the law, suppose that the attorney for Magnanimous offered to settle the case for $2,500 plus costs and attorney fees. Would you recommend acceptance of this settlement offer?

PROBLEM: READING PIPE AND THE WAIVER OF CONDITIONS

In *Jacob & Youngs v. Kent,* the court concluded that the installation of the particular brand of pipe, Reading pipe, was not a condition precedent to the duty of the owner to pay the balance due under the construction contract. But Judge Cardozo, speaking for the majority, did observe: "This is not to say that the parties are not free by apt and certain words to effectuate a purpose that performance of every term shall be a condition of recovery." What if, for some reason (e.g., it is intended as a showhouse for Reading pipe, or his wife once won a Miss Reading Pipe contest), the owner did indeed want the installation of this brand of pipe to be a condition? Could it be done? How?

Assume that installation of Reading pipe was thus made a condition precedent, but that the contractor cannot procure Reading pipe. He approaches the owner, advising him that Cohoes pipe, a brand of equal quality, is available. Owner is agreeable to the substitution, but after installation of the substitute, stands by the original contract provision making installation of Reading pipe a condition of recovery? Will owner prevail?

Assume instead that the owner does the totally unexpected; *viz.,* he says that not only is it all right to omit the installation of Reading pipe, there is no need to install any pipe at all or to even construct the building. The owner will pay anyway. Can contractor hold owner to this commitment?

As alternative to the above scenarios, suppose that contractor went ahead with the installation of Cohoes pipe without discussing the matter with the owner. Is the latter obligated to pay? Would it make a difference if the owner, after becoming aware of the substitution, indicated that he would still pay? Even if obliged to pay, could the owner still recover damages if the Cohoes pipe was inferior to the Reading pipe?

Finally, assume that the contractor did not install any pipe at all, but the owner (again, doing the unlikely thing) said that he would still pay? Would the owner be bound by this commitment?

(B) CONSTRUCTIVE CONDITIONS OF EXCHANGE

This section continues the study of a series of issues first raised or suggested by *Jacob & Youngs v. Kent*.

The first issue deals with the *order* in which the agreed exchange is to be performed. Which party is obligated to tender performance or to perform first? The question is important, for if Party A must perform first, Party B will have no duty under the contract until Party A has tendered or performed. Put differently, Party A's performance of the agreed exchange is a condition precedent to Party B's duty.

If Party A is obligated to go first, the second issue is quantitative: How much performance must Party A tender or render before Party B has a duty under the contract? Is literal performance required, or will "substantial" performance be sufficient? If the latter, by what standard will "substantial" performance be measured? Again, this is an important inquiry. If Party A's breach is substantial (material), Party B can cancel the contract and pursue remedies based upon Party A's total breach. If Party A's performance is substantial, Party B cannot cancel and must perform, subject to an offset for any damages caused by Party A's minor breach. (This latter alternative was the outcome in *Jacob & Youngs v. Kent*.) The question of what is a "material" breach will also be considered in Chapter 6, section 1.

A final problem involves restitution. If Party A has committed a material breach yet Party B's losses have been fully compensated, may Party A have restitution of any net benefits from Party A's part-performance retained by Party B? If so, how is restitution to be measured?

(1) HISTORICAL DEVELOPMENT

Suppose that an owner contracted to sell described land to a vendee for a stated price. The written agreement provided that the price was to be paid on June 1 but nothing was said about when the owner was to tender a deed. On June 1, the owner demanded payment but the vendee refused until a deed in proper form was tendered. The owner then sued for the price without tendering or alleging that the deed had been tendered. Can the vendor recover? Until the middle of the eighteenth century, the answer in England was yes, especially where the vendee ultimately had an action against the owner for failure to convey the land. See, e.g., Pordage v. Cole, 1 Wms. Saunders 319 (K.B.1669). In the absence of an agreement that the owner shall tender before the price was due, it was thought that the vendee "relied upon his remedy, and did not intend to make the performance a condition precedent." See Serjeant Williams' note to *Pordage v. Cole* in 1 Wms. Saunders 320. The legal result was that the exchange of promises, although mutual, was presumed to be independent rather than dependent. Professor Patterson explained this result by the interaction of three factors: (1) The literal-mindedness of the early law; (2) The failure of the common law courts to recognize the exchange function of many contracts; (3) The inhibiting effect of the forms of action available for contract litigation. Patterson, *Constructive Conditions in Contracts,* 42 Colum.L.Rev. 903, 907–910 (1943). According to Patterson, although the "courts were willing to seize upon any language which could be tortured into an express condition of exchange," in the absence of such language, they refused to "construct conditions of exchange." This was "serious because * * * procedure did not recognize the counterclaim; the defendant's remedy was to sue the plaintiff in a separate action for breach of contract." The practical effect of the rule was that the vendee was required to extend credit to the vendor and to rely upon his legal remedies if a tender of the deed was not forthcoming.

Kingston v. Preston*

King's Bench, 1773.
2 Doug. 689, 99 Eng.Rep. 437.

[This] was an action of debt for non-performance of covenants contained in certain articles of agreement between the plaintiff and the defendant. The declaration stated: That, by articles made the 24th of March, 1770, the plaintiff, for the considerations thereinafter mentioned, covenanted with the defendant to serve him for one year and a quarter next ensuing, as a covenant-servant, in his trade of a silk mercer, at 200 a year, and, in consideration of the premises, the defendant covenanted that, at the end of the year and a quarter, he would give up his business of a mercer to the plaintiff, and a nephew of the defendant, or some other person to be nominated by the defendant, and give up to them his stock in trade at a fair valuation; and that, between the young traders, deeds of partnership should be executed for fourteen years, and from and immediately after the execution of the said deeds the defendant would permit the said young traders to carry on the said business in the defendant's house. Then the declaration stated a covenant by the plaintiff, that he would accept the business and stock in trade, at a fair valuation, with the defendant's nephew, or such other person, & c., and execute such deeds of partnership, and, further, that the plaintiff should and would, at and before the sealing and delivery of the deeds, cause and procure good and sufficient security to be given to the defendant to be approved of by the defendant for the payment of 250 monthly to the defendant in lieu of a moiety of the monthly produce of the stock in trade, until the value of the stock should

---

* [The Report of the case is taken from the argument of counsel for the plaintiff in   Jones v. Barkley, 2 Doug. 689–92 (1781).]

be reduced to 4000. Then the plaintiff averred that he had performed and been ready to perform his covenants, and assigned for breach on the part of the defendant, that he had refused to surrender and give up his business at the end of the said year and a quarter. The defendant pleaded: 1. That the plaintiff did not offer sufficient security; and 2. That he did not give sufficient security for the payment of the 250 & c. And the plaintiff demurred generally to both pleas. On the part of the plaintiff, the case was argued by Mr. Buller, who contended that the covenants were mutual and independent, and therefore a plea of the breach of one of the covenants to be performed by the plaintiff was no bar to an action for a breach by the defendant of one which he had bound himself to perform, but that the defendant might have his remedy for the breach by the plaintiff in a separate action. On the other side, Mr. Grose insisted that the covenants were dependent in their nature, and therefore performance must be alleged. The security to be given for the money was manifestly the chief object of the transaction, and it would be highly unreasonable to construe the agreement so as to oblige the defendant to give up a beneficial business, and valuable stock-in-trade, and trust to the plaintiff's personal security (who might, and, indeed, was admitted to be worth nothing), for the performance of his part.

In delivering the judgment of the Court, Lord Mansfield expressed himself to the following effect: There are three kinds of covenants: 1. Such as are called mutual and independent, where either party may recover damages from the other for the injury he may have received by a breach of the covenants in his favor and where it is no excuse for the defendant to allege a breach of the covenants on the part of the plaintiff. 2. There are covenants which are conditions and dependent, in which the performance of one depends on the prior performance of another, and, therefore, till this prior condition is performed, the other party is not liable to an action on his covenant. 3. There is also a third sort of covenants, which are mutual conditions to be performed at the same time; and in these, if one party was ready and offered to perform his part, and the other neglected or refused to perform his, he who was ready and offered has fulfilled his engagement, and may maintain an action for the default of the other; though it is not certain that either is obliged to do the first act. His Lordship then proceeded to say, that the dependence or independence of covenants was to be collected from the evident sense and meaning of the parties, and that, however transposed they might be in the deed, their precedency must depend on the order of time in which the intent of the transaction requires their performance. That, in the case before the Court, it would be the greatest injustice if the plaintiff should prevail. The essence of the agreement was, that the defendant should not trust to the personal security of the plaintiff, but, before he delivered up his stock and business, should have good security for the payment of the money. The giving such security, therefore, must necessarily be a condition precedent. Judgment was accordingly given for the defendant, because the part to be performed by the plaintiff was clearly a condition precedent.

Goodison v. Nunn

King's Bench, 1792.
4 T.R. 762, 100 Eng.Rep. 1288.

■ LORD KENYON, CH.J.—This case is extremely clear, whether considered on principles of strict law or of common justice. The plaintiff engaged to sell an estate to the defendant, in consideration of which the defendant undertook to pay 210; and, if he did not carry the contract into execution, he was to pay 21; and now not having conveyed his estate, or offered to do so, or taken any one step towards it, the plaintiff has brought this action for the penalty. Suppose the purchase-money of an estate was 40,000 it would be absurd to say that the purchaser might enforce a conveyance without payment, and compel the seller to have recourse to him, who perhaps might be an insolvent person. The old cases, cited by the plaintiff's counsel, have been accurately stated; but the determinations in them outrage common sense. I admit the principle on which they profess to go: but I think that the Judges misapplied that principle. It is admitted in them all that where they are dependent covenants, no action will lie by one party unless he have performed, or offered to perform his covenant. Then the question is, whether these are, or are not, dependent covenants. I think they are; the one is to depend on the other; when the one party conveyed his estate he was to receive the purchase-money; and when the other parted with his money he was to have the estate. They were reciprocal acts, to be performed by each other at the same time. It seems, from the case in Strange, that the Judges were surprised at the old decisions; and in order to get rid of the difficulty, they said that a tender and refusal would amount to a performance: it is true they went farther, and said that "in consideration of the premises," meant only in consideration of the covenant to transfer, and not in consideration of the actual transferring of the stock: but to the latter part of that judgment I cannot accede. It is our duty, when we see that principles of law have been misapplied in any case, to overrule it. The principle is admitted in all the cases alluded to, that, if they be dependent covenants, performance, or the offer to perform, must be pleaded on the one part, in order to found the action against the other. The mistake has been in the misapplication of that principle in the cases cited; and I am glad to find that the old cases have been over-ruled; and that we are now warranted by precedent as well as by principle to say that this action cannot be maintained.

* * *

Judgment for the defendant.

NOTES

(1) In *Kingston*, the plaintiff failed to perform a material part of his promised performance; i.e., he committed a "material" breach. Yet he sought to enforce the contract against the defendant. On what theory? Upon what basis did the court protect the defendant? Did the result depend upon the intention

of the parties? Or on something else? See Patterson, *Constructive Conditions in Contracts,* 42 Colum.L.Rev. 903 (1942).

(2) Professor William McGovern rejects the "general consensus" that promises were treated as independent until the time of Lord Mansfield. See, e.g., K & G Construction Co. v. Harris, 223 Md. 305, 312–13, 164 A.2d 451, 454–55 (1960). He identified several types of contracts where promises were treated as dependent prior to *Kingston* and concluded that there was a fundamental similarity between medieval and modern law which was "obscured by the wide latitude given to medieval juries in deciding whether or not money was owed." McGovern, *Dependent Promises in the History of Leases and Other Contracts,* 52 Tulane L.Rev. 659, 703 (1978). McGovern also found that in "some early cases * * * promises were held to be independent, just as they are today" and concluded that, in the absence of agreement, this construction was sound so long as the remedies available to the aggrieved party, whether through setoff or counterclaim, were adequate. To construct a condition of dependency where none was agreed "violates the principle that parties to a contract should be put in the position they would have enjoyed if the contract had been performed." Id. at 703–704. For a broader, more complex study seeking to explain, among other things, the development of independent covenants in seventeenth-century English contract law, see Francis, *The Structure of Judicial Administration and the Development of Contract Law in Seventeenth–Century England,* 83 Colum.L.Rev. 35 (1983).

Palmer v. Fox

Supreme Court of Michigan, 1936.
274 Mich. 252, 264 N.W. 361.

■ Toy, J. This is an action at law to recover the balance of the purchase price due on a land contract, made on September 28, 1925, between the Louis G. Palmer & Company, a corporation, as vendor, and the defendant, as vendee, for the sale of a certain lot in Palmer Grove Park Subdivision Number Two, in the city of Detroit. The contract provided for a purchase price of $1,650, of which $247.50 was to be paid at the execution thereof, and the balance to be paid in monthly installments of $16.50 each; the entire amount to be paid "on or before five years from the date hereof." The defendant made the initial payment and also made the monthly payments as called for in the contract up to and including that of February 11, 1931.

The vendor assigned its interest in the contract to Grace H. Palmer, on March 1, 1930, and she commenced this action on February 7, 1933, for the balance of the purchase price due in the amount of $709.02, plus interest. In July, 1933, a trusteeship was created making Louis G. Palmer trustee for Grace H. Palmer, and another, and during the trial of this cause he was substituted as party plaintiff.

The defendant claimed that the vendor and its assignees failed to perform the covenants in the contract to make stated improvements in the subdivision, and especially, in failing to cinderize or gravel all the streets therein. Defendant further claimed that plaintiff could not recover because of the failure to tender a deed to the premises before commencement of this action.

The court below tried the case without a jury, and found for the plaintiff in the amount of $709.02 principal and $146.89 interest, or a total of $855.91, whereupon judgment was entered for that amount.

Defendant appeals to this court.

The land contract contained a covenant as follows:

"The vendor agrees at its own expense to furnish cement sidewalks and to grade all streets; and either cinderize or gravel the streets, except Plymouth Avenue, at its election, and to furnish water mains and lateral sewers in the streets or alleys of said subdivision. If the water and sewer are put in by the city, the assessment against the property shall be paid by the vendor."

The contract also provided that upon receiving payment of principal and interest in full and upon surrender of the contract, the vendor would execute and deliver to the vendee a warranty deed of the premises, subject to certain covenants and restrictions. The contract further provided, "that time is of the essence of this contract."

The lot contracted for fronts on a street in said subdivision known as Westwood avenue (formerly Martin avenue). The testimony showed that said street had been graded but never cinderized or graveled. The proof further showed that the other improvements called for in the contract had been made, although there is some dispute as to whether certain other streets in the subdivision had been fully cinderized or graveled. However, it is conceded by both parties that Westwood avenue in said subdivision was never cinderized or graveled as covenanted in the contract. Defendant contends that the failure to cinderize this street of the subdivision, on which the lot in question abuts, is a material breach of the covenant requiring this improvement, and that such covenant being a dependent one, plaintiff cannot recover in this action.

Plaintiff contends that the covenant by defendant to pay is independent of plaintiff's covenant to furnish improvements, and that whether the covenant to put in improvements "is dependent or independent, is immaterial in view of the fact that the plaintiff's failure to cinderize the street before the defendant's lot, under said covenant, is not a material breach."

Was the covenant of vendor to make improvements, in the instant case, a dependent covenant?

In Folkerts v. Marysville Land Co., 236 Mich. 294, this court conceded that:

"It appears to be a more or less difficult task in some cases to say whether the covenants are independent or dependent."

In that case the court set forth the language contained in 6 R.C.L. p. 861, as being the general rule for determining this question, and we quote therefrom, in part, as follows:

"But the modern rule is that stipulations are to be construed to be dependent or independent according to the intention of the parties and the good sense of the case. Technical words should give way to such intention. Courts will not and ought not to construe covenants and agreements as independent, and still enforce performance by the other party, unless there is no other mode of construing the instrument, and unless it clearly appears to have been the deliberate intention of the parties at the time the instrument was executed. In brief, the courts will construe covenants to be dependent, unless a contrary intention clearly appears. A party should not be forced to pay out his money, unless he can get that for which he stipulated. * * * Where the acts or covenants of the parties are concurrent, and to be done or performed at the same time, the covenants are dependent, and neither party can maintain an action against the other, without averring and proving performance on his part."

Were the covenants here concurrent? We think so.

It must be remembered that plaintiff brings this action to recover the balance due under the land contract. In the contract the defendant agreed to make payment "on or before five years from the date hereof." Plaintiff agreed to make certain improvements, and although no time was stated as to when such improvements were to be made, we think that the intention of the parties, in relation thereto, clearly appears from the language of the contract, as well as from extraneous facts contained in the record, that such improvements were to be made within the five-year period. Certainly they must be made within a reasonable time. Brow v. Gibraltar Land Co., 249 Mich. 662, 229 N.W. 604.

The contract contains a provision that *after* payment and "upon the surrender of this contract," the vendor will execute and deliver to the vendee a warranty deed to the premises. Logically, it would follow, then, that if the vendee must surrender the contract, every covenant of the contract, or at least every material covenant, must necessarily be effected before such surrender. Especially does such inference apply, where the contract itself does not provide for the performing of any of the agreements after the surrender of the contract. When the contract is surrendered by the vendee, it follows that any rights he has thereunder are likewise surrendered. So, if the vendee must surrender the contract before he may receive a deed, it must have been intended that all other covenants in the contract must necessarily be performed prior to such surrender. Therefore, the covenant to improve the property must have been intended by the terms of the contract to have run concurrently with the covenant to pay the full purchase price within five years.

It further appears from the record that plaintiff put in all the improvements called for by the contract during the period of five years, excepting the cinderizing or graveling of streets, or at least of one street, as hereinbefore stated. This partial performance by the vendor indicates its knowledge of the necessity of performing its covenants.

In the case of Folkerts v. Marysville Land Co., supra, this court, after quoting the statement from Ruling Case Law, hereinbefore in part set forth, said:

"Looking at the contracts which plaintiffs made, with these tests in mind, we are persuaded that the covenants to make improvements are dependent. The reasons which have moved us to this position are, in part, as follows: (a) The contract does not, upon its face, show that the covenants are independent. (b) The time stipulated for the performance by each party is concurrent. * * * (c) These plaintiffs purchased these lots for a home."

In the instant case, we have a contract that does not, upon its face, show that the covenants are independent; we also have the inferred intention of the parties that the covenants were to be performed concurrently. But here we do not have a vendee who purchased the lot for a home. On the contrary, the defendant testified that he purchased the property for investment purposes.

While, under the reasoning of this court in the case of Folkerts v. Marysville Land Co., supra, the fact that the vendees had purchased the property for a home was a circumstance considered in determining the intention of the parties, it was not conclusive. Nor does it appear that such circumstance was in and of itself decisive. While it is true that the defendant in the instant case purchased the lot for investment purposes, yet can it be consistently urged that he therefore intended that he should get less than that for which he bargained?

We infer from the record that at the time of the execution of the land contract there were no improvements in the subdivision. It does not seem plausible that defendant would have purchased the lot if it was to remain in that same condition. He had a right to expect, and in all probability did expect, that by the time he had the lot paid for, all of the improvements would be in, and that instead of owning a lot in a subdivision marked by surveyors' stakes, he would have a lot on a street in a subdivision with water mains, lateral sewers, cement sidewalks and graded and surfaced streets, all materially present and not merely outlined on a plat or prospectus. The agreed consideration was to be paid, not for the lot as it was when the contract was made, but as it would be when the stipulated improvements were completed.

The making of the improvements was an essential part of the consideration supporting defendant's agreement to pay the purchase price. That the defendant intended to buy, and that the vendor agreed to sell a lot in a subdivision with improvements, is clear from the provisions cf the contract. The defendant's covenant to pay the balance of the purchase price and to surrender the contract was dependent upon the vendor's covenant to make the specified improvements and to deliver a deed to the lot.

* * *

We therefore conclude that the covenant to improve and the covenant to pay the purchase price were dependent covenants.

But, contends plaintiff, it is immaterial whether or not the covenant to make improvements is dependent or independent "in view of the fact that the plaintiff's failure to cinderize the street before the defendant's lot, under said covenant, is not a material breach." On this point, in the trial court, plaintiff introduced testimony to the effect that the cost to cinderize the street in *front* of the lot in question would be only about $7. But the contract called for more than the cinderizing of the street in front of the lot purchased by defendant. It required the vendor to "either cinderize or gravel the streets." Merely to have cinderized or not to have cinderized that portion of the street in front of defendant's lot is beside the point.

The necessity of surfacing the streets in the subdivision, in order to improve the premises, is apparent, and insofar as defendant's rights are concerned, the surfacing of the entire street upon which his lot abutted was of paramount importance to him. The putting in of water mains, sidewalks, and sewers was of little avail, if the street remained unsurfaced so that he and others might not have a convenient way to and from his property. Merely to have surfaced the street in front of the one lot would be absurd. We think that the noncompliance by plaintiff in this respect amounts to a substantial and material breach of the covenant to improve.

The plaintiff and his assignors, therefore, being guilty of a substantial breach of a dependent covenant, cannot maintain this action.

It is not necessary to decide whether or not the tender of a deed to the property in question, made in the declaration of the plaintiff and again at the time of trial, is a sufficient tender, or whether any tender was necessary to be made before instituting this action, as decision has turned on the other questions presented.

The judgment is reversed, without new trial, with costs to defendant.

NOTES

(1) Review the agreement in *Palmer v. Fox*. When was the vendee to pay the price? When was the vendor to deliver a warranty deed? When was the vendor to complete the improvements? If the vendor did not agree to complete the improvements before the vendee's final payment, how does the court conclude that completion was a condition to payment?

(2) *Independent and Dependent Promises.* "Promises and counterpromises made by the respective parties to a contract have certain relations to one another, which determine many of the rights and liabilities of the parties. Broadly speaking, they are (1) independent of each other, or (2) mutually dependent, one upon the other. They are independent of each other if the parties intend that *performance* by each of them is in no way conditioned upon *performance* by the other. * * * In other words, the parties exchange promises for promises, not the *performance* of promises for the *performance* of promises. * * * A failure to perform an independent promise does not excuse non-performance on the part of the adversary party, but each is required to perform his promise, and, if one does not perform, he is liable to the adversary party for such nonperformance. * * * Promises are mutually dependent if the parties

intend *performance* by one to be conditioned upon *performance* by the other, and, if they be mutually dependent, they may be (a) precedent, i.e., a promise that is to be performed before a corresponding promise on the part of the adversary party is to be performed, (b) subsequent, i.e., a corresponding promise that is not to be performed until the other party to the contract has performed a precedent covenant, or (c) concurrent, i.e., promises that are to be performed at the same time by each of the parties, who are respectively bound to perform each. * * * In the early days, it was settled law that covenants and mutual promises in a contract were *prima facie* independent, and that they were to be so construed in the absence of language in the contract clearly showing that they were intended to be dependent. * * * In the case of Kingston v. Preston, 2 Doug. 689, decided in 1774, Lord Mansfield, contrary to three centuries of opposing precedents, changed the rule, and decided that performance of one covenant might be dependent on prior performance of another, although the contract contained no express condition to that effect. * * * The modern rule, which seems to be of almost universal application, is that there is a presumption that mutual promises in a contract are dependent and are to be so regarded, whenever possible." K & G Construction Company v. Harris, 223 Md. 305, 312–13, 164 A.2d 451, 454–55 (1960) (emphasis in original).

(3) *Presumption of Dependency.* Why is there a "presumption that mutual promises in a contract are dependent and are to be so regarded, whenever possible?" As Holmes put it: "You can always imply a condition in a contract. But why do you imply it?" Holmes, *The Path of the Law,* 10 Harv.L.Rev. 457, 466 (1897). According to one court, the "doctrine of constructive dependency of promises should * * * be rested solely on their fairness, and not on any intention of the parties where they express none." Thus, the determination of mutual dependency should arise from the "inherent justice of the situation and not the unexpressed intention of the parties." Giumarra v. Harrington Heights, Inc., 33 N.J.Super. 178, 191, 109 A.2d 695, 701 (1954). But, again, if the parties in *Palmer v. Fox* did not agree that the improvements should be completed before payment, what is the inherent injustice in requiring the vendee to pay before the improvements are completed? According to Restatement (Second), the answer turns on two general considerations: First, dependency "offers both parties maximum security against disappointment of their expectations of a subsequent exchange of performances by allowing each party to defer his own performance until he has been assured that the other will perform;" and Second, dependency "avoids placing on either party the burden of financing the other before the latter has performed." Section 234, Comment a. Do these considerations justify the result in *Kingston*? In *Goodison*? In *Palmer*? Compare Rowe v. Great Atlantic & Pacific Tea Co., Inc., 46 N.Y.2d 62, 412 N.Y.S.2d 827, 385 N.E.2d 566 (1978), where the court refused to "imply" a covenant limiting the lessee's power to assign the lease.

> [A] party who asserts the existence of an implied-in-fact covenant bears a heavy burden, for it is not the function of the courts to remake the contract agreed to by the parties, but rather to enforce it as it exists. Thus, a party making such a claim must prove not merely that it would have been better or more sensible to include such a covenant, but rather that the particular unexpressed promise sought to be enforced is in fact implicit in the agreement viewed as a whole. This is especially so where, as here, the implied covenant sought to be recognized and enforced is of a type not

favored by the courts. * * * Such a covenant is to be recognized only if it is clear that a reasonable landlord would not have entered into the lease without such an understanding, for it is only in such a situation that it can be said with the requisite certainty that to refuse to recognize such a covenant would be to deprive the landlord of the fruits of his bargain. 412 N.Y.S.2d at 831, 385 N.E.2d at 570.

(4) The modern view on the order of performance is stated in Restatement (Second) § 234:

> (1) Where all or part of the performances to be exchanged under an exchange of promises can be rendered simultaneously, they are to that extent due simultaneously, unless the language or the circumstances indicate the contrary.

> (2) Except to the extent stated in Subsection (1), where the performance of only one party under such an exchange requires a period of time, his performance is due at an earlier time than that of the other party, unless the language or the circumstances indicate the contrary.

In Bell v. Elder, 782 P.2d 545, 548 (Utah App.1989), the parties contracted to buy and sell real estate. The agreement did not provide a date for performance or state which party was to perform first. Before a reasonable time for performance had passed, the vendee, without first tendering payment, brought suit to cancel the contract and obtain restitution. The court dismissed the lawsuit.

> Although the contract . . . does not specify a precise deadline, performance was nevertheless due within a reasonable time . . . If neither party performed its exchanged promise within that time, both promises are discharged. . . . Neither of these parties argues that the time for performance exceeds a reasonable time. Since performance of these obligations was due concurrently, neither party could claim a breach by the other until the party claiming the breach tendered performance of its concurrent obligation. The rule requiring such a tender has been explained in a case in which a real estate purchaser and seller each demanded and awaited performance by the other of their respective obligations to pay the price and deliver the property. The Supreme Court's words in that case apply here as well: "This is precisely the sort of deadlock meant to be resolved by the requirement of tender . . . During the executory period of a contract whose time of performance is uncertain but which contemplates simultaneous performance by both parties, . . . neither party can be said to be in default . . . until the other party has tendered his performance. In other words, the party who desires to use legal process to exercise his legal remedies under such a contract must make a tender of his own agreed performance in order to put the other party in default."

(5) *Leases.* Under what circumstances can a lessee terminate a lease upon a "material" breach of a covenant by the lessor? At common law, a lease was regarded as a conveyance of property rather than a contract. Rent was regarded as a payment "yielded" by the land, not as a contract for the payment of money. See Jersey Boulevard Corp. v. Lerner Stores Corp., 168 Md. 532, 178 A. 707, 709 (1935). For this reason, covenants between lessor and lessee were regarded as independent unless otherwise expressly agreed. See, e.g., Rock

County Savings & Trust Co. of Janesville v. Yost's, Inc., 36 Wis.2d 360, 153 N.W.2d 594 (1967); Uniform Residential Landlord and Tenant Act § 1.102, Comment. But see McGovern, *Dependent Promises in the History of Leases and Other Contracts,* 52 Tul.L.Rev. 659, 703 (1978), who argues that the difference between modern and medieval law on dependency in leases has been "greatly exaggerated."

The modern view in both residential and commercial leases is that the promise to pay rent is dependent upon such lessor covenants as repair, habitability or assignability and that the lessee may withhold rent or terminate the lease if "deprived of a significant inducement to the making of the lease." Restatement (Second) of Property § 7.1 (1977). As one court put it, the "actual subject matter of most leases, commercial or residential, is the building leased, not the land upon which it stands, and that therefore contract law rather than property law should be applied to disputes between landlords and tenants." Pawco Inc. v. Bergman Knitting Mills, 283 Pa.Super. 443, 424 A.2d 891, 895 (1980). Thus, the duty of the lessee to pay rent or to remain in the lease is dependent upon "substantial performance" of the lessor's covenants, express or implied, with regard to the quality of the premises, thereby depriving the lessor of a traditional advantage when disputes over the lease arise. See, e.g., Teodori v. Werner, 490 Pa. 58, 415 A.2d 31 (1980); Shaw v. Mobil Oil Corp., 272 Or. 109, 535 P.2d 756 (1975), applying the "modern" view in commercial leases.

PROBLEM: THE CASE OF THE DEFAULTING PURCHASER

On March 1, Vendor contracted to sell land to Vendee for $8,000. Vendee paid $2,000 at the time of contracting and agreed to pay $1,000 by the first of each succeeding month until the total price was paid. Vendor agreed to convey the property on September 1, the day the final payment was due.

(a) Suppose Vendee failed to make the June 1 payment. Can Vendor recover the payment without tendering a deed?

(b) Assume that Vendee failed to make the July, August and September payments. Can Vendor recover these payments without tendering a deed? Can he recover the July and August payments alone? See Restatement (Second) § 234 and Illustrations 6, 7 and 12. See also Ideal Family and Youth Ranch v. Whetstine, 655 P.2d 429 (Colo.App.1982) (vendor agreed to put deed in escrow before vendee had duty to pay installments).

(2) THE AVOIDANCE OF FORFEITURE

Suppose a contractor agrees to construct a new garage for Owner for $25,000. Nothing is said about when payment should be made. Under the modern view of constructive conditions, "where the performance of only one party under an exchange requires a period of time, his performance is due at an earlier time than that of the other party, unless the language or the circumstances indicate the contrary." Restatement (Second) § 234(2). Contractor, then, must perform first. Suppose, however, that contractor demands part payment after 50% of the work has been completed and owner contends that contractor must either fully or substantially perform the work before any payment is due. Without more, owner is correct. Unless the contract is divisible or the parties have agreed upon installment payments or trade usage is to the contrary, contractor must first satisfy the constructive condition of exchange. As the court stated in Stewart v. Newbury, 220 N.Y. 379, 115 N.E. 984 (1917): "Where a contract is made to perform work and no agreement is made as to payment, the work must be substantially performed before payment can be demanded."

What is the "inherent fairness" in a rule that requires the construction contractor to extend credit to the owner? Is it enough to conclude that the operative rule is centuries old, the parties can, by agreement, mitigate its harshness and, in any event, "it is just as fair as the opposite rule would be?" See Section 234, Comment e. In this section, we will look at some of the ways that this harsh interpretation can be softened.

Jacob & Youngs v. Kent

Court of Appeals of New York, 1921.
Supra at 642.

O.W. Grun Roofing and Construction Co. v. Cope

Court of Civil Appeals of Texas, 1975.
529 S.W.2d 258.

■ CADENA, JUSTICE. Plaintiff, Mrs. Fred M. Cope, sued defendant, O.W. Grun Roofing & Construction Co., to set aside a mechanic's lien filed by defendant and for damages in the sum of $1,500.00 suffered by plaintiff as a result of the alleged failure of defendant to perform a contract calling for the installation of a new roof on plaintiff's home. Defendant, in addition to a general denial, filed a cross-claim for $648.00, the amount which plaintiff agreed to pay defendant for installing the roof, and for foreclosure of the mechanic's lien on plaintiff's home.

Following trial to a jury, the court below entered judgment awarding plaintiff $122.60 as damages for defendant's failure to perform the contract; setting aside the mechanic's lien; and denying defendant recovery on its cross-claim. It is from this judgment that defendant appeals.

The jury found (1) defendant failed to perform his contract in a good and workmanlike manner; (2) defendant did not substantially perform the contract; (3) plaintiff received no benefits from the labor performed and the materials furnished by defendant; the reasonable cost of performing the contract in a good and workmanlike manner would be $777.60. Although the verdict shows the cost of proper performance to be $777.60, the judgment describes this finding as being in the amount of $770.60, and the award of $122.60 to plaintiff is based on the difference between $770.60 and the contract price of $648.00.

* * *

The written contract required defendant to install a new roof on plaintiff's home for $648.00. The contract describes the color of the shingles to be used as "russet glow," which defendant defined as a "brown varied color." Defendant acknowledges that it was his obligation to install a roof of uniform color.

After defendant had installed the new roof, plaintiff noticed that it had streaks which she described as yellow, due to a difference in color or shade of some of the shingles. Defendant agreed to remedy the situation and he removed the nonconforming shingles. However, the replacement shingles do not match the remainder, and photographs introduced in evidence clearly show that the roof is not of a uniform color. Plaintiff testified that her roof has the appearance of having been patched, rather than having been completely replaced. According to plaintiff's testimony, the yellow streaks appeared on the northern, eastern and southern sides of the roof, and defendant only replaced the non-matching shingles on the northern and eastern sides, leaving the southern side with the yellow streaks still apparent. The result is that only the western portion of the roof is of uniform color.

When defendant originally installed the complete new roof, it used 24 "squares" of shingles. In an effort to achieve a roof of uniform color, five squares were ripped off and replaced. There is no testimony as to the number of squares which would have to be replaced on the southern, or rear, side of the house in order to eliminate the original yellow streaks. Although there is expert testimony to the effect that the disparity in color would not be noticeable after the shingles have been on the roof for about a year, there is testimony to the effect that, although some nine or ten months have elapsed since defendant attempted to achieve a uniform coloration, the roof is still "streaky" on three sides. One of defendant's experts testified that if the shingles are properly applied the result will be a "blended" roof rather than a streaked roof.

In view of the fact that the disparity in color has not disappeared in nine or ten months, and in view of the fact that there is testimony to the effect that it would be impossible to secure matching shingles to replace the nonconforming ones, it can reasonably be inferred that a roof of uniform coloration can be achieved only by installing a completely new roof.

The evidence is undisputed that the roof is a substantial roof and will give plaintiff protection against the elements.

The principle which allows recovery for part performance in cases involving dependent promises may be expressed by saying that a material breach or a breach which goes to the root of the matter or essence of the contract defeats the promisor's claim despite his part performance, or it may be expressed by saying that a promisor who has substantially performed is entitled to recover, although he has failed in some particular to comply with his agreement. The latter mode of expressing the rule is generally referred to as the doctrine of substantial performance and is especially common in cases involving building contracts, although its application is not restricted to such contracts.

It is difficult to formulate definitive rules for determining whether the contractor's performance, less than complete, amounts to "substantial performance," since the question is one of fact and of degree, and the answer depends on the particular facts of each case. But, although the decisions furnish no rule of thumb, they are helpful in suggesting guidelines. One of the most obvious factors to be considered is the extent of the nonperformance. The deficiency will not be tolerated if it is so pervasive as to frustrate the purpose of the contract in any real or substantial sense. The doctrine does not bestow on a contractor a license to install whatever is, in his judgment, "just as good." The answer is arrived at by weighing the purpose to be served, the desire to be gratified, the excuse for deviating from the letter of the contract and the cruelty of enforcing strict adherence or of compelling the promisee to receive something less than for which he bargained. Also influential in many cases is the ratio of money value of the tendered performance and of the promised performance. In most cases the contract itself at least is an indication of the value of the promised performance, and courts should have little difficulty in determining the cost of curing the deficiency. But the rule cannot be expressed in terms of a fraction, since complete reliance on a mathematical formula would result in ignoring other important factors, such as the purpose which the promised performance was intended to serve and the extent to which the nonperformance would defeat such purpose, or would defeat it if not corrected. See, generally, 3A Corbin, Contracts Secs. 700–07 (1960).

Although definitions of "substantial performance" are not always couched in the same terminology and, because of the facts involved in a particular case, sometimes vary in the recital of the factors to be considered, the following definition by the Commission of Appeals in Atkinson v. Jackson Bros., 270 S.W. 848, 851 (Tex.Comm.App.1925), is a typical recital of the constituent elements of the doctrine:

> To constitute substantial compliance the contractor must have in good faith intended to comply with the contract, and shall have substantially done so in the sense that the defects are not pervasive, do not constitute a deviation from the general plan contemplated for the work, and are not so essential that the object of the parties in making the contract and its purpose cannot, without difficulty, be accomplished by remedying them. Such performance permits only such omissions or deviations from the contract as are inadvertent and unintentional, are not due to bad faith, do not impair the structure as a whole, and are remediable without doing material damage to other parts of the building in tearing down and reconstructing.

See, also, Dupuy v. Shilling, 27 S.W.2d 323, 325 (Tex.Civ.App.—Beaumont 1930, writ dism'd); 10 Tex.Jur.2d, Building Contracts Sec. 21; 13 Am. Jur.2d, Building and Construction Contracts Secs. 41–43.

What was the general plan contemplated for the work in this case? What was the object and purpose of the parties? It is clear that, despite the frequency with which the courts speak of defects that are not "pervasive," which do not constitute a "deviation from the general plan," and which are "not so essential that the object of the parties in making the contract and its purpose cannot, without difficulty, be accomplished by remedying them," when an attempt is made to apply the general principles to a particular case difficulties are encountered at the outset. Was the general plan to install a substantial roof which would serve the purpose which roofs are designed to serve? Or, rather, was the general plan to install a substantial roof of uniform color? Was the object and purpose of the contract merely to furnish such a roof, or was it to furnish such a roof which would be of a uniform color? It should not come as a shock to anyone to adopt a rule to the effect that a person has, particularly with respect to his home, to choose for himself and to contract for something which exactly satisfies that choice, and not to be compelled to accept something else. In the matter of homes and their decoration, as much as, if not more than, in many other fields, mere taste or preference, almost approaching whimsy, may be controlling with the homeowner, so that variations which might, under other circumstances, be considered trifling, may be inconsistent with that "substantial performance" on which liability to pay must be predicated. Of mere incompleteness or deviations which may be easily supplied or remedied after the contractor has finished his work, and the cost of which to the owner is not excessive and readily ascertainable, present less cause for hesitation in concluding that the performance tendered constitutes substantial performance, since in such cases the owner can obtain complete satisfaction by merely spending some money and deducting the amount of such expenditure from the contract price.

In the case before us there is evidence to support the conclusion that plaintiff can secure a roof of uniform coloring only by installing a completely new roof. We cannot say, as a matter of law, that the evidence establishes that in this case that a roof which so lacks uniformity in color as to give the appearance of a patch job serves essentially the same purpose as a roof of uniform color which has the appearance of being a new roof. We are not prepared to hold that a contractor who tenders a performance so deficient that it can be remedied only by completely redoing the work for which the contract called has established, as a matter of law, that he has substantially performed his contractual obligation.

* * *

Finally, defendant argues that it was entitled to judgment at least on the theory of quantum meruit on its cross claim because the evidence establishes as a matter of law that defendant installed a good weatherproof roof which was guaranteed for 15 years, and that such roof was installed properly in accordance with factory specifications and was of use and benefit to plaintiff.

The evidence does not conclusively establish that the shingles were properly installed. There is evidence to the effect that if shingles of this type are properly installed the result will be a roof which "blends," rather than a roof with clearly discordant streaks. In any event, the evidence does not conclusively establish that plaintiff has received any benefit from defendant's defective performance. As already pointed out, there is evidence that plaintiff will have to install a completely new roof. Because of defendant's deficient performance, plaintiff is now in a position which requires that she pay for a new roof.

Nor does the evidence conclusively establish that plaintiff accepted the claimed benefit. She complained immediately and has expressed dissatisfaction at all times. We cannot infer an acceptance from the fact that plaintiff continued to live in the house. She was living in the house before defendant installed the new roof, and we know of no rule which would require that, in order to avoid a finding of implied acceptance, plaintiff was obligated to move out of her home.

The judgment of the trial court is affirmed.

NOTES

(1) *Jacob & Youngs v. Kent* and *O.W. Grun Roofing and Construction Co. v. Cope* squarely faced a question not considered in *Stewart v. Newbury*, namely, did the contractor satisfy the constructive condition that the work be substantially completed before the owner has a duty to pay? Consider the following questions:

(a) What was the agreement on payment in *Jacob & Youngs* and how does it differ from *O.W. Grun*?

(b) Why should the constructive condition ever be satisfied by less than a complete performance that conformed to the contract requirements? For example, if the contract required the construction of a "country house" with "standard pipe of Reading Manufacture," why should the owner be expected to pay for something different?

(c) If, at the time of contracting, the contractor did not know or have reason to know the owner's particular purpose in requiring "Reading" pipe and most "reasonable" owners would have been satisfied by either brand, how is the owner's particular purpose to be protected under the contract? By employment of a more attentive architect? By clearer and more complete contract drafting? Can you draft a clause that would protect Mr. Kent against the mitigating force of the doctrine of substantial performance? Compare Della Ratta, Inc. v. American Better Community Developers, Inc., 38 Md.App. 119, 380 A.2d 627 (1977), where the court held that in a wholly executory contract, the doctrine of substantial performance did not apply to the satisfaction of an express condition. The smaller the deviation and the greater the extent of forfeiture, however, the greater the odds that even an express condition will be excused. See Restatement (Second) § 229.

(3) *The Effect of Bad Faith.* Judge Cardozo, in *Jacob & Youngs v. Kent*, suggested that the quality of the breacher's conduct was relevant to the "substantial performance" question: The "willful transgressor must accept the penalty of his transgression" but the "transgressor whose default is unintentional and trivial may hope for mercy if he will offer atonement for his wrong." Section 241 of the Restatement (Second) is in accord: the "extent to which the behavior of the party failing to perform or to offer to perform comports with standards of good faith and fair dealing" is a circumstance relevant to the question. Which of the following cases would fall on the bad faith side of the line:

(a) P, with the intention of harming D, substituted Pipe X for Pipe Y knowing that the contract called for Pipe Y and that D strongly desired Pipe Y.

(b) P substituted Pipe X for Pipe Y by concealing the switch from the architect. P assumed that D was indifferent to which brand was used and hoped to save money for himself under the fixed-price contract by using Pipe X, which could be procured more cheaply.

(c) P substituted Pipe X for Pipe Y after honestly but carelessly concluding that the specifications called for "brand name or equal."

(4) *Trivial Breach*. In Foundation Dev. Corp. v. Loehmann's, Inc., 163 Ariz. 438, 788 P.2d 1189 (1990), Loehman's, the anchor tenant in a shopping center under a 20–year lease, failed by two days to pay a disputed charge within the ten days specified in the lease. Because of this tardy payment, the lessor exercised its contractual right to terminate the lease. The court finds that the lessor did not have the right to terminate for a "trivial breach" but does not explain what words would have been sufficient to make timely payment a condition of further rental. The court dismisses "stock phrases" such as "time is of the essence" as indicating an intent to create such a condition. What non-stock phrases would have been sufficient?

PROBLEM: THE CASE OF THE DEFICIENT VALVE TESTER

B manufactured valves for use in automobile engines. The valves were required to meet high performance standards before they could be used by automobile manufacturers. In order to increase the efficiency of its operation, B entered negotiations with S for the design and manufacture of a valve testing machine. B explained its needs to S, elaborating on the automobile manufacturer's requirements, and stated that it needed a machine that would test the valves with a 5% margin for error i.e., a minimum accuracy rate of 95%. In short, B expected that of every 100 valves tested by the machine, a 95% accuracy rate would be obtained. S agreed to this requirement and it appeared in the written contract. Six months later, the machine was completed and B put it through a rigorous inspection and test. The result was that the machine consistently achieved a 93–94% accuracy rate, with occasional batches testing out at 95%. B then claimed that S had breached an express warranty that the machine would achieve a 95% accuracy rate, see UCC 2–313(1), and that B could "reject" the goods, UCC 2–601, [UCC 2–703(a) (1997)] cancel the contract for breach, see UCC 2–711(1) [UCC 2–823 (1997)], and sue for damages. S concedes that the warranty was breached, but claimed that there was substantial performance. Thus, B was required to accept and pay for the goods, UCC 2–709(1) [UCC 2–822 (1997)], with an adjustment for any damages caused by the breach. See UCC 2–717 [UCC 2–828 (1997)]. B responded that the doctrine of substantial performance has been rejected by the UCC, and B was entitled to a "perfect" tender.

Consult the following Code sections from the unrevised article 2 and give us your opinion: UCC 2–601, 2–504, 2–508, 2–608, 2–612, 2–719 and the sections on good faith, UCC 1–203, 1–201(19) and 2–103(1)(b).

Lowy v. United Pacific Insurance Co.

Supreme Court of California, 1967.
67 Cal.2d 87, 60 Cal.Rptr. 225, 429 P.2d 577.

■ McComb, Associate Justice. Plaintiffs appeal from a judgment in favor of defendant Arnold Wolpin (hereinafter referred to as "defendant") on a cross-complaint for damages for breach of an excavation and grading contract.

Facts: Plaintiffs, owners and subdividers, entered into a contract with defendant, a licensed contractor, for certain excavation and grading work on lots and streets, together with street improvement work consisting of paving the streets and installing curbs and gutters, in a subdivision containing 89 residential lots.

After defendant had performed 98 percent of the contracted excavation and grading work, a dispute arose between the parties regarding payment of $7,200 for additional work, consisting of importing dirt for fills, necessitated by changes made by plaintiffs in the plans.

Defendant ceased performance. Plaintiffs immediately employed others to do street improvement work called for by the contract and thereafter sued defendant and his bonding company for breach of contract. Defendant answered and cross-complained for damages for breach of contract and reasonable services rendered. The trial court determined that plaintiffs were entitled to nothing against defendant and his bonding company and allowed defendant recovery on his cross-complaint.

Questions: First. *Was the contract between the parties divisible and the doctrine of substantial performance applicable?*

Yes.

The contract provided, in part, as follows: "[Defendant] agrees to provide and pay for all materials, labor, tools, equipment, light, transportation and other facilities necessary for the execution, in a good and workmanlike manner, of all the following described work: Excavation, Grading and Street Improvements in Tracts No. 26589 and 19517 in accordance with plans and specifications * * * and Exhibit 'A' attached hereto. * * *

"The price which [plaintiffs] shall pay [defendant] for performing his obligations, as aforesaid or as hereunder set forth, is at the following prices indicated: * * *

"See Exhibits *'A' and 'B'* attached hereto." (Italics added.)

Exhibit "A" states in part: "[Defendant] agrees to furnish all equipment, labor and material necessary for street improvements, onsite and offsite grading, grade and excavation and erosion control on Tracts 26589 and 19517 * * * for the lump sum price of Seventy–Three Thousand, Five Hundred Dollars ($73,500.00) including, without limitation, *all grading, compaction, cleaning, grade and erosion control and dumping,* all of which are to be performed to satisfaction of [plaintiffs]. * * *" (Italics added.)

The construction of pavement, curbs and gutters is not included in the list of specific items for which the sum of $73,500 is to be paid.

Exhibit "B" lists 45 unit prices ranging from $.04 to $4.50 per unit for use in the computation of the amount to be charged for the performance of that part of the street improvement work consisting of paving the streets and installing curbs and gutters. The unit prices are entirely unrelated to excavation and grading.

The contract further provides: "In invoicing [plaintiffs], multiply all the final quantities by the unit prices set forth in Exhibit 'B.' All quantities will be determined by Delta Engineering & Surveying Co. and approved by [defendant] and [plaintiffs], *with the exception of grading, etc., mentioned in Exhibit 'A' of this Agreement, which is a lump sum price for a complete job without any limitations.*" (Italics added.)

The latter paragraph of the contract shows clearly that the lump sum of $73,500 was not intended to include payment for paving the streets and installing curbs and gutters.

The trial court found that under the contract there were two phases of work to be performed, (1) grading and (2) street improvements; that defendant performed all the terms and conditions thereof relating to grading, except work which could be completed for $1,470, being 2 percent of the total grading cost contracted for; that defendant performed additional grading work, reasonably worth $7,200, necessitated by changes in plans on the part of plaintiffs and not attributable to defendant, which additional work was also authorized by plaintiffs through their superintendent; that plaintiffs breached the contract by employing others to do street improvement work and by not making payments to defendant for grading work done by him when due, thereby excusing further performance by defendant; and that defendant was entitled to recover on his cross-complaint for damages, as follows:

Contract price for grading	$73,500.00
Additional work	7,200.00
	80,700.00
Less amount paid defendant	− 60,227.50
	20,472.50
Less credit for uncompleted work	− 1,470.00
	19,002.50
Less credit for items paid for defendant's account	− 1,166.00
Balance owing defendant	$17,836.50

The trial court also found that defendant was entitled to reasonable attorney's fees in the sum of $4,000, the contract providing for reasonable attorney's fees to be awarded to the prevailing party in any action brought to enforce the terms and conditions thereof.

The trial court further found that defendant had breached that portion of the contract relating to street improvement work and was not entitled to recover damages for loss of profits in connection therewith.

As indicated above, the contract required the performance of two kinds of work. First, certain excavation and grading work was to be done on lots and streets. Thereafter, street improvement work, consisting of paving the streets and installing curbs and gutters, was required.

Plaintiffs agreed to pay defendant for the excavation and grading work (including street grading work) the sum of $73,500, as set forth in Exhibit "A" of the contract and they agreed to pay defendant for the paving of the streets and the installation of curbs and gutters (all commonly called "street improvement work") pursuant to the unit prices set forth in Exhibit "B" of the contract.

Accordingly, since the consideration was apportioned, the contract was a severable or divisible one.* (See Keene v. Harling, 61 Cal.2d 318, 323[5], 38 Cal.Rptr. 513, 392 P.2d 273; Simmons v. California Institute of Technology, 34 Cal.2d 264, 275[14], 209 P.2d 581.)

Before defendant commenced the excavation and grading work, for which a lump sum price of $73,500 was set by the contract, he gave a surety bond for $73,500. When the excavation and grading work was nearing completion, and it was almost time for work under the second phase to begin, plaintiffs requested that defendant provide a surety bond for "street improvements" in the sum of $125,000, stating that "no work should be performed on any portion of the street improvement portion of the contract until such bond is furnished." Thus, it is clear that the parties treated the contract as a divisible one.

Under the circumstances, the fact that defendant did not perform the second phase of the contract does not prevent his recovering for work done under the first phase.

Defendant did not entirely perform under the first phase of the contract. However, the doctrine of substantial performance, ordinarily applied to building contracts, is here applicable, since the evidence shows that defendant completed 98 percent of the work under the first phase and was prevented from completing the balance through the fault of plaintiffs.

Where a person agrees to do a thing for another for a specified sum of money, to be paid on full performance, he is not entitled to any part of the sum until he has himself done the thing he agreed to do, unless full performance has been excused, prevented, or delayed by the act of the other party. (Thomas Haverty Co. v. Jones, 185 Cal. 285, 288–289, 197 P. 105.)

---

* Williston defines a divisible contract, as follows: "A contract under which the whole performance is divided into two sets of partial performance, each part of each set being the agreed exchange for a corresponding part of the set of performances to be rendered by the other promisor, is called a divisible contract. Or, as expressed in the cases:

'A contract is divisible where by its terms, 1, performance of each party is divided into two or more parts, and 2, the number of parts due from each party is the same, and 3, the performance of each part by one party is the agreed exchange for a corresponding part by the other party.'" (6 Williston, Contracts (3d ed. 1962) § 860, pp. 252–254.)

In Thomas Haverty Co. v. Jones, supra, at page 289[1], 197 P. 105, we held that in the case of a building contract where the owner has taken possession of the building and is enjoying the fruits of the contractor's work in the performance of the contract, if there has been a substantial performance thereof by the contractor in good faith, if the failure to make full performance can be compensated in damages to be deducted from the price or allowed as a counterclaim, and if the omissions and deviations were not wilful or fraudulent and do not substantially affect the usefulness of the building or the purpose for which it was intended, the contractor may, in an action upon the contract, recover the amount of the contract price remaining unpaid, less the amount allowed as damages for the failure of strict performance.

Reference to the computation of items, both debit and credit, set forth in the findings in the present case, reveals an almost literal compliance with the formula approved in the *Haverty* case, supra; and there is substantial evidence to support the trial court's finding that plaintiffs themselves breached the contract and thus made impossible full performance on defendant's part.

* * *

The judgment is affirmed.

Plaintiffs are ordered to pay to defendant Wolpin additional attorney's fees on this appeal in an amount to be determined by the trial court.

NOTES

(1) Did the contractor in *Lowy* substantially perform the entire contract? If not, how did he recover the adjusted contract price for the excavation and grading work on the lots and streets?

(2) It is commonly stated that whether a contract is divisible depends upon the intention of the parties, and the intent to have a divisible contract may be inferred from such factors as the ease with which the agreed consideration can be apportioned to separate performances, the fungibility of those performances and the lack of evidence that the parties would have refused to deal for less than the whole. See Management Services Corp. v. Development Associates, 617 P.2d 406, 408 (Utah 1980) (contract to purchase eight lots divisible). Section 240 of Restatement (Second), however, states that the question is whether the "performances to be exchanged under an exchange of promises can be apportioned into corresponding pairs of part performances so that the parts of each pair are properly regarded as agreed equivalents. * * *" According to Comment d, the "process of apportionment is essentially one of calculation and the rule can only be applied where calculation is feasible." Even so, the contract is not divisible unless it is "proper to regard the parts of each pair as agreed equivalents" and, in many cases, the "parties * * * cannot even be said to have had any actual intention on the point." Comment e. Motivated by a desire to avoid forfeiture, the court's decision will "usually depend on considerations of fairness," such as the receipt by the aggrieved party of a part performance "worth to him roughly the same fraction of what full performance

would have been worth. * * *" Put another way, the "injured party will not be required to pay for a part of the performance that he has received if he cannot make full use of that part without the remainder of the performance" and, in making this determination, a court "must * * * take account of the possibility that the remainder of the performance can be easily obtained from some other source."

(3) UCC 2–307 provides: "Unless otherwise agreed all goods called for by a contract for sale must be tendered in a single delivery and payment is due only on such tender but where the circumstances give either party the right to make or demand delivery in lots the price if it can be apportioned may be demanded for each lot." Thus, where the circumstances indicate that a party has a right to delivery in lots, the price may be demanded for each lot if it is apportionable. 2–307, Comment 4. In the next chapter attention is given to the related problem of whether the breach of an installment discharges the other party from contractual obligation. [UCC 2–302 (1997)]

PROBLEMS: DIVISIBLE OR ENTIRE CONTRACT?

1. *The Case of the Unpaid Contractor.* Contractor and Owner entered into a home remodeling contract, containing the following provision respecting price and payment: "All above material, and labor to erect and install same to be supplied for $30,000 to be paid as follows: $1,500 on signing of contract, $10,000 upon delivery of materials and starting of work, $15,000 on completion of rough carpentry and rough plumbing, $3,500 on completion." C, upon completion of the rough work, demanded payment of the third installment and O refused. C then sued O for $15,000 and, at trial, failed to offer proof as to actual damages. O moved to dismiss. Although conceding that its failure to pay was a breach, O argued that C was not entitled to the third payment, but to only such amount as it could establish by way of actual loss sustained from the breach. Which view should prevail? See New Era Homes Corp. v. Forster, 299 N.Y. 303, 86 N.E.2d 757 (1949), infra at 875.

2. *The Case of the Defaulting Thresher.* Plaintiffs, owners of a threshing outfit, agreed with the defendant, a farmer, to thresh his grain at the following rates: wheat, $1.00 per bushel; oats, $.60 per bushel; flax, $1.50 per bushel. After threshing about 50% of the crop, P moved its equipment to another location because they were losing money on the job with D. D was obliged to complete the threshing of its grain at a higher price through other parties. Is P entitled to recover for the work done at the agreed price per bushel on the ground that the contract was "divisible"? See Johnson v. Fehsefeldt, 106 Minn. 202, 118 N.W. 797 (1908). If not, is there another basis upon which they might seek relief? See the cases that follow.

3. *The Case of the Failed Resort Bid.* Young and Tate agreed to invest in a proposed resort project. The first stage involved putting together a bid to be made to the State. Among other things, the agreement provided that Young, because of her better credit, was to provide $50,000 for this first stage, $25,000 on January 2, 1985, and the next $25,000 "as needed." The agreement also provided that Tate "will assume liability for the first $25,000." The first payment was made, but when Tate's agent requested the second payment, Young, without justification, refused to pay. Tate then spent $32,000 in furtherance of the bid, which was ultimately rejected by the State. Young sued

Tate to recover the $25,000 paid and Tate counterclaimed to recover $25,000 of the expenses incurred after Young refused to make the second payment. Assuming that Young's refusal was a breach of contract, what result? See Young v. Tate, 232 Neb. 915, 442 N.W.2d 865 (1989).

Britton v. Turner

Supreme Court of Judicature of New Hampshire, 1834.
6 N.H. 481.

Assumpsit for work and labour, performed by the plaintiff, in the service of the defendant, from March 9th, 1831, to December 27, 1831.

The declaration contained the common counts, and among them a count in *quantum meruit,* for the labor, averring it to be worth one hundred dollars.

At the trial in the C.C. Pleas, the plaintiff proved the performance of the labor as set forth in the declaration.

The defence was that it was performed under a special contract—that the plaintiff agreed to work one year, from some time in March, 1831, to March 1832, and that the defendant was to pay him for said year's labor the sum of one hundred and twenty dollars; and the defendant offered evidence tending to show that such was the contract under which the work was done.

Evidence was also offered to show that the plaintiff left the defendant's service without his consent, and it was contended by the defendant that the plaintiff had no good cause for not continuing in his employment.

There was no evidence offered of any damage arising from the plaintiff's departure, farther than was to be inferred from his nonfulfilment of the entire contract.

The court instructed the jury, that if they were satisfied from the evidence that the labor was performed, under a contract to labor a year, for the sum of one hundred and twenty dollars, and if they were satisfied that the plaintiff labored only the time specified in the declaration, and then left the defendant's service, against his consent, and without any good cause, yet the plaintiff was entitled to recover, under his *quantum meruit* count, as much as the labor he performed was reasonably worth, and under this direction the jury gave a verdict for the plaintiff for the sum of $95.

The defendant excepted to the instructions thus given to the jury.

■ PARKER, J. delivered the opinion of the court. It may be assumed, that the labor performed by the plaintiff, and for which he seeks to recover a compensation in this action, was commenced under a special contract to labor for the defendant the term of one year, for the sum of one hundred and twenty dollars, and that the plaintiff has labored but a portion of that time, and has voluntarily failed to complete the entire contract.

It is clear, then, that he is not entitled to recover upon the contract itself, because the service, which was to entitle him to the sum agreed upon, has never been performed.

But the question arises, can the plaintiff, under these circumstances, recover a reasonable sum for the service he has actually performed, under the count in *quantum meruit*.

Upon this, and questions of a similar nature, the decisions to be found in the books are not easily reconciled.

It has been held, upon contracts of this kind for labor to be performed at a specified price, that the party who voluntarily fails to fulfil the contract by performing the whole labor contracted for, is not entitled to recover any thing for the labor actually performed, however much he may have done towards the performance, and this has been considered the settled rule of law upon this subject. . . .

That such rule in its operation may be very unequal, not to say unjust, is apparent.

A party who contracts to perform certain specified labor, and who breaks his contract in the first instance, without any attempt to perform it, can only be made liable to pay the damages which the other party has sustained by reason of such non performance, which in many instances may be trifling—whereas a party who in good faith has entered upon the performance of his contract, and nearly completed it, and then abandoned the further performance—although the other party has had the full benefit of all that has been done, and has perhaps sustained no actual damage—is in fact subjected to a loss of all which has been performed, in the nature of damages for the nonfulfilment of the remainder, upon the technical rule, that the contract must be fully performed in order to [justify] a recovery of any part of the compensation.

By the operation of this rule, then, the party who attempts performance may be placed in a much worse situation than he who wholly disregards his contract, and the other party may receive much more, by the breach of the contract, than the injury which he has sustained by such breach, and more than he could be entitled to were he seeking to recover damages by an action.

The case before us presents an illustration. Had the plaintiff in this case never entered upon the performance of his contract, the damage could not probably have been greater than some small expense and trouble incurred in procuring another to do the labor which he had contracted to perform. But having entered upon the performance, and labored nine and a half months, the value of which labor to the defendant as found by the jury is $95, if the defendant can succeed in this defence, he in fact receives nearly five sixths of the value of a whole year's labor, by reason of the breach of contract by the plaintiff, a sum not only utterly disproportionate to any probable, not to say possible damage which could have resulted from the neglect of the plaintiff to continue the remaining two and a half months, but altogether beyond any damage which could have been recovered by the defendant, had the plaintiff done nothing towards the fulfilment of his contract.

* * *

It is said, that where a party contracts to perform certain work, and to furnish materials, as for instance, to build a house, and the work is done, but with some variations from the mode prescribed by the contract, yet if the other party has the benefit of the labor and materials he should be bound to pay so much as they are reasonably worth. . . .

Those cases are not to be distinguished, in principle, from the present, unless it be in the circumstance, that where the party has contracted to furnish materials, and do certain labor, as to build a house in a specified manner, if it is not done according to the contract, the party for whom it is built may refuse to receive it—elect to take no benefit from what has been performed—and therefore if he does receive, he shall be bound to pay the value—whereas in a contract for labor, merely, from day to day, the party is continually receiving the benefit of the contract under an expectation that it will be fulfilled, and cannot, upon the breach of it, have an election to refuse to receive what has been done, and thus discharge himself from payment.

But we think this difference in the nature of the contracts does not justify the application of a different rule in relation to them.

The party who contracts for labor merely, for a certain period, does so with full knowledge that he must, from the nature of the case, be accepting part performance from day to day, if the other party commences the performance, and with knowledge also that the other may eventually fail of completing the entire term.

If under such circumstances he actually receives a benefit from the labor performed, over and above the damage occasioned by the failure to complete, there is as much reason why he should pay the reasonable worth of what has thus been done for his benefit, as there is when he enters and occupies the house which has been built for him, but not according to the stipulations of the contract, and which he perhaps enters, not because he is satisfied with what has been done, but because circumstances compel him to accept it such as it is, that he should pay for the value of the house.

* * *

In fact we think the technical reasoning, that the performance of the whole labor is a condition precedent, and the right to recover any thing dependent upon it—that the contract being entire there can be no apportionment—and that there being an express contract no other can be implied, even upon the subsequent performance of service—is not properly applicable to this species of contract, where a beneficial service has been actually performed; for we have abundant reason to believe, that the general understanding of the community is, that the hired laborer shall be entitled to compensation for the service actually performed, though he do not continue the entire term contracted for, and such contracts must be presumed to be made with reference to that understanding, unless an express stipulation shows the contrary.

* * *

It is easy, if parties so choose, to provide by an express agreement that nothing shall be earned, if the laborer leaves his employer without having performed the whole service contemplated, and then there can be no pretence for a recovery if he voluntarily deserts the service before the expiration of the time.

The amount, however, for which the employer ought to be charged, where the laborer abandons his contract, is only the reasonable worth, or the amount of advantage he receives upon the whole transaction, . . . and, in estimating the value of the labor, the contract price for the service cannot be exceeded.

* * *

The benefit and advantage which the party takes by the labor, therefore, is the amount of value which he receives, if any, after deducting the amount of damage.

* * *

This rule, by binding the employer to pay the value of the service he actually receives, and the laborer to answer in damages where he does not complete the entire contract, will leave no temptation to the former to drive the laborer from his service, near the close of his term, by ill treatment, in order to escape from payment; nor to the latter to desert his service before the stipulated time, without a sufficient reason; and it will in most instances settle the whole controversy in one action, and prevent a multiplicity of suits and cross actions.

* * *

Applying the principles thus laid down, to this case, the plaintiff is entitled to judgment on the verdict.

The defendant sets up a mere breach of the contract in defence of the action, but this cannot avail him. He does not appear to have offered evidence to show that he was damnified by such breach, or to have asked that a deduction should be made upon that account. The direction to the jury was therefore correct, that the plaintiff was entitled to recover as much as the labor performed was reasonably worth, and the jury appear to have allowed a *pro rata* compensation, for the time which the plaintiff labored in the defendant's service.

* * *

Judgment on the verdict.

NOTES

The "constructive" condition dilemma facing Judge Parker in *Britton v. Turner* has been resolved by legislation in many states: the employer must pay the employee's wages at regular intervals regardless of "substantial" performance. See, e.g., Ill.Rev.Stat., ch. 48, §§ 39m–3 (all wage earners other than executives, administrators, professionals and commission agents must be paid on a semi-monthly basis.) The employer's failure to pay as required may be a crime. See Holmes v. Tradigrain, Inc., 411 So.2d 1132 (La.App.1982); Putnam v. Oregon Department of Justice, 58 Or.App. 111, 647 P.2d 949 (1982). For an illustration of the type of question that can arise under these statutes, see Suastez v. Plastic Dress–Up Co., 31 Cal.3d 774, 183 Cal.Rptr. 846, 647 P.2d 122 (1982), where the California Supreme Court held that a proportionate right to a paid vacation vested in the employee as labor was rendered and, once vested, was protected from forfeiture by the applicable legislation.

Maxton Builders, Inc. v. Lo Galbo

Court of Appeals of New York, 1986.
68 N.Y.2d 373, 509 N.Y.S.2d 507, 502 N.E.2d 184.

■ WACHTLER, CHIEF JUDGE.

The plaintiff contracted to sell a house to the defendants and accepted a check for the down payment. When the defendants canceled the contract and stopped payment on the check, the plaintiff sued for a breach claiming a right to the down payment—a right traditionally allowed in this State under the rule set forth in Lawrence v. Miller, 86 N.Y. 131. The trial court denied plaintiff's motion for summary judgment holding that a fact question was presented as to whether recovery of the down payment would constitute a penalty under the circumstances. The Appellate Division modified and granted summary judgment to the plaintiff for the amount of the down payment.

The defendants appealed claiming there was no breach because they effectively exercised a contractual right to cancel. In the alternative, defendants urge that plaintiff's recovery should be limited to actual damages, and that we should, therefore, reexamine the rule of *Lawrence v. Miller* (supra), which permits a vendor on a real estate contract to retain the down payment when the purchaser willfully defaults.

[The amount at stake was $21,000, the 10% down payment on the contract to purchase a newly constructed house. The court first held that the purchaser had breached by not notifying the vendor that it had canceled within the three day period stated in the contract and then refusing to perform. The court stated: "In short, the defendants bargained for and obtained a limited right to cancel which they failed to exercise within the time agreed upon. The cancellation was, therefore, ineffective and the defendants' refusal to perform constituted a breach ...."]

* * *

The defendants' alternative argument is that the Appellate Division erred in permitting the plaintiff to recover the entire down payment, and should instead have limited recovery to actual damages. On the basis of existing law it is clear that the defendants cannot prevail. For more than a century it has been well settled in this State that a vendee who defaults on a real estate contract without lawful excuse, cannot recover the down payment.... The rule, however, has been criticized as being out of harmony with the general principle that actual damages is the proper measure of recovery for a breach of contract and, it has been abandoned by several jurisdictions.... The defendants' argument on this appeal presents the question as to whether the long-standing rule should be retained in this State.

II.

In the leading case, Lawrence v. Miller, 86 N.Y. 131, supra, decided by this court in 1881, we denied the assignee of the defaulting vendee recovery of a $2,000 down payment, reasoning that the vendor acquired the money rightfully, failed in no duty to the vendee, and the money would have been his but for the vendee's breach. We stated (at p. 140): "To allow a recovery of this money would be to sustain an action by a party on his own breach of his own contract, which the law does not allow * * * Nor can the specious view be taken, presented by the plaintiff, that the defendant is entitled to no more than he has actually been damaged."

Much of the criticism of *Lawrence v. Miller* (supra) is directed at the rule on which it is based, which broadly holds that a party who defaults on a contract cannot recover the amount or value of part performance (Corbin, *Right of a Defaulting Vendee to the Restitution of Installments Paid*, 40 Yale L.J. 1013; 1942 Report of N.Y. Law Rev.Commn., at 179). This parent rule is applicable to contracts generally, and has been applied to a wide variety of circumstances including the sale of goods, employment contracts for a fixed term, construction contracts, and installment land sales (Corbin, op. cit.). In all of these cases the common law would deny any relief to the defaulting party even when there had been substantial, or nearly complete performance. It was these holdings especially which prompted the criticism calling for reform of the parent rule on the ground that it produced a forfeiture "and the amount of the forfeiture increases as performance proceeds, so that the penalty grows larger as the breach grows smaller." (Corbin, ibid., at 1029;....)

The "modern rule" advocated by the critics permits the party in default to recover for part performance in excess of actual damages, but places the burden on him to prove the net benefit conferred ... The rule was designed primarily to protect the party who had made a number of payments or substantial performance before default, and provides little relief to the defaulting purchaser seeking to recover a down payment or first installment. Corbin notes: "In such cases, it is unlikely that the amount retained by the vendor was greater than the injury suffered by the plaintiff's breach. Whatever the amount, the plaintiff must show that it is greater than the injury done. In most cases that injury is wholly unliquidated and difficult of accurate estimation; and in few cases does the plaintiff attempt to show how much it was." (Corbin, op. cit., at 1024–1025.)

The Restatement (Second) of Contracts adopts the "modern rule", but recognizes an exception for liquidated damages, and also for "money paid" under an understanding or "usage" that it be retained in the event of a breach (§ 374 comment c). The illustration involves the right of a seller on a real estate contract to retain the first installment equal to 10% of the contract price, upon the buyer's default.

In 1834 New Hampshire became the first State to reject the parent rule and permit a defaulting party to recover for part performance in a case involving a laborer who had defaulted on a one-year employment contract after working for nine and one-half months (Britton v. Turner, 6 N.H. 481). In most areas of the law the Legislature and the courts, have now adopted rules generally permitting a party in default to recover for part performance to the extent of the net benefit conferred (see, e.g., Williston, Contracts § 1473; Amtorg Trading Corp. v. Miehle Print. Press & Mfg. Co., 206 F.2d 103 [summarizing New York law]; Jacob & Youngs v. Kent, 230 N.Y. 656, 130 N.E. 933 [permitting contractor to recover for substantial performance]; U.C.C. 2–718; Act, Recommendation and Study Relating to Recovery for Benefits Conferred by Party in Default Under Contract, 1942 Report of N.Y.Law Rev.Commn., at 179; but also see, Comment, Forfeiture: The Anomaly of the Land Sale Contract, 41 Alb.L.Rev. 71). However in cases dealing with recovery of down payments on real estate contracts, a majority of jurisdictions still follow the principle of Lawrence v. Miller (supra), especially where the down payment does not exceed 10% of the contract price ...

Several years ago the Law Revision Commission proposed that the Legislature of this State abrogate Lawrence v. Miller (supra), and adopt a "more equitable" rule (Act, Recommendation and Study Relating to Recovery for Benefits Conferred by Party in Default Under Contract, 1942 Report of N.Y.Law Rev.Commn., at 179, 188, 237–239). The proposed law was not adopted. It is interesting to note, however, that although the proposed reform would generally have permitted the defaulting buyer to recover the net benefit conferred, it would also have allowed the seller, in any event, to retain "twenty percent of the value of the total performance for which the buyer is obligated under the contract" (ibid., at 183).** A similar proposal was later made, and adopted by the Legislature, with respect to the right of a buyer to recover for part performance after defaulting on a contract for the sale of goods (Act, Recommendation and Study Relating to Right of Buyer of Goods to Restitution for Benefits Conferred Under a Contract of Sale on Which He Has Defaulted, 1952 Report of N.Y.Law Rev.Commn, at 83, 643; Personal Property Law former

---

** On this point, the report states (at p. 188): "While it may be argued that the defaulting buyer should be allowed complete restitution for the benefit conferred, the Commission recognizes the practical difficulties which would result from the adoption of such a principle. Because of the difficulty of establishing the damages in many cases or because provable injury is sometimes not included within the rules of damages, and because a rule permitting complete restitution would encourage the breaking of contracts, the seller should be allowed to retain in any event a reasonable part of the net benefit conferred."

§ 145–a, now U.C.C. 2–718[2] [permitting seller to withhold 20% of the value of the total performance up to a limit of $500]).

III.

We have previously noted that a court should not depart from its prior holdings "unless impelled by *'the most cogent reasons'* " (Baker v. Lorillard, 4 N.Y. 257, 261). This standard is particularly apt in cases involving the legal effect of contractual relations. In fact, when contractual rights are at issue, "where it can reasonably be assumed that settled rules are necessary and necessarily relied upon, stability and adherence to precedent are generally more important than a better or even a 'correct' rule of law" (Matter of Eckart, 39 N.Y.2d 493, 500, 384 N.Y.S.2d 429, 436, 348 N.E.2d 905, 913). The rule permitting a party in default to seek restitution for part performance has much to commend it in its general applications. But as applied to real estate down payments approximating 10% it does not appear to offer a better or more workable rule than the long-established "usage" in this State with respect to the seller's right to retain a down payment upon default.***

In cases, as here, where the property is sold to another after the breach, the buyer's ability to recover the down payment would depend initially on whether the agreement expressly provides that the seller could retain it upon default. If it did, the provision would probably be upheld as a valid liquidated damages clause in view of the recognized difficulty of estimating actual damages and the general acceptance of the traditional 10% down payment as a reasonable amount.

If the contract itself is deemed to pose no bar, then the buyer would bear the burden of proving that the amount retained exceeded the actual damages. As the authorities note, this is a difficult burden in any case involving real estate sales, and is not likely to be met in suits on down payments or first installments where the actual damages will generally be very close to the amount of the traditional 10% retained. Thus, in most cases, a change in the law will provide a forum for the disputants to further dispute their differences, but cannot be reasonably expected to save any party from true financial loss. Indeed in the case now before us the defendants made no effort to show that the actual damages were less than the plaintiff alleged or that there was, in fact, a net benefit conferred.

Finally, real estate contracts are probably the best examples of arm's length transactions. Except in cases where there is a real risk of over-reaching, there should be no need for the courts to relieve the parties of the consequences of their contract. If the parties are dissatisfied with the rule of *Lawrence v. Miller* (supra), the time to say so is at the bargaining table.

Accordingly, the order of the Appellate Division should be affirmed.

*** It should be emphasized that we do not have before us any question concerning installment payments beyond a 10% down payment and thus we express no view concerning the parties' rights with respect to such payments following the vendee's default.

Comment: Recovery in Restitution by a Plaintiff in Default

Britton v. Turner permitted a plaintiff who had arguably committed a material breach to recover the reasonable value of work done up to the breach, "less whatever damages the other party has suffered." See also Kulseth v. Rotenberger, 320 N.W.2d 920 (N.D.1982); Kirkland v. Archbold, 113 N.E.2d 496 (Ohio App.1953); Pinches v. Swedish Evangelical Lutheran Church, 55 Conn. 183, 10 A. 264 (1887). Put another way, although a plaintiff cannot recover "on the contract," he or she can recover in restitution the net benefit retained by the defendant after full compensation for plaintiff's breach of contract. That benefit, however, is limited by the contract price. Section 357 of the first Restatement adopted the "net benefit" test, stating that the "measure of the defendant's benefit from the plaintiff's part performance is the amount by which he has been enriched as a result of such performance * * *." Section 357(3).

The first Restatement, however, provided that restitution was not available if the plaintiff's breach was "wilful and deliberate." Section 357(1). The apparent purpose of this limitation was to direct attention to the moral justification for the breach: an intentional breach is not regarded as wilful and deliberate if it was "due to hardship, insolvency, or circumstances that tend appreciably toward moral justification." Comment e. See G. Palmer, Law of Restitution § 5.1 (1978). Section 374(1) of Restatement (Second), however, does not make restitution turn upon the morality of the plaintiff's breach. If the defendant is justified in refusing to perform because of the plaintiff's material breach, the "party in breach is entitled to restitution for any benefit that he has conferred by way of part performance or reliance in excess of the loss that he has caused by his own breach." See Section 370, for the general requirement that a benefit be conferred for restitution. Section 371 provides the "measure" of the restitution interest. If money rather than specific restitution is sought, "it may as justice requires be measured by either (a) the reasonable value to the other party of what he received in terms of what it would have cost him to obtain it from a person in the claimant's position, or (b) the extent to which the other party's property has been increased in value or his other interests advanced." In no case, however, "will the party in breach be allowed to recover more than a ratable portion of the total contract price where such a portion can be determined." Section 374, Comment b. Does this approach rule out consideration of the moral justification for the breach? The answer is probably no when judicial discretion in measuring the restitution interest is taken into account. The measurement is made "as justice requires" and when the "party seeking restitution has himself committed a material breach * * * uncertainties as to the amount of the benefit may properly be resolved against him." Section 371, Comment a. See Illustration 1. This open-endedness is consistent with Professor Palmer's conclusion that although restitution should not always be denied when the breach is in bad faith, it "does mean that it should be allowed less readily." In short, "the retention of some enrichment may well be just when it is brought about by plaintiff's willful and deliberate breach." G. Palmer at § 5.15, p. 685.

In light of this, are you persuaded by the result in *Maxton Builders?*

PROBLEMS: RESTITUTIONARY RELIEF AND THE WRONGDOER

(1) A contracted with B to construct a swimming pool on B's land for $15,000. The specifications required a designated system for the walls and floor that was guaranteed for 20 years. A, in order to shave costs on the fixed-price contract, deliberately installed a different and somewhat inferior system, which was guaranteed for 10 years. B refused to pay the contract price and A sued for either the price or restitution. The trial court determined that although B had a functional pool for at least 10 years, A had committed a material breach. The trial court also determined that the cost to replace the system would be $20,000 and that the difference in value of the land with a pool as promised by A and the pool actually constructed was $5,000. In order to avoid "economic waste," the trial court then awarded B $5,000 damages for breach of contract. In considering A's claim for restitution, the trial court determined that: (a) the reasonable value to B of the pool constructed in terms of what it would have cost to obtain it from another pool contractor was $12,000; and (b) the difference in value of B's land with the pool actually constructed and without a pool was $5,000. What, if anything, should A recover in restitution from B?

(handwritten margin note: nothing because of breach in bad faith)

(2) Attorney and Client entered into a contingent fee contract for the prosecution of a tort claim against a third party. The agreement stipulated that Attorney's compensation was to be 20% of any amount recovered before trial and 25% if the action proceeded to trial. The agreement also provided: "This contract covers our understanding through the conclusion of the case in the trial court and, at Client's option, in any of the higher courts." An action was then brought against the third party and, after trial, a judgment was entered for Client in the amount of $100,000. The defendant then filed an appeal and Client advised Attorney that he wished him to handle the appeal under "our contract." Attorney stated that he would not handle the appeal unless Client paid him an additional $10,000. Client refused, discharged Attorney and retained another lawyer for the appeal. On appeal, the trial judgment was affirmed and Client paid the substitute attorney $7,500 for her services. Attorney now sues Client. What should he recover:

(a) $25,000;

(b) $15,000, the reasonable value of his services through trial;

(c) Nothing;

(d) None of the above.

(handwritten margin note: 25,000 / -7,500 / $17,500)

(C)   REPRESENTATIONS AND WARRANTIES OF QUALITY

In re Carter, supra at 649, highlighted the difference between warranties and conditions precedent as methods of insuring the other side's performance. Modern corporate contracts (involving, inter alia, mergers and acquisitions or sales of assets) are carefully structured around (1) conditions precedent to each side's performance and (2) the representations and warranties of each side. This section explores the latter. By warranting that an existing fact is true or promising that a future event will happen, a party can expose itself to breach of contract damages if the warranty fails—and thus can better assure the other side of its performance.

To begin, students should remember that representations are not promises, but representations *of fact*. Misrepresentations of fact, however, can give rise to contractual liability, because parties implicitly warrant (i.e. promise) that all representations are true. Thus, UCC § 2–313 establishes:

> (1) Express warranties by the seller are created as follows:

> (a) Any affirmation of fact or promise made by the seller to the buyer which relates to the goods and becomes part of the basis of the bargain creates an express warranty that the goods shall conform to the affirmation or promise.

> (b) Any description of the goods which is made part of the basis of the bargain creates an express warranty that the goods shall conform to the description.

> (c) Any sample or model which is made part of the basis of the bargain creates an express warranty that the whole of the goods shall conform to the sample or model.

> (2) It is not necessary to the creation of an express warranty that the seller use formal words such as "warrant" or "guarantee" or that he have a specific intention to make a warranty, but an affirmation merely of the value of the goods or a statement purporting to be merely the seller's opinion or commendation of the goods does not create a warranty.

Thus, representations ("affirmations of fact") or simply descriptions of the goods create express warranties that the representations are true. Why does the section exclude "an affirmation merely of the value of the goods"? What is the meaning of "merely" in this context?

(1) IMPLIED WARRANTIES

Besides express warranties, the common law has long enforced implicit warranties. For example, a seller implicitly represents that she owns the goods subject to the contract (and implicitly warrants that this implicit representation is true). Compare UCC 2–312. The UCC has created two important additional implied warranties: the implied warranty of merchantability and the implied warranty of fitness for a particular purpose:

§ 2–314. Implied Warranty: Merchantability;

> (1) Unless excluded or modified (Section 2–316), a warranty that the goods shall be merchantable is implied in a contract for their sale if the seller is a merchant with respect to goods of that kind. . . .

§ 2–315. Implied Warranty: Fitness for Particular Purpose

> Where the seller at the time of contracting has reason to know any particular purpose for which the goods are required and that the buyer is relying on the seller's skill or judgment to select or furnish suitable

goods, there is unless excluded or modified under the next section an implied warranty that the goods shall be fit for such purpose.

Notice that a warranty of merchantability is only implied for merchants of "goods of that kind," while an implied warranty of fitness for a particular purpose could potentially apply to non-merchants as well.

The concept of "merchantability" is not self-defining, and while UCC 2–314(2) provides a 6–part disjunctive definition, the core representation is that the goods "are fit for the ordinary purposes for which such goods are used." UCC 2–314(2)(c).

Thus, we see that unless disclaimed, merchants implicitly warrant that goods are fit for "ordinary purposes" and other sellers fulfilling the requirements of UCC 2–315 implicitly warrant that goods are fit for a "particular purpose." The official comment explains the distinction:

> A "particular purpose" differs from the ordinary purpose for which the goods are used in that it envisages a specific use by the buyer which is peculiar to the nature of his business whereas the ordinary purposes for which goods are used are those envisaged in the concept of merchantability and go to uses which are customarily made of the goods in question. For example, shoes are generally used for the purpose of walking upon ordinary ground, but a seller may know that a particular pair was selected to be used for climbing mountains. UCC 2–315, Comment 2.

Why does the implied warranty of merchantability only apply to merchants? Why is the implied warranty of fitness for a particular purpose limited to occasions where the buyer is relying on the seller's skill or judgment?

(2) LIMITATIONS OF WARRANTIES AND REMEDIES: CONTRACTS OF ADHESION?

The *implicit* warranties of UCC 2–314 and UCC 2–315 are default rules (presumed in the absence of express agreement to the contrary) which the parties are free to contract around. But the UCC (and other statutes governing consumer contracts) govern the method that the parties must use to contract and at times the extent to which the warranties or the remedies for breach of the warranties can be disclaimed. UCC 2–316 says in part:

> (2) Subject to subsection (3), to exclude or modify the implied warranty of merchantability or any part of it the language must mention merchantability and in case of a writing must be conspicuous, and to exclude or modify any implied warranty of fitness the exclusion must be by a writing and conspicuous. Language to exclude all implied warranties of fitness is sufficient if it states, for example, that "There are no warranties which extend beyond the description on the face hereof."

> (3) Notwithstanding subsection (2)

(a) unless the circumstances indicate otherwise, all implied warranties are excluded by expressions like "as is", "with all faults" or other language which in common understanding calls the buyer's attention to the exclusion of warranties and makes plain that there is no implied warranty; and

(b) when the buyer before entering into the contract has examined the goods or the sample or model as fully as he desired or has refused to examine the goods there is no implied warranty with regard to defects which an examination ought in the circumstances to have revealed to him . . . .

Thus, to disclaim the implied warranty of merchantability, a seller must either conspicuously use the shibboleth, "merchantability" or use words which clearly disclaim all implicit warranties.

The underlying premise that both buyer and seller are freely consenting to the warranty disclaimer may be belied by the pre-printed, non-negotiable nature of the seller's offer. Nowhere is concerns about "contracts of adhesion" greater than with provisions disclaiming warranties and/or limiting remedies. See Todd D. Rakoff, *Contracts of Adhesion: An Essay in Reconstruction*, 96 Harv. L. Rev. 1174 (1983).

Remember, in Revised Article 2 (1997), the warranty sections are renumbered and put in a new Part 4. The substance, however, is essentially the same.

Henningsen v. Bloomfield Motors

Supreme Court of New Jersey, 1960.
32 N.J. 358, 161 A.2d 69.

[Helen Henningsen, the wife of the purchaser, Claus Henningsen, was held to be entitled to recover for personal injury against both the dealer, Bloomfield Motors, and the manufacturer, Chrysler Corporation. In a landmark decision, the court held that lack of privity would not bar Mrs. Henningsen's suit. The influence of the case would have been even greater had there not emerged a short time later a nonwarranty alternative for those injured by a defective product unreasonably dangerous to the user or consumer or to his or her property. See Restatement (Second) of Torts, 402A (strict liability in tort). The court also invalidated a disclaimer of warranty clause in the contract, a clause which purported to limit warranty protection to the purchaser and to the replacement of defective parts. In concluding that Chrysler's attempted disclaimer of an implied warranty of merchantability is so inimical to the public good as to compel an adjudication of its invalidity, the court spoke as follows:]

* * *

[W]hat effect should be given to the express warranty in question which seeks to limit the manufacturer's liability to replacement of defective parts, and which disclaims all other warranties, express or implied? In assessing its significance we must keep in mind the general principle that, in the absence of fraud, one who does not choose to read a contract before signing it, cannot later relieve himself of its burdens. Fivey v. Pennsylvania R.R. Co., 67 N.J.L. 627, 52 A. 472 (E. & A.1902). And in applying that principle, the basic tenet of freedom of competent parties to contract is a factor of importance. But in the framework of modern commercial life and business practices, such rules cannot be applied on a strict doctrinal basis. The conflicting interests of the buyer and seller must be evaluated realistically and justly, giving due weight to the social policy evinced by the Uniform Sales Act, the progressive decisions of the courts engaged in administering it, the mass production methods of manufacture and distribution to the public, and the bargaining position occupied by the ordinary consumer in such an economy. This history of the law shows that legal doctrines, as first expounded, often prove to be inadequate under the impact of later experience. In such case, the need for justice has stimulated the necessary qualifications or adjustments. . . .

* * * As we have said, warranties originated in the law to safeguard the buyer and not to limit the liability of the seller or manufacturer. It seems obvious in this instance that the motive was to avoid the warranty obligations which are normally incidental to such sales. The language gave little and withdrew much. In return for the delusive remedy of replacement of defective parts at the factory, the buyer is said to have accepted the exclusion of the maker's liability for personal injuries arising from the breach of the warranty, and to have agreed to the elimination of any other express or implied warranty. An instinctively felt sense of justice cries out against such a sharp bargain. But does the doctrine that a person is bound by his signed agreement, in the absence of fraud, stand in the way of any relief?

In the modern consideration of problems such as this, Corbin suggests that practically all judges are "chancellors" and cannot fail to be influenced by any equitable doctrines that are available. And he opines that "there is sufficient flexibility in the concepts of fraud, duress, misrepresentation and undue influence, not to mention differences in economic bargaining power" to enable the courts to avoid enforcement of unconscionable provisions in long printed standardized contracts. 1 Corbin on Contracts (1950) § 128, p. 188. Freedom of contract is not such an immutable doctrine as to admit of no qualification in the area in which we are concerned. * * *

The traditional contract is the result of free bargaining of parties who are brought together by the play of the market, and who meet each other on a footing of approximate economic equality. In such a society there is no danger that freedom of contract will be a threat to the social order as a whole. But in present-day commercial life the standardized mass contract has appeared. It is used primarily by enterprises with strong bargaining power and position. * * * Such standardized contracts have been described as those in which one predominant party will dictate its law to an undetermined multiple rather than to an individual. They are said to resemble a law rather than a meeting of the minds. Siegelman v. Cunard White Star, 221 F.2d 189, 206 (2 Cir.1955). * * *

The warranty before us is a standardized form designed for mass use. It is imposed upon the automobile consumer. He takes it or leaves it, and he must take it to buy an automobile. No bargaining is engaged in with respect to it. In fact, the dealer through whom it comes to the buyer is without authority to alter it; his function is ministerial—simply to deliver it. The form warranty is not only standard with Chrysler but, as mentioned above, it is the uniform warranty of the Automobile Manufacturers Association. * * *

The gross inequality of bargaining position occupied by the consumer in the automobile industry is thus apparent. There is no competition among the car makers in the area of the express warranty. Where can the buyer go to negotiate for better protection? Such control and limitation of his remedies are inimical to the public welfare and, at the very least, call for great care by the courts to avoid injustice through application of strict common-law principles of freedom of contract. Because there is no competition among the motor vehicle manufacturers with respect to the scope of protection guaranteed to the buyer, there is no incentive on their part to stimulate good will in that field of public relations. Thus, there is lacking a factor existing in more competitive fields, one which tends to guarantee the safe construction of the article sold. Since all competitors operate in the same way, the urge to be careful is not so pressing. . . .

Although the courts, with few exceptions, have been most sensitive to problems presented by contracts resulting from gross disparity in buyer-seller bargaining positions, they have not articulated a general principle condemning, as opposed to public policy, the imposition on the buyer of a skeleton warranty as a means of limiting the responsibility of the manufacturer. They have endeavored thus far to avoid a drastic departure from age-old tenets of freedom of contract by adopting doctrines of strict construction, and notice and knowledgeable assent by the buyer to the attempted exculpation of the seller . . . .

The rigid scrutiny which the courts give to attempted limitations of warranties and of the liability that would normally flow from a transaction is not limited to the field of sales of goods. Clauses on baggage checks restricting the liability of common carriers for loss or damage in transit are not enforceable unless the limitation is fairly and honestly negotiated and understandingly entered into. If not called specifically to the patron's attention, it is not binding. It is not enough merely to show the form of a contract; it must appear also that the agreement was understandingly made. . . . The same holds true in cases of such limitations on parcel check room tickets, . . . and on storage warehouse receipts, . . . on automobile parking lot or garage tickets or claim checks; . . . as to exculpatory clauses in leases releasing a landlord of apartments in a multiple dwelling house from all liability for negligence where inequality of bargaining exists, see Annotation, 175 A.L.R. 8 (1948). * * *

It is true that the rule governing the limitation of liability cases last referred to is generally applied in situations said to involve services of a public or semi-public nature. Typical, of course, are the public carrier or storage or parking lot cases. Kuzmiak v. Brookchester, 33 N.J.Super. 575, 111 A.2d 425 (App.Div.1955); Annotation, supra, 175 A.L.R. at pp. 14–17. But in recent times the books have not been barren of instances of its application in private contract controversies, witness, e.g., Kuzmiak v. Brookchester, supra; Fairfax Gas & Supply Co. v. Hadary, 151 F.2d 939 (4 Cir.1945); and Cutler Corp. v. Latshaw, supra. In the last named matter, which has been noted earlier, the court relied upon the public interest cases as authority. It said:

"Although these cases have to do with limitation on the liability of common carriers, their reasoning applies with equal force to the facts in the case at bar. When a party to a contract seeks to bind the other party with the unyielding thongs of a warrant of attorney-confession of judgment, a device not ordinarily expected by a homeowner in a simple agreement for alterations and repairs, the inclusion of such a self-abnegating provision must appear in the body of the contract and cannot be incorporated by casual reference with a designation not its own." 97 A.2d at page 238.

Basically, the reason a contracting party offering services of a public or *quasi*-public nature has been held to the requirements of fair dealing, and, when it attempts to limit its liability, of securing the understanding consent of the patron or consumer, is because members of the public generally have no other means of fulfilling the specific need represented by the contract. Having in mind the situation in the automobile industry as detailed above, and particularly the fact that the limited warranty extended by the manufacturers is a uniform one, there would appear to be no just reason why the principles of all of the cases set forth should not chart the course to be taken here.

The task of the judiciary is to administer the spirit as well as the letter of the law. On issues such as the present one, part of that burden is to protect the ordinary man against the loss of important rights through what, in effect, is the unilateral act of the manufacturer. The status of the automobile industry is unique. Manufacturers are few in number and strong in bargaining position. In the matter of warranties on the sale of their products, the Automotive Manufacturers Association has enabled them to present a united front. From the standpoint of the purchaser, there can be no arms length negotiating on the subject. Because his capacity for bargaining is so grossly unequal, the inexorable conclusion which follows is that he is not permitted to bargain at all. He must take or leave the automobile on the warranty terms dictated by the maker. He cannot turn to a competitor for better security.

Public policy is a term not easily defined. Its significance varies as the habits and needs of a people may vary. It is not static and the field of application is an ever increasing one. A contract, or a particular provision therein, valid in one era may be wholly opposed to the public policy of another. ... Courts keep in mind the principle that the best interests of society demand that persons should not be unnecessarily restricted in their freedom to contract. But they do not hesitate to declare void as against public policy contractual provisions which clearly tend to the injury of the public in some way.

NOTES

(1) Was the court correct in concluding that there was no competition among the car makers in the area of the express warranty?

(2) Did the consumer have an opportunity to avoid bearing the risk—possibly by contracting with a third party?

(3) Does the uniform usage of a clause among all car manufacturers tend to establish unconscionability or is it a sign of a competitive market?

(4) "Sellers of 'hard goods'—appliances, machines—supply warranty clauses whose central features vary little across industries. These standard clauses (i) disclaim all implied warranties; (ii) expressly warrant the goods against defects in material and workmanship; (iii) limit the buyer's remedies, should the express warranty be breached, to the repair or replacement of defective parts, with the seller having the option of which remedy to use; (iv) limit the time within which claims under the express warranty can be made; (v) exclude liability for consequential damages." Alan Schwartz & Robert E. Scott, Commercial Transactions: Principles and Policies 204 (2d ed. 1991). Are these "central features" efficient? Equitable? See Chapter Six, Section 5(B) for a case dealing with this standard "warranty package."

(5) *Personal injury resulting from breach of warranty.* Article 2 includes as consequential damages resulting from a seller's breach "injury to person and property proximately resulting from any breach of warranty." UCC 2–715(2)(b) [UCC 2–806 (1997)]. Beyond that, two other sections deal with personal injury claims, UCC 2–719(3) [UCC 2–810(c) (1997)], providing that agreements excluding liability for personal injuries are "prima facie unconscionable," and UCC 2–318, providing three alternative limitations on the defense of "no privity of contract" where foreseeable users (Mrs. Henningsen) or subpurchasers are involved. Thus, Mrs. Henningsen would have a personal injury claim in strict tort liability in most states and, to the extent that tort law is not preemptive, a warranty claim under Article 2. Whether the seller's effort to disclaim warranties, express or implied is enforceable (as opposed to excluding liability for personal injury damages), would be tested under UCC 2–316(2) [UCC 2–407 (1997)], and the general section on Unconscionability. UCC 2–302 [UCC 2–105 (1997)].

As this edition goes to press, the American Law Institute has nearly completed a Restatement (Third) Torts, Products Liability and the revision of Article 2 should be completed by the Summer of 1998. How the overlap between warranty and tort law will be accommodated where personal injuries and property are involved has not been finally resolved. From the perspective of Article 2, the following outcome is likely: (1) If the condition in the goods causing damage to person or property is a "defect" under tort law, then tort law rather than Article 2 will apply; (2) Whether the goods are defective or not, the buyer will still have an opportunity to establish that the condition also breached an express or implied warranty, i.e., that the expectations created by express or implied representations were disappointed; and (3) If a breach of warranty is established, the buyer must satisfy the usual conditions in Article 2 for the proof of that claim, i.e., reasonable notice, privity of contract, statute of limitations and the absence of a valid disclaimer, except that agreements excluding liability for personal injuries are still "prima facie" unconscionable. A leading but controversial case supporting this approach in general is Denny v. Ford Motor Co., 87 N.Y.2d 248, 639 N.Y.S.2d 250, 662 N.E.2d 730 (1995).

Murray v. Holiday Rambler, Inc.

Supreme Court of Wisconsin, 1978.
83 Wis.2d 406, 265 N.W.2d 513.

■ CONNOR T. HANSEN, J. On January 23, 1974, the plaintiffs purchased a 22–foot 1973 Avenger motor home for a total sales price, including sales tax, license fees and trade-in allowance on another motor home owned by the plaintiffs, of $11,007.15. * * *

The document signed by Mr. Murray purported to exclude all warranties, express or implied.... The reverse side of this document stated:

MANUFACTURER'S UNDERTAKING—AVENGER CORPORATION

THERE ARE NO WARRANTIES EXPRESSED OR IMPLIED AND PARTICULARLY THERE ARE NO WARRANTIES OF MERCHANT-ABILITY OR FITNESS FOR A PARTICULAR PURPOSE MADE BY AVENGER CORPORATION FOR ITS PRODUCTS.

AVENGER CORPORATION, as the manufacturer, in lieu thereof undertakes and agrees that the product identified on the Pre–Delivery and Acceptance Declaration (reverse side) was free of defects in material and workmanship at the time of its delivery to the dealer and the initial user and owner; and * * *

If such Avenger product or its component parts (other than tires) shall fail within one year from the date of delivery to the original user because the product or component part was defective when installed; and

If the owner-user will return the trailer to a service facility authorized by Avenger Corporation within fifty-two (52) weeks after initial delivery, *Avenger Corporation will in the method it determines to be necessary replace, or repair, at its sole option any such defective product or component at its own cost and expense.*

THERE ARE NO OTHER WARRANTIES OF ANY KIND, EXPRESS OR IMPLIED, AND NO OTHER OBLIGATIONS, EITHER EXPRESS OR IMPLIED, INCLUDING SPECIFICALLY ANY OBLIGATION FOR INCIDENTAL EXPENSES OF ANY NATURE UNDERTAKEN BY AVENGER CORPORATION AS THE MANUFACTURER. (Emphasis added.)

* * * [W]here the limited remedy fails of its essential purpose, the limitation will be disregarded and ordinary UCC remedies will be available. Sec. 402.719(2), Stats. The purpose of an exclusive remedy of repair or replacement, from the buyer's standpoint, is to give him goods which conform to the contract—in this case, a motor home substantially free of defects—within a reasonable time after a defect is discovered.

> [E]very buyer has the right to assume his new car, with the exception of minor adjustments, will be 'mechanically new and factory furnished, operate perfectly, and be free of substantial defects' ... After the purchase of an automobile, the same should be put in good running condition; that is the seller does not have an unlimited time for the performance of the obligation to replace and repair parts. The buyer of an automobile is not bound to permit the seller to tinker with the article indefinitely in the hope that it may ultimately be made to comply with the warranty. 46 Am. Jur. Sales @ 732; 77 C.J.S. Sales @ 340. At some point in time, if major problems continue to plague the automobile, it must become obvious to all people that a particular vehicle simply cannot be repaired or parts replaced so that the same is made free of defect...." Orange Motors of Coral Gables v. Dade Co. Dairies, 258 So.2d 319, 320, 321 (Fla.App.1972).

Although individual nonconformities may not be substantial in and of themselves, the obligation to repair or replace parts may fail of its essential purpose where the cumulative effect of all the nonconformities substantially impairs the value of the goods to the buyer. Zoss v. Royal Chevrolet, Inc., 11 U.C.C. Rep. 527, 532 (Ind.Super.1972).

Where the seller is given reasonable opportunity to correct the defect or defects, and the vehicle nevertheless fails to operate as should a new vehicle free of defects, the limited remedy fails of its essential purpose. See, Soo Line Railroad Co. v. Fruehauf Corp. (8th Cir.1977), 547 Fed.2d 1365. The buyer may then invoke any of the remedies available under the UCC, including the right to revoke acceptance of the goods, under sec. 2–608 of the UCC (sec. 402.608, Stats.). * * *

The testimony favorable to the verdict showed the following: Mr. Murray experienced problems with the lights and battery of the vehicle on the day he took possession and, although repairs were attempted, the lights continued to dim, the electrical system went dead on several occasions, and the generator did not charge the battery properly. The wiring of an outdoor light short-circuited where it passed through a sharp-edged metal wall. There were problems with the clock. There was an exposed, allegedly non-energized, 120–volt wire coming from the main electrical panel. Plaintiffs' expert witness testified that the wiring in the 12–volt electrical system was of an insufficient gauge for the type of fuses used by the manufacturer, that this wiring was not in conformity with the applicable electrical code, and that there was a danger of overheating in the electrical system.

The original gas tank and an auxiliary gas tank, installed by KOA [the authorized Holiday Rambler dealer from who Murray bought the motor home] at the Murrays' request prior to delivery, were both apparently improperly vented. As a result, it was extremely difficult to fill the tanks; gasoline would spew out of the tanks when the caps were removed; and gasoline fumes came up into the passenger compartment. Mr. Murray testified that on one occasion, service station attendants were able to put only twenty cents' worth of gasoline into both tanks. Apparently as a result of problems with the carburetor, the vehicle would stall. Dirt and soldering flux were found in the fuel filter, which was replaced, as was the fuel pump.

There were problems with the air suspension system. There was testimony that this resulted in uneven distribution of weight on the tandem set of wheels in the rear of the vehicle, putting insufficient weight on the front wheels and causing steering problems. Repairs were made to the suspension system, but the steering problems persisted. Mr. Murray complained that the front brakes were not operating properly, and despite adjustments, had difficulty with the front wheels.

KOA apparently remedied various problems with the furnace and refrigerator, with an oil filter, and with a rattling engine cowling. KOA corrected the LP fuel tank gauge, which, as installed at the factory, indicated "full" when the tank was empty, and vice versa; KOA also supplied a missing handle for the tank and drained water which was inside the tank when it left the factory.

Unusual pressure caused a water line to come uncoupled. Mr. Murray advised KOA about this problem but repaired it himself.

There was also testimony regarding problems with folding seats, the furnace fan, the exhaust fan above the stove, a splash board which came unfastened, and the oven door, which fell off. Although there was conflicting testimony as to whether these parts were defective, the testimony of the Murrays with regard to these problems was not inherently incredible. * * *

Although the Murrays agreed that KOA had never refused to attempt a requested repair, this testimony does not affect their right to revoke acceptance. The limited remedy of repair or replacement of defective parts fails of its essential purpose whenever, despite reasonable opportunity for repair, the goods are not restored to a nondefective condition within a reasonable time, whether or not the failure to do so is willful. * * *

The jury awarded the plaintiffs $2,500 for loss of use of the motor home from the date of revocation of acceptance, August 15, 1974, to the date of the verdict. KOA argues that the plaintiffs were precluded by the terms of the limited warranty from recovering any incidental or consequential damages, including any damages for loss of use of the vehicle.

Where the exclusive limited remedy of the contract fails of its essential purpose, however, the buyer is entitled to invoke any of the remedies available under the UCC. Sec. 402.719(2), Stats. This includes the right to recover consequential damages under sec. 402.715.

Consequential damages include any loss caused by general or particular needs of the buyer of which the seller had reason to know at the time of contracting and which could not reasonably be prevented by cover or otherwise. Sec. 402.715(1), Stats. Consequential damages have specifically been held to include damages for loss of use of an inoperable motor vehicle. Bob Anderson Pontiac, Inc. v. Davidson (Ind.App.1973), 293 N.E.2d 232. * * *

The defendant, KOA, relies upon Russo v. Hilltop Lincoln–Mercury, Inc. (Mo.App.1972), 479 S.W.2d 211. There, defective wiring had caused an automobile to be totally burned. The Missouri Court of Appeals held that, because the car could not be repaired, the limited warranty remedy of repair or replacement of defective parts was inapplicable. Accordingly, the buyer was allowed to recover, not merely the replacement cost of the defective wiring, but rather the full value of the car.

Implicit in this holding was a determination that the limited warranty remedy had failed of its essential purpose. Nevertheless, when the Missouri court turned to the buyer's claim for damages for the rental cost of a replacement car, the court held that such damages were excluded by the terms of the warranty and that this exclusion had not failed of its essential purpose.

This result is inconsistent with the many decisions which have held that consequential damages may be recovered where a limited contractual remedy excluding such damages has failed. . . . Moreover, the result of the Russo Case, supra, which permitted the buyer to recover some UCC damages but not others, is inconsistent with the apparent intention of the drafters. Sec. 402.719(2), Stats., provides that once a limited remedy fails of its essential purpose "remedy may be had as provided in this code." In such a case the exclusive contractual remedy " . . . must give way to the general remedy provision of this Article [chapter 402, Stats.]." Official Comment 1, sec. 2–719 UCC.

Thus, although an express warranty excludes consequential damages, when the exclusive contractual remedy fails, the buyer may recover consequential damages under sec. 402.715, Stats., as though the limitation had never existed. [The court found, however, that plaintiff failed to prove that the loss of use caused $2500 in damages and awarded plaintiffs $500.]

NOTES

(1) Was the seller unreasonable in not replacing the motor home? Should good faith attempts to repair be a defense? For a case dealing with similar problems in a commercial rather than a consumer contract, see Lewis Refrigeration Co. v. Sawyer Fruit, Vegetable and Cold Storage Co., infra at Chapter Six, Section 5(B).

(2) *Research exercise.* A number of states have either amended the UCC or enacted separate legislation to prohibit warranty disclaimers in consumer sales. Even more states have passed immutable "lemon laws" that permit consumers to return new cars that dealers cannot repair. Check the relevant statutes of the state where you intend to practice and report your findings.

(3) The Magnuson–Moss Warranty Act provides that "No supplier may disclaim . . . any implied warranty to a consumer . . . [if] such supplier makes

any written warranty...." 15 U.S.C. § 2808(a) (1976). Section (b), however, provides that "implied warranties may be limited in duration to the duration of a written [express] warranty of reasonable duration, if such limitation is conscionable and is set for in clear and unmistakable language and prominently displayed on the face of the warranty."

Magnuson Moss also requires sellers to disclose whether their warranties are "full" or "limited." A "full" warranty does not limit the duration of implied warranties; requires the warrantor to remedy defects within a reasonable time at no extra charge to the consumer; permits consumers to rescind or obtain a new product if the item sold cannot be conveniently repaired; and requires any exclusion of consequential damages to be stated in conspicuous language. All other warranties are "limited." 15 U.S.C. §§ 2303–2304 (1976):

> This disclosure requirement seeks to increase the warranty coverage available to consumers in two ways. First, Congress hoped that firms would be embarrassed to describe their warranties as "limited" and so would make "full" warranties. Almost all firms, however, offer only "limited" warranties, apparently interpreting "full" to mean "too much." Second, if the concise labels "full" and "limited" would succinctly communicate to consumers the scope of warranty coverage, consumers could compare the coverage of different firms at greatly reduced cost.... But because almost all firms use limited warranties, ... [There is] no more information than existed before passage of the Act.

Alan Schwartz & Robert E. Scott, Commercial Transactions: Principles and Policies 226 (2d ed. 1991).

(4) In consumer contracts, Article 2 occupies an uneasy position between federal law, the Magnuson–Moss Warranty Act, and the state lemon laws: The former is inadequate unless a "full" warranty is offered and the latter is limited to new car sales. Section 2–811(b)(1997), in an attempt to bolster consumer protection in the gap, provides: "If, because of a breach of contract or other circumstances, an exclusive, agreed remedy fails substantially to achieve the intended purposes of the parties, the following rules apply:.... (2) In a consumer contract, an aggrieved party may reject the goods or revoke acceptance and, to the extent of the failure, may resort to all remedies under this Article."

SECTION 3. CHANGED CIRCUMSTANCES: IMPRACTICABILITY

The risk allocation problems treated in this section are suggested by a familiar hypothetical. Suppose that S has sold goods to B and agreed to have them transported to a port on the Gulf of Aden by a specified date. S then contracts with C, a shipping company, to pick up the goods in Galveston, Texas and transport them to the Gulf of Aden by the specified date for a fixed price of $50,000. After the ship was underway and just as it was entering the Mediterranean Sea, word was received that due to a flare up of hostilities in the Middle East, the Suez Canal had been closed indefinitely. C informed S of this event and offered to transport the goods to their destination via the Cape of Good Hope, a trip that would cost C

$100,000 more than the agreed contract price and would delay delivery by two weeks. S refused the offer to modify the contract and insisted that C complete the contract of carriage via the Cape at the original contract price and pay any damages caused by the delay. C then broke off discussions and returned to Galveston with the goods. S sued for damages caused by C's alleged breach of contract and C countered with the defense that performance was excused by a changed circumstance, the closing of the Suez Canal. How should this case be resolved?

In approaching this question, analysis is aided if the following questions are asked and answered.

First, what was the nature of the risk event and what was its impact on the contractual relationship? Was the "event" a condition which existed at the time of contracting or a circumstance which arose thereafter? Was the impact of the event that performance as agreed was prevented or made more costly, or that the incentive of one party to perform was impaired because its purpose in entering the contract was frustrated?

Second, was the party seeking relief at "fault" in that it caused the event or failed to take reasonable steps either to avoid it or to minimize the impact?

Third, if the party seeking relief was not at "fault," did the agreement allocate the risk of the event to one or the other or both parties? The form of agreement may include an express condition, an "excuse" or *force majeure* clause[1] or a more elaborate risk allocation system, including insurance. Or it may be concluded that because the risk was discussed or foreshadowed in the negotiations, it was "tacitly" agreed to by the promisor who made an unconditional promise to perform at a fixed price.[2]

Fourth, if there was no agreement, express or implied, allocating the risk, how is the court to fill the "gap" in risk allocation? One method is for the court to refuse to impose any risk allocation terms on the parties. In short, the maker of an unconditional promise bears the full risk of the event and its impact. A more flexible test, adopted by Section 261 of Restatement (Second), is as follows:

1. Here is an example of such a clause:
EXCUSABLE DELAY:

Shipper shall not be responsible nor deemed to be in default on account of delays in performance of this Agreement due to causes beyond Shipper's control and not occasioned by its fault or negligence, including but not being limited to civil war, insurrections, strikes, riots, fires, floods, explosions, earthquakes, serious accidents, and any act of government, acts of God or the public enemy, failure of transportation, epidemics, quarantine restrictions, failure of vendors or other shippers to perform their contracts or labor troubles causing cessation, slowdown, or interruption of work, provided such cause is beyond Shipper's control.

See Eastern Air Lines, Inc. v. McDonnell Douglas Corp., 532 F.2d 957, 988 (5th Cir. 1976).

2. See UCC 2–615, Comment 8; Barbarossa & Sons, Inc. v. Iten Chevrolet, Inc., 265 N.W.2d 655 (Minn.1978) (seller tacitly assumes a material risk foreseen at the time of contracting as a "real possibility" by failing explicitly to provide against it in the agreement); Harper & Associates v. Printers, Inc., 46 Wash.App. 417, 730 P.2d 733 (1986).

> Where, after a contract is made, a party's performance is made impracticable without his fault by the occurrence of an event the non-occurrence of which was a basic assumption on which the contract was made, his duty to render that performance is discharged, unless the language or the circumstances indicate the contrary.

Note that the test applies in the absence of "fault" by the party seeking relief or "language or circumstances" to the contrary. Note, also, that the test has two parts: (1) The non-occurrence of the event must have been a basic assumption on which the contract was made; and (2) the event must make performance "impracticable." The Restatement (Second) test, derived from UCC 2–615(a), governs whether the event existed at the time of contracting, Section 266, occurred after contract formation, Section 261, or frustrated the purpose of the party seeking relief rather than made performance impracticable, Section 265.

Fifth, what is the nature and scope of relief when the conditions of Section 261 or UCC 2–615(a) are satisfied? Is relief limited to discharge of the contract with appropriate restitution or must the parties continue performance under terms adjusted by the court to reflect the risk? Is there a remedial middle ground?

Sixth, suppose, in our hypothetical, that S accepted C's offer to modify the contract by agreement. Would that modification be enforceable? Suppose that the advantaged party refused to negotiate over a proposed modification. Would that ever be bad faith?

Keep these questions in mind as you search for answers in the following materials. Remember that the problem is far more complex and controversial than the effort to excuse a condition for unjust forfeiture or to determine what is bad faith in the exercise of performance discretion. To some, too much excuse undermines the stability of contracts, reallocates risks already insured against in an inefficient manner and invites courts to "make" contracts that the parties could and should have made for themselves. Thus, despite sound analysis and a flexible test for excuse, you should not be surprised to discover that there is considerable judicial talk about granting relief but precious little evidence that relief has been granted. This was the sad lesson learned by the carriers in the litigation that followed the two occasions when, due to hostilities, the Suez Canal was closed.[3]

---

3. The litigation following two earlier Suez Canal closings produced results against the interest of the ship owner. In short, they were held to have assumed the risk of the event and the extra costs that ensued. See, e.g., American Trading & Production Corp. v. Shell International Marine Ltd., 453 F.2d 939 (2d Cir.1972); Transatlantic Financing Corp. v. United States, 124 U.S.App.D.C. 183, 363 F.2d 312 (1966). The general problem, English cases and the special problems of international trade are well discussed in Birmingham, *A Second Look at the Suez Canal Cases: Excuse for Nonperformance of Contractual Obligations in the Light of Economic Theory,* 20 Hastings L.J. 1393 (1969); Schlegal, *Of Nuts, and Ships and Sealing Wax, Suez and Frustrating Things—The Doctrine of Impossibility of Performance,* 23 Rutgers L.Rev. 419 (1969); Berman, *Excuse for Nonperformance in the Light of Contract Practices in International Trade,* 63 Colum.L.Rev. 1413 (1963).

(A) EXISTING IMPRACTICABILITY

Mineral Park Land Co. v. Howard

Supreme Court of California, 1916.
172 Cal. 289, 156 P. 458.

■ SLOSS, J. The defendants appeal from a judgment in favor of plaintiff for $3,650. The appeal is on the judgment roll alone.

The plaintiff was the owner of certain land in the ravine or wash known as the Arroyo Seco, in South Pasadena, Los Angeles county. The defendants had made a contract with the public authorities for the construction of a concrete bridge across the Arroyo Seco. In August, 1911, the parties to this action entered into a written agreement whereby the plaintiff granted to the defendants the right to haul gravel and earth from plaintiff's land, the defendants agreeing to take therefrom all of the gravel and earth necessary in the construction of the fill and cement work on the proposed bridge, the required amount being estimated at approximately 114,000 cubic yards. Defendants agreed to pay 5 cents per cubic yard for the first 80,000 yards, the next 10,000 yards were to be given free of charge, and the balance was to be paid for at the rate of 5 cents per cubic yard.

The complaint was in two counts. The first alleged that the defendants had taken 50,131 cubic yards of earth and gravel, thereby becoming indebted to plaintiff in the sum of $2,506.55, of which only $900 had been paid, leaving a balance of $1,606.55 due. The findings support plaintiff's claim in this regard, and there is no question of the propriety of so much of the judgment as responds to the first count. The second count sought to recover damages for the defendants' failure to take from plaintiff's land any more than the 50,131 yards.

It alleged that the total amount of earth and gravel used by defendants was 101,000 cubic yards, of which they procured 50,869 cubic yards from some place other than plaintiff's premises. The amount due the plaintiff for this amount of earth and gravel would, under the terms of the contract, have been $2,043.45. The count charged that plaintiff's land contained enough earth and gravel to enable the defendants to take therefrom the entire amount required, and that the 50,869 yards not taken had no value to the plaintiff. Accordingly the plaintiff sought, under this head, to recover damages in the sum of $2,043.45.

The answer denied that the plaintiff's land contained any amount of earth and gravel in excess of the 50,131 cubic yards actually taken, and alleged that the defendants took from the said land all of the earth and gravel available for the work mentioned in the contract.

As Judge Mulligan put it: "Matters involving impossibility or impracticability of performance of contract are concededly vexing and difficult. One is even urged on the allocation of such risks to pray for the 'Wisdom of Solomon.' . . . [and rely upon] the efficacy of prayer." 453 F.2d at 944.

The court found that the plaintiff's land contained earth and gravel far in excess of 101,000 cubic yards of earth and gravel, but that only 50,131 cubic yards, the amount actually taken by the defendants, was above the water level. No greater quantity could have been taken "by ordinary means," or except by the use, at great expense, of a steam dredger, and the earth and gravel so taken could not have been used without first having been dried at great expense and delay. On the issue raised by the plea of defendants that they took all the earth and gravel that was available the court qualified its findings in this way: It found that the defendants did take all of the available earth and gravel from plaintiff's premises, in this, that they took and removed "all that could have been taken advantageously to defendants, or all that was practical to take and remove from a financial standpoint"; that any greater amount could have been taken only at a prohibitive cost, that is, at an expense of 10 or 12 times as much as the usual cost per yard. It is also declared that the word "available" is used in the findings to mean capable of being taken and used advantageously. It was not "advantageous or practical" to have taken more material from plaintiff's land, but it was not impossible. There is a finding that the parties were not under any mutual misunderstanding regarding the amount of available gravel, but that the contract was entered into without any calculation on the part of either of the parties with reference to the amount of available earth and gravel on the premises.

The single question is whether the facts thus found justified the defendants in their failure to take from the plaintiff's land all of the earth and gravel required. This question was answered in the negative by the court below. The case was apparently thought to be governed by the principle—established by a multitude of authorities—that where a party has agreed, without qualification, to perform an act which is not in its nature impossible of performance, he is not excused by difficulty of performance, or by the fact that he becomes unable to perform.

It is, however, equally well settled that, where performance depends upon the existence of a given thing, and such existence was assumed as the basis of the agreement, performance is excused to the extent that the thing ceases to exist or turns out to be nonexistent. 1 Beach, Contr. § 217; 9 Cyc. 631. Thus, where the defendants had agreed to pasture not less than 3,000 cattle on plaintiff's land, paying therefor $1 for each and every head so pastured, and it developed that the land did not furnish feed for more than 717 head, the number actually put on the land by defendant, it was held that plaintiff could not recover the stipulated sum for the difference between the cattle pastured and the minimum of 3,000 agreed to be pastured. Williams v. Miller, 68 Cal. 290, 9 Pac. 166. Similarly, in Brick Co. v. Pond, 38 Ohio St. 65, where the plaintiff had leased all the "good No. 1 fire clay on his land," subject to the condition that the lessees should mine or pay for not less than 2,000 tons of clay every year, paying therefor 25 cents per ton, the court held that the lessees were not bound to pay for 2,000 tons per year, unless there was No. 1 clay on the land in such quantities as would justify its being taken out. In Ridgely v. Conewago Iron Co. (C.C.) 53 Fed. 988, the holding was that a mining lease requiring the lessee to mine 4,000 tons of ore annually, and to pay therefor a fixed sum per ton, or, failing to take out such quantity, to pay therefor, imposed no obligation on the lessee to pay for such stipulated quantity after the ore in the demised premises had become exhausted. There are many other cases dealing with mining leases of this character, and the general course of decision is to the effect that the performance of the obligation to take out a given quantity or to pay royalty thereon, if it be not taken out, is excused if it appears that the land does not contain the stipulated quantity.

We think the findings of fact make a case falling within the rule of these decisions. The parties were contracting for the right to take earth and gravel to be used in the construction of the bridge. When they stipulated that all of the earth and gravel needed for this purpose should be taken from plaintiff's land, they contemplated and assumed that the land contained the requisite quantity, available for use. The defendants were not binding themselves to take what was not there. And, in determining whether the earth and gravel were "available," we must view the conditions in a practical and reasonable way. Although there was gravel on the land, it was so situated that the defendants could not take it by ordinary means, nor except at a prohibitive cost. To all fair intents then, it was impossible for defendants to take it.

"A thing is impossible in legal contemplation when it is not practicable; and a thing is impracticable when it can only be done at an excessive and unreasonable cost." 1 Beach on Contr. § 216. We do not mean to intimate that the defendants could excuse themselves by showing the existence of conditions which would make the performance of their obligation more expensive than they had anticipated, or which would entail a loss upon them. But, where the difference in cost is so great as here, and has the effect, as found, of making performance impracticable, the situation is not different from that of a total absence of earth and gravel.

On the facts found, there should have been no recovery on the second count.

The judgment is modified by deducting therefrom the sum of $2,043.45, and, as so modified, it stands affirmed.

■ We concur: SHAW, J.; LAWLOR, J.

NOTES

(1) Section 456 of the first Restatement, entitled "Existing Impossibility," provided that, unless a contrary intention was manifested, a "promise imposes no duty if performance of the promise is impossible because of facts existing when the promise is made of which the promisor neither knows nor has reason to know." The word "impossibility" was defined to include both "strict impossibility" and "impracticability because of extreme and unreasonable difficulty, expense, injury of loss involved." Section 460(1) provided that where the "existence of a specific thing * * * is, either by the terms of a bargain or in the contemplation of both parties necessary for the performance of a promise in the bargain, a duty to perform the promise (a) never arises if at the time the

bargain is made the existence of the thing within the time for seasonable performance is impossible * * *." Which of these sections catches the essence of *Mineral Park v. Howard?* Is it correct to conclude in *Mineral Park* that it was irrelevant which party assumed the risk of the subsurface conditions and that the real question was whether the performance was impracticable?

(2) For modern counterparts of *Mineral Park,* see Mat–Su/Blackard/Stephan & Sons v. State, 647 P.2d 1101 (Alaska 1982) (risk of inadequate gravel allocated by contract to contractor); Beck v. J.M. Smucker Co., 277 Or. 607, 561 P.2d 623 (1977) (subsurface sand).

United States v. Wegematic Corp.

United States Court of Appeals, Second Circuit, 1966.
360 F.2d 674.

■ Before LUMBARD, CHIEF JUDGE, and FRIENDLY and ANDERSON, CIRCUIT JUDGES.

■ FRIENDLY, CIRCUIT JUDGE. The facts developed at trial in the District Court for the Southern District of New York, fully set forth in a memorandum by Judge Graven, can be briefly summarized: In June 1956 the Federal Reserve Board invited five electronics manufacturers to submit proposals for an intermediate-type, general-purpose electronic digital computing system or systems; the invitation stressed the importance of early delivery as a consideration in determining the Board's choice. Defendant, a relative newcomer in the field, which had enjoyed considerable success with a smaller computer known as the ALWAC III–E, submitted a detailed proposal for the sale or lease of a new computer designated as the ALWAC 800. It characterized the machine as "a truly revolutionary system utilizing all of the latest technical advances," and featured that "maintenance problems are minimized by the use of highly reliable magnetic cores for not only the high speed memory but also logical elements and registers." Delivery was offered nine months from the date the contract or purchase order was received. In September the Board acted favorably on the defendant's proposal, ordering components of the ALWAC 800 with an aggregate cost of $231,800. Delivery was to be made on June 30, 1957, with liquidated damages of $100 per day for delay. The order also provided that in the event the defendant failed to comply "with any provision" of the agreement, "the Board may procure the services described in the contract from other sources and hold the Contractor responsible for any excess cost occasioned thereby." Defendant accepted the order with enthusiasm.

The first storm warning was a suggestion by the defendant in March 1957 that the delivery date be postponed. In April it informed the Board by letter that delivery would be made on or before October 30 rather than as agreed, the delay being due to the necessity of "a redesign which we feel has greatly improved this equipment"; waiver of the stipulated damages for delay was requested. The Board took the request under advisement. On August 30 defendant wrote that delivery would be delayed "possibly into 1959"; it suggested use of ALWAC III–E equipment in the interim and waiver of the $100 per day "penalty." The Board also took this request under advisement but made clear it was waiving no rights. In mid-October defendant announced that "due to engineering difficulties it has become impracticable to deliver the ALWAC 800 Computing System at this time"; it requested cancellation of the contract without damages. The Board set about procuring comparable equipment from another manufacturer; on October 6, 1958, International Business Machines Corporation delivered an IBM 650 computer, serving substantially the same purpose as the ALWAC 800, at a rental of $102,000 a year with an option to purchase for $410,450.

In July 1958 the Board advised defendant of its intention to press its claim for damages; this suit followed. The court awarded the United States $46,300 for delay under the liquidated damages clause, $179,450 for the excess cost of the IBM equipment, and $10,056 for preparatory expenses useless in operating the IBM system—a total of $235,806, with 6% interest from October 6, 1958.

The principal point of the defense, which is the sole ground of this appeal, is that delivery was made impossible by "basic engineering difficulties" whose correction would have taken between one and two years and would have cost a million to a million and a half dollars, with success likely but not certain. Although the record does not give an entirely clear notion what the difficulties were, two experts suggested that they may have stemmed from the magnetic cores, used instead of transistors to achieve a solid state machine, which did not have sufficient uniformity at this stage of their development. Defendant contends that under federal law, which both parties concede to govern, see Cargill, Inc. v. Commodity Credit Corp., 275 F.2d 745, 751–753 (2 Cir.1960), the "practical impossibility" of completing the contract excused its defaults in performance.

* * *

We find persuasive the defendant's suggestion of looking to the Uniform Commercial Code as a source for the "federal" law of sales. . . .

Section 2–615 of the UCC, entitled "Excuse by failure of presupposed conditions," provides that:

> "Except so far as a seller may have assumed a greater obligation * * * delay in delivery or non-delivery * * * is not a breach of his duty under a contract for sale if performance as agreed has been made impracticable by the occurrence of a contingency the nonoccurrence of which was a basic assumption on which the contract was made * * *."

The latter part of the test seems a somewhat complicated way of putting Professor Corbin's question of how much risk the promisor assumed. Recent Developments in the Law of Contracts, 50 Harv.L.Rev. 449, 465–66 (1937); 2 Corbin, Contracts § 1333, at 371. We see no basis for thinking that when an electronics system is promoted by its manufacturer as a revolutionary breakthrough, the risk of the revolution's occurrence falls on the purchaser; the reasonable supposition is that it has already occurred or, at least, the manufacturer is assuring the purchaser that it will be found to have when the machine is assembled. As Judge Graven said: "The Board in its invitation for bids did not request invitations to conduct a development program for it. The Board requested invitations from manufacturers for the furnishing of a computer machine." Acceptance of defendant's argument would mean that though a purchaser makes his choice because of the attractiveness of a manufacturer's representation and will be bound by it, the manufacturer is free to express what are only aspirations and gamble on mere probabilities of fulfillment without any risk of liability. In fields of developing technology, the manufacturer would thus enjoy a wide degree of latitude with respect to performance while holding an option to compel the buyer to pay if the gamble should pan out. See Austin Co. v. United States, 314 F.2d 518, 521, 161 Ct.Cl. 76, cert. denied, 375 U.S. 830, 84 S.Ct. 75, 11 L.Ed.2d 62 (1963). We do not think this the common understanding—above all as to a contract where the manufacturer expressly agreed to liquidated damages for delay and authorized the purchaser to resort to other sources in the event of non-delivery. Contrast National Presto Industries, Inc. v. United States, 338 F.2d 99, 106–112, 167 Ct.Cl. 749 (1964), cert. denied, 380 U.S. 962 (1965). If a manufacturer wishes to be relieved of the risk that what looks good on paper may not prove so good in hardware, the appropriate exculpatory language is well known and often used.

Beyond this the evidence of true impracticability was far from compelling. The large sums predicted by defendant's witnesses must be appraised in relation not to the single computer ordered by the Federal Reserve Board, evidently for a bargain price, but to the entire ALWAC 800 program as originally contemplated. Although the record gives no idea what this was, even twenty-five machines would gross $10,000,000 if priced at the level of the comparable IBM equipment. While the unanticipated need for expending $1,000,000 or $1,500,000 on redesign might have made such a venture unattractive, as defendant's management evidently decided, the sums are thus not so clearly prohibitive as it would have them appear. What seemingly did become impossible was on-time performance; the issue whether if defendant had offered prompt rectification of the design, the Government could have refused to give it a chance and still recover not merely damages for delay but also the higher cost of replacement equipment, is not before us.

Affirmed.

NOTES

(1) Excuse issues arise under government contracts when a contractor performing a fixed-price contract claims that it is "impossible" or impracticable to achieve the promised result under the specifications. Normally, the contractor will not be excused under the contract "default" clause or other standard risk allocation clauses. See, e.g., 32 C.F.R. 7:12, § 7.103(11) (fixed-price supply contract). See also Austin Co. v. United States, 161 Ct.Cl. 76, 314 F.2d 518 (1963), cert. denied 375 U.S. 830, 84 S.Ct. 75, 11 L.Ed.2d 62 (1963), holding that the contractor assumed the risk if the default clause did not provide an excuse and the contractor agreed to produce a particular result at a fixed-price. As Judge Friendly indicated in *Wegematic,* however, appropriate sections of the Uniform Commercial Code may be used as a source of federal contract law. See

Note, *Federal Common Law and Article 2 of the U.C.C.: A Working Relationship,* 20 B.C.L.Rev. 680 (1979). What "test" for excuse did Judge Friendly adopt in *Wegematic?* If the risk of not achieving the promised result was properly on the contractor, was the court correct in considering whether "performance as agreed" was made impracticable?

(2) If the government has furnished detailed specifications which the contractor must follow ("performance" specifications) or specifications which require a particular result ("design" specifications) and the contractor is unable to perform on time, the risk is placed upon the government if the specifications were "defective" or an implied warranty of "suitability" was made. Here, if the "technical impossibility" makes performance "impracticable, or unfeasible or commercially senseless," the contractor will be excused. J.A. Maurer, Inc. v. United States, 202 Ct.Cl. 813, 485 F.2d 588, 594–96 (1973). Similarly, if the contractor actually completes performance at a cost in excess of the contract price, it will be excused for any delay and compensated for additional costs under the Changes Clause in the contract. See Foster Wheeler Corp. v. United States, 206 Ct.Cl. 533, 513 F.2d 588 (1975). Finally, the government may be liable for extra costs incurred in achieving promised results when contracting officials have failed to disclose material information about performance at the time of contracting under circumstances where the government knew that the contractor was unaware of the information and not likely to find out. See, e.g., Broad Ave. Laundry & Tailoring Co. v. United States, 681 F.2d 746, 750–51 (Ct.Cl.1982). For a useful overview, see Vogel, *Impossibility of Performance—A Closer Look,* 9 Pub.Contract L.J. 110 (1977).

(3) *Subsurface Conditions.* When a contractor encounters unexpected subsurface conditions upon the land of another which delay or increase the cost of performance, the usual rule is that the contractor assumes the risk unless the owner, whether a private party or the government, has agreed to assume the risk, misrepresented the conditions or failed to disclose known difficulties. See, e.g., Carnegie Steel Co. v. United States, 240 U.S. 156, 36 S.Ct. 342, 60 L.Ed. 576 (1916); Rolin v. United States, 142 Ct.Cl. 73, 160 F.Supp. 264 (1958); Stees v. Leonard, 20 Minn. 494 (1874). See also Restatement (Second) § 266, Illus. 8. Impracticability alone is not an excuse: both parties must assume that the conditions did not exist. Compare *Mineral Park v. Howard,* supra. In order to avoid "padded" prices by contractors and the delays incident to disputes over subsurface conditions, the government has developed a standard clause dealing with these risks:

DIFFERING SITE CONDITIONS

(a) The Contractor shall promptly, and before such conditions are disturbed, notify the Contracting Officer in writing of: (1) subsurface or latent physical conditions at the site differing materially from those indicated in this contract, or (2) unknown physical conditions at the site, of an unusual nature, differing materially from those ordinarily encountered and generally recognized as inhering in work of the character provided for in this contract. The Contracting Officer shall promptly investigate the conditions, and if he finds that such conditions do materially so differ and cause an increase or decrease in the Contractor's cost of, or the time required for, performance of any part of the work under this contract, whether or not changed as a result of such conditions, an equitable adjustment shall be made and the contract modified in writing accordingly.

(b) No claim of the Contractor under this clause shall be allowed unless the Contractor has given the notice required in (a) above; *provided,* however, the time prescribed therefor may be extended by the Government.

(c) No claim by the Contractor for an equitable adjustment hereunder shall be allowed if asserted after final payment under this contract.

32 C.F.R. § 7.602.4.

For an excellent discussion of this clause in operation, see Gaskins, *Practical Aspects of the Changed Conditions Clause under Government Construction Contracts,* 5 B.C.Ind. & Com.L.Rev. 79 (1963).

(4) *Existing Impracticability v. Mutual Mistake.* Section 266(1) of Restatement (Second) provides:

> Where, at the time a contract is made, a party's performance under it is impracticable without his fault because of a fact of which he has no reason to know and the non-existence of which is a basic assumption on which the contract is made, no duty to render that performance arises, unless the language or circumstances indicate the contrary.

Section 152(1), on the other hand, provides that a contract is "voidable" by an adversely affected party "where a mistake of both parties at the time the contract was made has a material effect on the agreed exchange of performances" unless he bears the risk under the agreement, or has proceeded with limited knowledge of the facts to which the mistake relates but "treats his limited knowledge as sufficient" or the risk is allocated to him "by the court on the ground that it is reasonable in the circumstances to do so." Section 154. See Roy v. Stephen Pontiac–Cadillac, Inc., 15 Conn.App. 101, 543 A.2d 775, 776–79 (1988) (buyer "had reason to know" that seller could not deliver truck actually ordered). Suppose that you represented the contractor in *Mineral Park v. Howard* and Restatement (Second) was available. Which theory of risk allocation would you pursue, "Existing Impracticability" or "Mutual Mistake"? A question to consider is whether either theory should be applied to circumstances which arise after the contract is formed.

(5) *The Basic Assumption Test.* As revealed in *Wegematic,* UCC 2–615(a) provides that a seller in a contract for the sale of goods is excused for "delay in delivery or non-delivery * * * if performance as agreed has been made impracticable by the occurrence of a contingency the non-occurrence of which was a basic assumption on which the contract was made * * *." Without question, Restatement (Second) has jumped upon the "basic assumption" bandwagon. Whether an existing or supervening event makes performance impracticable or "frustrates" the purpose of one party to the contract, the *"non-occurrence"* of that event or fact must have been "a basic assumption on which the contract was made." See, e.g., Sections 261–66. If it was not, the promisor bears the risk of any impracticability unless the risk was otherwise allocated by agreement. How, then, does one come to grips with this crucial risk allocation test? The Reporter of Restatement (Second), Professor E. Alan Farnsworth, has offered the following guide:

Determining whether the non-occurrence of a particular event was or was not a basic assumption involves a judgment as to which party assumed the risk of its occurrence. In contracting for the manufacture and delivery of goods at a price fixed in the contract, for example, the seller assumes the risk of increased costs within the normal range. If, however, a disaster results in an abrupt tenfold increase in cost to the seller, a court might determine that the seller did not assume this risk by concluding that the non-occurrence of the disaster was a "basic assumption" on which the contract was made. In making such determinations, a court will look at all circumstances, including the terms of the contract. The fact that the event was unforeseeable is significant as suggesting that its non-occurrence was a basic assumption. However, the fact that it was foreseeable, or even foreseen, does not, of itself, argue for a contrary conclusion, since the parties may not have thought it sufficiently important a risk to have made it a subject of their bargaining. Another significant factor may be the relative bargaining positions of the parties and the relative ease with which either party could have included a clause. Another may be the effectiveness of the market in spreading such risks as, for example, where the obligor is a middleman who has an opportunity to adjust his prices to cover them.

Restatement (Second), ch. 11, p. 311.

As we shall see, most courts have focused upon (and become confused by) the "foreseeability" factor. If both parties could neither reasonably foresee the risk event nor its impact or could foresee them as *unlikely* to occur, a court might conclude that the basic assumption test has been satisfied. In short, the event was outside both parties' circle of risk assumption and the question of "impracticability" is now ripe for decision. But both parties may not have equal foresight or lack of it. The promisor may conclude that a risk event is not likely to occur and the promisee may conclude it is highly probable. Or, the event and its impact might be foreshadowed for both during the negotiations. In these cases, the court is likely to conclude that the promisor should have contracted against the risk and a failure to do so means that it was assumed. In either of these situations, it is hard to conclude that both parties assumed that the risk would not occur. Why, then, didn't it contract against the risk? Was it precluded by the other party's superior bargaining power? Or, did it simply "self insure" by devices other than a clause in the particular contract? Look for these issues in the cases that follow. Is Restatement (Second) very helpful? Or, does the "Superior Risk Bearer" analysis, presented in the next note, provide more assistance?

(6) *The "Superior Risk Bearer" Test.* Professor (now Judge) Richard Posner has argued that in all cases of impracticability, the key question is "who should bear the loss resulting from an event that has rendered performance uneconomical" and that the answer, provided by economic analysis, is the party who is the "most efficient bearer of the particular risk in the particular circumstances." Posner and Rosenfield, *Impossibility and Related Doctrines in Contract Law: An Economic Analysis*, 6 J.Leg.Stud. 83, 86, 90 (1977).

The discharge question arises only in those cases where the contract does not assign the risk in question and the event giving rise to the discharge claim was not avoidable by any cost justified precautions. When these threshold conditions have been satisfied, economic analysis suggests that the loss should be placed on the party who is the superior (that is, lower-cost) risk bearer. To determine which party is the superior risk bearer three factors are relevant—knowledge of the magnitude of the loss, knowledge of the probability that it will occur, and (other) costs of self-or market-insurance.

Id. at 117. Risk appraisal costs are incurred in acquiring knowledge of the probability that the event will occur and the magnitude of the loss if it does occur. These costs must be known "in order for the insurer to know how much to ask for from the other party to the contract as compensation for bearing the risk in question." Transaction costs are the "costs involved in eliminating or minimizing the risk through pooling it with other uncertain events * * * either through self-insurance or through the purchase of an insurance policy (market insurance)." Id. at 91–92. Thus, the promisee may be the superior risk bearer when the promisor could not "reasonably have prevented" the event and the promisee could have "insured against the occurrence of the event at a lower cost than the promisor" because it was in the best position to appraise the probability and magnitude of the loss. Id. at 92. Presumably, if the promisor is found to be the superior risk bearer, enforcement of the contract will be both efficient and fair—there is no undue hardship for a superior risk bearer to absorb the extra costs since it was in the best position ex ante to minimize or to avoid them. For an argument that it is less costly to identify and protect against existing rather than supervening risk events, see Kronman, *Mistake, Disclosure, Information, and the Law of Contracts*, 7 J.Leg.Stud. 1, 2–9 (1978) (information is the antidote to mistake). See also Sykes, *The Doctrine of Commercial Impracticability in a Second–Best World*, 19 J.Legal Stud. 43 (1990).

(B) SUPERVENING IMPRACTICABILITY

Taylor v. Caldwell

King's Bench, 1863.
3 B. & S. 826, 122 Eng.Rep. 309.

■ BLACKBURN, J. In this case the plaintiffs and defendants had, on the 27th May, 1861, entered into a contract by which the defendants agreed to let the plaintiffs have the use of The Surrey Gardens and Music Hall on four days then to come, viz., the 17th June, 15th July, 5th August and 19th August, for the purpose of giving a series of four grand concerts, and day and night fetes at the Gardens and Hall on those days respectively; and the plaintiffs agreed to take the Gardens and Hall on those days, and pay £100 for each day.

The parties inaccurately call this a "letting," and the money to be paid a "rent"; but the whole agreement is such as to shew that the defendants were to retain the possession of the Hall and Gardens so that there was to be no demise of them, and that the contract was merely to give the plaintiffs the use of them on those days. Nothing however, in our opinion, depends on this. The agreement then proceeds to set out various stipulations between the parties as to what each was to supply for these concerts and entertainments, and as to the manner in which they should be carried on. The effect of the whole is to shew that the existence of the Music Hall in the Surrey Gardens in a state fit for a concert was essential for the fulfilment of the contract,—such entertainment as the parties contemplated in their agreement could not be given without it.

After the making of the agreement, and before the first day on which a concert was to be given, the Hall was destroyed by fire. This destruction, we must take it on the evidence, was without the fault of either party, and was so complete that in consequence the concerts could not be given as intended. And the question we have to decide is whether, under these circumstances, the loss which the plaintiffs have sustained is to fall upon the defendants. The parties when framing their agreement evidently had not present to their minds the possibility of such a disaster, and have made no express stipulation with reference to it, so that the answer to the question must depend upon the general rules of law applicable to such a contract.

There seems no doubt that where there is a positive contract to do a thing, not in itself unlawful, the contractor must perform it or pay damages for not doing it, although in consequence of unforeseen accidents, the performance of his contract has become unexpectedly burdensome or even impossible. . . . But this rule is only applicable when the contract is positive and absolute, and not subject to any condition either express or implied; and there are authorities which, as we think, establish the principle that where, from the nature of the contract, it appears that the parties must from the beginning have known that it could not be fulfilled unless when the time for the fulfilment of the contract arrived some particular specified thing continued to exist, so that, when entering into the contract, they must have contemplated such continuing existence as the foundation of what was to be done; there, in the absence of any express or implied warranty that the thing shall exist, the contract is not to be construed as a positive contract, but as subject to an implied condition that the parties shall be excused in case, before breach, performance becomes impossible from the perishing of the thing without default of the contractor.

There seems little doubt that this implication tends to further the great object of making the legal construction such as to fulfill the intention of those who entered into the contract. For in the course of affairs men in making such contracts in general would, if it were brought to their minds, say that there should be such a condition.

Accordingly, in the Civil law, such an exception is implied in every obligation of the class which they call obligatio de certo corpore. The rule is laid down in the Digest, lib. xlv., tit. 1, d verborum obligationibus, 1. 33. "Si Stichus certo die dari promissus, ante diem moriatur: non tenetur promissor." The principle is more fully developed in 1. 23. "Si ex legati causa, aut ex stipulatu hominem certum mihi debeas: non aliter post mortem ejus tenearis mihi, quam si per te steterit, quominum vivo eo eum mihi dares: quod ita fit, si aut interpellatus non didisti, aut occidisti eum." The examples are of contracts respecting a slave, which was the common illustration of a certain subject used by the Roman lawyers, just as we are apt to take a horse; and no doubt the propriety, one might almost say necessity, of the implied condition is more obvious when the contract relates to a living animal, whether man or brute, than when it relates to some inanimate thing (such as in the present case a theatre) the existence of which is not so obviously precarious as that of the live animal, but the principle is adopted in the Civil law as applicable to every obligation of which the subject is a certain thing. The general subject is treated of by Pothier, who in his Traite des Obligations, partie 3, chap. 6, art. 3, § 668 states the result to be that the debtor corporis certi is freed from his obligation when the thing has perished, neither by his act, nor his neglect, and before he is in default, unless by some stipulation he has taken on himself the risk of the particular misfortune which has occurred.

Although the Civil law is not of itself authority in an English Court, it affords great assistance in investigating the principles on which the law is grounded. And it seems to us that the common law authorities establish that in such a contract the same condition of the continued existence of the thing is implied by English law.

There is a class of contracts in which a person binds himself to do something which requires to be performed by him in person; and such promises, e.g. promises to marry, or promises to serve for a certain time, are never in practice qualified by an express exception of the death of the party; and therefore in such cases the contract is in terms broken if the promisor dies before fulfilment. Yet it was very early determined that, if the performance is personal, the executors are not liable; Hyde v. The Dean of Windsor (Cro.Eliz. 552, 553). See 2 Wms.Exors. 1560, 5th ed., where a very apt illustration is given. "Thus," says the learned author, "if an author undertakes to compose a work, and dies before completing it, his executors are discharged from this contract: for the undertaking is merely personal in its nature, and, by the intervention of the contractor's death, has become impossible to be performed." For this he cites a dictum of Lord Lyndhurst in Marshall v. Broadhurst (1 Tyr. 348, 349), and a case mentioned by Patteson J. in Wentworth v. Cock (10 A. & E. 42, 45–46). In Hall v. Wright (E.B. & E. 746, 749), Crompton J., in his judgment, puts another case. "Where a contract depends upon personal skill, and the act of God renders it impossible, as, for instance, in the case of a painter employed to paint a picture who is struck blind, it may be that the performance might be excused."

It seems that in those cases the only ground on which the parties or their executors, can be excused from the consequences of the breach of the contract is, that from the nature of the contract there is an implied condition of the continued existence of the life of the contractor, and, perhaps in the case of the painter of his eyesight. In the instances just given, the person, the continued existence of whose life is necessary to the fulfilment of the contract, is himself the contractor, but that does not seem in itself to be necessary to the application of the principle; as is illustrated by the following example. In the ordinary form of an apprentice deed the apprentice binds himself in unqualified terms to "serve until the full end and term of seven years to be fully complete and ended,'' during which term it is covenanted that the apprentice his master "faithfully shall serve," and the father of the apprentice in equally unqualified terms binds himself for the performance by the apprentice of all and every covenant on his part. (See the form, 2 Chitty on Pleading, 370, 7th ed. by Greening.) It is undeniable that if the apprentice dies within the seven years, the covenant of the father that he shall perform his covenant to serve for seven years is not fulfilled, yet surely it cannot be that an action lie against the father? Yet the only reason why it would not is that he is excused because of the apprentice's death.

These are instances where the implied condition is of the life of a human being, but there are others in which the same implication is made as to the continued existence of a thing. For example, where a contract of sale is made amounting to a bargain and sale, transferring presently the property in specific chattels, which are to be delivered by the vendor at a future day; there, if the chattels, without fault of the vendor, perish in the interval, the purchaser must pay the price and the vendor is excused from performing his contract to deliver, which has thus become impossible.

* * *

It may, we think, be safely asserted to be now English law, that in all contracts of loan of chattels or bailments if the performance of the promise of the borrower or bailee to return the things lent or bailed, becomes impossible because it has perished, this impossibility (if not arising upon the fault of the borrower or bailee from some risk which he has taken upon himself) excuses the borrower or bailee from the performance of his promise to redeliver the chattel.

The great case of Coggs v. Bernard (1 Smith's L.C. 171, 5th ed.; 2 L.Raym. 909) is now the leading case on the law of bailments, and Lord Holt, in that case, referred so much to the Civil law that it might perhaps be thought that this principle was there derived direct from the civilians, and was not generally applicable in English law except in the case of bailments; but the case of Williams v. Lloyd (W. Jones, 179), above cited, shews that the same law had been already adopted by the English law as early as The Book of Assizes. The principle seems to us to be that, in contracts in which the performance depends on the continued existence of a given person or thing, a condition is implied that the impossibility of performance arising from the perishing of the person or thing shall excuse the performance.

In none of these cases is the promise in words other than positive, nor is there any express stipulation that the destruction of the person or thing shall excuse the performance; but that excuse is by law implied, because from the nature of the contract it is apparent that the parties contracted on the basis of the continued existence of the particular person or chattel. In the present case, looking at the whole contract, we find that the parties contracted on the basis of the continued existence of the Music Hall at the time when the concerts were to be given; that being essential to their performance.

We think, therefore, that the Music Hall having ceased to exist, without fault of either party, both parties are excused, the plaintiffs from taking the gardens and paying the money, the defendants from performing their promise to give the use of the Hall and Gardens and other things. Consequently the rule must be absolute to enter the verdict for the defendants.

Rule absolute.

NOTES

(1) Upon what theory does the court excuse the defendant? Does "implied condition" mean that the court is seeking the intention of the parties or providing a term regardless of that intention? See Patterson, *Constructive Conditions in Contracts*, 42 Colum.L.Rev. 903, 943–954 (1942). As Lord Wright put it eighty years later: "[T]he court has to decide not what the parties actually intended, but what as reasonable men they should have intended. The court personifies for this purpose the reasonable man." Joseph Constantine S.S. Line v. Imperial Smelting Corp. (1942) A.C. 154, 185. See Kinzer Construction Co. v. State, 125 N.Y.S. 46, 54 (1910) (provisions are implied in contract by force of law and not because parties had them in mind). For a more recent analysis, see Birmingham, *Why is There Taylor v. Caldwell?: Three Propositions About Impracticability*, 23 U.S.F.L.Rev. 379 (1989).

(2) How is it determined that the "parties contracted on the basis of the continued existence of the Music Hall"? Suppose the defendant had another hall of similar quality and offered it to the plaintiff without additional cost. Would the plaintiff be required to accept it? Suppose the fire destroyed part of the hall but, in the judgment of the plaintiff, would not substantially affect the suitability of the hall for the proposed concerts and fetes. Is the defendant excused from the contract? If the fire destroyed the concert stage but the defendant, at a cost of 10,000, could effect repairs in time for the concert, would he be obligated to do so? If the particular hall was necessary for performance, the probable answers to the last three questions are "no," "no," and "no." See Restatement (Second) § 263, which provides:

> If the existence of a specific thing is necessary for the performance of a duty, its failure to come into existence, destruction, or such deterioration as makes performance impracticable is an event the non-occurrence of which was a basic assumption on which the contract was made.

(3) *Death or Incapacity of an Essential Person.* Restatement (Second) § 262 provides:

> If the existence of a particular person is necessary for the performance of a duty, his death or such incapacity as makes performance impracticable is an event the non-occurrence of which was a basic assumption on which the contract was made.

As with Restatement (Second) § 263, the "basic assumption" question is answered by determining whether the "particular person is necessary for the performance of a duty." The question of who is "necessary" may be determined by the agreement or, if the agreement is silent, an assessment of whether the performance was a "personal matter requiring personal experience, ability, skill and judgment...." Kelley v. Thompson Land Co., 112 W.Va. 454, 164 S.E. 667, 669 (1932) (formation of a going corporation deemed personal on facts of case). Under this test, the death of an artist employed to paint a portrait would discharge the contract but the death of the subject of the portrait would not discharge a duty to pay the agreed price.

Another way to determine who is necessary is to ask whether the person who dies or was incapacitated could have delegated his or her duty to a third party without the other party's consent. The question is whether the other party has a "substantial interest" in having the contract performed by the particular person. See UCC 2–210(1) [UCC 2–503(a) (1997)]. If so, the contract is discharged. Compare Seitz v. Mark–O–Lite Sign Contractors, Inc., 210 N.J.Super. 646, 510 A.2d 319 (1986) (death of contractor does not excuse contract to do sheet metal work) with Cazares v. Saenz, 208 Cal.App.3d 279, 256 Cal.Rptr. 209 (1989) (death of attorney discharges contract with law firm). But since people rather than corporations die or become incapacitated, the question remains whether the performance to be rendered was "so personal in nature, calling for a peculiar skill or special exercise of discretion, as to make it nondelegable." *Seitz,* supra, 510 A.2d at 313.

Canadian Industrial Alcohol Co. v. Dunbar Molasses Co.

Court of Appeals of New York, 1932.
258 N.Y. 194, 179 N.E. 383.

■ CARDOZO, C.J. A buyer sues a seller for breach of an executory contract of purchase and sale.

The subject-matter of the contract was "approximately 1,500,000 wine gallons Refined Blackstrap [molasses] of the usual run from the National Sugar Refinery, Yonkers, N.Y., to test around 60% sugars."

The order was given and accepted December 27, 1927, but shipments of the molasses were to begin after April 1, 1928, and were to be spread out during the warm weather.

After April 1, 1928, the defendant made delivery from time to time of 344,083 gallons. Upon its failure to deliver more, the plaintiff brought this action for the recovery of damages. The defendant takes the ground that, by an implied term of the contract, the duty to deliver was conditioned upon the production by the National Sugar Refinery at Yonkers of molasses sufficient in quantity to fill the plaintiff's order. The fact is that the output of the refinery, while the contract was in force, was 485,848 gallons, much less than its capacity, of which amount 344,083 gallons were allotted to the defendant and shipped to the defendant's customer. The argument for the defendant is that its own duty to deliver was proportionate to the refinery's willingness to supply, and that the duty was discharged when the output was reduced.

The contract, read in the light of the circumstances existing at its making, or more accurately in the light of any such circumstances apparent from this record, does not keep the defendant's duty within boundaries so narrow. We may assume, in the defendant's favor, that there would have been a discharge of its duty to deliver if the refinery had been destroyed . . . or if the output had been curtailed by the failure of the sugar crop . . . or by the ravages of war . . . or conceivably in some circumstances by unavoidable strikes . . . . . We may even assume that a like result would have followed if the plaintiff had bargained not merely for a quantity of molasses to be supplied from a particular refinery, but for molasses to be supplied in accordance with a particular contract between the defendant and the refiner, and if thereafter such contract had been broken without fault on the defendant's part. . . . The inquiry is merely this, whether the continuance of a special group of circumstances appears from the terms of the contract, interpreted in the setting of the occasion, to have been a tacit or implied presupposition in the minds of the contracting parties, conditioning their belief in a continued obligation. . . .

Accepting that test, we ask ourselves the question what special group of circumstances does the defendant lay before us as one of the presuppositions immanent in its bargain with the plaintiff? The defendant asks us to assume that a manufacturer, having made a contract with a middleman for a stock of molasses to be procured from a particular refinery, would expect the contract to lapse whenever the refiner chose to diminish his production, and this in the face of the middleman's omission to do anything to charge the refiner with a duty to continue. Business could not be transacted with security or smoothness if a presumption so unreasonable were at the root of its engagements. There is nothing to show that the defendant would have been unable by a timely contract with the refinery to have assured itself of a supply sufficient for its needs. There is nothing to show that the plaintiff, in giving the order for the molasses, was informed by the defendant that such a contract had not been made, or that performance would be contingent upon obtaining one thereafter. If the plaintiff had been so informed, it would very likely have preferred to deal with the refinery directly, instead of dealing with a middleman. The defendant does not even show that it tried to get a contract from the refinery during the months that intervened between the acceptance of the plaintiff's order and the time when shipments were begun. It has wholly failed to relieve itself of the imputation of contributory fault (3 Williston on Contracts, § 1959). So far as the record shows, it put its faith in the mere chance that the output of the refinery would be the same from year to year, and finding its faith vain, it tells us that its customer must have expected to take a chance as great. We see no reason for importing into the bargain this aleatory element. The defendant is in no better position than a factor who undertakes in his own name to sell for future delivery a special grade of merchandise to be manufactured by a special mill. The duty will be discharged if the mill is destroyed before delivery is due. The duty will subsist if the output is reduced because times turn out to be hard and labor charges high. . . .

* * *

The judgment should be affirmed with costs.

NOTES

(1) "A party may not, by its own conduct, create the event causing the impracticability of performance, ...; in fact it must make all reasonable efforts to avoid the 'impossibility,' ...; and, once the event occurs, it must employ any practicable means of fulfilling the contract, even if it had originally expected to meet its obligation in a particular way, ..." Chemetron Corp. v. McLouth Steel Corp., 381 F.Supp. 245, 257 (N.D.Ill.1974), affirmed 522 F.2d 469 (7th Cir. 1975). See also Neal–Cooper Grain Co. v. Texas Gulf Sulphur Co., 508 F.2d 283 (7th Cir.1974).

(2) Suppose, in the *Dunbar Molasses* case, that the contract between the plaintiff and the defendant contained the following clause:

> If the failure to perform is caused by the default of a supplier, and if such default arises out of causes beyond the control of both the seller and the supplier, and without the fault or negligence of either of them, the seller shall not be liable for any excess costs for failure to perform, unless the supplies or services to be furnished by the supplier were obtainable from other sources in sufficient time to permit the seller to meet the delivery schedule.

Would this clause alter the result in *Dunbar?*

(3) Under UCC 2–615(a) [UCC 2–716 (1997)], if the parties specify a particular source of supply in the contract and that source fails, the seller will be excused if (1) both parties assumed that the source was exclusive, (2) the seller employed all due measures to assure that the source would perform, and (3) the seller turned over to the buyer any rights against the supplier corresponding to the seller's claim of excuse. UCC 2–615, Comment 5. See Zidell Explorations, Inc. v. Conval International, Ltd., 719 F.2d 1465 (9th Cir.1983). On the other hand, if excuse is predicated upon a *force majeure* clause in the contract for sale rather than UCC 2–615(a), the seller need not turn over its rights against the supplier to the buyer. See InterPetrol Bermuda Ltd. v. Kaiser Aluminum International Corp., 719 F.2d 992 (9th Cir.1983). Finally, as Judge Cardozo indicated in *Dunbar Molasses,* the seller's responsibility, both before and after the exclusive source failure, to avoid or mitigate the loss, exists as a condition to excuse. See InterPetrol Bermuda Ltd. v. Kaiser Aluminum Intern., Corp., Occidental Crude Sales, Inc., 719 F.2d 992 (9th Cir.1983).

PROBLEM: A BUILDER IN THE QUAGMIRE OF IMPRACTICABILITY

Here is a review problem. Fenstermacher, a builder, contracted with Harry, a homeowner, to construct a residence on Harry's land. The contract price was $300,000, and the home was to be constructed according to detailed plans and specifications prepared by Harry's architect. The home was to be constructed on the only feasible spot on the lot. In the following situations, assess the probability that F will be discharged or obtain some relief in performing the contract.

(1) F started bulldozing and quickly discovered a massive and unforeseen (by F) rock formation some four feet under the surface. F had performed no tests before commencing performance. F estimates that it will cost an extra $100,000 to remove the rock.

(2) When F had laid the foundations and completed the home up to the first floor, it became clear that one corner was sinking. Unknown to F and H, the soil under that corner turned to "jelly" after a hard rain. After spending $25,000 to remedy the situation, the house was still subsiding. Experts will testify that the problem, if detected in advance, could have been avoided with an expenditure of about $50,000 and that another $50,000 will be required to remedy the problem at this stage. F refuses to continue performance unless H agrees to adjust the contract price.

(3) After construction began, a new county zoning ordinance was adopted. The county attorney claimed that Harry's proposed residence was now on a lot that was too small and obtained an injunction against continued construction. F stopped work. Six months later, the injunction was dissolved after H, through his attorney, obtained a final ruling that the ordinance did not have retroactive effect. By this time, F had his building crew on other projects and refused to continue performance. Evidence will support the claim that F's overall construction costs have increased 10% in the six month period.

(4) After the home was 60% completed and without the fault or negligence of either party, a fire burned the structure to the ground. F had been paid $50,000 as progress payments. F was not insured, although it was customary for the builder to obtain insurance on the structure until closing. Is F excused or must he rebuild under the contract without a price adjustment? What about the progress payments?

(5) When the house was 60% completed, F died of a heart attack. F had been paid $50,000 up to that time. H contracted with C to complete the work for $300,000 and, when the work was done, sued F's executor for $50,000—damages for "breach" of contract. You may assume that F's executor had, upon H's request, refused to complete performance after F's death.

PROBLEMS: CASUALTY TO IDENTIFIED GOODS

(1) F, a farmer, has 100 acres of bottom land in which he regularly plants corn. On May 1, F contracted to sell 20,000 bushels of # 1 yellow corn to B, a grain dealer, for $2.40 per bushel. Delivery was expected after harvest. At the time of contracting, 50% of the land had been planted and the balance was completed within 10 days. In early July, a severe drought began and it intensified until after the usual harvest date. The crop was so bad that F ground it up for fodder. At that time, # 1 yellow corn was selling at $5 per bushel. B demanded delivery of 20,000 bushels and F refused, claiming excuse under UCC 2–613 through 2–616 [UCC 2–714 through 2–717 (1997)]. B claims damages of $2.60 per bushel. Should he collect them? See Alimenta (U.S.A.), Inc. v. Gibbs, Nathaniel (Canada) Ltd., 802 F.2d 1362 (11th Cir.1986) (regional drought excuses supplier of peanuts); Bugg, *Crop Destruction and Forward Grain Contracts: Why Don't Sections 2–613 & 2–615 of the U.C.C. Provide More Relief?*, 12 Hamline L.Rev. 669 (1989).

(2) B contracted to sell 11,000 combat boots of a stated quality to a country in Africa. The price was $158,000. On July 1, B contracted with S to procure those boots from a Korean manufacturer for $95,000, with delivery no later than November 1. S immediately placed the order with the manufacturer and the boots arrived in San Francisco on October 15. The boots conformed to the contract requirements, but contained no markings identifying their origin. S immediately shipped the boots to B in New York by rail under the shipment term "FOB point of Destination." The goods were totally destroyed by fire while in the carrier's possession, and S was unable to obtain substitutes in time to meet the November 1 delivery date. B then canceled the contract for breach, and sued S for damages. S claims that performance was excused under Sections 2–612 through 2–616 of the UCC [UCC 2–714 through 2–717 (1997)]. What result? You may assume that the goods were first identified to the contract between S and B when they were shipped to B from San Francisco, see UCC 2–501(1) [UCC 2–501(a) (1997)], and that the risk of loss was on S at the time of the fire. See UCC 2–319(1)(b) & 2–509(1)(b) [UCC 2–612 (1997)]. See also Bende & Sons, Inc. v. Crown Recreation, Inc., 548 F.Supp. 1018 (E.D.N.Y. 1982).

Dills v. Town of Enfield

Supreme Court of Connecticut, 1989.
210 Conn. 705, 557 A.2d 517.

■ PETERS, CHIEF JUSTICE.

The principal issue in this appeal is whether the doctrine of commercial impracticability excuses a developer from submitting construction plans when he discovers that necessary financing has become unavailable. The plaintiffs, Timothy E. Dills and the Neecon Corporation, sued the defendants, the town of Enfield (town) and the Enfield development agency (agency), to recover a $100,000 deposit Dills had paid the agency under an option and contract for sale. The trial court referred the case to Attorney J. Read Murphy, a state trial referee appointed pursuant to General Statutes § 52–434(a)(4). Following a hearing and the parties' submission of briefs, the referee reported his findings of fact and recommended that judgment enter for the plaintiffs. The trial court rejected the referee's recommendation, instead rendering judgment for the defendants. The plaintiff Neecon Corporation appealed to the Appellate Court and we transferred the case here pursuant to Practice Book § 4023. We find no error.

The relevant facts reported by the referee, accepted by the trial court and supported by the record, are as follows. The town of Enfield instructed its development agency to solicit private developers for the Enfield Memorial Industrial Park to be constructed on town property. Pursuant to an earlier option agreement, on May 1, 1974, the plaintiff Dills and the development agency entered into a contract for the sale of the land to be developed. Dills at that time paid a $100,000 deposit toward the contract price of $985,900. The plaintiff Neecon Corporation, owned by Dills, was to perform the necessary work, and has become, by virtue of an assignment from Dills, the only remaining plaintiff in this appeal.

Under the terms of the contract, the development agency agreed to convey the property to the developer sixty days after the fulfillment of two conditions: (1) the submission and approval of construction plans in accordance with section 301 of the contract; and (2) the submission of evidence of financial capacity in accordance with section 304 of the contract. The contract also included provisions for its termination by either party. Section 702(b) of the contract allowed the developer to withdraw and to reclaim his deposit if, after the preparation of construction plans satisfactory to the agency, the developer could not obtain the necessary mortgage financing. Section 703(b) of the contract allowed the agency to terminate the contract, retaining the deposit as liquidated damages, if the developer failed to submit acceptable construction plans.

Dills never submitted construction plans that were acceptable to the agency. A set of plans denominated "preliminary" was rejected by the agency on June 24, 1974. The agency accepted a revised set of "preliminary plans" and drawings three months later, but demanded the submission of full construction plans and specifications by early December. The referee found that the preliminary sets of plans did not themselves meet the definition of "construction plans" in section 301. The referee agreed with the agency's interpretation of section 301 of the contract as requiring the developer to submit full construction plans within 210 days of the agency's approval of preliminary plans.

The reason Dills failed to submit construction plans was that, despite diligent efforts, he was unable to obtain mortgage financing. Thereafter, both parties attempted, with proper notification, to invoke the contract's termination clauses. On December 19, 1974, the agency, having been informed by Dills of his financial difficulties, voted to terminate the agreement pursuant to section 703(b) of the contract of sale and to retain the $100,000 deposit as liquidated damages. On December 22, 1974, Dills' attorney notified the agency that, because of Dills' inability to obtain financing within the time specified in the contract, Dills was terminating the agreement pursuant to section 702(b) of the contract of sale.

* * *

[The referee found, among other things, that Dills' duty to provide full construction plans by December, 1974 was discharged by supervening impracticability. The trial court, however, rejected the referee's recommendation that judgment be entered for Dills, concluding that unless there was impracticability in preparing and submitting construction plans rather than obtaining financing for them there was no basis for excuse.]

B

Finally we must decide whether the trial court erred as a matter of law in rejecting the referee's determination, endorsed by the plaintiff on appeal, that the impracticability doctrine excused Dills' failure to deliver construction plans to the agency. The plaintiff contends that Dills' inability to obtain such financing made submitting the construction plans a "futile" and "useless act," and therefore the doctrine of supervening impracticability discharged his duty to submit the plans. We hold, as did the trial court, that "[t]he doctrine of impracticability and impossibility ... [is] not relevant to this case."

The impracticability[16] doctrine represents an exception to the accepted maxim of *pacta sunt servanda,* in recognition of the fact that certain conditions cannot be met because of unforeseen occurrences. Cf. Aetna Casualty & Surety Co. v. Murphy, 206 Conn. 409, 413, 538 A.2d 219 (1988). A party claiming that a supervening event or contingency has prevented, and thus excused, a promised performance must demonstrate that: (1) the event made the performance impracticable; (2) the nonoccurrence of the event was a basic assumption on which the contract was made; (3) the impracticability resulted without the fault of the party seeking to be excused; and (4) the party has not assumed a greater obligation than the law imposes. 2 Restatement (Second), Contracts § 261; E. Farnsworth, Contracts (1982) § 9.6, p. 678. We discuss only the first two prongs of this test in disposing of the plaintiff's argument.

Although courts in recent years have liberalized the requirements for such an excuse; see G. Gilmore, The Death of Contract (1972) pp. 80–81; H. Berman, "Excuse for Nonperformance in Light of Contract Practices in International Trade," 63 Colum.L.Rev. 1413, 1414 (1963); only in the most exceptional circumstances have courts concluded that a duty is discharged because additional financial burdens make performance less practical than initially contemplated. See, e.g., Neal–Cooper Grain Co. v. Texas Gulf Sulphur Co., 508 F.2d 283, 294 (7th Cir.1974) (party not allowed "to escape a bad bargain merely because it is burdensome"); American Trading & Production Corporation v. Shell International Marine, Ltd., 453 F.2d 939, 942 (2d Cir.1972) (closing of Suez Canal requiring charterer to sail nearly twice as many miles at a cost of nearly one-third more than the contract price does not excuse performance); United States v. Wegematic Corporation, 360 F.2d 674, 676–77 (2d Cir.1966) (duty of manufacturer to produce revolutionary computer system not excused because of "engineering difficulties" requiring two years and $1.5 million to correct); Peerless Casualty Co. v. Weymouth Gardens, 215 F.2d 362, 364 (1st Cir.1954) (increased costs caused by the unexpected outbreak of war does not constitute superior force ending obligation of contract); Matter of Westinghouse Electric Corporation, 517 F.Supp. 440, 452–53 (E.D.Va.1981) (duty to remove spent fuel not excused merely because reprocessing of the fuel became unprofitable); see also Connecticut General Statutes Annotated § 42a–2–614, comment 4; E. Farnsworth, supra, p. 680; 6 A. Corbin, Contracts (1962) § 1333; 16 S. Williston, Contracts (3d Ed. Jaeger 1978) § 1968; J. White & R. Summers, Uniform Commercial Code (2d Ed.1980) § 3–9, pp. 131–32. Thus, the fact

---

16. The doctrine of "impossibility" has come to include "physical impossibility," "frustration of purpose" and "impracticability" because of contingencies rendering performance more costly. See 6 A. Corbin, Contracts (1962) § 1325; 16 S. Williston, Contracts (3d Ed. Jaeger 1978) § 1932; G. Gilmore, The Death of Contract (1972) pp. 80–82. This case concerns only the last of these.

that preparing the construction plans would have cost Dills a great deal of money (more than the deposit he sought to recover) did not excuse him from submitting them as the contract provided.

Furthermore, the event upon which the obligor relies to excuse his performance cannot be an event that the parties foresaw at the time of the contract. We have previously held that "[t]he regular enforcement of conditions is ... subject to the competing but equally well established principle that the occurrence of a condition may be excused in the event of impracticability *'if the occurrence of the condition is not a material part of the agreed exchange* and forfeiture would otherwise result.' 2 Restatement (Second), Contracts § 271; 6 Corbin, Contracts (1962) § 1362; 5 Williston, Contracts (3d Ed.1961) § 793." (Emphasis added.) Grenier v. Compratt Construction Co., 189 Conn. 144, 148–49, 454 A.2d 1289 (1983); see also West Haven Sound Development Corporation v. West Haven, 201 Conn. 305, 313, 514 A.2d 734 (1986). Thus, the "central inquiry" is whether the nonoccurrence of the alleged impracticable condition "was a basic assumption on which the contract was made." General Statutes § 42a–2–615(a);[17] 2 Restatement (Second), Contracts § 261;[18] E. Farnsworth, supra, § 9.6, pp. 679–84.

In this case the contingency upon which fulfilling the contract allegedly depended was Dills' obtaining the requisite financing. We cannot conclude, however, that Dills' failure to obtain financing was "an event the non-occurrence of which was a basic assumption on which the contract was made." Indeed, section 702(b) of the contract of sale demonstrates that the parties expressly contemplated that Dills might encounter financial difficulties. The contract allowed Dills to terminate for this reason "after preparation of Construction Plans satisfactory to the Agency." If "an event is foreseeable, a party who makes an unqualified promise to perform necessarily assumes an obligation to perform, even if the occurrence of the event makes performance impracticable." E. Farnsworth, supra, p. 686.[19]

---

17. General Statutes § 42a–2–615(a) provides in pertinent part: "Delay in delivery or nondelivery in whole or in part by a seller ... is not a breach of his duty under a contract for sale if performance as agreed has been made impracticable by the occurrence of a contingency *the nonoccurrence of which was a basic assumption on which the contract was made* or by compliance in good faith with any applicable foreign or domestic governmental regulation or order whether or not it later proves to be invalid." (Emphasis added.) While the instant case does not concern the sale of goods, and therefore the Uniform Commercial Code does not apply, § 2–615 has been adopted by the Restatement and "promises to have a substantial influence on the law of contract generally...." E. Farnsworth, Contracts (1982) § 9.6, p. 677.

18. The Restatement (Second) of Contracts § 261 provides: "Where, after a contract is made, a party's performance is made impracticable without his fault by the occurrence of an event *the non-occurrence of which was a basic assumption on which the contract was made,* his duty to render that performance is discharged, unless the language or the circumstances indicate the contrary." (Emphasis added.)

19. Significantly, the defendants never conceded that the promised plans would have been of no use to them. Thus, it is far from certain that submitting the plans would have been a "futile act" from the defendants' point of view.

This case, like virtually every case involving discharge from an obligation to perform, concerns the issue of which party bears the loss resulting from an event that renders performance by one party uneconomical. See R. Posner, Economic Analysis of Law (3d Ed.1986) pp. 93–94; R. Posner & A. Rosenfield, "Impossibility and Related Doctrines in Contract Law: An Economic Analysis," 6 J. Legal Stud. 83, 86–87 (1977). "Determining whether the non-occurrence of a particular event was or was not a basic assumption involves a judgment as to which party assumed the risk of its occurrence.... In making such determinations, a court will look at all circumstances, including the terms of the contract." 2 Restatement (Second), Contracts, c. 11, introductory note. "Since impossibility and related doctrines are devices for shifting risk in accordance with the parties' presumed intentions, which are to minimize the costs of contract performance, one of which is the disutility created by risk, they have no place when the contract explicitly assigns a particular risk to one party or the other." Northern Indiana Public Service Co. v. Carbon County Coal Co., 799 F.2d 265, 278 (7th Cir.1986); see also Wasserman Theatrical Enterprise, Inc. v. Harris, 137 Conn. 371, 374–75, 77 A.2d 329 (1950). Where, as in this case, sophisticated contracting parties have negotiated termination provisions, courts should be slow to invent additional ways to excuse performance. We exercise such caution in this case.

There is no error.

In this opinion the other Justices concurred.

NOTES

(1) For exactly what reason did the court conclude that Dills was not excused from the contract: (a) The parties assigned the risk to Dills in the contract; or (b) Obtaining financing was *not* a basic assumption of the contract; or (c) The extra cost of performance did not make performance impracticable? Is the conclusion sound if the court relies on *all three* reasons?

(2) Can you develop a scenario (hypothetical) where Justice Peters would grant excuse?

(3) *The Foreseeability Test.* The court, in *Dills*, states that the "event upon which the obligor relies to excuse his performance cannot be an event that the parties foresaw at the time of the contract." Later, the court states that the "central inquiry" is whether the nonoccurrence of the event was a "basic assumption on which the contract was made." 557 A.2d at 524. What is the relationship between foreseeability and the "basic assumption"? Can an event be foreseeable at the time of contracting and still be an event that both parties assume will not occur? See Waldinger Corp. v. CRS Group Engineers, Inc., 775 F.2d 781 (7th Cir.1985) (if a contingency is foreseeable, the § 2–615 defense is not available because the party disadvantaged by the occurrence of the contingency might have contractually protected itself).

The answer, we think, is yes. Most modern courts concede that the foreseeability of some risk and its impact on performance does not necessarily prove its allocation to the promisor. As Judge Friendly recognized, the parties cannot provide for all the possibilities of which they are aware, "sometimes because they cannot agree, often simply because they are too busy." Transatlantic Financing Corp. v. United States, 363 F.2d 312, 319 (D.C.Cir.1966). Moreover, if the occurrence of the foreseen event is improbable, it is less likely that the parties intended to allocate its risk to one or the other. See Restatement (Second) § 261, Comment c. Thus, the key to the analysis is the probability that the foreseen event will occur or, if it does occur, certain consequences will follow. As one court put, "was the contingency which developed one which the parties could reasonably be thought to have foreseen as a *real possibility* which could affect performance"? Mishara Construction Co., Inc. v. Transit–Mixed Concrete Corp., 365 Mass. 122, 310 N.E.2d 363, 367 (1974). If so, the court is unlikely to conclude that both parties assumed that the event would not occur. See also Aluminum Co. of America v. Essex Group, Inc., 499 F.Supp. 53, 70 (W.D.Pa.1980) ("The proper question is not simply whether the parties to a contract were conscious of uncertainty with respect to a vital fact, but whether they believed that uncertainty was effectively limited within a designated range so that they would deem outcomes beyond that range to be highly unlikely"); Joskow, *Commercial Impossibility, the Uranium Market and the Westinghouse Case*, 6 J.Legal Stud. 119, 153–62 (1977) (foreseeability test should be used to delineate the boundary between those contingencies that are reasonably part of the decision-making process and those that are not).

(4) *Changes in Market Price or Cost of Performance.* In cases where the market price at the time for performance is either dramatically higher or lower than the contract price but the cost of performance is relatively stable, the courts have refused relief. See, e.g., R.N. Kelly Cotton Merchant, Inc. v. York, 494 F.2d 41 (5th Cir.1974) (market 300% higher than contract price); Hancock Paper Co. v. Champion Intern. Corp., 424 F.Supp. 285 (E.D.Pa.1976) (market price drops). As Comment 4 to UCC 2–615 states, this is "exactly the type of risk which business contracts made at a fixed price are intended to cover." See Schwartz, *Sales Law and Inflations*, 50 S.Cal.L.Rev. 1 (1976).

A similar result—no excuse—is reached when promisor's cost of performance dramatically exceeds the contract price due to supervening events beyond its control and without its fault or negligence. For example, in Louisiana Power & Light v. Allegheny Ludlum Industries, 517 F.Supp. 1319 (E.D.La., 1981), a seller refused to perform contract for nuclear condenser tubing after increase in metal price would have caused seller to lose $428,500 on a $1.3 million contract. The court found that seller's non-performance was not excused by impracticability. Commercial impracticability requires an "especially severe and unreasonable loss" and seller's plant even after loss on contract would have still cleared $589,000.

In cases involving increased costs of performance however, the risk event, whether it be an Act of God, war, extreme inflation, or an oil embargo, may, unlike market price fluctuations, be a "contingency the non-occurrence of which was a basic assumption on which the contract was made." UCC 2–615(a). In this case, the court should consider whether "performance as agreed has been made impracticable" by the risk event. The leading cases in this area, which deny relief, consider both the "basic assumption" and the "impracticability" questions. *Allegheny* ducked the "basic assumption" question on the ground that, in any event, the increased cost did not make performance as agreed impracticable. In no case was relief granted, basically on the ground that no extraordinary circumstance made performance so vitally different from what was reasonably to be expected as to alter the essential nature of that performance. See Restatement (Second), Chapter 11, page 309; UCC 2–615, Comment 4 (increased cost alone does not excuse performance unless the rise in cost is due to some unforeseen contingency which alters the essential nature of the performance). Accord: Bernina Distributors, Inc. v. Bernina Sewing Machine Co., 646 F.2d 434, 438–39 (10th Cir.1981) (cost increase must cause "especially severe and unreasonable" loss). But see Florida Power & Light Co. v. Westinghouse Elec. Corp., 826 F.2d 239 (4th Cir.1987), cert. denied 485 U.S. 1021, 108 S.Ct. 1574, 99 L.Ed.2d 890 (1988) (defendant excused from obligation to remove and dispose of spent nuclear waste after government unexpectedly discontinued waste processing and use of alternative source would increase cost by $80,000,000).

Comment: ALCOA Can't Wait!

In Aluminum Company of America v. Essex Group, Inc., 499 F.Supp. 53 (W.D.Pa.1980), a case whose length and complexity belie simple analysis, the parties signed in 1967 a 17–year contract under which ALCOA was to process alumina supplied by Essex into molten aluminum to be used by Essex in the manufacture of aluminum wire products. The long-term contract, called a "toll conversion service contract," was to be performed at a plant owned by ALCOA in Indiana. As part of the pricing mechanism, the parties agreed upon an escalation clause, prepared by the noted economist (who would later become Federal Reserve chief) Alan Greenspan, which varied with production costs at the plant. The clause was developed in light of past cost patterns and reflected a projected variation of costs that would give ALCOA a high of $.07 and a low of $.01 profit per pound. ALCOA's target profit was $.04 per pound. In 1973, at the time of the energy crisis, electricity costs at the Indiana plant began to escalate well beyond the projections of the contract clause. Although ALCOA had earned a profit of $27.6 million by the end of 1974 (the profit was down to $9 million at the time of trial), it was now projected that ALCOA would lose $60 million over the balance of the contract because of a 500% variation of actual to indexed costs. Should we trust Greenspan to set our monetary policy? At the same time, Essex was reaping a so-called "windfall" gain by reselling converted aluminum for which it paid ALCOA $.364 per pound on the open market for $.733 per pound. When efforts by ALCOA to obtain an agreed adjustment of the contract price failed, ALCOA sued to obtain relief from the escalation clause and a reformation of the contract so that Essex must pay the actual costs incurred at the plant. When Essex counterclaimed for breach damages, the issue was joined.

The court concluded that ALCOA was, on the facts, entitled to "some relief" but that the remedy should be "equitable reformation" of the price term rather than discharge of the contract. The court devised a complicated adjustment formula without the agreement of the parties, who, subsequently, reached an agreement on an adjustment and settled the dispute before an appeal to the United States Court of Appeals for the Third Circuit could be decided. The district court's unique reasoning and result on the question of liability and remedy took the following path.

First, the court seemed to conclude that the case was not governed by UCC 2–615. Rather, the court discussed the law of Indiana which governed, the common law doctrines of mistake, impracticability and frustration and Tentative Drafts of the Restatement (Second), as well as Section 2–615.

Second, the court concluded that both parties assumed at the time of contracting that the production cost index was realistic, but they were wrong due to changed circumstances which were not foreseeable as likely to occur. The court stressed that the parties had undertaken a closely calculated rather than a limitless risk and concluded that neither party had assumed the risk of events which caused such a severe imbalance in the exchange.

Third, without discounting ALCOA's profit up to the time of trial, the court concluded that the projected $60 million loss over the balance of the commercial contract made continued performance under the contract "commercially senseless." The point was bolstered by the so-called "windfall" profits enjoyed by Essex. In short, the case had gone beyond the point where the community interest in predictable contract enforcement should prevail and, because continued performance would be "commercially senseless and unjust," the contractor was entitled to "some relief."[1]

Fourth, although the court's conclusions were consistent with relief under the "basic assumption-impracticability" test, the court made a finding that the parties had made a "mistake * * * of fact rather than one of simple prediction of future events." 499 F.Supp. at 63. Thus, the court

---

1. In 1975, Westinghouse repudiated its promise to deliver some 70 million tons of uranium under long-term supply contracts with 27 utility companies. The claim was that dramatic, unprecedented and unforeseen events had occurred which increased the price of uranium to Westinghouse from between $6.50 to $9.00 per pound at the times of contracting to $40 per pound at the time of repudiation. Assuming that Westinghouse could actually obtain uranium to perform the contracts, the projected loss under the contracts with the utilities was in excess of $2 billion. The legal effect of all of this was, according to Westinghouse, that the agreed performance had become impracticable under UCC 2–615(a) and that the contracts should be discharged. Suits by thirteen utilities for breach of contract were consolidated for trial in the Eastern District of Virginia, see In re Westinghouse Elec. Corp. Uranium Contracts Lit., 405 F.Supp. 316 (J.P.M.L.1975), and the breach claims were ultimately settled without a published decision on the merits. See N.Y. Times, § 3, p. 1 (March 15, 1981). Before the settlements were reached, however, the district court judge decided that Westinghouse was not excused under UCC 2–615(a) and was liable for damages. For a brief summary of the Bench Opinion of Judge Mehrige, see Speidel, *Court-Imposed Price Adjustments Under Long–Term Supply Contracts*, 76 Nw. L.Rev. 369, 413, n. 181 (1981). For the decision in a related case, see Matter of Westinghouse Elec. Corp., Etc., 517 F.Supp. 440 (E.D.Va.1981). More detailed analyses of the issues in context can be found in Goldberg, *Price Adjustment in Long–Term Contracts*, 1985 Wis.L.Rev. 527; Eagan, *The Westinghouse Uranium Contracts: Commercial Impracticability and Related Matters*, 18 Am. Bus.Law J. 281 (1980); Joskow, *Commercial Impossibility: The Uranium Market and the Westinghouse Case*, 6 J.Leg.Stud. 119 (1977). See also Prance, *Energy Contract Planning: Allocating the Risks and Consequences of Commercial Impracticability*, 3 Hast.Int. Comp.L.Rev. 435 (1980); Comment, 47 U.Mo. K.City L.Rev. 650 (1979).

seemed to view the basis for relief as "existing" rather than "supervening" impracticability.

Plainly the mistake is not wholly isolated from predictions of the future or from the searching illuminations of painful hindsight. But this is not the legal test. At the time the contract was made both parties were aware that the future was unknown, and their agreed contract was intended to bind them for many years to come. Both knew that Essex sought an objective pricing formula and that ALCOA sought a formula which would cover its out of pocket costs over the years and which would yield it a return of around four cents a pound. Both parties to the contract carefully examined the past performance * * * (of production costs indices) * * * before agreeing to its use. The testimony was clear that each assumed the Index was adequate to fulfill its purpose. This mistaken assumption was essentially a present actuarial error. 499 F.Supp. at 63.

Fifth, the remedy of "equitable" reformation adjusted the price for future performance under the contract rather than for past performance. In short, the court deleted the existing cost index and imposed a new term in the "gap." The usual remedy of discharge was rejected in the interest of avoiding hardship and preserving expectations and the court-imposed adjustment was justified by what the court called a "new spirit" of contract. This "new spirit" reflected the "need for a body of law compatible with responsible practices and understandings" and the obligation of courts to give "close attention to the legitimate business aims of the parties, to their purpose of avoiding the risks of great losses, and to the need to frame a remedy to preserve the essence of the agreement." 499 F.Supp. at 91–92.

Kaiser–Francis Oil Co. v. Producer's Gas Co.

United States Court of Appeals, Tenth Circuit, 1989.
870 F.2d 563.

■ BALDOCK, CIRCUIT JUDGE.

Appellee and seller, Kaiser–Francis Oil Co. (Kaiser–Francis), sought to enforce the provisions of two similar gas purchase contracts (the "Ellis" and "Cronin" contracts) against appellant and buyer, Producer's Gas Co. (PGC). Under the contracts, PGC was required to take or pay for certain minimum quantities of gas from wells in which Kaiser–Francis had a percentage interest. When the resale price for natural gas declined, PGC did not pay Kaiser–Francis for gas taken on the theory that it was purchasing the gas from Kaiser–Francis' co-owners at reduced prices. PGC also declined to pay for the minimum contract quantities of the gas which were not taken. PGC's actions were based on various defenses to the contracts. The district court granted summary judgment on the issue of liability in favor of Kaiser–Francis, thereby rejecting all of PGC's defenses. The parties thereafter stipulated as to the appropriate damages, interest and attorney's fees that would accrue upon the liability determination. Thus, we consider only issues of liability under the contracts, whether the district court improperly rejected any or all of PGC's defenses to the contract.

On appeal, PGC contends that the district court erred in granting partial summary judgment in favor of Kaiser–Francis because 1) the force majeure provision in the contracts extends to a partial lack of demand caused by market forces, 2) the gas to be supplied by Kaiser–Francis failed to meet the quality specifications of the contract, 3) PGC was not purchasing gas from Kaiser–Francis, but rather from Kaiser–Francis' co-owners in various wells, and 4) any take-or-pay payments required under the contract would violate ceiling prices set by the Natural Gas Policy Act [NGPA]. We find each of these contentions without merit and affirm. Our jurisdiction to review this diversity case arises under 28 U.S.C. § 1291. Consistent with the choice of law provision in each contract, we apply Oklahoma substantive law.

* * *

I.

PGC first contends that the force majeure provision[1] in each contract extends to a lack of demand for gas, thereby providing relief in this case from the take-or-pay obligation[2] contained in each contract. PGC suggests

---

1. *14.1* Except for Buyer's obligations to make payment due for gas delivered hereunder, neither party shall be liable for failure to perform this agreement when such failure is due to "force majeure." "Force majeure" shall mean acts of God, strikes, lockouts, or industrial disputes or disturbances, civil disturbances, arrests and restraints, interruptions by government or court orders, present and future valid order of any regulatory body having proper jurisdiction, acts of the public enemy, wars, riots, insurrections, inability to secure labor or inability to secure materials, including inability to secure materials by reason of allocations promulgated by authorized governmental agencies, epidemics, fires, explosions, breakage or accident to machinery or lines of pipe, freezing of wells or pipelines, inability to obtain easements, right-of-way or other interests in realty, the making of repairs, replacements or alterations to lines of pipe or plants, partial or entire failure of gas supply or demand over which neither Seller nor Buyer have [sic] control or any other cause, whether of the kind herein enumerated or otherwise, not reasonably within the control of the party claiming "force majeure." Events of "force majeure" shall, so far as possible, be remedied with all reasonable dispatch. The settlement of industrial difficulties shall be within the discretion of the party having the difficulty, and the requirement that "force majeure" be remedied with all reasonable dispatch shall not require the settlement of industrial difficulties by acceding to the demands of any opposing party when such course is inadvisable in the discretion of the party having the difficulty.

Rec. vol. II (Attachment to Brief In Support of Kaiser–Francis Oil Company's Motion for Partial Summary Judgment—1980 Ellis & 1982 Cronin contracts) (emphasis added).

2. *4.1* Subject to all terms and conditions of this Agreement, Seller shall sell and deliver during each Accounting Year from the lands and leases covered hereby, and Buyer shall purchase and receive from Seller or pay for if available but not taken, a quantity of gas equal to the Daily Contract Quantities herein specified.

4.7 If at the end of any Accounting Year, Buyer shall have failed to purchase during such Year the sum the applicable Daily Contract Quantities, after credit is allowed for (i) deficiency existing by *force majeure*, ..., Buyer shall pay for the remaining deficiency as if taken.

Rec. vol. II (Attachment to Brief in Support of Kaiser–Francis Oil Company's Motion for Partial Summary Judgment—1980 Ellis and 1982 Cronin contracts).

that there is an issue of fact concerning the extent of the failure of demand for gas. Essentially, PGC contends that a force majeure event occurred because the demand for gas sharply decreased, with a corresponding decrease in the resale price of gas that PGC was obligated to take or pay for under the contracts. Unfortunately for PGC, however, the Oklahoma Supreme Court, in interpreting a similar force majeure provision, has determined that neither a decline in demand, nor an inability to sell gas at or above the contract price, constitutes a force majeure event. Golsen v. ONG Western, Inc., 756 P.2d 1209, 1213 (Okl.1988) (interpreting force majeure provision extending to "failure of gas supply or markets"). That decision applies to this case.

PGC's interpretation of the force majeure provision is antithetical to the take-or-pay provision. Under its interpretation, PGC could be expected to take only when the demand for gas resulted in a resale price at or above the contract price. PGC could never be expected to take or pay when the demand for gas resulted in a resale price below the contract price. Rather than taking or paying under the take-or-pay provision, PGC would rely on the force majeure provision. Thus, Kaiser–Francis would be shut in during any drop in demand, for up to twenty years, without any ability to sell in other markets. Such a one-sided interpretation is suspect.

The purpose of the take-or-pay clause is to apportion the risks of natural gas production and sales between the buyer and seller. The seller bears the risk of production. To compensate the seller for that risk, the buyer agrees to take, or pay for if not taken, a minimum quantity of gas. The buyer bears the risk of market demand.

Universal Resources Corp. v. Panhandle E. Pipe Line Co., 813 F.2d 77, 80 (5th Cir.1987); see also Golsen, 756 P.2d at 1213; 4 H. Williams & C. Meyers, Oil & Gas Law § 724.5 (1988) (take-or-pay provision assures the seller "of a minimum annual return and that his premises will be permitted to produce in paying quantities"). Should the resale price decline below the contract price, PGC could still take the gas and sell it, albeit at a loss, or pay for the gas without taking it, also at a loss. The change in the general or relative resale price of gas does not constitute a "partial failure of gas demand" which would relieve PGC of its obligation to take or pay. The force majeure provision cannot substitute for a price redetermination or market-out provision which would allow PGC to reduce the price paid to Kaiser–Francis for gas, thereby ameliorating PGC's take-or-pay obligation when the resale price of natural gas declined.

* * *

NOTES

(1) Are you persuaded by the court's reasoning on why the *force majeure* clause should not excuse the defendant? Suppose the clause, as in *Golsen,* had included "failure of gas supply or markets" as a ground for excuse? What contract provision would best protect the defendant from the particular events that occurred? See generally Lewis, *Allocating Risk in Take-or-Pay Contracts:*

Are Force Majeure and Commercial Impracticability the Same Defense?, 42 Sw.L.J. 1047 (1989).

(2) *Judge Posner on Force Majeure Clauses.*

A *force majeure* clause is not intended to buffer a party against the normal risks of a contract. The normal risk of a fixed-price contract is that the market price will change. If it rises, the buyer gains at the expense of the seller (except insofar as escalator provisions give the seller some protection); if it falls * * * the seller gains at the expense of the buyer. The whole purpose of a fixed-price contract is to allocate risk in this way. A *force majeure* clause interpreted to excuse the buyer from the consequences of the risk he expressly assumed would nullify a central term of the contract. Northern Indiana Public Service Co. v. Carbon County Coal Co., 799 F.2d 265, 275 (7th Cir.1986) (the *NIPSCO* case). The opinion is reprinted in part, infra at 965.

(3) *Judge Posner on Fixed Price Contracts.* The essence of the outcome in take-or-pay contracts, to be discussed below, was expressed in the *NIPSCO* case, supra, 799 F.2d at 278, where the court, speaking through Judge Posner, stated:

> Since impossibility and related doctrines are devices for shifting risk in accordance with the parties' presumed intentions, which are to minimize the costs of contract performance, one of which is the disutility created by risk, they have no place when the contract explicitly assigns a particular risk to one party or the other. [A] fixed-price contract is an explicit assignment of the risk of market price increases to the seller and the risk of market price decreases to the buyer, and the assignment of the latter risk to the buyer is even clearer where * * * the contract places a floor under price but allows for escalation. If * * * the buyer forecasts the market incorrectly and therefore finds himself locked into a disadvantageous contract, he has only himself to blame and so cannot shift the risk back to the seller by invoking impossibility or related doctrines. * * * Since "the very purpose of a fixed price agreement is to place the risk of increased costs on the promisor (and the risk of decreased costs on the promisee)," the fact that costs decrease steeply * * * cannot allow the buyer to walk away from the contract.

Comment: Take-or-Pay Contracts

In the 1970's, producers entered long-term contracts with pipelines for the sale of natural gas. The pipelines agreed to "take or pay" for a portion of the producer's output at an agreed price, subject to escalation. The base price was set at an agreed dollar amount per unit, called MMBTU. In essence, the pipeline could either "take" the gas when produced and pay for it or pay without taking and expect the producer to "make up" deliveries in the future. Under this arrangement, the pipeline secured a long-term source of supply at a predictable price and the producer obtained a reliable source of cash with which to finance production and the development of reserves. In addition, the contract might contain a *force majeure* clause or other provisions allocating risk, such as a "market out" or a "matching price" clause. Under these clauses, the pipeline could terminate the contract if a lower long-term price for gas could be found from another source and the producer was unwilling or unable to match it. See Caggiano, *Understanding Natural Gas Contracts,* 38 Oil & Gas Q. 267, 267–278 (1989).

By 1983, the price of most gas at the "wellhead" had been deregulated under the Natural Gas Policy Act of 1978. At the same time, a depressed economy and lower demand for natural gas at the retail level put the pipelines in a bind. They did not need the gas they had agreed to "take" and the contract price that they had agreed to "pay" was substantially above that now available under either new long-term contracts or on the "spot" market. With large volumes of gas at stake, the dollar amount involved in a single contract could exceed $500,000,000. To no one's surprise, the pipelines began to search for ways to adjust or to terminate the contracts.

Without attempting here to exhaust the possibilities for agreed settlement, a survey of litigation under the UCC suggests that the pipelines have been singularly unsuccessful in avoiding these contracts. A summary of the judicial outcomes appears below.

(1) A long-term contract for the sale of natural gas is subject to Article 2 of the UCC if the gas is to be "severed by the seller." UCC 2–107(1) [UCC 2–107(a) (1997)];

(2) Take-or-Pay provisions are not unconscionable at the time the contract is made;

(3) Take-or-Pay provisions do not provide for liquidated damages. Rather, they give the buyer a choice between alternative performances under the contract;

(4) *Force majeure* clauses are not intended to excuse the buyer from changes in the market, no matter how dramatic;

(5) UCC 2–615 [UCC 2–716 (1997)] will not be applied to excuse the buyer from the contract, even though government action in deregulating natural gas prices played an important role in the market decline.

In addition to *Kaiser–Francis Oil Co.,* supra, the following decisions support the brief summary above: Universal Resources Corp. v. Panhandle Eastern Pipe Line Co., 813 F.2d 77 (5th Cir.1987); Sabine Corp. v. ONG Western, Inc., 725 F.Supp. 1157 (W.D.Okl.1989); Resources Investment Corp. v. Enron Corp., 669 F.Supp. 1038 (D.Colo.1987); Golsen v. ONG Western, Inc., 756 P.2d 1209 (Okl.1988). See also Medina, *The Take-or-Pay Wars: A Further Status Report,* 41 Okl.L.Rev. 381 (1988); Greenwald, *Natural Gas Contracts Under Stress: Price, Quantity and Take or Pay,* 5 J.Energy & Nat.Resources L. 1 (1987); Smith, *How the UCC Applies to Natural Resources Transactions,* 33 Rocky Mtn.Min.L.Inst. 5 (1987); Note, *Deregulation and Natural Gas Purchase Contracts—Neoclassical and Relational Contract Theories,* 25 Washburn L.Rev. 43 (1986).

Comment: Reopener Clauses in Long–Term Supply Contracts

The uncertainties involved when a court develops and imposes a price adjustment, see, e.g., Comment, 47 Mo.L.Rev. 79, 102–110 (1982), could be partially resolved if the parties included a "gross inequities" or a "reopener" clause in the contract. These clauses operate in three stages: *first,* a "gross inequity" under the existing contract resulting from "unusual economic conditions not contemplated by the parties at the time of contracting" must exist; *second,* the parties agree to negotiate in good faith to correct or to adjust the inequity by agreement and to cooperate with each other in the process; *third,* if negotiations fail to produce an agreed adjustment, the dispute is submitted to arbitration, where the decision of the arbitrator is final and conclusive. These clauses, when included, preserve both the relative equities of the parties over time and the contract. Normally, the parties agree to continue performance under the original terms while the dispute is being resolved. See, e.g., Georgia Power Co. v. Cimarron Coal Corp., 526 F.2d 101, 103–04 (6th Cir.1975), cert. denied 425 U.S. 952, 96 S.Ct. 1727, 48 L.Ed.2d 195 (1976) (dispute under "gross inequities" clause subject to arbitration); Scott, *Coal Supply Agreements,* 23 Rky.Mtn.Min.L.Inst. 107, 131–39 (1977). These clauses will vary in scope and detail with the particular industry. As one commentator has noted, contract solutions "are not self-operative and depend, in large measure, upon the good faith of both the purchaser and the seller." Snyder, *Geothermal Sales Contracts,* 13 Land & Water L.Rev. 259, 288 (1977).

Here is an edited example of a "Fair Clause" which has been used in long-term international sales contracts in the copper industry.

Fair Clause

"§ **15.1** In entering into this long-term Agreement the parties hereto recognize that it is impracticable to make provision for every contingency which may arise during the term of this Agreement and the parties declare it to be their intention that this Agreement shall operate between them with fairness.

§ **15.2** Based on the foregoing principle the provisions of this Article 15 shall apply if during the term of this Agreement a new situation arises which is beyond the reasonable control of either party and which is not covered by any of the provisions of this Agreement and if such situation results in (a) a material disadvantage to one party and a corresponding material advantage to the other or (b) severe hardship to one party without an advantage to the other party.

* * *

§ **15.4** (a) In situations described under § 15.2(a) a solution shall be found in order to restore a fair balance of advantages and disadvantages as between the parties.

(b) In situations described under § 15.2(b) a solution shall be found in order to remove the severe hardship for the party affected; provided, however, that the provisions of this Agreement, as changed or modified by such solution and considered as a whole, shall remain commensurate with those of other international contracts between copper mines and independent smelters/refineries at the time of such change or modification and

(i) in case [buyer] invokes the Fair Clause, shall be no less favorable to [seller] than the provisions of any other comparable international contract between [buyer] and any independent copper mine other than [seller]; and

(ii) in case [seller] invokes the Fair Clause, shall be no less favorable to [buyer] than the provisions of any other comparable international contract between [seller] and any independent copper smelter/refinery other than [buyer].

The comparison of provisions as aforesaid shall serve as a valuation basis for the adjustment of the particular provisions of this Agreement which are involved, for instance the smelting/refining charge, but shall not result in replacing the provisions of this Agreement by the provisions of any compared contract, unless agreed upon between [seller] and [buyer].

(c) In arriving at solutions for either of the situations described in § 15.2, due consideration shall be given to such benefits as may have been obtained by each party as a result of a prior invocation of this Article 15.

§ 15.5 If either party hereto shall believe that a new situation described in § 15.2 shall have arisen, then, at the request of either party hereto, the parties shall promptly consult with a view toward reaching a mutually acceptable agreement dealing with such situation. In the event that within six months after the date of such request the parties shall not reach agreement with respect to such situation, either party shall have the right, exercisable within three months after the expiration of such six-month period, to refer the matter to arbitration pursuant to § 19.1. The arbitrator or arbitrators shall determine whether the particular situation is a "new situation" described in § 15.2(a) or in § 15.2(b) and, if so, shall, in any award entered, specify the section involved and unless the parties come to a prompt solution themselves, thereafter on the request of either party also establish a solution in conformity with § 15.4. Such arbitrator or arbitrators may obtain, for the purpose of establishing such solution, the opinion of an impartial expert of recognized standing in the international copper business, who shall not be domiciled in either the United States or Germany unless the parties hereto shall otherwise consent. Promptly after the entering of such award the parties hereto shall enter into a written agreement incorporating the terms of such award and making such changes or modifications in this Agreement as may be required in order to give effect to such award."

Practice in international trade has influenced the Unidroit Principles of International Commercial Contracts, which recognize that events subsequent to the contract may cause hardship and require that upon request of the disadvantaged party the other party must, at a minimum, negotiate in good faith toward an equilibrium. Articles 6.2.2 and 6.2.3, Comment 5. If the parties fail to reach agreement within a reasonable time, a court, if it finds hardship, "may, if reasonable, (a) terminate the contract at a date and on terms to be fixed, or (b) adapt the contract with a view to restoring its equilibrium." Article 6.2.3(4).

For an excellent analysis of the dynamics of adjustment, see Scott, *Conflict and Cooperation in Long-term Contracts,* 75 Calif.L.Rev. 2005 (1987).

(C) FRUSTRATION OF PURPOSE

Paradine v. Jane

King's Bench, 1647.
Aleyn, 26, 82 Eng.Rep. 897.

In debt the plaintiff declares upon a lease for years rendering rent at the four usual feasts; and for rent behind for three years, ending at the Feast of the Annunciation, 21 Car. brings his action; the defendant pleads, that a certain German prince, by name Prince Rupert, an alien born, enemy to the King and kingdom, had invaded the realm with an hostile army of men; and with the same force did enter upon the defendant's possession, and him expelled, and held out of possession from the 19 of July 18 Car. till the Feast of the Annunciation, 21 Car. whereby he could not take the profits; whereupon the plaintiff demurred, and the plea was resolved insufficient.

1.   Because the defendant hath not answered to one quarters rent.

2.   He hath not averred that the army were all aliens, which shall not be intended, and then he hath his remedy against them; and Bacon cited 33 H. 61 1. e. where the gaoler in bar of an escape pleaded, that alien enemies broke the prison & c. and exception take to it, for that he ought to shew of what countrey they were, viz. Scots, &c.

3.   It was resolved, that the matter of the plea was insufficient; for though the whole army had been alien enemies, yet he ought to pay his rent. And this difference was taken, that where the law creates a duty or charge, and the party is disabled to perform it without any default in him, and hath no remedy over, there the law will excuse him. As in the case of waste, if a house be destroyed by tempest, or by enemies, the lessee is excused. Dyer, 33. a. Inst. 53. d. 283. a. 12 H. 4. 6. so of an escape. Co. 4. 84. b. 33 H. 6. 1. So in 9 E. 3. 16. a supersedeas was awarded to the justices, that they should not proceed in a cessavit upon a cesser during the war, but when the party by his own contract creates a duty or charge upon himself, he is bound to make it good, if he may, notwithstanding any accident by inevitable necessity, because he might have provided against it by his contract. And therefore if the lessee covenant to repair a house, though it be burnt by lightning, or thrown down by enemies, yet he ought to repair it. Dyer 33. a. 40 E. 3. 6. h. Now the rent is a duty created by the parties upon the reservation, and had there been a covenant to pay it, there had been no question but the lessee must have made it good, notwithstanding the interruption by enemies, for the law would not protect him beyond his

own agreement, no more than in the case of reparations; this reservation then being a covenant in law, and whereupon an action of covenant hath been maintained (as Roll said) it is all one as if there had been an actual covenant. Another reason was added, that as the lessee is to have the advantage of casual profits, so he must run the hazard of casual losses, and not lay the whole burthen of them upon his lessor; and Dyer 56. 6. was cited for this purpose, that though the land be surrounded, or gained by the sea, or made barren by wildfire, yet the lessor shall have his whole rent: and judgment was given for the plaintiff.

Krell v. Henry

Court of Appeal, 1903.
[1903] 2 K.B. 740.

Appeal from a decision of DARLING, J. The plaintiff, Paul Krell, sued the defendant, C.S. Henry, for 50*l.*, being the balance of a sum of 75*l.*, for which the defendant had agreed to hire a flat at 56A, Pall Mall on the days of June 26 and 27, for the purpose of viewing the processions to be held in connection with the coronation of His Majesty. The defendant denied his liability, and counterclaimed for the return of the sum of 25*l.*, which had been paid as a deposit, on the ground that, the processions not having taken place owing to the serious illness of the King, there had been a total failure of consideration for the contract entered into by him.

[The defendant was induced to contract by an announcement in the window of plaintiff's flat renting windows to view the coronation, but the contract itself contained no express reference to the coronation.]

Darling J., held, upon the authority of *Taylor v. Caldwell* ... that there was an implied condition in the contract that the procession should take place, and gave judgment for the defendant on the claim and counterclaim. The plaintiff appealed.

■ VAUGHAN WILLIAMS L.J. read the following written judgment:—The real question in this case is the extent of the application in English law of the principle of the Roman law which has been adopted and acted on in many English decisions, and notably in the case of *Taylor v. Caldwell*. That case at least makes it clear that

> where, from the nature of the contract, it appears that the parties must from the beginning have known that it could not be fulfilled unless, when the time for the fulfilment of the contract arrived, some particular specified thing continued to exist, so that when entering into the contract they must have contemplated such continued existence as the foundation of what was to be done; there, in the absence of any express or implied warranty that the thing shall exist, the contract is not to be considered a positive contract, but as subject to an implied condition that the parties shall be excused in case, before breach, performance becomes impossible from the perishing of the thing without default of the contractor.

Thus far it is clear that the principle of the Roman law has been introduced into the English law. The doubt in the present case arises as to how far this principle extends. * * *

I do not think that the principle of the civil law as introduced into the English law is limited to cases in which the event causing the impossibility of performance is the destruction or non-existence of some thing which is the subject-matter of the contract or of some condition or state of things expressly specified as a condition of it. I think that you first have to ascertain, not necessarily from the terms of the contract, but, if required, from necessary inferences, drawn from surrounding circumstances recognised by both contracting parties, what is the substance of the contract, and then to ask the question whether that substantial contract needs for its foundation the assumption of the existence of a particular state of things. If it does, this will limit the operation of the general words, and in such case, if the contract becomes impossible of performance by reason of the nonexistence of the state of things assumed by both contracting parties as the foundation of the contract, there will be no breach of the contract thus limited. . . .

In my judgment the use of the rooms was let and taken for the purpose of seeing the Royal procession. It was not a demise of the rooms, or even an agreement to let and take the rooms. It is a license to use rooms for a particular purpose and none other. And in my judgment the taking place of those processions on the days proclaimed along the proclaimed route, which passed 56A, Pall Mall, was regarded by both contracting parties as the foundation of the contract; and I think that it cannot reasonably be supposed to have been in the contemplation of the contracting parties, when the contract was made, that the coronation would not be held on the proclaimed days, or the processions not take place on those days along the proclaimed route; and I think that the words imposing on the defendant the obligation to accept and pay for the use of the rooms for the named days, although general and unconditional, were not used with reference to the possibility of the particular contingency which afterwards occurred. It was suggested in the course of the argument that if the occurrence, on the proclaimed days, of the coronation and the procession in this case were the foundation of the contract, and if the general words are thereby limited or qualified, so that in the event of the non-occurrence of the coronation and procession along the proclaimed route they would discharge both parties from further performance of the contract, it would follow that if a cabman was engaged to take some one to Epsom on Derby Day at a suitable enhanced price for such a journey, say 10l., both parties to the contract would be discharged in the contingency of the race at Epsom for some reason becoming impossible; but I do not think this follows, for I do not think that in the cab case the happening of the race would be the foundation of the contract. No doubt the purpose of the engager would be to go to see the Derby, and the price would be proportionately high; but the cab had no special qualifications for the purpose which led to the selection of the cab for this particular occasion. Any other cab would have done as well. Moreover, I think that, under the cab contract, the hirer, even if the race went off, could have said, "Drive me to Epsom; I will pay you the agreed sum; you have nothing to do with the purpose for which I hired the cab," and that if the cabman refused he would have been guilty of a breach of contract, there being nothing to qualify his promise to drive the hirer to Epsom on a particular day. Whereas in the case of the coronation, there is not merely the purpose of the hirer to see the coronation procession, but it is the coronation procession and the relative position of the rooms which is the basis of the contract as much for the lessor as the hirer; and I think that if the King, before the coronation day and after the contract, had died, the hirer could not have insisted on having the rooms on the days named. It could not in the cab case be reasonably said that seeing the Derby race was the foundation of the contract, as it was of the license in this case. Whereas in the present case, where the rooms were offered and taken, by reason of their peculiar suitability from the position of the rooms for a view of the coronation procession, surely the view of the coronation procession was the foundation of the contract, which is a very different thing from the purpose of the man who engaged the cab—namely, to see the race—being held to be the foundation of the contract. Each case must be judged by its own circumstances. In each case one must ask oneself, first, what, having regard to all the circumstances, was the foundation of the contract? Secondly, was the performance of the contract prevented? Thirdly, was the event which prevented the performance of the contract of such a character that it cannot reasonably be said to have been in the contemplation of the parties at the date of the contract? If all these questions are answered in the affirmative (as I think they should be in this case), I think both parties are discharged from further performance of the contract. I think that the coronation procession was the foundation of this contract, and that the non-happening of it prevented the performance of the contract; and, secondly, I think that the non-happening of the procession ... was an event "of such a character that it cannot reasonably be supposed to have been in the contemplation of the contracting parties when the contract was made, and that they are not to be held bound by general words which, though large enough to include, were not used with reference to the possibility of the particular contingency which afterwards happened." The test seems to be whether the event which causes the impossibility was or might have been anticipated and guarded against. * * *

I myself am clearly of opinion that in this case, where we have to ask ourselves whether the object of the contract was frustrated by the non-happening of the coronation and its procession on the days proclaimed, parol evidence is admissible to shew that the subject of the contract was rooms to view the coronation procession, and was so to the knowledge of both parties. . . .

This disposes of the plaintiff's claim for 50*l.* unpaid balance of the price agreed to be paid for the use of the rooms. The defendant at one time set up a cross-claim for the return of the 25*l.* he paid at the date of the contract. As that claim is now withdrawn it is unnecessary to say anything about it.

[The concurring opinions of Romer, L.J. and Stirling, L.J. are omitted.]

Appeal dismissed.

NOTES

The Development of Frustration under English Law. After tracing the development of frustration in English law, G. H. Treitel concludes:

"From a practical point of view, the doctrine of frustration gives rise to two related difficulties. The first is that it may scarcely be more satisfactory to hold that the contract is totally discharged than to hold that it remains in force; often some compromise may be a more reasonable solution. * * * In the absence of * * * express provisions, this kind of solution is not open to the courts; they have no power to *modify* contracts in the light of supervening events. The second difficulty is that the allocation of risks produced at common law by the doctrine of frustration is not always entirely satisfactory. In a case like *Taylor v. Caldwell* it may be reasonable that neither party should be liable for loss of the benefit that the other expected to derive from performance * * * [b]ut it does not follow that loss suffered by one party as a result in acting in reliance on the contract should equally lie where it falls. In *Taylor v. Caldwell* the plaintiffs did not in fact make any claim for lost profits, but only one for expenses thrown away in advertising the concerts. It is by no means self-evident that the owners of the hall (who had presumably insured it) should escape all liability for this loss; and it might be more satisfactory if loss of this kind could be apportioned. At common law this was only possible where the contract expressly so provided; * * *. A more general, but nevertheless limited power of apportionment now exists by statute, but it does not cover all cases in which some form of apportionment would seem to be desirable. * * * (citing the Frustrated Contracts Act.)" G.H. Treitel, The Law of Contract 651–52 (6th ed. 1983). See also Price, *The Doctrine of Frustration and Leases,* 10 J.Legal Hist. 90, 92–101 (1989).

Washington State Hop Producers, Inc. v. Goschie Farms, Inc.

Supreme Court of Washington, 1989.
112 Wash.2d 694, 773 P.2d 70.

[From 1965 until 1985, the U.S. Department of Agriculture required hop growers to obtain federal allotments in order to market their hops. This was called "hop base." Growers could transfer excess allotments to other growers. Over time, "hop base" became a scarce, expensive commodity and a secondary market developed for trading. Plaintiff, the Trust, was organized in 1979 to acquire, lease and sell federal hop base.

Because the system restricted market entry, legal efforts to change the marketing order were commenced in 1981. The USDA considered various changes, but as late as June, 1985, substantial changes in the marketing order were not anticipated. On May 31, 1985, the Trust mailed invitations to bid on two pools of "hop base" for sale. Pool A of 633,500 pounds was available for use in 1985 and Pool B of 432,639 pounds was available for use in 1986. On June 16, 1985, bids were received ranging from $0.05 per pound to $0.76 per pound. On June 21, 1985, the Trust mailed notices of award to bids in the $0.50 to $0.76 range, including Goschie and other respondents in this case. On June 27, 1985, however, the USDA terminated the marketing order, effective December 31, 1985. All of the respondents refused to perform the contracts for sale. The Trust was able to sell nearly 50% of the "hop base" in Pool B for an average price of $0.07 per pound, compared with earlier successful bids of $0.60 per pound.

In an action by the Trust to enforce the contracts, the trial court granted summary judgment to the respondents. This was affirmed in the court of appeals which, in essence, held that the respondent's contracts were excused by the rule of supervening frustration. The Trust appealed.]

* * *

Perhaps the earliest case clearly recognizing frustration of purpose as a defense in a breach of contract action is Krell v. Henry, 2 K.B. 740 (C.A.1903). There, a lease was made to rent use of a window overlooking the route for the coronation parade of Albert Edward when he succeeded his mother, Queen Victoria. After the agreement, Edward became ill, the parade was canceled, and the purpose of renting the window was frustrated. The lessee refused to pay the agreed rent. The court held that his duty was discharged and that he was therefore not liable for breach. Both parties were capable of performing the terms of their contracts, and there was arguably still some market value in the vendor's performance. But the lessee's ultimate purpose was frustrated and he was released from his contract nonetheless.

The doctrine of "Discharge by Supervening Frustration" is recited in Restatement (Second) of Contracts § 265 (1979):

> Where, after a contract is made, a party's principal purpose is substantially frustrated without his fault by the occurrence of an event the non-occurrence of which was a basic assumption on which the contract was made, his remaining duties to render performance are discharged, unless the language or the circumstances indicate the contrary.

Comment (a) to the section further explains:

> This Section deals with the problem that arises when a change in circumstances makes one party's performance virtually worthless to the other, frustrating his purpose in making the contract ... First, the purpose that is frustrated must have been a principal purpose of that party in making the contract ... The object must be so completely the basis of the contract that, as both parties understand, without it the transaction would make little sense. Second, the frustration must be substantial. It is not enough that the transaction has become less profitable for the affected party or even that he will sustain a loss. The frustration must be so severe that it is not fairly to be regarded as within the risks that he assumed under the contract. Third, the non-occurrence of the frustrating event must have been a basic assumption

on which the contract was made ... The foreseeability of the event is ... a factor in that determination, but the mere fact that the event was foreseeable does not compel the conclusion that its non-occurrence was not such a basic assumption.

This is the rule and test recited and applied by the Court of Appeals. ... However, Washington has not before now adopted the doctrine of supervening frustration as recited in Restatement (Second) of Contracts § 265 (1979).

Under the restatement formula, "the purpose that is frustrated must have been a principal purpose of that party in making the contract ... without [which] the transaction would make little sense." Restatement (Second) of Contracts § 265, comment (a) (1979). The Court of Appeals found "the principal purpose of this contract was to purchase a hop allotment base provided and created pursuant to a hop marketing agreement." Washington State Hop Producers, Inc. Liquidation Trust v. Goschie Farms, Inc., 51 Wash.App. 484, 754 P.2d 139 (1988). We agree.

Under the conditions prevailing for nearly 20 years before the termination order, ownership of hop base provided permanent access to the hop market otherwise unavailable. After the termination, what was available to "purchase" was at most access to the 1985 crop year market. The Trust had formerly been in the business of renting 1–year access to the hop market. The Growers did not seek single-year market access, nor did they bid prices in the range of the 1–year rental (6 cents ($0.06) per pound). Without the federal requirement of hop base, there would have been no subject matter for the contracts nor any consideration from the Trust to support the transactions. Because the Growers sought to *purchase* hop base instead of renting it, the inference is that *future* market access was their principal purpose in entering the transactions. This purpose was understood by both parties. Purchase, as opposed to rental, of the hop base made little sense without future market access. The record provides sufficient undisputed facts to sustain the Court of Appeals' determination on this point.

The Court of Appeals relied upon the decline in value of hop allotments in determining that the purpose of the contracts had been frustrated by termination of the hop marketing order. The pertinent language from the appellate opinion is:

> Here, we find the principal purpose of this contract was to purchase a hop allotment base provided and created pursuant to a hop marketing agreement. As is evident when the marketing order was terminated, effective December 31, 1985, the value of that allotment decreased [in June 1985 when the termination was announced], assuming a bid of $.50 fell to $.05, i.e., one-tenth the bid price. We consider that a substantial frustration falling within the rule.

Washington State Hop Producers, Inc. Liquidation Trust v. Goschie Farms, Inc., 51 Wash.App. 484, 489, 754 P.2d 139 (1988). It is not clear from the language employed whether the "frustration" is the 90 percent decline in market price, or whether the decline in value is merely evidence of the substantiality of the frustration.

The decline in price was great. Before the Termination Order, hop base was a prerequisite to the sale of hops. The annual *rental* price of hop base for 1985 was 6 cents per pound before the Termination Order. Successful bids to *purchase* Pool "A" hop base before termination ranged up to 76 cents per pound. After termination, hop base would be unnecessary following the 1985 crop year. Pool "B" hop base that had commanded a pre-termination price of not less than 50 cents (when it could be sold at all after the termination was announced) commanded an average price of just $\frac{7}{10}$ of one cent ($0.007)—a 98 percent decrease in value.

[A] rational market should have valued post-termination Pool "A" base at about 6 and $\frac{7}{10}$ cents ($0.067) per pound.... [T]he post-termination decrease remains in the range of 92 percent....

If the decline in price alone is considered to be substantial frustration, then the decision of the Court of Appeals cannot be affirmed without doing violence to established principles of contract law. See, e.g., Restatement (Second) of Contracts § 265, comment (a) (1979) ("It is not enough that the transaction has become less profitable for the affected party or even that he will sustain a loss."). The decision may be affirmed on other grounds, however. * * *

If the decline in price is regarded merely as evidence of substantiality of frustration of the purpose of the contract, then the Court of Appeals' reasoning, as well as its decision, may stand.... [I]t is not the decline in market price, but the irrelevance of control of hop base after the 1985 crop year that supplies the frustration justifying rescission.

Application of the doctrine of frustration is a question of law and not a question of fact. 2 Restatement (Second) of Contracts 310 (1979); See Columbian National Title Insurance Company v. Township Title Services, Inc., 659 F.Supp. 796 (D.Kan.1987). Whether, as appellant states, "the value of the [Trust's] performance is ... totally or nearly totally destroyed by supervening events," as evidenced by the decline in price, seems a matter well within the sound judgment of the trial court. We will not disturb that court's determination.

In this case appellant Trust makes repeated references to "foreseeability" of the market order termination as invalidating the rescission granted by the trial court. However, as the Court of Appeals noted, "[w]hile the Trust seeks to hold the growers to knowledge that the order could be terminated at any time, it takes no responsibility for the same knowledge." Washington State Hop Producers, Inc. Liquidation Trust v. Goschie Farms, Inc., 51 Wash.App. 484, 488, 754 P.2d 139 (1988). The court noted that the Trust had incorporated no language in its bid form allocating the risk to the growers. The court also noted that the growers had not included any allocating language in their "acceptance." This latter reference seems not to be made to any particular document. All documents and exhibits in the record comprising the transactions between the parties consist of forms provided by the Trust. The growers simply filled in blanks on bid forms provided by the Trust. There is no indication that any restrictive language could have been added by the growers. By contrast, the Trust had every opportunity to draft the language to its own advantage. It did not do so.

Moreover, the inference is that, even to the Trust, the termination was unforeseeable or at least not foreseen.... In its own brief, the Trust states, "[a]s late as June, 1985 ... it was not anticipated that any substantial change in the Marketing Order would be proposed by the Secretary of Agriculture." In its introduction to Chapter 11, the Restatement notes the significance of the "relative ease with which either party could have inserted a clause" 2 Restatement (Second) of Contracts 311 (1979). In context, this factor is equivalent to foreseeability in affecting the application of the doctrine.

Under the Restatement formula, foreseeability is merely a relevant factor in determining whether nonoccurrence of the frustrating event was a basic assumption of the frustrated party in entering the transaction. If that basic assumption is found, as it was here, the "issue" of foreseeability becomes irrelevant.... The trial court, implicitly, and the Court of Appeals, explicitly, found that continued need to own or control hop base in order to sell hops was an assumption central to the subject matter of the contract. The Court of Appeals concluded that "[w]e find without this basic assumption there would neither have been an offer nor an acceptance." 51 Wash.App. 484, 490, 754 P.2d 139.

By repeating its position, the Restatement is emphatic on the role of foreseeability. The introductory note to Chapter 11 reads:

> The fact that the [frustrating] event was unforeseeable is significant as suggesting that its non-occurrence was a basic assumption. However, the fact that it was foreseeable, or even foreseen, does not, of itself, argue for a contrary conclusion, since the parties may not have thought it sufficiently important a risk to have made it a subject of their bargaining. Another significant factor may be the relative bargaining positions of the parties and the relative ease with which either party could have included a clause.

2 Restatement (Second) of Contracts 311 (1979).

Appellant refers to the Restatement (Second) of Contracts § 261 in support of its contention that foreseeability avoids the defense of commercial frustration. The section is inapposite because it concerns the defense of supervening impracticability. Frustration is covered in § 265. However, even if the reference did apply, the language does not advance appellant's argument.

> A commercial practice under which a party might be expected to insure or otherwise secure himself against a risk also militates against shifting it to the other party. If the supervening event was not reasonably foreseeable when the contract was made, the party claiming discharge can hardly be expected to have provided against its occurrence. However, if it was reasonably foreseeable, or even foreseen, the

opposite conclusion [i.e., that the party should not be discharged] does not necessarily follow.

Restatement (Second) of Contracts § 261 at comment (c), p. 315. Cross reference is made to § 265, comment (a), quoted above, and § 261, comment (c). Pertinent language from this latter reference includes the following: "The fact that the event was foreseeable *or even foreseen,* does not necessarily compel a conclusion that its non-occurrence was not a basic assumption." (Italics ours.) Restatement (Second) of Contracts § 261, comment (b), p. 314.

* * *

Although language suggesting that unforeseeability is a prerequisite of supervening frustration has found its way into the case law of this state, see, e.g., Weyerhaeuser Real Estate Co. v. Stoneway Concrete, Inc., 26 Wash.App. 882, 889, 614 P.2d 249 (1980) (Dore, J., dissenting) overruled, 96 Wash.2d 558, 637 P.2d 647 (1981), the basis for this rule does not apply to this case. The Growers did not receive an estate in land, such as would be provided by a commercial lease, see Lloyd v. Murphy, 25 Cal.2d 48, 153 P.2d 47 (1944), nor did they ever have the beneficial use of the subject matter of the contracts for which they request rescission. The Restatement (Second) of Contracts repeatedly refers to foreseeability as only a factor in determining whether the non-occurrence of the frustrating event was an assumption basic to the contract. Moreover, foreseeability of a possible frustrating event is meaningful only where the party seeking relief could have controlled the language of the contract to the extent of allocating the risk. Here, exclusive control of the contract language was in the hands of the Trust and the Trust did not include disclaimers in its contracts until after the termination order.

[Footnotes omitted.]

NOTES

(1) *Goschie Farms* is one of the rare American decisions granting relief under the doctrine of "frustration of purpose." For some other examples, see Aluminum Company of America v. Essex Group, Inc., 499 F.Supp. 53, 76–77 (W.D.Pa.1980) (supplier's "principal purpose" to make a profit substantially frustrated by changed economic conditions); Western Properties v. Southern Utah Aviation, Inc., 776 P.2d 656, 659 (Utah App.1989) (sublessee's duty to pay rent and improve premises frustrated by government act which left property without value); Matter of Fontana D'Oro Foods, Inc., 122 Misc.2d 1091, 472 N.Y.S.2d 528 (1983) (purpose of one party to settlement frustrated by unforeseen conduct of insurance company which rendered assets valueless); Molnar v. Molnar, 110 Mich.App. 622, 313 N.W.2d 171 (1981) (death of child frustrates purpose in divorce property settlement). But see Arabian Score v. Lasma Arabian, Ltd., 814 F.2d 529 (8th Cir.1987) (death of stallion shortly after delivery to buyer did not discharge seller's duty to pay a fixed price for advertising and promotion over a five year period).

(2) *Judge Posner on Frustration of Purpose.* In the NIPSCO case, supra at 744, the buyer, an Indiana electric utility, entered into a 20–year contract to purchase a fixed quantity of coal, some 1.5 million tons per year, at a fixed price of $24 per ton, subject only to upward escalation, from a producer in Wyoming. When the market for energy turned down, the Indiana Public Service Commission directed NIPSCO to make a good faith effort to buy electricity from other utilities at prices lower than the cost of producing it and warned that, because the coal contract was imprudent, permission to pass its high costs through to consumers might be disallowed. Later, NIPSCO stopped taking deliveries of coal and sought a declaratory judgment that it was excused from the contract. The producer, claiming breach, counterclaimed for damages and obtained a verdict in the amount of $181,000,000. On appeal, the verdict was affirmed.

One of the issues on appeal was whether the contract was unenforceable by virtue of the doctrines of "frustration or impracticability." After reviewing the excuse standards under UCC 2–615 and the Restatement, Judge Posner for the court stated:

> The leading case on frustration remains *Krell v. Henry* ... Krell rented Henry a suite of rooms for watching the coronation of Edward VII, but Edward came down with appendicitis and the coronation had to be postponed. Henry refused to pay the balance of the rent and the court held that he was excused from doing so because his purpose in renting had been frustrated by the postponement, a contingency outside the knowledge, or power to influence, of either party. The question was, to which party did the contract (implicitly) allocate the risk? Surely Henry had not intended to insure Krell against the possibility of the coronation's being postponed, since Krell could always relet the room, at the premium rental, for the coronation's new date. So Henry was excused.

The court noted that since NIPSCO "is a buyer in the present case ... its defense is more properly frustration than impracticability." The court, however, avoided having to decide whether Indiana recognized the doctrine of frustration by concluding that "the facts of the present case do not bring it within the scope of the frustration doctrine...." 799 F.2d at 277.

Do you agree with (1) Judge Posner's analysis of *Krell v. Henry* and (2) the court's result on the frustration question? If so, must you then disagree with the Supreme Court of Washington's decision in *Goschie Farms?* See Comment, *NIPSCO: Risk Assumption, Claims or Impossibility, Impracticability, and Frustration of Purpose,* 50 Ohio St.L.J. 163 (1989).

(3) *Frustration in Leases.* In England until 1981, *Paradine v. Jane,* supra, was still thought to be good law. Lessees to whom an interest in land was conveyed were thought to have an absolute duty to pay the rent regardless of alleged frustrating events. See G. Treitel, The Law of Contracts 583–86 (4th ed. 1975). In 1981, the House of Lords, in National Carriers Ltd. v. Panal Pina (Northern) Ltd., A.C. 675, 2 W.L.R. 45, [1981] 1 All E.R. 161, held that a lease could be discharged by frustration, but concluded that relief was not justified on the facts of the particular case. In *National Carriers,* the tenant, under a 10–year lease of a warehouse, was denied relief even though the only access road was closed by local authority four and one-half years before the end of the term and remained closed for 20 months. The interruption was not deemed

sufficiently serious to justify discharge. See Price, *The Doctrine of Frustration and Leases,* 10 J.Legal Hist. 90 (1989).

Courts in the United States have frequently noted the possibility that a lessee might be discharged due to frustration, but have rarely granted relief. In the well known case of Lloyd v. Murphy, 25 Cal.2d 48, 153 P.2d 47 (1944), Justice Traynor recognized that a lease might be frustrated in a proper case. Nevertheless, the court refused to discharge the lessee of prime commercial property when a governmental wartime order prevented use of the property for the sole purpose of the lease, the sale of new cars. The lessor, however, had modified the restriction to permit other uses and, although there were still restrictions, the lease was still valuable to the lessee. In short, in the absence of proof that the value of the lease was "totally destroyed," relief was denied.

More recently, a court discharged the duty of a sublessee to pay rent on the following facts. Cedar City leased undeveloped land near the municipal airport to Western Properties for a 15–year–term. Western, with Cedar City approval, subleased the land for part of that term to Southern Utah Aviation. Southern agreed to pay rent and to construct a maintenance building on the land, which would revert to Western at the end of the lease. Cedar City, however, had not developed a master plan for the airport and, because of this, failed to approve Southern's application for a site plan to construct the building. Southern abandoned the site without constructing the building or paying the rent due. Western sued for damages for failure to construct and for rent due. Concluding that both parties assumed that the City would approve the site plan, the court excused the duty to construct on grounds of impracticability and excused the duty to pay rent on grounds of frustration. Without confronting the common law rule restricting discharge of a duty to pay rent, the court discharged the lessee and stated: "Without a way of productively using the land, the purpose of the leasehold was effectively frustrated. * * * There was no point in leasing this land once its development became impossible." Western Properties v. Southern Utah Aviation, Inc., 776 P.2d 656, 659 (Utah App.1989).

(4) *ALCOA Revisited*: ALCOA's claim of frustration requires more discussion. ALCOA's "principal purpose" in making the contract was to earn money. This purpose has plainly been severely disappointed. The gravity of ALCOA's loss is undisputably sufficient to meet the stern standard for relief. But the question remains whether the law will grant relief for the serious frustration of this kind of purpose, i.e., for the conversion of an expected profit into a serious loss. All of the new Restatement illustrations center on purposes other than making a profit. However most of them bear on some stage of a profit oriented activity. Illustrations 2–7 describe profit oriented business activities which contribute to the success of enterprises though they are not themselves directly profitable. In each, the question is whether the immediate end of this discrete contract is frustrated, without regard to the impact of the frustration on the more remote end of earning profits. Thus illustration 4 involves a lease of a neon sign to a business. A subsequent governmental regulation prohibits illuminating the sign. The Restatement declares the lessee's duty to pay rent to be discharged. Here the lessee's most immediate principal purpose is night time advertising.

Illustration 6 involves a gasoline station lease. A change in traffic regulations reduces the lessee's business that he can operate only at a substantial loss. The Restatement declares: "If B can still operate a station ... his principal purpose of operating a gasoline station is not substantially frustrated." Here the profit is not deemed the principal purpose of the lessee. The operation of the gas station is that purpose. Why should a court or the Restatement prefer one characterization to the other? Perhaps it is due to the fact that the dispute involves a lease. Professor Corbin notes that this result is generally supported by the leasehold cases but that the reason for the result has changed over the years.

It was formerly thought to be a sufficient reason for making the lessee pay the agreed rent that he promised in general and unlimited terms, when he might have provided against such contingencies in his contract. He has "assumed the risk" by not having the foresight to exclude it in express terms. This reason has long since ceased to be convincing, as is shown by the multitude of cases holding that a promisor's duty is discharged by the supervening events that make his performance impossible. Whether the frustration of the tenant's purposes operates in discharge of his duty depends upon all the circumstances, especially upon the extent of that frustration and the prevailing practices of men in like cases. Professor Corbin clearly associates the result in such cases with the concept of judicial risk allocation. Among the factors entitled to serious consideration by the courts are the lessee's alternative uses of the premises, whether the lease is for a long term or a short term; whether the lessee's special intended use was known to the lessor, and whether that special use was reflected in the rental terms. The common understanding of business people who enter such leases is also important. A business lease is, among other things, the conveyance of a possessory interest in property for a term. Lessors are not commonly understood to insure the success of the business to be conducted on the premises. Williston does not wholly disagree, though he insists that relief should be granted only for "the total or nearly total destruction of the purpose for which, in the contemplation of both parties, the transaction was entered into." Williston on Contracts §§ 1955, 1961 (3d ed. 1978) (Jaeger). In light of this commentary, the Court infers that illustration 6 rests on the particular circumstances of the lease rather than on an implicit limitation of the general language of § 285 which precludes the earning of profits and avoidance (or limitation) of losses from being "the principal purpose" of a party.

In § 1360 Professor Corbin demonstrates that at times courts should treat loss avoidance as a principal purpose of a party. That section deals with frustration of purpose caused by inflationary depreciation of money. Corbin demonstrates that the decisions are not uniform on this subject, but he rejects as reprehensible the nominalist rule that a dollar's a dollar no matter how small. The injustice of the nominalist position was clearly recognized in the case of Anderson v. Equitable Life Assurance Society, 134 L.T. 557, 42 T.L.R. 302 (1926). The facts in *Anderson* were these: In 1887 an Englishman in Russia took out a life insurance policy with premiums and benefits payable in German marks. The policy benefit was 60,000 marks. The premiums were paid from 1887 to 1907 and were converted, as both parties understood they would be, into pounds. Their value came to £ 2,377. The insured died in 1922 at the height of the German hyperinflation. At that time the value of 60,000 marks was less than an English penny. The insurer argued that it owed nothing on the contract, for it could not be required to pay a fraction of a cent. Astonishingly, the court agreed. Under English law the obligation to pay in foreign currency was absolute and unqualified by variations in exchange rates. The judges noted the harshness of the result and pressed upon the company its moral obligation to make some payment which they held the law would not compel.

Happily some American cases and the law of many foreign countries take a different view of the problem. The problem of serious, sustained inflation is not unique to modern America. During the Revolution and the Civil War, America witnessed serious inflation. And several other nations have recently experienced more severe inflation than America has. When the problem has arisen, here and abroad, courts and legislatures have repeatedly acted to relieve parties from great and unexpected losses. See Mann, The Legal Aspect of Money (1938); Corbin on Contracts § 1360 and cases there cited. The exact character of the relief granted is not important here. Neither is the exact explanation of the decisions found in the cases, because even the Civil War cases antedate the evolution of the distinct doctrine of frustration. What is important is this: first, the results of those decisions would be readily explained today in terms of frustration of purpose. Corbin discusses them in his chapter on Frustration of Purpose. And second, the frustration which they involved was a frustration of the purpose to earn money or to avoid losses. Thus it appears that there is no legitimate doctrinal problem which prevents relief for frustration of this sort. There remain the customary strictures concerning risk allocation and gravity of injury. Those have been addressed above and need not be considered again here. The Court holds ALCOA is entitled to relief on its claim of frustration of purpose. [499 F.Supp. at 76–77. Footnotes omitted.]

Comment: Forms of Relief after Impracticability

If a claim of "existing" or "supervening" impracticability is raised during performance, the parties may agree upon an appropriate modification or adjustment of the contract and complete performance without knowing whether the promisor was entitled to "some relief" as a matter of law. The enforceability of these agreed adjustments will be considered in Chapter Five, Section 4(c). The courts are unanimous that in the absence of an agreement a promisee has no duty to negotiate with the promisor in good faith over any proposed adjustment. We will also consider the soundness of this position in the next section.

If the court determines that the promisor is not entitled to relief (and there is no agreed adjustment), the legal situation is reasonably clear. If the promisor has failed to complete performance, it has breached the contract and is liable for damages to the promisee. If the promisor has completed performance despite the difficulty it must bear the burden of any costs incurred in excess of the contract price. See, e.g., Transatlantic Financing Corp. v. United States, 363 F.2d 312 (D.C.Cir.1966).

If the court determines that the promisor is entitled to "some relief" from impracticability, exactly what form should that relief take? First, let us assume that despite the existing or supervening difficulty, the promisor has completed performance at additional costs but without any default. This is risky business. Even if the promisee has requested the continued performance in light of the difficulty, some courts have denied recovery for any costs incurred after the promisor knew or had reason to know that performance was impracticable. See, e.g., the "Chugach Trilogy," Northern Corp. v. Chugach Electric Ass'n, 518 P.2d 76 (Alaska 1974), modified 523 P.2d 1243 (1974), judgment of the trial court affirmed, Chugach Elec. Ass'n v. Northern Corp., 562 P.2d 1053 (1977). For the final word, see 563 P.2d 883 (1977). A unique exception is National Presto Indus., Inc. v. United States, 338 F.2d 99 (Ct.Cl.1964), cert. denied 380 U.S. 962, 85 S.Ct. 1105, 14 L.Ed.2d 153 (1965), where the Court of Claims granted one-half of the contractor's claim for extra costs incurred in overcoming difficulties inhering in a new, experimental manufacturing process. In holding that the United States must share the excess costs, the court stressed that (1) both parties assumed that an essential step in the process would not be required but understood that time and expense would be needed to determine this with certainty, (2) the government was anxious to perfect the new process, (3) the government benefited from the perfected process and (4) if asked, the government would have agreed at the beginning of performance to share some but not all of the extra costs. As Judge Davis put it:

> For such a case it is equitable to reform the contract so that each side bears a share of the unexpected costs, instead of permitting the whole loss to remain with the party on whom it chanced to light. ... Reformation, as the child of equity, can mold its relief to attain any fair result within the broadest perimeter of the charter the parties have established for themselves. Where that arrangement has allocated the risk to neither side, a judicial division is fair and equitable.

338 F.2d at 112. Despite the potential, reformation in this context has not been embraced in disputes in private contracts and has been limited in government contracts to a "joint enterprise" experiment where the government is more concerned with process than end product and also benefits from the contractor's trial and error. Even without loss sharing, however, a contractor whose performance is delayed by impracticability will be excused. See UCC 2–615(a).

Second, suppose the promisor, upon encountering claimed impracticability, refuses to continue performance. If the court determines that performance was excused, a traditional statement of the form of relief goes something like this. The promisor is discharged from the unexecuted portion of the contract. Neither party can recover damages for breach of contract. If there has been some part performance prior to discharge, either party can recover at the contract rate for a divisible or severable part of that performance. If part performance is not divisible, either party can recover in restitution for any benefit conferred on the other. But expenditures incurred in reliance on the contract, whether in preparation or part performance, are not recoverable unless they have met the "divisibility" or "benefit" tests.

The limited scope of this traditional position prompted parliament to enact the "Frustrated Contracts" Act in 1944. This statute, which is reprinted below,* gave limited protection to the pre-discharge reliance interest. See Comment, *Restitutionary Principles and the Frustrated Contracts Act of 1944,* 4 Auckland L.Rev. 56 (1980).

A bolder solution is proposed in Section 272 of Restatement (Second). Subsection (1) states the classic view. Paraphrasing, in "any case" where relief from impracticability or frustration of purpose is justified, "either party may have a claim for relief including restitution" under the rules stated in Section 240, dealing with "divisible" contracts, and Section 377, dealing with restitution in cases of impracticability. There is not much change here. Subsection (2), however, provides:

> In any case governed by the rules stated in this Chapter, if those rules together with the rules stated in Chapter 16 will not avoid injustice, the court may grant relief on such terms as justice requires including protection of the parties' reliance interests.

Thus, if the contract is discharged because of impracticability, the court, in the interest of justice, may supply a term to protect the reliance interest regardless of whether the contract was properly divisible or whether the

---

* The Law Reform (Frustrated Contracts), Act 1943 (6 & 7 Geo. 6 c. 40)

1. Adjustment of rights and liabilities of parties to frustrated contracts

(1) Where a contract governed by English law has become impossible of performance or been otherwise frustrated, and the parties thereto have for that reason been discharged from the further performance of the contract, the following provisions of this section shall, subject to the provisions of section two of this Act, have effect in relation thereto.

(2) All sums paid or payable to any party in pursuance of the contract before the time when the parties were so discharged (in this Act referred to as "the time of discharge") shall, in the case of sums so paid, be recoverable from him as money received by him for the use of the party by whom the sums were paid, and, in the case of sums so payable, cease to be so payable:

Provided that, if the party to whom the sums were so paid or payable incurred expenses before the time of discharge in, or for the purpose of, the performance of the contract, the court may, if it considers it just to do so having regard to all the circumstances of the case, allow him to retain or, as the case may be, recover the whole or any part of the sums so paid or payable, not being an amount in excess of the expenses so incurred.

(3) Where any party to the contract has, by reason of anything done by any other party thereto in, or for the purpose of, the performance of the contract, obtained a valuable benefit (other than a payment of money to which the last foregoing subsection applies) before the time of discharge, there shall be recoverable from him by the said other party such sum (if any), not exceeding the value of the said benefit to the party obtaining it, as the court considers just, having regard to all the circumstances of the case and, in particular,—

(*a*) the amount of any expenses incurred before the time of discharge by the benefited party in, or for the purpose of, the performance of the contract, including any sums paid or payable by him to any other party in pursuance of the contract and retained or recoverable by that party under the last foregoing subsection, and

(*b*) the effect, in relation to the said benefit, of the circumstances giving rise to the frustration of the contract.

(4) In estimating, for the purposes of the foregoing provisions of this section, the amount of any expenses incurred by any party to the contract, the court may, without prejudice to the generality of the said provisions, include such sum as appears to be reasonable in respect of overhead expenses and in respect of any work or services performed personally by the said party.

other party has benefited from the part-performance. An American court following the Restatement (Second), therefore, would have far more flexibility than an English court under the Frustrated Contracts Act to "mop up" after the discharge.

In *ALCOA*, however, the court imposed a price adjustment as a form of "equitable" reformation rather than to discharge the contract as a response to the conclusion that ALCOA was entitled to "some relief" from commercial impracticability. The court, in effect, deleted the original cost escalation clause and filled the "gap" with a new clause intended to respond to the changed circumstances. The parties did not agree to this move and there was no "equitable adjustment" clause in the contract beyond the escalation provision which had failed its intended purpose. The criticisms of this remedy have ranged from the pious assertion that it is an unprecedented and improper exercise of judicial power to "make" a contract for the parties to the more practical concern about the feasibility of a court undertaking to provide a realistic pricing mechanism in a complex case where the parties have been unable or unwilling to agree. See Dawson, *Judicial Revision of Frustrated Contracts,* 1982 Jurid.Rev. 86, 101–05. On the other hand, the case has been applauded as a recognition of the realities of long-term contracts and as responsive to the dilemmas posed by the either-or approach of the common law—either the contract is discharged or it is not. In addition, the case is seen as a healthy move toward the legal requirement of cooperation rather than competition where unanticipated events produce gains and losses that have not been "paid for" in the bargaining process. See, e.g., Speidel, *Court-Imposed Price Adjustments Under Long–Term Supply Contracts,* 76 Nw.L.Rev. 369 (1981). Depending on your point of view, *ALCOA* is either the golden herald of the "new spirit of contract," see McGinnis v. Cayton, 173 W.Va. 102, 312 S.E.2d 765, 770 (1984) (concurring opinion of Harshbarger, J.), or another dark cloud confirming the "death" of contract.

For representative articles, see Mark P. Gergen, *A Defense of Judicial Reconstruction of Contract,* 71 Ind.L.J. 45 (1995); Legrand, *Judicial Revision of Contracts in French Law: A Case Study,* 62 Tul.L.Rev. 963 (1988); White, *Contract Breach and Contract Discharge Due to Impossibility: A Unified Theory,* 17 J.Legal Stud. 353 (1988); Wladis, *Common Law and Uncommon Events: The Development of the Doctrine of Impossibility of Performance in English Contract Law,* 75 Geo.L.J. 1575 (1987); Scott, *Conflict and Cooperation in Long–Term Contracts,* 75 Calif.L.Rev. 2005 (1987); Halpern, *Application of the Doctrine of Commercial Impracticability: Searching for the Wisdom of Solomon,* 135 U.Pa.L.Rev. 1123 (1987); Hillman, *Court Adjustment of Long–Term Contracts: An Analysis Under Modern Contract Law,* 1987 Duke L.J. 1 (1987); Trakman, *Winner Take Some: Loss Sharing and Commercial Impracticability,* 69 Minn.L.Rev. 471 (1985); Dawson, *Judicial Revision of Frustrated Contracts: The United States,* 64 B.U.L.Rev. 1 (1984); Dawson, *Judicial Revision of Frustrated Contracts: Germany,* 63 B.U.L.Rev. 1039 (1983).

Could a court find support for the imposed price adjustment in Restatement (Second) § 272(2)? The seeds may be there. Comment c states that in "some instances" the "just solution is to 'sever' the agreement and require that some unexecuted part of it be performed on both sides, rather than to relieve both parties of all of their duties." So far, this is *ALCOA*. The Comment also states that the question is "whether the court can salvage a part of the agreement that is still executory on both sides" and to supply a term which is "reasonable in the circumstances." Again, this is *ALCOA*. But Section 272(2) was drafted before *ALCOA* was decided and the illustrations do not clearly support the excision by the court of an existing contract term and the substitution of a more reasonable one.** But, the seed is there and, as Professor Young has observed, Section 272 may be one of the most important changes in Restatement (Second). See Young, *Half-Measures,* 81 Colum.L.Rev. 19 (1981). See also Harrison, *A Case for Loss Sharing,* 56 S.Cal.L.Rev. 573 (1983).

SECTION 4. THE DUTY OF GOOD FAITH

(A) SCOPE AND CONTENT OF GOOD FAITH DUTY

If the parties have, at the time of contracting, allocated a foreseeable risk by an agreed express condition, a court will normally enforce the condition if the promisor insists upon it. But, as we have seen, the court may review that decision and, in theory, excuse the condition if there is extreme forfeiture. Thus, if the promisee has performed to the benefit of the promisor and, at the time the decision is made, the risk foreseeable at the time of contracting no longer has a material impact on the exchange, the court should excuse the condition whether the promisor likes it or not. Otherwise, the promisor would have no duty in contract or quasi-contract to pay for the part-performance under circumstances where an insistence upon the condition smacks of exploitation or opportunism.

In this section, we will examine cases where the parties have, at the time of contracting, identified risks or stated performance objectives but have been unable or unwilling to define them with particularity. Rather than leave the term "open" or "agree to agree" in the future, they adopt a general standard that confers performance discretion on one or both parties. Thus, the promisor may agree to pay if the other's performance is "satisfactory," or a buyer may agree to purchase "requirements," or a distributor may agree to use "best efforts" to market a product. In these

---

** See Freidco of Wilmington, Del., Ltd. v. Farmers Bank, etc., 529 F.Supp. 822, 830, n. 9 (D.Del.1981), where the court conceded that if commercial impracticability were established, the reformation remedy would be proper. Citing *ALCOA* and Restatement (Second) § 272, the court stated that "reformation serves the purpose of filling a gap in the parties' agreement." But see Helms Const. & Development Co. v. State, etc., 97 Nev. 500, 634 P.2d 1224, 1225–26 (1981), where the court concluded that reformation for mutual mistake was limited to a party "seeking to alter a written instrument which, because of mutual mistake of fact, fails to conform to the parties' previous understanding or agreement."

situations, the contract does not lack consideration because the party with discretion must act in good faith. But suppose the other party claims that the party with discretion acted in bad faith or failed to exercise best efforts? Again, the court will be asked to review the promisor's exercise of discretion under the contract and the focus will be upon the circumstances at the time of exercise rather than the time of contracting. The question is whether that party has exceeded the permissible range of conferred discretion and, therefore, breached the contract.

It is now well established that "every contract imposes upon each party a duty of good faith and fair dealing in its performance and its enforcement." Restatement (Second) § 205; UCC 1–203. What is not always clear is (1) what is good faith performance and (2) what remedies are available when one party performs in bad faith? To put the matter more practically, what is bad faith and what can the other party do about it?

All would agree that good faith, at a minimum, means "honesty in fact in the conduct or transaction involved," UCC 1–201(19), and, since the duty of good faith must be met "in a variety of contexts," its meaning should vary "somewhat with the context." Section 205, Comment a. Moreover, in the case of merchant buyers and sellers, UCC 2–103(1)(b) [2–102(a) (1997)] states that good faith means both "honesty in fact and the observance of reasonable commercial standards of fair dealing in the trade." Thus, the duty of "fair dealing" means more than just honesty in fact. According to Comment a:

> Good faith performance or enforcement of a contract emphasizes faithfulness to an agreed common purpose and consistency with the justified expectations of the other party; it excludes a variety of types of conduct characterized as involving "bad faith" because they violate community standards of decency, fairness or reasonableness. The appropriate remedy for a breach of the duty of good faith also varies with the circumstances.

And, according to Comment d:

> Subterfuges and evasions violate the obligation of good faith in performance even though the actor believes his conduct to be justified. But the obligation goes further: bad faith may be overt or may consist of inaction, and fair dealing may require more than honesty. A complete catalogue of types of bad faith is impossible, but the following types are among those which have been recognized in judicial decisions: evasion of the spirit of the bargain, lack of diligence and slacking off, willful rendering of imperfect performance, abuse of power to specify terms, and interference with or failure to cooperate in the other party's performance.

Professor Robert S. Summers, in a careful article, has applauded the Restatement (Second) approach to the duty of good faith, primarily because it permits examples of bad faith to emerge over time from context to context. Put another way, the meaning of good faith is best determined by the conduct excluded rather than through an *a priori,* structured definition.

Summers, *The General Duty of Good Faith—Its Recognition and Conceptualization,* 67 Cornell L.Rev. 810, 829 (1982). He then criticizes as "misguided" three attempts to define good faith:

> (1) Good faith is an absence of intention to harm a legally protected pecuniary interest;

> (2) Good faith performance occurs when a party's discretion is exercised for any purpose within the reasonable contemplation of the parties at the time of formation to capture opportunities that were preserved upon entering the contract, interpreted objectively;*

> (3) Good faith and fair conduct consists of action according to reasonable standards set by customary practices and by known individual expectations.

Professor Summers concedes that the "general duty of good faith and fair dealing is no more than a minimal requirement (rather than a high ideal,)" but applauds it as an explicit recognition of the need for "contractual morality," the increased recognition of which "is one of the hallmarks of the law of our time." 67 Cornell L.Rev. at 811.

Centronics Corporation v. Genicom Corporation

Supreme Court of New Hampshire, 1989.
132 N.H. 133, 562 A.2d 187.

■ SOUTER, JUSTICE.

A contract between the buyer and seller of business assets provided for arbitration of any dispute about the value of the property transferred, to which the purchase price was pegged, and required an escrow deposit of a portion of the price claimed by the seller pending final valuation. The seller has charged the buyer with breach of an implied covenant of good faith in

---

* For development of the "foregone opportunities" thesis, see Burton, *Breach of Contract and the Common Law Duty to Perform in Good Faith,* 94 Harv.L.Rev. 369 (1980); *Good Faith Performance of a Contract Within Article 2 of the Uniform Commercial Code,* 67 Ia.L.Rev. 1 (1981). Burton asserts:

> "Contract formation principles require that each party undertake to forgo in some way its future freedom to pursue opportunities alternative to the contract. A party who acts after formation to recapture a forgone opportunity often is in breach of the contract by failing to perform in good faith. .... (F)oregone opportunities (are) those alternative opportunities that would be regarded as forgone at formation by reasonable business persons operating in a commercial setting— an objective standard. Whether a party

acted after formation to recapture foregone opportunities is a question of subjective intention."

67 Ia.L.Rev. at 24. Another way of shooting at the same target is through the concept of "opportunism," defined by Professor Oliver Williamson to be a "variety of self-interest seeking" that "extends simple self-interest seeking to include self-interest seeking with guile." Williamson, *Transaction Cost Economics: The Governance of Contractual Relations,* 22 J.L. & Econ. 233, 234, n. 3 (1979). See Muris, *Opportunistic Behavior and the Law of Contracts,* 65 Minn.L.Rev. 521 (1981), where opportunism is defined as behavior by party A which is contrary to party B's understanding but not necessarily contrary to the explicit terms of the agreement and which results in a transfer of resources.

refusing, during arbitration, to release a portion of the escrow fund claimed to be free from "dispute." The Superior Court (Hollman, J.) granted summary judgment to the buyer, which we affirm.

* * *

Distribution from the escrow fund was to be governed by two sets of provisions. Insofar as the escrow agreement relates to the issue before us, it simply provided that "[i]n accordance with Section 2.07 of the Purchase Agreement, the Escrow Agent shall hold the Escrow Fund in its possession until instructed in writing" by respective New York counsel for Centronics and Genicom "to distribute the same or some portion thereof to Centronics or [Genicom] as the case may be," whereupon the escrow agent was to make the distribution as ordered. Section 2.07 of the Purchase Agreement, entitled "Final Payment of Purchase Price," began with a provision that "[f]inal settlement and payment of the Purchase Price shall be made not later than ten days after determination of [CCNBV, consolidated closing net book value] and computation of the Purchase Price," whether by agreement of the parties or decision of the arbitrator. There followed detailed instructions for payment out of escrow and final settlement between the parties, which are of no significance in the matter before us, being intended to provide for the payment to Centronics of whatever balance it might be owed on the purchase price, and the distribution to Genicom of any amount it might be found to have overpaid.

* * *

Genicom moved for summary judgment on the theory that, given the dispute over CCNBV, the terms of the parties' agreements required payments out of escrow only upon completion of arbitration, thus barring the implication of any duty to authorize a distribution before that event. Centronics objected and sought its own summary judgment, grounded on affidavits said to indicate that Genicom's refusal was meant to pressure Centronics into conceding a disputed item worth a substantial amount.

The trial court ruled for Genicom, after construing the contract to provide that the "only way funds can be released is upon final determination of the purchase price, which, as the parties agree, is in the hands of the arbitrator.

"The instant suit is no more than [an] attempt on the part of [Centronics] to rewrite the contract. Essentially, [Centronics] asks this Court to read between the lines of § 2.07 and insert therein a provision regarding partial disbursal of funds from escrow in light of the protracted arbitration. While it is true that the parties contemplated a short time period for resolution of disputes through binding arbitration, the Court cannot insert a provision in the contract for partial payments where such provision does not exist.

[Centronics] should have demanded a mechanism for partial payments from the Escrow Fund if the arbitration process lagged, or if the factual situation regarding adjustments to the final purchase price occurred as it did. The Court will not renegotiate the contract between the parties to obtain this result. To the extent [Centronics] made a less advantageous contract, it must now abide by the terms of that contract as originally agreed.''

Centronics reads the foregoing order as denying that any obligation of good faith is implied in the parties' contract. We read it differently, as concluding that the express terms of the contract are inconsistent with the claim that an obligation of good faith and fair dealing, or any other sort of implied obligation, either requires Genicom to agree to an interim distribution or bars Genicom from refusing to agree except in return for Centronics's concession on a disputed item. We consequently view this appeal as raising the related questions of whether the trial judge misunderstood the implied obligation of good faith or misconstrued the contract. We conclude that he did neither.

Although an obligation of good faith is imposed by statute in the performance and enforcement of every contract or duty subject to the Uniform Commercial Code, see RSA 382–A:1–203; 382–A:1–201(19), the parties before us have addressed the implied contractual obligation of good faith at common law, and our first concern in this case is to identify the jurisdiction whose common law is to be applied. Although the parties agreed that their contractual relations were to be governed by New York law, and although Centronics's brief cites two cases from the Second Circuit applying the law of that State, Centronics's principal reliance is on New Hampshire cases. Since the New York decisions are not at odds with our own, as we will indicate below, and since neither party has suggested that the relevant substantive law differs between the two jurisdictions, we will assume that to whatever extent the governing foreign law has not been proven it is identical to our own. See Adams v. Thayer, 85 N.H. 177, 179, 155 A. 687, 689 (1931).

Our own common law of good faith contractual obligation is not, however, as easily stated as we might wish, there being not merely one rule of implied good faith duty in New Hampshire's law of contract, but a series of doctrines, each of them speaking in terms of an obligation of good faith but serving markedly different functions. Since the time of our first contract decision couched in terms of good faith, Griswold v. Heat Corporation, 108 N.H. 119, 229 A.2d 183 (1967), we have relied on such an implied duty in three distinct categories of contract cases: those dealing with standards of conduct in contract formation, with termination of at-will employment contracts, and with limits on discretion in contractual performance, which is at issue in the instant case. Although decisions in the first and second categories are not directly relevant here, a short detour through their cases will serve clarity by indicating the categorical distinctions.

In our decisions setting standards of conduct in contract formation, the implied good faith obligations of a contracting party are tantamount to the traditional duties of care to refrain from misrepresentation and to correct subsequently discovered error, insofar as any representation is intended to induce, and is material to, another party's decision to enter into a contract in justifiable reliance upon it.

By way of contrast, the good faith enforced in the second category of our cases is an obligation implied in the contract itself, where it fulfills the distinctly different function of limiting the power of an employer to terminate a wage contract by discharging an at-will employee. Under the rule evolved from Monge v. Beebe Rubber Co., 114 N.H. 130, 316 A.2d 549 (1974) through Howard v. Dorr Woolen Company, 120 N.H. 295, 414 A.2d 1273 (1980), and Cloutier v. Great A. & P. Tea Co., Inc., 121 N.H. 915, 436 A.2d 1140 (1981), an employer violates an implied term of a contract for employment at-will by firing an employee out of malice or bad faith in retaliation for action taken or refused by the employee in consonance with public policy, *Cloutier,* supra at 921–22, 436 A.2d at 1143–44. Although good faith in this context has not been rigorously defined, bad faith has been spoken of as equivalent to malice, *Cloutier* supra, and treated virtually as a subject of equitable estoppel in labor relations, *Cloutier,* supra at 921, 436 A.2d at 1143. Indeed, the concepts of good and bad faith applied in these cases are best understood not as elements of general contract law as such, but as expressions of labor policy. See *Monge,* supra 114 N.H. at 133, 316 A.2d at 551.

The differences between the obligations of good faith exemplified even in these first two groups of cases are enough to explain why the commentators despair of articulating any single concept of contractual good faith, even after the more than fifty years of litigation following in the wake of the American common law's first explicit recognition of an implied good faith contractual obligation in Kirke La Shelle Co. v. Paul Armstrong Co., 263 N.Y. 79, 87, 188 N.E. 163, 167 (1933). See Summers, *"Good Faith" in General Contract Law and the Sales Provisions of the Uniform Commercial Code,* 54 Va.L.Rev. 195, 196 (1968); Summers, *The General Duty of Good Faith—Its Recognition and Conceptualization,* 67 Cornell L.Rev. 810, 819 (1982); Burton, *More on Good Faith Performance of a Contract: A Reply to Professor Summers,* 69 Iowa L.Rev. 497, 511 (1984); Restatement, supra at § 205, comments a, d, e.

Even within the narrower confines of the third category of cases, those governing discretion in contractual performance, the one notable attempt to conceptualize implied good faith in a single, general definition, Burton, *Breach of Contract and the Common Law Duty to Perform in Good Faith,* 94 Harv.L.Rev. 369 (1980), discussed infra, is opposed by the view that the obligation of good faith performance is better understood simply as excluding behavior inconsistent with common standards of decency, fairness, and reasonableness, and with the parties' agreed-upon common purposes and justified expectations, see Summers, 67 Cornell L.Rev. at 820, 826; Restatement, supra at § 205, comment a. This view is consonant with our own cases in the third category, a canvass of which should inform our consideration of what good faith may or may not demand of Genicom in the circumstances before us.

[The court reviewed the New Hampshire cases.]

* * *

Despite the variety of their fact patterns, these cases illustrate a common rule: under an agreement that appears by word or silence to invest one party with a degree of discretion in performance sufficient to deprive another party of a substantial proportion of the agreement's value, the parties' intent to be bound by an enforceable contract raises an implied obligation of good faith to observe reasonable limits in exercising that discretion, consistent with the parties' purpose or purposes in contracting. A claim for relief from a violation of the implied covenant of good faith contractual performance therefore potentially raises four questions:

1.   Does the agreement ostensibly allow to or confer upon the defendant a degree of discretion in performance tantamount to a power to deprive the plaintiff of a substantial proportion of the agreement's value? Contracts may be broken in a multitude of ways and theories of relief are correspondingly numerous, but the concept of good faith in performance addresses the particular problem raised by a promise subject to such a degree of discretion that its practical benefit could seemingly be withheld.

2.   If the ostensible discretion is of that requisite scope, does competent evidence indicate that the parties intended by their agreement to make a legally enforceable contract? * * *

3.   Assuming an intent to be bound, has the defendant's exercise of discretion exceeded the limits of reasonableness? The answer to this question depends on identifying the common purpose or purposes of the contract, against which the reasonableness of the complaining party's expectations may be measured, and in furtherance of which community standards of honesty, decency and reasonableness can be applied.

4.   Is the cause of the damage complained of the defendant's abuse of discretion, or does it result from events beyond the control of either party, against which the defendant has no obligation to protect the plaintiff? Although this question is cast in the language of causation, it may be seen simply as the other face of question three. Suffice it to say here that its point is to emphasize that the good faith requirement is not a fail-safe device barring a defendant from the fruits of every plaintiff's bad bargain, or empowering courts to rewrite an agreement even when a defendant's discretion is consistent with the agreement's legally contractual character.

Applying this analytical sequence to the instant case takes us no further than the first of the four questions, whether the agreement effectively confers such discretion on Genicom over the timing of distributions from the escrow fund that, in the absence of some good faith limitation, Genicom could deny Centronics a substantial proportion of the contract's benefit. Was Genicom, that is, given authority to deprive Centronics indefinitely of a portion of the agreed consideration for the business assets previously transferred? The answer is obviously no * * * [This contract] contains express and unequivocal provisions governing the timing of payment, which must occur no later than ten days after final resolution of the purchase price, presumably on conclusion of the mandatory arbitration. . . . Genicom has no discretion to withhold approval for pay-out beyond that time, or to affect the timing of the arbitration itself. If, indeed, either party were dragging its heels in the conduct of the arbitration, it should go without saying that the dilatory conduct would be seen as a breach of contract, whether expressed in the language of bad faith or in traditional terms of the obligation to act within a reasonable time. See Restatement, supra at § 205, comment d. In short, because contractual provisions mandating payment on conclusion of the valuation process determine the date on which Centronics will get its due, it is clear that what Centronics claims to be Genicom's discretion over the timing of distribution is in reality a power that each party may exercise, but only jointly with the other, to agree to remove some or all of the escrowed funds from the ambit of the otherwise mandatory pay-out provisions.

Although this discussion reflects the analytical structure of the prior good faith performance cases cited by Centronics and followed here, we should also note that the same result would obtain from applying an alternative analysis proposed by Professor Burton, referred to above, which Centronics has also urged us to employ. Burton's functional analysis of the obligation to observe good faith in discretionary contract performance applies objective criteria, see Burton, 94 Harv.L.Rev. at 390–91, to identify the unstated economic opportunities intended to be bargained away by a promisor as a cost of performance, and it identifies bad faith as a promisor's discretionary action subjectively intended, id. at 386, 389, to recapture such an opportunity, thereby refusing to pay an expected performance cost, id. at 373. Centronics argues that its uncontradicted summary judgment affidavits establish that Genicom showed bad faith in Burton's sense, because its refusal to authorize distribution of the so-called undisputed amounts was an "attempt to recapture [the] degree of control concerning the amount of the final purchase price [which] it had agreed to place . . . in the arbitrator's hands . . . and thereby unjustifiably attain funds to which it was not entitled."

Genicom, of course, denies the uncontradicted evidentiary force that Centronics claims for its affidavits. But even assuming, *arguendo,* that the affidavits are uncontradicted and tend to prove what Centronics asserts, there are two respects in which the facts would fail the Burton test of bad faith as an exercise of discretion meant to recapture an opportunity foregone at the creation of the contract.

It is significant, first, that Genicom's refusal to consent to the distribution from escrow neither recaptures nor gains Genicom anything. In and of itself, the refusal removes no issue from the contingencies of arbitration and gives Genicom no present or future right to the money it wishes to obtain. Genicom's behavior thus contrasts sharply with examples of bad faith given by Burton, in which the discretionary delay preserved the actual use of funds or other valuable resources to the party exercising the discretion. See Burton, 94 Harv.L.Rev. at 394–402. The point is that only when the discretionary act recaptures an economic opportunity does the exercise of discretion pass from the realm of applying leverage for the sake of inducing further agreement into the sphere of bad faith, in which no agreement is necessary to realize the offending party's advantage.

* * *

A second and more fundamental flaw infects Centronics's reliance on the Burton analysis, however. It will be recalled that Burton's conception of bad faith in performance is the exercise of discretion for the purpose of recapturing opportunities foregone or bargained away at the time of contracting, with the identification of such foregone opportunities depending on objective analysis of the parties' "[e]xpectations [as they] may be inferred from the express contract terms in light of the ordinary course of business and customary practice...." Burton, 94 Harv.L.Rev. at 389. Hence, if an objective basis exists to infer that the parties never bargained away the right of either of them to condition any distribution on completing the arbitration of any disputes, then Genicom can not be guilty of bad faith by so insisting, whatever its subjective motive may be. We infer that the opportunity for such insistence never was bargained away.

Although the contract documents do not concisely state there will be no interim distribution, the texts come very close to such a provision. We have previously quoted the language of the escrow agreement that "[i]n accordance with Section 2.07 of the Purchase Agreement," the escrow agent shall hold the fund until instructed by the buyer's and seller's counsel to make a distribution. Section 2.07 was also quoted above. Its topic heading is "Final Payment of Purchase Price," and it provides that final payment and settlement shall be made within ten days of the final determination of net book value and purchase price, which will presumably be at the close of arbitration. "Final Payment ..." is apparently so called to distinguish it from the "Payment to Sellers on Closing Date," required by § 2.03 of the agreement, since there is no other provision calling for any payment or distribution. The text thus supports the claim that the parties intended the escrow agent to leave the fund intact until the point of the final payment, if any, that would be due to Centronics ten days after the final price determination.

This reading is confirmed by an understanding of the evident business purposes to be served by such a restriction on payout. We explained above that the original escrow of $5,000,000 was to be increased by Genicom's deposit of an Adjustment Amount, which in effect was equal to the amount of Centronics's proposed revision of the final purchase price in excess of the preliminary purchase price. Although Centronics was obligated to follow accepted accounting procedures when it revised the balance sheet to calculate any adjustment, the revision was to be unaudited and Genicom had no control over the setting of this amount.

Genicom, however, was not left entirely subject to Centronics's natural temptation to state a higher, rather than a lower, Adjustment Amount. It is reasonable to suppose each party appreciated that the extent of disagreement and the resulting duration of arbitration would be roughly proportional to the size of the Adjustment Amount. If Centronics had to wait upon the outcome of arbitration before it received any escrowed funds, then Genicom would be able to rely on Centronics's own self-interest to limit the probable length of arbitration by limiting the amount of the adjustment potentially subject to arbitration.

It is also reasonable to assume that neither party expected the other to emerge from arbitration with the whole escrow fund. Each therefore had reason to seek some mechanism for inducing the other side to promote speedy arbitration and the prompt distribution of escrowed money. Such a mechanism would be provided by a scheme conditioning any distribution on completing arbitration, since each would thus be induced to hasten the process for their common benefit.

The probability is, therefore, that each party expected the escrow to remain intact throughout arbitration, as the reason for Genicom's agreement that Centronics would have discretion to state the amount of the adjustment, and as the inducement to a prompt effectuation of their common object of obtaining whatever would be due to each from the fund so escrowed. Whether, therefore, we rely on the analysis underlying our own prior cases, or on the rule as espoused by Burton, we affirm the trial judge's conclusion that Centronics is seeking a revision of the contract, not the enforcement of good faith in its performance.

Affirmed.

All concurred.

NOTES

(1) In *Centronics Corporation,* Judge Souter (now Mr. Justice) discussed the "good faith" scholarship of Robert Summers and Steven Burton. Exactly how do Summers and Burton differ in determining bad faith? Which view prevailed in *Centronics?* See Burton & Andersen, Contractual Good Faith 38–40 (1995), wherein Professor Burton claims victory.

(2) Suppose Genicom had been in bad faith in refusing to release the escrow funds. What remedy would be available to Centronics? Is bad faith simply another way to describe a breach by failing to perform an agreed part of the bargain?

(3) *Breach by Prevention and Hindrance.* Some forms of bad faith conduct by one party constitute a breach of contract by preventing or hindering or failing to cooperate with the other party's performance. See Patterson, *Constructive Conditions in Contracts,* 42 Colum.L.Rev. 903, 928–42 (1942). Typically, the agreement fails to deal with the particular conduct at issue, whether it involves active conduct of prevention or simply the failure to take affirmative action that might facilitate the exchange. These problems, their relationship

with tort and the available remedies will be treated in Chapter 6, Section 2(c)(3).

(4) *Good Faith Duty in Formation.* Judge Souter suggested that implied duty of good faith in formation is "tantamount to the traditional duties of care to refrain from misrepresentation and to correct subsequently discovered error," but there are fitful signs that some courts will impose more substantive duties of good faith in precontractual negotiations. See Hoffman v. Red Owl Stores, supra at 421.

(B) RESERVED DISCRETION

Omni Group, Inc. v. Seattle–First National Bank

Court of Appeals of Washington, 1982.
Supra at 125.

Neumiller Farms, Inc. v. Cornett

Supreme Court of Alabama, 1979.
368 So.2d 272.

■ SHORES, JUSTICE.

Jonah D. Cornett and Ralph Moore, Sellers, were potato farmers in DeKalb County, Alabama. Neumiller Farms, Inc., Buyer, was a corporation engaged in brokering potatoes from the growers to the makers of potato chips. The controversy concerns Buyer's rejection of nine loads of potatoes out of a contract calling for twelve loads. A jury returned a verdict of $17,500 for Sellers based on a breach of contract. Buyer appealed. We affirm.

From the evidence, the jury could have found the following:

On March 3, 1976, the parties signed a written contract whereby Sellers agreed to deliver twelve loads of chipping potatoes to Buyer during July and August, 1976, and Buyer agreed to pay $4.25 per hundredweight. The contract required that the potatoes be United States Grade No. 1 and "chipt [sic] to buyer satisfaction." As the term was used in this contract, a load of potatoes contains 430 hundredweight and is valued at $1,827.50.

Sellers' potato crop yielded twenty to twenty-four loads of potatoes and Buyer accepted three of these loads without objection. At that time, the market price of chipping potatoes was $4.25 per hundredweight. Shortly thereafter, the market price declined to $2.00 per hundredweight.

When Sellers tendered additional loads of potatoes, Buyer refused acceptance, saying the potatoes would not "chip" satisfactorily. Sellers responded by having samples of their crop tested by an expert from the Cooperative Extension Service of Jackson County, Alabama, who reported that the potatoes were suitable in all respects. After receiving a letter demanding performance of the contract, Buyer agreed to "try one more load." Sellers then tendered a load of potatoes which had been purchased from another grower, Roy Hartline. Although Buyer's agent had recently purchased potatoes from Hartline at $2.00 per hundredweight, he claimed dissatisfaction with potatoes from the same fields when tendered by Sellers at $4.25 per hundredweight. Apparently the jury believed this testimony outweighed statements by Buyer's agents that Sellers' potatoes were diseased and unfit for "chipping."

Subsequently, Sellers offered to purchase the remaining nine loads of potatoes from other growers in order to fulfill their contract. Buyer's agent refused this offer, saying "... 'I'm not going to accept any more of your potatoes. If you load any more I'll see that they're turned down.' ... 'I can buy potatoes all day for $2.00.' " No further efforts were made by Sellers to perform the contract.

At the time of Buyer's final refusal, Sellers had between seventeen and twenty-one loads of potatoes unharvested in their fields. Approximately four loads were sold in Chattanooga, Tennessee; Atlanta, Georgia; and local markets in DeKalb County. Sellers' efforts to sell their potato crop to other buyers were hampered by poor market conditions. Considering all of the evidence, the jury could properly have found that Sellers' efforts to sell the potatoes, after Buyer's final refusal to accept delivery, were reasonable and made in good faith.

This case presents three questions: 1) Was Buyer's refusal to accept delivery of Sellers' potatoes a breach of contract? 2) If so, what was the proper measure of Sellers' damages? and 3) Was the $17,500 jury verdict within the amount recoverable by Sellers under the proper measure of damages?

§ 7–2–703, Code of Alabama 1975 (UCC), specifies an aggrieved seller may recover for a breach of contract "Where the buyer *wrongfully* rejects ... goods...." (Emphasis Added) We must determine whether there was evidence from which the jury could find that the Buyer acted wrongfully in rejecting delivery of Sellers' potatoes.

A buyer may reject delivery of goods if either the goods or the tender of delivery fails to conform to the contract. § 7–2–601, Code of Alabama 1975. In the instant case, Buyer did not claim the tender was inadequate. Rather, Buyer asserted the potatoes failed to conform to the requirements of the contract; i.e., the potatoes would not chip to buyer satisfaction.

The law requires such a claim of dissatisfaction to be made in good faith, rather than in an effort to escape a bad bargain. Shelton v. Shelton, 238 Ala. 489, 192 So. 55 (1939); Jones v. Lanier, 198 Ala. 363, 73 So. 535 (1916); Electric Lighting Co. v. Elder Bros., 115 Ala. 138, 21 So. 983 (1896).

Buyer, in the instant case, is a broker who deals in farm products as part of its occupation and, therefore, is a "merchant" with respect to its dealings in such goods. § 7–2–104, Code of Alabama 1975. In testing the good faith of a merchant, § 7–2–103, Code of Alabama 1975, requires "... honesty in fact and the observance of reasonable commercial standards of fair dealing in the trade." A claim of dissatisfaction by a merchant-buyer of fungible goods must be evaluated using an objective standard to determine whether the claim is made in good faith. Because there was evidence that the potatoes would "chip" satisfactorily, the jury was not required to accept Buyer's subjective claim to the contrary. A rejection of goods based on a claim of dissatisfaction, which is not made in good faith, is ineffectual and constitutes a breach of contract for which damages are recoverable.

* * *

[The court concluded that the trial court had properly applied the measure of damages in UCC 2–708 and affirmed the jury verdict for the seller in the amount of $17,500.]

NOTES

(1) As *Omni Group* indicates, where the agreement reserves discretion in performance to one party, the first question may be whether there is a contract at all. If, because of the reserved discretion, the apparent promise is found to be illusory, there is no consideration. The combination, however, of a commitment to do something and the general duty of good faith in performance, is normally enough to provide consideration. See, e.g., Bleecher v. Conte, 173 Cal.Rptr. 278, 626 P.2d 1051 (1981), where, in a complicated land transaction, the court found consideration in the buyer's promise to "do everything in their power to expedite the recordation of the final map" and to "proceed with diligence." But see Artex, Inc. v. Omaha Edible Oils, Inc., 231 Neb. 281, 436 N.W.2d 146 (1989) (contract interpreted to give defendant absolute discretion to refuse work).

(2) *Condition of Personal Satisfaction: Subjective or Objective Standard?* When a promisor conditions a duty to perform upon being satisfied with the other party's performance or "with respect to something else," see Restatement (Second) § 228, the expression of dissatisfaction must be in good faith. A common example of bad faith is where the promisor is dissatisfied with the overall bargain rather than the other party's performance. If, for example, the market price for goods has dropped well below the contract price, the buyer may claim dissatisfaction with the seller's performance in order to wriggle out of a bad deal. A more complex problem is the standard of good faith to be insisted upon—should it be "subjective" or "objective"? What was the test applied in *Mattei v. Hopper*, discussed in *Omni Group*, and *Neumiller Farms?* In either *Omni Group* or *Neumiller*, could an expression of honest dissatisfaction have avoided liability under the contract? Under Restatement (Second) § 228, if it is "practicable to determine whether a reasonable person in the position of the obligor would be satisfied, an interpretation is preferred under which the condition occurs if such a reasonable person in the position of the obligor would be satisfied."

For cases applying the "objective" test for measuring conditions of satisfaction, see Kennedy Associates, Inc. v. Fischer, 667 P.2d 174 (Alaska 1983) (trial court erred in applying subjective good faith standard to lender's dissatisfaction with condition of commercial rental property under clause making property "subject to approval"); Empire South, Inc. v. Repp, 51 Wn.App. 868, 756 P.2d 745, 748–750 (1988) (reasonable person in buyer's position would have been satisfied with used goods); Hall v. W.L. Brady Investments, Inc., 684 S.W.2d 379, 387 (Mo.App.1984) (question whether reasonable person would be satisfied with value of collateral for security).

In *Kennedy Associates,* supra, the court stated:

"The question of whether a court should utilize an objective rather than a subjective standard of good faith in gauging the validity of reliance upon a satisfaction clause dependent upon commercial judgment is one of first impression in this jurisdiction. It is well-established that where the condition requires satisfaction as to commercial value or quality, operative fitness, or mechanical utility, an objective standard is to be used in determining whether the clause has been satisfied ... On the other hand, if a judgment dependent upon personal taste or fancy, such as design of a dress or execution of a portrait is involved, a subjective test is appropriate ... The difficulty of the case before us lies in the fact that it arises in a commercial context but involves a judgment dependent upon consideration of a multiplicity of factors.... We conclude that the superior court should have applied an objective standard in determining whether the paragraph 14(i) condition was satisfied. Our choice of standard is predicated on the principle that a forfeiture of contractual rights is to be avoided, whenever possible. Therefore, just as 'conditions' are to be construed as covenants, unless the parties have clearly agreed otherwise, so must a preference be given to application of an objective test of reasonable satisfaction whenever practicable and not precluded by the express terms of the parties' agreement." 667 P.2d at 181–82.

(3) If, in *Neumiller,* the buyer's dissatisfaction had been in good faith, the seller would have failed to deliver conforming goods. The buyer, then, could reject the tender of delivery, UCC 2–601 [UCC 2–703(a) (1997)], cancel the contract and pursue remedies for breach. See UCC 2–711(1) [UCC 2–823 (1997)]. Since the dissatisfaction was in bad faith, the rejection was "wrongful," enabling the seller to pursue remedies for breach under UCC 2–703 [UCC 2–815 (1987)]. We will have more to say about the buyer's remedies of rejection and revocation of acceptance later on.

(4) See generally Brook, *Conditions of Personal Satisfaction in the Law of Contracts,* 27 N.Y.L.Sch.L.Rev. 103 (1981).

Reid v. Key Bank of Southern Maine, Inc.

United States Court of Appeals, First Circuit, 1987.
821 F.2d 9.

■ BOWNES, CIRCUIT JUDGE.

Plaintiffs Paul and Mary J. Reid brought a seventeen-count action in United States District Court for the District of Maine against Key Bank of Southern Maine, Inc., defendant. Plaintiffs alleged various federal and state claims resulting from the actions of Depositors Trust Co. of Southern Maine (Depositors), Key Bank's predecessor in interest. The suit grew out of the circumstances surrounding the termination by Depositors of plaintiffs' credit arrangement with it. A jury trial resulted in a verdict for plaintiffs on one of the counts and an award of damages. Both parties have appealed.

I. SUMMARY OF THE FACTS

In mid–1975, Paul Reid approached Depositors to obtain financing for the establishment of a painting business. From 1976 through 1979, Depositors granted Reid a series of loans which Reid used for the operation of his business, Pro Paint and Decorating. During this period, Peter H. Traill was the loan officer responsible for Reid's accounts, Marco F. DeSalle was the president of the bank, and Henry Lawson was, for a time, an assistant vice-president.

On March 2, 1979, Reid and Depositors entered into a $25,000 commercial credit agreement. The agreement was variously explained at trial as a "line of credit" and an "incomplete loan." However defined, it was the largest amount of credit Depositors had yet extended to Reid. Reid sought the credit primarily to finance work he was performing at the Bucksport Housing Project for Nickerson & O'Day, Inc., a general contractor.

In mid-May, 1979, Traill telephoned Reid and informed him that Depositors would not grant him any further advances under the March agreement. Reid had thought at the time that this halt of further advances might only be temporary. Defendant claimed that Traill sent Reid a follow-up letter on May 18, 1979, stating that Depositors would no longer honor overdrafts on Reid's accounts and suggesting that Reid restructure his debts with another lender. Reid denied receiving the letter and alleged that it was never, in fact, sent to him.

On May 29, 1979, Nickerson & O'Day sent a check to Depositors as payment for Reid's work at the Bucksport Housing Project. The check was for $6,507.90. It was made out to Depositors and to Pro Paint pursuant to an agreement between Depositors and Reid whereby Reid assigned his accounts receivable to Depositors as security for the March loan. Depositors credited $2,500 to the account of Pro Paint and applied the remaining $4,007.90 to offset part of the outstanding balance on Reid's March loan. Reid claimed that Depositors undertook this action without his authorization.

Reid claimed that another check was also inappropriately handled by Depositors. He testified that on June 8, 1979, he gave Traill a check for an amount somewhere between eleven and fifteen thousand dollars. Reid contended that this check represented the proceeds for work he performed at Brunswick Naval Air Station. He alleged that Depositors converted the check and used it to offset part of the balance on the March loan. Defendant strongly contested this claim and implied at trial that the check in question existed only in Reid's imagination.

On September 20, 1979, Reid received a past-due notice on the March loan. The notice requested payment of $694.84 in interest and stated that the payment had been due on September 5, 1979. Reid testified that this was the first notice he had received concerning the March loan.

On November 5, 1979, Depositors repossessed Reid's personal automobile and one of his vans. Reid discovered one of the vehicles in a lot and attempted to drive it away. He testified that he did not know it had been repossessed and thought it had been stolen. On a complaint by Lawson, Reid was arrested in connection with this incident and was placed for a time in jail.

Reid's business collapsed and he lost his four vehicles and his home. On November 7, 1979, Reid filed a Chapter 13 bankruptcy proceeding which was converted to a Chapter 11 proceeding in January, 1980. Mrs. Reid suffered emotional problems and drug dependency. The couple separated for a period of a year and a half.

The Reids, who are black, claimed that Depositors acted in bad faith to limit and then terminate their credit. They also claimed that Depositors' actions were motivated by racial prejudice. Defendant claimed that Depositors acted in good faith to secure its financial interests when it learned of Reid's personal difficulties and mismanagement of his business; it denied that its actions were racially motivated.

At trial, the district court directed a verdict for defendant on plaintiffs' claims for violations of the Fair Credit Reporting Act and for breach of fiduciary duties. Plaintiffs withdrew their claims for interference with contractual relations and wrongful dishonoring of checks. The jury found for defendant on plaintiffs' claims for violation of the express terms of the credit agreement, racial discrimination, two counts for infliction of emotional distress, and failure to comply with Article 9 of the Uniform Commercial Code. The jury found for plaintiffs on their pendent state claim for breach of the March loan agreement based on violation of an implied covenant of good faith and fair dealing. It awarded plaintiffs $100,000 in compensatory and $500,000 in exemplary damages; the exemplary damages award was struck by the court. Both parties have appealed. In Part II, we address defendant's arguments on appeal; in Parts III–VI we address those of plaintiffs.

II.   IMPLIED COVENANT OF GOOD FAITH AND FAIR DEALING

A.   *The Existence of the Cause of Action in Maine*

Plaintiffs' recovery in contract was based on the theory that when Depositors, in May 1979, and thereafter, shut off Reid's credit and took steps to realize upon its collateral, it violated an implied covenant of good faith contained in the March loan agreement between plaintiffs and Depositors. The district court took as self-evident the proposition that Maine contract law required good faith performance. *See generally* Burton, *Breach of Contract and the Common Law Duty to Perform in Good Faith,* 94 Harv.L.Rev. 369 (1980). The Uniform Commercial Code, as adopted by Maine, states: "Every contract or duty within this Title imposes an obligation of good faith in its performance or enforcement." 4 Me.Rev.Stat. Ann. tit. 11, § 1–203 (1964). That this obligation carries with it a cause of action seems clear from another provision of the Code: "Any right or obligation declared by this Title is enforceable by action unless the provision declaring it specifies a different and limited effect." Id. at § 1–106(2). See also Restatement (Second) of Contracts § 205 (1979).

We interpret the Maine cases making reference to the general duty of good faith in light of this general acceptance of the principle. The Maine Supreme Judicial Court has explicitly recognized the U.C.C.'s "broad requirements of good faith, commercial reasonableness and fair dealing." Schiavi Mobile Homes, Inc. v. Gironda, 463 A.2d 722, 724–25 (Me.1983) (citing U.C.C. §§ 1–203, 2–103 & 1–106, Comment 1). In addition, some aspects of the present case concern the handling of Reid's bank accounts with Depositors and would thus be governed by the standard of "good faith" and "ordinary care" under section 4–103 of the U.C.C. See C–K Enterprises v. Depositors Trust Co., 438 A.2d 262, 265 (Me.1981).

* * *

[The court held that Maine would recognize a cause of action for breach of the duty of good faith.]

B.   *The "Demand" Provision*

Defendant argues that the "demand" provision of the note establishing the credit agreement precludes a good faith requirement in this case, even if such a requirement is recognized in general. Defendant contends that this exception to the general good faith requirement is mandated by section 1–208 of the U.C.C., as interpreted by the U.C.C. Comment to the section. Section 1–208 states:

§ 1–208. Option to accelerate at will

A term providing that one party or his successor in interest may accelerate payment or performance or require collateral or additional collateral "at will" or "when he deems himself insecure" or in words of similar import shall be construed to mean that he shall have power to do so only if he in good faith believes that the prospect of payment or performance is impaired. . . .

The U.C.C. Comment observes:

> Obviously this section has no application to demand instruments or obligations whose very nature permits call at any time with or without reason.

We turn, therefore, to the documents establishing the loan to see whether they clearly gave Depositors the right to demand payment or terminate the relationship on demand and without cause. The "Secured Interest Note," dated March 2, 1979, states in its opening paragraph:

> On Demand, after date, for value received, [Paul Reid d/b/a Pro Paint & Decorating] . . . promise[s] to pay to the order of [Depositors] . . . Twenty-five Thousand and no/100 DOLLARS with interest at 13.75 per cent per annum payable quarterly.

This provision appears, at first glance, to be an unambiguous demand clause. It cannot, however, possibly be read literally in the context of the kind of agreement entered into here. Although the note seems to grant Depositors the right to immediate repayment of $25,000 "on demand," Reid had not yet received that sum of money from the bank. Indeed, he was never to receive the full amount. The "demand" provision thus cannot represent the beginning and end of the inquiry into the time term of the contract.

DeSalle, president of Depositors, testified to similar effect at trial, based on his knowledge of banking practices. He said that the "demand" provision in such an agreement is to be interpreted in light of the other conditions in the note and that a bank could not simply terminate the agreement capriciously. He also thought that the absence of a time term in such a note indicated the likelihood that the schedule for repayment of the principal was governed by a verbal agreement between the loan officer and the debtor. In view both of our reading of the document and of DeSalle's testimony about banking practices, we find that the "demand" provision in the note should not be understood as a completely integrated agreement on the time term of the contract. See Astor v. Boulos Co., 451 A.2d 903, 905 (Me.1982); Restatement (Second) of Contracts § 209 (1979).

Furthermore, the documents establishing the loan place conditions on the acceleration of payment or termination of the agreement. The "Secured Interest Note" provides for various conditions which would "render" the obligation "payable on demand." The "Security Agreement," also signed March 2, 1979, lists a series of events whose occurrence would signify that Reid would be in "default." The presence of such conditions in both documents indicates that the agreement could not simply be terminated at the whim of the parties; rather, the right of termination or acceleration was subjected to various limitations. The detailed enumeration of events that would *"render"* the note "payable on demand," or which would put Reid in "default," shows the qualified and relative nature of any "demand" provision. It would be illogical to construe an agreement, providing for repayment or default in the event of certain contingencies, as permitting the creditor, in the absence of the occurrence of those contingencies, to terminate the agreement without any cause whatsoever. Under such a construction, the enumerated conditions would be rendered meaningless. We find, therefore, that the documents establishing the loan defeat neither the legal obligation nor the justifiable expectation of the parties that the contract be performed in good faith.

C. *The Standard*

Defendant challenges the district court's formulation of the test of "good faith" in its instruction to the jury. Defendant claims that the judge instructed the jury that the test for good faith comprises both an objective and a subjective component. Defendant argues that under Maine law an objective standard, such as a "reasonable man" test, may only be applied in cases involving the sales of goods that fall under Article 2 of the U.C.C. Otherwise, defendant claims, any consideration of "good faith" should be limited to its subjective definition in section 1–201(19) as "honesty in fact."

* * *

We find * * * that the judge ultimately instructed the jury to decide the issue of good faith under the subjective standard. "Honesty in fact" is required under all interpretations of the duty of good faith under section 1–203. Thus, even if we agreed with defendant that the Maine courts would limit an objective standard for good faith to Article 2 cases, we would not find a fatal error in the judge's instructions here.[2]

D.   *Sufficiency of Evidence*

Finally, defendant contends that there was insufficient evidence to support a finding of an absence of good faith, particularly in view of the jury's failure to find that racial discrimination had been an "effective factor" in the termination of Reid's credit at Depositors. We disagree. We affirm the district court's holding that evidence concerning the manner in which Depositors conducted their dealings with Reid was sufficient to support a jury verdict of bad faith and was not based on mere speculation. The standard for defendant's motion for a judgment notwithstanding the verdict was whether the evidence, viewed in the light most favorable to plaintiffs, would lead to the conclusion that no reasonable jury could have found for plaintiffs on the good faith issue. This heavy burden was not met by defendant.

We think the jury could have reasonably inferred that Depositors' actions were not taken in good faith. The March, 1979, credit agreement represented the largest amount of credit extended to Reid by the bank, and could be seen as the culmination of an ongoing and mutually beneficial relationship. The jury could have found that by mid-May, when Reid's line of credit was abruptly shut off, he was not in default and his overall position had not changed that significantly, especially as the bank did not first register complaints to him or ask him to alter his conduct in some manner. The bank's president testified that it was customary before cutting off a customer's line of credit to send notices in advance and call the customer to the bank for discussion. This was not done as to Reid, nor was any convincing reason advanced by the bank for not doing so. (The bank, indeed, did not even call as a witness the officer who had dealt directly with Reid and could have best explained why the bank acted as it did.) The jury could have found that in restricting Reid's credit when and

---

2. Moreover, we think there are strong indications that such a limitation would not represent the Maine court's future, or even current, thinking on this matter. First, we note that many courts have construed the "good faith" provision of § 1–208 as including an objective component. See, e.g., K.M.C. Co. v. Irving Trust Co., 757 F.2d 752, 760–61 (6th Cir.1985). This construction was supported by the views of Professor Gilmore, one of the drafters of the U.C.C. See 2 G. Gilmore, Security Interests in Personal Property § 43.4 at 1197 (1965). See also J. White and R. Summers, Uniform Commercial Code 1088 (2d ed. 1980) ("The draftsmen apparently intended an objective standard."). Moreover, as many commentators have shown, the difference between so-called "objective" and "subjective" standards is often minimal in practice. See, e.g., J. White and R. Summers at 1088–90. Finally, we note the following pronouncement of the Maine court, broadly paraphrasing § 4–103 of the U.C.C.: "[I]n fact the Uniform Commercial Code imposes a duty of ordinary care and good faith on banks in their dealings with customers." C–K Enterprises v. Depositors Trust Co., 438 A.2d 262, 264 (1981). The use of the sweeping phrase, "in their dealings with customers," arguably extends the protection of "ordinary care" in Maine beyond those bank transactions specifically covered in Article 4.

as it did the bank was motivated by ulterior considerations, not a good faith concern for its financial security. The jury could have found that the bank decided in bad faith and without notice to terminate the credit relationship as a whole. The jury might have viewed the bank's actions to restrict and terminate Reid's credit to be in bad faith in part because they were taken only a short time after the bank had shown confidence in Reid and had given him grounds to rely on the continuation of the relationship. The jury might have inferred bad faith from these actions of the bank, even if it did not believe that racial prejudice was the effective factor that motivated the bank's bad faith. In sum, the jury could have reasonably found that the bank acted in bad faith in precipitously and without warning halting further advances on which it knew Reid's business depended, in failing to make a sufficient effort to negotiate alternative solutions to any problems it perceived in its relationship with Reid, and in failing to give notice that it intended to terminate the relationship entirely. The evidence concerning these and other aspects of Depositors' actions provided a sufficient basis for a jury finding that the bank's actions were not taken in good faith.

* * *

[The court held that exemplary damages were not available in Maine for breach of contract and that there were "no recoverable torts to which the exemplary damages could attach."]

Affirmed. No costs to either party.

Comment: Lender Liability and the Duty to Act in Good Faith

A specialized context from which good faith disputes arise is the relationship between a lender and its customers. As *Reid v. Key Bank* illustrates, the termination of a line of credit by the lender may be bad faith, subjecting the lender to liability for the customer's commercial losses but not exemplary damages. Two of the leading cases in the development of bad faith "lender liability" are K.M.C. Co., Inc. v. Irving Trust Co., 757 F.2d 752 (6th Cir.1985) (bad faith refusal to make advance under "discretionary" clause) and 999 v. C.I.T. Corp., 776 F.2d 866 (9th Cir.1985) (bad faith refusal to honor commitment to finance).

Assuming that a contract exists between the parties and the contract does not clearly give the lender power to take action at any time for any reason, recurring questions include the standard of good faith to be applied and whether bad faith has been proved in the particular case. See, e.g., United States v. H & S Realty Co., 837 F.2d 1 (1st Cir.1987) (no proof that bank had dishonest motives or intent to harm customer); Garrett v. BankWest, Inc., 459 N.W.2d 833 (S.D.1990) (refusal to make payment not bad faith where agreement not breached and refusal neither violated the spirit of the contract nor the justified expectations of the parties); Gilbert Central Corp. v. Overland National Bank, 232 Neb. 778, 442 N.W.2d 372 (1989) (refusal of lender to perform commitment raises genuine issue of material fact on good faith); United States National Bank of Oregon v. Boge, 102 Or.App. 262, 794 P.2d 801 (1990) (delay in responding to customer's request for information not bad faith); Price v. Wells Fargo Bank, 213 Cal.App.3d 465, 261 Cal.Rptr. 735 (1989) (absent fiduciary duty, "hard line" in repayment negotiations with informed customer not bad faith). See generally Patterson, *Good Faith, Lender Liability and Discretionary Acceleration: Of Llewellyn, Wittgenstein, and the Uniform Commercial Code*, 68 Tex.L.Rev. 169 (1989); Griffin & Ebke, *Good Faith and Fair Dealing in Commercial Lending Transactions: From Covenant to Duty and Beyond*, 49 Ohio St.L.J. 1237 (1989); Lawrence, *Lender Control Liability: An Analytical Model Illustrated with Applications to the Relational Theory of Secured Financing*, 62 S.Cal.L.Rev. 1387 (1989). See also Chaitman, *The Ten Commandments for Avoiding Lender Liability*, 22 U.C.C.L.J. 3 (1989).

At issue in these cases is the scope of the lender's duty to act in good faith. Should the duty be subjective or objective? If objective, should it incorporate community standards of fair dealing, including concerns about racial discrimination, see Burton, *Racial Discrimination in Contract Performance: Patterson and a State Law Alternative*, 25 Harv.Civ.Rights–Civ. Lib.L.Rev. 431 (1990), or should the test be limited to an interpretation of the contract terms, allowing the market to resolve other aspects of the dispute? See Comment, *What's So Good About Good Faith? The Good Faith Performance Obligation in Commercial Lending*, 55 U.Chi.L.Rev. 1335 (1988). Or, is there a middle ground?

Consider the argument of Professor Fischel, which follows

Courts faced with a lender liability case must decide whether the challenged conduct of the lender was consistent with the agreement between the parties. This inquiry is primarily a matter of contract interpretation. What remains unclear, however, is whether courts should look beyond the contract itself and the usual tools of contract interpretation to some other body of authority in order to define the rights and duties between the parties. This question is important because borrowers in recent lender liability cases have argued that lenders' conduct violated the duty of good faith and fiduciary duties to the borrower. However, precisely what these concepts mean and what their relationship is to contract law is not clearly understood....

The doctrine of good faith has a long history in contract law. Section 1–203 of the Uniform Commercial Code provides that "[e]very contract or duty within this Act imposes an obligation of good faith in its performance or enforcement." Similarly, Section 205 of the Restatement (Second) of Contracts states that a duty of good faith should be imposed in all contracts.

However, notwithstanding the extensive literature on the subject, no consensus exists on precisely what the duty of good faith means. At one extreme, some commentators have argued that the duty should be limited to a prohibition of intentional dishonesty. Under this view, the duty of good faith adds little to the prohibition against fraud other than a vague exhortation for moral behavior. At the other extreme, several commentators have concluded that good faith should be interpreted expansively to incorporate community standards of fairness and decency. The obvious difficulty with this position is the lack of any accepted understanding of the meaning of these terms. Moreover, this lack of content creates an added risk that the fairness and decency standard will be applied arbitrarily to the detriment of lenders and borrowers alike. For example, a borrower-plaintiff might be able to invalidate default provisions used by borrowers to obtain more favorable credit terms on the grounds that they are "unfair," but this act would ultimately hurt borrowers as a class by raising the cost of credit.

An intermediate position is to interpret the duty of good faith as equivalent to a prohibition of opportunistic behavior. Under this view, lenders are entitled to the benefit of their bargain but are precluded from using contractual terms as a pretense for extracting benefits for which they have not bargained. For example, a lender.... could terminate funding if the default risk increased, but, absent a risk increase, the duty of good faith would prevent the same lender from threatening to terminate funding in order to force the borrower to pay a higher interest rate.

Once again, the rationale for imposing a duty of good faith on lenders relates to the impossibility of drafting a contract covering every possible contingency. If contracts could be negotiated and enforced without any cost, the parties could negotiate an agreement which would preclude attempts by the lender to behave opportunistically. Because of the costs of negotiating and enforcing agreements, however, the parties cannot prevent all opportunistic behavior by contract. Thus the duty of good faith acts as an implied contractual term to achieve what the parties themselves cannot given the costs involved.

While this interpretation of the duty of good faith has a certain appeal, it is not without difficulty. The problem is that distinguishing opportunistic from non-opportunistic behavior can be very complicated if not impossible. A lender will never concede that its actions were designed to obtain a benefit not bargained for in the initial agreement. On the contrary, the lender will claim that its refusal to continue funding was based on its assessment of the debtor and the probability of default. Moreover, not only will distinguishing between these two explanations be difficult, but also the attempt to distinguish them will impair the contractual protection given to the lender in the first instance.

Recall that provisions giving the lender sole discretion whether to continue funding and to call any amounts outstanding are best understood as bonding mechanisms used by the borrower to obtain more favorable credit terms. The strength of the bond, however, is weakened if the borrower can argue to a court that the exercise of discretion granted to the lender by the agreement was not done in good faith. This recourse defeats one of the key features of the bond: that the lender, and not a court, decides whether to continue the relationship with a particular borrower. On the other hand, allowing the lender absolute discretion, as discussed above, creates an incentive for the lender to behave opportunistically.

Thus there is a trade-off. The more absolute the discretion of the lender, the stronger the bond of the borrower but the greater the incentive of the lender to behave opportunistically. Conversely, the more expansive the interpretation of the duty of good faith to control opportunistic behavior by the lender, the weaker is the bond of the borrower and the less able the borrower is to use the bond to obtain more favorable credit terms. [Footnotes omitted.]

Fischel, *The Economics of Lender Liability,* 99 Yale L.J. 131, 140–42 (1989). [Reprinted by permission of the Yale Law Journal Company and Fred B. Rothman & Company from the Yale Law Journal, vol. 99, pp. 131–154.]

Feld v. Henry S. Levy & Sons, Inc.

Court of Appeals of New York, 1975.
37 N.Y.2d 466, 373 N.Y.S.2d 102, 335 N.E.2d 320.

■ COOKE, JUDGE.

Plaintiff operates a business known as the Crushed Toast Company and defendant is engaged in the wholesale bread baking business. They entered into a written contract, as of June 19, 1968, in which defendant agreed to sell and plaintiff to purchase "all bread crumbs produced by the Seller in its factory at 115 Thames Street, Brooklyn, New York, during the period commencing June 19, 1968, and terminating June 18, 1969," the agreement to "be deemed automatically renewed thereafter for successive renewal periods of one year" with the right to either party to cancel by giving not less than six months notice to the other by certified mail. No notice of cancellation was served. Additionally, pursuant to a contract stipulation, a faithful performance bond was delivered by plaintiff at the inception of the contractual relationship, and a bond continuation certificate was later submitted for the yearly term commencing June 19, 1969.

Interestingly, the term "bread crumbs" does not refer to crumbs that may flake off bread; rather, they are a manufactured item, starting with stale or imperfectly appearing loaves and followed by removal of labels, processing through two grinders, the second of which effects a finer granulation, insertion into a drum in an oven for toasting and, finally, bagging of the finished product.

Subsequent to the making of the agreement, a substantial quantity of bread crumbs, said to be over 250 tons, were sold by defendant to plaintiff but defendant stopped crumb production on about May 15, 1969. There was proof by defendant's comptroller that the oven was too large to accommodate the drum, that it was stated that the operation was "very uneconomical," but after said date of cessation no steps were taken to obtain more economical equipment. The toasting oven was intentionally broken down, then partially rebuilt, then completely dismantled in the summer of 1969 and, thereafter, defendant used the space for a computer room. It appears, without dispute, that defendant indicated to plaintiff at different times that the former would resume bread crumb production if the contract price of 6 cents per pound be changed to 7 cents, and also that, after the crumb making machinery was dismantled, defendant sold the raw materials used in making crumbs to animal food manufacturers.

Special Term denied plaintiff's motion for summary judgment on the issue of liability and turned down defendant's counter-request for a summary judgment of dismissal. From the Appellate Division's order of affirmance, by a divided court, both parties appeal.

Defendant contends that the contract did not require defendant to manufacture bread crumbs, but merely to sell those it did, and, since none were produced after the demise of the oven, there was no duty to then deliver and, consequently from then on, no liability on its part. Agreements to sell all the goods or services a party may produce or perform to another party are commonly referred to as "output" contracts and they usually serve a useful commercial purpose in minimizing the burdens of product marketing (see 1 Williston, Contracts [3d ed.], § 104A). The Uniform Commercial Code rejects the ideas that an output contract is lacking in mutuality or that it is unenforceable because of indefiniteness in that a quantity for the term is not specified (6 Encyclopedia New York Law, Contracts, § 442, 1974–1975 Supp. by Professor Schwartz, p. 43). Official Comment 2 to section 2–306 (McKinney's Cons.Laws of N.Y., Book 62½, Uniform Commercial Code, pp. 206–207) states in part: "Under this Article, a contract for output * * * is not too indefinite since it is held to mean the actual good faith output * * * of the particular party. Nor does such a contract lack mutuality of obligation since, under this section, the party who will determine quantity is required to operate his plant or conduct his business in good faith and according to commercial standards of fair dealing in the trade so that his output * * * will proximate a reasonably foreseeable figure." (See, also, Matter of United Cigar Stores Co. of Amer., D.C., 8 F.Supp. 243, 244, affd., 2 Cir., 72 F.2d 673, cert. den. sub nom., Consolidated Dairy Prods. Co. v. Irving Trust Co., 293 U.S. 617, 55 S.Ct. 210, 79 L.Ed. 706; 9 N.Y.Jur., Contracts, § 10, p. 531.)

The real issue in this case is whether the agreement carries with it an implication that defendant was obligated to continue to manufacture bread crumbs for the full term. Section 2–306 of the Uniform Commercial Code, entitled "Output, Requirements and Exclusive Dealings" provides:

"(1) A term which measures the quantity by the output of the seller or the requirements of the buyer means such actual output or requirements as may occur in good faith except that no quantity unreasonably disproportionate to any stated estimate or in the absence of a stated estimate to any normal or otherwise comparable prior output or requirements may be tendered or demanded.

"(2) A *lawful agreement* by either the seller or the buyer *for exclusive dealing* in the kind of goods concerned *imposes* unless otherwise agreed an obligation *by the seller to use best efforts to supply the goods* and by the buyer to use best efforts to promote their sale." (Emphasis supplied.)

The Official Comment thereunder reads in part: "Subsection (2), on exclusive dealing, makes explicit the commercial rule embodied in this Act under which the parties to such contracts are held to have impliedly, even when not expressly, bound themselves to use reasonable diligence as well as good faith in their performance of the contract. * * * An exclusive dealing agreement brings into play all of the good faith aspects of the output and requirement problems of subsection (1). It also raises questions of insecurity and right to adequate assurance under this Article."

Section 2–306 is consistent with prior New York case law (Buerger and O'Connor, Practice Commentaries, McKinney's Cons.Laws of N.Y., Book 62½, Uniform Commercial Code, § 2–306, p. 206). Every contract of this type imposes an obligation of good faith in its performance (Uniform Commercial Code, § 1–203; see Wigand v. Bachmann–Bechtel Brewing Co., 222 N.Y. 272, 277, 118 N.E. 618, 619; New York Cent. Ironworks Co. v. United States Radiator Co., 174 N.Y. 331, 335, 66 N.E. 967, 968). Under the Uniform Commercial Code, the commercial background and intent must be read into the language of any agreement and good faith is demanded in the performance of that agreement (Official Comment 1, McKinney's Cons.Laws of N.Y., Book 62½, Uniform Commercial Code, § 2–306), and, under the decisions relating to output contracts, it is clearly the general rule that good faith cessation of production terminates any further obligations thereunder and excuses further performance by the party discontinuing production (Du Boff v. Matam Corp., 272 App.Div. 502, 71 N.Y.S.2d 134; HML Corp. v. General Foods Corp., 365 F.2d 77, 83 [applying New York law]; Matter of United Cigar Stores Co. of Amer., supra; see Neofotistos v. Harvard Brewing Co., 341 Mass. 684, 171 N.E.2d 865; 6 Encyclopedia New York Law, Contracts, § 442, 1974–1975 Supp. by Professor Schwartz, p. 44).

This is not a situation where defendant ceased its main operation of bread baking (see *Neofotistos v. Harvard Brewing Co.*, supra). Rather, defendant contends in a conclusory fashion that it was "uneconomical" or "economically not feasible" for it to continue to make bread crumbs. Although plaintiff observed in his motion papers that defendant claimed it was not economically feasible to make the crumbs, plaintiff did not admit that as a fact. In any event, "economic feasibility," an expression subject to many interpretations, would not be a precise or reliable test.

There are present here intertwined questions of fact, whether defendant performed in good faith and whether it stopped its manufacture of bread crumbs in good faith, neither of which can be resolved properly on this record. The seller's duty to remain in crumb production is a matter calling for a close scrutiny of its motives (1 Hawkland, A Transactional Guide to the Uniform Commercial Code, p. 52, see, also, p. 48), confined here by the papers to financial reasons. It is undisputed that defendant leveled its crumb making machinery only after plaintiff refused to agree to a price higher than that specified in the agreement and that it then sold the raw materials to manufacturers of animal food. There are before us no componential figures indicating the actual cost of the finished bread crumbs to defendant, statements as to the profits derived or the losses sustained, or data specifying the net or gross return realized from the animal food transactions.

The parties by their contract gave the right of cancellation to either by providing for a six months' notice to the other. The apparent purpose of such a stipulation was to provide an opportunity to either the seller or buyer to conclude their dealings in the event that the transactions were not as profitable or advantageous as desired or expected, or for any other reason. Correspondingly, such a notice would also furnish the receiver of it a chance to secure another outlet or source of supply, as the case might be. Short of such a cancellation, defendant was expected to continue to perform in good faith and could cease production of the bread crumbs, a single facet of its operation, only in good faith. Obviously, a bankruptcy or genuine imperiling of the very existence of its entire business caused by the production of the crumbs would warrant cessation of production of that item; the yield of less profit from its sale than expected would not. Since bread crumbs were but a part of defendant's enterprise and since there was a contractual right of cancellation, good faith required continued production until cancellation, even if there be no profit. In circumstances such as these and without more, defendant would be justified, in good faith, in ceasing production of the single item prior to cancellation only if its losses from continuance would be more than trivial, which, overall, is a question of fact.

The order of the Appellate Division should be affirmed, without costs.

NOTES

(1) The *Feld* case was governed by Section 2–306(1) [UCC 2–304(a) (1997)] of the UCC. To what extent is the exercise of discretion by an "output" seller and a "requirements" buyer governed by circumstances existing at the time of contracting? What test(s) does the court use to define bad faith at the time of performance? In any case, is the approach consistent with the view that bad faith exists when either the seller or buyer exercises discretion to recapture opportunities foregone at the time of contracting? See Burton, *Breach of Contract and the Common Law Duty to Perform in Good Faith,* 94 Harv.L.Rev. 369, 381–84, 395–97 (1980). Compare Muris, *Opportunistic Behavior and the Law of Contracts,* 65 Minn.L.Rev. 521, 556–65 (1981).

(2) For a sampling of the literature on "requirements" and "output" contracts, see, e.g., Weistart, *Requirements and Output Contracts: Quantity Variations under the Uniform Commercial Code,* 1973 Duke L.J. 599; Havighurst & Berman, *Requirements and Output Contracts,* 27 Ill.L.Rev. 1 (1932); Comments: 33 Rutgers L.Rev. 105 (1980); 78 Harv.L.Rev. 1212 (1965); 102 U.Pa.L.Rev. 654 (1954).

(3) *The Case of Good Faith but Disproportionate Demand.* Seller and Buyer enter a five-year "requirements" contract. During the first three years, Buyer ordered and Seller supplied an average of 10,000 units. Thereafter, there was a sharp turndown in the market. During the fourth year, Buyer ordered 1,000 units and in the fifth year, no units were ordered. Seller, conceding that Buyer was in good faith, argues that the orders in both years were "substantially disproportionate" to orders during the first three years. Accordingly, under UCC 2–306(1), Buyer was in breach for the last two years. How should the court rule? See Posner, J. in Empire Gas Corp. v. American Bakeries Co., 840 F.2d 1333 (7th Cir.1988) (suggesting buyer has no liability because good faith is not limited by substantial disproportion language); Orange & Rockland v.

Amerada Hess Corp., 59 A.D.2d 110, 397 N.Y.S.2d 814 (1977) (buyer's decision under requirements contract to take advantage of its cheap supply of oil by dramatically increasing its requirements was not made in good faith). Comment, *And Then There Were None: Requirements Contracts and the Buyer Who Does Not Buy,* 64 Wash.L.Rev. 871 (1989).

PROBLEM: THE CASE OF THE URANIUM OXIDE DEBACLE

In May, 1976, S, a manufacturer, and B, a utility, entered into a ten year contract for the supply of uranium oxide, a fuel source for nuclear reactors. B agreed to purchase 50% of the annual output of S's plant at the higher of two prices, either a fixed price of $35 per pound subject to escalation based upon production costs, or an adjusted market price, then $37 per pound, whichever was higher. S's factory had a capacity of 600,000 pounds per year. During the first five years of the contract, S averaged 500,000 pounds per year in output. B took and paid for an average of 250,000 pounds per year. The balance of the output went to meet the "requirements" of C, a prime contractor with the United States. In the "requirements" contract with C, it was estimated that the government would need and C would order from S between 200,000 and 250,000 pounds per year. In May, 1981, the market price of uranium oxide, after a 12 month steady decline, bottomed out at $20 per pound. The escalated price in the contract between S and B, however, was at $39 per pound. At the same time, B's requirements for uranium oxide had dropped off due to a slow down in the construction of nuclear reactors. In effect, B was paying $39 per pound for goods worth $20 on the open market and could use only 100,000 of the 250,000 delivered. In June, 1981, the United States terminated its contract with C for convenience under a clause in the government contract. C informed S that, since it no longer had requirements, it was cancelling its contract. At the same time, B had requested S either to reduce the quantity of goods produced or to grant an adjustment in the price. S refused and, from June, 1981 until June, 1982, S continued to produce uranium oxide at previous levels, some 500,000 pounds per year. S shipped 50% of the output to B and stored the excess against a time when the market would improve. S claimed that it was more efficient to continue production at the previous output even though it had no current customers who would take the excess over B's contract. Consider the following questions.

(1) S is considering a suit against C for breach of contract. If suit were filed, what are the probabilities of success?

(2) B, upon learning that C had cancelled, refused to take and pay for 50% of S's output, claiming that S's maintaining the precancellation level of output was a breach of contract. Is B correct?

Comment: Effect of "Best Efforts" Agreement on Contracts for Indefinite Quantity

The fact that the parties have entered an "output" or a "requirements" does not necessarily mean that one party must use "best efforts" to have output or requirements. The parties must agree to use "best efforts" in addition to satisfying their obligation to perform the contract in good faith. See HML Corp. v. General Foods Corp., 365 F.2d 77 (3d Cir.1966) (court refuses to imply "best efforts" obligation). That agreement may be found in the bargain of the parties, see Perma Research and Development

v. Singer Co., 542 F.2d 111 (2d Cir.1976), cert. denied 429 U.S. 987, 97 S.Ct. 507, 50 L.Ed.2d 598 (1976) ("best efforts" obligation implied), or presumed from the fact that the parties have entered into an "exclusive dealing" contract. Thus, UCC 2–306(2) provides that a "lawful agreement by either the seller or the buyer for exclusive dealing in the kind of goods concerned imposes unless otherwise agreed an obligation by the seller to use best efforts to supply the goods and by the buyer to use best efforts to promote their sale."

The question whether a party has used "best efforts" in a particular dispute has bothered the courts and commentators. See Farnsworth, *On Trying to Keep One's Promises: The Duty of Best Efforts in Contract Law,* 46 U.Pitt.L.Rev. 117 (1983); Comment, *Best Efforts as Diligence Insurance: In Defense of "Profit Uber Alles,"* 86 Colum.L.Rev. 1728 (1986). If the parties have not specified the level of "best efforts" in the contract, the courts have, in most cases, applied an objective standard and asked whether the defendant has made reasonable efforts in the circumstances. See, e.g., Bloor v. Falstaff Brewing Corp., 601 F.2d 609 (2d Cir.1979); Goetz & Scott, *Principles of Relational Contracts,* 67 Va.L.Rev. 1089, 1149–50 (1981) (arguing that "best efforts" should require that level of effort "necessary to maximize the joint net product flowing from the ... relationship"). This is an important inquiry for both questions of liability and remedy. Thus, if the defendant has no duty to use "best efforts" or has satisfied that duty and is otherwise in good faith, there is no breach of contract. If, however, the defendant is in good faith but has not used "best efforts," the plaintiff should recover damages. As Judge Posner put it in Agfa–Gevaert, A.G. v. A.B. Dick Co., 879 F.2d 1518, 1523–24 (7th Cir.1989):

> When a distributor obligates himself to use his best efforts to promote a product and then breaks his contract, the remedial question is indeed how much he would have sold had he used his best efforts, implying diligent and energetic promotion.... But when he agrees merely to take his requirements of a particular product from his seller, and breaks his contract by satisfying those requirements elsewhere, the question is how much he bought from his alternative supplier(s) ... What he required, he bought; what he did not buy, he must not have required.

(C) MODIFICATION

Angel v. Murray

Supreme Court of Rhode Island, 1974.
Supra at 110.

Roth Steel Products v. Sharon Steel Corp.

United States Court of Appeals, Sixth Circuit, 1983.
705 F.2d 134.

[In November, 1972, Roth contracted to purchase 200 tons of "hot rolled" steel per month from Sharon through December, 1973. The price was $148 per ton. Sharon also "indicated" that it could sell "hot rolled" steel on an "open schedule" basis for $140 and discussed the "probability" that Sharon could sell 500 tons of "cold rolled" steel at prices varying with the type ordered. At that time, the steel industry was operating at 70% of capacity, steel prices were "highly competitive" and Sharon's quoted prices to Roth were "substantially lower" than Sharon's book price for steel. In early 1973, market conditions changed dramatically due to the development of an attractive export market and an increased domestic demand for steel. During 1973 and 1974, the steel industry operated at full capacity, steel prices rose and nearly every producer experienced substantial delays in filling orders. In March, 1973, Sharon notified all purchasers, including Roth, that it was discontinuing price concessions given in 1972. After negotiations, the parties agreed that Roth would pay the agreed price until June 30, 1973 and a price somewhere between the agreed price and Sharon's published prices for the balance of 1973. Roth was initially reluctant to agree to this modification, but ultimately agreed "primarily because they were unable to purchase sufficient steel elsewhere to meet their production requirements." Sharon was supplying one-third of Roth's requirements and all other possible suppliers were "operating at full capacity and ... were fully booked." The parties proceeded under this modification during the balance of 1973, although Sharon experienced difficulties in filling orders on time. During 1974, the parties did business on an entirely different basis. Roth would order steel, Sharon would accept the order at the price "prevailing at the time of shipment." During 1974 and 1975, Sharon's deliveries were chronically late, thereby increasing the price to Roth in a rising market. Roth, however, acquiesced in this pattern because it believed Sharon's assurances that late deliveries resulted from shortages of raw materials and the need for equitable allocation among customers and because there was "no practical alternative source of supply." This acquiescence was jolted in May, 1974 when Roth learned that Sharon was allocating substantial quantities of rolled steel to a subsidiary for sale at premium prices. After several more months of desultory performance on both sides, Roth sued Sharon for breach of contract, with special emphasis upon the modified contract for 1973. Sharon raised several defenses, including impracticability and, in the alternative, the agreed modification. The district court, after a long trial, held, *inter alia,* that Sharon was not excused from the 1973 contract on the grounds of impracticability and that the modification was unenforceable. A judgment for $555,968.46 was entered for Roth.

On appeal, the court of appeals affirmed the district court's decision on the impracticability, modification and other issues, but remanded the case for factual findings on whether Roth gave Sharon timely notice of breach. On the impracticability defense under UCC 2–615(a), the court held that "Sharon's inability to perform was a result of its policy accepting far more orders than it was capable of fulfilling, rather than a result of the existing shortage of raw materials." In refusing to enforce the modification of the 1973 contract, the court had this to say.]

■ CELEBREZZE, SENIOR CIRCUIT JUDGE.

* * *

C.   In March, 1973, Sharon notified its customers that it intended to charge the maximum permissible price for all of its products; accordingly, all price concessions, including those made to the plaintiffs, were to be rescinded effective April 1, 1973. On March 23, 1973, Guerin indicated to Metzger that the plaintiffs considered the proposed price increase to be a breach of the November, 1972 contract. In an effort to resolve the dispute, Guerin met with representatives of Sharon on March 28, 1973 and asked Sharon to postpone any price increases until June or July, 1973. Several days later, Richard Mecaskey, Guerin's replacement, sent a letter to Sharon which indicated that the plaintiffs believed that the November, 1972 agreement was enforceable and that the plaintiffs were willing to negotiate a price modification if Sharon's cost increases warranted such an action. As a result of this letter, another meeting was held between Sharon and the plaintiffs. At this meeting, Walter Gregg, Sharon's vice-president and chairman of the board, agreed to continue charging the November, 1972 prices until June 30, 1973 and offered, for the remainder of 1973, to charge prices that were lower than Sharon's published prices but higher than the 1972 prices. Although the plaintiffs initially rejected the terms offered by Sharon for the second half of 1973, Mecaskey reluctantly agreed to Sharon's terms on June 29, 1973.

Before the district court, Sharon asserted that it properly increased prices because the parties had modified the November, 1973 contract to reflect changed market conditions. The district court, however, made several findings which, it believed, indicated that Sharon did not seek a modification to avoid a loss on the contract. The district court also found that the plaintiffs' inventories of rolled steel were "alarmingly deficient" at the time modification was sought and that Sharon had threatened to cease selling steel to the plaintiffs in the second-half of 1973 unless the plaintiffs agreed to the modification. Because Sharon had used its position as the plaintiffs' chief supplier to extract the price modification, the district court concluded that Sharon had acted in bad faith by seeking to modify the contract. In the alternative, the court concluded that the modification agreement was voidable because it was extracted by means of economic duress; the tight steel market prevented the plaintiffs from obtaining steel elsewhere at an affordable price and, consequently, the plaintiffs were forced to agree to the modification in order to assure a continued supply of steel. See e.g. Oskey Gasoline & Oil Co. v. Continental Oil Co., 534 F.2d 1281 (8th Cir.1976). Sharon challenges these conclusions on appeal.

The ability of a party to modify a contract which is subject to Article Two of the Uniform Commercial Code is broader than common law, primarily because the modification needs no consideration to be binding. ORC § 1302.12 (UCC § 2–209(1)). A party's ability to modify an agreement is limited only by Article Two's general obligation of good faith. ... In determining whether a particular modification was obtained in good faith, a court must make two distinct inquiries: whether the party's conduct is consistent with "reasonable commercial standards of fair dealing in the trade," ... and whether the parties were in fact motivated to seek modification by an honest desire to compensate for commercial exigencies; ... ORC § 1302.01(2) (UCC § 2–103). The first inquiry is relatively straightforward; the party asserting the modification must demonstrate that his decision to seek modification was the result of a factor, such as increased costs, which would cause an ordinary merchant to seek a modification of the contract. See Official Comment 2, ORC § 1302.12 (UCC § 2–209) (reasonable commercial standards may require objective reason); J. White & R. Summers, Handbook of Law under the UCC at 41. The second inquiry, regarding the subjective honesty of the parties, is less clearly defined. Essentially, this inquiry requires the party asserting the modification to demonstrate that he was, in fact, motivated by a legitimate commercial reason and that such a reason is not offered merely as a pretext. ... Moreover, the trier of fact must determine whether the means used to obtain the modification are an impermissible attempt to obtain a modification by extortion or overreaching. ...

Sharon argues that its decision to seek a modification was consistent with reasonable commercial standards of fair dealing because market exigencies made further performance entail a substantial loss. The district court, however, made three findings which caused it to conclude that economic circumstances were not the reason that Sharon sought a modification: it found that Sharon was partially insulated from raw material price increases, that Sharon bargained for a contract with a slim profit margin and thus implicitly assumed the risk that performance might come to involve a loss, and that Sharon's overall profit in 1973 and its profit on the contract in the first quarter of 1973 were inconsistent with Sharon's position that the modification was sought to avoid a loss. Although all of these findings are marginally related to the question whether Sharon's conduct was consistent with reasonable commercial standards of fair dealing, we do not believe that they are sufficient to support a finding that Sharon did not observe reasonable commercial standards by seeking a modification. In our view, these findings do not support a conclusion that a reasonable merchant, in light of the circumstances, would not have sought a modification in order to avoid a loss. For example, the district court's finding that Sharon's steel slab contract[26] insulated it from industry wide cost increases is correct, so far as it goes. Although Sharon was able to purchase steel slabs at pre–1973 prices, the district court's findings also indicate that it was not able to purchase, at those prices, a sufficient

---

26. Sharon was a party to a contract with United States Steel which allowed it to make monthly purchases of slab steel ranging from a minimum of 25,000 tons per month to a maximum of 45,000 tons per month. It was also a party to a contract with Wierton Steel which allowed it to purchase slab steel in amounts varying between 10,000 to 20,000 tons per month. Both of these contracts were entered prior to 1973, at a very attractive price. When the market strengthened in 1973, however, Sharon was unable to obtain the maximum monthly tonnages permitted under these contracts: U.S. Steel delivered only 30,000 tons per month and Wierton 10,000 tons per month.

tonnage of steel slabs to meet its production requirements.[27] The district court also found that Sharon experienced substantial cost increases for other raw materials, ranging from 4% to nearly 20%. In light of these facts, the finding regarding the fixed-price contract for slab steel, without more, cannot support an inference that Sharon was unaffected by the market shifts that occurred in 1973. Similarly, the district court's finding that Sharon entered a contract in November, 1972 which would yield only a slim profit does not support a conclusion that Sharon was willing to risk a loss on the contract. Absent a finding that the market shifts and the raw material price increases were foreseeable at the time the contract was formed—a finding which was not made—Sharon's willingness to absorb a loss cannot be inferred from the fact that it contracted for a smaller profit than usual. Finally, the findings regarding Sharon's profits are not sufficient, by themselves, to warrant a conclusion that Sharon was not justified in seeking a modification. Clearly, Sharon's initial profit on the contract[28] is an important consideration; the district court's findings indicate, however, that at the time modification was sought substantial future losses were foreseeable.[29] A party who has not actually suffered a loss on the contract may still seek a modification if a future loss on the agreement was reasonably foreseeable. Similarly, the overall profit earned by the party seeking modification is an important factor; this finding, however, does not support a conclusion that the decision to seek a modification was unwarranted. The more relevant inquiry is into the profit obtained through sales of the product line in question. This conclusion is reinforced by the fact that only a few product lines may be affected by market exigencies;[30] the opportunity to seek modification of a contract for the sale of goods of a product line should not be limited solely because some other product line produced a substantial profit.

In the final analysis, the single most important consideration in determining whether the decision to seek a modification is justified in this context is whether, because of changes in the market or other unforeseeable conditions, performance of the contract has come to involve a loss. In this case, the district court found that Sharon suffered substantial losses by

27. The district court found that Sharon suffered a continuing shortage of slab steel. It found that in 1972 (when Sharon was operating at substantially less than full capacity) it received 602,277 tons of slab steel; that in 1973, it received 506,596 tons of slab steel; and that in 1974 it received 373,898 tons. Thus, the record is clear that Sharon was in a difficult position. As demand for steel increased, and as Sharon's mills began to work at a higher capacity, its supply of slab steel steadily diminished.

28. The district court noted that in the first three months of 1973, Sharon made $3,089.00 on sales to Roth and lost $263.00 on steel sold to Toledo. Although Sharon lost

significant sums of money on its contract with the plaintiffs, Sharon enjoyed overall profits in 1973, with net earnings of $11,566,000 on net sales of $338,205,000.

29. The evidence indicates, and the district court found, that with the exception of hot rolled sheets Sharon absorbed a loss on every rolled steel product which it sold to the defendants in 1973, even though the modified prices were in effect during the third and the fourth quarters.

30. Apparently, Sharon's record overall profit was the result of other operations. It obtained a pre-tax profit of less than one percent on its total sales of rolled steel.

performing the contract *as modified*. See note 29, supra. We are convinced that unforeseen economic exigencies existed which would prompt an ordinary merchant to seek a modification to avoid a loss on the contract; thus, we believe that the district court's findings to the contrary are clearly erroneous. . . .

The second part of the analysis, honesty in fact, is pivotal. The district court found that Sharon "threatened not to sell Roth and Toledo any steel if they refused to pay increased prices after July 1, 1973" and, consequently, that Sharon acted wrongfully. Sharon does not dispute the finding that it threatened to stop selling steel to the plaintiffs. Instead, it asserts that such a finding is merely evidence of bad faith and that it has rebutted any inference of bad faith based on that finding. We agree with this analysis; although coercive conduct is evidence that a modification of a contract is sought in bad faith, that prima facie showing may be effectively rebutted by the party seeking to enforce the modification. . . . Although we agree with Sharon's statement of principles, we do not agree that Sharon has rebutted the inference of bad faith that rises from its coercive conduct. Sharon asserts that its decision to unilaterally raise prices was based on language in the November 17, 1972 letter which allowed it to raise prices to the extent of any general industry-wide price increase. Because prices in the steel industry had increased, Sharon concludes that it was justified in raising its prices. Because it was justified in raising the contract price, the plaintiffs were bound by the terms of the contract to pay the increased prices. Consequently, any refusal by the plaintiffs to pay the price increase sought by Sharon must be viewed as a material breach of the November, 1972 contract which would excuse Sharon from any further performance. Thus, Sharon reasons that its refusal to perform absent a price increase was justified under the contract and consistent with good faith.

This argument fails in two respects. First, the contractual language on which Sharon relies only permits, at most, a price increase for cold rolled steel; thus, even if Sharon's position were supported by the evidence, Sharon would not have been justified in refusing to sell the plaintiffs hot rolled steel because of the plaintiffs' refusal to pay higher prices for the product. More importantly, however, the evidence does not indicate that Sharon ever offered this theory as a justification until this matter was tried. Sharon's representatives, in their testimony, did not attempt to justify Sharon's refusal to ship steel at 1972 prices in this fashion. Furthermore, none of the contemporaneous communications contain this justification for Sharon's action. In short, we can find no evidence in the record which indicates that Sharon offered this theory as a justification at the time the modification was sought. Consequently, we believe that the district court's conclusion that Sharon acted in bad faith by using coercive conduct to extract the price modification is not clearly erroneous. Therefore, we hold that Sharon's attempt to modify the November, 1972 contract, in order to compensate for increased costs which made performance come to involve a loss, is ineffective because Sharon did not act in a manner consistent with Article Two's requirement of honesty in fact when it refused to perform its remaining obligations under the contract at 1972 prices.[31]

* * *

NOTES

(1) In *Roth Steel Products,* the court held that Sharon was *not* entitled to any relief under UCC 2–615(a). If, as in the *ALCOA* case, Sharon had been entitled to "some relief," would the modification have been enforceable under UCC 2–209(1)?

(2) Would the modification have been enforceable under Section 89 of Restatement (Second), discussed and applied in *Angel v. Murray*? How does one draw the line between "circumstances not anticipated by the parties when the contract was made," Section 89(a), and the "occurrence of an event the non-occurrence of which was basic assumption on which the contract was made," Section 261?

(3) Note that *Roth Steel Products* invalidated the modification because of Sharon's bad faith rather than because of economic duress. The court suggests that proof of coercive means will not invalidate a modification made in good faith. See Note 31. What, then, was the bad faith in *Roth Steel Products*? Is this concept consistent with the view that a modification is in bad faith when one party uses a refusal to perform as a lever to recapture an opportunity foregone at the time of contracting? See Burton, *Good Faith Performance of a Contract Within Article 2 of the Uniform Commercial Code,* 67 Ia.L.Rev. 1 (1981).

(4) Some courts have relied exclusively upon concepts of economic duress when evaluating modifications. See, e.g., Austin Instrument, Inc. v. Loral Corp., 29 N.Y.2d 124, 324 N.Y.S.2d 22, 272 N.E.2d 533 (1971), supra at 499, where the court said:

> The applicable law is clear and, indeed, is not disputed by the parties. A contract is voidable on the ground of duress when it is established that the party making the claim was forced to agree to it by means of a wrongful threat precluding the exercise of his free will. ... The existence of economic duress or business compulsion is demonstrated by proof that 'immediate possession of needful goods is threatened' ... or ... by proof that one party to a contract has threatened to breach the agreement by withholding goods unless the other party agrees to some further demand. ... However, a mere threat by one party to breach the contract by not delivering the required items, though wrongful, does not in itself constitute

---

31. The district court also found, as an alternative ground, that the modification was voidable because the plaintiffs agreed to the modification due to economic duress. See, e.g., Oskey Gasoline & Oil Co. v. Continental Oil, 534 F.2d 1281 (8th Cir.1976). Because we conclude that the modification was ineffective as a result of Sharon's bad faith, we do not reach the issue whether the contract modification was also voidable because of economic duress. We note, however, that proof that coercive means were used is necessary to establish that a contract is voidable because of economic duress. Normally, it cannot be used to void a contract modification which has been sought in good faith; if a contract modification has been found to be in good faith, then presumably no wrongful coercive means have been used to extract the modification.

economic duress. It must also appear that the threatened party could not obtain the goods from another source of supply and that the ordinary remedy of an action for breach of contract would not be adequate.

324 N.Y.S.2d at 24, 272 N.E.2d at 535. The "economic duress" approach is strongly favored by some commentators. See, e.g., Hillman, *Contract Modification Under the Restatement (Second) of Contracts,* 67 Cornell L.Rev. 680 (1982); Mather, *Contract Modification under Duress,* 33 S.Car.L.Rev. 615 (1982). In *Roth Steel Products,* Roth was clearly unable to obtain the promised steel from another source and ordinary damage remedies would appear to have been inadequate. Was Sharon's refusal (which was not excused under UCC 2–615(a)) to deliver steel unless Roth agreed to a price modification "wrongful"?

Comment: The Duty to Modify

Most courts and the commentators agree that neither contract law nor the UCC imposes a duty on the parties to negotiate in response to changed circumstances. See Bermingham, *Extending Good Faith: Does the U.C.C. Impose a Duty of Good Faith Negotiation Under Changed Circumstances?* 61 St. Johns L.Rev. 217 (1987). One of your co-authors, however, has argued for such a duty: What do you think?

"It is now time to return to *ALCOA.* The basic problem was not new. ALCOA claimed that the occurrence of events not anticipated at the time of contracting as likely to occur had made performance of the long-term contract impracticable. The court agreed and held that ALCOA was entitled to "some relief". In moves quite consistent with the neo-classical model, the court employed standards to assist in determining risk allocation and "gap" filling and was responsive to the hardship that ALCOA would suffer if compelled by specific performance to perform the contract under the original price term. * * * ALCOA did not seek to take advantage of an opportunity foregone at contracting, because ALCOA did not assume the risk. Further, neither party attempted to exercise discretion, whether in performance or enforcement, expressly reserved to it in the contract. However, the changed circumstances caused extreme economic hardship to ALCOA and produced windfall or unbargained for gains to Essex. Given this combination of hardship to ALCOA and gain to Essex, was it bad faith for Essex to seek specific performance of the contract as originally agreed without accepting a proposed modification which was fair and reasonable under the circumstances? If the answer is yes, then Essex, indeed, has a duty to become a "commercial good Samaritan."[48]

This complex question has parallels in the "duty to rescue" problem in the law of torts.[49] To date, no court has held that there is such a contractual duty, especially where the advantaged party has not caused the

---

48. In *ALCOA,* the court did not evaluate the parties' efforts to reach an agreed adjustment. After concluding that the parties had failed to agree, the court stated: "Essex was under no duty or pressure to agree to revise the contract." 499 F.Supp. at 81.

49. See, e.g., M. Shapo, The Duty to Act (1977); Weinreb, *The Case for a Duty to Rescue,* 90 Yale L.J. 247 (1980).

peril and the disadvantaged party has, for one reason or another, assumed the risk.[50] Beyond a narrow band of affirmative responsibilities associated with breach of contract by failure to cooperate,[51] "freedom from" in this area is well preserved.

One justification for this result is a philosophical and moral aversion to the imposition of non-consensual duties in support of a generalized principle of altruism, the effect of which is to restrict liberty and accomplish a redistribution of resources.[52] If altruism is the "new" spirit of contract, then contract, indeed, has become a tort devoted to an egalitarian, collectivist spirit. A more focused justification has recently been advanced by Professor Clayton Gillette.[53] He argues that good faith does not include a duty to be a "commercial good Samaritan" where the economic peril was not created by the obligor and the contract does not create a duty to be concerned by an allocation of risks. His reasons, derived from commercial policy, are that the imposition of a duty here "subjects bargains to inconsistent and uncertain enforcement, and does not produce offsetting benefits in commercial conduct."[54]

Further, he argues that the vagueness of the good faith standard mitigates its independent force and that the lack of certainty in appropriate remedies impairs the predictability which ought to exist in commercial transactions.[55] Although cooperation, generosity and altruism should be encouraged, they should not be required.[56] Presumably, Gillette would conclude in the *ALCOA* case that Essex had no duty to aid ALCOA by adjustment or otherwise and, similarly, that the court had no power to impose a price adjustment without Essex' consent.

---

50. See, e.g., Iowa Elec. Light and Power Co. v. Atlas Corp., 467 F.Supp. 129, 134 (N.D.Iowa 1978), reversed on other grounds 603 F.2d 1301 (8th Cir.1979).

51. See UCC 2–311; Restatement (Second) of Contracts § 205 (1979), comment (d) (bad faith performance includes "interferences with or failure to cooperate in the other party's performance"); Patterson, Constructive Conditions in Contracts 903, 928–42 (1942) (arguing that a duty to cooperate exists when failure to act produces unjust enrichment).

52. See C. Fried, Contract as Promise: A Theory of Contractual Obligation 85–91 (1981) (arguing that good faith as honesty is compatible with the "promise principle" but good faith as "loyalty" is not); Kronman, *Contract Law and Distributive Justice*, 89 Yale L.J. 472 (1980). See also Gordley, *Equality in Exchange*, 69 Cal.L.Rev. 1587 (1981).

53. Gillette, *Limitations on the Obligation of Good Faith*, 1981 Duke L.J. 619.

54. Id. at 620.

55. The predictability is important to insure efficiency in the *ex ante* bargaining of the parties.

56. Drawing a parallel between the duty to act in tort law and the "commercial good Samaritan," Gillette argues that if the contract does not create a duty to be concerned or the advantaged party has not caused the need for intervention, the duty to act in commercial cases must be justified on the ground that the contract creates a special relationship from which that duty flows. He concludes that no support for that result is found in the U.C.C. Gillette, supra note 53, at 634–37. Fried also opposes deriving such a duty from some "undefined relationship" unless the agreement deals with the problem. Otherwise, its imposition "becomes despotism" and its enforcement "tends to tyranny." C. Fried supra note 52, at 85–91.

This position, bolstered by philosophical and policy grounds, is the underpinning of the spirit of "freedom from" in classical contract law and libertarian philosophy. But can a case be made for imposing a duty on the advantaged party to accept a "fair and equitable" adjustment proposal made by the disadvantaged party? If so, what remedies are appropriate? Keeping the *ALCOA* facts in mind, a tentative case can be made that does not convert the law of contracts into a pervasive duty to be altruistic.

First, the disadvantaged party must propose a modification that would be enforceable if accepted by the advantaged party. Under Restatement (Second), this occurs if the disrupted contract is not "fully performed on either side" and if the modification is "fair and equitable in view of circumstances not anticipated by the parties when the contract was made."[57] The changed circumstances are similar to but less than those required to discharge a contract for impracticability. This first requirement both neutralizes any opportunism by the disadvantaged party, e.g., duress, and affirms that agreed adjustments are preferred—that contract is available to resolve the dilemma and has been employed by the disadvantaged party.

Second, it must be clear that the disadvantaged party did not assume the risk of the unanticipated event by agreement, or under the test stated in the UCC in section 2–615(a), or otherwise. If the disadvantaged party did assume the risk, then the advantaged party has no duty to accept any proposed modification. The risk assumption question is complicated, and the answer will probably not be clear at the time that the adjustment is proposed. Why should the advantaged party be held to reject at his peril? Because it is in this precise situation—where there are substantial unbargained-for gains and losses caused by unanticipated events—that a case for the duty to rescue can be made. In this setting where the risk of changed circumstances has not been allocated to either party, a refusal to adjust by the advantaged party leaves all of the loss on the disadvantaged party and permits the advantaged party to salt away all of the gains. Short of discharging the contract and leaving the parties to restitution, a duty to adjust is necessary to avoid opportunism.

Thus, imposing the duty here is consistent with emerging notions of good faith performance and *ALCOA*'s second peg in the "new" spirit, loss avoidance.[58] More importantly, it is an imposition with little damage to the

---

57. Restatement (Second) of Contracts § 89 (1979). See UCC 2–209(1) and comment 2, where it states that a modification "needs no consideration to be binding" but that the "extortion of a 'modification' without legitimate commercial reason is ineffective as a violation of the duty of good faith." The extensive literature on this problem focuses exclusively upon the enforceability of an agreed modification rather than the duty, if any, of the advantaged party to negotiate or to agree. See, e.g., Muris, *Opportunistic Be-havior and the Law of Contracts*, 65 Minn. L.Rev. 521, 532–52 (1981). See Hillman, *A Study of Uniform Commercial Code Methodology: Contract Modification Under Article Two*, 59 N.C.L.Rev. 335 (1981).

58. Concededly, if the advantaged party honestly believes that the disadvantaged party assumed the risk, the refusal to negotiate or to adjust is understandable. Ideally, a procedure for first determining who should bear what risk and then proceeding to the adjustment issues should be devised.

requirement of consent in contract law. Since there is a "gap" in the agreement on risk allocation, even that staunch defender of the "promise principle," Professor Charles Fried, argues that the parties have "some obligation to share unexpected benefits and losses in the case of an accident" in the course of a joint enterprise where they are not strangers to each other.[59] This "sharing principle" is derived from a more general principle of altruism and is similar to what has been called the duty of "easy rescue" in the law of torts.[60]

Last, this conclusion is bolstered by what might be the imperatives of an emerging theory of relational contract law. In *ALCOA,* the parties, at the time of contracting, were unable adequately to deal with certain changed circumstances over the duration of a seventeen-year contract. Yet preserving the contract was important to the parties and to third parties dependent upon its performance but not represented in the litigation. Ian Macneil has argued that in situations such as this there are relational norms that the contract should be preserved and conflict harmonized by adjustment. These norms put a high premium upon developing mechanisms for adjustment over time and good faith efforts to adjust in the light of change.[61] Thus, if in an *ALCOA*-type case, the court concludes that the disadvantaged party is entitled to "some relief" but not discharge, and the advantaged party has refused to accept a reasonable adjustment in light of risks that the disadvantaged party did not assume, relational theory also supports a court imposed adjustment to preserve the contract, to adjust the price and to avoid the twin devils of unbargained-for hardship and unjust enrichment."

Speidel, *The New Spirit of Contract,* 2 J.Law & Commerce 193, 202, 205–08 (1982).

(D) MUTUAL TERMINATION OF CONTRACTUAL RELATIONS: DISCHARGE

The legal controls imposed upon the power of the parties to agree to a modification (in response to changed circumstances or a dispute over performance) are most often expressed in terms of good faith and duress rather than consideration.

The parties may also agree to *discharge* some or all of the duties created by the contract. Here, the duty to pay money is usually at stake. A creditor accepts a payment from the debtor in "full satisfaction" of the claimed obligation. Later, the creditor sues to recover the original amount promised and is met with the defense that the duty was discharged by an

59. C. Fried, supra note 52, at 72–73. See Coons, *Compromise as Precise Justice,* 68 Calif.L.Rev. 250 (1980).

60. The "easy rescue" duty is as follows:

> Persons who can use energy, ability, or information to aid others in serious peril without significant inconvenience or harm to themselves should do so.

M. Shapo, supra note 49, at xii.

61. [See, generally I. Macneil, The New Social Contract 36–70 (1980).]

"accord and satisfaction." The response may be that the "accord and satisfaction" was not supported by consideration, especially if the debtor paid a lesser amount than was originally promised in the contract. If the accord and satisfaction was bargained for, the courts have readily found sufficient consideration if the debtor gives the creditor something in addition to the agreed payment. See, e.g., Jaffray v. Davis, 124 N.Y. 164, 26 N.E. 351 (1891), where the court found sufficient consideration because the debtor gave the creditor negotiable notes in amount of $3,462 and a security interest in personal property in exchange for discharge of a $7,714 unsecured debt due for goods delivered. Similarly, consideration for an accord and satisfaction is normally found when a payment is tendered and accepted to discharge an unliquidated debt or a disputed claim. See Murray, Chapter 12.

Many authorities have questioned the extension of consideration doctrine to cover the discharge of contractual obligations. For example, Sir Frederick Pollock maintained that "[t]he doctrine of consideration . . . has been extended with not very happy results far beyond its proper scope, which is to govern the formation of contracts, and has been made to regulate and restrain the discharge of contracts." F. Pollock, Principles of Contract 165 (1881). Likewise, Professor Corbin was outspoken in his criticism of this extension. Corbin § 1240. On occasion, the courts have avoided the consideration requirement by utilizing gift theory, Gray v. Barton, 55 N.Y. 68 (1873), or promissory estoppel, Fried v. Fisher, 328 Pa. 497, 196 A. 39 (1938).

In other instances, courts intent on finding discharge can find legislative support. There are statutes in some states which to some extent dispense with the necessity of consideration in the making of binding contracts. These statutes substitute the formality of a signed writing for consideration and usually encompass discharge as well as the creation of obligations. See supra at 185. A significant UCC provision, Section 1–107, deals with the discharge of obligations as follows: "Any claim or right arising out of an alleged breach can be discharged in whole or in part without consideration by a written waiver or renunciation signed and delivered by the aggrieved party." See also UCC 3–605 relative to the discharge of liability on a negotiable instrument by a holder's cancellation or renunciation.

Still, when the discharge is by agreement, one must usually be prepared to meet the demands of consideration. This may, of course, not be at all difficult. For example, if there is a mutual rescission, with each party surrendering rights under the original contract, there is obviously sufficient consideration. Likewise, if the parties effect a novation, as where a new party replaces one of the original parties with the consent of both. Finally, where there is an accord and satisfaction, it is usually the liquidation of an unliquidated claim or the existence of a good faith dispute that provides consideration. For a discussion of the various contractual methods for discharge, see Calamari and Perillo §§ 21–1 through 21–11.

Lurking in the background, however, are concerns that one party, perhaps even the debtor, may have imposed duress or acted in bad faith.

AFC Interiors v. DiCello

Supreme Court of Ohio, 1989.
46 Ohio St.3d 1, 544 N.E.2d 869.

* * *

■ SWEENEY, JUSTICE.

The dispositive question presented in this cause is whether an accord and satisfaction has taken place with regard to the debt owed by DiCello to AFC. The appellee DiCello, contends that an accord and satisfaction has taken place under the instant facts. The appellant, AFC, argues however that R.C. 1301.13, which embodies Section 1–207 of the Uniform Commercial Code ("UCC"), should supersede the doctrine of accord and satisfaction in the "full payment" or "conditional check" situation where the payee reserves his or her rights to pursue the balance of the debt alleged to be owed.

Accord and satisfaction is a common-law doctrine where there is a contract between a creditor and debtor for settlement of a claim by some performance other than that which is due. See Grosse & Goggin, Accord and Satisfaction and the 1–207 Dilemma (1984), 89 Comm.L.J. 537. Satisfaction takes place when the creditor accepts the accord. Id.; see, also, State, ex rel. Shady Acres Nursing Home, Inc. v. Rhodes (1983), 7 Ohio St.3d 7, 7 OBR 318 455 N.E.2d 489.

In the cause *sub judice,* DiCello tendered a check for an amount apparently less than what AFC expected. The check carried the notation that it constituted payment in full for any and all claims that AFC may have against DiCello. AFC crossed out the notation and inserted the words "Payment on Account" and further negotiated the check. Under Ohio law, it has been held that in such a situation the creditor had "* * * but one alternative; he must accept the amount tendered upon the terms of the condition, unless the condition be waived, or he must reject it entirely, or if he has received the amount by check in a letter, he must return it." Seeds, Grain & Hay Co. v. Conger (1910), 83 Ohio St. 169, 93 N.E. 892, paragraph one of the syllabus. See, also, Inger Interiors v. Peralta (1986), 30 Ohio App.3d 94, 30 OBR 193, 506 N.E.2d 1199. Thus, the precise question before this court is whether the special endorsement of the check by AFC with knowledge of a dispute as to the amount due, and with knowledge of the conditional statement on the check, constituted an acceptance of the conditional check, i.e., an accord and satisfaction. In light of the language of R.C. 1301.13, we do not believe that the special endorsement by AFC reserving its rights and subsequent negotiation of the check should continue to be recognized as an accord and satisfaction. Therefore, we reverse the decision of the court of appeals below and remand the cause for further proceedings.

R.C. 1301.13 (UCC 1–207) provides:

"A party who with explicit reservation of rights performs or promises performance or assents to performance in a manner demanded or offered by the other party does not thereby prejudice the rights reserved. Such words as 'without prejudice,' 'under protest,' or the like are sufficient."

The Official Comment to this section provides in part:

"1. This section provides machinery for the continuation of performance along the lines contemplated by the contract despite a pending dispute, by adopting the mercantile device of going ahead with delivery, acceptance, *or payment* 'without prejudice,' 'under protest,' 'under reserve,' 'with reservation of all our rights,' and the like. All of these phrases completely reserve all rights within the meaning of this section. The section therefore contemplates that limited as well as general reservations and acceptance by a party may be made 'subject to satisfaction of our purchaser,' 'subject to acceptance by our customers,' or the like." (Emphasis added.)

The issue of whether UCC 1–207 should apply to supersede the doctrine of accord and satisfaction has been the subject of much scholarly debate. Courts in different jurisdictions are split with regard to the effect of UCC 1–207 in this context. See, e.g., White & Summers, Uniform Commercial Code (3 Ed.1988) 689–692, Section 13–24; Note, Contracts—Section 1–207 of the Uniform Commercial Code Not Intended to Apply to Doctrine of Accord & Satisfaction (1980), 15 Land & Water Review 737–748; and Hawkland, The Effect of UCC Section 1–207 on the Doctrine of Accord and Satisfaction by Conditional Check (1969), 74 Comm.L.J. 329.

We are of the opinion, however, that the drafters of the UCC, and Ohio's General Assembly, promulgated UCC 1–207 in response to a perceived injustice to creditors that occurs where a creditor, under protest, deposits a check marked "paid in full" or the like, and later discovers that an accord and satisfaction has taken place which extinguished the right to demand further payment on the debt.

While this court has not applied R.C. 1301.13 (UCC 1–207) in factual situations similar to the case at bar, it appears that a discernible trend has developed whereby UCC 1–207 is used to supersede the common-law doctrine of accord and satisfaction in "full payment" or "conditional check" situations. * * *

More recently, in Horn Waterproofing Corp. v. Bushwick Iron & Steel Co., Inc. (1985), 66 N.Y.2d 321, 497 N.Y.S.2d 310, 488 N.E.2d 56, the debtor sent the creditor a check for less than the amount owed with a "full payment" notation. The creditor endorsed the check and added the notation "Under Protest," and brought an action to recover the balance alleged to be due. The court applied the UCC and held that a creditor may preserve his right to the balance of a disputed claim by explicit reservation in his endorsement of the check tendered by the debtor as full payment under UCC 1–207. See Majestic Bldg. Material Corp. v. Gateway Plumbing, Inc. (Mo.App.1985), 694 S.W.2d 762.

In addition to the above-cited precedents, it appears that four other jurisdictions (Delaware, Florida, Massachusetts and New Hampshire) have embraced the view that the UCC 1–207 supersedes the common-law doctrine of accord and satisfaction in the local comments to their respective versions of UCC 1–207. See White & Summers, supra, at 691, fn. 4.

While the issue is far from settled in other jurisdictions, the competing viewpoints regarding the appropriateness of applying UCC 1–207 were best summarized by White & Summers, supra, at 691–692:

"* * * Those arguing that 1–207 does not alter the common law rule typically start with the position, generally unassailable, that the offeror is 'master of his offer.' They point out that the drawer has made an offer, namely that of full payment, and they argue that allowing the payee to accept the money without the other terms of the offer is not only unfair, but also in direct conflict with the traditional notions of contract formation. Those who apply 1–207 and readily reject the common law outcome characterize the offeror as a chisler [*sic*]. He knows that he owes $10,000 and hopes to get away with $9,000. While we have no empirical basis for concluding the typical offeror is a chiseler as opposed to a legitimately aggrieved debtor, we are inclined to that view."

While we disdain characterizing any of the parties to the instant action in such a manner, we believe that the framers of the UCC drafted Section 1–207 in order to balance the interests of debtors and creditors in a more equitable manner. In any event, we are persuaded that UCC 1–207 was intended to apply in the situation confronting us in the cause *sub judice.* * * *

In applying the provisions of R.C. 1301.13 to the facts of the cause *sub judice,* we find that appellant explicitly reserved its rights by crossing out DiCello's notation on the back of the check and substituting its own notation, "Payment on Account." By putting DiCello on notice in such a manner, AFC reserved its rights to collect the balance alleged to be due.

Therefore, based on the foregoing, we hold that R.C. 1301.13, which embodies UCC 1–207, supersedes the common-law doctrine of accord and satisfaction in the "full payment" or "conditional check" situation.

* * *

NOTES

(1) *The Case for the Common Law Rule. AFC Interiors* was a 4–3 decision. In a strong dissent, not reprinted here, Justice Brown advanced the following arguments in favor of preserving the common law accord and satisfaction rule within the language of UCC 1–207.

First, the facts of the case satisfied the elements of accord and satisfaction. There was a good faith dispute and the tender of an accord and satisfaction was made and accepted.

Second, a proper reading of UCC 1–207 reveals that the common law rule was not displaced. The statute refers to one who "performs or promises performance or assents to performance in a manner demanded or offered by the other party." One who cashes a check given in full payment neither performs nor promises to perform anything. Moreover, a creditor who protests the tender, as by crossing out the "full payment" notation, is not really assenting to performance in a manner demanded or offered by the debtor. As indicated in the comments, the section "provides machinery for the continuation of performance along the lines contemplated by the contract despite a pending dispute." UCC 1–207, comment 1. If an accord and satisfaction is effectuated through the check cashing process, there is a new contract which discharges the old, not a continuation of the old. Thus, UCC 1–207 should be limited to situations to which it is clearly applicable, i.e., where a party is wary of proceeding with performance for fear of waiving a breach by the other. See Rosenthal, *Discord and Dissatisfaction: Section 1–207 of the Uniform Commercial Code,* 78 Colum.L.Rev. 48 (1978) (legislative history does not support broad interpretation).

Third, the narrow interpretation is supported by a strong majority of the cases and by most commentators. For more discussion, see Grosse & Goggin, *The 1–207 Dilemma Revisited (Accord and Satisfaction),* 16 No.Ky.L.Rev. 425 (1989).

Fourth, the court noted that the majority's decision impaired UCC Article 3, which governs when checks are issued to pay and discharge underlying obligations. In short, Article 3 does not permit a creditor-drawee to alter a check by unilaterally changing a material term. Such an alteration provides a defense to the drawer and could discharge the obligation. See County Fire Door Corp. v. C.F. Wooding Co., 202 Conn. 277, 520 A.2d 1028 (1987).

Finally, the common law rule makes good policy. The full payment check is a convenient and valuable private dispute settlement mechanism, and the law should help facilitate this process. To permit a creditor to accept payment but reject the terms on which it is offered might lessen the likelihood of settlement and, thus, prolong the dispute.

(2) *Law Reform?* In 1990, the American Law Institute and the National Conference of Commissioners on Uniform State Law approved amendments of the UCC designed to resolve the disagreement over UCC 1–207. First, UCC 1–207 was amended to state that it did not apply to an accord and satisfaction. Second, a new section, placed in Article 3, has been drafted to deal with an accord and satisfaction when a negotiable instrument is involved.

As you read the proposal below, consider how it addresses the concerns of the majority in *AFC Interiors.*

§ 3–311. ACCORD AND SATISFACTION BY USE OF INSTRUMENT

(a) This section applies if a person against whom a claim is asserted proves that (i) that person in good faith tendered an instrument to the claimant as full satisfaction of the claim, (ii) the amount of the claim was unliquidated or subject to a bona fide dispute, and (iii) the claimant obtained payment of the instrument.

(b) Unless subsection (c) applies, the claim is discharged if the person against whom the claim is asserted proves that the instrument or an accompanying written communication contained a conspicuous statement to the effect that the instrument was tendered as full satisfaction of the claim.

(c) Subject to subsection (d), a claim is not discharged under subsection (b) if the claimant is an organization and proves that within a reasonable time before the tender, the claimant sent a conspicuous statement to the person against whom the claim is asserted that communication concerning undisputed debts, including an instrument tendered as full satisfaction of a debt, are to be sent to a designated person, office or place, and the instrument or accompanying communication was not received by that designated person, office, or place.

(d) Notwithstanding subsection (c), a claim is discharged under subsection (b) if the person against whom the claim is asserted proves that within a reasonable time before collection of the instrument was initiated, an agent of the claimant having direct responsibility with respect to the disputed obligation knew that the instrument was tendered in full satisfaction of the claim, or received the instrument and any accompanying communication.

(E) UNILATERAL TERMINATION OF CONTRACTUAL RELATIONS

Zapatha v. Dairy Mart, Inc.

Supreme Judicial Court of Massachusetts, 1980.
Supra at 529.

NOTES

(1) In *Zapatha,* Dairy Mart had reserved broad power to terminate the franchise without regard to cause. How did the court justify imposing a duty of good faith on the exercise of that power? But see Corenswet, Inc. v. Amana Refrigeration, Inc., 594 F.2d 129, 138 (5th Cir.1979), cert. denied 444 U.S. 938, 100 S.Ct. 288, 62 L.Ed.2d 198 (1979), where the court refused to impose a good faith limitation upon the power to terminate an exclusive distributorship where the contract permitted termination by either party "at any time for any reason" on the giving of ten days notice. The court thought that the good faith duty always required the evaluation of the terminating party's motives and that a termination "without cause will almost always be characterizable as 'bad faith' termination." Are you persuaded? For more on the termination problem, see Hillman, *An Analysis of the Cessation of Contractual Relations,* 68 Cornell L.Rev. 617, 642–57 (1983); Note, *Franchise Termination: An Analysis of the Implied Covenant of Good Faith in Franchise Agreements,* 12 Am.J.Trial Advoc. 325 (1988).

(2) Federal and state laws have increasingly regulated the power to terminate a franchise relationship. For example, the Automobile Dealer's Day in Court Act, 15 U.S.C.A. § 1221 et seq., provides that a dealer may sue for damages "by reason of the failure of said automobile manufacturer ... to act in good faith in performing or complying with any of the terms and provisions of the franchise or in terminating, canceling or not renewing the franchise with said dealer...." Id. at § 1222. Good faith, however, is narrowly defined as the

"duty of each party . . . to guarantee . . . freedom from coercion, intimidation, or threat of coercion or intimidation from the other party . . ." Id. at § 1221(e). See Hubbard Chevrolet Co. v. General Motors Corp., 873 F.2d 873, 876–77 (5th Cir.1989) (federal good faith duty does not override or contradict clear reservation of power in contract). For an analysis of federal law and the effect of state "franchise relationship laws," see Pitegoff, *Franchise Relationship Laws: A Minefield for Franchisors,* 45 Bus.Law. 289 (1989). See also Sutherland, *The Risks and Exposures Associated with Franchise Noncompliance,* 42 Bus.Law. 369 (1987).

Seubert v. McKesson Corporation

Court of Appeals of California, 1990.
223 Cal.App.3d 1514, 273 Cal.Rptr. 296.

[In 1981, defendant hired Seubert to sell a stand-alone computer system to retail pharmacies in several eastern states. Prior to being offered employment, Seubert signed an employment application which stated, in part: "I understand and agree, if hired, my employment is for no definite period and may, regardless of the date of payment of my wages and salary, be terminated at any time without any prior notice."

In November, 1982, Seubert accepted a substantial promotion to regional sales manager for the western United States. He relied upon defendant's representations that the stand alone computer system was in place and operational in California and was backed by customer service. Subsequently, Seubert learned from customers that a basic ingredient of the system was not in place. Defendant made unsuccessful efforts to correct the matter and Seubert lost commissions when the systems were returned.

In December, 1983, Seubert was directed to sell on-line systems in Hawaii, even though the basic ingredient was not in place. Despite Seubert's efforts to correct problems, most systems sold were returned and Seubert lost more commissions. In December, 1984, defendant adopted a personnel policy, not intended to be retroactive, that sales people were to be terminated "if not at quota for two full quarters or letter of explanation is required." In March, 1985, Seubert was fired because he was not at quota for two successive fiscal quarters. There was evidence that he would have been at quota if there were no problems with the returned systems.

Seubert sued defendant, among other things, for breach of the implied covenant of good faith and fair dealing. The jury returned a verdict for Seubert and the trial court entered a judgment against defendant in the sum of $240,000.]

■ PERLEY, ASSOCIATE JUSTICE.

DISCUSSION

I

1. Implied Covenant of Good Faith and Fair Dealing

Appellants contend that Seubert was an at-will employee and that therefore there could be no breach of the implied covenant of good faith and fair dealing because Seubert could be terminated with or without cause.

Appellants argue that Seubert's application for employment expressly indicates that his employment was at will. That application, however, was a standardized two page form and it did not contain an integration clause. In McLain v. Great American Ins. Companies (1989) 208 Cal.App.3d 1476, 1484–1485, 256 Cal.Rptr. 863, the court found these factors significant in determining that there was an implied contract that the employee could only be discharged for cause. There, the court held that an employment application form which provided that employment could be terminated with or without cause was not an integrated agreement because the application was a standardized form, it did not cover either the employee's salary or position, it did not contain an integration clause and it stated that the terms and conditions could be changed at any time by the employer.

Appellants, however, rely on Slivinsky v. Watkins–Johnson Company (1990) 221 Cal.App.3d 799, 806, 270 Cal.Rptr. 585 where the court held that a written employment agreement which defined the employment as at will precluded a cause of action for breach of the implied covenant of good faith and fair dealing. There, the employee signed an employment application and an employment agreement which stated that there was no express or implied agreement between the parties for any specific period of employment and the agreement stated that the parties each had the right to terminate employment with or without cause. The court determined that unlike the application form in McLain, these documents constituted an integrated employment contract.

Appellants' reliance on Slivinsky is misplaced. Here, there was no express employment agreement but only an application form. As in McLain supra, the application form did not state Seubert's salary or position[2] and was a standardized two page form. While it stated that employment was for no definite period and could be terminated at any time, it did not contain an integration clause and it did not state that employment could be terminated for any reason. (Cf. Gerdlund v. Electronic Dispensers International (1987) 190 Cal.App.3d 263, 271, 235 Cal.Rptr. 279 [court emphasized that the language "for any reason" in the termination clause of an employment agreement precluded a separate collateral agreement regarding reasons for termination].) Hence, despite the termination at-will language in the employment application, other factors indicate that the application was not intended to be the entire employment agreement between the parties.

While there is a presumption that employment is terminable at will, that presumption may be superseded by a contract, express or implied, which limits the employer's right to discharge the employee. (Labor Code, § 2922; Foley v. Interactive Data Corp. (1988) 47 Cal.3d 654, 665, 254

---

2. We note that Seubert's salary and position were listed on the application in the section labeled "DO NOT WRITE BELOW THIS LINE" which was initialed and dated by an interviewer subsequent to Seubert's filing of the application.

Cal.Rptr. 211, 765 P.2d 373.) The evidence here supports the existence of an implied contract requiring cause for termination. Prior to Seubert's termination, an express personnel policy governing termination of sales personnel was instituted. The policy provided that a salesperson could be terminated "if not at quota for two full quarters ..." The existence of the policy supports Seubert's position that he could only be terminated for cause. (See *McLain,* supra, 208 Cal.App.3d at p. 1486, 256 Cal.Rptr. 863) [personnel manual which provided that " 'new hires during their initial three months may be terminated for cause, providing they have received written warning....' " supports jury's finding of implied contract.] While there was testimony that this policy was not to be applied retroactively, the record indicates that there had been an informal practice of terminating sales personnel if they were not at quota. There is therefore support for the jury's implied finding here that the employment contract between appellants and Seubert was not at-will.

Appellants also argue that the jury's award of damages for breach of the implied covenant must be reversed in light of *Foley.* Contrary to appellants' argument, however, *Foley* does not preclude inquiry into an employer's motive for discharging an employee, but simply holds that tort damages are not available for breach of the implied covenant of good faith and fair dealing. (Foley v. Interactive Data Corp., supra, 47 Cal.3d at p. 700, 254 Cal.Rptr. 211, 765 P.2d 373.) Here, the jury was asked to determine in its special verdict whether appellants had a legitimate reason to terminate Seubert's employment and whether appellants acted in good faith on an honest but mistaken belief that they had a legitimate business reason to terminate Seubert's employment. Neither inquiry was inappropriate under *Foley.* The jury was also permitted to award economic damages for breach of the implied covenant.[3] As the *Foley* court specifically approved of contract damages for breach of the implied covenant, we discern no error.

NOTES

The *Seubert* case is but an ice cube on the surface of the turbulent sea of "termination at will." It reflects, however, the influence of Foley v. Interactive Data Corp., 47 Cal.3d 654, 254 Cal.Rptr. 211, 765 P.2d 373 (1988), a decision that belies simple description. In *Foley,* the employee sought punitive damages for an alleged wrongful discharge. The majority first rejected the contention that a public policy external to the contract barred the termination, 47 Cal.3d at 665–72, 254 Cal.Rptr. at 214–19. Next, the court concluded that the presumption favoring termination at will, found in Section 2922 of the California Labor Code, was overcome by the allegation of facts from which a jury might conclude that the employer had impliedly agreed to discharge only for cause. Id.

3. The jury was instructed in the language of BAJI 10.54 that "[i]f you find defendants in breach of the implied covenant of good faith and fair dealing, you will award to plaintiff such damages as you find were legal- ly caused to plaintiff by such breach. Such damages include: The value of the loss of compensation and benefits under the employment contract and consequentialy [sic] economic damages."

at 674–82, 254 Cal.Rptr. at 221–26. Next, the court held that although the employer was subject to a covenant of good faith, a bad faith discharge did not constitute a tort. [Accord: Noye v. Hoffmann–La Roche, Inc., 238 N.J.Super. 430, 570 A.2d 12 (1990).] Rather, since the duty of good faith facilitated performance of contract duties, express or implied, bad faith (a discharge for other than cause) was a breach of contract for which contract remedies were available. Id. at 683–700, 254 Cal.Rptr. at 227–39. A careful reading of the majority, concurring and dissenting opinions reveals sharp disagreements on where the line between contract and tort should be drawn in disputes outside of the insurance area.

Exactly how does *Seubert* play the game within the parameters of *Foley?* Suppose the clause in the job application had become part of the contract? Suppose that the personnel policy, subsequently adopted, had not provided the basis for an implied contract? See Pine River State Bank v. Mettille, 333 N.W.2d 622 (Minn.1983) (employee handbook distributed subsequent to employment limits employer's power to terminate at will).

Comment: Erosion of "Employment at Will" Doctrine

For more than a century, American courts firmly adhered to the view that an employment contract of no fixed duration was terminable "at will." This meant that an employee who was not subject to a collective bargaining agreement could quit or be fired for a good reason, a bad reason, or no reason at all. See Epstein, *In Defense of the Contract at Will,* 51 U.Chi. L.Rev. 947 (1984).

In recent years, the employer's power to discharge has been limited significantly by both statute and judicial opinion. For example, federal and some state statutes protect an employee against discriminatory discharges based upon race, sex and age. See Kauff and Silverstein, Recent Developments in the Law of Unjust Dismissal 7–26 (1988). Kauff and Silverstein summarize the results as follows:

> Today approximately thirty states have held that the presumption of at-will employment can be contractually altered through statements made in employee handbooks or manuals. Other contract theories, such as promissory or equitable estoppel, independent consideration, and implied covenant of good faith and fair dealing, have also been found to rebut the at-will presumption and thus impair the employer's otherwise unfettered right to discharge. In tort, a majority of states now recognize that an at-will employee cannot be terminated where the reason to termination contravenes some express or implied public policy. Id. at 26.

See also Weisenberger, *Remedies for Employer's Wrongful Discharge of an Employee from Employment of an Indefinite Duration,* 21 Ind.L.Rev. 547 (1988).

In light of these developments, one can speculate on the impact of *Foley.* As a precedent, *Foley* holds only that a breach of the covenant of good faith is not a tort. It does not preempt legislative regulation of the termination process or foreclose finding a tort associated with other conduct of the employer. For example, an independent tort might be found where the discharge was in retaliation for certain socially preferred conduct by the employee, see, e.g., Palmateer v. International Harvester Co., 85 Ill.2d 124, 52 Ill.Dec. 13, 421 N.E.2d 876 (1981) (employee gave information to local law enforcement officers about a fellow employee's possible criminal activities) or where the employer libeled the employee at the time of or shortly after the termination.

Foley does, however, put the employee's protection (and the employer's rights) in the hands of contract law. If the employee has assented to an "at will" termination, neither the covenant of good faith nor an "implied" agreement to terminate only for cause will be much help. Absent legislative intervention, is this a sound outcome?

CHAPTER SIX

BREACH OF CONTRACT AND PERMISSIBLE REMEDIAL RESPONSES

SECTION 1.   RIGHT TO SUSPEND PERFORMANCE OR CANCEL UPON PROSPECTIVE INABILITY OR BREACH

A promisor commits a "breach" of contract when he or she fails without justification to perform when a promised performance is due. If the promisee has fully performed the agreed exchange, the remedy for breach is limited to an action for damages or specific performance. If the promisee still has duties to perform under the agreed exchange, the breach, if material, may also discharge those remaining duties. Thus, for a "material" breach by the promisor, the promisee has both affirmative (sue for damages for total breach) and defensive (cancel the contract) remedies. These general principles are elaborated in Sections 235–249 of Restatement (Second) and form a backdrop for our extended discussion of risk allocation in contract performance in Chapter Five. See also Farnsworth, Ch. 8.

In addition, it is recognized that a promisor commits a breach of contract when, by words or conduct, he or she repudiates a performance not yet due under the agreed exchange. If both parties still have obligations under the contract and the promisor's repudiation is of a material part of the agreed exchange and the repudiation has not been effectively nullified by a retraction or otherwise, the promisee, again, has both affirmative and defensive remedies and these remedies can be invoked *before* the time set for performance. See generally Restatement (Second) §§ 250–57, dealing with the effect of "Prospective Non–Performance." See also Farnsworth, Ch. 8(E); Andersen, *A New Look at Material Breach in the Law of Contracts,* 21 U.C.Davis L.Rev. 1073 (1988).

Finally, it is recognized that when the circumstances or the promisor's words or conduct create doubt whether the performance will be forthcoming as agreed but do not amount to a breach, the promisee has a more limited remedy. In the proper circumstances, the promisee may suspend performance and demand adequate assurance from the promisor. If assurance of due performance is not forthcoming, the promisee may treat it as a repudiation and resort to the usual affirmative and defensive remedies. Even if the promisor has breached, the promisee may decide just to suspend performance, reserving any claims for damages, and seek to resolve the dispute by agreement. If so, this action is justified and increases the chance that the dispute can be resolved and the bargain preserved.

In this section, we will look more closely at the content of breach of contract, particularly "prospective non-performance," and what might be called the promisee's defensive remedies, cancellation and suspension of performance. The issue frequently arises because the promisor asserts that the promisee's defensive reaction was not justified and was, therefore, a breach. In subsequent sections, we will examine the promisee's affirmative remedies, damages and specific performance.

Hochster v. De La Tour

Queen's Bench, 1853.
2 E. & B. 678, 118 Eng.Rep. 922.

* * * On the trial, before Erle, J., at the London sittings in last Easter Term, it appeared that plaintiff was a courier, who, in April, 1852, was engaged by defendant to accompany him on a tour, to commence on June 1st, 1852, on the terms mentioned in the declaration. On May 11th, 1852, defendant wrote to plaintiff that he had changed his mind, and declined his services. He refused to make him any compensation. The action was commenced on May 22d. The plaintiff, between the commencement of the action and June 1st, obtained an engagement with Lord Ashburton, on equally good terms, but not commencing till July 4th. The defendant's counsel objected that there could be no breach of the contract before June 1st. The learned judge was of a contrary opinion, but reserved leave to enter a non-suit on this objection. The other questions were left to the jury, who found for plaintiff.

* * *

■ LORD CAMPBELL, C.J. On this motion in arrest of judgment, the question arises, whether if there be an agreement between A and B whereby B engages to employ A on and from a future day for a given period of time, to travel with him into a foreign country as a courier, and to start with him in that capacity on that day, A being to receive a monthly salary during the continuance of such service, B may, before the day, refuse to perform the agreement and break and renounce it, so as to entitle A before the day to commence an action against B to recover damages for breach of the agreement; A having been ready and willing to perform it, till it was broken and renounced by B. The defendant's counsel very powerfully contended that, if the plaintiff was not contented to dissolve the contract, and to abandon all remedy upon it, he was bound to remain ready and willing to perform it till the day when the actual employment as courier in the service of the defendant was to begin; and that there could be no breach of the agreement, before that day, to give a right of action. But it cannot be laid down as a universal rule that, where by agreement an act is to be done on a future day, no action can be brought for a breach of the agreement till the day for doing the act has arrived. If a man promises to marry a woman on a future day, and before that day marries another woman, he is instantly liable to an action for breach of promise of marriage; Short v. Stone, 8 Q.B. 358. If a man contracts to execute a lease on and from a future day for a certain term, and, before that day, executes a lease to another for the same term, he may be immediately sued for breaking the contract. Ford v. Tiley, 6 B. & C. 325. So, if a man contracts to sell and deliver specific goods on a future day, and before the day he sells and delivers them to another, he is immediately liable to an action at the suit of the person with whom he first contracted to sell and deliver them. Bowdell v. Parsons, 10 East, 359. One reason alleged in support of such an action is, that the defendant has, before the day, rendered it impossible for him to perform the contract at the day; but this does not necessarily follow; for, prior to the day fixed for doing the act, the first wife may have died, a surrender of the lease executed might be obtained, and the defendant might have repurchased the goods so as to be in a situation to sell and deliver them to the plaintiff. Another reason may be that, where there is a contract to do an act on a future day, there is a relation constituted between the parties in the meantime by the contract, and that they impliedly promise that in the meantime neither will do anything to the prejudice of the other inconsistent with that relation. As an example, a man and woman engaged to marry are affianced to one another during the period between the time of the engagement and the celebration of the marriage. In this very case, of traveller and courier, from the day of the hiring till the day when the employment was to begin, they were engaged to each other; and it seems to be a breach of an implied contract if either of them renounces the engagement. This reasoning seems in accordance with the unanimous decisions of the Exchequer Chamber in Elderton v. Emmens, 6 C.B. 160, which we have followed in subsequent cases in this court. The declaration in the present case, in alleging a breach, states a great deal more than a passing intention on the part of the defendant which he may repent of, and could only be proved by evidence that he had utterly renounced the contract, or done some act which rendered it impossible for him to perform it. If the plaintiff has no remedy for breach of contract unless he treats the contract as in force, and acts upon it down to the 1st June, 1852, it follows that, till then, he must enter into no employment which will interfere with his promise "to start with the defendant on such travels on the day and year," and that he must then be properly equipped in all respects as a courier for a three months' tour on the continent of Europe. But it is surely much more rational, and more for the benefit of both parties, that, after the renunciation of the agreement by the defendant, the plaintiff should be at liberty to consider himself absolved from any future performance of it, retaining his right to sue for any damage he has suffered from the breach of it. Thus, instead of remaining idle and laying out money in preparations which must be useless, he is at liberty to seek service under another employer, which would go in mitigation of the damages to which he would otherwise be entitled for a breach of the contract. It seems strange that the defendant, after renouncing the contract, and absolutely declaring that he will never act under it, should be permitted to object that faith is given to his assertion, and that an opportunity is not left to him of changing his mind. If the plaintiff is barred of any remedy by entering into an engagement inconsistent with starting as a courier with the defendant on the 1st

June, he is prejudiced by putting faith in the defendant's assertion: and it would be more consistent with principle, if the defendant were precluded from saying that he had not broken the contract when he declared that he entirely renounced it. Suppose that the defendant, at the time of his renunciation, had embarked on a voyage for Australia, so as to render it physically impossible for him to employ the plaintiff as a courier on the continent of Europe in the months of June, July and August 1852: according to decided cases, the action might have been brought before the 1st June; but the renunciation may have been founded on other facts, to be given in evidence, which would equally have rendered the defendant's performance of the contract impossible. The man who wrongfully renounces a contract into which he has deliberately entered cannot justly complain if he is immediately sued for a compensation in damages by the man whom he has injured: and it seems reasonable to allow an option to the injured party, either to sue immediately, or to wait till the time when the act was to be done, still holding it as prospectively binding for the exercise of this option, which may be advantageous to the innocent party, and cannot be prejudicial to the wrongdoer. An argument against the action before the 1st of June is urged from the difficulty of calculating the damages: but this argument is equally strong against an action before the 1st of September, when the three months would expire. In either case, the jury in assessing the damages would be justified in looking to all that had happened, or was likely to happen, to increase or mitigate the loss of the plaintiff down to the day of trial. We do not find any decision contrary to the view we are taking of this case. * * *

If it should be held that, upon a contract to do an act on a future day, a renunciation of the contract by one party dispenses with a condition to be performed in the meantime by the other, there seems no reason for requiring that other to wait till the day arrives before seeking his remedy by action: and the only ground on which the condition can be dispensed with seems to be, that the renunciation may be treated as a breach of the contract.

Upon the whole, we think that the declaration in this case is sufficient. It gives us great satisfaction to reflect that, the question being on the record, our opinion may be reviewed in a Court of Error. In the meantime we must give judgment for the plaintiff.

Judgment for plaintiff.

NOTES

(1) What was the underlying theory of the court in *Hochster v. De La Tour?* Accepting that theory, why was it necessary to give the plaintiff both an excuse for non-performance and an immediate cause of action for damages? See Williston, *Repudiation of Contracts,* 14 Harv.L.Rev. 421, 432–41 (1901), rejecting *Hochster.*

(2) *When a Statement or an Act is a Repudiation.* Section 250 of Restatement (Second) provides:

A repudiation is (a) a statement by the obligor to the obligee indicating that the obligor will commit a breach that would of itself give the obligee a claim for damages for total breach under § 243, or (b) a voluntary affirmative act which renders the obligor unable or apparently unable to perform without such a breach.

Comment a recites the consequences of repudiation:

"A statement by a party to the other that he will not or cannot perform without a breach, or a voluntary affirmative act which renders him unable or apparently unable to perform without a breach may impair the value of the contract to the other party. It may have several consequences under this Restatement. If it accompanies a breach by non-performance that would otherwise give rise to only a claim for damages for partial breach, it may give rise to a claim for damages for total breach instead. ... Even if it occurs before any breach by non-performance, it may give rise to a claim for damages for total breach ..., discharge the other party's duties ..., or excuse the non-occurrence of a condition. ...."

(3) *Repudiation in the Uniform Commercial Code.* The 1990 Text of Article 2 of the UCC contained no comprehensive definition of repudiation. Rather, it carefully set out the options available to the aggrieved party when the other "repudiates the contract with respect to a performance not yet due the loss of which will substantially impair the value of the contract to the other. ...." UCC 2–610. One option was to "suspend his own performance" and "for a commercially reasonable time await performance by the repudiating party." UCC 2–610(a) & (c). This has the advantage of preserving the contract for a possible settlement and the disadvantage that the repudiating party may retract the repudiation before "the aggrieved party has * * * canceled or materially changed his position or otherwise indicated that he considers the repudiation final." UCC 2–611(1). Another option, consistent with *Hochster v. De La Tour,* was to suspend performance and "resort to any remedy for breach" under UCC 2–703 or 2–711. Suppose that the seller has repudiated a promise to deliver goods on December 1. The date of the repudiation was November 18. The buyer had, under the contract, paid one-half of the price on November 15 and agreed to pay the balance upon delivery. Under UCC 2–711, the buyer may "where the seller * * * repudiates * * * with respect to any goods involved * * * cancel and whether or not he has done so may in addition to recovering so much of the price as has been paid" seek damages under UCC 2–712 or 2–713. Under UCC 2–106(4), cancellation occurs "when either party puts an end to the contract for breach by the other." The effect of cancellation is to discharge "all obligations which are still executory on both sides" except that the cancelling party retains "any right based on prior breach or performance" and "any remedy for breach of the whole contract or any unperformed balance." UCC 2–106(3) & (4). See UCC 1–107 and 2–720. The decision to cancel may be manifested either by notice to the breaching party or conduct inconsistent with continuing the contract. See National Cash Register Co. v. Unarco Industries, Inc., 490 F.2d 285 (7th Cir.1974) (written notice); Goldstein v. Stainless Processing Co., 465 F.2d 392 (7th Cir.1972). See generally Wallach, *Anticipatory Repudiation and the Uniform Commercial Code,* 13 U.C.C.L.J. 48 (1980).

Section 2–712(b) (1997) provides that repudiation "includes but is not limited to language that one party will not or cannot make a performance still due under the contract or voluntary affirmative conduct that reasonably appears to the other party to make a future performance impossible or apparently impossible.'' The aggrieved party's options are preserved in UCC 2–712(a). The seller's options are stated in UCC 2–815 and the buyer's options are stated in UCC 2–823. The power to cancel for breach is stated in those sections and cancellation procedures and effect are stated in UCC 2–808.

(4) *Retraction of Repudiation.* Under a contract with Plaintiff to supply natural gas, Defendant agreed to purchase its requirements and a specified minimum amount at $.30 per unit. Plaintiff repudiated the contract but Defendant insisted the contract was in effect and demanded performance. Thereafter, Plaintiff offered to supply some gas at $.35 per unit. Defendant, still insisting that the original contract was in effect, accepted gas but refused to pay more than $.30 per unit. Finally, Plaintiff stopped all deliveries of gas. At this time, Defendant was 181,982 units short on the minimum amount of gas to be purchased under the original agreement. Plaintiff dropped its claim for $.05 per unit for gas supplied after the repudiation and sued for damages for breach of the agreement to purchase a minimum amount of gas. Defendant, for the first time, asserted that the contract was cancelled when Plaintiff repudiated. *Held,* the district court's judgment for Plaintiff is affirmed. At all times subsequent to the repudiation and before the trial, Defendant took the position that the contract was in effect and insisted that the Plaintiff perform under it. Thus, the parties agreed neither to rescind nor to modify the repudiated contract. Even though Plaintiff did not, in light of Defendant's election to treat the contract in force, alter its position in reliance, the court held that Defendant's election to preserve the contract was final and that ''the party who has made such declaration can not alter his position even though the party who was in default has not acted in reliance thereon.'' Neither party was misled and Plaintiff, in effect, retracted the repudiation when at the trial it withdrew its demand for the higher price and limited the claim to damages for breach of the minimum obligation. ''Inasmuch as defendant had not prior to that time brought action for nonperformance but had insisted upon performance and had not materially changed its position in reliance on the attempted cancellation, the act of plaintiff in attempting to repudiate was 'nullified.' '' Kentucky Natural Gas Corp. v. Indiana Gas & Chemical Corp., 129 F.2d 17 (7th Cir.1942). See Lowe v. Beaty, 145 Vt. 215, 485 A.2d 1255 (1984) (retraction effective); UCC 2–611 (1990) [UCC 2–713 (1997) remains unchanged]; Restatement (Second) § 256 (effect of retraction).

Taylor v. Johnston

Supreme Court of California, 1975.
15 Cal.3d 130, 123 Cal.Rptr. 641, 539 P.2d 425.

■ SULLIVAN, JUSTICE. In this action for damages for breach of contract defendants Elizabeth and Ellwood Johnston, individually and as copartners doing business as Old English Rancho, appeal from a judgment entered after a non-jury trial in favor of plaintiff H.B. Taylor and against them in the amount of $132,778.05 and costs.

Plaintiff was engaged in the business of owning, breeding, raising and racing thoroughbred horses in Los Angeles County. Defendants were engaged in a similar business, and operated a horse farm in Ontario, California, where they furnished stallion stud services. In January 1965 plaintiff sought to breed his two thoroughbred mares, Sunday Slippers and Sandy Fork to defendants' stallion Fleet Nasrullah. To that end, on January 19 plaintiff and defendants entered into two separate written contracts—one pertaining to Sunday Slippers and the other to Sandy Fork. Except for the mare involved the contracts were identical. We set forth in the margin the contract covering Sunday Slippers.[1]

The contract provided that Fleet Nasrullah was to perform breeding services upon the respective mares in the year 1966 for a fee of $3,500, payable on or before September 1, 1966. If the stud fee was paid in full and the mares failed to produce a live foal (one that stands and nurses without assistance) from the breeding a return breeding would be provided the following year without additional fee.

On October 4, 1965, defendants sold Fleet Nasrullah to Dr. A.G. Pessin and Leslie Combs II for $1,000,000 cash and shipped the stallion to Kentucky. Subsequently Combs and Pessin syndicated the sire by selling various individuals 36 or 38 shares, each share entitling the holder to breed one mare each season to Fleet Nasrullah. Combs and Pessin each reserved three shares.

On the same day defendants wrote to plaintiff advising the latter of the sale and that he was "released" from his "reservations" for Fleet Nasrullah. Unable to reach defendants by telephone, plaintiff had his attorney write to them on October 8, 1965, insisting on performance of the contracts. Receiving no answer, plaintiff's attorney on October 19, wrote a second letter threatening suit. On October 27, defendants advised plaintiff by letter that arrangements had been made to breed the two mares to Fleet Nasrullah in Kentucky. However, plaintiff later learned that the mares

---

1. "Original

IMPORTANT

PLEASE SIGN ORIGINAL AND RETURN AS QUICKLY AS POSSIBLE RETAINING DUPLICATE FOR YOUR OWN FILE.

January 8, 1965

"OLD ENGLISH RANCHO
Route 1, Box 224–A
Ontario, California 91761

"Gentlemen:
I hereby confirm my reservation for one services to the stallion FLEET NASRULLAH for the year 1966.
"TERMS: $3,500.00—GUARANTEE LIVE FOAL.
"FEE is due and payable on or before Sept. 1, 1966.
"IF stud fee is paid in full, and mare fails to produce a live foal (one that stands and nurses without assistance) from this breeding, a

return breeding the following year to said mare will be granted at no additional stallion fee.
"FEE is due and payable prior to sale of mare or prior to her departure from the state. If mare is sold or leaves the state, no return breeding will be granted.
"STUD CERTIFICATE to be given in exchange for fees paid.
"VETERINARIAN CERTIFICATE due in lieu of payment if mare is barren.
"I hereby agree that OLD ENGLISH RANCHO shall in no way be held responsible for accident of any kind or disease.

"Mare: SUNDAY SLIP-PERS	Mr. H.B. Taylor
	112 North Evergreen Street
Roan filly 1959	
MOOLAH BUX-MAOLI-ORMESBY	Burbank, California 91505

"(Veterinary certificate must accompany all barren mares.)

"Stakes winner of $64,000.00
last raced in 1962   /s/Mr. H.B. Taylor"

could not be boarded at Spendthrift Farm where Fleet Nasrullah was standing stud and accordingly arranged with Clinton Frazier of Elmhurst Farm to board the mares and take care of the breeding.

In January 1966 plaintiff shipped Sunday Slippers and Sandy Fork to Elmhurst Farm. At that time, however, both mares were in foal and could not be bred, since this can occur only during the five-day period in which they are in heat. The first heat period normally occurs nine days, and the second heat period thirty days, after foaling. Succeeding heat periods occur every 21 days.

On April 17, 1966, Sunday Slippers foaled and Frazier immediately notified Dr. Pessin. The latter assured Frazier that he would make the necessary arrangements to breed the mare to Fleet Nasrullah. On April 26, the ninth day after the foaling, Frazier, upon further inquiry, was told by Dr. Pessin to contact Mrs. Judy who had charge of booking the breedings and had handled these matters with Frazier in the past. Mrs. Judy, however, informed Frazier that the stallion was booked for that day but would be available on any day not booked by a shareholder. She indicated that she was acting under instructions but suggested that he keep in touch with her while the mare was in heat.

Sunday Slippers came into heat on May 13, 1966. Frazier telephoned Mrs. Judy and attempted to book the breeding for May 16. She informed him that Fleet Nasrullah had been reserved by one of the shareholders for that day, but that Frazier should keep in touch with her in the event the reservation was cancelled. On May 14 and May 15 Frazier tried again but without success; on the latter date, Sunday Slippers went out of heat.

On June 4, the mare went into heat again. Frazier again tried to book a reservation with Fleet Nasrullah but was told that all dates during the heat period had been already booked. He made no further efforts but on June 7, on plaintiff's instructions, bred Sunday Slippers to a Kentucky Derby winner named Chateaugay for a stud fee of $10,000.

Sandy Fork, plaintiff's other mare awaiting the stud services of Fleet Nasrullah, foaled on June 5, 1966. Frazier telephoned Mrs. Judy the next day and received a booking to breed the mare on June 14, the ninth day after foaling. On June 13, 1966, however, she cancelled the reservation because of the prior claim of a shareholder. Frazier made no further attempts and on June 14 bred Sandy Fork to Chateaugay.

Shortly after their breeding, it was discovered that both mares were pregnant with twins. In thoroughbred racing twins are considered undesirable since they endanger the mare and are themselves seldom valuable for racing. Both mares were therefore aborted. However, plaintiff was not required to pay the $20,000 stud fees for Chateaugay's services because neither mare delivered a live foal.

The instant action for breach of contract proceeded to trial on plaintiff's fourth amended complaint, which alleged two causes of action, the first for breach of the two written contracts, the second for breach of an oral agreement. Defendants cross-complained for the stud fees. The court found the facts to be substantially as stated above and further found and concluded that by selling Fleet Nasrullah defendants had "put it out of their power to perform properly their contracts," that the conduct of defendants and their agents Dr. Pessin and Mrs. Judy up to and including June 13, 1966, constituted a breach and plaintiff "was then justified in treating it as a breach and repudiation of their contractual obligations to him," and that defendants unjustifiably breached the contracts but plaintiff did not. The court awarded plaintiff damages for defendants' breach in the sum of $103,122.50 ($99,800 net damage directly sustained plus $3,322.50 for reasonable costs and expenses for mitigation of damages). "Because of defendants' wholly unwarranted, high-handed, and oppressive breach of their contractual obligation to plaintiff, the plaintiff is entitled to recover from the defendants pre-judgment interest at the rate of 7% per annum on the sum of $99,800.00 from August 1, 1968...." It was concluded that defendants should take nothing on their cross-complaint. Judgment was entered accordingly. This appeal followed.

Defendants' main attack on the judgment is two-pronged. They contend: First, that they did not at any time repudiate the contracts; and second, that they did not otherwise breach the contracts because performance was made impossible by plaintiff's own actions. To put it another way, defendants argue in effect that the finding that they breached the contracts is without any support in the evidence. Essentially they take the position that on the uncontradicted evidence in the record, as a matter of law there was neither anticipatory nor actual breach. As will appear, we conclude that the trial court's decision was based solely on findings of anticipatory breach and that we must determine whether such decision is supported by the evidence.

Nevertheless both aspects of defendants' argument require us at the outset to examine the specifications for performance contained in the contracts. (See fn. 1, ante). We note that the reservation for "one services" for Fleet Nasrullah was "for the year 1966." As the evidence showed, a breeding is biologically possible throughout the calendar year, since mares regularly come into heat every 21 days, unless they are pregnant. The contracts therefore appear to contemplate breeding with Fleet Nasrullah at any time during the calendar year 1966. The trial court made no finding as to the time of performance called for by the contracts. There was testimony to the effect that by custom in the thoroughbred racing business the breeding is consummated in a "breeding season" which normally extends from January until early July, although some breeding continues through August. It is possible that the parties intended that the mares be bred to Fleet Nasrullah during the 1966 breeding season rather than the calendar year 1966.

However, in our view, it is immaterial whether the contract phrase "for the year 1966" is taken to mean the above breeding season or the full calendar year since in either event the contract period had not expired by June 7 and June 14, 1966, the dates on which Sunday Slippers and Sandy Fork respectively were bred to Chateaugay and by which time, according to the findings ... defendants had repudiated the contracts. There can be no *actual* breach of a contract until the time specified therein for performance has arrived. (Gold Min. & Water Co. v. Swinerton (1943) 23 Cal.2d 19, 29, 142 P.2d 22; 1 Witkin, Summary of Cal.Law (8th ed.) § 629, p. 536; see Rest.2d Contracts (Tent.Draft No. 8, 1973) § 260.) Although there may be a *breach by anticipatory repudiation*; "[b]y its very name an essential element of a true anticipatory breach of a contract is that the repudiation by the promisor occur before his performance is due under the contract." (Gold Min. & Water Co. v. Swinerton, supra, 23 Cal.2d at p. 29, 142 P.2d at p. 27.) In the instant case, because under either of the above interpretations the time for performance had not yet arrived, defendants' breach as found by the trial court was of necessity an anticipatory breach and must be analyzed in accordance with the principles governing such type of breach. To these principles we now direct our attention.

Anticipatory breach occurs when one of the parties to a bilateral contract repudiates the contract. The repudiation may be express or implied. An express repudiation is a clear, positive, unequivocal refusal to perform (Guerrieri v. Severini (1958) 51 Cal.2d 12, 18, 330 P.2d 635; Gold Min. & Water Co. v. Swinerton, supra, 23 Cal.2d 19, 29, 142 P.2d 22; Whitney Inv. Co. v. Westview Dev. Co. (1969) 273 Cal.App.2d 594, 602–603, 78 Cal.Rptr. 302; Atkinson v. District Bond Co. (1935) 5 Cal.App.2d 738, 743–744, 43 P.2d 867); an implied repudiation results from conduct where the promisor puts it out of his power to perform so as to make substantial performance of his promise impossible (Zogarts v. Smith (1948) 86 Cal. App.2d 165, 194 P.2d 143; 1 Witkin, Summary of Cal.Law (8th ed.) § 632, pp. 538–539; 4 Corbin, Contracts (1951) § 984, pp. 949–951).

When a promisor repudiates a contract, the injured party faces an election of remedies: he can treat the repudiation as an anticipatory breach and immediately seek damages for breach of contract, thereby terminating the contractual relation between the parties, or he can treat the repudiation as an empty threat, wait until the time for performance arrives and exercise his remedies for actual breach if a breach does in fact occur at such time. ... However, if the injured party disregards the repudiation and treats the contract as still in force, and the repudiation is retracted prior to the time of performance, then the repudiation is nullified and the injured party is left with his remedies, if any, invocable at the time of performance. ...

As we have pointed out, the trial court found that the whole course of conduct of defendants and their agents Dr. Pessin and Mrs. Judy from the time of the sale of Fleet Nasrullah up to and including June 13, 1966, amounted to a repudiation which plaintiff was justified in treating as an anticipatory breach. ... However, when the principles of law governing repudiation just described are applied to the facts constituting this course of conduct as found by the trial court, it is manifest that such conduct cannot be treated as an undifferentiated continuum amounting to a single repudiation but must be divided into two separate repudiations.

First, defendants clearly repudiated the contracts when, after selling Fleet Nasrullah and shipping him to Kentucky, they informed plaintiff "[y]ou are, therefore, released from your reservations made to the stallion." However, the trial court additionally found that "[p]laintiff did not wish to be 'released' from his 'reservations' ... insist[ed] on performance of the stud service agreements ... [and] threaten[ed] litigation if the contracts were not honored by defendants ..." Accordingly defendants arranged for performance of the contracts by making Fleet Nasrullah available for stud service to plaintiff in Kentucky through their agents Dr. Pessin and Mrs. Judy. Plaintiff elected to treat the contracts as in force and shipped the mares to Kentucky to effect the desired performance. The foregoing facts lead us to conclude that the subsequent arrangements by defendants to make Fleet Nasrullah available to service plaintiff's mares in Kentucky constituted a retraction of the repudiation. Since at this time plaintiff had not elected to treat the repudiation as an anticipatory breach and in fact had shipped the mares to Kentucky in reliance on defendants' arrangements, this retraction nullified the repudiation. Thus, plaintiff was then left with his remedies that might arise at the time of performance.

The trial court found that after the mares had arrived in Kentucky, had delivered the foals they were then carrying and were ready for servicing by Fleet Nasrullah, plaintiff was justified in concluding from the conduct of defendants, their agent Dr. Pessin, and their subagent Mrs. Judy, that "defendants were just giving him the runaround and had no intention of performing their contract in the manner required by its terms" and in treating such conduct "as a breach and repudiation of their contractual obligation to him." ... Since, as we have explained, defendants retracted their original repudiation, this subsequent conduct amounts to a finding of a second repudiation.

There is no evidence in the record that defendants or their agents Dr. Pessin and Mrs. Judy ever stated that Sunday Slippers and Sandy Fork would not be serviced by Fleet Nasrullah during the 1966 breeding season or that they ever refused to perform. Frazier, plaintiff's agent who made arrangements for the breeding of the mares admitted that they had never made such a statement to him. Accordingly, there was no *express* repudiation or unequivocal refusal to perform. ...

The trial court's finding of repudiation, expressly based on the "conduct of the defendants" and their agents suggests that the court found an implied repudiation. However, there is no implied repudiation, i.e., by conduct equivalent to an unequivocal refusal to perform, unless "the promisor *puts it out of his power to perform.*" (Zogarts v. Smith, supra, 86 Cal.App.2d 165, 172–173, 194 P.2d 143; 1 Witkin, Summary of Cal.Law (8th ed.) § 632, p. 538; 4 Corbin, Contracts, supra, § 984, pp. 949–951; Rest.2d Contracts (Tent.Draft No. 8, 1973) §§ 268, 274.) Once the mares arrived in Kentucky, defendants had the power to perform the contracts; Fleet Nasrullah could breed with the mares. No subsequent conduct occurred to render this performance impossible. Although plaintiff was subordinated to the shareholders with respect to the priority of reserving a breeding time with Fleet Nasrullah, there is no evidence in the record that this subordination of reservation rights rendered performance impossible. Rather it acted to postpone the time of performance, which still remained within the limits prescribed by the contracts. It rendered performance more difficult to achieve; it may even have cast doubt upon the eventual accomplishment of performance; it did not render performance impossible.[2]

Because there was no repudiation, express or implied, there was no anticipatory breach. Plaintiff contends that defendants' conduct, as found by the trial court, indicated that "defendants were just giving him the runaround and had no intention of performing their contract" and therefore that this conduct was the equivalent of an express and unequivocal refusal to perform. Plaintiff has not presented to the court any authority in California in support of his proposition that conduct which has not met the test for an implied repudiation, i.e. conduct which removed the power to perform, may nonetheless be held to amount to the equivalent of an express repudiation and thus constitute an anticipatory breach. Without addressing ourselves to the question whether some conduct could ever be found equal to an express repudiation, we hold that defendants' conduct in this case as a matter of law did not constitute an anticipatory breach.

To constitute an express repudiation, the promisor's statement, or in this case conduct, must amount to an unequivocal refusal to perform: "A mere declaration, however, of a party of an intention not to be bound will not of itself amount to a breach, so as to create an effectual renunciation of the contract; for one party cannot by any act or declaration destroy the binding force and efficacy of the contract. To justify the adverse party in treating the renunciation as a breach, the refusal to perform must be of the whole contract ... and must be distinct, unequivocal, and absolute." (Atkinson v. District Bond Co., supra, 5 Cal.App.2d 738, 743, 43 P.2d 867, 869.)

To recapitulate, Sandy Fork was in foal in January 1966, the commencement of the 1966 breeding season, and remained so until June 5, 1966. Throughout this period Fleet Nasrullah could not perform his services as contracted due solely to the conduct of plaintiff in breeding Sandy Fork in 1965. Biologically the first opportunity to breed Sandy Fork was on June 14, 1966, nine days after foaling. Frazier telephoned Mrs. Judy on June 6, 1966, and received a booking with Fleet Nasrullah for June 14,

---

2. Plaintiff suggests that this conduct, namely delaying plaintiff's breeding until a day not reserved by a shareholder, amounted to an anticipatory breach because Mrs. Judy inserted a condition to defendants' performance, which as the trial court found was not contemplated by the contracts. Assuming arguendo that this conduct might have amounted to a breach of contract by improperly delaying performance, at most it would have constituted only a partial breach—insufficiently material to terminate the contracts (see Rest.2d Contracts (Tent.Draft No. 8, 1973) §§ 262, 266, 268, 274). It did not constitute a repudiation of the contracts which was the sole basis of the trial court's decision since "[t]o justify the adverse party in treating the renunciation as a breach, the refusal to perform must be of the whole contract or of a covenant going to the whole consideration. ..." (Atkinson v. District Bond Co., supra, 5 Cal.App.2d 738, 743, 43 P.2d 867, 869.)

1966. On June 13 Mrs. Judy telephoned Frazier and informed him she would have to cancel Sandy Fork's reservation for the following day because one of the shareholders insisted on using that day. Mrs. Judy gave no indication whatsoever that she could not or would not breed Sandy Fork on any of the following days in that heat period or subsequent heat periods. Frazier made no further attempts to breed Sandy Fork with Fleet Nasrullah. Thus, plaintiff, who delayed the possibility of performance for five months, asserts that the delay of performance occasioned by defendants' cancellation of a reservation on the first day during the six-month period that plaintiff made performance possible amounts to an unequivocal refusal to perform, even though there was adequate opportunity for Fleet Nasrullah to perform within the period for performance specified in the contract and even though defendants never stated any intention not to perform. We conclude that as a matter of law this conduct did not amount to an unequivocal refusal to perform and therefore did not constitute an anticipatory breach of the contract covering Sandy Fork.

Sunday Slippers foaled on April 17, 1966, first came into heat on April 26 and then successively on May 13 and June 4, 1966. Mrs. Judy informed Frazier that she would breed Sunday Slippers on any day that one of the shareholders did not want to use the stallion. Frazier unsuccessfully sought to breed the mare on April 26, May 14, May 15 and June 4, 1966, Fleet Nasrullah being reserved on those dates. Mrs. Judy continued to assure Frazier that the breeding would occur. Sunday Slippers was due to come into heat again twice during the breeding season: June 25 and July 16, 1966. At most this conduct amounts to delay of performance and a warning that performance might altogether be precluded if a shareholder were to desire Fleet Nasrullah's services on all the remaining days within the period specified for performance in which Sunday Slippers was in heat. We conclude that as a matter of law this conduct did not amount to an unequivocal refusal to perform and therefore did not constitute an anticipatory breach of the contract covering Sunday Slippers.

In sum, we hold that there is no evidence in the record supportive of the trial court's finding and conclusion that defendants repudiated and therefore committed an anticipatory breach of the contracts.

In view of the foregoing conclusion we need not consider defendants' remaining contentions.

The judgment is reversed.

[Some footnotes omitted. Those retained have been renumbered.]

NOTES

(1) In *Taylor,* the defendants never made a "statement" to the plaintiff "indicating that * * * (they) * * * will commit a breach that would of itself give the obligee a claim for damages for total breach. ..." Restatement (Second) § 250(1). But were there "voluntary affirmative" acts which rendered the defendant "unable or apparently unable to perform" without a material breach? Section 250(2).

(2) Restatement (Second) § 251(1) provides that "where reasonable grounds arise to believe that the obligor will commit" a material breach, the "obligee may demand adequate assurance of due performance and may, if reasonable, suspend any performance for which he has not already received the agreed exchange until he receives such assurance." Section 251(2) then provides that the "obligee may treat as a repudiation the obligor's failure to provide within a reasonable time such assurance of due performance as is adequate in the circumstances of the particular case." Should the plaintiff have pursued this strategy in *Taylor?* See Rosett, *Partial, Qualified, and Equivocal Repudiation of Contract,* 81 Colum.L.Rev. 93, 106–07 (1981), who argues that § 251 should be available where equivocal behavior is not the equivalent of a refusal to perform.

(3) *Use of Declaratory Judgment.* What options are available to parties who have honest but substantial disagreements about the meaning of their contract? Between the extremes of a negotiated settlement and a unilateral termination with all of its risks, lies the possibility of a declaratory judgment. The Federal Declaratory Judgment Act, 28 U.S.C.A. § 2201 provides:

> In a case of actual controversy within its jurisdiction * * * any court of the United States, upon the filing of an appropriate pleading, may declare the rights and other legal relations of any interested party seeking such declaration, whether or not further relief is or could be sought. Any such declaration shall have the force and effect of a final judgment or decree and shall be reviewable as such.

If there is a genuine controversy, this form of relief is available to clarify and stabilize and to eliminate uncertainty as to the scope and content of existing or prospective rights. This includes the interpretation of contract rights so that a party need not risk liability for breach if he or she is wrong. The court has discretion to deny this remedy where, for example, the decree "would not terminate the uncertainty or controversy giving rise to the proceeding," Uniform Declaratory Judgment Act § 6, or where relief depends upon future hypothetical events.

PROBLEM: THE "SAFE HARBOR" DEFENSE

In the *Kaiser–Francis Oil* case, supra at 741, after deregulation and the market collapse, the pipeline (PGC) claimed that its performance was excused (1) under the *force majeure* clause and (2) because the gas produced did not meet the quality specification provision concerning allowable water vapor in the gas. The pipeline also proposed a contract amendment that would replace the take-or-pay arrangement with a system of flexible well-head prices that responded to changing market conditions. See 870 F.2d at 567. Consider the following questions.

(1) Suppose that after some discussion, Kaiser rejected PGC's offer to modify the contract and insisted upon performance under the take-or-pay provision. PGC came back with a counterproposal, more favorable to Kaiser, and stated: "We will not make the next payment unless you negotiate with us in good faith over this proposal." What is Kaiser's legal position? What would you advise Kaiser to do?

(2) Suppose, instead, that PGC filed a declaratory judgment action to have the court determine whether PGC was excused under either the *force majeure* clause or because the gas had too much water. Kaiser demanded that PGC continue to make payments during the course of the litigation, estimated to take twelve months. PGC responded that there was a "good faith" dispute over the interpretation of the contract, and that PGC would not make another payment until the dispute was finally resolved by the court. At that time, PGC would perform the contract under the court's interpretation. What is Kaiser's legal position? What would you advise Kaiser to do?

AMF, Inc. v. McDonald's Corp.

United States Court of Appeals, Seventh Circuit, 1976.
536 F.2d 1167.

■ CUMMINGS, CIRCUIT JUDGE. AMF, Incorporated, filed this case in the Southern District of New York in April 1972. It was transferred to the Northern District of Illinois in May 1973. AMF seeks damages for the alleged wrongful cancellation and repudiation of McDonald's Corporation's ("McDonald's") orders for sixteen computerized cash registers for installation in restaurants owned by wholly-owned subsidiaries of McDonald's and for seven such registers ordered by licensees of McDonald's for their restaurants. In July 1972, McDonald's of Elk Grove, Inc. sued AMF to recover the $20,385.28 purchase price paid for a prototype computerized cash register and losses sustained as a result of failure of the equipment to function satisfactorily. Both cases were tried together during a fortnight in December 1974. A few months after the completion of the bench trial, the district court rendered a memorandum opinion and order in both cases in favor of each defendant. The only appeal is from the eight judgment orders dismissing AMF's complaints against McDonald's and the seven licensees. We affirm.

The district court's memorandum opinion and order are unreported. Our statement of the pertinent facts is culled from the 124 findings of fact contained therein or from the record itself.

In 1966, AMF began to market individual components of a completely automated restaurant system, including its model 72C computerized cash register involved here. The 72C cash register then consisted of a central computer, one to four input stations, each with a keyboard and cathode ray tube display, plus the necessary cables and controls.

In 1967, McDonald's representatives visited AMF's plant in Springdale, Connecticut, to view a working "breadboard" model 72C to decide whether to use it in McDonald's restaurant system. Later that year, it was agreed that a 72C should be placed in a McDonald restaurant for evaluation purposes.

In April 1968, a 72C unit accommodating six input stations was installed in McDonald's restaurant in Elk Grove, Illinois. This restaurant was a wholly-owned subsidiary of McDonald's and was its busiest restaurant. Besides functioning as a cash register, the 72C was intended to enable counter personnel to work faster and to assist in providing data for accounting reports and bookkeeping. McDonald's of Elk Grove, Inc. paid some $20,000 for this prototype register on January 3, 1969. AMF never gave McDonald's warranties governing reliability or performance standards for the prototype.

At a meeting in Chicago on August 29, 1968, McDonald's concluded to order sixteen 72C's for its company-owned restaurants and to cooperate with AMF to obtain additional orders from its licensees. In December 1968, AMF accepted McDonald's purchase orders for those sixteen 72C's. In late January 1969, AMF accepted seven additional orders for 72C's from McDonald's licensees for their restaurants. Under the contract for the sale of all the units, there was a warranty for parts and service. AMF proposed to deliver the first unit in February 1969, with installation of the remaining twenty-two units in the first half of 1969. However, AMF established a new delivery schedule in February 1969, providing for deliveries to commence at the end of July 1969 and to be completed in January 1970, assuming that the first test unit being built at AMF's Vandalia, Ohio, plant was built and satisfactorily tested by the end of July 1969. This was never accomplished.

During the operation of the prototype 72C at McDonald's Elk Grove restaurant, many problems resulted, requiring frequent service calls by AMF and others. Because of its poor performance, McDonald's had AMF remove the prototype unit from its Elk Grove restaurant in late April 1969.

At a March 18, 1969, meeting, McDonald's and AMF personnel met to discuss the performance of the Elk Grove prototype. AMF agreed to formulate a set of performance and reliability standards for the future 72C's including "the number of failures permitted at various degrees of seriousness, total permitted downtime, maximum service hours and cost." Pending mutual agreement on such standards, McDonald's personnel asked that production of the twenty-three units be held up and AMF agreed.

On May 1, 1969, AMF met with McDonald's personnel to provide them with performance and reliability standards. However, the parties never agreed upon such standards. At that time, AMF did not have a working machine and could not produce one within a reasonable time because its Vandalia, Ohio, personnel were too inexperienced. After the May 1st meeting, AMF concluded that McDonald's had cancelled all 72C orders. The reasons for the cancellation were the poor performance of the prototype, the lack of assurances that a workable machine was available and the unsatisfactory conditions at AMF's Vandalia, Ohio, plant where the twenty-three 72C's were to be built.

On July 29, 1969, McDonald's and AMF representatives met in New York. At this meeting it was mutually understood that the 72C orders were cancelled and that none would be delivered.

In its conclusions of law, the district court held that McDonald's and its licensees had entered into contracts for twenty-three 72C cash registers but that AMF was not able to perform its obligations under the contracts. ... Citing Section 2–610 of the Uniform Commercial Code (Ill.Rev.Stats.

(1975) ch. 26, § 2–610) and Comment 1 thereunder, the court concluded that on July 29, McDonald's justifiably repudiated the contracts to purchase all twenty-three 72C's.

Relying on Sections 2–609 and 2–610 of the Uniform Commercial Code (Ill.Rev.Stats. (1975) ch. 26, §§ 2–609 and 2–610), the court decided that McDonald's was warranted in repudiating the contracts and therefore had a right to cancel the orders by virtue of Section 2–711 of the Uniform Commercial Code (Ill.Rev.Stats. (1975) ch. 26, § 2–711). Accordingly, judgment was entered for McDonald's.

The findings of fact adopted by the district court were a mixture of the court's own findings and findings proposed by the parties, some of them modified by the court. AMF has assailed ten of the 124 findings of fact, but our examination of the record satisfies us that all have adequate support in the record and support the conclusions of law.

Whether in a specific case a buyer has reasonable grounds for insecurity is a question of fact. Comment 3 to UCC § 2–609; Anderson, Uniform Commercial Code, § 2–609 (2d Ed.1971). On this record, McDonald's clearly had "reasonable grounds for insecurity" with respect to AMF's performance. At the time of the March 18, 1969, meeting, the prototype unit had performed unsatisfactorily ever since its April 1968 installation. Although AMF had projected delivery of all twenty-three units by the first half of 1969, AMF later scheduled delivery from the end of July 1969 until January 1970. When McDonald's personnel visited AMF's Vandalia, Ohio, plant on March 4, 1969, they saw that none of the 72C systems was being assembled and learned that a pilot unit would not be ready until the end of July that year. They were informed that the engineer assigned to the project was not to commence work until March 17th. AMF's own personnel were also troubled about the design of the 72C, causing them to attempt to reduce McDonald's order to five units. Therefore, under Section 2–609 McDonald's was entitled to demand adequate assurance of performance by AMF.*

However, AMF urges that Section 2–609 of the UCC ... is inapplicable because McDonald's did not make a written demand of adequate assurance of due performance. In Pittsburgh–Des Moines Steel Co. v. Brookhaven Manor Water Co., 532 F.2d 572, 581 (7th Cir.1976), we noted that the Code should be liberally construed and therefore rejected such "a formalistic

---

* McDonald's was justified in seeking assurances about performance standards at the March 18th meeting. The parts and service warranty in the contracts for the twenty-three 72C's was essentially a limitation of remedy provision. Under UCC § 2–719(2) (Ill.Rev.Stats. (1975) ch. 26, § 2–719(2)) if the 72C cash registers failed to work or could not be repaired within a reasonable time, the limitation of remedy provision would be invalid, and McDonald's would be entitled to pursue all other remedies provided in Article

2. See Riley v. Ford Motor Co., 442 F.2d 670, 673 (5th Cir.1971); Earl M. Jorgensen Co. v. Mark Construction Co., 540 P.2d 978, 985–987 (Hawaii 1975). Because McDonald's would have a right to reject the machines if they proved faulty after delivery and then to cancel the contract, it was consistent with the purposes of § 2–609 for McDonald's to require assurances that such eventuality would not occur. See Comment 1 to UCC § 2–719.

approach" to Section 2–609. McDonald's failure to make a written demand was excusable because AMF's Mr. Dubosque's testimony and his April 2 and 18, 1969, memoranda about the March 18th meeting showed AMF's clear understanding that McDonald's had suspended performance until it should receive adequate assurance of due performance from AMF (Tr. 395; AMF Exhibit 79; McD. Exhibit 232).

After the March 18th demand, AMF never repaired the Elk Grove unit satisfactorily nor replaced it. Similarly, it was unable to satisfy McDonald's that the twenty-three machines on order would work. At the May 1st meeting, AMF offered unsatisfactory assurances for only five units instead of twenty-three. The performance standards AMF tendered to McDonald's were unacceptable because they would have permitted the 72C's not to function properly for 90 hours per year, permitting as much as one failure in every fifteen days in a busy McDonald's restaurant. Also, as the district court found, AMF's Vandalia, Ohio, personnel were too inexperienced to produce a proper machine. Since AMF did not provide adequate assurance of performance after McDonald's March 18th demand, UCC Section 2–609(1) permitted McDonald's to suspend performance. When AMF did not furnish adequate assurance of due performance at the May 1st meeting, it thereby repudiated the contract under Section 2–609(4). At that point, Section 2–610(b) ... permitted McDonald's to cancel the orders pursuant to Section 2–711 ... as it finally did on July 29, 1969.

In seeking reversal, AMF relies on Pittsburgh–Des Moines Steel Co. v. Brookhaven Manor Water Co., supra, 532 F.2d at 581. There we held a party to a contract could not resort to UCC Section 2–609 since there was no demonstration that reasonable grounds for insecurity were present. That case is inapt where, as here, McDonald's submitted sufficient proof in that respect. But that case does teach that McDonald's could cancel the orders under Sections 2–610 and 2–711 because of AMF's failure to give adequate assurance of due performance under Section 2–609.

* * *

Judgment affirmed. [Some footnotes omitted.]

NOTES

(1) *Right to Adequate Assurance of Performance.* UCC 2–609 [UCC 2–711 (1997)] provides:

> (1) A contract for sale imposes an obligation on each party that the other's expectation of receiving due performance will not be impaired. When reasonable grounds for insecurity arise with respect to the performance of either party the other may in writing demand adequate assurance of due performance and until he receives such assurance may if commercially reasonable suspend any performance for which he has not already received the agreed return.

(2) Between merchants the reasonableness of grounds for insecurity and the adequacy of any assurance offered shall be determined according to commercial standards.

* * *

(4) After receipt of a justified demand failure to provide within a reasonable time not exceeding thirty days such assurance of due performance as is adequate under the circumstances of the particular case is a repudiation of the contract.

According to Professor James J. White, the *AMF* case is not a conventional application of UCC 2–609:

> First, the court brushed aside section 2–609's explicit requirement that the demand be written. Second, nothing in the opinion indicates that there was even a formal oral demand. In effect, the court applied section 2–609 to one party's routine negotiating behavior and gave it significant legal consequence—namely, repudiation by the other.

White, *Eight Cases and Section 251*, 67 Cornell L.Rev. 841, 846 (1982). White's study of eight cases where either UCC 2–609 or Restatement (Second) § 251 were involved leads to the conclusion that the adequate assurance strategy was less a weapon in the hands of lawyers and more a discrete, subtle tool in the hands of courts to "give legal consequences to acts taken in the course of negotiations by parties who never considered those consequences." 67 Cornell L.Rev. at 859.

> My eight cases tell me that one who acts in bad faith, appears incapable of performing, or breaches his contract in even a limited way commits a repudiation or a material breach by much more equivocal and less egregious behavior than the black letter would lead one to believe. If the courts continue down this path, it is possible that Restatement Third will read:
>
> > One has committed a material breach or a repudiation when his acts or other circumstances make it appear likely that he is either incapable of performing or unwilling to do so.

67 Cornell L.Rev. at 860. For more on the relationship between UCC 2–609 and Restatement (Second) § 251, see Robertson, *The Right to Demand Adequate Assurance of Due Performance: UCC § 2–609 and Restatement of Contracts § 251*, 38 Drake L.Rev. 305 (1988–89); Comment, 50 Fordham L.Rev. 1292 (1982).

(2) As a buyer of goods, McDonald's route to victory in the *AMF* case involved the following steps: UCC 2–609(1) [UCC 2–711(a) (1997)]; UCC 2–609(4) [UCC 2–711(d) (1997)]; UCC 2–610(b) [UCC 2–712(b) (1997)]; and UCC 2–711(1) [UCC 2–823(a) (1997)].

(3) In government contracts, a "failure to make progress" clause, protecting the government's interest, is included in the standard Default Clause for fixed-price supply contracts. See 41 C.F.R. § 1–16.901–32 cl. 11(19). Paragraph (a) provides:

> The Government may, subject to the provisions of paragraph (c) below, by written notice of default to the Contractor, terminate the whole or any part of this contract in any one of the following circumstances: (i) if the

Contractor fails to make delivery of the supplies or to perform the services within the time specified herein or any extension thereof; or (ii) if the Contractor fails to perform any of the other provisions of this contract, or so fails to make progress as to endanger performance of this contract in accordance with its terms, and in either of these two circumstances does not cure such failure within a period of 10 days (or such longer period as the Contracting Officer may authorize in writing) after receipt of notice from the Contracting Officer specifying such failure.

If a termination under paragraph (a) is proper and the default is not excused under paragraph (c) because it arose "out of causes beyond the control and without the fault or negligence of the Contractor," the government's remedies are spelled out in paragraph (b): "The Government may procure, upon such terms and in such manner as the Contracting Officer may deem appropriate, supplies or services similar to those so terminated, and the Contractor shall be liable to the Government for any excess costs for such similar supplies or services." On the other hand, if the termination under paragraph (a) is premature or a default termination is excused under paragraph (c), the contractor's remedies are limited under paragraph (e) to costs incurred plus profit on work done up to the time of termination. One may not recover profits prevented by the improper termination.

PROBLEMS: FINANCIAL INABILITY TO PERFORM

(1) In October, 1990, S and B entered a contract for sale under which S was to manufacture and deliver "on or before" February 1, 1991, 10,000 fiber cartons and B was to pay $20,000, $10,000 on December 1, 1990 and the balance upon delivery. In late November, 1990, B obtained reliable information that S was in financial difficulty. Several creditors of S had obtained judgments. The electricity to S's plant had been turned off for nonpayment of the utility bill. The workforce had been cut back from fifty full-time employees to three and they had not been paid since October 15. A bank holding the mortgage on the land had commenced foreclosure for default. S's bank account was depleted and, to avoid creditor claims, S had not sent invoices for payment to other customers for goods delivered. S's response to B's expressed concern was, in effect, "not to worry, the cartons will be delivered on time." It is now December 1, 1990 and the $10,000 installment is due. The market price for similar fiber cartons has increased 5% since the time of contracting and, because of problems obtaining raw materials, fiber carton manufacturers are experiencing delays in delivery. B wants out of the contract *NOW* and comes to you for advice. What would you recommend?

(2) M, a manufacturer of goods, sells on credit to a number of buyers. To secure the obligation to pay, M normally creates and perfects a security interest in the goods under Article 9. This provides some help if the buyer defaults (M can repossess the goods, resell them and apply the proceeds to the debt), but the process is costly and there may be deficiencies. On the other hand, if M insisted on cash on delivery, it would lose 30% of its customers. From past experience, M knows that if a buyer is insolvent, i.e., unable to meet obligations in the ordinary course of business, M may refuse to deliver goods until the buyer pays cash. See UCC 2–702(1) [UCC 2–816(a) (1997)]. Compare Restatement (Second) § 252. Also, for financial difficulties short of insolvency, M

knows that it can demand adequate assurance under UCC 2–609 [UCC 2–712 (1997)]. But M is concerned about the difficulty of determining when a buyer is insolvent and the legal conditions imposed upon the use of the adequate assurance procedure. So M comes to you with the following clause and asks whether you would recommend inclusion in written contracts for the sale of goods on credit.

> If at any time in the sole opinion of the Seller, the financial responsibility of the Purchaser shall become impaired or unsatisfactory to the Seller, cash payments in advance of delivery may be required. Upon failure to pay any amount due to the Seller under this contract, the Seller may at its option terminate this contract as to further deliveries, and no forbearance or course of dealings shall affect this right of the Seller.

What would you recommend? See UCC 1–208.

(3) Suppose, in (1), above, that S agreed in October, 1990 to manufacture and deliver to B 10,000 fiber cartons on July 1, 1991 at a fixed-price of $20,000. Due to unanticipated bad weather and a government embargo, the cost to S of obtaining the raw fiber increased 500%. On May 1, S knew that the total cost of performing the contract would be $50,000. On that date, S telephoned B and said: "We have encountered severe cost problems in obtaining raw materials. Given these circumstances, I would like to suggest that you agree to pay us $40,000 for the cartons. Otherwise we might not be able to deliver. That won't cover our costs but it seems like a sensible solution." B "snorted," hung up the telephone and, on the advice of counsel, immediately sent S a written demand for adequate assurance of due performance. S did not respond. On June 15, B cancelled the contract, repurchased the containers from C for $55,000 and, on June 20, 1991, sued S for breach of contract.

(a) Was B's cancellation proper?

(b) Suppose that the court ultimately decides that S was excused for "impracticability" under UCC 2–615(a)[UCC 2–716 (1997)]. What effect on your answer to 3(a), above? See Restatement (Second) § 254(2).

(c) Suppose the court ultimately determines that B, because of insolvency, would have been unable to pay for the cartons if they had been delivered on July 1. What effect on your answer to 3(a), above? See Restatement (Second) § 254(1).

Plotnick v. Pennsylvania Smelting & Refining Co.

United States Court of Appeals, Third Circuit, 1952.
194 F.2d 859.

■ HASTIE, CIRCUIT JUDGE. This litigation arises out of an installment contract for the sale of quantities of battery lead by a Canadian seller to a Pennsylvania buyer. The seller sued for the price of a carload of lead delivered but not paid for. The buyer counterclaimed for damages caused by the seller's failure to deliver the remaining installments covered by the contract. The district court sitting without a jury allowed recovery on both claim and counterclaim. This is an appeal by the seller from the judgment against him on the counterclaim. The ultimate question is whether the buyer had committed such a breach of contract as constituted a repudiation justifying rescission by the seller.

Suit was brought in the District Court for the Eastern District of Pennsylvania. Federal jurisdiction is based on diversity of citizenship. Consequently, the conflict of laws rules of the forum, Pennsylvania, are invoked to solve the choice of law problem. Klaxon Co. v. Stentor Electric Mfg. Co., 1941, 313 U.S. 487, 61 S.Ct. 1020, 85 L.Ed. 1477. This involves no difficulty since familiar conflict of laws doctrine accepted generally and in Pennsylvania tells us that legal excuse for the non-performance or avoidance of a contract is to be determined in accordance with the law of the place of performance. Restatement, Conflict of Laws, Pa.Annot. § 358 (1936). Beyond this, the parties agree, and correctly so, that Pennsylvania is the place of performance in this case. Therefore, we apply the substantive law of Pennsylvania, particularly the Uniform Sales Act, to determine the legal consequences of the operative facts.

Uncontested findings of fact show that the contract in question was the last of a series of agreements, several of them installment contracts, entered into by the parties between June and October, 1947. Under these contracts, numerous shipments of lead were made by the seller in Canada to the buyer in Philadelphia. The seller frequently complained, and with justification, that payments were too long delayed. On the other hand, several shipments were not made at the time required by the contracts. However, by the end of March 1948, all contracts other than the one in suit had been fully performed by both parties. In this connection, it was the unchallenged finding of the district court that both parties waived the delays which preceded the buyer's breach involved in this suit. The earlier delays are relevant only insofar as they may reasonably have influenced either party in its interpretation of subsequent conduct of the other party.

The contract in suit was executed October 23, 1947 and called for deliveries aggregating 200 tons of battery lead to be completed not later than December 25, 1947. The agreed price was 8.1 cents per pound, or better if quality warranted. The court found that it was the understanding of the parties that at least 63 percent of the price should be paid shortly after each shipment was delivered and the balance within four weeks after that delivery. This finding is not contested.

Under this contract a first carload was delivered November 7, 1947. About 75 percent of the price was paid six days later. A second carload was received January 8, and about 75 percent of the price was paid 10 days later. Final adjustments and payments of small balances due on these two carloads were completed March 30, and these shipments are not now in dispute. The earliest shipment immediately involved in this litigation, the third under the contract, was a carload of lead received by the buyer on March 23, 1948. This delivery followed a March 12 conference of the parties. They disagree on what transpired at that conference. However, about 290,000 pounds of lead were then still to be delivered under the contract which stated December 25, 1947 as the agreed time for the completion of performance. And shortly after the conference, one carload of

43,000 pounds was delivered. No part of the price of this third carload has been paid. It is not disputed that plaintiff is entitled to the price of this shipment and his recovery on his claim in this suit vindicates that right.

On April 7, the buyer, who had been prodding the seller for more lead for some time, notified the seller that unless the balance of the lead should be delivered within thirty days he would buy in the open market and charge the seller any cost in excess of 8.1 cents per pound. On April 10, the seller replied refusing to ship unless the recently delivered third carload should be paid for. On May 12, buyer's attorney threatened suit unless the undelivered lead should be shipped promptly and at the same time promised to pay on delivery 75 percent of the price of this prospective shipment together with the full price of the third installment already received. Seller's solicitor replied on May 22 that seller regarded the contract as "cancelled" as a result of buyer's failure to pay for lead already delivered. At the same time the letter stated the seller's willingness to deliver at the originally agreed price if the overdue payment should be made by return mail and a letter of credit established to cover the price of the lead not yet shipped. Buyer's attorney replied on May 25 that buyer had withheld the price of the third carload "only as a set-off by reason of the failure of your client to deliver" and that buyer would place the overdue payment in escrow and would accept the remaining lead if shipped to Philadelphia "sight draft attached for the full invoice price of each car." On May 27, seller's solicitors reiterated the position stated in their March 22 letter and on June 2 seller notified buyer that the Canadian government had imposed export control on lead. The district court found, and it is here admitted, that between October 1947 and May 1948 the market price of battery lead increased from 8.1 cents to 11½ cents per pound.

The court concluded that the failure of defendant to make a down payment of at least 63 percent of the price of the third carload constituted a breach of contract but "not such a material breach of the contract as to justify plaintiff in refusing to ship the balance due under the contract within the meaning of section 45 of The Sales Act." This was the decisive conclusion of law which the seller has challenged.

Section 45 of the Sales Act as in force in Pennsylvania provides in relevant part as follows: "Where there is a contract to sell goods to be delivered by stated instalments, which are to be separately paid for, and * * * the buyer neglects or refuses to * * * pay for one or more instalments, it depends in each case on the terms of the contract, and the circumstances of the case, whether the breach of contract is so material as to justify the injured party in refusing to proceed further * * * or whether the breach is severable, giving rise to a claim for compensation, but not to a right to treat the whole contract as broken." Pa.Stat.Ann. Tit. 69, § 255 (Purdon, 1931).

We are dealing, therefore, with a situation in which the controlling statute explicitly makes the circumstances of the particular case determine whether failure to pay the price of one shipment delivered under an installment contract justifies the seller in treating his own obligation with reference to future installments as ended. Our problem is how to determine the legal effect of non-payment in a particular case.

We think the key is to be found in the rational basis of the statute itself. The flexibility of the statute reflects the impossibility of generalization about the consequences of failure to pay promptly for installments as delivered. Yet, the commercial sense of the statute yields two guiding considerations. First, nonpayment for a delivered shipment may make it impossible or unreasonably burdensome from a financial point of view for the seller to supply future installments as promised. Second, buyer's breach of his promise to pay for one installment may create such reasonable apprehension in the seller's mind concerning payment for future installments that the seller should not be required to take the risk involved in continuing deliveries. If any such consequence is proved, the seller may rescind. Moreover, the Pennsylvania decisions indicate that these embarrassments and apprehensions are normal consequences of non-payment; but the cases also make it clear that they are not necessary consequences. American Tube & Stamping Co. v. Erie Iron & Steel Co., 1924, 281 Pa. 10, 125 A. 304; G.B. Hurt, Inc. v. Fuller Canneries Co., 1920, 269 Pa. 85, 112 A. 148; Cf., Helgar Corp. v. Warner's Features, Inc., 1918, 222 N.Y. 449, 119 N.E. 113.

In this case there is no evidence that the delay in payment for one carload made it difficult to provide additional lead. To the contrary, seller admits that throughout the period in controversy he had sufficient lead on hand for the full performance of this contract. He could have delivered had he chosen to do so. His excuse, if any, must be found in reasonable apprehension as to the future of the contract engendered by buyer's behavior.

The district court's finding number 16, with which seller takes issue, is a direct negation of the claim of reasonable apprehension upon which seller seeks to establish under Section 45 of the Sales Act his asserted "right to treat the whole contract as broken." It reads as follows: "Plaintiff's claim of fear that the defendant would not pay for the balance of battery lead due under Contract No. 5794 at the contract price was without foundation and unreasonable."

In considering the propriety of this finding, it is to be borne in mind that the point here is not the absence of legal justification for the withholding of an overdue payment but rather whether, under the circumstances, that withholding gave the seller reason to believe that there was likelihood of continuing or additional default when and after he should deliver the rest of the lead in accordance with his promise. The substantiality of this alleged apprehension must be judged in the light of the uncontroverted finding that no impairment of buyer's credit had been shown. Moreover, the market was rising and all of the evidence indicates that buyer needed and urgently requested the undelivered lead. Indeed, as early as March 1, before the delivery of the carload for which payment was withheld, the buyer had complained quite urgently of the non-delivery of the entire balance of some 290,000 pounds overdue since December. Thereafter, when the seller shipped 43,000 pounds, about one-seventh of what was due, the buyer insisted that he was withholding payment because of the delay in delivery of the overdue balance. The court's finding that buyer had waived any claim for damages for delay up to that time does not alter this factual picture or its rational implications. In these circumstances, the trial court was justified in concluding that buyer's explanation of his conduct merited belief and that seller had no valid reason to be fearful that payment would not be forthcoming upon full delivery.

The clincher here is provided by the additional evidence concerning the possibility of delivery with sight draft attached. While there is no specific finding on the point, the evidence, including testimony tendered on behalf of seller, shows without dispute that at the beginning of this series of contracts, the seller had the privilege of shipping on sight draft but elected not to do so. And just before the collapse of the efforts of the parties to work out their difficulties amicably, the buyer specifically proposed that the seller assure himself of prompt payment by the use of sight drafts accompanying shipments. It is again important that at this time the market was substantially higher than the contract price and that seller was advised of buyer's urgent need for lead to meet his own commitments. In such circumstances it is incredible that the buyer would refuse to honor sight drafts for the contract price. These facts considered together leave no basis for reasonable apprehension concerning payment.

There is one other relevant and important fact. Throughout the controversial period the seller, with a stock of lead on hand adequate for the full performance of this contract, was using this lead in a rising market for sales to other purchasers at prices higher than agreed in the present contract. The inference was not only allowable but almost inescapable that desire to avoid a bad bargain rather than apprehension that the buyer would not carry out that bargain caused the seller to renounce the agreement and charge the buyer with repudiation. Recission for such cause is not permissible. See Truitt v. Guenther Lumber Co., 1920, 73 Pa.Super. 445, 450.

It follows that the seller has failed to establish justification for recission under Section 45 of the Sales Act and that judgment for the buyer on the counterclaim was proper.

The judgment will be affirmed.

NOTES

(1) In *Plotnick,* the seller canceled an installment contract because of a breach by the buyer and the court held that the cancellation was improper under Section 45 of the Uniform Sales Act. Section 45 is now superseded by UCC 2–612 [UCC 2–710 (1997)]. Under the Code, the seller may cancel where the buyer "fails to make a payment due on or before delivery * * * if the breach is of the whole contract (Section 2–612) * * *." UCC 2–703(f) [UCC 2–815(8) (1997)]. Section 2–612(1) [UCC 2–710(a) (1997)] defines an installment contract and, in subsection (2) states when the buyer (but not the seller) may

reject a non-conforming installment. Subsection (3) then provides: "Whenever non-conformity or default with respect to one or more installments substantially impairs the value of the whole contract there is a breach of the whole." [UCC 2–710(c) (1997)].

Would the reasoning and result of *Plotnick* be the same under UCC 2–703(f) and 2–612(3)? [UCC 2–815(8) and 2–710(c) (1997)]. For a case upholding the seller's cancellation in light of an "undenied and uncured stoppage of a check given to comply with the buyer's promise to reduce significantly the amount of its outstanding arrearages," see Cherwell–Ralli, Inc. v. Rytman Grain Co., Inc., 180 Conn. 714, 433 A.2d 984 (1980). The court stated that "what constitutes impairment of the value of the whole contract is a question of fact" and held that in case of such impairment the seller may cancel without invoking the adequate assurance procedure of UCC 2–609 [UCC 2–711 (1997)]. See Patterson, *UCC 2–612(3): Breach of an Installment Contract and a Hobson's Choice for the Aggrieved Party,* 48 Ohio St.L.J. 177 (1987).

(2) *Were Buyers Excused From Performance?* "The essence of the buyers' contentions is that the bringing of the suit for total breach of the contract in October 1958 terminated any obligation on their part to perform the contract. They purport to reach this position (1) by asserting that the sellers, by bringing suit in 1958, elected to treat the contract at an end and 'thereafter seek redress through the medium of litigation;' and (2) by insisting that they justifiably relied on this election to their detriment.

"Their argument can best be understood by casting it in hypothetical form. Assume S conveyed Blackacre to B in exchange for B's promise to farm Blackacre and to pay S an annual sum, equal to one half the gross value of the crops derived therefrom for a period of ten years, or until the sum of $50,000 had been paid, whichever occurs first. Following his conveyance, S became dissatisfied with B's methods of farming and the amounts he was receiving. S brought suit against B alleging a total breach of the contract by B and seeking to recover damages in an amount equal to the present value of B's entire future performance. B responded by denying that a total breach had occurred and that the breach, if any, was only partial. In the course of the litigation it was determined that B was correct as of the date suit was initiated—i.e., only a partial breach had occurred. During the pendency of the litigation, B did not repudiate the contract but ceased all performance and retained Blackacre. It is the contention of the buyers in this case that B is entitled to cease such performance, retain the land, and be liable thereafter in damages only for the partial breach.

"This should not be the law; nor do we think that it is the law. The line between a partial and a total breach is not so plain as to visit such a severe forfeiture upon a plaintiff who exaggerates his injury. Under the circumstances of our hypothetical, it was the duty of B to continue his performance or to offer to restore S substantially to his antecedent position. Failure to do either amounts to a total breach by B which entitles S either to amend his complaint to include a prayer for relief with respect to such breach or, if the case has proceeded to final judgment in which only damages for partial breach have been recovered, to bring a new suit seeking damages for the total breach. In this latter case, the initial proceeding is not *res judicata;* the second suit is upon a different and distinct injury." Riess v. Murchison, 503 F.2d 999, 1007–08 (9th Cir.1974), cert. denied 420 U.S. 993, 95 S.Ct. 1430, 43 L.Ed.2d 674 (1975).

(3) A "partial" breach coupled with a repudiation of the "whole" contract justifies cancellation of the entire contract. See, e.g., Kirkwood Agri–Trade v. Frosty Land Foods International, Inc., 650 F.2d 602 (5th Cir.1981).

(4) *A New Look at Material Breach.*

The idea of constructive conditions of exchange is among the most important in all of contract law, for it establishes a conceptual mechanism for the exercise of the power of cancellation. The material-breach doctrine qualifies constructive conditions. Its function is to control that power, to mitigate the harshness that would follow if it routinely were put into the hands of one injured by any breach, however slight. Effective control requires a coherent and intelligible theory of material breach. Unfortunately, such a theory has eluded the law of contract. The *Restatements* have not offered a satisfactory approach to materiality and the courts have found nothing to supplement or replace them other than the vacuous "essence of the contract" notion.

Material breach can be brought into sharp focus by viewing it from the perspective of the cancellation remedy. Basic remedial principles already are in place that make materiality comprehensible. The most important is that a remedy for breach should protect the victim's expectation interest at the least cost to the breaching party. To apply that principle to material breach, one must recognize that the expectation interest consists of two components: the interest in present performance and the interest in future performance. The cancellation remedy protects only the latter, which is one party's contractually-based sense of security that the other will perform its executory duties as and when agreed. Cancellation should be invoked only when a breach so impairs the interest in future performance that the victim has reasonable cause to bring the contract to an end, so that the bargained-for security, or its economic equivalent, may be acquired elsewhere.

When cancellation is appropriately invoked, its costs for the party in breach must not be unnecessarily high. The costs of cancellation, however, even if substantial, must not deprive the victim of access to the cancellation remedy when the interest in future performance is genuinely threatened. Rather, needless costs should be avoided by awarding the breaching party a post-cancellation settlement of accounts that is as generous as possible, consistent with giving first priority to the victim's expectation interest. Specifically, the recovery of the defaulting party need not be restricted to the value of the benefit conferred on the victim, and during the time between cancellation and resolution of the dispute the victim should be entitled to retain from the unpaid contract price no more than an honest estimate of the damages owed on account of the breach.

When material breach is so understood and administered, the cancellation power is effectively harnessed. It may be exercised only when the interest it protects is seriously at risk. Even then, it preserves for the one in breach what remains of the benefit of that party's bargain.

Andersen, *A New Look at Material Breach in the Law of Contracts,* 21 U.C.Davis L.Rev. 1073, 1139–40 (1988). [Copyright 1988 by the Regents of University of California. Reprinted by permission.]

Comment: Post–Breach Conduct Affecting the Cancellation Remedy

In Chapter Five, Section 2(A)(2), we saw that a promisor could "waive" a condition included in the bargain for his or her benefit. Without the express condition, the promisor's power to avoid a duty of performance and, ultimately, to obtain a discharge was impaired. In the materials now under consideration, we have assumed that a promisor's duty to render a performance was expressly or "constructively" conditioned upon performance by the other party. See Chapter Five, Section 2(B). Thus, if the other party repudiated or failed to perform a material part of the agreed exchange, the promisor's duty to perform is, at a minimum, suspended and, at a maximum, discharged. In short, the promisor can "cancel" the contract because of the other party's material breach. Under what circumstances can the promisor, by action or inaction, "waive" or alter the effect of the other's breach and thereby lose the cancellation remedy?

First, it is important to distinguish a claim for damages arising from breach from the cancellation remedy. In point of law, it is harder to waive the former than the latter. The damage claim can be discharged by an agreement supported by consideration or by a "written waiver or renunciation" when "signed and delivered by the aggrieved party." UCC 1–107. See Restatement (Second) §§ 273, 277. A renunciation may also be effective without consideration or a formality if it has "induced such action or forbearance as would make a promise enforceable." Restatement (Second) § 273(c). In the absence of consideration, reliance or a formality, therefore, one would expect the damage claim to survive even though the aggrieved party has lost the cancellation remedy through inaction or election. [See UCC 2–808 (1997)].

Second, there are a number of situations, difficult to classify, where the aggrieved party's action or inaction will foreclose a subsequent cancellation. In each case, assume that the cancellation remedy would have been available but for the aggrieved party's conduct.

1.   A repudiates the whole contract on October 1. B decides to wait a reasonable time before cancelling the contract. A then retracts the repudiation before B has canceled or "materially changed its position or otherwise indicated that it considers the repudiation final." The retraction nullifies the breach and, of course, forecloses any remedy for breach of contract. UCC 2–611(1)[UCC 2–713(1) (1997)]; Restatement (Second) § 256.

2.   S tenders goods to B on October 1. B inspects them on that date and finds a non-conformity. On November 1, B notifies S that it is rejecting the goods, UCC 2–601 [UCC 2–703 (1997)] and cancelling the contract. UCC 2–711(1)[UCC 2–823(a) (1997)]. On these facts, B has lost the cancellation remedy by failing to reject the goods within a reasonable time. UCC 2–602(1)[UCC 2–703(b) (1997)]. Cancellation is available for a "rightful"

rejection. Under the UCC, B has accepted the goods by failing to make an "effective rejection," UCC 2–606(1)(b) [UCC 2–706(a) (1997)], but still could cancel if it justifiably revokes acceptance under UCC 2–608 [UCC 2–708 (1997)]. See UCC 2–711(1) [UCC 2–823(a) (1997)]. Revocation of acceptance, however, requires action within a reasonable time, and it is probable that this remedy is also foreclosed. Thus, B is left with a claim for damages to accepted goods. UCC 2–714 [UCC 2–827 (1997)]. See UCC 2–607(3)(a) [UCC 2–707(c)(1) (1997).] Has B, through inaction, lost its damages claim as well?

3.   C completes a construction project and O finds two breaches, one material and one not. O rejects the work and gives only the non-material breach as a reason. C "cures" the defect and O then attempts to avoid payment by citing the material breach. If C has relied to its detriment on the stated objection without reason to know about the unstated objection, O may not assert the material breach as a basis for cancellation. See New England Structures, Inc. v. Loranger, 354 Mass. 62, 234 N.E.2d 888, 891–92 (1968); UCC 2–605(1) [UCC 2–703 (1997)]; Restatement (Second) § 248.

4.   S agrees to deliver goods to B in installments over a two-year period. At the end of the first year, S was substantially behind in deliveries and this substantially impaired the value of the whole contract. UCC 2–612(3). Although B could cancel the contract for breach, that remedy would be lost in the following situations: (a) B sues S "with respect only to past installments or demands performance as to future installments," UCC 2–612(3) [UCC 2–710(c) (1997)]; (b) B continues to perform its part of the exchange without objecting to S's breach, see Dangerfield v. Markel, 252 N.W.2d 184 (N.D.1977); or (c) B "accepts a non-conforming installment without seasonably notifying of cancellation." UCC 2–612(3) [UCC 2–710(c) (1997)]; Restatement (Second) §§ 246, 247. This conduct "reinstates" the contract.

As one court put it:

> Waiver of strict performance may be inferred from the circumstances or course of dealings between the parties. . . . A waiver may result from one party's express or implied assent to the continued performance of the other party without objection to the delay. . . . In addition, express representations by one party that strict compliance with a deadline will not be required, or other actions that reasonably lead the other party to believe such, will also cause an effective waiver of a time provision in a contract. Finally, a party may effectively waive a breach of agreement by the other party by continuing to insist on performance by the other party even after the breach. . . . In our case, Seismic waived the contract provision as to time of performance through its failure to object to the delay, its failure to reject the software programs when delivered, and its subsequent conduct in both assenting to the delay and requesting additional word from Digital on the completed programs.

Seismic & Digital Concepts, Inc. v. Digital Resources Corp., 590 S.W.2d 718, 721 (Tex.Civ.App.1979).

See, generally, Comment, *Fairness, Flexibility and the Waiver of Remedial Rights by Contract*, 87 Yale L.J. 1057 (1978).

SECTION 2.   COMPENSATORY DAMAGES

(A) BASIC POLICIES

If one party to an enforceable bargain has repudiated or failed without justification to perform and the other has properly either suspended performance or canceled the contract, the question of what affirmative remedies are available for breach of contract is posed. What relief is available to the aggrieved party, and what policies seem to be involved as the courts work to secure that protection? Some rather general responses to these broad questions are contained in Comment: An Introduction to Contract Remedies, supra at 40. Please review that Comment.

References:

Cohen, *The Fault Lines in Contract Damages*, 80 Va. L. Rev. 1225 (1994).

Kull, *Restitution as a Remedy for Breach of Contract*, 67 S. Cal. L. Rev. 1465 (1994).

Eisenberg, *The Principle of Hadley v. Baxendale*, 80 Cal. L. Rev. 563 (1992).

Scott, *The Case for Market Damages: Revisiting the Lost Profits Puzzle*, 57 U.Chi.L.Rev. 1155 (1990).

Slawson, *The Role of Reliance in Contract Damages*, 76 Cornell L. Rev. 197 (1990).

Andersen, *Good Faith in the Enforcement of Contracts*, 73 Ia.L.Rev. 299 (1988);

Sebert, *Punitive and Nonpecuniary Damages in Actions Based Upon Contract: Toward Achieving the Objective of Full Compensation*, 33 U.C.L.A.L.Rev. 1565 (1986);

Cooter & Eisenberg, *Damages for Breach of Contract*, 73 Calif.L.Rev. 713 (1986);

Farnsworth, *Your Loss or My Gain: The Dilemma of the Disgorgement Principle in Breach of Contract*, 94 Yale L.J. 1339 (1985);

Tomain, *Contract Compensation in Non–Market Transactions*, 46 U.Pitt.L.Rev. 867 (1985);

Ulen, *The Efficiency of Specific Performance: Toward A Unified Theory of Contract Remedies*, 83 Mich.L.Rev. 341 (1984);

Goetz & Scott, *The Mitigation Principle: Toward A General Theory of Contractual Obligation*, 69 Va.L.Rev. 967 (1983);

Yorio, *In Defense of Money Damages for Breach of Contract*, 82 Colum.L.Rev. 1365 (1982);

Sebert, *Remedies Under Article Two of the Uniform Commercial Code: An Agenda for Review,* 130 U.Pa.L.Rev. 360 (1981);

Farnsworth, *Legal Remedies for Breach of Contract,* 70 Colum.L.Rev. 1145 (1970);

Leff, *Injury, Ignorance and Spite—The Dynamics of Coercive Collection,* 80 Yale L.J. 1 (1970);

Fuller & Perdue, *The Reliance Interest in Contract Damages,* 46 Yale L.J. 52, 373 (1936–37).

Sullivan v. O'Connor

Supreme Judicial Court of Massachusetts, 1973.
Supra at 32.

NOTES

(1) *Protected Interests of Promisee.* The court in *Sullivan* identified and Restatement (Second) elaborates upon three interests of the promisee that might be protected upon breach by the promisor: expectation, reliance and restitution. "Expectation" refers to the gain or profit that would have been made on full performance and "reliance" and "restitution" refer to the post-contract investment made by the promisee to earn that gain. Why did the court refuse to protect Ms. Sullivan's "expectation" interest? What expenditures of Ms. Sullivan fit into her "restitution" interest? Her "reliance" interest? How would you classify a claim for pain and suffering or mental anguish caused by the breach?

As the court indicates, promises by doctors and other providers of professional services to achieve a particular result are rare indeed. In the absence of an enforceable promise, the law requires the exercise of that skill and judgment which can be reasonably expected from similarly situated professionals, not perfect results. See Note, *Contorts: Patrolling the Borderland of Contract and Tort in Legal Malpractice Actions,* 22 B.C.L.Rev. 545 (1981).

(2) *Why Protect The Expectation Interest?* Why should contract remedies ever protect the expectation interest? One set of reasons involves the perceived need to support "efficient" exchange in competitive markets. Protecting expectations (1) rewards risk taking in market transactions and, therefore, contributes to allocative efficiency, and (2) deters the inefficient breach, i.e., a breach where the value derived when the breaching party reemploys resources committed to the contract is equaled or exceeded by the loss to the promisee. Put affirmatively, when contract law clearly protects the expectation interest, the parties can plan more effectively at the time of contracting and the breacher can better assess at the time of breach when the gains through breach will exceed the cost of compensating the aggrieved party. See Goetz & Scott, *Enforcing Promises: An Examination of the Basis of Contract,* 89 Yale L.J. 1261 (1980). The assumption here is that the efficient breach is a good thing, so long as the expectation interest of the aggrieved party is fully protected. There are, of course, skeptics. See, e.g., Friedman, *The Efficient Breach Fallacy,* 18

J.Leg.Stud. 1 (1989); Macneil, *Efficient Breach of Contract: Circles in the Sky*, 68 Va.L.Rev. 947 (1982).

Another set of reasons involves the asserted need to protect the reliance interest. The argument is that reliance is the primary interest to be protected but that proof of reliance, whether by action or forbearance, is costly and uncertain. There is a real risk that reliance that is "hidden" in opportunities foregone by the promisee will not be compensated. The solution is to award expectation damages, when provable with reasonable certainty, as a "surrogate" for accurate measurement of reliance. Thus, expectation recovery is viewed as an outer limit of recovery for actual but unprovable costs incurred and opportunities foregone in reliance on the promise. See Farnsworth 18–19; Eisenberg, *The Bargain Principle and Its Limits,* 95 Harv.L.Rev. 741, 785–98 (1982). In the latter view, the importance of protecting expectations has more to do with fairness in the particular transaction than overall market efficiency. See Pettit, *Private Advantage and Public Power: Reexamining the Expectation and Reliance Interests in Contract Damages,* 38 Hast.L.J. 417 (1987). Compare C. Fried, Contract as Promise: A Theory of Contractual Obligation 17–21 (1981), where both expectation and reliance are rejected as the basis of a theory of moral obligation.

Allen v. Jones

Court of Appeals of California, 1980.
104 Cal.App.3d 207, 163 Cal.Rptr. 445.

[Plaintiff entered an oral contract with Defendant to cremate the remains of Plaintiff's deceased brother and to ship the cremated remains from California to Illinois. Plaintiff paid the Defendant mortuary $516 for its services. Plaintiff alleged that as a result of Defendant's negligence in packaging, the package arrived empty and the remains were lost, "causing plaintiff to suffer great nervous shock, mental anguish and humiliation." Plaintiff also alleged intentional infliction of emotional distress and deceit on Defendant's part and, for these causes of action, sought both emotional damages and punitive damages. The trial court sustained demurrers to the complaints. On appeal, the court of appeals reversed on the negligent performance claim but affirmed the decision on the other two claims on the ground that the "allegations of intentional infliction of emotional distress and deceit were too vague and conclusory to state a cause of action * * *."]

■ TAMURA, ASSOCIATE JUSTICE.

I

In an action for breach of contract the measure of damages is "the amount which will compensate the party aggrieved for all the detriment proximately caused thereby, or which, in the ordinary course of things would be likely to result therefrom" (Civ.Code, § 3300), provided, however, that the damages are "clearly ascertainable in both their nature and origin" (Civ.Code, § 3301). These statutory provisions have been interpreted by our courts to mean that damages for breach of contract are ordinarily confined to those which would naturally arise from the breach or which

846 BREACH OF CONTRACT AND PERMISSIBLE REMEDIAL RESPONSES

might have been reasonably contemplated or foreseen by the parties at the time they contracted, as the probable result of the breach. . . .

The great majority of contracts involve commercial transactions in which it is generally not foreseeable that breach will cause significant mental distress as distinguished from mere mental agitation or annoyance. Accordingly, the rule has developed that damages for mental suffering or injury to reputation are generally not recoverable in an action for breach of contract. . . .

There are, however, certain contracts which so affect the vital concerns of the individual that severe mental distress is a foreseeable result of breach. For many years, our courts have recognized that damages for mental distress may be recovered for breach of a contract of this nature. . . .

A contract whereby a mortician agrees to prepare a body for burial is one in which it is reasonably foreseeable that breach may cause mental anguish to the decedent's bereaved relations. "One who prepares a human body for burial and conducts a funeral usually deals with the living in their most difficult and delicate moments. . . . The exhibition of callousness or indifference, the offer of insult and indignity, can, of course, inflict no injury on the dead, but they can visit agony akin to torture on the living. So true is this that the chief asset of a mortician and the most conspicuous element of his advertisement is his consideration for the afflicted. A decent respect for their feelings is implied in every contract for his services." (Fitzsimmons v. Olinger Mortuary Assn. (1932) 91 Colo. 544, 17 P.2d 535, 536–537.) In a similar vein, another court has stated: "The tenderest feelings of the human heart center around the remains of the dead. When the defendants contracted with plaintiff to inter the body of her deceased husband in a workmanlike manner they did so with the knowledge that she was the widow and would naturally and probably suffer mental anguish if they failed to fulfill their contractual obligation in the manner here charged. The contract was predominantly personal in nature and no substantial pecuniary loss would follow its breach. Her mental concern, her sensibilities, and her solicitude were the prime considerations for the contract, and the contract itself was such as to put the defendants on notice that a failure on their part to inter the body properly would probably produce mental suffering on her part. It cannot be said, therefore, that such damages were not within the contemplation of the parties at the time the contract was made." (Lamm v. Shingleton (1949) 231 N.C. 10, 55 S.E.2d 810, 813–814.)

* * *

The leading case on the same subject in this state is Chelini v. Nieri, supra, 32 Cal.2d 480, 196 P.2d 915, in which the plaintiff recovered $10,000 general damages for a mortician's breach of contract to preserve the body of the plaintiff's mother. The only significant distinction between *Chelini* and the instant case is that in *Chelini* the plaintiff's emotional suffering was manifested in physical illness, whereas in the present case plaintiff has alleged only mental distress.

To date all of the cases in this state in which mental distress damages have been awarded for breach of contract have been cases in which the mental distress caused physical illness, and it is not clear whether mental distress damages alone can ever support an action for breach of contract in this state. We need not address that question in the present case, however, because plaintiff alleged that the cremated remains were lost because of defendants' negligence in preparing them for shipment. Plaintiff has thereby pleaded an action in tort as well as in contract. . . .

In tort actions courts have traditionally been reluctant to allow recovery for mental distress not accompanied by physical injury. However, as Prosser states: "It is now more or less generally conceded that the only valid objection against recovery for mental injury is the danger of vexatious suits and fictitious claims, which has loomed very large in the opinions as an obstacle." (Prosser, Law of Torts (4th ed.) p. 328, fns. omitted.) Prosser observes that the majority of jurisdictions now permit recovery for negligent mishandling of corpses, and explains that this particular situation presents "an especial likelihood of genuine and serious mental distress, arising from the special circumstances, which serves as a guarantee that the claim is not spurious." (Ibid., at pp. 329–330. See also, Leavitt, *The Funeral Director's Liability for Mental Anguish,* 15 Hastings L.J. 464, 482–494.)

Section 868 of the Restatement Second of Torts recognizes a cause of action for intentional, reckless, or negligent conduct which prevents proper interment of a dead body.[1] The official comment to the section states: "The technical basis of the cause of action is the interference with the exclusive right of control of the body, which frequently has been called by the courts a 'property' or a 'quasi-property' right. This does not, however, fit very well into the category of property, since the body ordinarily cannot be sold or transferred, has no utility and can be used only for the one purpose of interment or cremation. In practice the technical right has served as a mere peg upon which to hang damages for the mental distress inflicted upon the survivor; and in reality the cause of action has been exclusively one for the mental distress. . . . There is no need to show physical consequences of the mental distress."

We conclude that damages are recoverable for mental distress without physical injury for negligent mishandling of a corpse by a mortuary. Public policy requires that mortuaries adhere to a high standard of care in view of the psychological devastation likely to result from any mistake which upsets the expectations of the decedent's bereaved family. As mental distress is a highly foreseeable result of such conduct and in most cases the only form of damage likely to ensue, recovery for mental distress is a useful

---

1. Section 868 provides: "One who intentionally, recklessly, or negligently removes, withholds, mutilates or operates upon the body of a dead person or prevents its proper interment or cremation is subject to liability to a member of the family of the deceased who is entitled to the disposition of the body."

and necessary means to maintain the standards of the profession and is the only way in which the victims may be compensated for the wrongs they have suffered. The nature of the wrongful conduct that must be present in this type of case provides sufficient assurance of the genuineness of a claim for emotional distress. As to this form of negligence action, therefore, we hold that plaintiff may recover for mental distress without accompanying physical injury.

It is neither necessary nor appropriate for us in this case to take that giant leap for mankind espoused by the concurring opinion. We need only take the modest step, consistent with common law tradition, of declaring the law applicable to the case at hand. Our decision today hopefully clarifies California law on liability for negligent mishandling of corpses by bringing it into conformity with the views expressed by Professor Prosser, the Restatement and modern decisions from sister states.

* * *

We conclude that the court below erred in sustaining the demurrer to the cause of action for negligent breach of contract, but we conclude also that the ruling was correct as to plaintiff's other causes of action. It follows, of course, that plaintiff may not recover punitive damages. (See Walker v. Signal Companies, Inc. (1978) 84 Cal.App.3d 982, 996, 149 Cal.Rptr. 119.)

The judgment of dismissal is reversed with directions to overrule defendants' demurrer to plaintiff's first cause of action.

[Presiding Justice Gardner, concurring, advocated the recovery of damages for "purely mental and emotional" distress caused by the negligent mishandling of a corpse, whether or not there was an accompanying physical manifestation, and in ordinary negligence actions.]

NOTES

(1) *Recovery for Emotional Disturbance: Contract or Tort? Allen v. Jones* resides in the borderland between contract and tort. The emotional disturbance is caused by a breach of contract but the injury is to what might be called a "tort" rather than a "contract" interest. In addition to losing the value of the bargain, the plaintiff is worse off physically than before the contract. See W. Prosser & P. Keeton, The Law of Torts § 12 (5th ed. 1984). The *Allen* decision appears to fall on the "tort" side of the line; liability was imposed for the "negligent" performance of a cremation contract. The emphasis was on the type of breach (negligent) rather than the type of contract (burial services). See Note, *Burial of a Tort: The California Supreme Court's Treatment of Tortious Mishandling of Remains in Christensen v. Superior Court [820 P.2d 181]*, 26 Loyola (L.A.) L. Rev. 909 (1993).

Suppose that there was no negligent breach in *Allen v. Jones*. Section 353 of Restatement (Second) provides:

Recovery for emotional disturbance will be excluded unless the breach also caused bodily harm or the contract or the breach is of such a kind that serious emotional disturbance was a particularly likely result.

How would *Allen v. Jones* come out under this test? What about *Sullivan v. O'Connor? See* Gaglidari v. Denny's Restaurants, Inc., 117 Wash.2d 426, 815 P.2d 1362 (1991), where the court concluded that emotional distress damages were not available for breach of an employment contract. The court emphasized that an employment contract did not have "elements of personality" and that the parties had not agreed to protect those losses. According to the court, the type of contract involved rather than the nature of the breach or whether the loss was foreseeable was the critical issue.

Is the failure to perform a promise with reason to know of a high probability that emotional harm will result any different than the intentional infliction of emotional harm? Restatement (Second) of Torts § 46(1) provides:

> One who by extreme and outrageous conduct intentionally or recklessly causes severe emotional distress to another is subject to liability for such emotional distress, and if bodily harm to the other results from it, for such bodily harm.

See generally Whaley, *Paying for the Agony: The Recovery of Emotional Distress Damages in Contract Actions,* 26 Suffolk U.L. Rev.935 (1992); Tomain, *Contract Compensation in Non–Market Transactions,* 46 U.Pitt.L.Rev. 867 (1985); Kastely, *Compensation for Lost Aesthetic and Emotional Enjoyment: A Reconsideration of Contract Damages for Nonpecuniary Loss,* 8 U.Haw.L.Rev. 1 (1986); Goldberg, *Emotional Distress Damages and Breach of Contract: A New Approach,* 20 U.C.Davis L.Rev. 57 (1986).

(2) Suppose the plaintiff alleged that because of defendant's willful and malicious failure to pay money when due the "plaintiff suffered grave humiliation and severe mental distress." Assuming that the alleged damage is provable and caused by the breach, does the petition state a cause of action? According to Professor Corbin, when the anguish is caused wholly by "mere pecuniary loss and disappointment, it is believed that damages for such suffering should always be refused" even though pecuniary deprivation may "reduce one to poverty and bankruptcy, and the humiliation and mental discomfort may be very great." Corbin § 1076. See Smith v. Sanborn State Bank, 147 Iowa 640, 126 N.W. 779 (1910) (damages for mental anguish growing out of a contract for payment of money not recoverable). But in Crisci v. Security Insurance Co. of New Haven, Conn., 66 Cal.2d 425, 58 Cal.Rptr. 13, 426 P.2d 173 (1967), the plaintiff insured sought damages for mental suffering caused by the defendant's unwarranted refusal to settle a third party's claim within the policy limits. The court characterized the claim as sounding in contract or tort, emphasized the insurer's good faith duty in settlement and the special nature of insurance protection and upheld recovery. According to the court, more was involved than obtaining a commercial advantage: one consideration in buying insurance "is the peace of mind and security it will provide in the event of an accidental loss, and recovery of damages has been permitted for breach of contracts which directly concern the comfort, happiness or personal esteem of one of the parties." See generally Rea, *Non-Pecuniary Loss and Breach of Contract,* 11 J.Leg.Stud. 35 (1982); Yates, *Damages for Non–Pecuniary Loss,* 36 Mod.L.Rev. 535 (1973).

PROBLEM: THE CASE OF THE DISTRESSED NEWLYWEDS

Fred and Joyce were engaged in January and set the wedding date for June 21. Among other things, the couple entered a written agreement, dated February 21, with a local band, the High Flyers, to play at the wedding reception. The couple paid $300 down and agreed to pay $700 more after the reception. The agreement said nothing about the consequences of a breach. Since the High Flyers were in great demand, Joyce called on June 1 to confirm the engagement and was told by the leader, "Hey man, no problem." The High Flyers, however, did not show up at the reception. On June 14, they took another job for the big evening (the fee was $2,000) and neglected to notify either Fred or Joyce. After an hour of no music, Fred induced his younger brother John to rig up a stereo system and play disc jockey for the rest of the evening. Fred paid his brother $75 for the job.

The couple consulted their attorney, claiming that the quality of the substitute music was inferior to that promised by the High Flyers and that they both suffered extreme anxiety and distress resulting from the breach.

How much, if anything, should Fred and Joyce recover from the High Flyers? If the High Flyers offered $375 to settle the case, would you recommend that the newlyweds accept?

F.D. Borkholder Co. v. Sandock

Supreme Court of Indiana, 1980.
274 Ind. 612, 413 N.E.2d 567.

■ Hunter, Justice.

This case is before this Court upon the petition to transfer of plaintiffs-appellees B. & S. Sandock, Inc., et al. The trial court awarded the plaintiffs compensatory and punitive damages arising out of a breach of contract by the defendant-appellant F.D. Borkholder Company, Inc. The Court of Appeals, Third District, affirmed the award of compensatory damages but reversed the punitive damages award in an opinion authored by Judge Staton. *Sandock v. F.D. Borkholder Co.* (1979), Ind.App., 396 N.E.2d 955. Judge Garrard dissented from the majority's treatment of the punitive damages issue.

Transfer is now granted, and the decision and opinion of the Court of Appeals are hereby vacated. The relevant facts were summarized by Judge Staton as follows:

"B. & S. Sandock, Inc. (Sandock) and F.D. Borkholder Company, Inc. (Borkholder), entered into a contract for the construction by Borkholder of a concrete block addition to Sandock's pre-existing structure. The addition was to be used as a retail showroom and warehouse in furtherance of Sandock's furniture and carpet business. Sandock was unable to use the addition for its intended use, however, because of a recurring moisture problem on the inside of one of the walls. Sandock filed suit seeking both compensatory and punitive damages. After trial by the court, Sandock was awarded compensatory damages in the amount of $8,711.69 and punitive damages in the amount of $6,500.00."

[After rejecting the defendant's contentions that the judgment was not supported by sufficient evidence and that the trial court erred in not granting Borkholder's motion for an involuntary dismissal, the Court addressed the punitive damage issue.]

The Court of Appeals cited our decision in Hibschman Pontiac, Inc. v. Batchelor, (1977) 266 Ind. 310, 362 N.E.2d 845, for the proposition that punitive damages are recoverable in breach of contract actions only when a separate tort accompanies the breach or tort-like conduct mingles in the breach. Here, prior to the execution of the contract, Sandock representatives expressed their concern about moisture on the walls. Under the terms of the contract, they were to pay $200 for plans to be drawn up by Borkholder's architect. The contract provided that all labor and material would be furnished in accordance with specifications. Sandock was given a copy of the plans. However, contrary to these plans, the top and bottom courses of block forming the one wall were not filled with concrete, thus constituting latent variances. Furthermore, the roofline was shortened which represented an additional deviation from the plans.

There was testimony that the cut-off roofline enabled water to leak down into the top of the block wall. Other evidence indicated that the wetness problem resulted from this water percolating down through the inside of the wall, collecting at the bottom, and then rising again by capillary action. Sandock made numerous complaints but was constantly reassured by several Borkholder representatives that the problem was caused by simple condensation, a theory ultimately disproved by an on-site test conducted by the Borkholder firm. Sam Sandock testified that Freeman Borkholder, president of the company, promised that the situation would be remedied whereupon Sandock tendered all but $1,000 of the contract price. The problem was never corrected. The Borkholder people knew, of course, that the blocks in the wall were not filled with concrete. Also, Borkholder himself conceded that the roofline adjustment increased the likelihood of water running down into the core of the wall.

We believe that there is cogent and convincing proof that the Borkholder firm engaged in intentional wrongful acts constituting fraud, misrepresentation, deceit, and gross negligence in its dealings with Sandock. *Hibschman Pontiac, Inc.*, supra. Accordingly, we agree with the Court of Appeals that the trial court could have concluded that separate torts accompanied the breach. Next, relying on *Hibschman*, the Court of Appeals attempted to identify the public interest to be served by imposing punitive damages. However, the majority could not perceive any such interest and refused to let the award stand. We disagree. As Judge Garrard stated in his dissent:

> "I have no problem identifying the public interest to be served in requiring that the builders of public buildings be deterred from fraudulently disregarding building code requirements or those contained in the plans and specifications they have agreed to comply with." *Sandock v. Borkholder*, supra, at 959.

The purpose of punitive damages generally is to punish the wrongdoer and to deter him and others from engaging in similar conduct in the future. *Indiana & Michigan Electric Co. v. Stevenson,* (1977) Ind.App., 363 N.E.2d 1254; *Jos. Schlitz Brewing Co. v. Central Beverage Co.,* (1977) Ind.App., 359 N.E.2d 566. An award of such damages is particularly appropriate in proper cases involving consumer fraud. *Jones v. Abriani,* (1976) 169 Ind.App. 556, 350 N.E.2d 635; *Capitol Dodge, Inc. v. Haley,* (1972) 154 Ind.App. 1, 288 N.E.2d 766.

The building contractor occupies a position of trust with members of the public for whom he agrees to do the desired construction. Few people are knowledgeable about this industry, and most are not aware of the techniques that must be employed to produce a sound structure. Necessarily, they rely on the expertise of the builder. Here, the builder has been found to have engaged in fraudulent or deceptive practices by constructing a building with latent deviations from the plans which resulted in damage to the owner. Further, the builder has attempted to disclaim responsibility for such damage when it may be inferred that it knew or should have known that its work was the cause. Under these circumstances, certainly the imposition of punitive damages furthers the public interest.

We find no reversible error in the judgment of the trial court and the judgment should be affirmed.

Judgment affirmed.

■ GIVAN, C.J., and PIVARNIK, J., concur.

■ DeBRULER, J., dissents with opinion in which PRENTICE, J., concurs.

■ DeBRULER, JUSTICE, dissenting.

The elements of a claim for fraud include false representation of a present or past fact by defendant, knowledge of falsity in the defendant, action in reliance thereupon by plaintiff, and injury resulting to plaintiff from such misrepresentation. *Automobile Underwriters v. Rich,* (1944) 222 Ind. 384, 53 N.E.2d 775. A false representation of fact may take the form of an opinion depending upon the surrounding circumstances. *Rochester Bridge Co. v. McNeill,* (1919) 188 Ind. 432, 122 N.E. 662. The evidence most favorable to the finding of fraud in this case is that there were several deviations between the plans and specifications for the building and the actual building as erected. These deviations were discovered by the plaintiff before the contract price was paid. Defendant was confronted with the deviations and stated that he would correct them. Upon the representation plaintiff paid the major portion of the contract price reserving a minor portion as security for corrections. The corrections were not made. This evidence establishes no more than one, perhaps two, breaches of contract by defendant. There is nothing beyond the breaches upon which to predicate a finding of fraud.

There is no false representation of fact by defendant, with scienter, resulting in injurious action in reliance. The damages awarded plaintiff on the count for breach of contract were complete. That award made plaintiff whole. It healed all wounds to plaintiff resulting as the natural consequences of the defendant's breach of contract. That award fulfilled plaintiff's expectancies legitimately arising from the contract it made, to the extent that the recovery of money in the aftermath of a breach can do so.

I likewise dissent on the basis of the opinion of Justice Prentice in Vernon Fire & Casualty Insurance Co. v. Sharp, (1976) 264 Ind. 599, 349 N.E.2d 173, in which I concurred. The law should treat torts occurring in the season of a breach of contract as separate wrongs. Furthermore, I continue to be troubled with the absence of an express limitation of the extent of punitive damages. Hibschman Pontiac, Inc. v. Batchelor, (1977) 266 Ind. 310, 362 N.E.2d 845 (Concurring Opinion). They should be no more than is necessary to deter unwanted behavior. In this regard it may be noted that the Legislature has made the judgment that the crime of theft in its class D felony manifestation should carry a penalty of two (2) years imprisonment and a fine of not more than $10,000.

Boise Dodge, Inc. v. Clark

Supreme Court of Idaho, 1969.
92 Idaho 902, 453 P.2d 551.

[Clark purchased an automobile from Boise Dodge with 165 miles showing on the odometer and described by a salesman as "new." In fact, the car was a "demonstrator" and the general manager knew that the odometer had been set back from 6,968 miles. Clark traded in a car valued at $1,100 and issued checks for $500 and $1,562 for the balance of the purchase price. Payment was stopped when Clark discovered that the car was "used." Boise sued on the checks and Clark counterclaimed for damages for breach of contract and deceit as well as punitive damages. The court, after trial, instructed the jury that it might find damages for breach of contract (the difference between the car's value as represented and its actual value) or for deceit (the difference between the price paid for the car and its actual value). On the theory that the contract had been affirmed rather than rescinded, the jury found for Boise in the amount of the checks, some $2,062, and for Clark in the amount of $350, the difference between the value of the car as represented, $2,400, and its actual value, $2,050. This award was not contested on appeal. The court also instructed the jury that it could award punitive damages if it found Boise's actions to have been willful, wanton, gross or outrageous but that the punitive damages must bear a reasonable relation to any actual damages found. The jury awarded punitive damages to Clark in the amount of $12,500. On appeal, respondent Boise presented a single ultimate issue: whether or not the award of punitive damages was proper. The Court affirmed the judgment, holding first that the plaintiff was entitled to an award of some punitive damages.]

■ McQUADE, JUSTICE.

* * *

Appellant complains mainly about the amount of punitive damages awarded. The court gave its Instruction No. 18 as follows:

"There is no fixed or mathematical proportion, ratio, or relation between amount of actual damages and amount of exemplary or punitive damages, which in a proper case may be awarded, but such an award must not be so disproportionate to actual damages sustained as to be result of passion or prejudice rather than reason, and such an award must bear some reasonable relation or proportion to actual damages, and exemplary damages must bear some relation to damages complained of and cause thereof." (Tr. 104).

This instruction also correctly stated the law relevant to the determination of an amount of punitive damages in an action at law. The question thus becomes whether the jury can be said as a matter of law to have exceeded the bounds of its discretion in making the award of damages.

We note preliminarily that, under the instructions of the court on the measure of actual damages sustained by respondent Clark, the jury apparently applied the standard for breach of contract rather than that for the tort of deceit. We do not view that course of action by the jury as indicating a negation of the elements of misrepresentation, fraud or deceit present in the case. In any event, from the legal point of view of the imposition of punitive damages in this case, it does not matter whether respondent's counterclaim technically sounded in contract or tort. The rule established in Idaho is that punitive damages may be assessed in contract actions where there is fraud, malice, oppression or other sufficient reason for doing so. This rule recognizes that in certain cases elements of tort, for which punitive damages have always been recoverable upon a showing of malice, may be inextricably mixed with elements of contract, in which punitive damages generally are not recoverable. In such cases, punitive damages are allowed according to the substance of a showing of willful fraud.

The assessment of punitive damages, like the assessment of all damages, is in the first instance for the discretion of the jury. Though the existence of punitive damages has been denounced as anomalous in the law, "[d]espite such denunciations the great majority of states retain the doctrine of exemplary damages in full force." The criticism that punitive damages are superfluous in view of the criminal law fallaciously assumes complete identity of criminal and civil punishment. The existence of such a remedy serves useful, if limited, functions in the law as a means of punishing conduct which consciously disregards the rights of others and as a means of deterring tortious conduct generally.

Various jurisdictions, including Idaho, have limited the discretion of juries in imposing punitive damages by declaring that the amount of punitive damages must bear a "reasonable relation" to the amount of actual damages. It is never made clear precisely upon what basis an amount of punitive damages will be declared "reasonable" or "unreasonable" in relation to the amount of actual damages, especially in view of the often-repeated statement that no strict mathematical ratio is to be applied. Of course, the ratios of punitive to actual damages which may be gleaned from the cases have little precedential value when excised from their respective factual settings. This is true because the culpability of a defendant's conduct and the sociological significance of damages as a deterrent vary from case to case. Thus, the true basis for an award of one amount of punitive damages as opposed to another amount lies in an overall appraisal of the circumstances of the case.

The amount of actual damages sustained by a plaintiff is one indication of the culpability of the defendant's acts, but it cannot be the sole criterion for the assessment of punitive damages. Also relevant is the prospective deterrent effect of such an award upon persons situated similarly to the defendant, the motives actuating the defendant's conduct, the degree of calculation involved in the defendant's conduct, and the extent of the defendant's disregard of the rights of others. These are legitimate concerns of the law, and the application of any fixed arithmetic ratio to all cases in which punitive damages are assessed would be arbitrary. It therefore must be recognized that the requirement of a "reasonable relation" between actual and punitive damages serves as a rough device available to trial and appellate courts for the purpose of paring down plainly extreme awards of punitive damages.

Applying these principles to the case at bar, we are satisfied that the jury's award of $12,500 punitive damages against Boise Dodge, Inc., was justified, and [the] court below did not commit error in refusing to set aside that verdict. This is a case of calculated commercial fraud in broad disregard of the rights not only of respondent Clark but the consuming public generally. It occurs in an area of sales in which consumers are unable to gain accurate information about the product. On this basis we find particularly appropriate the reasoning used in the case of Walker v. Sheldon* in which the New York Court of Appeals determined that punitive damages would be allowed in fraud and deceit actions. That case involved the fraudulent commercial activities of Comet Press which were characterized as a " 'virtually larcenous scheme to trap generally the unwary.' " That court, in a thoughtful opinion by Judge Fuld, stated:

"Exemplary damages are more likely to serve their desired purpose of deterring similar conduct in a fraud case, such as that before us, than in any other area of tort. One who acts out of anger or hate, for instance, in committing assault or libel, is not likely to be deterred by the fear of punitive damages. On the other hand, those who deliberately and coolly engage in a far-flung fraudulent scheme, systematically conducted for profit, are very much more likely to pause and consider the consequences if they have to pay more than the actual loss suffered by an individual plaintiff. An occasional award of compensatory damages against such parties would have little deterrent effect. A judgment simply for compensatory damages would require the offender to do no more than return the money which he had taken from the plaintiff. In the calculation of his expected profits, the wrongdoer is likely to allow

---

* 10 N.Y.2d 401, 223 N.Y.S.2d 488, 179 N.E.2d 497 (1961).

for a certain amount of money which will have to be returned to those victims who object too vigorously, and he will be perfectly content to bear the additional cost of litigation as the price for continuing his illicit business. It stands to reason that the chances of deterring him are materially increased by subjecting him to the payment of punitive damages."

Those considerations are fully applicable to the case at bar.

* * *

The judgment of the court below is affirmed. Costs to respondent. [Some footnotes omitted.]

NOTES

(1) *Punitive Damages for Breach of Contract?* The traditional rule was that "punitive damages are not recoverable for breach of contract." Restatement (First) § 342. Section 355 of Restatement (Second) has opened the door just a crack: "Punitive damages are not recoverable for a breach of contract unless the conduct constituting the breach is also a tort for which punitive damages are recoverable." A common statement of the "rule" is that the breach must constitute an "independent and wilful tort accompanied by fraud, malice, wantonness or oppression." McIntosh v. Magna Systems, Inc., 539 F.Supp. 1185, 1190 (N.D.Ill.1982). How does the *Borkholder* case square with this rule? See Miller Brewing Co. v. Best Beers of Bloomington, Inc., 608 N.E.2d 975, 982 (Ind.1993)(punitive damages not available in contract actions unless plaintiff establishes "each element of a recognized tort for which Indiana law would permit the recovery of punitive damages"). See also Hill, *Breach of Contract as a Tort,* 74 Colum.L.Rev. 40 (1974).

(2) The purposes of punitive damages may involve punishment, deterrence and, to a lesser extent, compensation. [The O.J. Factor.]

Often, the function of punitive damages * * * is to legitimate the jury's giving vent to a sense of outrage at the conduct of the defendant and to relieve it of the sometimes difficult task of quantifying the degree to which the plaintiff has literally been harmed. Further, punitive damages are assessed to deter conduct of a serious antisocial or irresponsible nature.

Madisons Chevrolet, Inc. v. Donald, 109 Ariz. 100, 505 P.2d 1039, 1042–43 (1973). In commercial transactions, however, the courts have resisted imposing punitive damages even though the breach was "knowing and wilful." As one court put it, compensatory damages are sufficient for the plaintiff "without the necessity of assuaging his feelings or allaying community outrage" and that the award of punitive damages for a "pure" breach of contract would "seriously jeopardize the stability and predictability of commercial transactions, so vital to the smooth and efficient operation of the modern American economy." General Motors Corp. v. Piskor, 281 Md. 627, 381 A.2d 16, 20–23 (1977). Accord: Pogge v. Fullerton Lumber Co., 277 N.W.2d 916, 918–20 (Iowa 1979) (award of punitive damages creates uncertainty and confusion in commercial transactions); J.G.S., Inc. v. Lifetime Cutlery Corp., 87 A.D.2d 810, 448 N.Y.S.2d 780 (1982).

Apart from the "independent" tort exception, punitive damages are sometimes awarded when the breach is accompanied by fraudulent conduct, involves breach of a fiduciary duty or arises in a specialized contract, such as a consumer sale or insurance. But even in insurance contracts, an allegation of breach plus gross negligence may not be enough. See Rocanova v. Equitable Life Assurance Soc. of U.S., 83 N.Y.2d 603, 612 N.Y.S.2d 339, 343, 634 N.E.2d 940, 944 (1994)(private party must "not only demonstrate egregious tortious conduct by which he or she was aggrieved, but also that such conduct was part of a pattern of similar conduct directed at the public generally"); Paiz v. State Farm Fire & Cas. Co., 118 N.M. 203, 880 P.2d 300, 305 (1994)(bad faith or malice). For criticisms of this restrained approach, see Cavico, *Punitive Damages for Breach of Contract—A Principled Approach,* 22 St. Mary's L.J. 357 (1990); Coleman, *Punitive Damages for Breach of Contracts: A New Approach,* 11 Stet.L.Rev. 250 (1982).

(3) The reluctance of courts to award punitive damages for breach of contract parallels recent attacks upon the power of courts to award punitive damages in tort law. In BMW of North America, Inc. v. Gore, ___ U.S. ___, 116 S.Ct. 1589, 134 L.Ed.2d 809 (1996), the Supreme Court held that the 14th Amendment prohibits a state protecting its legitimate interests from imposing "grossly excessive" punitive damages on a tortfeasor. The discretion of state courts to award punitive damages is limited by the state interest to be protected and the reprehensibility of the defendant's conduct. Assuming a legitimate state interest, the award of punitive damages must not be grossly out of proportion to the severity of the offense.

Comment: The Rise and Fall of Punitive Damages for Breach of Non-Insurance Contracts in California

California, like many states, recognizes that every contract is subject to an implied covenant of good faith and fair dealing. The question is when, if ever, a breach of the implied covenant may constitute a tort. California courts have held that in contracts for insurance, the insurer's refusal to settle within the terms of an insurance policy or to pay an undisputed claim of an insured may be a bad faith tort, for which the insured can recover damages for mental anguish and punitive damages. The bases for such a tort consist of the following "special circumstances":

> (1) One of the parties to the contract enjoys a superior bargaining position to the extent that it is able to dictate the terms of the contract; (2) the purpose of the weaker party in entering into the contract is not primarily to profit but rather to secure an essential service or produce financial security or peace of mind; (3) the relationship of the parties is such that the weaker party places trust and confidence in the larger entity; and (4) there is conduct on the part of the defendant indicating an intent to frustrate the weaker party's enjoyment of the contract rights.

Louderback & Jurika, *Standards for Expanding the Tort of Bad Faith Breach of Contract,* 16 U.San.F.L.Rev. 187, 227 (1982).

The question whether tort liability for a "bad faith breach" would be extended beyond insurance or other contracts where "special circumstances" exist was presented in Seaman's Direct Buying Service, Inc. v. Standard Oil Co. of California, Inc., 36 Cal.3d 752, 206 Cal.Rptr. 354, 686 P.2d 1158 (1984). The answer was a qualified yes.

Seaman's, a small dealer in ship supplies and equipment, asked the City of Eureka for a long-term lease of waterfront property, which was in the process of redevelopment. The City was interested, but stipulated that Seaman's must agree to operate a modern marine fuel dealership and to obtain written evidence of a binding agreement with an oil supplier before the lease would be signed. After extensive negotiations with Standard Oil, a letter of intent, which contemplated additional negotiation and a formal dealership agreement, was assented to by Seaman's and Standard and presented to the City. Shortly thereafter, the City and Seaman's entered into a 40–year lease of waterfront property and Seaman's began plans to construct a new marina.

During 1973, however, the so-called OPEC oil crisis developed and the market advantage shifted dramatically from oil buyers to oil producers. Standard, no longer enthusiastic about the letter of intent, informed Seaman's that under a new federal mandatory allocation program, oil could not be supplied to Seaman's because Seaman's had not been a customer in 1972. Seaman's contested this decision and, despite Standard's opposition, ultimately obtained an administrative ruling that a federal order directing Standard to perform would issue upon the filing of a copy of a court decree that a valid contract existed between the parties under state law. Seaman's, however, doubted that it could remain in business during the judicial proceeding and requested Standard to stipulate the existence of a contract. Standard refused. Its agent, according to the court, "laughed" and said "see you in court." As a result, Seaman's went out of business and lost the lease with the City.

At trial, Seaman's obtained, inter alia, compensatory damages of $397,050 for breach of contract (Standard had clearly repudiated the contract) and punitive damages of $1,000,000 (after reduction) for tortious breach of the implied covenant of good faith and fair dealing. The supreme court affirmed the judgment for breach of contract but reversed the judgment for breach of the implied covenant, since the trial court had committed reversible error in failing to charge the jury on bad faith.

The Supreme Court first concluded that the letter of intent was enforceable and that Standard committed a breach by repudiation. The implied covenant, however, provided additional protection by requiring that "neither party do anything which will deprive the other of the benefits of the agreement." Conceding that breach of the implied covenant is not always a tort, the court stated that it was moving "into largely uncharted and potentially dangerous waters" when it moved from contexts where there was a " 'special relationship' between insurer and insured, characterized by elements of public interest, adhesion, and fiduciary responsibility."

Here, parties of roughly equal bargaining power are free to shape the contours of their agreement and to include provisions for attorney fees and liquidated damages in the event of breach. They may not be permitted to disclaim the covenant of good faith but they are free, within reasonable limits at least to agree upon the standards by which application of the covenant is to be measured. In such contracts, it may be difficult to distinguish between breach of the covenant and breach of contract, and there is the risk that interjecting tort remedies will intrude upon the expectations of the parties. This is not to say that tort remedies have no place in such a commercial context, but that it is wise to proceed with caution in determining their scope and application.

For the purposes of this case it is unnecessary to decide the broad question which Seaman's poses. Indeed, it is not even necessary to predicate liability on a breach of the implied covenant. It is sufficient to recognize that a party to a contract may incur tort remedies when, in addition to breaching the contract, it seeks to shield itself from liability by denying, in bad faith and without probable cause, that the contract exists.

It has been held that a party to a contract may be subject to tort liability, including punitive damages, if he coerces the other party to pay more than is due under the contract terms through the threat of a lawsuit, made " 'without probable cause and with no belief in the existence of the cause of action.' " (Adams v. Crater Well Drilling, Inc. (1976) 276 Or. 789, 556 P.2d 679, 681.) There is little difference, in principle, between a contracting party obtaining excess payment in such manner, and a contracting party seeking to avoid all liability on a meritorious contract claim by adopting a "stonewall" position ("see you in court") without probable cause and with no belief in the existence of a defense. Such conduct goes beyond the mere breach of contract. It offends accepted notions of business ethics. (See Jones v. Abriani (1976) 169 Ind.App. 556, 350 N.E.2d 635.) Acceptance of tort remedies in such a situation is not likely to intrude upon the bargaining relationship or upset reasonable expectations of the contracting parties.

Turning to the facts of this case, the jury was instructed that "where a binding contract [has] been agreed upon, the law implies a covenant that neither party will deny the existence of a contract, since doing so violates the legal prohibition against doing anything to prevent realization of the promises of the performance of the contract."

According to Standard, this instruction erroneously allowed the jury to hold Standard liable if it found that Standard denied the existence of a valid contract, regardless of whether that denial was in good or bad faith.

Of course, "it is not a tort for a contractual obligor to dispute his liability under [a] contract" ... if the dispute is honest and undertaken in good faith. Similarly, it is not a tort for one party to deny, in good faith, the existence of a binding contract.

Since Standard's denial of the existence of a binding contract would not have been tortious if made in good faith, the trial court erred in failing to so instruct the jury. It is then necessary to decide whether this error requires that the judgment be reversed.

206 Cal.Rptr. at 363, 686 P.2d at 1167.

In the aftermath of critical reactions to *Seaman's,* see e.g., Comment, *Tort Remedies for Breach of Contract: The Expansion of Tortious Breach of the Implied Covenant of Good Faith and Fair Dealing into the Commercial Realm,* 86 Colum.L.Rev. 377 (1986); Note, *Damage Measurement for Bad Faith Breach of Contract: An Economic Analysis,* 39 Stan.L.Rev. 160 (1986), the California Supreme Court initiated a retreat in Foley v. Interactive Data Corp., 47 Cal.3d 654, 254 Cal.Rptr. 211, 765 P.2d 373 (1988) that culminated in the overruling of *Seaman's* in Freeman & Mills, Inc. v. Belcher Oil Co., 11 Cal.4th 85, 44 Cal.Rptr.2d 420, 430, 900 P.2d 669, 679 (1995) "in favor of a general rule precluding tort recovery for noninsurance contract breach, at least in the absence of violation of 'an independent duty arising from principles of tort law' ... other than the bad faith denial of the existence of, or liability under, the breached contract."

Seaman's had been sharply criticized and its overruling urged by Judge Alexander Kozinski, concurring in Oki America, Inc. v. Microtech Intern., Inc., 872 F.2d 312, 314–17 (9th Cir.1989). He reasoned:

Nowhere but in the Cloud Cuckooland of modern tort theory could a case like this have been concocted. One large corporation is complaining that another obstinately refused to acknowledge they had a contract. For this shocking misconduct it is demanding millions of dollars in punitive damages. I suppose we will next be seeing lawsuits seeking punitive damages for maliciously refusing to return telephone calls or adopting a condescending tone in interoffice memos. Not every slight, nor even every wrong, ought to have a tort remedy. The intrusion of courts into every aspect of life, and particularly into every type of business relationship, generates serious costs and uncertainties, trivializes the law, and denies individuals and businesses the autonomy of adjusting mutual rights and responsibilities through voluntary contractual agreement.

* * *

The eagerness of judges to expand the horizons of tort liability is symptomatic of a more insidious disease: the novel belief that any problem can be ameliorated if only a court gets involved. Not so. Courts are slow, clumsy, heavy-handed institutions, illsuited to oversee the negotiations between corporations, to determine what compromises a manufacturer and a retailer should make in closing a mutually profitable deal, or to evaluate whether an export-import consortium is developing new markets in accordance with the standards of the business community. See generally Snyderman, *What's So Good About*

Good Faith? The Good Faith Performance Obligation in Commercial Lending, 55 U.Chi.L.Rev. 1335, 1361 (1988).

Moreover, because litigation is costly, time consuming and risky, judicial meddling in many business deals imposes onerous burdens. It wasn't so long ago that being sued (or suing) was an unthinkable event for many small and medium-sized businesses. Today, legal expenses are a standard and often uncontrollable item in every business's budget, diverting resources from more productive areas of entrepreneurship. Nor can commercial enterprises be expected to flourish in a legal atmosphere where every move, every innovation, every business decision must be hedged against the risk of exotic new causes of action and incalculable damages. See generally P. Huber, *Liability: The Legal Revolution and its Consequences* 153–71 (1988).

Perhaps most troubling, the willingness of courts to subordinate voluntary contractual arrangements to their own sense of public policy and proper business decorum deprives individuals of an important measure of freedom. The right to enter into contracts—to adjust one's legal relationships by mutual agreement with other free individuals—was unknown through much of history and is unknown even today in many parts of the world. Like other aspects of personal autonomy, it is too easily smothered by government officials eager to tell us what's best for us. The recent tendency of judges to insinuate tort causes of action into relationships traditionally governed by contract is just such overreaching. It must be viewed with no less suspicion because the government officials in question happen to wear robes.

Comment: Enforcement of Money Judgments

The successful plaintiff in a breach of contract action will normally obtain a money judgment against the defendant. That judgment will evidence a right to compensatory damages for breach of contract plus interest and costs. Except where a confession of judgment is authorized (see *Cutler Corp. v. Latshaw,* supra at 512), or the defendant fails to answer the complaint, judgment will be entered after litigation resolves disputes arising out of a variety of transactions, involving both professional business people and consumers. What must the plaintiff do to secure what the late Professor Garrard Glenn called the "first principle of creditor's rights," a "satisfied" judgment? Glenn, Cases on Creditor's Rights 4 (1940).

A judgment does not order the defendant to pay any particular sum. Rather it orders that the plaintiff shall recover "of the defendant" the stated sum and have "execution" therefor. If the defendant pays, the matter is settled. If the defendant does not pay, the plaintiff must proceed by the process of execution to obtain satisfaction from the defendant's real and personal property.

Execution involves a number of steps and procedures, the details of which vary from state to state. The basic objectives are to impose by attachment, levy, garnishment or docketing of the judgment, i.e., by operation of law, a lien upon the defendant's non-exempt property and, through the sheriff or other public official, to conduct a public sale the proceeds of which are used to satisfy the judgment. If the proceeds are sufficient, the judgment is discharged and any excess paid to the defendant. However, there is many a slip between the docketing and satisfaction of a judgment. For example, the defendant may not have any property in the jurisdiction, the sheriff may not be able to find that which is there, other creditors may have liens with priority, the proceeds from the public sale may be insufficient or bankruptcy may intervene. Further, the concern for consumer protection has produced further pressure to limit the traditional rights enjoyed by creditors. Nevertheless, unless the claim reduced to judgment is discharged in bankruptcy, the plaintiff normally has a 20–year renewable period to obtain satisfaction.

Suppose, then, that a seller has tendered and a buyer has accepted goods on credit. If the buyer fails to pay on time the seller is entitled to a judgment for the agreed price. UCC 2–709(1) [UCC 2–822 (1997)]. (In the absence of an agreement on security, however, the seller is rarely able upon breach to take possession of the goods sold. But see UCC 2–702 [UCC 2–816 (1997)].) Further, "self help" to other of the buyer's property is not permitted. Finally, even with a judgment, satisfaction is not automatic. The various risks in the enforcement procedure, therefore, may help to explain some of the doctrines of contract law and the practices of professional business people. For example, one way to avoid the need for enforcement is to demand payment before the goods are delivered. Constructive "concurrent" conditions of exchange implement this non-credit transaction in the absence of agreement to the contrary. Similarly, many business people will extend unsecured credit only if convinced that the buyer is willing and able to pay on time. If substantial doubts exist, credit is not extended or security is demanded.

A brief word on the secured transaction might here be in order. Under Article 9 of the UCC, sellers of goods on credit or other lenders may easily create by agreement with the buyer or borrower a security interest in personal property and "perfect" it by filing a financing statement in the appropriate public office. Security interest means an "interest in personal property * * * which secures payment or performance of an obligation." UCC 1–201(37). The written agreement creating the security interest (called a security agreement) is often accompanied by a negotiable promissory note which evidences the debtor's obligation to pay in a lump sum or installments. See UCC 3–104. Upon default by the debtor either on the note or as defined in the security agreement, the secured party may take possession of the property subject to the security interest if no breach of the peace is involved. Subject to a limited right of redemption and the possible claims of other lien or secured creditors, the property will usually be sold by the secured creditor at a public or private sale. The proceeds of this sale will be used to reimburse the secured creditor for expenses incurred in repossessing, to satisfy the underlying obligation and to satisfy the security interests of those subordinate to the repossessing creditor. If a surplus exists, it is paid to the debtor. If an inadequate sum is produced, the secured party is entitled to seek a deficiency judgment for the balance due and, in effect, becomes unsecured. The entire process, which can occur without the need for direct intervention by a court or sheriff, is closely regulated by Article 9. For example, any public or private sale must be accomplished in a commercially reasonable manner; basic debtor rights cannot be eroded by agreement with the creditor; the debtor is given extensive private remedies if the creditor fails to comply with Article 9. Even so, many feel that this protection is inadequate for the consumer. Efforts for reform are manifested in the 1972 revision of Article 9 and legislation such as the Uniform Consumer Credit Code. A more extensive treatment of financing patterns and problems where personal property or real estate is involved (whether by mortgage or installment sales contract) must be reserved for another time and another course.

PROBLEM: REMEDIES FOR BAD FAITH BREACH OF CONTRACT TO PAY MONEY

Filbert, a self-employed carpenter, contracted with MedServ, Inc. for the protection of a major medical insurance plan. The annual premium was $2,500. In July of 1990, Filbert was injured on a job and spent sixty days in the hospital. The total cost of that visit was $250,000. Filbert had no other applicable insurance, although the Owner of the project where Filbert was injured was insured by the Magnanimous Insurance Company against liability to third persons caused by negligence. The Owner and Magnanimous have denied liability and Filbert's lawyer has advised that there is only a 20% chance that Filbert could obtain a judgment against Owner. Under the contract with MedServ, Filbert was clearly entitled to $200,000 for medical expenses. Med-Serv, without any justification in the contract, refused to pay either Filbert or the hospital until Filbert had exhausted his claim against Owner. Filbert's lawyer has advised that there is a 100% chance that MedServ's refusal to pay is a breach of contract and that it is highly probable that MedServ knew that its demand was improper. MedServ, however, continued to insist that Filbert first pursue his claim against Owner and that if he wanted payment now he would have to sue. Pressed by creditors, Filbert sued MedServ for $200,000 plus interest from the date of demand. In addition, Filbert sought damages for emotional distress in the amount of $50,000 and punitive damages in the amount of $250,000. In the pre-trial maneuvering, MedServ conceded that its refusal to pay was wrongful and offered to pay $200,000 plus interest. It moved, however, to dismiss the claims for special and punitive damages. MedServ argued that although the breach was deliberate, it did not amount to an independent, aggravated tort. Furthermore, special and punitive damages were not appropriate for breach of a contract to pay money. In arguing against the motion to dismiss, Filbert claimed that special and punitive damages should be granted for the following reasons:

1. The dominant purpose of the transaction was not commercial;

2. MedServ, as a health insurer, has quasi-public responsibilities;

3. Emotional distress was foreseeable at the time of contracting;

4. Filbert was dependent upon MedServ's skill and judgment in a continuing relationship where trust and confidence were important;

5.   MedServ took advantage of Filbert's weakness by deliberately refusing to pay a valid claim under circumstances where Filbert needed the money and was left with litigation as the only recourse; and

6.   MedServ enjoyed a superior bargaining position in that it was able both to dictate the terms of the contract and, after the dispute arose, to refuse payment without financial hardship.

How would you rule on the motion?

(B) BREACH OR REPUDIATION BY PAYOR

In most bargains, one party has agreed to render a performance, e.g., transfer and sell goods or land, construct a home, perform professional services, in exchange for an agreed price. As we have seen, unless the parties have agreed upon a time for payment (either before or after performance) the duty to pay, whether in a lump sum or in installments, does not arise until the performer has tendered or completed all or part of its portion of the exchange. If this is done without a breach, the performer, with one notable exception, is entitled to enforce the contract for the full amount promised plus interest. Even if the performer has breached, the duty to pay is enforceable with an adjustment for damages caused by the immaterial breach.

If, however, a non-breaching performer has not completed its part of the exchange before the payor repudiates the contract or fails to make a payment due, the remedial problems become more complex. If the performer cannot recover the agreed price (arguably the best remedy), what are the alternatives?

We have already explored the performer's defensive remedy of being able to withhold her own performance, see supra at 814. We will now explore the distinct problems confronting the performer in achieving affirmative protection upon breach or repudiation by the payor. Look carefully for the interaction between remedial objectives and policy and the position of the performer. In the next subsection, we will reverse the coin to consider the remedial posture of the payor upon breach or repudiation by the performer.

John Hancock Mutual Life Insurance Co. v. Cohen

United States Court of Appeals, Ninth Circuit, 1958.
254 F.2d 417.

[The insured, who died in February, 1945, was protected by a life insurance policy issued by the defendant. The policy contained a provision for "family income benefit" under which, in lieu of a lump sum payment, the plaintiff-beneficiary was to receive monthly payments for 20 years from the date that the policy was issued, 1939, and a final lump sum of $5,000. The defendant made monthly payments for 15 years and at the end of that time tendered the final lump sum payment. The defendant refused to make any further monthly payments on the ground that the policy was issued for

20 years by mistake and that both parties intended protection for 15 years. The lower court found for the plaintiff on the mistake issue and held that the defendant had breached the contract by anticipatory repudiation. Accordingly, an $8,000 judgment was entered for the plaintiff which included the installments due and to become due under the policy and the final payment. On appeal, the court of appeals, speaking through Judge Barnes, affirmed the lower court on the mistake issue and then treated the anticipatory breach question.]

■ BARNES, CIRCUIT JUDGE.

* * *

Appellant's sixth alleged error is the finding that the appellant committed an anticipatory breach of said contract on or about May 13th 1954.[1]

Appellant cites Cobb v. Pacific Mut. Life Ins. Co., 1935, 4 Cal.2d 565, 51 P.2d 84; 12 Cal.Juris. 2nd Contracts, § 250, and Restatement of Contracts, § 318. Cal.Juris. 2d cites the Cobb case as authority for the rule there can be no anticipatory breach of a unilateral contract in California, and Flinn v. Mowry, 1901, 131 Cal. 481, 63 P. 724, 1006, and Brix v. People's Mut. Life Ins. Co., 1935, 2 Cal.2d 446, 41 P.2d 537, (as well as Cobb, supra) for the proposition that

"'* * * notwithstanding the failure or refusal to pay the installment, the other party cannot treat the contract as repudiated and demand payment in full, contrary to the terms of the contract providing for payment in installments.''

Appellee here urges that there yet remains a condition to be performed by the plaintiff—the surrender of the policy to the defendant in Boston. This being so, and relying on Corbin on Contracts § 967, he states that the plaintiff can maintain an action at once for anticipatory repudiation. Corbin divided his discussion of repudiation of unilateral insurance contracts into two classes: First, "those in which the insurer undertakes to pay a definite sum of money at a specified future time or on the happening of a future event that is certain to occur, but the time of which is uncertain. * * * A second class consists of disability and annuity policies. * * *" ("Annuity" here is used, we presume, in its usual sense and not as an "annuity certain" in length of time as it was in the instant case.) In reference to the first class of cases, Corbin states:

"It is well settled by ample authority that an action lies at once for anticipatory repudiation by an insurer, either for the recovery of premiums paid or for damages." Corbin, § 968.

1. Finding 14: "On or about May 13, 1954 defendant notified plaintiff in writing that it 'does not consider it is liable for any further monthly payments under the family income provision,' and that it would pay a final payment of $4,993.59 but only upon surrender of the policy. Thereby defendant committed an anticipatory breach of the said contract entered into between it and said Troutfelt." [Tr. p. 104].

We need not go into Corbin's "ample authority," nor determine if this action falls within the limited type of actions which Corbin states can be filed, for recovery of premiums or damages.

The contract here under consideration is a "payment certain" insurance contract. It has become, in effect, an unconditional unilateral contract for the payment of money in future installments. There were no contingencies which might occur to give the company a right to refuse payment. Even should the beneficiary have died, the "payment certain" would have been payable to her heirs. Particularly, after the insured's death and the company's endorsement on July 26, 1945 is this true. The insurer then undertook to pay certain sums each month and a larger certain sum at a later date.

This contract falls neither into Corbin's first class—a definite sum or sums payable on a future event certain to occur, but uncertain as to the time of occurrence—nor into his second class—"the disability and annuity policies providing for periodic payments for an indefinite time." It is a contract wherein the time for payment is certain and there remains no condition or covenant for performance by the plaintiff.

Corbin does not like the "dicta" to the effect that there can be no anticipatory breach of a unilateral contract because in the *first* class of cases the doctrine is in fact applied. (See cases cited at Corbin, § 968, n. 35.) Nor does he care for the rule that the doctrine of anticipatory breach is inapplicable to a case of an unconditional unilateral contract for the payment of money in installments, but he cites no authority to the contrary. (Corbin, §§ 965, 969.)

We are in essence here asked to hold that the doctrine of anticipatory breach applies to an unconditional unilateral insurance contract in a case where the insurer has promised to pay definite sums of money at specified future dates and that this should be declared by the Federal Court to be the law of New Mexico because an eminent writer and authority on contracts disagrees with the more recent New York cases and the Massachusetts rule and two Supreme Court cases. (Corbin, § 968, n. 34.)

We are asked to so rule in a case where the "present value" of future payments was not raised below, nor apparently considered by the trial court. Corbin states:

"Some of the courts denying that the insurer has committed a total breach of anticipation base their decision upon the ground that the contract is a unilateral contract for the payment of money. That this is not a good reason has already been argued in a previous section. The decision of the Supreme Court does not rest upon it; indeed, in the opinion rendered it is in part, at least, rejected. We differ with the court in holding that there was no total breach by anticipatory repudiation; but its reasoning and analysis may be otherwise approved. The decision itself need not be regretted, if it leads to the granting of the truly 'appropriate relief' in all such cases. This is a single decree that money already overdue shall be paid, with interest, and that future instalments shall be paid as they fall due. * * *" Corbin, § 969, pp. 893–94.

Williston on Contracts states the general rule to be "that no unilateral promise for an executed agreed exchange to pay money at a future time can be enforced until that day arrives." (Williston, § 1328; accord, Restatement, Contracts § 318). With respect to the applicability of the doctrine of anticipatory breach to future disability payments, he says: "[T]here remained divided opinions until two recent decisions of the Supreme Court of the United States," citing Mobley v. New York Life Ins. Co., 1935, 295 U.S. 632, 55 S.Ct. 876, 79 L.Ed. 1621; New York Life Ins. Co. v. Viglas, 1936, 297 U.S. 672, 56 S.Ct. 615, 80 L.Ed. 971; the Brix and Cobb cases, supra; and, 24 Calif.L.Rev. 216.

Williston goes on:

"The only argument for allowing immediate recovery of a future payment due under such a (disability) policy is the hardship supposedly imposed on the insured of bringing successive suits." (§ 1330A.) He then points out how this can be avoided by the courts' "full exercise of equitable powers." He quotes from Mobley v. New York Life Ins. Co., supra, to the effect that if the insured is

"* * * allowed a present recovery for all future benefits, the calculations on which insurance business is done would be upset, and the purposes for which the benefits were made payable only in installments would often be defeated." (Ibid.)

Williston then criticizes as "extreme" the application of the doctrine to a non-insurance case in Texas,[2] although "the present value" was therein determined, after use of expectancy tables—a value not herein considered by the trial court.

We conclude the general rule to be that the doctrine of anticipatory breach has no application to suits to enforce contracts for future payment of money only, in installments or otherwise. . . .

* * *

It is our conclusion that the theory of anticipatory breach is not here applicable—to make it so where the defendant insurer has disputed liability in good faith would change the terms of the contract executed by the insurer and force him to pay now what he contracted to pay later; that the court should decree that money already overdue shall be paid now with interest; and that future installments shall be paid as they fall due, including the final payment.

What we have said with respect to the alleged error in holding an anticipatory breach controls the seventh specification of error, and requires us to hold the judgment as given to be error.

* * *

2. Pollack v. Pollack, Tex.Civ.App., 23 S.W.2d 890, Tex.Com.App., 39 S.W.2d 853. [Texas law still rejects the distinction between executory and fully executed contracts in connection with the doctrine of anticipatory breach. Pitts v. Wetzel, 498 S.W.2d 27 (Tex.Civ.App.1973) Ed.]

The cause is remanded, with directions to award plaintiff an amount equal to payments due to the date of judgment, plus interest; decreeing that future installments shall be paid when they fall due, together with the final lump sum payment; and, that appellee be awarded her costs, both below and on this appeal.

Remanded with directions.

NOTES

(1) *Repudiation of Promise to Pay Money When Other Party Has Fully Performed.* A has fully performed his obligations under the contract. All express and implied conditions have been satisfied except that the agreed time for payment, whether in installments or a lump sum, has not yet arrived. B unequivocally repudiates her obligation to pay. May A bring suit for damages and obtain a judgment *before* the time for payment has arrived? Professor Corbin's answer was an emphatic yes. His argument was: 1) It is wrong to limit the doctrine of anticipatory repudiation, as announced in *Hochster v. de la Tour,* supra at 815, to cases where the plaintiff still has part of the exchange to perform. Its need for affirmative protection against repudiation is no less just because full performance has occurred; 2) The amount to be paid is certain and time is the only contingency involved; 3) Judgment for the plaintiff will neither "accelerate" the obligation nor grant specific performance. Rather, the plaintiff will recover damages for breach of a promise to pay money measured by the present value of that promise. In other words, the full amount promised must be "discounted" to reflect the defendant's loss of use. The fact that the damage amount resembles specific performance is fortuitous since, when full performance by the plaintiff has occurred, there are no savings to deduct from the total recovery. See Corbin §§ 962–70. With regard to the *Cohen* case, Professor Corbin stated that justice would also have been achieved "if the beneficiary had been given judgment for the full amount of the future installments properly discounted to 'present value.' " "These were definite in number and amount and could be adequately discounted. This would be a judgment for 'damages' and not accelerated specific performance." 4 Corbin § 968 (1964 Pocket Part). Do you agree? Other than the possibility of multiple litigation when installments are involved, what special hardship is involved in requiring the plaintiff to wait for the money?

(2) Would the problem posed in the *Cohen* case be alleviated by a contract clause authorizing "acceleration" of the obligation in the event of default, defined to include "repudiation"? Acceleration clauses, which are standard in most loan and credit transactions, are drafted to permit the remedy denied in *Cohen.*

(3) Despite criticism, see, e.g., Wiesner, *Anticipatory Breach and the Unilateral Contract: A Decade of the Status Quo,* 8 U. Dayton L.Rev. 61 (1982), the "unilateral" contract exception to the doctrine of anticipatory breach or repudiation persists. Section 253(1) of Restatement (Second) states that where an "obligor repudiates a duty before he has committed a breach by non-performance and before he has received all of the agreed exchange for it, his repudiation alone gives rise to a claim for damages for total breach." In Comment c, it is noted that "one of the established limits on the doctrine of

'anticipatory breach' " is that the obligor's "repudiation alone * * * gives rise to no claim for damages at all if he has already received all of the agreed exchange for it." In Comment d, however, it is conceded that the "degree to which the limitation might yield on a showing of manifest injustice, as where the refusal to pay is not in good faith, is unclear." Suppose the obligor is in default on one installment and then repudiates the balance of the contract? The Restatement (Second) answer is found in Section 243(3):

> Where at the time of the breach the only remaining duties of performance are those of the party in breach and are for the payment of money in installments not related to one another, his breach by non-performance as to less than the whole, whether or not accompanied or followed by a repudiation, does not give rise to a claim for damages for total breach.

(4) One of the recurring objections to permitting an immediate suit upon repudiation is the supposed difficulty of putting a present value on a promise to pay to be performed in future installments. This uncertainty is eliminated, however, where the promise is to pay a fixed sum of money and the duty to pay is not hedged with contingencies. In these cases, the plaintiff may be relying upon installment payments for support and be put to great expense and frustration if required separately to enforce each installment. How did the *Cohen* case deal with this problem? What is the effect of its decree that "future installments shall be paid when they fall due"? Is it tantamount to a declaratory judgment that the policy is still in effect and a decree reinstating the policy? See Federal Declaratory Judgment Act, 28 U.S.C.A. §§ 2201–02. What about a judgment that the defendant shall pay in installments so long as the conditions for liability last? What about equitable relief? With the exception of one or two isolated cases, courts have been reluctant to grant conditional installment judgments or equitable relief where the plaintiff seeks to recover money.

(5) *Adjusting Damage Award For Inflation.* Suppose that P has fully performed his side of the bargain in exchange for D's promise to pay $10,000 per year for the next 10 years, a total of $100,000. D then commits a material breach and the court is willing to give P a lump sum judgment for the total amount due over the ten-year period. At least two things are clear: (1) D will be relieved from paying any agreed interest on the principal, and (2) the lump sum of $100,000 must be discounted to present value. The discount rate is the interest rate which is assumed to be available for future investments of the capital sum awarded as damages. Assume a rate of 10%. Thus, a $100,000 award is subject to a discount rate of 10% when it is reduced to a sum which, if invested for 10 years at an interest rate of 10%, would produce a total of principal and interest equal to $100,000. On these facts, that discounted amount is $50,000. D is not penalized by paying interest on principal he cannot use and P is not overcompensated by having an opportunity to invest principal that would not otherwise have been available. See Comment, *Adjusting Damage Awards for Future Inflation*, 1982 Wis.L.Rev. 397, 397–98. But if P's lump sum must be discounted downward, is he entitled to an upward adjustment for inflation or projected price increases over the ten-year period? If, over time, the $100,000 award would buy less and less, isn't P undercompensated unless inflation or deflation factors are employed for an adjustment? Most courts have held yes, but there is considerable disagreement over the fairest and most efficient way to accomplish the adjustment. One line of cases requires a total

offset of the discount rate by the inflation rate as a matter of law, e.g., Beaulieu v. Elliott, 434 P.2d 665 (Alaska 1967), see Comment, 49 U.Chi.L.Rev. 1003 (1982), while other courts apply more flexible offsets. See Note, 57 St. Johns L.Rev. 316 (1983). The issue is of considerable importance in tort law, where judgments are frequently for injuries which extend into the future and efforts are now underway to "structure" judgments into periodic payments. See, e.g., Henderson, *Periodic Payments of Personal Injury Awards,* 66 A.B.A.J. 733 (1980); Corboy, *Structured Injustice: Compulsory Periodic Payment of Judgments,* 66 A.B.A.J. 1524 (1980). For Dean Henderson's reply to Mr. Corboy, see 67 A.B.A.J. 301 (1981).

(7) *Damages for Breach of Contract to Pay or Lend Money: Consequential Damages.* Increasingly, banks and other financial institutions have been sued for breach of a contract to lend money or to finance a particular venture. What is the lender's liability in these cases? The courts, relying upon Restatement (Second) § 351, Comment e, agree that the presumptive measure is the difference between the interest rate plaintiffs contracted to pay and the actual rate plaintiffs were compelled to pay to secure substitute financing. Thus, if the bank agreed to finance at 9% and the substitute rate was 10%, the 1% spread would be the base rate for damages. But suppose the borrower is unable to obtain substitute financing and suffers other consequential damages. For example, the venture to be financed may fall through. Again, most courts agree that where it is foreseeable to the lender that substitute financing will be unavailable, the lender may be liable for the foreseeable actual damages resulting from the breach. Whether the foreseeability requirement is satisfied and the amount of loss resulting from the breach are questions of fact to be resolved in each case. See, e.g., Hill v. Ben Franklin Sav. & Loan Ass'n, 177 Ill.App.3d 51, 126 Ill.Dec. 462, 531 N.E.2d 1089 (1988) (foreseeability for the jury); Doyle v. Oregon Bank, 94 Or.App. 230, 764 P.2d 1379 (1988) (failure to allege damages were foreseeable precludes recovery). See also UCC 2–806 (1997), which now permits a seller to recover consequential damages for breach by the buyer of a promise to pay the price.

PROBLEM: SELLER'S RESALE REMEDY UNDER THE UCC

Slick Shoe Company entered into a contract with Bobo's Sports for the sale of 200 pairs of basketball shoes. The shoes were a current fad among teenagers since being popularized by several stars in the National Basketball Association. The agreed price was $12,000. Under the contract, Slick was to ship the goods to Bobo "fob destination" (which meant that Slick was to pay the transportation costs) as follows: 100 pairs in three months, June 1, and the balance on September 1. Bobo agreed to pay the full price for each installment within 30 days after delivery. In establishing a price of $60 per pair, Slick took the following costs into account:

1.	leather, rubber and other materials for manufacturing	$30.00
2.	labor	10.00
3.	fixed costs, e.g., overhead, etc.	10.00
4.	transportation to buyer	4.00
	Total variable and fixed costs	54.00
	Expected net profit per pair	6.00
		$60.00

Slick shipped and Bobo accepted the first installment of shoes. On June 15, Bobo telephoned and repudiated the contract. Apparently a new shoe style had emerged with the signing by the Bulls of the next "Michael" and sales of the "contract" shoes had slumped. At the time of the repudiation, Slick had completed the second installment and had identified them as intended for Bobo. Also, it is stipulated that at all relevant times the market price for the "contract" shoes was $30.00 per pair at the point of shipment and $20.50 per pair at the point of delivery. Bobo refused to retract the repudiation. Slick then canceled the contract and consulted an attorney. The questions posed are as follows (please consult your UCC):

1. Will there be any problems because I canceled the contract before consulting with you? See UCC 2–610, 2–703 & 2–612 [UCC 2–712, 2–803 & 2–710 (1997)].

2. If I sue *before* July 1, can I recover the full price for those goods delivered? See UCC 2–607(1), 2–709 & 2–723 [UCC 2–708(a), 2–822 & 2–812 (1997)]. In any event, can I recover the full price for the completed shoes sitting in my warehouse?

3. If I can't recover the price on the second installment, I have found a local "second hand" retail outlet which is willing to buy them for $28 per pair. Nobody else in this area is interested. If I sell them now for $28, how much can I recover from Bobo? The buyer says that he will pick them up at my plant. See UCC 2–706 [UCC 2–819 (1997)].

4. It will cost me $100 to arrange this resale. Can I recover this from Bobo? See UCC 2–710 [UCC 2–805 (1997)].

5. Suppose I decide to hold rather than to resell the second installment of shoes. What can I recover from Bobo? See UCC 2–708 [UCC 2–821 (1997)]. If I recover damages under UCC 2–708 [UCC 2–821 (1997)], and later these sandals come back into style and I sell them for $70 per pair, do I have any duty to account to Bobo?

American Mechanical Corp. v. Union Machine Co. of Lynn, Inc.

Appeals Court of Massachusetts, 1985.
21 Mass.App.Ct. 97, 485 N.E.2d 680.

[On October 16, 1976, American contracted with Union to sell its real estate and business equipment for $135,000. Union knew that American was in financial difficulty, that it was in arrears on mortgage payments to Saugus Bank and that Saugus was pressing American to sell. Union issued a $5,000 check as a down payment, to be held in escrow until closing. On November 1, 1976, Union repudiated the contract. Saugus Bank took possession of the property and, after American was unable to find another purchaser, the equipment was sold by Saugus for $35,000. On June 1, 1977, Saugus conducted a foreclosure sale and purchased the real estate for $55,000. American sued Union for breach of contract. After trial, the superior court concluded that although there was a breach of contract,

American had not proved the "right to recover damages, beyond nominal damages." Upon appeal, the judgment was vacated and a final judgment was entered in favor of American in the amount of $46,000 with interest.]

■ FINE, JUSTICE.

* * *

Damages for Breach of Contract.

The judge ruled that the contract was one for the sale of the real estate for $100,000 and for the sale of the personal property for $35,000. Since $35,000 was obtained by the Saugus Bank & Trust Company when it sold the equipment and machinery, and that amount presumably was credited to American's account with the bank, the judge ruled that American had sustained no loss unless it did so with respect to the real estate. We need not decide whether a breakdown of the contract price between the real estate and the personalty was called for, or whether the price should be viewed as a lump sum for the entire sale. In our view, the result is not affected by any such determination. The judge ruled that the measure of damages for the breach of the agreement to purchase the real estate was the difference between the contract price and the fair market value on the date of the breach. Because he did not believe that the price obtained at the foreclosure sale, seven months after the breach, represented the fair market value of the property on the date of the breach, and because the plaintiff had produced no other evidence of the market value of the real estate on the date of the breach, the judge ruled that American had failed to prove actual damages.

The judge correctly stated the traditional rule generally applicable in measuring damages for breach of an agreement to purchase real estate ... He was also correct in his conclusion that the foreclosure sale price, even if some evidence of the market value, was not binding on him as establishing the market value of the property on the date of the breach. The actual sale of a piece of property normally provides strong evidence of market value, although the "evidentiary value of such sales in less than arms-length transactions is diminished." New Boston Garden Corp. v. Assessors of Boston, 383 Mass. 456, 469, 420 N.E.2d 298 (1981) ... We assume that the bank in conducting the sale complied with its duty of due diligence, observing the procedural requirements of both the mortgage and the statute (G.L. c. 244, § 14), and acted in good faith ... It does not follow, however, that a sale so conducted will necessarily yield a price reflecting the full market value ...

Based upon his view of the applicable rule for measuring damages, and his disbelief of American's evidence of market value, the judge awarded American nominal damages only. The rule relied upon by the judge for measuring damages for breach of an agreement to purchase real estate, however, does not apply in all cases.

Consistent with general principles of contract law, the aim in measuring damages in the event of a breach is to place the injured party in as good a position as he would have been in had the contract been performed ... An important aspect of this principle is that if a party suing for breach of contract has sustained a loss as a result of a breach, and the loss is of such a nature that it was reasonably foreseeable by the parties or actually within their contemplation at the time the contract was entered into, then that loss may be recovered in an action for damages ...

There is no logical basis for treating real estate purchase and sale agreements differently from other purchase and sale agreements, or from contracts generally, for purposes of measuring damages. See 11 Williston, Contracts § 1399 (3d ed. 1968). The usual formula for measuring damages for breach of a real estate purchase and sale agreement—the difference between the contract price and the market value on the date of the breach—is merely a different formulation of the general rule for measuring contract damages. In the usual case, the contract price less the market value represents the seller's actual loss, and the formula, therefore, affords the injured seller an adequate remedy. In some cases, however, the actual loss suffered as a result of a breach exceeds the amount yielded by that formula. The question is whether, because the contract involves the sale of real estate, we may not, in such cases, refer to that aspect of the general rule of contract damages which gives recognition to actual losses sustained as a result of a breach when the losses are reasonably foreseeable or within the contemplation of the parties. That principle has been applied to contracts which are exclusively for the sale of real estate when the particular circumstances are such that the usual rule produces an inadequate remedy. Cobb v. Wood, 8 Cush. 228, 230 (1851). Roper v. Milbourn, 93 Neb. 809, 142 N.W. 792 (1913). Taefi v. Stevens, 53 N.C.App. 579, 281 S.E.2d 435 (1981), aff'd as modified, 305 N.C. 291, 287 S.E.2d 898 (1982). Brewer v. Vanek, No. 84–CA–56, Slip Op. (Ohio Ct.App., Feb. 21, 1985). Senior Estates, Inc. v. Bauman Homes, Inc., 272 Or. 577, 539 P.2d 142 (1975). Borton v. Medicine Rock Land Co., 275 Or. 59, 549 P.2d 1122 (1976). See Lynch v. Andrew, 20 Mass.App. 623, 627–628, 481 N.E.2d 1383 (1985).[3]

American proved that it sustained a loss in the amount of $45,000, the difference between the contract price of $135,000 and the $90,000 received from the mortgagee bank's sale of the real estate, machinery, and equipment. The judge's findings make it clear that at the time the contract was entered into, Union knew that, if the sale of the property did not go through, the result would be that the bank would enforce its rights under the mortgage and that a foreclosure sale was likely. On almost identical facts, an Ohio court recently ruled that the correct measure of damages, on traditional contract principles, was the full amount of the actual loss, the contract price less the amount received for the property at the foreclosure sale. Brewer v. Vanek, supra. We do not hesitate to reach the same result on the facts of this case. It does not seem to us to be a departure from established principles.

3. In some jurisdictions, the usual rule for measuring damages for a buyer's breach of a real estate purchase and sale agreement is the difference between the contract price and the price obtained on resale. Green v. Ansley, 92 Ga. 647, 19 S.E. 53 (1893). Clever v. Clever, 38 Pa.Super. 66, 75 (1909). Harris v. Dawson, 479 Pa. 463, 466, 388 A.2d 748 (1978). Tator v. Salem, 81 App.Div.2d 727, 439 N.Y.S.2d 497 (N.Y.1981). See also Uniform Land Transactions Act § 2–504 (1980).

Union would, of course, be entitled to have American's damages reduced to the extent that American could reasonably have avoided the loss. Restatement (Second) of Contracts § 350 (1979). Thus, if, once it knew of the breach, American could reasonably have sold the property to someone else, it would be entitled to damages in an amount no greater than the difference between the contract price and the price for which it could have sold the property. Union established through cross-examination of Beckett that, following notification of the breach, no attempt was made by American to put the property back on the market. The judge found as a fact, however, that "American was unable to secure another purchaser for the realty and equipment." There is evidence in the record to support that finding. The evidentiary support consists principally of Beckett's recitation of what transpired between him and the Saugus Bank & Trust Company during the period immediately following notice of the breach. The bank moved relatively quickly to take possession, and the property was not of the kind for which one could assume there would be a ready market. Thus, it is not clear, as a practical matter, that American could have done anything to avoid the foreclosure. In any event, the burden of proving that losses could have been avoided by reasonable effort rests with the party in breach. See Maynard v. Royal Worcester Corset Co., 200 Mass. 1, 6, 85 N.E. 877 (1908); Food Specialties, Inc. v. John C. Dowd, Inc., 339 Mass. 735, 748, 162 N.E.2d 276 (1959); Clark v. General Cleaning Co., 345 Mass. 62, 65, 185 N.E.2d 749 (1962); National Med. Care, Inc. v. Zigelbaum, 18 Mass.App. 570, 581, 468 N.E.2d 868 (1984); Hedgecock v. Stewart Title Guar. Co., 676 P.2d 1208, 1210 (Colo.App.1983); Farnsworth, Contracts § 12.12 (1982); Restatement (Second) of Contracts § 350, comment c (1979). Union's showing on this point was insufficient to establish that American failed to act reasonably to avoid the loss. Accordingly, there is no basis for reducing the damages to which American would otherwise be entitled because of any failure on its part to act reasonably to avoid the loss.

* * *

NOTES

(1) At what time was the market value of the real estate relevant? Suppose there was evidence that the market value was $75,000 at the date of breach and $70,000 at the date set for closing. What result under the court's reasoning? Are you persuaded that the price produced in a foreclosure sale some seven months later at which the mortgagee, Saugus, was the purchaser reflects a "fair" market value?

Problems of proof aside, the contract price/market price standard used by the court is common in contracts for the sale of improved real estate, e.g., Frank v. Jansen, 303 Minn. 86, 226 N.W.2d 739 (1975), and contracts for the lease of realty, improved or unimproved. See F. Enterprises, Inc. v. Kentucky Fried Chicken Corp., 47 Ohio St.2d 154, 351 N.E.2d 121 (1976) (measure of damages for breach by lessee is difference between the fair market rental of the property proposed to be leased and the agreed rental to be paid in the proposed lease, such sum discounted to present value, together with any special damages arising from the breach.) A similar approach is taken under UCC 2–708(1) [UCC 2–821 (1997)] whether or not the seller has completed goods on hand.

(2) Note that the real estate in the *American Mechanical* case was sold at a foreclosure sale by the mortgagee, Saugus Bank, rather than by the vendor, American. From the proceeds, Saugus is entitled to satisfy its claim against American, including expenses incurred in enforcement. If there is a surplus, it must be paid to American. If there is a deficit, American still owes that amount to Saugus, who becomes an unsecured creditor. Similar principles are employed where a creditor with a security interest in goods repossesses them and conducts a public or private resale. See UCC 9–504.

(3) *Mitigation and Leases.* If an estate has "vested" in the lessee by a lease, the lessor's remedy upon breach by the lessee is no different than that of a vendor of land after title has passed to the vendee or a seller of goods after the buyer has accepted them: an action for the agreed rent is proper. See *Kentucky Fried Chicken Corp.,* supra. But suppose the lessee has vacated the premises. Does the lessor have any "duty" to mitigate damages by reletting the premises to another? At common law the answer was no, on the theory that an interest in land had been sold. If the lessor in fact relet the premises, the lessee's obligation would be credited by the amount obtained, but the lessor had no duty to make a reasonable effort to relet. More recently, some cases have treated the problem as if it were a contract to lease and required the lessor to made reasonable efforts to relet. The effect of this is that if the lessor fails to make these efforts, the lessee's obligation will be credited with the amount of rent that the lessor reasonably could have obtained. See D. Dobbs, Remedies § 12.6 (1973), Restatement (Second) § 350, Comment b. See also Farmers and Bankers Life Insurance Co. v. St. Regis Paper Co., 456 F.2d 347 (5th Cir.1972), holding that the lessor may elect to treat failure to pay rent under a lease as a contract to lease and seek damages based upon the difference between the lease price and the market price.

In contracts for the sale of goods, if the seller, after breach by the buyer, unreasonably fails to resell goods still in his or her possession and identified to the contract, the buyer has some protection in the "market" damage formula in UCC 2–708(1) [UCC 2–821 (1997)]. The seller gets no more than the difference between the contract price and the market price at the time and place for tender. See Restatement (Second) § 350, Comment c. See also Neumiller Farms, Inc. v. Cornett, 368 So.2d 272, 275–77 (Ala.1979), supra at 775. Thus, a mitigation principle is built into the UCC damage formula.

Lowy v. United Pacific Insurance Co.

Supreme Court of California, 1967.
Supra at 686.

New Era Homes Corp. v. Forster

Court of Appeals of New York, 1949.
299 N.Y. 303, 86 N.E.2d 757.

■ DESMOND, JUDGE. Plaintiff entered into a written agreement with defendants, to make extensive alterations to defendants' home, the reference therein to price and payment being as follows:

"All above material, and labor to erect and install same to be supplied for $3,075.00 to be paid as follows:

$150.00 on signing of contract,

$1,000.00 upon delivery of materials and starting of work,

$1,500.00 on completion of rough carpentry and rough plumbing,

$425.00 upon job being completed."

The work was commenced and partly finished, and the first two stipulated payments were made. Then, when the "rough work" was done, plaintiff asked for the third installment of $1,500 but defendants would not pay it, so plaintiff stopped work and brought suit for the whole of the balance, that is, for the two last payments of $1,500 and $425. On the trial plaintiff stipulated to reduce its demand to $1,500, its theory being that, since all the necessary "rough carpentry and rough plumbing" had been done, the time had arrived for it to collect $1,500. It offered no other proof as to its damages. Defendants conceded their default but argued at the trial, and argue here, that plaintiff was entitled not to the $1,500 third payment, but to such amount as it could establish by way of actual loss sustained from defendants' breach. In other words, defendants say the correct measure of damage was the value of the work actually done, less payments made, plus lost profits. The jury, however, by its verdict gave plaintiff its $1,500. The Appellate Division, Second Department, affirmed the judgment, and we granted defendants leave to appeal to this court.

The whole question is as to the meaning of so much of the agreement as we have quoted above. Did that language make it an entire contract, with one consideration for the doing of the whole work, and payments on account at fixed points in the progress of the job, or was the bargain a severable or divisible one in the sense that, of the total consideration, $1,150 was to be the full and fixed payment for "delivery of materials and starting of work", $1,500 the full and fixed payment for work done up to and including "completion of rough carpentry and rough plumbing", and $425 for the rest. We hold that the total price of $3,075 was the single consideration for the whole of the work, and that the separately listed payments were not allocated absolutely to certain parts of the undertaking, but were scheduled part payments, mutually convenient to the builder and the owner. That conclusion, we think, is a necessary one from the very words of the writing, since the arrangement there stated was not that separate items of work be done for separate amounts of money, but that the whole alteration project, including material and labor, was "to be supplied for $3,075". There is nothing in the record to suggest that the parties had intended to group, in this contract, several separate engagements, each with its own separate consideration. They did not say, for instance, that the price for all the work up to the completion of rough carpentry and plumbing was to be $1,500. They did agree that at that point $1,500 would be due, but as a part payment on the whole price. To illustrate: it is hardly conceivable that the amount of $150, payable "on signing of contract" was a reward to plaintiff for the act of affixing its corporate name and seal.

We would, in short, be writing a new contract for these people if we broke this single promise up into separate deals; and the new contract so written by us might be, for all we know, most unjust to one or the other party.

We find no controlling New York case, but the trend of authority in this State, and elsewhere, is that such agreements express an intent that payment be conditioned and dependent upon completion of all the agreed work. Tompkins v. Dudley, 25 N.Y. 272, 82 Am.Dec. 349; Ming v. Corbin, 142 N.Y. 334, 37 N.E. 105; United States v. United States Fidelity & Guaranty Co., 236 U.S. 512, 35 S.Ct. 298, 59 L.Ed. 696; Integrity Flooring v. Zandon Corp., 130 N.J.L. 244, 32 A.2d 507; Peist v. Richmond, 97 Vt. 97; 17 C.J.S., Contracts, §§ 331–334; 1 Restatement, Contracts, § 266, illustration 4 on p. 386. We think that is the reasonable rule—after all, a householder who remodels his home is, usually, committing himself to one plan and one result, not a series of unrelated projects. The parties to a construction or alteration contract may, of course, make it divisible and stipulate the value of each divisible part. But there is no sign that these people so intended, see Integrity Flooring v. Zandon, supra. It follows that plaintiff, on defendants' default, could collect either in quantum meruit for what had been finished, Heine v. Meyer, 61 N.Y. 171, or in contract for the value of what plaintiff had lost—that is, the contract price, less payments made and less the cost of completion. Witherbee v. Meyer, 155 N.Y. 446, 50 N.E. 58; Washburne v. Property Owners' Cooperative Ass'n of Middlesex County, 209 App.Div. 365, 205 N.Y.S. 36, affirmed 240 N.Y. 663, 148 N.E. 749.

The judgments should be reversed, and a new trial granted, with costs to abide the event.

■ LEWIS, JUDGE (dissenting).

A contract is entire or divisible depending upon the intention of the parties to be gathered from the agreement itself and the circumstances surrounding its execution. Portfolio v. Rubin, 233 N.Y. 439, 444–445, 135 N.E. 843, 844–845; Ming v. Corbin, 142 N.Y. 334, 341, 37 N.E. 105, 107; Pierson v. Crooks, 115 N.Y. 539, 555, 22 N.E. 349, 354, 12 Am.St.Rep. 831. See, also, 3 Williston on Contracts [Rev. ed.], §§ 860A, 862.

The parties to the written agreement here in suit were careful to provide that the contract price was to be paid in specified installments which, after the initial payment, were in varying amounts payable upon completion of designated stages of the work. The contracting parties thus indicated their intent to be that the part to be performed by the plaintiff was to consist of several distinct and separate items and that the price to be paid by the defendants was to be apportioned accordingly to fall due when each specified stage of the work should be completed. Ming v. Corbin, supra, 142 N.Y. at page 340, 37 N.E. at page 107.

Concluding, as I do, that such a contract is divisible in character, see Foshay v. Robinson, 137 N.Y. 134, 137, 32 N.E. 1041; Tipton v. Feitner, 20 N.Y. 423, 430, I would affirm the judgment.

NOTES

(1) In government supply and construction contracts, there is often a long "lead time" between the beginning of work and final delivery or completion where the contractor is uncompensated for partial performance expenditures. To alleviate the impact of this on the contractor's financial position, the government will make progress payments based upon costs incurred. In construction contracts the contractor will be paid 80% of its costs incurred at various stages of performance (compare *New Era Homes*), and in supply contracts the payments are made "as work progresses, from time to time upon request." The payments are liquidated from amounts due as construction is completed or the supplies are delivered.

(2) Suppose, in *New Era Homes,* the owner had agreed to pay 80% of the contractor's total cost at each stage of completion rather than a fixed amount. Would the contract have been divisible? Should the contractor be satisfied by an action "on the contract" to recover just 80% of his cost incurred?

Comment: Breach of Construction Contract and the "Components" Approach

New Era Homes presents a classic case of breach by the Owner while a Contractor is in the midst of performing a construction contract. Unless the contract is divisible or Contractor has "substantially" performed, an action for the agreed price for the job will not lie. Furthermore, any performance by Contractor after the breach is normally out of the question (the work is being done on Owner's land) and, in any event, would probably run afoul of the mitigation principle. See, e.g., Rockingham County v. Luten Bridge Co., 35 F.2d 301 (4th Cir.1929)(unreasonable expenditures in performance incurred after the breach not recoverable). Put another way, Contractor would probably be unable to recover for any work done after the breach. What damages can Contractor recover?

1. *A Useful Formula. New Era Homes* stated that the plaintiff "could collect either in quantum meruit for what had been finished ... or in contract for what plaintiff had lost—that is, the contract price, less payments made and less the cost of completion." Leaving the quantum meruit or "restitution" recovery aside for the moment, the damage recovery can be illustrated as follows. If the contract price was $3,075 and, at the time of the breach, the estimated cost to complete the project was $425 (savings realized by breach, SR), and Contractor had been paid $2,000 in progress payments, the damages for breach would be $3,075 (KP) less $425 (SR) less $2,000 (PP) = $650. This figure will be enhanced if Contractor can prove other losses, including incidental or consequential damages, and, of course, Owner can always attack Contractor's attempt to prove the savings realized by the breach, here $425. See generally Patterson, *Builder's Measure of Recovery for Breach of Contract,* 31 Colum.L.Rev. 1286 (1931).

Note that the remainder above, $650, covers both the gain prevented by the breach and performance expenditures incurred up to the breach. Assume, in our example, that Owner had made no payments under the contract and that the cost to complete (SR) was $425. The remainder, after subtracting $425 from $3,075, $2,650, should be broken down into components for a more through analysis, i.e., what part of the $2,650 represents net profit prevented, what part represents costs incurred up to the breach and, of those costs incurred, what part is variable and what part is fixed (overhead) costs? Suppose, then, that the value of the total costs incurred (TCI) at the time of breach was $2,500. The net profit prevented should be determined by subtracting from $3,075 (KP) the sum of $425 (SR) and $2,500 (TCI) for a profit figure of $150. When this is added to the TCI figure of $2,500, the total recovery for breach of contract is still $2,650. A more thorough breakdown might try to distinguish between fixed and variable costs in the $2,500 TCI figure, especially since Owner may claim that Contractor did not exercise reasonable efforts to salvage materials purchased or to reallocate labor after the breach. If Owner is correct, the TCI figure might be reduced in the amount that would have been realized if a reasonable salvage had been effected. For a fuller exploration of these complexities, see Colorado Environments, Inc. v. Valley Grading Corp., 105 Nev. 464, 779 P.2d 80 (1989).

In the example above, the damages, whether expressed in a lump sum or components, protect both the expectation and the reliance interests. Put more directly, Contractor cannot be put in the place Owner's full performance would have put it unless it recovers both net gains prevented and unreimbursed expenses in part performance. In addition, Contractor should have the opportunity to plead and prove consequential damages resulting from the breach which were foreseeable to the defendant at the time of contracting. See Independent Mechanical Contractors, Inc. v. Gordon T. Burke & Sons, Inc., 138 N.H. 110, 635 A.2d 487 (1993)(profits lost in other ventures).

Comment: Reliance Damages or Restitution as Alternatives to Expectation Damages

Because of difficulties of proof or otherwise, a contractor or other performer may prove expenditures in part performance up to the breach but not try to prove lost profits. In this situation, the evidence will include the total cost incurred (TCI) but not savings realized (SR). Without more, Contractor can, as an alternative, recover reliance expenditures. See, e.g., United States v. Behan, 110 U.S. 338, 4 S.Ct. 81, 28 L.Ed. 168 (1884); Restatement (Second) § 349 (includes reliance expenses in preparation or part-performance); Fuller & Perdue, *The Reliance Interest in Contract Damages*, 46 Yale L.J. 52, 76–80 (1936). See also Crespi, *Recovering Pre-contractual Expenditures as an Element of Reliance Damages*, 49 S.M.U. L.Rev. 43 (1995)(supports recovery of pre-contract reliance expenditures).

The defendant, however, may prove that if Contractor had completed performance there would have been a loss. For example, in the construction hypothetical above Owner may prove that Contractor's savings realized by the breach were $2,000 and that the total costs of performing a $3,075 contract would have been $4,500. In that case, there would have been a losing contract. Contractor is obviously foreclosed from recovering any profit and the reliance expenditures should be adjusted downward in proportion to the projected loss. See Bausch & Lomb Inc. v. Bressler, 977 F.2d 720, 729 (2d Cir.1992), where the court stated: "If the breaching party establishes that the plaintiff's losses upon full performance would have equalled or exceeded its reliance expenditures, the plaintiff will recover nothing under a reliance theory."

It is at this point that the "quantum meruit" or restitution alternative becomes relevant. If the plaintiff can cancel the contract for material breach and prove that the defendant has been benefited by part performance, can the plaintiff recover the value of that part performance without limitation by the contract price?

In a provocative article, Professor Robert Childres argued that use of the term "restitution" obscures the fact that the plaintiff is frequently seeking to recover for reliance in part performance of the breached contract rather than to disgorge benefits unjustly retained by the defendant. If the latter were true, such as the case where money was paid or property delivered, no one suggests that the plaintiff ought to receive less than the full amount retained. The same is generally true where the defendant has benefited from services actually rendered and retained; restitution here is in the form of a quantum meruit. But when the plaintiff seeks the reasonable value of reliance expenditures and that value exceeds the contract price, there is no apparent reason why the contract price should not control the outer limits of that recovery. Childres said:

> There is no justification for the position that the terms of the promise do not regulate the recovery of reliance damages in some cases which may be twisted into an "action in *quantum meruit*." A promise excites expectations and causes reliance, for both of which the law should justly give protection. The crucial question * * * is whether or not the promise which was relied upon, being the *provocateur* of the reliance, will regulate the damages recoverable in event of a breach. * * * By way of example, a firm agrees to manufacture X number of rifles for the government at Y unit price. After the government requires that performance cease, the firm seeks five times Y for each rifle delivered, saying that this was the reasonable value of what it did. The argument is an attempt to entirely upset the parties' original business arrangement. If freedom of contract means freedom to deviate from the standards of reasonable men, fully informed, and enjoying levels of knowledge and intelligence to be expected in the situation, it can have no more fertile field than that of allocating market and other relevant risks in a business transaction. Specifically, the parties' own allocation of the market and other risks should be upset, if at all, by substantive doctrine and not by whether one chooses the label "quantum meruit" * * * on the one hand, or "reliance damages" on the other.

On the relevant "substantive doctrine," Professor Childres states:

> There is no reason why "aggrieved" persons should, by the contract law of damages, be put in a better position than they would have occupied had they performed; secondly, the agreed market and risk allocations should not be upset by the often unclear question of who was in breach; and thirdly, the law should not encourage those who misspeculate to escape obligation by claiming that the other person is, for some contrived reason, in breach.

Childres & Garmella, *The Law of Restitution and the Reliance Interest in Contract*, 64 Nw.L.Rev. 433, 439–41, 445–46 (1969). See also Mather, *Restitution as a Remedy for Breach of Contract: The Case of the Partially Performing Seller*, 92 Yale L.J. 14 (1982), who argues that the partially performing "seller's" recovery should be "limited" to expectancy damages, a conclusion which is "derived from liberal principles of justice, which usually impel courts to protect personal liberty and minimize coercion * * *." 92 Yale L.J. at 48. Another case which struggles with the contract price as a limitation upon restitution recovery is Constantino v. American S/T Achilles, 580 F.2d 121 (4th Cir.1978).

Under the Restatement (Second) one of the interests protected upon breach is called the "restitution" interest, which is the aggrieved party's interest "in having restored to him any benefit that he has conferred on the other party." Restatement (Second) § 344(c). In protecting this interest, a court might enter a judgment or order "requiring restoration of a specific thing to prevent unjust enrichment" or "awarding a sum of money to prevent unjust enrichment." Restatement (Second) § 345(c) & (d). But the plaintiff is entitled to restitution "only to the extent that he has conferred a benefit on the other party by way of part performance or reliance." Section 370. This is in sharp contrast to the measure of damages designed to protect the expectation interest, e.g., the "loss in the value to him of the other party's performance caused by its failure or deficiency." Section 347(a). See Simon, *A Critique of the Treatment of Market Damages in the Restatement (Second) of Contracts*, 81 Colum.L.Rev. 80 (1981). Compare Hudec, *Restating the Reliance Interest*, 67 Cornell L.Rev. 704 (1982). When, then, is a contractor or seller of goods and services entitled to restitution as a remedy for breach by the other? Section 373(1) provides that "on a breach by nonperformance that gives rise to a claim for damages for total breach or on a repudiation, the injured party is entitled to restitution for any benefit that he has conferred on the other party by way of part performance or reliance."

Are there any limitations? Here is one: "The injured party has no right to restitution if he has performed all of his duties under the contract and no performance by the other party remains due other than payment of a definite sum of money for that performance." See John T. Brady & Co. v. City of Stamford, 220 Conn. 432, 599 A.2d 370, 376–79 (1991). The contract price is not otherwise a limitation, however, and, in theory at least, the plaintiff can recover the full amount of the benefit conferred even though it would have been a losing contract had there been no breach. See Section

373, Comment d. A possible limitation, however, lies in the measure of the restitution interest. Section 371 provides:

> If a sum of money is awarded to protect a party's restitution interest, it may as justice requires be measured by either (a) the reasonable value to the other party of what he received in terms of what it would have cost him to obtain it from a person in the claimant's position, or (b) the extent to which the other party's property has been increased in value or his other interests advanced.

How is a court to exercise this choice when, say, the market price to have similar work done is $2,000 and the increase in value to the property is $1,500? One suggestion is that the court should award the smaller amount when the plaintiff is in breach. See Section 374 and Illustration 1 to Section 371. Another suggestion is that in making the choice in a losing contract, the court should "take account of standards of good faith and fair dealing during any negotiations leading up to the rupture of contractual relations." Restatement (Second) § 373, Comment d. The question is whether the plaintiff provoked a breach in a losing contract "in order to avoid having to perform." For a concise summary, see Perillo, *Restitution in the Second Restatement of Contracts*, 81 Colum.L.Rev. 37 (1982). For striking evidence of disagreement with the Restatement position, see *Kull, Restitution as a Remedy for Breach of Contract*, 67 S. Cal. L. Rev. 1465 (1994)(distinguishing between remedies of rescission and restitution) and Andersen, *The Restoration Interest and Damages for Breach of Contract*, 53 Md. L. Rev. 1 (1994)(restoration in excess of expectation depends upon clear proof of benefit retained).

Bernstein v. Nemeyer

Supreme Court of Connecticut, 1990.
213 Conn. 665, 570 A.2d 164.

[Plaintiffs invested $1,050,000 as limited partners in a partnership formed to purchase and renovate two apartment complexes in Houston, Texas. The plaintiffs' objectives were capital appreciation and a tax shelter for assets previously acquired. As an inducement to invest, the defendants made a negative cash flow guaranty: They promised to lend to the partnership the amount by which defined operating and financing expenses exceeded the cash receipts from normal business operations. The guaranty was limited in time and provisions were made for the defendants to recover loans made from income or the proceeds of any sale of the complexes. The plaintiffs were informed of the risk of foreclosure in a weak real estate market.

Despite good faith efforts and after loans to the partnership of $3,000,-000 under the guaranty, the defendants defaulted on their obligations to the financiers of the project. No further loans to the partnership were made. The mortgages were ultimately foreclosed and both the plaintiffs and defendants lost their entire investment.

The plaintiffs sued for rescission of the contract and restitution of their investment. The trial court denied relief, concluding inter alia that the defendant's breach of the negative cash flow guaranty was not material. The trial court also found that the plaintiff's losses resulted from a bad market rather than the defendant's breach and that, despite the breach, the plaintiffs had fully realized their tax advantages.

On appeal, the decision was affirmed. The court, speaking through Chief Justice Peters, first held that the defendant's breach was material. In short, the trial court had not given sufficient consideration to the fact that the plaintiffs had lost the substantial benefit of the bargain and that the defendant's breach was not curable.]

* * *

II

The conclusion that the defendants' nonperformance of the negative cash flow guaranty was a material breach of the partnership agreement does not, however, end our inquiry. It follows from an uncured material failure of performance that the other party to the contract is discharged from any further duty to render performances yet to be exchanged ... It does not follow that the party so discharged is automatically entitled to restitution rather than to a claim for damages. We must still determine whether, in the circumstances of this case, the trial court correctly rendered judgment in favor of the defendants because the plaintiffs have failed to prove a right to restitution of the payments that they made to the partnership. We conclude that the record sustains the judgment of the trial court on this alternate ground.

"When a court grants [the remedy of restitution] for breach, the party in breach is required to account for a benefit that has been conferred on him by the injured party.... In contrast to cases in which the court grants specific performance or awards damages as a remedy for breach, the effort is not to enforce the promise by protecting the injured party's expectation or reliance interest, but to prevent unjust enrichment of the party in breach by protecting the injured party's restitution interest. The objective is not to put the *injured* party in as good a position as he would have been in if the contract had been performed, nor even to put the injured party back in the position he would have been in if the contract had not been made; it is, rather, to put the party in breach back in the position he would have been in if the contract had not been made." (Emphasis in original.) E.A. Farnsworth, Contracts (1982) § 12.19, p. 905; 1 G. Palmer, The Law of Restitution (1978) § 4.1, p. 369; 3 Restatement (Second), Contracts §§ 344(c) and 370 (1981);[11] and see Monarch Accounting Supplies, Inc. v.

---

11. Section 344 of the Restatement (Second) of Contracts provides in relevant part: "Judicial remedies under the rules stated in this Restatement serve to protect one or more of the following interests of a promisee...."

"(c) his 'restitution interest,' which is his interest in having restored to him any benefit that he has conferred a benefit on the other party."

Prezioso, 170 Conn. 659, 665–67, 368 A.2d 6 (1976); Franks v. Lockwood, 146 Conn. 273, 278, 150 A.2d 215 (1959). When an injured party seeks an award of money to protect his restitutionary interest, any award "may as justice requires be measured by either (a) the reasonable value to the other party of what he received ... or (b) the extent to which the other party's property has been increased in value or his other interests advanced." 3 Restatement (Second), Contracts § 371 (1981).[12]

The principles of the law of restitution demonstrate that the defendants' non-performance of the negative cash loan guaranty, although a material breach of the partnership agreement, does not automatically and unconditionally entitle the plaintiffs to recover their investment in the partnership. The award of a restitutionary remedy for breach of contract depends upon a showing of what justice requires in the particular circumstances.... The decision to award a particular restitutionary remedy thus necessarily rests in the discretion of the court.

In the present litigation, the trial court could reasonably have concluded that the plaintiffs had failed to establish their right to the return of their investments. We have regularly held that it is a condition of rescission and restitution that the plaintiff offer, as nearly as possible, to place the other party in the same situation that existed prior to the execution of the contract.... The record in this case is entirely unclear about what efforts the plaintiffs made to tender back their partnership interests to the defendants before bringing this law suit. The record likewise contains no finding that the financial condition of the partnership, at the time the plaintiffs learned of the defendants' breach, was already so impoverished that a restitutionary tender would have been pointless.

Even more damaging to the plaintiffs' claim for restitution is the trial court's affirmative finding that the defendants "suffered a great loss of their own, about three million dollars, in attempting to satisfy their obligations under the contract and, specifically, the guaranty provision." This unchallenged finding of fact supports the conclusion that the plaintiffs could not have restored the defendants to their position prior to their execution of the partnership agreement. Further, it demonstrates that, despite the defendants' material breach of the partnership agreement, the defendants' property interests have not been "increased in value or [their] other interests advanced." 3 Restatement (Second), Contracts § 371(b) (1981). In short, the plaintiffs have not proven that the defendants have been unjustly enriched.

Section 370 provides: "A party is entitled to restitution under the rules stated in this Restatement only to the extent that he has conferred a benefit on the other party by way of part performance or reliance."

12. Section 371 of the Restatement (Second) of Contracts provides: "If a sum of money is awarded to protect a party's restitution interest, it may as justice requires be measured by either

"(a) the reasonable value to the other party of what he received in terms of what it would have cost him to obtain it from a person in the claimant's position, or

"(b) the extent to which the other party's property has been increased in value or his other interests advanced."

There is no error.

PROBLEM: RESTITUTION AS A REMEDY FOR BREACH

C contracted with O to construct a three-foot stone wall around three sides of O's residential lot for $30,000. It is stipulated that the contract was "entire" rather than divisible and that C was to be paid the full amount upon completion. When the wall was completed on one side of the lot, O, without warning, repudiated the contract. O claimed that C's work had increased the value of the lot by $5,000 and offered C that amount to discharge the contract. C, who had encountered unexpected problems in construction, the risk of which he assumed, had incurred costs of $25,000 up to the breach. Given the unexpected difficulties, these costs were reasonable. Experts will testify, however, that O would have had to pay $20,000 to obtain the same work from a contractor who was aware of the difficulties. C estimates that it will cost at least $25,000 to complete the project. On these facts, C should:

(a) Take the $5,000 and run;

(b) Sue "on the contract" for $25,000, his "reliance" interest;

(c) Sue in "restitution" for $20,000;

(d) None of the above.

PROBLEM: SELLER'S REMEDIES UNDER THE UCC—UCC 2–708(2) [UCC 2–821 (1997)]

Return with us now to the controversy between Slick Shoe Company and Bobo's Sports. See supra at 870. Suppose that Bobo repudiated the whole contract for 200 pairs before any of the shoes had been manufactured. Keeping in mind that the total contract price was $12,000, which included the cost of shipment to Bobo, you, as Slick's attorney, have ascertained that the following situation existed at the time Slick learned of the repudiation:

a. Slick operated in a highly competitive market. Slick manufactured several "lines" of basketball shoes and possessed an expansible and highly flexible production capacity. Even though the shoes for Bobo were a relatively new "line," Slick's production capacity could easily respond to increased demand. On the other hand, if demand slacked off, Slick could, with minimum disruption, discontinue a particular "line" and reallocate production resources to other contracts.

b. Of the total fixed costs or overhead of operating the plant, Slick had, using generally accepted accounting principles, allocated $2,000 to Bobo's contract, or, $10 per pair. These costs would have been incurred regardless of whether a contract had been entered into with Bobo.

c. The leather and other materials needed for production had been purchased for $6,000 and were being processed. Using reasonable efforts to reallocate the materials to other jobs or to sell for scrap, it appears that the materials could be salvaged for $3,500.

d. If work is stopped, Slick will "save" $8 per pair in variable costs, mostly direct labor, or $1,600, and $4 per pair, or $800, in not having to incur any costs in shipping the goods to Bobo.

e. If Slick completed performance under the repudiated contract, the shoes could be sold to a local buyer for $35 per pair, excluding transportation costs and costs incurred in arranging a resale. At no time will the general market price for these goods exceed $30 per pair.

Based upon these facts, consider the following questions:

(a) Suppose Slick wanted to complete the manufacturing process and resell the shoes to the local buyer for $35 per pair. Would this action be a failure to mitigate damages? Could Slick recover under UCC 2–706 [UCC 2–819 (1997)]? See UCC 2–704 [UCC 2–817 (1997)].

(b) Suppose that Slick completed the manufacturing and, due to a shift in demand, the shoes were now worth $60 per pair on the market. Slick then resold them for $60 and sued Bobo for $32, the "profit (including reasonable overhead) which the seller would have made from full performance by the buyer." UCC 2–708(2)[UCC 2–821(b) (1997)]. Bobo argued that since Slick had already sold the 200 pairs of shoes for $12,000, the claimed $3,200 would amount to a double recovery. On these facts, how would you counter this argument? The question is whether a court would treat Slick as a "lost volume" seller. See next case.

Locks v. Wade

Superior Court of New Jersey, Appellate Division, 1955.
36 N.J.Super. 128, 114 A.2d 875.

■ CLAPP, S.J.A.D. Defendant appeals from a county district court judgment taken against him for breach of contract. Contract and breach are admitted or assumed on appeal; the only issue is damages.

Under the contract plaintiff leased to defendant an automatic phonograph, a juke box, for two years and agreed to supply records and replace parts wearing out. Proceeds of the operation were to be shared on a specified basis, but with a minimum of $20 per week to be paid plaintiff by defendant. Defendant, it is claimed, repudiated the contract; and plaintiff never installed the machine.

The court gave plaintiff judgment for $836—that is, the sum of $20 per week for two years, less apparently the costs plaintiff would have been put to, had he performed the contract, less also depreciation on the machine.

Defendant makes two points. The first rests on plaintiff's testimony that the component parts of the very machine he had intended to lease defendant were, after the breach, rented to others. Defendant argues that the amount plaintiff thus realized should have been credited on the claim sued upon.

Defendant would have us apply here the rule obtaining on the breach of an agreement to lease realty; that is, he claims the measure of the lessor's damages here is the difference between the agreed rental and the rental value of the property. His contention further is that even though under the agreement before us, the lessor is obliged to perform some personal services, he, in order to establish the rental value, has the burden of proving what he received on a reletting. . . .

Plaintiff, passing the questions (or most of them), meets the argument by referring to his testimony, not contradicted, that:

"The equipment called for by this agreement was readily available in the market. But locations were very hard to get."

We think the position plaintiff takes on the matter is sound. Where, as here, a plaintiff lessor agrees to lease an article of which the supply in the market is for practical purposes not limited, then the law would be depriving him of the benefit of his bargain if on the breach of the agreement, it required his claim against the lessee to be reduced by the amount he actually did or reasonably could realize on a reletting of the article. For if there had been no breach and another customer had appeared, the lessor could as well have secured another such article and entered into a second lease. In case of the breach of the first lease, he should have the benefit of both bargains and not—in a situation where the profit on both would be the same—be limited to the profit on the second of them.

An illustration with figures may make this more graphic. If the agreed rental under the lease amounts to $2,040, the cost of installation and of furnishing records and parts to $500, and the depreciation on the juke box over the period of the lease to $700, the lessor stands to make $840 on the deal. If another customer presents himself, the lessor will buy another juke box, which he is entitled to enter on his books at cost and depreciate in the same way as he does with the first. Thus, if he makes the same agreement with the second customer, he will make another $840 on the second lease. If the first lessee repudiates his agreement, the purchase of an additional machine will, of course, be unnecessary, because the first machine can be leased to the second customer. In such a situation, under defendant's theory, the lessor would receive as damages for this repudiation only the $2,040 rental agreed on under the first lease, less the $2,040 rental for the same machine under the second lease, or nothing. This would leave the lessee only the $840 profit he will make under the second lease; whereas had the first lessee lived up to his bargain, the lessor's profits would have been $840 on each of two leases, or $1,680.

We conclude that the proper measure of damages here is the difference between the contract price and the cost of performing the first contract, as the court apparently held below. In the case of realty which (unlike the juke box) is specific and not to be duplicated on the market, the lessor could not properly lease it to another for the same period unless the first lease were broken or terminated. In such a case the lessor should not be awarded two profits merely because of the first lessee's default.

So in general we may say that gains made by a lessor on a lease entered into after the breach are not to be deducted from his damages unless the breach enabled him to make the gains. The recoverable damages in the case of a contract are such as may reasonably be within the contemplation of the parties at the time of the contract, Patco Products v. Wilson, 5 N.J. 543, 547, 76 A.2d 677 (1950); and with that in view, we should not in the present case deny lessor the benefit of his bargain. Contrast Zeliff v. Sabatino, 15 N.J. 70, 104 A.2d 54 (1954), referring to the rule obtaining in case of a fraud.

Restatement of Contracts § 336(c) and Illustrations 6 and 7, and 5 Corbin, Contracts, § 1041 (1951) support these propositions. Cf. 3 Williston, Sales (rev.ed.1948), § 583a. The principles, however, seem not to be widely recognized, but there are cases dealing with various sorts of contracts, which can be said to sustain them. . . .

These principles lead us logically into questions with which we have no concern here—in particular, the question as to a seller's remedy on a sale of goods where he (like the plaintiff here) has for practical purposes the capacity to supply all probable customers—a matter as to which the law may perhaps be governed by statute, R.S. 46:30–70, N.J.S.A., or by precedent, 3 Williston, Sales (rev. ed. 1948), § 583a. But see 5 Corbin, Contracts, §§ 1100, 1039 (1951). Note, too, the change in the Sales Act proposed by the Uniform Commercial Code—Sales § 2–708 (1952), also Comment 2 thereon—a matter apparently overlooked in the 1955 amendment to the section. We limit our opinion to the situation at hand.

* * *

NOTES

(1) In Neri v. Retail Marine Corp., 30 N.Y.2d 393, 334 N.Y.S.2d 165, 285 N.E.2d 311 (1972), the seller, a retailer, and the buyer, a consumer, entered into a contract for the sale of a pleasure boat at an agreed price of $12,587.40. After the seller had ordered the boat from the manufacturer, the buyer repudiated the contract. Shortly thereafter, the seller, upon taking delivery of the boat from the manufacturer, resold it to a third party for $12,587.40. In the meantime, the buyer sued to recover the initial deposit of $4,250. The seller counterclaimed to recover the profit that would have been made on the sale to the buyer, some $2,579, and incidental damages in the amount of $674. The lower courts, among other things, rejected the lost profits claim as "untenable" since the boat was later sold for the same price that the buyer had contracted to pay. On appeal, this part of the decision was reversed by the New York Court of Appeals. The retail dealer had an unlimited supply of "fixed-price" goods, i.e., goods where the price is essentially fixed by the manufacturer. In this setting, the buyer's breach "costs the dealer a sale" even though the same goods are resold to a third party without any apparent loss. Had the buyer performed the contract, the seller would have made two sales instead of one. Since the breach depletes the dealer's sales to the extent of one, he should recover the lost profit from the buyer under UCC 2–708(2). Accord: Teradyne, Inc. v. Teledyne Industries, Inc., 676 F.2d 865, 868 (1st Cir.1982); Snyder v. Herbert Greenbaum & Associates, 38 Md.App. 144, 380 A.2d 618, 624–26 (1977). See Hitz v. First Interstate Bank, 38 Cal.App.4th 274, 44 Cal.Rptr.2d 890, 895–96 (1995)(gains made on other transactions after the breach not

deductible from damages "unless such gains could not have been made, had there been no breach").

(2) *Proving Lost Volume.* Professor Robert Harris has this to say about the general problem posed in *Locks v. Wade:*

"When plaintiff resells the entity in completed form he usually deprives himself of something of value—the sale to a new buyer of another similar entity. Had there been no breach, and consequently no resale, plaintiff would have sold two similar entities—one to defendant and one to the resale purchaser. The breach and resale have reduced plaintiff's total volume of sales by the quantity rejected by defendant.

"Where there has been an actual resale of the entity prior to the trial with attendant lost volume, the value of the lost volume can be taken into account in either of two ways: (1) by adjusting the value of the subtrahend to reflect it, or (2) by treating the lost volume as incidental damage. Where there has been no such resale before trial, but damages are computed at resale value, only the first approach should be used. As will be shown shortly, the value of the lost volume is the profit plaintiff would have made on the additional sale. Plaintiff should have the burden of proving this value, but some latitude should be allowed him in proving with reasonable certainty his profit per unit.

"To take a simplified example, plaintiff is a car retailer who sells all his cars of a certain model at $3,000 and defendant-customer repudiates his contract to purchase one. Assume that resale would be attended by lost volume. The minuend is the unpaid balance of the price—$3,000 if defendant has paid nothing. The subtrahend is the resale value of the entity ($3,000), reduced by the profit plaintiff would have made on the additional sale—hypothetically $500. Deducting the adjusted subtrahend, $2,500, from the minuend, $3,000, plaintiff should recover $500 plus any incidental expenses. In this instance his recovery is identical with the profit he would have made on the contract with defendant had there been no breach, but this is not always the case. Recovery would be different from the amount of profit lost if (1) part of the price had been prepaid, (2) there were incidental damages in addition to the lost volume, or (3) resale did not occur at the same price as the contract price.

"Resale results in loss of volume only if three conditions are met: (1) the person who bought the resold entity would have been solicited by plaintiff had there been no breach and resale; (2) the solicitation would have been successful; and (3) the plaintiff could have performed that additional contract.

"The notion that 'the person who bought the resold entity would have been solicited by plaintiff to buy other wares had there been no breach and resale' can be broken down into two aspects. One is the likelihood that plaintiff would have solicited someone to buy other wares at all. If plaintiff is not a commercial seller, absent other evidence he probably would not have solicited anyone and should not get a lost volume adjustment. If he is a commercial seller, absent other facts he probably would have attempted other sales. However, even if plaintiff is a commercial seller, if he had decided to go out of business before receiving notice of defendant's breach, he would not have solicited anyone to buy other wares. Alternatively, he might have reached the limits of the volume he planned to sell. Plaintiff may have reached his limit of volume because he could not handle more business without expansion of his plant or drastic revision of his mode of doing business. Under these circumstances the court should presume that he did not intend to solicit another order. Of course, the presumption should be rebuttable by evidence that plaintiff in fact planned such expansion or revision.

"The other aspect of this first condition is the identity of the person whose business plaintiff intended to solicit. If he would not have solicited the person who actually purchased the resold entity, the condition is not met. For example, if plaintiff resold the entity in a market in which he did not ordinarily operate, the probabilities are that the resale purchaser was not someone whom plaintiff otherwise would have solicited.

"The second condition—that the resale purchaser would have purchased the entity absent breach and resale—may be evidentially supported by his actual purchase upon resale. This has probative value where the resold entity is fungible. If the purchaser had not bought this entity from plaintiff, presumably he would have purchased another like one from him. Once we depart from fungibles, however, the problem becomes more difficult. If the wares plaintiff claims he otherwise would have sold this purchaser differ in some respects from the resold entity, the court must determine whether the purchaser would have bought these other wares despite the differences.

"The car retailer situation furnishes an illustration. If a defendant refused to accept a 1966 Chevrolet of a certain color and model and it was resold to X, and plaintiff is the only Chevrolet dealer accessible to X, plaintiff probably could have sold X another 1966 Chevrolet of that model and color had X not bought the car rejected by defendant. But if plaintiff could not have obtained another Chevrolet of that color and model, and another Chevrolet dealer accessible to X could have done so, it is less likely that X would have bought a different car from plaintiff. Assuming for the moment that price and other terms would be identical, it is more likely that X would have purchased his car from the other Chevrolet dealer. Of course, if X is identified, there may be other evidence that he would have preferred to deal with plaintiff rather than another dealer, even if this meant buying a different model or color. But absent such other evidence, the second condition is not satisfied.

"Where it is shown that plaintiff was unable to perform an additional contract with X—that is, the third condition is not met—obviously no volume has been lost that would not have been lost even without breach and resale."

Harris, *A Radical Restatement of the Laws of Seller's Damages: Sales Act and Commercial Code Results Compared*, 18 Stan.L.Rev. 66, 80–83 (1965). [Copyright 1965 by the Board of Trustees of the Leland Stanford Junior University.]

Comment: The Lost Volume Seller Under UCC Article 2

Suppose that Seller contracts to manufacture and sell a specified piece of medical diagnosis equipment to Buyer for $500,000. After the goods were finished and identified to the contract, Buyer breached by refusing to accept delivery. What are Seller's remedial options under the 1995 Official Text of Article 2?

First, since Buyer did not accept the goods, Seller cannot recover the price unless a reasonable resale is not available. Seller must prove that it is "unable after reasonable effort to resell them at a reasonable price or the circumstances reasonably indicate that such effort will be unavailing." UCC 2–709(1)(b)[UCC 2–822(a) (1997)(same)].

Second, Seller could resell the goods under UCC 2–706 [UCC 2–819(a) (1997)]. Assuming that the resale conditions are satisfied, Seller "may recover the difference between the resale price and the contract price together with any incidental damages ... but less expenses saved in consequence of the buyer's breach."

Third, whether or not the goods are resold, Seller can claim damages under UCC 2–708(1) [UCC 2–821(a) (1997)] measured by the "difference between the market price at the time and place for tender and the unpaid contract price, together with any incidental damages ... but less expenses saved in consequence of the buyer's breach."

Fourth, Seller can claims that damages under UCC 2–708(1) [UCC 2–821(a) (1997)] are "inadequate" to put it "in as good a position as performance would have done" and that it is entitled to damages measured by the "profit (including reasonable overhead) which the seller would have made from full performance by the buyer, together with any incidental damages ..., due allowance for costs reasonably incurred and due credit for payments or proceeds of resale" under UCC 2–708(2).

As suggested by the *Neri* case, supra, the lost volume problem arises when Seller resells the goods for roughly the contract price. There is, in fact, no difference between the resale price or its surrogate the relevant market price. Invoking the lost volume principle, Seller claims that neither the resale nor the contract price-market price measure are adequate to protect the expectation interest and that damages for Buyer's breach should be measured under UCC 2–708(2).

This argument has been accepted by the courts. See *R.E. Davis Chemical Corp. v. Diasonics, Inc.*, 826 F.2d 678 (7th Cir.1987), a leading case which reviews the authorities. *Davis*, however, is less strict than some in determining when there is a lost volume seller: "[A] lost volume seller ... has a predictable and finite number of customers and ... has the capacity either to sell to all new buyers or to make the one additional sale represented by the resale the breach." If the seller "would have made the sale represented by the resale whether or not the breach occurred, damages measured by the difference between the contract price and the market price cannot put the lost volume seller in as good a position as it would have been in had the buyer performed." On the other hand, Davis adds a restriction found in the law and economics literature but not in the other cases. In addition to whether Seller could have produced the additional item is the question "whether it would have been profitable for the seller to produce both units." Thus, the case was remanded for Seller to establish "not only that it had the capacity to produce the breached unit in addition to the unit resold, but also that it would have been profitable for it to have produced and sold both." See R.E. Davis Chemical Corp. v. Diasonics, Inc., 924 F.2d 709 (7th Cir.1991).

How does one measure the profit on the breached contract under UCC 2–708(2) and whether it would have been profitable to produce and sell both units? Here is a suggestion. First, determine the profit from the breached contract by subtracting the total variable costs of performance from the contract price. The resulting "profit (including reasonable overhead) from full performance" is not adjusted by deducting any "proceeds of resale." As the cases, including *Davis*, have held, the "proceeds of resale" language in UCC 2–708(2) does not apply to the lost volume calculation. Next, subtract the total variable costs that would have been incurred in producing the next unit from the contract price of that unit. This measures the profit including overhead from the second sale. Finally, if the profit on the second sale is less than the profit on the first, make an appropriate adjustment in the first sale profit. For example, an appropriate adjustment is made if the contract prices for both sales are added together and the total variable costs from producing two units are subtracted. If variable costs for the second unit are higher, they will reduce the profit figure. See John M. Breen, *The Lost Volume Seller and Lost Profits Under UCC 2–708(2): A Conceptual, Linguistic Critique*, 50 U. Miami L. Rev. 779 (1996).

Lost Volume under Revised Article 2. Under UCC 2–821, dealing with Seller's Damages for Nonacceptance, Failure to Pay or Repudiation, the seller can choose between damages measured by the contract price less the market price under subsection (a) or lost profits under subsection (b). There is no requirement that damages under (a) must be inadequate before the seller can claim damages under (b). Under UCC 2–803(c), however, a court may deny or limit the remedy chosen "if, under the circumstances, it would put the aggrieved party in a substantially better position than if the other party had fully performed." If the choice of (b) is appropriate, there is no attempt to solve the "lost volume" problem. Rather, damages are measured as follows: "(b) A seller may recover damages measured by other than the market price including: (1) lost profits, including reasonable overhead, resulting from the breach of contract determined in any reasonable manner, together with incidental and consequential damages; and (2) reasonable expenditures made in preparing for or performing the contract if, after the breach, the seller is unable to obtain reimbursement by salvage, resale, or other reasonable measures."

PROBLEM: SELLER'S REMEDIES UNDER UCC 2–708(2) CONTINUED

In the case of Bobo's Sports, suppose that Bobo repudiated while Slick was in the middle of performing the $12,000 contract to manufacture shoes. The resale market was very bad and Slick, in the exercise of commercial judgment under UCC 2–704 [UCC 2–817 (1997)], stopped work. At this point, the following facts are clear:

1. Slick's accountant had allocated $2,000 in fixed costs or overhead to the contract.

2.   Slick will save $800 in not having to ship the goods to Bobo.

3.   Slick had incurred $6,000 in expenses at the time of the breach, all in leather and materials needed for production. Slick can sell the materials on hand to a third party for $3,500.

4.   Slick estimated that he would have spent $2,000 more to perform the contract, most of it on labor.

5.   The market price for the shoes at the time and place for tender was $6,000.

(a) Would Bobo be successful in a claim that Slick's damages were determined by UCC 2–708(1)[UCC 2–821(a) (1997)]? Why not?

(b) How much should Slick recover under UCC 2–708(2) [UCC 2–821(b)]? Professor Sebert has suggested that the formula in this case (no lost volume) should be: "Unpaid contract price less total variable costs, plus incidental damages, plus costs reasonably incurred, less proceeds of resale, and less the market value of goods retained." 130 U.Pa.L.Rev. 360 at 412. Doesn't this make sense?

PROBLEM: THE SCOPE OF UCC 2–708(1)

Seller, a middleman or jobber, agrees on January 2, 1991 to supply 9,000 units of goods to Buyer in six semi-annual installments over a three-year period. The parties agree on a fixed price of $100 per unit and the first delivery was scheduled for July 1, 1991. At the time of contracting, Seller had neither units on hand nor forward contracts to purchase them from manufacturers. Seller delivered and Buyer paid for 1,500 units on July 1, 1991. At that time, the retail market price at the place of tender was $95 per unit. Shortly thereafter, the market started a steep decline and, by December 1, 1991, the retail price per unit was $45. On that date, Buyer repudiated the contract. At that time, Seller had a forward contract with a manufacturer to purchase 1,500 units for the next installment at $75 per unit. Seller had no other goods on hand or forward contracts. On January 2, 1992, when the retail market price per unit was $40, Seller tendered but Buyer rejected the second installment. Buyer reiterated that it would take no more deliveries under the contract. Seller sued Buyer for damages in March, 1992. On July 1, 1992, the relevant retail market price per unit was $50, but economists were hopeful that it would gradually recover over the next two years. The case came to trial in September, 1992. Seller's attorney insisted that it was entitled to use UCC 2–708(1) [UCC 2–821(a) (1997)] as a basis for recovery.

You are Buyer's attorney and are persuaded that UCC 2–708(1) [UCC 2–821(a) (1997)] will overcompensate Seller. Prepare a memo for the court that defends that position and presents an alternative approach. See UCC 1–106(1), 2–711 through 2–723. See also UCC 2–803(c) (1997).

Comment: Employee's Remedies for Breach of Employment Contract

If, in a contract for personal services, the employee has done the work and the employer fails to pay, the remedy is clear: the employee may sue for the agreed price. But suppose the employer repudiates the contract before work commences or terminates employment while work is under-way. In the absence of a divisible contract, what damages may be recovered here? In all probability, the employee will stop work after the termination and consider or make some effort to find substitute employment. Does this mean that the employee's claim for damages will be treated like that in a construction contract or a contract for the sale of goods?

The answer is "not quite." Most courts have rejected the "constructive" service doctrine, which stated that a wrongfully discharged employee who remained ready and able to perform could recover the full amount of the agreed wage without any "duty" to mitigate damages. See Howard v. Daly, 61 N.Y. 362, 19 Am.Rep. 285 (1875); Murray § 12.12. But a vestige of this rule remains.

> The general rule is that the measure of recovery by a wrongfully discharged employee is the amount of salary agreed upon for the period of service, less the amount which the employer affirmatively proves the employee has earned or with reasonable effort might have earned from other employment.

Parker v. Twentieth Century–Fox Film Corp., 3 Cal.3d 176, 89 Cal.Rptr. 737, 474 P.2d 689, 692 (1970). This varies from the usual rule, which allows damages based upon the "loss in the value to him of the other party's performance . . . less . . . any cost or other loss that he has avoided by not having to perform." Restatement (Second) § 347. In short, the discharged employee is not required to prove what savings were realized by the breach in order to establish damages. The employer, on the other hand, has the burden of proving that the employee failed to mitigate damages. Assuming that the employee will be paid for any work done, the amount that he or she reasonably could have obtained from other employment will be the measure of any savings realized over the balance of the contract.

There are a number of interesting problems around the fringes of this rule.

First, under what circumstances will the employee's failure to look for or refusal to take substitute employment constitute a failure to mitigate damages? According to the *Parker* case:

> However, before projected earnings from other employment opportunities not sought or accepted by the discharged employee can be applied in mitigation, the employer must show that the other employment was comparable, or substantially similar, to that of which the employee has been deprived; the employee's rejection of or failure to seek other available employment of a different or inferior kind may not be resorted to in order to mitigate damages. 89 Cal.Rptr. at 740, 474 P.2d at 692.

Whether the possible substitute employment was "different or inferior" or the employee's efforts to find it were reasonable are, in the main, questions of fact for each case. See, e.g., Ryan v. Superintendent of Schools of Quincy, 374 Mass. 670, 373 N.E.2d 1178 (1978) (failure of discharged art teacher to find work justified on facts).

Second, suppose, after the discharge, the employee actually finds and takes another job. Is the employer automatically entitled to deduct that income from the damages? Although the answers are not entirely clear, if "but for" the breach the employee would not have had the time, capacity or energy to take the second job, the answer is yes. This will turn on the nature and demands of the job from which the employee was discharged and whether the second job could have been undertaken without interfering with the employment promised by the defaulting employer. It goes without saying that if the employee is already "moonlighting" or engaged in some business at the time of discharge, the income from those existing activities should not be deducted.

Third, suppose the employee is not able to find suitable employment and is paid unemployment or similar benefits. Should those payments, which are a form of employment substitute, be deducted from damages? Restatement (Second) § 347, Comment e properly identifies this as a problem of collateral source, suggests that deducting the benefits from "collateral sources is less compelling in the case of a breach of contract than in the case of tort" and concludes that the answer "will turn on the court's perception of legislative policy rather than on the rule stated" in Section 347. Professor Fleming, however, has argued that legislative policy will invariably be inconclusive and that tort policies argue against deduction even for breach of contract.

> Wrongful dismissal is simply not a breach of contract which courts will view with the detachment advocated by apologists of the 'efficient' breach; its potentially devastating effect on the employee is attested by the pejorative use of the term 'wrongful' from the tort vocabulary; and the collateral source rule is justified both by the need for deterrence and by the feeling that mere indemnity for his net economic loss does not compensate the employee for all his injury, emotional as well as pecuniary.

Fleming, *The Collateral Source Rule and Contract Damages,* 71 Cal.L.Rev. 56, 81 (1983). For a well reasoned case refusing to deduct from damages the disability payments made to a wrongfully discharged employee, see Seibel v. Liberty Homes, Inc., 305 Or. 362, 752 P.2d 291 (1988).

Finally, can the employee recover punitive damages for a wrongful discharge? The answer to this question is probably no in most states. See Chapter Six Section 2A, supra.

(C) Breach or Repudiation by Performer

We now turn to the "flip" side, i.e., where the breach is of a promise to sell and deliver goods or land, construct a home or perform personal or professional services rather than a promise to accept and pay for the performance. Here the statement of remedial policy remains constant, but its application may vary in the different contexts. For example, the plaintiff may have a greater opportunity to obtain specific performance of the defendant's promise to perform. Furthermore, the recovery of consequential losses becomes more important where the failure to deliver goods or to perform services prevents or disrupts a planned profitable use of the performance. Thus, if a seller has failed to deliver goods that the buyer had planned to use in an operating business, the damages may include both the extra costs incurred in obtaining substitute goods from a third party ("direct" damages) and any profits lost because of the delay in obtaining the substitute ("consequential" damages). These issues lurked in *The Case of the Recalcitrant Manufacturer,* supra at 40. At this point, please review your analysis and conclusions in that problem, paying particular attention to the relevant UCC damage provisions. We will use the problem as a model throughout this subsection.

(1) DIRECT DAMAGES

Reliance Cooperage Corp. v. Treat

United States Court of Appeals, Eighth Circuit, 1952.
195 F.2d 977.

[On July 12, 1950, Reliance and Treat entered a written contract under which Treat agreed to produce and deliver 300,000 "white oak bourbon staves" not later than December 31, 1950. The price was $450 per thousand, f.o.b. freight cars "nearest millsite where staves were produced." Between the middle and the end of August, 1950, Treat, by letter* and over the telephone, apparently repudiated the contract. On October 6, 1950, Reliance informed Treat by letter that they were not "confident" that Treat would perform and that they would hold him to "strict compliance with the contract." Treat never replied and, in fact, delivered no staves to Reliance under the contract.

Reliance sued Treat for damages. At the trial, Treat, over Reliance's objection, testified that the price of bourbon staves began to advance beyond $450 a thousand around the last of August. On cross-examination, however, Treat conceded that a more accurate August price for staves was

---

* It was admitted that the defendant had on August 12, 1950, sent to Ralph Ettlinger, an officer of the plaintiff, the following letter:

"Marshall, Arkansas

August 12, 1950

"Dear Mr. Ralph Ettlinger:

"I have been trying to get a letter to you for some time but they return to me. I went to Harrison yesterday and got Tom Burns Co. adress trying to get in touch with you. We got a mill at Hallaster, Mo. trying to get started. Have a few Bolts will have a time getting any more. I can't make these staves up there or any where else at the price I haft to pay for Bolts. Every one else are paying $475.00 to $500.00 per M. You see I can't compete with them so if you want those staves I will haft to get around what ever the market is from time to time. You can see you seff that I can get bolts say 70a price when others paying $100.00 per foot. I think the boys can make a lot of staves fast up there if they can pay as much as others are paying if not they will haft to quit. Now you can see where I am at. The other to co. that I am making for with my other 3 mills have raised from $75.00 to $100.00 on the 1000 4½" staves and said they would cancel out as the market raises. So you do just what you want to. I can't make them unless I can buy the timber so let me hear at once. I will have a car before long.

"Yours as ever,

A.R. Treat."

$525 per thousand. Treat also testified that he got $625 per thousand for staves toward the end of December. The evidence, however, would sustain a finding that the market price for staves on December 31, 1950 was more than the contract price but not in excess of $750 a thousand.]

■ SANBORN, CIRCUIT JUDGE.

* * *

At the close of the evidence, the court was requested by the plaintiff to instruct the jury that the plaintiff was entitled to recover the difference between the contract price of the staves the defendant had promised to deliver on or before December 31, 1950, and the market price of similar staves on that date. The court denied the request.

The jury was instructed substantially as follows: That the undisputed facts made a prima facie case of liability against the defendant for damages based upon the difference, if any, between the contract price of $450.00 per thousand staves and the market price as of December 31, 1950. That the defendant contended that he had repudiated the contract prior to that date and that it was the plaintiff's duty to mitigate its damages by purchasing the staves elsewhere. That the burden of proving his contentions was upon the defendant. That the jury was to determine whether the defendant did in fact repudiate his contract prior to December 31, 1950, and, if so, when the repudiation occurred, and whether, after such repudiation, the plaintiff by a reasonable effort could have mitigated its damages by the purchase of the staves on the open market, and whether the damages could have been completely or partially mitigated. That if, on a date prior to December 31, 1950, the defendant definitely and unequivocally advised the plaintiff that he would not deliver any staves under the contract, this would be a breach of the contract by him as of that date; and that if, after the repudiation, the plaintiff, by a reasonable effort and without undue risk or expense, could have purchased the staves on the open market at a price equal to the contract price, it was the plaintiff's duty to do so, and that the plaintiff would, in that event, be entitled to nominal damages only. That if the plaintiff by a reasonable effort and without undue risk or expense, after the repudiation, if any, by the defendant of the contract prior to December 31, 1950, could have purchased the staves on the open market at a price in excess of the contract price, then it was the plaintiff's duty to do that and mitigate its damages so far as possible, and the plaintiff would then be entitled to damages only for the difference between the market price of the staves at that time and the contract price. That if the jury failed to find that there was a breach of the contract by the defendant prior to December 31, 1950, the plaintiff was entitled to the difference between the market price of the staves on that date and the contract price.

The plaintiff objected to the instructions relating to the duty of the plaintiff to mitigate damages, and to the right of the defendant to repudiate the contract prior to December 31, 1950.

The jury returned a verdict for the plaintiff and assessed its damages at $500.00. The plaintiff appealed from the judgment entered on the verdict.

We gather from the court's instructions that its opinion was that if the defendant had definitely notified the plaintiff prior to December 31, 1950, that he would not produce and deliver staves under the contract, and that if the plaintiff, notwithstanding its insistence that the contract be fulfilled, by a reasonable effort and without undue risk or expense could then have bought similar staves on the market, the measure of its damages would be the difference between what the plaintiff would have had to pay for staves at the time the defendant announced his refusal of performance and the contract price of such staves.

* * *

There is no doubt that a party to an executory contract such as that in suit may refuse to accede to an anticipatory repudiation of it and insist upon performance, and, if he does so, the contract remains in existence and is binding on both parties, and no actionable claim for damages arises until the time for performance expires. . . .

It is our opinion that, under the undisputed facts in this case, the unaccepted anticipatory renunciation by the defendant of his obligation to produce and deliver staves under the contract did not impair that obligation or affect his liability for damages for the nonperformance of the contract, and that the measure of those damages was no different than it would have been had no notice of renunciation been given by the defendant to the plaintiff. If there had been no anticipatory repudiation of the contract, the measure of damages for nonperformance by the seller would have been the difference between the contract price and the market price of the staves on the date when delivery was due, and that is the measure which should have been applied in assessing damages in this case.

Moreover, the measure of damages would have been the same had the plaintiff accepted the anticipatory repudiation as an actionable breach of the contract. The plaintiff would still have been entitled to recover what it had lost by reason of the defendant's failure to produce and deliver by December 31, 1950, the staves contracted for, namely, the difference between the market price and the contract price of the staves on that date. The Comment in Restatement of the Law of Contracts, § 338, Measure of Damages for Anticipatory Breach, contains the following statement (page 549): "The fact that an anticipatory repudiation is a breach of contract (see § 318) does not cause the repudiated promise to be treated as if it were a promise to render performance at the date of the repudiation. Repudiation does not accelerate the time fixed for performance; nor does it change the damages to be awarded as the equivalent of the promised performance." See, also, Williston on Contracts, Rev.Ed. Vol. 5, § 1397; 46 Am.Jur., Sales, § 688.

It seems safe to say that ordinarily no obligation to mitigate damages arises until there are damages to mitigate. No damages for the nonperformance of the contract in suit accrued before December 31, 1950. Until that time the defendant, notwithstanding his anticipatory repudiation of the contract, was obligated and was at liberty to produce and deliver the staves, and had he done so the plaintiff would have been required to take and to pay for them. There is no justification for ruling that, after the plaintiff was advised that the defendant did not intend to perform, it must hold itself in readiness to accept performance from him and at the same time, at its own risk and expense, buy the staves contracted for upon the open market in the hope of reducing the defendant's liability for damages in case he persisted in his refusal to fulfill his obligations. The plaintiff did nothing to enhance its damages and seeks no special damages.

This same question as to mitigation of damages by a purchaser who insisted upon performance of a contract after a seller's anticipatory repudiation, arose in Continental Grain Co. v. Simpson Feed Co., D.C.E.D.Ark., 102 F.Supp. 354 (tried in the Eastern District of Arkansas). In that case Judge Lemley, we think, correctly decided that the purchaser was not required to attempt to mitigate his damages by buying the commodity contracted for upon the open market. Judge Lemley said, page 363 of 102 F.Supp.:

"* * * There are two reasons for this rule. First, to require the innocent party to make an immediate purchase or sale upon receipt of notice of the other's repudiation would encourage such repudiation on the part of the seller or of the buyer as the market rose or fell. See Fahey v. Updike Elevator Co., supra. Second, the immediate action of the innocent party might not have the effect of mitigating his damages, but might, on the other hand, enhance them. Williston on Contracts, Section 1397, Callan v. Andrews, and Missouri Furnace Co. v. Cochran, both supra."

The doctrine of anticipatory breach by repudiation is intended to aid a party injured as a result of the other party's refusal to perform his contractual obligations, by giving to the injured party an election to accept or to reject the refusal of performance without impairing his rights or increasing his burdens. Any effort to convert the doctrine into one for the benefit of the party who, without legal excuse, has renounced his agreement should be resisted.

The plaintiff is entitled to recover as damages the amount by which on December 31, 1950, the market price of the staves contracted for exceeded their contract price. What the market price of such staves was on that date is a question of fact which has not as yet been determined.

The judgment is reversed and the case is remanded with directions to grant a new trial limited to the issue of the amount of damages.

NOTES

(1)(a) Suppose Reliance, on September 1, 1950, had canceled the contract for breach and purchased 300,000 barrel staves at $525 per thousand from another producer. On December 31, 1950, the market price had dropped back to $450 per thousand. What damages? See UCC 2–712 [UCC 2–825 (1997)].

Note that the cost of "cover" rather than the relevant market price determines the damages. If the buyer does not cover in fact, should damages be limited to the market price when the buyer should have covered? What policies support this result?

(b) Suppose, above, that the market price had risen to $750 per thousand on December 31, 1950. Instead of suing for "cover" damages under UCC 2–712 [UCC 2–825 (1997)], Reliance sued under UCC 2–713(1) [UCC 2–826(a) (1997)]. What result? What is the strongest argument for Treat?

(2) Evaluate the following analysis of the *Treat* case from the standpoint of the 1995 Official Text of Article 2 of the UCC:

(a) The UCC does not define what a repudiation is. This is presumably left to other principles of contract law in the state. UCC 1–103. But see UCC 2–609(4). The UCC does, however, prescribe the remedial alternatives available to the buyer upon a repudiation by the seller. UCC 2–610 & 2–711(1).

(b) The seller did not retract his repudiation before the time for performance arrived. Cf. UCC 2–611(1). Since the buyer is seeking direct rather than consequential damages, there is no affirmative UCC requirement that it seek to mitigate damages by "covering" on the open market. Even so, "covering" in an unstable market might not be a reasonable responsibility to impose because of the risk involved. Cf. UCC 2–715(2)(a). However, after repudiation by the seller, the buyer is privileged to await performance by the seller for only "a commercially reasonable time." UCC 2–610(a). What does this mean?

(c) The answer to this question depends upon how you read UCC 2–713, dealing with buyer's damages for repudiation. First, the special rule for measuring repudiation damages set out in UCC 2–723(1) does not apply here. The action did not come to trial before the time for performance arose. Thus, the measure must be determined from UCC 2–713(1). Second, the measure for repudiation by the seller is "the difference between the market price at the time when the buyer learned of the breach and the contract price * * *." The use of the phrase "learned of the breach" rather than "learned of the repudiation" is critical. Given the policy of UCC 2–610(a) and the language of UCC 2–723(1), choice of the word "breach" suggests a time for measurement *later* than the time when the buyer first heard of the repudiation. Third, without more, since the buyer elected not to treat the repudiation as a breach, it first "learned of the breach" when the seller failed to deliver the goods in December. Market price, therefore, should be measured as of the December delivery date at the "place for tender." UCC 2–713(2). This result is consistent with the *Treat* case. See J. White & R. Summers, Uniform Commercial Code § 6–7 (4th ed. 1995).

(d) This analysis, however, flies in the face of the language in UCC 2–610(a). Permitting a buyer to wait a commercially reasonable time affords time to assess the seriousness of the seller's repudiation and legitimate business needs of the aggrieved party. Once that time has expired, the buyer's losses should be measured at the time when it *should* have covered on the open market. While not required actually to risk covering, the buyer should not be permitted to profit or to lose on a shifting market between the time that the commercially reasonable time expired and the agreed time for performance. Otherwise, speculation and unrealistic measurement of loss would be encouraged and the objective of efficient loss avoidance would be undercut. Accord: Cosden Oil v. Karl O. Helm Aktiengesellschaft, 736 F.2d 1064 (5th Cir.1984); Jackson, *"Anticipatory Repudiation" and the Temporal Element of Contract Law: An Economic Inquiry into Contract Damages in Cases of Prospective Nonperformance,* 31 Stan.L.Rev. 69 (1978) (damages should be measured at or near time the buyer "learned" of repudiation).

(e) On the other hand, if the buyer decides to "cover" before a commercially reasonable time expires, damages will be measured under UCC 2–712(1).

(f) **Revised Article 2.** See UCC 2–826(a)(2) (1997): "Subject to Section 2–812 [proof of market price], if a seller breaches a contract, the buyer may recover damages based on market price as follows: . . . If the case comes to trial before the agreed time for performance, the measure of damages is the market price of comparable goods at the time the buyer learned of the breach less the contract price, together with any incidental and consequential damages, but less expenses avoided in consequence of the seller's breach." Notes to the November, 1996 Draft state that subsection (a)(2) "simplifies by selecting the time when the buyer learned of the breach (invariably a repudiation) regardless of whether the buyer had a valid reason for not covering or cover was reasonable on that date. There are no nuances here and the tool for combatting strategic behavior is that valiant soldier, good faith."

PROBLEM: THE CASE OF THE RECALCITRANT MANUFACTURER—A REPRISE

1. Review your analysis and conclusions in *The Case of the Recalcitrant Manufacturer,* supra at 40, a case where the seller failed to deliver.

2. To what extent is there a doctrine of "substantial" performance under Article 2 of the UCC? What are the buyer's non-judicial remedies? Consider the following variations in the case of *Smirgo v. Bisko:*

(a) Smirgo tendered delivery of the two ovens three days late. In addition, one of the ovens failed to conform to the specifications (a minor deviation which could be corrected for $100). Bisko wants to reject the goods, cancel the contract and sue Smirgo for damages. Would you recommend this course of action? See UCC 2–601, 2–602, 2–711(1) & 2–713 [UCC 2–703, 2–823 & 2–826 (1997)]. Or, should Bisko accept the goods and seek damages for breach of warranty? See UCC 2–606 & 2–714(2) [UCC 2–707 & 2–827 (1997)].

(b) Would your analysis in (a), above, be altered by the following factual changes: (1) Bisko in fact has suffered no damage and has found another manufacturer who can supply the same ovens at 20% less. See UCC 1–103, 1–203, & 2–103(1)(b) [UCC 2–102(a)(8) (1997)]; see also Neumiller Farms, Inc. v. Cornett, supra at 775. (2) Smirgo delivered the defective oven on October 15 rather than November 4. See UCC 2–508(1) [UCC 2–608 (1997)]. (3) The delay of three days was caused by Smirgo's failure promptly to notify Bisko of the shipment. See UCC 2–504 [UCC 2–603 (1997)]. (4) Smirgo was to deliver the ovens in two installments, the first of which was defective. See UCC 2–612 [UCC 2–710 (1997)]. (5) Bisko accepted delivery of both ovens, subsequently discovered the defect and now seeks to cancel the contract. See UCC 2–608 [UCC 2–708 (1997)].

(c) Do any discernible commercial policies emerge from the foregoing rules? How does the factual pattern differ from construction contracts where the requirement of substantial performance is well established? Should UCC 2–601 be revised? See Sebert, *Rejection, Revocation, and Cure Under Article 2 of the Uniform Commercial Code: Some Modest Proposals*, 84 Nw.U.L.Rev. 375 (1990).

3. Suppose Bisko had paid Smirgo $15,000 upon signing the contract and agreed to pay the balance upon delivery. Consider the following questions:

(a) If Smirgo repudiated the contract before any deliveries were made, would Bisko be entitled to cancel the contract, recover the down payment *and* seek compensatory damages for breach of contract? See UCC 2–711 [UCC 2–823 (1997)].

(b) Suppose Bisko repudiated the contract before delivery and it is clear that Smirgo suffered no damage from the breach. May Bisko recover the $15,000 down payment? (Assume there has been no effort to liquidate damages.) See UCC 2–718(2) & (3) [UCC 2–809(b) & (c) (1997)].

Jacob & Youngs v. Kent

Court of Appeals of New York, 1921.
Supra at 642.

Rivers v. Deane

Supreme Court of New York, Appellate Division, 1994
209 A.D.2d 936, 619 N.Y.S.2d 419

MEMORANDUM.

Defendant appeals from a judgment of Supreme Court awarding plaintiffs damages for defendant's breach of contract for the construction of an addition to plaintiffs' home. Defendant in his brief challenges only that aspect of the judgment that awarded damages to plaintiffs for the difference between the market value of the structure had it been completed pursuant to the terms of the contract and the market value of the structure as actually completed. We agree with defendant's assertion that the record does not support the court's award for diminution in value, because no such proof was presented.

At trial plaintiffs produced two experts who testified that defendant failed to construct the addition in a good and workmanlike manner. They further testified that the inadequate structural support of the addition rendered unusable the third floor of the addition, which plaintiffs had intended to use as a master bedroom and bathroom. The appeal by defendant, as limited by his brief (see, Ciesinski v. Town of Aurora, 202 A.D.2d 984, 609 N.Y.S.2d 745; Hodge v. LoRusso, 181 A.D.2d 1009, 582 N.Y.S.2d 575), does not contest those findings of fact.

The general rule in cases of faulty construction is that the measure of damages is the market value of the cost to repair the faulty construction (see, American Std. v. Schectman, 80 A.D.2d 318, 439 N.Y.S.2d 529, lv. denied 54 N.Y.2d 604, 443 N.Y.S.2d 1027, 427 N.E.2d 512). The court erred in applying the "difference in value rule," as initially set forth by Justice Cardozo in Jacob & Youngs v. Kent, 230 N.Y. 239, 241, 129 N.E. 889, which is limited to instances where the builder's failure to perform under a construction contract is "both trivial and innocent", such that damages may be measured by the diminution in value of the building rather than the cost of tearing apart the structure and properly completing the project. Where, as here, the defect arising from the breach of the contract "is so substantial as to render the finished building partially unusable and unsafe, the measure of damage is 'the market price of completing or correcting the performance'" (Bellizzi v. Huntley Estates, 3 N.Y.2d 112, 115, 164 N.Y.S.2d 395, 143 N.E.2d 802, quoting 5 Williston, Contracts § 1363, at 3825 [rev. ed.]). Thus, on the facts found by the court, plaintiffs are entitled to the market value of the cost of correcting the deficiencies in the addition arising from defendant's breach.

The trier of fact is in the best position to evaluate the credibility of the witnesses, who gave conflicting testimony concerning the cost of repair to the addition. Therefore, we modify the judgment appealed from by vacating the court's award of $10,000 for diminution in value due to inadequate structural support, and we remit the matter to Supreme Court for further findings of fact on the actual cost of repair for inadequate structural support and direct that judgment be entered accordingly.

Judgment unanimously modified on the law and as modified affirmed without costs and matter remitted to Supreme Court for further proceedings.

NOTES

(1) Section 346 of the first Restatement of Contracts provided that for "defective or unfinished construction" the plaintiff can get judgment for "the reasonable cost of construction and completion in accordance with the contract, if this is possible and does not involve unreasonable economic waste." In Prier v. Refrigeration Engineering Co., 74 Wash.2d 25, 442 P.2d 621 (1968) the court relied upon this section and the following excerpt from Corbin on Contracts in holding that the cost to repair deficiencies in a new ice skating rink, which were around 30% of the original contract price, were not unreasonable: "The modifications were necessary, not only to provide a usable ice sheet, but also to protect the very foundations of the building."

"This treatise supports the rule that the damages should be measured in the same way whether the breach be large or small; it should be determined by the cost of completion (the cost of curing the defects) except in a case in which actual completion (the actual curing of the defects) would cause unreasonable economic waste. In the latter case the damages should be the difference between the value of full performance as promised and the value of the defective performance actually rendered. Any reasonable doubt as to whether curing defects would cause such economic waste should be resolved against the contractor guilty of the breach; and on him should be put the burden of proof if there is dispute on the issue. It is true that the phrase 'unreasonable economic waste' is no more definite and certain in its meaning and application than is the phrase 'substantial performance.' It too raises a question of fact. Whether the 'economic waste' involved in any specific tearing down and rebuilding is 'unreasonable' cannot be resolved by the application of any rule of law; prevailing practices and opinions (the mores) of men, involving their emotions as well as reason and logic, must be taken into account. 5 A. Corbin, Contracts § 1089 (1964) at 491. See also § 1090.''

(2) Restatement (Second) adopts a subjective test for the measurement of damages based upon the expectation interest. Section 347 provides, in part, that the damages are the ''loss in the value to him of the other party's performance caused by the failure or deficiency'' plus incidental and consequential damages less ''any cost or other loss that he has avoided by not having to perform.'' This approach contrasts with the more objective contract price ''market'' price or ''cover'' price comparison adopted by UCC 2–712 & 2–713, and its illusory character has been criticized. See Simon, *A Critique of the Treatment of Market Damages in the Restatement (Second) of Contracts,* 82 Colum.L.Rev. 80 (1982). Section 348, however, provides an alternative measure where the breach ''results in defective or unfinished construction and the loss in value to the injured party is not proved with sufficient certainty.'' Here the plaintiff ''may recover damages based on (a) the diminution in the market price of the property caused by the breach, or (b) the reasonable cost of completing performance or of remedying the defects if that cost is not clearly disproportionate to the probable loss in the value to him.'' Section 348(2). How should *Jacob & Youngs v. Kent* and the *Rivers* case be decided under this test?

(3) In discussing Sections 347 and 348 of Restatement (Second), the court in Douglass v. Licciardi Const. Co., Inc., 386 Pa.Super. 292, 296–97, 562 A.2d 913, 915–16 (1989), in affirming a jury verdict for cost-to-complete damages in the defective construction of a home, stated:

> Sometimes, especially if the performance is defective as distinguished from incomplete, it may not be possible to prove the loss in value to the injured party with reasonable certainty. In that case he can usually recover damages based on the cost to remedy the defect.... Sometimes, however, such a large part of the cost to remedy the defects consists of the cost to undo what has been improperly done that the cost to remedy the defects will be clearly disproportionate to the probable loss in value to the injured party. Damages based on the cost to remedy the defects would then give the injured party a recovery greatly in excess of the loss in value to him and result in a substantial windfall. Such an award will not be made. It is sometimes said that the award would involve ''economic waste,'' but this is a misleading expression since the injured party will not, even if awarded an excessive amount of damages, usually pay to have the defects remedied if to do so will cost him more than the resulting increase in value to him. If an award based on the cost to remedy the defects would clearly be excessive and the injured party does not prove the actual loss in value to him, damages will be based instead on the difference between the market price that the property would have had without the defects and the market price

of the property with the defects. This diminution in market price is the least possible loss in value to the injured party, since he could always sell the property on the market even if it had no special value to him.... It is only where the cost of completing performance or of remedying the defects is clearly disproportionate to the probable loss in value to the injured party that damages will be measured by the difference between the market price that the property would have had without the defects and the market price of the property with the defects.

See also Anuszewski v. Jurevic, 566 A.2d 742 (Me.1989), where the court approved an award that included both the cost to complete defective construction and a reasonable markup or profit for the general contractor. Otherwise, the plaintiff's expectation interest would not be fully protected.

American Standard, Inc. v. Schectman

Supreme Court of New York, Appellate Division, 1981.
80 A.D.2d 318, 439 N.Y.S.2d 529, motion for leave to appeal denied 54 N.Y.2d 604, 443 N.Y.S.2d 1027, 427 N.E.2d 512.

■ HANCOCK, JUSTICE.

Plaintiffs have recovered a judgment on a jury verdict of $90,000 against defendant for his failure to complete grading and to take down certain foundations and other subsurface structures to one foot below the grade line as promised. Whether the court should have charged the jury, as defendant Schectman requested, that the difference in value of plaintiffs' property with and without the promised performance was the measure of the damage is the main point in his appeal. We hold that the request was properly denied and that the cost of completion—not the difference in value—was the proper measure. Finding no other basis for reversal, we affirm.

Until 1972, plaintiffs operated a pig iron manufacturing plant on land abutting the Niagara River in Tonawanda. On the 26-acre parcel were, in addition to various industrial and office buildings, a 60-ton blast furnace, large lifts, hoists and other equipment for transporting and storing ore, railroad tracks, cranes, diesel locomotives and sundry implements and devices used in the business. Since the 1870's plaintiffs' property, under several different owners, had been the site of various industrial operations. Having decided to close the plant, plaintiffs on August 3, 1973 made a contract in which they agreed to convey the buildings and other structures and most of the equipment to defendant, a demolition and excavating contractor, in return for defendant's payment of $275,000 and his promise to remove the equipment, demolish the structures and grade the property as specified.

We agree with Trial Term's interpretation of the contract as requiring defendant to remove all foundations, piers, headwalls, and other structures, including those under the surface and not visible and whether or not shown on the map attached to the contract, to a depth of approximately one foot below the specified grade lines.[2] The proof from plaintiffs' witnesses and the exhibits, showing a substantial deviation from the required grade lines and the existence above grade of walls, foundations and other structures, support the finding, implicit in the jury's verdict, that defendant failed to perform as agreed. Indeed, the testimony of defendant's witnesses and the position he has taken during his performance of the contract and throughout this litigation (which the trial court properly rejected), viz., that the contract did not require him to remove all subsurface foundations, allow no other conclusion.

We turn to defendant's argument that the court erred in rejecting his proof that plaintiffs suffered no loss by reason of the breach because it makes no difference in the value of the property whether the old foundations are at grade or one foot below grade and in denying his offer to show that plaintiffs succeeded in selling the property for $183,000—only $3,000 less than its full fair market value. By refusing this testimony and charging the jury that the cost of completion (estimated at $110,500 by plaintiffs' expert), not diminution in value of the property, was the measure of damage the court, defendant contends, has unjustly permitted plaintiffs to reap a windfall at his expense. Citing the definitive opinions of Chief Judge Cardozo in Jacob & Youngs, Inc. v. Kent, 230 N.Y. 239, 129 N.E. 889, he maintains that the facts present a case "of substantial performance" of the contract with omissions of "trivial or inappreciable importance" (p. 245, 129 N.E. 889), and that because the cost of completion was "grossly and unfairly out of proportion to the good to be attained," (p. 244, 129 N.E. 889), the proper measure of damage is diminution in value.

The general rule of damages for breach of a construction contract is that the injured party may recover those damages which are the direct, natural and immediate consequence of the breach and which can reasonably be said to have been in the contemplation of the parties when the contract was made. . . . In the usual case where the contractor's performance has been defective or incomplete, the reasonable cost of replacement or completion is the measure. . . . When, however, there has been a substantial performance of the contract made in good faith but defects exist, the correction of which would result in economic waste, courts have measured the damages as the difference between the value of the property as constructed and the value if performance had been properly complet-

---

2. Paragraph 7 of the Agreement states in pertinent part:

7. After the Closing Date, Purchaser shall demolish all of the Improvements on the North Tonawanda Property included in the sale to Purchaser, cap the water intake at the pumphouse end, and grade and level the property, all in accordance with the provisions of Exhibit "C" and "C1" attached hereto.

Exhibit "C" (Notes on demolition and grading) contains specifications for the grade levels for four separate areas shown on Map "C1" and the following instruction:

Except as otherwise excepted all structures and equipment including foundations, piers, headwalls, etc. shall be removed to a depth approximately one foot below grade lines as set forth above. Area common to more than one area will be faired to provide reasonable transitions, it being intended to provide a reasonably attractive vacant plot for resale.

ed.... *Jacob & Youngs* is illustrative. There, plaintiff, a contractor, had constructed a house for the defendant which was satisfactory in all respects save one: the wrought iron pipe installed for the plumbing was not of Reading manufacture, as specified in the contract, but of other brands of the same quality. Noting that the breach was unintentional and the consequences of the omission trivial, and that the cost of replacing the pipe would be "grievously out of proportion" (Jacob & Youngs, Inc. v. Kent, supra, 230 N.Y. p. 244, 129 N.E. 889) to the significance of the default, the court held the breach to be immaterial and the proper measure of damage to the owner to be not the cost of replacing the pipe but the nominal difference in value of the house with and without the Reading pipe.

Not in all cases of claimed "economic waste" where the cost of completing performance of the contract would be large and out of proportion to the resultant benefit to the property have the courts adopted diminution in value as the measure of damage. Under the Restatement rule, the completion of the contract must involve "unreasonable economic waste" and the illustrative example given is that of a house built with pipe different in name from but equal in quality to the brand stipulated in the contract as in *Jacob & Youngs, Inc. v. Kent* (supra) (Restatement, Contracts, § 346, subd. [1], par. [a], cl. [ii], p. 573; Illustration 2, p. 576). In Groves v. John Wunder Co., 205 Minn. 163, 286 N.W. 235, plaintiff had leased property and conveyed a gravel plant to defendant in exchange for a sum of money and for defendant's commitment to return the property to plaintiff at the end of the term at a specified grade—a promise defendant failed to perform. Although the cost of the fill to complete the grading was $60,000 and the total value of the property, graded as specified in the contract, only $12,160 the court rejected the "diminution in value" rule, stating:

> The owner's right to improve his property is not trammeled by its small value. It is his right to erect thereon structures which will reduce its value. If that be the result, it can be of no aid to any contractor who declines performance. As said long ago in Chamberlain v. Parker, 45 N.Y. 569, 572: "A man may do what he will with his own, * * * and if he chooses to erect a monument to his caprice or folly on his premises, and employs and pays another to do it, it does not lie with a defendant who has been so employed and paid for building it, to say that his own performance would not be beneficial to the plaintiff."

(Groves v. John Wunder Co., supra, 205 Minn., p. 168, 286 N.W. 235).

The "economic waste" of the type which calls for application of the "diminution in value" rule generally entails defects in construction which are irremediable or which may not be repaired without a substantial tearing down of the structure as in *Jacob & Youngs*....

Where, however, the breach is of a covenant which is only incidental to the main purpose of the contract and completion would be disproportionately costly, courts have applied the diminution in value measure even where no destruction of the work is entailed (see, e.g., Peevyhouse v. Garland Coal & Min. Co., 382 P.2d 109 [Okla.], cert. den. 375 U.S. 906, 84

S.Ct. 196, 11 L.Ed.2d 145, holding [contrary to *Groves v. John Wunder Co.*, supra] that diminution in value is the proper measure where defendant, the lessee of plaintiff's lands under a coal mining lease, failed to perform costly remedial and restorative work on the land at the termination of the lease. The court distinguished the "building and construction" cases and noted that the breach was of a covenant incidental to the main purpose of the contract which was the recovery of coal from the premises to the benefit of both parties; and see Avery v. Fredericksen & Westbrook, 67 Cal.App.2d 334, 154 P.2d 41).

It is also a general rule in building and construction cases, at least under *Jacob & Youngs* in New York (see *Groves v. John Wunder Co.*, supra; Ann. 76 A.L.R.2d 805, § 6, pp. 823–826), that a contractor who would ask the court to apply the diminution of value measure "as an instrument of justice" must not have breached the contract intentionally and must show substantial performance made in good faith (Jacob & Youngs, Inc. v. Kent, supra, 230 N.Y. pp. 244, 245, 129 N.E. 889).

In the case before us, plaintiffs chose to accept as part of the consideration for the promised conveyance of their valuable plant and machines to defendant his agreement to grade the property as specified and to remove the foundations, piers and other structures to a depth of one foot below grade to prepare the property for sale. It cannot be said that the grading and the removal of the structures were incidental to plaintiffs' purpose of "achieving a reasonably attractive vacant plot for resale" (compare *Peevyhouse v. Garland Coal & Min. Co.*, supra). Nor can defendant maintain that the damages which would naturally flow from his failure to do the grading and removal work and which could reasonably be said to have been in the contemplation of the parties when the contract was made would not be the reasonable cost of completion (see 13 N.Y.Jur., Damages, §§ 46, 56; *Hadley v. Baxendale*, supra). That the fulfillment of defendant's promise would (contrary to plaintiffs' apparent expectations) add little or nothing to the sale value of the property does not excuse the default. As in the hypothetical case posed in Chamberlain v. Parker, 45 N.Y. 569, supra (cited in *Groves v. John Wunder Co.*, supra), of the man who "chooses to erect a monument to his caprice or folly on his premises, and employs and pays another to do it," it does not lie with defendant here who has received consideration for his promise to do the work "to say that his own performance would not be beneficial to the plaintiff[s]" (*Chamberlain v. Parker*, supra, p. 572).

Defendant's completed performance would not have involved undoing what in good faith was done improperly but only doing what was promised and left undone (compare *Jacob & Youngs, Inc. v. Kent*, supra; Restatement, Contracts, § 346, Illustration 2, p. 576). That the burdens of performance were heavier than anticipated and the cost of completion disproportionate to the end to be obtained does not, without more, alter the rule that the measure of plaintiffs' damage is the cost of completion. Disparity in relative economic benefits is not the equivalent of "economic waste" which will invoke the rule in *Jacob & Youngs, Inc. v. Kent* (supra) (see *Groves v.*

John Wunder Co., supra). Moreover, faced with the jury's finding that the reasonable cost of removing the large concrete and stone walls and other structures extending above grade was $90,000, defendant can hardly assert that he has rendered substantial performance of the contract or that what he left unfinished was "of trivial or inappreciable importance" (Jacob & Youngs, Inc. v. Kent, supra, 230 N.Y. p. 245, 129 N.E. 889). Finally, defendant, instead of attempting in good faith to complete the removal of the underground structures, contended that he was not obliged by the contract to do so and, thus, cannot claim to be a "transgressor whose default is unintentional and trivial [and who] may hope for mercy if he will offer atonement for his wrong" (Jacob & Youngs, Inc. v. Kent, supra, p. 244, 129 N.E. 889). We conclude, then, that the proof pertaining to the value of plaintiffs' property was properly rejected and the jury correctly charged on damages.

The judgment and order should be affirmed.

Judgment and Order unanimously affirmed with costs.

■ SIMONS, J.P., and DOERR, DENMAN and SCHNEPP, JJ., concur.

NOTES

(1) Note, in *American Standard,* that the plaintiff's purpose was to obtain a clear, graded industrial lot for resale and that the plaintiff actually sold the lot as cleared and graded by the defendant for $183,000, "only $3,000 less than its full market value." The outcome of the case was that the plaintiff had a judgment for $90,000 *after* the property had been sold and that the difference in market value of the property in the condition at the time of sale and the property if defendant had fully performed the contract was only $3,000. How does the court justify this result? Has the plaintiff been awarded a "windfall" in a case where the value of the bargain to it can easily be measured in market terms? Or, would the award of diminished value rather than the cost of completion improperly reallocate a performance risk assumed by the defendant, especially since defendant intentionally refused to conform to the contract requirements? These and other problems are well discussed in Muris, *Cost of Completion or Diminution in Market Value: The Relevance of Subjective Value,* 12 J.Leg.Stud. 379 (1983). Muris suggests that an award of "cost to complete" damages protects the plaintiff's "subjective" value and should be made in cases where diminution is too difficult or costly to calculate and where "subjective" value is relevant and the cost to complete does not "grossly exceed" the "subjective" value. These conditions are most likely to be met when the plaintiff is a government agency or a consumer and the property is retained for use after the breach. See also Marschall, *Willfulness: A Crucial Factor in Choosing Remedies for Breach of Contract,* 24 Ariz.L.Rev. 733, 760 (1982), who argues that the key factor is whether the breach was willful or nonwillful. If the breach was willful and not excused, the objective of deterring breaches justifies granting the plaintiff either specific performance or the "highest possible measure of expectation damages." For a more general study, see Polinsky, *Risk Sharing Through Breach of Contract Remedies,* 12 J.Leg.Stud. 427 (1983). For evidence that the contractor's willful breach tipped the balance in favor of a

cost-to-complete remedy protecting the plaintiff's "subjective" value, see Laurin v. De Carolis Const. Co., Inc., 372 Mass. 688, 363 N.E.2d 675, 678–79 (1977) (plaintiff entitled to reasonable value of gravel taken from land rather than diminished value of land); Kaiser v. Fishman, 138 A.D.2d 456, 525 N.Y.S.2d 870 (1988) (cost-to-complete in defective construction of residence); Kangas v. Trust, 110 Ill.App.3d 876, 65 Ill.Dec. 757, 441 N.E.2d 1271 (1982) (nonconforming construction of residence).

(2) The *Peevyhouse* case, discussed in *American Standard,* has been criticized on the ground that the diminished value award undercut both the landowner's "subjective" value in having his land reclaimed and a broader "public interest" in achieving the same results. See, e.g., Note, 49 Iowa L.Rev. 597 (1964). In 1967, the Oklahoma legislature imposed a duty upon mine operators to reclaim the land after work was done and authorized the State to contract for the work to be done if the operator defaulted. The operator must, at the start of work, post a bond covering the estimated cost of reclamation and there is no exception for cases where the cost of reclamation is disproportionate to any resulting increase in the value of the land. See 45 Okl.Stat.Ann. §§ 721–92. Section 722 provides in part:

> It is hereby declared to be the policy of this State to provide, after mining operations are completed, for the reclamation and conservation of land subjected to surface disturbance by open cut mining and thereby to preserve natural resources, to aid in the protection of wildlife and aquatic resources, to establish recreational, home and industrial sites, to protect and perpetuate the taxable value of property, and to protect and promote the health, safety, and general welfare of the people of this State.

The United States Court of Appeals for the Tenth Circuit has concluded that, in light of subsequent legislative changes, the Oklahoma Supreme Court would probably no longer follow *Peevyhouse.* Rock Island Improvement Co. v. Helmerich & Payne, Inc., 698 F.2d 1075 (10th Cir.1983). Not so, at least where the breach results in damages to real property: The plaintiffs may recover the reasonable costs of repairing the damage to property so long as the recovery does not "exceed the depreciated value of the land itself." Schneberger v. Apache Corp., 890 P.2d 847, 849 (Okl.1994)(breach of settlement agreement requiring reduction in level of water pollution caused by oil and gas drilling).

For a "deep background" study, see Judith L. Maute, *Peevyhouse v. Garland Coal & Mining Co. Revisited: The Ballad of Willie and Lucille,* 89 Nw. U. L. Rev. 1341 (1995).

Comment: Buyer's Remedies for Seller's Breach of Warranty under the UCC

A frequent source of disputes in contracts for the sale of goods is whether the seller has met the obligation of quality under the contract. The buyer may claim, either before or after the goods have been accepted, that the goods do not conform to the contract description, or that they do not conform to expectations about basic attributes or that they are not suitable for general or particular purposes that the buyer had in mind. Since the agreement rarely details all of these aspects of quality, the UCC provides three types of warranty that may help to fill the "gap," an express warranty, UCC 2–313, an implied warranty of merchantability, UCC 2–314, and an implied warranty of fitness for particular purpose, UCC 2–315 [UCC 2–403, 2–405 & 2–406 (1997)]. Based upon what the agreement contains, what the seller has said, what the buyer has communicated as to needs, the commercial or consumer setting and the relative knowledge of the parties, to name a few factors, the court will try to determine from a mix of agreement, inference and policy what in fact the seller agreed to sell. See Chapter Five, Section 2(C).

Suppose, then, that the seller has described the goods as a RXB 450 Disc Computer System and stated in the agreement that the system will perform six basic functions. This description and the affirmations are express warranties under UCC 2–313. [UCC 2–403 (1997)] When the goods are tendered, the buyer has a right to inspect them to determine whether they conform to the express warranty. UCC 2–513(1) [UCC 2–609 (1997)]. A certain amount of testing may be required. If a non-conformity is discovered, the buyer may reject the goods under UCC 2–601 and 2–602(2)[UCC 2–703 (1997)]. After a "rightful" rejection, the seller has a limited "right" to cure the defects, see UCC 2–508 [UCC 2–709 (1997)], and, beyond this, the buyer may encourage the cure effort. If the defects are not remedied, the buyer may pursue remedies for "rightful" rejection, which include cancellation, "cover" or damages, including consequential damages. See UCC 2–711 and 2–715(2) [UCC 2–823 & 2–806 (1997).]

Suppose, however, that the buyer has accepted the goods before the defects are discovered. See UCC 2–606 [UCC 2–706 (1997)] for what constitutes an acceptance. Acceptance of the goods precludes the remedy of rejection, makes the buyer liable for the price and puts the burden of proving a breach of warranty on the buyer. See UCC 2–607 [UCC 2–707 (1997)]. But UCC 2–608 [UCC 2–708 (1997)] provides a special remedy called "revocation" of acceptance which, if properly exercised, gives the buyer the same remedial options as if the goods had been rejected. UCC 2–608(3) [UCC 2–708(c) (1997)]. "Revocation" of acceptance, however, is a complicated remedy and will be denied if the defect was insubstantial, or the buyer should have discovered it before acceptance or notice is given after an unreasonable time has elapsed since the defect was or should have been discovered. Again, if the revocation is "justifiable," the buyer can cancel the contract, obtain a substitute system through "cover" and seek any consequential damages resulting from the breach.

Finally, suppose the buyer, for one reason or another, can neither "rightfully" reject the goods nor "justifiably" revoke acceptance. Is that the end of the remedial road? The answer is no. If timely notice of the breach has been given, see UCC 2–607(3)(a) [UCC 2–707(c)(1) (1997)], the buyer may recover damages for "breach in regard to accepted goods" under UCC 2–714 [UCC 2–827 (1997)] and, where appropriate, for incidental and consequential damages under UCC 2–715 [UCC 2–806 (1997)]. In this situation, the buyer must keep the goods and pay the agreed price, but the price will be adjusted downward to reflect the loss of bargain from the breach. UCC 2–717 [UCC 2–828 (1997)].

One last note. All of this may change if the parties have agreed to remedies which are in addition to or differ from the usual Code scheme. For example, the buyer may give up the right to reject in exchange for the seller's promise to "cure" certain defects after acceptance. Or, the seller may attempt to "disclaim" certain warranties or exclude liability for consequential damages. We will look at the effectiveness of these efforts in the next subsection. See, e.g., UCC 2–316 and 2–719 [UCC 2–407 & 2–806 (1997)].

PROBLEM: SELLER'S POST–ACCEPTANCE LIABILITY FOR DEFECTIVE GOODS

(1) Suppose, in *Bisko v. Smirgo,* supra at 40, that Smirgo tendered delivery of the ovens on November 1 and that Bisko, after a reasonable inspection, accepted and put them into operation. Bisko paid the full contract price 90 days later. Thereafter, Bisko discovered a defect in the ovens which impaired their overall capacity to bake bread. This defect constituted a breach of warranty by Smirgo. Smirgo, however, refused either to correct the defect or to replace the ovens. Assume that at the time of delivery the value of the ovens as warranted was $29,500 and the value of the ovens as actually delivered was $25,000. Assume, also, that the reasonable cost to correct the defect would be $8,000. Bisko has rejected the option of "revoking" the acceptance under UCC 2–608 [UCC 2–708 (1997)] and pursuing remedies under UCC 2–711 [UCC 2–823(1997)] in favor of correcting the defect and keeping the goods. If Bisko does so, how much may Bisko recover from Smirgo for breach of warranty?

(a) $5,000

(b) $8,000

(c) $4,500

(d) None of the above.

See UCC 2–714 [UCC 2–827 (1997)].

(2) Suppose that Smirgo had expressly warranted that the ovens were fit for Bisko's particular needs and purposes. As delivered, the ovens were fine for ordinary baking but did not satisfy Bisko's particular needs. In fact, it is clear that an oven of that design could not conform to the express warranty and that a different type of oven which cost $75,000 would be required. Bisko would like to recover $50,000, the difference in value between the oven that would have conformed to the warranty and the oven actually delivered. Smirgo argues that this recovery is not permitted under UCC 2–714(2)[UCC 2–827(b) (1997)], which limits recovery to the "value of the goods accepted" not some hypothetical oven. Otherwise, Bisko would be put in a better position than promised by Smirgo. What argument should Bisko make? Should it be accepted? See Chatlos Systems, Inc. v. National Cash Register Corp., 670 F.2d 1304 (3d Cir.1982), cert. dismissed sub nom., 457 U.S. 1112, 102 S.Ct. 2918, 73 L.Ed.2d 1323 (1982)(finding "special circumstances" showing "proximate damages of a different amount").

Comment: Restitution of Down Payment by Payor

Under what circumstances can a buyer or vendee choose restitution of a down payment as a remedy for the seller's or vendor's breach?

Under UCC 2–711(1) [UCC 2–823(a) (1997)], a buyer who cancels after a seller's breach may recover "so much of the price as has been paid. . . . " More importantly, the non-breaching buyer can have restitution of the price paid in addition to damages measured by the expectation interest. To illustrate, suppose that the buyer paid $50 down on a contract to purchase goods for $100. If the seller failed to deliver and the buyer "covered" for $120, the total recovery under would be $50 (restitution under UCC 2–711(1) [UCC 2–823(a) (1997)]) plus $20 (expectation under UCC 2–712(2) [UCC 2–825(b) (1997)]), adjusted for savings realized and incidental damages. On the other hand, UCC 2–711(1) [UCC 2–823(a) (1997)] does not say that the price recovery should be adjusted for a losing contract. Thus, if the market price at the time and place of delivery was $80, the buyer could recover $50 in restitution without any downward adjustment for the losing contract. See Bausch & Lomb Inc. v. Bressler, 977 F.2d 720, 729–730 (2d Cir.1992)(down payment to seller adjusted for value of benefit to buyer from part performance). Other than this, Article 2 is relatively silent on the restitution interest. But see UCC 2–718(2) [UCC 2–809(b) (1997)] (permitting a breaching buyer to recover in restitution the amount that payments made exceed the seller's damages); Barco Auto Leasing Corp. v. House, 202 Conn. 106, 520 A.2d 162 (1987) (dictum that the formula in UCC 2–718(3)(b) should be extended to cover restitution by a breaching seller as well).

The scope of restitution by a vendee of realty upon breach by the vendor is illustrated by Potter v. Oster, 426 N.W.2d 148 (Iowa 1988). After the vendee was in possession of a farm for six years under a contract to sell, the vendor, who had financial reverses, was unable to convey good title. The land involved, along with related tracts, had been mortgaged and, because of declining land values, the vendor had defaulted and lost his equitable title to all of the land. The vendee, who had paid a total of $65,169 in principal, interest, improvements, taxes, insurance and other reliance, was unable to pay the $27,900 still due under the contract to save his property from foreclosure. The vendee then brought a suit against the vendor to rescind the contract and to recover $65,169 in restitution. The trial court endorsed the restitution theory and, after deducting $10,800 for the value of six years' rental, awarded the vendee $54,369.

On appeal, the judgment was affirmed. The court first stated that in order to obtain rescission and restitution, the vendee must establish that (1) he was not in default, (2) the breach was material, and (3) legal remedies were inadequate. There was little dispute that the first two conditions were satisfied. Oster, however, argued that Potter should be limited in damages to the difference between the market value of the land at the time of forfeiture, $35,000, and the contract balance of $27,900. Oster claimed that the risk of declining land values should be shared by Potter and that restitution would give Potter a windfall.

The court rejected this argument, stating that Oster had tried to limit damages by an "expectation" theory even though Potter sued only for restitution. Even if declining land values motivated Potter's selection of remedies, restitution was still proper where the first two conditions were satisfied and the legal remedies were inadequate.

> [L]egal remedies are considered inadequate when the damages cannot be measured with sufficient certainty ... [E]xpectation damages are correctly calculated as the difference between the contract price and market value at the time for performance ... Since the time of performance in this case would have been March 1990, the market value of the homestead and acreage cannot be predicted with any certainty, thus rendering such a formulation inadequate. More importantly, the fair market value of the homestead at the time of forfeiture is an incorrect measure of the benefit Potters lost. It fails to account for the special value Potters placed on the property's location and residential features that uniquely suited their family. For precisely this reason, remedies at law are presumed inadequate for breach of a real estate contract ... His characterization of the transaction as a mere market loss for Potters, compensable by a sum which would enable them to make a nominal down payment on an equivalent homestead, has no legal or factual support in this record.

426 N.W.2d at 152. Accord: Kim v. Conway & Forty, Inc., 772 S.W.2d 723 (Mo.App.1989) (vendees get restitution of earnest money when vendors fail to convey good title to condominium).

(2) CONSEQUENTIAL DAMAGES: FORESEEABILITY; MITIGATION; CERTAINTY; INCIDENTAL RELIANCE

Up to now we have considered remedies which measure the direct or immediate loss to the plaintiff-payor upon breach by the defendant. To employ a few weasel words, the courts are trying to determine the "natural and usual value of the contract under ordinary circumstances." This is normally determined by the difference in either the contract price and the cost which was or would have been incurred in purchasing substitutes on the open market at the time of breach or the value of what was promised and what was received. See UCC 2–714(1) [UCC 2–827 (1997)]; Hawkins v. McGee, 84 N.H. 114, 146 A. 641 (1929). When the plaintiff's lost bargain is measured in this way, no consequential damages are involved, problems of certainty are minimized, and mitigation of damage policies are often built into standardized formulas for measuring loss. Cf. UCC 2–712(1) [UCC 2–825(a) (1997)].

More complex problems, however, are posed by the now familiar *Case of the Recalcitrant Manufacturer.* Note that Bisko purchased the ovens for the purpose of expanding a well established business. They were not purchased for resale. Also, Bisko expended $7,500 in preparation for using the ovens upon delivery. While this expenditure was in reliance upon Smirgo's promise to deliver, it was not part of or in preparation for the performance of Bisko's part of the bargain, i.e., to accept and pay for the goods. Expenditures of this sort have been called "incidental" reliance since they are not necessary to the perfection of Bisko's rights under the contract. Nor will they be fully reimbursed if Smirgo performs the contract.

See Fuller & Perdue, *The Reliance Interest in Contract Damages,* 46 Yale L.J. 52, 78 (1936). They are, however, "necessary" if Bisko is to use the ovens to expand the business and would be reimbursed from the gross return, if any, from that expansion. Upon breach by Smirgo, therefore, possible items of additional damage to Bisko include loss of profits that might have been earned in the expanded business or the $7,500 reliance expenditure, or both.

There are four basic problems involved in compensating Bisko for these additional losses: (1) Were the losses a foreseeable consequence of the breach at the time of contracting? (2) Could Bisko have reasonably "mitigated" damages by purchasing substitute goods on the open market or continuing to deal with Smirgo? (3) Could Bisko prove what profits were lost with reasonable certainty? (4) If profits are too speculative, could Bisko recover the reliance expenditures as an alternative? Could Bisko recover both lost profits and reliance expenditures? The following materials are organized around these questions and should provide plenty of ammunition for discussion. In addition, we will examine the enforceability of clauses "excluding" consequential damages caused by a breach. For an interesting critique, see Epstein, *Beyond Foreseeability: Consequential Damages in the Law of Contracts,* 18 J.Legal Stud. 105 (1988).

Hadley v. Baxendale

Court of Exchequer, 1854.
9 Exch. 341, 156 Eng.Rep. 145.

At the trial before Crompton, J., at the last Gloucester Assizes, it appeared that the plaintiffs carried on an extensive business as millers at Gloucester; and that, on the 11th of May, their mill was stopped by a breakage of the crank shaft by which the mill was worked. The steam-engine was manufactured by Messrs. Joyce & Co., the engineers, at Greenwich, and it became necessary to send the shaft as a pattern for a new one to Greenwich. The fracture was discovered on the 12th, and on the 13th the plaintiffs sent one of their servants to the office of the defendants, who are the well-known carriers trading under the name of Pickford & Co., for the purpose of having the shaft carried to Greenwich. The plaintiffs' servant told the clerk that the mill was stopped, and that the shaft must be sent immediately; and in answer to the inquiry when the shaft would be taken, the answer was, that if it was sent up by twelve o'clock any day, it would be delivered at Greenwich on the following day. On the following day the shaft was taken by the defendants, before noon, for the purpose of being conveyed to Greenwich, and the sum of £2, 4s. was paid for its carriage for the whole distance; at the same time the defendants' clerk was told that a special entry, if required, should be made to hasten its delivery. The delivery of the shaft at Greenwich was delayed by some neglect; and the consequence was, that the plaintiffs did not receive the new shaft for several days after they would otherwise have done, and the working of their mill was thereby delayed, and they thereby lost the profits they would otherwise have received.

On the part of the defendants, it was objected that these damages were too remote, and that the defendants were not liable with respect to them. The learned Judge left the case generally to the jury, who found a verdict with £25 damages beyond the amount paid into Court.

Whateley, in last Michaelmas Term, obtained a rule nisi for a new trial on the ground of misdirection.

* * *

■ ALDERSON, B. We think that there ought to be a new trial in this case; but, in so doing, we deem it to be expedient and necessary to state explicitly the rule which the Judge, at the next trial, ought, in our opinion, to direct the jury to be governed by when they estimate the damages.

It is, indeed, of the last importance that we should do this; for, if the jury are left without any definite rule to guide them, it will in such cases as these, manifestly lead to the greatest injustice. The Courts have done this on several occasions; and, in Balke v. Midland Railway Company, 18 Q.B. 93, the Court granted a new trial on this very ground that the rule had not been definitely laid down to the jury by the learned Judge at Nisi Prius.

* * *

Now we think the proper rule in such a case as the present is this:— Where two parties have made a contract which one of them has broken, the damages which the other party ought to receive in respect of such breach of contract should be such as may fairly and reasonably be considered either arising naturally, i.e., according to the usual course of things, from such breach of contract itself, or such as may reasonably be supposed to have been in the contemplation of both parties, at the time they made the contract, as the probable result of the breach of it. Now, if the special circumstances under which the contract was actually made were communicated by the plaintiffs to the defendants, and thus known to both parties, the damages resulting from the breach of such a contract, which they would reasonably contemplate, would be the amount of injury which would ordinarily follow from a breach of contract under these special circumstances so known and communicated. But, on the other hand, if these special circumstances were wholly unknown to the party breaking the contract, he, at the most, could only be supposed to have had in his contemplation the amount of injury which would arise generally, and in the great multitude of cases not affected by any special circumstances, from such a breach of contract. For, had the special circumstances been known, the parties might have specially provided for the breach of contract by special terms as to the damages in that case; and of this advantage it would be very unjust to deprive them. Now the above principles are those by which we think the jury ought to be guided in estimating the damages arising out of any breach of contract. It is said, that other cases such as breaches of contract in the non-payment of money, or in the not making a good title to land, are to be treated as exceptions from this, and as governed by a conventional rule. But as, in such cases, both parties must be supposed to be cognizant of that well-known rule, these cases may, we think, be more properly classed under the rule above enunciated as to cases under known special circumstances, because there both parties may reasonably be presumed to contemplate the estimation of the amount of damages according to the conventional rule. Now, in the present case, if we are to apply the principles above laid down, we find that the only circumstances here communicated by the plaintiffs to the defendants at the time the contract was made, were, that the article to be carried was the broken shaft of a mill, and that the plaintiffs were the millers of that mill. But how do these circumstances shew reasonably that the profits of the mill must be stopped by an unreasonable delay in the delivery of the broken shaft by the carrier to the third person? Suppose the plaintiffs had another shaft in their possession put up or putting up at the time, and that they only wished to send back the broken shaft to the engineer who made it; it is clear that this would be quite consistent with the above circumstances, and yet the unreasonable delay in the delivery would have no effect upon the intermediate profits of the mill. Or, again, suppose that, at the time of the delivery to the carrier, the machinery of the mill had been in other respects defective, then, also the same results would follow. Here it is true that the shaft was actually sent back to serve as a model for a new one, and that the want of a new one was the only cause of the stoppage of the mill, and that the loss of profits really arose from not sending down the new shaft in proper time, and that this arose from the delay in delivering the broken one to serve as a model. But it is obvious that, in the great multitude of cases of millers sending off broken shafts to third persons by a carrier under ordinary circumstances, such consequences would not, in all probability, have occurred; and these special circumstances were here never communicated by the plaintiffs to the defendants. It follows, therefore, that the loss of profits here cannot reasonably be considered such a consequence of the breach of contract as could have been fairly and reasonably contemplated by both the parties when they made this contract. For such loss would neither have flowed naturally from the breach of this contract in the great multitude of such cases occurring under ordinary circumstances, nor were the special circumstances, which, perhaps, would have made it a reasonable and natural consequence of such breach of contract, communicated to or known by the defendants. The Judge ought, therefore, to have told the jury, that, upon the facts then before them, they ought not to take the loss of profits into consideration at all in estimating the damages. There must therefore be a new trial in this case.

Rule absolute.

NOTES

(1) *Hadley v. Baxendale and the English Courts.* Since *Hadley v. Baxendale,* the English courts have invested considerable energy in fine-tuning the test of foreseeability that excludes liability for consequential damages. See, e.g.,

Victoria Laundry (Windsor) Limited v. Newman Industries Limited, 2 K.B. 528 (1949); The Heron II (Kaufos v. C. Czarnikow, Limited), 3 All E.R. 686 (House of Lords 1967). In Parsons Limited v. Uttley Ingham & Co. (C.A.), 1 Q.B. 791, 802 (1978), Lord Denning summarized the results of that effort when the breach caused lost profits or "economic" loss.

> [T]he defaulting party is only liable for the consequences if they are such as, at the time of the contract, he ought reasonably to have contemplated as a serious possibility or a real danger. You must assume that, at the time of the contract, he had the very kind of breach in mind—such a breach as afterwards happened, as for instance, delay in transit—and you must ask: ought he reasonably to have contemplated that there was a serious possibility that such a breach would involve the plaintiff in a loss of profit. If yes, the contractor is liable for the loss unless he has taken care to exempt himself from it by a condition in the contract—as, of course, he is able to do if it was the sort of thing which he could reasonably contemplate.

In Parsons, however, the plaintiff's pigs died after eating moldy nuts stored in a bulk food storage hopper supplied by the defendant. The cause of the mold was an improperly installed ventilator. The judge below gave judgment for the plaintiff even though concluding that at the time of contracting the parties could not have reasonably contemplated that there would be a serious possibility of moldy pignuts causing serious illness in the pigs. The appeal was denied by the Court of Appeal. Lord Denning distinguished the case where breach of contract caused lost profits from that where it caused physical injury. In the latter case, "the defaulting party is liable for any loss or expense which he ought to have foreseen at the time of the breach as a possible consequence, even if it was only a slight possibility. You must assume that he was aware of his breach, and then you must ask: ought he reasonably to have foreseen, at the time of the breach, that something of this kind might happen in consequence of it?" 1 Q.B. at 803. This is similar to the test applied by the English courts in tort. Lords Orr and Scarman concurred in the judgment but rejected the distinction between economic and physical harm. For them it was enough that at the time of contracting that physical injury to the pigs was a serious possibility if the hopper was unfit for storing nuts suitable to be fed to them. Lord Denning's distinction is criticized in Bishop, *The Contract–Tort Boundary and the Economics of Insurance,* 12 J.Leg.Stud. 241, 254–60 (1983). The question, according to Bishop, is whether the relationship between the parties provided the opportunity and incentive for a low-cost sharing of information. If so, the *Hadley* test should be applied. If not, the tort test is proper. The objective is to avoid doctrines that allow "potential victims to refrain from disclosing important information to potential injurers in cases where they have such information and could easily provide it." 12 J.Leg.Stud. at 259. See Chesire, Fifoot & Furmston, Law of Contract 595–612 (12th ed.1991).

(2) *American Tests of Foreseeability.* Two American statements of the "foreseeability" test in *Hadley v. Baxendale* are UCC 2–715(2) (1995) and Restatement (Second) § 351.

UCC 2–715(2) provides:

> Consequential damages resulting from the seller's breach include (a) any loss resulting from general or particular requirements and needs of which the seller at the time of contracting had reason to know and which could

not reasonably be prevented by cover or otherwise; and (b) injury to person or property proximately resulting from any breach of warranty.

See Note, *Lost Profits and Hadley v. Baxendale,* 19 Wash.L.Rev. 488 (1980).

Restatement (Second) § 351 provides:

(1) Damages are not recoverable for loss that the party in breach did not have reason to foresee as the probable result of the breach when the contract was made.

(2) Loss may be foreseeable as a probable result of a breach because it follows from the breach (a) in the ordinary course of events, or (b) as a result of special circumstances, beyond the ordinary course of events, that the party in breach had reason to know.

(3) A court may limit damages for foreseeable loss by excluding recovery for loss of profits, by allowing recovery only for loss incurred in reliance, or otherwise if it concludes that in the circumstances justice so requires in order to avoid disproportionate compensation.

On the potential of Restatement (Second) § 351(3), see Kniffen, *A Newly Identified Contract Unconscionability: Unconscionability of Remedy,* 63 Notre Dame L.Rev. 247 (1988); Harvey, *Discretionary Justice Under the Restatement (Second) of Contracts,* 67 Cornell L.Rev. 666 (1982).

Here are some questions to consider:

(1) How does the American test of "foreseeability" differ from the English? Is there an American distinction between "economic" loss and physical damage to property?

(2) How does Restatement (Second) § 351 differ from UCC 2–715(2), i.e., is it easier or harder to get consequential damages under Restatement (Second)? [See UCC 2–806 (1997)]

(3) Why shouldn't the *Hadley* principle limit lost-profit damages where a buyer breaches?

Spang Industries, Inc., Fort Pitt Bridge Division v. Aetna Casualty & Surety Co.

United States Court of Appeals, Second Circuit, 1975.
512 F.2d 365.

■ MULLIGAN, CIRCUIT JUDGE: Torrington Construction Co., Inc. (Torrington), a Connecticut corporation, was the successful bidder with the New York State Department of Transportation for a highway reconstruction contract covering 4.47 miles of road in Washington County, New York. Before submitting its bid Torrington received an oral quotation from Spang Industries, Inc., Fort Pitt Bridge Division (Fort Pitt), a Pennsylvania corporation, for the fabrication, furnishing and erection of some 240 tons of structural steel at a unit price of 27.5 cents per pound; the steel was to be utilized to construct a 270 foot long, double span bridge over the Battenkill River as part of the highway reconstruction. The quotation was confirmed in a letter from Fort Pitt to Torrington dated September 5, 1969, which stated in part: "Delivery to be mutually agreed upon." On November 3, 1969, Torrington, in response to a request from Fort Pitt, advised that its requirements for delivery and erection of the steel would be late June, 1970. On November 12, 1969, Fort Pitt notified Torrington that it was tentatively scheduling delivery in accordance with these requirements. On January 7, 1970, Fort Pitt wrote to Torrington asking if the June, 1970 erection date was still valid; Torrington responded affirmatively on January 13, 1970. However, on January 29, 1970, Fort Pitt advised that it was engaged in an extensive expansion program and that "[d]ue to unforeseen delays caused by weather, deliveries from suppliers, etc., it is our opinion that the June date cannot be met." On February 2, 1970, Torrington sent a letter requesting that Fort Pitt give a delivery date and, receiving no response, wrote again on May 12, 1970 requesting a written confirmation of the date of delivery and threatening to cancel out if the date was not reasonably close to the originally scheduled date. On May 20, 1970, Fort Pitt responded and promised that the structural steel would be shipped early in August, 1970.

Although some 25 tons of small steel parts were shipped on August 21, 1970, the first girders and other heavy structural steel were not shipped until August 24, 26, 27, 31 and September 2 and 4, 1970. Fort Pitt had subcontracted the unloading and erection of the steel to Syracuse Rigging Co. but neglected to advise it of the August 21st shipment. The steel began to arrive at the railhead in Shushan, New York about September 1st and the railroad demanded immediate unloading. Torrington was therefore compelled to do the unloading itself until Syracuse Rigging arrived on September 8, 1970. Not until September 16 was there enough steel delivered to the job site to permit Syracuse to commence erection. The work was completed on October 8, 1970 and the bridge was ready to receive its concrete deck on October 28, 1970. Because of contract specifications set by the State requiring that concrete be poured at temperatures of 40° Fahrenheit and above, Torrington had to get special permission from the State's supervising engineer to pour the concrete on October 28, 1970, when the temperature was at 32°.

Since the job site was in northern New York near the Vermont border and danger of freezing temperatures was imminent, the pouring of the concrete was performed on a crash basis in one day, until 1 a.m. the following morning, which entailed extra costs for Torrington in the form of overtime pay, extra equipment and the protection of the concrete during the pouring process.

In July, 1971, Fort Pitt instituted an action against Aetna Casualty and Surety Co., which had posted a general contractor's labor and material bond, in the United States District Court for the Western District of Pennsylvania, seeking to recover the balance due on the subcontract, which at that point was $72,247.37 with interest. Thereafter in 1972 Torrington made two further payments totalling $48,983.92. That action was transferred pursuant to 28 U.S.C. § 1406(a) to the United States District Court for the Northern District of New York by order dated December 9, 1971. In the interim, Torrington had commenced suit in New York Supreme Court, Washington County, seeking damages in the sum of $23,290.81 alleged to be caused by Fort Pitt's delay in furnishing the steel. Fort Pitt then removed the case to the United States District Court for the Northern District of New York (where the two cases were consolidated), and counterclaimed for the balance due on the contract. From May 29 to 31, 1973, the cases were tried without a jury before Hon. James S. Holden, Chief Judge of the United States District Court for the District of Vermont, who was sitting by designation. On September 12, 1973, Judge Holden filed his findings of fact and conclusions of law in which he held that Fort Pitt had breached its contract by its delayed delivery and that Torrington was entitled to damages in the amount of $7,653.57. He further held that Fort Pitt was entitled to recover from Torrington on the counterclaim the sum of $23,290.12, which was the balance due on its contract price plus interest, less the $7,653.57 damages sustained by Torrington. He directed that judgment be entered for Fort Pitt against Torrington and Aetna on their joint and several liability for $15,636.55 with interest from November 12, 1970.[1]

Fort Pitt on this appeal does not take issue with any of the findings of fact of the court below but contends that the recovery by Torrington of its increased expenses constitutes special damages which were not reasonably within the contemplation of the parties when they entered into the contract.

I

While the damages awarded Torrington are relatively modest ($7,653.57) in comparison with the subcontract price ($132,274.37), Fort Pitt urges that an affirmance of the award will do violence to the rule of Hadley v. Baxendale, 156 Eng.Rep. 145 (Ex.1854), and create a precedent which will have a severe impact on the business of all subcontractors and suppliers.

While it is evident that the function of the award of damages for a breach of contract is to put the plaintiff in the same position he would have been in had there been no breach, Hadley v. Baxendale limits the recovery to those injuries which the parties could reasonably have anticipated at the time the contract was entered into. If the damages suffered do not usually flow from the breach, then it must be established that the special circumstances giving rise to them should reasonably have been anticipated at the time the contract was made.[2]

1. A third party action by Fort Pitt against Syracuse Rigging Co. was resolved by judgment for Syracuse with costs. No appeal from that judgment has been taken and it is not before this court.

2. The rule of Hadley v. Baxendale was stated by Alderson, B., as follows:

Where two parties have made a contract which one of them has broken, the damages which the other party ought to receive in respect of such breach of contract should be such as may fairly and reasonably be considered either arising naturally, i.e., according to the usual course of things, from such breach of

There can be no question but that Hadley v. Baxendale represents the law in New York and in the United States generally. E.g., Hughes Tool Co. v. United Artists Corp., 279 App.Div. 417, 110 N.Y.S.2d 383 (1st Dep't 1952), aff'd, 304 N.Y. 942, 110 N.E.2d 884 (1953); J. Calamari & J. Perillo, Contracts 329 (1970); C. McCormick, Damages § 138 (1935); 11 S. Williston, Contracts § 1356 (3d ed. (W. Jaeger) 1968); Restatement of Contracts § 330 (1932). There is no dispute between the parties on this appeal as to the continuing viability of Hadley v. Baxendale and its formulation of the rule respecting special damages, and this court has no intention of challenging or questioning its principles, which Chief Judge Cardozo characterized to be, at least in some applications, "tantamount to a rule of property," Kerr S.S. Co. v. Radio Corporation of America, 245 N.Y. 284, 291, 157 N.E. 140, 142 (1927).

The gist of Fort Pitt's argument is that, when it entered into the subcontract to fabricate, furnish and erect the steel in September, 1969, it had received a copy of the specifications which indicated that the total work was to be completed by December 15, 1971. It could not reasonably have anticipated that Torrington would so expedite the work (which was accepted by the State on January 21, 1971) that steel delivery would be called for in 1970 rather than in 1971. Whatever knowledge Fort Pitt received after the contract was entered into, it argues, cannot expand its liability, since it is essential under Hadley v. Baxendale and its Yankee progeny that the notice of the facts which would give rise to special damages in case of breach be given at or before the time the contract was made. The principle urged cannot be disputed. Czarnikow–Rionda Co. v. Federal Sugar Refining Co., 255 N.Y. 33, 41, 173 N.E. 913, 915 (1930); 11 S. Williston, supra, § 1357; Restatement, supra, § 330. We do not, however, agree that any violence to the doctrine was done here.

Fort Pitt also knew from the same specifications that Torrington was to commence the work on October 1, 1969. The Fort Pitt letter of September 5, 1969, which constitutes the agreement between the parties, specifically provides: "Delivery to be mutually agreed upon." On November 3, 1969, Torrington, responding to Fort Pitt's inquiry, gave "late June 1970" as its required delivery date and, on November 12, 1969, Fort Pitt stated that it was tentatively scheduling delivery for that time. Thus, at the

contract itself, or such as may reasonably be supposed to have been in the contemplation of both parties, at the time they made the contract, as the probable result of the breach of it. Now, if the special circumstances under which the contract was actually made were communicated by the plaintiffs to the defendants, and thus known to both parties, the damages resulting from the breach of such a contract, which they would reasonably contemplate, would be the amount of injury which would ordinarily follow from a breach of contract under these special circumstances so known and communicated. But, on the other hand, if these special circumstances were wholly unknown to the party breaking the contract, he, at the most, could only be supposed to have had in his contemplation the amount of injury which would arise generally, and in the great multitude of cases not affected by any special circumstances, from such a breach of contract.

156 Eng.Rep. at 151.

time when the parties, pursuant to their initial agreement, fixed the date for performance which is crucial here, Fort Pitt knew that a June, 1970 delivery was required. It would be a strained and unpalatable interpretation of Hadley v. Baxendale to now hold that, although the parties left to further agreement the time for delivery, the supplier could reasonably rely upon a 1971 delivery date rather than one the parties later fixed. The behavior of Fort Pitt was totally inconsistent with the posture it now assumes. In November, 1969, it did not quarrel with the date set or seek to avoid the contract. It was not until late January, 1970 that Fort Pitt advised Torrington that, due to unforeseen delays and its expansion program, it could not meet the June date. None of its reasons for late delivery was deemed excusable according to the findings below, and this conclusion is not challenged here. It was not until five months later, on May 20, 1970, after Torrington had threatened to cancel, that Fort Pitt set another date for delivery (early August, 1970) which it again failed to meet, as was found below and not disputed on this appeal.

We conclude that, when the parties enter into a contract which, by its terms, provides that the time of performance is to be fixed at a later date, the knowledge of the consequences of a failure to perform is to be imputed to the defaulting party as of the time the parties agreed upon the date of performance. This comports, in our view, with both the logic and the spirit of Hadley v. Baxendale. Whether the agreement was initially valid despite its indefiniteness or only became valid when a material term was agreed upon is not relevant. At the time Fort Pitt did become committed to a delivery date, it was aware that a June, 1970 performance was required by virtue of its own acceptance. There was no unilateral distortion of the agreement rendering Fort Pitt liable to an extent not theretofore contemplated.

Having proceeded thus far, we do not think it follows automatically that Torrington is entitled to recover the damages it seeks here; further consideration of the facts before us is warranted. Fort Pitt maintains that, under the Hadley v. Baxendale rubric, the damages flowing from its conceded breach are "special" or "consequential" and were not reasonably to be contemplated by the parties. Since Torrington has not proved any "general" or "direct" damages, Fort Pitt urges that the contractor is entitled to nothing. We cannot agree. It is common place that parties to a contract normally address themselves to its performance and not to its breach or the consequences that will ensue if there is a default. See J. Calamari & J. Perillo, supra, at 331; C. McCormick, supra, at 580; 11 S. Williston, supra, at 295. As the New York Court of Appeals long ago stated:

> [A] more precise statement of this rule is, that a party is liable for all the direct damages which both parties to the contract would have contemplated as flowing from its breach, if at the time they entered into it they had bestowed proper attention upon the subject, and had been fully informed of the facts. [This] may properly be called the fiction of law . . .

Leonard v. New York, Albany & Buffalo Electro–Magnetic Telegraph Co., 41 N.Y. 544, 567 (1870).[3]

It is also pertinent to note that the rule does not require that the direct damages must necessarily follow, but only that they are likely to follow; as Lord Justice Asquith commented in Victoria Laundry, Ltd. v. Newman Industries, Ltd., [1949] 2 K.B. 528, 540, are they "on the cards"? We believe here that the damages sought to be recovered were also "in the cards."

It must be taken as a reasonable assumption that, when the delivery date of June 1970 was set, Torrington planned the bridge erection within a reasonable time thereafter. It is normal construction procedure that the erection of the steel girders would be followed by the installation of a poured concrete platform and whatever railings of superstructure the platform would require. Fort Pitt was an experienced bridge fabricator supplying contractors and the sequence of the work is hardly arcane. Moreover, any delay beyond June or August would assuredly have jeopardized the pouring of the concrete and have forced the postponement of the work until the spring. The work here, as was well known to Fort Pitt, was to be performed in northern New York near the Vermont border. The court below found that continuing freezing weather would have forced the pouring to be delayed until June, 1971. Had Torrington refused delivery or had it been compelled to delay the completion of the work until the spring of 1971, the potential damage claim would have been substantial. Instead, in a good faith effort to mitigate damages, Torrington embarked upon the crash program we have described. It appears to us that this eventuality should have reasonably been anticipated by Fort Pitt as it was experienced in the trade and was supplying bridge steel in northern climes on a project requiring a concrete roadway.

Torrington's recovery under the circumstances is not substantial or cataclysmic from Fort Pitt's point of view. It represents the expenses of unloading steel from the gondola due to Fort Pitt's admitted failure to notify its erection subcontractor, Syracuse Rigging, that the steel had been shipped, plus the costs of premium time, extra equipment and the cost of protecting the work, all occasioned by the realities Torrington faced in the wake of Fort Pitt's breach. In fact, Torrington's original claim of $23,-290.81 was whittled down by the court below because of Torrington's failure to establish that its supervisory costs, overhead and certain equipment costs were directly attributable to the delay in delivery of the steel.

Professor Williston has commented:

---

3. A second fiction, added as an embellishment to Hadley v. Baxendale by Mr. Justice Holmes as federal common law in Globe Ref. Co. v. Landa Cotton Oil Co., 190 U.S. 540, 23 S.Ct. 754, 47 L.Ed. 1171 (1903), would require not only knowledge of the special circumstances but a tacit agreement on the part of the party sought to be charged to accept the liability imposed by the notice. This second test has generally been rejected by the courts and commentators. Krauss v. Greenbarg, 137 F.2d 569, 571 (3d Cir.), cert. denied 320 U.S. 791, 64 S.Ct. 207, 88 L.Ed. 477 (1943); J. Calamari & J. Perillo, supra, at 331, 32; 11 S. Williston, supra, § 1357.

The true reason why notice to the defendant of the plaintiff's special circumstances is important is because, just as a court of equity under circumstances of hardship arising after the formation of a contract may deny specific performance, so a court of law may deny damages for unusual consequences where the defendant was not aware when he entered into the contract *how serious an injury would result from its breach.*

11 S. Williston, supra, at 295 (footnote omitted) (emphasis added).

In this case, serious or catastrophic injury was avoided by prompt, effective and reasonable mitigation at modest cost.[7] Had Torrington not acted, had it been forced to wait until the following spring to complete the entire job and then sued to recover the profits it would have made had there been performance by Fort Pitt according to the terms of its agreement, then we might well have an appropriate setting for a classical Hadley v. Baxendale controversy.[8] As this case comes to us, it hardly presents that situation. We therefore affirm the judgment below permitting Torrington to offset its damages against the contract price. [Some footnotes omitted.]

* * *

NOTES

(1) To what extent is the *Spang Industries* case consistent with the "logic and spirit" of *Hadley v. Baxendale,* as amplified in Note (1) at 917. Are the policy bases for this limitation upon damages any clearer in the "Yankee progeny"?

(2) *Hadley v. Baxendale and the UCC.* UCC 2–715(2)(a) [UCC 2–806 (1997)] provides that "consequential damages resulting from the seller's breach include (a) any loss resulting from general or particular requirements and

---

7. It is well understood that expenses incurred in a reasonable effort, whether successful or not, to avoid harm that the defendant had reason to foresee as a probable result of the breach when the contract was made may be recovered as an item of damage flowing from the breach. Elias v. Wright, 276 F. 908, 910 (2d Cir.1921); C. McCormick, supra, § 42; Restatement, supra, § 336(2).

8. In Hadley v. Baxendale a miller sought to recover the profits lost from the closing of the mill as a result of a carrier's failure to make timely delivery of a broken crank shaft to an engineering firm where it was to be used as a model for a replacement. A recovery of those profits was disallowed on the ground that it was not reasonably foreseeable that profits would be lost as a result of the breach of the contract of carriage. Lord Justice Asquith pointed out in Victoria Laundry, Ltd. v. Newman Indus., Ltd., supra, that the headnote in Hadley v. Baxendale is mis-

leading in stating that the clerk of the defendant carrier knew that the mill was stopped and that the broken shaft had to be delivered immediately. The *Victoria* court stated that the Court of Exchequer must have rejected this statement and decided to deny the loss of profits from the closing of the mill because the only knowledge possessed by the defendant was that the mill shaft was broken and that the plaintiffs were the millers. Otherwise, "the court must, one would suppose, have decided the case the other way round...." [1949] 2 K.B. at 537. The misleading headnote, however, was considered to reflect the actual facts by at least two scholarly articles on the famous case. Bauer, Consequential Damages in Contract, 80 U.Penn. L.Rev. 687, 689 (1932); McCormick, Damages for Breach of Contract, 19 Minn.L.Rev. 497, 500 (1935).

needs of which the seller at the time of contracting had reason to know and which could not reasonably be prevented by cover or otherwise." Comment 2 states that the "tacit agreement" test for the recovery of consequential damages is rejected and the "older rule at common law which made the seller liable for all consequential damages of which he had 'reason to know' in advance is followed." This rather expansive approach was ignored in an "early" Code case, Keystone Diesel Engine Co. v. Irwin, 411 Pa. 222, 191 A.2d 376 (1963), but the oversight was later corrected. R.I. Lampus Co. v. Neville Cement Products Corp., 474 Pa. 199, 378 A.2d 288 (1977). Most decisions have followed the spirit of UCC 2–715(2)(a). Thus, in Lewis v. Mobil Oil Corp., 438 F.2d 500, 510 (8th Cir.1971), the court rejected the restrictive "tacit agreement" test and stated:

> Where a seller provides goods to a manufacturing enterprise with knowledge that they are to be used in the manufacturing process, it is reasonable to assume that he should know that defective goods will cause a disruption of production, and loss of profits is a natural consequence of such disruption. Hence, loss of profits should be recoverable under those circumstances.

See also J. White & R. Summers, Uniform Commercial Code § 10–4 (4th ed. 1995). But Comment 2 also provides that the "liberality" of the foreseeable consequences rule is "modified by refusing to permit recovery unless the buyer could not reasonably have prevented the loss by cover or otherwise." In other words, the "duty" to mitigate damages rather than the "tacit agreement" test provides the primary control upon the scope of liability. For a sample of the mix of issues, see Draft Systems, Inc. v. Rimar Manufacturing, Inc., 524 F.Supp. 1049 (E.D.Pa.1981).

(3) *Foreseeability in Tort.* The foreseeable consequences test has been used to limit the scope of liability in tort as well as contract. The critical point is the time of the alleged negligent conduct. If, given the nature of the conduct and the circumstances, the defendant could not reasonably foresee the risk of any harm to the plaintiff or a class of persons similarly situated, there is no duty of care owed to the plaintiff. Palsgraf v. Long Island Railroad, 248 N.Y. 339, 162 N.E. 99 (1928). See Semler v. Psychiatric Institute of Washington, D.C., 538 F.2d 121 (4th Cir.1976), cert. denied 429 U.S. 827, 97 S.Ct. 83, 50 L.Ed.2d 90. If, however, the defendant has breached a duty of care owed to the plaintiff and the negligence has been the cause in fact of varied and extensive damage to person and property, the unforeseeability of that damage does not necessarily insulate the defendant from full liability. The test, according to Judge Friendly, is whether the "very risks" that made the conduct negligent produced "other and more serious consequences to such persons that were fairly foreseeable when he fell short of what the law demanded." If so, there is full liability. If, however, the "injury sprang from a hazard different from that which was improperly risked" the defendant might not be liable for the full consequences caused. Petition of Kinsman Transit Co., 338 F.2d 708, 724 (2d Cir.1964), cert. denied 380 U.S. 944, 85 S.Ct. 1026, 13 L.Ed.2d 963 (1965). See generally Prosser, Torts § 43 (4th ed. 1971); Morris on Torts 179–85 (2d ed. 1980), for a more complete discussion. The English cases, which use a test of foreseeability to determine both the existence and scope of liability, are discussed in Bishop, *The Contract–Tort Boundary and the Economics of Insurance,* 12 J.Leg.Stud. 241 (1983). See also Adams *"Hadley v. Baxendale" and the Contract Tort*

Dichotomy, 8 Anglo–Amer.L.Rev. 147 (1978). For a decision applying both foreseeability and mitigation ideas borrowed from contracts to protect a bank from economic loss caused by the negligent failure to transfer funds, see Evra Corp. v. Swiss Bank Corp., 673 F.2d 951 (7th Cir.1982). In *Evra,* Judge Posner stated that the "rule" in *Hadley v. Baxendale* is that "consequential damages will not be awarded unless the defendant was put on notice of the special circumstances giving rise to them" and that its "animating principle" is that the "costs of the untoward consequence of a course of dealings should be borne by that party who was able to avert the consequence at least cost and failed to do so." 673 F.2d 951 at 955–56, 957. In *Evra,* which was litigated on a negligence theory, the "animating principle" borrowed from contracts required conduct in avoidance by the injured party both before and after the tort. See also Rardin v. T & D Mach. Handling, Inc., 890 F.2d 24, 26–27 (7th Cir.1989) (Posner, J.); McDowell, *Foreseeability in Contract and Tort: The Problems of Responsibility and Remoteness,* 36 Case W.Res.L.Rev. 286 (1986).

(4) *Smirgo v. Bisko Visited Again.* Assuming that Smirgo's breach by non-delivery "caused" the losses and that all damages can be proved with reasonable certainty, has Bisko satisfied the "foreseeability" test of UCC 2–715(2)(a)? Put another way, did Bisko communicate enough information to Smirgo so as to enable it to take precautions or to insure against the harm? If so, has Bisko, after the breach, mitigated damages by taking reasonable action to "prevent" the consequential losses "by cover or otherwise"? UCC 2–715(2)(a).

Would Bisko have any "duty" to deal with Smirgo, the breaching party, if that effort would avoid a six–month delay in repurchasing from a third party? The pre-Code answer was yes, unless the offer was accompanied by a condition operating as an abandonment of the contract or a waiver of any right of action for damages for breach. As one court put it, the "rule" of mitigation "has never been regarded as requiring one to yield to a wrongful demand that he may thereby save the wrongdoer from the legal consequences of his own error." Lurton, J. in Hirsch v. Georgia Iron & Coal Co., 169 Fed. 578, 581 (C.C.A.6 1909). See Gilson v. F.S. Royster Guano Co., 1 F.2d 82 (3d Cir.1924); Lawrence v. Porter, 63 Fed. 62 (6th Cir.1894). See also Schatz Distributing Co., Inc. v. Olivetti Corp. of America, 7 Kan.App.2d 676, 647 P.2d 820 (1982) (buyer of defective computer did not fail to mitigate by refusing seller's offer to resell the goods on buyer's behalf and to substitute new goods).

PROBLEM: JUDGE POSNER'S HYPOTHETICAL

In the *Rardin* case, supra, note 3, Judge Posner posed the following hypothetical. Try your hand at it.

A takes his watch to a retail store, B, for repair. B sends it out to a watchmaker, C. Through negligence, C damages the watch, and when it is returned to A via B it does not tell time accurately. As a result, A misses an important meeting with his creditors. They petition him into bankruptcy. He loses everything. Can he obtain damages from C, the watchmaker, for the consequences of C's negligence? 890 F.2d at 26.

PROBLEM: RECOVERY OF LOST RESALE PROFITS

(1) Bob, a retailer, entered into a contract with Sam, a manufacturer, for the purchase of goods at $100 per unit. Before the goods were delivered, Bob

contracted to sell the goods to Carl, located 1,000 miles away, for $125 a unit. Sam knew at the time of contracting that Bob resold goods of this kind in the ordinary course of business but knew nothing about the prospective contract with Carl. Sam failed to deliver the goods. Bob, after considerable effort, was unable to "cover" on the open market and so informed Carl. Carl released Bob from any liability on the resale contract. Bob, however, sued Sam for lost profits, to be measured by the difference between the contract price and the resale price, some $25 per unit. Sam denied liability on the ground that he had no reason to foresee the particular resale contract with Carl or that Bob would be unable to cover on the open market. Therefore, there was no liability for consequential damages. What result?

(2) Suppose that Bob could have "covered" at $110 per unit but failed to do so. What are Bob's damages here? Do you have enough information?

Hydraform Products Corp. v. American Steel & Aluminum Corp.

Supreme Court of New Hampshire, 1985.
127 N.H. 187, 498 A.2d 339.

■ SOUTER, JUSTICE.

The defendant, American Steel & Aluminum Corporation, appeals from the judgment entered on a jury verdict against it. The plaintiff, Hydraform Products Corporation, brought this action for direct and consequential damages based on claims of negligent misrepresentation and breach of a contract to supply steel to be used in manufacturing woodstoves. American claims that prior to trial, the Superior Court (Nadeau, J.) erroneously held that a limitation of damages clause was ineffective to bar the claim for consequential damages. American further claims, inter alia, that the Trial Court (Dalianis, J.) erred (a) in allowing the jury to calculate lost profits on the basis of a volume of business in excess of what the contract disclosed and for a period beyond the year in which the steel was to be supplied; (b) in allowing the jury to award damages for the diminished value of the woodstove division of Hydraform's business; (c) in failing to direct a verdict for the defendant on the misrepresentation claim; and (d) in allowing Hydraform's president to testify as an expert witness. We hold that the trial court properly refused to enforce the limitation of damages clause, but we sustain the other claims of error and reverse the judgment.

Hydraform was incorporated in 1975 and began manufacturing and Selling woodstoves in 1976. During the sales season of 1977–78 it sold 640 stoves. It purchased steel from a number of suppliers until July 1978, when it entered into a "trial run" contract with American for enough steel to manufacture 40 stoves. Upon delivery of the steel, certain of Hydraform's agents and employees signed a delivery receipt prepared by American, containing the following language:

> "Seller will replace or refund the purchase price for any goods which at the time of delivery to buyer were damaged, defective or not in conformance with the buyer's written purchase order, provided that

the buyer gives seller written notice by mail of such damage, defect or deviation within 10 days following its receipt of the goods. In no event shall seller be liable for labor costs expended on such goods or other consequential damages.''

UCC 2-207

(Emphasis added.)

When some of the deliveries under this contract were late, Hydraform's president, J.R. Choate, explained to an agent of American that late deliveries of steel during the peak season for manufacturing and selling stoves could ruin Hydraform's business for a year. In response, American's agent stated that if Hydraform placed a further order, American would sheer and stockpile in advance, at its own plant, enough steel for 400 stoves, and would supply further steel on demand. Thereafter Hydraform did submit a purchase order for steel sufficient to manufacture 400 stoves, to be delivered in four equal installments on the first days of September, October, November and December of 1978.

American's acceptance of this offer took the form of deliveries accompanied by receipt forms. The forms included the same language limiting American's liability for damages that had appeared on the receipts used during the trial run agreement. Hydraform's employees signed these receipts as the steel was delivered from time to time, and no one representing Hydraform ever objected to that language.

Other aspects of American's performance under the trial run contract reoccurred as well. Deliveries were late, some of the steel delivered was defective, and replacements of defective steel were tardy. Throughout the fall of 1978 Mr. Choate protested the slow and defective shipments, while American's agent continually reassured him that the deficient performance would be corrected. Late in the fall, Mr. Choate finally concluded that American would never perform as agreed, and attempted to obtain steel from other suppliers. He found, however, that none could supply the steel he required in time to manufacture stoves for the 1978–79 sales season. In the meantime, the delays in manufacturing had led to cancelled orders, and by the end of the season Hydraform had manufactured and sold only 250 stoves. In September, 1979, Hydraform sold its woodstove manufacturing division for $150,000 plus royalties.

In December, 1979, Hydraform brought an action for breach of contract, which provoked a countersuit by American. In January, 1983, American moved to dismiss Hydraform's claims for consequential damages to compensate for lost profits and for loss on the sale of the business. American based the motion on the limitation of damages clause and upon its defense that Hydraform had failed to mitigate its damages by cover or otherwise. In February, 1983, Hydraform's pretrial statement filed under Superior Court Rule 62 disclosed that it claimed $100,000 as damages for lost profits generally and $220,000 as a loss on the sale of the business. Later in February, 1983, the superior court permitted Hydraform to amend its writ by adding further counts, which included claims for fraudulent and negligent misrepresentation. Hydraform did not, however, proceed to trial on the claim of fraud.

In April, 1983, Nadeau, J., denied American's motion to dismiss the claims for consequential damages. He relied on the Uniform Commercial Code as adopted in New Hampshire, RSA chapter 382–A, in ruling that the limitation of damages clause was unenforceable on the alternative grounds that the clause would have been a material alteration of the contract, see RSA 382–A:2207(2)(b), or was unconscionable or was a term that had failed of its essential purpose, see RSA 382–A:2–719(2) and (3). He further concluded that, under the circumstances of the case, the failure to cover, if proven, would not bar consequential damages.

The case was tried to a jury before Dalianis, J. American's exceptions at trial are discussed in detail below. At the close of the evidence, American objected to the use of a verdict form with provision for special findings, and the case was submitted for a general verdict, which the jury returned for Hydraform in the amount of $80,245.12.

American's first assignment of error for our consideration challenges the trial court's refusal to recognize the provision insulating American from liability for consequential damages caused by defective goods. We hold that the trial court was correct.

* * *

Since the clause was not enforceable, the trial court allowed the jury to consider Hydraform's claims for lost profits in the year of the contract, 1978, and for the two years thereafter, as well as its claim for loss in the value of the stove manufacturing business resulting in a lower sales price for the business in 1979. American argues that the court erred in submitting such claims to the jury, and rests its position on three requirements governing the recovery of consequential damages.

First, under RSA 382–A:2–715(2)(a) consequential damages are limited to compensation for "loss resulting from general or particular requirements and needs of which the seller at the time of contracting had reason to know . . ." This reflection of Hadley v. Baxendale, 156 Eng.Rep. 145 (1854) thus limits damages to those reasonably foreseeable at the time of the contract. See Gerwin v. Southeastern Cal. Ass'n of Seventh Day Adventists, 14 Cal.App.3d 209, 220, 92 Cal.Rptr. 111, 118 (1971); Petrie–Clemons v. Butterfield, 122 N.H. 120, 124, 441 A.2d 1167, 1170 (1982). To satisfy the foreseeability requirement, the injury for which damages are sought "must follow the breach in the natural course of events, or the evidence must specifically show that the breaching party had reason to foresee the injury." Salem Engineering & Const. Corp. v. Londonderry School Dist., 122 N.H. 379, 384, 445 A.2d 1091, 1094 (1982). Thus, peculiar circumstances and particular needs must be made known to the seller if they are to be considered in determining the foreseeability of damages. Lewis v. Mobil Oil Corporation, 438 F.2d 500, 510 (8th Cir.1971).

Second, the damages sought must be limited to recompense for the reasonably ascertainable consequences of the breach. See RSA 382–A:2–715, comment 4. While proof of damages to the degree of mathematical certainty is not necessary, Smith v. State, 125 N.H. 799, 805, 486 A.2d 289,

294 (1984), a claim for lost profits must rest on evidence demonstrating that the profits claimed were "reasonably certain" in the absence of the breach. Whitehouse v. Rytman, 122 N.H. 777, 780, 451 A.2d 370, 372 (1982). Speculative losses are not recoverable.

Third, consequential damages such as lost profits are recoverable only if the loss "could not reasonably be prevented by cover or otherwise." § 2–715(2)(a). See § 2–712(1) (i.e., by purchase or contract to purchase goods in substitution for those due from seller). In summary, consequential damages must be reasonably foreseeable, ascertainable and unavoidable.

Applying these standards, we look first at the claim for lost profits for the manufacturing season beginning in September, 1978. There is no serious question that loss of profit on sales was foreseeable up to the number of 400 stoves referred to in the contract, and there is a clear evidentiary basis for a finding that Hydraform would have sold at least that number. There was also an evidentiary basis for the trial court's ruling that Hydraform acted reasonably even though it did not attempt to cover until the season was underway and it turned out to be too late. American had led Hydraform on by repeatedly promising to take steps to remedy its failures, and the court could find that Hydraform's reliance on these promises was reasonable up to the time when it finally and unsuccessfully tried to cover.

Lost profits on sales beyond the 400 stoves presents a foreseeability issue, however. Although American's agent had stated that American would supply steel beyond the 400 stove level on demand, there is no evidence that Hydraform indicated that it would be likely to make such a demand to the extent of any reasonably foreseeable amount. Rather, the evidence was that Mr. Choate had told American's agent that the business was seasonal with a busy period of about four months. The contract referred to delivery dates on the first of four separate months and spoke of only 400 stoves. Thus, there appears to be no basis on which American should have foreseen a volume in excess of 400 for the season beginning in 1978. Lost profits for sales beyond that amount therefore were not recoverable, and it was error to allow the jury to consider them.

Nor should the claims for profits lost on sales projected for the two subsequent years have been submitted to the jury. The impediment to recovery of these profits was not total unforeseeability that the breach could have effects in a subsequent year or years, but the inability to calculate any such loss with reasonable certainty. In arguing that a reasonably certain calculation was possible, Hydraform relies heavily on Van Hooijdonk v. Langley, 111 N.H. 32, 274 A.2d 798 (1971), a case that arose from a landlord's cancellation of a business lease. The court held that the jury could award damages for profits that a seasonal restaurant anticipated for the three years that lease should have run. It reasoned that the experience of one two-month season provided sufficient data for a reasonably certain opinion about the extent of future profits. The court thus found sufficient certainty where damages were estimated on the basis of one year of operation and profit, as compared with no operation and hence no profit in the later years.

Hydraform's situation, however, presents a variable that distinguishes it from Van Hooijdonk. In our case the evidence did not indicate that American's breach had forced Hydraform's stove manufacturing enterprise out of business, and therefore the jury could not assume that there would be no profits in later years. Without that assumption the jury could not come to any reasonably certain conclusion about the anticipated level of sales absent a breach by American. The jury could predict that Hydraform would obtain steel from another source and would be able to manufacture stoves; but it did not have the evidence from which to infer the future volume of manufacturing and sales. Thus, it could not calculate anticipated lost profits with a reasonable degree of certainty.

There is, moreover, a further reason to deny recovery for profits said to have been lost in the later years. Although Hydraform's pretrial statement disclosed that Hydraform claimed $100,000 in lost profits, it did not indicate that the claim related to the seasons beginning in 1979 and 1980. Since the pretrial statement also listed a claim for loss of the value of the business at the time of its sale in 1979, we believe that the statement could reasonably be read as claiming lost profit only for the one year before the business was sold. Therefore the claim for profits in 1979 and 1980 should have been disallowed for failure to disclose the claim as required by Superior Court Rule 62.

We consider next the claim for loss in the value of the business as realized at the time of its sale in 1979. As a general rule, loss in the value of a business as a going concern, or loss in the value of its good will, may be recovered as an element of consequential damages. See Salem Engineering & Const. Corp. v. Londonderry School Dist., 122 N.H. at 384, 445 A.2d at 1094; Salinger v. Salinger, 69 N.H. 589, 591–92, 45 A. 558, 559–60 (1899); see also J. Story, Partnership § 99, at 169–70 (6th ed. 1868).

In this case, however, it was error to submit the claim for diminished value to the jury, for three reasons. First, to the extent that diminished value was thought to reflect anticipated loss of profits in future years, as a capitalization of the loss, it could not be calculated with reasonable certainty for the reasons we have just discussed. Second, even if such profits could have been calculated in this case, allowing the jury to consider both a claim for diminished value resting on lost profits and a claim for the lost profits themselves would have allowed a double recovery. See Westric Battery Co. v. Standard Electric Co., Inc., 522 F.2d 986, 989 (10th Cir.1975). Third, to the extent that diminished value was thought to rest on any other theory, there was no evidence on which it could have been calculated. There was nothing more than Mr. Choate's testimony that he had sold the business in September of 1979 for $150,000 plus minimum royalties, together with his opinion that the sales price was less than the business was worth. This testimony provided the jury with no basis for determining what the business was worth or for calculating the claimed loss, and any award on this theory rested on sheer speculation.

In summary, we hold that the jury should not have been allowed to consider any contract claim for consequential damages for lost profits beyond those lost on the sale of 150 stoves, the difference between the 400 mentioned in the contract and the 250 actually sold. Nor should the trial court have allowed the jury to consider the claim for loss in the value of the business.

* * *

Reversed.

NOTES

(1) *"New Business" Rule.* The ease with which lost profits can be proved may depend upon whether the plaintiff is a new or an established business. Where did the plaintiff fit in *Hydraform*? What limitations did the court impose upon recovery of the claimed lost profits.

Here is a traditional statement of the so-called "new business" or *per se* rule:

> When the business that is interfered with as a result of a breach of contract is a new business or venture, or one merely in contemplation, the anticipated profits from such business cannot be recovered as an item of damages because it cannot be rendered reasonably certain that there would have been any profits at all from the conduct of the business.

Coastland Corporation v. Third National Mortgage Co., 611 F.2d 969, 978 (4th Cir.1979) (Virginia law). For a collection of the authorities and arguments for and against the *per se* rule, see Note, 67 Va.L.Rev. 431 (1981) (for); Comment, 56 N.Car.L.Rev. 693 (1978) (against). See generally Schaefer, *Uncertainty and the Law of Damages,* 19 Wm. & Mary L.Rev. 719 (1979). Most decisions under the UCC, however, have rejected the *per se* rule. The crucial issue is not whether the plaintiff is a new business but whether the lost profits are proven with reasonable certainty. See, e.g., Hawthorne Industries, Inc. v. Balfour Maclaine International, Limited, 676 F.2d 1385 (11th Cir.1982); Deaton, Inc. v. Aeroglide Corp., 99 N.M. 253, 657 P.2d 109 (1982) (B fails to prove damages with reasonable certainty in new business); El Fredo Pizza, Inc. v. Roto–Flex Oven Co., 199 Neb. 697, 261 N.W.2d 358 (1978). See also Note, *The New Business Rule and the Denial of Lost Profits,* 48 Ohio St.L.J. 855 (1987).

(2) *Causation Issue.* Proof issues are frequently mixed with the question of whether the breach "caused" the lost consequential profits. Thus, a buyer was denied lost profits when a delay was attributable to a tactical business decision by the buyer rather than to a defect in the seller's product. Duracote Corp. v. Goodyear Tire & Rubber Co., 2 Ohio St.3d 160, 443 N.E.2d 184 (1983). Similarly, reduced profits attributable to the plaintiff's capital structure rather than to defendant's breach of warranty were also denied. Lewis v. Mobil Oil Corp., 438 F.2d 500 (8th Cir.1971). See also Dura–Wood Treating Co. v. Century Forest Industries, Inc., 675 F.2d 745 (5th Cir.1982) (P ties up production facilities by decision to manufacture product which D had failed to deliver rather than by covering); Overstreet v. Norden Laboratories, Inc., 669 F.2d 1286 (6th Cir.1982) (breach of warranty regarding vaccine did not cause brood mares to abort foals). As one court has put it, the "rule preventing recovery of 'speculative' damages referred 'more especially to the uncertainty as to the

cause rather than uncertainty as to the measure or extent of damages.' " Hawthorne Industries, Inc. v. Balfour Maclaine International, Limited, 676 F.2d 1385, 1387 (11th Cir.1982). See also Redgrave v. Boston Symphony Orchestra, Inc., 855 F.2d 888, 891–94 (1st Cir.1988) (claim that reputation damaged by breach is unduly speculative and too remote).

L. Albert & Son v. Armstrong Rubber Co.

United States Court of Appeals, Second Circuit, 1949.
178 F.2d 182.

■ L. HAND, CHIEF JUDGE. Both sides appeal from the judgment in an action brought by the Albert Company, which we shall speak of as the Seller, against the Armstrong Company, which we shall call the Buyer. The action was to recover the agreed price of four "Refiners," machines designed to recondition old rubber; the contract of sale was by an exchange of letters in December, 1942, and the Seller delivered two of the four "Refiners" in August, 1943, and the other two on either August 31st or September 8th, 1945. Because of the delay in delivery of the second two, the Buyer refused to accept all four in October, 1945—the exact day not being fixed—and it counterclaimed for the Seller's breach. The judge dismissed both the complaint and the counterclaim; but he gave judgment to the Seller for the value without interest of a part of the equipment delivered—a 300 horse-power motor and accessories—which the Buyer put into use on February 20th, 1946. * * *

[The court affirmed the judgment for the Seller with a modification as to interest and a limited set-off possibility for the Buyer.]

Coming next to the Buyer's appeal, it does not claim any loss of profit, but it does claim the expenses which it incurred in reliance upon the Seller's promise. These were of three kinds: its whole investment in its "reclaim department," $118,478; the cost of its "rubber scrap," $27,555.63; the cost of the foundation which it laid for the "Refiners," $3,000. The judge in his opinion held that the Buyer had not proved that "the lack of production" of the reclaim department "was caused by the delay in delivery of plaintiffs' refiners"; but that was "only one of several possible causes. Such a possibility is not sufficient proof of causation to impose liability on the plaintiffs for the cost of all machinery and supplies for the reclaim department." The record certainly would not warrant our holding that this holding was "clearly erroneous"; indeed, the evidence preponderates in its favor. The Buyer disposed of all its "scrap rubber" in April and May, 1945; and, so far as appears, until it filed its counterclaim in May, 1947, it never suggested that the failure to deliver two of the four "Refiners" was the cause of the collapse of its "reclaim department." The counterclaim for these items has every appearance of being an afterthought, which can scarcely have been put forward with any hope of success.

The claim for the cost of the foundation which the Buyer built for the "Refiners," stands upon a different footing. Normally a promisee's damages for breach of contract are the value of the promised performance, less his outlay, which includes, not only what he must pay to the promisor, but any expenses necessary to prepare for the performance; and in the case at bar the cost of the foundation was such an expense. The sum which would restore the Buyer to the position it would have been in, had the Seller performed, would therefore be the prospective net earnings of the "Refiners" while they were used (together with any value they might have as scrap after they were discarded), less their price—$25,500—together with $3,000, the cost of installing them. The Buyer did not indeed prove the net earnings of the "Refiners" or their scrap value; but it asserts that it is nonetheless entitled to recover the cost of the foundation upon the theory that what it expended in reliance upon the Seller's performance was a recoverable loss. In cases where the venture would have proved profitable to the promisee, there is no reason why he should not recover his expenses. On the other hand, on those occasions in which the performance would not have covered the promisee's outlay, such a result imposes the risk of the promisee's contract upon the promisor. We cannot agree that the promisor's default in performance should under this guise make him an insurer of the promisee's venture; yet it does not follow that the breach should not throw upon him the duty of showing that the value of the performance would in fact have been less than the promisee's outlay. It is often very hard to learn what the value of the performance would have been; and it is a common expedient, and a just one, in such situations to put the peril of the answer upon that party who by his wrong has made the issue relevant to the rights of the other. On principle therefore the proper solution would seem to be that the promisee may recover his outlay in preparation for the performance, subject to the privilege of the promisor to reduce it by as much as he can show that the promisee would have lost, if the contract had been performed.

The decisions leave much to be desired. There is language in United States v. Behan[1] which, read literally, would allow the promisee to recover his outlay in all cases: the promisor is said to be "estopped" to deny that the value of the performance would not equal it. We doubt whether the Supreme Court would today accept the explanation, although the result was right under the rule which we propose. Moreover, in spite of the authority properly accorded to any decision of that court, we are here concerned only with Connecticut law; and the decisions in that state do not seem to be in entire accord. In the early case of Bush v. Canfield[2] the buyer sued to recover a payment of $5,000 made in advance for the purchase of 2,000 barrels of flour at $7.00 a barrel. Although at the time set for delivery the value of the flour had fallen to $5.50, the seller for some undisclosed reasons failed to perform. The action was on the case for the breach, not in indebitatus assumpsit, and the court, Hosmer, J., dissenting, allowed the buyer to recover the full amount of his payment over the seller's objection that recovery should be reduced by the buyer's loss. The chief justice gave the following reason for his decision which we take to be that of the court, 2 Conn. page 488: "The defendant has violated his contract; and it is not

---

1. 110 U.S. 338, 345, 346 (1884).   **2.** 2 Conn. 485.

for him to say that if he had fulfilled it, the plaintiffs would have sustained a great loss, and that this ought to be deducted from the money advanced." If there is no difference between the recovery of money received by a promisor who later defaults, and a promisee's outlay preparatory to performance, this decision is in the Buyer's favor. However, when the promisor has received any benefit, the promisee's recovery always depends upon whether the promisor has been "unjustly enriched"; and, judged by that nebulous standard, there may be a distinction between imposing the promisee's loss on the promisor by compelling him to disgorge what he has received and compelling him to pay what he never has received. It is quite true that the only difference is between allowing the promisee to recover what he has paid to the promisor and what he has paid to others; but many persons would probably think that difference vital.

[The court discussed several other decisions and found them "inconclusive" on the recoverability of reliance expenditures paid to others.]

It appears to us therefore that the reported decisions leave it open to us to adopt the rule we have stated. Moreover, there is support for this result in the writings of scholars. The Restatement of Contracts allows recovery of the promisee's outlay "in necessary preparation" for the performance, subject to several limitations, of which one is that the promisor may deduct whatever he can prove the promisee would have lost, if the contract had been fully performed. Professor McCormick thinks[3] that "the jury should be instructed not to go beyond the probable yield" of the performance to the promisee, but he does not consider the burden of proof. Much the fullest discussion of the whole subject is Professor Fuller's in the Yale Law Journal.[4] The situation at bar was among those which he calls cases of "essential reliance," and for which he favors the rule we are adopting. It is one instance of his "very simple formula: We will not in a suit for reimbursement of losses incurred in reliance on a contract knowingly put the plaintiff in a better position than he would have occupied, had the contract been fully performed."

The judgment will therefore be affirmed with the following modifications. To the allowance for the motor and accessories will be added interest from February 20th, 1946. The Buyer will be allowed to set off $3,000 against the Seller's recovery with interest from October, 1945, subject to the Seller's privilege to deduct from that amount any sum which upon a further hearing it can prove would have been the Buyer's loss upon the contract, had the "Refiners" been delivered on or before May 1st, 1945.

Judgment modified as above, and affirmed as so modified.

[Some footnotes are omitted. Those retained have been renumbered.]

NOTES

(1) If the $3,000 was spent in preparation for using the refiners rather than performing the contract, how can this be "essential" reliance as Judge

---

3. McCormick on Damages, 142, p. 584.   **4.** 46 Yale Law Journal, 52, 75–80.

Hand suggests? *United States v. Behan,* discussed by the court, clearly involved essential reliance since the expenditures were necessary for the contractor to earn the price. Not so the expenditure in *Albert.* Professor Fuller maintained that claims for "essential" reliance should be limited by the full contract price or its equivalent in market terms while reimbursement for "incidental" reliance should be limited by the expectation interest "measured in terms of its utility to the plaintiff in his particular situation." Fuller & Perdue, 46 Yale L.J. at 78. Which limitation did Judge Hand utilize in the *Albert* case?

(2) Another difference between "essential" and "incidental" reliance may find expression in the difference between "general" and "consequential" damages. Did somebody forget about *Hadley v. Baxendale* in the *Albert* case? See Atlan Industries, Inc. v. O.E.M., Inc., 555 F.Supp. 184 (W.D.Okl.1983) (court allows consequential, foreseeable reliance expenditures when lost profits not provable with reasonable certainty). Compare Restatement (Second) § 349.

(3) In sum, consequential damages result from the inability of the plaintiff to use the defendant's promised performance, either because the defendant failed to perform or because the performance did not conform to the contract. Loss of use may result in lost profits or, in the alternative, expenditures in reliance on the promised performance. But these losses are subject to the limitations of foreseeability, cause in fact, proof with reasonable certainty and the requirements of damage mitigation. If all of these obstacles are overcome, are there any other limitations that should be imposed? According to Section 351(3) of the Restatement (Second) of Contracts, the answer is yes: "A court may limit damages for foreseeable loss by excluding recovery for loss of profits, by allowing recovery only for loss incurred in reliance, or otherwise if it concludes that in the circumstances justice so requires in order to avoid disproportionate compensation."

PROBLEM: SMIRGO AND BISKO—ONE MORE TIME!

Assume that after Smirgo's breach, Bisko elected not to expand the bakery. After salvage, Bisko had $5,000 in unreimbursed expenses in preparing to receive the ovens. In addition, Bisko can prove with reasonable certainty that it would have grossed $150,000 in new business between the time that Smirgo promised to deliver and the time that the ovens could have been replaced by an effective cover. Bisko can also prove that the costs saved by Smirgo's breach were $100,000. Bisko claims $55,000 in consequential damages, including $50,000 in lost profits ($150,000 gross less $100,000 in costs saved) and $5,000 in reasonable reliance. Evaluate the arguments of Smirgo in response:

1. $55,000 puts Bisko in a better position than full performance would have because Bisko elected after the breach to discontinue the expansion. You can't recover lost profits on a project that was discontinued.

2. $55,000 gives Bisko a double recovery for reliance expenditures. At best, Bisko should recover the "net" profit prevented by the breach plus any unreimbursed reliance. "Net" profit is determined by subtracting costs saved ($100,000) plus reliance incurred ($5,000) from the gross prevented ($150,000), for a figure of $45,000. When reliance is added in, the amount of recovery should be $50,000, not $55,000.

3. The substantial cause of the lost revenues, if Bisko had continued, would have been the competition from Caraway rather than the breach by Smirgo. Thus, Bisko's recovery is limited to $5,000.

4. In any event, the cumulative effect of these factors plus the relatively small contract price, justify the application by a court of Restatement (Second) § 351(3), supra.

To what extent will a court enforce an agreement excluding consequential damages for breach of contract? For the answer, see Chapter Six, Section 5(B).

SECTION 3.   PREVENTION, HINDRANCE AND THE DUTY OF COOPERATION

In a very real sense, the principles governing non-performance of a promise are principles of strict liability. If the bargain is enforceable and the defendant's non-performance is not justified by such things as the failure of an express condition, some recognized excuse or the plaintiff's misconduct, liability for "breach" does not require the plaintiff to establish fault. True, a negligent or deliberate breach may induce a court to characterize it as material rather than immaterial and could influence the measure or amount of damages recoverable. But although it may be accurate to conclude that someone who fails to perform an enforceable promise without justification is at "fault," the plaintiff is not required to prove either negligence or willful misconduct to establish liability.

Saying this, one might speculate about the relationship between contract and tort. In tort, the primary question concerns the responsibility of individuals and entities for acts or omissions which cause damage to someone else's person, property or economic opportunities. When these duties are imposed and for what reasons and the scope of the protection available are key issues in dispute. In contract, the rights and duties arise from the exchange relationship—a relationship that requires a certain quantity and quality of agreement before liability can attach and rewards informed consent by the parties. It is fashionable to say that in tort the duties are imposed regardless of consent and in contract the duties arise because of consent. But as you well know, the instances where consent (or the intention of the parties) is fully expressed are limited in many bargains and, even so, the principles of liability and remedy frequently apply in spite of expressed intention. And there are those troublesome areas, such as products liability and fraudulent misrepresentation, where things seem to overlap in a confused jumble. Conduct which is tortious is also part of the exchange relationship—the "breach" of contract may also be a tort. Whether the overlap features minimum duties of a seller of defective products regardless of consent or tort-like duties imposed upon an exchange relationship in the absence of agreement, the similarity of the problems argues against any assertion that tort and contract can and should be compartmentalized. See, e.g., Epstein, *Medical Malpractice: The Case for Contract,*

1976 A.B.F. Research J. 87; Speidel, *The Borderland of Contract,* 10 N.Ky.L.Rev. 163 (1983).

A useful way to think about the problem posed in this section—prevention, hindrance and the duty of cooperation—is in terms of duties imposed by the courts upon parties to exchange relationships in the absence of and, maybe, in spite of an expression of contrary agreement. Whether you say that these duties are implied or imposed is not as important as understanding when and why these relational duties will be found and enforced by the courts. Thus, the doctrines of "prospective inability" to perform and "anticipatory" repudiation both emerge from the perception that the defendant has done something to impair the plaintiff's expectation of receiving due performance, and that the plaintiff's interests, whether you call them expectation, reliance or restitution, should have some protection, be it defensive, affirmative or both. Despite the "implied promise" terminology, Lord Campbell put it very well when he said "where there is a contract to do an act on a future day, there is a relation constituted between the parties in the meantime by the contract and that they impliedly promise that * * * neither will do anything to the prejudice of the other inconsistent with that relation." *Hochster v. De La Tour*, supra at 41. This basic notion has been particularized in a contemporary decision which does not improve too much on the original:

> It is a fundamental principle of law that in every contract there exists an implied covenant of good faith and fair dealing. ... Furthermore, each contract contains an implicit understanding that neither party will intentionally do anything to prevent the other party from carrying out his part of the agreement. * * * "It is likewise implied in every contract that there is a duty of cooperation on the part of both parties. *Thus, whenever the cooperation of the promisee is necessary for the performance of the promise, there is a condition implied that the cooperation will be given.*"

Lowell v. Twin Disc., Inc., 527 F.2d 767, 770 (2d Cir.1975) (New York law; emphasis in original). As with a repudiation or breach by a material nonperformance, breach by prevention or hindrance or a failure to cooperate both excuses the aggrieved party from any duty to continue performance and gives a cause of action for damages.

Blandford v. Andrews

Queen's Bench, 1599.
78 Eng.Rep. 930.

Debt on an obligation of eighty pounds, conditioned, that if the defendant procured a marriage to be had between the plaintiff, and one Bridget Palmer, at or before the Feast of St. Bartholomew then next following; that then the defendant pleaded, that the plaintiff, before that feast, came to the said Bridget Palmer, and called her whore; and told her, that if he married her, he would tie her to a post; and used other opprobrious words unto her; by reason whereof the defendant could not procure the said marriage before the said feast. Whereupon the plaintiff demurred.—Williams, Serjeant, moved that this was not any plea; for he hath not shewn that he used his endeavour to procure the marriage; for it may be that, notwithstanding these words, they would have intermarried.—And of that opinion was all the Court; for the defendant ought to shew that there was not any default in him, and that he did as much as in him lay to procure it; otherwise he doth not save his obligation; and these words spoken before the day, at one time only, are not such an impediment but that the marriage might have taken effect. Wherefore it was adjudged for the plaintiff.

Patterson v. Meyerhofer

Court of Appeals of New York, 1912.
204 N.Y. 96, 97 N.E. 472.

■ WILLARD, BARTLETT, J. The parties to this action entered into a written contract whereby the plaintiff agreed to sell and the defendant agreed to buy four several parcels of land with the houses thereon for the sum of $23,000, to be paid partly in cash and partly by taking title subject to certain mortgages upon the property. When she executed this contract, the defendant knew that the plaintiff was not then the owner of the premises which he agreed to sell to her but that he expected and intended to acquire title thereto by purchasing the same at a foreclosure sale. Before this foreclosure sale took place the defendant stated to the plaintiff that she would not perform the contract on her part but intended to buy the premises for her own account without in any way recognizing the said contract as binding upon her, and this she did, buying the four parcels for $5,595 each. The plaintiff attended the foreclosure sale, able, ready and willing to purchase the premises, and he bid for the same, but in every instance of a bid made by him the defendant bid a higher sum. The result was that she acquired each lot for $155 less than she had obligated herself to pay the plaintiff therefor under the contract or $620 less in all.

In the foreclosure sale was included a fifth house, which the defendant also purchased. This was not mentioned in the written contract between the parties, but according to the complaint there was a prior parol agreement which provided that the plaintiff should buy all five houses at the foreclosure sale and should convey only four of them to the defendant, retaining the fifth house for himself.

Upon these facts the plaintiff brought the present action demanding judgment that the defendant convey to him the fifth house and declaring that he had a lien upon the premises purchased by her at the foreclosure sale and that she holds the same in trust for the plaintiff subject to the contract. The complaint also prays that the plaintiff be awarded the sum of $620 damages, being the difference between the price which the defendant paid at the foreclosure sale for the four houses mentioned in the contract and the price which she would have had to pay the plaintiff thereunder.

The learned judge who tried the case at Special Term rendered judgment in favor of the defendant, holding that under the contract of sale there was no relation of confidence between the vendor and vendee. "In the present case," he said, "each party was free to act for his own interest, restricted only by the stipulations of the contract." He was, therefore, of the opinion that "the defendant had a right to buy in at the auction and that she is entitled to hold exactly as though she had been a stranger and that the plaintiff is not entitled to recover the difference between the price paid at the auction and the contract price."

I am inclined to agree with the trial court that no relation of trust can be spelled out of the transactions between the parties. There is no finding of any parol agreement in respect to the fifth house which has been mentioned, and even if there had been such an agreement resting merely in parol, I do not see that it would have been enforceable. As to the four parcels which constituted the subject-matter of the written contract, the defendant avowed her intention to ignore that contract before bidding for them, and cannot be regarded as having gone into possession *under* the plaintiff as vendor, but did so rather in defiance of any right of his; hence, there is no likeness to the cases of Galloway v. Finley (12 Peters, [U.S.], 264) and Bush v. Marshall (6 How. [U.S.], 284) relied upon by the appellant. In those cases, it is true, vendees who had bought up better titles than those of their vendors were treated as trustees for the latter; but the contracts of sale had been carried out and the vendees were in full possession of the lands before they acquired the superior outstanding title; and both decisions were expressly placed on the ground that under such circumstances the vendor and vendee stand in the relation of landlord and tenant and the vendee cannot disavow the vendor's title.

There is no need of judicially declaring any trust in the defendant, however, to secure to the plaintiff the profit which he would have made if the defendant had not intervened as purchaser at the foreclosure sale and had fulfilled the written contract on her part. This is represented by his claim for $620 damages. That amount, under the facts as found, I think the plaintiff was entitled to recover. He has demanded it in his complaint and he should not be thrown out of court because he has also prayed for too much equitable relief.

In the case of every contract there is an implied undertaking on the part of each party that he will not intentionally and purposely do anything to prevent the other party from carrying out the agreement on his part.

This proposition necessarily follows from the general rule that a party who causes or sanctions the breach of an agreement is thereby precluded from recovering damages for its non-performance or from interposing it as a defense to an action upon the contract. (Young v. Hunter, 6 N.Y. 203; Barton v. Gray, 57 Mich. 622, and cases there cited.)

"Where a party stipulates that another shall do a certain thing, he thereby impliedly promises that he will himself do nothing which may hinder or obstruct that other in doing that thing." (Gay v. Blanchard, 32 La.Ann. 497.)

By entering into the contract to purchase from the plaintiff property which she knew he would have to buy at the foreclosure sale in order to convey it to her, the defendant impliedly agreed that she would do nothing to prevent him from acquiring the property at such sale. The defendant violated the agreement thus implied on her part by bidding for and buying the premises herself. Although the plaintiff bid therefor she uniformly outbid him. Presumably if she had not interfered he could have bought the property for the same price which she paid for it. He would then have been able to sell it to her for the price specified in the contract (assuming that she fulfilled the contract), which was $620 more. This sum, therefore, represents the loss which he has suffered. It is the measure of the plaintiff's damages for the defendant's breach of contract.

I see no escape from this conclusion. It is true that the contract contemplated that the four houses should go to the defendant and they have gone to her; but that is not all. The contract contemplated that they should go to the plaintiff first. In that event the plaintiff would have received $620 which he has not got. This would have had to be paid by the defendant if she had fulfilled her contract; and she should be required to pay it now unless she can present some better defense than is presented in this record. This will place both parties in the position contemplated by the contract. The defendant will have paid no more than the contract obligated her to pay; the plaintiff will have received all to which the contract entitled him. I leave the fifth house out of consideration because as to that it seems to me there was no enforceable agreement.

For these reasons the judgments of the Appellate Division and the Special Term should be reversed and a new trial granted, with costs to abide the event.

Iron Trade Products Co. v. Wilkoff Co.

Supreme Court of Pennsylvania, 1922.
272 Pa. 172, 116 A. 150.

■ OPINION BY MR. JUSTICE WALLING. In July, 1919, plaintiff entered into a written contract with defendant for the purchase of twenty-six hundred tons of section relaying rails, to be delivered in New York harbor at times therein specified, for $41 a ton. Defendant failed to deliver any of the rails and plaintiff brought this suit, averring, by reason of such default, it had been compelled to purchase the rails elsewhere (two thousand tons thereof at $49.20 per ton and six hundred tons at $49 per ton), also that the market or current price of the rails at the time and place of delivery was approximately $50 per ton, and claiming as damages the difference between what it had been compelled to pay and the contract price. Defendant filed an affidavit of defense and a supplement thereto, both of which the court below held insufficient and entered judgment for plaintiff; from which defendant brought this appeal.

In effect, the affidavit of defense avers the supply of such rails was very limited, there being only two places in the United States (one in Georgia and one in West Virginia) where they could be obtained in quantities to fill the contract, and that, pending the time for delivery, defendant was negotiating for the required rails when plaintiff announced to the trade its urgent desire to purchase a similar quantity of like rails, and, in fact, bought eight hundred and eighty-seven tons and agreed to purchase a much larger quantity from the parties with whom defendant had been negotiating; further averring this conduct on behalf of plaintiff reduced the available supply of relaying rails and enhanced the price to an exorbitant sum, rendering performance by defendant impossible. The affidavit, however, fails to aver knowledge on part of plaintiff that the supply of rails was limited or any intent on its part to prevent, interfere with or embarrass defendant in the performance of the contract; and there is no suggestion of any understanding, express or implied, that defendant was to secure the rails from any particular source, or that plaintiff was to refrain from purchasing other rails; hence, it was not required to do so. The true rule is stated in Williston on Contracts, p. 1308, as quoted by the trial court, viz: "If a party seeking to secure all the merchandise of a certain character which he could, entered into a contract for a quantity of the required goods, and subsequently made performance of the contract by the seller more difficult by making other purchases which increased the scarcity of the available supply, his conduct would furnish no excuse for refusal to perform the prior contract." Mere difficulty of performance will not excuse a breach of contract: Corona C. & C. v. Dickinson, 261 Pa. 589; Janes v. Scott, 59 Pa. 178; 35 Cyc. 245. Defendant relies upon the rule stated in United States v. Peck, 102 U.S. 64, that, "The conduct of one party to a contract which prevents the other from performing his part is an excuse for nonperformance." The cases are not parallel; here, plaintiff's conduct did not prevent performance by defendant, although it may have added to the difficulty and expense thereof. There is no averment that plaintiff's purchases exhausted the supply of rails, and the advance in price caused thereby is no excuse. The Peck case stands on different ground, there Peck contracted to sell the government a certain quantity of hay for the Tongue River station, and the trial court found it was mutually understood the hay was to be cut on government lands called "the Big Meadows," in the Yellowstone Valley, which was the only available source of supply; also that thereafter the government caused all of that hay to be cut for it by other parties. In view of this Peck was relieved from his contract.

[The court held that the plaintiff was entitled to damages measured by the difference between the contract price and the price paid to obtain substitute goods on the market.]

The assignments of error are overruled and the judgment is affirmed.

NOTES

(1) *Implied Covenant of Good Faith.* Whether the inquiry concerns discharge of duty, excuse for failure of condition, or action for breach, cases of this type are said to apply, in the last analysis, the principle that "in every contract there is an implied covenant that neither party shall do anything which will

have the effect of destroying or injuring the right of the other party to receive the fruits of the contract, which means that in every contract there exists an implied covenant of good faith and fair dealing." Kirke La Shelle Co. v. Paul Armstrong Co., 263 N.Y. 79, 87, 188 N.E. 163, 167 (1934). See UCC 1–203 ("Every contract or duty within this Act imposes an obligation of good faith in its performance or enforcement."); UCC 2–103(1)(b) (" 'Good faith' in the case of a merchant means honesty in fact and the observance of reasonable commercial standards of fair dealing in the trade."); Restatement (Second) § 205 ("Every contract imposes upon each party a duty of good faith and fair dealing in its performance and its enforcement."). Here also the strictness of the older cases, typified by *Blandford*, has been mitigated by later decisions "making a contract for the parties" by the implication or construction of conditions. See, in general, Patterson, *Constructive Conditions in Contracts*, 42 Colum.L.Rev. 903, 928–42 (1942).

(2) In both *Patterson v. Meyerhofer* and *Iron Trade Products Co. v. Wilkoff Co.* and in *United States v. Peck*, discussed in *Wilkoff*, one party to the contract actively competed with the other to obtain what was promised under the contract. In each instance, the competition, which was in the defendant's best interest, was successful, either preventing or hindering the other party in performance. But liability was imposed only in *Patterson*. Can the cases be reconciled? Is the difference to be found in the motive behind the conduct or, perhaps, the knowledge possessed by the defendant at the time? Or, does the answer lie in a theory of risk assumption, based upon the language of the contract, the capacity of the parties, the nature of the performance, market conditions and what both parties knew or had reason to know about the exchange? For a critique of these cases, set in the context of a broad study of "opportunistic behavior" in contract performance, see Muris, *Opportunistic Behavior and the Law of Contracts*, 65 Minn.L.Rev. 521, 553–56 (1981).

(3) *The Case of the Opportunistic Tenant.* Landlord leased premises to Tenant for use as a gasoline station at a rental of five cents for each gallon of gasoline sold. Midway during the five-year term, Tenant purchased adjoining property upon which he built and operated a new station. Prior to operation of the new station gallonage totaled approximately 40,000 per month; since that time the average has declined to around 4,000. There was no covenant in the lease prohibiting operation of a new station. Landlord consults you relative to his right, if any, to cancel the lease. What do you advise? Cf. Seggebruch v. Stosor, 309 Ill.App. 385, 33 N.E.2d 159 (1941).

(4) *The Case of the Interfering Homeowner.* Builder and Mr. and Mrs. Homeowner contracted for the construction of a new house, to be built according to certain plans and specifications at a cost of $100,000. Work began one week later. Almost at once Mrs. Homeowner began making daily visits to the site, each time contacting the foreman in charge relative to what, how, why, etc. was going on. After enduring this for a week, the foreman reported to Builder that he simply "couldn't stand having her around all the time, yakking and getting in the way." Builder asked if she had interfered with the work, to which he replied: "Well, yes, in a way—but the main thing is she's just a damned nuisance." Builder consults you, asking: "What can I do about this?" Advise him. Cf. Livolsi Construction Co., Inc. v. Shepard, 133 Conn. 133, 48

A.2d 263 (1946); Gamble v. Woodlea Construction Co., 246 Md. 260, 228 A.2d 243 (1967).

Comment: Tort Liability for Inducing Breach of Contract

Suppose, in *Patterson v. Meyerhofer,* that Defendant was late to the auction and Plaintiff was able to purchase the parcels at the expected price. Suppose, further, that Defendant was able to induce Auctioneer to deed over the parcels to her for a total payment $620 more than Plaintiff had bid. Plaintiff would, at a minimum, have two contract claims in these circumstances: 1) against Auctioneer for repudiation of the contract to sell the parcels; and 2) against Defendant for breach by prevention of her contract to purchase from Plaintiff. (Surely the acceptability of the defendant's conduct does not improve simply because she missed the auction.) In addition, Plaintiff, in all probability, has a claim in tort against Defendant for inducing Auctioneer to breach the contract with Plaintiff. What are the elements of this tort?

First, there must be either an existing contract or a protected expectancy of a future economic benefit between Plaintiff and the Auctioneer of which Defendant had knowledge. It is generally recognized that a "voidable or unenforceable" contract (e.g., one within the Statute of Frauds) or one that is terminable at will is protected. See Noller v. GMC Truck and Coach Div., GMC, 13 Kan.App.2d 13, 760 P.2d 688, 698–700 (1988); Lorenz v. Dreske, 62 Wis.2d 273, 214 N.W.2d 753 (1974) (liability for inducing employee to leave contract terminable at will); Restatement (Second) of Torts § 766 (1979).

Second, Defendant's inducement must actually cause Auctioneer to breach the contract, and Plaintiff must be damaged by the breach.

Third, Defendant's conduct must be intentional rather than inadvertent or careless. Actual malice is not required. Rather, an intentional act occurs when Defendant has reason to know or to anticipate that its conduct will induce Auctioneer to breach the contract. See, e.g., Texaco, Inc. v. Pennzoil, Co., 729 S.W.2d 768, 796–809 (Tex.App.Houston [1st Dist.] 1987, writ ref'd n.r.e.), cert. denied 485 U.S. 994, 108 S.Ct. 1305, 99 L.Ed.2d 686 (1988) (Defendant had knowledge of agreement and actively induced breach); Law Research Service of Mo., Inc. v. Western Union Telegraph Co., 336 F.Supp. 510, 512 (E.D.Mo.1971); McDonough v. Kellogg, 295 F.Supp. 594 (W.D.Va.1969); A.S. Rampell, Inc. v. Hyster Co., 3 N.Y.2d 369, 165 N.Y.S.2d 475, 144 N.E.2d 371 (1957).

Fourth, if Plaintiff establishes the three elements just listed, liability attaches unless Defendant can establish that the conduct was "privileged," that is, taken in good faith to protect a legally protected interest of its own which it believes may otherwise be impaired or destroyed by the performance of the contract. See Restatement (Second) of Torts § 773 (1979). A good faith effort to protect self-interest supposedly neutralizes "wrongful" motives and shifts the focus to what is a properly protectible interest. See Zoby v. American Fidelity Co., 242 F.2d 76, 80 (4th Cir.1957) (defendant protected if "impetus for his conduct lies in a proper business interest rather than in wrongful motives"). In drawing this illusory line, Dean Prosser suggested that if the conduct was intended to protect an existing contract of Defendant it might be privileged, but if it was intended to preserve competition and to protect a prospective advantage not yet realized it would not. Prosser, Torts § 129, pp. 942–946 (4th ed. 1971).

Finally, if the elements are established and the conduct is not privileged, a wide range of remedies, including injunction, damages for loss of bargain, consequential damages, including mental anguish and damage to reputation, and even punitive damages, are available. See American Air Filter Co., Inc. v. McNichol, 527 F.2d 1297, 1299–1300 (3d Cir.1975) (loss of bargain); Morgan's Home Equipment Corp. v. Martucci, 390 Pa. 618, 136 A.2d 838 (1957) (injunction); Clements v. Withers, 437 S.W.2d 818 (Tex. 1969) (punitive damages where actual malice). See also Price v. Sorrell, 784 P.2d 614 (Wyo.1989).

For additional reading, see Restatement (Second) of Torts §§ 766–774 (1979); W. P. Keeton, Prosser & Keeton on Torts §§ 129–30 (5th Ed. 1984); Annot., *Liability for Procuring Breach of Contract,* 26 A.L.R.2d 1227 (1952); Epstein, *Intentional Harms,* 4 J.Leg.Studies 391 (1975); Stevens, *Interference with Economic Relations—Some Aspects of the Turmoil in Intentional Torts,* 12 Osgoode Hall L.Rev. 595 (1974); Perlman, *Interference with Contract and Other Economic Interests: A Clash of Tort and Contract Doctrine,* 49 U.Chi.L.Rev. 61 (1982); Mark P. Gergen, *Tortious Interference: How it is Engulfing Commercial Law, Why This is Not Entirely Bad, and a Prudential Response,* 38 Ariz.L.Rev. 1175 (1996). See also Ansaldi, *Texaco, Pennzoil and the Revolt of the Masses: A Contracts Postmortem,* 27 Hous.L.Rev. 733 (1990).

Billman v. Hensel

Court of Appeals of Indiana, Third District, 1979.
181 Ind.App. 272, 391 N.E.2d 671.

■ GARRARD, PRESIDING JUDGE.

The Hensels, as sellers, entered into a contract to sell their home to the Billmans (the buyers) for $54,000 cash. A condition of the contract was the ability of the buyers to secure a conventional mortgage on the property for not less than $35,000 within thirty (30) days. When the buyers did not complete the purchase, the sellers commenced this suit to secure a thousand dollars ($1,000) earnest money/liquidated damage deposit required by the contract. The buyers defended upon the basis that they were relieved from performing. The case was tried by the court and judgment was entered in favor of the sellers. The sole question raised on appeal is whether the court properly determined that the buyers were not excused from performance. We affirm.

The parties do not dispute, nor do we, that the "subject to financing" clause constituted a condition precedent in the contract. See, e.g., Blakley v. Currence (1977), Ind.App., 361 N.E.2d 921; Capitol Land Co. v. Zorn

(1962), 134 Ind.App. 431, 184 N.E.2d 152. It is also undisputed that the buyers did not, in fact, secure a mortgage loan commitment within the contractual period.

The evidence at trial disclosed that on September 30, the day following execution of the contract, Mr. Billman met with an agent of the Lincoln National Bank and Trust Company of Fort Wayne. Billman was told that he could not obtain a mortgage loan of $35,000 unless he could show he had the difference between the purchase price and the amount of the mortgage. After totaling his available resources, including a 90 day short term note for $10,000 representing the proceeds from the sale of his present home, Billman was $6,500 short of the required $19,000 balance. On October 1st, the Hensels deposited the earnest money check into their account. Billman called Mr. Hensel to tell him that he was close on the financing and requested permission to show the home to his parents on October 3rd.

The Billmans and Mr. Billman's parents went through the house by themselves. The Hensels overheard Mr. Billman's father tell Mr. Billman that "I think I'd be careful with this ... I'm afraid of it." The Billmans returned without the parents later that same day. Mr. Billman told the Hensels that the deal was off because his parents were unable to loan him the $5,000 needed to complete his financing. The next day, Mr. Hensel told Mr. Billman that he would reduce the price of the home by $5,000. Mr. Billman refused to consider such a reduction, stating that he still needed another $1,500. The Billmans did not deposit funds to cover the check given as earnest money, and Mrs. Billman stopped payment on the check on October 4th.

The Billmans contacted only one financial institution concerning a mortgage loan, and made no formal loan application whatever. They limited discussion to a loan of $35,000 although they subsequently claimed to have required more. When Billman told Hensels he was canceling the sale, he stated the reason was that his parents would not give him $5,000 for the purchase. However, prior to that time he had not mentioned relying upon any assistance and had instead assured Hensels they had all the money needed to complete the sale. Then when Hensels offered to reduce the price by the figure Billman had mentioned, he stated he needed yet an additional $1,500.

We believe the better view to be that such subject to financing clauses impose upon the buyers an implied obligation to make a reasonable and good faith effort to satisfy the condition. See, e.g., Fry v. George Elkins Co. (1958), 162 Cal.App.2d 256, 327 P.2d 905; Lach v. Cahill, et al. (1951), 138 Conn. 418, 85 A.2d 481; Stabile v. McCarthy (1957), 336 Mass. 399, 145 N.E.2d 821; Rand v. B.G. Pride Realty (Me.1976), 350 A.2d 565; Reese v. Walker (1958), 6 Ohio Op.2d 55, 77 Ohio Law Abst. 583, 151 N.E.2d 605; Anaheim Co. v. Holcombe (1967), 246 Or. 541, 426 P.2d 743; 1 Corbin Contracts (3rd Ed. 1963), § 95; Anno. 78 A.L.R.3d 880.

Such an interpretation not only comports with the reasonable expectations of the parties, but is a logical extension of the sound rule of contract law that a promisor cannot rely upon the existence of a condition precedent to excuse his performance where the promisor, himself, prevents performance of the condition. See 5 Williston On Contracts (3rd Ed.) § 677, p. 224; Gulf Oil Corp. v. American Louisiana Pipe Line Co. (6th Cir.1960), 282 F.2d 401.

We recognize that the First District's decision in Blakley v. Currence (1977), Ind.App., 361 N.E.2d 921 refused to impose such an obligation where the condition was not expressed in terms of the *ability* of the buyers to secure financing. We need not reach that question on the facts before us, although we believe the rule in *Blakley* should be limited to the facts there present.

Here the condition imposed was that the buyers be *able* to secure a conventional mortgage of *not less than* $35,000. From the evidence recited above the court was justified in concluding that the sellers had carried their burden of proof by establishing that the buyers did not make a reasonable and good faith effort to secure the necessary financing,[1] and therefore could not rely upon the condition to relieve their duty to perform.

Affirmed.

NOTES

A Prevention–Hindrance Sampler: It's Bad Faith Stupid.

Market Street Associates v. Frey, 941 F.2d 588, 597 (7th Cir.1991)(question of fact whether lessee, during performance of contract, was in bad faith in failing to point out to lessor a term in the lease which gave the lessee a right to purchase the property when negotiations over financing improvements broke down: "To be able to correct your contract partner's mistake at zero cost to yourself and decide not to do so, is a species of opportunistic behavior that the parties would have expressly forbidden in the contract had they foreseen it.") Guess who wrote this opinion.

Ashland Management Inc. v. Janien, 82 N.Y.2d 395, 604 N.Y.S.2d 912, 624 N.E.2d 1007 (1993)(firm's refusal to negotiate confidentiality agreement in contract with employee is bad faith).

R.J. Kuhl Corp. v. Sullivan, 13 Cal.App.4th 1589, 17 Cal.Rptr.2d 425 (1993)(collusive acts to avoid broker's fee).

Beck v. Mason, 580 N.E.2d 290 (Ind.App.1991)(vendees failed to fulfill good faith duty to obtain financing).

Cenac v. Murry, 609 So.2d 1257 (Miss.1992)(bizarre behavior by vendor who, under installment contract containing a forfeiture clause to sell country store, interferes with operation of store; bad faith is breach for which damages are recoverable).

---

1. Note that ordinarily this burden will fall upon the buyer who must bring suit seeking return of his earnest money.

Anthony's Pier Four, Inc. v. HBC Associates, 411 Mass. 451, 583 N.E.2d 806 (1991)(unreasonable refusal by owner under a development contract to approve developer's master plan).

United States National Bank of Oregon v. Boge, 311 Or. 550, 814 P.2d 1082 (1991)(question of fact whether bank's refusal to give payoff information to borrower in order to prevent him from paying notes was in bad faith).

Larson v. Larson, 37 Mass.App.Ct. 106, 636 N.E.2d 1365 (1994)(where separation agreement calculates support obligation on husband's earned income, bad faith for husband to retire prematurely without making some other provision for support).

Comment: Outer Fringes of the Duty to Cooperate

A breach by prevention, hindrance or the failure to cooperate is a form of bad faith under the general duty of "good faith and fair dealing" in the performance and enforcement of the contract. Restatement (Second) § 205, Comment (d). The duty of good faith in this setting, as well as those previously considered, is generally imposed to protect exchange interests rather than to create a tort. Thus, a court is likely to conclude that there was no prevention or hindrance where no contract was formed between the parties, Garrett v. BankWest, Inc., 459 N.W.2d 833, 841–44 (S.D.1990), or where an existing contract permitted the very conduct claimed to be a breach, see Super Valu Stores v. D–Mart Food Stores, 146 Wis.2d 568, 431 N.W.2d 721, 725–26 (App.1988) (decision to cease marketing products permitted by contract). The issues in these latter cases overlap with those posed when one party allegedly exercises reserved discretion or terminates a contract in bad faith.

Breach by prevention and hindrance, however, has overtones of misfeasance. Party A has actively interfered with the performance of Party B or with the occurrence of a material condition precedent. As one court put it:

> It is well settled that nonoccurrence of a condition precedent to a promisor's performance is normally excused when fairly attributable to the promisor's own conduct. An express promise to perform on the happening of an event warrants implication of a promise to refrain from actively impeding its happening, and breach of the implied promise is legally as serious as breach of the express. This rule is properly invoked not only when the promisor completely forecloses occurrence of the condition but also when he substantially hinders its occurrence.

R.A. Weaver & Assoc., Inc. v. Haas & Haynie Corp., 663 F.2d 168, 176 (D.C.Cir.1980). Accord: Unit Trainship, Inc. v. Soo Line R. Co., 905 F.2d 160, 162–63 (7th Cir.1990) (hinders occurrence of condition); Shear v. National Rifle Association of America, 606 F.2d 1251 (D.C.Cir.1979) (condition); Canterbury Realty and Equipment Corp. v. Poughkeepsie Sav. Bank, 135 A.D.2d 102, 524 N.Y.S.2d 531, 535 (1988) (promised performance); Hais v. Smith, 547 A.2d 986 (D.C.App.1988) (duty recognized, but no breach on facts).

Breach of the duty to cooperate also has overtones of nonfeasance. Party A has failed to do something that would facilitate the performance of Party B or the occurrence of a condition precedent. But Party A has not agreed to do that "something" and therein lies the rub. Three questions must be answered.

(a) Will the duty to cooperate be imposed in every contract? The probable answer is no: The duty to take affirmative action will not be imposed in most cases.

(b) If there is a duty, how much must Party A do to cooperate? In Bonanza, Inc. v. McLean, 242 Kan. 209, 747 P.2d 792, 799–800 (1987), the court stated that "whenever cooperation of the promisee is necessary for performance of the promisee, there is a condition implied that the cooperation will be given." On the facts, the court held that the landlord had failed to cooperate by refusing to affirm that the lease was valid or assist in removing restrictive covenants when such actions were necessary for the lessee to use the premises in a lawful business enterprise.

(c) What remedies are available for breach of the duty to cooperate? Does the "breach" simply excuse a condition or does it form the basis for an action in damages? The answer will depend on the facts of each case.

In resolving these questions, an excellent reference is Steven J. Burton & Eric G. Andersen, Contractual Good Faith: Formation, Performance, Breach, Enforcement (1995). See also Richard E. Speidel, *The "Duty" of Good Faith in Contract Performance and Enforcement*, 46 J. Legal Ed. ____ (#4, 1996).

PROBLEM: THE CASE OF THE ACQUIESCENT OWNER

On October 1, Amos Watts, owner of Metropolis real estate, engaged Charles Fisher, a broker, to find a purchaser for the property at the price of $150,000, pursuant to an agreement providing, *inter alia,* as follows:

Seller (Watts) agrees to pay Broker (Fisher) a commission of five (5) per cent of the gross sale price of any sale made during the life of this contract, whether made by Broker or not. In the event Broker arranges a sale thereof in accordance herewith, and said sale is not consummated by reason of any default of Seller, Seller agrees to pay Broker for his services a sum equal to such commission had the sale been consummated.

One week later, Fisher was successful in finding a prospective purchaser, Carl Anderson. On October 8, Watts as seller and Anderson as purchaser executed a written contract for sale of the property, purchase price stipulated at $150,000 payable on or before November 15, the date set for closing.

On October 15 Anderson informed Fisher and Watts that he did not propose to "go through with the deal." Despite Fisher's urging, Watts acquiesced in this repudiation of the contract and refused to take any legal action against Anderson. Actually, for personal reasons, Watts was not displeased by Anderson's refusal. Evaluate Fisher's legal position and state whether, in your opinion, he would be likely to succeed in recovering the stipulated commission.

PROBLEM: THE CASE OF THE UNCOOPERATIVE VENDOR

In the process of negotiating a contract for the sale of land, Vendee indicated that he hoped to secure a loan on the property to be guaranteed by the Veterans Administration. Vendor, on the other hand, was opposed to dealing with the VA and preferred other financing arrangements. The issue was resolved by the insertion of the following clauses in the contract:

"(18) It is understood and agreed that this home is to be bought and financed under the G.I. Bill of Rights and is subject to approval by Veterans Administration of purchase price not to exceed Twenty One Thousand Nine Hundred Fifty ($21,950.00); said Eighteen Thousand Dollar First Deed of Trust herein mentioned has already been committed by the First Federal Savings & Loan Assoc. of Washington, D.C., and said loan must be placed with this company, otherwise secondary financing will be arranged.

"(21) The purchaser agrees to accept the following financing in the event the house is not financed under the aforementioned G.I. financing * * *."

Shortly before the agreed closing date, the VA issued a certificate of "reasonable value" which appraised the property at some $4,450 less than the contract price. Since the purchase price exceeded valuation, it appeared that the VA guarantee would not be available. Vendor then informed Vendee that since the VA had disapproved the loan they should proceed in making settlement under the agreed alternative financing. Vendee then requested that Vendor furnish a schedule of his actual construction costs as a basis of appealing to the VA for a higher appraisal. Vendor refused and Vendee subsequently canceled the contract. After the settlement date passed without a closing, Vendor declared the 10% deposit forfeited and retained it as liquidated damages. Vendee sues to recover the deposit. What result?

Comment: The Failure to Act Where There Is No Promise to Act

[The following is reprinted from the Northern Kentucky Law Review.]

The ultimate question in this "borderland" inquiry, is this: To what extent in a bargain do the parties have a duty in either Contract or Tort to take affirmative action to cooperate with or to "rescue" the other when such action has not been promised? Is there such a duty? If so, when should it be satisfied and what are the consequences of failure? To date, the nose of the "good Samaritan" camel has not appeared in the contract tent, although its hot breath can be felt on the side.

There is a strong historical correlation between the outcome in Contract and Tort: neither imposes exacting duties upon one party to be a good Samaritan, commercial or otherwise. In Contract, an "implied duty of cooperation" is imposed upon the bargain relationship and has occasionally been breached where A's failure to cooperate with B is necessary for the occurrence of a condition or to effectuate the exchange. In Tort, A may have a duty to act or to "rescue" where his conduct has created the risk to B or he occupies a special relationship with B. In both Contract and Tort, a relationship may create a dependence by B upon A's assistance and the circumstances may give A power to render that assistance at very little cost. But if A has not promised to assist and there are no special relational features, such as a fiduciary duty, or the assistance would be risky or costly to A, the failure to act is neither a breach of contract nor a tort.

This result should surprise no one. A has not promised to act, so no reasonable expectations are created. B's dilemma was not caused by A's conduct. A's decision not to act, although motivated by self interest rather than altruism, has moral justification, especially if B can be said to have assumed the risk of the accident. Thus, imposing the duty to act on A is tantamount to a forced exchange exacted by government. Although this exchange might be justified by some broader conception of the social contract, it is inconsistent with both Tort and Contract doctrine, not to mention Aristotle's theory of Commutative Justice. Nevertheless, there is some argument for a more expansive concept of the duty to act, either as the duty to effect an "easy" rescue in the law of Torts or as the duty to negotiate in good faith toward the adjustment of a contract where, beyond the bounds of clear risk allocation, a commercial "accident" has occurred. Good arguments notwithstanding, however, there is no evidence that Tort and Contract have joined forces to increase the legal duty to rescue within the bargain relationship.

Speidel, *The Borderland of Contract,* 10 N.Ky.L.Rev. 163, 193–95 (1983)(footnotes omitted).

SECTION 4. EQUITABLE REMEDIES FOR BREACH OF CONTRACT: PROHIBITORY INJUNCTION AND SPECIFIC PERFORMANCE

Some General Comments

In the materials just considered, a primary objective has been to determine the amount of compensatory damages due to the plaintiff because of the defendant's breach, whether that breach be of a contract to pay money or render some other performance, such as the sale of goods or stock, the conveyance of interests in land, construction or personal or professional services. If the court decides that the defendant is liable for damages and enters a money judgment against the defendant, that judgment is enforced against the defendant's property, that is, *in rem.* If the property is insufficient, the enforcement process may be renewed until the judgment is satisfied or the obligation is discharged. But the defendant will not be imprisoned for failure to pay the obligation represented by the judgment. See Note, *Imprisonment for Debt: In the Military Tradition,* 80 Yale L.J. 1679 (1971). For all practical purposes, the defendant has a choice whether to perform the contract or "pay damages," that is, run the risk that the plaintiff will sue and ultimately recover the full amount of the claim from the defendant's personal assets. This, then, is the plaintiff's remedy "at law" for breach of contract. Subject to the possibility of declaratory relief for an anticipatory breach, it remains remarkably consistent with Holmes' view that the "only universal consequence of a legally binding promise is, that the law makes the promisor pay damages if the promised event does not come to pass * * * [and] * * * leaves him free from interference until the time for fulfillment has gone by, and therefore free to break his contract if he chooses." O.W. Holmes, The Common Law 235–36 (Howe ed. 1963).

Equitable remedies make it possible for the plaintiff to obtain the actual performance promised by the defendant rather than damages. The court has power to issue a personal order to the defendant, directing conduct of a specified sort, and to punish noncompliance by either a fine or imprisonment for contempt. An injunction is the main form of this personal, coercive order issued by the court. In a breach of contract action, the injunction may prohibit the defendant from taking a specified course of action or compel specific performance of the contract or both. See Kaiser Trading Co. v. Associated Metals & Minerals Corp., 321 F.Supp. 923 (N.D.Cal.1970), appeal dismissed 443 F.2d 1364 (9th Cir.1971) (seller ordered to deliver goods sold and enjoined from selling them to others). Here, then, the order is directed to the person, that is, *in personam,* and denies the defendant the choice to perform the contract or pay damages. Although the contempt power appears to punish the defendant's refusal to comply, the real purpose is to coerce performance. In the words of some immortal bard, the defendant has "the keys to the jailhouse in his own pocket."

When is the plaintiff entitled to an equitable remedy for breach of contract? Professor A.W.B. Simpson informs us that although the origin of the principle "equity treats as done that which ought to be done" remains uninvestigated, specific performance was granted by the English Court of Chancery in land cases by the mid-fifteenth century. Since that time, specific enforcement of contracts for the sale of land has been the rule rather than the exception, the reason being "that land is assumed to have a peculiar value, so as to give an equity for a specific performance, without reference to its quality or quantity." 5A Corbin § 1143 (1964). See Berryhill v. Hatt, 428 N.W.2d 647, 657–58 (Iowa 1988). Simpson also states that before the development of the writ of assumpsit in the seventeenth century, the Chancery Court regularly issued *in personam* orders in a wide range of contract disputes. A.W.B. Simpson, A History of the Common Law of Contract 595–98 (1975). What happened next is too long and complicated to relate here in full. But as the adequacy and availability of contract remedies improved, the scope of the common law expanded and England's market system developed and diversified, it became more difficult for plaintiffs to demonstrate that contract remedies in the law courts were so inadequate that invocation of the power of the Chancery Court was justified. So in matters other than land contracts, it became customary to say that specific performance was the exception rather than the rule or that equitable remedies were "extraordinary." Compare Dawson, *Specific Performance in France and Germany,* 57 Mich.L.Rev. 495 (1959), where a preference for specific performance is noted in the civil law tradition. As an American court put it, specific performance is "largely a discretionary remedy to prevent substantial injury where no adequate remedy at law obtains. ...." Stokes v. Moore, 262 Ala. 59, 77 So.2d 331 (1955). What, more specifically, must the plaintiff show to persuade the court to exercise that discretion and grant equitable relief?

The following materials are designed to provide some insight into this important question. As you read them, keep the following questions in mind:

1. What was the inadequacy in the legal remedy asserted by the plaintiff to justify equitable relief? The focus here should be upon the ease with which the plaintiff can obtain a substitute performance from the available market and the impact upon the plaintiff if that substitute is costly or not readily available.

2. What, if any, are the practical problems involved in enforcing an *in personam* order in the particular case? Can and should the court order an artist to paint, a singer to sing or a builder to build? How is the court to supervise the mandated performance when the standards are aesthetic or, perhaps, the agreement is indefinite? As you will see, courts have found it easier to order the defendant in a personal service contract to refrain from doing rather than to perform.

3. Are there any questions of fairness associated with enforcing the contract or problems of morality associated with the plaintiff's conduct? For example, would specific enforcement of the contract be unconscionable because of disproportion in the exchange? Or, to quote some choice maxims, must the plaintiff "do equity to receive equity" or "come into equity with clean hands"?

4. May the plaintiff recover damages in addition to equitable relief? Suppose the requested equitable remedy is not available—may the court award damages in lieu of specific performance or must it remand the case for further consideration?

Although the plaintiff must struggle uphill to obtain equitable remedies for breach of contract, the test applied by the courts is flexible and, presumably, expandable as market conditions and attitudes change. With the merger in most states of the previously separate systems of law and equity and a condition of increasing scarcity in some relevant markets, one should not be surprised to find that equitable relief is increasingly available for breach of contract.

References:

5A Corbin §§ 136–1213 (1964); 11 Williston §§ 1418–1453A; D. Dobbs, Remedies §§ 2.1–2.12 (1973); Chesire, Fifoot & Furmston, Law of Contract 628–36 (12th ed. 1991); McClintock, Equity (2d Ed.1948); Farnsworth, *Legal Remedies for Breach of Contract,* 70 Colum.L.Rev. 1145, 1149–56 (1970); Peters, *Remedies for Breach of Contracts Relating to the Sale of Goods under the Uniform Commercial Code: A Roadmap for Article Two,* 73 Yale L.J. 199, 231–39 (1964); Van Hecke, *Changing Emphasis in Specific Performance,* 40 N.Car.L.Rev. 1 (1961). For a developing debate on when specific performance should be granted, see, Kornhauser, *An Introduction to the Economic Analysis of Contract Remedies,* 57 U. Colo.L.Rev. 683, 711–17 (1986); Ulen, *The Efficiency of Specific Performance: Toward a*

Unified Theory of Contract Remedies, 83 Mich.L.Rev. 341 (1984); Kronman, *Specific Performance,* 45 U.Chi.L.Rev. 351 (1978); Linzer, *On the Amorality of Contract Remedies—Efficiency, Equity and the Second Restatement,* 81 Colum.L.Rev. 111 (1981); Schwartz, *The Case for Specific Performance,* 89 Yale L.J. 271 (1979); Muris, *The Costs of Freely Granting Specific Performance,* 1982 Duke L.J. 1053. See also Narasimhan, *Modification: The Self–Help Specific Performance Remedy,* 97 Yale L.J. 61 (1987).

Curtice Brothers Co. v. Catts

Court of Chancery of New Jersey, 1907.
72 N.J.Eq. 831, 66 A. 935.

Complainant is engaged in the business of canning tomatoes and seeks the specific performance of a contract wherein defendant agreed to sell to complainant the entire product of certain land planted with tomatoes. Defendant contests the power of this court to grant equitable relief.

■ LEAMING, V.C. The fundamental principles which guide a court of equity in decreeing the specific performance of contracts are essentially the same whether the contracts relate to realty or to personalty. By reason of the fact that damages for the breach of contract for the sale of personalty are, in most cases, easily ascertainable and recoverable at law, courts of equity, in such cases withhold equitable relief. Touching contracts for the sale of land the reverse is the case. But no inherent difference between real estate and personal property controls the exercise of the jurisdiction. Where no adequate remedy at law exists specific performance of a contract touching the sale of personal property will be decreed with the same freedom as in the case of a contract for the sale of land. Professor Pomeroy, in referring to the distinction, says:

"In applying these principles, taking into account the discretionary nature of the jurisdiction, an agreement for the sale of land is *prima facie* presumed to come within their operation so as to be subject to specific performance, but a contrary presumption exists in regard to agreements concerning chattels." Pom. on Const. § 11.

Judge Story urges that there is no reasonable objection to allowing the party who is injured by the breach of any contract for the sale of chattels to have an election either to take damages at law or to have a specific performance in equity. 2 Story Eq.Jur. (13th Ed.) § 717a. While it is probable that the development of this branch of equitable remedies is decidedly toward the logical solution suggested by Judge Story, it is entirely clear that his view can not at this time be freely adopted without violence to what has long been regarded as accepted principles controlling the discretion of a court of equity in this class of cases. The United States Supreme Court has probably most nearly approached the view suggested by Judge Story. In Mechanics Bank of Alexandria v. Seton, 1 Pet. (U.S.) 299, 305, Mr. Justice Thompson, delivering the opinion of that court, says: "But notwithstanding this distinction between personal contracts for goods and contracts for lands is to be found laid down in the books as a general rule, yet there are many cases to be found where specific performance of contracts relating to personalty have been enforced in chancery, and courts will only view with greater nicety contracts of this description than such as relate to land." See also, Barr v. Lapsley, 1 Wheat. (U.S.) 151. In our own state contracts for the sale of chattels have been frequently enforced and the inadequacy of the remedy at law, based on the characteristic features of the contract or peculiar situation and needs of the parties, have been the principal grounds of relief. . . .

I think it clear that the present case falls well within the principles defined by the cases already cited from our own state. Complainant's factory has a capacity of about one million cans of tomatoes. The season for packing lasts about six weeks. The preparations made for this six weeks of active work must be carried out in all features to enable the business to succeed. These preparations are primarily based upon the capacity of the plant. Cans and other necessary equipments, including labor, must be provided and secured in advance with reference to the capacity of the plant during the packing period. With this known capacity and an estimated average yield of tomatoes per acre the acreage of land necessary to supply the plant is calculated. To that end the contract now in question was made, with other like contracts, covering a sufficient acreage to insure the essential pack. It seems immaterial whether the entire acreage is contracted for to insure the full pack, or whether a more limited acreage is contracted for and an estimated available open market depended upon for the balance of the pack; in either case a refusal of the parties who contract to supply a given acreage to comply with their contracts leaves the factory helpless except to whatever extent an uncertain market may perchance supply the deficiency. The condition which arises from the breach of the contracts is not merely a question of the factory being compelled to pay a higher price for the product; losses sustained in that manner could, with some degree of accuracy, be estimated. The condition which occasions the irreparable injury by reason of the breaches of the contracts is the inability to procure at any price at the time needed and of the quality needed the necessary tomatoes to insure the successful operation of the plant. If it should be assumed as a fact that upon the breach of contracts of this nature other tomatoes of like quality and quantity could be procured in the open market without serious interference with the economic arrangements of the plant, a court of equity would hesitate to assume to interfere, but the very existence of such contracts proclaims their necessity to the economic management of the factory. The aspect of the situation bears no resemblance to that of an ordinary contract for the sale of merchandise in the course of an ordinary business. The business and its needs are extraordinary in that the maintenance of all of the conditions prearranged to secure the pack are a necessity to insure the successful operation of the plant. The breach of the contract by one planter differs but in degree from a breach by all.

The objection that to specifically perform the contract personal services are required will not divest the court of its powers to preserve the benefits of the contract. Defendant may be restrained from selling the crop to others, and if necessary, a receiver can be appointed to harvest the crop.

A decree may be devised pursuant to the prayer of the bill. By reason of the manner in which the facts on which the opinion is based were stipulated, no costs will be taxed.

Laclede Gas Co. v. Amoco Oil Co.

United States Court of Appeals, Eighth Circuit, 1975.
522 F.2d 33.

■ Ross, Circuit Judge. The Laclede Gas Company (Laclede), a Missouri corporation, brought this diversity action alleging breach of contract against the Amoco Oil Company (Amoco), a Delaware corporation. It sought relief in the form of a mandatory injunction prohibiting the continuing breach or, in the alternative, damages. The district court held a bench trial on the issues of whether there was a valid, binding contract between the parties and whether, if there was such a contract, Amoco should be enjoined from breaching it. It then ruled that the "contract is invalid due to lack of mutuality" and denied the prayer for injunctive relief. The court made no decision regarding the requested damages. Laclede Gas Co. v. Amoco Oil Co., 385 F.Supp. 1332, 1336 (E.D.Mo.1974). This appeal followed, and we reverse the district court's judgment.

On September 21, 1970, Midwest Missouri Gas Company (now Laclede), and American Oil (now Amoco), the predecessors of the parties to this litigation, entered into a written agreement which was designed to provide central propane gas distribution systems to various residential developments in Jefferson County, Missouri, until such time as natural gas mains were extended into these areas. The agreement contemplated that as individual developments were planned the owners or developers would apply to Laclede for central propane gas systems. If Laclede determined that such a system was appropriate in any given development, it could request Amoco to supply the propane to that specific development. This request was made in the form of a supplemental form letter, as provided in the September 21 agreement; and if Amoco decided to supply the propane, it bound itself to do so by signing this supplemental form.

Once this supplemental form was signed the agreement placed certain duties on both Laclede and Amoco. Basically, Amoco was to "[i]nstall, own, maintain and operate ... storage and vaporization facilities and any other facilities necessary to provide [it] with the capability of delivering to [Laclede] commercial propane gas suitable ... for delivery by [Laclede] to its customers' facilities." Amoco's facilities were to be "adequate to provide a continuous supply of commercial propane gas at such times and in such volumes commensurate with [Laclede's] requirements for meeting the demands reasonably to be anticipated in each Development while this Agreement is in force." Amoco was deemed to be "the supplier," while Laclede was "the distributing utility."

For its part Laclede agreed to "[i]nstall, own, maintain and operate all distribution facilities" from a "point of delivery" which was defined to be "the outlet of [Amoco] header piping." Laclede also promised to pay Amoco "the Wood River Area Posted Price for propane plus four cents per gallon for all amounts of commercial propane gas delivered" to it under the agreement.

Since it was contemplated that the individual propane systems would eventually be converted to be natural gas, one paragraph of the agreement provided that Laclede should give Amoco 30 days written notice of this event, after which the agreement would no longer be binding for the converted development.

Another paragraph gave Laclede the right to cancel the agreement. However, this right was expressed in the following language:

> This Agreement shall remain in effect for one (1) year following the first delivery of gas by [Amoco] to [Laclede] hereunder. Subject to termination as provided in Paragraph 11 hereof [dealing with conversions to natural gas], this Agreement shall automatically continue in effect for additional periods of one (1) year each unless [Laclede] shall, not less than 30 days prior to the expiration of the initial one (1) year period or any subsequent one (1) year period, give [Amoco] written notice of termination.

There was no provision under which Amoco could cancel the agreement.

For a time the parties operated satisfactorily under this agreement, and some 17 residential subdivisions were brought within it by supplemental letters. However, for various reasons, including conversion to natural gas, the number of developments under the agreement had shrunk to eight by the time of trial. These were all mobile home parks.

During the winter of 1972–73 Amoco experienced a shortage of propane and voluntarily placed all of its customers, including Laclede, on an 80% allocation basis, meaning that Laclede would receive only up to 80% of its previous requirements. Laclede objected to this and pushed Amoco to give it 100% of what the developments needed. Some conflict arose over this before the temporary shortage was alleviated.

Then, on April 3, 1973, Amoco notified Laclede that its Wood River Area Posted Price of propane had been increased by three cents per gallon. Laclede objected to this increase also and demanded a full explanation. None was forthcoming. Instead Amoco merely sent a letter dated May 14, 1973, informing Laclede that it was "terminating" the September 21, 1970, agreement effective May 31, 1973. It claimed it had the right to do this because "the Agreement lacks 'mutuality.' "[1]

---

1. While Amoco sought to repudiate the agreement, it resumed supplying propane to the subdivisions on February 1, 1974, under the mandatory allocation guidelines promulgated by the Federal Energy Administration under the Federal Mandatory Allocation Program for propane. It is agreed that this is now being done under the contract.

The district court felt that the entire controversy turned on whether or not Laclede's right to "arbitrarily cancel the Agreement" without Amoco having a similar right rendered the contract void "for lack of mutuality" and it resolved this question in the affirmative. We disagree with this conclusion and hold that settled principles of contract law require a reversal.

[The court held that Laclede's restricted right to terminate did not make the agreement unenforceable for lack of "mutuality," i.e., consideration. Further, the agreement, fairly construed, was nothing more than a requirements contract under which Laclede agreed to order all of its requirements for the subdivision from Amoco. The district court, therefore, erred in holding that there was no enforceable contract.]

II.

Since he found that there was no binding contract, the district judge did not have to deal with the question of whether or not to grant the injunction prayed for by Laclede. He simply denied this relief because there was no contract. Laclede Gas Co. v. Amoco Oil Co., supra, 385 F.Supp. at 1336.

Generally the determination of whether or not to order specific performance of a contract lies within the sound discretion of the trial court. Landau v. St. Louis Public Service Co., 364 Mo. 1134, 273 S.W.2d 255, 259 (1954). However, this discretion is, in fact, quite limited; and it is said that when certain equitable rules have been met and the contract is fair and plain "specific performance goes as a matter of right." Miller v. Coffeen, 365 Mo. 204, 280 S.W.2d 100, 102 (1955), quoting, Berberet v. Myers, 240 Mo. 58, 77, 144 S.W. 824, 830 (1912). (Emphasis omitted.)

With this in mind we have carefully reviewed the very complete record on appeal and conclude that the trial court should grant the injunctive relief prayed. We are satisfied that this case falls within that category in which specific performance should be ordered as a matter of right. ...

Amoco contends that four of the requirements for specific performance have not been met. Its claims are: (1) there is no mutuality of remedy in the contract; (2) the remedy of specific performance would be difficult for the court to administer without constant and long-continued supervision; (3) the contract is indefinite and uncertain; and (4) the remedy at law available to Laclede is adequate. The first three contentions have little or no merit and do not detain us for long.

There is simply no requirement in the law that both parties be mutually entitled to the remedy of specific performance in order that one of them be given that remedy by the court. Beets v. Tyler, 365 Mo. 895, 290 S.W.2d 76, 80 (1956); Rice v. Griffith, 349 Mo. 373, 161 S.W.2d 220, 225 (1942).

While a court may refuse to grant specific performance where such a decree would require constant and long-continued court supervision, this is merely a discretionary rule of decision which is frequently ignored when the public interest is involved. See, e.g., Joy v. St. Louis, 138 U.S. 1, 47, 11 S.Ct. 243, 34 L.Ed. 843 (1891); . . .

Here the public interest in providing propane to the retail customers is manifest, while any supervision required will be far from onerous.

Section 370 of the Restatement of Contracts (1932) provides:

Specific enforcement will not be decreed unless the terms of the contract are so expressed that the court can determine with reasonable certainty what is the duty of each party and the conditions under which performance is due. We believe these criteria have been satisfied here. As discussed in part I of this opinion, as to all developments for which a supplemental agreement has been signed, Amoco is to supply all the propane which is reasonably foreseeably required, while Laclede is to purchase the required propane from Amoco and pay the contract price therefor. The parties have disagreed over what is meant by "Wood River Area Posted Price" in the agreement, but the district court can and should determine with reasonable certainty what the parties intended by this term and should mold its decree, if necessary accordingly. Likewise, the fact that the agreement does not have a definite time of duration is not fatal since the evidence established that the last subdivision should be converted to natural gas in 10 to 15 years. This sets a reasonable time limit on performance and the district court can and should mold the final decree to reflect this testimony.

It is axiomatic that specific performance will not be ordered when the party claiming breach of contract has an adequate remedy at law. Jamison Coal & Coke Co. v. Goltra, 143 F.2d 889, 894 (8th Cir.), cert. denied, 323 U.S. 769, 65 S.Ct. 122, 89 L.Ed. 615 (1944). This is especially true when the contract involves personal property as distinguished from real estate.

However, in Missouri, as elsewhere, specific performance may be ordered even though personalty is involved in the "proper circumstances." Mo.Rev.Stat. § 400.2–716(1); Restatement of Contracts, supra, § 361. And a remedy at law adequate to defeat the grant of specific performance "must be as certain, prompt, complete, and efficient to attain the ends of justice as a decree of specific performance." National Marking Mach. Co. v. Triumph Mfg. Co., 13 F.2d 6, 9 (8th Cir.1926). Accord, Snip v. City of Lamar, 239 Mo.App. 824, 201 S.W.2d 790, 798 (1947).

One of the leading Missouri cases allowing specific performance of a contract relating to personalty because the remedy at law was inadequate is Boeving v. Vandover, 240 Mo.App. 117, 218 S.W.2d 175, 178 (1949). In that case the plaintiff sought specific performance of a contract in which the defendant had promised to sell him an automobile. At that time (near the end of and shortly after World War II) new cars were hard to come by, and the court held that specific performance was a proper remedy since a new car "could not be obtained elsewhere except at considerable expense, trouble or loss, which cannot be estimated in advance."

We are satisfied that Laclede has brought itself within this practical approach taken by the Missouri courts. As Amoco points out, Laclede has propane immediately available to it under other contracts with other suppliers. And the evidence indicates that at the present time propane is readily available on the open market. However, this analysis ignores the fact that the contract involved in this lawsuit is for a long-term supply of propane to these subdivisions. The other two contracts under which Laclede obtains the gas will remain in force only until March 31, 1977, and April 1, 1981, respectively; and there is no assurance that Laclede will be able to receive any propane under them after that time. Also it is unclear as to whether or not Laclede can use the propane obtained under these contracts to supply the Jefferson County subdivisions, since they were originally entered into to provide Laclede with propane with which to "shave" its natural gas supply during peak demand periods.[4] Additionally, there was uncontradicted expert testimony that Laclede probably could not find another supplier of propane willing to enter into a long-term contract such as the Amoco agreement, given the uncertain future of worldwide energy supplies. And, even if Laclede could obtain supplies of propane for the affected developments through its present contracts or newly negotiated ones, it would still face considerable expense and trouble which cannot be estimated in advance in making arrangements for its distribution to the subdivisions.

Specific performance is the proper remedy in this situation, and it should be granted by the district court.[5]

CONCLUSION

For the foregoing reasons the judgment of the district court is reversed and the cause is remanded for the fashioning of appropriate injunctive relief in the form of a decree of specific performance as to those developments for which a supplemental agreement form has been signed by the parties.

NOTES

(1) *Buyer's Right to Specific Performance or Replevin.* UCC 2–716 [UCC 2–807 (1997)] provides:

(1) Specific performance may be decreed where the goods are unique or in other proper circumstances.

(2) The decree for specific performance may include such terms and conditions as to payment of the price, damages, or other relief as the court may deem just.

(3) The buyer has a right of replevin for goods identified to the contract if after reasonable effort he is unable to effect cover for such goods or the

---

4. During periods of cold weather, when demand is high, Laclede does not receive enough natural gas to meet all this demand. It, therefore, adds propane to the natural gas it places in its distribution system. This practice is called "peak shaving."

5. In fashioning its decree the district court must take into account any relevant rules and regulations promulgated under the Federal Mandatory Allocation Program.

circumstances reasonably indicate that such effort will be unavailing
* * *.

The Comments state that UCC 2–716 furthers a "more liberal attitude than some courts have shown in connection with the specific performance of contracts of sale" through emphasis upon the "commercial feasibility of replacement." Specific performance is "no longer limited to goods which are already specific or ascertained at the time of contracting." Further:

> The test of uniqueness under this section must be made in terms of the total situation which characterizes the contract. Output and requirements contracts involving a particular or peculiarly available source or market present today the typical commercial specific performance situation, as contrasted with contracts for the sale of heirlooms or priceless works of art which were usually involved in the older cases. However, uniqueness is not the sole basis of the remedy under this section for the relief may also be granted "in other proper circumstances" and inability to cover is strong evidence of "other proper circumstances."

Some questions:

1.   Would *Curtice Brothers v. Catts* be decided the same way under UCC 2–716 [UCC 2–807 (1997)]?

2.   Do you think that the *Laclede* case takes the "liberal" attitude of UCC 2–716 a bit too far? See Greenberg, *Specific Performance Under Section 2–716 of the Uniform Commercial Code: "A More Liberal Attitude" in the "Grand Style,"* 17 N.Eng.L.Rev. 321, 344–52 (1982). See also King Aircraft Sales, Inc. v. Lane, 68 Wash.App. 706, 846 P.2d 550, 556–57 (1993) (specific performance proper even though legal remedy not absent and goods not "absolutely" unique).

3.   In either *Curtice* or *Laclede,* would replevin under UCC 2–716(3) have been successful? See Putnam Ranches, Inc. v. Corkle, 189 Neb. 533, 203 N.W.2d 502 (1973) (replevin denied where no evidence that goods were ever identified to the contract). See generally Comment, 33 U.Pitt.L.Rev. 243 (1971).

(2) *"Unique" or in "Other Proper Circumstances."* When are goods "unique" within the meaning of UCC 2–716(1)? In the now famous cotton fiasco in 1973, growers of cotton made contracts to sell cotton to be planted on their land to middlemen for roughly $.30 per pound. Delivery was to be made after the cotton was harvested, ginned and bailed. Between the time of contracting and the time of delivery, the price of cotton rose to roughly $.90 per pound. Cotton was available on the market, but in uncertain quantities. When the growers refused to deliver, the buyers brought suit for specific performance. In R.L. Kimsey Cotton Co., Inc. v. Ferguson, 233 Ga. 962, 214 S.E.2d 360 (1975), the parties stipulated in the contract that the cotton was "unique." The court, without extended discussion, granted specific performance. But in Duval & Co. v. Malcom, 233 Ga. 784, 214 S.E.2d 356 (1975), the same court held that, in the absence of a stipulation of uniqueness, a dramatic price rise not accompanied by an inability to cover in the open market did not constitute "other proper circumstances" under UCC 2–716(1). The court stated that "other proper circumstances" was not a "license to afford specific performance for all commercial goods and turn the courts into referees in commerce." Presumably the court was swayed by the fungibility of cotton. But if a blight

had ruined the cotton to be grown by the seller, presumably he would have been excused under UCC 2–613—the cotton involved was "required" by the contract. See supra at 732. If the cotton was "required" by the contract, should not that mean that the goods were unique? What about replevin in the cotton cases?

(3) *Injunction Against Breach.* In an action for specific performance, when may the plaintiff, in order to preserve the *status quo,* obtain a temporary or permanent injunction restraining the defendant from breaching the contract? Traditionally, the courts have considered four flexible and interdependent factors: 1) Without such relief, will the plaintiff suffer irreparable harm; 2) Is there a substantial probability of success on the merits; 3) Will others be injured by the injunction; and 4) Will the injunction be inconsistent with or further the public interest? In addition, the injunction may be denied unless the facts as stated justify a specific performance decree. Thus, in Kaiser Trading Co. v. Associated Metals & Minerals Corp., 321 F.Supp. 923 (N.D.Cal. 1970), appeal dismissed 443 F.2d 1364 (9th Cir.1971), the court first determined that California courts would grant specific performance under UCC 2–716(1) "when goods cannot be covered or replaced" and then determined on the particular facts that a failure to enjoin the seller from disposing of the goods in litigation would cause irreparable harm to the buyer. The court stressed that the supply of goods on the open market was "very scarce" in relation to what the seller had promised to deliver, the price of the goods had more than doubled in the past year and the goods were "indispensable" in the buyer's manufacturing process. See also Petereit v. S.B. Thomas, Inc., 63 F.3d 1169 (2d Cir.1995)(injunction inappropriate where expectancy damages can be computed); Simpson v. Lee, 499 A.2d 889, 892–93 (D.C.App.1985); Pickerign v. Pasco Marketing, Inc., 303 Minn. 442, 228 N.W.2d 562 (1975); Division of Triple T Service, Inc. v. Mobil Oil Corp., 60 Misc.2d 720, 304 N.Y.S.2d 191, 195–196 (1969), affirmed 34 A.D.2d 618, 311 N.Y.S.2d 961 (1970) (injunction against unwarranted franchise termination). See D. Dobbs, Remedies § 2.10 (1973); Nussbaum, *Temporary Restraining Orders and Preliminary Injunctions—The Federal Practice,* 26 Sw.L.J. 265 (1972); Note, *Developments in the Law—Injunctions,* 78 Harv.L.Rev. 994 (1965). See also Rendleman, *The Inadequate Remedy at Law Prerequisite for an Injunction,* 33 U.Fla.L.Rev. 346 (1981).

(4) *The "Clean Up" Problem.* In a case where specific performance is, for any reason, denied but the contract is not otherwise illegal or unenforceable at law, the plaintiff still has "remedies at law." See McKinnon v. Benedict, 38 Wis.2d 607, 157 N.W.2d 665 (1968). In the days of the separation between law and equity courts, this frequently meant that the plaintiff was remanded to the law courts for relief and there was some evidence that parties rarely took advantage of that opportunity. See Frank & Endicott, *Defenses in Equity and "Legal Rights,"* 14 La.L.Rev. 380 (1954). In a time of an increasing merger of law and equity into one court, what is the status of the plaintiff's claim for damages? If the plaintiff is entitled to equitable relief, the court may, in the specific performance decree, "clean up" the litigation by including "such terms and conditions as to payment of the price, damages, or other relief as the court may deem just." UCC 2–716(2). And even if specific performance is denied, some courts, where legal and equitable powers are merged, have retained the case to grant the legal remedy, provided that the action does not impinge upon

the defendant's right to a jury trial and the evidence adduced in the hearing otherwise supports the claimed legal remedy. See, e.g., Ziebarth v. Kalenze, 238 N.W.2d 261 (N.D.1976) (court ignores "technicalities" to avoid a needless waste of time and money involved in remand).

(5) *Mutuality of Remedy.* The *Laclede* court rejects summarily the contention that the buyer cannot have specific performance against the seller unless the seller could have specific performance against the buyer. For additional cases in accord, see Pallas v. Black, 226 Neb. 728, 414 N.W.2d 805, 810 (1987); Safeway System, Inc. v. Manuel Brothers Inc., 102 R.I. 136, 228 A.2d 851 (1967); Ellis v. Mihelis, 60 Cal.2d 206, 32 Cal.Rptr. 415, 384 P.2d 7 (1963). The alleged remedial inequality is balanced by the court's power in equity to condition the decree to insure that the defendant receives the agreed exchange. The issue is both illuminated and resolved in Section 3386 of the California Civil Code, as amended in 1969:

> Notwithstanding that the agreed counter performance is not or would not have been specifically enforceable, specific performance may be compelled if:
>
> (a) Specific performance would otherwise be an appropriate remedy, and
>
> (b) The agreed counter performance has been substantially performed or its concurrent or future performance is assured or, if the court deems necessary, can be secured to the satisfaction of the court.

Accord: Restatement (Second) § 363.

(6) *Specific Performance in Restatement (Second).* Under Restatement (Second), specific performance of a contract or an order enjoining its nonperformance are remedies available for breach. See §§ 345(b), 357. The relief may be granted at the discretion of the court, the order "will be drawn as best to effectuate the purposes for which the contract was made and on such terms as justice requires," § 358(1), and "damages or other relief may be awarded in the same proceeding" in addition to specific performance or an injunction. § 358(3). But "specific performance or an injunction will not be ordered if damages would be adequate to protect the expectation interest of the injured party," § 359(1). Section 360 provides the "factors" affecting the adequacy of damages, viz., "(a) the difficulty of proving damages with reasonable certainty, (b) the difficulty of procuring a suitable substitute performance by means of money awarded as damages, and (c) the likelihood that an award of damages could not be collected." Comment a to Section 359, however, notes the "tendency to liberalize the granting of equitable relief by enlarging the classes of cases in which damages are not regarded as an adequate remedy" and concludes:

> Adequacy is to some extent relative, and the modern approach is to compare remedies to determine which is more effective in serving the ends of justice. Such a comparison will often lead to the granting of equitable relief. Doubts should be resolved in favor of the granting of specific performance or injunction.

Professor Linzer has stated that this comment is "vague" and that Restatement (Second) adopts an "equivocal approach to the availability of specific performance." Linzer, *On the Amorality of Contract Remedies—Efficiency, Equity and the Second Restatement,* 81 Colum.L.Rev. 111, 120 (1981). Linzer argues for the general use of specific performance on grounds of both efficiency and fairness. Id. at 138–39.

(7) *Unconscionable Bargains.* Specific performance may be denied for reasons other than the adequacy of the legal remedy. See, e.g., Da Silva v. Musso, 53 N.Y.2d 543, 444 N.Y.S.2d 50, 428 N.E.2d 382 (1981) (mistake). One such control is that the plaintiff must come into equity with "clean hands." But the conduct that sullies the hands must relate to the subject matter of the litigation and affect the "equitable" relations between the litigants. See, e.g., New York Football Giants, Inc. v. Los Angeles Chargers Football Club, Inc., 291 F.2d 471 (5th Cir.1961). Cf. Washington Capitols Basketball Club, Inc. v. Barry, 304 F.Supp. 1193, 1200–01 (N.D.Cal.1969), affirmed 419 F.2d 472 (9th Cir. 1969).

Another general limitation is that equity will not specifically enforce an inequitable or unconscionable bargain, see Campbell Soup Co. v. Wentz, 172 F.2d 80 (3d Cir.1948), and that a "shockingly" inadequate consideration may be sufficient to deny relief. But whether the consideration is inadequate or the bargain otherwise unfair "must be viewed prospectively, not retrospectively." Tuckwiller v. Tuckwiller, 413 S.W.2d 274, 278 (Mo.1967). See Leff, *Unconscionability and the Code: The Emperor's New Clause,* 115 U.Pa.L.Rev. 485, 528–41 (1967). Thus, where agreed prices for the purchase of cotton were fair at the time of contracting, a subsequent and dramatic price increase the risk of which the seller was held to assume did not foreclose specific performance. R.L. Kimsey Cotton Co., Inc. v. Ferguson, 233 Ga. 962, 214 S.E.2d 360, 363 (1975). See also, Wittick v. Miles, 274 Or. 1, 545 P.2d 121, 125–26 (1976) (gross inadequacy of consideration without fraud or knowing advantage not enough to deny specific performance); Restatement (Second) § 364(1)(c)(specific performance or an injunction "will be refused if such relief would be unfair because * * * the exchange is grossly inadequate or the terms of the contract are otherwise unfair".

Northern Indiana Public Service Co. v. Carbon County Coal Co.

United States Court of Appeals, Seventh Circuit, 1986.
799 F.2d 265.

[In 1978, NIPSCO and Carbon County entered a 20–year contract under which Carbon County, the owner and operator of a coal mine in Wyoming, agreed to sell and NIPSCO agreed to buy approximately 1.5 million tons of coal every year for 20 years, at a price of $24 a ton, subject to upward escalation. By 1985, the contract price had escalated to $44 per ton, but, because of changed economic circumstances, NIPSCO was able to buy electricity at prices below the cost of generation. Under pressure from the Indiana Public Service Commission, NIPSCO sought a declaratory judgment that it was excused from the contract. Carbon County counterclaimed for breach of contract and moved for a preliminary injunction and specific performance. The district court granted the preliminary injunction but, after a jury verdict for Carbon County in the amount of $181 million, the court denied specific performance. NIPSCO, inter alia, appealed from the verdict and Carbon County appealed from the denial of specific performance. The court, speaking through Judge Posner, first affirmed the verdict against NIPSCO.]

This completes our consideration of NIPSCO's attack on the damages judgment and we turn to Carbon County's cross-appeal, which seeks specific performance in lieu of the damages it got. Carbon County's counsel virtually abandoned the cross-appeal at oral argument, noting that the mine was closed and could not be reopened immediately—so that if specific performance (i.e., NIPSCO's resuming taking the coal) was ordered, Carbon County would not be able to resume its obligations under the contract without some grace period. In any event the request for specific performance has no merit. Like other equitable remedies, specific performance is available only if damages are not an adequate remedy, Farnsworth, supra, § 12.6, and there is no reason to suppose them inadequate here. The loss to Carbon County from the breach of contract is simply the difference between (1) the contract price (as escalated over the life of the contract in accordance with the contract's escalator provisions) times quantity, and (2) the cost of mining the coal over the life of the contract. Carbon County does not even argue that $181 million is not a reasonable estimate of the present value of the difference. Its complaint is that although the money will make the owners of Carbon County whole it will do nothing for the miners who have lost their jobs because the mine is closed and the satellite businesses that have closed for the same reason. Only specific performance will help them.

But since they are not parties to the contract their losses are irrelevant. Indeed, specific performance would be improper as well as unnecessary here, because it would force the continuation of production that has become uneconomical. Cf. *Farnsworth,* supra, at 817–18. No one wants coal from Carbon County's mine. With the collapse of oil prices, which has depressed the price of substitute fuels as well, this coal costs far more to get out of the ground than it is worth in the market. Continuing to produce it, under compulsion of an order for specific performance, would impose costs on society greater than the benefits. NIPSCO's breach, though it gave Carbon County a right to damages, was an efficient breach in the sense that it brought to a halt a production process that was no longer cost-justified. See Lake River Corp. v. Carborundum Co., 769 F.2d 1284, 1289 (7th Cir.1985); Thyssen, Inc. v. S.S. Fortune Star, 777 F.2d 57, 63 (2d Cir.1985) (Friendly, J.). The reason why NIPSCO must pay Carbon County's loss is not that it should have continued buying coal it didn't need but that the contract assigned to NIPSCO the risk of market changes that made continued deliveries uneconomical. The judgment for damages is the method by which that risk is being fixed on NIPSCO in accordance with its undertakings.

With continued production uneconomical, it is unlikely that an order of specific performance, if made, would ever actually be implemented. If, as a finding that the breach was efficient implies, the cost of a substitute supply (whether of coal, or of electricity) to NIPSCO is less than the cost of producing coal from Carbon County's mine, NIPSCO and Carbon County can both be made better off by negotiating a cancellation of the contract and with it a dissolution of the order of specific performance. Suppose, by way of example, that Carbon County's coal costs $20 a ton to produce, that the contract price is $40, and that NIPSCO can buy coal elsewhere for $10. Then Carbon County would be making a profit of only $20 on each ton it sold to NIPSCO ($40–$20), while NIPSCO would be losing $30 on each ton it bought from Carbon County ($40–$10). Hence by offering Carbon County more than contract damages (i.e., more than Carbon County's lost profits), NIPSCO could induce Carbon County to discharge the contract and release NIPSCO to buy cheaper coal. For example, at $25, both parties would be better off than under specific performance, where Carbon County gains only $20 but NIPSCO loses $30. Probably, therefore, Carbon County is seeking specific performance in order to have bargaining leverage with NIPSCO, and we can think of no reason why the law should give it such leverage. We add that if Carbon County obtained and enforced an order for specific performance this would mean that society was spending $20 (in our hypothetical example) to produce coal that could be gotten elsewhere for $10—a waste of scarce resources.

As for possible hardships to workers and merchants in Hanna, Wyoming, where Carbon County's coal mine is located, we point out that none of these people were parties to the contract with NIPSCO or third-party beneficiaries. They have no legal interest in the contract. Cf. Local 1330, United Steel Workers of America v. United States Steel Corp., 631 F.2d 1264, 1279–82 (6th Cir.1980); Serrano v. Jones & Laughlin Steel Co., 790 F.2d 1279, 1289 (6th Cir.1986). Of course the consequences to third parties of granting an injunctive remedy, such as specific performance, must be considered, and in some cases may require that the remedy be withheld.... The frequent references to "public interest" as a factor in the grant or denial of a preliminary injunction invariably are references to third-party effects. See, e.g., Punnett v. Carter, 621 F.2d 578, 587–88 (3d Cir.1980). But even though the formal statement of the judicial obligation to consider such effects extends to orders denying as well as granting injunctive relief, see, e.g., Kershner v. Mazurkiewicz, 670 F.2d 440, 443 (3d Cir.1982) (en banc), the actuality is somewhat different: when the question is whether third parties would be injured by an order denying an injunction, always they are persons having a legally recognized interest in the lawsuit, so that the issue really is the adequacy of relief if the injunction is denied. In Mississippi Power & Light Co. v. United Gas Pipe Line Co., 760 F.2d 618 (5th Cir.1985), for example, a public utility sought a preliminary injunction against alleged overcharges by a supplier. If the injunction was denied and later the utility got damages, its customers would be entitled to refunds; but for a variety of reasons explained in the opinion, refunds would not fully protect the customers' interests. The customers were the real parties in interest on the plaintiff side of the case, and their interests had therefore to be taken into account in deciding whether there would be irreparable harm (and how much) if the preliminary injunction was denied. See id. at 623–26. Carbon County does not stand in a representative relation to the workers and businesses of Hanna, Wyoming. Treating them as real parties in interest would evade the limitations on the concept of a third-party beneficiary and would place the promisor under obligations potentially far heavier than it had thought it was accepting when it signed the contract. Indeed, if we are right that an order of specific performance would probably not be carried out—that instead NIPSCO would pay an additional sum of money to Carbon County for an agreement not to enforce the order—it becomes transparent that granting specific performance would make NIP-SCO liable in money damages for harms to nonparties to the contract, and it did not assume such liability by signing the contract. Cf. H.R. Moch Co. v. Rensselaer Water Co., 247 N.Y. 160, 159 N.E. 896 (1928).

Moreover, the workers and merchants in Hanna assumed the risk that the coal mine would have to close down if it turned out to be uneconomical. The contract with NIPSCO did not guarantee that the mine would operate throughout the life of the contract but only protected the owners of Carbon County against the financial consequences to them of a breach. As Carbon County itself emphasizes in its brief, the contract was a product of the international oil cartel, which by forcing up the price of substitute fuels such as coal made costly coal-mining operations economically attractive. The OPEC cartel is not a source of vested rights to produce substitute fuels at inflated prices.

* * *

Walgreen Co. v. Sara Creek Property Co.

United States Court of Appeals, Seventh Circuit, 1992.
966 F.2d 273.

■ POSNER, CIRCUIT JUDGE.

This appeal from the grant of a permanent injunction raises fundamental issues concerning the propriety of injunctive relief 775 F.Supp. 1192 (E.D.Wis.1991). The essential facts are simple. Walgreen has operated a pharmacy in the Southgate Mall in Milwaukee since its opening in 1951. Its current lease, signed in 1971 and carrying a 30–year, 6–month term, contains, as had the only previous lease, a clause in which the landlord, Sara Creek, promises not to lease space in the mall to anyone else who wants to operate a pharmacy or a store containing a pharmacy....

In 1990, fearful that its largest tenant—what in real estate parlance is called the "anchor tenant"—having gone broke was about to close its store, Sara Creek informed Walgreen that it intended to buy out the anchor tenant and install in its place a discount store operated by Phar–Mor Corporation, a "deep discount" chain, rather than, like Walgreen, just a "discount" chain. Phar–Mor's store would occupy 100,000 square feet, of which 12,000 would be occupied by a pharmacy the same size as Walgreen's. The entrances to the two stores would be within a couple of hundred feet of each other.

Walgreen filed this diversity suit for breach of contract against Sara Creek and Phar–Mor and asked for an injunction against Sara Creek's letting the anchor premises to Phar–Mor. After an evidentiary hearing, the judge found a breach of Walgreen's lease and entered a permanent injunction against Sara Creek's letting the anchor tenant premises to Phar–Mor until the expiration of Walgreen's lease. He did this over the defendants' objection that Walgreen had failed to show that its remedy at law—damages—for the breach of the exclusivity clause was inadequate. Sara Creek had put on an expert witness who testified that Walgreen's damages could be readily estimated, and Walgreen had countered with evidence from its employees that its damages would be very difficult to compute, among other reasons because they included intangibles such as loss of goodwill.

Sara Creek reminds us that damages are the norm in breach of contract as in other cases. Many breaches, it points out, are "efficient" in the sense that they allow resources to be moved into a more valuable use. Patton v. Mid–Continent Systems, Inc., 841 F.2d 742, 750–51 (7th Cir. 1988). Perhaps this is one—the value of Phar–Mor's occupancy of the anchor premises may exceed the cost to Walgreen of facing increased competition. If so, society will be better off if Walgreen is paid its damages, equal to that cost, and Phar–Mor is allowed to move in rather than being kept out by an injunction. That is why injunctions are not granted as a matter of course, but only when the plaintiff's damages remedy is inadequate. Northern Indiana Public Service Co. v. Carbon County Coal Co., 799 F.2d 265, 279 (7th Cir.1986). Walgreen's is not, Sara Creek argues; the projection of business losses due to increased competition is a routine exercise in calculation. Damages representing either the present value of lost future profits or (what should be the equivalent, Carusos v. Briarcliff, Inc., 76 Ga.App. 346, 351–52, 45 S.E.2d 802, 806–07 (1947)) the diminution in the value of the leasehold have either been awarded or deemed the proper remedy in a number of reported cases for breach of an exclusivity clause in a shopping-center lease.... Why, Sara Creek asks, should they not be adequate here?

Sara Creek makes a beguiling argument that contains much truth, but we do not think it should carry the day. For if, as just noted, damages have been awarded in some cases of breach of an exclusivity clause in a shopping-center lease, injunctions have been issued in others.... The choice between remedies requires a balancing of the costs and benefits of the alternatives.... The task of striking the balance is for the trial judge, subject to deferential appellate review in recognition of its particularistic, judgmental, fact-bound character....

The plaintiff who seeks an injunction has the burden of persuasion—damages are the norm, so the plaintiff must show why his case is abnormal. But when, as in this case, the issue is whether to grant a permanent injunction, not whether to grant a temporary one, the burden is to show that damages are inadequate, not that the denial of the injunction will work irreparable harm. "Irreparable" in the injunction context means not rectifiable by the entry of a final judgment....

The benefits of substituting an injunction for damages are twofold. First, it shifts the burden of determining the cost of the defendant's conduct from the court to the parties. If it is true that Walgreen's damages are smaller than the gain to Sara Creek from allowing a second pharmacy into the shopping mall, then there must be a price for dissolving the injunction that will make both parties better off. Thus, the effect of upholding the injunction would be to substitute for the costly processes of forensic fact determination the less costly processes of private negotiation. Second, a premise of our free-market system, and the lesson of experience here and abroad as well, is that prices and costs are more accurately determined by the market than by government. A battle of experts is a less reliable method of determining the actual cost to Walgreen of facing new competition than negotiations between Walgreen and Sara Creek over the price at which Walgreen would feel adequately compensated for having to face that competition.

That is the benefit side of injunctive relief but there is a cost side as well. Many injunctions require continuing supervision by the court, and that is costly. . . . A more subtle cost of injunctive relief arises from the situation that economists call "bilateral monopoly," in which two parties can deal only with each other: the situation that an injunction creates. . . . The sole seller of widgets selling to the sole buyer of that product would be an example. But so will be the situation confronting Walgreen and Sara Creek if the injunction is upheld. Walgreen can "sell" its injunctive right only to Sara Creek, and Sara Creek can "buy" Walgreen's surrender of its right to enjoin the leasing of the anchor tenant's space to Phar–Mor only from Walgreen. The lack of alternatives in bilateral monopoly creates a bargaining range, and the costs of negotiating to a point within that range may be high. Suppose the cost to Walgreen of facing the competition of Phar–Mor at the Southgate Mall would be $1 million, and the benefit to Sara Creek of leasing to Phar–Mor would be $2 million. Then at any price between those figures for a waiver of Walgreen's injunctive right both parties would be better off, and we expect parties to bargain around a judicial assignment of legal rights if the assignment is inefficient. R.H. Coase, "The Problem of Social Cost," 3 J. Law & Econ. 1 (1960). But each of the parties would like to engross as much of the bargaining range as possible—Walgreen to press the price toward $2 million, Sara Creek to depress it toward $1 million. With so much at stake, both parties will have an incentive to devote substantial resources of time and money to the negotiation process. The process may even break down, if one or both parties want to create for future use a reputation as a hard bargainer; and if it does break down, the injunction will have brought about an inefficient result. All these are in one form or another costs of the injunctive process that can be avoided by substituting damages.

The costs and benefits of the damages remedy are the mirror of those of the injunctive remedy. The damages remedy avoids the cost of continuing supervision and third-party effects, and the cost of bilateral monopoly as well. It imposes costs of its own, however, in the form of diminished accuracy in the determination of value, on the one hand, and of the parties' expenditures on preparing and presenting evidence of damages, and the time of the court in evaluating the evidence, on the other.

The weighing up of all these costs and benefits is the analytical procedure that is or at least should be employed by a judge asked to enter a permanent injunction, with the understanding that if the balance is even the injunction should be withheld. The judge is not required to explicate every detail of the analysis and he did not do so here, but as long we are satisfied that his approach is broadly consistent with a proper analysis we shall affirm; and we are satisfied here. The determination of Walgreen's damages would have been costly in forensic resources and inescapably inaccurate. . . . The lease had ten years to run. So Walgreen would have had to project its sales revenues and costs over the next ten years, and then project the impact on those figures of Phar–Mor's competition, and then discount that impact to present value. All but the last step would have been fraught with uncertainty.

* * *

Damages are not always costly to compute, or difficult to compute accurately. In the standard case of a seller's breach of a contract for the sale of goods where the buyer covers by purchasing the same product in the market, damages are readily calculable by subtracting the contract price from the market price and multiplying by the quantity specified in the contract. But this is not such a case and here damages would be a costly and inaccurate remedy; and on the other side of the balance some of the costs of an injunction are absent and the cost that is present seems low. The injunction here, like one enforcing a covenant not to compete . . . is a simple negative injunction—Sara Creek is not to lease space in the South-gate Mall to Phar–Mor during the term of Walgreen's lease—and the costs of judicial supervision and enforcement should be negligible. There is no contention that the injunction will harm an unrepresented third party. It may harm Phar–Mor but that harm will be reflected in Sara Creek's offer to Walgreen to dissolve the injunction. (Anyway Phar–Mor is a party.) The injunction may also, it is true, harm potential customers of Phar–Mor—people who would prefer to shop at a deep-discount store than an ordinary discount store—but their preferences, too, are registered indirectly. The more business Phar–Mor would have, the more rent it will be willing to pay Sara Creek, and therefore the more Sara Creek will be willing to pay Walgreen to dissolve the injunction.

The only substantial cost of the injunction in this case is that it may set off a round of negotiations between the parties. In some cases, illustrated by Boomer v. Atlantic Cement Co., 26 N.Y.2d 219, 309 N.Y.S.2d 312, 257 N.E.2d 870 (1970), this consideration alone would be enough to warrant the denial of injunctive relief. The defendant's factory was emitting cement dust that caused the plaintiffs harm monetized at less than $200,000, and the only way to abate the harm would have been to close down the factory, which had cost $45 million to build. An injunction against the nuisance could therefore have created a huge bargaining range (could, not would, because it is unclear what the current value of the factory was), and the costs of negotiating to a point within it might have been immense. If the market value of the factory was actually $45 million, the plaintiffs would be tempted to hold out for a price to dissolve the injunction in the tens of millions and the factory would be tempted to refuse to pay anything more than a few hundred thousand dollars. Negotiations would be unlikely to break down completely, given such a bargaining range, but they might well be protracted and costly. There is nothing so dramatic here. Sara Creek does not argue that it will have to close the mall if enjoined from leasing to Phar–Mor. Phar–Mor is not the only potential anchor tenant. Liza Danielle, Inc. v. Jamko, Inc., 408 So.2d 735, 740 (Fla.App.1982), on which Sara Creek relies, presented the converse case where the grant of the injunction would have forced an existing tenant to close its store. The size of the bargaining range was also a factor in the denial of injunctive relief in Gitlitz v. Plankinton Building Properties, Inc., 228 Wis. 334, 339–40, 280 N.W. 415, 418 (1938).

To summarize, the judge did not exceed the bounds of reasonable judgment in concluding that the costs (including forgone benefits) of the damages remedy would exceed the costs (including forgone benefits) of an injunction. We need not consider whether, as intimated by Walgreen, exclusivity clauses in shopping-center leases should be considered presumptively enforceable by injunctions. Although we have described the choice between legal and equitable remedies as one for case-by-case determination, the courts have sometimes picked out categories of case in which injunctive relief is made the norm. The best-known example is specific performance of contracts for the sale of real property. Anderson v. Onsager, 155 Wis.2d 504, 455 N.W.2d 885 (1990); Okaw Drainage District v. National Distillers & Chemical Corp., 882 F.2d 1241, 1248 (7th Cir.1989); Anthony T. Kronman, "Specific Performance," 45 U.Chi.L.Rev. 351, 355 and n. 20 (1978). The rule that specific performance will be ordered in such cases as a matter of course is a generalization of the considerations discussed above. Because of the absence of a fully liquid market in real property and the frequent presence of subjective values (many a homeowner, for example, would not sell his house for its market value), the calculation of damages is difficult; and since an order of specific performance to convey a piece of property does not create a continuing relation between the parties, the costs of supervision and enforcement if specific performance is ordered are slight. The exclusivity clause in Walgreen's lease relates to real estate, but we hesitate to suggest that every contract involving real estate should be enforceable as a matter of course by injunctions. Suppose Sara Creek had covenanted to keep the entrance to Walgreen's store free of ice and snow, and breached the covenant. An injunction would require continuing supervision, and it would be easy enough if the injunction were denied for Walgreen to hire its own ice and snow remover and charge the cost to Sara Creek. Cf. City of Michigan City v. Lake Air Corp., 459 N.E.2d 760 (Ind.App.1984). On the other hand, injunctions to enforce exclusivity clauses are quite likely to be justifiable by just the considerations present here—damages are difficult to estimate with any accuracy and the injunction is a one-shot remedy requiring no continuing judicial involvement. So there is an argument for making injunctive relief presumptively appropriate in such cases, but we need not decide in this case how strong an argument.

AFFIRMED.

NOTES

(1) In City Stores Co. v. Ammerman, 266 F.Supp. 766 (D.D.C.1967), aff'd, 394 F.2d 950 (D.C.Cir.1968), the plaintiff obtained specific performance of defendant's agreement to grant a lease as a major tenant in a shopping center under construction despite the fact that numerous complex details were still to be agreed and that a great deal of supervision by the court would be required. The district court concluded that since "money damages would in no way compensate the plaintiff for loss of the right to participate in the shopping center enterprise and for the almost incalculable future advantages that might accrue to it as a result of extending its operations into the suburbs" equity required specific performance even though some supervision of both future construction and the terms of the lease would be required. In a *per curiam* affirmance, the Court of Appeals for the District of Columbia narrowed somewhat the district court's grounds for decision. The court stressed that specific performance was available because the obligation involved a commitment to lease in addition to construction and that the work was to be done on the defendant's land, making it impossible for the plaintiff to have the job done.

(2) "We do not imply that in all cases where a landlord has contracted to construct a building on its property, the landlord will be required to perform on the ground that interests in land are always specifically enforceable. If the record shows that at the time the landlord breached its contract, other properties were available to the tenant that offered business advantages comparable to those offered by the landlord's property—except for differences in rent and overhead costs for which an adequate remedy at law exists—a Chancellor might properly deny the tenant's prayer for specific performance. Such a denial might be particularly appropriate in a case where the tenant has failed to lease comparable property that he knew or should have known was available, and where the costs arising from the delay in construction are such that the landlord will no longer get his part of the bargain if the lease is specifically enforced. A plaintiff seeking equitable relief must have acted in good faith; and if the court of equity finds that a tenant could have reasonably protected his interests but failed to do so, relief may be withheld. In the present case, however, the Chancellor made no such findings, and on appeal, Wells Fargo has not raised the issue of Easton's good faith." Easton Theatres v. Wells Fargo Land & Mortg., 265 Pa.Super. 334, 401 A.2d 1333, 1345 (1979).

(3) "It is not unusual for parties involved in complicated business transactions to allow subsidiary details to remain unspecified until such time as the need for agreement actually arises. Indeed, it would be impossible to foresee in advance and presently agree upon all the details of a project as far-reaching as the development and construction of a P.U.D. [Planned Unit Development] Therefore, we do not believe that the fact that some terms pertaining to the future performance of this joint venture contract remain unspecified at this time is alone sufficient to prevent the specific enforcement of the agreement. We are no more ready to assume that the parties will breach their obligation to

negotiate in good faith than we are to assume that they will breach any other contractual obligation. See City Stores Co. v. Ammerman, 266 F.Supp. 766 (D.D.C.1967), affirmed 129 U.S.App.D.C. 325, 394 F.2d 950, 38 A.L.R.3d 1042 (1968). . . .

"Finally, plaintiffs have already expended considerable time and money in performing their obligations under the joint venture agreement. These efforts have inured to the benefit of defendants by enhancing the value of the property of which they are now the legal owners. At this stage, defendants can hardly expect an equity court to be too favorably disposed toward the argument that the instrument which they themselves drafted should not be specifically enforced—in order to allow plaintiffs to continue with their own performance—solely because it is somewhat incomplete and indefinite. See J. Pomeroy, Specific Performance of Contracts 378–79, § 145 (3d ed. 1926):

"'* * * [W]hen a *contract has been partly performed* by the plaintiff, and the defendant has received and enjoys the benefits thereof, and the plaintiff would be virtually remediless unless the contract were enforced, the court, from the plainest considerations of equity and common justice, does not regard with favor any objections raised by the defendant merely on the ground of the incompleteness or uncertainty of the agreement. Even if the agreement be incomplete, the court will then, in furtherance of justice and to prevent a most inequitable result, decree a performance of its terms as far as possible, although, perhaps, with compensation or allowance. In fact * * * one ground of the equitable jurisdiction to decree a specific performance is the incompleteness of the contract, which would prevent an action at law, but which exists to such a limited extent and under such circumstances that a refusal to grant any relief would be plainly inequitable.' (Emphasis in original; footnotes omitted.)

"See also 5A Corbin, supra § 1174 at 287; 11 Williston, supra § 1424 at 819 & n. 15:

'[I]t seems probable that the difficulty regarding uncertainty has been overemphasized; certainly, it should not be allowed to hamper or restrict equitable relief further than necessity requires. * * *

'The decisions reveal a trend toward great liberality in enforcement * * *.' '" Van v. Fox, 278 Or. 439, 564 P.2d 695, 701–02 (1977). See Restatement (Second) § 362.

American Broadcasting Companies v. Wolf

Court of Appeals of New York, 1981.
52 N.Y.2d 394, 438 N.Y.S.2d 482, 420 N.E.2d 363.

■ COOKE, CHIEF JUDGE.

* * *

I.

Warner Wolf, a sportscaster who has developed a rather colorful and unique on-the-air personality, had been employed by ABC since 1976. In February, 1978, ABC and Wolf entered into an employment agreement which, following exercise of renewal option, was to terminate on March 5, 1980. The contract contained a clause, known as a good-faith negotiation and first-refusal provision, that is at the crux of this litigation: "You agree, if we so elect, during the last ninety (90) days prior to the expiration of the extended term of this agreement, to enter into good faith negotiations with us for the extension of this agreement on mutually agreeable terms. You further agree that for the first forty-five (45) days of this renegotiation period, you will not negotiate for your services with any other person or company other than WABC–TV or ABC. In the event we are unable to reach an agreement for an extension by the expiration of the extended term hereof, you agree that you will not accept, in any market for a period of three (3) months following expiration of the extended term of this agreement, any offer of employment as a sportscaster, sports news reporter, commentator, program host, or analyst in broadcasting (including television, cable television, pay television and radio) without first giving us, in writing, an opportunity to employ you on substantially similar terms and you agree to enter into an agreement with us on such terms." Under this provision, Wolf was bound to negotiate in good faith with ABC for the 90–day period from December 6, 1979 through March 4, 1980. For the first 45 days, December 6 through January 19, the negotiation with ABC was to be exclusive. Following expiration of the 90–day negotiating period and the contract on March 5, 1980, Wolf was required, before *accepting* any other offer, to afford ABC a right of first refusal; he could comply with this provision either by refraining from accepting another offer or by first tendering the offer to ABC. The first-refusal period expired on June 3, 1980 and on June 4 Wolf was free to accept any job opportunity, without obligation to ABC.

Wolf first met with ABC executives in September, 1979 to discuss the terms of a renewal contract. Counterproposal were exchanged, and the parties agreed to finalize the matter by October 15. Meanwhile, unbeknownst to ABC, Wolf met with representatives of CBS in early October. Wolf related his employment requirements and also discussed the first refusal-good faith negotiation clause of his ABC contract. Wolf furnished CBS a copy of that portion of the ABC agreement. On October 12, ABC officials and Wolf met, but were unable to reach agreement on a renewal contract. A few days later, on October 16 Wolf again discussed employment possibilities with CBS.

Not until January 2, 1980 did ABC again contact Wolf. At that time, ABC expressed its willingness to meet substantially all of his demands. Wolf rejected the offer, however, citing ABC's delay in communicating with him and his desire to explore his options in light of the impending expiration of the 45–day exclusive negotiation period.

On February 1, 1980, after termination of that exclusive period, Wolf and CBS orally agreed on the terms of Wolf's employment as sportscaster for WCBS–TV, a CBS-owned affiliate in New York. During the next two days, CBS informed Wolf that it had prepared two agreements and divided his annual compensation between the two: one covered his services as an on-the-air sportscaster, and the other was an off-the-air production agreement for sports specials Wolf was to produce. The production agreement contained an exclusivity clause which barred Wolf from performing "services of any nature for" or permitting the use of his "name, likeness, voice or endorsement by, any person, firm or corporation" during the term of the agreement, unless CBS consented. The contract had an effective date of March 6, 1980.

Wolf signed the CBS production agreement on February 4, 1980. At the same time, CBS agreed in writing, in consideration of $100 received from Wolf, to hold open an offer of employment to Wolf as sportscaster until June 4, 1980, the date on which Wolf became free from ABC's right of first refusal. The next day, February 5, Wolf submitted a letter of resignation to ABC.

Representatives of ABC met with Wolf on February 6 and made various offers and promises that Wolf rejected. Wolf informed ABC that they had delayed negotiations with him and downgraded his worth. He stated he had no future with the company. He told the officials he had made a "gentlemen's agreement" and would leave ABC on March 5. Later in February, Wolf and ABC agreed that Wolf would continue to appear on the air during a portion of the first-refusal period, from March 6 until May 28.[1]

ABC commenced this action on May 6, 1980, by which time Wolf's move to CBS had become public knowledge. The complaint alleged that Wolf, induced by CBS breached both the good-faith negotiation and first-refusal provisions of his contract with ABC. ABC sought specific enforcement of its right of first refusal and an injunction against Wolf's employment as a sportscaster with CBS.

After a trial, Supreme Court found no breach of the contract, and went on to note that, in any event, equitable relief would be inappropriate. A divided Appellate Division, while concluding that Wolf had breached both the good-faith negotiation and first-refusal provisions, nonetheless affirmed on the ground that equitable intervention was unwarranted. There should be an affirmance.

II.

Initially, we agree with the Appellate Division that defendant Wolf breached his obligation to negotiate in good faith with ABC from December, 1979 through March 1980. When Wolf signed the production agreement with CBS on February 4, 1980, he obligated himself not to render services "of any nature" to any person, firm or corporation on and after March 6, 1980. Quite simply, then, beginning on February 4 Wolf was unable to extend his contract with ABC; his contract with CBS precluded him from

---

1. The agreement also provided that on or after June 4, 1980, Wolf was free to "accept an offer of employment with anyone of [his] choosing and immediately begin performing on-air services." The parties agreed that their rights and obligations under the original employment contract were in no way affected by the extension of employment.

legally serving ABC in any capacity after March 5. Given Wolf's existing obligation to CBS any negotiations he engaged in with ABC, without the consent of CBS, after February 4 were meaningless and could not have been in good faith.

At the same time, there is no basis in the record for the Appellate Division's conclusion that Wolf violated the first-refusal provision by entering into an oral sports casting contract with CBS on February 4. The first-refusal provision required Wolf, for a period of 90 days after termination of the ABC agreement, either to refrain from accepting an offer of employment or to first submit the offer to ABC for its consideration. By its own terms, the right of first refusal did not apply to offers accepted by Wolf prior to the March 5 termination of the ABC employment contract. It is apparent, therefore, that Wolf could not have breached the right of first refusal by accepting an offer during the term of his employment with ABC.[2] Rather, his conduct violates only the good-faith negotiation clause of the contract. The question is whether this breach entitled ABC to injunctive relief that would bar Wolf from continued employment at CBS.[3] To resolve this issue, it is necessary to trace the principles of specific performance applicable to personal service contracts.

III.

–A–

Courts of equity historically have refused to order an individual to perform a contract for personal services (e.g., 4 Pomeroy, Equity Jurisprudence [5th ed.], § 1343, at pp. 943–944; 5A Corbin, Contracts, § 1204; see Haight v. Badgeley, 15 Barb. 499; Willard, Equity Jurisprudence, at pp. 276–279). Originally this rule evolved because of the inherent difficulties courts would encounter in supervising the performance of uniquely personal efforts[4] (e.g., 4 Pomeroy, Equity Jurisprudence, § 1343; 5A Corbin,

---

2. In any event, the carefully tailored written agreement between Wolf and CBS consisted only of an option prior to June 4, 1979. Acceptance of CBS's offer of employment as a sportscaster did not occur until after the expiration of the first-refusal period on June 4, 1979.

3. In its complaint, ABC originally sought specific enforcement of the right of first refusal. ABC now suggests that Wolf be enjoined from performing services for CBS for a two-year period. Alternatively, ABC requests this court to "turn the clock back to February 1, 1980" by: (1) setting aside Wolf's agreement with CBS and enjoining CBS from enforcing the agreement; (2) ordering Wolf to enter into good-faith negotiations with ABC for at least the period remaining under the negotiation clause when Wolf breached it; (3) ordering Wolf to honor the 90–day first-refus-

al period should the parties fail to reach agreement; and (4) enjoining CBS from negotiating with Wolf "for a period sufficient to render meaningful the above-described relief".

4. The New York Court of Chancery in De Rivafinoli v. Corsetti (4 Paige Chs. 264, 270) eloquently articulated the traditional rationale for refusing affirmative enforcement of personal service contracts: "I am not aware that any officer of this court has that perfect knowledge of the Italian language, or possesses that exquisite sensibility in the auricular nerve which is necessary to understand, and to enjoy with a proper zest, the peculiar beauties of the Italian opera, so fascinating to the fashionable world. There might be some difficulty, therefore, even if the defendant was compelled to sing under the direction and in the presence of a master

Contracts, § 1204; see, also, De Rivafinoli v. Corsetti, 4 Paige Chs. 264, 270). During the Civil War era, there emerged a more compelling reason for not directing the performance of personal services: the Thirteenth Amendment's prohibition of involuntary servitude. It has been strongly suggested that judicial compulsion of services would violate the express command of that amendment[5] (Arthur v. Oakes, 63 F. 310, 317; Stevens, Involuntary Servitude by Injunction, 6 Corn.L.Q. 235; Calamari & Perillo, The Law of Contracts [2d ed.], § 16–5). For practical policy and constitutional reasons, therefore, courts continue to decline to affirmatively enforce employment contracts.

Over the years, however, in certain narrowly tailored situations, the law fashioned other remedies for failure to perform an employment agreement. Thus, where an employee refuses to render services to an employer in violation of an existing contract, and the services are unique or extraordinary, an injunction may issue to prevent the employee from furnishing those services to another person for the duration of the contract (see, e.g., Shubert Theatrical Co. v. Gallagher, 206 App.Div. 514, 201 N.Y.S. 577). Such "negative enforcement" was initially available only when the employee had expressly stipulated not to compete with the employer for the term of the engagement (see, e.g., Lumley v. Wagner, 1 De G.M. & G. 604, 42 Eng.Rep. 687; Shubert Theatrical Co. v. Rath, 271 F. 827, 830–833; 4 Pomeroy, Equity Jurisprudence [5th ed.], § 1343, at p. 944). Later cases permitted injunctive relief where the circumstances justified implication of a negative covenant (see, e.g., Montague v. Flockton, L.R. 16 Eq. 189 [1873], 4 Pomeroy, Equity Jurisprudence [5th ed.], § 1343; 5A Corbin, Contracts, § 1205). In these situations, an injunction is warranted because the employee either expressly or by clear implication agreed not to work elsewhere for the period of his contract. And, since the services must be unique before negative enforcement will be granted, irreparable harm will befall the employer should the employee be permitted to labor for a competitor (see 5A Corbin, Contracts, § 1206, at p. 412).

–B–

After a personal service contract terminates, the availability of equitable relief against the former employee diminishes appreciably. Since the period of service has expired, it is impossible to decree affirmative or negative specific performance. Only if the employee has expressly agreed not to compete with the employer following the term of the contract, or is threatening to disclose trade secrets or commit another tortious act, is

in chancery, in ascertaining whether he performed his engagement according to its spirit and intent. It would also be very difficult for the master to determine what effect coercion might produce upon the defendant's singing, especially in the livelier airs; although the fear of imprisonment would unquestionably deepen his seriousness in the graver parts of the drama. But one thing at least is certain; his songs will be neither comic, or even semi-serious, while he remains confined in that dismal cage, the debtor's prison of New York."

5. It is well established that legislative enactments may not coerce performance of services by penalizing nonperformance (e.g., People v. Lavender, 48 N.Y.2d 334, 338–339, 422 N.Y.S.2d 924, 398 N.E.2d 530).

injunctive relief generally available at the behest of the employer. ... Even where there is an express anticompetitive covenant, however, it will be rigorously examined and specifically enforced only if it satisfies certain established requirements. ... Indeed, a court normally will not decree specific enforcement of an employee's anticompetitive covenant unless necessary to protect the trade secrets, customer lists or good will of the employer's business, or perhaps when the employer is exposed to special harm because of the unique nature of the employee's services[6] .... And, an otherwise valid covenant will not be enforced if it is unreasonable in time, space or scope or would operate in a harsh or oppressive manner. ... There is, in short, general judicial disfavor of anticompetitive covenants contained in employment contracts....

Underlying the strict approach to enforcement of these covenants is the notion that, once the term of an employment agreement has expired, the general public policy favoring robust and uninhibited competition should not give way merely because a particular employer wishes to insulate himself from competition.... Important, too, are the "powerful considerations of public policy which militate against sanctioning the loss of a man's livelihood" (Purchasing Assoc. v. Weitz, 13 N.Y.2d at p. 272, 246 N.Y.S.2d 600, 196 N.E.2d 245, supra). At the same time, the employer is entitled to protection from unfair or illegal conduct that causes economic injury. The rules governing enforcement of anticompetitive covenants and the availability of equitable relief after termination of employment are designed to foster these interests of the employer without impairing the employee's ability to earn a living or the general competitive mold of society.

–C–

Specific enforcement of personal service contracts thus turns initially upon whether the term of employment has expired. If the employee refuses to perform during the period of employment, was furnishing unique services, has expressly or by clear implication agreed not to compete for the duration of the contract and the employer is exposed to irreparable injury, it may be appropriate to restrain the employee from competing until the agreement expires. Once the employment contract has terminated, by contrast, equitable relief is potentially available only to prevent injury from unfair competition or similar tortious behavior or to enforce an express and valid anticompetitive covenant. In the absence of such circumstances, the general policy of unfettered competition should prevail.

IV.

Applying these principles, it is apparent that ABC's request for injunctive relief must fail. There is no existing employment agreement between

---

6. Although an employee's anticompetitive covenant may be enforceable where the employee's services were special or unique (Reed, Roberts Assoc. v. Strauman, 40 N.Y.2d 303, 308, 386 N.Y.S.2d 677, 353 N.E.2d 590, supra; Purchasing Assoc. v. Weitz, 13 N.Y.2d 267, 272–273, 246 N.Y.S.2d 600, 196 N.E.2d 245, ...) no New York case has been found where enforcement has been granted, following termination of the employment contract, solely on the basis of the uniqueness of the services.

the parties; the original contract terminated in March, 1980. Thus, the negative enforcement that might be appropriate during the term of employment is unwarranted here. Nor is there an express anticompetitive covenant that defendant Wolf is violating, or any claim of special injury from tortious conduct such as exploitation of trade secrets. In short, ABC seeks to premise equitable relief after termination of the employment upon a simple, albeit serious, breach of a general contract negotiation clause.[7] To grant an injunction in that situation would be to unduly interfere with an individual's livelihood and to inhibit free competition where there is no corresponding injury to the employer other than the loss of a competitive edge. Indeed, if relief were granted here, any breach of an employment contract provision relating to renewal negotiations logically would serve as the basis for an open-ended restraint upon the employee's ability to earn a living should he ultimately choose not to extend his employment.[8] Our public policy, which favors the free exchange of goods and services through established market mechanisms, dictates otherwise.

Equally unavailing is ABC's request that the court create a noncompetitive covenant by implication. Although in a proper case an implied-in-fact covenant not to compete for the term of employment may be found to exist, anticompetitive covenants covering the postemployment period will not be implied.[9] Indeed, even an express covenant will be scrutinized and enforced only in accordance with established principles.

This is not to say that ABC has not been damaged in some fashion or that Wolf should escape responsibility for the breach of his good-faith negotiation obligation.[10] Rather, we merely conclude that ABC is not

---

7. Even if Wolf had breached the first-refusal provision, it does not necessarily follow that injunctive relief would be available. Outside the personal service area, the usual equitable remedy for breach of a first-refusal clause is to order the breaching party to perform the contract with the person possessing the first-refusal right (e.g., 5A Corbin, Contracts, § 1197, at pp. 377–378). When personal services are involved, this would result in an affirmative injunction ordering the employee to perform services for plaintiff. Such relief, as discussed, cannot be granted.

8. Interestingly, the negative enforcement ABC seeks—an injunction barring Wolf from broadcasting for CBS—is for a two-year period. ABC's request is premised upon the fact that Wolf and CBS entered into a two-year agreement. Had the agreement been for 10 years, presumably ABC would have requested a 10-year restraint. In short, since it lacks an express anticompetitive clause to enforce, plaintiff seeks to measure its relief in a manner unrelated to the breach or the injury. This well illustrates one of the rea-

sons why the law requires an express anticompetitive clause before it will restrain an employee from competing after termination of the employment.

9. Of course, as discussed, tortious interference with the employer's business by a former employee may sometimes be enjoined absent a noncompetitive covenant.

10. It should be noted that the dissenter would ground relief upon the first-refusal clause, a provision of the contract that defendant did not breach. The dissenting opinion fails to specify why the first-refusal clause—or for that matter any other provision of the contract that defendant did not breach—is relevant in determining the availability of equitable relief. And, while the dissent correctly noted the flexibility of equitable remedies, this does not mean that courts of equity totally dispense with governing rules. Our analysis of the relevant principles, guided by important underlying policy considerations, reveals that this case falls well beyond the realm where equitable intervention would be permissible.

entitled to equitable relief. Because of the unique circumstances presented, however, this decision is without prejudice to ABC's right to pursue relief in the form of monetary damages, if it be so advised.

Accordingly, the order of the Appellate Division should be affirmed.

■ FUCHSBERG, JUDGE (dissenting).

I agree with all the members of this court, as had all the Justices at the Appellate Division, that the defendant Wolf breached his undisputed obligation to negotiate in good faith for renewal of his contract with ABC. Where we part company is in the majority's unwillingness to mold an equitable decree, even one more limited than the harsh one the plaintiff proposed, to right the wrong.

Central to the disposition of this case is the first-refusal provision. Its terms are worth recounting. They plainly provided that, in the 90–day period immediately succeeding the termination of his ABC contract, before Wolf could accept a position as sportscaster with another company, he first had to afford ABC the opportunity to engage him on like terms. True, he was not required to entertain offers, whether from ABC or anyone else, during that period. In that event he, of course, would be off the air for that 90 days, during which ABC could attempt to orient its listeners from Wolf to his successor. On the other hand, if Wolf wished to continue to broadcast actively during the 90 days, ABC's right of first refusal put it in a position to make sure that Wolf was not doing so for a competitor. One way or the other, however labeled, the total effect of the first refusal agreement was that of an express conditional covenant under which Wolf could be restricted from appearing on the air other than for ABC for the 90–day posttermination period.

One need not be in the broadcasting business to understand that the restriction ABC bargained for, and Wolf granted, when they entered into the original employment contract was not inconsequential. The earnings of broadcasting companies are directly related to the "ratings" they receive. This, in turn, is at least in part dependent on the popularity of personalities like Wolf. It therefore was to ABC's advantage, once Wolf came into its employ, especially since he was new to the New York market, that it enhance his popularity by featuring, advertising and otherwise promoting him. This meant that the loyalty of at least part of the station's listening audience would become identified with Wolf, thus enhancing his potential value to competitors, as witness the fact that, in place of the $250,000 he was receiving during his last year with ABC, he was able to command $400,000 to $450,000 per annum in his CBS "deal." A reasonable opportunity during which ABC could cope with such an assault on its good will had to be behind the clause in question.

The dissenting opinion would now create a new agreement for the parties, and apply the first-refusal clause backwards into the period of the ABC employment, under the guise of equitable interpretation. Although the reach of equity may be broad, so far as we are aware equitable principles have never sanctioned the creation of a new and different contract between sophisticated parties merely to condemn conduct which was permissible under an actual written agreement.

Moreover, it is undisputed that, when in late February Wolf executed the contract for an extension of employment during the 90–day hiatus for which the parties had bargained, ABC had every right to expect that Wolf had not already committed himself to an exclusivity provision in a producer's contract with CBS in violation of the good-faith negotiation clause (see majority opn. at pp. 397–398, at p. 483 of 438 N.Y.S.2d, at p. 364 of 420 N.E.2d). Surely, had ABC been aware of this gross breach, had it not been duped into giving an uninformed consent, it would not have agreed to serve as a self-destructive vehicle for the further enhancement of Wolf's potential for taking his ABC-earned following with him.

In the face of these considerations, the majority rationalizes its position of powerlessness to grant equitable relief by choosing to interpret the contract as though there were no restrictive covenant, express or implied. However, as demonstrated, there is, in fact, an express three-month negative covenant which, because of Wolf's misconduct, ABC was effectively denied the opportunity to exercise. Enforcement of this covenant, by enjoining Wolf from broadcasting for a three-month period, would depart from no entrenched legal precedent. Rather, it would accord with equity's boasted flexibility (see 11 Williston, Contracts [3d ed.], § 1450, at pp. 1043–1044; 6A Corbin, Contracts, § 1394, at p. 100; see, generally, 20 N.Y.Jur. [rev.], Equity, §§ 79, 83, 84).

That said, a few words are in order regarding the majority's insistence that Wolf did not breach the first-refusal clause. It is remarkable that, to this end, it has to ignore its own crediting of the Appellate Division's express finding that, as far back as February 1, 1980, fully a month before the ABC contract was to terminate, "Wolf and CBS orally agreed on the terms of Wolf's employment as sportscaster for WCBS–TV" (majority opn., at p. 399, at p. 484 of 438 N.Y.S.2d, at p. 365 of 420 N.E.2d; see American Broadcasting Co. v. Wolf, 76 A.D.2d 162, 166, 170–171, 430 N.Y.S.2d 275). It follows that the overt written CBS–Wolf option contract, which permitted Wolf to formally accept the CBS sports casting offer at the end of the first-refusal period, was nothing but a charade.

Further, on this score, the majority's premise that Wolf could not have breached the first-refusal clause when he accepted the producer's agreement, exclusivity provision and all, *during* the term of his ABC contract, does not withstand analysis. So precious a reading of the arrangement with ABC frustrates the very purpose for which it had to have been made. Such a classical exaltation of form over substance is hardly to be countenanced by equity....

For all these reasons, in my view, literal as well as proverbial justice should have brought a modification of the order of the Appellate Division to include a 90–day injunction—no more and no less than the relatively short and certainly not unreasonable transitional period for which ABC and Wolf struck their bargain.

■ JASEN, GABRIELLI, JONES, WACHTLER and MEYER, JJ., concur with COOKE, C.J.

■ FUCHSBERG, J., dissents in part and votes to modify in a separate opinion.

Order affirmed, with costs.

NOTES

(1) *Specific Performance of Personal Service Contract.* Suppose that ABC and Wolf had, in 1978, signed a five-year contract under which Wolf was to render "exclusive" sports casting services. In 1980, Wolf repudiated and signed a five-year contract with CBS. ABC can prove that because of Wolf's unique style and ability he will be "difficult if not impossible" to replace. Further, ABC can prove that damages to it in the New York area from Wolf's competition at CBS will be "substantial and extremely difficult to measure." ABC sues in 1980, seeking specific performance of the contract. Should it be granted?

The traditional answer is no. See Restatement (Second) § 367(2). What justifications are there for this result? According to Comment a, the reasons fall into three overlapping categories: (1) It is undesirable to compel the continuation of a personal relationship after a dispute has undercut confidence and loyalty; (2) The difficulties inherent in passing judgment on the quality of what frequently is a subjective performance are too great; and (3) An award requiring performance may impose a form of involuntary servitude that is prohibited by the 13th Amendment to the Constitution. See In re A.P. Johnson, 178 B.R. 216, 221–22 (BAP 9th Cir.1995); Read v. Wilmington Senior Center, Inc., 1992 WL 296870 (Del.Ch.1992); Robert S. Stevens, *Involuntary Servitude by Injunction*, 6 Cornell L.Q. 235 (1921). See also Restatement (Second) §§ 365, 366.

(2) *Availability of Injunctive Relief.* If specific performance is not available, could ABC enjoin Wolf from sports casting with CBS or anyone else for the balance of the five-year contract? The answer is probably yes, and the "probably" relates to the question whether the injunction will, in effect, compel a performance "involving personal relations the enforced continuance of which is undesirable or will be to leave the employee without other reasonable means of making a living." Restatement (Second) § 367(2). The starting point for the analysis is Lumley v. Wagner, 42 Eng.Rep. 687 (Ch.1852), where a famous opera singer agreed to a three-month engagement at the plaintiff's theater and promised not to appear in any other theater or concert during that period without the plaintiff's written approval. The defendant was induced by a third person to breach the negative covenant and, at the plaintiff's request, the English Court of Chancery, among other things, enjoined the defendant from appearing at the third party's theater. The Lord Chancellor was of the opinion that the total agreement necessarily excluded the defendant from singing elsewhere and that a denial of the injunction would leave the plaintiff "to the mere chance of any damages which a jury may give." Conceding that the court had no power to compel the defendant to sing, the Lord Chancellor stated that the defendant had "no cause of complaint, if I compel her to abstain from the commission of an act which she has bound herself not to do, and thus possibly cause her to fulfill her engagement." He disclaimed "doing indirectly what I cannot do directly." According to Professor Treitel, English courts will enforce an express covenant not to work elsewhere, but only if the breaching party has some other reasonable means of earning a living. G. Treitel, The Law of Contract 691–95 (4th ed. 1975). The defendant must not be given a choice

between starving and working for the plaintiff. Accord: Restatement (Second) § 362(2).

The *Lumley* principle was adopted in America, see McCaull v. Braham, 16 Fed. 37 (S.D.N.Y.1883), and expanded equity jurisdiction in two ways: first, by enforcing the negative covenant where the direct promise was not specifically enforceable, and second, by granting the plaintiff an injunction where comparable relief was not available to the defendant. See, e.g., Philadelphia Ball Club v. Lajoie, 202 Pa. 210, 51 A. 973 (1902) (absence of mutual remedy not fatal to injunction). And the injunction, whose primary purpose is to protect the plaintiff from unfair competition from a contract breacher whose unique services cannot easily be replaced, is available whether or not an express negative covenant has been made. As Professor Corbin put it, an injunction against competition is proper if the competition "will do additional irreparable injury to the plaintiff, and if the injunction may induce proper performance of the entire contract by economic pressure without at the same time creating harmful personal relations." 5A Corbin § 1206, p. 412.

Although there are many variables to consider, the *Lumley* principle has survived in the United States and found its home in the domain of professional sports and entertainment. See Yeam, *New Remedial Developments in the Enforcement of Personal Service Contracts for the Entertainment and Sports Industries: The Rise of Tortious Bad Faith Breach and the Fall of the Speculative Damage Defense*, 7 Loy.Ent.L.J. 27 (1987). At times the papers have been full of reports about players and coaches of exceptional and not so exceptional talent who have joined other teams in violation of contracts or "reserve" clauses and have been enjoined from competing until the period of commitment to the plaintiff team has expired. For a typical example, see Nassau Sports v. Peters, 352 F.Supp. 870 (E.D.N.Y.1972) (hockey). See also Note, *Professional Athletic Contracts and the Injunctive Dilemma*, 8 J. Marshall J. of Prac. & Proc. 437 (1975), where the author asserts that injunctive relief has become the ordinary rather than the extraordinary relief and that this is based upon a misguided assumption that such relief is necessary to protect the plaintiff's large investment in acquiring and developing talented players. Be this as it may, professional sports is big business and such restraints on player mobility raise important questions concerning the scope of federal antitrust and labor policy. See, e.g., Flood v. Kuhn, 407 U.S. 258, 92 S.Ct. 2099, 32 L.Ed.2d 728 (1972); Winter & Jacobs, *Antitrust Principles and Collective Bargaining by Athletes: Of Superstars in Peonage*, 81 Yale L.J. 1 (1971); McCormick, *Baseball's Third Strike: The Triumph of Collective Bargaining in Professional Baseball*, 35 Vand.L.Rev. 1131 (1982); Zollers, *From Gridiron to Courtroom to Bargaining Table: The New National Football League Agreement*, 17 Am.Bus. L.J. 133 (1979); Comment, *National Hockey League Reserve System: A Restraint of Trade?*, 56 U.Det.Urb.L. 467 (1979).

Professor Lea VanderVelde has shown that negative injunctions were only issued against women for nearly the first century of the *Lumley* doctrine. Vander Velde, *The Gendered Origins of the Lumley Doctrine*, 101 Yale L.J. 775 (1992). Simply put, without injunctions against women, there would have been no *Lumley* rule in the United States in the nineteenth century.

Comment: Remedies for Breach of Valid Restrictive Covenant in Employment Contracts

It is common in many industries for employment contracts to contain a restrictive covenant. The covenant, in essence, states that if the employee leaves the company for any reason, the employee agrees not to compete with the employer for a stated time in a defined area. Although one purpose of the restriction is to protect the employer against harmful competition, other objectives are to protect the employer's confidential information and the investment in the employee's training. See Comment, *Post–Employment Restraint Agreements: A Reassessment,* 50 U.Chi.L.Rev. 703 (1985). The employee's freedom and the public's interest in competition, however, must be weighed in the balance. Thus, a court will not enforce the restriction unless it is "reasonable," which in turn depends upon such factors as whether the employees services are "special, unique or extraordinary," or there is a risk that the employee will disclose trade secrets or solicit the employer's customers. The duration and scope of the restraint are also relevant to the inquiry. See, e.g., Data Management, Inc. v. Greene, supra at 560; Purchasing Associates, Inc. v. Weitz, 13 N.Y.2d 267, 246 N.Y.S.2d 600, 196 N.E.2d 245 (1963) (restraint unreasonable). See also Handler & Lazerof, *Restraint of Trade and the Restatement (Second) of Contracts,* 57 N.Y.U.L.Rev. 669 (1982); Kniffen, *Employee Noncompetition Covenants: The Perils of Performing Unique Services,* 10 Rut.Cam.L.J. 25 (1978); Note, *Economic and Critical Analyses of the Law of Covenants Not to Compete,* 72 Geo.L.J. 1425 (1984). See also Christopher T. Wonnell, The Contractual Disempowerment of Employees, 46 Stan. L. Rev. 687, 92–95 (1993); Stewart E. Sterk, Restraints on Alienation of Human Capital, 79 Va. L. Rev. 383, 401–03 (1993).

If the restriction passes the test of reasonableness, in whole or in part, the probabilities are that normal damage remedies will be inadequate. There is a risk of irreparable harm that cannot be measured with reasonable certainty. Without more, a court should enforce the employee's promise not to compete through an injunction. In some contracts, however, there may be a clause attempting to liquidate the probable damages in the event of breach. For example, the contract may provide that in the event of breach the employee will pay the employer $100,000 as "liquidated damages and not a penalty" for the breach.

We will consider when liquidated damage provisions are enforceable in the next section. For now, remember this. If the liquidated damage provision is valid and the contract provides that is the *exclusive* remedy, the employer is not entitled to injunctive relief. It must take the money and run. In the absence of an exclusive remedy clause, however, the employer has a choice: Enforce the liquidated damage clause or seek an injunction. The employer cannot have both (Do you see why?) If the employer obtains an injunction, however, the employer may recover any actual damages caused between the time of the breach and the date the injunction issues. See Karpinski v. Ingrasci, 28 N.Y.2d 45, 320 N.Y.S.2d 1, 268 N.E.2d 751

(1971); Restatement (Second) § 361 (provision for liquidated damages will not bar injunctive relief).

SECTION 5.   EFFECT OF AGREEMENT LIQUIDATING DAMAGES OR ALTERING THE SCOPE OF LIABILITY OR REMEDY

(A) LIQUIDATED DAMAGES

As we have seen, punitive damages are not recoverable in the ordinary action for breach of contract. This is true, generally, even though the defendant's breach is willful, malicious or in bad faith. Courts insist that the remedial objective is to compensate the plaintiff, not to punish the defendant. But what if the parties provide in their contract what the damages are to be in the event of breach, and they set a figure which is greatly in excess of probable harm? Suppose, for example, in a building contract (to cost $100,000) it is agreed that for every day's delay in completion the builder is to pay the owner $5,000. Is such a provision, from the standpoint of fairness and justice, objectionable? Would it likely be upheld in court? Consider the following statements of Judge Irving Kaufman and Professor Lewis Kornhauser.

[Judge Kaufman.] More than three centuries ago, in *The Merchant of Venice,* Shakespeare tellingly illustrated the evil of agreements which exact a "pound of flesh." Since that time, courts have grappled with the problem of oppressive contracts through the doctrine of unconscionability. Originating in Equity as a form of relief against the harshness of penal bonds, this doctrine has been employed by courts to deny enforcement to harsh and unreasonable contract terms. Today we are asked to determine whether the liquidated damages provisions of several commercial leasing agreements are unconscionable as a matter of law. In reaching our decision, we must resolve a significant tension between two important goals served by rules governing the enforceability of liquidated damages clauses: rejecting clauses which operate as a penalty or forfeiture while upholding provisions which are reasonable attempts by parties to estimate the probable damages which would flow from a breach. This tension is an example of a more general conflict between contract law as a system of private ordering and contract law as an expression of the public interest. * * *

Determining the enforceability of a liquidated damages clause or other contractual provision governing a lessor's remedies upon default reveals a tension between two often conflicting goals. On the one hand, courts will not enforce such a provision if it operates as a penalty or forfeiture clause. ... The law is clear that contractual terms providing for the payment of a sum disproportionate to the amount of actual damages exact a penalty and are unenforceable. ... The rationale for this principle is that contractual terms fixing damages in an amount clearly disproportionate to actual loss seek to deter breach through compulsion and have an *in terrorem* effect: fearing severe economic loss, the promisor is compelled to continue performance, while the promisee may reap a windfall well in excess of his just compensation. . . .

On the other hand, courts uphold contractual provisions fixing damages for breach when the terms constitute a reasonable mechanism for estimating the compensation which should be paid to satisfy any loss flowing from the breach. . . . These provisions have value in situations where it is difficult to estimate the amount of actual damages. From these principles, the standards for evaluating appellants' claim that the challenged lease terms are unconscionable are easily discernible. Contractual provisions fixing liquidated damages in the event of breach will not be voided as unconscionable or contrary to public policy if the amount liquidated bears a reasonable proportion to the probable loss and the amount of actual loss is incapable or difficult of precise estimation. . . . If the amount fixed by contract is plainly or grossly disproportionate to the probable loss, the contractual provisions exact a penalty and will not be enforced. . . .

Leasing Service Corp. v. Justice, 673 F.2d 70, 73 (2d Cir.1982).

[Professor Kornhauser.] *Liquidated Damages Clause.* The judicial attitude towards contract clauses that specify the amount to be paid in the event of breach is one of the few areas of contract law that has received generally adverse criticism from economic analysts. The traditional rule against the enforcement of "penalty" clauses runs strongly counter to the elaboration of the efficiency criterion, particularly in commercial contexts.

Several reasons account for the economists' antagonism. First, the assumption of rationality entails that a party will not accept a clause for which he is inadequately compensated. When the promisee demands a "penalty clause," the promisor will agree only if the price is increased sufficiently to cover any increase in the cost of performance. Thus, if parties are "rational," no contract should require performance when the (expected) costs to party A of performing exceed the (expected) benefits to party B of receiving it. Of course, the parties may have different expectations as to the likelihood of some contingency occurring, and one may be more accurate than the other. Moreover, the occurrence of the contingency may impose some inequality of costs and benefits between the parties. But, since it seems plausible that commercial contractors act largely in their "rational" self-interest, it is likely that both parties initially saw a benefit even in a clause which a court later terms a penalty. This benefit might simply be to trade a risk that one party perceives as high to a second party who perceives it as low. Such trades may be "efficient" because trading the risk may be cheaper for the first party than correcting or improving his estimate of the risk to which he was exposed. In that event, judicial intervention after the fact would only serve to induce excessively costly gathering of information. Alternatively, the benefits to the parties may be more "substantial" than those arising from different perceptions. For instance, a new entrant into a market may be willing to accept a clause imposing a penalty in the event his product fails to meet some quality standard precisely because he has no other means of credibly assuring quality and thereby successfully entering the market.

A second reason economists criticize limitations on liquidated damage clauses lies in the informational advantage that the parties themselves are presumed to have; at the time of contracting the parties are likely to have better information about any idiosyncratic damages that might be incurred than a court will have at or after the time of breach. Particularly in markets where substitute performance is difficult to obtain, this informational advantage argues strongly for liberal enforcement of liquidated damage clauses. An analogous argument derives from the widespread belief that expectation damages are in fact undercompensatory. If the law seeks to promote efficient decisions to perform or not, then allowing parties to estimate damages in advance will induce more appropriate decisions in this respect than court-imposed rules.

A third problem with the current proscription of "penalty" clauses lies in its implicit distributional bias; it forces the parties to allocate some risks in a particular way. Suppose the breach is caused by the appearance of a third party willing to pay more for the good than the first buyer agreed to pay. The ban on penalties (together with a rule of expectation damages) effectively allocates the entire gain from the appearance of the third party to the seller, while the parties might rationally have wished to divide this risk differently. On the other hand, if the breach is prompted by an uneconomic increase in costs, expectation damages allocates all of the loss to the breaching party, while contractors, negotiating before the breach, might knowingly have chosen to share this risk differently.

These arguments suggest that the current rules governing liquidated damage clauses are too restrictive. They do not necessarily contend that every liquidation clause, whether it appears to be a "penalty" or not, should be permitted. Most commentators would make exceptions for clauses that resulted from defective bargaining procedures (akin to those covered by unconscionability). These defects, however, seem unlikely to occur in commercial contexts, where one can presume that the parties are sophisticated and rational in their negotiations. Other commentators suggest that liquidated damage clauses be policed for more than fraud or oppression in bargaining. In some circumstances, a clause which unduly benefitted one party might stimulate it to induce a breach by the other; in that case, these commentators suggest the clause should not be enforced. [Footnotes omitted.]

Kornhauser, *An Introduction to the Economic Analysis of Contract Remedies,* 57 U.Colo.L.Rev. 683, 720–21 (1986) [Reprinted with permission].

Southwest Engineering Co. v. United States

United States Court of Appeals, Eighth Circuit, 1965.
341 F.2d 998, cert. denied 382 U.S. 819, 86 S.Ct. 45, 15 L.Ed.2d 66.

■ VAN OOSTERHOUT, CIRCUIT JUDGE. Plaintiff Southwest Engineering Company, hereinafter called Southwest, has appealed from summary judgment dismissing its complaint against the United States for recovery of $8,300 withheld as liquidated damages for delay in performance on four construction contracts entered into between Southwest and the United States.

This appeal is before us upon an agreed statement of the record. Four contracts entered into between Southwest and the Government called for the construction by Southwest of three V.O.R. radio facilities at Readsville, Blackwater, and Maryland Heights, Missouri, and for a high intensity approach light lane at Lambert Field, Missouri. Each of the contracts fixed a completion date and provided for liquidated damages on a per diem basis for each day's delay beyond the agreed completion date. The agreed liquidated damage on the Lambert Field project was $100 per day, and $50 per day on each of the other projects. Each contract contained the general provisions set forth in Standard Form 23–A (March 1953) prescribed by the General Services Administration, including, among others, a provision that plaintiff was not to be charged with delays "due to unforeseeable causes beyond the control and without the fault or negligence of the Contractor, including, but not restricted to, acts of God or of the public enemy, acts of the Government, in either its sovereign or contractual capacity, acts of another contractor in the performance of a contract with the Government, fires, floods, epidemics, quarantine restrictions, strikes, freight embargoes, and unusually severe weather, or delays of subcontractors or suppliers due to such causes." Within ten days from the beginning of any such delay, plaintiff was to notify the contracting officer in writing of the causes of delay. The contracting officer was to ascertain the facts and extent of the delay, and extend the time for completing the work when "in his judgment the findings of fact justify such an extension." His findings of fact were to be final, subject only to appeal to the "head of the department."

The Blackwater project was completed 97 days late. Plaintiff requested time extensions, alleging the delay resulted from causes for which it was not responsible, including acts and omissions of defendant. Administrative appeals resulted in extensions by the C.A.A. because of delays by the Government, and, later on, a remission of an additional $4,200 liquidated damages by the Comptroller General under the authority of 41 U.S.C. § 256a, because of late delivery of Government-furnished material. This left $550 (11 days) withheld as liquidated damages on the Blackwater project.

The Readsville project was completed 84 days late. Administrative appeals resulted in a three-days extension, leaving liquidated damages for 81 days totalling $4,050.

The Maryland Heights project was completed 48 days late. On administrative appeal, a fourteen-days extension was allowed resulting in liquidated damages of $1,700 for 34 days delay.

The Lambert Field project was completed 54 days late, 34 days extension was granted, leaving $2,000 as liquidated damages for 20 days delay.

The parties stipulated "although each project was not completed until after the date prescribed in its contract, defendant suffered no actual damage on any project." The Government withheld the liquidated damages for delays provided in the contracts after giving credit for the extensions of time administratively allowed. This suit by Southwest is for recovery of the $8,300 so withheld as liquidated damages. The Government counterclaimed for the liquidated damages here involved. Plaintiff by reply admitted the projects were not completed within the time limits as administratively extended but denied the Government was entitled to liquidated damages because the Government caused and contributed to the delays and because the Government suffered no actual damages.

The trial court determined that the Government was entitled to liquidated damages in the amount claimed, offset such damages which equaled the amount of payments withheld, sustained the motion for summary judgment, and dismissed the complaint.

Southwest as a basis for reversal urges the trial court's decision was induced by two erroneous views of the law, either of which requires reversal. The points relied upon for reversal are thus stated:

* * *

2.   "The court erred in awarding the Government liquidated damages because a contract provision for liquidated damages is clearly a penalty and not enforceable where the party seeking to enforce it formally admits he sustained no actual damage."

At the outset, we observe that the contracts here involved were entered into pursuant to federal law by an authorized federal agency. Federal law controls in the construction and determination of rights under federal contracts. Priebe & Sons, Inc. v. United States, 332 U.S. 407, 411, 68 S.Ct. 123, 92 L.Ed. 32; Clearfield Trust Co. v. United States, 318 U.S. 363, 63 S.Ct. 573, 87 L.Ed. 838; United States v. Le Roy Dyal Co., 3 Cir., 186 F.2d 460, 461.

In the Priebe case, the Supreme Court states:

"It is customary, where Congress has not adopted a different standard, to apply to the construction of government contracts the principles of general contract law. United States v. Standard Rice Co., 323 U.S. 106, 111, [65 S.Ct. 145, 147, 89 L.Ed. 104] and cases cited. That has been done in other cases where the Court has considered the enforceability of 'liquidated damages' provisions in government contracts." 332 U.S. 407, 411, 68 S.Ct. 123, 125.

* * *

Southwest's second point in substance is that the parties' stipulation that the Government suffered no actual damage bars any recovery of liquidated damages. Such stipulation was made. It relates to the situation as it existed at the time of the completion of the work. The stipulation does not go to the extent of agreeing that the parties at the time of contracting did not reasonably contemplate that damages would flow from a delay in performance.

The contracts prescribe the payments to be made for delays as liquidated damages. Southwest urges that such provision is a penalty provision. The agreed record is highly condensed and does not show the contract price for the various projects, but such projects appear to be substantial. There is no showing that the liquidated damages for delay provided for are beyond damages reasonably contemplated by the parties at the time of the contract.

Two requirements must be considered to determine whether the provision included in the contract fixing the amount of damages payable on breach will be interpreted as an enforceable liquidated damage clause rather than an unenforceable penalty clause: First, the amount so fixed must be a reasonable forecast of just compensation for the harm that is caused by the breach, and second, the harm that is caused by the breach must be one that is incapable or very difficult of accurate estimation. See J.D. Streett & Co. v. United States, 8 Cir., 256 F.2d 557, 559; United States v. Le Roy Dyal Co., supra; Restatement, Contracts § 339.

Whether these requirements have been complied with must be viewed as of the time the contract was executed rather than when the contract was breached or at some other subsequent time. Courts presently look with candor upon provisions that are deliberately entered into between parties and therefore do not look with disfavor upon liquidated damage stipulations. Rex Trailer Co. v. United States, 350 U.S. 148, 151, 76 S.Ct. 219, 100 L.Ed. 149; Priebe & Sons, Inc. v. United States, supra; United States v. Bethlehem Steel Co., 205 U.S. 105, 119, 27 S.Ct. 450, 51 L.Ed. 731; Sun Printing & Publishing Ass'n v. Moore, 183 U.S. 642, 660, 22 S.Ct. 240, 46 L.Ed. 366.

In the Bethlehem Steel case, the Court sets out the standard to be applied for determining whether a liquidated damage provision can be upheld as follows: "The question always is, What did the parties intend by the language used? When such intention is ascertained it is ordinarily the duty of the court to carry it out." 205 U.S. 105, 119, 27 S.Ct. 450, 455.

Here Southwest has failed to establish that the intention of the parties was to do anything other than execute a valid liquidated damage provision.

Priebe & Sons, Inc. v. United States, supra, involved a Government contract for purchase of dried eggs for foreign shipment. The Court observes the contract contains two provisions for liquidated damages. The one involved in the case related to failure to have eggs inspected and ready for delivery for the date specified in the order. The court construed the contract to mean that performance was not due until demand for delivery and held that since inspection was made before such demand, the provision for liquidated damages could not possibly be a reasonable forecast of just compensation for breach of contract. The Court further observes that the contract contains a provision for liquidated damages for delay in delivery upon demand and with respect to such provision, breach of which was not involved, states: "It likewise is apparent that the only thing which could possibly injure the Government would be failure to get prompt performance when delivery was due. We have no doubt of the validity of the provision for 'liquidated damages' when applied under those circumstances." 332 U.S. 407, 412, 68 S.Ct. 123, 126.

The Court also speaks of standards applicable to allowance of liquidated damages, stating:

"Today the law does not look with disfavor upon 'liquidated damages' provisions in contracts. When they are fair and reasonable attempts to fix just compensation for anticipated loss caused by breach of contract, they are enforced. * * * They serve a particularly useful function when damages are uncertain in nature or amount or are unmeasurable, as is the case in many government contracts. * * * And the fact that the damages suffered are shown to be less than the damages contracted for is not fatal. These provisions are to be judged as of the time of making the contract." 332 U.S. 407, 411–412, 68 S.Ct. 123, 126.

In Rex Trailer Co. v. United States, supra, recovery was allowed upon the statutory penalty imposed for fraud in obtaining a Government contract. The Court states: "Liquidated-damage provisions, when reasonable, are not to be regarded as penalties, * * * "350 U.S. 148, 151, 76 S.Ct. 219, 221. And then says:

"The Government's recovery here is comparable to the recovery under liquidated-damage provisions which fix compensation for anticipated loss. As this Court recognized in Priebe & Sons v. United States, 332 U.S. 407, 411–412, [68 S.Ct. 123, 126, 92 L.Ed. 32] liquidated damages 'serve a particularly useful function when damages are uncertain in nature or amount or are unmeasurable, as is the case in many government contracts. * * *' And the fact that no damages are shown is not fatal." 350 U.S. 148, 153, 76 S.Ct. 219, 222.

In United States v. J.D. Streett & Co., E.D.Mo., 151 F.Supp. 469, 472, Judge Harper, in upholding a claim for liquidated damages, states:

"Although it is clear that a finding that a provision is one for liquidated damages requires that damages could be anticipated at the time of execution of the contract, whether actual damage did or did not occur or was not proved to have occurred does not prevent recovery." We affirmed upon appeal. J.D. Streett & Co. v. United States, 8 Cir., 256 F.2d 557.

The late Judge Goodrich in United States v. Le Roy Dyal Co., supra, in a well-considered opinion dealing with numerous aspects of the liquidated damage issue, states:

"If a provision for liquidated damages is upheld the fact that actual damage did or did not occur or was not proved to have occurred does not prevent the recovery of the stipulated sum. There is some dissent on this point, but the statement just made represents the great weight of decided cases." 186 F.2d 460, 462.

In Frick Co. v. Rubel Corp., 2 Cir., 62 F.2d 765, 768, the late Judge Learned Hand allowed liquidated damages, stating inter alia:

"My brothers think, though I do not, that evidence as to the *actual* loss was not material to the issue of the losses in *contemplation,* though we all agree that it is the comparison of the liquidated damages with the last, not the first, which can raise the point at all."

C.J.S. Damages § 115d; 15 Am.Jur., Damages, § 263, and 34 A.L.R. 1336, 1341, and supporting cases cited in such authorities, indicate that the majority view is that proof of actual damages is not required to sustain an action for liquidated damages, unless the contracts so provide, at least in situations where damages could reasonably be anticipated at the time of contracting.

We recognize that there are cases, including Massman Const. Co. v. City Council of Greenville, 5 Cir., 147 F.2d 925, Rispin v. Midnight Oil Co., 9 Cir., 291 F. 481, 34 A.L.R. 1331, and Northwest Fixture Co. v. Kilbourne & Clark Co., 9 Cir., 128 F. 256, cited by Southwest, which reach a contrary result.

We believe that the cases holding that the situation existing at the time of the contract is controlling in determining the reasonableness of liquidated damages are based upon sound reasoning and represent the weight of authority. Where parties have by their contract agreed upon a liquidated damage provision as a reasonable forecast of just compensation for breach of contract and damages are difficult to estimate accurately, such provision should be enforced. If in the course of subsequent developments, damages prove to be greater than those stipulated, the party entitled to damages is bound by the liquidated damage agreement. It is not unfair to hold the contractor performing the work to such agreement if by reason of later developments damages prove to be less or nonexistent. Each party by entering into such contractual provision took a calculated risk and is bound by reasonable contractual provisions pertaining to liquidated damages.

Southwest has completely failed to demonstrate that the court committed an error of law in determining that absence of actual damages at the time of breach of the contract or thereafter does not bar recovery of liquidated damages. The court at least impliedly found that the liquidated damage provisions of the contracts here involved were reasonable when viewed in the light of circumstances existing at the time the contract was entered into. We find nothing in the record which would compel a contrary conclusion. The court committed no error in allowing liquidated damages.

The judgment appealed from is affirmed.

NOTES

(1) *"Time of Contracting" Test.* The courts adhere to the "time of contracting" test, which is undoubtedly the prevailing rule. See Watson v. Ingram,

124 Wash.2d 845, 881 P.2d 247 (1994); Taos Const. Co. v. Penzel Const. Co., 750 S.W.2d 522, 526–27 (Mo.App.1988) (construction delay); Manufacturers Casualty Insurance Co. v. Sho–Me Power Corp., 157 F.Supp. 681 (W.D.Mo. 1957). This approach makes the most sense when both parties, in negotiations, have addressed themselves to the inability of standard damages to provide adequate compensation under the peculiar facts of their case. On the other hand, liquidated damage clauses usually serve the interest of one party more than the other and may be the product of superior bargaining power. Put another way, the ability of one party—the plaintiff—to overstate remedies may raise the same problems posed when a defendant has attempted to limit liability through disclaimer clauses or other "agreed" remedies. See Melodee Lane Lingerie Co. v. American District Telephone Co., 18 N.Y.2d 57, 271 N.Y.S.2d 937, 218 N.E.2d 661 (1966); Fritz, *"Underliquidated" Damages as a Limitation of Liability*, 33 Tex.L.Rev. 196 (1954). Arguably, the "hindsight" rule, i.e., the power of a court to assess the liquidation in light of actual damage caused by the breach, becomes more appealing when the plaintiff has been able to impose the clause on the defendant with little or no actual bargaining. See UCC 2–718(1) [UCC 2–809 (1997)]. In view of this, how well does *Southwest Engineering* fit the realities of most government contracting? Do you suppose the contractor had any say about inclusion of the liquidated damage clause or its amount? Did the contractor fail to satisfy its burden of proof in attacking the clause? See generally Gantt & Breslauer, *Liquidated Damages in Federal Government Contracts*, 47 Boston U.L.Rev. 71 (1967). For an economic argument supporting the enforcement of reasonable *ex ante* forecasts of damages, see Rea, *Efficiency Implications of Penalties and Liquidated Damages*, 13 J.Legal Stud. 147 (1984).

(2) Might one be able to disguise an impermissible penalty by phrasing it in terms of an "alternative performance" or as a "premium" for timely performance? See Blank v. Borden, 11 Cal.3d 963, 115 Cal.Rptr. 31, 524 P.2d 127 (1974). For example, how would you classify a "take-or-pay" commitment, as an alternative performance or a liquidated damage clause? See Universal Resources Corp. v. Panhandle Eastern Pipe Line Co., 813 F.2d 77 (5th Cir. 1987) (alternative performance).

(3) Where, at the time of the breach, the plaintiff has fully performed and the defendant has failed to pay money due, efforts to liquidate damages are more difficult to sustain. As one court put it: "In this context [breach by lessee of a covenant to pay rent] it is a relevant general rule that a failure to pay a sum of money due will rarely, if ever, justify a further sum, in excess of interest, to be paid by way of liquidated damages. On the contrary, such a requirement is likely to be condemned as a penal forfeiture which the law will not recognize." Breitel, J. in Manhattan Syndicate, Inc. v. Ryan, 14 A.D.2d 323, 220 N.Y.S.2d 337, 340–41 (1961). But see United Merchants and Manufacturers, Inc. v. Equitable Life Assurance Society, 674 F.2d 134 (2d Cir.1982) (Applying New York law, court upheld provision in loan agreement that upon default the principal of the note plus interest would be due, together with an amount equal to the pre-payment charges that would be payable if the borrower were pre-paying the note). See also Garrett v. Coast & Southern Federal Savings & Loan Association, 9 Cal.3d 731, 108 Cal.Rptr. 845, 511 P.2d 1197 (1973) (late charge assessed at 2% of unpaid balance of due notes is void because parties "failed to make a reasonable endeavor to estimate a fair

compensation which would be sustained on the default"); A–Z Servicenter v. Segall, 334 Mass. 672, 138 N.E.2d 266 (1956) (acceleration clause permitting creditor upon default to demand substantial amounts of unpaid interest as liquidated damages is void).

(4) *Liquidated Damages under the UCC and Restatement (Second)*. UCC 2–718(1) provides: "Damages for breach by either party may be liquidated in the agreement but only at an amount which is reasonable in the light of the anticipated or actual harm caused by the breach, the difficulties of proof of loss, and the inconvenience or nonfeasibility of otherwise obtaining an adequate remedy. A term fixing unreasonably large liquidated damages is void as a penalty." How does this approach differ from that adopted in *Southwest Engineering*? Does the Code appear to be more supportive or less supportive of the power of contracting parties to fix the amount of damage in advance of breach? See Note, 72 Nw.L.Rev. 1055 (1978). Restatement (Second) § 356(1), drafted so as to harmonize with the Code, reads: "Damages for breach by either party may be liquidated in the agreement but only at an amount that is reasonable in the light of the anticipated or actual loss caused by the breach and the difficulties of proof of loss. A term fixing unreasonably large liquidated damages is unenforceable on grounds of public policy as a penalty." See Note, 67 Cornell L.Rev. 862 (1982).

The focus upon the time of breach as well as the time of contracting raises a number of questions. For example, what if the agreed upon figure is unreasonable in the light of anticipated loss but reasonable in the light of actual loss? Or what if it is reasonable in the light of anticipated harm, but not reasonable in terms of actual harm caused by the breach? See Anderson, *Liquidated Damages Under the Uniform Commercial Code*, 41 Sw.L.J. 1083 (1988). See also Irving Tire Co., Inc. v. Stage II Apparel Corp., ___ A.D.2d ___, 646 N.Y.S.2d 528, 530 (1996), where the court refused to enforce a purported liquidated damage clause where the damages actually arising from the breach were readily ascertainable and the "sum fixed is disproportionate to the landlord's loss."

(5) *Revised Article 2*. Revised Section 2–718(1), now Section 2–809(a) (Jan. 1997) provides: "(a) Damages for breach of contract may be liquidated but only in an amount that is reasonable in light of either the actual loss or the then anticipated loss caused by the breach and the difficulties of proof of loss in the event of breach. If a term liquidating damages in unenforceable under this subsection, the aggrieved party has the remedies provided in this article." What changes are made in this revision?

What if the damage clause fixes an unreasonably *small* amount? Would it constitute a "penalty"? Is there a basis for invalidating such a provision?

United Air Lines, Inc. v. Austin Travel Corp.

United States Court of Appeals, Second Circuit, 1989.
867 F.2d 737.

■ MINER, CIRCUIT JUDGE:

Defendant-appellant Austin Travel Corp. ("Austin") appeals from a summary judgment entered in the United States District Court for the

Southern District of New York (Pollack, J.) awarding plaintiff-appellee United Air Lines, Inc. ("United") $408,375 in liquidated damages and unpaid debt plus interest and costs. United sued Austin to recover (i) damages for breach of leases obligating Austin to use a United computerized reservation system ("CRS") called Apollo and a United business and accounting system known as Apollo Business System ("ABS"), and (ii) unpaid accrued rentals. Austin claimed that the liquidated damages clauses of its Apollo contracts with United were unreasonable and unenforceable. * * *

The district court held that the liquidated damages clauses were reasonable and enforceable. * * * 681 F.Supp. 176 (S.D.N.Y.1988). On appeal, Austin reasserts its liquidated damages [claim]. Because we hold that the liquidated damages provisions of the United–Austin contracts were at the time of execution a reasonable forecast of damages in case of breach * * *, we affirm the entry of summary judgment in United's favor.

BACKGROUND

United owns and markets to travel agents and others the Apollo CRS. A CRS provides subscribers access to a vast data bank through which they may make airline reservations, issue tickets, reserve car rentals and hotel rooms and perform other travel-related functions. By licensing this system, United earns income in two ways: First, the travel agent pays United a monthly subscription fee, either fixed or based on use, and second, each time the travel agent uses Apollo to book a flight on an airline other than United, United charges that airline a booking fee. United flights booked through Apollo do not generate booking fees. United's Apollo contracts require an agent to book a minimum of 50% of that agent's average monthly bookings through Apollo. United also markets its ABS, a back-office accounting and management system for travel agents.

Competing nationwide with Apollo are four other CRS systems, SystemOne, PARS, DATAS II and SABRE, each owned by separate air carriers. SABRE, owned by American Airlines, is used as a principal CRS by approximately 28% of the more than 28,000 travel agency locations across the country. SABRE also holds the largest share of CRS transactions nationally, more than 45% in the years 1983–1985. Nationally, Apollo is the second largest CRS, used by approximately 25% of travel agency locations in the United States, and, according to Austin, accounting for 31% of all CRS transactions in this country. On Long Island, New York, Apollo ranks fourth, used by 3% of Long Island travel agency locations and earning 8% of all Long Island CRS revenues.

Austin is a travel agency with thirteen offices on Long Island. Prior to mid–1985, Austin used a variety of CRSs, but it never used Apollo. In 1985, Austin acquired two smaller Long Island agencies, Karson Travel and Fantasy Adventures, both of which subscribed to Apollo. By separate agreements with United, Austin assumed Karson's ABS contract and Fantasy's Apollo contract. Austin then executed a five-year Apollo contract covering two of its other locations in Oceanside and Mitchell Field.

Each of the Apollo contracts that Austin signed provided for payment of liquidated damages upon premature termination of the contract. In the contract for the Oceanside and Mitchell Field locations, the liquidated damages consist of: (i) 80% of the remaining monthly fees due under the contract, (ii) 80% of variable charges, accrued by generation of tickets and itineraries, for the month preceding termination, multiplied by the number of months remaining in the contract term and (iii) 50% of the average monthly booking fee revenues, using the first six months of the contract as a basis for calculation, multiplied by the number of months remaining in the contract term. In the contract assuming Fantasy's Apollo obligation, only the first two elements are used to define liquidated damages. The contracts specify that Illinois law governs disputes; for the contract issues raised by this case, the law of Illinois is the same as that of New York, the state where the claim arose, and virtually all other states.

Austin then moved the SABRE CRS into its three locations covered by Apollo, using the two systems side by side at each location. Austin later notified United that it wished to discontinue use of the ABS system at the Karson Travel location. United agreed to the discontinuance and to forego the $90,511.43 in liquidated damages Austin owed under the Karson ABS agreement provided that Austin continue to use Apollo until November 30, 1989. Austin accepted the condition and discontinued use of ABS.

Thereafter, representatives of the rival SystemOne CRS, owned and operated by Texas Air Corp., offered Austin indemnity against any damages incurred for breach of the existing Apollo agreements if Austin would contract for use of SystemOne. In June 1986, Austin adopted the System-One CRS at Mitchell Field, its principal Apollo location, and abandoned all of its Apollo obligations before the expiration of the term of the contracts. At Austin's request, United removed all Apollo equipment from Austin premises. Austin had never paid United for the use of Apollo equipment and services provided by the contracts.

United brought this breach of contract action on the two Apollo contracts and the ABS agreement. Austin defended and counterclaimed on two grounds relevant to this appeal: first, that the liquidated damages clauses included in the Apollo contracts were unenforceable penalties; * * *

The district court rejected Austin's defenses and counterclaims. It held that the liquidated damages clauses were reasonable and enforceable. * * *

On appeal, Austin argues that the district court erred by enforcing liquidated damages that are penalties, * * * and abused summary judgment standards by deciding in plaintiff's favor issues of fact that should have been submitted to a jury.

DISCUSSION

A.   Liquidated Damages

It is commonplace for contracting parties to determine in advance the amount of compensation due in case of a breach of contract. 5 Corbin on

Contracts § 1054, at 319 (1964). A liquidated damages clause generally will be upheld by a court, unless the liquidated amount is a penalty because it is plainly or grossly disproportionate to the probable loss anticipated when the contract was executed. Lake River Corp. v. Carborundum Co., 769 F.2d 1284, 1289–90 (7th Cir.1985) (applying Illinois law); Truck Rent–A–Center, Inc. v. Puritan Farms 2nd, Inc., 41 N.Y.2d 420, 424, 361 N.E.2d 1015, 1018, 393 N.Y.S.2d 365, 369 (1977). Liquidated damages are not penalties if they bear a "reasonable proportion to the probable loss and the amount of actual loss is incapable or difficult of precise estimation." Leasing Service Corp. v. Justice, 673 F.2d 70, 73 (2d Cir.1982).

The liquidated damages fixed in the Apollo contracts[1] were, as the district court found, reasonable at the time the contracts were executed. Most of United's costs when providing Apollo service are either fixed or determined in the early stages of the contractual relationship. The few costs that United would avoid by an early termination of an Apollo contract are estimated to be "less than 20 percent of the amount of revenue from the monthly fixed usage fees and variable charges." 681 F.Supp. at 187 (emphasis omitted). The Apollo contracts' liquidated damages clauses provide for recovery by United of only 80% of the fixed and variable charges. Austin is thus provided with better than adequate credit for the costs United is able to avoid by the early removal of the Apollo CRSs from Austin premises.

* * *

Austin complains that the 20% discount incorporated by the liquidated damages provisions underestimates the savings realized by United in the event of early contract termination. Austin points to testimony by a representative of a competing CRS vendor that United's avoidable costs likely equal 40% to 50% of United's total costs. The testimony of a competitor about United's costs and savings is inherently suspect, and United presented sufficient evidence to justify the 20% figure. The appropriate analysis is not whether a better quantification of damages could have been drafted by the contracting parties, but whether the amount of

---

1. The Apollo Subscriber Lease Agreement between United and Austin for the Oceanside and Mitchell Field locations includes the following paragraphs:

12.   TERMINATION FOR CAUSE

If either party (the "Defaulting Party") shall refuse, neglect, or fail to perform, observe or keep any of the covenants, agreements, terms or conditions contained herein on its part to be performed, observed and kept, and such refusal, neglect or failure shall continue for a period of thirty (30) days after written notice (except in the case of any payments due where the period to cause such nonpayment shall be five (5) days

after notice) to the Defaulting Party thereof, then without prejudice to any other rights or remedies of the other party, this Agreement shall terminate at the expiration of the notice period.

21.   LIQUIDATED DAMAGES

In the event that prior to the expiration of the term of this Agreement, as specified in Article 11 ..., this Agreement is terminated by Subscriber, except pursuant to Article 12, or by United pursuant to the provisions of this Agreement, then Subscriber will pay to United liquidated damages....

The other contract at issue contains substantially the same language.

liquidated damages actually inserted in the contract is reasonable. "[T]he disputable analysis of presumed costs savings belatedly submitted by Austin does not discredit the reasonableness of United's anticipatory estimate in light of anticipated or actual loss caused by the breach and the difficulties of proof." 681 F.Supp. at 188. We note as well, as the district court did, that CRS contracts of United's competitors often call for 100% of rent due on the unexpired term of the contract; United obligated Austin for only 80%. There is no indication that the estimate of probable loss, identified in the contracts as liquidated damages, is either unfair or unreasonable. Indeed, the liquidated damages provisions edge closer toward over-generousness to Austin than they do toward unreasonableness.

Austin complains that in the disputed contract covering its Oceanside and Mitchell Field locations the liquidated damages formula, which envisions repayment for all potential booking fees, fails to account for the fact that United does not receive booking fees for United flights booked on the Apollo CRS. The booking fees reimbursement, however, is based on a lenient minimum usage level of Apollo—future monthly bookings are estimated as 50% of the average level of all bookings Austin made on Apollo in the early months of the contract. Any unfairness suggested by a failure to exclude United bookings from the liquidated damages formula is negated by the low level of Apollo usage employed for estimation of future bookings.

Austin further depicts the liquidated damages clauses as imposing penalties because they provide the same amount of damages for each possible breach of the contract, no matter how insignificant. Austin argues that establishing a single liquidated damages amount for any breach indicates that a fair estimation of probable loss for each breach was not conceived when the contract was drafted and executed.

Austin, however, ignores basic tenets of contract law. "A party may terminate a contract only because of substantial nonperformance by the other party so fundamental 'as to defeat the objects of the parties in making the agreement.'" Maywood Sportservice, Inc. v. Maywood Park Trotting Ass'n, Inc., 14 Ill.App.3d 141, 302 N.E.2d 79, 84 (1973) (quoting Wright v. Douglas Furniture Corp., 98 Ill.App.2d 137, 143, 240 N.E.2d 259, 262 (1968)); see John F. Trainor Co. v. G. Amsinck & Co., 236 N.Y. 392, 394, 140 N.E. 931, 931 (1923). Neither United nor Austin can terminate the contracts because of a non-material breach. Thus, liquidated damages can only be owed to United in the event of a material breach by Austin.

Furthermore, the presumed intent of the parties is that a liquidated damages provision will apply only to material breaches. Hackenheimer v. Kurtzmann, 235 N.Y. 57, 66, 138 N.E. 735, 738–39 (1923). Additionally, for a non-material breach to allow an aggrieved party to abrogate the contract, it must be explicitly stated in the agreement of the parties. See Seidlitz v. Auerbach, 230 N.Y. 167, 129 N.E. 461 (1920) (liquidated damages clause applies to trivial breaches because contract stated as to its many obligations that "all and every one of which the tenant covenants to keep and perform"); Hackenheimer, 235 N.Y. at 66–67, 138 N.E. at 739 (warning not to extend Seidlitz to an extreme conclusion for fear of rendering liquidated damages impossible to draft); Brecher v. Laikin, 430 F.Supp. 103, 106 (S.D.N.Y.1977) (according to New York law, liquidated damages clause can only apply to material breaches); see also Restatement (Second) of Contracts § 237 comment a (1981).

We are not persuaded that the liquidated damages outlined in the Apollo contracts were meant to apply to trivial breaches. Article 12 of the Lease Agreement states in unexceptional language that liquidated damages are to be awarded for a failure of "any of the covenants, agreements, terms or conditions." We take this language to refer to material breach. Absent a more explicit demonstration of intent to apply the termination provisions to trivial breaches, the liquidated damages clauses must be enforced.[2]

The parties to the contracts negotiated at arms length and without misinformation. Since summary judgment is rendered appropriately when there exists no genuine issue as to any material fact, Fed.R.Civ.P. 56(c), the district court was correct to enforce the liquidated damages clauses by summary judgment. See Katz v. Goodyear Tire & Rubber Co., 737 F.2d 238, 244 (2d Cir.1984).

* * *

Leeber v. Deltona Corp.

Supreme Judicial Court of Maine, 1988.
546 A.2d 452.

■ Clifford, Justice.

Defendants, The Deltona Corporation and Marco Surfside, Inc., appeal from a judgment for the plaintiffs, Donald A. Leeber, Jeremy Morton and Jan Drewry, on Count I of their complaint entered in the Superior Court, Cumberland County, following a jury-waived trial. The plaintiffs cross-appeal from a judgment against them on the remaining two counts in their complaint.

This case arises out of a dispute involving a Florida real estate transaction. Defendant Marco Surfside, Inc., a wholly owned subsidiary of defendant The Deltona Corporation,[1] was the developer of a condominium real estate development on Marco Island in Florida. The plaintiffs, Portland area residents, decided to invest as a group in one of the condominium units being constructed by Deltona. On May 14, 1980, the plaintiffs, dealing with defendant Maine–Florida Properties, the exclusive sales agent in

---

2. Professor Corbin writes that in a case where the liquidated damages specified in the contract are a reasonable estimate of the injury actually caused, but would not have been so for injuries caused by other possible breaches, and the extent of the injury is difficult to estimate, the liquidated damages clause should be enforced. 5 Corbin on Contracts § 1066, at 383–84.

1. Because Marco Surfside and Deltona have acted as one entity during this litigation and at all other relevant times, they will frequently be treated as one entity in this opinion and will be referred to collectively as "Deltona."

Maine for Deltona, signed a Subscription and Purchase Agreement ("the Agreement") to buy a condominium unit in the Marco Island project, designated as unit 711. The price for the unit was $150,200, with 15% of this amount, $22,530, paid at the time the Agreement was signed and the balance due at the closing date, to be specified by Deltona within four years from the time of the Agreement. Under the express terms of the Agreement, the $22,530 was to be retained by Deltona as liquidated damages in the event of a breach by the plaintiffs.

Beginning in May 1982, Deltona notified the plaintiffs several times that they would be required to close on the condominium on certain dates or the liquidated damages deposit would be retained by Deltona. After each notice, the plaintiffs were able to obtain an extension from Deltona. Deltona sent the plaintiffs a final closing notice on July 8, 1982, which set a closing date of July 20, 1982. The July 8 letter advised the plaintiffs that the Agreement would be canceled if they did not close on unit 711. The plaintiffs did not close on the July 20 date. On July 27, 1982, Deltona informed the plaintiffs in writing that the Agreement had been canceled and the liquidated damages deposit would be retained by Deltona. Deltona then sold unit 711 to another party on July 31, 1982, for what the trial court found to be $167,500.[2] That party paid a 15% deposit of $25,125.

Deltona refused to return the plaintiffs' deposit, and this suit was initiated in the Superior Court. Plaintiffs' complaint contained three counts: Count I, directed against Deltona and Marco Surfside, alleged that the liquidated damages provision was unenforceable. * * *

At the close of the plaintiffs' evidence in the nonjury trial in this case, the trial justice granted the defendants' motion for dismissal with respect to Counts II and III, * * *. As to Count I, the trial justice determined that the enforcement of the liquidated damages provision was unconscionable. The trial justice found that Deltona had proved it incurred actual damages consisting of some administrative costs and a $5,704 commission paid to Maine–Florida from the deposit and awarded plaintiffs $15,020—the balance of the deposit. * * * Defendants Deltona and Marco Surfside then appealed on Count I to this court in timely fashion. The plaintiffs cross-appealed on Counts II and III. We vacate the judgment as to Count I of the complaint, and affirm as to Counts II and III.

I.

The defendants contend that the liquidated damages provision in the Agreement was valid and enforceable under Florida law.[3] The Agreement provided for the retention by Deltona of the 15% deposit in the event of a breach of the Agreement on the part of the plaintiffs. The validity of a liquidated damages clause is assessed in the following way under Florida law:

2. The Superior Court rejected the contention of defendants that the actual resale price was $150,000.

3. All parties agree with the determination of the trial justice that Florida law controls the substantive issue of liquidated damages.

> If the damages are ascertainable on the date of the contract, the clause is a penalty and unenforceable; if they are not so ascertainable, the clause is truly one for liquidated damages and enforceable; however, if subsequent circumstances demonstrate it would be unconscionable to allow the seller to retain the sum in question as liquidated damages, equity may relieve against the forfeiture.

Bruce Builders, Inc. v. Goodwin, 317 So.2d 868, 869–70 (Fla.Dist.Ct.App. 1975)....

The plaintiffs do not dispute that damages were not ascertainable at the time the Agreement was entered into. Thus, the issue placed before us in this case is whether the Superior Court erred in its determination that retention of money by the sellers under an otherwise valid liquidated damage provision was unconscionable under the standard set out in *Bruce Builders*.

A determination of unconscionability cannot be made unless the circumstances of the case truly "shock the conscience" of the court. See Beatty v. Flannery, 49 So.2d 81, 82 (Fla.1950); .... The factual findings upon which the conclusion of unconscionability is based are reviewed on a clearly erroneous basis....

Under Florida law, if the liquidated damages provision is not a penalty, it is enforceable unless the plaintiff proves the existence of one or more of the following factors:

> (1) an intimation of fraud on the seller's part; (2) misfortune beyond his control accounting for the buyer's failure to fulfill the contract; (3) a mutual rescission of the contract; or (4) a benefit to the seller "the retention of which [when compared to the total contract price would be] shocking to the conscience of the court."

Johnson v. Wortzel, 517 So.2d 42, 43 (Fla.Dist.Ct.App.1987) (per curiam) (alteration by court in *Johnson* opinion) (quoting Beatty, 49 So.2d at 82).[4] Here, there was no showing of fraud on Deltona's part, nor evidence that plaintiffs' failure to buy was caused by misfortune beyond their control, nor evidence of mutual rescission. Only Deltona's retention of $22,530, 15% of

---

4. Plaintiffs cite Multitech Corp. v. St. Johns Bluff Inv. Corp., 518 So.2d 427, 433 (Fla.Dist.Ct.App.1988), for the proposition that another factor to be considered in an unconscionability analysis under Florida law is "whether or not the sellers actually suffered any damage as a result of the breach." We are reluctant to accept this as a valid factor for assessing unconscionability under Florida law. The *Multitech* court, only one of several District Courts of Appeal in Florida, failed to cite any precedent for that holding and we can find no case decided by Florida's highest court, the Florida Supreme Court, that incorporates this factor. Moreover, to routinely allow such a consideration in determining unconscionability would unduly undermine one of the purposes of liquidated damages, namely to avoid the difficulties and uncertainties of proof of actual damages. Restatement (Second) of Contracts § 356 comment a (1981); 5 A. Corbin, Corbin on Contracts §§ 1054, 1062 (1964). See Dairy Farm Leasing Co., Inc. v. Hartley, 395 A.2d 1135, 1139 (Me.1978). In any event, *Multitech* is distinguishable from the instant case because the court found unconscionability in a case where the liquidated damage amount was $120,000 and the seller suffered no damage.

the purchase price, examined under a "shocking to the conscience" standard, is properly considered by the court. Id.

Liquidated damages are favored under Florida law, Hutchison, 259 So.2d at 132, and Florida courts have uniformly viewed liquidated damage sums in the range of 15% as reasonable. Wortzel, 517 So.2d at 43 (18.2% not unconscionable); Dade Nat'l Dev. Corp. v. Southeast Invs. of Palm Beach County, Inc., 471 So.2d 113, 116 (Fla.Dist.Ct.App.1985) (18%); Hooper v. Breneman, 417 So.2d 315, 318 (Fla.Dist.Ct.App.1982) (13.3%); O'Neill, 112 So.2d at 281–83 ($1500 deposit on $10,440 contract).

The Superior Court, despite its recitation that it found defendants' retention of the liquidated damages to be unconscionable, did not apply a true "shock the conscience" standard in overriding the liquidated damage provision in this case. The court considered the fact of the resale of the condominium unit by Deltona several days after the default but several months after the originally designated closing date, and allowed the plaintiff buyers to recover from Deltona all of the previously paid deposit except what Deltona convinced the court were its actual out of pocket losses resulting from plaintiffs' breach.[5] Such an approach nullified the effect of the liquidated damages provision and made this case indistinguishable from one of ordinary breach of contract. This result undercut the traditional role of liquidated damages provisions, which have always served as an economical alternative to the costly and lengthy litigation involved in a conventional breach of contract action. Restatement (Second) of Contracts § 356 comment a (1981); 5 A. Corbin, Corbin on Contracts §§ 1054, 1062 (1964). See Dairy Farm Leasing Co., Inc. v. Hartley, 395 A.2d 1135, 1139 (Me. 1978).

Efforts by contracting parties to avoid litigation and to equitably resolve potential conflicts through the mechanism of liquidated damages should be encouraged.... Prompt resale of real estate units by sellers upon breach of contract by buyers likewise should be encouraged. However, the Superior Court ruling in this case, if allowed to stand, would have the opposite effect.

Florida law provides that, under a real estate contract containing a liquidated damages clause similar in language to the instant contract, sellers are denied the remedy of specific performance.... Moreover, their damage recovery is limited to the liquidated damage amount. ... Buyers breaching such contracts, not being subject to specific performance nor to liability for excess damages should the sellers' losses exceed the amount of liquidated damages, would have nothing to lose in challenging the amount of liquidated damages retained or sought to be recovered by the sellers in every case where the buyers suspected the actual losses of the sellers to be less than the liquidated damage amount.

Under Florida law, the determination of the unconscionability of allowing a seller to retain liquidated damages under an otherwise valid

---

5. The court was unpersuaded by evidence presented by defendants that plaintiffs' delays in closing the transaction resulted in substantial losses to defendants.

liquidated damage provision should be based on the circumstances existent "at the time of breach." Hutchinson, 259 So.2d at 132.[6] A case of liquidated damages, when the liquidated damage amount is not unreasonable on its face, is not converted as a matter of course to one of ordinary breach of contract by the seller's fortuitous resale of the contract real estate subsequent to the buyer's breach. Sellers are inescapably bound by the liquidated damage provisions in such contracts. Buyers should be bound as well unless the plaintiff proves that the circumstances are so extraordinary that the sellers' retention of the liquidated damage amount would truly shock the conscience of the court. Beatty, 49 So.2d at 82.

It is undisputed that this liquidated damage amount of $22,530, 15% of the total contract price of the Florida real estate, was reasonable on its face and not a penalty. The retention of that sum by the sellers in this case, when plaintiff buyers delayed closing on the project for several months before breaching the contract, and sellers subsequently were able to resell the real estate through their own efforts and in doing so reduced their actual losses flowing from plaintiffs' breach, is not so extraordinary or unfair as to shock the conscience of the court. Id. The plaintiffs having failed to demonstrate circumstances sufficiently extraordinary to meet the shock the conscience test of Beatty, defendants must be allowed to retain the liquidated damage amount.

* * *

NOTES

1. In Lake Ridge Academy v. Carney, 66 Ohio St.3d 376, 613 N.E.2d 183, 188 (1993), the court, in upholding a clause in a school "reservation agreement" that imposed liability for full tuition if the reservation was not canceled after a stated date, used a three-point step to determine whether the parties had agreed upon liquidated damages or a penalty: "Where the parties have agreed on the amount of damages, ascertained by estimation and adjustment, and have expressed this agreement in clear and unambiguous terms, the amount so fixed should be treated as liquidated damages and not as a penalty, if the damages would be (1) uncertain as to amount and difficult of proof, and if (2) the contract as a whole is not so manifestly unconscionable, unreasonable, and disproportionate in amount as to justify the conclusion that it does not express the true intention of the parties, and if (3) the contract is consistent with the conclusion that it was the intention of the parties that damages in the amount stated should follow the breach thereof." Is this helpful?

(2) For recent cases enforcing liquidated damage clauses, see Wallace Real Estate Investment, Inc. v. Groves, 124 Wash.2d 881, 881 P.2d 1010 (1994)(pay-

---

6. Some states, including Maine, measure the soundness of a liquidated damage provision as of the time the contract is made and not at the time of the breach. Dairy Farm Leasing, 395 A.2d at 1137; Walter E. Heller & Co. v. American Flyers Airline Corp., 459 F.2d 896, 898 (2d Cir.1972) (N.Y. law); Pembroke v. Gulf Oil Corp., 454 F.2d 606, 611 (5th Cir.1971) (La. law); Babbitt Ford, Inc. v. Navajo Indian Tribe, 519 F.Supp. 418, 432 (D.Ariz.1981); Monsen Eng'g Co. v. Tami–Githens, Inc., 219 N.J.Super. 241, 530 A.2d 313 318–19 (App.Div. 1987).

ment of $15,000 for each 30 day delay in settlement under contract), and Reliance Insurance Co. v. Utah Department of Transportation, 858 P.2d 1363 (Utah 1993)(liquidated damages for delay in construction contract). See also Space Master Int'l, Inc. v. Worcester, 940 F.2d 16 (1st Cir.1991), Wasserman's Inc. v. Township of Middletown, 137 N.J. 238, 645 A.2d 100 (1994), Sutton v. Epperson, 631 So.2d 832 (Ala.1993), and Shallow Brook Assoc. v. Dube, 135 N.H. 40, 599 A.2d 132 (1991) for useful analysis and discussion.

Comment: Exculpation and Underliquidated Damage Clauses

In commercial transactions, contract clauses exculpating one party from the consequences of negligence are enforceable if they clearly and conspicuously set out the purpose of the drafter. See, e.g., Neville Chemical Co. v. Union Carbide Corp., 422 F.2d 1205 (3d Cir.1970); Mayfair Fabrics v. Henley, 48 N.J. 483, 226 A.2d 602 (1967); Goldman v. Ecco–Phoenix Electric Corp., 62 Cal.2d 40, 41 Cal.Rptr. 73, 396 P.2d 377 (1964) (indemnification clause). See Gates Rubber Co. v. USM Corp., 508 F.2d 603 (7th Cir.1975) (valid exculpation need not mention negligence). The exculpation effort may, however, be against public policy when attempted by a party who is "under a public duty entailing the exercise of care," such as common carriers or public utilities, or is in a position of superior bargaining power, such as a hospital exacting a release from an entering patient. Mayfair Fabrics v. Henley, supra, 226 A.2d at 605. See also Weaver v. American Oil Co., supra at 525. A more subtle exculpation takes the form of a liquidated damage clause but, in effect, states a limit almost always under the amount of actual damage caused by negligence or breach of contract. A classic example is the case where one party agrees to install and maintain, in connection with the telephone company, a system designed promptly to detect and report fires or burglary. If there is defective equipment or negligent maintenance, the delay in reporting the critical event can contribute to substantial loss of life, property and economic opportunity. These contracts invariably contain a clause providing that if the contractor "should be found liable for loss or damage due to a failure of service in any respect, its liability shall be limited to a sum equal to ten percent of the annual service charge or $250, whichever is the greater." If the contractor is negligent and this negligence causes losses of, say, $50,000, will the limitation clause be enforced?

The answer appears to be yes. In California, the issue has been treated as involving liquidated damages and the limitation has been enforced under Cal.Civ.Code §§ 1670 & 1671. See Better Food Markets v. American District Telephone Co., 40 Cal.2d 179, 253 P.2d 10 (1953); Feary v. Aaron Burglar Alarm, Inc., 32 Cal.App.3d 553, 108 Cal.Rptr. 242 (1973). In New York, the clause is treated as an effort to limit liability rather than to liquidate damages and is enforced where the limitation is conspicuous and the other party could have obtained "more coverage . . . for a negotiable fee." See Melodee Lane Lingerie Co. v. American District Telephone Co., 18 N.Y.2d 57, 271 N.Y.S.2d 937, 218 N.E.2d 661 (1966). If the other party has a choice to pay more for greater protection and selects less, it would be "unfair to hold the defendant liable for the grossly disproportionate losses sustained by the plaintiff." Rinaldi & Sons v. Wells Fargo Alarm Service, 47 A.D.2d 462, 367 N.Y.S.2d 518, 522 (1975). In New Jersey, such limitations are not *per se* against public policy and will be enforced if conscionable at the time of contracting. Abel Holding Co., Inc. v. American District Telephone Co., 138 N.J.Super. 137, 350 A.2d 292 (Law Div.1975). When all is said and done, which approach do you prefer?

For a study of the underliquidated damage problem, see Warren, *Formal and Operative Rules under Common Law and Code,* 30 U.C.L.A.L.Rev. 898 (1983).

PROBLEM: THE CASE OF THE "BIG SHIP" DEAL

Big Sugar Company, owner of a sugar plantation in Hawaii, was in need of a ship to transport "raw sugar," the crushed cane in the form of coarse brown crystal, from the islands to the mainland. Sugar is a seasonal crop, and Big Sugar had storage capacity in Hawaii for no more than a quarter of the crop. It was, therefore, imperative to have assured transportation. To this end, Big Sugar entered into extensive negotiations with Tall Ships, Inc. for the construction and sale of a ship specially designed for this purpose. Eventually, the parties executed a written contract for a sale of such a ship for $24,000,000. The agreed delivery date was April 30, with a provision for payment by Tall Ships of $17,000 for each day's unexcused delay in delivery.

The ship was not delivered until October 30, some 150 days late. Fortunately for Big Sugar, it was able to avoid catastrophic losses by utilizing older equipment and renting from others. A fair estimate of the loss actually caused by Tall Ship's breach is $250,000.

(A) What, if anything, should Big Sugar recover from Tall Ships? Cf. California and Hawaiian Sugar Co. v. Sun Ship, Inc., 794 F.2d 1433 (9th Cir.1986).

(B) Suppose that Big Sugar's actual loss, after reasonable efforts to mitigate damages, was $7,500,000. What, if anything, should Big Sugar recover from Tall Ships?

(C) Suppose that at the time of contracting, Tall Ships had stated, "We don't care about estimating actual damages if we breach. We won't pay more than $5,000 per day under any circumstances." Big Sugar agreed to a clause limiting the per diem liability to $5,000. If Big Sugar's actual loss was $17,000, what if, anything, can be recovered?

(B) AGREED REMEDIES

Through proper use of a liquidated damage clause the parties may fashion their own remedy. UCC 2–718(1) [UCC 2–809 (1997)] prescribes the Code standards. There are, in addition, other ways in which the parties may attempt to settle in advance what the remedy is to be in the event of breach. They might, for example, provide that in the event of breach the seller's obligation is to repair or replace the goods. The applicable Code provision is Section 2–719 [UCC 2–810 (1997)], which provides as follows:

(1) Subject to the provisions of subsection (2) and (3) of this section and of the preceding section on liquidation and limitation of damages,

(a) the agreement may provide for remedies in addition to or in substitution for those provided in this Article and may limit or alter the measure of damages recoverable under this Article, as by limiting the buyer's remedies to return of the goods and repayment of the price or to repair and replacement of non-conforming goods or parts; and

(b) resort to a remedy as provided is optional unless the remedy is expressly agreed to be exclusive, in which case it is the sole remedy.

(2) Where circumstances cause an exclusive or limited remedy to fail of its essential purpose, remedy may be had as provided in this Act.

(3) Consequential damages may be limited or excluded unless the limitation or exclusion is unconscionable. Limitation of consequential damages for injury to the person in the case of consumer goods is prima facie unconscionable but limitation of damages where the loss is commercial is not.

The materials which follow deal with aspects of this "agreed remedy" problem. See also Chapter Five, Section 2(C)(2).

Lewis Refrigeration Co. v. Sawyer Fruit, Vegetable and Cold Storage Co.

United States Court of Appeals, Sixth Circuit, 1983.
709 F.2d 427.

■ NEWBLATT, DISTRICT JUDGE.

I FACTS

This is an appeal in a diversity action originally brought on March 18, 1974 by Lewis Refrigeration Co. (hereinafter Lewis) against Sawyer Fruit, Vegetable and Cold Storage Cooperative Co. (hereinafter Sawyer). Lewis sued Sawyer to collect a balance allegedly due under an agreement in which Lewis sold Sawyer a freezer. Sawyer counterclaimed against Lewis asserting counts of breach of contract, breach of warranty and misrepresentation.

The case arose out of a 1970 contract between Sawyer and Lewis. The contract provided for Lewis to sell Sawyer an individually quick-frozen freezer. The typed portion of the contract covered contract pages 2–7; the printed portion covered contract pages 7–12.

The typed portion of the contract contained warranties that the freezer was capable of processing six thousand pounds of various fruits per hour and that the freezer would use no more than 1.8 liquid pounds of Freon per one hundred pounds of frozen products. Paragraph 6A of the typewritten portion of the contract contained a clause setting out a guarantee obligating Lewis to supply, for a given period of time, the Freon that the freezer consumed over the warranted rate. Paragraph B3 of the printed portion of the agreement provided that, in the event the machine failed to perform at the warranted rates, Lewis would have the right to repair or replace promptly the malfunctioning part of the machine. Paragraph B3 provided that rescission was the only other available remedy.

In addition to paragraph B3, the contract contained another remedy limitation. This limitation, found at paragraph B4 of the handwritten portion of the contract, excluded consequential damages.

A consent judgment eventually was entered in favor of Lewis for the claim for the balance due on the contract. Trial on Sawyer's counterclaim began on April 4, 1978. After denying Lewis's motions for a directed verdict and for judgment notwithstanding the verdict, the district court instructed and then sent the case to the jury. A verdict was returned for Sawyer in the amount of $25,823 in lost profits and $27,080 in excess Freon costs.

In this appeal, Lewis advances four arguments: (1) the district court erroneously allowed the jury to consider whether, under the state of Washington version of UCC § 2–719(2), the paragraph B3 repair and rescission limitation failed its essential purpose; (2) the district court erred by not generally disallowing consequential damages in favor of benefit of the bargain damages under Washington's version of UCC § 2–714(2); (3) the district court should have granted a new trial on the ground that Sawyer failed to amend and supplement discovery responses as required by Rule 26(e)(2) of the Federal Rules of Civil Procedure; (4) the district court erroneously omitted making a judicial determination of whether the B3 consequential damages exclusion was unconscionable—in the absence of such a determination the consequential damages exclusion should have blocked the jury from awarding consequential damages.

We shall now consider each of the four arguments advanced by Lewis. For the reasons to follow, we affirm the district court as to the first three arguments and vacate and remand as to the fourth argument.

II LEGAL ANALYSIS

A.   Failure of Repair and Rescission Remedy to Achieve its Essential Purpose.

The first argument raised by Lewis involves the district court's treatment of RCW § 62A.2–719(2), the state of Washington's statutory version of UCC § 2–719(2). The statute provides:

"Where circumstances cause an exclusive or limited remedy to fail of its essential purpose, remedy may be had as provided in this Title."

Lewis argues that the district court erroneously allowed the jury to reach the issue of whether the paragraph B3 repair and rescission exclusive remedy failed its essential purpose as described in section 2–719(2). Lewis contends that its motions for directed verdict and judgment notwithstanding the verdict should have been granted as to the issue of the repair and rescission remedy barring the award of any other damages. Lewis thus urges us to vacate the jury's verdict to the extent that it includes $25,823 in lost profit consequential damages.

In opposing this argument, Sawyer contends that it presented enough evidence to permit a reasonable fact finder to determine that the exclusive remedy contractual provision failed its essential purpose. In deciding this issue, we shall separately consider the repair and rescission portions of the exclusive remedy.

Lewis appears to concede that the repair remedy failed its essential purpose. . . . We agree. In any event, there can be no doubt but that the record contains trial evidence adequate to support the conclusion that Lewis was unable to repair promptly the freezer to meet performance warranties. . . .

Furthermore, we note that Washington appellate decisions clearly hold that a seller's inability to repair fully a product causes the repair and rescission remedy to fail of its essential purpose under RCW 62A.2–719(2). See Lidstrand v. Silvercrest Industries, 28 Wash.App. 359, 623 P.2d 710 (1981); Melby v. Hawkins Pontiac, 13 Wash.App. 745, 537 P.2d 807 (1975). We thus conclude that a jury could reasonably have determined that the repair remedy failed its essential purpose under section 2–719(2).

A much closer question obtains with respect to the rescission remedy. Sawyer contends that the jury could reasonably have determined that the rescission remedy failed its essential purpose because of either of the following two reasons: (1) Lewis would have been extremely reluctant to rescind the transaction or (2) Sawyer would have experienced severe financial loss in the event the contract was rescinded.

Sawyer's first contention must be rejected outright. The section 2–719(2) "essential purpose" language refers to circumstances that make it exceedingly impractical to carry out the essence of an agreed-upon remedy. Given that Lewis had categorically refused to rescind the transaction, the rescission provision could have been enforced in a court action, and thus the essence of the remedy could have been carried out.

As to the rescission remedy, Sawyer contends that there was enough evidence in the record to permit a reasonable jury to conclude that Lewis deliberately concealed the machine's inability to meet cherry processing warranties until sometime in 1972. By this time, Sawyer contends, it had made significant commitments with respect to frozen products. Sawyer further asserts that rescission and the concomitant removal of the freezer in 1972 would have been financially destructive in that it would have caused Sawyer to lose revenues and breach important commitments.

Having studied the record below, we believe that there was adequate evidence to support Sawyer's version as set out above. Letters and trial testimony indicate that Lewis was either unable or reluctant to promptly and effectively administer performance tests on the cherries. This well could have prevented Sawyer from making an intelligent decision on rescission until 1972, by which time Sawyer had made numerous frozen product commitments. . . .

We believe it was appropriate for the jury to consider these circumstances in connection with the issue of whether the rescission remedy failed of its essential purpose. Washington cases hold that an exclusive remedy fails its essential purpose where a conceded defect is not detectable until it is impractical to effectuate the exclusive remedy. While the latent defect theory is most often applied in cases involving the repair remedy, and while the facts of this case are not nearly as strong as Sawyer seems to believe, we find that it was not erroneous for the district court to allow the jury to consider whether Lewis concealed the facts until such time as a rescission would have caused severe financial damages to Sawyer. And given that this factual version was true, it was within the ambit of section 2–719(2) for the jury to find that the rescission remedy failed of its essential purpose. Thus, we reject appellant's contention that the district court erred by allowing the jury to consider the evidence in this case as applied to the issue of whether the repair and rescission remedy failed its essential purpose under RCW 62A.2–719(2).

B. Lewis's General Argument Against Consequential Damages.

Lewis next contends that, assuming arguendo that the repair and rescission remedy failed of its essential purpose, the district court should generally have prohibited the jury from awarding consequential damages. This argument is bottomed on Lewis's apparent belief that damages in breach of warranty actions are confined to the benefit of the bargain measure of damages set out in RCW 62A.2–714(2).

This contention is patently incorrect. RCW 62A.2–714(3) authorizes consequential damages in appropriate cases. RCW 62A.2–715(2) then provides that consequential damages from a seller's breach include losses reasonably foreseeable that cannot be mitigated by cover.

Cover is not an issue in this appeal. And since there is a good deal of evidence in the record indicating that the freezer was to be an important part of Lewis's production, we conclude that a reasonable jury easily could have determined that Lewis should have foreseen that its breach of warranty would cause consequential damages. . . . Thus, it certainly was not erroneous for the district court to not generally preclude damages for lost profits.

C. Sawyer's Failure to Supplement Discovery Responses.

* * *

[The Court rejected Lewis' argument for a new trial based on alleged discovery abuses of Sawyer.]

D. District Court's Failure to Make a Separate Determination of Unconscionability Under RCW § 62A.2–719(3).

Lewis's final argument centers on the district court's treatment of the paragraph B4 exclusion of consequential damages. This paragraph excludes consequential damages apparently under the authority of RCW 62A.2–719(3), the Washington version of UCC § 2–719(3). RCW 62A.2–719(3) provides in pertinent part:

> Limitation of consequential damages for injury to the person in the case of goods purchased primarily for personal, family or household use or of any services related thereto is invalid unless it is proved that the limitation is not unconscionable ... Limitation of other consequential damages is valid unless it is established that the limitation is unconscionable.[8]

The district court did not give a separate instruction on the paragraph B4 consequential damages exclusion. Instead, the district court merely instructed that lost profits could be awarded.

> "if you find that circumstances not caused by Sawyer Fruit ... caused the exclusion of lost profits to deprive Sawyer Fruit of the substantial value of its bargain under the Agreement." ...

Apparently, the district court believed that if the jury determined that the exclusive repair and rescission remedy failed of its essential purpose, the exclusion of consequential damages provision automatically became unconscionable under section 2–719(3). Alternatively, the district court may have believed that the "remedy may be had as provided in the act" phrase of RCW 62A.2–719(2) authorizes all UCC damages—including consequential damages—upon a finding of unconscionability.

While a number of courts have taken the general approach of the district court,[9] a larger number of courts—including the Courts of Appeals of the Third and Ninth Circuits—have construed subsection (3) of UCC 2–719 as the governing provision on the issue of consequential damages.[10] We believe that this is the correct approach.

In arriving at this conclusion, we are mindful that Washington law governs this case. And while the Washington appellate courts have not squarely decided this issue, it is notable that in 1955 the Washington Supreme Court indicated that analogous provisions in the Uniform Sales Act should be dealt with separately and distinctly. See Ketel v. Hovick, 47 Wash.2d 368, 287 P.2d 739 (1955). Furthermore, for several reasons, we

---

8. The text of RCW § 62A.2–719(3) differs slightly from UCC § 2–719(3). The two statutes are, however, almost identical in that [exclusion of] consequential damages are prima facie unconscionable as applied to consumer goods—but not as applied to commercial goods.

9. See e.g., Deere v. Hand, 33 UCC Rep. 1369, 211 Neb. 549, 319 N.W.2d 434 (1982); KKO Inc. v. Honeywell, 517 F.Supp. 892 (N.D.Ill., 1981); Soo Line RR Co. v. Fruehauf, 547 F.2d 1365 (C.A.8, 1977); Bosway Tube & Steel Co. v. Michigan Machine Co., 65 Mich. App. 426, 237 N.W.2d 488 (1975).

10. See Chatlos Systems v. National Cash Register Corp., 635 F.2d 1081 (C.A.3, 1980); S.M. Wilson & Co. v. Smith International, 587 F.2d 1363 (C.A.9, 1978). See also Excavation Constr. v. Mack Trucks, 31 UCC Rep. 1386 (D.C.Md.1981); Williams v. Hyatt Chrysler, 30 UCC Rep. 90, 48 N.C.App. 308, 269 S.E.2d 184 (1980); Johnson v. Deere, 31 UCC Rep. 992, S.D., 306 N.W.2d 231 (1981). Garden State Food Distributiors v. Sperry Rand, 512 F.Supp. 975 (D.C.N.J.1981); Stutts v. Green Ford, 29 UCC Rep. 1241, 47 N.C.App. 503, 267 S.E.2d 919 (1980).

believe that sound statutory construction leads to the conclusion that subsection (3) of RCW 62A.2–719 must be viewed as the governing provision on the issue of consequential damages exclusion.

In this respect it should first be noted that, absent the specific language of subsection (3), the general language of subsection (2) would seem to cover the issue of consequential damages. Since it is a basic principle of statutory construction that the particular governs over the general,[11] we believe that the section 2–719 drafters intended subsection (3) to deal with the issue of consequential damages.

Second, the distinctly different substantive content of subsections (2) and (3) must be considered. Subsection (2) turns on the failure of essential purpose; subsection (3) turns on a judicial determination of unconscionability. Unconscionability deals with grossly unequal bargaining power at the time of the contracts formation. As numerous decisions have pointed out, unconscionability rarely exists unless the buyer is a consumer. Indeed, the consumer orientation of subsection (3) is reflected in the subsection's different allocations of proof. Where the transaction involves a consumer buyer, the limitation is prima facie unconscionable. Where the transaction does not involve a consumer, however, the exclusion of consequential damages is not prima facie unconscionable.

Thus, subsection (3) is a powerful provision designed to protect against abuse of consumers in contract formation. The Official UCC comment to UCC 2–719(3) indicates, however, that another basic purpose of subsection (3) is to allow merchants to allocate business risks. This purpose is consonant with the general UCC philosophy of freedom in commercial transactions. Taking these two statutory policies together, we believe that section 2–719(3) is meant to allow freedom in excluding consequential damages unless a consumer is involved in the contract. This freedom would be abridged by the sweeping interpretation of subsection (2) applied by the district court.

We thus hold that the district court had an obligation to take evidence and then determine whether the consequential damages exclusion clause was unconscionable. In the absence of an unconscionability determination, the district court should have allowed the paragraph B2 consequential damages exclusion to stand. Accordingly, we must vacate the portion of the judgment reflecting the jury's award of $25,283 in lost profits and remand this case to the district court for a judicial determination of whether the consequential damages exclusion clause was unconscionable. In the event the district court determines that the consequential damages clause was not unconscionable, the jury's award of $25,823 in lost profits must be voided.[19]

---

11. See Roth Steel Products v. Sharon Steel Co., 705 F.2d 134, 141 (C.A.6, 1983).

19. The jury's award of $27,080 in Freon costs should not be disturbed even if the consequential damages limitation is upheld. This is because the Freon costs are incidental damages rather than consequential damages. See Lewis v. Mobil Oil Corp., 438 F.2d 500 (C.A.8, 1971). See generally White & Summers, *Uniform Commercial Code*, pp. 312–314.

III CONCLUSION AND ORDER

We hereby affirm the district court as to the issues discussed in Parts IIA–IIC of the foregoing Opinion. We hereby Vacate the jury's award of $25,823 in lost profits and Remand to the district court for the reasons stated in Part IID of this Opinion. On remand, the district court is to conduct the proceedings specified in part IID of this Opinion.

[Some footnotes omitted. Ed.]

NOTES

(1) *Integral Part of Commercial Warranty Package.* A clause attempting to exclude liability for consequential damages is an integral part of a commercial warranty package which (1) *gives* the buyer an express warranty that the goods are free from defects in material and workmanship, (2) *disclaims* all other warranties, express or implied, (3) *limits* the remedy for breach of the express warranty to repair or replacement of the defective part or workmanship, and (4) *excludes* consequential damages from the scope of liability. This "package" is supported by the UCC, see UCC 2–313(1), 2–316, 2–719(1) & 2–719(3), and has been virtually unstoppable in commercial disputes. See, e.g., McNally Wellman & Co. v. New York State Electric & Gas Corp., 63 F.3d 1188 (2d Cir.1995); International Financial Services, Inc. v. Franz, 534 N.W.2d 261 (Minn.1995); Canal Elec. Co. v. Westinghouse Elec. Corp., 406 Mass. 369, 548 N.E.2d 182 (1990) (exclusion of consequential damages enforceable even though limited remedy fails essential purpose); Envirotech Corp. v. Halco Engineering, Inc., 234 Va. 583, 364 S.E.2d 215 (1988) (clause excluding consequential damages treated as an independent provision); Kearney & Trecker v. Master Engraving, 107 N.J. 584, 527 A.2d 429 (1987) (exclusion clause independent of limited remedy); Cayuga Harvester, Inc. v. Allis–Chalmers Corp., 95 A.D.2d 5, 465 N.Y.S.2d 606 (1983) (excluder clause conscionable even though limited remedy fails). See also Foss, *Failure of Essential Purpose: An Objective Approach*, 25 Duq.L.Rev. 551 (1987); Mather, *Consequential Damages When Exclusive Repair Remedies Fail: UCC § 2–719*, 38 S.Car.L.Rev. 673 (1987); Eddy, *On the "Essential" Purpose of Limited Remedies: The Metaphysics of U.C.C. Section 2–719(2)*, 65 Cal.L.Rev. 28 (1977). Compare UCC 2–719(3); Matthews v. Ford Motor Co., 479 F.2d 399 (4th Cir.1973) (exclusion clause prima facie unconscionable where product defects cause personal injuries to consumers).

(2) "NCR repeatedly attempted to correct the deficiencies in the system, but nevertheless still had not provided the product warranted a year and a half after Chatlos had reasonably expected a fully operational computer. In these circumstances, the delay made the correction remedy ineffective, and it therefore failed of its essential purpose. Consequently, the contractual limitation was unenforceable and did not preclude recovery of damages for the breach of warranty.

"This conclusion, however, does not dispose of the contractual clause excluding consequential damages. * * *

"Several cases have held that when a limited remedy fails of its purpose, an exclusion of consequential damages also fails, but approximately the same number of decisions have treated that preclusion as a separate matter. * * *

"It appears to us that the better reasoned approach is to treat the consequential damage disclaimer as an independent provision, valid unless unconscionable. This poses no logical difficulties. A contract may well contain no limitation on breach of warranty damages but specifically exclude consequential damages. Conversely, it is quite conceivable that some limitation might be placed on a breach of warranty award, but consequential damages would expressly be permitted.

"The limited remedy of repair and a consequential damages exclusion are two discrete ways of attempting to limit recovery for breach of warranty. . . . The Code, moreover, tests each by a different standard. The former survives unless it fails of its essential purpose, while the latter is valid unless it is unconscionable. We therefore see no reason to hold, as a general proposition, that the failure of the limited remedy provided in the contract, without more, invalidates a wholly distinct term in the agreement excluding consequential damages. The two are not mutually exclusive.

"Whether the preclusion of consequential damages should be effective in this case depends upon the circumstances involved. The repair remedy's failure of essential purpose, while a discrete question, is not completely irrelevant to the issue of the conscionability of enforcing the consequential damages exclusion. The latter term is 'merely an allocation of unknown or undeterminable risks.' U.C.C. § 2–719, Official Comment 3, N.J.Stat.Ann. § 12A:2–719, at 537 (West 1962). Recognizing this, the question here narrows to the unconscionability of the buyer retaining the risk of consequential damages upon the failure of the essential purpose of the exclusive repair remedy.

"One fact in this case that becomes significant under the Code is that the claim is not for personal injury but for property damage. Limitations on damages for personal injuries are not favored, but no such prejudice applies to property losses. It is also important that the claim is for commercial loss and the adversaries are substantial business concerns. We find no great disparity in the parties' bargaining power or sophistication. Apparently, Chatlos, a manufacturer of complex electronic equipment, had some appreciation of the problems that might be encountered with a computer system. Nor is there a 'surprise' element present here. The limitation was clearly expressed in a short, easily understandable sales contract. This is not an instance of an ordinary consumer being misled by a disclaimer hidden in a 'linguistic maze.' Cf. Gladden v. Cadillac Motor Car Division, 83 N.J. 320, 416 A.2d 394 (1980).

"Thus, at the time the contract was signed there was no reason to conclude that the parties could not competently agree upon the allocation of risk involved in the installation of the computer system." Chatlos Systems v. National Cash Register Corp., 635 F.2d 1081, 1086–87 (3d Cir.1980).

(3) Section 2–810(b) (1997) of revised Article 2 proposes the following solution to the problems posed above:

"(b) If, because of a breach of contract or other circumstances, an exclusive, agreed remedy fails substantially to achieve the intended purposes of the parties, the following rules apply:

(1) In a contract other than a consumer contract, the aggrieved party may resort to all remedies provided in this article, but an agreement expressly providing that consequential damages, including those resulting from the failure to provide the limited remedy, are excluded is enforceable to the extent permitted under subsection (c) [old UCC 2–719(3), which is not revised].

(2) In a consumer contract, an aggrieved party may reject the goods or revoke acceptance and, to the extent of the failure, may resort to all remedies provided in this article.''

PROBLEM: FAILURE OF ESSENTIAL PURPOSE UNDER UCC 2–719

Seller, a manufacturer, sold and delivered a complex machine to Buyer for use in its plant. The contract for sale incorporated by reference detailed specifications to which the machine was to conform. Within six months after delivery, a serious "latent" defect was discovered in the machine. Despite persistent and honest efforts by Seller, the defect could not be corrected either by correction of deficiencies or replacement of parts. Six months later, Seller conceded defeat and offered to replace the machine without additional cost to Buyer. Although Buyer had incurred no costs in attempting to repair the machine, the alleged profits lost while the machine was out of operation amounted to $100,000. Buyer argued that since the exclusive remedy had failed its essential purpose, it was entitled to normal remedies under the UCC, including consequential damages under UCC 2–715(2)(a). Seller, pointing to the following contract clause, argued that Paragraph (2), Limitation of Liability, survived the breach and, subject to UCC 2–719(3), excluded the consequential damages. As counsel for Buyer, would you recommend that it accept Seller's offer to replace the machine?

WARRANTY/LIMITATION OF LIABILITY

1. WARRANTY—The Corporation warrants that the equipment to be delivered will be of the kind and quality described in the order or contract [and] will be free of defects in workmanship or material. Should any failure to conform to this warranty appear within one year after the initial date of synchronization, the Corporation shall, upon notification thereof and substantiation that the equipment has been stored, installed, maintained and operated in accordance with the Corporation's recommendations and standard industry practice, correct such nonconformities, including nonconformance with the specifications, at its option, by suitable repair or replacement at the Corporation's expense. This warranty is in lieu of all warranties of merchantability, fitness for purpose, or other warranties, express or implied, except of title and against patent infringement. Correction of nonconformities, in the manner and for the period of time provided above, shall constitute fulfillment of all liabilities of the Corporation to the Purchaser, whether based on contract, negligence or otherwise with respect to, or arising out of such equipment.

2. LIMITATION OF LIABILITY—The Corporation shall not be liable for special, or consequential damages, such as, but not limited to, damage or loss of other property or equipment, loss of profits or revenue, loss of use of power system, cost of capital, cost of purchased or replacement power, or claims of customers of Purchaser for service interruption. The remedies of the Purchaser set forth herein are exclusive, and the liability of the Corporation with respect

to any contract, or anything done in connection therewith such as the performance or breach thereof, or from the manufacture, sale, delivery, resale, installation or use of any equipment covered by or furnished under this contract whether in contract, in tort, under any warranty, or otherwise, shall not, except as expressly provided herein, exceed the price of the equipment or part on which such liability is based.

PROBLEM: THE CASE OF THE DISAPPOINTED FANS

A fervent group of California Bears football fans, living in Davis, decided to charter a bus to "Big Game," played this year at Stanford. "Rabid" Ron was authorized by the group to negotiate the charter. In negotiating the matter with Mr. Smith, president of the Reliable Transit Co. (and a Stanford graduate), Ron stressed how important it was to his "fans" that they arrive in plenty of time for "Big Game"—it would not be televised this year, this group was exceptionally "interested" in the rivalry and would be terribly disappointed if anything went wrong. In short, Ron stated that his group would want damages if a charter were arranged and the bus did not go. Mr. Smith stated that he would be glad to arrange the charter (there were six weeks to go) for a flat fee of $750, round trip, but that the usual practice was to expressly limit liability of the Company for failure "to go" to a return of any amount paid on the charter. This was unsatisfactory to Ron. After more negotiations and consultation with the other "fans," Ron made the following proposition to Smith: "Look, I've talked with my group and here's the way it is. We will pay you $1,500 for the charter if you will agree to pay us $15,000 as liquidated damages if, for any reason, the bus fails to go and we miss the game. We are willing to pay $750 extra to know that our disappointment will be well compensated if we don't go. Take it or leave it." Smith "took it" and an appropriate written contract was prepared which included the "liquidated damage" clause. The "group" paid $750 on the charter and were told to assemble at a specified point in Davis no later than 9:30 AM on the day of "Big Game." As by now you have suspected, the bus did not show at 9:30 AM or at anytime on the day of "Big Game." In fact, Smith chartered the bus to a group of Stanford fans in Davis who paid $3,000 for the charter. By the time it was clear what had happened, it was not possible for Ron to arrange another method of transportation and none of the Cal fans saw the game.

Ron has demanded $15,000 from Smith and been politely refused. Smith, however, did tender back to Ron the $750, which Ron, so far, has refused. Ron and a few of his fans are in your law office and have asked your assessment of their chances. What would you advise?

See Goetz and Scott, *Liquidated Damages: Penalties and the Just Compensation Principle: Some Notes on an Enforcement Model and a Theory of Efficient Breach,* 77 Colum.L.Rev. 554 (1977).

SECTION 6. RESOLUTION OF CONTRACT PERFORMANCE DISPUTES: SOME ALTERNATIVES TO COURTS

(A) THE LEGAL FRAMEWORK FOR SETTLEMENT

A variety of disputes may arise during the course of contract performance. Most involve one of more of the following: the meaning of contract language; the existence and effect of conditions; the order and extent of the agreed exchange; whether the contractor's performance conformed to the contract and promisee's permissible responses; prospective inability to perform; the responsibility for conduct by one party which prevents or hinders performance by the other or alters the character of the agreed exchange; and the effect of unforeseen conditions or events which materially alter the ability or incentives of one party to perform.

In some cases, the aggrieved party may elect promptly to treat conduct by the other as a breach of contract, cancel the contract and seek affirmative remedies in the court. See Chapter Six, Section 1. In other cases, some effort may be made by both parties to modify the contract by agreement. See Chapter Five, Section 4(C). In still others, a form of modification or adjustment from action or inaction by one party rather than a bilateral modification may occur. This conduct often answers to the name of "waiver" or "estoppel." In general, contract law both permits the parties considerable latitude for settlement and readily supports *bona fide* efforts to resolve disputes and complete the exchange. Yet contract law, as such, has no direct contact with the dispute until settlement efforts break down and one party seeks judicial assistance by filing a lawsuit. One can only speculate how much the presence of contract law and courts actually influences behavior in the countless disputes which are settled, in one way or another, without formal adjudication or intervention by the legal system.[1]

It is important, of course, to understand the extent to which efforts to adjust or settle contract disputes by agreement or otherwise will "stand

---

1. A few examples from Article 2 of the UCC illustrate how modern contract law supports and facilitates the process of private dispute settlement. First, as we have seen, a seller and buyer of goods have considerable latitude to fashion their own remedies by agreement, and this includes consent to commercial arbitration. See UCC 2–718 & 2–719 [UCC 2–809 & 2–810 (1997)]. Second, it is fairly easy to achieve a binding modification by agreement. UCC 2–209(1) & 2–208(1) [UCC 2–209 & 2–210 (1997)]. Third, uncertainty over whether cancellation requires a "material" breach and a lack of precision on the content of "materiality" tend to restrain precipitous cancellation and induce discussion. Fourth, in a number of situations an aggrieved party may properly suspend his or her own performance or elect to ignore a repudiation in the hope that uncertainty will be allayed, breach cured or repudiation retracted. See UCC 2–609(1); 2–612, comment 7; 2–610(a); 2–611(1) [UCC 2–710, 2–711 & 2–712 (1997)]. Fifth, in some cases a seller may "cure" a breach of contract whether the buyer likes it or not. UCC 2–508(1) [UCC 2–

709 (1997)]. Finally, if contract rights or remedial claims have not been "waived" under UCC 2–209(5) [UCC 2–210(d) (1997)], they can be "discharged in whole or in part without consideration by a written waiver or renunciation signed and delivered by the aggrieved party." UCC 1–107. In short, these illustrations reflect a pervasive policy which supports and sometimes requires private efforts to settle disputes and complete the agreed exchange. As Chief Justice Peters put it: "[A]rticle 2 urges the contracting parties to engage in a continuing dialogue about what will constitute acceptance performance of their sales contract.... It is entirely consistent with this article 2 policy to provide, as does [1–207], a statutory methodology for the effective communication of objections." County Fire Door Corp. v. C.F. Wooding Co., 202 Conn. 277, 520 A.2d 1028, 1035 (1987). See generally Hillman, *Keeping the Deal Together After Material Breach—Common Law Mitigation Rules, the UCC and the Restatement (Second) of Contracts*, 47 U.Colo.L.Rev. 553 (1976).

up" in court. However, a vital function of the commercial lawyer may well be in the area of "preventive law." Put another way, the lawyer who by creative planning and drafting can avoid contract disputes and who by skillful negotiation can settle once they have arisen may perform a more valuable service for his client than the victorious litigator. See Brown, *The Law Office—A Preventive Law Laboratory,* 104 U.Pa.L.Rev. 940 (1956).[2] Without question, modern lawyers will have more rather than less opportunity to put the skills of planner, negotiator and drafter to work. Litigation is costly, time consuming and often delays justice. It is a last-ditch recourse after a variety of nonlegal options and sanctions have broken down. See Havighurst, The Nature of Private Contract 45–92 (1961). In a similar vein, a study by Professor Stewart Macaulay reveals that business people and, to a lesser extent, their attorneys, pay little attention in planning and dispute settlement to the supposed sanctions for breach of contract imposed by courts. Often contract law is not needed because its functions are performed by other devices, e.g., both sides understand primary obligations, little room exists for honest misunderstanding, trade usage fills gaps, and sophisticated product testing can be accomplished. Similarly, informal sanctions or values in the trade substitute for those imposed by courts, e.g., commitments are to be honored, one "ought" to produce a good product and stand behind it, business is organized to perform not litigate and one desiring to remain in business will avoid conduct which might interfere with attaining this goal. Macaulay, *Non-Contractual Relations in Business: A Preliminary Study,* 28 Am.Soc.Rev. 55 (1963). See also White, *Contract Law in Modern Commercial Transactions, An Artifact of Twentieth Century Business Life,* 22 Wash.L.J. 1 (1982).

But when careful planning and good faith settlement efforts fail,[3] must the parties always go to court to obtain a final resolution of their dispute? And if a lawsuit is filed, must every dispute proceed to a final judgment?

The answer to both questions, of course, is no. Increasingly, the parties to disputes are taking advantage of alternative practices and techniques for dispute resolution. A good working definition of alternative dispute resolution (ADR) has been suggested: "ADR is a set of practices and techniques that aim (1) to permit legal disputes to be resolved outside the courts for the benefit of all disputants; (2) to reduce the cost of conventional litigation and the delays to which it is ordinarily subject; or (3) to prevent legal disputes that would otherwise likely be brought to the courts." Lieberman & Henry, *Lessons From the Alternative Dispute Resolution Movement,* 53 U.Chi.L.Rev. 424, 425–26 (1986). But see Brunet, *Questioning the Quality of Alternate Dispute Resolution,* 62 Tul.L.Rev. 1 (1987).

According to Eric Green, there are "primary" and "hybrid" dispute resolution processes. "Primary" processes include adjudication, arbitration,

2. See also Macneil, *A Primer of Contract Planning,* 48 S.Cal.L.Rev. 627 (1975).

3. See Eisenberg, *Private Ordering through Negotiation: Dispute–Settlement and Rulemaking,* 89 Harv.L.Rev. 637 (1976); Full-er, *Mediation—Its Forms and Functions,* 44 S.Cal.L.Rev. 305 (1971). See also Cover, *Foreward: Dispute Resolution,* 88 Yale L.J. 905, 910 (1979); Sander, *Varieties of Dispute Processing,* 70 F.R.D. 111 (1976).

mediation and conciliation, and traditional negotiation. "Hybrid" processes include private judging, neutral expert fact finding, minitrial, and settlement conferences. Green, *A Comprehensive Approach to the Theory and Practice of Disputes Resolution,* 34 J.Legal Ed. 245 (1984). Except for adjudication, all other processes are, in large part, voluntary. Thus, consent is necessary and careful planning for dispute resolution is well advised. See Bush, *Dispute Resolution Alternatives and the Goals of Civil Justice: Jurisdictional Principles for Process Choice,* 1984 Wis.L.Rev. 893 (1984).

In order to highlight the similarities and differences between "primary" and "hybrid" dispute resolution processes, we have reprinted with permission a chart prepared by Eric Green. See Green, supra, 34 J.Legal Ed. at 257–58.

"PRIMARY" DISPUTE RESOLUTION PROCESSES

ADJUDICATION	ARBITRATION	MEDIATION/ CONCILIATION	TRADITIONAL NEGOTIATION
Nonvoluntary	Voluntary unless contractual or court centered	Voluntary	Voluntary
Binding, subject to appeal	Binding (usually), no appeal	Nonbinding	Nonbinding (except through use of adjudication to enforce agreement)
Imposed, third-party neutral decision maker, with no specialized expertise in dispute subject	Party-selected third-party decision maker, usually with specialized subject expertise	Party-selected outside facilitator, often with specialized subject expertise	No third-party facilitator
Highly procedural; formalized and highly structured by predetermined, rigid rules	Procedurally less formal; procedural rules and substantive law may be set by parties	Usually informal, unstructured	Usually informal, unstructured
Opportunity for each party to present proofs supporting decision in its favor	Opportunity for each party to present proofs supporting decision in its favor	Presentation of proofs less important than attitudes of each party; may include principled argument	Presentation of proofs usually indirect or nonexistent; may include principled argument
Win/Lose result	Compromise result possible (probable?)	Mutually acceptable agreement sought	Mutually acceptable agreement sought
Expectation of reasoned statement	Reason for result not usually required	Agreement usually embodied in contract or release	Agreement usually embodied in contract or release
Process emphasizes attaining substantive consistency and predictability of results	Consistency and predictability balanced against concern for disputants' relationship	Emphasis on disputants' relationship, not on adherence to or development of consistent rules	Emphasis on disputants' relationship, not on adherence to or development of consistent rules
Public process: lack of privacy of submissions	Private process unless judicial enforcement sought	Private process	Highly private process

"HYBRID" DISPUTE RESOLUTION PROCESSES

PRIVATE JUDGING	NEUTRAL EXPERT FACT FINDING	MINITRIAL	SETTLEMENT CONFERENCE
Voluntary	Voluntary or nonvoluntary under FRE 706	Voluntary	Voluntary or mandatory
Binding but subject to appeal and possibly review by trial court	Nonbinding but results may be admissible	Nonbinding (except through use of adjudication to enforce agreement)	Binding or nonbinding
Party-selected third-party decision maker; may have to be former judge or lawyer	Third-party neutral with specialized subject matter expertise may be selected by the parties	Third-party neutral advisor with specialized subject expertise	Judge, other judge, or third-party neutral selected by parties
Statutory procedure (see, e.g., Cal.Code Civ. Proc. § 638 et seq.) but highly flexible as to timing, place and procedures	Informal	Less formal than adjudication and arbitration but procedural rules and scope of issues may be set by the parties and implemented by neutral advisor	Informal, off-the-record
Opportunity for each party to present proofs supporting decision in its favor	Investigatory	Opportunity and responsibility to present proofs supporting result in its favor	Presentation of proofs may or may not be allowed
Win/lose result (judgment of court)	Report or testimony	Mutually acceptable agreement sought	Mutually acceptable agreement sought; binding conference is similar to arbitration
Findings of fact and conclusions of law possible but not required	May influence result or settlement	Agreement usually embodied in contract or release	Agreement usually embodied in contract or release
Adherence to norms, laws and precedent	Emphasis on reliable fact determination	Emphasis on sound, cost-effective and fair resolution satisfactory to both parties	Emphasis on resolving the dispute
Private process unless judicial enforcement sought	May be highly private or discussed in court	Highly private process	Private process but may be discovered

(B) DISPUTE RESOLUTION IN CONSTRUCTION CONTRACTS

(1) ROLE OF ARCHITECT OR ENGINEER

In construction contracts, the interwoven doctrines of "constructive" conditions of exchange, express conditions precedent and contract interpretation frequently converge around payment and coordination decisions by the architect, who acts as the owner's representative during the construction period. If the contract between the owner and contractor is based upon forms prepared by the American Institute of Architects, the architect is typically installed as the person in charge of the general administration of the contract and through whom the owner shall issue all instructions to the contractor. As one might expect, an important aspect of this authority relates to payments. Assume that the contract authorizes progress payments. The owner's obligation to pay depends upon an application for payment submitted to the architect by the contractor and a certificate for payment issued by the architect. Based upon observation of the work and the application for payment, the architect, who is a party to the contract, agrees to issue the certificates for payment unless he or she finds the following: 1) defective work not remedied, 2) claims filed, 3) failure of the contractor to make payments properly to subcontractors or for labor, materials, or equipment, 4) damage to another contractor, or 5) unsatisfactory prosecution of the work by the contractor. Final payment shall not be made until these conditions have occurred and the contractor has delivered a complete release of liens arising out of the contract, or receipts in full covering work for which a lien could be filed, or a satisfactory indemnity bond. A typical clause provides that the architect will be "in the first instance, the interpreter of the requirements of the Contract Documents" and "will make decisions on all claims and disputes between the Owner and the Contractor." In many cases, the architect's decisions are subject to arbitration, and an arbitration clause is included in the contract. There are AIA forms for varying situations, and the parties using them are encouraged to make modifications to fit particular circumstances. For a useful discussion, see Fabyanske & Halverson, *Arbitration: Is It an Acceptable Method of Resolving Construction Contract Disputes?*, 16 Forum 281 (1980); Trapasso, *The Lawyer's Use of AIA Construction Contracts,* 19 Prac.Law 37 (# 5, 1973). See also McCormick, *Representing the Owner in Contracting with the Architect and Contractor,* 8 The Forum 435 (1973).

The following materials first focus on the architect's or engineer's payment and coordination decision under the contract. It must be noted, however, that the architect's responsibilities may carry beyond the three-party contract. The architect may be liable in tort to third persons for such things as the negligent preparation of plans and specifications or defective supervision of the work. See Jay M. Feinman, Economic Negligence: Liability of Professionals and Businesses to Third Parties for Economic Loss § 15.5 (1995) for an excellent analysis. The materials will then consider the role of arbitration in private construction contracts.

Comment: Judicial Review of Architect's Refusal to Issue Certificate

In *Jacob & Youngs v. Kent,* supra at 642, the court, after concluding that the defendant's duty to make the final payment was constructively conditioned upon the plaintiff completing the work under the contract, held that the constructive condition was satisfied by substantial performance. But an architect was involved in the project, and it is clear from the opinion that the architect refused to issue the certificate of payment when the plaintiff refused to "do the work anew." Except for noting that the architect failed to notice the discrepancy in the pipe until after the house was completed, the court did not consider the effect of substantial performance upon the express condition that issuance of the certificate was to precede the duty to pay. One reason for this may be the case of Nolan v. Whitney, 88 N.Y. 648 (1882), where the court held that when a contractor has substantially performed the contract the architect is "bound" to issue the certificate. An unreasonable and wrongful refusal excuses the necessity that the certificate be issued. This is evidently still the law in New York. Arc Electrical Construction Co. v. George A. Fuller Co., 24 N.Y.2d 99, 104–105, 299 N.Y.S.2d 129, 131–33, 247 N.E.2d 111, 113 (1969). See Van Iderstine Co. v. Barnet Leather Co., 242 N.Y. 425, 433, 152 N.E. 250, 252 (1926).

Most states, however, have followed the principle of review set forth in Section 303 of the first Restatement: "Where a certificate of an architect, surveyor or engineer is a condition precedent to a duty of immediate payment for work, the condition is excused if the architect, surveyor or engineer (a) dies or becomes incapacitated, or (b) refuses to give a certificate because of collusion with the promisor, or (c) refuses to give a certificate after making examination of the work and finding it adequate, or (d) fails to make proper examination of the work, or (e) fails to exercise an honest judgment, or (f) makes a gross mistake with reference to facts on which a refusal to give a certificate is based."

An assumption here is that the architect, as a professional, should have more room for the exercise of honest judgment than that permitted if the decision were reviewable under standards of reasonableness. Other policies are also involved:

> Agreements to submit specific determinations of controversies and disputes arising under a contract to a third party chosen by the contracting parties are valid. * * * The decision of the third party as to matters entrusted to him, like the award of an arbitrator, is final and binding upon the parties unless the decision is impeached for fraud, accident, or gross mistake of such a nature that fraud may be inferred. * * * Parties competent to enter into this construction contract are competent to agree that the architect, even though he is the agent of one of the contracting parties, shall determine the question of claimed losses and damages. They are also competent to agree that said designated person's determination shall be final and binding on them. * * * Anticipatory provisions for settlements of disputes are favored and have the approval of the courts. United States v. Moorman, 338 U.S. 457, 70 S.Ct. 288, 94 L.Ed. 256 (1950).

E.H. Marhoefer, Jr., Co. v. Mount Sinai, Inc., 190 F.Supp. 355, 359–60 (E.D.Wis.1961). See Laurel Race Course, Inc. v. Regal Construction Co., Inc., 274 Md. 142, 333 A.2d 319, 325–28 (1975); Restatement (Second) § 227, Illus. 5–8.

But even an honest judgment may collide with the policy against forfeiture. Restatement (Second) § 229 provides:

> To the extent that the non-occurrence of a condition would cause extreme forfeiture, a court may excuse the non-occurrence of a condition unless its occurrence was a material part of the agreed exchange.

Could *Jacob & Youngs v. Kent* also be explained under the anti-forfeiture policy? Should the same approach be followed where the question is the binding effect on the owner of an issued certificate? Suppose, for example, that the architect in *Kent* had issued a certificate approving pipe that was substantially inferior to that specified. Although the answer is not free from doubt, the certificate can be set aside if there was a gross mistake of fact or a failure to exercise honest judgment on the part of the architect or engineer. See James I. Barnes Construction Co. v. Washington Township, 134 Ind.App. 461, 184 N.E.2d 763 (1962).

Bolton Corp. v. T.A. Loving Co.

Court of Appeals of North Carolina, 1989.
94 N.C.App. 392, 380 S.E.2d 796, review denied 325 N.C. 545, 385 S.E.2d 496 (1989).

This "delay damages" case arises from a multiple-prime contract pursuant to N.C.G.S. § 143–128, to build a multi-million dollar central library on the UNC–Chapel Hill campus. Bolton, the heating and ventilating contractor, sued the general contractor and "project expediter," Loving, in negligence, and as a third-party beneficiary for breach of Loving's contract with the State. Bolton claims that Loving breached its contract with the State by causing Bolton "undue delay" which prevented Bolton from performing its contract in a timely way. Bolton initiated claims against Loving for delay damages and against the State of North Carolina. The claim against the State is before this panel in a connected case.

* * *

In large public construction projects many factors may combine to prevent timely completion:

> [T]he complexity of design and quality construction which may be required, the myriad of necessary reviews and approvals, the number of changes required throughout the design/construction cycle, and the possibility of one or more of the contractors becoming delayed in performance.... Clearly, the necessity for effective scheduling, supervision, and coordination is at the heart of the phased design and construction method; and without it, the result may be akin to [a] "battlefield"....

Conner, *Construction and Management Services* 46 Law & Contemp.Prob. 5, 14 (1983).

* * *

N.C.G.S. § 143–128 requires that when a public building project's expected costs exceed $50,000.00 "separate specifications must be prepared, and separate bids must be received, and separate contracts must be awarded for each of four branches of work[:]" heating, ventilating and air conditioning (HVAC); plumbing and gas fittings; electrical wiring and installation; and general work not included in the first three branches. A.F. Bell, *Construction Law* North Carolina Bar Foundation IV–1 (Institute of Government 1988). The rationale in favor of multiple-prime contracts has been stated:

While there can be additional bidding expenses, proponents of separate contracts also see cost advantages. Breaking down the project into specialty segments generates more bidders and more competition. Finally, some owners believe that they can reduce their costs by performing less expensively and at least as efficiently as the prime contractor. The latter earns part of her compensation for selection, policing, and coordination of the specialty trades.

J.   Sweet, Sweet On Construction Industry Contracts § 19.2 at 372 (1987).

* * *

We interpret N.C.G.S. § 143–128 to mean that a prime contractor may be sued by another prime contractor working on a construction project for economic loss foreseeably resulting from the first prime contractor's failure to fully perform "all duties and obligations due respectively under the terms of the separate contracts."

A directed verdict in favor of Loving on the negligence claim was correct; however, Bolton does have a claim pursuant to the statute. On retrial, Bolton must provide sufficient evidence to support a cause of action under N.C.G.S. § 143–128.

To identify the extent of Loving's potential liability to Bolton it is necessary to understand what Loving's "duties and obligations" were under the terms of its separate contract. N.C.G.S. § 143–128. On appeal, both parties question the significance of the "project expediter" provisions of Loving's contract to Bolton's claim for delay damages. On cross-appeal Loving argues that the trial court erred in refusing to grant its motion for a directed verdict on the ground that Loving could not be liable for failure to expedite because it "cannot be held liable for breach of a duty to coordinate the work of contractors." We disagree.

Loving's argument ignores the terms of the contract which separate the duty to coordinate from the duty to expedite, and assigns the duty to coordinate to the architect. The duty to coordinate derives from the owner's duty to "furnish a work site," and to cooperate to allow the contractor to perform. Goldberg, *The Owner's Duty to Coordinate Multi-Prime Construction Contractors, A Condition of Cooperation*, 28 Emory L.J. 377, 380–81 (1979). At common law "one who contracts to render a performance or produce a result for which it is necessary to obtain the co-operation of third persons is not excused by the fact that they will not co-operate." 6 Corbin § 1340 (1962). However an owner's duty to cooperate and its ancillary duty to coordinate may be delegated in a contract. *Broadway Maintenance Corporation v. Rutgers*, 90 N.J. 253, 265, 447 A.2d 906, 912 (1982).

At Articles 14 and 31 of the contract in the instant case each prime contracts to cooperate with the other primes in the execution of the project. In addition, Loving specifically contracted to assume the "project control responsibility" of project expediter:

Article 14—Construction Supervision

The Owner may designate a "Project Expediter" for State-owned projects involving two or more prime contractors. . . .

It shall be the responsibility of the Project Expediter to schedule the work of all prime contractors; to maintain a progress schedule for all prime contractors for this project; and to notify the designer of any changes in the progress schedule.

By its terms the contract defines the project expediter as the entity which schedules the work of all primes and maintains the progress schedule. The project expediter is charged with using proper procedures to obtain information to evaluate the progress of the project. See Goldberg at 385–87. In Article 31 the contract states that the responsibility to coordinate work schedules remains with the engineer or architect. Article 14 contemplates that the project expediter's scheduling of the project will assist the architect, who has the power to sanction contractors who do not keep up with their work. See Conner at 14.

As General Contractor, Loving was responsible for "General work relating to the erection [and] construction" of the building not included in the three other prime contracts. N.C.G.S. § 143–128. As project expediter Loving's work was to facilitate and assist in the smooth and efficient production of the building. By statute Bolton may sue Loving for breach of these contract duties.

To prove Loving's liability Bolton attempted to establish that the architect's allocation of responsibility for delay was final, absent bad faith. By its order dated 2 November 1987, the trial judge denied Bolton's motion for partial summary judgment which, among other claims, stated that "[t]he architect was designated by the contract to rule on requests for extensions of time." Bolton's motion was denied, and it is not appealable. "Improper denial of a motion for summary judgment is not reversible error when the case has proceeded to trial and has been determined on the merits by the trier of facts, either judge or jury." Harris v. Walden, 314 N.C. 284, 286, 333 S.E.2d 254, 256 (1985).

At trial, Bolton's attempt to introduce the project architect's testimony concerning responsibility for delay was refused by the trial judge because he saw the testimony as going to the ultimate issue for the jury. The testimony should have been allowed for two reasons: First, "the admissibility of expert opinion testimony does not depend on whether it invades the province of the jury, but whether it will aid the jury's understanding of the issue. . . ." . . . Second, the parties had agreed by contract that the project architect's opinion would be determinative on the issue.

An authority on construction law posits that when a contract assigns the project architect or engineer responsibility to make decisions on all claims of contractors, as in this case, the architect's decision on responsibility for delay should control unless it is shown to be dishonestly made or to be clearly wrong. J. Sweet, Legal Aspects of Architecture, Engineering, and the Construction Process § 33.09 (3rd edition 1985). The rule is adopted from cases concerned with conditions precedent to payment. See, e.g., Laurel Race Course, Inc. v. Regal Construction Co., 274 Md. 142, 333 A.2d

319 (1975) (engineer's certificate required before owner obligated to make payment); Barnes Construction Co. v. Washington Township, 134 Ind.App. 461, 184 N.E.2d 763 (1962); see Restatement 2nd Contracts § 227 comment c.

In Laurel, the contractor sued the owner for amounts allegedly due under the contract. Owner defended that contractor had failed to produce the certification of the project engineer which would entitle it to payment under the terms of the contract. Id. Finding for the owner, the court stated:

> "By this contract, which is perfectly lawful, the parties expressly agreed to submit the question ... to the judgment of [a] third party, ... [whose] judgment, no matter how erroneous or mistaken it may be, or how unreasonable it may appear to others, is conclusive between the parties, unless it be tainted with fraud or bad faith. To substitute for it the opinions and judgments of other persons, whether judge, jury or witnesses, would be to annul the contract, and make another in its place."

Id. at 151, 333 A.2d at 325 (quoting Lynn v. B. & O.R.R. Co., 60 Md. 404, 415 (1883)).

* * *

Articles 31 and 35 of Loving's contract allocates to the architect the authority to determine responsibility for delay among the prime contractors. Article 31 of the contract concerns "Separate Contracts and Contractor Relationships":

> Chapter 143, Article 8, General Statutes of North Carolina requires that separate contracts will be awarded for General Construction, Heating and Ventilating and Air Conditioning, Plumbing, and Electrical installations. The Owner reserves the right to prepare separate specifications, receive separate bids, and award separate contracts for such other major items of work as may seem to the best interest of the State.
>
> All Contractors shall cooperate in the execution of their work, and shall plan their work in such manner as to avoid conflicting schedules or delay of the work. The Engineer or Architect shall coordinate work schedules.
>
> If any part of a Contractor's work depends upon the work of another Contractor, defects which may affect that work shall be reported to the Architect or Engineer in order that prompt inspection may be made and the defects corrected. Commencement of work by a Contractor where such condition exists will constitute acceptance of the other Contractor's work as being satisfactory in all respects to receive the work commenced except as to defects which may later develop. The Engineer or Architect shall be the judge as to the quality of work, and shall settle all disputes on the matter between Contractors.

Whether the architect's allocation of responsibility for delay is final absent bad faith is largely answered by the last paragraph of Article 31. The subject of the paragraph as set out in the topic sentence is plain: when one prime's work depends on the work of another. When problems develop a report is to be made to the architect, otherwise the complaining prime will be deemed to have accepted the work of the prime whose work necessarily came first. Reading the paragraph as a whole, the last sentence explains that when the work of one prime depends on the work of another the "Architect shall be the judge as to the quality of work, and shall settle all disputes on the matter between Contractors." In this instance, to preclude the architect's testimony "would be to annul the contract."

Article 35 of the contract guides us in our determination of the proper weight to be accorded the architect's decisions:

> Art. 35—Architect's or Engineer's Decisions
>
> The Architect or Engineer is charged with the responsibility of interpretation of the contract documents and general directions of the work. He shall make decisions on all claims of the Contractor or the Owner, or on any matter dealing with the execution of the work. His decisions relating to artistic effect and technical matters shall be final, provided such decisions are within the limitations of the contract terms.

The architect interprets the contract which governs the relationship of the parties, and makes decisions on all claims of contractors "on any matter dealing with the execution of the work." Finality is accorded only to decisions relating to artistic effect and technical matters.

As in any construction project, contractors in a multiple-prime situation co-exist in a delicate state of symbiosis. Each prime's ability to maintain timely progress is as much a part of their work, and is as important to the other primes, as their ability to perform more tangible tasks. We hold that judgment of the quality of a prime's ability to perform its jobs and to maintain timely progress in those jobs is delegated to the architect by the contract. The architect's determination is *"prima facie* correct, and the burden is upon the other parties to show fraud or mistake." *Barnes,* 134 Ind.App. at 466, 184 N.E.2d at 764–65.

* * *

Loving's argument that the Uniform Arbitration Act, N.C.G.S. § 1–567.1 et seq., somehow lessens the power of the architect to settle disputes concerning cause for delay is also without merit. Loving correctly observes that the architect is not specifically made an arbitrator. The contract does not contemplate arbitration, and the parties are in no way bound to that procedure by the contract. However, the parties have agreed to be bound by the architect's judgments made under the powers given the architect in Articles 18, 31, and 35, and the correct forum to introduce such evidence is in a court of law.

* * *

NOTES

As the court in *Bolton Corp.* correctly states, unless some or all of the parties have agreed to arbitration, the legal effect of a contract conferring some decision-making authority on the architect is not affected by any arbitration legislation enacted in the state. Put differently, the decision process is not arbitration, the architect is not an arbitrator, and the finality of the architect's decisions will be determined by the court under contract and common law standards. See, e.g., Thomas Crimmins Contracting Co. v. City of New York, 74 N.Y.2d 166, 544 N.Y.S.2d 580, 542 N.E.2d 1097 (1989) (contract did not clearly give chief engineer power to make final legal determinations).

The construction contract, however, may contain an arbitration clause. An example of a typical provision is found in Article 10 of Document A107 of the American Institute of Architects (1987):

> § 10.5 The Architect will interpret and decide matters concerning performance under and requirements of the Contract Documents on written request of either the Owner or Contractor. The Architect will make initial decisions on all claims, disputes or other matters in question between the Owner and Contractor, but will not be liable for results of any interpretations or decisions rendered in good faith. The Architect's decision in matters relating to aesthetic effect will be final if consistent with the intent expressed in the Contract Documents. All other decisions of the Architect, except those which have been waived by making or acceptance of final payment, shall be subject to arbitration upon the written demand of either party. * * *

> § 10.8 All claims or disputes between the Contractor and the Owner arising out or relating to the Contract, or the breach thereof, shall be decided by arbitration in accordance with the Construction Industry Arbitration Rules of the American Arbitration Association currently in effect unless the parties mutually agree otherwise and subject to an initial presentation of the claim or dispute to the Architect as required under Paragraph 10.5. Notice of the demand for arbitration shall be filed in writing with the other party to this Agreement and with the American Arbitration Association and shall be made within a reasonable time after the dispute has arisen. The award rendered by the arbitrator shall be final and judgment may be entered upon it in accordance with applicable law in any court having jurisdiction thereof. * * *

Under the dispute resolution system noted above, the architect's decision is final on "matters relating to aesthetic effect." See NSC Contractors v. Borders, 317 Md. 394, 564 A.2d 408 (1989) (architect's power to make final decision not subject to arbitration limited to aesthetic considerations). The decision on non-aesthetic issues will be final, however, if the losing party fails to demand arbitration within the time stated in the contract. See Huntington Woods v. Ajax Paving Industries, Inc., 177 Mich.App. 351, 441 N.W.2d 99 (1989).

Let us now briefly consider the nature of arbitration and the enforceability of agreements to arbitrate and arbitral awards.

(2) ARBITRATION

Comment: The Nature and Characteristics of Arbitration

[The following is reprinted from the Ohio State Journal of Dispute Resolution.]

Arbitration: The Classic Model

Let us start with the basics. Arbitration is a form of Alternative Dispute Resolution (ADR). Unlike other methods of ADR, however, arbitration is a private adjudicatory process invoked as an alternative to filing a law suit. The classic model of arbitration can be reduced to three essential elements. First, arbitration depends upon consent. The parties must agree, either before or after the dispute arises, to arbitrate the dispute. In most cases, that agreement will be evidenced by mutual assent to a commercial or consumer contract which contains a written arbitration term.

Second, arbitration is a less formal adjudicatory process that has assumed advantages over litigation in courts or other forms of ADR. The parties expect that an unbiased and competent private arbitrator will conduct a relatively expeditious, informal, inexpensive, and private hearing and decide the merits of the dispute fairly between them.

Third, the arbitrator is empowered by the agreement and applicable arbitration rules to make a final decision on the merits of the dispute, i.e., to decide both questions of fact and of law and to provide appropriate remedies.

Unlike the judicial process, there is no review of the merits of this primary decision by the arbitrator. In the absence of fraud, bias, or process defects, the court is empowered to confirm and enforce the award as if it were a final judgment. There are, of course, incentives for negotiated settlement within the arbitral process and the arbitrator's decision will frequently contain an element of compromise. Nevertheless, in whatever contexts arbitration is invoked, the parties participate in the decisional process by presenting evidence and reasoned arguments to an arbitrator whose final decision should be responsive to the dispute as presented. As a practical matter, finality is achieved when both parties acquiesce in the arbitrator's decision with or without seeking limited judicial review.

Characteristics of Arbitration

Although an objective of arbitration is to achieve justice between the parties through less formal adjudication, the quality of justice may be different (if not less) than that achieved in civil litigation. As one court warned, arbitration is "not the most perfect alternative to adjudication" in the courts. It is "an inferior system of justice, structured without due process, rules of evidence, accountability of judgment or rules of law." In short, "parties should be aware that they get what they bargain for and that arbitration is far different from adjudication."*

What do the parties get when they bargain for arbitration? The characteristics of the classic model of arbitration, along with its potential strengths and limitations, emerge when it is contrasted with the judicial process. For emphasis, the differences will be stated in the extreme.

---

* Stroh Container Co. v. Delphi Indus.,   denied, 476 U.S. 1141 (1986).
783 F.2d 743, 751, n. 12 (8th Cir.), cert.

1. *Control Over Scope, Content and Arbitrator Selection.* As a voluntary dispute resolution technique, one party can avoid arbitration by refusing to agree to arbitrate an existing or future dispute. But if a decision to arbitrate is made, the parties have an opportunity to define the scope and content of the process as well as to control its procedures in the agreement. The same cannot be said for civil litigation. Similarly, the arbitrator is selected by or through procedures agreed to by the parties while the judge is imposed upon them by law and local allocation practices.

2. *Less Formality and Complexity.* Arbitration procedures and fact finding processes are not clearly defined or required by arbitration statutes. They depend upon the agreement, relevant arbitration practice or institutional procedures, such as the American Arbitration Association (AAA) Arbitration Rules, and are usually less formal than those in court. The arbitrator has less authority than a judge to order discovery or to compel the attendance of witnesses or the production of evidence. The parties have less power to engage in pretrial discovery. The parties, however, may define by agreement the procedures and the powers of and even the substantive law and remedies to be applied by the arbitrator. In the absence of such agreement, arbitration procedures may be attended with a great deal of uncertainty.

3. *Duration of Proceedings.* In arbitration, the arbitrator and the parties control the timing, duration, and complexity of the hearings. In judicial proceedings, these matters may be beyond the parties' control. The potential for savings in time and cost, therefore, differs. In short, arbitration is expected (and assumed) to be quicker, less formal and less expensive than litigation in court.

4. *Arbitrator Expertise.* In arbitration, the arbitrator is expected to be an expert in or familiar with the context within which the dispute arose while a judge will, normally, have no special expertise. Furthermore, an arbitrator is not required to produce a written opinion with reasons for the decision. Presumably, this reduces the risk of disagreement over reasons by parties otherwise satisfied with the result. In court, a reasoned opinion by a judge is required.

5. *Confidentiality.* Arbitration is touted as a private process where confidence is normally maintained while the opposite is true in court.

6. *Justice Between the Parties.* A primary objective in arbitration is to achieve a just result between the parties. But arbitration seeks particularized justice rather than to foster substantive consistency and predictable results for the future. Courts, on the other hand, are concerned both about just results and announced precedent and the effect of the decision on third persons who are not parties to the litigation.

Furthermore, in arbitration, a compromise decision is possible while judicial decisions tend to be either win all or lose all. According to some observers: "The arbitration process frequently resembles three-party negotiation or mediation, with many arbitrators consciously or unconsciously identifying outside parameters of possible settlement and endeavoring to reach a decision that will at least be minimally acceptable to both parties."**

In sum, arbitration is a form of consensual, relatively informal, personalized adjudication where the primary objective is to obtain less expensive justice between the parties. The challenge is to obtain particularized justice in an extra-legal adjudicatory process which has potential strengths and weakness when compared to civil litigation.

[Reprinted with permission from Richard E. Speidel, *Arbitration of Statutory Rights Under the Federal Arbitration Act: The Case for Reform,* 4 Ohio St.J.Disp.Res. 157, 158–61 (1989). Some footnotes omitted.]

Uniform Arbitration Act

§ 1. Validity of Arbitration Agreement

A written agreement to submit any existing controversy to arbitration or a provision in a written contract to submit to arbitration any controversy thereafter arising between the parties is valid, enforceable and irrevocable, save upon such grounds as exist at law or in equity for the revocation of any contract. * * *

§ 2. Proceedings to Compel or Stay Arbitration

(a) On application of a party showing an agreement described in Section 1, and the opposing party's refusal to arbitrate, the Court shall order the parties to proceed with arbitration, but if the opposing party denies the existence of the agreement to arbitrate, the Court shall proceed summarily to the determination of the issue so raised and shall order arbitration if found for the moving party, otherwise, the application shall be denied.

(b) On application, the court may stay an arbitration proceeding commenced or threatened on a showing that there is no agreement to arbitrate. Such an issue, when in substantial and bona fide dispute, shall be forthwith and summarily tried and the stay ordered if found for the moving party. If found for the opposing party, the court shall order the parties to proceed to arbitration.

(c) If an issue referable to arbitration under the alleged agreement is involved in an action or proceeding pending in a court having jurisdiction to hear applications under subdivision (a) of this Section, the application shall be made therein. Otherwise and subject to Section 18, the application may be made in any court of competent jurisdiction.

(d) Any action or proceeding involving an issue subject to arbitration shall be stayed if an order for arbitration or an application therefor has been made under this section or, if the issue is severable, the stay may be

** E. Johnson, V. Kantor & E. Schwartz,   Alternatives in Civil Cases 55 (1977). Outside the Courts: A Survey of Diversion

with respect thereto only. When the application is made in such action or proceeding, the order for arbitration shall include such stay.

(e) An order for arbitration shall not be refused on the ground that the claim in issue lacks merit or bona fides or because any fault or grounds for the claim sought to be arbitrated have not been shown.

§ 3.   Appointment of Arbitrators by Court

If the arbitration agreement provides a method of appointment of arbitrators, this method shall be followed. In the absence thereof, or if the agreed method fails or for any reason cannot be followed, or when an arbitrator appointed fails or is unable to act and his successor has not been duly appointed, the court on application of a party shall appoint one or more arbitrators. An arbitrator so appointed has all the powers of one specifically named in the agreement.

§ 4.   Majority Action by Arbitrators

The powers of the arbitrators may be exercised by a majority unless otherwise provided by the agreement or by this act.

§ 5.   Hearing

Unless otherwise provided by the agreement:

(a) The arbitrators shall appoint a time and place for the hearing and cause notification to the parties to be served personally or by registered mail not less than five days before the hearing. Appearance at the hearing waives such notice. The arbitrators may adjourn the hearing from time to time as necessary and, on request of a party and for good cause, or upon their own motion may postpone the hearing to a time not later than the date fixed by the agreement for making the award unless the parties consent to a later date. The arbitrators may hear and determine the controversy upon the evidence produced notwithstanding the failure of a party duly notified to appear. The court on application may direct the arbitrators to proceed promptly with the hearing and determination of the controversy.

(b) The parties are entitled to be heard, to present evidence material to the controversy and to cross-examine witnesses appearing at the hearing.

(c) The hearing shall be conducted by all the arbitrators but a majority may determine any question and render a final award. If, during the course of the hearing, an arbitrator for any reason ceases to act, the remaining arbitrator or arbitrators appointed to act as neutrals may continue with the hearing and determination of the controversy.

§ 6.   Representation by Attorney

A party has the right to be represented by an attorney at any proceeding or hearing under this act. A waiver thereof prior to the proceeding or hearing is ineffective.

§ 7. Witnesses, Subpoenas, Depositions

(a) The arbitrators may issue (cause to be issued) subpoenas for the attendance of witnesses and for the production of books, records, documents and other evidence, and shall have the power to administer oaths. Subpoenas so issued shall be served, and upon application to the Court by a party or the arbitrators, enforced, in the manner provided by law for the service and enforcement of subpoenas in a civil action.

(b) On application of a party and for use as evidence, the arbitrators may permit a deposition to be taken, in the manner and upon the terms designated by the arbitrators, of a witness who cannot be subpoenaed or is unable to attend the hearing.

(c) All provisions of law compelling a person under subpoena to testify are applicable.

(d) Fees for attendance as a witness shall be the same as for a witness in the _____ Court.

§ 8. Award

(a) The award shall be in writing and signed by the arbitrators joining in the award. The arbitrators shall deliver a copy to each party personally or by registered mail, or as provided in the agreement.

(b) An award shall be made within the time fixed therefor by the agreement or, if not so fixed, within such time as the court orders on application of a party. The parties may extend the time in writing either before or after the expiration thereof. A party waives the objection that an award was not made within the time required unless he notifies the arbitrators of his objection prior to the delivery of the award to him.

* * *

§ 11. Confirmation of an Award

Upon application of a party, the Court shall confirm an award, unless within the time limits hereinafter imposed grounds are urged for vacating or modifying or correcting the award, in which case the court shall proceed as provided in Sections 12 and 13.

§ 12. Vacating an Award

(a) Upon application of a party, the court shall vacate an award where:

(1) The award was procured by corruption, fraud or other undue means;

(2) There was evident partiality by an arbitrator appointed as a neutral or corruption in any of the arbitrators or misconduct prejudicing the rights of any party;

(3) The arbitrators exceeded their powers;

(4) The arbitrators refused to postpone the hearing upon sufficient cause being shown therefor or refused to hear evidence material

to the controversy or otherwise so conducted the hearing, contrary to the provisions of Section 5, as to prejudice substantially the rights of a party; or

(5) There was no arbitration agreement and the issue was not adversely determined in proceedings under Section 2 and the party did not participate in the arbitration hearing without raising the objection;

but the fact that the relief was such that it could not or would not be granted by a court of law or equity is not ground for vacating or refusing to confirm the award.

(b) An application under this Section shall be made within ninety days after delivery of a copy of the award to the applicant, except that, if predicated upon corruption, fraud or other undue means, it shall be made within ninety days after such grounds are known or should have been known.

(c) In vacating the award on grounds other than stated in clause (5) of Subsection (a) the court may order a rehearing before new arbitrators chosen as provided in the agreement, or in the absence thereof, by the court in accordance with Section 3, or if the award is vacated on grounds set forth in clauses (3) and (4) of Subsection (a) the court may order a rehearing before the arbitrators who made the award or their successors appointed in accordance with Section 3. The time within which the agreement requires the award to be made is applicable to the rehearing and commences from the date of the order.

(d) If the application to vacate is denied and no motion to modify or correct the award is pending, the court shall confirm the award.

§ 13.   Modification or Correction of Award

(a) Upon application made within ninety days after delivery of a copy of the award to the applicant, the court shall modify or correct the award where:

(1) There was an evident miscalculation of figures or an evident mistake in the description of any person, thing or property referred to in the award;

(2) The arbitrators have awarded upon a matter not submitted to them and the award may be corrected without affecting the merits of the decision upon the issues submitted; or

(3) The award is imperfect in a matter of form, not affecting the merits of the controversy.

(b) If the application is granted, the court shall modify and correct the award so as to effect its intent and shall confirm the award as so modified and corrected. Otherwise, the court shall confirm the award as made.

(c) An application to modify or correct an award may be joined in the alternative with an application to vacate the award.

§ 14. Judgment or Decree on Award

Upon the granting of an order confirming, modifying or correcting an award, judgment or decree shall be entered in conformity therewith and be enforced as any other judgment or decree. Costs of the application and of the proceedings subsequent thereto, and disbursements may be awarded by the court.

* * *

§ 19. Appeals

(a) An appeal may be taken from:

(1) An order denying an application to compel arbitration made under Section 2;

(2) An order granting an application to stay arbitration made under Section 2(b);

(3) An order confirming or denying confirmation of an award;

(4) An order modifying or correcting an award;

(5) An order vacating an award without directing a rehearing; or

(6) A judgment or decree entered pursuant to the provisions of this act.

(b) The appeal shall be taken in the manner and to the same extent as from orders or judgments in a civil action.

Michael–Curry Co. v. Knutson Shareholders

Supreme Court of Minnesota, 1989.
449 N.W.2d 139.

■ KEITH, JUSTICE.

The central issue in this case is whether an arbitration clause which provides for arbitration of, *inter alia,* "[a]ny controversy or claim arising out of or relating to * * * the making" of a contract, compels arbitration of a claim that an amendment to the contract was fraudulently induced. The trial court held in the negative. The court of appeals reversed, holding that the clause was sufficiently broad to comprehend that the issue of fraud in the inducement be submitted to arbitration. 434 N.W.2d 671. We affirm.

* * *

1. The issue of arbitrability is to be determined by ascertaining the intention of the parties through examination of the language of the arbitration agreement. State v. Berthiaume, 259 N.W.2d 904, 909 (Minn. 1977). A reviewing court is not bound by the trial court's interpretation of the arbitration agreement and independently determines whether the trial court correctly interpreted the clause. See Berthiaume, 259 N.W.2d at 910 n. 8.

The purchase and sale agreement in this case provided that "this Agreement shall be construed in accordance with, and governed by, the laws of the State of Minnesota." Both parties agree that Minnesota law governs the agreement and the amendment, which incorporates the terms of the agreement.

Minn.Stat. § 572.08 (1988) provides that written agreements or contract provisions to arbitrate are valid, enforceable, and irrevocable absent grounds for revocation of the contract. Under the procedural rules of Minn.Stat. § 572.09, if one party refuses to arbitrate, the court must order arbitration. A party wishing to stay arbitration must show that there is no agreement to arbitrate. "Such an issue, when in substantial bona fide dispute, shall be forthwith and summarily tried and the stay ordered if found for the moving party." Minn.Stat. § 572.09(b) (1988). Otherwise the court must order arbitration. Id.

A claim of fraud in the inducement puts the "making" of the contract itself in issue. This court has said that "that issue is more properly determined by those trained in the law." Atcas v. Credit Clearing Corp., 292 Minn. 334, 350, 197 N.W.2d 448, 457 (1972). Minnesota has ruled that fraud which vitiates a contract also vitiates an arbitration clause within the contract. Atcas v. Credit Clearing Corp., 292 Minn. at 349, 197 N.W.2d at 457 (1972); Minn.Stat. § 572.08. By claiming fraud in the inducement, the Trust is asserting that no valid agreement to arbitrate exists under Minn.Stat. § 572.09. The court must therefore determine whether the parties agreed to arbitrate the issue of fraud in the inducement.

Parties may validly choose to arbitrate all controversies, including fraud in the inducement. Atcas, 292 Minn. at 342, 197 N.W.2d at 453. To determine intent to arbitrate fraud in the inducement, the court must look to the language of the arbitration clause. The language in the clause must either (1) specifically show that the parties intended to arbitrate fraud in the inducement, or (2) be "sufficiently broad to comprehend that the issue of fraudulent inducement be arbitrated." Id., 292 Minn. at 347, 197 N.W.2d at 456. If the clause does not specifically include fraud in the inducement and is not sufficiently broad to comprehend it, then a trial must be had on the issue of fraud in the inducement. Atcas, 292 Minn. at 348, 197 N.W.2d at 456.

The arbitration clause in the instant case states:

> 13.01 *Arbitration.* Any controversy or claim arising out of, or relating to, this Agreement, or the making, performance, or interpretation thereof, shall be settled by arbitration * * *. (Emphasis supplied).

The clause does not specifically mention fraud. We find, however, that it meets the second prong of the Atcas test.

The clause in this case is broader than the clauses in previous cases this court has considered. First, it provides for arbitration of controversies relating to "the making" of the contract, which clauses Atcas and later cases did not contain. The word "making" refers to circumstances surrounding formation of the contract. See Atcas, 292 Minn. at 350, 197

N.W.2d at 457 (a claim of fraudulent inducement puts "the making of the agreement itself * * * in issue"). See also Two Sisters, Inc. v. Gosch & Co., 171 Conn. 493, 497, 370 A.2d 1020, 1022 n. 2, 1022–23 (1976) (clause including claims "arising under" the contract or "with respect to the making or validity" of it showed the parties' intent to arbitrate all disputes, including fraud in the inducement); Prima Paint v. Flood & Conklin Mfg., 388 U.S. 395, 403–04, 87 S.Ct. 1801, 1805–06, 18 L.Ed.2d 1270 (1967) (under the FAA, a fraud in the inducement claim "goes to the 'making' of the agreement"). It is difficult to see how the parties in this case could have drafted a "broader" agreement.

The Trust attempts to circumvent the Atcas "broadly worded" option by arguing that specificity is always required. The Trust argues that the word "fraud" must appear in the arbitration clause. The Minnesota Uniform Arbitration Act changed "the common law policy of judicial hostility toward arbitration to one favoring arbitration." Layne–Minnesota Co. v. Regents of Univ. of Mn., 266 Minn. 284, 288, 123 N.W.2d 371, 374 (1963). This policy requires the court to give effect to parties' arbitration agreements, and weighs against the Trust's assertion. The Trust's suggested standard would render meaningless the second alternative of the Atcas test. Requiring a specific list of all possible claims constituting grounds for rescission would be impractical, defeating the policy favoring arbitration. Further, given the realities of commercial dealings, parties would hesitate to enter into a contract when fraud is mentioned at the outset. Michael–Curry Companies v. Knutson Shareholders Liquidating Trust, 434 N.W.2d 671, 676 (Minn.App.1989), pet. for review granted, (Minn. filed March 17, 1989).[2]

2. We are also concerned that parties often allege fraud in the inducement as a final attempt to avoid arbitration. We therefore emphasize that, where a party applies for a stay of arbitration, "circumstances constituting fraud * * * shall be stated with particularity." See Atcas, 292 Minn. at 348, 197 N.W.2d at 456 (citing Minn.R.Civ.P. 9.02). Minn.Stat. §§ 572.09(a) and (b) should not be invoked without such particularity.

For the reasons stated above, we affirm the judgment of the court of appeals and remand to the district court for an order compelling arbitration pursuant to the arbitration clause in the parties' purchase agreement.

2. In a related area, this court has held that parties who fashion a "broad" arbitration clause must enumerate specifically whatever they wish to exclude from the powers of the arbitrators.

In David Co. v. Jim W. Miller Constr., Inc., 444 N.W.2d 836 (Minn.1989), this court upheld an "innovative and unique" award fashioned by arbitrators as authorized by a broad arbitration clause, even though "it may be correct to surmise that initially neither party specifically contemplated" that such an award could be made. Id. at 840, 842. The parties were experienced in construction; therefore they should have been aware of the extent of the liability and possible awards involved. Thus, if the parties had desired to limit the powers of the arbitrators, they should have specifically expressed this in the broadly-worded arbitration clause. Supporting this conclusion is the "long-established policy favoring expansion of the arbitration remedy." Id. at 842.

NOTES

(1) Minnesota, like many states, has enacted legislation based upon the Uniform Arbitration Act, reprinted supra. In *Michael–Curry,* what legal questions were before the court under UAA §§ 1 & 2? Make a list of the statutory conditions that must be satisfied before the petitioner is entitled to an order compelling arbitration. These conditions determine the arbitrability of the dispute. How is the agreement to arbitrate enforced?

(2) *Preemptive Effect of Federal Arbitration Act.* The Federal Arbitration Act, 9 U.S.C.A. §§ 1–15, was enacted by Congress in 1925. The FAA, with some exceptions, applies to "[A] written provision in any maritime transaction or a contract evidencing a transaction involving commerce to settle by arbitration a controversy thereafter arising out of such contract or transaction, or the refusal to perform the whole or any part thereof, or an agreement in writing to submit to arbitration an existing controversy arising out of such a contract, transaction, or refusal." FAA § 2. Thus, under both the FAA and the Uniform Arbitration Act, written agreements to arbitrate existing and future disputes are enforceable.

Suppose, however, that state arbitration law denied enforcement to agreements to arbitrate future disputes and the "contract evidenced a transaction involving commerce" under FAA § 2. In Allied–Bruce Terminix Companies, Inc. v. Dobson, 513 U.S. 265, 115 S.Ct. 834, 130 L.Ed.2d 753 (1995), the Court held that the FAA's scope extended to the limits of Congress's power to regulate interstate commerce and that state law conflicting with the enforceability of the federal contract to arbitrate was preempted. Thus, Alabama law, which did not enforce agreements to arbitrate future disputes, could not preclude the enforcement of such an agreement within the scope of the FAA. Similarly, state law that imposes conditions on the enforcement of the federal contract to arbitrate not found in the FAA (and not applicable to other contracts) is preempted, Doctor's Associates, Inc. v. Casarotto, ___ U.S. ___, 116 S.Ct. 1652, 134 L.Ed.2d 902 (1996), unless the parties have clearly agreed to be bound by those conditions by a choice of law clause or other terms. Volt Information Sciences, Inc. v. Board of Trustees of Leland Stanford Junior University, 489 U.S. 468, 109 S.Ct. 1248, 103 L.Ed.2d 488 (1989)(choice of California law). What law was chosen in *Michael-Curry?*

For more discussion of these and other cases interpreting the FAA, see Stephen L. Hayford, *Commercial Arbitration in the Supreme Court, 1983–1995: A Sea Change*, 31 Wake Forest L. Rev. 1 (1996).

(3) *Who Decides Arbitrability?* FAA § 2 states that written agreements to arbitrate within its scope "shall be valid, irrevocable, and enforceable, save upon such grounds as exist at law or in equity for the revocation of any contract." UAA § 1 and Minnesota law are in accord. In *Michael–Curry,* the claim was that an amendment to the contract containing the arbitration clause was induced by fraud. There was no claim that the arbitration clause itself was induced by fraud. The court, however, held that fraud that vitiates the underlying contract "also vitiates an arbitration clause within the contract" and proceeded to decide whether the fraud claim was within the scope of the agreement to arbitrate. Why? According to the court, the issue was "more

properly determined by those trained in law." Once the arbitrability issue is decided, however, whether there was fraud or not is for the arbitrators.

Under the FAA, arbitrability issues (i.e., was there a written agreement to arbitrate, was the dispute within the scope of the agreement, was the arbitration agreement induced by fraud) are for the court unless the parties have expressly agreed to have the arbitrator decide them. First Options of Chicago, Inc. v. Kaplan, ___ U.S. ___, 115 S.Ct. 1920, 131 L.Ed.2d 985 (1995). On the other hand, the better view under the FAA is that a claim that the underlying contract or an amendment was induced by fraud does not constitute a direct attack on the arbitration clause, even though invalidation of the underlying contract might vitiate the arbitration clause. Under Prima Paint Corp. v. Flood & Conklin Mfg. Co., 388 U.S. 395, 87 S.Ct. 1801, 18 L.Ed.2d 1270 (1967) and its better reasoned progeny, a fraud attack on the underlying contract is for the arbitrator to decide unless the claim was beyond the scope of the agreement to arbitrate. This approach expands the scope of the arbitrator's power and, of course, assumes that the arbitrator is capable of resolving fraud and similar claims. For a full discussion, see II Ian R. Macneil, Richard E. Speidel & Thomas J. Stipanowich, Federal Arbitration Law: Agreements, Awards, and Remedies Under the Federal Arbitration Act Ch. 15 (1994, supp. 1996).

Container Technology Corp. v. J. Gadsden Pty., Ltd.

Court of Appeals of Colorado, 1989.
781 P.2d 119.

■ Opinion by JUDGE METZGER.

Plaintiff, Container Technology Corporation (Container), appeals the summary judgment confirming an arbitration award entered in favor of defendant, J. Gadsden Pty., Ltd. (Gadsden). We affirm.

The parties' contract dispute was submitted to arbitration and the arbitrators awarded Gadsden $44,937. Container filed an application to set aside the award, asserting that the arbitrators failed to follow the terms of the parties' contract, gave undue weight to hearsay testimony, and thus, violated the Uniform Arbitration Act (the Act). Sections 13–22–201, et seq., C.R.S. (1987 Repl.Vol. 6A).

Container then sought to depose the arbitrators, and Gadsden objected, contending that Container's proposed inquiry into the thought processes of the arbitrators was not authorized by the Act. The trial court refused to allow the arbitrators to be deposed and granted summary judgment confirming the arbitration award in favor of Gadsden. This appeal followed.

It has long been the policy of this state to foster and encourage the use of arbitration as a method of dispute resolution. See Colo. Const. art. XVIII, § 3; Judd Construction Co. v. Evans Joint Venture, 642 P.2d 922 (Colo. 1982). The Uniform Arbitration Act, adopted to establish a statutorily based scheme of arbitration, states as its purpose: "To validate voluntary written arbitration agreements, make the arbitration process effective, provide necessary safeguards, and provide an efficient procedure when judicial assistance is necessary." Section 13–22–202, C.R.S. (1987 Repl.Vol. 6A).

Judicial confirmation of an arbitration award is an often-used method of judicial assistance and usually includes only a few, relatively simple procedures. See C.R.C.P. 109. And, for several reasons, confirmation is the rule rather than the exception.

An arbitration award is tantamount to a judgment and is entitled to be given such status by the court which reviews it. Columbine Valley Construction Co. v. Board of Directors, 626 P.2d 686 (Colo.1981). Thus, when a party attacks the validity of an arbitration award, he bears the burden of sustaining the attack. Ormsbee Development Co. v. Grace, 668 F.2d 1140 (10th Cir.1982).

The issues before the court in a confirmation proceeding are limited by the terms of the Act. Judd Construction Co. v. Evans Joint Venture, supra. Parties who agree to submit matters to arbitration are presumed to have agreed that everything, both as to law and fact, necessary to render an ultimate decision, is included in the authority of the arbitrator. Continental Materials Corp. v. Gaddis Mining Co., 306 F.2d 952 (10th Cir.1962).

Thus, an arbitration award is not open to review on the merits. Checkrite of San Jose, Inc. v. Checkrite, Ltd., 640 F.Supp. 234 (D.Colo. 1986). This includes asserted errors in determining the credibility of witnesses, the weight to be given to their testimony, and the determination of factual issues. Sterling Colorado Beef Co. v. United Food & Commercial Workers, 767 F.2d 718 (10th Cir.1985).

Also, the merits of the award include the arbitrators' interpretation of the contract. The rationale for vesting contract interpretation in the province of the arbitrators is expressed in United Steelworkers v. Enterprise Wheel & Car Corp., 363 U.S. 593, 80 S.Ct. 1358, 4 L.Ed.2d 1424 (1960): "It is the arbitrator's construction which was bargained for; and so far as the arbitrator's decision concerns construction of the contract, the courts have no business overruling him because their interpretation of the contract is different from his."

With these principles in mind, we address Container's assertions of error.

Relying on Twin Lakes Reservoir & Canal Co. v. Platt Rogers, Inc., 112 Colo. 155, 147 P.2d 828 (1944), Container first argues that the trial court erred in prohibiting it from taking the depositions of the arbitrators. We disagree.

The court in Twin Lakes Reservoir & Canal Co. v. Platt Rogers, Inc., supra, held that the testimony of arbitrators may be admitted in a confirmation hearing to determine "what took place before the arbitrators, what was in controversy and what matters entered into the decision." Container asserts that this language authorizes it to inquire into the arbitrators' assessment of the evidence and their thought processes in reaching the award. We do not agree.

In *Twin Lakes,* after both parties had completed the presentation of their respective cases, the arbitrators determined that the evidence was insufficient to allow them to reach a decision. Accordingly, they hired an engineer to do a survey, had several conversations with him and his staff outside the presence of the parties, and also hired a private legal advisor without furnishing reports of their consultations with him to the parties. Thus, the court allowed the arbitrators to be deposed and to testify in order to ascertain the information they obtained in these various meetings held outside the presence of the parties.

Here, the facts are quite different. All evidence was presented to the arbitrators during a five-day hearing at which both parties were present. The parties did not dispute what occurred during the arbitration so they did not need to depose the arbitrators to ascertain what occurred.

We conclude that deposing arbitrators for the purpose of essentially reconstructing a record of arbitration proceedings bears no similarity to an inquiry into the arbitrators' thought processes. Container freely admits that the latter was the purpose of its proposed depositions, and it is that purpose which is uniformly disallowed since it, of necessity, involves a review on the merits. Checkrite of San Jose, Inc. v. Checkrite, Ltd., supra. See generally Annot., 80 A.L.R.3d 155 (1977). Consequently, we conclude that the trial court correctly prohibited Container from deposing the arbitrators.

Container next contends that the trial court erred in entering summary judgment in Gadsden's favor. Again, we disagree.

In its motion to set aside the arbitration award, Container asserted the arbitrators had exceeded their powers by allowing credits to which Gadsden was not entitled, disregarding the contract terms, substituting costs for contract price on various items, rewriting the contract, and allowing credits for which there was no contract provision.

The grounds for setting aside an arbitration award are limited by the Act; an unfavorable interpretation of a contract is not a basis to set aside an arbitration award. See §§ 13–22–214(1) and 13–22–215(1), C.R.S. (1987 Repl.Vol. 6A); see also Judd Construction Co. v. Evans Joint Venture, supra. Moreover, because an inquiry into arbitrators' interpretation of a contract is an inquiry into the merits, it is not allowed. United Steelworkers v. Enterprise Wheel & Car Corp., supra.

Since all of Container's allegations are predicated upon the arbitrators' unfavorable interpretation of the contract, it failed to state a valid ground to set aside the award. Therefore, entry of summary judgment was correct.

The judgment is affirmed.

NOTES

(1) "A few prefatory comments concerning the nature of arbitration and the role of the court are appropriate. 'The ancient practice of arbitration [i]n its broad sense * * * is a substitution by consent of the parties, of another

tribunal for the tribunal provided by the ordinary processes of law. The object of arbitration is the final disposition, in a speedy, inexpensive, expeditious, and perhaps less formal manner, of the controversial differences between the parties. "The submission * * * is the commission of the arbitrator. By force of it he becomes a judge, with absolute power *over the things submitted to his judgment.* . . . Submission to arbitration is contractual, the parties being bound by the arbitration only to the extent they have so agreed. . . . Likewise, the scope of the arbitrator's jurisdiction and authority is delineated by the terms of the parties' agreement . . . and the arbitrator may not rewrite contract terms for the parties. . . . Where properly functioning within the agreement terms, however, 'the essence of arbitration is . . . that the arbitrators decide *both the facts* and the law. . . . The forum chosen by the parties operates as a trial court, and judicial review of the awards rendered by it is extremely narrow and restricted to ascertaining whether one of the situations set forth in N.J.S.A. § 2A:24–8 exists. . . . N.J.S.A. 2A:24–8 pertinently reads:

> The court shall vacate the award in any of the following cases:
>
> a. Where the award was procured by corruption, fraud or undue means;
>
> b. Where there was either evident partiality or corruption in the arbitrators, or any thereof * * *
>
> d. Where the arbitrators exceed or so imperfectly executed their powers that a mutual, final and definite award upon the subject was not made.

Clearly, the arbitrators' factual determinations concerning the merits of the controversy are not reviewable as such by the court. Further, only issues of fact bearing on a statutory criteria will suffice for withholding of summary judgment." Harsen v. Board of Education of West Milford Township in Passaic County, 132 N.J.Super. 365, 333 A.2d 580, 583–84 (1975). For other decisions upholding awards under the UAA, see, e.g., Granger Northern, Inc. v. Cianchette, 572 A.2d 136 (Me.1990); Breeze v. Sims, 778 P.2d 215 (Alaska 1989).

(2) The FAA and the UAA agree on the limited scope by which a court may review or modify an arbitration award. See FAA §§ 10 & 11. For a more complete discussion, see IV Macneil, et. al., Chapters 40–43.

(3) *Is Arbitration an Acceptable Method of Resolving Construction Contract Disputes?* Here is the conclusion of Fabyanske and Halverson.

> By now, it should be clear that the question posed in the title of this paper, has not been answered and is not susceptible to a categorical answer. It simply is not possible to say whether arbitration, in general, is better than, worse than, or as good as litigation. It is even difficult to say whether one or the other means of resolving disputes is better in any particular case.
>
> A few things can be said with certainty. Arbitration is fundamentally different than litigation in several key respects. First, it is primarily a fact finding forum; it is not well suited to deal with complex legal issues. Second, the procedural framework of arbitration is substantially less rigid than that of litigation. Depending on one's perspective, this can be an advantage or a disadvantage. While there are fewer procedural burdens for parties, there are also correspondingly fewer procedural safeguards. A decision of an arbitrator, basically, is final and conclusive, and carries with it both the benefits and burdens of that characteristic. Third, parties may

agree upon both the limit of the arbitrator's jurisdiction and the appropriate venue. Parties should consider (carefully) the scope of the arbitration clause in their contracts, if they decide that they want their disputes resolved by arbitration. By careful drafting of the arbitration clause, it should be possible to limit the scope of arbitrable controversies to select a suitable place for the hearing and to provide whatever procedural framework is deemed desirable. * * *

In the last analysis, arbitration is an effective disputes' resolution mechanism only if all the parties involved genuinely want it to work. Both the basis and strength of arbitration is consent. If it is lacking, arbitration becomes ineffective and resort to the courts is almost inevitable.

Fabyanske & Halverson, *Arbitration: Is It An Acceptable Method of Resolving Construction Contract Disputes?*, 16 The Forum 281, 295 (1980). See also Thomas J. Stipanowich, *Beyond Arbitration: Innovation and Evolution in the United States Construction Industry*, 31 Wake Forest L. Rev. 65 (1996); Hayford & Peeples, *Commercial Arbitration in Evolution: An Assessment and Call for Dialogue*, 10 Ohio St.J. Dispute Res. 343 (1995).

CHAPTER SEVEN

THIRD PARTY INTERESTS

We turn now to two issues that are often given short shrift in first-year courses: (i) contractor's ability subsequent to an initial contract to assign the benefits or delegate the duties of performance to third-parties (not in privity with the initial contractors); and (ii) contractor's ability as part of the initial contract to assign benefits to so-called "third-party beneficiaries" (who do not themselves provide any consideration for these benefits).

SECTION 1. ASSIGNMENT AND DELEGATION

Once a contract right exists, can it be sold or given to another? Can one delegate duties or performance to someone else?

There are two common transactions that produce assignments. First, A sells and delivers goods to or performs services for B who promises to pay the price at some future time. A's right against B is commonly called an account receivable. Second, C agrees to construct a home for D who promises to pay as work progresses. Since C, unlike A, has not yet earned payment by performance under the contract, the right against D is commonly called a contract right. But see UCC 9–106, which defines accounts to include both rights that have been earned by full performance and those that have not. Note that both A and C have extended credit. If they need cash before B's and D's duties mature, they may try to assign or sell the account or contract right to a third party for an immediate but discounted cash payment. If there is a willing third party and contract law will permit enforcement of A's and C's contract rights against B and D, A and C can convert a promise of future payment into present cash. This ability is the hallmark of a credit economy, for it permits the third party immediately to finance A and C on the strength of B's and D's promises.

Occasionally, a contractor in the position of C will attempt to transfer the contract to the third party, i.e., assign the rights and delegate the duties. More frequently a construction contractor will assign rights to a bank for immediate financing and delegate some performance duties to subcontractors. As you might imagine, the risks involved to the third party who pays value for rights or assumes the responsibility for performance are considerable and vary from transaction to transaction. See Gilmore, *The Assignee of Contract Rights and His Precarious Security*, 74 Yale L.J. 216 (1964). For example, the rights of an assignee are, in general, subject to all the terms of the contract between the assignor and the account debtor and any claim or defense arising therefrom. See UCC 9–318; Restatement (Second) §§ 334–339.

Since assignments are commonplace today—indeed one cannot imagine our complex credit structure existing without them—it may come as a surprise to learn that at one time common law courts refused to recognize the assignability of a "chose in action," including a right arising *ex contractu*.[1] The emphasis upon the personal relationship of the contracting parties, discernible also in the development of third party beneficiary contracts, tended to make the lack of privity an insurmountable obstacle to the third party's right of action. However, at a time when common law courts steadfastly refused to recognize assignments, the law merchant, presumably in response to commercial demand, developed a considerable body of assignment doctrine. As the economy expanded, the common law courts, spurred on by courts of equity, came to fashion legal doctrine which, in effect, permitted the assignment of a contract right.[2]

More recently, however, Article 9 of the UCC—the secured transactions article—has preempted a considerable chunk of assignments law. Article 9 applies to "any transaction (regardless of its form) which is intended to create a security interest in personal property * * * including * * * general intangibles * * * or accounts; and also * * * to any sale of accounts." UCC 9–102(1). Expressly excluded from Article 9, however, is a "sale of accounts * * * which is for the purpose of collection only, or a transfer of a right to payment under a contract to an assignee who is also to do the performance under the contract * * *." UCC 9–104(f). Our emphasis here is on assignment law which is not preempted by Article 9.[3]

For the sale of goods, the assignment of contractual rights are presumptively "unless otherwise agreed" or unless "the assignment would

---

1. The severe proscription of maintenance and champerty, the unlawful interference in or purchase of an interest in another's lawsuit, helped create a climate of judicial disfavor to the notion of one suing to enforce a right arising out of a transaction to which one was not privy.

2. This was accomplished ostensibly within the framework of settled law, but actually amounted to a sharp departure from precedent. The "owner" of the right could appoint another as agent for collection and agree that the latter would keep the proceeds. As time went on, even if the transaction was formally denominated an assignment, courts would say the effect was to create a power of attorney, enabling the "assignee" to sue in the name of the "assignor." There were serious drawbacks to this agency evasion, however. The "assignor" could revoke the agency, and revocation was effected automatically by death or bankruptcy. To

overcome this defect in the process, litigants appealed, characteristically, to the Chancery court. And, again characteristically, equity responded. If the "assignee" gave value, he or she would be treated as "owner" of the claim, which ownership could not be divested by the "assignor's" attempted revocation or by death or bankruptcy. At this point the future of assignment doctrine was assured. While there persisted for years a language which described choses in action as assignable in equity but not at law, the subsequent merger of law and equity caused even this terminology to all but disappear. The result is that the power of assignment is firmly embedded in the law, and judicial attention has been given to the implications and ramifications of this power. Fuller, Basic Contract Law 585–92 (1947); Corbin § 856.

3. For collateral reading, see Farnsworth §§ 11.1–11.11; Calamari and Perillo §§ 18.1–18.32; Murray §§ 135–142.

materially change the duty of the other party or increase materially the burden or risk imposed on him by his contract." UCC 2–210 [UCC 2–503 (1997)]. Accord: Restatement (Second) § 317(2).

There are relatively few cases where the assignment of a contract right alone has been held to materially increase the obligor's risk, especially where the right is to the payment of money. For a few examples, see Crane Ice Cream Co. v. Terminal Freezing & Heating Co., 147 Md. 588, 128 A. 280 (1925); Kingston v. Markward & Karafilis, Inc., 134 Mich.App. 164, 350 N.W.2d 842 (1984) (assignment of right to indemnification materially increases risk). But see Collins Co., Ltd. v. Carboline Co., 125 Ill.2d 498, 127 Ill.Dec. 5, 532 N.E.2d 834 (1988) (assignment by buyer of right to express warranty does not materially increase seller's risk); Evening News Association v. Peterson, 477 F.Supp. 77 (D.D.C.1979) (assignment of right to services of newscaster does not materially increase risk); Tennell v. Esteve Cotton Co., 546 S.W.2d 346 (Tex.Civ.App.1976) (buyer's assignment of cotton contract does not materially increase seller's risk).

Once a promise is due, the UCC also allows promisees to assign their rights even if the initial contract prohibits assignment—thus giving promisees an immutable option to assign rights which are no longer executory such as a right to damages for breach or a right to payment of an "account." UCC 2–210(2) [UCC 2–503 (1997)].

(A) ASSIGNMENT OF RIGHTS

Fitzroy v. Cave

Court of Appeal, 1905.
[1905] 2 K.B. 364.

■ COZENS-HARDY L.J. read the following judgment:—This is an appeal from the judgment of Lawrance J. in favour of the defendant. The plaintiff is the assignee of five debts amounting together to over 50*l*. due from the defendant to five creditors resident in Ireland. The assignment is effected by a deed dated October 13, 1904.

[The deed provided: "And the assignee hereby covenants with the assignors, and with each of them, that, in case he shall be able to recover and realize the amount of the said debts from the said Arthur Oriel Singer Cave, he will immediately thereupon pay over to them, the assignors, their executors, administrators, and assigns, the said respective amounts, or so much thereof as he may be able to recover or realize, after payment of all costs necessarily incurred by him." Notice in writing of this assignment had been given to the defendant.]

It appeared in evidence that the plaintiff was interested in, and a director of, a company called the Cork Mineral Development Company. The defendant was a co-director and the local manager of the company. The plaintiff, being dissatisfied with the action of the defendant as a director of the company, had, acting under the advice of a solicitor, taken the assignment of the before-mentioned debts with the view of procuring an adjudication in bankruptcy against the defendant, and so getting him removed from the directorate of the company.]

It is desirable to consider the limits of the doctrine of maintenance as applied to choses in action. There are undoubtedly many choses in action which are not and never were assignable either at law or in equity. * * *

There are, however, other choses in action which, though not assignable at common law, were always regarded as assignable in equity. A debt presently due and payable is an instance. At common law such a debt was looked upon as a strictly personal obligation, and an assignment of it was regarded as a mere assignment of a right to bring an action at law against the debtor. Hence the assignment was, with some exceptions which need not be referred to (see 1 Hawkins' Pleas of the Crown, p. 458), looked upon as open to the objection of maintenance. After a time the Common Law Courts recognized the right of any one who had a pecuniary interest in the debt to sue in the name of the creditor. This, however, was the limit of their departure from the old strict rule, so far as I have been able to discover. But the Courts of Equity took a different view: . . . They admitted the title of an assignee of a debt, regarding it as a piece of property, an asset capable of being dealt with like any other asset, and treating the necessity of an action at law to get it in as a mere incident. They declined to hold such a transaction open to the charge of maintenance. * * *

A Court of Equity recognised not merely transactions which amounted to sales or mortgages of debts, under which the assignee took a beneficial interest in the debt, but also the creation of trusts, under which the trustee took no interest. Thus A., the creditor, might assign the debt to B., with or without a power of attorney, upon trust for C. Or A. might simply declare himself a trustee of the debt for C. In either case the trustee would take no beneficial interest, and would, by virtue of his position as trustee, be entitled to be indemnified out of the moneys recovered against all costs of the action brought in the name of A. against the debtor. If the debt were secured by a promissory note or bill or other negotiable instrument, A. might deliver the instrument to B. upon trust for C., and B. could sue at law on it. Or A. might create a trust in favour of himself by delivering the instrument to B. upon trust for himself. It would, I apprehend, in this case be no objection to say that B. had no interest in the debt. It has never, so far as I am aware, been suggested that a trustee to whom a debt is assigned is exposed to a charge of maintenance. Mortgages are every day dealt with in this fashion, including an assignment of the debt. From time to time particular classes of obligation have by statute been rendered assignable at law, and by the Judicature Act, 1873, s. 25, sub-s. 6, any debt is made assignable at law by an absolute assignment in writing, of which notice is given to the debtor. Henceforth in all Courts a debt must be regarded as a piece of property capable of legal assignment in the same sense as a bale of goods. And on principle I think it is not possible to deny the right of the owner of any property capable of legal assignment to vest that property in a trustee for himself, and thereby to confer upon such trustee a right of indemnity. It is not easy to see how the doctrine of maintenance can be applied to a case like the present. * * * It is said that the plaintiff does not really desire to be paid and can take nothing for his own benefit under the judgment. For the reasons above stated I think this is of no moment. It is further urged that his only object is to obtain a judgment which may serve as the foundation of bankruptcy proceedings, the ultimate result of which will be the removal of the defendant from his position as director of a company in which the plaintiff is largely interested. But I fail to see that we have anything to do with the motives which actuate the plaintiff, who is simply asserting a legal right consequential upon the possession of property which has been validly assigned to him. If the defendant pays, no bankruptcy proceedings will follow. If he does not pay, bankruptcy is a possible result. In my opinion this appeal must be allowed.

Appeal allowed. [Footnotes omitted.]

NOTES

(1) Is not the effect of the decision, in *Fitzroy* to obligate the defendant to do something which he had not agreed to do; *viz.,* pay the plaintiff rather than the "five tradesmen in Ireland"? Does this holding improperly impinge freedom of contract? For a treatment of assignment in English law, see G. Treitel, The Law of Contract, ch. 16 (6th Ed. 1983).

(2) What policy justification is there for the recognition of a power to assign a contract right? Cozens–Hardy, L.J., states that "a debt must be regarded as a piece of property capable of legal assignment in the same sense as a bale of goods." Do you agree? With what qualification(s), if any?

(3) Does the fact that the assignee is *persona non grata* with the debtor bar an action? Should it?

(4) *On the Making of an Irrevocable Gratuitous Assignment.* Restatement (Second) Contracts § 332(1) provides: "(1) Unless a contrary intention is manifested, a gratuitous assignment is irrevocable if (a) the assignment is in a writing either signed or under seal that is delivered by the assignor; or (b) the assignment is accompanied by delivery of a writing of a type customarily accepted as a symbol or as evidence of the right assigned." In both parts, one expressly and the other impliedly, the pattern adopted is consistent with the requirement respecting gifts of chattels that a symbolic or constructive "delivery" is required. See Brown, The Law of Personal Property § 7.2 (3d ed. 1975).

(5) *On the Assignment of "Future Accounts" and "Future Wages."* If one "owns" something—a tract of land, an automobile, a chose in action—one has a legal and practical advantage, an "asset." With this asset one can, for example, obtain money, either by transferring ownership (as in a sale) or by using the asset as security for a loan (as in a mortgage or pledge). But what if this something has no present existence in the ordinary sense, such as fish to be caught, gears to be manufactured, crops to be grown, accounts receivable from future sales? Can there be a present sale or assignment of whatever there is— the "expectancy," or "hope"? Why should not one be able to sell "anything" which another is willing to buy, providing of course the transaction is not violative of public policy?

It became particularly useful for sellers to assign their expected accounts receivable for future sales as security to help the seller receive credit. The financing of accounts receivable has developed into a major industry. Indeed, the transfer of these rights may be the most notable contemporary implementation of the power of assignment. A serious difficulty encountered in the operation of receivables financing was the problem of handling future accounts. Early in this century courts were hostile to the assignment of future accounts. See, e.g., Taylor v. Barton–Child Co., 228 Mass. 126, 117 N.E. 43 (1917). To circumvent such precedents, it was deemed necessary for the debtor/seller to execute supplementary assignments as the accounts came into existence.

Restatement (Second) § 321, however, reflects a much more congenial attitude toward the assignment of future accounts: "(1) Except as otherwise provided by statute, an assignment of a right to payment expected to arise out of an existing employment or other continuing business relationship is effective in the same way as an assignment of an existing right. (2) Except as otherwise provided by statute and as stated in Subsection (1), a purported assignment of a right expected to arise under a contract not in existence operates only as a promise to assign the right when it arises and as a power to enforce it." A critical section of the UCC goes even further in facilitating the sale of future accounts. UCC 9–204(1) provides:

"[A] security agreement may provide that any or all obligations covered by the security agreement are to be secured by after-acquired collateral."

Under this provision, the secured party may include in the security agreement an "after-acquired property" clause, file a financing statement with the proper officer, give value to the debtor and be assured of a perfected security interest at the time when the debtor obtains rights in the described collateral— including any "accounts receivable" subsequently acquired. No further agreement or filing is required.

Modern legislation, however, has limited the assignability of "future wages." A few States proscribe all such assignments; most regulate the practice, as by restricting the amount of wages subject to assignment, etc. See Statutory Note, Restatement (Second) Ch. 15.

Allhusen v. Caristo Construction Corp.

Court of Appeals of New York, 1952.
303 N.Y. 446, 103 N.E.2d 891.

■ FROESSEL, JUDGE. Defendant, a general contractor, subcontracted with the Kroo Painting Company (hereinafter called Kroo) for the performance by the latter of certain painting work in New York City public schools. Their contracts contained the following prohibitory provision: "The assignment by the second party [Kroo] of this contract or any interest therein, or of any money due or to become due by reason of the terms hereof without the written consent of the first party [defendant] shall be void." Kroo subsequently assigned certain rights under the contracts to Marine Midland Trust Company of New York, which in turn assigned said rights to plaintiff. These rights included the "moneys due and to become due" to Kroo. The *contracts* were not assigned, and no question of improper delegation of contractual duties is involved. No written consent to the assignments was procured from defendant.

Plaintiff as assignee seeks to recover, in six causes of action, $11,650 allegedly due and owing for work done by Kroo. Defendant answered with denials, and by way of defense set up the aforementioned prohibitory clause, in addition to certain setoffs and counterclaims, alleged to have existed at the time of the assignments. It thereupon moved for summary judgment under rule 113 of the Rules of Civil Practice, and demanded dismissal of plaintiff's several causes of action on the sole ground that the prohibitory clause constituted a defense sufficient as a matter of law to defeat each cause of action. Special Term dismissed the complaint, holding that the prohibition against assignments "must be given effect." The Appellate Division affirmed, one Justice dissenting on the ground that the "account receivable was assignable by nature, and could not be rendered otherwise without imposing an unlawful restraint upon the power of alienation of property." 278 App.Div. 817, 104 N.Y.S.2d 565, 566.

Whether an anti-assignment clause is effective is a question that has troubled the courts not only of this State but in other jurisdictions as well. . . .

Our courts have not construed a contractual provision against assignments framed in the language of the clause now before us. Such kindred clauses as have been subject to interpretation usually have been held to be either (1) personal covenants limiting the covenantee to a claim for damages in the event of a breach as e.g., Manchester v. Kendall, 19 Jones & Sp. 460, affirmed 103 N.Y. 638; Sacks v. Neptune Meter Co., 144 Misc. 70, 258 N.Y.S. 254, affirmed 238 App.Div. 82, 263 N.Y.S. 462, or (2) ineffectual because of the use of uncertain language, State Bank v. Central Mercantile Bank, 248 N.Y. 428, 162 N.E. 475, 59 A.L.R. 1473. But these decisions are not to be read as meaning that there can be no enforcible [sic] prohibition against the assignment of a claim; indeed, they are authority only for the proposition that, in the absence of language clearly indicating that a contractual right thereunder shall be nonassignable, a prohibitory clause will be interpreted as a personal covenant not to assign.

In the Manchester case, supra, it was held, 103 N.Y. at page 463, that the words, " 'This contract not to be assigned, or any part thereof, or any installments to grow due under the same,' " must be construed as an agreement not to assign, the breach of which would give rise to a claim for damages by the covenantee. The court stated 103 N.Y. at page 463, that the quoted words "would not make the assignment void." In the clause now before us, however, it is expressly provided that the "assignment * * * shall be void." In the State Bank case, supra, 248 N.Y. at page 431, 162 N.E. at page 476, 59 A.L.R. 1473, which involved the assignment of certificates of deposit which were "not subject to check" and were "payable only to himself [depositor] * * * on return of this Certificate properly endorsed," we held that such language did not make the certificates nonassignable, and that nonnegotiable certificates of deposit are assignable *in the absence of an agreement to the contrary.* Judge Pound, writing for a unanimous court, added, however, 248 N.Y. at page 435, 162 N.E. at page 477: "Clear language should therefore be required to lead to the conclusion that the certificates are not assignable. 1 Williston on Contracts, § 422. We cannot deduce such consequences from uncertain language. Scheffer v. Erie County Sav. Bank, 229 N.Y. 50, 127 N.E. 474. The plainest words should have been chosen so that he who runs could read, in order to limit the freedom of alienation of rights and prohibit the assignment. It might have been stipulated on the face of the certificates that they should be 'nontransferable' or 'nonassignable.' " * * *

In the light of the foregoing, we think it is reasonably clear that, while the courts have striven to uphold freedom of assignability, they have not failed to recognize the concept of freedom to contract. In large measure they agree that, where appropriate language is used, assignments of money due under contracts may be prohibited. When "clear language" is used, and the "plainest words * * * have been chosen," parties may "limit the freedom of alienation of rights and prohibit the assignment." State Bank v. Central Mercantile Bank, supra, 248 N.Y. at page 435, 162 N.E. at page 477, 59 A.L.R. 1473. We have now before us a clause embodying clear, definite and appropriate language, which may be construed in no other way but that any attempted assignment of either the contract or any rights created thereunder shall be "void" as against the obligor. One would have to do violence to the language here employed to hold that it is merely an agreement by the subcontractor not to assign. The objectivity of the language precludes such a construction. We are therefore compelled to conclude that this prohibitory clause is a valid and effective restriction of the right to assign.

Such a holding is not violative of public policy. Professor Williston, in his treatise on Contracts, states (Vol. 2 § 422, p. 1214): "The question of the free alienation of property does not seem to be involved." The New York cases do not hold otherwise, State Bank v. Central Mercantile Bank, supra, 248 N.Y. at page 435, 162 N.E. at page 477, 59 A.L.R. 1473. Plaintiff's claimed rights arise out of the very contract embodying the provision now sought to be invalidated. The right to moneys under the contracts is but a companion to other jural relations forming an aggregation of actual and potential interrelated rights and obligations. No sound reason appears why an assignee should remain unaffected by a provision in the very contract which gave life to the claim he asserts.

Nor is there any merit in plaintiff's contention that section 41 of the Personal Property Law, Consol.Laws, c. 41, requires that the prohibitory clause be denied effect. Because the statute provides that a person may transfer a claim, it does not follow that he may not contract otherwise. Countless rights granted by statutes are voluntarily surrendered in the everyday affairs of individuals. In Rosenthal Paper Co. v. National Folding Box & Paper Co., 226 N.Y. 313, 325–326, 123 N.E. 766, 770, we noted: "The general rule now prevailing * * * that any property right, not necessarily personal, is assignable, *is overcome only by agreement of the contracting parties* or a principal of law or public policy. [Citing cases.] In this jurisdiction the statute, in effect, so provides [referring to the predecessor of section 41 of the Personal Property Law]." (Emphasis supplied.)

The judgment should be affirmed, with costs.

NOTES

(1) In terms of legal consequence, what is the difference between saying the prohibition deprived Kroo of the power to assign rather than merely created a duty on his part not to do so? See Wellington Green Apartments, Ltd. v. B & D Investment Corp., 693 F.2d 748 (8th Cir.1982) (unless restriction expressly states assignment void, remedy for breach is damages).

(2) What policy conflicts are discernible in a case of this type?

(3) *Contractual Prohibition of Assignment and the UCC.* Section 9–318(4) of the Uniform Commercial Code provides: "A term in any contract between an account debtor and an assignor is ineffective if it prohibits assignment of an account." The official comments for this provision note:

> Subsection (4) breaks sharply with the older contract doctrines by denying effectiveness to contractual terms prohibiting assignment of accounts and contract rights—that is, sums due and to become due under contracts of sale, construction contracts and the like. Under the rule as stated an assignment would be effective even if made to an assignee who took with full knowledge that the account debtor had sought to prohibit or restrict assignment of the account or of the money to be earned under the contract.

UCC 9–318, Comment 4. The obligor's interest in prohibiting assignment is grounded in a concern that assignment might render the obligor's performance more difficult. But once the obligor's performance is due, this concern is attenuated.[4]

(4) *Assignment of Claims Against the United States.* There has been legislation prohibiting the assignment of executory contract claims against the United States since 1792. See 41 U.S.C.A. § 15 and 31 U.S.C.A. § 203. The basic purposes of this prohibition are to "protect the government against harassment caused by a multiplication of the firms with which it has to deal; prevent collusive bidding; prevent persons of influence from buying up claims against the government which then might be used against government officials; preserve for the government any defense it might have against the assignor by way of set-off or counterclaim; and secure for the government the performance of the firm with which it contracts." Cuneo, Government Contracts Handbook 7 (1962). In 1940, however, an amendment was approved by Congress permitting contractors to assign money due or to become due from the United States under a contract providing for payments aggregating $1,000 or more to a "bank, trust company, or other financing institution." The purpose of this amendment

---

4. It will be noted that the blanket proscription of Section 9–318(4) appears to conflict somewhat with Section 2–210(2), which allows for assignment of rights "unless otherwise agreed." For a discussion of how the provisions may be reconciled, see Murray § 138(c).

was to assist government contractors in obtaining private financing on the security of the government's promise to pay for work done or to be done. See Speidel, *"Stakeholder" Payments under Federal Construction Contracts: Payment Bond Surety vs. Assignee*, 47 Va.L.Rev. 640 (1961).

Continental Purchasing Co. v. Van Raalte Co., Inc.

Supreme Court of New York, Appellate Division, 1937.
251 App.Div. 151, 295 N.Y.S. 867.

■ EDGCOMB, JUSTICE. This action is brought by the plaintiff, as assignee of Ethel L. Potter, to recover from the Van Raalte Company, Inc., the employer of Mrs. Potter, the sum of $19.20, wages earned by her while employed by the company. The defendant claims exoneration from liability by reason of having paid the amount involved direct to the assignor.

It is conceded that on April 21, 1934, Mrs. Potter assigned to the plaintiff all wages, or claims for wages, salary, or commission earned, or to be earned, and all claims or demands due her from any person, firm, or corporation by whom she was employed, or who might owe her money, as security for the payment of an account which the Steckler Sporting Goods Store had against her, and which account had been purchased by and assigned to the plaintiff.

This assignment, having been made prior to July 1, 1934, when section 46 was added to the Personal Property Law by chapter 738 of the Laws of that year (section 1), is not void by reason of any statutory prohibition relating to wage assignments. Neither is such transfer contrary to public policy. Messina v. Continental Purchasing Co., 272 N.Y. 125, 126, 5 N.E.2d 62.

While the assignee of a chose in action succeeds to all the rights of the assignor, a debtor is not affected by the assignment until he has notice thereof. If he pays his indebtedness to the assignor in ignorance of the assignment, he is relieved from all liability to the assignee. He may set up against the claim of the assignee any defense acquired prior to notice which would have been available against the assignor had there been no assignment. . . .

After notice of the transfer, however, the debtor is put on his guard, and if he pays the assignor any money which, under the assignment, belongs to the assignee, or if he does anything prejudicial to the rights of the latter, he is liable for the resulting damage. . . .

No set form of notice is required. It is sufficient if such information is given the debtor as will fully inform him that the alleged assignee is the owner of the chose in action, or as will serve to put him on inquiry. . . .

Here the plaintiff protected itself against any bona fide payments made by the debtor to its employee by giving the defendant a written notice of this assignment on September 12, 1934. Seven days later defendant acknowledged receipt of the notice, and suggested that, inasmuch as Mrs. Potter had no other income except her weekly earnings, it would be a great accommodation if a deduction of $2 per week could be made until the total amount of plaintiff's claim was paid. Plaintiff consented to this adjustment, and withdrew its formal notice. But defendant still knew of the assignment, and on six occasions during the following two months deducted $1.50 from Mrs. Potter's wages, and forwarded the same to the plaintiff. This arrangement was discontinued after November 20th. Plaintiff then gave defendant another formal notice of the assignment, and demanded payment direct to it of the wages due Mrs. Potter, and called attention to the fact that any sums paid to the employee would not relieve the defendant from its obligation to the plaintiff. With full knowledge that the plaintiff was entitled to receive Mrs. Potter's wages, defendant has chosen to pay them to Mrs. Potter. In so doing, defendant acted at its peril.

Defendant claims immunity from liability in this action because of the fact that neither the original assignment, nor a copy thereof, was ever filed with or exhibited to it. This defense has found favor in the courts below. Such a requirement is not necessary to render a debtor liable to the assignee of a chose in action for the failure to pay him a debt owed to the assignor. Especially is that so where, as here, no such demand or request has ever been made. . . . The cases relied upon by the respondent do not lay down any different rule.

Here a full and complete notice of the assignment was given to the defendant, and a demand was made that the assignor's wages be paid to the plaintiff. Defendant never questioned the existence or validity of the transfer, nor asked for any additional proof thereof. On the contrary, it acknowledged its validity, and made six separate payments to the assignee, totaling $9, in reliance thereon. Later it utterly ignored plaintiff's rights in the premises, and paid the assignor her wages as they became due, notwithstanding the fact that it knew this money belonged to the plaintiff. Its only excuse for so doing was the fact that Mrs. Potter was receiving aid from a local charitable organization, and that the matter had been referred to that organization for a decision. Under these circumstances, defendant cannot escape its liability to the plaintiff because it paid Mrs. Potter's wages to her.

For the reasons stated, we think that the judgments of the City Court of Dunkirk, and of the County Court of Chautauqua county, should be reversed with costs, and that judgment should be ordered in favor of the plaintiff for the sum of $19.20, with interest thereon from the 21st day of November, 1934.

Judgments reversed on the law with costs in all courts and judgment directed in favor of the plaintiff in the sum of $19.20 with interest thereon from the 21st day of November, 1934, with costs. All concur.

NOTES

(1) If, after April 21, 1934, the defendant, without notice of the assignment, had paid Ethel Potter, would the plaintiff here have been successful

against the defendant? Does the answer depend upon whether the assignment was operative at that time or when notification was given to the obligor?

(2) *Modification of Contract After Notification of Assignment.* Since the obligor, after notice of the assignment, cannot secure a discharge by payment thereafter to the assignor, it would seem to follow as well that one cannot thereafter be discharged by obtaining a release from the assignor, or by executing an accord and satisfaction or a novation. One must get a discharge from the assignee. See Corbin § 894. It also follows that the original parties could not then modify the contract. The consent of the assignee would be essential to a modification. It has been argued that this may be commercially inconvenient, especially where a prime contractor must make adjustments with subcontractors as the work progresses. To an extent the Uniform Commercial Code permits modification without securing the assignee's consent. Section 9–318(2) provides: "So far as the right to payment or a part thereof under an assigned contract has not been fully earned by performance and notwithstanding notification of the assignment, any modification of or substitution for the contract made in good faith and in accordance with reasonable commercial standards is effective against an assignee unless the account debtor has otherwise agreed but the assignee acquires corresponding rights under the modified or substituted contract. The assignment may provide that such modification or substitution is a breach by the assignor." For a discussion of this provision, see Note, 105 U.Pa.L.Rev. 836, 918–20 (1957).

(3) UCC 9–318(3): "The account debtor is authorized to pay the assignor until the account debtor receives notification that the amount due or to become due has been assigned and that payment is to be made to the assignee. A notification which does not reasonably identify the rights assigned is ineffective. If requested by the account debtor, the assignee must seasonably furnish reasonable proof that the assignment has been made and unless he does so the account debtor may pay the assignor." For elaboration upon this notification requirement as it pertained to an assignment of royalties for the television showing of "Gone with the Wind," see Estate of Haas v. Metro–Goldwyn–Mayer, Inc., 617 F.2d 1136 (5th Cir.1980). Even after acquiring knowledge of the assignment, if an account debtor continues to make payments to the assignor, and if the assignee does not object to this practice, the account debtor is protected. See UCC 9–318, Comment 3; Ertel v. Radio Corp. of America, 261 Ind. 573, 575, 307 N.E.2d 471, 473 (1974).

(4) *Counterclaims and Set–Offs.* Clearly the assignee must be concerned about defenses available to the obligor, such as fraud, failure of consideration and the like. But account must also be taken of possible counterclaims and set-offs which the obligor might assert against the assignor, whether growing out of the original transaction or collateral transactions. UCC 9–318(1) provides: "Unless an account debtor has made an enforceable agreement not to assert defenses or claims arising out of a sale as provided in Section 9–206 the rights of an assignee are subject to (a) all the terms of the contract between the account debtor and assignor and any defense or claim arising therefrom; and (b) any other defense or claim of the account debtor against the assignor which accrues before the account debtor receives notification of the assignment." See Restatement (Second) § 336.

(5) *Assignor's Liability to Assignee.* If the assignee, when suing the obligor, is met with a valid defense, he or she must then consider the possibility of recourse against the assignor. Even absent the assignor's promise or representation that no defense was available, thereby furnishing the basis for an express warranty, the assignee may still be successful. "[T]he assignor of a chose in action, for a valuable consideration, impliedly warrants to the assignee that the chose assigned is a valid, subsisting obligation in his favor against the debtor to the extent to which it purports to be such, and as a general rule the assignor of a claim impliedly warrants that it is valid and that the debtor or obligator is liable to pay it, and if in fact the claim is invalid, the assignor is liable to the assignee for the amount paid for the assignment." Friedman v. Schneider, 238 Mo.App. 778, 186 S.W.2d 204, 206 (1945). See Corbin § 904; Williston § 445. It will be noted that an assignor does not warrant that the obligor is solvent or will perform the obligation. Restatement (Second) § 333(2). This points up another difference between assignment and negotiation. Unless otherwise specified in the indorsement, the indorser of a negotiable note is obliged to pay the amount due upon the instrument to a person entitled to enforce the instrument. UCC 3–415(a). In addition to liability on this indorsement contract, the indorser, if a transferor, gives the warranties stated in UCC 3–416.

(6) *Priority of Successive Assignees of the Same Right.* Suppose that AR assigned a contract right against D to AE #1 for value. Later, AR assigned the same contract right to AE #2, who takes for value and without notice. AE #2 notified D of the assignment but AE #1 did not. When the debt is due, both AE #1 and AE #2 demand full payment from D. Who should D pay? Put differently, which assignee should have priority?

American courts have rejected the English rule that priority goes to the assignee who first notified the debtor. See, e.g., Salem Trust Co. v. Manufacturers' Finance Co., 264 U.S. 182, 44 S.Ct. 266, 68 L.Ed. 628 (1924). Unless modified by statute, priority goes to the assignee whose enforceable assignment is first in time unless the second assignee, in good faith and without reason to know of the prior assignment, "gives value and obtains (i) payment or satisfaction of the obligation, (ii) judgment against the obligor, (iii) a new contract with the obligor by novation, or (iv) possession of a writing of a type customarily accepted as a symbol or as evidence of the right assigned." Restatement (Second) § 342. See Murray § 142. See generally Axelrod, *Successive Assignments—Conflicting Priorities,* 14 U.Dayton L.Rev. 295 (1989).

Under Article 9, however, priority usually goes to the first party to perfect a security in accounts by filing a financing statement. See UCC 9–312.

Comment: A Comparison of the Assignment Process and the Negotiation Process

In the assignment process the assignor transfers a contract right to the assignee. The assignor's right of performance from the obligor is thereby extinguished, in whole or in part depending upon whether it is a total or partial assignment, and the assignee acquires a right to such performance. Restatement (Second) § 317(1). A corollary is that the right is not somehow transformed in the process; it is subject to the same imperfections as before. Thus, if the obligor, when sued by the assignor, could have successfully asserted a defense (e.g., lack of consideration), this defense is also available against the assignee. Restatement (Second) § 336. Cf. UCC 9–318(1).

By contrast, a holder in due course of a negotiable instrument may obtain in the negotiation process a right superior to that of the one from whom he or she receives the instrument. One does not simply "step into the shoes" of the other. The extraordinary legal effect given to a negotiable instrument derives from the law merchant and is carefully delineated by statute. The writing must meet certain formal requirements, UCC 3–104, and must be transferred in prescribed ways. UCC 3–203. If the one to whom the instrument is transferred qualifies as a holder in due course, UCC 3–302(a), he or she takes the instrument free of many defenses. UCC 3–305. For example, in exchange for merchandise, the maker executes and delivers to the payee a negotiable promissory note for the purchase price. The payee indorses the note and delivers it to a third person, the holder, in repayment of an outstanding loan. Even though the maker is able to assert against the payee a number of ordinary defenses, such as lack or failure of consideration, the maker is not able to so defend against one who is a holder in due course.

The emergence in our legal system of the concept of negotiability has been of inestimable value in facilitating commercial transactions. It is an important part of "the triumph of the good faith purchaser," aptly characterized as "one of the most dramatic episodes in our legal history." Gilmore, *The Commercial Doctrine of Good Faith Purchase,* 63 Yale L.J. 1057 (1954). A high-energy economic system is dependent upon the free flow of commerce; accordingly, impediments to voluntary exchange should be kept to a minimum. Allowing purchaser of a right evidenced by a negotiable note to prevail, despite the availability of so-called "personal defenses" of the maker, enhances the value of negotiable paper.

It is now, however, an "unfair or deceptive act or practice" under Section 5 of the Federal Trade Commission Act for a seller who ordinarily sells or leases goods or services to consumers to enter into a consumer credit contract which does not contain the following provision in at least ten point, bold-face type:

> ANY HOLDER OF THIS CONSUMER CREDIT CONTRACT IS SUBJECT TO ALL CLAIMS AND DEFENSES WHICH THE DEBTOR COULD ASSERT AGAINST THE SELLER OF GOODS OR SERVICES OBTAINED PURSUANT HERETO OR WITH THE PROCEEDS HEREOF. RECOVERY HEREUNDER BY THE DEBTOR SHALL NOT EXCEED AMOUNTS PAID BY THE DEBTOR HEREUNDER.

16 C.F.R. § 433.2. See Sturley, *The Legal Impact of the Federal Trade Commission's Holder in Due Course Notice on a Negotiable Instrument: How Clever Are the Rascals at the FTC?,* 68 N.C.L.Rev. 953 (1990).

(B) DELEGATION OF DUTIES

To what extent can one party delegate the duty of performance created by a contract to a third party without the consent of the other party? For example, can an artist delegate a contractual duty to paint a portrait to another artist without consent of the client? If so (and this is highly dubious), suppose the other artist fails to paint. What, if anything, is the liability of the delegator?

The test for delegation under Restatement (Second) § 318 and UCC 2–210(1) [2–503(b) (1997)] turns crucially on the phrase "substantial interest":

> Restatement (Second) § 318: "(1) An obligor can properly delegate the performance of his duty to another unless the delegation is contrary to public policy or the terms of his promise. (2) Unless otherwise agreed, a promise requires performance by a particular person only to the extent that the obligee has a substantial interest in having that person perform or control the acts promised. (3) Unless the obligee agrees otherwise, neither delegation of performance nor a contract to assume the duty made with the obligor by the person delegated discharges any duty or liability of the delegating obligor."

> UCC 2–210(1): "A party may perform his duty through a delegate unless otherwise agreed or unless the other party has a substantial interest in having his original promisor perform or control the acts required by the contract. No delegation of performance relieves the party delegating of any duty to perform or any liability for breach."

Sally Beauty Co. v. Nexxus Products Co., Inc.

United States Court of Appeals, Seventh Circuit, 1986.
801 F.2d 1001.

■ CUDAHY, CIRCUIT JUDGE.

Nexxus Products Company ("Nexxus") entered into a contract with Best Barber & Beauty Supply Company, Inc. ("Best"), under which Best would be the exclusive distributor of Nexxus hair care products to barbers and hair stylists throughout most of Texas. When Best was acquired by and merged into Sally Beauty Company, Inc. ("Sally Beauty"), Nexxus cancelled the agreement. Sally Beauty is a wholly-owned subsidiary of Alberto–Culver Company ("Alberto–Culver"), a major manufacturer of hair care products and a competitor of Nexxus. Sally Beauty claims that Nexxus breached the contract by canceling; Nexxus asserts by way of defense that the contract was not assignable or, in the alternative, not assignable to Sally Beauty. The district court granted Nexxus' motion for summary judgment, ruling that the contract was one for personal services and therefore not assignable. We affirm on a different theory—that this contract could not be assigned to the wholly-owned subsidiary of a direct competitor under section 2–210 of the Uniform Commercial Code.

[The court held that the sales aspect of the distributorship dominated and that the transaction was governed by Article 2 of the UCC.]

The fact that this contract is considered a contract for the sale of goods and not for the provision of a service does not, as *Sally Beauty* suggests, mean that it is freely assignable in all circumstances. The delegation of performance under a sales contract (whether in conjunction with an assignment of rights, as here, or not) is governed by UCC section 2–210(1), Tex.Bus. & Com.Code § 2–210(a) (Vernon 1968). The UCC recognizes that in many cases an obligor will find it convenient or even necessary to relieve himself of the duty of performance under a contract, see Official Comment 1, UCC § 2–210 ("[T]his section recognizes both delegation of performance and assignability as normal and permissible incidents of a contract for the sale of goods."). The Code therefore sanctions delegation except where the delegated performance would be unsatisfactory to the obligee: "A party may perform his duty through a delegate unless otherwise agreed to or unless the other party has a substantial interest in having his original promisor perform or control the acts required by the contract." UCC § 2–210(1), Tex.Bus. & Com.Code Ann. § 2–210(a) (Vernon 1968). Consideration is given to balancing the policies of free alienability of commercial contracts and protecting the obligee from having to accept a bargain he did not contract for.

We are concerned here with the delegation of Best's duty of performance under the distribution agreement, as Nexxus terminated the agreement because it did not wish to accept Sally Beauty's substituted performance.[6] Only one Texas case has construed section 2–210 in the context of a party's delegation of performance under an executory contract. In McKinnie v. Milford, 597 S.W.2d 953 (Tex.Civ.App.1980, writ ref'd, n.r.e.), the court held that nothing in the Texas Business and Commercial Code prevented the seller of a horse from delegating to the buyer a pre-existing contractual duty to make the horse available to a third party for breeding. "[I]t is clear that Milford [the third party] had no particular interest in not allowing Stewart [the seller] to delegate the duties required by the contract. Milford was only interested in getting his two breedings per year, and such performance could only be obtained from McKinnie [the buyer] after he bought the horse from Stewart." Id. at 957. In *McKinnie,* the Texas court recognized and applied the UCC rule that bars delegation of duties if there is some reason why the non-assigning party would find performance by a delegate a substantially different thing than what he had bargained for.

---

6. If this contract is assignable, Sally Beauty would also, of course, succeed to Best's rights under the distribution agreement. But the fact situation before us must be distinguished from the assignment of contract rights that are no longer executory (e.g., the right to damages for breach or the right to payment of an account), which is considered in UCC section 2–210(2), Tex.Bus. & Com.Code Ann. § 2–210(b) (Vernon 1968), and in several of the authorities relied on by appellants. The policies underlying these two situations are different and, generally, the UCC favors assignment more strongly in the latter. See UCC § 2–210(2) (non-executory rights assignable even if agreement states otherwise).

In the exclusive distribution agreement before us, Nexxus had contracted for Best's "best efforts" in promoting the sale of Nexxus products in Texas. UCC § 2–306(2), Tex.Bus. & Com.Code Ann. § 2–306(b) (Vernon 1968), states that "[a] lawful agreement by either buyer or seller for exclusive dealing in the kind of goods concerned imposes unless otherwise agreed an obligation by the seller to use best efforts to supply the goods and by the buyer to use best efforts to promote their sale." This implied promise on Best's part was the consideration for Nexxus' promise to refrain from supplying any other distributors within Best's exclusive area. See Official Comment 5, UCC § 2–306. It was this contractual undertaking which Nexxus refused to see performed by Sally.

In ruling on Nexxus' motion for summary judgment, the district court noted: "Unlike Best, Sally Beauty is a subsidiary of one of Nexxus' direct competitors. This is a significant distinction and in the court's view, it raises serious questions regarding Sally Beauty's ability to perform the distribution agreement in the same manner as Best." Memorandum Opinion and Order at 7. In Berliner Foods Corp. v. Pillsbury Co., 633 F.Supp. 557 (D.Md.1986), the court stated the same reservation more strongly on similar facts. Berliner was an exclusive distributor of Haagen–Dazs ice cream when it was sold to Breyer's, manufacturer of a competing ice cream line. Pillsbury Co., manufacturer of Haagen–Dazs, terminated the distributorship and Berliner sued. The court noted, while weighing the factors for and against a preliminary injunction, that "it defies common sense to require a manufacturer to leave the distribution of its products to a distributor under the control of a competitor or potential competitor." Id. at 559–60.[7] We agree with these assessments and hold that Sally Beauty's position as a wholly-owned subsidiary of Alberto–Culver is sufficient to bar the delegation of Best's duties under the agreement. * * *

At oral argument, Sally Beauty argued that the case should go to trial to allow it to demonstrate that it could and would perform the contract as impartially as Best. It stressed that Sally Beauty is a "multi-line" distributor, which means that it distributes many brands and is not just a conduit for Alberto–Culver products. But we do not think that this creates a material question of fact in this case.[8] When performance of personal services is delegated, the trier merely determines that it is a personal services contract. If so, the duty is *per se* nondelegable. There is no inquiry into whether the delegate is as skilled or worthy of trust and confidence as the original obligor: the delegate was not bargained for and the obligee

---

7. The effort by the dissent to distinguish *Berliner* merely because the court there apparently assumed in passing that distributorship agreements were a species of personal service contracts must fail. The *Berliner* court emphasizes that the sale of a distributorship to a competitor of the supplier is by itself a wholly sufficient reason to terminate the distributorship.

8. We do not address here the situation in which the assignee is not completely under the control of a competitor. If the assignee were only a partially-owned subsidiary, there presumably would have to be fact-finding about the degree of control the competitor-parent had over the subsidiary's business decisions.

need not consent to the substitution. * * * The judgment of the district court is AFFIRMED.

■ POSNER, CIRCUIT JUDGE, dissenting.

[Judge Posner could find no support for the Majority's *per se* rule in either the UCC or the case law.]

My brethren find this a simple case—as simple (it seems) as if a lawyer had undertaken to represent the party opposing his client. But notions of conflict of interest are not the same in law and in business, and judges can go astray by assuming that the legal-services industry is the pattern for the entire economy. The lawyerization of America has not reached that point. Sally Beauty, though a wholly owned subsidiary of Alberto–Culver, distributes "hair care" supplies made by many different companies, which so far as appears compete with Alberto–Culver as vigorously as Nexxus does. * * *

Selling your competitor's products, or supplying inputs to your competitor, sometimes creates problems under antitrust or regulatory law—but only when the supplier or distributor has monopoly or market power and uses it to restrict a competitor's access to an essential input or to the market for the competitor's output, ... There is no suggestion that Alberto–Culver has a monopoly of "hair care" products or Sally Beauty a monopoly of distributing such products, or that Alberto–Culver would ever have ordered Sally Beauty to stop carrying Nexxus products. Far from complaining about being squeezed out of the market by the acquisition, Nexxus is complaining in effect about Sally Beauty's refusal to boycott it!

How likely is it that the acquisition of Best could hurt Nexxus? Not very. Suppose Alberto–Culver had ordered Sally Beauty to go slow in pushing Nexxus products, in the hope that sales of Alberto–Culver "hair care" products would rise. Even if they did, since the market is competitive Alberto–Culver would not reap monopoly profits. Moreover, what guarantee has Alberto–Culver that consumers would be diverted from Nexxus to it, rather than to products closer in price and quality to Nexxus products? In any event, any trivial gain in profits to Alberto–Culver would be offset by the loss of goodwill to Sally Beauty; and a cost to Sally Beauty is a cost to Alberto–Culver, its parent. Remember that Sally Beauty carries beauty supplies made by other competitors of Alberto–Culver; Best alone carries "hair care" products manufactured by Revlon, Clairol, Bristol–Myers, and L'Oreal, as well as Alberto–Culver. Will these powerful competitors continue to distribute their products through Sally Beauty if Sally Beauty displays favoritism for Alberto–Culver products? Would not such a display be a commercial disaster for Sally Beauty, and hence for its parent, Alberto–Culver? * * *

Another relevant consideration is that the contract between Nexxus and Best was for a short term. Could Alberto–Culver destroy Nexxus by failing to push its products with maximum vigor in Texas for a year? In the unlikely event that it could and did, it would be liable in damages to Nexxus for breach of the implied best-efforts term of the distribution contract. Finally, it is obvious that Sally Beauty does not have a bottleneck position in the distribution of "hair care" products, such that by refusing to promote Nexxus products vigorously it could stifle the distribution of those products in Texas; for Nexxus has found alternative distribution that it prefers—otherwise it wouldn't have repudiated the contract with Best when Best was acquired by Sally Beauty.

Not all businessmen are consistent and successful profit maximizers, so the probability that Alberto–Culver would instruct Sally Beauty to cease to push Nexxus products vigorously in Texas cannot be reckoned at zero. On this record, however, it is slight. And there is no principle of law that if something happens that trivially reduces the probability that a dealer will use his best efforts, the supplier can cancel the contract. * * * At most, so far as the record shows, Nexxus may have had grounds for "insecurity" regarding the performance by Sally Beauty of its obligation to use its best efforts to promote Nexxus products, but if so its remedy was not to cancel the contract but to demand assurances of due performance. See UCC § 2–609; Official Comment 5 to § 2–306. No such demand was made.

NOTES

(1) In the assignment of an executory bilateral contract, is the "probable intention of the assignee" to assume duties as well as rights?

(2) UCC 2–210(4) [UCC 2–503 (1997)]: "An assignment of 'the contract' or of 'all my rights under the contract' or an assignment in similar general terms is an assignment of rights and unless the language or the circumstances (as in an assignment for security) indicate the contrary, it is a delegation of performance of the duties of the assignor and its acceptance by the assignee constitutes a promise by him to perform those duties. This promise is enforceable by either the assignor or the other party to the original contract." See Continental Can Co. v. Poultry Processing, Inc., 649 F.Supp. 570, 573 (D.Me. 1986) (phrase is "term of art"); Restatement (Second) § 328(1).

(3) *The Case of "All in the Family."* Tandem Productions, Inc., producer of "All in the Family," and Columbia Broadcasting System, Inc. entered into a contract covering the distribution and syndication of the series. In a "Memorandum of Agreement," it was provided that "CBS may assign its rights hereunder in full or in part to any person, firm or corporation provided, however, that no such assignment shall relieve CBS of its obligations hereunder." Later CBS purported to assign to Viacom International, Inc. the rights it possessed to distribute and syndicate television programs, including "All in the Family." Tandem maintained that this transcended the power of assignment granted by the written agreement, insisting that CBS could only assign the right to receive distribution and syndication fees called for by the contract but not relinquish or delegate obligations. Do you agree? See Viacom International, Inc. v. Tandem Productions, Inc., 526 F.2d 593 (2d Cir.1975).

SECTION 2. THIRD PARTY BENEFICIARIES

For a consideration furnished by B (e.g., delivery of merchandise), A promises to render a performance (e.g., payment of $1,000) to T. If A refuses to abide by the commitment, may T successfully sue A for breach of contract? Have A and B conferred a contract right upon T, who was not privy to the transaction? Stated another way, is T a protected third party beneficiary of the A–B contract?

It may first be wondered why A and B would ever so agree. A's apparent purpose is the receipt of the merchandise, but what of B's? B may in this way pay a debt owed to T or may simply wish to give T the $1,000. In either situation, what objections would you expect to be asserted as a bar to recovery? That T did not pay for A's promise; i.e., did not furnish the consideration? That T was a stranger to the transaction; i.e., was not the promisee? Are these sound objections? In short, ought A and B be recognized as having the power to confer a contract right upon T?

Assuming a general willingness to recognize third party beneficiary contracts, how is a court in a particular case to determine when the third party acquires a right against the promisor? Surely one ought not be able to sue in every case where performance of the contract would somehow inure to his or her benefit. But where is the line to be drawn? What are properly to be regarded as elements of judgment?

Granted the right of a beneficiary to sue in a particular case, what is the nature of that right? What defenses can A assert against T? Moreover, after execution of the contract may A and B so act as to deprive T of any rights in the transaction?

(A) CREATION OF RIGHTS

(1) *Giving Birth to a New Principle of Law.* "The question of determining what rights one who is not a party to a contract has in its performance is one which is not free from difficulty. [T]he first recognition of such rights was in the cases now called the donee beneficiary type. Here the courts protected the interest of the person for whose benefit the performance was intended to prevent a failure of justice. The party to the contract would have no action for its breach except for nominal damages since he was not one who suffered by the promisor's default. If the beneficiary could not sue there could be no adequate recovery even though the breach was established. The next extension was made, with hesitancy on the part of some courts, to the creditor beneficiary situation." Goodrich J., in Isbrandtsen Co. v. Local 1291 of International Longshoremen's Association, 204 F.2d 495, 96–7 (3d Cir.1953).

(2) *Restatement Categories.* The first Restatement defined contract beneficiaries as follows in § 133(1): "Where performance of a promise in a contract will benefit a person other than the promisee that person is * * * (a) a donee beneficiary if it appears from the terms of the promise in view of the accompanying circumstances that the purpose of the promisee in obtaining the promise of all or part of the performance thereof is to make a gift to the beneficiary or to confer upon him a right against the promisor to some performance neither due nor supposed or asserted to be due from the promisee to the beneficiary; (b) a creditor beneficiary if no purpose to make

a gift appears from the terms of the promise in view of the accompanying circumstances and performance of the promise will satisfy an actual or supposed or asserted duty of the promisee to the beneficiary, * * * (c) an incidental beneficiary if neither the facts stated in Clause (a) nor those stated in Clause (b) exist."

(3) *The Concept of Privity and the Third Party Beneficiary Contract.* The third party beneficiary contract involves judicial recognition of the power of contracting parties to vest rights in others. The recognition of the power to assign a contract right both paves the way for validation of third party beneficiary contracts and enables one to properly analyze the so-called lack of privity objection. "Privity, in the law of contracts, is merely the name for a legal relation arising from right and obligation. For example, A, by contract, secures a promise from B. A may transfer his right of enforcement to C. C thereby succeeds to A's right of action, and, in consequence, comes into the relationship with A and B which we call privity of contract. Instead of waiting to do it by assignment, A may, at the outset, extract from B the same promise in favor of C." La Mourea v. Rhude, 209 Minn. 53, 56, 295 N.W. 304, 307 (1940).

(4) *Weakening Resistance.* For over a century Massachusetts resisted the movement in this country recognizing third party beneficiary contracts. In 1979, however, the Supreme Judicial Court of Massachusetts joined ranks with the other jurisdictions in a forthright opinion that acknowledged "the handwriting has long been on the wall." Choate, Hall & Stewart v. SCA Services, Inc., 378 Mass. 535, 546, 392 N.E.2d 1045, 1051 (1979).

Third party claimants have not fared as well in other common law jurisdictions. For example, despite the initiative in *Dutton,* the English courts, since at least the middle of the nineteenth century, have rejected third party recovery. Tweddle v. Atkinson (1861) I.B. 7 S. 393. The courts have, however, managed to fashion various "exceptions," so as to allow recovery in certain situations. Treitel, The Law of Contract 458–467 (6th ed. 1983). For a discussion of Canadian resistance, see Comment, 59 Can.B.Rev. 549 (1981).

Johnson v. Holmes Tuttle Lincoln–Mercury, Inc.

Court of Appeals of California, 1958.
160 Cal.App.2d 290, 325 P.2d 193.

■ VALLÉE, JUSTICE. Appeal from a judgment for plaintiffs as third party beneficiaries of an oral agreement to procure public liability and property damage insurance.

The agreement is alleged to have been entered into between Holmes Tuttle Lincoln–Mercury, Inc., called defendant, and Phillip R. Caldera and his wife, Ruth, in connection with the purchase by the Calderas of a new Mercury automobile from defendant on November 23, 1953.

On December 11, 1953, about three weeks after the Calderas purchased the car, Phillip Caldera was involved in an accident with the

Mercury. Plaintiffs, Willie Mae Johnson and Fletcher Jones, a passenger, were injured and Johnson's car was damaged.

Separate actions were filed by plaintiffs against Phillip Caldera. Judgments were entered May 23, 1955 in favor of plaintiff Johnson for $4,413.89, and in favor of plaintiff Jones for $2,070. These judgments remain unsatisfied.

Plaintiffs allege defendant, by its salesman Harry Rozany, had agreed with Caldera at the time the Mercury was purchased to procure "full coverage" insurance for Caldera, including public liability and property damage, for the operation of the Mercury; both Caldera and defendant understood the insurance was to be obtained for the usual term and for no less than the minimum legal limits; defendant failed to obtain the public liability and property damage insurance after Caldera had performed all of the terms of the agreement on his part. The prayer is for the amounts of the judgments obtained against Caldera with interest. In a jury trial the verdict was for plaintiffs as prayed. Defendant appeals from the judgment which followed.

On November 23, 1953 Caldera appeared with his wife, Ruth, at the showroom of defendant for the purpose of purchasing a new Mercury. One of defendant's salesmen, Harry Rozany, approached the Calderas and discussed with them the prospective purchase of a new Mercury like the one then in the showroom. After about five minutes Rozany took them to a "closing room" where terms were discussed for about an hour and the purchase consummated. The Calderas told Rozany they had a 1948 Chevrolet as a trade-in and $900 cash as a down payment. They indicated they could not afford to make payments of over $80 a month on the balance. During the discussion Caldera told Rozany he wanted "full coverage insurance," and Rozany replied, "Oh, yes you are getting it." Rozany made out the papers and sold them "another insurance," a policy by which the insurer engaged to pay the balance of the purchase price of the car in the event of the death or disability of Caldera. The premium of $2.50 to $3.00 a month was to be included in the installment payments. Rozany computed the figures in the transaction on "scratch paper." He had Caldera sign the car order and the conditional sale contract in blank. Rozany took the papers "upstairs," saying he was going to complete filling them out.

About December 2, 1953 Mrs. Caldera received by mail a copy of the conditional sale contract dated December 1, 1953 which showed fire, theft, comprehensive, and $50 deductible collision insurance thereon, but which made no reference to public liability and property damage insurance. Mrs. Caldera read only the figures. * * * Caldera first learned he had no public liability and property damage insurance after his wife went to the office of Olympic Insurance Company "to find out about the insurance." * * *

Defendant first asserts the evidence does not support the implied finding of the jury that there was a contract to procure public liability and property damage insurance between Caldera and defendant; nor does the evidence support the implied finding that plaintiffs were third party beneficiaries of a contract between Caldera and defendant. It is argued there was no consideration paid by Caldera for defendant's agreement to procure full coverage insurance, including public liability and property damage. The agreement alleged and proved was that in consideration of Caldera's purchasing the Mercury defendant would procure full coverage insurance, including public liability and property damage.

[The court found "contrary to defendant's claim" sufficient evidence of "a meeting of minds" that "full coverage" insurance meant insurance against damage cause by insured's car.]

Defendant contends plaintiffs were not third party beneficiaries. "A contract, made expressly for the benefit of a third person, may be enforced by him at any time before the parties thereto rescind it." Civ.Code, § 1559. Where one person for a valuable consideration engages with another to do some act for the benefit of a third person, and the agreement thus made has not been rescinded, the party for whose benefit the contract or promise was made, or who would enjoy the benefit of the act, may maintain an action against the promisor for the breach of his engagement. While the contract remains unrescinded, the relations of the parties are the same as though the promise had been made directly to the third party. Although the party for whose benefit the promise was made was not cognizant of it when made, it is, if adopted by him, deemed to have been made to him. He may sue on the promise. Where a promise is made to benefit a third party on the happening of a certain contingency, the third party may enforce the contract on the occurrence of that contingency. 12 Cal.Jur.2d 493, § 261. The action by a third party beneficiary for the breach of the promisor's engagement does not rest on the ground of any actual or supposed relationship between the parties but on the broad and more satisfactory basis that the law, operating on the acts of the parties, creates the duty, establishes a privity, and implies the promise and obligation on which the action is founded. Washer v. Independent M. and D. Co., 142 Cal. 702, 708–709, 76 P. 654.

It is not necessary that the beneficiary be named and identified as an individual; a third party may enforce a contract if he can show he is a member of a class for whose benefit it was made. ... It is no objection to the maintenance of an action by a third party that a suit might be brought also against the one to whom the promise was made. ...

The test for determining whether a contract was made for the benefit of a third person is whether an intent to benefit a third person appears from the terms of the contract. ... If the terms of the contract necessarily require the promisor to confer a benefit on a third person, then the contract, and hence the parties thereto, contemplate a benefit to the third person. The parties are presumed to intend the consequences of a performance of the contract. It is held that a person injured may sue on a contract for the benefit of all members of the public who are so injured since the happening of the injury sufficiently determines his identity and right of action. Levy v. Daniels' U–Drive Auto Renting Co., 108 Conn. 333, 143 A. 163, 165, 61 A.L.R. 846. * * *

There is no escape from the conclusion that the agreement between defendant and Caldera was not for the sole benefit of the latter but that it was intended to inure to the benefit of third persons who might be protected by a full coverage policy. The intent to confer a benefit on anyone to whom Caldera might become liable as a result of a hazard incident to ownership and operation of the Mercury is obvious. This is precisely what Caldera wanted as a means of obtaining a benefit to himself. It must have been in the contemplation of the parties when Rozany agreed to procure public liability and property damage insurance that injury to third persons might result from ownership and operation of the Mercury. It was reasonable for the jury to infer that Caldera, in making the agreement with defendant, desired and intended that such persons be protected in the event of an accident with the Mercury. The jury's finding that there was a third party beneficiary contract breached by defendant to plaintiffs' damage is amply supported by the record. * * *

Affirmed.

NOTES

(1) *"A Key Which Unlocks Many of the Cases."* Professors Calamari and Perillo suggest the following as "a key which unlocks many of the cases": the determination of to whom the performance is to be rendered. They elaborate: "If the performance is to run directly to the promisee, the third party is ordinarily an unprotected incidental beneficiary, but if it is to run to the third party, he is ordinarily an intended beneficiary with enforceable rights. Thus, for example, if a bank promised A a loan to pay his creditors, the creditors would most probably be deemed incidental beneficiaries; but if the bank promised to pay the money directly to creditors they generally would be classified as intended beneficiaries." Calamari & Perillo, Contracts § 17–2 (2d ed. 1977). Does this "key" work in the instant case?

(2) *"Donee" and "Creditor" Beneficiaries: Categorical Imperatives?* The first Restatement distinction between "creditor" and "donee" beneficiaries is not preserved in the revised Restatement. Definition of donees as recipients of a "gift promise" and creditors as recipients of "a promise to discharge the promisee's duty" arguably compels courts to restrict recovery to cases in which a "gift" or "debt" moving from promisee to third party exists in a legal or quasi-legal sense. The creditor category is on its face limited, since it includes only third parties who either possess a legal "right ... against the promisee" presently barred by technicalities or to whom the promisee owes an "actual or supposed or asserted duty." Although the donee category is more open-ended, use of the terms "donee" and "gift" at least provides opportunities for courts to restrict recovery to cases where traditional "donative intent" is clear. See, e.g., United States v. Inorganics, Inc., 109 F.Supp. 576, 579–80 (E.D.Tenn. 1952), where the court denied relief because no "beneficial impulse" existed.

Restatement (Second) § 302 provides: "(1) Unless otherwise agreed between promisor and promisee, a beneficiary of a promise is an intended beneficiary if recognition of a right to performance in the beneficiary is appropriate to effectuate the intention of the parties and either (a) the performance of the promise will satisfy an obligation of the promisee to pay money to the beneficiary; or (b) the circumstances indicate that the promisee intends to give the beneficiary the benefit of the promised performance. (2) An incidental beneficiary is a beneficiary who is not an intended beneficiary." See generally Note, *Third Party Beneficiaries and the Restatement (Second) of Contracts,* 67 Cornell L.Rev. 880 (1982).

Was the desired avoidance of the old categories complete? It seems the drafters did not come up with an entirely "new" test; many courts have long employed variations on the intent theme to resolve third party beneficiary problems. See Corbin § 776.

(3) *The Use, Misuse and Limitations of the "Intention to Benefit" Standard.* The "travail" experienced during the emergence of the third party beneficiary contract is mild compared to that accompanying the efforts at delineation. The task of differentiating the protected and the unprotected (or incidental) beneficiary has proven to be extraordinarily difficult.

Ostensibly the courts seek to ascertain the manifested "intention" of the contracting parties. But in the litigated cases there is rarely any clear manifestation of intention; no explicit provision is made, one way or the other, relative to rights of third persons who may in some way benefit from performance of the contract. Moreover, the emphasis upon an elusive "intention" criterion, often to the exclusion of all other considerations, precludes an analysis that is responsive to what might otherwise be regarded as appropriate policy considerations. Because of the imprecision of the intent to benefit approach, one writer maintains that "[t]he major need of third party beneficiary law is to expand the scope of inquiry and thereby bring decisions in line with both the commercial needs and policies of the market in which the parties are functioning and more general concepts of equity and justice." Note, *Third Party Beneficiaries and the Intention Standard: A Search for Rational Contract Decision–Making,* 54 Va. L.Rev. 1166, 1172 (1968).

Hale v. Groce

Supreme Court of Oregon, 1987.
304 Or. 281, 744 P.2d 1289.

■ LINDE, JUSTICE.

Defendant, who is an attorney, was directed by a client to prepare testamentary instruments and to include a bequest of a specified sum to plaintiff. After the client's death, it was discovered that the gift was not included either in the will or in a related trust instrument. After an unsuccessful attempt to obtain judicial reformation of the will and trust, plaintiff brought the present action for damages against the attorney.

The complaint alleged as two separate claims, first, that defendant was negligent in a number of particulars and, second, that he failed to carry out a contractual promise to his client, the decedent, which the decedent had intended specifically for the benefit of plaintiff. In other states plaintiffs in such cases have sometimes been allowed to recover on one or both of these theories, as negligently injured parties or as third-party beneficiaries under a contract. It is a new question in this court. * *. *

We agree that the beneficiary in [this type of case] is not only a plausible but a classic "intended" third-party beneficiary of the lawyer's promise to his client within the rule of Restatement section 302(1)(b) and may enforce the duty so created, as stated id. section 304. See, e.g., Johnson v. Doughty, 236 Or. 78, 83, 385 P.2d 760 (1963), Parker v. Jeffery, 26 Or. 186, 189, 37 P. 712 (1894) (stating rule that a contract may be enforced by one for whose benefit it was intended). The promise, of course, was not that the lawyer would pay plaintiff the stipulated sum, and it is too late for the lawyer to perform the promise that he did make, but this does not preclude an action for damages for the nonperformance. In principle, such an action is available to one in plaintiff's position. * * *

[W]e reverse so much of the decision of the Court of Appeals as affirmed the dismissal of the contract claim.

NOTES

(1) *"The Assault Upon the Citadel of Privity is Proceeding in These Days Apace."* One of the most dramatic legal developments in recent decades has involved the enlargement of the rights of third parties not in "privity" with the defendant. One facet is the growing enlargement of the category of protected beneficiaries of third party beneficiary contracts. Even more spectacular has been the expansion of tort recovery by third persons. See, e.g., Prosser, *The Assault on the Citadel (Strict Liability to the Consumers)*, 69 Yale L.J. 1099 (1960); Prosser, *The Fall of the Citadel (Strict Liability to the Consumer)*, 50 Minn.L.Rev. 791 (1966). In the area of contracted-for services there has been scant recognition of strict liability to third persons, but there has been a pronounced extension of liability predicated upon the contractor's negligence in performing promised service. For example, in an attorney malpractice case, the court emphasized the special status of an attorney: "Public policy requires that the attorney exercise his position of trust and superior knowledge responsibly so as not to affect adversely persons whose rights and interests are certain and foreseeable." Heyer v. Flaig, 70 Cal.2d 223, 227, 74 Cal.Rptr. 225, 229, 449 P.2d 161, 165 (1969) (intended beneficiaries recovered where attorney failed to revise will in accordance with decedent's instructions). Moreover, the court pointed out that if the third parties could not recover, no one could do so.

What are the competing policy considerations? California courts have balanced the following factors: (1) the extent to which the transaction was intended to affect the plaintiff; (2) the foreseeability of harm to plaintiff; (3) the degree of certainty that plaintiff suffered injury; (4) the closeness of connection between the defendant's conduct and injuries suffered; (5) the moral blame attached to the defendant's conduct; (6) the policy of preventing future harm. Biakanja v. Irving, 49 Cal.2d 647, 650, 320 P.2d 16, 19 (1958).

(2) *The Case of Alleged Referee Malpractice.* In a basketball game between Purdue and Iowa on March 6, 1982, James C. Bain, a referee, called a foul on an Iowa player, which resulted in free throws that gave Purdue a last-minute victory. John and Karen Gillispie operated a store, known as Hawkeye John's

Trading Post, that specialized in University of Iowa sports memorabilia. Alleging that Bain's performance was below the standard of competence required of a professional referee, they sought damages for malpractice (asserting that the Iowa loss eliminated it from the Big Ten championship and destroyed a potential market for Gillispies' memorabilia touting Iowa as a Big Ten champion) and as beneficiaries of a contract between Bain and the Big Ten. In rejecting both tort and contract claims, the trial judge observed: "Heaven knows what uncharted morass a court would find itself in if it were to hold that an athletic official subjects himself to liability every time he might make a questionable call. The possibilities are mind boggling." The Court of Appeals affirmed. Bain v. Gillispie, 357 N.W.2d 47 (Iowa App.1984).

(3) *The Privity Barrier and Economic Loss.* In J'Aire Corp. v. Gregory, 24 Cal.3d 799, 157 Cal.Rptr. 407, 598 P.2d 60 (1979), a contractor agreed with Owner to renovate a building. Tenant, operator of a restaurant in the building, sued Contractor, based upon alleged negligence of Contractor in delaying completion of the work and resulting in loss of business by Tenant. Applying the "special relationship" factors referred to in note 1, the court concluded: "Where the risk of harm is foreseeable, as it was in the present case, an injury to the plaintiff's economic interests should not go uncompensated merely because it was unaccompanied by any injury to his person or property." 24 Cal.3d at 805, 157 Cal.Rptr. at 411. Tenant chose to sue Contractor rather than Owner, because it "did not wish to upset its friendly relations with the building owner and thereby jeopardize the continuation of the lease arrangement." Schwartz, *Economic Loss in American Tort Law: The Examples of J'Aire and of Products Liability,* 23 San Diego L.Rev. 37, 41 (1986).

The privity barrier has been lowered for tort actions, whether negligence or strict liability, where the plaintiff seeks compensation for personal injury or property damage, but, by and large, the citadel still stands where the plaintiff seeks recovery of economic loss. See, e.g., East River S.S. Corp. v. Transamerica Delaval, Inc., 476 U.S. 858, 106 S.Ct. 2295, 90 L.Ed.2d 865 (1986). For an argument that the privity defenses should be abolished in economic loss cases, see Speidel, *Warranty Theory, Economic Loss, and the Privity Requirement: Once More Into the Void,* 67 B.U.L.Rev. 9 (1987).

(4) *Owner as Beneficiary of Contract between Subcontractor and Contractor.* In the ordinary case an owner is not recognized as a protected beneficiary of the contract between the general contractor and a subcontractor. See, e.g., Vogel v. Reed Supply Co., 277 N.C. 119, 177 S.E.2d 273 (1970). The most frequently assigned reason is that it is the contractor's duty to erect and deliver the complete structure according to plans and specifications; the subcontractor's work does not discharge that duty to any extent. Corbin § 787. Courts may be persuaded to depart from the usual rule because of special language in the contract between the contractor and the subcontractor manifesting an intention to benefit the owner. See, e.g., Oliver B. Cannon & Son, Inc. v. Dorr–Oliver, Inc., 336 A.2d 211 (Del.1975).

(5) *Interrelationship of Third Party Beneficiary and Promissory Estoppel.* The law pertaining to promissory estoppel and to the rights of third persons to sue on contracts made for their benefit when combined has the potential for dramatic growth. Two types of situations come to mind. First, the promisor makes a promise in a contract that would not normally be regarded as being for

the third party's benefit, but the latter nonetheless relies on the promise. See Restatement § 90 (covering reliance "on the part of the promisee *or a third person*"). Second, a gratuitous promise causes the promisee to rely, and a third party claims as beneficiary of the legal relationship thereby created.

Zigas v. Superior Court, Etc.

California Court of Appeal, 1981.
120 Cal.App.3d 827, 174 Cal.Rptr. 806.

■ FEINBERG, ASSOCIATE JUSTICE.

Petitioners are tenants of an apartment building at 2000 Broadway in San Francisco, which was financed with a federally insured mortgage in excess of $5 million, pursuant to the National Housing Act (12 U.S.C. § 1701 et seq.) (the Act) and the regulations promulgated thereunder (24 C.F.R. § 207 et seq.). They seek in a class action, inter alia, damages for the landlords' (real parties in interest) violation of a provision of the financing agreement which requires that the landlords charge no more than the Department of Housing and Urban Development (HUD) approved schedule of rents. The trial court has sustained demurrers without leave to amend to 5 causes of action of 15 alleged, apparently on the ground that there is no right in the tenants to enforce the provisions of an agreement between their landlords and the federal government.

Petitioners allege that their landlords were required under their contract with HUD to file a maximum rental schedule with HUD and to refrain from charging more than those rents without the prior approval of the Secretary of HUD. Petitioners further allege that real parties are, and have been, charging rent in excess of the maximums set out in the rental schedule; the complaint avers that real parties have collected excessive rents and fees in an amount exceeding $2 million.

In addition to sustaining demurrers as to the third-party causes of action, the trial court granted real parties' motion to strike all references to the Act, the regulations promulgated thereunder, and the terms of the agreement between HUD and real parties. It is these orders sustaining the demurrers and granting the motion to strike that petitioners seek to have set aside. * * *

At this juncture, we conclude as follows: Granted that the National Housing Act does not create a *federal* statutory right of action in petitioners, nevertheless, they may have standing to sue based on a cause of action under applicable state law.

We turn now to the question of whether petitioners have a cause of action under California law. * * *

California law clearly allows third-party suits for breaches of contract where no government agency is a party to the contract. (Civ.Code, § 1559.) Whether such suits are allowed when the government contracts with a private party depends upon analysis of the decisions in Shell v. Schmidt

(1954) 126 Cal.App.2d 279, 272 P.2d 82, and Martinez v. Socoma Companies, Inc., supra, 11 Cal.3d 394, 113 Cal.Rptr. 585, 521 P.2d 841.

In *Shell,* plaintiffs sued as third-party beneficiaries to defendant's contract with the Federal Housing Authority (FHA). The contract entailed an agreement by the defendant to build homes for sale to veterans according to plans and specifications submitted by the defendant to FHA in return for which FHA gave priorities to the defendant to secure the materials necessary for the building.

In deciding that plaintiffs had standing to enforce the terms of the contract between the defendant and the FHA, the *Shell* court relied on common law principles as embodied in Civil Code section 1559, which states: "A contract, made expressly for the benefit of a third person, may be enforced by him at any time before the parties thereto rescind it." Applying this provision to the facts before it, the *Shell* court observed: "Once it is established that the relationship between the contractor and the government is contractual, it follows that veterans purchasing homes, that is, the class intended to be protected by that contract, are third party beneficiaries of that contract. As already pointed out, the statute and the regulations passed thereunder resulting in the contract were passed to aid and assist veterans and for their benefit. Purchasing veterans constitute the class intended to be benefitted, and the contract must therefore be for their benefit." (Id., 126 Cal.App.2d at p. 290, 272 P.2d 82.)

It is evident that petitioners are entitled to maintain a third-party cause of action under the *Shell* rationale. Real parties do not dispute the contractual nature of their relationship with HUD. And it is clear that a requirement of HUD approval of rent increases could *only* benefit the tenants.

Furthermore, even the most cursory review of the statutes and regulations which resulted in the contract in the present case leads to the conclusion that the tenants constitute the class which Congress intended to benefit. As stated in 12 United States Code section 1701t: "The Congress affirms the national goal, as set forth in section 1441 of Title 42, of 'a decent home under a suitable living environment for every American family.'" Section 1713(b) of Title 12, United States Code, also provides, in part: "*The insurance of mortgages under this section is intended to facilitate particularly the production of rental accommodations, at reasonable rents,* . . . The Secretary is, therefore, authorized . . . to take action, by regulation or otherwise, which will direct the benefits of mortgage insurance hereunder primarily to those projects which make adequate provision for families with children, and *in which every effort has been made to achieve moderate rental charges.*" (Emphasis added, see also 24 C.F.R. § 207.19(e)). * * *

In the subsequent case of Martinez v. Socoma Companies, Inc., supra, 11 Cal.3d 394, 113 Cal.Rptr. 585, 521 P.2d 841, the court approved of the result in *Shell* but, at the same time, applied a different standard.[2]

---

2. The *Martinez* court approved of the result in *Shell,* based upon a finding that the legislation under which the homes in *Shell* were built included a provision empowering

Plaintiffs in *Martinez* sought to enforce the terms of a contract between Socoma Companies, Inc. and the Secretary of Labor. Under this agreement, defendants received government funds in exchange for a promise to hire and train "hard core unemployed" residents of a "Special Impact Area" in East Los Angeles. Defendants failed to perform, and plaintiffs, who were residents of East Los Angeles and members of the class which the government intended to benefit, sought to recover under the contract.

In holding that the plaintiffs had no standing to sue as third-party beneficiaries, the *Martinez* court adopted a more restrictive standard than that embodied in Civil Code section 1559, choosing instead to be guided by the principles set forth in section 145 of the Restatement of Contracts: " 'A promisor bound to the United States or to a State or municipality by contract to do an act or render a service to some or all of the members of the public, is subject to no duty under the contract to such members to give compensation for the injurious consequences of performing or attempting to perform it, or of failing to do so, unless, ... *an intention is manifested in the contract,* as interpreted in the light of the circumstances surrounding its formation, *that the promisor shall compensate members of the public for such injurious consequences....*' " (Martinez v. Socoma Companies, Inc., supra, at pp. 401–402, 113 Cal.Rptr. 585, 521 P.2d 841; City & County of San Francisco v. Western Air Lines, Inc. (1962) 204 Cal.App.2d 105, 121, 22 Cal.Rptr. 216; Rest., Contracts, *supra,* § 145.)[3]

Thus, under *Martinez,* standing to sue as a third-party beneficiary to a government contract depends on the intent of the parties as manifested by the contract and the circumstances surrounding its formation. "Insofar as intent to benefit a third person is important in determining his right to bring an action under a contract, it is sufficient that the promisor must have understood that the promisee had such intent. No specific manifestation by the promisor of an intent to benefit the third person is required." (Lucas v. Hamm (1961) 56 Cal.2d 583, 591, 15 Cal.Rptr. 821, 364 P.2d 685.) We therefore must determine, from the terms of the contract between HUD and real parties and the attendant circumstances, whether there was manifested an intention that petitioners be compensated in the event of real parties' nonperformance. Mindful of the rule that "[w]hen a complaint is based on a written contract which it sets out in full, a general demurrer

the government to obtain payment by the contractor to the veteran purchasers for deficiencies resulting from failure to comply with specifications. (*Martinez, supra,* at p. 403, 113 Cal.Rptr. 585, 521 P.2d 841.) Thus, the intent to compensate which Restatement, Contracts, section 145 requires was present. However, the *Shell* court made no mention of section 145.

3. It has been suggested that section 145 was meant only to preclude lawsuits for *consequential* damages arising out of government contracts, because the resulting potential liability may be disproportionately burdensome in relation to the value of the promised performance. (See Rest., Contracts, *supra,* § 145, illus. 1 and 2; 44 A.L.I. Proceedings 331 (1967).) Thus, the underlying rationale of section 145 is inapplicable where, as here, the money sought is not a *consequence* of the breach, it is the breach. In such a situation, standard third-party beneficiary doctrines should apply. (See Note 88 Harv.L.Rev. 646, 650–651.)

to the complaint admits not only the contents of the instrument but also any pleaded meaning to which the instrument is reasonably susceptible". (Martinez v. Socoma Companies, Inc., supra, 11 Cal.3d at p. 400, 113 Cal.Rptr. 585, 521 P.2d 841) and focusing upon the precepts of *Martinez* as to standing, we are of the view that the case falls within *Shell;* that is to say, appellants were direct beneficiaries of the contract and have standing, and not, as in *Martinez,* incidental beneficiaries without standing.

We explicate:

1.   In *Martinez,* the contract between the government and Socoma provided that if Socoma breached the agreement, Socoma would refund to the government that which the government had paid Socoma pursuant to the contract between them. Thus, it is clear in *Martinez* that it was the government that was out of pocket as a consequence of the breach and should be reimbursed therefor, not the people to be trained and given jobs. In the case at bench, as in *Shell,* the government suffered no loss as a consequence of the breach, it was the renter here and the veteran purchaser in *Shell* that suffered the direct pecuniary loss.

2.   Unlike *Martinez,* too, in the case at bench, no governmental administrative procedure was provided for the resolution of disputes arising under the agreement. Thus, to permit this litigation would in no way affect the "efficiency and uniformity of interpretation fostered by these administrative procedures." (Martinez v. Socoma Companies, Inc., supra, 11 Cal.3d at p. 402, 113 Cal.Rptr. 585, 521 P.2d 841.) On the contrary, as we earlier noted, lawsuits such as this promote the federal interest by inducing compliance with HUD agreements.

3.   In *Martinez,* the court held that "To allow plaintiffs' claim would nullify the limited liability for which defendants bargained and which the Government may well have held out as an inducement in negotiating the contracts." (At p. 403, 113 Cal.Rptr. 585, 521 P.2d 841, fn. omitted.) Here, there is no "limited liability." As we shall point out, real parties are liable under the agreement, *without limitation,* for breach of the agreement.

4.   Further, in *Martinez,* the contracts "were designed not to benefit individuals as such but to utilize the training and employment of disadvantaged persons as a means of improving the East Los Angeles neighborhood." (At p. 406, 113 Cal.Rptr. 585, 521 P.2d 841.) Moreover, the training and employment programs were but one aspect of a "broad, long-range objective" (*id.*) contemplated by the agreement and designed to benefit not only those to be trained and employed but also "other local enterprises and the government itself through reduction of law enforcement and welfare costs." (*Id.*) * * *

5.   Finally, we believe the agreement itself manifests an intent to make tenants direct beneficiaries, *not* incidental beneficiaries, of real parties' promise to charge no more than the HUD approved rent schedule.

Section 4(a) and 4(c) of the agreement, providing that there can be no increase in rental fees, over the approved rent schedule, without the prior approval in writing of HUD, were obviously designed to protect the tenant against arbitrary increases in rents, precisely that which is alleged to have occurred here. Certainly, it was not intended to benefit the Government as a guarantor of the mortgage.

Furthermore, the provision in section 11(d) of the agreement, authorizing the Secretary of HUD to "[a]pply to any court . . . for specific performance . . ., for an injunction against any violation . . . or *for such other relief as may be appropriate*" (emphasis added) would entitle the secretary to seek restitution on behalf of the tenants overcharged, for such relief would surely be "appropriate." (See Porter v. Warner Co. (1946) 328 U.S. 395, 66 S.Ct. 1086, 90 L.Ed. 1332.) Thus, there was an intent upon the part of the government in executing the agreement with real parties, to secure the return of any rents exacted in excess of the rent schedule.

We are supported in our view by section 17 of the Agreement which specifically provides that real parties are personally liable, "(a) for funds . . . of the project coming into their hands which, by the provisions [of the Agreement] *they are not entitled to retain;* and (b) for their own acts and deeds or acts and deeds of other [sic] which they have authorized in violation of the provisions [of the Agreement]." (Emphasis added.)

By the allegations of the complaint, real parties have "retained" in excess of two million ($2,000,000) dollars in violation of the Agreement. Therefore, they are liable for that sum. To whom should they be liable? To ask the question is to answer it. It is not the government from whom the money was exacted; it was taken from the tenants. Therefore, it should be returned to the tenants.

In the face of this evidence of intent to direct the benefits of mortgage insurance to the tenants of the facilities involved, real parties argue that petitioners have no standing to sue because enforcement of the agreement is vested solely in the Secretary. They point to 12 United States Code section 1731a, which empowers the Secretary to refuse the benefits of participation to any mortgagor who violates the terms of the agreement. However, section 1731a's authorization does not constitute the exclusive remedy for enforcement of the agreement by the Secretary or by third parties. As stated by the court in Shell v. Schmidt, supra, 126 Cal.App.2d at p. 287, 272 P.2d 82: "This fundamental purpose would, in many cases, be defeated if the statute were interpreted so as to deprive the veterans of their normal remedies to the benefit of defaulting contractors—the very class it was the purpose of the statute to protect the veterans against. It must be held, therefore, that the enumeration of remedies in the statute merely created new enumerated remedies and was not intended to and did not deprive the veterans of any action for fraud or breach of contract that they might have under general contract principles." * * *

Thus, for reasons we have set forth, appellants are entitled to maintain a third-party beneficiary action against real parties.

NOTES

(1) One writer, in commenting upon *Martinez,* underscores a particular difficulty in utilizing the "intention to benefit" standard when the Federal

government is one of the contracting parties: "The relevant intent to be divined is no longer that of a single individual or entity, but rather that of an amalgam of legislative bodies, administrative agencies, and government officials—each of whom may have differing expectations and objectives with regard to the contract." Recent Cases, 88 Harv.L.Rev. 646, 651–52 (1975). Since the government's decision to benefit a certain group through a contract is usually based on broad policy objectives, it is urged that these objectives be taken into account in determining the rights of the various beneficiaries. The author draws an analogy to the question of whether a court should imply a private right of action from a statute: "When implying a private right of action, courts have carefully considered the impact of an additional remedy in the hands of private parties on the legislative policy underlying the statute. Courts tend to imply a right of action when there is evidence that existing remedies are inadequate and that additional remedies would increase the likelihood of compliance and afford direct relief to a class which the legislature wished to protect. Strong arguments against allowing such a right arise when it would interfere with the policy goals of the legislature by imposing disproportionate liability or impinging excessively on administrative discretion." Id. at 653.

(2) *Problems: Varieties of Third Party Beneficiary Controversy.* (a) *The Case of the Ingested Birds.* A jet crashed because of the ingestion of a large number of birds swarming over the airport and an adjacent garbage dump. Are injured passengers entitled to sue as third party beneficiaries of a contract between the Federal Aviation Administration and the County under which the latter agreed "to restrict the use of land adjacent to or in the vicinity of the airport to activities and purposes compatible with normal airport operations including landing and take-off of aircraft"? See Miree v. United States, 538 F.2d 643 (5th Cir.1976).

(b) *The Case of the Striking Ferry Workers.* Union ferry workers went out on strike in violation of a collective bargaining agreement with a State agency, thereby causing a cessation of normal ferry service during a holiday weekend. Could a resort owner, who lost bookings, sue as third party beneficiary of this contract? See Burke & Thomas, Inc. v. International Organization of Masters, Mates & Pilots, 92 Wn.2d 762, 600 P.2d 1282 (1979).

(c) *The Case of the Unimproved Roads.* Developer, in order to obtain approval of subdivision plat, agreed with County to construct certain road improvements. Developer failed to keep its commitment. Can lot owners in the subdivision sue as third party beneficiaries of the Developer/County contract? See Vale Dean Canyon Homeowners Association v. Dean, 100 Or.App. 158, 785 P.2d 772 (1990).

(d) *The Case of the Parking Meter Contract.* City entered into a contract with Company for the maintenance of parking meters, the contract specifying certain minimum wages and working conditions. Employees of Company seek to persuade the court that they are third party beneficiaries of this contract. Will they succeed? See Alicea v. City of New York, 145 A.D.2d 315, 534 N.Y.S.2d 983 (1988).

(e) *The Case of the Ungrateful Medical Student.* A scholarship fund agreed to pay a medical student $200 monthly during his time in medical school, in exchange for his promise to practice upon graduation in a specified area. Are the residents of the area third party beneficiaries of this contract? See Suthers v. Booker Hospital District, 543 S.W.2d 723 (Tex.Civ.App.1976).

(f) *The Case of the Cable Television Subscribers.* City granted franchise to television cable company, prescribing a rate schedule. Could subscribers bring an action as third party beneficiaries to recover damages for violation of the schedule? See Bush v. Upper Valley Telecable Co., 96 Idaho 83, 524 P.2d 1055 (1973).

(g) *The Case of the Bank's Loan Commitment.* Vendor contracts to sell land to Purchaser, conditional upon Purchaser securing loan. Bank makes the loan commitment to Purchaser and then reneges. Is Vendor an intended beneficiary of the Bank–Purchaser contract? See Khabbaz v. Swartz, 319 N.W.2d 279 (Iowa 1982).

(h) *The Case of the Undelivered Machine.* Company A, in need of a particular type of machine, contacts Company B. B learns that yet another company, Company C, owns such a machine. B asks A to examine the machine on C's premises. A does so and thereafter enters into a contract with B to buy the machine. B then contracts with C for the purchase of the machine, the contract providing that shipment is to be direct to A and the latter is to pay the freight. Later A, B and C enter into negotiations whereby the delivery date specified in the contracts is extended. Thereafter, A and B get into a dispute (on an unrelated matter) and B directs C to ship the machine to yet another party. C does so. Is A a protected beneficiary of the B/C contract? See Corrugated Paper Products, Inc. v. Longview Fibre Co., 868 F.2d 908 (7th Cir.1989).

(i) *The Case of the Federal Tax Lien.* Taxpayer underpaid federal income taxes, and the United States secured a tax lien. Thereafter, Taxpayer and his wife executed a property settlement in contemplation of their impending divorce. The agreement required the taxpayer to convey certain property to his wife, who was required, in turn, to sell the property and was authorized to retain any proceeds of sale after existing liens and mortgages were paid off. Was the United States a third party beneficiary of this agreement? See United States v. Wood, 877 F.2d 453 (6th Cir.1989).

(j) *The Case of the Pre–Paid Legal Plan.* The Fraternal Order of Police made available to "a member and his eligible dependents" a pre-paid legal plan. One of the services under the plan was described as "[d]omestic problems— including divorce, legal separation, adoption of children, change of name." A law firm servicing the plan represented a member in a divorce action. His wife also requested representation by the firm, but was refused on grounds of conflict of interest. She then retained other counsel and later claimed reimbursement from the plan for her lawyer's fees as a third party beneficiary of the contract. What result? See Baltimore City Lodge No. 3 of Fraternal Order of Police, Inc. v. Mantegna, 61 Md.App. 694, 487 A.2d 1252 (1985).

(k) *The Case of the Injured Tenant.* Was a tenant, who was injured during an electrical blackout, an intended beneficiary of contract between electric company and landlord? See Shubitz v. Consolidated Edison Co., 59 Misc.2d 732, 301 N.Y.S.2d 926 (1969). Cf. Koch v. Consolidated Edison Co., 62 N.Y.2d 548, 479 N.Y.S.2d 163, 468 N.E.2d 1 (1984) (suit by city and public benefit corporations to recover damages allegedly sustained from utility's gross negligence that caused citywide blackout).

(*l*) *The Case of the Stranded Motorist.* An oil company had a contract with the New York State Thruway Authority, under which it had the exclusive right to service cars on the thruway. The company promised to provide roadside automobile service to disabled vehicles within thirty minutes from the time called. The decedent's car had a flat tire at about 3:00 P.M. About an hour later a state trooper stopped by and radioed a request for assistance to the oil company. Not having received any assistance by 6:00 P.M., the decedent attempted to change the tire himself. In doing so he experienced difficulty and complained of chest pains. He was taken to a hospital and died 28 days later. Was the decedent, as user of the thruway, a third party beneficiary of the contract between the oil company and the thruway authority? See Kornblut v. Chevron Oil Co., 62 A.D.2d 831, 407 N.Y.S.2d 498 (1978).

(m) *The Case of the Housing Project Tenants.* The owners of a housing project entered into a contract with the Secretary of Housing and Urban Development. One of the provisions of this "Regulatory Agreement" obligated the owners to maintain the premises in good repair and condition. Citing numerous failures to properly maintain the premises, tenants asserted rights as third party beneficiaries. What result? See Little v. Union Trust Co. of Maryland, 45 Md.App. 178, 412 A.2d 1251 (1980); Falzarano v. United States, 607 F.2d 506 (1st Cir.1979). Cf. Holbrook v. Pitt, 643 F.2d 1261 (7th Cir.1981) (project tenants sue for housing assistance payments under contract between owner and Department of Housing and Urban Development); Ayala v. Boston Housing Authority, 404 Mass. 689, 536 N.E.2d 1082 (1989) (tenants sue city housing authority for failing to inspect for lead paint hazards and for failing to enforce elimination of those hazards).

(n) *The Case of the Defective Appraisal.* Purchaser signed a contract to purchase certain property, conditional upon his obtaining a loan. Upon applying for a loan, a bank officer informed him that there would have to be an appraisal of the property before the loan could be approved. The purchaser paid the bank $100 for the appraisal, and the bank arranged for the defendant to do the appraisal. If the defendant-appraiser negligently failed to discover, and to disclose in his report, serious structural defects in the property, what are the purchaser's prospects of recovery? Upon what theory? See Alva v. Cloninger, 51 N.C.App. 602, 277 S.E.2d 535 (1981).

(o) *The Case of the Undelivered Body.* The children of Rozena Neal, deceased, arranged with Inman Nationwide Shipping to transport their mother's body to Alabama for burial. Inman, in turn, contracted with Republic Airlines, which, through some error, delayed the shipment. Could the children claim as third party beneficiaries of the Inman/Republic contract? See Neal v. Republic Airlines, Inc., 605 F.Supp. 1145 (N.D.Ill.1985).

(p) *The Case of the Fake Diamond Ring.* Fiance buys "diamond" ring from Jeweler and gives it to his prospective bride as an engagement ring. The ring turns out to be nothing more than "cut glass or cubic zirconia." Can she maintain a suit for breach of contract as a third party beneficiary? See Warren v. Monahan Beaches Jewelry Center, Inc., 548 So.2d 870 (Fla.App.1989).

(B) NATURE OF RIGHTS

Tweeddale v. Tweeddale

Supreme Court of Wisconsin, 1903.
116 Wis. 517, 93 N.W. 440.

[The defendant, Daniel Tweeddale, in exchange for consideration received from his mother, gave the latter a bond for support secured by a mortgage on certain land. The bond indebtedness was $1,350, conditioned, among other things, that in case the defendant should sell the land, $1,200 should immediately become due from him to his mother, $50 should likewise become due to his sister, and $100 to his brother, the plaintiff Edward Tweeddale. Subsequently, the defendant did sell the land, making operative the foregoing promises. The defendant made a settlement with his mother, fully discharging him of all obligation to her, and she released the mortgage. The plaintiff brought a foreclosure action, insisting that such release did not bar him from recovery. Neither the plaintiff nor his sister knew that the bond and mortgage made any provision for them until after the mortgage was discharged. The trial court held that plaintiff had no cause of action, and ordered the complaint dismissed.]

■ MARSHALL, J. * * * [T]he turning point in the case, in the mind of the circuit judge, we apprehend, was that the beneficiaries did not know of the agreement and did not accept the same or in any way become parties thereto till their mother, with the consent of Daniel Tweeddale, rescinded the transaction. * * * Whether the benefit secured to the third person is a gift, strictly so called, or one intended, when realized, to discharge some liability of such promisee to the third person does not change the situation. It is the exchange of promises between the immediate parties, and the operation of law thereon, that binds the promisor to the third person. The idea which ruled this case,—that where a person for a consideration paid to him by another agrees to pay a sum of money to a third person, a stranger to the transaction, the latter does not thereby become possessed of the absolute right to the benefit of the promise, nor until he accepts the same in some way; and that while he is ignorant of the promise, or thereafter, at any time before he assents to the transaction, it may be rescinded,—we must admit is well supported in the books. The authorities so holding, in the main, go upon the ground that privity between parties is absolutely essential to a liability of one to another of a contractual nature, and that until the third person brings himself into privity with the one who has promised to be his debtor by at least assenting thereto, he has at least no legal right to the benefit of the promise; and that, till then, the parties to the transaction may rescind it or change it as they see fit. There is also much authority to the effect that, while the element of privity between the promisor and the third person is essential to render the promise absolutely binding upon the former, no act of the latter is necessary thereto; that the law, operating upon the acts of the parties to the transaction, creates the privity immediately upon its being consummated between them, and that neither one nor both of them can thereafter, without the third person's consent, enforce the promise. * * * It is useless to endeavor to review the authorities touching the subject before us with a view of harmonizing them upon any one single theory as to the principle upon which the liability to the third person is based or as to what are the essential elements to effect it. * * *

Without further discussion of the matter we adhere to the doctrine that where one person, for a consideration moving to him from another, promises to pay to a third person a sum of money, the law immediately operates upon the acts of the parties, establishing the essential of privity between the promisor and the third person requisite to binding contractual relations between them, resulting in the immediate establishment of a new relation of debtor and creditor, regardless of the relations of the third person to the immediate promisee in the transaction; that the liability is, as binding between the promisor and the third person as it would be if the consideration for the promise moved from the latter to the former and such promisor made the promise directly to such third person, regardless of whether the latter has any knowledge of the transaction at the time of its occurrence; that the liability being once created by the acts of the immediate parties to the transaction and the operation of the law thereon, neither one nor both of such parties can thereafter change the situation as regards the third person without his consent. It is plainly illogical to hold that immediately upon the completion of the transaction between the immediate parties thereto, the law operates upon their acts and creates the element of privity between the promisor and the third person, and at the same time to hold that such third person's status as regards the promise may be changed thereafter without his consent. The idea that privity between the promisor and the third person is necessary to render the transaction between the original parties thereto beyond the reach of either of them to revoke it, or both acting together to rescind it, springs from the supposed necessity of contractual relations between the promisor and the third person, binding upon the promisor at law. The moment such essential is established, it seems clear that such third person's right accrues and becomes absolute.

NOTES

(1) *When Should the Third Party's Right "Vest"?* "Suppose A and B enter into a contract for the benefit of C. Suppose further that C never knew of the agreement between A and B, and therefore had placed no reliance on such contract, and in nowise had changed his position. Is the contract between A and B, the moment executed, like the laws of the Medes and Persians—no longer subject to change? * * * Is the contractual status of the parties immutably fixed? Before A and B are permitted to change or abrogate their agreement must they of necessity secure consent of the third party C, who, until then, is a stranger to the contract, and at all times a mere windfall volunteer? To hold that the moment A and B enter into an agreement for the benefit of C, that such third party C has at that moment and under all circumstances acquired an interest in the contract which is indefeasibly vested, is an affront to common

sense." Stanfield v. W.C. McBride, Inc., 149 Kan. 567, 88 P.2d 1002, 1005–06 (1939).

(2) *Vesting and the Restatement.* The Restatement of Contracts, § 142, recognized the right of a donee beneficiary as vesting immediately upon execution of the contract, but the Restatement did not accord the creditor beneficiary such favorable treatment. Is there a sound basis for the differentiation? Cf. Restatement (Second) § 311: "(1) Discharge or modification of a duty to an intended beneficiary by conduct of the promisee or by a subsequent agreement between promisor and promisee is ineffective if a term of the promise creating the duty so provides. (2) In the absence of such a term, the promisor and promisee retain power to discharge or modify the duty by subsequent agreement. (3) Such a power terminates when the beneficiary, before he receives notification of the discharge or modification, materially changes his position in justifiable reliance on the promise or brings suit on it or manifests assent to it at the request of the promisor or promisee. * * *" The Supreme Court of Pennsylvania recently refused to abandon its long-held adherence to Restatement § 142 which makes a contractual gift to a donee beneficiary irrevocable upon execution of the contract, in contrast with Restatement (Second) § 311 which postpones vesting until a beneficiary "materially changes his position in justifiable reliance on the promise or brings suit on it or manifests assent to it at the request of the promisor or promisee." Biggins v. Shore, 523 Pa. 148, 565 A.2d 737 (1989).

(3) *"Acceptance" by Beneficiary.* The Indiana Supreme Court has affirmed that the right to rescind or modify a third party beneficiary contract, without the assent of the beneficiary, ceases once the contract is *accepted, adopted or acted upon* by the third party. In re Estate of Fanning, 263 Ind. 414, 333 N.E.2d 80 (1975). This has been characterized as the "majority view." Detroit Bank and Trust Co. v. Chicago Flame Hardening Co., Inc., 541 F.Supp. 1278, 1283 (N.D.Ind.1982). But what is meant by "acceptance"? Is a beneficiary's knowledge of the contract, coupled with a failure to object, sufficient to "vest" the right? *Detroit Bank*, applying Indiana law, said it was not. The court did indicate that there would be such a "presumption of acceptance" in the case of an infant beneficiary, a view not supported by the drafters of the revised Restatement. See Restatement (Second) § 311, Comment d.

*

INDEX

References are to Pages

†

1–56662–468–1

90000